COUNTY AND MUNICIPAL GOVERNMENT IN NORTH CAROLINA

Second Edition 2014

Edited by Frayda S. Bluestein

UNC
SCHOOL OF
GOVERNMENT

The School of Government at the University of North Carolina at Chapel Hill works to improve the lives of North Carolinians by engaging in practical scholarship that helps public officials and citizens understand and improve state and local government. Established in 1931 as the Institute of Government, the School provides educational, advisory, and research services for state and local governments. The School of Government is also home to a nationally ranked graduate program in public administration and specialized centers focused on information technology and environmental finance.

As the largest university-based local government training, advisory, and research organization in the United States, the School of Government offers up to 200 courses, webinars, and specialized conferences for more than 12,000 public officials each year. In addition, faculty members annually publish approximately 50 books, manuals, reports, articles, bulletins, and other print and online content related to state and local government. Each day that the General Assembly is in session, the School produces the *Daily Bulletin Online*, which reports on the day's activities for members of the legislature and others who need to follow the course of legislation.

The Master of Public Administration Program is offered in two formats. The full-time, two-year residential program serves up to 60 students annually. In 2013 the School launched MPA@UNC, an online format designed for working professionals and others seeking flexibility while advancing their careers in public service. The School's MPA program consistently ranks among the best public administration graduate programs in the country, particularly in city management. With courses ranging from public policy analysis to ethics and management, the program educates leaders for local, state, and federal governments and nonprofit organizations.

Operating support for the School of Government's programs and activities comes from many sources, including state appropriations, local government membership dues, private contributions, publication sales, course fees, and service contracts. Visit www.sog.unc.edu or call 919.966.5381 for more information on the School's courses, publications, programs, and services.

Printed in the United States of America

23 22 21 20 19 5 6 7 8 9

ISBN 978-1-56011-767-4

Summary Contents

Part 9. Education

Contents

Part 9. Education

Chapter 45

Chapter 46

Preface

Counties and municipalities are the primary forms of local government in North Carolina. The state has 100 counties and 553 cities. Everyone in the state lives in a county, and just over half of the people in the state live in a city (municipalities in North Carolina may be called cities, towns, or villages, but these different names do not denote any legal or structural differences). North Carolina cities range in population from 22 to 732,422, and 421 of the 553 cities have populations of less than 5,000. While the issues they face and their administration and policies may vary, the legal framework that governs counties and cities, respectively, is the same all across the state, regardless of the size of the unit. This book describes that legal framework and common administrative practices that are currently in use. It explains what counties and cities in North Carolina do, and how they do it.

The book is designed primarily to meet the needs of elected and appointed county and city board members and the employees who, on a day-to-day basis, carry out the functions mandated and authorized for North Carolina local governments. We hope that it will also appeal to a broader audience, including citizens, civic leaders, high school and college students, state employees, legislators, members of the media, and any others who need basic information about the legal authority and responsibilities of North Carolina counties and cities.

Subjects included in this book are described in general rather than detailed terms, in keeping with its purpose of providing an overview and basic information. Most of the chapters include references to additional materials and resources related to the topic. More detailed treatments of many of the book's topics are available in other School of Government publications, including *Public Records Law for North Carolina Local Governments, Open Meetings and Local Governments in North Carolina, Fundamentals of Property Tax Collection Law in North Carolina, Introduction to Local Government Finance,* and *A Legal Guide to Purchasing and Contracting for North Carolina Local Governments.*

The law governing county and municipal government changes constantly. New cases are handed down by state and federal courts, and state laws, which define and control local government authority, are constantly evolving. Legislative developments affecting North Carolina local governments are particularly in flux as this edition is being released. For that reason, some content that has appeared in previous editions has been omitted. Most notably, there is no chapter on environmental regulation, as this area of statutory and administrative law will be substantially reshaped over the next several years.

The School of Government has developed several resources to help public officials and others interested in local government stay informed. Its local government law blog, *Coates' Canons* (canons.sog.unc.edu), provides legislative and case updates; answers to frequently asked questions; and other short, substantive explanations of local government law issues. In addition, the School publishes several bulletin series, including *Local Government Law Bulletin, Property Tax Bulletin,* and *Local Finance Bulletin.* Interested readers may subscribe to the blog and may view the bulletins online to learn about recent developments in the law. They may also subscribe to a listserv to receive information about new School of Government publications. Visit the School's website at www.sog.unc.edu for details.

The first versions of these materials were created for use in courses for newly elected county and city officials in 1969, and previous versions of this publication have included multiple editions of separate books on county and municipal government in North Carolina. In 2007, the separate publications were merged and released as one book for the first time. The chapters in the earlier versions were primarily authored by Institute and School of Government faculty members along with several outside authors, all of whom generously contributed their knowledge and experience to the effort. This second edition of the combined county and municipal government book reflects, and in some cases incorporates, the earlier work of previous authors. We are indebted to them for their contributions to this important resource.

I want to especially acknowledge the contributions of the previous editors of the earlier versions of this publication: Warren Jake Wicker, Joseph S. Ferrell, David M. Lawrence, and A. Fleming Bell, II. These former faculty members epitomize the best of what the Institute and School of Government has sought and valued in its faculty. They were experts in their fields, generous with their time, committed to the mission of service to the State of North Carolina and its people, and dedicated to high quality, responsive, practical scholarship. This edition includes the work of many new faculty members who are continuing in the tradition of excellence modeled by those who came before.

This publication also would not have been possible without the incredible work of the School's publications staff: Nancy Dooly, Owen DuBose, Jennifer Henderson, Katrina Hunt, Kevin Justice, Daniel Soileau, Melissa Twomey, Leslie Watkins, and Lisa Wright. This book, and the process of creating it, was significantly improved by their creativity, professional expertise, attention to detail, flexibility, and patience.

Frayda S. Bluestein
David M. Lawrence Professor of Public Law and Government
UNC School of Government
Chapel Hill
Fall 2014

Part 1

Local Government Basics

Chapter 1

An Overview of Local Government

David M. Lawrence

Under the American federal system, state governments are primarily responsible for all governmental functions not delegated to the federal government by the U.S. Constitution. Each of the fifty state governments has divided responsibility for all activities under its control between itself and its local units of government: cities and towns, counties, townships, school districts, other special districts, and authorities. The pattern of responsibility differs from state to state depending on that state's traditions, circumstances, and political judgments, but the state and one or more units of local government are collectively responsible for most of the governmental activities that affect citizens directly and often, such as the following:

Administration of the courts
Airports
Conduct of elections
Fire protection
Law enforcement
Mental health
Parks and recreation
Prisons and jails
Public education
Public health
Public libraries
Public water supply and distribution
Recording of documents
Regulation of land use and development
Regulation of individual conduct
Sewage collection and disposal
Social services
Solid waste collection and disposal
Streets and highways

This list is not comprehensive, but it does indicate the scope of responsibilities that are met by state government and the various kinds of local governments.

The Primacy of State Government

In North Carolina's governmental system some governmental activities are the responsibility of state government alone, such as regulation of insurance or provision of four-year public colleges and universities. Other activities are provided concurrently or collaboratively by state and local government, activities such as social services, public health, election administration, K-12 education, community colleges, and parks and recreation. Still other activities are provided only by local governments, such as water distribution and sewage collection and disposal, fire protection, and zoning and subdivision regulation. Even with this latter group of activities, however, there is frequently some degree of state supervision or coordination.

The decisions that have created the basic framework for local government in North Carolina, for example, what kinds of local governments there are; how those local governments are created, are structured, and may expand; what activities local governments are permitted to engage in, what activities they are required to engage in; and how they may raise the revenues necessary to pay for it all, have all been made at the state level. One source is the North Carolina Constitution. Although this document is mostly concerned with establishing certain rights guaranteed to the state's citizens and creating the basic structure of state government, it also includes a few provisions that directly affect local government, such as that each county will have an elected sheriff and that certain forms of local government borrowing require voter approval. More important to the day-to-day operations of local government, however, are the many decisions made over time by the North Carolina General Assembly, the entity with the primary constitutional power to structure and modify the provision of governmental activities within the state. In the absence of state constitutional or federal constitutional, statutory, or regulatory restriction, the General Assembly is free under North Carolina's governmental system to create, abolish, and govern cities, counties, and other local governments as it sees fit.[1] As the North Carolina Supreme Court stated in a case involving a county, local governments in this state "are subject to almost unlimited legislative control, except when the power is restricted by constitutional provisions."[2]

A corollary to this primacy of the General Assembly in establishing the system of local government in a state like North Carolina is the understanding the local governments are entities with delegated powers only. Unlike some states, North Carolina is not a *home rule* state, which means that only the General Assembly can empower local governments to act. They have no constitutional capacity to empower themselves in the absence of state legislative action. The mere lack of any prohibition on any specific local government action is not sufficient to allow that action; it must be grounded upon some sort of legislative authorization. It should be stressed, though, that the General Assembly has been generous in its authorizations to local government, and as a result there is ample statutory authority for almost any initiative a local government wishes to take.

The necessary legislative authorizations may take either of two forms: *general laws* that apply statewide or *local or special acts* that pertain exclusively to named counties, cities, or other local government entities.[3] North Carolina General Statutes (hereinafter G.S.) Chapter 160A, which governs the structure and operations of city governments, is an example of a general law; the legislative act creating a particular city, which contains its operating "constitution" or charter, is an example of a local act. One use of local acts is to permit local variation and experimentation. This activity was once denounced by students of government but is now seen as a useful device for exploring new ideas and approaches to government problems, although it occasionally is used by legislators to override decision making by a specific local government. Given this legislative flexibility, any discussion of city or county powers and responsibilities

1. See N.C. Const. art. VII, sec. 1, first sentence: "The General Assembly shall provide for the organization and government and the fixing of boundaries of counties, cities and towns, and other governmental subdivisions, and, except as otherwise prohibited by this Constitution, may give such powers and duties to counties, cities and towns, and other governmental subdivisions as it may deem advisable."

2. Martin v. Comm'rs of Wake Cnty., 208 N.C. 354 (1935).

3. The North Carolina Constitution contains a number of topical limitations on legislative authority to enact local acts. *See, e.g.,* N.C. Const. art. II, sec. 24; art. V, sec. 2(2) and 2(3); and art. VI, sec. 3. N.C. Const. art. XIV, sec. 3, explains some of the constitutional formulations that restrict the enactment of local or special acts.

must always be prefaced with a caution that what is being said about cities or counties in general may not hold true for any particular jurisdiction.

The Current System of Local Government

County and City Governments

The dominant forms of local government in North Carolina are counties and cities. In North Carolina there is no legal distinction between a *city*, a *town*, or a *village*. Each is a *municipality*, and in this state a municipality may call itself by whichever designation it chooses, making that choice in its charter. Although *city* usually refers to a large municipality and *town* or *village* to a small one, there is no requirement that a particular municipality follow that general practice. The *Town* of Cary, for example, is now the seventh largest municipality in the state, while the *City* of High Shoals has a population of less than 700. In this volume *city* refers to municipalities of all sizes, both large and small.

Both counties and cities are general-purpose local governments, which means

- their governing boards are elected by the qualified voters of the county's or city's geographic area.
- they have the power to levy taxes.
- they may regulate conduct through adoption of *ordinances* (this ability is called the police power and is discussed in Chapter 5, "General Ordinance Authority."
- they are authorized and, especially with counties, sometimes required to provide a broad range of services to their citizens.

Although some other types of local governments in the state have at least one of the previously listed characteristics (for example, sanitary district boards and boards of education are elected; boards of health may enact regulations related to health and airport authorities may enact rules governing conduct on airport property; and a wide range of entities from water and sewer districts to hospital authorities provide services), no other local governments combine all of these attributes in the way that counties and cities do. (Types of local governments beyond counties and cities are briefly described at the end of this section.)

Counties and cities historically served very different purposes. Originally, counties were established to serve state purposes, that is, to carry out government on behalf of the state. Sheriffs enforced the state's criminal laws and collected its taxes; registers of deeds recorded the state's deeds and other documents; justices of the peace and clerks of court presided over the lowest rung of the state's judicial system, and the justices established and maintained the state's roads. Over time, counties came to be seen as the local government that provided services that were needed by all citizens, regardless of where they lived. Therefore, as government began to provide statewide public education, public health services, and welfare services, it was counties that were given the responsibility. Cities, by contrast, were created to adopt regulations and provide services more appropriate to built-up or urban areas. Over time, this meant that cities provided water distribution or sewage collection and disposal, solid waste collection, fire protection, recreation, and similar services, and it was cities that first began to regulate land use and development.

Around the middle of twentieth century, citizens living outside cities began to request some of the governmental services characteristic of cities but not of counties. They wanted community water or sewer systems, organized fire protection, and recreational spaces or programs. They wanted to be able to dispose of their trash in some way other than dumping or burning. And they wanted the protection of zoning. The General Assembly's response, over time, was to empower counties to engage in these city-like activities. As a result, although counties continue to serve a crucial role in the provision of state government services, they also have been given the opportunity to provide a range of services almost comparable to those provided by cities. The current authorizations for county and city functions and activities is set out in Table 1.1, below.

TABLE 1.1. Chief Services and Functions Authorized for City and County Government in North Carolina

Services and Functions Authorized for Counties Only

1. Agricultural extension
2. Community colleges
3. County home
4. Court system support
5. Drainage of land
6. Forest protection
7. Juvenile detention homes
8. Medical examiner/coroner
9. Public health
10. Public schools
11. Register of deeds
12. Social services
13. Soil and water conservation

Services and Functions Authorized for Both Cities and Counties

1. Aging programs
2. Air pollution control
3. Airports
4. Alcoholic rehabilitation
5. Ambulance services
6. Animal shelters
7. Armories
8. Art galleries and museums
9. Auditoriums and coliseums
10. Beach erosion control and hurricane protection
11. Bus lines and public transportation systems
12. Civil defense and emergency management
13. Community action
14. Community appearance
15. Community development
16. Drug abuse programs
17. Economic development
18. Fire protection
19. Historic preservation
20. Hospitals
21. Human relations
22. Industrial promotion
23. Inspections
24. Jails
25. Law enforcement
26. Libraries
27. Manpower
28. Mental health
29. National Guard
30. Off-street parking
31. Open space
32. Parks
33. Planning
34. Ports and harbors
35. Public housing
36. Railroad revitalization
37. Recreation
38. Rescue squads
39. Senior citizens' programs
40. Sewage collection and disposal
41. Solid waste collection and disposal
42. Storm drainage
43. Urban redevelopment
44. Veterans' services
45. Water
46. Watershed improvement

Services and Functions Authorized for Cities Only

1. Cable television and communication services
2. Cemeteries
3. Electric systems
4. Gas systems
5. Sidewalks
6. Street lighting
7. Streets
8. Traffic engineering

As general purpose local governments, counties and cities have many similarities, and as the General Assembly has authorized counties to provide many of the services once provided by cities only, those similarities have grown. But there remain important differences between counties and cities.

Geographic Extent

All the land in North Carolina is within one or another of the one hundred counties, and, therefore, all the citizens of North Carolina live in a county. But not all live in a city. The municipal population of the state, as estimated by the State's Office of State Management and Budget, is only slightly more than 55 percent of the total state population.[4] Therefore, as noted above, if there is a local government service that is needed by all the state's citizens, it will almost certainly be one that is provided—probably exclusively—by county government.

Because the state's entire territory is allocated among the one hundred counties, those local governments have no need for any sort of annexation power. Cities do, however, have the capacity to grow territorially, and, therefore, over

4. The Office of State Management and Budget estimated the state's total population as of 2013 as 9,861,952 and estimated the total municipal population in North Carolina on that date as 5,488,775. These estimates are available at the office's website, www.osbm.state.nc.us/ncosbm/facts_and_figures/socioeconomic_data/population_estimates.shtm.

the years the general assembly has given cities various sorts of annexation powers. The current annexation laws are summarized in Chapter 2, "Incorporation, Annexation, and City–County Consolidation."[5]

Authorized Activities

Although in recent years counties have gained authority to provide many of the services traditionally provided by cities, there remain a number of city functions for which there is no comparable county authority, as is set out in Table 1.1, above. That table also demonstrates that there are a number of important county functions that cities are not authorized to provide. As the preceding paragraphs have discussed, these by and large are activities that the general assembly has determined should be provided to all the citizens of North Carolina and, therefore, should be provided by counties, the one form of general purpose local government that covers the entire state. County responsibility for these services is a continuing reminder of the counties' historical role as an agency of state government.

Mandated Activities

As the General Assembly has turned to counties as the instrumentalities to provide certain services over the entire state, it has recognized that its goal of statewide provision of those services cannot be met unless the counties are required to provide the services. Therefore, counties are subject to a number of service mandates, which in total comprise well over half of any county's annual budget. For many of these mandated activities, there is also a substantial degree of state government supervision of county operations. The following are the most important mandated activities for counties:

- Public education
- Social services
- Public health
- Mental health
- Jails
- Sheriff
- Medical examiner
- Support of the court system
- Emergency management
- Register of deeds
- Elections administration
- Building code enforcement
- Tax listing and assessment
- Emergency medical services

By contrast, the only mandated activity for cities is building code enforcement, and many smaller cities meet this obligation by contracting with the county to take responsibility for the function.[6] (Federal law requires that some larger cities engage in stormwater management.)

Governmental Structure

Counties are highly decentralized organizations. Two department heads, the sheriff and the register of deeds, are elected, and several important functions—including public education, community colleges, social services, public health, and mental health—are controlled by elected or appointed boards other than the board of county commissioners. These other boards appoint their own employees and make policy for the entities or county departments under their control.

5. Although most cities are located within only one county, there is no legal reason for that to be so. Rather, city boundaries tend to follow development, which often pays no attention to county lines. There are at least thirty-four different cities in North Carolina that are in two or more counties; one, the city of High Point, is in four counties.

6. Cities that have been incorporated after 1999 are required to provide at least four services from a statutory list of eight in order to receive certain state-shared revenues, N.C. Gen. Stat. § 136-41.2(c), but such cities may choose to forego the revenues and a few have.

In addition, some members of some appointed boards are appointed by persons or entities other than the board of county commissioners.

Cities, on the other hand, are centralized organizations, with almost all employees reporting either to the manager or the governing board. A city manager has a great deal more day-to-day control over city-funded operations than does a county manager over county-funded operations.

Partisan versus Nonpartisan

All elected county officials in North Carolina—commissioners, sheriff, and register of deeds—are chosen through partisan elections. Almost all city elected officials, on the other hand, are elected in nonpartisan elections.[7] As a result, county elections are held in even-numbered years, at the same time as statewide and national elections, while city elections are held in odd-numbered years.

Other Types of Local Governments

School Administrative Units

Substantially independent school districts in North Carolina were abolished in 1931. In their place the General Assembly created geographically defined school administrative units overseen by locally elected boards of education with no taxing power. These units are funded by counties and by the state and federal governments. (Elementary and secondary education is discussed in detail in Chapter 45, "The Governance and Funding Structure of North Carolina Public Schools.")

Special Districts and Authorities

Special purpose governments also exist in North Carolina, but they have never been as widely used here as elsewhere in the nation. Generally, *special districts* are special purpose governments with taxing power, and *authorities* are such governments without taxing power. The two most common special districts in the state are the sanitary district and the rural fire protection district. North Carolina also has several types of authorities, the most common being

- housing authorities, created under G.S. Chapter 157.
- water and sewer authorities, created under G.S. Chapter 162A.
- airport authorities, usually created by local act of the General Assembly.

A few authorities are also involved in operating hospitals, public transportation, off-street parking facilities, and a variety of recreational facilities and activities. Many other states make much more extensive use of authorities, especially to operate revenue-producing enterprise activities.

Townships

North Carolina undertook a relatively brief experiment with township government after 1868, the township being a subdivision of the county with independent governmental powers and responsibilities. The experiment was mostly abandoned later in the nineteenth century, although townships remained involved in road construction and maintenance through the 1920s. Unlike some other states, townships exist today in North Carolina only as convenient administrative areas within counties, chiefly for tax-listing and sometimes to provide convenient boundary lines in the drawing of census districts and voting precincts. G.S. 153A-19 allows the board of commissioners to establish, abolish, and name townships, as long as specified procedures are followed.

7. Cities can choose to use partisan elections, but only 7 out of more than 550 of the cities and towns do so.

A Brief History of Local Government in North Carolina

We now turn to a discussion of the history of North Carolina counties, cities, and other local governmental units, followed by a summary of the current characteristics of local government in the state.

Colonial Times through the Civil War

Counties

It was accepted from the earliest days of colonial government in North Carolina that governmental administration could not be efficiently centralized in the colonial capital. Therefore, following the English tradition, the colony established county governments for the local administration of many of the functions of government considered essential throughout the colony: administration of the court system, law enforcement, the conduct of elections, care of the poor, and maintenance of roads. Justices of the peace, as a body or court, administered the county's affairs, exercising both judicial and administrative powers. Independence from England brought no wrenching changes to this system. The county justices of the peace were appointed by the governor to serve at the pleasure of the governor, but in making his appointments the governor relied on recommendations from the General Assembly. Thus, as a matter of practical politics, the members of the legislature from a given county had a powerful voice in the selection of its justices of the peace and, therefore, in its government.

At first the justices appointed the sheriff, the coroner, and the constables; later, these offices were made elective. The sheriff and coroner were from the county at large and the constables from captains' districts (militia-mustering areas). The justices were also responsible for appointing a clerk of court, register of deeds, county attorney, county trustee (treasurer), surveyor, and overseers or wardens of the poor. In sum it was a system with very little direct control by the county's voters.

Cities

In contrast to the county, the colonial and early 1800s North Carolina towns, serving several hundred people, had few functions. They organized a town watch, established a volunteer fire department, built public wells, kept the streets in repair, occasionally (as in Fayetteville and Wilmington) built a town market, and passed ordinances to protect the public health and safety. The early towns supported their activities from fees, charges, fines and penalties, and revenue from the sale of lots.

North Carolina towns remained largely small trading centers and county seats until after 1865. They did not grow with industrialization during the antebellum period, as many northern cities did. Indeed, by 1850 only one North Carolina city, Wilmington, had a population as great as 5,000. As a result, North Carolina cities were a full half-century or more delayed in encountering a demand for such major municipal functions as water systems and paid police departments. Property, poll, and license taxes were introduced around 1800, but tax levies for cities and towns were very small until after the Civil War.

Local Government from 1868 until 1900

The 1868 Reconstruction Constitution of North Carolina attempted a fundamental restructuring of county government. The justices of the peace were restricted to judicial functions, with county government administration transferred to newly constituted—and locally elected—boards of county commissioners. The constitution also added township governments, additional elected officials with limited responsibilities. When the so-called Conservatives regained political power in the 1870s, these constitutional changes were reversed. Township government was essentially abolished, and commissioners were made subservient to the reinstituted justices of the peace.

This arrangement lasted for twenty years. In 1895 the ability of the people to elect commissioners was restored in most counties, and the requirement that the boards' decisions be approved by the justices of the peace was repealed. Popular election of the commissioners was finally restored in all counties in 1905.

The history of city government in this period was more tranquil. Between 1865 and 1900, city water and sewer systems were first introduced, largely through franchised private companies. Public transportation, such as streetcar systems, was introduced under similar franchises, as were electric and telephone systems. Street lighting first became common. The large cities began to spend a lot of money on paving streets, just as the large counties began to pave the roads that led out from the cities. With the demand for paved streets and utilities came special assessments and water charges. Public health regulations also received an increased emphasis. Schools came to be operated by school districts, with better and more expensive schools in the cities and the towns. Wilmington reached a population of 10,000 in 1870, followed by Asheville, Charlotte, and Raleigh in 1880.

Cities and Counties in the Twentieth and Early Twenty-First Centuries

From 1900 through World War II

The first three decades of the twentieth century continued the growth of North Carolina local government that had begun in the final decades of the nineteenth. Streets and roads were paved as the automobile became commonplace. Water and sewer systems came under public ownership as private companies found it difficult to maintain high-quality systems and still produce a profit. A number of cities acquired their own electric systems. Full-time city police departments were established, and full-time paid fire brigades began to supplement the efforts of volunteer companies. The first building codes were adopted. Public support for city and county libraries began, largely in response to Carnegie Foundation grants-in-aid for library construction. Public health departments were first established by counties.

In the 1920s the statewide system of primary highways connecting county seats and other principal cities and towns was established. Zoning was introduced, and the first county and city managers were appointed. The prosperity of the 1920s encouraged a significant growth of local government.

The Great Depression broke the expansion bubble. All services were cut back, and debt service obligations became a heavy burden. With no one to advise or warn them in marketing their securities, many cities and counties had overextended their obligations and saw their credit ratings drop so low that they had to pay crippling rates of interest; eventually, some faced bankruptcy. Defaults on bond obligations led the legislature to establish the County Government Advisory Commission in 1927 and to give it the supervisory powers necessary to correct the situation. This commission effected a reversal in local government financing. Its successor, the Local Government Commission, remains a bulwark of North Carolina government today. In addition, poor property tax collections threatened continued operation of county road systems and public schools. As a result, the state assumed responsibility for non-city roads in 1931 and for a minimum level of public education in 1933. Independent school districts were abolished.

With all of these changes, state and federal financial aid, virtually unknown until the Great Depression, became a significant source of local government revenue. Federal public works programs built many local government improvements, including the first water and sewer systems in many small towns. Federal aid led to uniform county responsibility for public welfare and encouraged development of health departments.

1945 to the Present

The immediate postwar period was a time of rapid urban growth and a very rapid expansion of local government facilities, first to make up deficiencies left from the depression and later to meet new demands, and there has been steady growth in the decades since. In most of this growth, counties and cities could rely and build upon their existing powers, but there were a number of major episodes of significant expansion in local government powers in the latter half of the twentieth century.

The 1959 General Assembly enacted a number of important pieces of legislation, some of which remains important today. The leading product of 1959 legislation was a city annexation procedure that remained in place until 2011, permitting cities to unilaterally annex areas that had become or were in the process of becoming urban in nature. Thoroughfare planning and land use planning and zoning enabling statutes were also passed in 1959, and both laws still exist in modified form. The thoroughfare statute places joint responsibility for thoroughfare planning and for adoption of a major thoroughfare plan on city councils and the state's Department of Transportation. The planning legislation significantly expanded on the prior powers of cities and counties to plan, zone, and regulate land development, and it provided for increased joint and cooperative activities by city and county governments. Finally, 1959 also saw the beginnings of today's extraterritorial jurisdiction (ETJ) statute that gives cities an ability to regulate development outside their boundaries. Although smaller cities were not originally given ETJ authority, the extraterritorial jurisdiction law applies statewide today.

In 1967 the General Assembly established a Local Government Study Commission. It operated for six years, successfully proposing significant modernization in the constitutional provisions affecting local government finance, revising and modernizing the basic local government statutes, and transferring important decisions from the General Assembly to county commissioners and city councils. It also continued strengthening legal powers delegated to county government, for example, by extending to counties a general ordinance-making power.

The most significant change in city and county revenues in many years also came in 1967, when Mecklenburg County was authorized to "piggyback" a 1 percent local sales and use tax on the state's general sales tax. The success of this tax in Mecklenburg quickly led to its authorization across the state. Since then, the rate has increased several times, and the tax is levied in all one hundred counties under arrangements by which the proceeds in each county are shared between the county government and the cities within it. The sales and use tax revenues have become especially important to local governments, because the past forty years have also witnessed a significant narrowing of the property tax base by the General Assembly.

The past several decades have seen the continued spread of the council–manager form of city government and the county manager form of county government in North Carolina. Nearly all cities with more than 10,000 citizens and many with lower populations use the council–manager form. About ninety-nine of North Carolina's counties currently have a manager (the number varies slightly from year to year), although the powers of county managers, particularly over hiring and firing, may be restricted by the board of county commissioners in ways that are not possible under the city–manager system. In addition, an elected county commissioner can and sometimes does serve as the county manager. This is forbidden for cities.[8]

Changes have also occurred in local governing bodies and in city and county workforces. There has been some movement to various forms of district election of city council members and county commissioners, although the at-large method retains great popularity. There have also been marked increases in the numbers of women and African Americans elected to city and county offices.

The growth of North Carolina's population and economic changes have created an increasing need for city and county governments to cooperate. Hundreds of cooperative arrangements have developed since 1970, varying from one unit contracting with another to the merger of functions. (See Chapter 11, "Interlocal Cooperation, Shared Services, and Regional Councils," for a more detailed discussion.)

North Carolina Local Government in the National Context

This chapter ends with a summary of important distinctions between North Carolina's current pattern of local government and the patterns commonly found elsewhere. At least nine general distinguishing features can be identified:

1. *Primary state responsibility for financing education and highways.* Two functions for which state and local financial outlays are large—education and highways—are both financed primarily at the state level in North Carolina, and from taxes imposed by the state. All states support these two functions from the state treasury to some extent, but few to the degree that North Carolina does. In most states the local share of financial

8. In the council–manager form of government, the city council makes planning and policy decisions, leaving the day-to-day administration of city affairs to a professional manager. In jurisdictions without a manager, all decisions concerning the city are entrusted to the council. The manager in cities operating under the council–manager plan has statutory hiring and firing authority for all city employees except those appointed directly by the council. Arrangements are more complex in counties, even with a manager, both for the reasons noted in the text and because of the existence of several boards besides the county commissioners with a role in making policy and choosing employees (e.g., the boards of health, mental health, and social services; the board of education; and the board of elections). For more information, see Chapter 3, "County and City Governing Boards"; Chapter 4, "County and City Managers"; and Part 8 describing county budgeting and particular county government functions.

responsibility is much greater, and in almost all states, but not North Carolina, county (or township) governments bear a major portion of the responsibility for roads outside municipalities. Moreover, in North Carolina the property tax is less important in financing these two functions than in the nation at large, because of the major state government responsibility.

2. *Primary county responsibility for areawide, or "human," services at the local level.* A number of major services and functions, especially health, education, and welfare, are needed by people in both rural areas and urban areas. In North Carolina the local responsibility for these services and functions is vested in the county, the one type of unit that covers the entire state, and the county commissioners have limited discretion in whether or how much to fund them. In contrast, in other states these services and functions may be carried out at the state level or vested locally in cities, counties, special districts, or a combination thereof.
3. *Primary city responsibility for the high levels of some services that are needed in urban areas.* Fire protection, law enforcement, solid waste collection, water and sewer services, and street maintenance and improvement are all key city responsibilities in North Carolina, much as they are in many states. However, some states are more likely to use local authorities or special districts to provide water and sewer services, fire protection, and so forth.
4. *County authority to provide urban types of services.* North Carolina counties have extensive authority to provide water and sewer services, solid waste collection and disposal, fire protection, recreation, and other services needed by citizens. (As noted previously, counties still have no authority to build or maintain streets.) A county government may, if it chooses, provide urban types of services throughout the county's unincorporated areas as may be necessary. Counties also frequently cooperate with cities in providing some of these services within city limits (see number 6). In some other states urban functions could be undertaken in unincorporated areas only by forming special districts or authorities.
5. *Extensive city and county authority to regulate and direct urban development.* Both cities and counties in North Carolina are broadly authorized to undertake planning programs and to regulate land use through zoning and subdivision control. Most cities have ETJ with respect to these controls. Local governmental units in other states also have such powers, but not all states grant such broad authority.
6. *Flexibility in city–county and multi-unit arrangements.* Cities and counties in North Carolina also have broad authority to take joint or parallel action or to contract with one another for performance of functions that both are authorized to undertake. Such agreements may range from the joint financing of a water line to the merging of tax collection or other offices.
7. *A model system for major thoroughfare planning.* Under a procedure established in 1959, each municipality and the state's Department of Transportation jointly develop and adopt a major thoroughfare plan for the municipality and its surrounding area. North Carolina's system is a nationally recognized approach that has served as a model for procedures adopted elsewhere.
8. *A state–local revenue system that relies on four main taxes.* The major taxes in North Carolina are the property tax, the general sales tax, the individual and corporate income taxes, and the gasoline tax. The property tax is levied by local governments only, the general sales tax by local and state governments, and the income and gasoline taxes by the state only (although the gasoline tax is shared with cities). Rates for the sales and income taxes are average to high compared to rates for the same types of taxes in some other states, whereas rates for the property tax are low compared with those found in many other places. In terms of responsiveness to the economy, the property tax everywhere tends to lag economic growth more than taxes tied directly to economic activity, such as income and sales taxes. Because the property tax is relatively less important in North Carolina than it is elsewhere, while income and sales taxes have greater significance, North Carolina's total revenue structure tends to be somewhat more sensitive than most states' tax programs to changes, positive or negative, in the economic environment.
9. *Reliance on general-purpose local governments.* At the local level in North Carolina, almost all governmental responsibilities have been vested in city and county governments, two general-purpose types of governmental units. The vast majority of expenditures of local governmental units in North Carolina are also made through

cities and counties. In many other states, special districts, school districts, and authorities are relatively much more important. The result is that North Carolina's urban areas generally do not have the multitude of overlapping units frequently found elsewhere.

Summary

North Carolina's pattern of local government reflects an arrangement that is flexible and provides for much local control. The pattern has resulted in a relatively simple governmental structure, with few types of local government and limited overlapping jurisdictions and with both state and local financing being important. At least three main roles have been defined for local governments in this state.

The first major function of cities and counties is protection of the individual and the public as a whole. They carry out this responsibility through fire services and law enforcement (police and sheriff's departments), ordinances that protect the safety of individuals and the public at large from the acts of other persons, and ordinances that protect the use and value of property.

Local governments are also providers of many other services. Most cities provide a local street system, and some build and operate essential facilities such as electric and gas distribution systems. Counties support school systems and health, mental health, and social services programs. Both cities and counties operate water and sewer systems; collect solid waste; sometimes build and operate airports and auditoriums; and contribute to their citizens' cultural and leisure-time activities by supporting libraries, parks, and recreation programs.

Finally, local governments are a major factor in the continued economic development of the community. Cities, for example, share responsibility with the state for the street and highway system that is the key to effective transportation. Cities, counties, and some independent districts and authorities build and operate the water and sewer systems without which urban development is impossible. Local governments often directly support economic and industrial development bodies, sometimes alone and at other times in cooperation with other local governments. Cities, counties, and in some cases special local authorities provide the civic facilities such as parking, auditoriums, and airports that make an area attractive as an economic center. Local governments help to improve housing. Through all of these activities, local governments are involved in helping to build attractive, convenient, and appealing communities.

Local governments in North Carolina play a major role in providing the services and functions that are needed in an increasingly urbanized state that also contains large rural areas. They are created by the state legislature, and their powers and functions are authorized by that body. Although many North Carolina cities and counties provide similar kinds of services to other jurisdictions of the same type, each city and to a lesser extent each county has considerable flexibility in determining what functions it will undertake and at what level. Within the limitations prescribed by the state legislature and the courts, city councils and boards of county commissioners have discretion to provide the services and functions that will best serve the needs of their communities.

Additional Resources

Adrian, Charles R. "Forms of City Government in American History." In *The Municipal Yearbook 1988*, 3–12. Washington, D.C.: International City Management Association, 1988.

Adrian, Charles R., and Ernest S. Griffith. *A History of American City Government: The Formation of Tradition, 1775–1870.* New York: Praeger Publishers, for the National Municipal League, 1976.

Corbitt, David L. *Formation of North Carolina Counties, 1663–1943.* Raleigh, N.C.: North Carolina Department of Archives and History, 1950.

Griffith, Ernest S. *A History of American City Government: The Progressive Years and Their Aftermath, 1900–1920.* New York: Praeger Publishers, for the National Municipal League, 1974.

Liner, Charles D., ed. *State and Local Government Relations in North Carolina: Their Evolution and Current Status.* 2nd ed. Chapel Hill, N.C.: School of Government, 1995.

About the Author

David M. Lawrence is a retired School of Government faculty member who specializes in local government law.

This chapter updates and revises the previous versions authored by A. Fleming Bell, II, Joseph S. Ferrell, and Warren Jake Wicker. The author is indebted to Professors Bell and Ferrell and to the late Professor Wicker for their work.

Chapter 2

Incorporation, Annexation, and City–County Consolidation

Frayda S. Bluestein

In North Carolina, the General Assembly creates cities and counties and defines their initial boundaries.[1] County boundaries are established in local acts of the General Assembly and may from time to time be modified. The current one hundred counties are listed in Section 153A-10 of the North Carolina General Statutes (hereinafter G.S.). The legislature has delegated to cities the authority to expand their boundaries through annexation subject to statutory requirements. Annexation initiated by the city must be approved in a referendum by a majority of residents in the area to be annexed. Annexation may also occur upon petition by the property owner or by the General Assembly by local act. The General Assembly has also authorized city–county consolidation, which has been attempted several times but has not been accomplished in North Carolina to date. This chapter provides an overview of the process for creating, expanding, dissolving, and consolidating counties and cities in North Carolina.

Municipal Incorporation

In North Carolina a city is created—that is, incorporated—in only one way: by an act of the General Assembly. Such an act establishes the initial borders of the city and enacts its charter. No standards restrict the legislature's discretion in

1. The North Carolina Constitution, Article VII, Section 1, provides, "The General Assembly shall provide for the organization and government and the fixing of boundaries of counties, cities and towns, and other governmental subdivisions, and, except as otherwise prohibited by this Constitution, may give such powers and duties to counties, cities and towns, and other governmental subdivisions as it may deem advisable."

incorporation. It may incorporate an area with very few people or with a largely rural character; it may even incorporate an area in anticipation of development, before any city in fact exists. The single constitutional restriction on the General Assembly's power of incorporation is found in Article VII, Section 1, of the North Carolina Constitution. That provision stipulates that if a community lies within one mile of the limits of an existing city of 5,000 people or more, within three miles of a city of 10,000 or more, within four miles of a city of 25,000 or more, or within five miles of a city of 50,000 or more, the General Assembly may incorporate that community only on approval of three-fifths of the members of each house. This provision reflects the assumption that cities will expand as areas near their boundaries grow and develop. The supermajority vote requirement is rarely significant. Most incorporation bills are passed unanimously, following the General Assembly's practice of deferring to the local delegation on local matters. Furthermore, as noted later in this chapter, the legislature's recent changes in the annexation laws will likely limit the extent to which the cities will continue to expand into the areas around their current boundaries.

The support of the legislators who represent an area that is proposed for incorporation is an essential element in the process. The legislature has established a procedure for considering proposed incorporations, but a legislator is also free to introduce a bill to incorporate an area without going through the statutory procedure. As set out in G.S. Chapter 120, Article 20, Part 2,[2] the statutory process starts with a petition signed by 15 percent of the registered voters in the area to be incorporated. The petition is submitted to the Municipal Incorporations Subcommittee of the Joint Legislative Committee on Local Government. The subcommittee reviews the proposal and makes a recommendation to the General Assembly on whether or not the area should be incorporated. The statute contains a number of standards—pertaining, for example, to proximity to existing cities, size, urban character, and economic resources—and if an area fails to meet all the standards, the subcommittee is required to make a negative recommendation. In addition, in order to obtain a positive recommendation from the subcommittee, the petition must propose that the new city levy a property tax of at least five cents and provide at least four of eight listed services. Those eight services are police protection, fire protection, solid waste collection or disposal, water distribution, street maintenance, street construction or right-of-way acquisition, street lighting, and zoning. Even if a negative recommendation is made, however, the General Assembly may still incorporate the community; the subcommittee's recommendation in no way binds the legislature.

The General Assembly incorporates an area by enacting a local bill consisting of a charter for the new city and a description of the city's initial boundaries. The bill may take effect upon ratification, or it may include a requirement for a referendum by the residents of the area to be incorporated. The decision as to whether or not to require residents' approval rests with the General Assembly; local voters have no inherent constitutional right to approve an incorporation.

North Carolina has experienced periods of rapid growth, as reflected in the number of requests to the General Assembly to incorporate communities as cities. From the 1981 session through the 1994 session, the General Assembly enacted incorporation legislation for forty-nine communities. Of these, thirty-nine have become active cities, while voters in ten communities voted incorporation down. Similarly, from the 1995 session through the 2005 session, the General Assembly enacted incorporation legislation for an additional thirty-eight communities, twenty-nine of which in fact became active cities. From 2005 to 2013 the legislature enacted incorporation bills for nine communities, of which six have become active cities.

Since 2000, newly incorporated cities have been subject to a tax levy and service requirement that conditions their eligibility for various shared revenues. In order for a city incorporated after January 1, 2000, to receive local government sales tax proceeds, state street assistance, state beer and wine tax proceeds, state utility tax proceeds, or other state-shared revenues, it must levy a property tax of at least five cents per $100 of valuation and it must provide at least four of the following eight services: police protection, fire protection, solid waste collection or disposal, water distribution, street maintenance, street construction or right-of-way acquisition, street lighting, and zoning.[3] In addition, such a city must open at least a majority of its street mileage to the general public. These changes were intended to

2. N.C. Gen. Stat. (hereinafter G.S.) §§ 120-163 through -174.

3. This requirement is set out in G.S. 136-41.2(c) for street assistance and is cross-referenced in other statutes for each of the other affected revenues.

discourage the incorporation of paper towns (cities that did not provide city services) and the incorporation as cities of gated communities.

Repealing City Charters and Dissolving Counties

Just as only the General Assembly may incorporate a community or create a county, only the General Assembly may unincorporate, dissolve, or merge them. The legislature does this by repealing a city charter or by repealing or amending a local act creating a county. In practice, the General Assembly rarely takes such an action, and it does so usually only on the request of the affected community. A 1971 omnibus act repealed the charters of ninety-five inactive towns,[4] but numerous others are technically still in existence. Since 1971, the General Assembly has repealed the charters of only two towns.[5] The General Assembly also has merged local governments—for example, by incorporating one city into another[6] or by incorporating the charters of two cities into a newly created city.[7]

Annexation

North Carolina's annexation laws have been a significant component of the state's policies for providing government services in urban areas. These policies have favored the expansion of existing cities over other ways of providing those services by facilitating the orderly expansion of the state's cities. Only cities are authorized by law to provide the full range of basic urban services: water supply and distribution, sewage collection and treatment, law enforcement, fire protection, solid waste collection and disposal, and street maintenance and improvement. Counties are not authorized to provide street maintenance and improvement, and no types of special districts are authorized to provide either law enforcement or street maintenance and improvement. Furthermore, as is noted in the discussion on incorporation, the law favors expansion of existing cities over incorporation of new ones.

Prior to 1947, annexation required action by the General Assembly. In 1947, in order to avoid the controversy often accompanying annexation bills, the legislature delegated to cities the authority to annex by local ordinance. That law did not include specific standards for urbanization as a prerequisite to annexation. The delegation of local authority to annex did not end the controversy over the issue and the legislature commissioned a study in 1957, which produced revisions enacted in 1959. The revised law, which remained in place until 2011, limited annexation to areas that meet urban development standards and required cities to provide services as set out in the statute. Affected property owners often challenged city-initiated annexations (also called involuntary annexations) in court, usually on procedural grounds. Courts generally upheld annexations so long as the statutory procedures were substantially met. During this period, the law served to facilitate the orderly expansion of the state's cities. In some cases, however, cities annexed without providing significant services.[8] In addition, existing policies requiring property owners to pay fees for extension of water and sewer services to their property, while lawfully imposed, were unpopular.

In 2011, frustrated property owners once again brought their concerns to the attention of their legislators in Raleigh. Complaints included not having a voice in the decision to annex as well as the cost of and delay in receiving services, particularly water and sewer services. The legislature considered enacting a moratorium on annexation but ultimately revised the law to require water and sewer services to be provided without cost to the property owners and to allow

4. 1971 N.C. Sess. Laws ch. 740.

5. S.L. 1995-119 (repealing the charter for the Town of Sandyfield, subject to a referendum); S.L. 1998-54 (repealing the charter for the Town of Sloop Point).

6. See, for example, S.L. 2001-16 (Jonesville and Arlington merged).

7. S.L. 1999-66 (creating the Town of Oak Island out of the Towns of Yaupon Beach and Long Beach).

8. In *Nolan v. City of Marvin*, 360 N.C. 256 (2006), the North Carolina Supreme Court invalidated an annexation because the city failed to provide meaningful services to the annexed area.

property owners to file petitions to deny the annexation.[9] (The law also amended the procedures for voluntary annexation, making it easier for economically distressed areas to receive city services. These provisions are still in place and are discussed below.) The petition to deny process was to be administrated by the county board of elections, much like a referendum; if petitions were signed by the owners of 60 percent of the properties to be annexed, the annexation would not become effective. The petition process was also applied, in a series of local acts, to particular annexations that had already been completed.[10] Several cities challenged the petition process on constitutional and other grounds, and a superior court judge invalidated the petition process in the local acts as well as in the general law. The legislature responded to the ruling by replacing the petition process with a referendum.[11] Under the current law, a majority of voters in the area to be annexed must vote to approve the annexation.

The referendum requirement, combined with the requirement for the city to pay for water and sewer service as a condition of annexation, will very likely reduce, if not eliminate, city-initiated annexations. It may also alter local government finances, as residents living near the city will continue to use and demand city services but may not willingly agree to be annexed. The change may also alter service delivery polices in cities, counties, and special districts, and it may affect land development patterns across the state.[12]

Overview of Current Annexation Methods

There are four methods by which territory may be annexed to a nearby city. Three methods are delegated to cities and do not require action by the state legislature. These are (1) annexation by petition (hereinafter referred to as voluntary annexation) of areas contiguous to the city; (2) voluntary annexation of areas not contiguous to the city but nearby (also called satellite annexation); and (3) annexation at the city's initiative of contiguous areas that are developed for urban purposes (hereinafter referred to as involuntary annexation). The fourth method is legislative annexation, which is not subject to any standards or procedural requirements other than those applicable to local acts of the General Assembly. With only very minor exceptions, these methods are available to all the state's cities.[13]

In general, a city may annex any territory qualifying under the various procedures as long as that territory is not part of another, active city. (Under G.S. 160A-1(2), which defines *city* and *incorporated municipality* for purposes of G.S. Chapter 160A, to be considered active in this context, the other city must have held its most recent election for council.) A city may annex territory that is within a sanitary district or another special district[14] or territory that is within another city's extraterritorial jurisdiction for land use planning. In addition, a city may by ordinance annex property owned by the city itself.[15] Finally, county boundaries are not a bar to annexation; some fifty-three cities lie within two or more counties.

Historically, most annexations in North Carolina have been by petition of the property owners under one of the two voluntary procedures. These annexations typically are relatively small, however, often comprising the property of only one person or very few persons. The greatest number of persons and the greatest amount of property has been annexed under the involuntary, city-initiated procedures. As noted earlier, the recent changes in the involuntary annexation law will likely reduce the frequency and size of this type of annexation.

Voluntary Annexation of Contiguous Areas

G.S. 160A-31 authorizes a city to annex any area contiguous to its borders on receipt of a petition signed by all the owners of real property within the area proposed for annexation. The procedure is simple. Once a petition is presented and certified by the city clerk as sufficient, the council holds a public hearing on whether or not the statutory requirements—contiguity and signatures by all the owners of the subject property—have been met. If the council determines that the

9. S.L. 2011-396.

10. S.L. 2011-173; 2011-177.

11. S.L. 2012-11.

12. For an overview of North Carolina annexation policy and analysis of the effects of the 2011 legislative changes, see Judith Welch Wegner, *North Carolina's Annexation Wars: Whys, Wherefores, and What Next,* 91 N.C. L. Rev. 165 (2012).

13. Charter provisions in several small towns contain exceptions to the general annexation laws.

14. *See* State *ex rel.* E. Lenoir Sanitary Dist. v. City of Lenoir, 249 N.C. 96 (1958).

15. G.S. 160A-31(g) (contiguous); 160A-58.7 (satellite).

requirements have been met, it may adopt an ordinance annexing the property. This method is especially suited to annexations of small areas, new subdivisions (before lots have been sold), and tracts with a limited number of property owners.

Two points should be made about the procedure. First, the petition must contain the signature of all the owners of each lot or tract included in the petition. If a married couple owns a property, for example, both must sign. Second, the North Carolina Supreme Court has held that a property owner may withdraw his or her signature at any time before the council has adopted the annexation ordinance.[16] If that happens, the council may not simply annex the remaining property listed in the petition. Rather, because the council no longer has before it a petition signed by all the owners of the property listed in the petition, such a withdrawal invalidates that petition, and a new petition must be submitted including only property whose owners still desire annexation. The same is true if ownership of some of the property changes between the time the petition is signed and the time the city seeks to act. Again the council no longer has before it a petition signed by all the owners of the property listed in the petition, and submission of a new petition is necessary.

Voluntary Annexation of Noncontiguous (Satellite) Areas

Areas near an existing city often develop in an urban manner but are separated from the city by undeveloped territory, so they are not subject to annexation by methods that limit annexation to contiguous areas. Frequently these areas are in the normal path for city growth, and property owners in the area desire the advantages of city services—water and sewer systems, police and fire protection, solid waste collection, and street maintenance. Also, early annexation of the areas is an advantage to the city because it enables the city to plan for the orderly expansion of basic facilities to serve both these areas and the intervening areas that will develop in time.

North Carolina has responded to this situation by permitting voluntary annexation of such noncontiguous, or satellite, areas. The procedure was first developed and authorized for Raleigh by local act in 1967. Over the next several years, eleven other cities secured similar local act authority from the legislature. In 1974, in response to the likelihood of further requests for local acts, the General Assembly enacted general enabling authority for satellite annexation (G.S. 160A-58 through -58.8), repealing the various local acts.

The procedure for satellite annexation is similar to that for voluntary annexation of contiguous areas. Once a petition signed by all the owners of the listed property has been received and certified by the city clerk, the council holds a public hearing on the petition's sufficiency and the annexation's desirability. (G.S. 160A-58.1(a) provides that the petition need not be signed by owners of property exempt from property taxation, by railroad companies, by public utilities, or by electric or telephone membership corporations.) If the council determines that the petition is adequate and the property involved qualifies under the statutory standards, it may adopt an ordinance annexing the property. The statute sets out the following four standards that the property must meet:

1. The nearest point on the proposed satellite area must be no more than three miles from the city's primary limits.
2. No point within the proposed satellite area may be closer to another city than to the annexing city. (This standard does not apply if the property in question is subject to an annexation agreement between the two cities and is within the exclusive annexing authority of the city that received the petition.)
3. The total satellite area or areas of the city may not exceed 10 percent of the area of the city within its primary limits. (Many cities have obtained local legislation from the General Assembly waiving this standard.)
4. The city must be able to provide the full range of city services to the satellite area.

The fourth standard deserves elaboration. One situation in which satellite annexation is sometimes sought is when the annexing city allows the sale of beer and wine or mixed drinks and the surrounding county does not. Owners of restaurants or grocery or convenience stores then seek annexation of their single lot or tract in order to sell beer and wine or mixed drinks. Sometimes these owners will assure the annexing city that they do not care about receiving city services and indeed will sign a waiver of such services. City officials need to understand that such a waiver probably

16. Cunningham v. City of Greensboro, 212 N.C App. 86 (2011); Conover v. Newton, 297 N.C. 506 (1979).

does not obviate the statutory responsibility of the city to be able to provide services and actually to provide them, and such a waiver most certainly does not bind subsequent owners of the property.

Voluntary Annexation of High Poverty and Distressed Areas

Amendments to the annexation laws enacted in 2011 addressed a common problem with the voluntary annexation procedures. Some areas outside of cities are developed and need services but are not attractive prospects for annexation because they have low property values. In addition, they tend to have high percentages of residents who rent rather than own their property, and property owners are required to petition for annexation. Neither the city nor the property owners are enthusiastic about annexation in these situations. The legislature amended the statute to *require* annexation of high poverty areas upon petition of the owners of 75 percent of the parcels in the area to be annexed.[17] This relaxes the usual requirement for 100 percent of the property owners to sign the petition. It also removes the discretion of the city to deny the petition, so long as the area and the petition meet the requirements in the statute. The statute defines a *high poverty* area as an area in which 51 percent of the households have incomes that are 200 percent or less than the most recent U.S. Census Bureau poverty thresholds. In addition, the population in the area to be annexed must not exceed 10 percent of the existing city population, and one-eighth of the external boundary of the area to be annexed must be contiguous to the existing city boundary. A city is not required to annex more than one of these areas within a thirty-six-month period.

A second provision allows residents (rather than property owners) in *distressed areas*—defined the same way as high poverty areas in the provision described above to petition for voluntary annexation.[18] Under this provision, the city may consider annexation if it receives petitions signed by at least one adult resident of at least two-thirds of the resident households in the area to be annexed. The statute allows the city to require reasonable proof that the petitioner actually resides at the address indicated. The area must be contiguous, but no minimum amount of contiguity is specified. This provision *does not require* the city to annex upon receipt of a valid petition.

Cities annexing under either of these provisions must provide services to the annexed areas in accordance with the provisions of the involuntary annexation statute, described below. This means that if the annexing city provides water and sewer services, lines must be extended at no cost to the annexed property owners. The voluntary annexation statute does allow a city to deny a petition from high poverty area property owners if the cost of extending lines is too high, as determined by a formula set out in the statute (G.S. 160A-31(d2)), and subject to review by the Local Government Commission. If a petition is denied, another request may not be filed within the next thirty-six months, but during that time, the law requires the city to make ongoing efforts to secure funding sufficient to make the extension feasible. The law also requires the relevant state agencies to give priority consideration to grant requests for water and sewer projects in these areas.

Involuntary Annexation

North Carolina's involuntary annexation statute, first enacted in 1959, was designed to balance the state's interest in the orderly expansion of city boundaries to include developed and developing urban territory against residents' and property owners' interest in receiving services equitably. The statute permits a city to annex an area that is developed in an urban manner if the city can demonstrate plans to provide adequate services to the area on the same basis as it provides services within the existing city. As noted earlier, amendments enacted in 2011 and 2012 added requirements for the city to pay for the cost of extending water and sewer services and a requirement for voter approval.

Minimum Standards for Areas to Be Annexed

To be subject to involuntary annexation, an area must meet three general conditions:

1. It must be contiguous to the existing city. Satellite annexations are not permitted under this procedure.

17. G.S. 160A-31(b1).
18. G.S. 160A-31(j).

2. One-eighth of the external boundary of the area to be annexed must coincide with the existing city boundary. This requirement is intended to avoid "shoestring" or "balloon" annexations, in which a large developed area is connected to the city by only a thin string of land, such as a road right-of-way.[19]
3. The area may not be part of an existing, active city.

In addition to these general standards, the area must be developed for *urban purposes* as defined in the statute. The statute sets out five standards under which an area meets the requirement that it be developed for urban purposes:[20]

1. Population Density Test: This standard looks solely to population and defines as urban any area with a population density of at least 2.3 persons per acre.
2. Subdivision and Density Test: This standard measures urban character by a combination of population and degree of land subdivision. It first requires a population of at least one person per acre. It then requires that at least 60 percent of the *acreage* be subdivided into lots and tracts of three acres or less in size and that at least 65 percent of the *lots and tracts* be no more than one acre in size.
3. Use and Subdivision Test: This standard measures urban character by the uses to which land is put and the degree to which land has been subdivided. In order to qualify, at least 60 percent of the area's *lots and tracts* must be in urban uses: residential, commercial, industrial, institutional, or governmental. The remaining non-urban properties must meet the *subdivision test,* which requires that at least 60 percent of the total *acreage* of land that is vacant or in agricultural, forest, or residential use be subdivided into lots or tracts of three acres or less in size.
4. Urban Use Test: This standard requires that *every lot or tract* in the annexation area be in one of four urban uses: commercial, industrial, institutional, or governmental.
5. Donut Holes: This standard allows annexation of areas that are completely surrounded by the city's primary corporate limits.

A city may qualify sub-areas within the total area to be annexed under any one of these tests such that the entire area to be annexed may comprise a combination of types of urbanized areas. In addition, a city may annex a limited number of non-urban areas when they are necessary bridges for providing services to the urban portions of the annexation area or because a non-urban area meets the following numerical test: at least 60 percent of the circumference of the non-urban area coincides with some combination of the borders of the existing city and the remainder of the annexation area.

Service Requirements to Annexed Areas

The city must be able to provide major services to the annexation area on the same basis as it provides these services to the existing city. The statute defines *major services* as police protection, fire protection, street maintenance, solid waste collection, water distribution, and sewerage collection and treatment. The city must extend the first four services—police, fire, street maintenance, and solid waste—into the annexation area immediately when the annexation becomes effective. If a city does not provide a particular service, it is not prohibited from annexing, nor is it required to offer it to newly annexed areas.

Water and Sewer Service Requirements

If a city provides water and sewer service, its obligation, effective with the passage of the 2011 revisions to the law, is to provide water and sewer service to each individual property at no cost to the property owner for the installation.[21]

---

19. Even meeting the one-eighth requirement may not be enough if a court considers the resulting annexation to be shoestring in nature. In *Amick v. Town of Stallings,* 95 N.C. App. 64 (1989), the court invalidated an annexation that met the one-eighth requirement by proposing to annex a thin strip (50 to 150 feet wide) along more than 7,400 feet of existing city boundary, thus extending a shoestring to annex two outlying subdivisions. The court held that the resulting annexation would have contravened the contiguity requirements of the annexation law. *Hughes v. Town of Oak Island,* 158 N.C. App. 175, *aff'd,* 357 N.C. 653 (2003), is a similar case.

20. G.S. 160A-58.54. Prior to 2011, cities under 5,000 in population were subject to slightly different requirements for qualifying areas for annexation and for providing services. The 2011 changes eliminated these separate requirements, replacing them with a single set of requirements that apply to all cities.

21. G.S. 160A-58.56.

Under this provision, at an early stage of the annexation procedure—just after the adoption of the resolution of intent to annex—the city must provide notice to the property owners in the annexed area describing their right to have water and sewer lines and connections installed and extended to their property at no cost to them (other than user fees). Property owners have sixty-five days to request service. The city's obligation to extend lines to these properties at no cost applies only if the owners of a majority of parcels in the area to be annexed request service. (If the owners of a majority of parcels opt in, the law requires a second notice to those who didn't, in case they want to opt in as well.) If the obligation to extend service is triggered, the city must complete all of the improvements necessary to provide water and sewer service to each property within three and a half years of the effective date of the ordinance. The language of the statute indicates that the required improvements include service to and within the property, including the part of the extension that becomes the private property of the owner.

If the owners of a majority of parcels do not request service within the initial time frame, the city is not required to extend service. If the city does extend the lines, and property owners later request service, the law sets a sliding scale (based on how much later the requests come in) that limits how much the city may charge these customers, expressed as a percentage of the total cost of connecting under the policies then in effect. This limitation on the amounts that may be charged applies to requests received within the first five years following annexation, after which property owners requesting service may be charged according the policies in effect at the time of the request.

The obligation to provide water and sewer services relates back to the provision that requires provision of services "on substantially the same basis and in the same manner as such services are provided in the rest of the municipality." So if a city doesn't provide or contract for the provision of water and sewer services, it does not apply.[22]

Procedure for Annexation; Referendum Requirement

The annexation procedures start when the city adopts a resolution of consideration identifying the area under consideration for annexation and provides notice of the resolution as provided in the statute.[23] At least one year after the resolution, a city may adopt a resolution of intent, which officially begins the annexation process for some or all areas identified in the resolution of consideration, as specified in the resolution of intent. The resolution of intent triggers the requirement to schedule the referendum.[24] Effective with the 2012 amendments to the statute, a city must place the question of annexation on the ballot at the next general municipal election. (As a practical matter this means that for most cities, annexation can occur only at one time every other year.) The annexation must be approved by a majority of voters in the area to be annexed. If the area has no residents, the statutory language suggests that involuntary annexation is simply not possible. If the annexation fails in the referendum, the city must wait at least thirty-six months before proceeding with involuntary annexation of the same area.

Following the notice of intent, and before the referendum, the process requires notice to owners of property who are eligible to receive water and sewer service. The city then must prepare a report that demonstrates how the area to be annexed meets the urbanization standards and describes the city's plans for extending and financing major services to the area. After notice to the residents and the property owners of the area, the city council holds a public information meeting on the proposal, at which citizens may ask questions about the annexation, and a public hearing, at which the council listens to public comment. If the statutory standards are met, the city is able to extend and finance the necessary services, the procedures have been followed, and the voters have approved the annexation, the city may adopt an ordinance to annex the property.

Annexation by Legislative Act

The General Assembly always has the authority to enlarge the boundaries of a city by local act. This was the original method used to effect annexations, and before 1947, it was the only method available. Although the legislature has essentially complete discretion in annexing territory to existing cities and no standards guide its decision making, in

22. G.S. 160A-58.56(a). The statute also provides that the city has no financial responsibility for the extension of lines if water and sewer services are provided under contract with another water or sewer system and the contract does not require the city to pay for extensions to annexed areas.

23. G.S. 160A-58.55.

24. G.S. 160A-58.64. Only residents in the area to be annexed may vote in the referendum.

practice it almost never does so except at the request of the city involved. Legislative annexation is especially useful for areas that need annexation but for some reason cannot be annexed under any of the other procedures. Annexation of public facilities surrounded by areas of limited development, annexation of areas involving lakes or rivers, and realignment of existing boundaries to match service areas all fall into this class. The General Assembly also has authority to de-annex, as described later in this chapter.

The Effect of Annexation on Existing Public Services

When a city annexes an area, in the absence of a statute protecting private service providers, the city becomes entitled to be the primary provider of municipal services in the annexation area. A case involving a Winston-Salem annexation illustrates this point.[25] Forsyth County had franchised a number of private solid waste collectors to collect residential and commercial solid waste in the area annexed. Upon annexation, and in conformity to its duties under the annexation statutes, Winston-Salem itself began to collect solid waste in the area. Because the city service was financed from taxes, which the residents had to pay in any event, the effect was to put the private haulers out of business in the annexation area. When they sued the city, the North Carolina Supreme Court held that the county franchises expired on annexation and that the city had no duty to cooperate with the private collectors or to compensate them for lost business. In the absence of a statute, the same rules would apply for other privately provided services.

A number of statutes have been adopted that modify this basic principle. These statutes protect volunteer fire departments and private solid waste collectors. They do not apply evenly to all annexation procedures, however.

Contracts with Fire Departments

If an area being annexed under the involuntary procedure is served by a volunteer fire department, the annexing city must make a good-faith effort to negotiate a contract with the fire department for the latter to continue to provide fire protection in the annexation area for five years. The statute defines what constitutes a *good-faith effort* and permits the fire department, if its officials think it has not received a good-faith offer, to appeal the matter to the state's Local Government Commission.[26] If the commission agrees with the fire department, it must delay the annexation until the city makes the necessary offer.

If a city annexes property under the voluntary procedures, however, or if the annexation is effected by legislative act, there is no statutory requirement to contract with a volunteer fire department.

Fire Department Debt

If a city has annexed territory under any of the *statutory* procedures, voluntary or involuntary, and has not contracted with a volunteer fire department, or if it has contracted with a volunteer fire department and the contract has expired, the city may be responsible for a portion of the outstanding indebtedness of the volunteer department.[27] The city's responsibility extends to any fire department debt that existed when the city began the annexation proceeding. The city's share of the debt repayment obligation is determined by the assessed valuation of the area annexed and served by the fire department in relation to the assessed valuation of the total area served by the fire department. Thus, if the city's annexation area represents 5 percent of the valuation of the fire district served by the fire department, the city must pay 5 percent of the department's debt obligation. This requirement does not apply to legislative annexations.

Contracts with Solid Waste Collectors

The result of the Winston-Salem case, described earlier, has been reversed by statute, but only in legislative annexations and in involuntary annexations.[28] If a private solid waste collector has been doing a substantial amount of business—at least fifty customers in the county in which the city is located—in an area annexed by a city, the collector is entitled either to have the city contract with it to continue collecting solid waste on the city's behalf for two years or to have the

25. Stillings v. City of Winston-Salem, 311 N.C. 689 (1984).
26. G.S. 160A-58.57.
27. *See* G.S. 160A-31.1 (voluntary contiguous); 160A-58.2A (voluntary satellite); 160A-58.58 (involuntary).
28. G.S. 160A-58.59 (involuntary); 160A-324 (legislative).

city make good the losses occasioned by the annexation (defined as fifteen times the firm's average monthly revenues in the annexation area). Like fire departments, the private firm enjoys a right to appeal to the state's Local Government Commission if the city does not offer a contract or compensation. This requirement does not apply to any voluntary annexations.

Taxation of Newly Annexed Property

G.S. 160A-58.10 sets out the rules to be followed in extending property taxes to areas annexed under any of the statutory methods. (Annexations effected by legislative act are frequently made subject to G.S. 160A-58.10 as well.) These rules apply to taxes for the fiscal year during which the annexation becomes effective.

Basically, owners of annexed property are liable for city taxes for that fiscal year on a prorated basis. The city determines what each property owner's tax liability would have been had the property been in the city for the entire fiscal year, then prorates that amount based on the number of full months remaining in the fiscal year on the effective date of annexation. For example, an annexation becomes effective on March 17. At that time, there are three full months remaining in the fiscal year: April, May, and June. Therefore, an owner who would have been liable for $600 of city taxes had his or her property been in the city the entire year will be liable for three-twelfths of an entire year's taxes, or $150. After that first year, property in the annexation area is taxed in the same manner as all other property in the city.

The preceding paragraph sets out the rules for determining the *amount* of tax owed by property owners in the annexation area. There are additional rules about the *date* on which those taxes are due. If the annexation occurs on or after July 1 and before September 1, the taxes are due on September 1, in the same manner as all other property taxes in the city. But if the annexation occurs on September 1 or later in the fiscal year, the prorated taxes are not due until the next September 1.

Annexation Disputes between Cities

Sometimes more than one city is interested in annexing the same parcel or parcels of property, and sometimes the owners of property in the area much prefer annexation by one city over annexation by another. The courts have looked to the doctrine of *prior jurisdiction* to determine which of two such cities is entitled to carry out the annexation. Under this doctrine, the city that takes the first formal statutory step toward annexation is entitled to complete its procedure without interference by the other. If this results in a valid annexation, the other city no longer has any rights of annexation over the disputed area.

The first formal step differs depending on the nature of the annexation. If it is an involuntary annexation, the first formal step is the city's adoption of the resolution of intent. If it is a voluntary annexation, the first formal step is when the annexation petitions are presented to the city's governing board.[29]

The statutes also permit cities that would rather avoid annexation fights of this sort to enter into agreements under which each city is granted a zone of territory that it has exclusive authority to annex.[30] These agreements may extend for up to twenty years, and a city must give five years' notice to withdraw from one. If a city attempts to annex territory in violation of such an agreement, any other city party to the agreement may bring an action to enforce it and thereby invalidate the annexation. (These agreements between cities are the only kind of contract authorized by law by which a city may agree in advance not to annex a particular parcel of property.)

De-annexation

There are no statutory procedures under which a city may de-annex territory. Rather, if a city or a property owner wants to subtract some part of the city's existing territory, the only way it may do so is to seek a local act of the General Assembly effecting the de-annexation. Such acts were quite rare and were only enacted at the request of the affected city until 2011. The 2011 and 2012 legislative sessions saw a marked increase in de-annexations, which accompanied the changes in the state-wide annexation laws. The de-annexations were opposed by the affected cities. The General

29. *See, e.g.,* City of Burlington v. Town of Elon Coll., 310 N.C. 723 (1984).

30. G.S. 160A-58.21 through -58.28.

Assembly is subject to no standards when it decides to de-annex territory, in the same way that no standards condition its ability to incorporate an area or annex territory to an existing city.

City–County Consolidation

City–county consolidation is the merger of a county government with one or more city governments. As a general rule, the city government is abolished and the county government is legally transformed into one that has all the powers and functions previously held by both governments. Authority for counties and cities to create special commissions to study consolidation and other forms of cooperative action, including the drafting of a charter for a consolidated government, is found in Article 20 of G.S. Chapter 153A.

The History of City–County Consolidation

City–county consolidation has a long history in the United States. New Orleans City and Parish were consolidated in 1813; Boston and Suffolk County in 1821; and Philadelphia City and County in 1854.

In North Carolina, interest in city–county consolidation also has a long history, beginning with a 1927 plan (never submitted to the voters) to consolidate the City of Charlotte and Mecklenburg County. Since that time, consolidation plans have been placed before the electorate four times in Wilmington and New Hanover County, twice in Durham and Durham County, and once each in Charlotte and Mecklenburg County and Asheville and Buncombe County. All the plans were rejected, but the margins of defeat have decreased in the places that have had more than one consolidation attempt. The results of the eight referenda on consolidation are shown in Table 2.1.

In every case, voters inside the city proposed for consolidation were more favorable toward the merger than those outside the city but inside the county. However, only in the three most recent votes—Wilmington and New Hanover County in 1987 and 1995, and Asheville and Buncombe County in 1982—have a majority of the voters inside the city involved favored merger.

Other moves toward city–county consolidation in the four counties mentioned earlier have been made in the past sixty years, but they all stopped short of the referendum. There were efforts in Charlotte-Mecklenburg and in Durham in the 1990s that led to proposed charters, but the governing boards decided not to submit those charters to the county's voters. Interest in consolidation, as evidenced by the creation of study groups, has also been present in recent years in a number of other cities and counties, including Brevard and Transylvania County, Fayetteville and Cumberland County, Roxboro and Person County, Sanford and Lee County, and Elizabeth City and Pasquotank County.

Advantages and Disadvantages of City–County Consolidation

The people who have supported consolidation have done so on the grounds of efficiency. They note that the county is a single social and economic community and argue that it could be better served by one local government than by two. They see better coordination of all government services and improved management of growth flowing from consolidation. Merger would also result in greater equity in taxation, in their view, because it typically involves the use of service districts in which taxation is tied to service levels. Proponents also argue that a single governing board, serving all citizens for all local government purposes, would be more responsive and responsible. Furthermore, they assert, consolidation would eliminate city–county conflicts and the objections to municipal annexation decisions being made by a governing board not responsive to those being annexed.

The opponents of consolidation, for their part, have put forth a host of objections. Citizens outside the central city fear that merger would, in effect, result in their being "swallowed up" by the "big city." They note that a merged government would be a larger one and argue that this would mean a less responsive and less efficient government. The fear of higher taxes, especially among residents outside the city, has usually been a major objection to consolidation.

Most of the plans for consolidation proposed in North Carolina have called for changes in the manner in which the governing board was elected and for the merger of administrative departments and offices. These proposed changes

Table 2.1. Results of City–County Consolidation Referenda in North Carolina

Governmental Units Involved	Date of Referendum	Votes For / Against	Percentage For / Against
Wilmington and New Hanover County	March 28, 1933	1,189 / 4,128	22 / 78
	February 27, 1973	4,040 / 11,722	26 / 74
	October 6, 1987	7,051 / 10,337	41 / 59
	October 10, 1995	11,377 / 15,923	42 / 58
Durham and Durham County	January 28, 1961	4,115 / 14,355	22 / 78
	September 10, 1974	6,198 / 13,124	32 / 68
Charlotte and Mecklenburg County	March 22, 1971	17,313 / 39,464	31 / 69
Asheville and Buncombe County	November 2, 1982	12,642 / 20,883	38 / 62

Source: Official election returns

have caused some citizens to fear a loss of political influence or jobs or both. Members of rural fire departments and employees of sheriffs' offices, for example, have usually opposed consolidation.

Residents of small towns in counties proposed for merger with a central city have usually opposed consolidation, even though their towns would continue to exist after the merger. They have seen the initial consolidation as a first step that might lead eventually to the merger of their towns and a loss of their identity.

The efforts at city–county consolidation have not yet culminated in a merger of any city and county governments in North Carolina. Almost all of them, however, have been a factor in promoting city–county cooperation by the merger of functions or by an increase in the joint use of facilities. For more information about city–county collaboration and interlocal cooperation, see Chapter 11, "Interlocal Cooperation, Shared Services, and Regional Councils."

Additional Resources

Lawrence, David M. *Incorporation of a North Carolina Town.* 2nd ed. Chapel Hill, N.C.: Institute of Government, University of North Carolina at Chapel Hill, 1998.

______. *Annexation Law in North Carolina* (3 volumes); Volume 1. *General Topics.* Chapel Hill, N.C.: Institute of Government, University of North Carolina at Chapel Hill, 2003.

______. *Annexation Law in North Carolina* (3 volumes); Volume 2. *Voluntary Annexation.* Chapel Hill, N.C.: Institute of Government, University of North Carolina at Chapel Hill, 2004.

______. *Annexation Law in North Carolina* (3 volumes); Volume 3. *Involuntary Annexation.* Chapel Hill, N.C.: Institute of Government, University of North Carolina at Chapel Hill, 2006.

City-County Consolidation in North Carolina, School of Government Website: www.sog.unc.edu/node/1677.

Additional information can be found by searching *Coates' Canons: NC Local Government Law Blog* (http://sogweb.sog.unc.edu/blogs/localgovt) using the keyword "annexation."

About the Author

Frayda S. Bluestein is a School of Government faculty member whose interests include incorporation and annexation.

This chapter updates and revises the previous chapter authored by David M. Lawrence, whose expertise and contributions to the field and to this publication are gratefully acknowledged.

Chapter 3

County and City Governing Boards

Vaughn Mamlin Upshaw

This chapter describes the governance structures under which North Carolina's city and county governing boards organize and conduct their activities. It also discusses legal responsibilities of and common expectations for county and city governing boards and their presiding officers, the board chair or mayor. The chapter concludes with a description of how a county or city governing structure may be changed.

Background

A county's governing body is known as the *board of county commissioners*. What is commonly referred to as a *city council* may be alternatively designated as the city's *board of aldermen, board of commissioners*, or *village* or *town council*. The name used makes no difference from a statutory standpoint and is not tied to population or authority; it is likely to have been chosen based on custom and local preference. For ease of reference, this chapter uses the term *council* to refer to a city's or town's governing board, and both cities and towns are referred to herein as *cities*. The terms *local governing board* and *governing board member(s)* are used when discussing matters that apply equally to boards of commissioners and city councils.

Introduction

Counties and cities are the main forms of general-purpose local governments in North Carolina. The state's General Statutes (hereinafter G.S.) provide counties and cities with different options for operation: The local governing body can (1) carry out local government responsibilities itself or (2) hire a professional to administer local government affairs on its behalf.[1] The General Statutes also describe alternatives for the structure of a county commission or city council.[2]

County governments affect every person who resides within North Carolina in one way or another. All of the state's residents live in a county, while slightly more than half of the population lives within a city.

Units of Government in North Carolina

Counties

North Carolina created county governments in the seventeenth and eighteenth centuries to give people greater access to public services and make it easier for them to conduct official business. Initially, the governor appointed justices of the peace to oversee each county and carry out the mandated policies and services of state government. Following the civil war, North Carolina adopted the Constitution of 1868, which gave citizens more input into electing their local leaders. Under the new constitution, citizens in each county elected the sheriff, coroner, register of deeds, clerk of court, surveyor, treasurer, and board of commissioners. The newly created county commissioners replaced the state-appointed justices of the peace and assumed full financial responsibility for the county, including adopting the budget and setting the property tax rate.[3]

Cities

Generally

The *mayor–council* form of government (where, as the name implies, local government administration is handled by a mayor, while policy making is the realm of the city/county's governing body) is the original form of general-purpose local government, descended from the English borough mayor-and-council system and instituted in the first American colonies. Throughout its long history and in its many variations—such as a bicameral council, a weak versus a strong mayor's office, and an at-large or a ward system—it has been successfully employed from the smallest colonial town dependent on ferry tolls for operating expenses, to the modern megalopolis with a multi-billion-dollar budget.

Early in America's history, as cities grew in wealth, responsibility, and bureaucracy, a patronage system emerged. Popular dissatisfaction grew in cities that experienced corruption, inefficiency, and political favoritism. These dif-

1. *See* N.C. Gen. Stat. (hereinafter G.S.) § 153A-76 (counties); 160A-146 (cities).

2. *See* G.S. 153A-58 (counties); 160A-101 (cities).

3. For more about local government in North Carolina, see Chapter 1, "An Overview of Local Government." For more on the history of North Carolina county governments, see the N.C. Association of County Commissioners' web page, "What Is a County," at www.welcometoyourcounty.org/content/what_is_a_county.shtm.

ficulties may be blamed as much on the people in government—or on the size of the government—as on the form of government (mayor–council was the preferred form).

Due to these kinds of problems with government, in the first decade of the twentieth century the *council–manager* form of government emerged as an alternative to the prevailing norm (the mayor–council plan had up until then been the exclusive form of municipal government in the United States). The council–manager form has steadily increased in popularity since its inception, and it is now the principal form of municipal government in U.S. cities with populations between 2,500 and 250,000. The mayor–council form, in either its strong-mayor or weak-mayor variation, predominates in cities in both the smaller (less than 2,500) and larger (more than 250,000) population classes.

Means of Organizing

The form of government under which a North Carolina city may operate is set forth in the city's charter. An initial charter results from an act of the state legislature. Changing the form of city government requires the adoption of an ordinance or a change to the city's charter. The options for changing the form of city government are described in more detail later in this chapter.

Mentioned briefly above and in more detail below, the council–manager form of government is one option available to cities under the General Statutes (see Chapter 4, "County and City Managers"). As cities get larger and services more complex, communities often decide that a change is needed. Some cities change their form of government and hire a city manager (i.e., adopt the council–manager form of government), while others hire a chief administrator without immediately changing the form of government and then after some successful experience with that arrangement, make the full transition to the council–manager form. Under G.S. 160A-148, adoption of the council–manager form requires that the manager be given hiring and firing authority over all employees not otherwise hired by the council. As a result, councils that want to retain this authority but also want the help of a chief administrative officer retain the mayor–council form and hire an administrator. No charter amendment is required for a city council to hire an administrator, but if a city wants to adopt the council–manager form, it may do so only by amending its charter in one of four defined ways.

Organizing North Carolina Cities—By the Numbers

The mayor–council form remains the principal form of local government in North Carolina today. In 2014, it was used by 299 (or 54 percent) of the state's 553 cities. It predominates among cities with populations of less than 2,500. The council–manager plan has been the exclusive form in large (25,000+) cities in North Carolina since the late 1940s, and it is used by most cities with populations between 2,500 and 25,000. Cities in this range have also tended over the last forty years to shift from the mayor–council plan to the council–manager plan.

In 2014, only 18 percent (nine of fifty) of North Carolina cities with populations between 5,000 and 10,000 used the mayor–council form of government. The distribution of mayor–council cities in cities with populations under 5,000 in 2014 is shown in Table 3.1.

County and City Governing Boards in North Carolina

Generally

There is no typical structure for a county board of commissioners or a city council in North Carolina. Each county board's structure is set out in local legislation of the General Assembly, while each city board's structure is set out in the city charter. Both local acts and charters exhibit considerable variety as to governing body size; whether members are elected by district or at large; and whether terms are for two years or four. All 100 boards of county commissioners in North Carolina are elected in partisan elections, while almost all city council elections are nonpartisan. Despite the absence of a typical board structure, it is useful to examine the patterns found in the various board structures and also look at the trend of structural change in recent years. (Appendix 3.1A contains summary figures on the structures of the governing boards of North Carolina cities; comparable information on counties is tabulated by the North Carolina Association of County Commissioners and can be found at www.ncacc.org/index.aspx?nid=195.)

Table 3.1 Prevalence of Mayor–Council Form of Government in Small North Carolina Cities, by Population

Population Class	Under 500	500–1,000	1,000–2,500	2,500–5,000	Total
Number of Cities	127	93	111	90	421
Mayor–Council Cities	119	86	58	26	289
Percent Using Mayor–Council Form, by Pop. Class	94%	92%	52%	29%	68%

Source: "Forms of North Carolina City Government" (School of Government web page), www.sog.unc.edu/programs/cityfog.

Size of Board

County boards of commissioners range in size from three members to nine, although only five have more than seven members. By far the most popular county board size is five. City councils range in size from two members to eleven, although only two have more than eight members. As with county boards, five is the most popular size for city councils.

Length of Members' Terms

All terms, both for county commissioners and for city council members, are for two years or four, with the larger number of governing boards having four-year terms. Most boards with four-year terms stagger elections so that about half the members are elected every two years; of all the changes made to governing boards in recent years, instituting a staggered four-year term has been the most prevalent. This staggering ensures a degree of continuity in county and municipal affairs and a constant level of experience.

Election at Large or by District

Slightly more than half of the boards of county commissioners in North Carolina elect at least some of their members from specific districts. The remaining boards are elected from the county at large, although more than half of these counties require commissioners to reside in their respective districts. In contrast, nearly all city councils—more than 85 percent statewide—are elected from the city at large. Only twelve of the 330+ cities in the state with populations under 2,500 use any sort of electoral district.

Election on a Partisan or Nonpartisan Basis

As was noted above, all 100 boards of county commissioners in North Carolina are elected on a partisan basis, with the elections occurring in even-numbered years. On the other hand, more than 98 percent of city councils are elected on a nonpartisan basis. Most of these, particularly those in smaller cities, are elected on a plurality basis, without a primary. All but a few city elections take place in odd-numbered years.[4]

Designation and Composition

Smaller cities sometimes have three council members and a mayor responsible for local government operations, while larger cities will usually have five or six council members and a mayor. Most council members are elected on an at-large (meaning they represent/are voted in by qualified voters from the entire city, not merely one district therein), nonpartisan basis. However, two or more electoral districts may be established from which some or all of the council members are elected. The district candidates may be elected exclusively by residents of the district in which they live or by the electorate at large.

---

4. High Point, Archdale, Pilot Mountain, and Dobson currently hold elections in even-numbered years. High Point is moving back to odd-numbered years beginning in 2017. Those elected in High Point in 2014 will serve a three-year term until the next election in 2017.

Presiding Officers on Governing Boards

The Chair of the Board of Commissioners

In most counties, the board of commissioners itself selects its chair, who is to preside at all board meetings. Unless directly elected by the voters, the chair serves a term of one year. By law, this official has the same right—indeed duty—to vote on all questions before the board unless excused by a standing rule of the body. However, the chair may not vote to break a tie on any vote in which he or she participated.[5] The chair is generally recognized by law as the county's chief executive officer and may acquire considerable prestige and influence by virtue of the position. Although as a general rule chairs have no more legal power than other members of the board, they do have special authority to declare states of emergency under the state laws governing riots and civil disorders, and they have authority to call special meetings of the board on their own initiative.[6]

Unlike mayors of cities (who are expressly prohibited under G.S. 160A-151 from assuming the duties of the city manager on any basis), chairs of county boards of commissioners are able to perform county manager duties by action of the board in accordance with G.S. 153A-81.

The Mayor

Mayors in North Carolina enjoy very few formal powers. With a limited number of exceptions, their powers consist of presiding at governing board meetings, voting to break ties at those meetings (at no other time can they be tie-breakers), and signing documents on behalf of the city. The *strong-mayor system* used in many of the nation's large cities, under which the mayor is charged with actually running city government, is simply not found in this state. However, despite having so few formal powers, many North Carolina mayors do exercise great influence in the operation of their cities. It is common, for example, for the city council to delegate to the mayor responsibilities such as working with the clerk to create council agendas, representing the city on regional advisory boards, or serving as the primary contact for local media.

Most of the powers held by mayors in the state are created by individual city charters, by action of the particular mayor's city council, or by the mayor's own political stature. G.S. 160A-67 confers on a mayor all powers and duties enumerated in the General Statutes, as well as any others conferred on him or her by the city council. This statute recognizes the mayor as the official head of the city for purposes of serving civil process, and most federal and state agencies extend this same recognition for purposes of official correspondence or actions such as grant awards or enforcement of federal laws and regulations. G.S. 160A-69 requires the mayor to preside at council meetings, and G.S. 160A-71 gives the mayor the power to call special meetings of the council.

All but a few mayors in North Carolina are elected by the voters of a given city. In a few cities, the governing board elects the mayor from its own ranks. If the people elect the mayor, he or she may, by local charter or ordinance, be given the right under G.S. 160A-101 to vote on all matters before the council; alternatively, the mayor may only have the right to vote to break a tie. If the mayor is selected from the membership of the council, he or she does not give up his or her vote as a member of the council and may vote on all matters.

Much of the electorate of a city, along with those who serve in city office, may view the office of mayor as the chief political office in local government. By force of that perception, combined with the strength of their personalities, many mayors effectively lead their governing boards. In small cities without a manager, the mayor often serves as de facto chief administrator simply because he or she is willing to work long hours in the town hall. In council–manager cities, discussed in more detail later in this chapter, when there is a managerial vacancy, the mayor might seem like a natural choice as a stand-in until another manager can be found. However, G.S. 160A-151 expressly makes the mayor (and any member of the city council) ineligible to serve as manager, interim manager (temporarily filling a vacancy), or acting manager (serving in the manager's absence). Under this provision, the mayor could always resign his or her office and be appointed as manager, but he or she could not hold the elected and appointed offices at the same time.

---

5. G.S. 153A-39.
6. G.S. 153A-40.

Common Expectations of Board Chairs and Mayors

Expectation 1: The chair/mayor effectively manages governing board meetings by

- presiding at the meetings,
- being a good timekeeper,
- keeping governing board members' dialogue on track,
- focusing on the job at hand,
- staying on topic,
- paying attention to the board's feedback on the conduct of meetings, and
- avoiding introducing and making important decisions at the same meeting.

Expectation 2: The chair/mayor serves as liaison to the governing board by

- staying on top of matters coming before the board,
- overseeing relations with stakeholders in between board meetings,
- testing the board's preliminary ideas with key stakeholders between meetings, and
- asking external stakeholders to provide input on strategic issues.

Expectation 3: The chair/mayor facilitates communication by

- treating everyone in an even-handed and fair manner,
- managing governing board member contributions so that no one member dominates,
- encouraging board members to express opinions and perspectives,
- engaging more reticent members in discussion,
- fostering healthy participation, especially among those with different views, and
- employing effective group processes, making it safe to explore alternate views.

Expectation 4: The chair/mayor serves as spokesperson for the governing board by

- being a strong advocate and credible representative of local government and the board,
- honoring the "one voice" principle whereby a vote of a majority of council members is recognized as the board's final decision,
- speaking knowledgeably and energetically about the board's accomplishments and opportunities for the community,
- using the "Five F's" (**F**ast, **F**actual, **F**rank, **F**air, and **F**riendly),
- thinking before speaking (imagine what statements will sound like on the evening news before speaking—don't say more than necessary),
- staying on message,
- not answering questions "off the record,"
- remembering the role of the media and the part it plays in democratic government, and
- talking with the press in advance of a big issue to help reporters anticipate important stories.

Expectation 5: The chair/mayor helps in city/county government team-building by

- gaining the trust and respect of fellow team members,
- building positive and productive relationships with the manager or administrator,
- acknowledging the contributions of governing board members,
- developing and maintaining teamwork between board members and professional staff,
- being aware of and seeking to improve board dynamics,
- learning to "lead from behind" so that others can share in accomplishments, and
- creating a positive culture and establishing expectations that the board and management will work as a team.

Expectation 6: The chair/mayor manages conflict by

- increasing governing board consciousness of group dynamics—promoting desirable outcomes as to matters relating to group norms, value differences, diversity, honesty, questioning, conflict, and dialogue,
- suspending judgment until all perspectives have been shared,
- being independent (able to disagree without being disagreeable),
- modeling good listening and inquiry skills, and
- managing conflict on the board constructively.

Expectation 7: The chair/mayor shapes the governing board's agenda by

- actively working with board members and the manager or administrator to identify agenda items,
- working with the manager and others (as locally determined) to establish the board's agenda, and
- planning meetings to allow enough time for members to discuss and explore issues and viewpoints.

Expectation 8: The chair/mayor promotes a high-performing governing board by

- demonstrating an understanding of local government and the environment in which it operates,
- learning skills in managing group dynamics,
- using techniques to help the board look at things differently and from alternative points of view,
- giving the manager and senior staff opportunities to contribute to the board's dialogue,
- making sure members of the board read materials in advance and ask for necessary information in a timely and efficient manner,
- being prepared for meetings,
- offering and inviting constructive feedback,
- seeking out opportunities to develop the board's effectiveness,
- supporting the board–manager or board–administrator relationship, and
- mentoring newer members.

Responsibilities of the Governing Board

A county's or city's governing board holds ultimate authority to act for the local government. It decides what services the county or city will provide and at what level. It establishes the county's or city's fiscal policy by adopting the annual budget ordinance, and it levies the unit's taxes. It adopts the county's or city's ordinances. In addition to exercising these sorts of broad policy-making responsibilities, a governing board typically decides numerous separate administrative matters. Thus, it may authorize the local government to enter into a contract, buy or sell a parcel of property, award the successful bid on a purchase or a construction project, or accept the dedication of a street or utility easement.

As it takes all of these actions—among others—the county or city governing board must act as a collective body. A county or city has a legal existence separate from its residents; a board of county commissioners or city council is a body separate from its members. The members may act as the governing board only when properly convened, in a legal meeting. An individual member may not act on the board's behalf without specific authorization from the board. Moreover, a majority of the entire membership may act on the board's behalf only at a meeting of the board called and held pursuant to law. Legal procedures governing board meetings and actions are described in more detail in Chapter 9, "Open Meetings and Other Legal Requirements for Local Government Boards."

Statutory Duties—County Board of Commissioners

Regardless of the form of government, state law gives a county's board of commissioners broad authority to organize county government.[7] The board of commissioners may create, change, abolish, and consolidate offices, positions, departments, boards, commissions, and agencies of the county government; impose ex officio the duties of more than

7. County boards of commissioners' powers are described in G.S. 153A-76.

one office on a single officer; change the composition and manner of selection of boards, commissions, and agencies; and generally organize and reorganize county government in order to promote orderly and efficient administration of county affairs, subject to the following limitations:

1. The board of county commissioners may not abolish an office, position, department, board, commission, or agency established or required by law.
2. The board may not combine offices or confer certain duties on the same officer when law specifically forbids this action.
3. The board may not discontinue or assign elsewhere a function or duty assigned by law to a particular office, position, department, board, commission, or agency.
4. The board may not change the composition or manner of selection of local boards of education, boards of health, boards of social services, boards of elections, or boards of alcoholic beverage control. By law (G.S. 153A-77), these boards appoint their agency directors. A board of commissioners may create a consolidated health and human services board to which they appoint a director.

This seemingly broad grant of responsibility nonetheless leaves many county functions outside the commissioners' direct control. For example:

- The sheriff[8] and the register of deeds[9] are elected officers.
- Board of education members are separately elected and appoint the superintendent.[10]
- The state board of elections appoints the local board, which, in turn, appoints the director of elections.[11]
- In most counties, the directors of health and social services are appointed by their respective boards. County commissioners are authorized by law to appoint the director of a consolidated health and human services agency.[12]

These exceptions notwithstanding, the commissioners still have fairly broad authority to organize the administrative apparatus of county government to carry out the board's policies, including the option of appointing a county manager to oversee the administration of county services. This option is discussed further below.

Organizational Meeting—County Board of Commissioners

New boards of commissioners usually take their oaths of office, and the board as a whole selects its chair, at the board's first regular meeting in December in odd-numbered years or on the first Monday in December in even-numbered years.[13] In three counties, the chair is a separate office elected by the people; in a fourth county, the highest vote-getter among the commissioners is automatically designated chair.[14] In all counties in North Carolina, the board itself must choose a vice-chair at its organizational meeting to act in the absence or disability of the chair.[15]

8. Article VII, Section 2, of the North Carolina Constitution.

9. *See* G.S. 161-1.

10. *See* G.S. 115C-271.

11. G.S. 163-30.

12. See G.S. 153A-77, which authorizes boards of commissioners to create consolidated human services agencies, which may include public health, social services, or both. A consolidated human services agency is governed by a consolidated human services director, who is appointed by the county manager with the advice and consent of a consolidated human services board. If the consolidated agency includes public health or social services, the consolidated director acquires the powers and duties ordinarily exercised by the directors of those individual agencies. G.S. 153A-77 also authorizes boards of commissioners to directly assume the powers and duties of certain boards, potentially including the local board of health, social services board, or consolidated human services board. A board of commissioners that exercises this authority may thus acquire the power to appoint the directors of health or social services or to give advice and consent to the appointment of a consolidated human services director. For more information, see Chapter 38, "Public Health," and Chapter 39, "Social Services."

13. G.S. 153A-39.

14. Voters in three counties—Buncombe, Jackson, and Swain—elect the chair of the board directly. See http://ncacc.org/index.aspx?nid=195 for more information about county election methods.

15. G.S. 153A-39.

Appointment of County Officers, Boards, and Commissions

The law dictates many features of county government organization. For example, the people elect each county's sheriff and register of deeds. Each county has at least one board of education (and such boards are separate from county government) and a board of elections. A board of health, a social services board (or a consolidated human services agency board), and a mental health, developmental disabilities, and substance abuse board serves every county. Many counties have a community college board and a board of alcoholic beverage control, both separate from county government. The board of county commissioners participates in choosing at least some of the members of all of these boards, except for the board(s) of education (whose members are wholly elected by citizens) and the board of elections (whose members are appointed by the State Board of Elections). Because these excepted boards are established pursuant to the requirements of state law, a board of county commissioners has little or no power to alter their structure or authority, although the county board may exercise control over the budgets of some of them. (The roles of most of these other boards are discussed in later chapters.) A board of county commissioners has authority to organize other local boards, agencies, departments, and offices not mandated by state law in any way it sees fit.

Three principal officials serve the board of county commissioners, and the board itself appoints them directly: the county manager, the county attorney, and the clerk to the board. This power pertains whether the governing board is operating as a board of commissioners or under the county–manager plan. The process for adopting a county–manager plan is described below. (Chapter 4 outlines county and city manager statutory powers and duties and professional responsibilities. The powers and duties of the county attorney and the clerk to the board are discussed in Chapter 14.) Each of these appointed officials serves at the pleasure of the board. The county commissioners also appoint the tax assessor,[16] and county boards (in addition to city governing boards) are authorized to appoint a tax collector.[17] In practice, many cities contract with the county for tax collection. Each county (and city) in North Carolina is required by law to have a finance officer.[18] In many counties (and cities), the manager appoints the finance officer.[19] In counties (and cities) without a manager, the governing board usually makes the appointment; the finance officer serves at the pleasure of the appointing authority. See Chapter 22, "Accounting, Fiscal Control, and Cash Management."

Statutory Duties—City Council

Regardless of the form of government, G.S. 160A-67 states that "except as otherwise provided by law, the government and general management of the city shall be vested in the council." The city council has authority to confer powers and duties on both the mayor and the manager in addition to the duties conferred on each official by law. Further, under G.S. 160A-146, the council has authority to organize and reorganize city government. The council can, except when expressly prevented by other laws, ". . . create, change, abolish, and consolidate offices, positions, departments, boards, commissions, and agencies . . . to promote orderly and efficient administration of city affairs . . . ." Finally, G.S. 160A-147 provides that in a council–manager city (discussed more below), the council as a body appoints the city manager to serve at its pleasure. Thus, by statute, the city council has the primary responsibility for establishing the general framework under which the government can meet the needs of the community and, as the employer of the manager, the council is the body to which the manager is directly responsible and accountable.

Organizational Meeting—City Council

A new council usually takes office at its first regular meeting in December after the results of the city elections have been certified. At this time, the members take the oath of office and organize the government so that business may be conducted.[20] The council must appoint a mayor pro tempore to preside over it and to fulfill the other duties of the mayor when he or she is absent or incapacitated.[21]

16. G.S. 105-294.
17. G.S. 105-349.
18. G.S. 159-24.
19. G.S. 153A-82 (counties); 160A-148 (cities).
20. G.S. 160A-68.
21. G.S. 160A-70.

Appointment of City Officers, Employees, Boards, and Commissions

Generally

The city charter and state statutes spell out governing board appointments for the manager, the city attorney, and the city clerk. In some cases the charter may also provide for the appointment of a deputy clerk. In council–manager cities, the manager appoints all other city officers and employees. In a number of cities with managers, the board appoints the tax collector and the finance officer and, depending upon the city charter, the manager or the council appoints the clerk. In a city without a manager, the board appoints all department heads and normally delegates to them the appointment and the supervision of other employees, although in a few mayor–council cities the board delegates employee appointment and supervision to an administrator. For more on the options for appointing clerks, see Chapter 14 covering attorneys and clerks.

The board and the mayor are also responsible for appointments to the various boards and commissions of city government, such as the planning commission, boards of adjustment, the parks and recreation commission, and the civil service board. (In most cases the board makes the appointments; the mayor, however, is by statute the appointing official for the housing authority.) The number of board or commission members and their terms of office are established by general law authorizing such boards or by ordinance implementing the authority granted by statute. In addition, the council is authorized to create special citizen advisory committees, such as a human relations committee, and to appoint their members.[22]

Officers and Employees

A city's charter ordinarily states that certain officers and employees will be appointed by the city council and specifies each officer/employee's duties. The General Statutes (relevant sections are indicated in parentheses in the discussion below) require that the following officers be appointed and have, in addition to any other duties specified by the council, the general duties as described below.

City Clerk (G.S. 160A-171). The clerk is responsible for giving the proper notices of regular and special meetings of the council, keeping an accurate journal of the council's proceedings, and acting as custodian of city records. A *deputy clerk* may (but need not) be appointed to perform whatever duties of the clerk the council specifies (G.S. 160A-172).

City Budget Officer (G.S. 159-9). The budget officer receives budget requests and revenue estimates from the various city departments, prepares a proposed budget for submission to the council, and complies with other requirements concerning budget preparation and administration prescribed by the General Statutes. Unlike cities with a council–manager form of government—where the city manager is the budget officer—cities with the mayor–council plan may designate any city officer or employee (including the mayor, if he or she agrees) as budget officer.

City Finance Officer (G.S. 159-24). The finance officer may also be called the *accountant, treasurer,* or *finance director.* He or she has general responsibility for keeping the accounts and disbursing the city's funds in a manner consistent with General Statute provisions pertaining to the finance officer's duties (G.S. 159-25). These duties may be conferred on the budget officer or on another officer or employee who is eligible to perform the duties of budget officer.

City Attorney (G.S. 160A-173). The council must appoint a city attorney to be its legal advisor. He or she serves at the council's pleasure.

City Tax Collector (G.S. 105-349). The tax collector has the general responsibility for collecting property, privilege license, and all other taxes due the city and for fulfilling the other duties imposed by the General Statutes concerning tax collection (G.S. 105-350). Any officer or employee may be appointed tax collector, except a member of the governing body; the finance officer may be appointed to the office only with the Local Government Commission's consent. Many cities, both large and small, contract with the county to collect their taxes.

Department Heads and Employees

Under the mayor–council form of government, the council is responsible for (1) establishing the city operating departments deemed necessary or desirable (see next paragraph for examples) and (2) appointing, suspending, and removing department heads and all other city employees. It may delegate to an administrative officer or a department head the

22. For more information on this topic, see Vaughn Mamlin Upshaw, *Creating and Maintaining Effective Local Government Citizen Advisory Committees* (UNC School of Government, 2010).

authority to appoint, suspend, or remove employees assigned to that department (G.S. 160A-155). In mayor–council cities with populations of less than 5,000, the mayor and the members of the council may serve as department heads or as other city employees and may receive reasonable compensation. In mayor–council cities with populations of 5,000 or more, and in council–manager cities, they may not do so (G.S. 160A-158).

Typical city departments considered "necessary or desirable" are police, fire, water, streets, sanitation, recreation, planning, and inspections. The council may combine the responsibilities of departments or appoint one person to supervise several departments or to fill duties in more than one department (G.S. 160A-146). For example, a public works director may be appointed to supervise both the streets and sanitation departments, or the fire chief may also be assigned the duties of building inspector.

Vacancies on Governing Boards

When there is a vacancy on a board of county commissioners or city council (including a vacancy in the office of mayor),[23] state law gives the remaining members of the board or council the authority to fill the vacancy.[24] The statute pertaining to cities leaves the process fairly open to the council's discretion for the majority of cities that elect members on a nonpartisan basis. The statute for counties creates a role for political parties in recommending or choosing replacements, as described in more detail below.

In both counties and cities, if the vacancy occurs in an office carrying a two-year term or in the last two years of an office with a four-year term, the appointment is for the remainder of the unexpired term. If the vacancy takes place in the first two years of an office with a four-year term, the appointment runs only until the next general election, at which the office is filled for the unexpired term.[25] In addition, the statutes for both cities and counties set out contingency procedures for situations when the number of vacancies is such that a quorum is not possible.[26]

There are no public records or open meetings exceptions for the consideration of nominees or applicants for council or board vacancies. Indeed, the open meetings law specifically prohibits the consideration or evaluation of members or potential members of the governing board from being discussed in closed sessions of that board.[27]

Counties

A person appointed to fill a vacancy on a board of county commissioners must belong to the same political party as the person he or she is replacing, if the person being replaced was elected as the nominee of a political party. If the county is divided into electoral districts, the appointee must also reside in the same district as the person being replaced. The board is required to consult the executive committee of the relevant political party before making the appointment.[28] In many counties, the board is not required to follow any advice given by the executive committee. Nearly half of the state's counties are governed by a modified version of this procedure, however, under which the board *must* appoint the executive committee's nominee if the recommendation is made within thirty days after the seat becomes vacant.[29]

Occasionally, a majority of a board of county commissioners is unable to agree on which person to appoint to fill a vacancy. Since nearly all of these boards have an odd number of members, one vacancy means that the remaining

23. G.S. 160A-63 authorizes the city to fill a vacancy in any elective office of the city.

24. G.S. 160A-63 (cities); 153A-27, -27.1 (counties).

25. If the vacancy occurs at the very end of the first two years of an office with a four-year term, so that there is no time to file for the midterm election, the board fills the vacancy for the remainder of the unexpired term. In county government, this period is the sixty days before the general election, while in city government, it is the ninety days before the city election.

26. *See* G.S. 153A-27, -27.1 (for counties, the chair must appoint enough members to make a quorum, and the board then fills the remaining vacancies; if the office of chair is also vacant, the clerk of superior court may act in the chair's stead on petition of any remaining member of the board or any five registered voters of the county); 160A- 63 (for cities, the mayor must appoint enough members to make a quorum, and the council then fills the remaining vacancies; if there are not enough members for a quorum and the mayor's office is vacant, the governor may fill the vacancy upon request of any remaining council member or by petition of any five registered voters of the city).

27. *See* G.S. 143-318.11(a)(6).

28. G.S. 153A-27.

29. See G.S. 153A-27.1, which lists the affected counties.

members could become equally divided over two candidates, so that neither candidate could receive a majority vote. If for this or any other reason the board fails to fill a vacancy in its membership within sixty days, the clerk to the board must report it to the clerk of superior court, who must fill the vacancy within ten days after receiving the report.

Cities

In cities that hold nonpartisan elections, the council may appoint any person who is eligible to vote in city elections to fill a council vacancy. In cities whose councils are elected on a partisan basis, a person appointed to fill a vacancy must belong to the same political party as the person he or she is replacing, if that person was elected as the nominee of a political party.

In some cities, it is common to fill a council vacancy with the unsuccessful candidate in the most recent city election with the most votes, but there is no general statutory requirement to follow this practice. Unlike the statute covering counties, the statute for cities does not provide for an alternative method of filling the vacancy if the city council becomes deadlocked or for any other reason does not fill a vacancy.[30] For cities, there is no statutory requirement that a vacancy be filled within any particular time. A council has an obligation, nonetheless, to act in good faith to attempt to fill a vacancy within a reasonable period of time. In a representative government, the people deserve to have a full complement of lawmakers to engage in legislative debate and exercise communal wisdom on their behalf.

Organizing the Supervision of Officers and Employees in Mayor–Council Cities

In organizing, directing, and supervising the various functions or departments of municipal government, the city council may use one of several administrative or organizational plans, unless the city charter provides otherwise. Whatever type of administrative plan is used, it is important for the council to define clearly the responsibilities of each officer or department; to coordinate, as far as possible, the activities of each; to establish clear lines of authority between the council, the department heads, and employees; and in general, to establish a sound administrative plan that will enable the council to adequately supervise all municipal activities.

Three basic administrative plans are used in cities under the mayor–council form of government: (1) the entire council directly supervises all departments of city government; (2) one council member is assigned to supervise each department; and (3) committees of the council supervise one or more functions or departments. The specifics of each plan are discussed below.

1. Direct Supervision of All Departments by Council as a Whole

Under this organizational plan, the council appoints and removes all department heads and directs and supervises each in carrying out his or her duties. Each department head or officer reports directly to the council and is responsible to it for the operation of his or her department. This plan is widely used but can be cumbersome if the particular city has many departments. It is probably best suited to small cities with not more than three or four departments or functions that require the council's direct supervision.

2. Assignment of Council Members to Departments

Under this administrative arrangement, a designated city council member has charge of a specific department and may exercise such administrative control over the operation of the department and its head as the council may direct. The department head or officer is directly responsible to the selected council member rather than to the entire council, although personnel decisions for the department, such as hiring and termination, remain the responsibility of the entire council. The supervising member reports to and recommends measures to the entire council regarding the department's affairs. This system expedites the administration of departmental affairs, but council members may become more concerned with their respective departments than with the total operation and administration of all departments, which is the council's principal responsibility.

---

30. Depending upon the method used to submit nominees for consideration, the mayor may or may not be able to break a tie. The mayor has authority under G.S. 160A-69 to vote in the case of an equal number of "yes" and "no" votes. If a motion is made to nominate a particular person, and the votes are equally divided for and against, the mayor can break the tie as provided in the statute. If, however, multiple names are submitted for consideration and votes are taken using a ballot method, it's possible for two individual candidates to receive equal numbers of votes. Because of the wording of the statute, the mayor cannot break this type of tie vote.

3. Committee System

The city council in this organizational approach creates committees of the council to study and make recommendations concerning the operation of the respective city departments; in some places these committees are given the authority to supervise departmental operations. When this system is used, the committees are normally assigned general areas of responsibility that may include several departments. For example, supervision of police, fire, and inspection services might be assigned to a public safety committee that is comprised of several council members. Governing bodies should be aware that committees of the council are themselves considered public bodies under the open meetings law and thus must comply with that statute's requirements.

The number of committees and their membership will vary depending on the council's size, the number of departments, and other factors. If the city charter is silent regarding requirements for committees, the council itself may establish committees and assign them such duties, consistent with the charter and general laws of the state, as it deems best. Suggested committee structures for a council consisting of a mayor and five council members appear in Table 3.2A, below; a break-down of common assignments is shown in Table 3.2B, below.

Best Practices for County and City Governing Boards

County and city governing boards must operate transparently, in a public setting, and are entrusted to carry out their work legally and ethically. Local governing boards have a direct influence on the culture, effectiveness, and efficiency of county and city governments and function best when they adopt common expectations for their work, examples of which are provided below.

Expectation 1: The governing board sets direction by

- clarifying the local government's mission and purposes and setting goals for the short and long term,
- adopting policies to accomplish these purposes and employing professional public managers and administrators as needed for administrative functions and service operations,
- engaging regularly in strategy development (e.g., during an annual retreat), and
- routinely monitoring and evaluating local government's ability to administer and provide efficient and effective public services.

Expectation 2: The governing board acts as a body by

- focusing its discussion by using clear and consistent rules of procedure, following a planned agenda, and spending time on important topics,
- understanding its (the governing board's) own legal and ethical responsibilities, as well as those of the local government,
- making sure all board members have the same information with which to make decisions,
- working to master small-group decision-making techniques,
- respecting one another and abiding by the decisions of the board's majority, and
- making clear to the public that decision-making power rests with the majority, not with individual board members.

Expectation 3: The governing board serves citizens well by

- enhancing the local government's public image,
- providing citizens opportunities to respectfully comment on public issues,
- ensuring the success and viability of the community by convening and facilitating citizen engagement, and
- making sure that resources are adequate to serve the public and are used for their intended purposes.

Expectation 4: The governing board respects the role of the manager by

- channeling communications appropriately to the manager or other responsible person,
- depending upon employees to respond to citizen concerns and complaints as fully and as expeditiously as practical,

- expecting staff to make independent and objective recommendations,
- expecting the manager, administrator, and staff to support and advocate for adopted board policies,
- respecting the professionals who work in local government and following appropriate protocols for interacting with staff, and
- refraining from publicly criticizing an individual employee (where criticism is differentiated from questioning the facts or opinions of staff).

Expectation 5: The board takes responsibility for its members' behaviors by

- abstaining from seeking political support from staff,
- submitting questions about board agenda items ahead of the meeting,
- providing each member an opportunity to influence and respectfully dissent in board meetings,
- focusing on issues, not personalities,
- having members themselves address inappropriate behavior in their ranks rather than delegating this responsibility to the staff, and
- working as a team to jointly develop and hold itself accountable to a common code of conduct.

Expectation 6: The board gives the manager a chance to prove himself/herself by

- recruiting, selecting, and hiring the manager or administrator,
- promoting and encouraging a positive relationship between its members and the manager or administrator,
- treating and respecting the manager or administrator as a professional, and
- recognizing that the role of a professional manager or administrator is to serve the governing board as a whole.

Expectation 7: The board freely gives and seeks feedback by

- supporting the manager or administrator by providing clear direction and annually reviewing her or his performance,
- annually setting expectations for itself and assessing its own performance,
- inviting constructive feedback to improve its own performance, and
- regularly reviewing and monitoring the local government's finances, programs, and services.

Expectation 8: The board works with the manager or administrator to function as a high-performing governing body by

- Looking to the manager/administrator for assistance in
  - clearly defining roles and relationships,
  - thinking to the future and acting strategically on key issues,
  - operating in a culture of values and ethics,
  - regularly evaluating policy implementation,
  - developing and following protocols for board behavior and board–staff relations,
  - allocating time and energy appropriately,
  - setting clear rules and procedures for meetings,
  - getting regular assessments of citizen concerns and governing board performance,
  - recognizing the governing board's position in intergovernmental systems and in building productive partnerships, and
  - focusing on personal learning and developing as leaders.
- Having the board chair and manager or administrator orient new members to the governing board, providing expectations about how to be successful.
- Working with the manager or administrator to promote behavior that encourages citizen confidence in local government.

Table 3.2A Alternative Organizational Plans for a City Council Comprised of a Mayor and Five Council Members

THREE-COMMITTEE SYSTEM*

	Finance	*Public Works*	*Public Safety*
Plan 1	Mayor	Council Member 1	Council Member 2
	Council Member 2	Council Member 4	Council Member 3
	Council Member 3	Council Member 5	Council Member 4
Plan 2	Council Member 1	Council Member 4	Council Member 3
	Council Member 2	Council Member 5	Council Member 4
	Council Member 3	Council Member 2	Council Member 5
Plan 3	Mayor	Council Member 1	Council Member 4
	Council Member 2	Council Member 3	Council Member 5

TWO-COMMITTEE SYSTEM**

	Finance and Public Safety	*Public Works*
Plan 1	Mayor	Council Member 1
	Council Member 2	Council Member 4
	Council Member 3	Council Member 5
Plan 2	Council Member 1	Council Member 4
	Council Member 2	Council Member 5
	Council Member 3	Council Member 2

Author's Comments: Plan 1 requires the mayor to serve on the Finance Committee; this is often advantageous. Also, Plan 1 requires only three members to serve on two committees. Plan 2 requires four members to serve on two committees. Plan 3 requires that each member serve on only one committee; this is desirable, but a committee composed of only two members is often unworkable.

* The council is organized into three committees: Finance, Public Works, and Public Safety.
The committees' responsibilities are as follows:

- Finance: budgets, taxation, recreation, and library
- Public Works: streets, transportation, water and sewer, electric light and power, stormwater drainage, and solid waste
- Public Safety: police, fire, and health and sanitation

** The council is organized into two committees: Finance and Public Safety, and Public Works.
The committees' responsibilities are as follows:

- Finance and Public Safety: budgets, taxation, recreation, and library, police, fire, and health and sanitation
- Public Works: streets, transportation, water and sewer, electric light and power, stormwater drainage, and solid waste

Table 3.2B Number of Committee Assignments per Member, by Plan

	SYSTEM				
	Three-Committee			*Two-Committee*	
	Plan 1	Plan 2	Plan 3	Plan 1	Plan 2
Mayor	1	0	1	1	0
Council Member 1 (mayor pro tem)	1	1	1	1	1
Council Member 2	2	2	1	1	2
Council Member 3	2	2	1	1	1
Council Member 4	2	2	1	1	1
Council Member 5	1	2	1	1	1

Exercising Caution in Speaking for the Governing Board

Members of county commissions and city councils should be careful when talking with the news media, citizens' groups, and even individuals to make certain that their comments reflect the governing board's views rather than their own personal opinions. Opinions and statements of position expressed by elected board members are frequently taken to be those of the entire body. If a governing board member misstates the county or city's position, assumes a position that has not actually been taken by the full board, or incorrectly predicts a board position or action, the result can be embarrassment, mistrust, and resentment on the part of the listener and other governing board members, as well as on the part of the public at large.

Citizens do not always distinguish between the thoughts of an individual board member and those of the body as a whole, nor do they remember that other members of the board may not share one particular member's feelings. The listener may take what is actually only a personal expression of opinion to be an authoritative pronouncement of official policy. On important or sensitive matters requiring clarity and careful explanation, it may be desirable for the governing board to designate one of its members as spokesperson. In some situations it may be advisable to have a written statement, agreed on by the whole governing board, that is available for distribution if the need arises.

Role of the Manager in North Carolina Local Governments

As has been stated, the North Carolina General Statutes give boards of county commissioners and city councils the option of operating with or without a professional manager.[31] If the governing board decides to run local government on its own, it is said to use the *board of commissioner* (counties) or the *mayor–council form* (cities) of local government. A county or city that uses a professional manager is described as operating under the *county–manager* or *council–manager form*. For more information about the role and responsibilities of professional managers, see Chapter 4.

All 100 counties in the state have chosen to employ a full-time professional to administer county government. Under this county–manager plan, county commissioners have a choice in whether or not to grant the manager hiring and firing authority. Chairs of county boards of commissioners are able to serve as county managers by action of their respective boards in accordance with G.S. 153A-81. Mayors cannot so serve under the council–manager form.[32]

Use of an Administrator in Mayor–Council Cities

Some municipalities hire a chief administrative official while maintaining the mayor–council form of government.[33] A charter amendment is not required to have such an administrator in charge, although the municipality may wish to adopt an ordinance to create the position and specify its duties. Typically, "administrator" is the term used for this sort of employee, though "manager" is sometimes used, even though a municipality has not yet changed to the council–manager form of government.

In a council–manager form of government, managers are granted specific powers and responsibilities by statute, including the power to hire and fire. When the governing body in a mayor–council municipality is ready to grant the full powers of a manager to its administrator, that signals the need to change to the council–manager form.

Procedures for Adopting a County–Manager or Council–Manager Plan

As has been noted, counties in North Carolina may operate under different forms of government, including the county–manager form. If a county's board of commissioners does not choose this option, the county operates without a county manager under the authority of G.S. 153A-76, which permits the board to organize county government however it wishes, consistent with the law. Among other things, commissioners are permitted to hire an "administrator," whose

---

31. *See* G.S. 153A-76, -81 (counties); 160A-146, -101 (cities).

32. *See* G.S. 160A-151.

33. For additional information on this topic, see Frayda Bluestein, "About Town Administrators," *Coates' Canons: NC Local Government Law Blog* (UNC School of Government, Oct. 13, 2010), http://canons.sog.unc.edu/?p=3356.

duties might not include all of those granted by statute to a county manager but might be prescribed by the commissioners themselves. Unlike councils in small North Carolina cities, boards of county commissioners have seldom used this more circumscribed position.

When a governing board transitions to the county–manager or council–manager form of government, the manager's duties are derived from state statutes. Additional information about the legal responsibilities of county and city managers appears in Chapter 4.

Adopting the County–Manager Form of Government

When a county's board of commissioners chooses to use the county–manager plan, it proceeds by passing a resolution adopting the plan by authority of G.S. 153A-81. The plan can be carried out in any one of three ways:

1. The commissioners may employ a county manager, who holds no other office and who serves at the pleasure of the commissioners. In this alternative, the county manager must be appointed solely on the basis of his or her administrative qualifications.[34]
2. The board of commissioners may confer the duties of county manager upon its chair or some other commissioner, as was done in Jackson County until 2000.[35]
3. The commissioners may confer the duties of county manager upon any other county employee, as Brunswick County commissioners did when they appointed the county attorney to also serve as county manager.[36]

Unlike cities, counties are not required to continue to operate with or without the county–manager plan for any minimum period of time after passing a resolution to change from one arrangement to the other.[37]

Adopting the Council–Manager Form of Government

As has been mentioned, the council–manager plan is one form of municipal government operation available by general law and in use in North Carolina. A city's form of government is set forth in its charter. An initial charter is an act of the General Assembly. The Municipal Board of Control, a now-defunct state commission, originally chartered a few cities.

The General Assembly can amend a city's charter, but the General Statutes also allow a city to itself change its form of government by passing a local ordinance that amends the charter.[38] Thus, a city that has the council–manager form of government may adopt the mayor–council form (and vice versa) by following the statutory procedure for amending its charter. This procedure is discussed in more detail below.

Options for Amending a City Charter to Put Council–Manager Plan in Place

Amendment by Ordinance

A city council may alter its governmental form by amending its charter through the passage of an ordinance adopting the council–manager form of government.[39] This is the amendment option most commonly used by cities today. To exercise it, a council must adopt a resolution of intent that describes the proposed charter amendment and, at the same time, call a public hearing to be held within forty-five days. The council must publish a notice of this hearing and a summary of the amendment proposal at least ten days before the hearing date. After the hearing, the council may not take action before its next regular meeting, but it may act on the ordinance at that meeting or at any time after that.

---

34. *See* G.S. 153A-81(1).

35. See G.S. 153A-81(2), which is consistent with the provisions of G.S. 128-1.1(b), allowing any person holding an elective state or local government office to concurrently hold one other appointive office in either state or local government. This arrangement has been used only in Jackson County, until November 29, 2000, where the board chair was elected while also serving as county manager.

36. *See* G.S. 153A-81(3). This arrangement was used from 1990 until 1993, when the county manager/county attorney left the position and the commissioners chose not to continue to combine the offices.

37. Under G.S. 160A-107, if a city changes its charter to create or eliminate the council–manager plan, it must keep the change in effect for at least two years. This is discussed in the text below.

38. *See* G.S. 160A-101 through -111.

39. *See* G.S. 160A-102. The School of Government provides a web-based, question-and-answer resource summarizing the options for changing charters by local ordinance and covering related topics. See www.sog.unc.edu/node/428.

If the council adopts the ordinance, the council must publish a notice within ten days of such adoption summarizing the substance and effects of its action.

Under this amendment option, a council may simply adopt an ordinance after following the procedure outlined immediately above, without any vote by its citizens on the matter. However, amendment by this method may have to be confirmed by a referendum if enough voters call for it.[40] If a valid referendum petition is filed with the city clerk within thirty days after the council publishes notice of its adoption of the ordinance amending the city charter, an election must be held on the question between sixty and 120 days following receipt of the petition. To be valid, the petition must include the signatures of 10 percent, or 5,000, of the city's registered voters, whichever is less. If the election supports the ordinance, the ordinance takes effect; if not, it becomes void.

Amendment by Ordinance Subject to Referendum

A city council may on its own initiative make its amendment ordinance subject to a referendum.[41] This might happen because council members, while believing that the council–manager form is in the best interest of the community, may nonetheless want to give citizens an opportunity to confirm or deny that judgment. In such cases, the council will follow the same procedures described earlier for the simple passage of an ordinance without a referendum. However, on passage of the ordinance, the council will simultaneously adopt a resolution calling for a referendum election on the issue. The election must be held within ninety days of the ordinance's adoption. If the council takes the initiative to call an election in this manner, then it must publish a notice of the election at least thirty days before voter registration closes; it does not have to publish a separate notice of the ordinance's passage. If a majority of those voting in the election support the ordinance, it is put into effect; if not, it becomes void.

Amendment Following Initiative, Petition, and Referendum

Voters themselves may initiate a referendum to change their city's form of government.[42] If a petition that is valid by the same standards described above is initiated by citizens and submitted to the city council, the council must call a referendum election on the issue between sixty and 120 days after receiving the petition. The council need not pass any ordinance before this election, but it must publish a notice of the election, including a description of the issue to be voted on, thirty days before voter registration closes. If the election results favor the proposed changes, then the council must pass an ordinance putting them into effect. In this situation, the ordinance is immune to a petition to put it to a vote after the fact, as provided in G.S. 160A-102.

Amendment by Special Act

A city council may ask the General Assembly to enact a bill amending its city's charter. The special act may or may not require a referendum. This method is seldom used today because of the ease with which a city can decide the matter under the general law just described.

Requirement: Amendments to City Charters Must Remain in Effect for a Minimum of Two Years

A city that changes its charter by any one of the first three general law provisions discussed above must, under G.S. 160A-107, keep such changes in effect for at least two years after they are adopted. The purpose of this provision is to give the new arrangement an opportunity to get through the transition period and prove itself. In the case of a city moving to the council–manager form, this mandate gives the council, the mayor, and the manager a chance to develop and test new ways of doing things, clarify roles and responsibilities, and determine how to make their arrangement work well for everyone involved.

The transition to a council–manager plan is seldom easy. Old habits are difficult to break, and the powers and duties assigned to the city manager by statute are ones that the council or staff members may have been exercising for a long time, making them difficult to relinquish under the new arrangement. Adjustment to and acceptance of the roles that various elected and appointed officials will play under the new form of government is usually a more complex and difficult undertaking than was the process of effecting the change in the charter.

---

40. *See* G.S. 160A-103.
41. *See* G.S. 160A-102.
42. *See* G.S. 160A-104.

Advantages and Disadvantages of the Board of Commissioner and Mayor–Council Forms of Government

The primary advantage of both the board of commissioner (again, this is where no professional administrator has been hired to run local government) and mayor–council (this system of operating is self-explanatory) forms of government is that each brings government closer to the voters. The people directly elected by the citizens are responsible for formulating policy and operating the gears of government. The elected leaders are solely accountable for the direct administration and the oversight of local government functions.

On the other hand, there are two major weaknesses inherent in the board of commissioner and mayor–council plans as they are used in North Carolina. The first is the absence of any real concentration of executive authority and responsibility, as decision making ultimately rests with the board of commissioners or city council as a group. Responsibility for operating the local government is divided among and shared by all members of the governing board, making it administration by committee. Strong, consistent direction depends on maintaining general agreement, which may be difficult at times. (Note: This diffusion of authority and responsibility has been perceived by some as an advantage: the difficulty of concerted and decisive action makes it unlikely that the government can do much harm!)

The second weakness in the board of commissioner and mayor–council forms of government is the fact that good politicians are not necessarily good administrators. Those who are elected may be popular with the voters but may be amateurs when it comes to running a county or city. Thus, even if inept administration by a given board or council later brings rejection at the polls, the result is usually a new set of popular but inexperienced elected administrators.

The continued use of the mayor–council form of government in many of North Carolina's smaller jurisdictions belies these weaknesses and indicates that it can and does work where conscientious elected officials work together for the welfare of the city. As a practical matter, many small cities cannot afford to employ an experienced professional manager. The mayor–council form of government is best suited for and most often used by small towns, where municipal functions are fewer and less complex and can be well provided by an elected council and relatively few employees.

Procedures for Changing the Governing Board's Structure

County Board

A county governing board's structure may be changed through one of two methods. First, the General Assembly may enact a local act that is applicable to the county. Second, the governing board itself may propose a structure change by ordinance, subject to approval by the county's voters. Change by the latter method is limited to specific options set out in the applicable statutory provisions, G.S. 153A-58 through -64; as a practical matter, however, this second restructuring method is almost never used.

City Board

A city governing board's structure may be changed through any of four methods. First, as with a board of county commissioners, the General Assembly may change the structure of a city council by amending the city's charter, which amounts to a local act of the legislature. Although the General Assembly retains full legal control of the change process, as a practical matter any such amendment would normally be enacted only at the request of the affected board. Second, the governing board itself may change its structure simply by adopting an ordinance as authorized in Part 4 of G.S. Chapter 160A. Such an ordinance is adopted following a public hearing on the proposed change. Third, the governing board may adopt an ordinance on a change of structure but the city's voters may condition the ordinance's effectiveness upon approval. For example, the governing board itself might decide to require voter approval for the change to be effective or voters might force a referendum on a board ordinance by submitting petitions with a sufficient number of signatures, e.g., 10 percent of the city's registered voters or 5,000 such voters, whichever is less. Last, voters may initiate such a change in structure by submitting petitions that both propose the change and call for a referendum on the proposal. This method also requires the signatures of 10 percent of the city's registered voters, or 5,000 registered voters, whichever is less. Each of the methods that may be carried out locally is limited to specific options set out in the applicable statute's subsections, G.S. 160A-101(1)–(9).

Additional Resources

Adrian, Charles R., and Ernest S. Griffith. *A History of American City Government: The Formation of Traditions, 1775–1870.* New York: Praeger Publishers, for the National Municipal League, 1976.

Bell, A. Fleming, III. *Suggested Rules of Procedure for a City Council.* 3rd ed. Chapel Hill: UNC Institute of Government, 2000.

Ferrell, Joseph S. *Suggested Rules of Procedure for the Board of County Commissioners.* 3rd ed. Chapel Hill: UNC Institute of Government, 2002.

Griffith, Ernest S. *A History of American City Government: The Progressive Years and Their Aftermath, 1900–1920.* New York: Praeger Publishers, for the National Municipal League, 1974.

International City/County Management Association. *The Municipal Year Book.* Washington, D.C.: International City/County Management Association, published annually.

Lawrence, David M. *North Carolina City Council Procedures.* 2nd ed. Chapel Hill: UNC Institute of Government, 1997.

About the Author

Vaughn Mamlin Upshaw is a School of Government faculty member. Her areas of interest include public governance, leadership development and training for elected officials and public managers, organizational change, governing board development, board self-assessment, manager performance evaluation, strategic and critical thinking, and long-range planning and visioning.

Previous versions of this chapter were authored by School of Government faculty members Carl Stenberg, David Lawrence, Joseph S. Ferrell, and Warren Jake Wicker and North Carolina League of Municipalities attorneys Kimberly S. Hibbard, Andrew L. Romanet Jr., Fred P. Baggett, and S. Leigh Wilson, whose contributions to the field and to this publication are gratefully acknowledged.

Appendix 3.1A Summary Figures on the Structures, Forms of Governing Boards of North Carolina Cities

	CITY SIZE (Number in Size Class)							
	Under 500 (127)	500–1,000 (93)	1,000–2,500 (111)	2,500–5,000 (90)	5,000–10,000 (50)	10,000–25,000 (48)	Over 25,000 (34)	Total (553)
STYLE OF INCORPORATION								
City	0	3	0	7	14	22	24	70
Town	119	86	110	80	34	24	10	463
Village	8	4	1	3	2	2	0	20
STYLE OF GOVERNING BOARD								
Aldermen	12	13	19	10	5	3	3	65
Commissioners	71	54	65	37	12	8	4	251
Council Members	44	26	27	43	33	37	27	237
FORM OF GOVERNMENT								
Council–Manager	8	7	53	64	41	47	34	254
Mayor–Council	119	86	58	26	9	1	0	299
SELECTION OF MAYOR								
By and from Governing Board	10	9	5	6	2	0	1	33
Council Member with the Most Votes	1	1	0	0	0	0	0	2
Elected	116	83	106	84	48	48	33	518
MAYOR'S TERM								
2 Years	89	50	55	43	24	23	17	301
4 Years	33	37	54	45	25	25	17	236
At Pleasure of Board	5	6	2	2	1	0	0	16
NUMBER OF MEMBERS OF GOVERNING BOARD								
11 Members	0	0	0	0	0	0	1	1
9 Members	0	0	0	0	0	0	1	1
8 Members	0	0	0	0	1	6	4	11
7 Members	0	1	0	1	2	6	7	17
6 Members	1	3	9	16	6	10	14	59
5 Members	69	69	72	56	27	18	6	317
4 Members	27	16	28	16	14	8	1	110
3 Members	29	4	2	1	0	0	0	36
2 Members	1	0	0	0	0	0	0	1
TERM OF OFFICE OF GOVERNING BOARD								
2 Years	71	25	23	17	4	11	11	162
4 Years	12	7	5	1	5	0	5	35
4S (4 Yrs., Staggered)	42	59	81	69	40	36	18	345
4S/2 Years	2	2	0	3	1	1	0	9

Source: Compiled using data from "Forms of Government and Methods of Election in North Carolina Cities" (School of Government web page), www.iog.unc.edu/pubs/FOG/index.php.

Appendix 3.1B Summary Figures on The Mode, Type of Election of Governing Boards of North Carolina Cities

	POPULATION (Total Number of Cities)							
	Under 500 (127)	500–1,000 (93)	1,000–2,500 (111)	2,500–5,000 (90)	5,000–10,000 (50)	10,000–25,000 (48)	Over 25,000 (34)	Total (553)
MODE OF ELECTION OF GOVERNING BOARD								
AL	127	92	100	77	38	28	15	477
D	0	0	3	2	2	4	6	17
DAL	0	0	2	3	4	8	9	26
CDA	0	0	5	6	5	5	2	23
CDAL	0	1	1	2	1	3	2	10
TYPE OF ELECTION								
Majority	0	3	2	1	2	4	5	17
Partisan	0	0	1	0	0	3	4	8
Plurality	126	88	106	85	46	37	16	504
Primary	1	2	2	4	2	4	9	24

AL = Elected at large
D = Elected by and from districts
DAL = Elected at large but with requirement of district residence
CDA = Combination of at-large and district members
CDAL = Combination of at-large members and members elected at large by representing districts

Appendix 3.2A Numbers, Terms of North Carolina Boards of County Commissioners

County	TERMS OF OFFICE No. of Comms.	Years	Staggered?
Alamance	5	4	Yes
Alexander	5	4	Yes
Alleghany	5	4	Yes
Anson	7	4	Yes
Ashe	5	2/4	Yes
Avery	5	2/4	Yes
Beaufort	7	4	Yes
Bertie	5	4	Yes
Bladen	9	4	Yes
Brunswick	5	4	Yes
Buncombe	7	4	
Burke	5	4	Yes
Cabarrus	5	4	Yes
Caldwell	5	4	Yes
Camden	5	4	Yes
Carteret	7	4	Yes
Caswell	7	4	Yes
Catawba	5	4	Yes
Chatham	5	4	Yes
Cherokee	5	4	
Chowan	7	4	Yes
Clay	3	4	
Cleveland	5	4	Yes
Columbus	7	4	Yes
Craven	7	4	
Cumberland	7	4	Yes
Currituck	7	4	Yes
Dare	7	4	Yes
Davidson	7	4	Yes
Davie	5	4	Yes
Duplin	6	4	Yes
Durham	5	4	
Edgecombe	7	4	Yes
Forsyth	7	4	Yes
Franklin	7	4	Yes
Gaston	7	4	Yes
Gates	5	4	Yes
Graham	5	4	
Granville	7	4	Yes
Greene	5	4	Yes
Guilford	9	4	Yes
Halifax	6	4	Yes
Harnett	5	4	Yes
Haywood	5	4	Yes
Henderson	5	4	Yes
Hertford	5	4	Yes
Hoke	5	4	Yes
Hyde	5	4	Yes
Iredell	5	2/4	Yes
Jackson	5	4	Yes
Johnston	7	4	Yes
Jones	5	4	
Lee	7	4	Yes
Lenoir	7	4	Yes
Lincoln	5	4	Yes
Macon	5	4	Yes
Madison	5	4	Yes
Martin	5	4	Yes
McDowell	5	4	Yes
Mecklenburg	9	2	
Mitchell	5	2/4	Yes
Montgomery	5	4	Yes
Moore	5	4	Yes
Nash	7	4	Yes
New Hanover	5	4	Yes
Northampton	5	4	Yes
Onslow	5	4	
Orange	7	4	Yes
Pamlico	7	4	Yes
Pasquotank	7	4	Yes
Pender	5	4	Yes
Perquimans	6	4	Yes
Person	5	4	Yes
Pitt	9	4	Yes
Polk	5	2/4	Yes
Randolph	5	4	Yes
Richmond	7	4	Yes
Robeson	8	4	Yes
Rockingham	5	4	Yes
Rowan	5	4	Yes
Rutherford	5	4	Yes
Sampson	5	4	Yes
Scotland	7	4	Yes
Stanly	5	4	Yes
Stokes	5	4	Yes
Surry	5	4	Yes
Swain	5	4	
Transylvania	5	4	Yes
Tyrrell	5	4	Yes
Union	5	4	Yes
Vance	7	4	Yes
Wake	7	4	Yes
Warren	5	4	Yes
Washington	5	4	Yes
Watauga	5	2/4	Yes
Wayne	7	4	
Wilkes	5	4	Yes
Wilson	7	4	
Yadkin	5	2/4	Yes
Yancey	5	2/4	Yes
	580	**(Total No. of Comms.)**	

Appendix 3.2B Distribution of North Carolina County Commissioners by Mode of Election

County	Mode of Election	Number of Commissioners per Election Mode					
		AL	D	DAL	CDA	CDAL	L
Alamance	AL	5					
Alexander	AL	5					
Alleghany	AL	5					
Anson	D		7				
Ashe	AL	5					
Avery	AL	5					
Beaufort	L						7
Bertie	DAL			5			
Bladen	CDA; L	3	6				9
Brunswick	DAL			5			
Buncombe	CDA	1	6				
Burke	AL	5					
Cabarrus	AL	5					
Caldwell	AL	5					
Camden	DAL	2	3				
Carteret	DAL			7			
Caswell	CDA	2	5				
Catawba	AL	5					
Chatham	DAL			5			
Cherokee	CDA				5		
Chowan	CDA	1	6				
Clay	AL	3					
Cleveland	AL	5					
Columbus	D		7				
Craven	D		7				
Cumberland	CDA	2	5				
Currituck	CDAL	2		5			
Dare	CDA	1	6				
Davidson	AL	7					
Davie	AL	5					
Duplin	D		6				
Durham	AL	5					
Edgecombe	D		7				
Forsyth	CDA	1	6				
Franklin	CDA	2	5				
Gaston	DAL			7			
Gates	DAL			5			
Graham	AL	5					
Granville	D		7				
Greene	AL	5					
Guilford	D		9				
Halifax	CDA	3	3				
Harnett	D		5				
Haywood	AL	5					
Henderson	DAL			5			
Hertford	DAL			5			
Hoke	AL	5					
Hyde	AL	5					
Iredell	AL	5					
Jackson	DAL; L			4			1
Johnston	DAL			7			
Jones	AL	5					
Lee	CDA	3	4				
Lenoir	CDA	2	5				
Lincoln	AL	5					
Macon	DAL			5			
Madison	AL	5					
Martin	L						5
McDowell	AL	5					
Mecklenburg	CDA	3	6				
Mitchell	AL	5					
Montgomery	CDA	2	3				
Moore	DAL			5			
Nash	D		7				
New Hanover	AL	5					
Northampton	AL	5					
Onslow	AL	5					
Orange	CDAL	4	3				
Pamlico	CDAL	2	5				
Pasquotank	CDAL	3	4				
Pender	DAL			5			
Perquimans	L						6
Person	AL	5					
Pitt	D		9				
Polk	AL	5					
Randolph	DAL			5			
Richmond	AL	7					
Robeson	D		8				
Rockingham	AL	5					
Rowan	AL	5					
Rutherford	DAL			5			
Sampson	D		5				
Scotland	DAL			7			
Stanly	AL	5					
Stokes	AL	5					
Surry	L						5
Swain	AL	5					
Transylvania	AL	5					
Tyrrell	AL	5					
Union	AL	5					
Vance	D		7				
Wake	DAL			7			
Warren	D		5				
Washington	CDA	1	4				
Watauga	DAL			5			
Wayne	CDA	1	6				
Wilkes	AL	5					
Wilson	D		7				
Yadkin	AL	5					
Yancey	AL	5					

AL = Elected at large
D = Elected by and from districts
DAL = Elected at large but with requirement of district residence
CDA = Combination of at-large and district members
CDAL = Combination of at-large members and members elected at large by representing districts
L = Limited Voting Plan

Appendix 3.3 2014 Municipal Forms of Government in North Carolina

	CITY SIZE (Number in Size Class)							
FORM OF GOVERNMENT	0–499 (127)	500–999 (93)	1,000–2,499 (111)	2,500–4,999 (90)	5,000–9,999 (50)	10,000–24,999 (48)	Over 25,000 (34)	Total (553)
Council/Manager	8	7	53	64	41	47	34	254
Mayor/Council	104	64	28	11	2	0	0	209
Mayor/Council with Administrator	15	22	30	15	7	1	0	90

Chapter 4

County and City Managers

Carl W. Stenberg

In North Carolina, local governments may operate under different forms of government: (1) a county–manager or council–manager form; (2) a mayor–council or county commissioner form; or (3) an alternative form that complies with state law. While a county may choose to adopt the county–manager model, if the county board of commissioners takes no action in this respect, it then operates without a county manager under the authority of Section 153A-76 of the North Carolina General Statutes (hereinafter G.S.), which permits the board to organize county government however it wishes, consistent with the law. Similar provisions (G.S. 160A-101(9), 160A-146) govern cities in their selection of an organizational form. Under the mayor–council form of government (discussed in detail in Chapter 3, "County and City Governing Boards"), the governing board is not required to employ a professional manager, but it may do so. Any county or city that has not adopted the council–manager/county–manager form may hire an "administrator," whose duties might not include all of those granted by statute to the manager but may be prescribed by the governing body.

This chapter focuses on local governments that have adopted the county–manager or council–manager forms of government. As used in this chapter, the term *council–manager* includes both forms.

Council–Manager Form of Government under North Carolina Law

North Carolina's laws authorizing the council–manager form of government, like those of most states, drew on the provisions contained in the National Municipal League's (now the National Civic League) *Model City Charter.* The key provisions of the General Statutes relating to county and city managers are discussed in more detail below.

The County Manager

The powers and duties of the county manager specified in G.S. 153A-82 are fairly typical of those found in most state statutes and are, by and large, consistent with the general elements of the council–manager plan in North Carolina. The Introduction and first subsection of the law read as follows:

> **§ 153A-82. Powers and duties of manager.**
>
> The manager is the chief administrator of county government. He [or she] is responsible to the board of commissioners for the administration of all departments of county government under the board's general control and has the following powers and duties:
>
> (1) He [or she] shall appoint with the approval of the board of commissioners and suspend or remove all county officers, employees, and agents except those who are elected by the people or whose appointment is otherwise provided for by law. The board may by resolution permit the manager to appoint officers, employees, and agents without first securing the board's approval. The manager shall make his [or her] appointments, suspensions, and removals in accordance with any general personnel rules, regulations, policies, or ordinances that the board may adopt. . . .

Hiring, Firing, and Disciplinary Powers

Unlike the city manager in North Carolina, the county manager does not have automatic statutory authority to hire, fire, and discipline all employees not otherwise appointed by the governing board. The county manager may perform these actions only with the approval of the board of county commissioners, unless the commissioners take affirmative action to grant the county manager the power to do so without their approval.

The manager's hiring and firing authority does not extend to administrative officers who are elected by the citizens or to those who are appointed by authorities other than the commissioners. In addition, the board appoints the county clerk, the county attorney, the tax assessor, and the tax collector. Thus, county managers preside over an administrative apparatus in which they have less authority of appointment and removal than city managers. County managers are obligated to exercise whatever authority of appointment and removal they do have in accordance with personnel rules and regulations adopted by the board of commissioners.

Administrative Authority

Under G.S. 153A-82(2), the county manager

> . . . shall direct and supervise the administration of all county offices, departments, boards, commissions and agencies under the general control of the board of commissioners, subject to the general direction and control of the board.

This provision makes the county manager responsible for supervision of county operations in accordance with whatever laws, regulations, policies, direction, and guidance are decided upon by the board of commissioners. The commissioners' control is meant to be general in nature, leaving the manager to exercise professional judgment as to how to carry out the board's intent. This can be a difficult line to draw, and its actual practice varies from county to county, depending on a variety of factors, such as tradition, confidence in the person who serves as manager, individual personalities and styles, and the issues involved.

Because other individuals elect or appoint several key department heads, and because, as stated above, the commissioners usually appoint the county clerk, attorney, tax assessor, and tax collector (and in many counties the finance director), the extent of a county manager's authority over the administrative apparatus for which he or she is responsible is not always clear. To be successful, North Carolina county managers have to be more tolerant of ambiguity in their authority and more facilitative rather than directive in their management styles than their counterparts in North Carolina cities.

Duties Related to Governing Body Meetings

Under G.S. 153A-82(3), the county manager (or his or her designee)

> . . . shall attend all meetings of the board of commissioners and recommend any measures that he [or she] considers expedient.

This provision acknowledges that one of the manager's fundamental responsibilities is to give professional advice and counsel to the commissioners in their deliberations or, at the very least, to ensure that the board has access to and understands the information it needs to make informed choices in the matters coming before it. The expectation is that the commissioners will be able to access the advice of the manager or the manager's designee any time they gather. Most managers will not miss a meeting if they can help it and will be careful to secure the concurrence of the chair or the entire board if they must be absent. They will also make sure that an assistant or other designee chosen to act in their place is fully able and prepared to give the board the support it needs.

Oversight Regarding Proper Execution of Orders, Ordinances, etc.

Subsection (4) of G.S. 153A-82 mandates that the manager

> . . . shall see that the orders, ordinances, resolutions, and regulations of the board of commissioners are faithfully executed within the county.

This general supervisory role of the manager is self-explanatory.

Financial Duties

The manager's financial duties are addressed in G.S. 153A-82(5) and (6):

> (5) He [or she] shall prepare and submit the annual budget and capital program to the board of commissioners.
> (6) He [or she] shall annually submit to the board of commissioners and make available to the public a complete report on the finances and administrative activities of the county as of the end of the fiscal year.

In a county that adopts the county–manager form of government, the manager is also the budget officer (G.S. 159-9) and is required by G.S. 159-11 to prepare a budget for consideration by the commissioners in whatever form and detail the board might specify. This is, of course, a *recommended* budget and capital program; the commissioners may modify these items as they wish before adopting the budget ordinance (see Chapter 20, "Budgeting for Operating and Capital Expenditures"). Further, in addition to the statutorily required annual report (see G.S. 153A-82(6), above), the manager commonly makes periodic financial and administrative reports to the commissioners throughout the fiscal year.

Reports and Miscellaneous Duties

The county manager must, under G.S. 153A-82(7),

> . . . make any other reports that the board of commissioners may require concerning the operations of county offices, departments, boards, commissions, and agencies.

The eighth and final subsection of G.S. 153A-82 is a "catch-all," requiring that the manager

> . . . perform any other duties that may be required or authorized by the board of commissioners.

The City Manager

The powers and duties of the city manager are specified in G.S. 160A-148. Unless otherwise noted, they are similar to those of county managers. The introduction and first subsection of the statute read as follows:

> **§ 160A-148. Powers and duties of manager**
>
> The manager shall be the chief administrator of the city. He [or she] shall be responsible to the council for administering all municipal affairs placed in his [or her] charge by them, and shall have the following powers and duties:
>
> (1) He [or she] shall appoint and suspend or remove all city officers and employees not elected by the people, and whose appointment or removal is not otherwise provided for by law, except the city attorney, in accordance with general personnel rules, regulations, policies, or ordinances as the council may adopt.

Hiring and Firing Powers

As indicated in Chapter 3, the laws of North Carolina provide that the city council is to appoint a city attorney. Appointment of a city clerk is also a statutory requirement. Some city charters authorize the council to appoint the clerk, others specify that the manager makes this appointment, and still others are silent on the matter. In all cities, the clerk performs duties for the council, but some clerks report to the council and others to the manager.

A few council–manager cities have charters that require the council to appoint the chief of police, a very high-profile and sensitive position. The General Statutes provide for the council to appoint the tax collector, if such position exists, although some charters authorize the manager to make this appointment. Otherwise, except for these council appointments, the manager is responsible for the hiring, the disciplining, and the removal of all administrative personnel. Managers consider this authority to be of the utmost importance, because if the council is to hold them responsible and accountable for the performance of administrative units, they feel that they must, in turn, have hiring and firing authority over personnel directly responsible for the units' work. An important qualification to this authority of city managers is that it must be exercised in accordance with whatever personnel rules the council adopts.

Administrative Authority

G.S. 160A-148(2) states that the city manager

> . . . shall direct and supervise the administration of all departments, offices, and agencies of the city, subject to the general direction and control of the council, except as otherwise provided by law.

This language reflects the long-standing prohibition in the *Model City Charter* (referenced on page 54, above) on "Interference with Administration," which provides that council members should deal with employees through the city manager. To make sure that the non-interference tenet is honored, some managers have insisted that there be no contact between employees and council members without their permission. However, this can prove frustrating for everyone involved: employees may feel as if they are being deprived of their citizenship, the manager might find that he or she has to devote too much time to managing communications traffic, and council members could come to regard the contact-only-with-permission rule as unduly restrictive of their ability to keep track of the pulse of government or to get simple information. Most managers find it effective to have an understanding that prevents the council from issuing directives to employees but allows council members to freely seek information and keep up with employees' activities and outlooks. Managers also expect that employees will keep them informed of contacts with council members.

Research conducted in 2005 found that the charters of nine of the twenty-eight largest municipalities in North Carolina contained "work through the manager" language, while the remaining charters were silent on the matter of council–staff relations. In the latter cities, there was either an informal unwritten policy or no policy at all. The majority of managers interviewed in the 2005 survey agreed that the norm applicable to their city could be best described as "direct communication between council members/mayor and city employees is neither strongly discouraged nor prohibited, but city employees are advised to inform a supervisor when contacted by council members/mayor." They also stated that violations of the council member/staff contact policy or norm seldom occurred. More than three-fourths of the managers indicated that their councils were respectful of the manager's role as chief executive officer and that their city's policy on council member/staff contact was "about right." Reflecting the changing times, one manager stated: "Twenty-five years ago managers wanted everything to go through the manager's office, and that's just not practical today."[1]

Miscellaneous Duties

The remaining subsections of G.S. 160A-148, which outline various other city manager responsibilities, are reproduced below.

(3) [The manager] shall attend all meetings of the council and recommend any measures that he [or she] deems expedient.

(4) [The manager] shall see that all laws of the State, the city charter, and the ordinances, resolutions, and regulations of the council are faithfully executed within the city.

(5) [The manager] shall prepare and submit the annual budget and capital program to the council.

(6) [The manager] shall annually submit to the council and make available to the public a complete report on the finances and administrative activities of the city as of the end of the fiscal year.

(7) [The manager] shall make any other reports that the council may require concerning the operations of city departments, offices, and agencies subject to his [or her] direction and control.

(8) [The manager] shall perform any other duties that may be required or authorized by the council.

Origins and Reasons for the Growth of the Council–Manager Form

History—North Carolina

North Carolina has a long tradition of using professional managers to assist elected leaders in governing their respective communities and generally ensure that local governments operate efficiently and effectively. In 1917, Catawba and Caldwell counties each secured authorization by special acts of the General Assembly to appoint a county manager, although neither did so at the time.[2] In that same year, Buncombe County designated the chair of the board of commissioners as a full-time manager.[3] In 1927, following the success of a general law allowing cities to determine their form of government by local action, the General Assembly passed similar legislation to allow counties to choose their form of government without special legislation.[4] In 1929, Robeson County became the first county in the United States to adopt the county–manager form,[5] and in 1930, Durham County became the second.[6]

1. Parker Wiseman, "Examining Council Contact with Subordinate Staff in Large and Mid-Size North Carolina Municipalities," a paper submitted to the faculty of The University of North Carolina at Chapel Hill in partial fulfillment of the requirements for the degree of Master of Public Administration, March 11, 2005.

2. 1917 N.C. Pub.-Local Laws ch. 433 (Catawba); 1917 N.C. Pub.-Local Laws ch. 690 (Caldwell). More than two decades later, at its organizational meeting in 1936, the Catawba Board of County Commissioners, having decided that the county needed an executive to manage county affairs when the board was not in session, voted to hire Nolan J. Sigmon as county accountant with the intention of making him county manager. In March 1937, the commissioners passed a resolution adopting the county–manager form, which had by then been authorized by Chapter 91 of the Public Laws of 1929 (now Chapter 81 of the North Carolina General Statutes (hereinafter G.S.), and appointed Sigmon to the post of county manager.

3. This arrangement continued until December 1984, when the offices of county manager and chairman were separated pursuant to special legislation passed by the 1983 session of the General Assembly (1983 N.C. Sess. Laws ch. 129). This arrangement continues in effect today.

4. 1927 Pub. Laws ch. 91, §§ 5–8, modified and recodified in 1973; now G.S. 153A-81 (adoption of county manager plan; appointment or designation of manager) and 153A-82 (powers and duties of manager).

5. Robeson is the only county in the United States to have had the appointed-manager form of government continuously since the late 1920s.

6. The International City/County Management Association (ICMA) lists Durham County as having adopted the form in 1930.

Although they were ahead of their counterparts in other states, North Carolina counties were more cautious than cities in adopting this new form of government: Until 1960, only nine counties had used the general law to appoint county managers, and three other counties elected commissioners to serve in the capacity of county manager.[7] By 1970, thirty-five counties were using the county–manager form, and by 1980, eighty-two had adopted it. Today, all of North Carolina's 100 counties employ a full-time professional county manager.

The cities of Hickory and Morganton first adopted the council–manager plan as part of their charters in 1913, just one year after the first charter adoption of the plan in the country by Sumter, South Carolina. Another twenty-three North Carolina cities had adopted the plan by 1940, and two or three more adopted it each year from the 1940s through the 1960s. Between 1994 and 2002, twenty-four additional cities adopted the council–manager plan, while the number operating under the mayor–council form decreased by three cities.

By 2012, all but thirty-six of the 222 North Carolina cities with populations exceeding 2,500 had appointed a manager under their charters, including all of the thirty-four largest cities in the state. Small communities (with populations of less than 2,500) seem to favor the mayor–council form (see Chapter 3).

History—Generally

Exactly when did this growth in professional management begin? The form of government where there is a professional manager who is accountable to elected officials first appeared in the United States a century ago. It was created as part of a reform effort to eliminate the corruption in American local government that existed at the time. Nineteenth-century Jacksonian democracy—with its aversion to concentrated power in government—had created a system (the so-called long ballot) in which popularly elected officials filled not only the most critical administrative positions in government, but many others as well. Few of these officials had the requisite skills or incentives to cooperate with other officials to run an efficient or effective government.

This system created a leadership void that was quickly filled by party machines, whose political bosses controlled and manipulated voting. In return for delivering the vote, political bosses told elected officials how to run local operations, usually in a way that enriched them and their friends. Public affairs were organized and conducted on the basis of personal favors, political deals, and private profit. Party machine politics resulted in much inefficiency, laid waste to local government treasuries, and became a blatant affront to notions of a broader public good as the guiding principle of government. To remedy this, progressive reformers promoted widespread citizen access to accountable, elected officials through devices such as the short ballot, the strong executive, nonpartisan at-large elections, the initiative, the referendum, and the recall.

Reformers sought to apply to local government business and scientific management principles that were popular at the time. One such vehicle was the council–manager plan for cities, originated by reformer Richard Childs in 1910[8] and officially incorporated into the *Model City Charter* of the National Civic League (referenced above) in 1915. The plan sought to bring a balance of democratic political accountability and honest, competent administration to local government. In a move away from the reformers' previous support of a strong, elected executive, the new plan called for a small, accountable elected body with a presiding officer to employ a politically neutral, expert manager to serve at its pleasure. The manager would give objective, rational advice to the elected body and then faithfully execute whatever decisions the elected body made for the welfare of the citizens, using sound business practices to administer efficiently

7. In Catawba, Davidson, Durham, Forsyth, Gaston, Hertford, Rockingham, Guilford, and Robeson counties, commissioners appointed a separate county manager. In Buncombe, Haywood, and Mecklenburg counties, the board of commissioners' chair served as county manager.

8. Childs first articulated the plan in a proposal to combine the commission form of government with a professional city manager. (The commission form of government became popular after its successful use in resurrecting Galveston, Texas, from almost complete destruction from a hurricane in 1900.) Childs drafted a bill incorporating the plan and persuaded the Lockport (N.Y.) Board of Trade to sponsor its introduction in the New York State Legislature with the public support of reform organizations. Thus, the earliest version is known as the Lockport Plan. *See* Robert Paul Boynton, "The Council–Manager Plan: An Historical Perspective," *Public Management* (Oct. 1974): 3–5.

the day-to-day affairs of government. Many of the early managers were civil engineers by training, and much of their time was spent on public works problems.

While these reforms were initially employed in cities, the impetus to use measures aimed at increasing the efficiency of local government affected counties as well, as they grew in population and became more urbanized in some parts of the country. In 100 years, the main elements of the plan have changed very little.

ICMA Recognition

The International City/County Management Association (ICMA) officially recognizes jurisdictions ". . . that have established positions of professional authority. Recognition means the community is identified as one that provides a legal framework conducive to the practice of professional management." Criteria for ICMA recognition as a jurisdiction having a *council–manager position* (the term applies to both cities and counties) include that the manager

- be appointed by majority vote of the governing body, based on professional experience, administrative qualifications, and education, for a definite or indefinite term;
- serve at the pleasure of the entire governing body (not the chair or mayor alone) and be subject to termination by majority vote at any time;
- have direct responsibility for policy formulation on overall problems, especially developing and analyzing alternatives, and for implementation of policy approved by the governing body;
- have responsibility for budget preparation and presentation and direct responsibility for administration of the approved budget; and
- have full authority to appoint and remove, at minimum, most heads of principal departments and local government functions who are administratively responsible to the manager.[9]

Roles and Responsibilities of the Manager

Basics of the Council–Manager Plan

A few assumptions implicit in the council–manager plan have influenced North Carolina's (and other states') general laws regarding this form of government and affected the way in which elected officials and managers perceive their roles in relation to one another. The plan, for the most part, assumes that the governing body fairly represents the electorate, that competing public values can be reconciled, that a public interest can be discerned to guide most decisions, and that the governing body can, with some degree of consensus, give the manager clear direction for carrying out its policies. The plan promotes separation of the governing body's responsibility for political judgments and policy direction from the manager's responsibility for administration in accordance with the board or council's overall policy guidance and his or her own politically neutral expertise. In these ways, the plan seeks to create an effective balance between objective, honest, expert governmental operation and democratic access and control through the authority and the accountability of the elected body.

Realities of the Council–Manager Plan's Implementation

Unfortunately, the council–manager plan's underlying assumptions (discussed above) have, in reality, been difficult to implement and are becoming even more problematic in the political and social landscape of contemporary local government. In 1993, the ICMA convened a task force of city and county managers from across the country to examine council–manager relations. This panel began its work by examining the forces of change that were affecting the council–manager form of government. Managers suggested that citizens seemed to be losing respect for both politics

9. International City/County Management Association, "ICMA Local Government Recognition; Criteria for Recognition of a Council–Manager Position" (adopted Oct. 11, 1969, and revised July 22, 1989), www.icma.org/en/icma/about/overview/local_government_recognition.

and government itself and that the public was becoming increasingly fragmented into interest groups with competing narrow agendas, an unwillingness to cooperate, and a tendency to vie for absolute control. As a result, managers saw themselves faced with mixed signals and sometimes irresolvable conflicts of expectations from elected officials and citizens. Managers felt that directly elected mayors often viewed them as competitors in the arena of local leadership and that the business traditions of the profession had evolved into such a state of "thriving on chaos" that managers who played by the old rules might find themselves characterized as impediments to progress.[10]

Also in 1993, an article was published in the ICMA's monthly magazine, *Public Management*, presenting research findings on council members' perceptions of the council–manager relationship. It identified the following seven "unspoken" concerns and beliefs often held by governing body members that restrict ". . . the development of trust and meaningful partnerships in governing"[11]: (1) managers "hide" money amidst complex budget accounts, arcane language, and detailed provisions and are reluctant to inform governing bodies how much discretionary money is available; (2) managers have personal agendas that they advance, especially when the governing body is divided; (3) governing bodies will not acknowledge or deal with personality conflicts with their manager; (4) governing body members want to hire their own manager, so many newly elected officials are not committed to the current manager; (5) governing bodies do not take seriously the task of evaluating the manager, in part because they have not set clear goals and objectives for the community; (6) managers should be out in front of issues that are "lose-lose" for elected officials, like tax hikes and service cuts; and (7) elected officials expect the manager to discipline or coach controversial "mavericks" on the governing body.

A little more than ten years later, contributors to the third edition of the ICMA book *The Effective Local Government Manager* noted a number of trends that create tension in the relationships between managers and governing bodies and could even jeopardize the existence of the council–manager plan in some communities.[12] These include:

- an expectation by citizens and interest groups that local government can deliver "more for less" and provide customized services, sometimes without regard for due process, social equity, and other core values of deliberative democracy;
- perpetuation of antigovernment feelings among the public—even though opinion surveys reveal local governments are considered more honest, trustworthy, and efficient than other levels of government—leading to local candidates running against the government itself, including the professional "bureaucrat" in the manager's office;
- a shift from a "trustee" to a "delegate" or "activist" role for local elected officials, exemplified by increases in single-issue candidates who are more concerned about addressing their particular program or advancing the interests of special constituencies than working collaboratively with the governing body to address general needs or common problems;
- the steadily increasing power and visibility of directly elected mayors in areas such as budget-making, vetoes of governing body decisions, appointment of council committee chairs, and annual state of the city addresses, which creates competition with the manager for publicity and leadership;
- a growing tendency among elected officials to focus on implementation matters instead of policy, since their re-election hinges on constituent service, leading to micromanagement of administration;
- the emphasis that governing bodies demand managers place on privatization as a way of dealing with the citizenry's desire for "quicker, better, cheaper" services, making it difficult for a manager to introduce other more potentially useful tools; and
- the technology revolution, which, in addition to providing new ways for citizens to obtain services and receive information, has empowered citizens by enabling them to quickly and easily obtain data about local

10. The task force's conclusions were summarized in three parts in *ICMA Newsletter* 74, no. 10 (May 17, 1993); no. 11 (May 31, 1993); and no. 13 (June 28, 1993).

11. R. William Mathis, "What Councils Want from Managers . . . But Do Not Tell Them," *Public Management* 75 (Sept. 1993): 5–10.

12. *See* James H. Svara, "Achieving Effective Community Leadership," *in* Charldean Newell, ed., *The Effective Local Government Manager* 3rd ed. (Washington, D.C.: International City/County Management Association, 2004), 27–40.

> operations, register complaints to elected officials and administrators, monitor performance of agencies, and put an administration under the spotlight.

These changes—and managers' attempts to adjust to them—have led to confusion over what the absolutes of the council–manager plan are; i.e., which of the elements in the idealized version of the plan are essential to its integrity and which can be adapted to the political needs in a given community. Managers and elected officials must seek ways to forge a true partnership in leading their communities, one that recognizes that governing body members, chairs, mayors, and managers are mutually dependent on one another, share responsibility for most aspects of local government, yet need to divide some responsibility in order to make the system work for the benefit of the community.

Concept of Governance

The need for this type of awareness on the part of managers and elected officials has grown with the complexity of local government. Most important public problems, to be successfully addressed, require working across jurisdictional and sector boundaries—with other communities, nonprofit organizations, businesses, citizen groups, and volunteers. Since the 1990s, the term *governance* has been used to describe the reality that "governments" are only one of the players in local service delivery, albeit the key player. The need to manage within and work with a diverse array of vertical and horizontal networks of intergovernmental partners, public–private organizations, and regional and community groups has changed the traditional roles and authority of managers and governing bodies. They have come to act more as facilitators, brokers, networkers, and enablers and to operate less in a hierarchical, command-and-control, "we know best" model. While the responsibilities of managers and governing bodies have grown, their authority has become more shared.[13]

University of Kansas professor H. George Frederickson has observed that this notion of governance creates two fundamental paradoxes: (1) to serve a locality, elected and appointed officials must transcend the boundaries of their respective communities and share power with others; and (2) since local boundaries are meaningful mainly to elected officials for political purposes, increasingly interjurisdictional relationships, power-sharing arrangements, and other aspects of democratic governance must be handled by professional administrators.[14]

In a 2013 report, ICMA executive director Bob O'Neill noted five key drivers of local government: fiscal crisis, demographic changes, technology, polarized politics, and economic disparities. He predicted that ". . . this is the decade of local government" and observed that an important facilitating factor in addressing critical issues like jobs, education, safety, health care, the environment, and infrastructure is the trust citizens have in local government. In this context, O'Neill finds that

> [l]eadership will have to span the normal boundaries of the local government organization and the political boundaries of the jurisdiction: (1) to match the geography and scale of significant issues, and (2) to reach all of the sectors and disciplines necessary to make meaningful change. At the same time, local governments will need to preserve their own sense of "place" and what distinguishes their community and makes it special.[15]

Managers are spending more and more time with their governing bodies seeking to build partnerships that can respond to and survive the diverse, divisive, and difficult demands of contemporary governance. But such partnerships must often be formed and sustained in an arena in which personal interests, district interests, and political divisions make building political consensus and trust on governing bodies quite challenging.

---

13. Svara, "Achieving Effective Community Leadership," at 28.

14. H. George Frederickson, "Transcending the Community: Local Leadership in a World of Shared Power," *Public Management* 87 (Nov. 2005): 14. *See also* Eric S. Zeemering, "Governing Interlocal Cooperation: City Council Interests and the Implications for Public Management," *Public Administration Review* 68 (July/Aug. 2008): 731–41.

15. Bob O'Neill, "Leadership and the Profession: Where to From Here? Be Reformers or Be Reformed?" *Public Management* 95 (March 2013): 22.

The responsibilities of the manager that come from the law, from the managers' professional code of ethics, from realistic notions of roles in policy and administration, and from commonly understood expectations of behavior can be helpful in understanding how the manager–governing body partnership might work and how it is often challenged in the context of the council–manager form of government.[16]

ICMA Code of Ethics

The professional county or city manager has a specific set of expectations governing his or her behavior: a code of ethics originally developed in 1924 by the International City Managers' Association (the original name of the International City/County Management Association (ICMA)).[17] The code and related guidelines have been modified periodically since then; the former was most recently amended in 1998, and the latter in 2004.

The ICMA Code of Ethics is a point of pride among professional managers. Any manager admitted to the association is bound by its ethical tenets and subject to censure by or even expulsion from the association for violations of this professional code. The code seeks to enforce and balance what the ICMA believes to be the prerogatives a professional manager must have to do his or her job properly and the obligations the manager must meet in order to honor the authority of the governing body and promote the overall welfare of the citizens. The twelve tenets of the ICMA Code of Ethics are as follows:[18]

1. Be dedicated to the concepts of effective and democratic local government by responsible elected officials and believe that professional general management is essential to the achievement of this objective.
2. Affirm the dignity and worth of the services rendered by government and maintain a constructive, creative, and practical attitude toward local government affairs and a deep sense of social responsibility as a trusted public servant.
3. Be dedicated to the highest ideals of honor and integrity in public and personal relationships in order that the member may merit the respect and confidence of the elected officials, of other officials and employees, and of the public.
4. Recognize that the chief function of local government at all times is to serve the best interests of all of the people.
5. Submit policy proposals to elected officials; provide them with facts and advice on matters of policy as a basis for making decisions and setting community goals; and uphold and implement local government policies adopted by elected officials.
6. Recognize that elected representatives of the people are entitled to the credit for the establishment of local government policies; responsibility for policy execution rests with the members.
7. Refrain from political activities which undermine public confidence in professional administrators. Refrain from participation in the election of the members of the employing legislative body.
8. Make it a duty continually to improve the member's professional ability and to develop the competence of associates in the use of management techniques.
9. Keep the community informed on local government affairs; encourage communication between the citizens and all local government officers; emphasize friendly and courteous service to the public; and seek to improve the quality and image of public service.

---

16. John Nalbandian and Shannon Portillo, "Council–Manager Relations Through the Years," *Public Management* 88 (July 2006): 6–7; Gary O'Connell, "Council–Manager Relations: Finding Respectable Ground," *Public Management* 89 (Nov. 2007): 20–23.

17. In 1969, the ICMA changed the word "*Managers*" in its name to "*Management*" in order to recognize the inclusion of members who are deputies, assistants, directors of councils of governments, and local government chief administrative officers who do not have the title or the traditional authority of a manager. In 1991, the ICMA included a reference to county managers, who had by then become a significant proportion of its membership—thus the name International City/County Management Association. Because of tradition and widespread recognition of the original acronym, ICMA, the association decided to continue it in that form.

18. Adapted from International City/County Management Association, "ICMA Code of Ethics with Guidelines" (2004), downloadable at www.icma.org.

10. Resist any encroachment on professional responsibilities, believing the member should be free to carry out official policies without interference, and handle each problem without discrimination on the basis of principle and justice.
11. Handle all matters of personnel on the basis of merit so that fairness and impartiality govern a member's decisions pertaining to appointments, pay adjustments, promotions, and discipline.
12. Seek no favor; believe that personal aggrandizement or profit secured by confidential information or by misuse of public time is dishonest.

Roles and Relationships in Policy and Administration

Dichotomy Theory

Although both the law and the ICMA Code of Ethics and guidelines prescribe responsibilities for the manager and the governing body, these responsibilities are very general and do not describe in any detail how these officials should interact with one another to be effective in the division of labor set out in the code's twelve tenets (see above). Years ago, popular wisdom promoted the notion of a strict dichotomy between policy making and administration: the elected body should make policy, the thinking went, and the administration should carry it out, each without interference from the other as it performed its functions. The dichotomy concept probably arose originally from misinterpretation of a highly respected paper by Woodrow Wilson in which he advocated the use of appointed officials to relieve legislators of the burden of administrative functions.[19] The fact that the popular interpretation of this dichotomy theory reduced council–manager relations to a simple, easy-to-follow formula probably accounts for its perpetuation. However, as anyone who works in local government for very long soon realizes, matters are not that simple. For example, the manager often has training, analytical skills, experience in other jurisdictions, and in-depth knowledge of the county or city and its governmental operations that can be extremely helpful to the governing body in establishing policy. And when constituents complain about the quality of a service or the treatment they receive from local government employees, a member of the board or council is unlikely to feel that it is an administrative matter that does not concern him or her.

Dichotomy-Duality Model

John Nalbandian, a local government scholar who has served as council member and mayor of Lawrence, Kansas, has observed:

> The practical world of city management often suggests a more complicated view [than the dichotomy theory]. The manager is deeply involved in policy-making as well as implementation, responds to a multitude of community forces as well as to the governing body, and incorporates a variety of competing values into the decision-making process.[20]

A more realistic relationship between elected officials and managers in policy and administration has been depicted by Professor James H. Svara, as shown in Figure 4-1.[21]

19. Woodrow Wilson, "The Study of Administration," *Political Science Quarterly* 2 (June 1887): 197–222. When Wilson wrote that "administration lies outside the proper sphere of politics. Administrative questions are not political questions. Although politics sets the tasks for administration, it should not be suffered to manipulate its offices" (p. 210), he was arguing for the provision of administrative support to legislative bodies, not prescribing a strict separation of duties between the two.

20. John Nalbandian, *Professionalism in Local Government* (San Francisco: Jossey-Bass, 1991), xiii. *See also* Tansu Demir and Christopher G. Reddick, "Understanding Shared Roles in Policy and Administration: An Empirical Study of Council–Manager Relations," *Public Administration Review* 72 (July/Aug. 2012): 516–36; and Yahong Zhang and Richard C. Feiock, "City Managers' Policy Leadership in Council–Manager Cities," *Journal of Public Administration Research and Theory* 20 (April 2010): 461–76.

21. A more thorough discussion of the relationships among the council, the manager, and the mayor over a continuum from mission to management, as depicted in Figure 4.1, can be found in a series of articles by James H. Svara: "Understanding the Mayor's Office in Council–Manager Cities," *Popular Government* 51 (UNC Institute of Government, Fall 1985): 6–11; "Contributions of the City Council to Effective Governance," *Popular Government* 51 (UNC Institute of Government, Spring 1986): 1–8; and "The Responsible Administrator: Contributions of the City Manager to Effective Governance," *Popular Government* 52 (UNC Institute of Government, Fall 1986): 18–27. *See also* James H. Svara, "Mayors in the Unity of Powers Context: Effective Leadership

Figure 4.1 Dichotomy-Duality Model
Mission-Management Separation with Shared Responsibility for Policy and Administration

Dimensions of Government Process

ILLUSTRATIVE TASKS FOR COUNCIL

Determine purpose, scope of services, tax level, constitutional issues

Pass ordinances, approve new projects and programs, ratify budget

Make implementing decisions (e.g., site selection), handle complaints, oversee administration

Suggest management changes to manager, review organizational performance in manager's appraisal

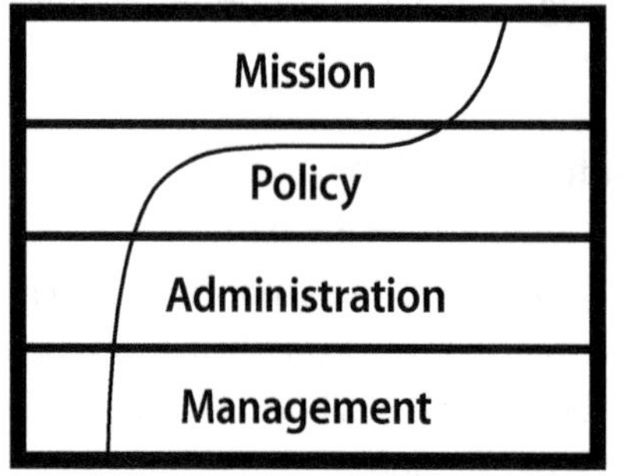

The division presented here is intended to approximate a proper degree of separation and sharing. Shifts to either the left or right would indicate improper incursions.

ILLUSTRATIVE TASKS FOR ADMINISTRATORS

Advise (what city "can" do may influence what it "should" do), analyze conditions and trends

Make recommendations on all decisions, formulate budget, determine service distribution formulae

Establish practices and procedures and make decisions for implementing policy

Control the human, material, and informational resources of organization to support policy and administrative functions

Source: Taken from James H. Svara, "Dichotomy and Duality: Reconceptualizing the Relationship between Policy and Administration in Council–Manager Cities," *Public Administration Review* 45 (Jan./Feb. 1985), 228.

Svara's depiction recognizes that there is no strict dichotomy; rather, there is involvement of both elected and administrative officials at all levels of policy and administration. The engagement and the responsibility of each are proportionately different depending on the level at which they occur. At the highest level, the governing body is responsible for setting the overall direction, or *mission*, of local government, including its purpose, scope, and philosophy. Figure 4.1 suggests that although the governing body has a clearly dominant role in this function, the manager can bring knowledge and experience to the table that enhances the elected official's ability to make informed choices and decisions. The governing body must enact *policy* to achieve the mission that it sets for local government. It does this through functions such as budgeting, capital improvement programming, comprehensive planning, and the making of laws and policies regarding county or city quality of life and governmental operations. Although the governing body has final responsibility for adopting budgets, plans, and ordinances, the manager and his or her staff play a major role in developing technical studies and estimates and analyzing the impact of alternative choices. These kinds of policy making are a shared responsibility in practice.

In government, how something is done is often as important to citizens' satisfaction with the outcome as what is done. Consequently, although the manager and the staff are responsible for implementing the policies adopted by the governing body, elected officials still have a stake in how those policies are carried out—that is, in *administration* and *management.* For example, after making a decision to build a new community center and budgeting funds for it, the

in Council–Manager Governments," *in* H. George Frederickson and John Nalbandian, eds., *The Future of Local Government Administration: The Hansell Symposium* (Washington, D.C.: International City/County Management Association, 2002), 43–54; "Exploring Structures and Institutions in City Government," *Public Administration Review* 65 (July/Aug. 2005): 500–506; "The Myth of the Dichotomy: Complementarity of Politics and Administration in the Past and Future of Public Administration," *Public Administration Review* 61 (March/April 2001): 176–83; "Effective Mayoral Leadership in Council–Manager Cities: Reassessing the Facilitative Model," *National Civic Review* 92 (Summer 2003): 57–72; and "Beyond Dichotomy: Dwight Waldo and the Intertwined Politics–Administration Relationship," *Public Administration Review* 68 (Jan./Feb. 2008): 46–52.

governing body will have a continued interest in how the facilities actually look and work. It will be concerned about how well the scheduling of work on a downtown streetscape project minimizes disruption of business for merchants. It will want to know how increases in public safety spending have affected reported crime rates and citizen perceptions of safety in their neighborhoods. And it will have an interest in how overall employee morale is affected by internal operating policies developed by the administration.

Figure 4.1 describes a partnership at every level of endeavor, with the elected body shouldering most of the responsibility, authority, and initiative at the mission level, the administration shouldering most of it in internal management, and the two sharing it significantly in policy. The line that is depicted in Figure 4.1 is symbolic; for the reasons described earlier, it would vary among jurisdictions, within a particular jurisdiction over time, and by the issue. Some governing bodies want the manager to push aggressively for policies that he or she deems necessary, while others want the manager to stay in the background and respond to the governing body's initiatives. Some elected officials feel the need to be intimately familiar with day-to-day occurrences in service delivery, while others want to concern themselves with administrative matters only when those matters might create public controversy or relate to special interests of constituents.

Other factors influencing where the line is drawn are the manager's experience and tenure and the degree of trust and confidence in his or her relationship with the governing body. Agreement between elected and appointed officials is an essential element of a good working relationship and, because the relationship is dynamic, its contours should be assessed frequently to ensure that everyone involved understands and is comfortable with where the line is drawn.

When it comes to these interrelationships, elected officials have to consider more than their own personal preferences and operating styles, taking into account, for example, how citizens perceive the relationship between elected and appointed officials. Citizens' most important expectation is that quality public services will be provided reliably and efficiently. If the professional staff does not satisfy this expectation by their service and behavior, citizens will expect the governing body to take a more dominant role. If citizens' needs are being met routinely, they may be satisfied with elected officials taking a more passive role on a day-to-day basis.

In the dynamic world of local government, it is hard for both the governing body and the administration to please everyone, hard for elected officials to achieve consensus on many issues that might have been routine in the past, and therefore hard for the governing body to continually give the manager clear direction. As a result, it is hard for the manager to perform his or her administrative duties in a way that satisfies the entire governing body.

As noted previously, some observers of local government bemoan the increase in confrontational politics on the part of constituents, the trend back to district representation on governing bodies, and the growing number of single-issue and antigovernment candidates for local elective office as undermining the principles of broad representation of the public good and efficient administration. Others, however, point out that these developments typify the reality of constituent politics and make for more transparent, fairer representation of all the diverse interests in the community, instead of just those of a powerful privileged few or an exclusive majority. Nalbandian has observed the implications of such matters for managers: "In the future the legitimacy of professional administrators in local government will be grounded in the tasks of community-building and enabling democracy—in getting things done collectively, while building a sense of inclusion."[22] Nevertheless, managers may feel it is more difficult than it used to be to obtain and maintain the kind of clear consensus and direction from the governing body that is one of the fundamental assumptions of the council–manager form of government.

Common Expectations among the Governing Body, the Chair or Mayor, and the Manager

Specific expectations and practices among the governing body, the chair or mayor, and the manager vary greatly from community to community, depending on social and political norms, traditions, and local codes. They can also vary over time in a particular community with changes in the personalities involved as elected offices turn over and managers come and go. However, experience and research have shown that in some critical aspects of these partnerships, there are fairly consistent expectations across jurisdictions and over time. For the most part, these expectations may be

22. John Nalbandian, "Facilitating Community, Enabling Democracy: New Roles for Local Government Managers," *Public Administration Review* 59 (May/June 1999): 189.

regarded as basic and necessary to defining roles and maintaining healthy relationships among the elected members of the governing body, the chair or mayor, and the manager.

Expectation 1: The Manager Is an Organization Capacity-Builder

From the inception of the council–manager form, governing bodies have expected their professional managers to see to it that county and city operations run smoothly, services are provided efficiently and effectively, and prudent fiscal practices are followed. This heritage continues. In order to meet citizen and governing body expectations, the manager must build a modern organization that has both capacity and competence. This entails implementing and updating business practices and processes for personnel administration, finance, purchasing, payroll, contracting, and other basic local systems. It also involves adept use of management tools like strategic planning, performance measurement, benchmarking, and program evaluation to ensure continuous improvement of operations as well as use of technologies like websites and social media to increase public outreach and access and reduce costs.

A critical component of this organization capacity-building is professional staff. The manager must attract and retain talented and motivated personnel for the systems of government to work well. This involves careful workforce and succession planning and investments in training and professional development. Increasingly, local government workforces are diverse and multigenerational, and strategies will need to be put in place to respond to the "changing faces" of the administrative staff, such as bilingual education, job rotation, job sharing, and flexible work hours.

When the processes and personnel perform as expected, local operations run smoothly and routinely. Their workings might be almost invisible to citizens and elected officials. If there is a breakdown in organizational capacity, however, managers and elected officials can be placed under a harsh public spotlight.

Expectation 2: The Manager Is a Valued Advisor to the Governing Body

While both the North Carolina General Statutes and the ICMA Code of Ethics require the manager to give policy advice to the governing body and carry out its policy decisions, neither tenet deals specifically with some subtle but important aspects of this advise-and-implement process. The General Statutes require the manager to "recommend any measures that he [or she] deems expedient," and the Code of Ethics requires him or her to "submit policy proposals" and provide "facts and advice" to help the governing body make policy decisions and set goals. Governing bodies expect the manager to offer balanced and impartial advice—to present alternatives and provide all relevant information that is reasonably available on the different options, assess the advantages and disadvantages of each option, explain the professional reasoning and analysis that leads him or her to a recommendation, and base that reasoning on established professional, technical, ethical, or legal principles and not on personal beliefs, no matter how strongly held, unless the governing body specifically solicits them. Even the appearance or the suspicion that the manager is being selective in the information he or she gives, personally biased in the judgment he or she renders, or manipulative of the governing body's decision in the way he or she presents material can severely damage the manager's credibility and undermine his or her effectiveness.

Most managers will express support (and perhaps push) for a course of action they believe in, no matter how unpopular it might be with the public, the board, or the council. This often means that managers must have the courage to make recommendations that might not have very good prospects of being accepted. On such occasions, managers must bear in mind the human propensity for "killing the messenger" who brings bad news. Elected officials or citizens who are upset over the facts that are presented by the manager or who disagree with the recommendations made might, at best, attack the validity of the manager's advice or, at worst, attack the competence, motives, or character of the manager himself or herself. One of the most difficult tests for a professional manager acting as policy advisor is to remain cool and nondefensive during heated debate over the information and the recommendations that he or she has brought to the governing body.

Once the governing body has made a decision, the manager must get behind it fully and ensure that the administration does the same. The General Statutes require the manager to see that all actions of the council are "faithfully executed," and the Code of Ethics requires him or her to "uphold and implement" all policies adopted by elected officials. This sometimes requires the manager to aggressively implement what he or she thinks is a bad idea. If the manager believes that the directive the governing body has given is illegal, or if the manager deems it professionally or personally repugnant, if the manager cannot dissuade the board or council from its action, he or she can, of course, resign. If the manager chooses to stay, however, he or she is obliged to assist the governing body in carrying out its will.

Sometimes the manager will be put in the awkward position of arguing strenuously for a course of action that the governing body subsequently rejects, and then having the media ask what he or she thinks of the decision. Unless reasoned debate has changed the manager's mind, to agree completely with the governing body will make the manager look weak. On the other hand, to criticize or denigrate the governing body for its decision will violate the Code of Ethics and invite censure. Most professional managers who find themselves in this situation will acknowledge the differences in judgment that were exhibited in the deliberations and try to explain the reasoning that brought the governing body to the decision it made. In other words, they will help elected officials explain their decision to the public and help the public understand the governing body's point of view. Carrying out this important responsibility often takes great emotional maturity and keen diplomatic and communications skills on the part of the manager.

Expectation 3: The Governing Body and the Manager Jointly Strive for Good Service to Citizens

Service to citizens is the litmus test of local operations, and it is one of the most obvious points where the dichotomy theory (discussed above) fails the test of reality. Regardless of what the governing body accomplishes or the capacity and competence of the administration, if the county or city does not satisfactorily deliver basic services to citizens, those citizens will be dissatisfied with the elected officials, and the governing body, in turn, will be dissatisfied with the manager and the administration. Everyone's fate rises or falls with citizen satisfaction with services. Therefore, tirelessly urging his or her administration to provide the very best service possible to the community is one of the key responsibilities of a manager.

Careful planning, budgeting, and management help in ensuring high-quality service delivery, but the manager cannot be everywhere at all times to supervise day-to-day execution. Thus, he or she has to create a culture of responsiveness and performance within the organization, both in providing routine service to citizens and in handling special requests and complaints. This usually involves (1) delegating to front-line service providers in the organization the responsibility and authority to make decisions and take action, (2) supporting staff who take initiative, and (3) helping staff learn from mistakes made in good faith. The manager must take personal risks on behalf of employees and fully accept responsibility with the governing body when things go wrong.

The manager should be able to expect that board or council members will give the system he or she has put in place a chance to work and will channel complaints through the manager. The sense of accomplishment an elected official might enjoy as a result of personally wading into a problem and doing something about it is ordinarily short-lived and transitory. More lasting credit usually comes from citizen recognition that the governing body has created and is maintaining a responsive, customer-service-oriented workforce—an essential ingredient of efficient and effective local government.

Even when an administration excels at responding to citizen needs, people will ask their elected officials for help, usually in good faith, but sometimes with manipulation in mind. Managers expect governing body members to determine whether a citizen seeking assistance has tried administrative remedies and expect members to steer the citizen into the system. If the administration has been unresponsive, then the manager expects to be informed of this and to have the opportunity to get the problem fixed. A manager in this situation will give the elected official(s) involved the necessary information to follow up with the citizen.

Expectation 4: Elected Officials' Relationships with Employees Are Carefully Managed

Observing a chain of command in answering service needs is desirable, especially from the standpoint of managing resources effectively. The problems that can arise when elected officials intervene directly in service operations include confusing employees with conflicting directives or priorities from supervisors and elected officials, weakening or destroying accountability for work results, wasting staff time and resources, and short-circuiting coordinated plans developed by the supervisor responsible for day-to-day operations. This does *not* mean that elected officials should not have regular, or even periodic, contact with county or city employees. To prohibit such contact would be to ask employees and elected officials to give up some of their basic rights as members of the community, and it would make it harder to build harmony among the critical players in local government operations. It would also be highly inefficient. Funneling all communication through the manager would fill his or her time up with unnecessary traffic and would be awkward and inconvenient for elected officials.

A common arrangement designed to protect planned workflow and still reap the benefits of regular interaction is to encourage direct contact between elected officials and employees for routine inquiries or requests that do not affect administrative workloads and to route more significant requests through the manager. This lets elected officials get the routine information they need quickly and accurately from the persons who are closest to the action and most informed about details; citizens should be able to do the same. This arrangement also provides the opportunity for regular informal communication between elected officials and employees, helping each group become more familiar with, more comfortable with, and more trusting of the other over time. Anything an elected official might want from employees that will involve significant and unplanned expenditures of time or money or that will disrupt agreed-upon work schedules is taken up with the manager so as not to put employees on the spot. The manager and the elected official can then make informed choices about whether the official's request should take precedence over existing commitments, whether something could be done that would meet the official's needs but not be disruptive, or whether it should not be done at all, given other commitments. The manager and the elected official who made the request might also agree to submit the question to the entire governing body for a vote by all as to whether a change in resource allocation would make sense.

Sometimes managers attempt to cut off direct contact between elected officials and employees in order to counteract council members who meddle with or harass employees or employees who are manipulative and disloyal. Like most treatments of a symptom alone, such an approach usually does little or nothing to solve the problems that underlie these dysfunctional behaviors. Often it makes matters worse by creating a siege mentality among administrators, anxiety among employees, and distrust and frustration among elected officials.

Expectation 5: The Governing Body Acts as a Body and Is Dealt with as a Body

By law, the governing body takes official action as a body, yet it is made up of two to eleven individual politicians (counting the chair or mayor) with various constituencies, personal interests, public values, political philosophies, and personalities. This can sometimes make dealing with the governing body a delicate proposition. Without benefit of consensus or at least formal support of a majority of the board or council, individual elected officials may seek to make their views known and impose their own personal agendas on the administration. Most managers will welcome, discuss, and frequently respond at any time to suggestions from individual members, as long as they do not conflict with the pleasure of the governing body as a whole. However, if a request sets new directions or requires allocation of funds or staff time not anticipated by the governing body, the manager will usually ask the member making the proposal to put it to the entire body for consideration. It is important for the manager to treat all members alike in this respect. Unless he or she is scrupulous in avoiding even the appearance of favoritism, the manager can seriously undermine his or her effectiveness by alienating members who feel slighted or barred from some inner circle, real or imagined. Even in the case of routine requests for information, most managers will keep all members informed of transactions with individuals by sending copies of written responses or summaries of opinions rendered or actions agreed to in conversation to all members for their information.

One area in which managers must be especially ardent is keeping members up to date on day-to-day events. Elected officials do not like surprises. It is embarrassing for an official to be asked about some newsworthy item of local business and have to admit that he or she does not know much about it. It is unforgivable for someone to be the *only* member of the governing body who is ignorant about such an item! Governing bodies expect their managers to be sensitive, alert, and responsive to their needs for current information, and this expectation includes the manager making occasional extraordinary efforts necessary to ensure that every member has the same level of information and understanding.

Expectation 6: The Manager and Members of the Governing Body Give One Another a Chance to Prove Themselves

One of the implicit foundations of the council–manager form of government is that a professional manager, who is dedicated to serving whatever elected governing body is seated by the people, will provide smooth transitions and institutional stability and memory and will make changes as different individuals or groups join and leave the governing body. Sometimes members—who sought election because they, too, want to make changes—may find it hard to trust the loyalty of the manager to new members or to have confidence in the ability of the manager to help bring about the changes they (the members) want. Even in communities where the manager routinely makes available to all candidates information about local operations and finances to help inform discussion and debate, this behavior could be viewed as defense of the status quo. In short, the manager is sometimes viewed by members as inextricably tied to the old way of doing things and assumed to be an impediment to progress. It should be noted, though, that managers strive to change the direction of administration in whatever way a majority of the governing body decides (though they can always resign if they feel they cannot serve the new governing body's agenda in good conscience). Therefore, managers are entitled to expect newly elected officials to give them a chance to prove that they can serve new members as well as veterans.

Sometimes after an election the manager finds himself or herself working for one or more board or council members who as candidates roundly criticized the way in which the community was governed and managed. During their campaigns, some of these members may have called for the manager's dismissal. Few elected officials would dispute that even if they had prior county or municipal involvement on volunteer boards or commissions, the view of government from the inside is very different than the view from the outside. Candidates, upon taking office, usually learn that the simplicity and surety of campaign rhetoric seldom stands up to the complexity of governing, leading, or managing. Realizing this, experienced managers will withhold judgment on members whose campaigning seems threatening and will set about to prove that they can serve the new governing body as well as they served the old one. They will hold out hope that, given a chance, they will eventually earn the trust and confidence of new members as those members learn the realities of governing, gain skill as legislators, and observe the manager's performance at close hand.

Expectation 7: The Manager and the Governing Body Freely Give and Seek Feedback

One of the main ingredients for building and maintaining any relationship of trust and confidence is open communication. Managers and elected officials find themselves caught up in a whirlwind of activity on a daily basis. There never seems to be enough time to do everything, let alone do it all just right. So both elected officials and managers make mistakes—they overlook side effects of actions taken in the heat of urgency and say or do things that convey unintended messages. Any/all of these occurrences can generate dissatisfaction, disappointment, offense, anger, and distrust if not acknowledged and resolved appropriately. The key to dealing effectively with such matters is maintaining clear and open communication between elected officials and the manager.

The nature of both the elected official and manager jobs can make the persons holding them feel very isolated. The manager, accountable to a body of citizens and responsible for a county or city workforce, might feel apart from both constituencies, a part of neither. The elected official, held accountable by fellow citizens for oversight of the county or city's administration, might feel that he or she has no real direct role to play in making sure things go well. Open communication is one effective cure for these feelings of isolation. Managers must provide all governing body members with accurate, relevant, and timely information, and members must take initiative to ask questions and make their interests, positions, and feelings known to the manager.

Most managers appreciate clear signals about how well they are satisfying the elected officials whom they serve, even when those signals are negative. Being criticized is never pleasant, but it is more comforting than having to infer dissatisfaction from elected officials' behavior (or not pick up on dissatisfaction at all due to silence). Many people find it easier to give faint compliments or remain silent than to confront others—even subordinates—with criticism. However, dissatisfaction is often hard to conceal for very long—it usually ends up being revealed indirectly by behavior or by rumor. This kind of indirect revelation almost always produces at least some inaccuracy and misinterpretation regarding facts, feelings, and underlying motivations; distracts the manager, who becomes unduly preoccupied with figuring out where he or she stands; and often has the effect of shutting down communication and producing a downward spiral of tension between the manager and the elected official involved. On the other hand, when a governing body member openly directs constructive criticism toward the manager—gets issues out on the table—the manager can ask questions, provide information the member might not have, and respond to his or her concerns. Such dialogue gives members the opportunity to clarify their expectations of the manager by means of concrete examples as they come up, and it gives the manager more certainty about what he or she has to do to satisfy the elected officials and how well he or she is succeeding. Each governing body and its manager must work out how publicly they are willing to give and receive this feedback. They should come to an agreement early in the manager's tenure and confirm or modify it when there is turnover on the governing body.

Many elected officials appreciate the same sort of candor from the manager when they (the officials) are behaving in a way that frustrates effective management. This attitude is by no means universal, however, and managers must be very careful in determining the comfort zone of a particular body and its individual members regarding the offering of constructive criticism. Nevertheless, the benefits of freely giving and accepting feedback can be as great for elected officials as they are for the manager.

Expectation 8: The Manager and the Governing Body Work Together to Develop a Highly Effective Governing Body

The ideological and political trends discussed earlier have sometimes produced dysfunctional effects on governing bodies. To the extent that elected officials are interested primarily in promoting particular causes or special constituencies, micromanaging administration, and criticizing their colleagues and the manager, prospects for responsible decision making in the public interest are diminished. Tensions on the governing body are exacerbated in such cases by a knowledge gap that separates a full-time professional staff from a body of part-time elected officials.[23] The usual lack of government expertise on the part of newer members is compounded by the frequency of turnover on boards and councils. In most communities, governing bodies are comprised of "amateurs," in the very best sense of the term, who function as civic-minded citizen-legislators. Although they may be interested in seeking re-election, they are not professional politicians. The vast majority of local elected officials do not derive the bulk of their income from serving on governing bodies. They see themselves individually and collectively as local government leaders and, as noted earlier, as trustees, delegates, and activists responsible for representing citizens and making public policy for their community.

Who is responsible for closing the gap, for giving the board or council the tools it needs to become a high-performing decision-making body and for developing a partnership with the professional staff? While some might answer "the chair or mayor" and others might respond "the veteran members on the board or council," the manager also has an obligation here. The nature of this obligation is discussed in the sections that follow.

Tips for Ensuring Peak Performance of Governing Bodies

What would a "high-performing" governing body look like? At least nine common habits have been identified: (1) thinking and acting strategically and with a vision for the community's future; (2) respecting the "shared constituency" with citizens, in horizontal and vertical relations with other jurisdictions; (3) demonstrating teamwork; (4) mastering small-group decision making; (5) honoring the council–staff partnership; (6) allocating governing body time and energy appropriately in four key areas—goal-setting retreats, study sessions, regular public hearings and meetings, and community relations; (7) having clear rules and procedures for board or council meetings; (8) obtaining objective feedback and conducting systematic and valid assessment of policy and implementation performance; and (9) practicing continuous personal learning and leadership development of individual elected officials.[24]

There are a number of practical steps a manager can take to help improve the efficiency of governing body deliberations. These include preparing the meeting agenda in a timely manner; scheduling meetings in a way that promotes good time management and the ability to focus on major topics; not overwhelming elected officials with highly detailed, lengthy technical reports; creating an annual policy calendar to identify and address long-range issues; and identifying

23. John Nalbandian, "Professionals and the Conflicting Forces of Administrative Modernization and Civic Engagement," *American Review of Public Administration* 35 (Dec. 2005): 311–26.

24. Carl H. Neu Jr., "The Manager as Coach: Increasing the Effectiveness of Elected Officials," *ICMA IQ Report*, Oct. 2003, 10.

and costing-out in advance possible alternative courses of action. Managers can also serve as "coaches" for their elected officials and governing bodies to help them develop high-performance habits.

One useful beginning point is for the manager to hold orientation sessions for new members of the governing body. At the same time, the chair or mayor should work with members to improve the conduct of the governing body's business, including encouraging colleagues to do their homework, ask good questions, and not make too many speeches or embarrass the staff by public comments that would be better said in private. The chair or mayor also should let the manager know if elected officials want other professional staff members to be present and contribute to the meeting and whether the agenda and related materials meet the governing body's expectations in terms of timeliness, priority, quantity, and quality of the information. In these respects, both the manager and the chair or mayor can play the important role of "coach" to the governing body.

Becoming a more high-performing board or council can pay important dividends beyond just the efficient and effective conduct of the public's business. Many governing bodies routinely televise their public hearings and deliberations. The image on a television screen of members of a deliberative body asking thoughtful questions of one another and the professional staff, listening carefully to the views expressed by citizens, treating all who are present with courtesy and respect, and making decisions after assessing options and alternatives goes a long way toward maintaining citizen confidence in local government, not to mention conveying a sense of genuine partnership between the governing body and manager in the governance process.

There is no set formula for building a high-performing governing body, but the above process improvements are important steps in this direction. While the lines between policy and administration will always be blurred, the desired outcome is for governing body members to be able and willing to successfully balance a number of competing interests—to focus on the vision and big picture for the community while dealing with concrete projects and programs, to think and act long-term and strategically while dealing with pressing immediate problems and needs, and to decide on the collective best interest while satisfying constituent expectations.

Searching for an Effective Manager

Hiring a county or city manager is one of the most important actions a governing body may be called upon to take. From the preceding discussion of how the manager and the governing body work together, it should be evident that the parties' relationship can have a significant influence on the effectiveness of the local government they serve. Whether a governing body is hiring its first manager or replacing one who has resigned or been dismissed, it can take the following basic steps to ensure that it makes a good choice.

1. *Determine the future needs of the community and the county or city government.* It is well worth the governing body's time to spend a few hours discussing what it thinks the future demands on the manager's position will look like. What will be happening in the community? What will be the prominent or controversial issues? What will the workforce be like and how will it change? The answers to questions like these are likely to be different for every community. By thinking about them, the governing body increases the probability of finding somebody for the manager's post who has the right talents and experience to deal with the issues facing its community.
2. *List the critical competencies and skills that are required to deal with those future needs.* More than 9,000 men and women are members of the International City/County Management Association (ICMA) and forty-two affiliated state associations, and there are many capable public administrators working in the public and private sectors who are not members. As of 2014, 1,326 managers had successfully completed the ICMA's Voluntary Credentialing Program and committed to an additional forty hours of professional development each year to retain their credentials.

   Many applicants for a county or city manager position will have educational credentials and experience that are at least adequate for the job and often are impressive, but no two of them will be exactly the same.

Each will have different strengths and weaknesses. The challenge facing the governing body involves having to choose from such a large pool of capable applicants the one person who comes closest to having the unique set of skills and abilities needed to deal with local issues and with the board or council's personality. The ICMA has identified the following eighteen manager competencies considered essential to effective local government management, and these competencies can guide governing boards in selecting a manager: staff effectiveness; policy facilitation; functional and operational expertise and planning; citizen service; performance measurement/management and quality assurance; initiative, risk taking, vision, creativity, and innovation; technological literacy; democratic advocacy and citizen participation; diversity; budgeting; financial analysis; human resources management; strategic planning; advocacy and interpersonal communication; presentation skills; media relations; integrity; and personal development.[25]

3. *Recruit and screen applicants.* This step typically includes setting a salary range within which the governing body is willing to negotiate, advertising the job to attract persons with the attributes the governing body seeks, screening applications, and deciding on and arranging to interview the top candidates. Normally the governing body needs a staff person or search consultant to assist with this process, and it is important that this be somebody who has the confidence of the entire membership. Care must be taken to preserve the confidentiality of the applications[26] unless and until the applicants release the county or city from that obligation. The governing body typically seeks such a release in the interview stage.

   Depending on the candidate pool, screening interviews will be arranged for five to ten semifinalists with a committee of the governing body or with a search consultant who will videotape the interviews, after which three to five finalists will each be invited for an interview with the entire governing body. Alternatively, it might be possible to narrow the field down to three to five finalists simply by reviewing and discussing the applications and talking to the candidates' references.
4. *Interview finalists.* The structure of the interview process can vary quite a bit in practice, ranging from (1) simply interviewing each candidate, to (2) having candidates participate in an assessment center and take various performance-related tests on key aspects of the manager's job, to (3) conducting highly structured interviews. At the very least, the interviews should be designed to allow governing body members to make reliable judgments about the important attributes they have agreed are needed in a manager and to make valid and consistent comparisons among the candidates. G.S. 143-318-11(6) (a section of the state open meetings law) allows these interviews to be conducted in a closed session.[27] Sometimes all of the candidates and their spouses are brought in together to see various aspects of the community and meet key people in and outside of county government.
5. *Hire the manager.* After the interviews have wrapped up, the governing body usually tries to reach consensus on one candidate, with, perhaps, a backup if the chosen candidate does not accept an offer of employment. Many managers insist on consensus before they will accept an offer, feeling that anything less would make their positions too tenuous to survive the stress and strain that the demands of leadership and management put on the relationship between them and the elected officials. Some managers, however, are willing to start with no more than the tentative security of support from a simple majority.

---

25. International City/County Management Association, "Practices for Effective Local Government Management," www.icma.org/en/university/about_management_practices_overview. For a detailed treatment of the hiring process, see Vaughn Mamlin Upshaw, John A. Rible IV, and Carl W. Stenberg, *Getting the Right Fit: The Governing Board's Role in Hiring a Manager* (Chapel Hill: UNC School of Government, 2011).

26. Elkin Tribune, Inc. v. Yadkin Cnty. Bd. of Comm'rs, 331 N.C. 735, (1992). The state supreme court held that applications for employment were confidential personnel records under G.S. 153A-98 and that, therefore, their disclosure was prohibited. *See also* Robert Joyce, "Confidentiality of Applicants' Names," *Coates' Canons: NC Local Government Law Blog* (UNC School of Government, Oct. 2, 2012), http://canons.sog.unc.edu/?p=6866.

27. The governing body must nevertheless follow all of the other procedural requirements contained in Article 33C of G.S. Chapter 143. While manager interviews are typically done in closed session, the law does not require that they be so conducted.

If the leading finalist is not an inside candidate, sometimes the governing body will choose to send one or more of its members (or will send its search consultant) to the candidate's community for confirmation of its impressions. Usually, however, the governing body simply arranges for a final background investigation while it negotiates the terms and conditions of employment with the prospective manager.

When these negotiations are complete, the other candidates are notified, and the governing body takes formal action in open session to hire the successful candidate. The entire recruitment, screening, selection, and hiring process can normally be completed in about six months.

6. *Conclude an employment agreement.* An increasing number of counties and cities in North Carolina have formal employment agreements with managers. Sometimes called *contracts,* these documents may set out a variety of conditions specific to the manager's employment. The ICMA has a model employment agreement that (1) covers optional and recommended approaches to items such as compensation; health, disability, and life insurance benefits; vacation, sick, and military leave; use of a car for official business; retirement fund contributions; expense accounts; participation in professional activities; moving and relocation expenses; home sale and purchase expenses; and other terms of employment and (2) seeks to establish a clear understanding between the governing body and the manager about the responsibilities, benefits, and privileges of the office. These types of agreements commonly include severance provisions, which, among other things, specify the manager's responsibilities for notifying the governing body in advance of his or her intention to resign and provide for a lump-sum severance payment in the event the manager's employment is involuntarily terminated for reasons other than illegal or improper behavior.[28] These agreements do not and cannot guarantee any tenure to the manager, inasmuch as G.S. 153A-81(1) and 160A-147(a) provide that the board or council shall appoint the manager to serve at its pleasure.

Evaluating the Manager—And the Governing Body

Generally

Evaluating the county or city manager is a task that governing bodies often find difficult and uncomfortable. Sometimes a manager's evaluation is done in the context of decisions on an annual salary increase and the feedback is general or even perfunctory. In other cases, the chair or mayor, outside of the yearly salary review, simply gives the manager feedback on how he or she is doing on behalf of the governing body. In still other communities, the fact that the manager continues to hold his or her job is a clear indication that performance is satisfactory to the majority of the governing body (i.e., it amounts to a positive evaluation). Why, then, should a governing body take valuable time to more formally evaluate the manager, especially if "things are going OK?"

Clearly Set Expectations

As has been stressed throughout this chapter, the relationship between a governing body and a manager can greatly enhance or impede the processes of governing, leading, and managing, so it is important that the parties devote time to properly establishing and maintaining it. As soon as possible, they should decide what they expect of one another beyond the general tenets of statutory and professional responsibilities. No two governing bodies are exactly alike, nor are any two managers. No matter how much previous experience a new manager has had or how many managers a particular community has had, the relationship between a particular board or council and a particular manager is certain to be different in some ways from any other relationship previously experienced by either party. Thus, it is critical for all parties to be clear and in agreement around priorities, performance, and process.

Soon after a new manager is hired, and again if a significant turnover in governing body membership occurs or a new chair or mayor is elected, all parties will find it useful to discuss their specific expectations of one another. Such

28. *See* International City/County Management Association, "ICMA Model Employment Agreement" (2003), http://icma.org/en/icma/career_network/career_resources/model_employment_agreement.

a discussion allows each party to discover what is needed from him/her and to express what he/she needs from the others to effectively carry out major responsibilities. The chair, mayor, and governing body's expectations of the manager inform their ability to both formally evaluate the manager and give him or her informal feedback about specific behavior and general performance.

Evaluation Process for Managers

Once the governing body and manager have reached agreement on performance expectations in the context of the vision, goals, and objectives for the community, they should agree on the purpose, procedure, and timing of the manager's evaluation. As indicated above, evaluations are often related to the governing body's decisions about adjustments in the manager's compensation.[29] Evaluations also are important tools for giving the manager feedback on strong points and weak points, which can be useful in strengthening his or her competencies and approaches. This regular dialogue can go a long way in avoiding surprises on the part of all parties and in building trust between the manager and governing body. The ICMA model employment agreement (referenced above) establishes the following minimum requirements for both the manager and the governing body: (1) a written evaluation, (2) a meeting to discuss the evaluation, (3) a written summary, and (4) delivery of the final written evaluation to the manager within thirty days of the evaluation meeting.

There are a variety of evaluation approaches—from "one-on-one" reviews with the chair or mayor to a complete 360-degree assessment of the manager by the governing body, professional staff, and community leaders. In accordance with the ICMA model employment agreement, elected officials are asked to complete a written form prior to the evaluation session with the manager, rating the manager on how well he or she exercises general organization management responsibilities, works with the governing body, carries out goals and objectives set by the board or council, develops and executes the budget, provides leadership, relates to the community, deals with the media and external audiences, communicates, delegates and supervises, and performs in other key areas. Usually the manager is also rated on personal characteristics, such as objectivity, integrity, productivity, judgment, initiative and risk-taking, ethics and morals, imagination, drive, self-assurance, stress management, and positive image. The manager normally does a self-assessment, which is shared with governing body members. These materials become the basis for a two-way conversation about the manager's performance and strong/weak points led by the chair or mayor or, in some cases, by an outside facilitator, in closed session. In addition to decisions on compensation and continuity, evaluation results are used by managers in their plan for personal and professional development prior to the next evaluation cycle.

More and more governing bodies are using retreats to set out these initial expectations between themselves and the manager and to address other issues that contribute to effective governance. The idea behind a retreat is for the governing body (and other parties invited by it) to convene at a time and a place different from its regular meeting time and place[30] to deliberate about matters that are difficult to fit into the routine formal business that fills its regular meeting agendas. Retreats are commonly used by governing bodies for the following purposes: to identify strategic goals, objectives, and priorities to advance the governing body's vision for the community; to identify agreements and differences among members in their beliefs about and goals for the community; to plan how to achieve common goals and accommodate differences; to understand one another's expectations about working together and learn individual leadership styles and behaviors; and to review progress in achieving previously agreed-upon goals.[31] Facilitators from outside the local government are often used to bring neutrality into the retreat proceedings and to enhance listening and communications among the participants. Annual retreats are an effective way to build and sustain a unity of effort that is difficult to develop in the course of a governing body's regular meetings and to help keep elected officials and the manager focused on the "big picture" for the community.

---

29. *See* Vaughn Mamlin Upshaw, *How Are We Doing? Evaluating Manager and Board Performance* (Chapel Hill, N.C.: UNC School of Government, 2014).

30. Note: A retreat must still meet all of the requirements set out in the open meetings law (G.S. Chapter 143, Article 33C).

31. For a more thorough discussion of retreats, see Kurt Jenne, "Governing Board Retreats," *Popular Government* 53 (UNC Institute of Government, Winter 1988): 20–26; Amy Cohen Paul, "The Retreat as Management Tool," *ICMA IQ Report* (Jan. 2001); and Robert Porter, "Secrets of a Successful Board Retreat," *Trustee* (May 2000): 26–27.

Evaluating the Governing Body

Increasingly, managers are giving feedback regarding the governing body's performance, and boards and councils are evaluating themselves as decision-making bodies and representatives of the citizens. As indicated in the previously discussed research by John Nalbandian and James Svara, managing, leading, and governing in council–manager communities are shared responsibilities. Just as the governing body expects the manager to conduct himself or herself in accordance with the General Statutes and the ICMA Code of Ethics, the manager has expectations of the governing body that impact upon his or her performance. These might include looking to the board or council to take ownership of its decisions, to recognize and uphold its role as policy maker not micromanager, to defend staff members when they are attacked for carrying out board or council policy, to be decisive and consistent, and to show respect and support for professional staff. Elected officials could fill out questionnaires assessing how the governing body as a unit sets goals, makes policy decisions, establishes priorities, understands the budget, engages the public, operates in a businesslike manner, handles information provided by the professional staff, and relates to the manager.[32]

For some governing bodies, annually evaluating the manager might seem to be a big step, and evaluating their own effectiveness could be viewed as potentially disruptive and dysfunctional. However, just as regular feedback can enhance the manager's performance, introspection by the governing body as to how it conducts its work and relates to professional staff can lead to improvements in its decision-making capacity and ability to represent the community.

Conclusion

The council–manager form of government has a long and successful history in the United States and especially in North Carolina. Like any governmental arrangement, it has potential advantages that are not automatically put into practice. However, many of these advantages can be realized if elected officials and managers work together in a good faith effort to observe the tenets on which the council–manager system is based. The General Statutes and the ICMA Code of Ethics constitute a solid foundation for this form of government, but they are only a starting point in a very complex working relationship. Success under the council–manager form depends, ultimately, on the governing body and the manager's ability to establish clear expectations, maintain good communication, and develop a sense of shared vision and teamwork on behalf of the community.

Additional Resources

Publications

International City/County Management Association. *The Effective Local Government Manager.* 3rd ed. Washington, D.C: ICMA, 2004.

______. *Managing Local Government: Cases in Effectiveness.* Washington, D.C.: ICMA, 2009.

______. *Leading Your Community.* Washington, D.C.: ICMA, 2008.

______. *Working Together: A Guide for Elected and Appointed Officials Training Workbook.* Washington, D.C.: ICMA, 1999.

Organizations

International City/County Management Association, 777 North Capitol St. NE, Suite 500, Washington, D.C., 20002, www.icma.org.

National League of Cities, 1301 Pennsylvania Ave. NW, Suite 550, Washington, D.C., 20004, www.nlc.org.

32. *See* Craig M. Wheeland, "Enhancing the Governing Body's Effectiveness," *in* Charldean Newell, ed., *The Effective Local Government Manager,* 3rd ed. (Washington, D.C.: International City/County Management Association, 2004), 57–69, 79–81.

National Association of Counties, 25 Massachusetts Ave. NW, Suite 500, Washington, D.C., 20001, www.naco.org.

North Carolina League of Municipalities, Albert Coates Local Government Center, 215 North Dawson St., Raleigh, NC, 27603, www.nclm.org.

North Carolina Association of County Commissioners, Albert Coates Local Government Center, 215 North Dawson St., Raleigh, NC, 27603, www.ncacc.org.

North Carolina City and County Management Association, P.O. Box 3069, Raleigh, NC, 27602-3069, www.ncmanagers.org.

About the Author

Carl W. Stenberg is a School of Government faculty member whose work includes directing the Public Executive Leadership Academy, serving as liaison with the North Carolina City and County Management Association, and teaching in the Master of Public Administration Program.

This chapter updates and revises previous chapters authored by former School of Government faculty members Kurt Jenne and Donald Hayman, whose contributions to the field and to this publication are gratefully acknowledged. The author also expresses appreciation to David Leonetti and Ebony Perkins for research assistance on this chapter.

Chapter 5

General Ordinance Authority

Trey Allen

The general ordinance authority of local governments in North Carolina is synonymous with their general police power. The term "police power" denotes much more than the enforcement of criminal laws.[1] In the American legal system, it refers in the first instance to the sovereign power retained by the states under the United States Constitution "to govern men and things within the limits of [their] dominion."[2] A state exercises its police power whenever it legislates, regardless of whether the law being enacted is "a quarantine law, or a law to punish offences, or to establish courts of justice, or requiring certain instruments to be recorded, or to regulate commerce within its own limits."[3]

The courts understand the police power to encompass anything touching the safety, health, welfare, or morals of the public.[4] While the potential scope of the police power is therefore vast, federal and state constitutional provisions substantially limit its reach. For instance, Article I, Section 19 of the North Carolina Constitution and the Fourteenth Amendment to the United States Constitution bar state and local officials from taking an individual's life, liberty, or property without due process of law.[5] Federal statutes and regulations further curtail the states' police power. No state,

1. The word "police" derives from the Latin *politia*, a term the ancient Romans used to refer to the civil administration of government. Santiago Legarre, *The Historical Background of the Police Power*, U. Pa. J. Const. L. 745, 748–49 (2007). *Politia*, in turn, descends from polis, the Greek work for city. *Id.*

2. Thurlow v. Commonwealth of Mass., 46 U.S. 504, 583 (1847) (footnote omitted).

3. *Id.* One influential treatise asserts that the police power's two main attributes are that "it aims directly to secure and promote the public welfare, and it does so by restraint and compulsion." Ernst Freund, *The Police Power, Public Policy and Constitutional Rights*, college ed. (Callaghan & Co., 1904), sec. 3.

4. *E.g.*, City of Concord v. Stafford, 173 N.C. App. 201, 205 (2005) ("The scope of the police power generally includes the public health, safety, morals and general welfare.").

5. While the phrase "due process" does not appear in Article I, Section 19, North Carolina's courts have long construed the phrase "law of the land" in Section 19 to encompass many of the requirements of the Fourteenth Amendment's due process clause. *See* John v. Orth & Paul Martin Newby, *The North Carolina State Constitution*, 2nd ed. (Oxford University Press, 2013), 68–72.

for example, may relieve employers of their legal obligation under Title VII of the Civil Rights Act of 1964 to refrain from discriminating against job applicants and employees based on race, color, gender, religion, or national origin.[6]

The police power is typically exercised by both the states and their various political subdivisions. The way in which this power is shared varies from state to state, depending on the relevant constitutional and statutory provisions in each jurisdiction. In North Carolina the General Statutes (hereinafter G.S.) delegate a portion of the police power to counties and cities in the form of their general ordinance authority.[7] This chapter explores the sources and scope of that general ordinance authority, including the extent to which local governments may enforce their ordinances through criminal and civil actions. It ends with a brief description of the legal rules concerning the adoption and filing of ordinances in North Carolina.

Defining the General Ordinance Authority of Counties and Cities in North Carolina

Sources of the General Ordinance Authority

The North Carolina Constitution declares that the General Assembly "shall provide for the organization and government and the fixing of boundaries of counties, cities and towns, and other governmental subdivisions, and, except as otherwise prohibited by th[e] Constitution, may give such powers and duties to counties, cities and towns, and other governmental subdivisions as it may deem advisable."[8] This constitutional language endows the General Assembly with almost unbridled power to create, abolish, or merge counties, cities, and other units of local government and to define and limit their authority.[9]

As creations of the legislature, local governments may act only as permitted by statute. The primary grants of power to local governments are found in G.S. Chapters 153A (counties) and 160A (cities). Strictly speaking, practically all of the statutes in Chapters 153A and 160A concern the police power in some manner. The statute conferring zoning authority on cities, for instance, explains that the purpose of zoning is to promote the "health, safety, morals, or the general welfare of the community."[10] The focus here, though, is on the general police power delegated to local governments by the statutory provisions located in Article 6 of G.S. Chapter 153A and Article 8 of G.S. Chapter 160A. (To avoid confusion, Articles 6 and 8 will be referred to collectively hereinafter as the "Police Power Statutes.")

The most important of the Police Power Statutes are G.S. 153A-121 and 160A-174. Together the statutes invest the governing boards of counties and cities with the power to adopt ordinances that define, regulate, prohibit, or abate "acts, omissions, or conditions detrimental to the health, safety, or welfare of [their] citizens" and "the peace and dignity" of their jurisdictions and to "define and abate nuisances."[11] This general ordinance authority is supplemented by other provisions in the Police Power Statutes that expressly authorize local regulation of designated matters, with abandoned automobiles (G.S. 153A-132.2, 160A-303.2), noise (G.S. 153A-133, 160A-184), and sexually oriented businesses (G.S. 160A-181.1) being but three examples.

---

6. *See* 42 U.S.C. § 2000e-2.

7. Counties and cities are not the only local government entities to which the General Assembly has delegated a portion of its police power. For example, state law grants local boards of health the authority to adopt rules necessary to protect and promote public health. N.C. Gen. Stat. (hereinafter G.S.) § 130A-39(a). The regulatory powers of boards of health are discussed further in Chapter 38, "Public Health."

8. N.C. Const. art VII, § 1.

9. In other words, North Carolina is not a "home rule" state, as that term is commonly understood; its local governments exist by legislative benevolence, not by constitutional mandate. In constitutional home rule states, the existence or powers of at least some of the state's units of local government are spelled out in the state constitution. To change such provisions, a constitutional amendment, rather than simply a legislative act, is required. *See generally* Frayda S. Bluestein, *Do North Carolina Local Governments Need Home Rule?* 84 N.C. L. Rev. 1983–2030 (2006) (comparing local government authority in home rule states with the powers granted to local governments in North Carolina).

10. G.S. 160A-381(a). Chapter 25 of this publication discusses zoning and other local development measures in detail.

11. *See* G.S. 153A-121(a), 160A-174(a).

Scope of the General Ordinance Authority

It is not always easy to tell whether a particular matter falls within the general ordinance authority. Grave threats to the public health, safety, or welfare are obviously subject to local control unless state or federal law dictates otherwise. The same is true of those matters expressly covered by the Police Power Statutes. Yet reasonable people can disagree over whether any number of other conditions qualify as "detrimental" to the public and, thus, constitute proper objects for local government action. It could be argued, for instance, that G.S. 153A-121 and 160A-174 do not allow local governments to regulate private property solely for the purpose of improving its appearance. The North Carolina Supreme Court, though, has upheld a county ordinance that required junkyards situated near public roads to be surrounded by fencing for purely aesthetic reasons.[12]

To a large degree, the reach of the general ordinance authority depends upon how broadly the courts interpret key terms like "detrimental" and "health, safety, or welfare." A brief review of the judiciary's approaches to questions of local government authority reveals that, while the courts have often narrowly construed statutes granting power to counties and cities, they can be expected to take an expansive view of G.S. 153A-121 and 160A-174 in future cases.

Judicial Approaches to Local Government Power

In 1874 the North Carolina Supreme Court endorsed "Dillon's Rule" for interpreting legislative grants of power to local governments.[13] Named for the Iowa judge who formulated it, Dillon's Rule holds that a local government has only those powers (1) expressly granted to it by the legislature, (2) necessarily or fairly implied in or incident to powers expressly granted, and (3) essential—not simply convenient, but indispensable—to accomplish its declared objects and purposes.[14] Under Dillon's Rule, any reasonable doubt concerning the lawfulness of a challenged action had to be resolved against the local government.

North Carolina's courts applied Dillon's Rule in cases disputing the authority of local governments until the 1970s, often with unpredictable results. Many of the inconsistent outcomes stemmed from judicial attempts to discern whether specific legislative grants of authority "necessarily or fairly implied" certain powers. It is fair to say that the judiciary generally seemed more willing to find implied authority when local governments engaged in historically unremarkable activities than when they embarked upon new, unusual, or controversial endeavors.[15] The courts also tended to disfavor local measures imposing taxes or fees during the Dillon's Rule era.[16]

In 1971 the General Assembly appeared to overrule Dillon's Rule for cities by enacting G.S. 160A-4. This law declares that the provisions of G.S. Chapter 160A "shall be broadly construed and grants of power shall be construed to include any additional and supplemental powers . . . reasonably necessary or expedient to carry them into execution and

12. State v. Jones, 305 N.C. 520, 530, (1982). The *Jones* case articulates a balancing test the courts apply when evaluating the legality of aesthetic regulations. In a nutshell, the court must determine whether the aesthetic purpose to which the regulation is reasonably related outweighs the burdens imposed on the private property owner. *Id.*

13. Smith v. City of Newbern, 70 N.C. 14, 70 (1874).

14. David W. Owens, *Local Government Authority to Implement Smart Growth Programs: Dillon's Rule, Legislative Reform, and the Current State of Affairs in North Carolina*, 35 Wake Forest L. Rev. 671, 680–81 (2000) (quoting John F. Dillon, *The Law of Municipal Corporations*, 2nd ed. (1873), sec. 55).

15. *Compare City of Newbern*, 70 N.C. at 14 (emphasis in original) (holding that a law granting the city power to *"appoint[] market places* and regulat[e] the same" implied authority to build a public market house) *with* State v. Gulledge, 208 N.C. 204, 208 (1935) (holding that neither the power "to regulate the use of automobiles" conferred by charter nor the authority "to license and regulate all vehicles operated for hire" and "to make . . . regulations for the better government" delegated by statute granted the city express or implied power to require taxicab operators to file proof of liability insurance in designated amounts). One explanation for the different outcomes in *City of Newbern* and *Gulledge* is that public marketplaces go back at least as far as ancient Greece, whereas at the time of *Gulledge* the requirement that taxicab operators have liability insurance was "a public policy hitherto unknown in the general legislation of the State." 208 N.C. at 208.

16. *See* Owens, *supra* note 14, at 683 (noting that the courts "strictly construed" local authority in the area of taxes and fees during the period between 1890 and 1910). In 1893, for instance, the North Carolina Supreme Court invalidated an assessment for sidewalks in Greensboro. *Id.* at 684 (citing City of Greensboro v. McAdoo, 112 N.C. 359, 367–78 (1893)).

effect." In 1973, by enacting G.S. 153A-4, the legislature endorsed a substantially identical rule of construction for G.S. Chapter 153A.

Although, taken at face value, G.S. 153A-4 and 160A-4 direct the judiciary to interpret the primary county and city statutes broadly, the North Carolina Supreme Court has not uniformly applied this mandate when reviewing the validity of local government actions. In 1994 the court held that a city may charge reasonable fees for regulatory services, such as commercial driveway permit reviews and rezoning reviews, even though no statute expressly authorized the fees in question.[17] In reaching this conclusion, the court opined that G.S. 160A-4 obliged it to construe the grants of power in G.S. Chapter 160A expansively.

Roughly five years later, the state supreme court invalidated both the ordinance establishing the City of Durham's stormwater management program and the fee schedule used to fund the program.[18] While cities had explicit statutory authority to operate stormwater and drainage systems, Durham's stormwater program incorporated components—hazardous waste collection was one—not directly tied to stormwater management. Moreover, G.S. 160A-314(a1) prohibited a city from imposing fees in excess of a stormwater and drainage system's cost. The court ruled that the city had exceeded statutory parameters by including the supplemental components in its stormwater management program and by charging fees to fund those components. The court made this determination without applying G.S. 160A-4 to the statutory provisions at issue in the case, reasoning that the provisions' clear and unambiguous wording eliminated the need for judicial interpretation.

In 2012 the North Carolina Supreme Court struck down an ordinance adopted to reduce the strain of residential development on public school capacity in Cabarrus County.[19] The ordinance permitted the county to deny or conditionally approve a developer's application when a proposed development would exceed unused school capacity. Developers frequently agreed to contribute funds for school expansion in amounts designated by the county in order to have their applications approved.

The court rejected the county's claim that the general zoning power supported the ordinance, even though one purpose of the zoning statutes is to promote the "efficient and adequate provision of . . schools."[20] According to the court, nothing in the "plain language" of the zoning laws allows counties to address inadequate school capacity through developer fees. The court declined to apply G.S. 153A-4 because it saw no need to go beyond the unambiguous wording of the zoning statutes to decide the case.

The apparent reluctance of the state supreme court to apply G.S. 153A-4 and 160A-4 prompted speculation that it remained disposed to rule against local governments in disputes over the lawfulness of ordinances. Prior to 2014, however, the court had not been squarely presented with the question of whether the broad construction mandates in G.S. 153A-4 and 160A-4 extend to the general ordinance authority. The court finally confronted this question in *King v. Town of Chapel Hill*,[21] a case brought by a tow truck operator to challenge the legality of towing and mobile phone ordinances adopted by Chapel Hill's town council. The towing ordinance prohibited the removal of automobiles from non-residential private lots without the vehicle owners' permission unless signs were posted at designated intervals warning that the lots were tow-away zones. It also capped towing and storage fees at amounts set annually by the council and directed towing companies to accept payment by credit card at no extra charge to the owners of involuntarily towed vehicles. The mobile phone ordinance barred individuals 18 years old or older from using mobile phones while driving, on pain of a $25 fine but no driver's license points.

The basic issue before the supreme court was whether the general ordinance authority conferred on cities by G.S. 160A-174 could sustain the towing and mobile phone ordinances. To resolve this issue, the court first had to

---

17. Homebuilders Ass'n of Charlotte v. City of Charlotte, 336 N.C. 37, 45–47 (1994).

18. Smith Chapel Baptist Church v. City of Durham, 350 N.C. 805, 815 (1999). The high court initially upheld the city's stormwater management program, but then reversed itself after granting the plaintiffs' petition for rehearing. *See id.* at 806; Smith Chapel Baptist Church v. City of Durham, 348 N.C. 632, 639 (1998).

19. Lanvale Props., LLC v. Cnty. of Cabarrus, 366 N.C. 142, 169 (2012).

20. G.S. 153A-341.

21. ____ N.C. ____, 758 S.E.2d 364 (2014).

determine whether G.S. 160A-174 must be interpreted expansively pursuant to G.S. 160A-4. The court explained that it had no choice but to apply G.S. 160A-4 because the police power "is by its very nature ambiguous" and "cannot be fully defined in clear and definite terms."[22] The court then held that, broadly construed, G.S. 160A-174 allows cities to regulate involuntary towing to prevent or mitigate conflicts between the owners of private lots and individuals who park there without permission and between tow truck operators and automobile owners. Turning to the disputed provisions of the towing ordinance, the court found that G.S. 160A-174 was expansive enough to support the ordinance's signage requirements. It further ruled that the town's interest in ensuring that owners have quick and easy access to towed vehicles justified forcing towing companies to take credit cards.

Unlike the signage and form-of-payment provisions, the ordinance's caps on towing and storage fees did not survive judicial scrutiny. The link between the public welfare and the fee caps was too "attenuated" in the court's view for the town to impose the caps without explicit statutory authorization.[23] Additionally, the court expressed concern that the caps would make it impossible for towing companies to recover the costs of complying with the ordinance's other mandates. It even suggested that the caps might violate the constitutional right to enjoy the fruits of one's labor.[24] The court also invalidated the ordinance's prohibition against passing credit card fees on to the owners of involuntarily towed vehicles, describing it as tantamount to a fee cap.

The mobile phone ordinance was struck down in its entirety. State law already prohibited individuals of all ages from texting while driving and barred school bus drivers and individuals under the age of 18 from using mobile phones while driving on public streets or highways.[25] The court regarded these laws as evidence that the General Assembly wanted all regulation of drivers' mobile phone usage to occur at the statewide level.

Impact of King v. Town of Chapel Hill *on the General Ordinance Authority*

The *King* decision could be the North Carolina Supreme Court's most significant treatment of the general ordinance authority. It will have a major impact on future lawsuits alleging that local governments have acted beyond the scope of their police power.

The most important aspect of *King* is its definitive pronouncement that the provisions of G.S. 160A-174, and by implication G.S. 153A-121, must be interpreted broadly. Obviously, the more expansively the general ordinance authority is construed, the more likely a court is to find that an issue falls within the scope of the police power and that the means a local government has chosen to address it are lawful.

Another valuable attribute of *King* is that it provides lower courts with a framework for analyzing whether an ordinance represents a valid exercise of the general ordinance authority. The state supreme court did not consider the lawfulness of the towing ordinance's individual provisions until after it concluded that the police power covers the practice of involuntary towing. Thus, when facing a claim that a local government has acted outside the bounds of G.S. 153A-121 or 160A-174, a court should begin by asking whether the contested ordinance targets a problem within the scope of the police power. So long as the ordinance concerns an activity or condition that threatens the health, safety, or welfare of the public in some way, the answer to this question will probably be yes.[26] If it is yes, the court should then consider whether the requirements imposed by the ordinance are reasonably calculated to deal

22. *King*, ____ N.C. at ____, 758 S.E.2d at 370.

23. *King*, ____ N.C. at ____, 758 S.E.2d at 371. As an example of such statutory authorization, the court pointed to G.S. 160A-304, which permits cities to set the rates charged by taxi cabs. *Id.*

24. *See* N.C. Const. art. I, § 1 (declaring "that all persons are created equal; that they are endowed by their Creator with certain inalienable rights; that among these are life, liberty, the enjoyment of the fruits of their own labor, and the pursuit of happiness").

25. *See* G.S. 20-137.3(b) (forbidding mobile phone use by minor drivers); 20-137.4(b) (outlawing the use of mobile phones by persons operating school buses); 20-137.4A(a) (banning drivers from text messaging while operating automobiles).

26. Minor threats to the public welfare can be enough to bring a matter within the police power's reach. Concerns about odor and noise problems, for example, have been held to justify a city's decision to regulate the number of dogs that could be kept per lot. State v. Maynard, 195 N.C. App. 757 (2009).

with the problem.[27] A finding that such requirements are reasonable will typically warrant a ruling in favor of the local government, even if the requirements are extensive. In *King* the signage provision regulated practically every aspect of "Tow Away" signs on nonresidential private lots, including their placement, exact wording, and size.[28] The supreme court nonetheless upheld the signage provision as a "rational attempt" to prevent or mitigate the risks posed by involuntary towing.

Of course, *King* was not a total win for Chapel Hill. The supreme court's rulings against the town highlight a few of the substantial restrictions on the police power of local governments. Although the court stopped short of saying that a county or city may never rely on the general ordinance authority to control the prices charged by companies in transactions to which the local government is not a party, *King* leaves the impression that explicit statutory authorization is usually needed for such action. The court's invocation of the right to the fruits of one's labor is a warning that local governments can violate constitutional rights when they simultaneously increase regulatory burdens on businesses and take steps to limit what the businesses may charge others. Likewise, the invalidation of the mobile phone ordinance reminds local governments that the police power granted by G.S. 153A-121 and 160A-174 is preempted when the General Assembly either expressly or implicitly removes a matter from local control. The principles of preemption and other limitations on the general ordinance authority are discussed in more detail below.

Other Provisions in the Police Power Statutes

G.S. 153A-121 and 160A-174 speak in broad terms, but the Police Power Statutes contain a number of provisions that address local government power over designated matters. Table 5.1 at the end of this chapter contains a partial list of the individual topics covered in the Police Power Statutes alongside the statutes pertaining directly to each.

The cumulative effect of the statutes cited in Table 5.1 is to confer express power on local governments to regulate a hodgepodge of subjects. Several of the statutes, though, establish procedural requirements a county or city must adhere to when exercising its general ordinance authority over certain matters, while others totally exclude some things from the local regulation.

Grants of Specific Authority

The grants of specific authority listed in Table 5.1 include the power to regulate, restrict, or prohibit amplified noises that tend to annoy, disturb, or frighten citizens (G.S. 153A-133, 160A-183); business activities of itinerant merchants and peddlers (G.S. 153A-125, 160A-178); and begging and other canvassing of the public for contributions (G.S. 153A-126, 160A-179). Local governments also have express statutory authority to prohibit the abuse of animals (G.S. 153A-127, 160A-182) and to restrict or prohibit the possession of dangerous animals (G.S. 153A-131, 160A-187). The Police Power Statutes invest counties and cities with the power to regulate places of amusement, such as coffee houses, cocktail lounges, night clubs, and beer halls, so long as their regulations are consistent with any permits or licenses issued by the state's Alcoholic Beverage Control Commission (G.S. 153A-135, 160A-181). Additionally, local governments may restrict or prohibit the discharge of firearms except in defense of persons or property or pursuant to the lawful instructions of law enforcement officials (G.S. 153A-129, 160A-189).

The particular grants of authority in the Police Power Statutes mostly reinforce rather than expand the general ordinance authority bestowed by G.S. 153A-121 and 160A-174. Venomous snakes, for instance, unquestionably pose potential health and safety risks to a city's inhabitants, and consequently, G.S. 160A-174 would allow cities to restrict or ban the possession of such animals, even if Article 8 lacked a "dangerous animals" provision.

On the other hand, merely because a matter is not expressly mentioned in the Police Power Statutes does not mean that local governments are powerless to regulate it under G.S. 153A-121 or 160A-174. G.S. 153A-124 states that the enumeration of specific powers in G.S. Chapter 153A "is not exclusive, nor is it a limit on the general authority [of a county] to adopt ordinances [pursuant to] G.S. 153A-121." Likewise, G.S. 160A-177 provides that the enumeration of specific powers in G.S. Chapter 160A is not a constraint on a city's general ordinance authority.

---

27. Of course, if an ordinance concerns a matter beyond the reach of the police power, then it is unlawful unless other statutory authority exists for its adoption.

28. *King*, ____ N.C. at ____, 758 S.E.2d at 370–71.

If the specific provisions in the Police Power Statutes do not really expand the general ordinance authority, why did the General Assembly pass them? Several of the statutes were enacted before—some long before—the adoption of the broad construction mandates in G.S. 153A-4 and 160A-4, when the judiciary commonly invoked Dillon's Rule to invalidate local measures. The statute allowing cities to prohibit the abuse of animals, for instance, dates from 1917, while the first version of the statute permitting counties to regulate solid waste (G.S. 153A-136) appeared in 1955. These older provisions could represent a legislative attempt to ensure that local regulation of certain matters would not fall victim to Dillon's Rule.

The legislature has delegated many of the same ordinance powers to counties and cities, but there are differences. Thus, while cities have explicit power under G.S. Chapter 160A, Article 8 to address "the emission or disposal of substances or effluents that tend to pollute . . [the] land" (G.S. 160A-185), no statute in G.S. Chapter 153A, Article 6 expressly grants comparable authority to counties. Similarly, Article 6 contains a provision allowing counties to mandate the annual registration of mobile homes used for living or business quarters (G.S. 153A-138), but Article 8 has no such statute for cities.

How should these disparities be interpreted? It would be a mistake to assume that, just because a provision appears in one article but not the other, the authority to regulate a subject is reserved exclusively to either counties or cities. As explained above, the general ordinance authority extends beyond the individual powers enumerated in the Police Power Statutes. The existence of specific authority could reflect nothing more than a legislative assumption that a problem is more acute in urban or rural areas.

Procedural Requirements

Some Police Power Statutes include procedural requirements that must be followed for ordinances dealing with designated subjects to be valid and enforceable. For example, separate statutes expressly allow a county or city to mandate removal of an off-premises outdoor advertisement that violates an outdoor advertising ordinance, but only after written notice of the intent to require removal has been communicated to the owners of the advertisement and of the property on which the advertisement is situated (G.S. 153A-143, 160A-199). Except in limited circumstances, the same statutes also prevent a local government from ordering the removal of a nonconforming outdoor advertisement without compensating the advertisement's owner. Other statutes explicitly authorize counties and cities to adopt ordinances prohibiting the abandonment of motor vehicles on public and private property and to enforce those ordinances through the removal and disposal of abandoned vehicles, provided the local government takes precise steps to notify the vehicle owners of the removals and to afford them the right to contest the removals at hearings (G.S. 153A-132, 160A-303).

When more than one statute authorizes an action, a local government usually has the choice of proceeding under any or all of them. This principle does not apply, however, when it is clear from the unambiguous text or level of detail in a statute that the General Assembly intended that law to guide local action on a particular matter. A governing board should consult its attorney whenever questions arise about whether to rely on G.S. 153A-121 or 160A-174 or on one of the grants of specific authority in the Police Power Statutes.

Restrictions on Ordinance Authority

A handful of the Police Power Statutes exclude things from the general ordinance authority of local governments. G.S. 153A-145 and 160A-202 collectively prohibit counties and cities from banning cisterns and rain barrel collection systems used to collect water for irrigation purposes. Still other provisions prevent local governments from halting the sale of soft drinks above a particular size (G.S. 153A-145.2, 160A-203).

Some grants of express authority implicitly restrict regulation that is not within the scope of the power granted. For example, by permitting counties and cities to impose curfews on persons under 18 years of age, G.S. 153A-142 and 160A-198 likely signal the legislature's disapproval of local curfews for adults in non-emergency situations.

Exercising General Ordinance Authority

Almost every provision in the Police Power Statutes requires a local government to exercise its general police power "by ordinance." The adoption of an ordinance is therefore usually necessary if a county or city wishes to regulate, restrict, or prohibit something. A few statutes permit a county or city to eliminate threats to public health or safety even in the absence of an ordinance. Those statutes are examined briefly in the "Public Nuisance Abatement" section below.

Territorial Limits of General Ordinance Authority

A county has the option of making an ordinance adopted pursuant to G.S. 153A-121 or another statute in G.S. Chapter 153A, Article 6 applicable to any part of the county not within a city.[29] A city's governing board may adopt a resolution allowing a county police power ordinance to apply inside the city.[30] If the governing board later changes its mind, it may by resolution withdraw its consent to enforcement of the ordinance within its borders. The governing board should promptly inform the county of its withdrawal resolution, as the ordinance will remain in effect inside the city until thirty days after the county receives the notice.

For the most part, a city's police power ordinances apply only within the corporate limits and to any city-owned property or right-of-way outside the city.[31] A city may enforce zoning and other development ordinances inside its corporate limits and within its extraterritorial jurisdiction (ETJ). Depending on a city's population, the ETJ can stretch as far as three miles beyond the corporate limits.[32] (More information about ETJs is available in Chapter 25 of this publication.) When a city chooses to enforce development ordinances in its ETJ, the county's development ordinances no longer apply there, but the county's police power ordinances continue in force. Thus, a county's noise ordinance applies within the ETJ, even though its zoning ordinances do not. Action by either the county or the city may therefore be proper in some circumstances. If, for instance, a dwelling located in the ETJ appears unfit for human habitation, the county might take remedial action under its nuisance ordinance or the city might take steps to have the house repaired or demolished in accordance with its minimum housing standards.

Preemption of Local Ordinances

It is not uncommon for state or federal law to deny local governments the power to regulate matters that would otherwise fall within their general ordinance authority. Local regulation is said to be "preempted" when this occurs.

The essential rules of preemption are codified in G.S. 160A-174(b). Nothing about preemption appears in the text of G.S. 153A-121, but the North Carolina Supreme Court has repeatedly held that G.S. 160A-174(b) applies to a county's exercise of its general ordinance authority.[33] G.S. 160A-174(b) describes six scenarios in which local ordinances are preempted.

- Counties and cities are prohibited from adopting ordinances that violate liberties guaranteed by the state or federal constitution. Thus, if a city council were to ban all religious speech in city parks but allow other categories of speech there, G.S. 160A-174(b) would render its action void as an infringement on the constitutional rights of individuals to free speech and religious liberty.
- Local governments have no power to prohibit acts, omissions, or conditions expressly made lawful by state or federal law. In a 1962 case, the North Carolina Supreme Court invalidated a Raleigh ordinance that absolutely banned the peddling of ice cream from vehicles on city streets. The plaintiff had obtained a privilege license from the state allowing it to peddle its ice cream products, and the supreme court viewed the city's total ban on the practice as an impermissible restriction on conduct approved by the General Assembly.[34]
- Ordinances may not make lawful an act, omission, or condition expressly prohibited by state or federal law. So, because state law criminalizes prostitution, no county or city may legalize prostitution within its borders.

---

29. G.S. 153A-122.

30. *Id.*

31. G.S. 160A-176.

32. More information about the legal rules concerning the extraterritorial jurisdiction of municipalities may be found in Chapter 25 of this publication

33. *E.g.*, Craig v. Cnty. of Chatham, 356 N.C. 40, 45 (2002) (citation omitted) ("This Court has held that [G.S.] 160A-174 is applicable to counties as well as cities.").

34. E. Carolina Tastee-Freez, Inc. v. City of Raleigh, 256 N.C. 208, 211–12 (1962).

- Local governments have no power to regulate subjects that state or federal law expressly forbids them to regulate. State law, for example, generally prohibits local governments from adopting ordinances that establish rules for the manufacture, sale, purchase, transport, possession, or consumption of alcoholic beverages which differ from those set forth in G.S. Chapter 18B.[35] (One noteworthy exception to Chapter 18B's prohibition on local regulation is G.S. 18B-300(c), which allows a county or city to regulate or prohibit the possession or consumption of malt beverages or unfortified wine on public streets by persons who are not occupants of motor vehicles and on property owned, occupied, or controlled by the local government.)
- Even when no state or federal law expressly deprives counties or cities of the power to regulate a matter, local governments may not regulate subject(s) for which state or federal statutes clearly evince a legislative intent to provide a complete and integrated regulatory scheme to the exclusion of local regulation. In other words, if federal or state laws regarding a subject are sufficiently comprehensive, the courts will assume that the U.S. Congress or the General Assembly meant to remove the matter from local control. In one case, the North Carolina Supreme Court struck down an ordinance designed to regulate large-scale hog farming operations in Chatham County.[36] The plaintiffs argued that comprehensive state-level swine farm laws preempted the local rules. The supreme court agreed, concluding that "North Carolina's swine farm regulations [and the applicable state statutes] are so comprehensive in scope that the General Assembly must have intended that they comprise a 'complete and integrated regulatory scheme' on a statewide basis, thus leaving no room for further local regulations."[37]
- No ordinance may define an offense using the same elements as an offense defined by state or federal law. State law, for instance, already criminalizes various forms of assault, including simple assault, simple assault and battery, and assault inflicting serious bodily injury.[38] Accordingly, counties and cities may not adopt ordinances that prohibit the very same misconduct covered by the assault statutes.

G.S. 160A-174(b) ends with a reminder that the preemption rules ordinarily do not stop local governments from adopting standards of conduct higher than those demanded by federal or state laws. In a case involving a challenge to local obscenity regulations, for example, the North Carolina Supreme Court observed that, "notwithstanding the existence of a general state-wide law relating to obscene displays and publications, a city may enact an ordinance prohibiting and punishing conduct not forbidden by such state-wide law."[39]

Ordinance Enforcement

Local governments have the ability to enforce their ordinances through any or all of the criminal and civil enforcement actions described below. A county or city may pursue criminal and civil enforcement actions against an offender for the same ordinance violation.[40] Moreover, an ordinance may specify that each day's continuing violation is a separate and distinct offense, thus exposing offenders to mounting criminal and civil penalties the longer they remain in violation of the ordinance. The main statutes concerning ordinance enforcement are G.S. 153A-123 and 160A-175.

---

35. G.S. 18B-100.

36. *Craig*, 356 N.C. at 50.

37. *Id.* The court also struck down board of health regulations and zoning amendments regulating hog farming operations, though for somewhat different reasons.

38. G.S. 14-33(a) (making simple assault and simple assault and battery Class 2 misdemeanors); G.S. 14-32.4 (making it a Class F felony to assault and inflict serious injury on another person).

39. State v. Tenore, 280 N.C. 238, 247 (1972). Of course, a local government may not impose a higher standard of conduct than state or federal law when such law indicates either expressly or by its comprehensiveness that local regulation of a given matter is entirely precluded.

40. *See* Sch. Dirs. v. City of Asheville, 137 N.C. 503, 510 (1905) ("A party violating a town ordinance may be prosecuted by the state for the misdemeanor, and sued by the town for the penalty.")

Criminal Actions

Anyone who violates a county or city ordinance commits a Class 3 misdemeanor and risks a fine of not more than $500.[41] There are two exceptions to this rule. First, if the ordinance regulates the operation or parking of vehicles, a violator is responsible for an infraction rather than a misdemeanor and any fines assessed may not exceed $50.[42] Second, a county or city governing board may expressly provide that the violation of an ordinance will not result in a misdemeanor or infraction or, alternatively, that the maximum punishment will be some number of days or amount of money less than the statutory maximum.[43]

Only a law enforcement officer or person expressly authorized by statute may issue a citation requiring an individual to answer to a misdemeanor charge or infraction.[44] Proving that a criminal misdemeanor has been committed requires local officials to secure the assistance of the district attorney's office to prosecute the crime, and the violation must be proved "beyond a reasonable doubt." Although the potential fine for a Class 3 misdemeanor is relatively small, a person convicted of an ordinance violation has a criminal record. Some local officials prefer to enforce ordinances through criminal actions, reasoning that the threat of a criminal record may help deter ordinance violations.

Civil Actions

Local governing boards have the option of enforcing their ordinances through a variety of civil measures, including civil penalties and court orders directing offenders to comply with particular ordinances. In most cases, such measures cannot be pursued unless the ordinance at issue contains language identifying them as potential methods of enforcement.[45]

Civil Penalties

To impose a civil penalty for an ordinance violation, the ordinance must specify the amount of the penalty to be charged per violation. The local government may pursue payment of the penalty through a civil action against the offender. There is no statutory cap on the amount of civil penalties, but the Eighth Amendment to the U.S. Constitution prohibits civil penalties which are grossly disproportionate to their corresponding offenses.[46] The courts are unlikely to rule that a civil penalty as high as several hundred dollars violates the Eighth Amendment, so long as the penalty is not exceptionally large compared with other civil penalties imposed by the county or city.[47]

Local governments may delegate the power to issue civil citations to personnel who are not law enforcement officers.[48] A county or city may have its attorneys pursue civil penalty actions in superior or district court, depending on the amount of penalty at issue. If the penalty amount is small enough, a local government may use non-attorney employees to seek a judgment against the offender in small claims court. A civil penalty action is one "in the nature of debt," which means that a person found responsible for violating an ordinance with a civil penalty provision owes a debt to the county or city. Furthermore, the standard of proof in civil penalty cases, as in most civil proceedings, is "by a preponderance of evidence," which is a lower burden of proof for the local government than the criminal "beyond a reasonable doubt" standard. All of these factors (who may issue citations, who may bring the action, the lack of a set

---

41. G.S. 14-4(a). No fine for an ordinance violation may exceed $50 "unless the ordinance expressly states that the maximum fine is greater than fifty dollars." *Id.*

42. An infraction is "a noncriminal violation of law not punishable by imprisonment." G.S. 14-3.1(a).

43. G.S. 153A-123(b), 160A-175(b).

44. David M. Lawrence, "Criminal versus Civil Enforcement of Local Ordinances—What's the Difference?" *Local Government Law Bulletin* No. 130 (UNC School of Government, Dec. 2012), http://sogpubs.unc.edu/electronicversions/pdfs/lglb130.pdf (citing G.S. 15A-302). The practical effect of G.S. 15A-302 is to limit the issuance of such citations to sworn law enforcement officers. *Id.*

45. Rather than include enforcement language in every ordinance, some jurisdictions have "remedies" sections in their codes of ordinances that cross-reference various ordinances and specify which remedies may be applied for violations of each ordinance.

46. David M. Lawrence, "Are There Limits on the Size of Penalties to Enforce Local Government Ordinances?" *Local Government Law Bulletin* No. 128 (UNC School of Government, July 2012), http://sogpubs.unc.edu/electronicversions/pdfs/lglb128.pdf.

47. Lawrence, *supra* note 46.

48. Lawrence, *supra* note 44.

dollar maximum on the penalty, and the evidentiary standard) lead some local officials to prefer civil actions to criminal prosecutions for ordinance violations.

The Setoff Debt Collection Act offers local governments an avenue for recovering civil penalties in excess of $50 without having to resort to litigation.[49] As authorized by the Act, the North Carolina Association of County Commissioners and the North Carolina League of Municipalities have set up the Local Government Debt Setoff Clearinghouse. Provided they give debtors the statutorily mandated notice, counties and cities may submit qualifying debts to the Clearinghouse to be recovered from debtors' state tax refunds or lottery winnings. According to its website, the Clearinghouse has collected more than $210 million for local governments since 2002.[50]

Local officials should not assume that incorporating a civil penalty provision into an ordinance will generate significant revenue for county or city coffers. Pursuant to Article IX, Section 7 of the North Carolina Constitution, the "clear proceeds" of moneys collected for many if not most ordinance violations must go to the public school system(s) of the county in which the local government is situated. See Chapter 45, "The Governance and Funding Structure of North Carolina Public Schools," for more information about the legal principles used to determine when and how much of the moneys collected for ordinance violations are owed to the public schools.

Equitable Remedies

The governing board of a county or city may include language in an ordinance providing for its enforcement through an appropriate equitable remedy. Language of this kind allows the county or city to obtain a court order directing an offender to comply with the ordinance. The offender who ignores such an order risks being held in contempt of court.

Public Nuisance Abatement

A public nuisance is "a condition or activity involving real property that amounts to an unreasonable interference with the health, safety, morals, or comfort of the community."[51] The authority of local governments to define and abate such nuisances is usually exercised through ordinances that prohibit certain conditions or uses of real property. One common example is the overgrown vegetation ordinance, which imposes minimum maintenance requirements on residential or commercial lots.

When a nuisance ordinance is violated, the local government may seek a court order directing the defendant to take whatever steps are necessary to comply with the ordinance, including the closure, demolition, or removal of structures; the removal of items such as fixtures or furniture; the cutting of grass or weeds; or the making of improvements or repairs to the property. If the offender fails to obey the order within the time set by the court, the local government can execute the order and automatically obtain a lien on the property for the cost of execution. The offender may be cited for contempt.

It is sometimes lawful for counties and cities to remedy nuisances without going to court. Indeed, local governments possess statutory authority to deal with dangerous nuisances even when the property owner involved has not actually violated an ordinance. G.S. 153A-140 allows a county "to remove, abate, or remedy everything that is dangerous or prejudicial to the public health or safety," though this authority does not extend to bona fide farms and is sharply limited with regard to other agricultural or forestry operations. For a county to exercise its power under G.S. 153A-140, it must provide the property owner with adequate notice, the right to a hearing, and the right to seek judicial review.

G.S. 160A-193 permits a city to "remove, abate, or remedy everything in the city limits, or within one mile thereof, that is dangerous or prejudicial to the public health or public safety." Consequently, nuisances that threaten the health or safety of the public anywhere within one mile of a city may be addressed by either the county or the city.

Unlike G.S. 153A-140, G.S. 160A-193 declares that the power it confers may be exercised "summarily," that is to say, without affording the property owner notice or a hearing. As interpreted by the North Carolina Court of Appeals,

---

49. G.S. 105A-1, -16.

50. *See* www.ncsetoff.org/index.html

51. Richard Ducker, "Nuisance Abatement and Local Governments: What a Mess," *Coates' Canons: NC Local Government Law Blog* (UNC School of Government, June 6, 2011), http://canons.sog.unc.edu/?p=4747.

however, G.S. 160A-193 does not authorize a city to demolish a building "without providing notice or a hearing to the owner [unless] the building constitutes an imminent danger to the public health or safety necessitating its immediate demolition."[52]

When a local government eliminates a nuisance pursuant to G.S. 153A-140 or 160A-193, it automatically obtains a lien for the expense of corrective action upon the land or premises where the nuisance occurred. A city also has a lien for the action's cost on any other real property—except a primary residence—owned by the offending property owner inside or within one mile of the city. (The owner can avoid a lien on other property by showing that the nuisance resulted solely from another's conduct).

Dangerous nuisances do not represent the only situations that can lead to local government action without a court order. In the case of an individual who qualifies as a chronic violator of a public nuisance ordinance, the local government may notify the person that, if his or her property is found to be in violation of the ordinance during the calendar year in which notice is given, the county or city will remedy the violation and the cost of corrective action will be a lien upon the property.[53] The same rules apply to chronic violators of a city's overgrown vegetation ordinance.[54]

Adoption and Filing of Local Ordinances

Adoption of Ordinances

Consistent with the notion that ordinances regulate important aspects of citizens' lives, special procedural rules govern the adoption of ordinances in most situations.[55] With certain exceptions, the only time a county's governing board may adopt an ordinance at the meeting at which it is introduced is when all board members are present and vote in favor of the ordinance.[56] If the ordinance passes with anything less than a unanimous vote of all members, the board may adopt the ordinance by majority vote at any time within 100 days of its introduction. For a city's governing board to adopt an ordinance on the date of its introduction, the ordinance must garner an affirmative vote equal to at least two-thirds of the board's membership, excluding vacant seats and not counting the mayor unless the mayor has the right to vote on all questions before the board.[57] (See Chapter 3 of this publication for an in-depth discussion of the voting rules for local governing boards.)

Many people mistakenly assume that a public hearing must be held any time an ordinance is proposed for adoption. In fact, only a few types of ordinances require a public hearing, such as those regulating land use and Sunday business closings.[58]

Filing of Ordinances

With certain exceptions, every ordinance enacted by the governing board of a county or city must appear in either an *ordinance book* or a *code of ordinances.* Local governments are under no legal obligation to post ordinances on their websites, though many do so anyway to improve public access to their ordinances.

52. Monroe v. City of New Bern, 158 N.C. App. 275, 278 (2003). The court also held that, if a city wishes to destroy a dwelling that does not pose an imminent threat to the public, it must follow the procedures set forth in the Minimum Housing Standards statutes (G.S. 160A-441 through -450). *Id.* at 279. Those statutes outline in significant detail the notice and hearing procedures a city has to satisfy prior to the demolition of a dwelling deemed unfit for human habitation.

53. G.S. 153A-140.2, 160A-200.1 (defining a chronic violator as "a person who owns property whereupon, in the previous calendar year, the [local government] gave notice of violation at least three times under any provision of the public nuisance ordinance").

54. G.S. 160A-200 (defining a chronic violator as "a person who owns property whereupon, in the previous calendar year, the municipality took remedial action at least three times under the overgrown vegetation ordinance," *id.* § -200(a)).

55. These procedural rules also apply to most ordinance amendments.

56. G.S. 153A-45.

57. G.S. 160A-75.

58. David Lawrence, "When Are Public Hearings Required," *Coates' Canons: NC Local Government Law Blog* (UNC School of Government, Aug. 21, 2009), http://canons.sog.unc.edu/?p=77.

The primary statutory provisions for ordinance books appear in G.S. 153A-48 and 160A-78, while those for codes reside in G.S. 153A-49 and 160A-77. Some of the county and city rules differ. To avoid confusion, they are considered separately below.

City Ordinance Book

A true copy of each city ordinance must be filed in an appropriately indexed ordinance book. This book is separate from the minutes book and is maintained for public inspection in the city clerk's office. If the city has adopted and issued a code of ordinances, its ordinances need to be filed and indexed in the ordinance book only until they are codified.

City Code of Ordinances

Every city with a population of 5,000 or more must adopt and issue a code of ordinances. A code is a bound or loose-leaf compilation of the local government's ordinances systematically arranged by topic into chapters or articles; it is the local parallel to the North Carolina General Statutes. In requiring larger cities to codify their ordinances, the law assumes that these cities will have so many ordinances that particular ones would be difficult to locate in a simple ordinance book. If a city of under 5,000 people finds itself in that situation, then it too should codify its ordinances.

The code must be updated at least annually unless there have been no changes. It may contain separate sections for general ordinances and technical ordinances, or the latter may be issued as separate books or pamphlets. Examples of technical ordinances are those pertaining to the following:

- building construction
- installation of plumbing and electric wiring
- installation of cooling and heating equipment
- zoning
- subdivision control
- privilege license taxes
- the use of public utilities, buildings, or facilities operated by the city

The governing board also has the option of classifying other specialized ordinances as technical ordinances for code purposes.

A city's governing board may omit from the code classes of ordinances that it designates as having limited interest or transitory value—the annual budget ordinance is one example—but the code should clearly describe what has been left out. The council may also codify certain ordinances pertaining to zoning district boundaries and traffic regulations by making appropriate entries upon official map books permanently retained in the clerk's office or in another city office generally accessible to the public.

The city is free to choose a code-preparation method that meets its needs. One acceptable method would be for the city attorney or a private code-publishing company to prepare the code in consultation with the clerk.

County Ordinance Book

The clerk to the board of commissioners must file each county ordinance in an appropriately indexed ordinance book, with the exception of certain kinds of ordinances discussed in the next paragraph. The ordinance book, kept separately from the minutes book, is stored for public inspection in the clerk's office. If the county has adopted and issued a code of ordinances, it must index its ordinances and maintain them in an ordinance book only until it codifies them.

The ordinance book need not include transitory ordinances—like the budget ordinance—and certain technical regulations adopted in ordinances by reference, although the law does require a cross-reference to the minutes book (at least for transitory ordinances). If the board of commissioners adopts technical regulations in an ordinance by reference, the clerk must maintain an official copy of the regulations in his or her office for public inspection.[59]

County Code of Ordinances

Counties may, but are not required to, adopt and issue codes of ordinances. A county that has codified its ordinances should update its code annually unless there have been no changes. Counties may reproduce their codes by any method

59. G.S. 153A-47.

that yields legible and permanent copies. A county, like a city, is free to select a code-preparation method that suits its needs.

A county may include separate sections in a code for general ordinances and for technical ordinances, or it may issue the latter as separate books or pamphlets. The governing board may omit from the code classes of ordinances designated by it as having limited interest or transitory value, but the code should clearly describe the classes of ordinances that have been left out. The board may also codify certain ordinances pertaining to zoning areas or district boundaries by making appropriate entries upon official map books permanently retained in the clerk's office or in some other county office generally accessible to the public.

Importance of Filing Ordinances

It is crucial for a local government to file and index or codify its ordinances as required by law. Pursuant to G.S. 160A-79, any ordinance not filed and indexed or codified is unenforceable.

Records Retention Considerations

Records retention schedules promulgated by the North Carolina Department of Cultural Resources mandate that local governments keep official copies of their ordinances permanently.[60] To the extent that they have funds available for the purpose, counties and cities likewise have to create "preservation duplicates" of their ordinances that are "durable, accurate, complete and clear."[61] The department's policy is that those duplicates must be maintained in paper form or on microfilm. Local governments should consult the website of the department's Office of Archives and History for more details concerning the permanent retention of ordinances.[62]

About the Author

Trey Allen is a School of Government faculty member who specializes in the general ordinance authority of local governments and governmental liability and immunity.

This chapter updates and revises previous chapters authored by former School of Government faculty member A. Fleming Bell, II, whose contributions to the field and to this publication are gratefully acknowledged.

60. *See* N.C. Department of Cultural Resources, Records and Retention Schedule: County Management (April 15, 2013), 8 (Standard 1, Item No. 38), www.ncdcr.gov/Portals/26/PDF/schedules/schedules_revised/County_Management.pdf; Records Retention and Disposition Schedule: Municipal (Sept. 10, 2012), 11 (Standard 1, Item No. 49), www.ncdcr.gov/Portals/26/PDF/schedules/schedules_revised/municipal.pdf.

61. G.S. 132-8.2.

62. *See* www.history.ncdcr.gov/.

Table 5.1 Selected Police Power Statutes for Local Governments

Subject Matter	City Statute (G.S.)	County Statute (G.S.)
Solicitation campaigns, flea markets, itinerant merchants	160A-178	153A-125
Begging/panhandling	160A-179	153A-126
Aircraft overflights	160A-180	—
Places of amusement	160A-181	153A-135
Sexually oriented businesses	160A-181.1	—
Abuse of animals	160A-182	153A-127
Explosive, corrosive, inflammable, or radioactive substances	160A-183	153A-128
Noise	160A-184	153A-133
Pollutants or contaminants	160A-185	—
Domestic animals	160A-186	—
Possession or harboring of dangerous animals	160A-187	153A-131
Bird sanctuaries	160A-188	—
Firearms	160A-189	153A-129
Pellet guns	160A-190	153A-130
Sunday closings	160A-191	—
Solid wastes	—	153A-136
Public health nuisance	160A-193	153A-140
Stream-clearing programs	160A-193.1	153A-140.1
Regulation/licensing of businesses, trades, etc.	160A-194	153A-134
Curfews	160A-198	153A-142
Outdoor advertising	160A-199	153A-143
Removal/disposal of abandoned and junked vehicles	160A-303*	153A-132
Abandonment of junked vehicles	160A-303.2*	153A-132.2
Removal/disposal of trash, garbage, etc.	160A-303.1*	153A-132.1
Registration of mobile homes, house trailers, etc.	—	153A-138

**Denotes a provision found outside of the Police Power Statutes.*

Chapter 6

Civil Liability of the Local Government and Its Officials and Employees

Anthony J. Baker

The expense and trouble of lawsuits are unavoidable costs of doing a local government's business. If a city or county operates a law enforcement department, a fire department, a park, or any other public service long enough, someone will cause damage to something or harm somebody. Indeed, even without any legitimate basis, a local government and its employees may still be made defendants to a civil lawsuit. The challenge for public servants is, therefore, not the impossible task of eliminating lawsuits. Rather, it is providing local services while minimizing the cost and the disruption that lawsuits bring. The first step in accomplishing that task is learning the basic legal principles that control the liability of local governments and their public servants. This chapter uses the term "public servants" to refer to all the people who do the local government's work, including elected members of the governing board, members of appointed boards, and staff. At times, however, the chapter distinguishes "employees" from "officials" and "elected officials" from "other municipal workers." In these cases the meanings of the terms used should be clear from the context.

This chapter deals with the two most common areas of liability for local governments: tort liability under North Carolina law and liability under federal law for violations of the Civil Rights Act of 1871[1] (often called Section 1983, which refers to its location in the United States Code).[2] As covered in this chapter, the state and federal rules governing these claims determine whether a local government and its public servants may be required to pay damages to someone harmed by official action. Some overlap between the two sets of rules means that certain official actions may violate both of them and make the local government and its public servants potentially liable under state and federal law. (However, the person who brings the lawsuit may be compensated only once for the injuries.)

The discussion that follows is an introduction to a complex subject. There are many twists and turns in this dynamic area of the law that cannot be and are not fully described here. Furthermore, there is a universe of both state and federal claims that this chapter cannot begin to address: environmental claims, tax claims, a variety of other civil rights claims, and contract claims, to mention a few.

Civil Procedure

All lawsuits begin with a complaint, filed by the plaintiff, in which the plaintiff alleges that the defendant has somehow harmed the plaintiff. Generally, the defendant will respond to a complaint with an answer in which the defendant admits or denies the plaintiff's allegations while also asserting relevant affirmative defenses and motions to dismiss. One such motion to dismiss asserts that the plaintiff has not stated a legal claim for which damages should be paid, even if the court assumes that the plaintiff's allegations are true. Attorneys call this a Rule 12(b) motion. If successful, a 12(b) motion will end a lawsuit very early in the process before either party spends funds or time on discovery.

If the motions to dismiss are unsuccessful, the parties will begin discovery. The process of discovery allows parties to share and to explore the evidence should the case go to trial. Common tools of discovery are interrogatories, requests for production of documents, and depositions. Depositions, especially, may be very expensive after both sides pay their attorneys to participate and pay a court reporter to record the deposition. Once discovery is completed, either party may file a motion for summary judgment. Again, simply stated, this motion means that the moving party does not believe any significant facts are in dispute, negating the need for a jury, and the judge can rule as a matter of law in favor of the moving party. Plaintiffs will commonly file a motion for summary judgment in which they ask the court to rule that the defendant is liable, thereby leaving the jury to decide only the amount of damages. Defendants file motions for summary judgment to show the court that the significant facts are not in dispute and to ask the court to rule, as a matter of law, that the defendants are not liable. Regardless of who files the motion for summary judgment, if the motion is denied, the case proceeds to trial before a jury, if a jury trial has been requested.

Civil cases are subject to mandatory mediated settlement efforts prior to trial. Cases may be mediated before or after the motion for summary judgment is heard. A successful mediation allows the parties to retain control of the case rather than relying on a jury to decide it. When a case settles, one party usually pays the other, general releases are signed, and the lawsuit is dismissed. Many experienced mediators will tell both parties that a mediation is successful when both parties are equally dissatisfied with the proposed settlement; rarely does a litigant receive everything that has been demanded.

Cases in which a local government is a defendant and the local government has lost a motion for summary judgment are often immediately appealed. These appeals are presented to the North Carolina Court of Appeals. If the court of appeals affirms the trial court's denial of the motion for summary judgment, the case usually proceeds to trial. The local government may then appeal the matter to the North Carolina Supreme Court only if one of the appellate judges filed a dissenting decision or if the supreme court permits the appeal to be heard.

---

1. 42 U.S.C.A. § 1983 (1988).

2. The question of what law applies to a particular claim is largely independent of the court in which the lawsuit is brought. State courts handle some claims brought under federal law, including Section 1983 claims, and federal courts handle some claims brought under state law. *See* Howlett v. Rose, 496 U.S. 356 (1990); 28 U.S.C. § 1332(a)(1).

The history of many cases cited in this chapter ends with the court of appeals either affirming or reversing the trial court's ruling on a motion for summary judgment. The result of the case (that is, who won) will not always be evident in the appellate cases. Thus, usually, either the case ended with the court of appeals ruling and the other party did not try to appeal to the supreme court, the case settled, or the case was tried and no later appeals arose after the trial. Since local governments are, more often than not, the defendants in lawsuits, winning a motion for summary judgment and having that decision affirmed by the appellate courts creates a general rule of law that local governments may not be held liable under the facts presented by that specific case. Losing a motion for summary judgment does not necessarily create a rule of law declaring that the local government is liable under the facts of the case but is a ruling that, based on these facts, the case should be submitted to a jury. If the appellate history of the case ends after the local government loses the motion for summary judgment, it often signals that the local government settled the claim.

Tort Liability under North Carolina Law

Tort law serves to protect a person's interest in his or her bodily security, tangible property, financial resources, or reputation. Unlike contract law, in which the standard of conduct is determined by mutual promises between parties, in tort law, the defendant is being held to a standard of conduct (or duty) imposed by law. To succeed in the lawsuit, the plaintiff must demonstrate that the defendant violated that duty and that the violation caused an injury.

Compensation is the primary concern of tort law. This area of law is premised on the belief that individuals who are harmed through no fault of their own should not be required to bear the loss; instead, the person whose wrongful act caused the harm must pay to restore the injured party to the condition before the harm. Another purpose of tort law is to deter people from engaging in conduct likely to cause personal injury or property damage. Tort law assumes that people will be more careful in conducting their day-to-day activities if they have to pay for any harm that results.

Three types of civil wrongs may be remedied by an award of damages in a civil tort lawsuit: intentional torts, negligence, and nuisances. Understanding these wrongs is important in comprehending how tort law affects the liability of local governments and their officials and employees.

Intentional Torts

Intentional torts are deliberate wrongful acts that cause personal injury or property damage. These acts give rise to civil liability for damages unless a special privilege or defense applies. To succeed in demonstrating liability, the plaintiff only has to show that the person causing the injury deliberately engaged in the wrongful act. The definition does not require that the defendant intended the consequences of the act, including the particular damages caused. For example, someone may have intended to hit another person. Even though they may not have intended to cause serious injury, if such injury occurs, they may be liable for an intentional tort.

There is a common misperception that local governments may not be held liable for the intentional torts of their public servants. As the examples below illustrate, however, local governments may be held liable for these intentional torts.

Battery

Battery is the intentional touching or striking of another person without either that person's consent or a legally recognized authorization. The local government's potential liability will depend, in part, on whether the battery occurred within the scope and course of the employee's duties.

In *Munick v. the City of Durham,*[3] a 1921 case, the North Carolina Supreme Court ruled that Durham was liable when the city's water department manager severely beat Munick for nothing more than paying his $4.50 water bill using paper bills and a wrapped roll of fifty pennies. The court found that Munick could recover damages from the City of

3. 181 N.C 188 (1921).

Durham where the water department manager was an "officer of the corporation and was acting in the discharge of his duty, and that the plaintiff was on the premises at the invitation of the corporation."[4]

Striking another person without that person's consent is not always a battery. For example, a law enforcement officer may use reasonable force to effect a legal arrest.[5] Therefore an officer who uses such force and strikes a suspect to prevent an escape does not commit a civil battery unless more force is employed than is reasonably necessary to make the arrest. If excess force is used, the officer may be sued in state court for the intentional tort of battery and be required to pay damages.[6] Absent the defenses discussed in the section on local government liability, the local government that employs the officer may also be held liable under state tort law.

Assault

An *assault* is legally defined as the placing of another person in reasonable apprehension of immediate harm or offensive contact.[7] An assault must include an "overt act or an attempt, or the unequivocal appearance of an attempt, with force and violence, to do some immediate physical injury to the person of another. . . ."[8] So, for example, an outraged municipal employee who approaches a customer with fists clenched and shouting angry threats has committed an assault if the customer perceives the threat to be serious and is reasonably fearful.

False Imprisonment

False imprisonment is restraining the movement of another without that person's permission or without a legally recognized authorization. This claim is frequently made against local government, especially in the law enforcement context. A common subset of the law enforcement cases involves claims that the plaintiff concealed merchandise. North Carolina General Statutes (hereinafter G.S.) Section 14-72.1(c) protects law enforcement officers from civil liability in this situation as long as the search is at or near the store and the officer has probable cause to believe the person committed the offense. Regarding warrantless arrests, the initial standard is whether the officer had probable cause to arrest.[9] Where an officer made an erroneous assumption about whether the plaintiff told the officer the truth and then compounded that error by ignoring the statements of two eye witnesses, the officer not only did not have probable cause to arrest but also voided the defense of qualified immunity.[10]

A less frequently litigated issue regarding false imprisonment involves holding a prisoner beyond the scheduled release date. In one case of false imprisonment, an inmate was held on work release for nearly six months following a contempt order issued after the inmate had failed to appear at an equitable distribution hearing in district court. There was apparently some ambiguity in the ordered release date—whether it was a time certain or when the inmate complied with an order to fulfill his equitable distribution obligation. The inmate brought an action against the Mecklenburg County sheriff, who was found not to be liable since no intent to unlawfully imprison the inmate could be found where

---

4. 181 N.C. at 196. See the section below titled "Scope of Employment" for a more in-depth discussion regarding an employer's liability for the intentional torts of its employees.

5. N.C. Gen Stat. (hereinafter G.S.) § 15A-401(d)(1).

6. State v. Mobley, 240 N.C. 476 (1954). In *Houston v. DeHerrodora*, 192 N.C. 749 (1926), for example, police officers who chased the plaintiff in their car and fired twenty shots at him before identifying themselves as police officers were held liable for battery and required to pay $2,000 in damages.

7. See Prosser and Keaton on Torts § 10, 43 (1984).

8. *See* Dickens v. Puryear, 302 N.C. 437, 445 (1981).

9. Sevigny v. Dicksey, 846 F.2d 953, 956 (1988). The additional issue of whether the officer retains his qualified immunity depends on the standard of "objective legal reasonableness"—whether a police officer acting under the circumstances at issue reasonably could have believed that he or she had probable cause to arrest (that is, the facts were such that a reasonable officer would have believed the arrestee was committing or had committed a criminal offense).

10. *Id.* at 956.

there was no clear mandate as to the inmate's release.[11] In another case, an inmate was kept in the county jail beyond the court-ordered release date.[12] The county was held liable.

Regarding the potential liability of non-sworn local government staff for false imprisonment, a mayor was found liable for false imprisonment for ordering a police officer to arrest and detain a man for thirty to forty minutes without legal justification.[13]

Defamation

Defamation is written or oral communication that injures a third party's reputation. Defamation in writing is called *libel*; oral defamation is called *slander*. Defamatory remarks might include accusations that a person is a criminal, statements that injure someone in his or her occupation, or claims that an individual has an offensive disease. For example, a false rumor spread by a city emergency medical services worker that a particular person has a sexually transmitted disease would be defamation. Defamation was also established against a city employee in a case in which the city manager falsely told a local newspaper that an employee had been dismissed for stealing.[14] However, establishing a defamation claim against the local government via respondeat superior (liability of the employer for the acts of its employees) has proven to be much more difficult in light of governmental immunity,[15] and rarely does a local governing body, collectively, make an official defamatory comment.[16]

A public servant sued for defamation may have available three defenses. First, the truth of a statement is an absolute defense to liability for damages in a defamation lawsuit. Second, a person may avoid liability for a false statement by showing that it was made under circumstances that gave rise to a qualified privilege.[17] A qualified privilege exists when (1) the person who makes a statement has a valid interest in making it or a legal duty to make it and (2) the person makes a statement to someone with a corresponding interest or duty. Public servants protected by a qualified privilege to make a particular statement will not be held liable for defamation unless they act with malice in making it. Finally, if the employee accused of defamation is a public official, that public official may also be protected from liability by governmental immunity if the immunity is available to the governing body and if the allegations against the public official do not give rise to intentional or malicious conduct.[18]

Negligence

Negligence involves unintentional torts. This area of law imposes a duty on all people, including public servants, to use reasonable care in conducting their daily affairs. If someone fails to use reasonable care and such conduct causes personal injury or property damage that was a predictable result of the carelessness, the person harmed is entitled to compensation. The main exception to this rule permits a person sued for negligence to invoke the defense of *contributory negligence*—a legal rule that bars recovery by any individual whose own negligence, however slight, contributes to his or her injury.

---

11. Emory v. Pendergragh, 154 N.C. App. 181 (2002).

12. *See* Williams v. State, 168 N.Y.S.2d 163 (Ct. Cl. 1957) (awarding damages for false imprisonment to prison inmate who had been detained for one and one-half years after his maximum sentence had expired).

13. Blackwood v. Cates, 297 N.C. 163 (1979); *see also* Hoffman v. Clinic Hosp., 213 N.C. 669 (1938) (per curiam).

14. *See* Jones v. Brinkley, 174 N.C. 23 (1917).

15. Houpe v. City of Statesville, 128 N.C. App. 334 (1998); Shuping v. Barber, 89 N.C. App. 242 (1988). The cities' respective liability policies excluded defamation as a covered tort and, thus, the cities retained governmental immunity.

16. Phillips v. Winston-Salem/Forsyth Cnty. Bd. of Educ., 117 N.C. App. 274 (1994). The court ruled that the board's vice-chairman was not acting as an agent of the board when he made allegedly defamatory comments to a newspaper reporter outside of a board meeting.

17. *See* Presnell v. Pell, 298 N.C. 715 (1979); Towne v. Cope, 32 N.C. App. 660 (1977). In some instances state statutes expressly extend this qualified privilege to designated public servants. For example, the 1987 General Assembly created a privilege for written communications made by members of nursing home advisory committees. *See* G.S. 131E-128(i).

18. *Shuping*, 89 N.C. App. 242. Police officer was not protected by governmental immunity as a public official where governmental immunity will protect a public official for mere negligence only and allegations gave rise to slander per se, creating the presumption of malice.

Negligence may occur in an infinite variety of situations. Whether particular conduct is negligent cannot be determined in the abstract; the jury must decide in each specific case whether the defendant acted as a reasonably prudent person would have under the same circumstances. Some examples may help illustrate these rules. In one case, two local government employees drove a truck that spewed a thick insecticide fog along a road.[19] The fog totally blocked the view of approaching traffic. No warning signs were displayed to give oncoming vehicles notice of the hazard. A man rounded a curve into the fog and slowed his truck, but he was blinded by the fog and sideswiped a car that had pulled off the road to wait for the fog to clear. The North Carolina Supreme Court held that a jury could find that the two employees were negligent—had not exercised reasonable care under the circumstances—in creating a hazardous condition likely to cause injury to highway travelers.

Another case involved a six-year-old boy who was riding his bike and was struck and killed by a drunk driver. The young boy was riding his bike down a steep hill toward a T-intersection at which there was a clearly visible stop sign and took a right turn, remaining in the right lane. Whether the young boy stopped at the stop sign is unknown. The drunk driver was driving in the wrong lane toward the intersection and struck the child just as he made the right turn. On the corner of this intersection, in the city's right-of-way (though not in the paved portion of the road), were bushes that the plaintiff alleged obscured the drunk driver's ability to see the child coming down the hill and obscured the young boy's ability to see the drunk driver proceeding in the wrong lane (the bushes did not, however, obscure the stop sign). In response to the trial court's denial of the city's motion for summary judgment, the North Carolina Court of Appeals ruled that a jury would need to decide whether the city knew or should have known that the bushes may have obscured the intersection, whether the city breached its duty to maintain the public rights-of-way by not removing the bushes, and finally, whether the bushes were a proximate cause of the accident.[20]

In another case, a county jailer took custody of a sick and helpless man who had been arrested and placed him in a cell with another man who was violently insane.[21] During the night the insane man used a leg torn from a table in the cell to beat the helpless inmate, and he died the next morning. The North Carolina Supreme Court ruled that a jury could find that the jailer had failed to act reasonably—in other words, that he was negligent—in placing a helpless individual in the same cell with a violent one.

In still another case, an employee was cutting grass in a rocky area of a government-owned park using a ten-year-old mower without a front guard.[22] The mower threw out a rock, which hit a man and fractured his skull. The park superintendent testified that he had seen rocks thrown from beneath the mower "thousands of times." The North Carolina Supreme Court found it unreasonable under the circumstances for the local government to allow operation of the mower without a guard because it should have anticipated that eventually someone would be injured.

Finally, a city was held not liable for a sewage backflow into a home caused by a baseball-sized rock lodged at a dislocated joint in the public sewer main where there was no evidence that the city knew or should have known of the impending blockage in the public sewer main.[23]

Nuisance and Inverse Condemnation

A local government that engages in an activity that substantially and unreasonably interferes with the use and enjoyment of someone's land commits a tort called *nuisance.* The local government may be required to pay damages caused by a nuisance even if the damage arises from the performance of a governmental function. For example, in one case a city's sewage treatment plant smelled so badly that the value of the plaintiff's nearby home was permanently reduced.

19. Moore v. Town of Plymouth, 249 N.C. 423 (1959).

20. Beckles-Palomares v. City of Winston-Salem, 202 N.C. App. 235, *cert. denied,* 364 N.C. 434 (2010). Governmental immunity was not an issue, as G.S. 160A-296 imposes a duty on cities to maintain streets. That statutory duty has been held to override governmental immunity. Kirkpatrick v. Town of Nags Head, 213 N.C. App. 132, 713 S.E.2d 151 (2011).

21. Dunn v. Swanson, 217 N.C. 279 (1940).

22. Glenn v. City of Raleigh, 246 N.C. 469 (1957).

23. Ward v. City of Charlotte, 48 N.C. App. 463, *cert. denied,* 301 N.C. 531 (1980). The court also rejected the arguments that the City of Charlotte was liable pursuant to breach of contract.

The state supreme court held that the plaintiff was entitled to recover damages from the city to compensate him for the reduction in value.[24]

In another sewer-related case, a homeowner's basement flooded with raw sewage from the city-maintained public sewer system during heavy rains. The city's investigation showed that the sewer main in front of the home was at least fifty years old, that the elevation of the basement was too low to properly work with the gravity-operated sewer system, and that the home required a check valve to prevent sewage from backing into the home. The homeowner claimed that the city's operation of the sewer system, which allowed stormwater to infiltrate the system, was a nuisance. The North Carolina Court of Appeals ruled that the evidence was sufficient to submit the issue of nuisance to the jury.[25]

A local government may also be liable for lowering someone's land values under federal and state constitutional provisions that prevent government from taking a person's private property without just compensation. If a local government's activities permanently and substantially reduce the value of land, a court may say that the locality has in effect taken the property and must compensate the property owner.[26] This kind of taking is sometimes called *inverse condemnation* to distinguish it from condemnation or outright appropriation of land for public use. For example, the state supreme court has ruled that inverse condemnation, not nuisance, provides the sole remedy available to a landowner for interference with his property by aircraft overflights involving a city-owned airport.[27] Inverse condemnation has also been pled where a zoning ordinance restricted the uses available to a property owner under the theory that the zoning ordinance had taken a property interest without just compensation. The North Carolina Supreme Court responded that the zoning ordinance in question must eliminate all reasonable uses of the property before the zoning authority will be liable for a taking of some property interest.[28]

Scope of Employment

Generally, a local government is liable for the torts of its employees if the harm occurs while they are acting within the scope of their employment, meaning in furtherance of the local government's business.[29] Determining what is inside and what is outside the scope of employment is sometimes difficult. In one case, for example, the Town of Black Mountain was sued when a boy died after falling from a town truck negligently driven by a town golf course employee.[30] The accident occurred while the employee drove the truck on a personal pleasure trip down a public road against the explicit orders of his supervisor. The North Carolina Supreme Court held that the town was not responsible for his negligence because at the time of the accident, he was acting outside the scope of his employment.[31] Another case took a broader view of the scope of employment, relying on *Munick v. City of Durham*, cited above, in reference to intentional torts. In *Edwards v. Akion*, Edwards alleged that Akion, a Raleigh sanitation employee, assaulted her after an argument arose between Edwards and Akion regarding how Akion had performed his duties at Edwards's residence. Without further provocation, Akion attacked Edwards. The North Carolina Court of Appeals ruled that the issue of whether Akion's actions were within the scope of his employment would be decided by a jury. Critical to the court's decision was that the argument between Edwards and Akion was apparently about how Akion performed his duties. The court stated

24. Glace v. Town of Pilot Mountain, 265 N.C. 181 (1965).

25. Hughes v. City of High Point, 62 N.C. App. 107, *cert. denied*, 309 N.C. 320 (1983).

26. *See* Gray v. City of High Point, 203 N.C. 756 (1932); *cf.* Williams v. Town of Greenville, 130 N.C. 93 (1902).

27. Long v. City of Charlotte, 306 N.C. 187 (1982). A related rule provides that a city does not enjoy governmental immunity if it undertakes to abate a nuisance on private property and the property owner can later prove that a nuisance did not in fact exist. *See* Rhyne v. Town of Mount Holly, 251 N.C. 521 (1960) (holding that city may be required to pay for trees wrongfully cut down by city workers enforcing local ordinance requiring landowners to cut weeds and brush twice a year).

28. Messer v. Town of Chapel Hill, 346 N.C. 259 (1997).

29. This rule assumes the local government has waived governmental immunity, as discussed below.

30. Rogers v. Town of Black Mountain, 224 N.C. 119 (1944).

31. *See also* Lertz v. Hughes Bros., 208 N.C. 490 (1935), in which the employer was held liable for an automobile accident that occurred when an employee took a joy ride while running an errand for the employer; Munick v. City of Durham, 181 N.C. 188 (1921).

that an act could be within the scope of employment "even if it is contrary to the employer's express instructions, when the act is done in the furtherance of the employer's business and in the discharge of the duties of employment."[32]

The North Carolina Supreme Court later distinguished *Munick* in *Medlin v. Bass and the Franklin Board of Education* when it ruled that a principal's sexual assault of a student was not within the scope of his employment. The court noted that "[w]hile [the principal] was exercising authority conferred upon him by defendant Franklin County Board of Education when he summoned the minor plaintiff to his office to discuss her truancy problem, in proceeding to assault her sexually he was advancing a completely personal objective. The assault could advance no conceivable purpose of defendant [the board of education]; [the principal] acted for personal reasons only, and his acts thus were beyond the course and scope of his employment as a matter of law."[33]

Liability of the Local Government

Governmental Immunity

Governmental versus Proprietary Activities

Because of governmental immunity, the law treats public employers very differently from private employers. However, a North Carolina local government's liability for the torts of its public servants depends on whether the employee was engaged in a governmental or a proprietary activity. The distinction is important because governmental immunity protects a local government from liability for the tort of an employee who harms someone while performing a government function; however, the government is liable if the employee commits a tort while engaged in a proprietary activity. Governmental immunity is granted to cities and counties by the state of North Carolina and is derived from the doctrine of sovereign immunity, which is inherited from the British system of government and means "the king can do no wrong." Sovereign immunity protects the state of North Carolina from paying damages for torts committed by state employees and officers. The state grants governmental immunity, a limited form of sovereign immunity, to cities, counties, and other municipal corporations, such as boards of education. Cities and counties may give up their protection under governmental immunity by obtaining liability insurance coverage or by funding a reserve expressly in lieu of insurance, even if such a waiver is limited.[34]

Courts have defined governmental activities as follows:

> Any activity . . . which is discretionary, political, legislative or public in nature and performed for the public good on behalf of the State, rather than to itself, comes within the class of governmental functions. When, however, the activity is commercial or chiefly for the private advantage of the compact community, it is private or proprietary.[35]

Unfortunately this distinction between governmental and proprietary activities is difficult to apply and often results in arbitrary characterizations of a local government's activities. The absence of a precise standard makes it difficult to predict whether a local government will be liable for the torts of employees engaged in particular activities. North Carolina courts rely heavily on earlier cases and certain public policies when distinguishing between governmental and proprietary activities. Some of the factors courts have considered in determining whether an activity is governmental

---

32. Edwards v. Akion, 52 N.C. App. 688, 693, *aff'd*, 304 N.C. 585 (1981) (per curiam). The court contrasted *Edwards* with *Robinson v. Sears, Roebuck & Co.*, 216 N.C. 322 (1939). In *Robinson*, the North Carolina Supreme Court relieved Sears, Roebuck & Co. of liability where the argument that instigated the assault was based on a personal matter and not related to the work of the Sears employee.

33. Medlin v. Bass, 327 N.C. 587, 594 (1990). See also *Young v. Great American Insurance Co. of New York*, 359 N.C. 58 (2004), in which the North Carolina Supreme Court ruled that a police officer acted outside of the scope of his employment when he sexually assaulted female drivers he had stopped for traffic violations while on duty.

34. G.S. 153A-435(a) (counties) and G.S. 160A-485(a) (cities). Not all municipal corporations are authorized to waive immunity through the purchase of insurance. Water and sewer districts, for example, are special-purpose municipal corporations that cannot waive immunity in this manner. *See* Thrash v. City of Asheville, 95 N.C. App. 457 (1989), *rev'd on other grounds*, 327 N.C. 251 (1990).

35. Millar v. Town of Wilson, 222 N.C. 340 (1942).

or proprietary include (1) who traditionally performs the service, (2) whether a fee is charged for the service, and (3) whether the primary beneficiaries of the service are community citizens or residents of the state as a whole.

Who Performs the Service?

Activities historically performed by governments but not ordinarily engaged in by private corporations have been held by the courts to be governmental activities.[36] Examples of activities that governments traditionally perform include operating traffic lights,[37] driving a police car,[38] using a police or fire alarm,[39] enforcing zoning regulations or ordinances,[40] furnishing water to firefighters,[41] condemning property,[42] granting franchises,[43] administering sanitation programs,[44] and operating a public park.[45] If the activity is one not traditionally performed only by cities and counties, courts have not allowed local governments to claim the protections of governmental immunity. For example, a young woman died when the doctors in a public hospital negligently gave her a transfusion with the wrong type of blood. The North Carolina Supreme Court held that operating a public hospital was a proprietary function because its operation was not a service traditionally performed only by local governments. As a result, the woman's survivors could recover damages from the hospital for the negligent acts of its employees.[46]

Even where the local government traditionally performs a specific function, the state may legislatively remove the protection afforded by governmental immunity. For example, G.S. 160A-296 imposes a duty on cities to maintain streets. That statutory duty has been held to override governmental immunity.[47] Similarly, cities do not enjoy governmental immunity for maintaining storm drains.[48]

Is a Fee Charged for the Service?

Collecting user fees is a popular method of paying for many local services but unfortunately can increase a local government's potential liability. Local government operations are more likely to be deemed proprietary if they involve a fee of some sort.[49] Examples of proprietary activities include charging a fee to maintain a landfill,[50] distributing water for profit,[51] distributing electricity for profit,[52] operating an airport,[53] operating a municipal golf course,[54] operating a public coliseum,[55] and maintaining a public park in which a fee was charged for admission into an amusement area of the park.[56] Charging a fee does not automatically render an activity proprietary. Services truly governmental in nature

---

36. Sides v. Cabarrus Mem'l Hosp., Inc., 287 N.C. 14, 29 (1975).

37. Hamilton v. Hamlet, 238 N.C. 741 (1953).

38. Lewis v. Hunter, 212 N.C. 504 (1937).

39. Cathey v. City of Charlotte, 197 N.C. 309 (1929).

40. Orange County v. Heath, 14 N.C. App. 44, *aff'd*, 282 N.C. 292 (1972).

41. Howland v. Asheville, 174 N.C. 749 (1917).

42. Dale v. City of Morganton, 270 N.C. 567 (1967).

43. Denning v. Goldsboro Gas Co., 246 N.C. 541 (1957).

44. James v. City of Charlotte, 183 N.C. 630 (1900); Koontz v. City of Winston-Salem, 280 N.C. 513 (1972).

45. Hickman v. Fuqua and City of Winston-Salem, 108 N.C. App. 80 (1992) (citing Hare v. Butler, 99 N.C. App. 693, 698, *disc. review denied*, 327 N.C. 634 (1990)).

46. Sides v. Cabarrus Mem'l Hosp., Inc., 287 N.C. 14 (1975); *see also* Casey v. Wake Cty., 45 N.C. App. 522, *discretionary review denied*, 300 N.C. 371 (1980) (holding that provision of birth control in county family planning clinic is governmental function).

47. Kirkpatrick v. Town of Nags Head, 713 S.E.2d 151 (2011).

48. Jennings v. City of Fayetteville, 198 N.C. App. 698 (2009). However, see *Stone v. City of Fayetteville*, 3 N.C. App. 261 (1968). For further distinction, see *Biggers v. John Hancock Mutual Life Insurance Co.*, 127 N.C. App. 199 (1997), in which the court of appeals ruled that Charlotte was protected by governmental immunity for assisting a private property owner to clear a storm drain pipe that was privately owned and maintained and that drained water that accumulated on private property.

49. Sides v. Cabarrus Mem'l Hosp., Inc., 287 N.C. 14 (1975).

50. Koontz v. City of Winston-Salem, 280 N.C. 513 (1972).

51. Foust v. Durham, 239 N.C. 306 (1954).

52. Rice v. Lumberton, 235 N.C. 227 (1952).

53. Rhodes v. City of Asheville, 230 N.C. 134 (1949).

54. Lowe v. Gastonia, 211 N.C. 564 (1937).

55. Aaser v. Charlotte, 265 N.C. 494 (1965).

56. Glenn v. Raleigh, 246 N.C. 469 (1957). Glenn was injured in a picnic area of the 42-acre park, an area used free of charge. The City of Raleigh charged admission to an amusement area of the same park. The North Carolina Supreme Court determined that

are not made proprietary merely because a local government charges fees for them.[57] The following cases illustrate the courts' approach to local government activities involving a fee. In one case, a woman was seriously injured when she was struck by a garbage truck negligently operated by an employee of the city's sanitation department.[58] The court held that garbage collection was a governmental function and the plaintiff therefore could not recover damages from the city. The fee charged for waste disposal did not make garbage collection a proprietary function because the fees covered only actual expenses. The court of appeals has also ruled that governmental functions include operating a county-owned ambulance service,[59] operating an emergency call center,[60] and providing inspections for building code violations,[61] even though local governments charge fees for these services. However, if the local government is making a profit on the activity, the court will consider such profit strong evidence that the activity is proprietary.[62]

Are the Primary Beneficiaries Community Citizens or Residents of the Entire State?
Some local government functions exist primarily for the benefit of that jurisdiction's residents. Other operations more broadly protect the health and welfare interests of the state as a whole. When a local government engages in an activity for the exclusive benefit of its residents, courts are more likely to find that the local government is acting within its proprietary nature.[63] For example, in 1909 the North Carolina Supreme Court ruled that maintaining a free public sewer was a governmental function and therefore the City of Asheville was not liable for causing cases of typhoid fever by negligently discharging sewage into a creek.[64] In 1980 the North Carolina Court of Appeals followed that rule when it decided that the City of Lenoir was not liable for sewage backing up into a resident's home.[65] In both cases the court was sensitive to the public health benefits of having municipal sewage systems. However, in 1991 the North Carolina Court of Appeals ruled the North Carolina legislature intended for sewage collection to be a proprietary function with the passage of Chapter 160A, Article 16, of the North Carolina General Statutes, entitled Public Enterprises, in which sewage collection and disposal is defined as a public enterprise and which authorizes a fee to be charged for this service.[66]

Operations with Both Proprietary and Governmental Elements

When an injury results from an activity that includes both governmental and proprietary characteristics, North Carolina courts sometimes isolate the particular part of the activity that caused the plaintiff's injury to determine whether governmental immunity applies to that part of the activity. So, to use a public works department as an example, sup-

---

the park operation was a proprietary function. In addition, Glenn was injured by a rock thrown from a city lawnmower from which the front guard had been removed. City staff acknowledged seeing debris previously ejected from beneath the lawnmower.

57. *See* Casey v. Wake Cnty., 45 N.C. App. 522, *review denied,* 300 N.C. 371 (1980).

58. James v. City of Charlotte, 183 N.C. 630 (1922). *See* Broome v. City of Charlotte, 208 N.C. 729 (1935).

59. McIver v. Smith, 134 N.C. App. 583 (1999). See *Childs v. Johnson,* 155 N.C. App. 381 (2002), in which the court of appeals held that Forsyth County did not have governmental immunity where the director of the Forsyth County EMS services was involved in an automobile accident while driving his assigned county-owned vehicle since the director was on a personal errand at the time of the accident. See also *Earp v. Peters,* No. 5:07CV31, 2010 WL 3895718 (W.D.N.C. Sept. 30, 2010), in which the federal district court judge for the Western District of North Carolina relied on *Beckles-Palomares v. City of Winston-Salem,* 202 N.C. App. 235 (2010), cited above, and ruled that, much like G.S. 160A-296, G.S. 20-156 creates a statutory duty for emergency vehicle drivers to drive with due regard for the safety of all persons using the highway and that this statutory duty preempts the doctrine of governmental immunity.

60. Wright v. Gaston Cnty., 205 N.C. App. 600 (2010). The fee involved is levied pursuant to G.S. 62A-43, which mandates a $0.70 monthly fee for each active voice communications service connection capable of accessing the 911 system.

61. Norton v. SMC Bldg, Inc. and Montgomery Cnty., 156 N.C. App. 564 (2003). Curiously, though most jurisdictions charge a fee for building permits and inspections, the court did not address the issue of charging fees.

62. Hare v. Butler, 99 N.C. App. 693, *review denied,* 327 N.C. 634 (1990); Waters v. Biesecker, 60 N.C. App. 253, *aff'd,* 309 N.C. 165 (1983) ("[a]lthough the term 'proprietary' denotes a profit motive, profit motive is not essential to the determination that a function by a governmental body is proprietary").

63. *See* Britt v. City of Wilmington, 236 N.C. 446 (1952).

64. Metz v. City of Asheville, 150 N.C. 748 (1909).

65. Roach v. City of Lenoir, 44 N.C. App. 608 (1980). *But cf.* Williams v. Town of Greenville, 130 N.C. 93 (1902) (holding city liable for tort of trespass when water backing up at clogged culvert causes property damage).

66. Pulliam v. City of Greensboro, 103 N.C. App. 748, *discretionary review denied,* 330 N.C. 197 (1991).

plying water to fight fires is distinguished as a governmental function,[67] whereas selling available water to the public for consumption is isolated as a proprietary activity.

It is not uncommon for a county or municipal building to house offices for several different departments, some of which perform governmental functions, while others undertake proprietary functions. The maintenance or repair of such a building is a governmental function, even though part of the building is devoted to proprietary activities. Consequently, governmental immunity may bar the claim of a plaintiff who was injured by a local government's negligent failure to keep the building in proper repair.[68]

Waiver of Governmental Immunity by the Purchase of Insurance

The General Assembly has authorized cities and counties to waive the defense of governmental immunity by purchasing liability insurance.[69] Local governments may be inclined to waive this defense for several reasons. First, as just illustrated, for many activities local governments cannot be certain in advance that governmental immunity will protect them from liability. Second, by purchasing liability insurance, a local government provides a remedy for citizens who otherwise could not be compensated for injuries caused by the negligence of the local government's employees in performing governmental activities. Third, the defense of governmental immunity is limited to tort claims. It does not extend to claims for violations of constitutional rights or federal or state statutes. The statutes under which the North Carolina General Assembly authorizes local governments to waive governmental immunity through the purchase of insurance make it clear that the local government's governing body—the board of county commissioners or city council—has full discretion in determining the specific torts to which the insurance policy applies and the officials or employees who will be covered under it. The governing body may decide not to purchase insurance at all.

If the local governing body purchases insurance, an injured person may not recover more than the policy amount for his or her injuries, even if the person's damages far exceed the policy limits. For example, if the policy is limited to $25,000 per occurrence, even if the plaintiff's injuries are $57,000, the plaintiff may recover only $25,000. Indeed, the waiver statute specifically provides that if a jury returns a verdict in excess of the insurance limits, the judge must reduce the award to the maximum limits of the policy before entering the judgment on the court docket. In other words, governmental immunity is waived only to the extent of insurance coverage. Similarly, when a local government's insurance policy involves a deductible, the local government retains governmental immunity for damages that fall within the amount of the deductible.[70]

A local government can waive its governmental immunity through insurance coverage in three basic ways. First, insurance includes liability coverage provided by companies licensed to execute insurance in the state. Second, participation in a local government risk pool is considered the equivalent of purchasing insurance. Third, a local government may expressly waive its immunity and set aside funds to cover claims against it.[71]

Local government risk pools are defined in G.S. 58-23 as agreements between two or more local governments either to jointly purchase insurance or to pool resources to pay claims for property losses or liability. Risk pools differ from self-insurance, wherein the local government does not pool resources with another entity. A city may share the costs of administering claims with other local governments and retain governmental immunity so long as each government entity is liable for its own claims.[72] Courts have also ruled that a city has not created a risk pool, and thereby waived its immunity, where the city creates, funds, contracts with, and operates a nonprofit corporation to manage claims against the city.[73]

---

67. Howland v. Asheville, 174 N.C. 749 (1917).
68. Bynum v. Wilson County, ____ N.C. ____, 758 S.E.2d 643 (2014).
69. G.S. 153A-435; G.S. 160A-485.
70. Jones v. Kearns, 120 N.C. App. 301, *review denied*, 342 N.C. 414 (1995) (plaintiffs may be required to submit statement of damages indicating that damages exceeded deductible).
71. G.S. 160A-485 and G.S. 153-435.
72. Lyles v. City of Charlotte, 344 N.C. 676 (1996).
73. Blackwelder v. City of Winston-Salem, 332 N.C. 319 (1992).

If a local government sets aside a self-insurance reserve, the court will find that it has waived its immunity if the governing board adopted a specific resolution indicating that the creation of the reserve serves the same function as the purchase of insurance. Adoption of the resolution waives the city's or county's governmental immunity only to the extent specified in the board's resolution, but in no event can a plaintiff recover an amount greater than the funds available in the funded reserve for the payment of claims.[74]

The Doctrine of Discretionary Immunity

The doctrine of discretionary immunity provides that North Carolina courts will not review decisions left by law to the discretion of a local legislative body. Although this type of immunity is sometimes characterized as one of the governmental functions included within the broader doctrine of governmental immunity,[75] it is more appropriately discussed as a separate category of immunity.

The power of cities and counties to enact ordinances offers a good example of how courts apply the discretionary immunity doctrine. A court will not substitute its judgment for that of a local governing body by imposing liability on the unit for the exercise or the nonexercise of the unit's ordinance-making power. For example, Charlotte's board of aldermen once temporarily suspended an ordinance against the use of fireworks inside the local government limits. A man's building was destroyed when fireworks landed on the roof and caught fire. He sued the city to recover damages, alleging that the board's negligence in suspending the ordinance caused his loss. The North Carolina Supreme Court denied recovery against the city on the grounds that a local government was not liable for the exercise or the nonexercise of a discretionary power, such as the power to enact ordinances.[76]

The Public Duty Doctrine

Generally, the public duty doctrine holds that local governments do not have a duty to protect individual members of the public from crime or from criminal third parties. Although the government may undertake a duty to protect the public at large, individual victims of crime are not entitled to recover damages for the failure of law enforcement officers to prevent a crime from happening. The duty to prevent crime extends to the public generally and cannot be enforced by individuals against a city.

The public duty doctrine has two exceptions. First, a special duty to a specific person can arise in certain circumstances, usually as a result of contact between a unit of local government and the specific person.[77] In most cases the contact involves a promise to protect a specific individual, the failure to protect that individual, and the individual's reliance on the promise of protection to the individual's detriment.[78] General words of comfort and assurance are not sufficient,[79] and simply providing public safety controls to a particular area or neighborhood does not create a special duty.[80]

The second exception to the public duty doctrine applies when a special relationship exists between the government and the plaintiff. The most often cited example is the relationship between the police and a witness or informant who has aided the police.[81]

The North Carolina Supreme Court, in *Lovelace v. City of Shelby*, has held that the public duty doctrine, as it applies to local governments, is limited to "law enforcement departments when they are exercising their general duty to pro-

---

74. G.S. 160A-485 and G.S. 153-435.

75. *See, e.g.*, Blackwelder v. Concord, 205 N.C. 792, 795 (1934) ("[t]he exercise of discretionary or legislative power is a governmental function, and for injury resulting from the negligent exercise of such power a municipality is exempt from liability").

76. Hill v. Board of Aldermen, 72 N.C. 55 (1875); *see* Moye v. McLawhorn, 208 N.C. 812 (1935).

77. *See* Braswell v. Braswell, 98 N.C. App. 231 (1990), *aff'd in part, rev'd in part, and remanded*, 330 N.C. 363 (1991).

78. *See id.*; *also see* Coleman v. Cooper, 89 N.C. App. 188, *review denied*, 322 N.C. 834 (1988); note that the public duty doctrine bars claims of gross negligence. Hedrick v. Rains, 121 N.C. App. 466, *aff'd*, 344 N.C. 729 (1996).

79. *Braswell*, 98 N.C. App. 231, *aff'd in part, rev'd in part, and remanded*, 330 N.C. 363.

80. Prevette v. Forsyth Cnty., 110 N.C. App. 754, *review denied*, 334 N.C. 622 (1993).

81. Stafford v. Baker, 129 N.C. App. 576, 580, *review denied*, 348 NC 695 (1998).

tect the public."[82] Lovelace alleged that the City of Shelby emergency operator negligently delayed in dispatching fire personnel to her home and that her child died as the result of that delay. On remand to the trial court, Shelby amended its pleading to clarify that the emergency operator was a sworn police officer and reasserted the public duty doctrine defense under the theory that, though the emergency call was for fire protection, the doctrine applied where a sworn officer was performing his duties to the general public by dispatching the fire department. The trial court dismissed the city's public duty doctrine defense and that dismissal was upheld by the North Carolina Court of Appeals, which clarified that the public duty doctrine did not provide protection for fire suppression.[83]

Before the North Carolina Supreme Court's limiting pronouncement in *Lovelace*, in addition to law enforcement, the lower courts had made the public duty doctrine available in cases involving building inspection,[84] safety inspection,[85] planning,[86] taxicab permitting,[87] animal control,[88] and fire protection.[89] These cases are no longer good law.

Since the supreme court's limitation of the public duty doctrine, North Carolina courts have refused to apply the public duty doctrine in cases involving the following facts: a school crossing guard,[90] a sewer line excavation,[91] the negligent repair of a stop sign,[92] a municipal housing authority,[93] the negligent inspection of residential construction,[94] negligent fire suppression,[95] an automobile accident with a police officer in pursuit,[96] an intentional tort committed by a police technician,[97] the intentional and negligent torts committed by a school resource officer,[98] the county sheriff's negligent hiring and supervision of a deputy sheriff,[99] and county employees sued in their individual capacity alone.[100]

Recently, North Carolina courts have ruled that a county was protected from liability pursuant to the public duty doctrine where a county employee alleged that the county negligently secured the county courthouse by contracting with a private security service that provided non-sworn security personnel.[101] In another case, a county was protected by the public duty doctrine where a shooting victim alleged that the county 911 emergency response operator negligently delayed in dispatching law enforcement to the scene of a domestic assault.[102]

---

82. 351 N.C. 458, 461, *reh'g denied,* 352 N.C. 157 (2000); *see* Thompson v. Waters, 351 N.C. 462, 465 (2000).

83. Lovelace v. City of Shelby, 153 N.C. App. 378 (2002). See *Jefferson v. County of Vance*, 153 N.C. App. 523 (2002), an unpublished opinion cited below, where the North Carolina Court of Appeals applied the public duty doctrine with regards to an allegation that the county's 911 emergency response system negligently dispatched law enforcement to the scene of a domestic assault.

84. Lynn v. Overlook Development, 98 N.C. App. 75 (1990); Sinning v. Clark, 119 N.C. App. 515 (1995).

85. Stone v. N.C. Dep't of Labor, 347 N.C. 473 (1998); Hunt v. N.C. Dep't of Labor, 348 N.C. 192 (1998).

86. Derwort v. Polk Cnty., 129 N.C. App. 789 (1998).

87. Clark v. Red Bird Cab Co., 114 N.C. App. 400, *review denied,* 336 N.C. 603 (1994).

88. Prevette v. Forsyth Cnty., 110 N.C. App. 754, *review denied,* 334 N.C. 622 (1993).

89. *See, e.g.,* Davis v. Messer, 119 N.C. App. 44 (1995).

90. Isenhour v. Hutto and City of Charlotte, 350 N.C. 601 (1999).

91. Hargrove v. Billings & Garrett, Inc., 137 N.C. App. 759 (2000).

92. Cucina v. Jacksonville, 138 N.C. App. 99 (2000).

93. Huntley v. Pandya, 139 N.C. App. 624 (2000).

94. Thompson v. Waters, 351 N.C. 462 (2000).

95. Willis v. Town of Beaufort, 143 N.C. App. 106 (2001).

96. Moses v. Young, 149 N.C. App. 613 (2002).

97. Walker v. City of Durham, 158 N.C. App. 747 (2003) (unpublished opinion). The doctrine shielded the city only from negligent behavior of the police technician, not the allegedly intentional behavior.

98. Smith v. Jackson Cnty. Bd. of Educ., 168 N.C. App. 452 (2005). See *Collum v. Charlotte–Mecklenburg Board of Education,* 614 F. Supp. 2d 598, 245 Ed. Law Rep. 48 (2008), in which the federal district court judge refused to apply a blanket exception to the public duty doctrine for all school resource officers and distinguished *Smith v. Jackson County Board of Education.*

99. *Smith,* 168 N.C. App. at 465.

100. Murray v. County of Person, 191 N.C. App. 575 (2008).

101. Wood v. Guilford Cnty., 355 N.C. 161 (2002).

102. Jefferson v. County of Vance, 153 N.C. App. 523 (2002) (unpublished opinion).

Liability of Public Servants

A local government does its work through the actions of its elected officials, appointed officials, and employees, and just as the local government may be held responsible for the actions of the public servants, so may the public servants be personally liable. A public servant may be sued for negligence in an official capacity—that is, as the representative of the local government—and also in a personal or individual capacity. Damages awarded in personal capacity suits, in the absence of insurance coverage or a local government policy to defend the employee, would be paid from the public servant's personal assets. A government that may otherwise be immune from suit may defend and settle a claim on behalf of a liable employee, pursuant to G.S. 160A-167, thereby providing relief to the claimant without waiving governmental immunity.[103]

A legal action brought against a public servant in his or her official capacity is, in all respects other than name, an action against the public entity for which he or she works.[104] Thus, the same defenses and immunities available to the entity are available to the public servant. On the other hand, an action against a public servant in his or her individual capacity represents the plaintiff's allegation that the public servant is personally liable to the plaintiff. Immunities separate and distinct from those available to the governmental entity often insulate public servants from liability for acts within the scope of their duties.

In ascertaining the capacity in which the plaintiff seeks to sue the defendant, the court typically looks first to the caption of the complaint. If the capacity is unclear from the caption, the court will look to the allegations of the complaint, to the relief sought, and then to the course of the proceedings. Absent some clear indication in the allegations or the procedural history of the case, the court will presume that the plaintiff is trying to impose only official-capacity liability.[105]

The immunities that may insulate a public servant sued in an individual capacity balance the need to protect particular persons involved in certain government functions from suit with the duty to compensate injured plaintiffs and to hold individuals accountable for wrongdoing. For example, all public servants are liable for damages caused by their intentional torts.[106] Both the highest-ranking local government official and the lowest-ranking employee are personally liable for damages if they assault someone.[107] No public policy interests are served by granting public servants immunity from liability for damages for intentional wrongful acts.

On the other hand, legitimate policy reasons exist for granting certain public officials immunity from liability for harm caused by their negligence. The main reason is that those whose duties involve the exercise of discretion might be hesitant to take necessary official actions if they could be held personally liable for harm caused by simple negligence. The result of this reluctance to act would be a less efficient government. The law of personal liability reflects this concern about the exercise of discretion: whether public servants may be held liable for the consequences of their negligent acts depends entirely on the nature of their responsibilities. The extent of immunity available to public servants sued in their individual capacities depends, therefore, on the particular function of government affected. Some immunities are absolute and protect "even conduct which is corrupt, malicious or intended to do injury."[108] Others are qualified and will protect only public servants who act reasonably and in good faith.

103. See "Defense of Employees, Payment of Judgments, and Settlements" below.

104. Dickens v. Thorne, 110 N.C. App. 39 (1993) (citing Whitaker v. Clark, 109 N.C. App. 379, *review denied*, 333 N.C. 795 (1993)).

105. Mullis v. Sechrest, 347 N.C. 548 (1998).

106. One exception to this rule concerns the intentional tort of defamation. As discussed earlier, public servants with a qualified privilege to make a particular statement will not be held liable for defamation unless they act with malice.

107. *See* Blackwood v. Cates, 297 N.C. 163 (1979) (holding mayor personally liable for intentional tort of false imprisonment).

108. Jacobs v. Sherard, 36 N.C. App. 60 (1978), *review denied*, 295 N.C. 466 (1978) (citing Foust v. Hughes, 21 N.C. App. 268, *review denied*, 285 N.C. 589 (1974)).

Absolute Immunities

Legislative Immunity

Legislative immunity protects local legislators and executives acting in a quasi-legislative function from personal liability for injuries caused by their acts. This type of immunity applies even if the plaintiff can prove that the defendant acted with bad faith.

Legislative immunity under state law was not recognized by the North Carolina Court of Appeals until 1996 in *Vereen v. Holden*.[109] Prior to that case, trial courts routinely applied the doctrine of legislative immunity looking to federal decisions for guidance. The court of appeals confirmed in *Vereen* that the parameters of legislative immunity are the same under both state and federal law. Legislative immunity applies if (1) the defendant was acting in a legislative capacity at the time of the alleged incident and (2) the defendant's acts were not illegal.[110]

Judicial Immunity

Judges and prosecutors are protected from civil liability for errors committed in the discharge of their judicial duties.[111] Members of local quasi-judicial boards, such as the planning board or board of adjustment, also have judicial immunity when acting in their quasi-judicial capacities. As in the case of legislative immunity, state courts often look to federal law for guidance in their determination of whether a public servant is acting in a judicial or quasi-judicial capacity.

Qualified Immunities

Public Official Immunity

Public official immunity protects public servants deemed to be public officers from liability for negligent activity unless they act with malice, for corrupt reasons, or outside the scope of their official duties.[112] A public employee, on the other hand, is not protected under public official immunity. Therefore, public employees may be held personally liable for injuries caused by their negligence during the course of performing their duties.[113]

Public Officers

The significant difference between the liability exposure of public officers and that of public employees means that the distinction between the two is an important one. In *Pigott v. City of Wilmington*,[114] the North Carolina Court of Appeals held that a public official is someone whose position was created by legislation, who normally takes an oath of office, who performs legally imposed duties, and who exercises a certain amount of discretion. The court directed that all these factors be taken into account in deciding whether someone is a public official. Since *Pigott*, however, the court of appeals has emphasized one factor—whether the position was created by statute—almost to the exclusion of all others.[115]

Based on one or some combination of those four factors, North Carolina courts have held the following public servants to be public officers: the county director of social services,[116] certain social workers with a county depart-

---

109. 121 N.C. App. 779 (1996).

110. *Id.* at 782 (citing Scott v. Greenville Cnty., 716 F.2d 1409, 1422 (4th Cir. 1983)).

111. Fugual Springs v. Rowland, 239 N.C. 299, 300 (1954) (judges); Sharp v. Gulley, 120 N.C. App. 878, 880 (1995) (court-appointed referee); *Jacobs*, 36 N.C. App. at 64 (citing *Foust*, 21 N.C. App. 268, *review denied*, 285 N.C. 589) (prosecutor); Greer v. Skyway Broadcasting Co., 256 N.C. 382 (1962) (does not apply to law enforcement officers).

112. Wiggins v. City of Monroe, 73 N.C. App. 44 (1985), *cert. denied*, 320 N.C. 178 (1987)).

113. Harwood v. Johnson, 92 N.C. App. 306, 309 (1988), *aff'd in part, rev'd in part on other grounds*, 326 N.C. 231 (1990).

114. 50 N.C. App. 401, *disc. review denied*, 303 N.C. 181 (1981); *see also* State v. Hord, 264 N.C. 149 (1965); Wiggins v. City of Monroe, 73 N.C. App. 44 (1985).

115. *See* Hare v. Butler, 99 N.C. App. 693, 700, *disc. review denied*, 327 N.C. 634 (1990); Harwood v. Johnson, 92 N.C. App. 306, 310–11 (1988), *aff'd in part, rev'd in part*, 326 N.C. 231 (1990); *see also* EEE-ZZZ Lay Drain Co. v. N.C. Dep't of Human Res., 108 N.C. App. 24 (1992).

116. Hobb v. N.C. Dep't of Human Res., 135 N.C. App. 412 (1999).

ment of social services,[117] notaries,[118] school trustees and park commissioners,[119] school district superintendents and principals,[120] coroners,[121] forensic pathologists,[122] the state banking commissioner,[123] the Commissioner of the North Carolina Division of Motor Vehicles,[124] an inspector with the North Carolina Division of Motor Vehicles,[125] the director of the county health department,[126] the chief building inspector,[127] a building inspector,[128] a code enforcement officer,[129] a police chief and police officers,[130] elected officials,[131] animal control officers,[132] correctional officers,[133] a county emergency medical services director and emergency medical services medical director,[134] a director of federal programs for a county school system,[135] a state probation officer,[136] and a fire chief.[137]

Public Employees

Public employee positions are those in which the court believes the person acts mostly at the direction of others and has duties that are more administrative than discretionary in nature. The basis for failing to cover these employees under public official immunity lies in the assumption that they have clearer, simpler responsibilities than policy-making officials and therefore are less likely to be made hesitant to act from fear that they might be held liable for possible negligence. In a case that provides an example of the operation of this rule, government employees negligently drove a street

---

117. *Id.* (social workers responsible for placing children in foster care pursuant to G.S. 108A-14(a)(12)); Dalenko v. Wake Cnty. Dep't of Human Services, 157 N.C. App. 495 (2003) (social workers responsible for receiving and evaluating reports of abuse, neglect, or exploitation of disabled adults and for taking appropriate action pursuant to G.S. 108A-14(a)(14)); and Hunter v. Transylvania Cnty. Dep't of Social Services, 207 N.C. App. 735 (2010) (social workers responsible for investigating abuse and neglect of children pursuant to G.S. 108A-14(a)(11)). However, see *Meyer v. Walls,* 122 N.C. App. 507, *reversed and remanded on other grounds by* 347 N.C. 97 (1996), in which the North Carolina Court of Appeals ruled that social workers acting pursuant to G.S. 108A-14(a)(14) regarding disabled adults are not public officials. The North Carolina Supreme Court noted in its reversal in *Meyer* that the issue of whether the social workers were public employees or officials was not appealed and, therefore, the court let stand the earlier ruling of the court of appeals. G.S. 108A-14(b), which allows the director of social services to delegate the authority to act as his or her representative, was enacted on October 1, 1995, and the facts giving rise to the *Meyer* case occurred prior to 1995.

118. McGee v. Eubanks, 77 N.C. App. 369 (1985), *review denied,* 315 N.C. 589 (1986).

119. Smith v. Hefner, 235 N.C. 1 (1952).

120. Gunter v. Anders, 114 N.C. App. 61, 67 (1994), *review denied,* 339 N.C. 611 (1995). See also *Jetton v. Caldwell County Board of Education,* 185 N.C. App. 159 (2007), an unpublished opinion in which public official immunity was extended to an assistant principal.

121. Gilikin v. United States Fid. & Guar. Co., 254 N.C. 247 (1961).

122. Cherry v. Harris, 110 N.C. App. 478, *review denied,* 335 N.C. 171 (1993).

123. Sansom v. Johnson, 39 N.C. App. 682 (1979).

124. Thompson Cadillac–Olds v. Silk Hope Automobile, Inc., 87 N.C. App. 467 (1987), *review denied,* 321 N.C. 480 (1988).

125. *Id.*

126. EEE-ZZZ Lay Drain Co. v. N.C. Dep't of Human Res., 108 N.C. App. 24 (1992), *overruled on other grounds by* Meyer v. Walls, 347 N.C. 97 (1997).

127. Pigott v. City of Wilmington, 50 N.C. App. 401, *review denied,* 303 N.C. 181 (1981).

128. McCoy v. Coker, 174 N.C. App. 311 (2005).

129. Al-Nasra v. Cleveland Cnty., 202 N.C. App. 584 (2010).

130. State v. Hord, 264 N.C. 149 (1965).

131. Town of Old Fort v. Harmon, 219 N.C. 241 (1941).

132. Kitchin v. Halifax Cnty., 192 N.C. App. 559 (2008), *discretionary review denied,* 363 N.C. 127 (2009).

133. Price v. Davis, 132 N.C. App. 556 (1999).

134. Dempsey v. Halford, 183 N.C. App. 637 (2007). But see *Fraley v. Griffin,* 217 N.C. App. 624, 720 S.E.2d 694 (2011), in which the court of appeals ruled that a county emergency medical technician is not a public official.

135. Farrell v. Transylvania Cnty. Bd. of Educ., 175 N.C. App. 689 (2006) (the court cited G.S. 115C-287.1(a)(3), which states, "[s]chool administrator[s]" include principals, assistant principals, supervisors, and directors "whose major function includes the direct or indirect supervision of teaching or of any other part of the instructional program" in support of the argument that school supervisors are public officials, though the case dealt specifically with the position of federal programs director.

136. Lambert v. Cartwright, 160 N.C. App. 73 (2003).

137. Willis v. Town of Beaufort, 143 N.C. App. 106 (2001).

sweeper past the open doors of a store and blew dirt into it.[138] Much of the merchandise was ruined. The state supreme court held that the sweeper operators could be required to pay for damage caused by their negligence, explaining:

> [A] mere employee doing a mechanical job . . . must exercise some sort of judgment in plying his shovel or driving his truck—but he is in no sense invested with a discretion which attends a public officer in the discharge of public or governmental duties, not ministerial in their character. . . . The mere fact that a person charged with negligence is an employee of others to whom immunity from liability is extended on grounds of public policy does not thereby excuse him from liability for negligence in the manner in which his duties are performed, or for performing a lawful act in an unlawful manner.[139]

Similarly, in another case the state supreme court held that a county jailer could be required to pay damages to an inmate whose thumb the jailer negligently caught in a cell door.[140] City employees are most often held responsible for negligence in the operation of city vehicles and other equipment. Courts have held the following positions to also be public employee positions: teachers,[141] an environmental health specialist and supervisor,[142] a school crossing guard,[143] an emergency medical technician,[144] staff members of an after-school enrichment program,[145] and a parole case analyst.[146]

Liability under Federal Law

Section 1983 of the Civil Rights Act of 1871 authorizes a person to sue and recover damages against a local government or its governing board members, officials, or employees for violating any of the person's federal constitutional or statutory rights, when the violation is caused by official conduct.[147] The provision remained dormant until 1961 when the Supreme Court held in *Monroe v. Pape*[148] that conduct by police officers, even when it violated state law, could be the basis of an action under Section 1983. By providing a remedy under federal law for the violation of rights protected by a federal statute or the U.S. Constitution, Section 1983 creates a framework of liability separate from state tort law. Section 1983 may allow for a finding of liability in some cases in which there is none under state law; in other cases, an official action may violate both sets of liability rules and expose the public servant and the local government to liability under state and federal law. However, Section 1983 does not create a cause of action where there is no violation of federal law or a federal constitutional right.[149]

Section 1983 serves many of the same functions as state liability rules. Compensation of victims is an example: a person who violates someone's federal rights may be required to compensate the injured party, just as an individual who commits a civil wrong under state law may be required to do. In addition, the federal rules, like state rules, are designed to deter local government public servants from violating someone's legal rights. The federal laws also allow the prevailing party to recover reasonable attorneys' fees.[150] In analyzing how the federal liability rules affect the civil liability of cities and their employees, one must first examine the type of official conduct that can give rise to liability under Section 1983.

---

138. Miller v. Jones, 224 N.C. 783 (1944).
139. *Id.* at 787.
140. Davis v. Moore, 215 N.C. 449 (1939).
141. Daniel v. City of Morganton, 125 N.C. App. 47 (1997).
142. Block v. Person, 141 N.C. App. 273 (2000).
143. Isenhour v. Hutto, 350 N.C. 601 (1999).
144. Fraley v. Griffin, 217 N.C. App. 624 (2011).
145. Schmidt v. Breeden, 134 N.C. App. 248 (1999).
146. Harwood v. Johnson, 326 N.C. 231 (1990).
147. 42 U.S.C.A. § 1983.
148. 365 U.S. 167 (1961).
149. Clayton v. Branson, 170 N.C. App. 438, (2005) (citing Baker v. McCollan, 443 U.S. 137, 144 n.3 (1979).
150. 42 U.S.C.A. § 1988.

Violation of Constitutional Rights

Section 1983 provides a remedy only for the deprivation of "rights, privileges, or immunities secured by the Constitution and laws" of the United States.[151] Several common constitutional violations are violations of the First Amendment rights of free speech and political affiliation, violation of the Fourth Amendment right of freedom from unreasonable searches and seizures, and violation of the Fourteenth Amendment right of due process and equal protection.

First Amendment Rights of Free Speech and Political Affiliation

The Constitution's First Amendment protects everyone's freedom of speech. A public servant violates this protection if, for example, he or she prevents a person from holding a non-obscene protest sign at a political rally.[152] The free speech right also protects public employees who speak out on matters of public concern.[153] A local government employee may sue under Section 1983 if, for example, he or she is fired or disciplined for writing a letter to the newspaper about the misuse of local government funds.[154]

The same principle also prohibits firing or otherwise punishing most local government employees because of their political party affiliation.[155] Grounds for a Section 1983 lawsuit may exist if, for example, the party controlling the governing board decided to dismiss the public works director because the director was a member of the other party.[156]

Fourth Amendment Rights of Freedom from Unreasonable Searches and Seizures

The Fourth Amendment to the U.S. Constitution guarantees everyone's right to be free from unreasonable searches and seizures. This right is violated if a law enforcement officer arrests (an arrest being one kind of seizure) someone without a solid basis, called "probable cause," for believing the person committed a crime. An officer may also violate Fourth Amendment rights by searching a person or a person's property without a search warrant or a valid exception to the warrant requirement. In one case, for example, the plaintiff alleged that a law enforcement officer had violated the plaintiff's constitutional rights when the officer broke into the plaintiff's home unannounced, searched the entire house without a warrant, shot and killed the family dog, arrested the plaintiff, and pushed him out into public with a gun pointed at his head. The federal district court held that the plaintiff could recover damages under Section 1983 for this violation of the Fourth Amendment.[157]

Fourteenth Amendment Right of Due Process

The Fourteenth Amendment to the Constitution provides that no person may be deprived of life, liberty, or property without due process of law. For the most part, due process concerns itself with the procedures the government must follow before depriving someone of life, liberty, or property. The complicated rules for criminal trials are one example of due process.

In other contexts the due process clause requires that those who are to be deprived of liberty or property receive prior notice of the reasons for the deprivation and an opportunity for a hearing to consider those reasons. *Property* and *liberty* are defined broadly for purposes of this guarantee. For example, under the personnel ordinances of some cities and counties, employees may not be fired without good cause.[158] Such an ordinance gives them a "property"

151. *Clayton*, 170 N.C. App. at 452 (citing Gonzaga Univ. v. Doe, 536 U.S. 273, 283 (2002)).

152. Glasson v. City of Louisville, 518 F.2d 899 (6th Cir.), *cert. denied*, 423 U.S. 930 (1975).

153. *See* Stephen Allred, *Employment Law: A Guide for North Carolina Public Employers* (Chapel Hill, N.C.: Institute of Government, The University of North Carolina at Chapel Hill, 1992), 190–203.

154. *See, e.g.*, Pickering v. Board of Educ., 391 U.S. 563 (1968).

155. Rutan v. Republican Party, 497 U.S. 62 (1990).

156. *See* Allred, *Employment Law*, 204–8.

157. Ellis v. City of Chicago, 478 F. Supp. 333 (N.D. Ill. 1979).

158. *See* Allred, *Employment Law*, 31.

interest in their jobs,[159] and the local government must give them a hearing on the grounds for discharge before they may be fired.[160]

Due process also protects persons from arbitrary government actions. For example, a developer was permitted to sue under Section 1983 for violations of due process when a local governing board intervened to prevent the routine issuance of a building permit to which he was entitled under state law.[161] Section 1983 may impose liability when a plaintiff can prove that the local government took away a liberty or property interest created by state or local law through arbitrary or capricious conduct or an abuse of discretion.[162]

Violation of Statutory Rights

Most claims under Section 1983 involve the Constitution. Section 1983 also authorizes a person to sue for and recover damages under a limited number of federal statutes.[163] Typically, those statutes create rights but do not themselves offer any remedy for the violation of those rights. In one case, for example, the Supreme Court held that an error in billing low-income housing tenants for utilities might violate the Housing Act of 1937 and result in a recovery of damages under Section 1983.[164] There are no remedial provisions in the Housing Act of 1937. Thus, without Section 1983, the tenants would have been left with no recourse for the violation. In another case, a man alleged that social service workers improperly reduced his Aid to Families with Dependent Children benefits because they misinterpreted the Social Security Act. The United States Supreme Court held that he could sue for damages in federal court under Section 1983.[165]

Liability of the Local Government

The rules that govern a local government's liability under federal law for violating federal constitutional or statutory rights differ from those that govern a local government's tort liability under state law. State tort law holds a local government liable for any actions of its employees performed within the scope of their employment whenever they are carrying out functions for which the local government does not have governmental immunity. In contrast, a local government may be required to pay money damages in a lawsuit brought under Section 1983 if the violation of federal rights is caused by the local government's official policy,[166] regardless of whether the local government would enjoy governmental immunity under state law.[167]

How can a violation of federal rights be caused by a local government's official policy? A local government may, for example, be held liable if someone's federal rights are violated by the implementation of an ordinance, a regulation, or a decision officially adopted by the local government's governing board.[168] Thus, a local government might be held liable if a city council were to enact an arbitrary zoning ordinance in violation of federally protected constitutional property rights. Acts less formal than passing an ordinance can also establish official policy, such as adopting personnel

---

159. Board of Regents v. Roth, 408 U.S. 564 (1972).

160. Cleveland Bd. of Educ. v. Loudermill, 470 U.S. 532 (1985); Bishop v. Wood, 426 U.S. 341 (1976). *See* Allred, *Employment Law*, 225–30.

161. Scott v. Greenville Cnty., 716 F.2d 1409 (4th Cir. 1983).

162. *Id.* at 1419.

163. There are two exceptions to the use of a Section 1983 lawsuit to remedy alleged violations of federal statutes by municipal public servants. First, a lawsuit under Section 1983 is not possible if the federal statute allegedly violated provides an exclusive remedy for its own enforcement. Middlesex Cnty. Sewerage Auth. v. National Sea Clammers Ass'n, 453 U.S. 1 (1981). Second, no Section 1983 lawsuit is permitted if the federal statute allegedly violated does not create an enforceable right. Pennhurst State Sch. & Hosp. v. Halderman, 451 U.S. 1 (1981).

164. Wright v. City of Roanoke Redevelopment & Hous. Auth., 479 U.S. 418 (1987).

165. Maine v. Thiboutot, 448 U.S. 1 (1980).

166. Monell v. Dep't of Social Servs., 436 U.S. 658 (1978). An extensive discussion of the principles of municipal liability under *Monell* and subsequent Supreme Court decisions appears in *Spell v. McDaniel*, 824 F.2d 1380 (4th Cir. 1987), *cert. denied sub nom.* City of Fayetteville v. Spell, 484 U.S. 1027 (1988).

167. Owen v. City of Independence, 445 U.S. 622 (1980).

168. *See, e.g.*, Matthias v. Bingley, 906 F.2d 1047, *modified*, 915 F.2d 946 (5th Cir. 1990) (per curiam).

policies, passing formal resolutions supporting particular persons or conduct, or issuing instructions to the local government manager.[169] In addition, a governing board's failure to act can establish official policy.[170] The most common lawsuit of this kind involves governing boards alleged to have failed to control persistent, widespread customs of police misconduct.

A local government may also be required to pay damages under Section 1983 if someone's federal rights are violated by a local government board or a public servant given decision-making authority under state or local law in the area involved[171] or if a violation of rights occurs after a governing body delegates its authority to another board or public servant. An isolated act of a public servant who has no authority to make policy for the local government does not establish official policy, and the local government is not liable for that act.[172] For example, a local government is not liable under Section 1983 every time a law enforcement officer makes an illegal arrest or conducts a warrantless search in violation of someone's Fourth Amendment rights. To recover damages from the local government, the person arrested or searched would have to prove that the arrest or the search represented the official policy of the local government. In essence, a plaintiff must establish fault on the part of the local government in order to recover damages from the entity.

Liability of Public Servants

Public servants may also be sued individually in a Section 1983 lawsuit if they violate someone's federal rights. In some cases, however, they may be entitled to the protection of either absolute or qualified immunity from personal liability for damages.

Liability of Governing Board Members

Members of local legislative bodies are absolutely immune from personal liability for damages if the body's legislative acts violate someone's federal rights.[173] Thus, local government governing board members may never be required to pay damages for acts taken within the scope of their legislative duties. However, local government board members may be held personally liable for acts taken within the scope of their administrative duties, although qualified immunity may sometimes protect them (see the discussion under "Liability of Other Public Servants").

The legal distinction between an administrative and a legislative act is difficult to draw, but an example may help.[174] Because passing an ordinance is a legislative action, local government board members are absolutely immune from personal liability if the board enacts a personnel ordinance that lists Republican political-party affiliation by a local government employee as cause for dismissal, even though the ordinance interferes with an employee's First Amendment right to affiliate freely with any political party. However, enforcing a personnel ordinance is an administrative action, and board members who vote to dismiss an employee under an unconstitutional ordinance are individually liable for that action.[175] These two examples make clear that how a local government conducts its business makes a difference in its liability exposure. In a case before the United States Supreme Court, a local government outside of North Carolina eliminated an employee's position as part of its budgetary process. The facts were uncontroverted that the governing board was attempting to fire this employee. However, because they used a legitimate legislative activity to accomplish the purpose, the court held that the individual members of the board could not be held personally liable.[176]

---

169. *See* S. Nahmod, *Civil Rights and Civil Liberties Litigation*, 3rd ed., vol. 1 (Colorado Springs: Shepard's/McGraw-Hill, 1991), 429–30.

170. *See* Avery v. Cnty. of Burke, 660 F.2d 111 (4th Cir. 1981).

171. Dotson v. Chester, 937 F.2d 920 (4th Cir. 1991).

172. As noted earlier, a city may be held liable under state law for torts committed by its employees solely because it is the employer, regardless of whether the employees were implementing official city policy. In fact, under state law the city may be liable even if the employee is acting contrary to official policy. Edwards v. Akion, 52 N.C. App. 688, 693, *aff'd*, 304 N.C. 585 (1981) (per curiam).

173. Bruce v. Riddle, 631 F.2d 272 (4th Cir. 1980).

174. On the legislative–administrative distinction, see *Scott v. Greenville County*, 716 F.2d 1409, 1422–23 (4th Cir. 1983).

175. *See*, e.g., Gross v. Winter, 876 F.2d 165 (D.C. Cir. 1989).

176. Gordon v. Katz, 934 F. Supp. 79 (S.D.N.Y.), *reconsideration denied*, *aff'd*, 101 F.3d 1393 (1995).

Liability of Other Public Servants

Public servants who are not members of a governing board and who violate someone's federal rights while performing their official duties (and city governing board members who are performing administrative tasks) are entitled to qualified immunity from personal liability.[177] Such immunity is necessary to ensure that public servants will make decisions without fear of personal liability for honest mistakes in judgment. The qualified immunity defense provides that public servants may not be held personally liable in a Section 1983 lawsuit unless their conduct violates clearly established statutory or constitutional rights about which a reasonable person in similar circumstances would have known.[178] In other words, public servants are shielded from Section 1983 liability if they could reasonably have thought their conduct was lawful. The qualified immunity defense protects public servants if the law governing their conduct is unclear at the time they act, even if a court later declares such conduct unconstitutional.[179]

For example, a local government manager has dismissed an employee. The personnel ordinance provides that employees may be dismissed only for cause (that is, for a good reason). The manager gave the dismissed employee neither a reason for the action nor a hearing to challenge it. A year before the dismissal the United States Supreme Court held that public employees who might be dismissed only for cause had a property interest in their jobs and had to be granted a due process hearing before they might be dismissed. When the employee brings a Section 1983 lawsuit against the manager on the basis of not receiving due process, the manager claims entitlement to qualified immunity from liability for damages on the basis of never having heard about the Supreme Court decision. The manager loses the argument because a reasonable person under the circumstances would have known about the constitutional requirement of a hearing. Although qualified immunity offers complete protection to public servants who violate someone's constitutional rights, it protects them only if they could not reasonably have predicted that their conduct was unlawful.

Insurance against Civil Liability

One prudent way to protect the local government treasury and municipal public servants from potentially crippling state or federal damage awards, and from the huge expenses that can result from defending a lawsuit, is to purchase liability insurance. The General Assembly has authorized counties and cities to purchase insurance to protect themselves and any of their officers, agents, or employees from civil liability for damages.[180] The governing board has absolute discretion in deciding which liabilities and which public servants, if any, will be covered by this insurance. If the governing board so chooses, insurance coverage may extend to claims of both state and federal liability. The coverage may also cover both the entity and its public servants sued in their individual capacities.

Defense of Employees, Payment of Judgments, and Settlements

Provision of Defense

Each local government is authorized, but not required, to provide for the defense of any civil or criminal action brought against current or former public servants in state or federal court on account of alleged acts or omissions committed in the scope and course of their employment.[181] A local government may provide a defense through the local government

177. *See* Wood v. Strickland, 420 U.S. 308 (1975). Absolute immunity is available to local government employees under narrow circumstances. An example is law enforcement officers who testify in criminal trials. *See* Briscoe v. LaHue, 460 U.S. 325 (1983).

178. Anderson v. Creighton, 483 U.S. 635 (1987). In *Anderson,* the Supreme Court stated that qualified immunity protected public servants from Section 1983 liability "so long as their actions could reasonably have been thought consistent with the rights they are alleged to have violated." *Id.* at 638.

179. Bryant v. Jones, 575 F.3d 1281, *reh'g and reh'g en banc denied,* 400 F. App'x 551 (11th Cir. 2009), *cert. denied,* 559 U.S. 940 (2010).

180. G.S. 160A-485.

181. G.S. 153A-97; G.S. 160A-167.

attorney or a private attorney. Also, as discussed earlier, the local government may purchase liability insurance that requires the insurer to defend lawsuits brought against certain public servants. Whether to provide a defense at all is of course the local government board's decision.

Payment of Judgments

Each local government is also authorized, but not required, to pay all or part of any settlements or judgments in lawsuits against public servants for acts committed in the scope and course of their employment.[182] No statutory limit is placed on the amount a local government may appropriate to pay a settlement or a judgment. However, funds may not be appropriated to pay a public servant's settlement or judgment if the governing board finds that the individual acted or failed to act because of fraud, corruption, or malice.

The local government must meet certain procedural requirements before it may pay a public servant's settlement or judgment. (No such requirements need be met before providing for the defense.) First, the local government board must have adopted a set of uniform standards under which claims against public servants will be paid. These standards must be available for public inspection. Also, notice of a claim or litigation must be given to the local government before a settlement is reached or a judgment is entered if the local government is to pay the settlement or the judgment.

Settlements

Local governments have broad authority to decide whether to settle particular lawsuits and under what terms. A North Carolina Court of Appeals opinion, *Dobrowolska v. Wall*,[183] raised concerns about consistency among settlement decisions. Dobrowolska was involved in a car accident with a Greensboro city police officer. The city relied on its governmental immunity defense and refused to settle the case. *Dobrowolska* alleged that Greensboro had a haphazard practice of refusing to settle some claims based on governmental immunity and paying other claims regardless of governmental immunity. The court of appeals ruled that there was sufficient evidence that the city's practices did not have a rational basis and remanded the case for a jury trial.

In reaction to the *Dobrowolska* decision, many cities reviewed and revised their settlement policies and practices so that the discretion allowed staff in settling claims was defined, clarified, or limited. When later plaintiffs raised similar constitutional claims against other cities based on settlement practices, those cities were able to point to settlement parameters that were more clearly defined than those of Greensboro. Also, in later cases, the court of appeals seems to clarify that the *Dobrowolska* decision did not create a new cause of action or strategy for circumventing the defense of governmental immunity. Rather, *Dobrowolska* reminded local governments that they may not act arbitrarily or capriciously and that they must have a rational basis for treating differently claimants who may be similarly situated.[184]

About the Author

Anthony J. Baker is an assistant city attorney and the risk manager for the City of Winston-Salem. Mr. Baker's office handles all general liability and workers' compensation claims against the City of Winston-Salem.

This chapter updates and revises previous chapters authored by Anita R. Brown-Graham and Michael R. Smith and Jeffrey Koeze, whose contributions to the field and to this publication are gratefully acknowledged. The author also thanks Jerry Kontos, assistant city attorney for the City of Winston-Salem, for his assistance in proofreading this chapter.

182. G.S. 160A-167.

183. 138 N.C. App. 1 (2000).

184. *See* Clayton v. Branson, 170 N.C. App. 438 (2005) *and* Jones v. Durham, 183 N.C. App. 57 (2007).

Chapter 7

Ethics and Conflicts of Interest

Frayda S. Bluestein and Norma R. Houston

Ethics in Government: Why It's Important

The conduct of local government officials and public employees affects public perceptions of and trust in government. Citizens expect local officials and public employees to act in the best interest of the public and not to use their office for their personal benefit. In some cases, laws restrict the conduct of local public officials, but in many cases they have a choice in how to act, for example, when deciding whom to hire, when to contract, and how to vote. North Carolina laws governing the conduct of local officials focus on financial interests in voting and contracting as well as on other ways in which government decision makers might personally benefit from the actions they take. In addition, constitutional due process requirements focus on the need for fair and unbiased decision making when certain types of private rights are at stake.

I. Requirements for Local Elected Officials

Ethics Education Requirement

North Carolina law requires elected members of the governing boards of cities and counties, unified governments, consolidated city–counties, sanitary districts, and local boards of education to receive at least two (2) clock hours of ethics education within twelve (12) months after each election or reelection (or appointment or reappointment) to office. The education program must cover laws and principles that govern conflicts of interest and ethical standards of conduct at the local government level; it is designed to focus on both the legal requirements and the ethical considerations so that key governmental decision makers will have the information and insight needed to exercise their authority appropriately and in the public interest. The ethics education requirement is an ongoing obligation triggered by re-election or reappointment to office.[1]

While state law does not require ethics education for local employees and members of local appointed boards (such as boards of adjustment or advisory committees), a local governing board may impose this requirement on these groups under the board's local ethics code or other ordinance or policy.

Local Codes of Ethics

North Carolina law also requires the governing boards subject to the ethics education requirement to adopt ethics resolutions or policies (often referred to as "codes of ethics") to guide board members in performing their duties.[2] The ethics resolution or policy must address at least five key responsibilities of governing board members enumerated by statute:

1. obey all applicable laws about official actions taken as a board member,
2. uphold the integrity and independence of the office,
3. avoid impropriety in the exercise of official duties,
4. faithfully perform duties,
5. act openly and publicly.

The statute does not impose or authorize sanctions for failure to comply with ethics codes. Boards have no explicit authority to sanction their members as a means of enforcing the ethics code or for other purposes. However, failure to adopt a code or to comply with its provisions may elicit citizen and media criticism and may itself be considered unethical.

As with the ethics education requirement, state law does not require that ethics codes be applied to local employees and members of local appointed boards (such as boards of adjustment or advisory committees), but a local governing board may choose to extend the provisions of its code of ethics to these groups.

Some state government officials and senior employees are subject to the State Government Ethics Act,[3] which establishes ethical standards of conduct for those covered under the act and regulates individuals and entities that seek to influence their actions. The North Carolina State Ethics Commission is responsible for enforcing the act, including investigating alleged violations. Most local government officials and employees are not subject to the State Government Ethics Act by virtue of their local government positions.[4] Consequently, the State Ethics Commission does not have the authority to investigate allegations of unethical conduct by local government officials.

---

1. N.C. Gen. Stat. (hereinafter G.S.) §§ 160A-87 and 153A-53.
2. G.S. 160A-86; G.S. 153A-53.
3. G.S. Chapter 138A.
4. Individual officials and employees may be subject to the act if they also serve in a state level capacity covered under it, such as serving on a covered state board or commission. In addition, voting members of the policy-making boards of Metropolitan Planning Organizations (MPOs) and Rural Transportation Planning Organizations (RPOs) (these boards are often referred to as "transportation advisory committees" or "TACs") are subject to ethics requirements specific to their service on the MPO or RPO TAC (G.S. 136-200.2(g)–(k) for MPOs and G.S. 136-211(f)–(k) for RPOs). For more information about the state ethics and lobbying

Censuring Board Members

Although state law does not provide specific authority for boards to sanction their members for ethical violations, elected boards do have general authority to pass resolutions or motions, and some boards use a motion or resolution of censure to address ethical or legal transgressions by board members, including violations of the board's code of ethics. This type of censure has no legal effect other than to express dissatisfaction or disapproval by the board (or a majority of the board) of the actions or behavior of one of its members. There are no specific procedural requirements for such an action. The School of Government's model code of ethics includes recommendations for a censure process.[5]

II. Conflicts of Interest in Voting

Ethical and conflict of interest issues often arise as questions about whether a board member may, must, or must not vote on a particular matter in which he or she has some personal interest. In general, a governing board member has a duty to vote and may be excused from voting only in specific situations as allowed by statute. North Carolina law does not explicitly authorize county or city board members to abstain or recuse themselves from voting. Instead, the statutes describe limited grounds for which a member may be excused from voting.

The statutes governing voting by county and city board members are slightly different, and especially for cities there is some ambiguity about the proper procedure for excusing a member. The county statute, G.S. 153A-44, provides that the board may excuse a member, whereas the city statute, G.S. 160A-75, simply says that a member "may be excused" without specifying who does the excusing. Another important difference is that the city statute enforces the duty to vote by providing that if a person is present at the meeting, does not vote, and has not been excused, the person is considered to have voted "yes." The county statute does not contain this provision. Both statutes are specific, however, about the reasons for which a person may be excused from voting. In addition, three other statutes prohibit board members from voting in situations involving contracting, land use decisions, and quasi-judicial decisions.

The Duty to Vote

Board members are often advised to avoid even the appearance of a conflict of interest, and in many situations and on many issues a board member may choose to act or to refrain from acting due to a concern about such an appearance. When it comes to voting, however, a board member's duty to vote overrides this choice, in some cases requiring a person to vote, while in only limited circumstances is a person required to refrain from voting. The general voting statutes—Sections 153A-44 (counties) and G.S. 160A-75 (cities) of the North Carolina General Statutes (hereinafter G.S.)—allow governing board members of cities and counties to be excused from voting *only* on matters

1. involving the consideration of the member's own official conduct or financial interest (board member compensation is not considered financial interest or official conduct) or
2. on which the member is prohibited from voting under the following statutes (discussed below):
   (1) exemptions to the prohibition against directly benefiting under a public contract (G.S. 14-234),
   (2) zoning matters (G.S. 153A-340(g); G.S. 160A-381(d)), and
   (3) quasi-judicial decisions (G.S. 153A-345.1; G.S. 160A-388(e2)).

---

laws that apply to state officials, see Norma R. Houston, "State Government Ethics and Lobbying Laws: What Does and Does Not Apply to Local Governments," *Local Government Law Bulletin* No. 135 (March 2014), http://sogpubs.unc.edu/electronicversions/pdfs/lglb135.pdf.

5. A. Fleming Bell, II, *A Model Code of Ethics for North Carolina Local Elected Officials* (Chapel Hill: UNC School of Government, 2010), http://shopping.netsuite.com/s.nl/c.433425/it.A/id.2531/.f.

When there is a question about whether a board member has a conflict of interest in voting, the first thing to determine is what type of matter is involved. Specific statutes govern the standard to be applied, depending on the nature of the matter before the board for decision. The following is a short list of circumstances that will help identify the appropriate standard to apply:

1. If the matter involves a legislative land use matter (such as a rezoning or text amendment), the standard is as follows: a board member *shall not* vote where the outcome of the matter is reasonably likely to have a direct, substantial, and readily identifiable personal financial impact. G.S. 160A-381(d); G.S. 153A-340(g).
2. If the matter involves a quasi-judicial function (such as the issuance of a special use permit or an appeal of a personnel decision), the standard is as follows: a board member *shall not participate or vote* if the member has a fixed opinion (not susceptible to change) prior to the hearing; undisclosed ex parte communications; a close familial, business, or other associational relationship with an affected person; or a financial interest in the outcome. G.S. 153A-345.1; G.S. 160A-388(e2). Note that this provision applies to any person (not just a governing board member) who serves on a board and exercises quasi-judicial functions.
3. If the matter involves a contract from which the member derives a direct benefit (this comes up only if the contract is allowed under an exception to the statute), the standard is as follows: the board member is *prohibited from participating or voting.* G.S. 14-234(b1).
4. For all other matters that come before the governing board for a vote, the standard is as follows: the board member *may be excused* if the matter involves the member's own financial interest or official conduct. G.S. 160A-75; G.S. 153A-44. As noted above, these general voting statutes specifically acknowledge a conflict under any of the other three statutes as grounds for being excused.

Note that each of the first three specific statutes *prohibits* the member from voting. Under the fourth statute, however, it is unclear whether the use of the word "may" in the general voting statutes is intended to make excusing a member from voting optional or whether it simply describes the permissible grounds for being excused.

What Constitutes Financial Interest

North Carolina courts have often ruled on matters involving conflicts of interest. School of Government Professor Fleming Bell fully explores the case law in *Ethics, Conflicts, and Offices: A Guide for Local Officials.* It's important to note, however, that some conflict of interest cases arise in the context of constitutional due process considerations or contracting issues, matters that are now governed by specific statutes that incorporate the standards from the cases. School of Government Professor David Owens analyzes the case law on conflicts of interest in land use matters in *Land Use Law in North Carolina.*

Other matters are governed by the general voting statutes, which contain the more broadly stated "own financial interest" standard. Several cases involving legislative and administrative decisions suggest that courts use a deferential standard when evaluating what constitutes a financial interest. For example, in *Kistle v. Randolph County,*[6] board members' ownership of property near the area in which a school site was located was considered insufficient to constitute conflict of interest. And in *City of Albermarle v. Security Bank and Trust,*[7] council members' direct ties to competing financial institutions did not require them to abstain from voting on a proposed condemnation of a portion of the bank's land. These holdings seem appropriate given the underlying obligation to vote as well as the usual judicial deference given to local government decisions in the absence of a clear abuse of discretion.

The following factors, based on case law and the statutes, may be useful in determining when a person may be excused from voting under the general voting statutes.

6. 233 N.C. 400 (1951).
7. 106 N.C. App. 75 (1993).

Number of People Affected

The range of financial impact on board members can be thought of as a continuum based on the extent to which the effect is unique to the board member, on one end of the spectrum, or experienced by many or most citizens, on the other end. If the effect on the board member is the same as the effect on a significant number of citizens, then it is fair to allow the individual to vote. The board member is affected as part of a larger group of citizens, and the vote can serve to represent that group. This is perhaps the most important factor. Even a significant financial effect may not be disqualifying if it is one that is universally or widely experienced by citizens in the jurisdiction.

Extent of the Financial Interest (Benefit or Detriment)

The general voting statutes refer to financial *interest,* not financial *benefit,* as some of the other statutes do. This means that a positive or a negative financial impact may be a basis for excusing a member from voting. An insignificant financial interest, however, whether positive or negative, is not enough to sway a person's vote and should not be used to avoid the duty to vote. Obviously, the significance of a financial interest must be considered in relation to the individual's particular situation, though it might be assessed based on what a reasonable person would do in that situation.

Likelihood That the Financial Impact Will Actually Occur

Sometimes several actions in addition to the specific vote in question are needed for an alleged financial interest to materialize. For example, a person who is a real estate agent votes in favor of a loan which will facilitate a project that the real estate agency might have the opportunity to offer for sale. Without more to suggest that the sales opportunity will actually arise and be available to the board member, such a chain of events is probably too speculative to form a basis for being excused from voting.

III. Conflicts of Interest in Contracting

Several state laws place limits on the ability of elected officials and public employees at the state and local government level[8] to derive personal benefit from contracts with the governmental units they serve. These laws reflect the public's need to ensure that contracting and other decisions are made in a neutral, objective way based on what is in the public interest and not in consideration of actual or potential benefit to the decision maker. However, these laws do not prohibit all activity that the public might consider improper. Instead, they identify particular activities that the legislature has identified as serious enough to constitute a criminal offense. Situations that are not illegal may nonetheless be inappropriate, so public officials should always consider the public perception of their actions in addition to the legal consequences.

Contracts for Personal Benefit

A criminal statute, G.S. 14-234, prohibits a public officer (elected or appointed) or a public employee from deriving a direct benefit from any contract in which he or she is involved on behalf of the public agency he or she serves. The statute contains two additional prohibitions. Even if a public official or employee is not involved in making a

8. While the statutes discussed in this section apply to all state and local government officials and employees, certain senior-level state officials and employees are subject to specific standards of conduct under the State Government Ethics Act, G.S. Chapter 138A. This act does not generally apply to local government officials and employees unless they also serve in a state capacity, such as serving on a state board or commission covered under the act. Similarly, local government officials and employees are generally exempt from G.S. Chapter 120C, which regulates lobbying senior-level state officials and employees.

contract from which he or she will derive a direct benefit, the official or employee is prohibited from influencing or attempting to influence anyone in the agency who is involved in making the contract. In addition, all public officers and employees are prohibited from soliciting or receiving any gift, reward, or promise of reward, including a promise of future employment, in exchange for recommending, influencing, or attempting to influence the award of a contract, even if they do not derive a direct benefit under the contract. Violation of this statute is a Class 1 misdemeanor. Key definitions contained in the statute, along with several important exceptions, are discussed below.

As defined in the statute, a person "derives a direct benefit" from a contract if the person or *his or her spouse* (1) has more than a 10 percent interest in the company that is a party to the contract, (2) derives any income or commission directly from the contract, or (3) acquires property under the contract.[9] Note that while the prohibition includes a direct benefit to a spouse, it does not extend to other family members or friends, or to unmarried partners. If the employee or official or his or her spouse does not derive a direct benefit from it, a contract between a public agency and a family member, friend, or partner of a board member or employee does not violate the law. Another important aspect of the statutory definition is that it does not make illegal a contract with an entity in which a county or city official is an employee as long as no commission or other direct benefit is derived from the contract.

Since the definition of direct benefit includes the acquisition of property, board members and employees who are involved in the disposal of surplus property are prohibited from purchasing that surplus property from their unit of government. Elected and appointed officials (but not employees) may be able to do so if the unit falls within the "small jurisdiction exception" described below.

The law also specifies what it means to be involved in "making or administering" the contract, which is a necessary element in the statutory prohibition. Individuals who are *not* involved in making or administering contracts are not legally prohibited from contracting with their unit of government. Activity that triggers the prohibition includes participating in the development of specifications or contract terms, or preparation or award of the contract, as well as having the authority to make decisions about or interpret the contract.[10] Performing purely ministerial duties is not considered "making or administering" the contract.[11] The statute also makes clear that a person is involved in making the contract when the board or commission on which he or she serves takes action on the contract, even if the official does not participate. Simply being excused from voting on the contract does not absolve a person with a conflict of interest from potential criminal liability. If an exception (discussed below) applies, the interested party may be excused from voting and legally contract with the unit. However, unless an exception applies, simply being excused from voting does not eliminate a conflict under the statute.

As noted above, public officials or employees may legally benefit from a contract with the unit of government they serve as long as they are not involved in making or administering it. Thus, for example, employees who are not involved in disposing of surplus property may legally purchase items from the unit, and the unit may legally contract to acquire goods or services from employees whose county or city job does not involve them in making or administering the contract.

The broad prohibition in G.S. 14-234 is modified by several exceptions. In any case where an exception applies, a public officer who will derive a direct benefit is prohibited from deliberating or voting on the contract or from attempting to influence any other person who is involved in making or administering the contract.[12] Contracts with banks, savings and loan associations, and regulated public utilities are exempt from the limitations in the statute,[13] as are contracts for reimbursement for providing direct assistance under state or federal public assistance programs under certain conditions.[14] An officer or employee may, under another exception, convey property to the unit but only through

9. G.S. 14-234(a1)(4).
10. G.S. 14-234(a1)(2), (3).
11. G.S. 14-234(a1)(5).
12. G.S. 14-234(b1).
13. G.S. 14-234(b)(1).
14. G.S. 14-234(b)(4).

a condemnation proceeding initiated by the unit.[15] An exception in the law also authorizes a county or city to hire as an employee the spouse of a public officer (this exception does not apply to public employees).[16]

A final exception applies only in cities with a population of less than 15,000 and in counties with no incorporated municipality with a population of more than 15,000.[17] In these jurisdictions, governing board members as well as certain members of the social services, local health, or area mental health boards, of the board of directors of a public hospital, and of the local school board may lawfully contract with the units of government they serve, subject to several limitations contained in the exception. First, the contract may not exceed $20,000 for medically related services and $40,000 for other goods or services in any twelve-month period (note this requirement specifically applies to any twelve-month period, not necessarily a fiscal year). In addition, the exemption does not apply to any contract that is subject to the competitive bidding laws, which includes purchase and construction or repair contracts with an estimated cost of $30,000 or more. Contracts made under this exception must be approved by special resolution of the governing board in open session. The statute imposes additional public notice and reporting requirements for these contracts and prohibits the interested board member from participating in the development of or voting on the contract. A contract entered into under the "small jurisdiction" exception that does not comply with all the procedural requirements applicable to this exception violates the statute.

Contracts entered into in violation of G.S. 14-234 violate public policy and are not enforceable. There is no authority to pay for or otherwise perform a contract that violates the statute unless the contract is required to protect the public health or welfare and limited continuation is approved by the Local Government Commission.[18] Prosecutions under the statute are not common (although some have occurred), but situations in which board members or public officials stand to benefit from contracts involving public funds often make headlines.

Gifts and Favors

Another criminal statute, G.S. 133-32, is designed to prevent the use of gifts and favors to influence the award and administration of public contracts. The statute makes it a Class 1 misdemeanor for a current contractor, a contractor who has performed under a contract with a public agency within the past year, or a person who anticipates bidding on a contract in the future to give any gift or favor to public officials and employees who have responsibility for preparing, awarding, or overseeing contracts, including inspecting construction projects. The statute also makes it a Class 1 misdemeanor for those officials to receive the gift or favor.

The statute does not define gift or favor. A reasonable interpretation is that the prohibition applies to anything of value acquired or received without fair compensation unless it is covered by a statutory exception. These exceptions include advertising items or souvenirs of nominal value, honoraria for participating in meetings, and meals at banquets. Inexpensive pens, mugs, and calendars bearing the name of the donor firm clearly fall within the exception for advertising items and souvenirs. Gifts of a television set, use of a beach cottage, or tickets to a professional sports event probably are prohibited. Although meals at banquets are allowed, free meals offered by contractors under other circumstances, such as lunch, should be refused. Some local governments have adopted local policies establishing a dollar limit for gifts that may be accepted; however, a gift allowed under a local policy must still be refused if it violates state law.

The statute also allows public officials and employees to accept customary gifts or favors from friends and relatives as long as the existing relationship, rather than the desire to do business with the unit, is the motivation for the gift. Finally, the statute specifically does not prohibit contractors from making donations to professional organizations to defray meeting expenses, nor does it prohibit public officials who are members of those organizations from partici-

15. G.S. 14-234(b)(2). The statute specifically authorizes the conveyance to be undertaken under a consent judgment, that is, without a trial, if approved by the court.

16. G.S. 14-234(b)(3).

17. G.S. 14-234(d1). Population figures must be based on the most recent federal decennial census.

18. G.S. 14-234(f).

pating in meetings that are supported by such donations and are open to all members (for example, sponsorship of a conference event that is open to all conference attendees).

It is important to distinguish between gifts to individuals and gifts to the government entity itself. A contractor may legally donate goods and services to the local government for use by the unit. For example, a local business can legally donate products to the unit for its own use or for the unit to raffle to employees for an employee appreciation event. Gifts or favors delivered directly to individuals for their personal use should be returned or, in some cases, may be distributed among employees such that each person's benefit is nominal. The latter approach is common for gifts of food brought to a department by a vendor. Public officials should inform contractors and vendors about the existence of the gifts-and-favors statute and about any local rules in effect within the unit addressing this issue.

Misuse of Confidential Information

G.S. 14-234.1 makes it a Class 1 misdemeanor for any state or local government officer or employee to use confidential information for personal gain, to acquire a pecuniary benefit in anticipation of his or her own official action, or to help another person acquire a pecuniary benefit from such actions. Confidential information is any non-public information that the officer or employee has learned in the course of performing his or her official duties.

IV. Conflicts of Interest for Specific Categories of Officials and Public Employees

In addition to the statutes discussed above that apply to all local officials and employees, specific conflict of interest prohibitions apply to certain groups of officials and employees, including those discussed briefly below.

Building Inspectors

Both city and county building inspectors are prohibited from having a financial interest in or being employed by a business that furnishes labor, materials, or appliances for building construction or repair within the city or county jurisdiction. All employees of city and county inspection departments, including individuals working under contract with those departments, are prohibited from engaging in any work that is inconsistent with their public duties. In addition to these general prohibitions, the statute requires a city or county to find a conflict of interest if the employee (including individuals working under contract with an inspection department) has a financial or business interest in the project being inspected or has a close relationship with or has previously worked within the past two years for the project's owner, developer, contractor, or manager.[19]

Project Designers

Architects and engineers performing work on public construction projects are prohibited from specifying any materials, equipment, or other items manufactured, sold, or distributed by a company in which the project designer has a financial interest.[20] Project designers are prohibited also from allowing manufacturers to draw specifications for public

19. G.S. 153A-355 (counties) and G.S. 160A-415 (cities).
20. G.S. 133-1.

construction projects.[21] A violation of these restrictions is punishable as a Class 3 misdemeanor; violators lose their licenses for one year and a pay a fine of up to five hundred dollars ($500).[22]

Public Hospital Officials and Employees

Boards of directors and employees of public hospitals and hospital authorities and their spouses are prohibited from acquiring a direct or indirect interest in any hospital facility, property planned to be included within a hospital facility, or a contract or proposed contract for materials or services provided to a hospital facility. Limited exceptions to this prohibition apply; a contract entered into in violation of these prohibitions is void and unenforceable.[23]

Local Management Entity (LME) Board Members

Local management entity (LME) board members cannot contract with their LME for the delivery of mental health, developmental disabilities, and substance abuse services while serving on the board (and are not eligible for board service so long as such a contract is in effect).[24] Nor can an individual who is a registered lobbyist serve on an LME board.

Housing Authorities

Commissioners and employees of a housing authority, or of a city or county when acting as a housing authority, are prohibited from having or acquiring any direct or indirect interest in any housing project, property included or planned to be included in any project, or a contract or proposed contract for materials or services to be furnished or used in connection with any housing project.[25]

V. Conflicts of Interest Applicable to Federal Grant Funds

The Grants Management Common Rule (GMCR) is a set of federal regulations that generally apply to the management of federal grant funds and include both specific procurement requirements as well as conflict of interest prohibitions that differ in some ways from state law. Grantees and subgrantees are required to adopt a written code of conduct that (1) addresses real and apparent conflicts of interest, (2) imposes prohibitions against accepting gifts and favors from vendors and contractors, and (3) establishes disciplinary actions for violations. In addition, the GMCR prohibits real or apparent financial or other interests in a contract funded with federal funds by officers, employees, and agents of grantees and subgrantees as well as their spouses, immediate family members, partners, and soon-to-be-employers. Finally, the GMCR prohibits all officers, employees, and agents of grantees and subgrantees from accepting gifts or favors from current or future contractors. A violation of these prohibitions can result in disciplinary action and loss of federal funding. Local governments should consult with the federal granting agency to ensure full compliance with the GMCR or any other federal regulations applicable to federal grant funds.

---

21. G.S. 133-2.
22. G.S. 133-4.
23. G.S. 131E-14.2 (public hospitals) and G.S. 131E-21 (hospital authorities).
24. G.S. 122C-118.1(b).
25. G.S. 157-7.

Additional Resources

Bell, A. Fleming, II. *Ethics, Conflicts, and Offices: A Guide for Local Officials.* 2nd ed. Chapel Hill: UNC School of Government, 2010.

_____. *A Model Code of Ethics for North Carolina Local Elected Officials.* Chapel Hill: UNC School of Government, 2010.

Bluestein, Frayda S. *A Legal Guide to Purchasing and Contracting for North Carolina Local Governments.* 2nd ed. with supplement. Chapel Hill: UNC School of Government, 2007.

Ethics for Local Government Officials, UNC School of Government webpage, www.sog.unc.edu/programs/ethics.

"Ethics & Conflicts." *Coates' Canons: NC Local Government Law Blog,* canons.sog.unc.edu/?cat=5.

Houston, Norma R. "State Government Ethics and Lobbying Laws: What Does and Does Not Apply to Local Governments." *Local Government Law Bulletin* No. 135 (Mar. 2014).

About the Authors

Frayda S. Bluestein is a School of Government faculty member specializing in local government law. Norma R. Houston is a faculty member of the School of Government and a fellow of the Parr Center for Ethics at UNC Chapel Hill.

Part 2

Transparency, Collaboration, and Citizen Involvement

Chapter 8

Public Records

Frayda S. Bluestein

Public Records Law Overview

North Carolina's public records law provides a broad right of access to records of public agencies. The main statutes that define the scope of the law are contained in Chapter 132 of the North Carolina General Statutes (hereinafter G.S.). Many exceptions and other laws that deal with public records can be found in other chapters. The School of Government publication *Public Records Law for North Carolina Local Governments* (2nd ed., 2009), by David M. Lawrence, provides a comprehensive guide to these laws and their interpretation by the courts.

As an introduction to this topic, the following list provides a summary of some of the most important basic concepts for understanding the law.

- The law applies to records made or received in connection with the transaction of public business.
- The law applies to all types of state and local government agencies, and all types of records, including paper and electronic records, recordings, films, videos, and photographs.
- A record that falls within the scope of the statute is subject to public access unless an exception provides otherwise.
- North Carolina courts have been unwilling to recognize exceptions to the law that are not found in existing statutes.

- The statutory exceptions to the right of access fall into one of two categories: (1) confidential records, which the public agency is *prohibited* from releasing except under specified conditions, or (2) nonpublic records, to which there is no right of access but which the public agency *may* release in its discretion.
- The status of a record under the law is determined based on its content, not its location.
- Personal records (not related to the transaction of public business) are not public records, even if they are created using government resources. Records related to the transaction of public business are public, even if they are created using private resources.
- The right of access includes the right to inspect and obtain copies (although a few specific provisions limit some element of access for particular types of records).[1]
- Anyone can request access; the right is not limited to citizens or constituents of the agency.
- State law limits a public agency's authority to charge for providing access to records, in most cases allowing a charge only for the actual cost of the paper or other medium, if any, on which copies are provided.
- Requirements for retention of public records are governed by rules promulgated by the State Division of Archives and History, Government Records Branch. These rules apply based on the content, not the form of the record. For example, there is no general rule for retention of email. Instead, the requirements for email records will vary depending on the content of the email.

Scope of the Public Records Law

G.S. 132-1 establishes a broad definition of "public record," and G.S. 132-6 entitles any person to examine and have a copy of any public record. The state supreme court has concluded that these statutory rights extend to all documents meeting the definition of public record, unless the General Assembly has enacted a statute that limits or denies public access to a category of record.[2] As a result, the great bulk of material held by local governments in North Carolina is public record and therefore open to public access. Financial records, leases and contracts, insurance policies, reports, agency minutes, permit applications, emails, and information in computer databases are all examples of records that generally must be made available to the public upon request.

The definition of public record under the statute is quite broad and generally not limited by the form of the material in question or by the circumstances under which it was received or created. The statute begins by including within the definition not only documents and other papers but also "maps, books, photographs, films, sound recordings, magnetic or other tapes, electronic data-processing records, [and] artifacts, . . . regardless of physical form or characteristics." It then goes on to state that the term includes the listed items "made or received pursuant to law or ordinance in connection with the transaction of public business." Litigants have sometimes argued that the latter part of the definition—"made or received pursuant to law or ordinance"—is limiting and that only those records whose receipt is specifically required by statute or local ordinance are public records. The court of appeals rejected such a limiting reading in *News and Observer Publishing Co. v. Wake County Hospital System, Inc.*,[3] holding instead that the term includes any material kept in carrying out an agency's lawful duties. Given its own public records decisions, the state supreme court has obviously accepted the same broad reading of the statute.[4] In addition, the supreme court has held that the term includes preliminary drafts of documents and that a person need not wait until a record is finalized in order to examine it or have a copy.[5]

G.S. 132-1 extends the reach of the public records statute to every agency of state and local government in North Carolina. The section defines the covered agencies to include "every public office, public officer or official (State or local, elected or appointed), institution, board, commission, bureau, council, department, authority or other unit of

1. *See, e.g.*, N.C. Gen. Stat. (hereinafter G.S.) § 132-1.13.
2. News and Observer Publ'g Co., Inc. v. Poole, 330 N.C. 465 (1992).
3. 55 N.C. App. 1 (1981).
4. *E.g., Poole, supra* note 2.
5. *Id.*

government of the State or of any county, unit, special district or other political subdivision of government." Thus at the local level the law extends to counties; cities; school administrative units; community colleges; special districts, such as sanitary districts and metropolitan sewerage districts; and public authorities, such as water and sewer authorities, housing authorities, and drainage districts. It also extends to joint entities, such as councils of government, district health departments, area mental health authorities, regional libraries, and joint agencies established by contracts between local governments.

Personal Records Distinguished

Public employees often create records at work and use government resources that do not relate to the transaction of public business. Most commonly, perhaps, these might include email communications with family members, calendar entries reflective of personal activities, and other records of a purely personal nature. Based on the definition of public record under North Carolina's statute, these types of records are not public records, since they are not made in connection with the transaction of public business. Under this definition, it is the subject and purpose of the record, rather than its location on a public or private medium, that governs its characterization as a public record. Although North Carolina case law has not addressed this issue to date, courts in other states have held that documents that are personal in nature do not become government records simply because they are found in a government office or on a government computer.

While personal records made on government-owned devices are not subject to general public access, they may be subject to access by the employer (the government agency). Inappropriate or excessive use of email for non-work-related purposes may violate local polices and could therefore become the basis for a personnel action. Policies governing use of government resources may provide the governmental employer (though not the general public at large) with legal access to material created by local government employees using public resources. Government access to and use of this personal information is limited by constitutionally protected privacy rights, which in turn are affected by the policies and practices in place within each specific jurisdiction.[6]

Records versus Information

The theory of the public records law is that when a government maintains records for its own operational purposes, the public enjoys a general right to inspect and copy those records (subject, of course, to statutory exceptions). But in general the public has no right to demand that a government maintain records that the government has no need for itself or to demand that a government maintain records in a way that facilitates use of the records by others if that use is unimportant to the government. Courts usually express this principle through the statement that the public records law does not require a government to create new records, and the General Assembly has affirmed this point in the statute itself.[7]

There are several important exceptions to this general rule. The first occurs when a government for its own reasons combines in a single document information that is exempt from public access and information that is not exempt. Simply because the document includes confidential information does not make the entire document exempt from public inspection. Rather, it is the government's responsibility to delete (or redact) the confidential information and then make the remaining information public. In a sense this is creating a new record, but the law requires that it be done, and it requires that the agency bear the cost of doing so.[8]

The second exception involves access to personnel information. As noted below, most of the information in government employee personnel files is confidential, and local governments are prohibited from releasing such information except in limited circumstances. The statutes that govern access to personnel files, however, contain a list of *information* within those files that is open to the public. Because of the specific wording of these statutes, the public agency's

6. *See* City of Ontario, California, et al. v. Quon et al., 560 U.S. 746 (2010).

7. *See* G.S. 132-6.2(e) ("Nothing in this section shall be construed to require a public agency to respond to a request for a copy of a public record by creating or compiling a record that does not exist.").

8. G.S. 132-6(c).

obligation is to provide the *information* requested (such as list of employee salaries or list of position changes for a particular employee), even if such a list does not exist as a separate record at the time of the request.

The Right of Access

Form of the Request

G.S. 132-6 accords the rights of inspection and copying to "any person," and there is no reason to think that the quoted words are limiting in any way. The rights extend both to natural persons and to corporations and other artificial persons (such as associations, partnerships, and cooperatives). And they extend both to citizens of the government holding the record and to noncitizens. Furthermore, as a general rule a person's intended use of the records is irrelevant to the right of access, and the records custodian may not deny access simply because of the intended use. Indeed, G.S. 132-6(b) *prohibits* custodians from requiring that persons requesting access to or a copy of a record disclose their purpose or motives in seeking access or the copy.

There is no specific authority to require that requests be in writing or that a requester identify himself or herself in order to obtain access. There are legitimate practical reasons to request and document requests in writing, but it is important for public agencies to recognize their lack of authority to condition access on the requester's completion of such documentation.[9]

Form in Which Records Are Provided

Public agencies must provide records in the form in which they are requested, so long as the agency has the capacity to do so. Under G.S. 132-6.2(a), persons requesting copies "may elect to obtain [the records] in any and all media in which the public agency is capable of providing them. No request for copies of public records in a particular medium shall be denied on the grounds that the custodian has made or prefers to make the public records available in another medium." The records may be certified or noncertified, at the option of the person making the request.

Time for Response

North Carolina's public records law requires custodians of records to allow public records to be inspected "at reasonable times and under reasonable supervision" and copies to be provided "as promptly as possible."[10] The law does not set a specific time within which an agency must respond. What constitutes a reasonable or prompt response will depend on the nature of the request and the available personnel and other resources available to the agency that receives the request. A prompt response to a fairly simple records request ranges from immediate, within a few hours, or within a day or two. As the request becomes more substantial, however, and the burden on the custodian becomes correspondingly greater, it seems reasonable to allow the custodian somewhat more time to locate and deliver the desired records. Among factors that might appropriately delay granting access are the number of records requested, whether they are located in multiple or remote sites, how large the public agency is, and whether any part of the records must be redacted. Unless a request is extraordinary, however, a custodian probably should respond within a week or two at most.

9. For a discussion of what policies and procedures may be implemented for responding to public records requests, see Frayda Bluestein, "Ask, Don't Compel: Local Government Authority to Establish Rules for Public Records Requests," *Coates' Canons: NC Local Government Law Blog* (UNC School of Government, June 15, 2011), sogweb.sog.unc.edu/blogs/local govt/?p=4806.

10. G.S. 132-6(a).

Electronic Records and Metadata

As previously noted, the public records law applies to electronic records of all kinds, including word documents, email, text and voice mail messages, spreadsheets, and other electronically stored data. An emerging and as yet unclear aspect of the law deals with the extent to which the right of access extends to information that is embedded in electronic records. The term "metadata" is used to describe this type of information, which can range from email information that is automatically created (such as date and time information) to changes that can be seen in earlier versions of a document, to file name and other embedded data automatically created by computers and applications.[11] Although it's clear that a public agency must provide records in electronic form if requested, it is not clear how much embedded information in an electronic record is considered part of the record that must be provided. For example, an email from a private citizen to a city official employee may contain the citizen's email address. Must this information be provided to a person who requests a copy of the email? Neither the statutes nor the courts have addressed this issue to date, but courts in other jurisdictions have begun to develop interpretations of these and other issues related to the status of electronic information in public records.[12]

While the North Carolina statutes do not yet address what metadata is subject to public access, the law is clear about access to programming or other information technology system data. G.S. 132-6.1(c) specifies that public agencies are *not* required to disclose security features of their computer or telecommunications systems, nor are the unit's computer passwords, system software, or codes subject to public access.

Custodians of Records

The public records law imposes a number of responsibilities on the *custodian* of public records. This official maintains public records, may bring actions to recover records improperly held by others, and is required to permit public inspection of records and provide copies of records to those who request them. G.S. 132-2 declares that the official in charge of an office that holds public records is the custodian of those records. Thus the register of deeds is the custodian of records in the register of deeds' office, the sheriff is the custodian of records held by the sheriff's department, the county assessor is the custodian of records held in the assessor's office, and so on. G.S. 160A-171, however, provides that the city clerk is the custodian of all city records. This provision should probably be interpreted as applying to general supervision over records management as well as responsibility for the official records of the unit (such as minutes and ordinances) rather than literally requiring the clerk to be responsible for all records within each department and office of the city government. Although the custodian has the legal responsibility to provide access, many records requests necessitate review by the agency attorney and other staff prior to their release.

Fees for Providing Copies

G.S. 132-6 and 132-6.2 expressly permit fees for *copies* of public records but are silent about fees for the right of *inspection* only. This silence is the common statutory pattern around the country, and courts in other states generally have held that custodians may not charge fees for mere inspection, when the custodian does no more than locate and retrieve the record and no copy is provided.

11. For more discussion of metadata and emerging case law involving e-discovery and public records, see Kara Millonzi, "Metadata, E-Discovery, and E-Public Records in North Carolina," *Coates' Canons: NC Local Government Law Blog* (UNC School of Government, Sept. 15, 2011), http://sogweb.sog.unc.edu/blogs/localgovt/?p=5432.

12. *See* O'Neill v. City of Shoreline, 240 P.3d 1149 (Wash. 2010) (Email address is part of the record and must be provided if specifically requested.); Kara Millonzi, "Is Metadata a Public Record? Case Law Update," *Coates' Canons: NC Local Government Law Blog* (UNC School of Government, Oct. 21, 2010), http://sogweb.sog.unc.edu/blogs/localgovt/?p=3417. Note that G.S. 132-1.13 limits access to emails of subscribers to local government email lists, allowing inspection of such lists but not copying.

The statutes do not establish the fees that a custodian may charge for making a copy but rather give direction about the proper amount that may be charged. G.S. 132-6.2 directs that the fee be based on the *actual cost* of making the copy. The statute limits "actual cost" to "direct, chargeable costs related to the reproduction of a public record . . . [not including] costs that would have been incurred by the public agency if a request to reproduce a public record had not been made." The statute's use of "direct, chargeable costs" seems to rule out inclusion of indirect costs in determining fees for a copy. In addition, because the costs may not include costs that the agency would have incurred whether the copy was made or not, in most instances the fee may not include personnel costs; the person making the copy would have been paid whether he or she made the copy or did other work.

G.S. 132-6.2(b) authorizes public agencies to charge a "special service charge" for requests involving extensive use of information technology resources, including labor costs of the personnel providing these services. This authority appears to be limited to resources and labor associated with information technology and may not be sufficient authority for large requests that do not involve extensive use of information technology resources. Furthermore, the provision does not appear to authorize a surcharge for the labor involved in reviewing records to determine what records or parts of records may be provided.

Categories of Records Not Subject to the Right of Access

The General Statutes comprise literally dozens of statutes that create exceptions to the general right of access to public records. The following summary lists those that seem most important to local governments.

Personnel Records

A number of separate statutes exempt from public access most of the records in the personnel files of public employees.[13] There is some variation among these statutes, but most permit the employee, as well as anyone with supervisory authority over the employee, to have access to almost everything in the employee's file; they also permit certain others access to the file in very limited circumstances. In addition, each statute contains a list of information about each employee that is public record. This list includes the employee's name, age, current salary and salary history, contract terms, original employment date, current position title and location, history of changes in position classification and disciplinary actions, and in the case of dismissal for disciplinary reasons, a copy of the final notice of dismissal, stating the reasons for the dismissal. Other information in the personnel file is confidential, and the public agency is prohibited from releasing it except under specified, limited circumstances. In addition, a number of statutes permit local governments to require criminal records checks of prospective employees, and G.S. 114-19.13 directs that the records provided by such a check are to be kept confidential.

Criminal Investigation Records

G.S. 132-1.4 establishes special rules of access to records generated while a law enforcement agency is investigating alleged or known violations of the criminal law. In general the statute denies the public any right of access to these records, with a few exceptions. The exceptions allow public access to records involving details of criminal incidents, information about persons arrested or charged, the circumstances of arrests, contents of 911 telephone calls (these may be provided with altered voice or transcribed to protect callers' identity), radio communications between law enforcement personnel, and information about victims of crime and persons who file complaints or report violations.

13. G.S. 153A-98 (county employees); 160A-168 (city employees); 115C-319 through -321 (public school employees); 115D-27 through -30 (community college employees); 130A-42 (district health department employees); 122C-158 (area authority employees); 131E-97.1 (public hospital employees); 162A-6.1 (water and sewer authority employees); and 126-22 through -30 (state employees).

Legal Materials

Two statutes exempt certain legal materials from public access, though both exemptions are limited in duration. First, G.S. 132-1.1 exempts communications from an attorney to a public body in state or local government when the communications involve (1) a claim by or against the public body or the government for which it acts or (2) a judicial action or administrative proceeding to which the public body is a party or by which is it affected. This exemption, however, expires three years after the date the public body receives the communication. Second, G.S. 132-1.9 exempts trial preparation materials, such as documents showing the mental impressions or legal theories of an attorney or reports from consultants to be used at trial or in support of trial. Once the litigation is completed, however, this exemption ends. In addition, G.S. 132-1.3 specifies that settlement documents in any suit or legal proceeding involving a government agency are to be open to the public unless closed by court order.

Trade Secrets

G.S. 132-1.2 prohibits a government from allowing access to business trade secrets that have been shared with the government, as long as the business has designated the material as confidential or a trade secret at the time it was disclosed to the government.

Local Tax Records

Two statutes prohibit cities or counties from making public local tax records that contain information about a taxpayer's income or gross receipts.[14] The kinds of local taxes that might generate such records are privilege license taxes, when measured by gross receipts; occupancy taxes; prepared food taxes; and cable television franchise taxes. In addition, some forms that must be filled out to qualify for property tax classifications—the homestead exemption and use-value taxation—also require taxpayers to reveal their income; and that information also is covered by these provisions.

Medical and Patient Records

A variety of statutes exempt from public access records about particular patients held by different sorts of health-related public agencies.[15] These include records held by public hospitals, public health departments, mental health agencies, and emergency medical services providers.

Closed-Session Minutes and General Accounts

G.S. 143-318.10(c) permits a public body to seal the minutes or the general account of any closed session "so long as public inspection would frustrate the purpose of a closed session."

Social Security Account Numbers and Other Personal Identifying and Personal Financial Information

Two statutes restrict or deny public access to information that can be used to steal a person's identity or that reveals certain sorts of financial information about a person. First, G.S. 132-1.10 prohibits government agencies from making public Social Security account numbers and other "identifying information" as defined in G.S. 14-113.20. This other information includes drivers' license numbers (except as they appear on law enforcement records), bank account numbers, bank card account numbers, fingerprints, and a few other types of similar information. Second, G.S. 132-1.1(c) exempts from public access billing information gathered or compiled as part of operating a public enterprise, such as a utility system. Billing information is defined as "any record or information, in whatever form, compiled or maintained with respect to individual customers."

---

14. G.S. 153A-148.1 (county tax records); 160A-208.1 (city tax records).

15. G.S. 131E-97 (medical records and financial records of patients at health care facilities); 130A-12 (patient medical records held by local health departments); 122C-52 (patient medical records held by area authorities); 143-518 (medical records held by EMS providers).

Records Involving Public Security

Several statutes exempt material from public access because of public security concerns. G.S. 132-1.7 exempts from public access the specific details of public security plans and detailed plans and drawings of public buildings and infrastructure. This section also exempts plans to prevent or respond to terrorist activity. G.S. 132-6.1 exempts from public access the security features of a government's electronic data-processing systems, information technology systems, telecommunications networks, and electronic security systems.[16]

Contract Bid Documents and Construction Diaries

G.S. 143-131 specifies that a government's record of informal construction or purchasing bids it has received is not open to the public until the contract for which the bids have been solicited has been awarded. In addition, G.S. 133-33 permits the state and local governments to adopt rules that make confidential the agency's cost estimates for a construction project and any list of contractors who have obtained proposals for bid purposes.

Economic Development Records

G.S. 132-6(d) exempts from public access records that relate to the proposed expansion or location of specific business or industrial projects. Once the project has been announced, however, or once the company has communicated a decision not to locate or expand in the state, the exemption ends.

Social Services Records

G.S. 108A-80 and 108A-3 prohibit any person from obtaining, disclosing, or using a list of names or other information about persons applying for or receiving public assistance or other social services.

Library Records

G.S. 125-19 prohibits a public library from disclosing any record that identifies a person as having requested or obtained specific materials, information, or services from the library.

Telephone Numbers Held by 911 Systems

Several statutes prohibit local governments operating 911 systems from releasing telephone numbers received from telephone companies, except in response to an emergency.[17]

Framework for Responding to Public Records Requests

As this chapter has described, the public records law creates a broad right of access to government records. Access to records must be allowed unless an exception applies. The following framework provides a set of questions to be considered when responding to public requests for public records. The questions are set out below, followed by a brief explanation of the issues involved in answering each question.

Framework Questions

1. **Does a record exist that corresponds to the request?** *If not, no disclosure is required. If so, continue to question 2.*
2. **Is the record "made or received in the transaction of public business"?** *If not, no disclosure is required. If so, continue to question 3.*

---

16. *See also* G.S. 132-1.6, which exempts from public access emergency response plans adopted by a constituent institution of the University of North Carolina, a community college, or a public hospital.

17. G.S. 62A-51 and 132-1.5.

3. **Is there an exception that applies?** *If not, the requested access must be provided. If so, continue to question 4.*
4. **Does the exception apply to the entire record or only to certain information, and does it prohibit disclosure or deny right of access?** *If a prohibition applies to the entire record, do not disclose; if it applies only to certain information, redact and disclose. If there is no right of access to some or all of the information, but release is not prohibited, determine whether or not to release the entire or a redacted record.*

Framework Answers

1. **Does a record exist that corresponds to the request?**
   Records can exist in many forms, but there will rarely be an issue about whether a particular record is of a type that is covered by the statute. The more significant aspect of this first question is whether a record actually exists that corresponds to the request. Sometimes public agencies receive requests for information that can be found in various records or which is known but not made part of any record. The obligation under the law is to provide access to or copies of records that exist, and the statute specifically says that a public agency is not required to respond to records requests by "creating or compiling a record that does not exist." As noted above, a request for public information from an employee's personnel file is an exception to this general rule.
2. **Is the record "made or received in the transaction of public business"?**
   Most of the records that a public agency has do relate to the business of the agency. Records that are personal, however, are not related to the work of the agency and are not subject to disclosure under the public records law, even if they are created using government email systems or devices. This can describe a great many records, including personal emails and text messages created by public employees or officials.
3. **Is there an exception that applies?**
   There are numerous exceptions to the public records law. The better part of David Lawrence's *Public Records Law for North Carolina Local Governments* explains the various exceptions, and it is the most complete resource for information on how to interpret them. A careful assessment must be made about whether an exception covers a particular record or category of record since there must be a legal basis for refusing to provide access to records.
4. **Does the exception apply to the entire record or only to certain information, and does it prohibit disclosure or deny right of access?**
   Some exceptions are described as exceptions to the right of access, though they do not prohibit the release of the records. The exceptions for criminal investigation information and economic development projects are examples of these types of exceptions. In these cases, the public agency is not required to provide the records, but it may choose to do so. Other exceptions, like those involving information in the personnel file and trade secrets, actually prohibit disclosure. In addition, there are some exceptions that have exceptions within them—that is, some exceptions identify specific information that would fall within the exception but that must nonetheless be made public. Both the personnel file and criminal investigation information exceptions contain these types of provisions. This part of the analysis requires careful attention to the various types of information that may be contained in a single record as well as a determination about whether all or part of the record is subject to public access. If an exception applies, the public agency may be allowed or even required to deny access to the entire record. In many cases, however, a particular record may contain a mix of public and nonpublic information. Depending on the wording of the particular exception, the public agency may be required to redact or separate confidential information from other information that is public. Although the public records law applies to records, not information, it also provides that a request for access to a record cannot be denied on the grounds that confidential information is commingled with nonconfidential information. Indeed, the law requires the public agency to bear the cost of separating the information in order to comply with the request. If an exception specifically prohibits disclosure of an entire record, redaction is not required.

Remedies for Denial of Access

Individuals who have been denied access to public records may attempt a mediated settlement under G.S. 7A-38.3E and may file an action under G.S. 132-9 to compel a public agency to provide the requested records. A claimant who substantially prevails in a claim under the statute may be allowed to recover attorneys' fees from the public agency. A court is prohibited from awarding attorneys' fees, however, if the public agency acted in reasonable reliance on (1) a court judgment or decision applicable to the agency involved, (2) a published opinion or order of any North Carolina court, or (3) a written opinion, decision, or letter of the North Carolina Attorney General.[18] Individuals may be personally liable for attorneys' fees only if they failed to follow advice of counsel.

Records Retention and Disposition

G.S. Chapter 132 and G.S. 121-5 together establish responsibilities for records protection and records management for two kinds of actors. The first is each custodian of one or more public records, and the second is the state Department of Cultural Resources. Together the custodians and the department are responsible for maintaining the integrity of public records and for developing a plan for the management of records in every public office or agency.

G.S. 132-3 prohibits any public official from destroying, selling, loaning, or otherwise disposing of any public record except in accordance with G.S. 121-5. That section in turn empowers the Department of Cultural Resources to decide how long particular categories of records are kept and whether and when they may be destroyed. In furtherance of that responsibility, the department has adopted a series of Records Retention and Disposition Schedules for almost all forms of records held by local governments. The department maintains current copies of its records schedules on its website.[19]

Once agreed to by the officials of a particular local government, these schedules govern whether various categories of records may be destroyed and when that may occur. For example, the original of all minutes of a city or county governing board must be retained permanently at the city or county offices, with a microfilmed duplicate set maintained by the department at the State Records Center. Local government contracts may be destroyed three years after their termination, if there is no outstanding litigation, while records of vehicles owned and maintained by the unit may be destroyed after one year. Records of "short-term value" need not be retained beyond their usefulness to the custodian. As such, most emails may be destroyed by the sender and recipient as they see fit and need be retained only if the substance of the communication is subject to retention under a specific provision as set out in the applicable schedule.

Additional Resources

Additional information can be found by searching *Coates' Canons: NC Local Government Law Blog* (http://sogweb.sog.unc.edu/blogs/localgovt) using the keyword "public records." A comprehensive guide to the state's public records laws and their interpretation by the courts is provided by David M. Lawrence, *Public Records Law for North Carolina Local Governments*, 2nd ed. (Chapel Hill: UNC School of Government, 2009).

About the Author

Frayda S. Bluestein is a School of Government faculty member specializing in local government law.

This chapter updates and revises the previous chapter authored by David M. Lawrence, whose contributions to the field and to this publication are gratefully acknowledged.

---

18. *See* G.S. 132-9(c).

19. See the Government Records Section webpage at www.records.ncdcr.gov/local/default.htm.

Chapter 9

Open Meetings and Other Legal Requirements for Local Government Boards

Frayda S. Bluestein

This chapter describes various legal requirements that affect elected and appointed local governing boards. In addition to the county and city elected governing boards, there are many other appointed boards that carry out important functions and activities at the local government level. The North Carolina open meetings law applies to all public bodies, including local elected and appointed boards, councils, and commissions, and to subcommittees of these bodies. County and city governing boards are subject to additional state statutory requirements regarding meetings and voting. There are numerous locally appointed boards as well. Some are governed by state statutory requirements, such as rules about voting and conflicts of interest for quasi-judicial boards. Many locally appointed boards are created by local ordinance and are governed primarily by the rules and requirements set out in those ordinances.

The first section of this chapter provides a summary of the open meetings law. The second section deals with procedures that apply only to governing boards of counties and cities. The final section outlines how to determine the procedures that apply to statutorily mandated and locally appointed boards and commissions.

Open Meetings Law Requirements for All Public Bodies

Overview

The North Carolina open meetings law[1] gives the general public a right to attend official meetings of public bodies, except in those cases where the law permits closed sessions. The law defines the types of public entities and meetings to which it applies and sets out mandatory forms and timing of notice that must be provided. If public officials conduct a meeting and do not comply with the notice and access requirements under the law, there is no immediate legal consequence. Rather, the law creates a legal remedy for a person who has been denied access to the meeting to seek redress in court, as further outlined below. Failure to comply with the open meetings law often does, however, create negative publicity for the public body and may diminish the public's trust and confidence in their local government representatives.

Public Right of Access to Open Meetings

The public's right to attend meetings of public bodies represents a strong policy in favor of transparency in local government decision making. Compliance with the notice requirements is an essential element of providing the mandated access. As part of the right of access, the law allows media broadcast of meetings and permits any person to photograph, film, tape-record or otherwise reproduce any part of an open meeting.[2] The open meetings law does not, however, provide the public any right to speak at public meetings. As noted later in this chapter, a separate statute requires regular public comment periods at certain governing board meetings. Public hearings also provide opportunities for public input and are required for some types of actions.[3] Other than these provisions, however, there is no general right for members of the public to be heard by, or to hear from, members of public bodies. It is up to each board to establish, in its discretion, additional opportunities for public input, either at meetings or through other channels. For a more complete discussion of citizen involvement in local government, see Chapter 10, "Citizen Involvement."

Official Meetings of Public Bodies

The notice and access requirements under the open meetings law are triggered when there is an "official meeting" of a "public body." The statute[4] defines the term *public body* as any elected or appointed board, commission, committee, council, authority, or other body in state or local government that (1) has at least two members and (2) exercises or is authorized to exercise any of these powers: legislative, policy-making, quasi-judicial, administrative, or advisory. This definition—and thus the scope of the statute—is very broad. Public bodies in county or city government include the elected governing board; each committee of that board, whether it is a standing committee or an ad hoc committee; boards created by statute, such as the board of health and the board of social services; and each body established by action of the governing board, such as a planning board, a zoning board of adjustment, a parks and recreation commission, or a human relations commission. Other local level governing boards include local boards of education, community college boards of trustees, and governing boards of public hospitals.

All official meetings of public bodies must be open to the public, unless the purpose of the meeting is one for which a closed session is allowed under the statute. As defined in the statute[5] an official meeting occurs whenever a *majority* of the members of a public body gather together to take action, hold a hearing, deliberate, or otherwise transact the business of the body. Even an informal gathering that includes a majority of the board triggers the statute if the members discuss or otherwise engage in the business of the public body.

Meetings solely among the professional staff of a public body and purely social gatherings among members of a public body are specifically excluded from the requirements of the law.

1. N.C. Gen. Stat. (hereinafter G.S.) Ch. 143, Art. 33C, §§ 143-318.9 through -318.18.
2. G.S. 143-318.14.
3. Public hearings are only required when a statute specifically calls for them. *See* David Lawrence, "When Are Public Hearings Required," *Coates' Canons: NC Local Government Law Blog* (UNC School of Government, Aug. 21, 2009), http://canons.sog.unc.edu/?p=77.
4. G.S. 143-318.10(b).
5. G.S. 143-318.10(d).

The definition of official meeting makes clear that an official meeting occurs by the simultaneous communication, in person *or electronically*, by a majority of the public body. Because the definition includes electronic communication, a telephone call or email communication that involves a simultaneous conversation among a majority of a public body would violate the open meetings law if notice and access are not provided.

Notice Requirements

A key component of the open meetings law is the requirement to provide advance notice of meetings. The statute requires that each public body give public notice of its official meetings, even those that will be conducted in closed session.[6] These requirements apply to meetings of the governing board, to meetings of each appointed board, and to meetings of each committee of any of these boards. The type of notice required depends on the nature of the meeting, as described below. Specific additional types of notice required for county and city *governing boards* are described later in this chapter.

Regular Meetings

If a public body holds regular meetings, it gives public notice of those meetings by filing its schedule of regular meetings in a central location. For public bodies that are part of a county government, that location is the office of the clerk to the board of commissioners. For public bodies that are part of a city government, that location is the office of the city clerk. For local public bodies not part of a county or city, such as a local board of education, that location is the office of its clerk or secretary. The law also requires the schedule of regular meetings to be posted on the public body's website, if it maintains one. Once this notice is properly filed and posted, no other public notice is required for regular meetings held pursuant to the schedule. Changes in the regular meeting schedule are made by filing and posting a revised schedule at least seven days before the first meeting to occur under the revised schedule.

Special Meetings

If a public body meets at some time or place other than that shown on its regular meeting schedule, or if the public body does not meet on a regular schedule, it must give special meeting notice. Such a notice sets out the time, place, and purpose of the meeting and is provided in three ways. First, it must be posted on the *principal bulletin board* of the public body (or on the meeting room door if there is no principal bulletin board). Second, it must be mailed, emailed, or delivered to any person who has made a written request for notice of special meetings. Third, it must be posted on the website of the public body, if it has one. Each of these forms of notice must occur at least forty-eight hours before the meeting. A public body may require media requests to be renewed annually. Non-media requesters may be required to renew quarterly and must be charged a fee of $10 per calendar year. No fee may be charged for email notices.

It is important to note that the statute requires the notice to specify the *purpose* of the meeting. Public bodies should be careful when conducting special meetings not to discuss or take action on matters not included in the scope of the notice.

Emergency Meetings

If the public body must meet within less than forty-eight hours, notice must be given to all *local* news media that have requested notice. Notice may be given by telephone or email or by the same method used to notify the members of the public body. An emergency meeting may be held only to address "generally unexpected circumstances that require immediate consideration by the public body," and only matters meeting this standard may be discussed at the meeting.[7] As noted later in this chapter, because of a separate notice requirement for city council members, a city council usually must allow at least six hours when scheduling an emergency meeting.[8]

6. G.S. 143-318.12.
7. G.S. 143-318.12(b)(3).
8. *See* G.S. 160A-71(b)(1).

Recessed Meetings

If a public body is in a properly noticed regular, special, or emergency meeting, it may recess that meeting to a time, date, and place certain. Notice of a recessed meeting is provided by announcing the time, date, and place of the recessed meeting in open session at the original meeting. In addition, the statute requires notice of the recessed meetings to be posted on the public body's website, if it has one.[9]

Closed Sessions

The open meetings law authorizes a public body to meet in closed session for any of nine specific reasons listed in the statute.[10] This authority applies to all public bodies (not just governing boards), although many appointed boards rarely have justification to meet in closed session.

Procedures for Closed Sessions

A closed session can be a part of any regular, special, or emergency meeting, and the applicable notice of the meeting must be given, even if the entire meeting consists of the closed session. If a public body wishes to hold a closed session, the body must first meet in open session and then vote to hold the closed session. It is not sufficient for the presiding officer simply to announce that a closed session will be held. Rather, there must be a motion to go into closed session, and the motion must identify the permissible purpose from among those authorized in the statute. (A specific citation is not necessary as long as it is clear from the motion which provision is being invoked.) Once the closed session is complete, the public body must return to the open session to complete its business or to adjourn.

A brief overview of the closed session purposes most commonly used by local governments is set out below. For more detail, see the School of Government publication *Open Meetings and Local Governments in North Carolina: Some Questions and Answers.*[11]

Confidential Records

A public body may meet in a closed session to discuss information that is part of a record that is confidential or otherwise not available to the public.[12] Thus, for example, a board of social services may have a closed session to discuss matters involving recipients of public assistance, because records about recipients are closed to public access. A motion to go into closed session under this provision must state the name or citation of the law that makes the information privileged or confidential.[13]

Attorney Consultations

A public body may meet in closed session with its attorney to discuss matters that are within the attorney–client privilege—that is, legal subjects.[14] While in the closed session, the public body may give instructions to the attorney about handling or settling claims, litigation, or other proceedings. If a board meets in closed session under this provision in order to receive advice about an existing lawsuit, the motion to go into closed session must identify the parties to the lawsuit.[15] The basis for this exception to the open meetings law is to preserve the attorney–client privilege. This means that the meeting cannot legally include any person who is not within that privilege.[16]

---

9. G.S. 143-318.12 (e).

10. G.S. 143-318.11(a)(1) through (9).

11. David M. Lawrence, *Open Meetings and Local Governments in North Carolina: Some Questions and Answers* (UNC School of Government, 7th ed. 2008).

12. G.S. 143-318.11(a)(1).

13. G.S. 143-318.11(c).

14. G.S. 143-318.11(a)(3).

15. *Id.*

16. For more detail on the scope of the attorney–client exception, see David M. Lawrence, "Closed Sessions Under the Attorney–Client Privilege," *Local Government Law Bulletin* No. 103 (Apr. 2002), www.sogpubs.unc.edu/electronicversions/pdfs/lglb103.pdf.

Economic Development

A public body may have a closed session to discuss matters relating to the location or expansion of businesses in the area served by the public body.[17] This is the authority under which a public body may in closed session develop an incentives package to attract a new business or encourage an existing business to expand.

Purchase of Real Property

A public body may hold a closed session to develop its negotiating position in the purchase of real property, and it may, while in closed session, give instructions to its bargaining agent in that transaction.[18] Note that this provision *does not* authorize a public body to meet in closed session when it is *selling* real property.[19]

Employment Contracts

A public body may hold a closed session to develop its position in the negotiating of an employment contract, and it may, while in closed session, give instructions to its negotiating agent in that transaction.[20]

Public Employees

A public body may hold a closed session to consider the qualifications, competence, performance, character, fitness, and conditions of appointment or employment of a public employee or public officer.[21] In addition, a public body may hold a closed session to hear or investigate a complaint, charge, or grievance by or against a public officer or employee.[22] A public body may not use this provision to discuss members of the public body itself or members of other public bodies. This provision does not allow closed session discussions of general personnel policies. It applies only to matters involving specific employees of the unit and does not extend to independent contractors or volunteers.

Criminal Investigations

A public body may hold a closed session to plan, conduct, or hear reports concerning an investigation of alleged criminal conduct.[23]

Minutes and General Accounts

The open meetings law requires public bodies to prepare "full and accurate minutes" of all meetings and a "general account" of closed sessions.[24] Separate statutes for county[25] and city[26] governing boards also require each board, through its clerk, to keep full and accurate minutes of its proceedings. Although the statutes do not detail what full and accurate minutes should include, the proper content of board minutes is suggested by their purpose, which is to provide an official record, or proof, of governing board actions. Therefore, at a minimum the minutes should include two sorts of material: (1) the actions taken by a board, stated specifically enough to be identified and proved; and (2) proof of any conditions necessary to action, such as the presence of a quorum. Additional detail about matters that were discussed or individuals who addressed the board is often included but is not legally required. Minutes should be approved by the public body. The statutes do not establish a specific time frame within which minutes must be prepared or approved.

---

17. G.S. 143-318.11(4).
18. G.S. 143-318.11(5).
19. Procedures for selling real property are governed by Article 12 of Chapter 160A of the North Carolina General Statutes and are described in Chapter 23 of this publication.
20. G.S. 143-318.11(a)(5).
21. G.S. 143-318.11(a)(6).
22. *Id.*
23. G.S. 143-318.11(a)(7).
24. G.S. 143-318.10(e).
25. G.S. 153A-42.
26. G.S. 160A-72.

As noted, the purpose of minutes is to provide an official record, or proof, of council action. In a judicial proceeding, the minutes are the only competent evidence of council action, and as such, they may not be attacked on the ground that they are incorrect. Once approved, minutes may be modified in only two ways: (1) a person may bring a legal action alleging that the minutes are incorrect and seeking a court order to correct them; and (2) much more common, a council may itself modify its minutes if they are found to be incorrect.

Since public bodies have limited authority to take action in closed sessions, minutes of closed sessions can be quite skeletal. For closed sessions, the open meetings law requires, in addition to minutes, a general account of the closed session. The statute requires that the general account be detailed enough "so that a person not in attendance would have a reasonable understanding of what transpired."[27] It is common for boards to combine the minutes and general account in a single document.

Minutes are generally open to the public under the public records law (see Chapter 8) and must be permanently retained. Closed session minutes, however, may be withheld from public access (sealed) for as long as is necessary to avoid frustrating the purpose of the closed session. Many public bodies initially seal all minutes and general accounts of closed sessions and then delegate to their attorney or other staff the responsibility for periodically reviewing these documents and opening them to public access when that is appropriate. Closed session minutes should be approved by the public body, and it may hold a closed session to do so.[28]

Remedies

There are two statutory remedies for correcting violations of the open meetings law. The first is an injunction.[29] Any person may seek an injunction to stop the recurrence of past violations of the law, the continuation of present violations, or the occurrence of threatened future violations. The second is the invalidation of any action taken or considered in violation of the law.[30] Action taken at a meeting held in violation of the open meetings law is not automatically invalid, but a trial judge does have the option of entering such an order if a lawsuit is filed seeking that remedy. The court may award attorneys' fees to the prevailing party in a lawsuit alleging a violation of the open meetings law, and it may order that they be paid personally by individual members of the public body if they are found to have knowingly or intentionally violated the law.[31] Individuals cannot be held liable for costs if they follow the advice of counsel.

Additional Meeting Requirements for County and City Governing Boards

Boards of county commissioners and city councils hold ultimate authority to act for the local government. Chapter 3, "County and City Governing Boards," describes the structure and roles of these important bodies. This section describes some of the specific meeting requirements that apply—in addition to those under the open meetings law—to these governing boards.

Governing Board Meetings

Specific statutes in Chapters 153A (counties) and 160A (cities) of the North Carolina General Statutes prescribe procedures for governing board meetings that supplement the requirements of the open meetings law. Both sets of requirements must be met.

---

27. G.S. 143-318.10(e). A case that sets out an acceptable general account is *Multimedia Publishing Co. of N.C., Inc. v. Henderson County*, 145 N.C. App. 365 (2001).

28. G.S. 143-318.11(a)(1).

29. G.S. 143-318.16.

30. G.S. 143-318.16A.

31. G.S. 143-318.16B.

Organizational Meetings

After each election the newly elected (or re-elected) members must qualify for office by taking and subscribing the oath of office. In addition, the governing board must organize itself. The meeting at which these events take place is known as the *organizational meeting.*

Counties

Section 153A-26 of the North Carolina General Statutes (hereinafter G.S.) directs that each commissioner elected or re-elected at the November election must take the oath of office on the first Monday in December following the election; at the same time, the board elects its chair and vice-chair for the ensuing year. If a commissioner is unable to take the oath at that time, he or she may take it later.

Cities

Unless a council sets an earlier date,[32] a city council's organizational meeting is held at the board's first regular meeting in December following the election. At the organizational meeting, all newly elected and re-elected members, and the mayor, if newly elected or re-elected, must take the oath of office. If the city is one in which the board elects the mayor, this is done at the organizational meeting. The board must also elect a mayor pro tempore.[33]

Regular Meetings

Counties

G.S. 153A-40 directs boards of county commissioners to hold at least one meeting each month, although they may meet more often if necessary. Many boards hold two regular meetings each month. The board may select any day of the month and any public place within the county for its regular meetings, but unless it selects some other time or place by formal resolution, the law requires the board to meet on the first Monday of the month at the courthouse.

Cities

G.S. 160A-71 directs each city's governing board to fix the time and the place of its regular meetings. If the board fails to act, the statute provides that meetings shall be held on the first Monday of each month at 10:00 a.m. Cities are not required to hold a meeting every month.

Special Meetings

Although both county commissioners and city councils may hold special meetings, the statutes under which they may do so are somewhat different. Under the county and city statutes governing meeting notice, a *special meeting* is any meeting other than a regular meeting.[34]

In general, a governing board may take any action at a special meeting that it may take at a regular meeting. A few exceptions do exist, however, as some statutes require action to be taken at a regular meeting. Examples include adoption of ordinances awarding or amending franchises and action on several procedures for selling property. (Even so, a board may *discuss* these matters at a special meeting; it simply may not act.) Because of these exceptions, before taking any action at a special meeting, a board should consult its attorney to ascertain whether it may properly take the action. As noted earlier, it is also important to limit actions taken at special meetings to those matters identified in the notice of the meeting.

Governing boards must comply with the separate requirements for notice to the public of special and emergency meetings under the open meetings law as well as the procedures for notice to the board members, as described below.

---

32. G.S. 160A-68 permits a board to establish an earlier date, which may be any date within the period beginning on the day that the election results are officially determined and published and ending on the day that the board holds its first regular meeting in December.

33. G.S. 160A-70 specifies that the mayor pro tempore is to serve at the pleasure of the governing board.

34. G.S. 153A-40(b); G.S. 160A-71(b)(1).

Counties

G.S. 153A-40 permits a special meeting to be called by the chair or by a majority of the other board members. The law sets specific rules for calling special meetings. They must be called by written notice stating the time, place, and subjects to be considered. This notice must be posted on the courthouse bulletin board and delivered to each board member at least forty-eight hours before the meeting. Unless all members attend the meeting or sign a written waiver, only business related to the subjects stated in the notice may be transacted at a special meeting. It is important to remember, however, that expansion of the subjects to be addressed in a special meeting, even if allowed under this statute, may violate the open meetings law.

Cities

G.S. 160A-71 permits special meetings of a city council to be called in either of two ways. First, if a board is convened in a regular meeting or a duly called special meeting, it may schedule a special meeting. Second, the mayor, the mayor pro tempore, or any two members of the board may call such a meeting. They may do so by preparing and signing a written notice of the meeting—setting out the time and place and the subjects to be considered—and causing this notice to be delivered to each board member (or to his or her home). The notice must be delivered at least six hours before the meeting, but as noted earlier, the open meetings law requires forty-eight hours' *public* notice of a special meeting.

Emergency Meetings

Counties

G.S. 153A-40 provides that notice to board members is not required for a special meeting that is called to deal with an emergency, but it requires the person or persons calling the meeting to take reasonable actions to inform the other board members and the public of the meeting.

Cities

The city statutes do not specifically address emergency meetings. This means that the six-hour notice for special meetings applies to these types of meetings. Even though there is no minimum time for public notice of emergency meetings under the open meetings law, the six-hour board member notice requirement will usually limit a city's ability to hold a meeting with less than six hours notice. If, however, an emergency meeting is set in a regular or duly called special meeting, the six-hour notice requirement does not apply.

Meeting Location

While county commissioners' meetings are generally held within the county, G.S. 153A-40 permits out-of-county meetings in four specific instances (and not otherwise):

1. In connection with a joint meeting of two or more public bodies, as long as the meeting is within the boundaries of the political subdivision represented by the members of one of the participating bodies;
2. In connection with a retreat, forum, or similar gathering held solely to provide the county commissioners with information relating to the performance of their public duties (no vote may be taken during this type of meeting);
3. In connection with a meeting between the board and its local legislative delegation while the General Assembly is in session, as long as no votes are taken except concerning matters directly relating to proposed or pending legislation;
4. While the commissioners are attending a convention, association meeting, or similar gathering, if the meeting is held solely to discuss or deliberate on the board's position concerning convention resolutions, association officer elections, and similar issues that are not legally binding.

There are no comparable statutory restrictions on the location of city council meetings.

Rules of Procedure

Each governing board has the power to adopt its own rules of procedure. Exercise of this power can help prevent arguments over procedure that cannot otherwise be satisfactorily resolved. Boards often base their rules on *Robert's Rules of Order* or similar sources. Boards should be careful, however, to adapt these models, which are primarily intended for large groups, to the special needs of a small board. The School of Government publishes two resources—*Suggested Rules of Procedure for the Board of County Commissioners*[35] and *Suggested Rules of Procedure for a City Council*[36]—that are adaptations of *Roberts Rules* designed specifically for North Carolina county and city governing boards.

Quorum

As noted earlier, a governing board may take action only during a legally constituted meeting. A meeting is legally constituted only when a quorum is present. As described below, the rules for determining a quorum are slightly different for counties and cities.

In both counties and cities, once a quorum has been attained and the meeting convened, a member may not destroy the quorum by simply leaving. G.S. 153A-43, for counties, and G.S. 160A-74, for cities, both provide that if a member withdraws from the meeting without being excused by a majority vote of the remaining members present, he or she is still counted as present for purposes of a quorum. In addition, the city statute provides that the member is counted as voting "yes" on all matters that come before the board after he or she leaves. There is no comparable provision in the county statute, but many boards of commissioners have adopted the same rule by board action.

Counties

G.S. 153A-43 defines a quorum as a majority of the membership of the board of commissioners, and it provides that the number is not affected by vacancies. Thus, if a board has six members, its quorum is four; and if there is a vacant seat, the quorum remains four.

Cities

G.S. 160A-74 defines a quorum as a majority of the actual membership of the council, including the mayor but excluding vacant seats. Thus, if a city is governed by a five-member board plus the mayor, the actual membership of the group is six, and a quorum is four. If one seat is vacant, however, the membership becomes five, and a quorum is three.

Governing Board Action

Governing boards take action in a variety of forms: ordinances, resolutions, motions, and orders. Textbooks usually define *ordinance* as a permanent rule of conduct imposed by a county or city on its citizens. Thus, ordinances may limit the amount of noise that citizens may make, regulate how they may use their land, or require their businesses to treat sewage before discharging it into the government's system. In North Carolina, local governments also appropriate money and levy taxes by ordinance.

The other sorts of actions are less precise in their meaning. Textbooks often define *resolutions* as expressions of board opinion on administrative matters and *motions* and *orders* as actions resulting in or expressing a decision. Thus, a board might set out the unit's policy on extension of utilities by resolution while approving specific extensions by motion or order. In practice, the distinction is not always so carefully drawn; often one board takes actions by order or motion that another takes by resolution.

Voting Rules

Both county commissions and city councils are subject to complicated rules that determine whether a measure has passed. In both counties and cities, the number of board members who must vote for a measure in order for that

---

35. Joseph S. Ferrell, *Suggested Rules of Procedure for the Board of County Commissioners* (UNC School of Government, 3d ed. 2002).

36. A. Fleming Bell, II, *Suggested Rules of Procedure for a City Council* (UNC School of Government, 3d ed. 2000).

measure to pass differs according to a number of factors: whether the measure is an ordinance or some other form of action, when the measure first comes before the governing board, and whether any members have been excused from voting on the measure. The actual provisions, however, differ between counties and cities.

Counties

The law does not regulate the manner in which orders and resolutions are adopted by a board of commissioners beyond the minimum requirement of a valid meeting at which a quorum is present, but several laws govern the adoption of ordinances.[37] An ordinance may be adopted at the meeting at which it is introduced only if it receives a unanimous affirmative vote, with all members of the board present and voting. If the ordinance passes at this meeting but with less than a unanimous vote, it may finally be passed by a majority of votes cast (a quorum being present) at any time within 100 days of its introduction. This rule does not apply to the following ordinances:

- The budget ordinance (which may be passed at any meeting at which a quorum is present);
- Any bond order (which always requires a public hearing before passage and in most cases requires approval by the voters as well);
- Any ordinance on which the law requires a public hearing before adoption (such as a zoning ordinance);
- A franchise ordinance (which must be passed at two separate regular meetings of the board).

City Ordinances

To be adopted on the day that it is introduced, a city ordinance must be approved by a vote of at least two-thirds of the actual membership of the council, excluding vacant seats. This rule applies to any city action that has the effect of an ordinance, no matter how it is labeled. In determining actual membership, the mayor is not counted unless he or she has the right to vote on all questions before the board. Thus, if a board has seven members and is presided over by a mayor who votes only to break ties, five members must vote in favor of an ordinance for it to be adopted on the day that it is introduced. If there is a vacant seat, however, the actual membership is then six, and only four votes are required to adopt the ordinance on that first day.

Given this special rule pertaining to the day of introduction, what constitutes introduction? The statute states that the day of introduction is the day on which the board *first votes on the subject matter* of the ordinance.[38] Examples of such a vote might include a vote to hold a hearing on the ordinance, refer it to committee, or try to pass it.

After the day on which it is introduced, an ordinance may be adopted by an affirmative vote equal to at least a majority of the board membership; vacancies do not affect the number necessary for approval. Members who have been properly excused from voting on a particular issue (see the discussion under the heading "Excusing of Members from Voting," below) are not included in the membership for a vote on that issue. For example, a six-member board normally requires an affirmative vote of four members to adopt an ordinance. But if one member is excused on a particular issue, the board is treated as having only five members on that issue, and only three need vote affirmatively for the measure to pass.

Nonvoting mayors are not counted in determining how many members constitute the board. If there is a tie, however, the mayor's vote is counted in determining whether the requisite majority vote has been attained. Thus, if a six-member board divides three to three on an issue and the mayor votes affirmatively to break the tie, the measure has received the four votes necessary for its adoption.

G.S. 160A-75 requires a majority vote of the board membership on a few other measures besides ordinances: (1) any action having the effect of an ordinance, no matter how it is labeled; (2) any measure that authorizes an expenditure of funds or commits a board to one, other than the budget ordinance or a project ordinance; and (3) any measure that authorizes, makes, or ratifies a contract.

37. G.S. 153A-45 through -47.
38. G.S. 160A-75.

With the exceptions just noted, the general law makes no special provision for the sort of city council vote necessary to adopt resolutions, motions, or measures other than ordinances. (Some charters do require that resolutions or other actions receive the same vote as ordinances.) For these actions the rule is that action may be taken by a majority of those present and voting, as long as a quorum is present. Thus, if a board has eight members, its quorum is five; and if only five members are present, a resolution or a motion may be adopted by a vote of only three of the five.

Excusing Members from Voting

G.S. 153A-44, for counties, and G.S. 160A-75, for cities, permit a board member to be excused from voting in two circumstances in which there is a potential conflict of interest: (1) when the question involves his or her own financial interest, and (2) when it involves his or her official conduct. In addition, these two statutes reference three other statutes that *prohibit* a board member from voting in certain circumstances because of a financial conflict: G.S. 14-234, when the board member may be interested in a contract being approved or considered by the board; G.S. 153A-340 or G.S. 160A-381, when the board is considering a zoning ordinance amendment that is likely to have a "direct, substantial, and readily identifiable financial impact on the member"; and G.S. 153A-345 or G.S. 160A-388, when the board is acting on a land use matter in a quasi-judicial capacity and the board member's participation would violate the constitutional requirement of an impartial decision maker. These statutes are discussed in more detail in Chapter 7, "Ethics and Conflicts of Interest."

In those situations in which the statutes do not expressly prohibit the interested board member from voting, the county statute specifies that the board must vote to excuse a member. The city statute is silent as to procedure, but unless the board has adopted a procedural rule authorizing a member to be excused by the mayor or to excuse himself or herself, such an abstention should be allowed only by vote of the remaining board members. If a member is excused, that member should neither vote nor participate in any way in the deliberations leading up to the vote.

Unless a board member is excused, he or she must vote; the statutes do not authorize unexcused abstentions. If a council member persists in abstaining without being excused, G.S. 160A-75 directs that the member be counted as voting "yes." There is no comparable provision in the county statute, but many boards of county commissioners have adopted such a provision by rule.

The rules for mayors are slightly different than for commissioners or council members. If a mayor is elected by and from the board, he or she remains a board member and must vote. But a mayor who may vote only to break a tie has the option of not voting at all. The statute allows, but does not require, the mayor to break a tie. If he or she refuses to break a tie, the measure is defeated.

Public Hearings and Public Comment

As noted earlier, the open meetings law allows the public to attend meetings but does not provide a right to be heard. The public has opportunities for public comment through hearings and public comment periods. Some hearings are required,[39] such as the hearing on the budget ordinance, a bond ordinance, or a zoning ordinance or amendment. Others are held on the board's own initiative to give interested citizens an opportunity to make their views known to the board on a controversial issue, such as a noise-control or towing ordinance.

State statutes also require boards of county commissioners, city councils, and school boards to offer at least one public comment period each month during a regular meeting, at which members of the public may comment on local government affairs more broadly.[40] This public comment period is discussed in more detail in Chapter 10's discussion of citizen involvement.

The laws that require public hearings do not specify the manner in which they must be conducted; the laws only require that they be held. Nevertheless, G.S. 153A-52 and -52.1, for counties, and G.S. 160A-81 and -81.1, for cities, allow

---

39. Public hearings are required only when a statute specifically calls for them. *See* David Lawrence, "When Are Public Hearings Required," *Coates' Canons: North Carolina Local Government Law Blog* (UNC School of Government, Aug. 21, 2009), http://canons.sog.unc.edu/?p=77.

40. G.S. 153A-52.1 (counties); G.S. 160A-81.1 (cities); G.S. 115C-51 (schools).

the board to adopt reasonable rules governing the conduct of public hearings and public comment periods. These rules may regulate such matters as allotting time to each speaker, designating who will speak for groups, selecting delegates from groups when the hearing room is too small to hold everyone who wants to attend, and maintaining order as well as decorum. The statutes requiring public hearings and comment periods create constitutionally protected rights of expression for members of the public. Governing boards must be careful when regulating conduct to avoid restricting speakers based on the opinion or point of view they are expressing.

Rules for Quasi-Judicial Proceedings

County and city governing boards, as well as some types of appointed boards, sometimes function in a quasi-judicial capacity. Examples include decisions on certain types of land use permits or zoning variances and appeals of personnel actions. In these settings, boards are limited in their process and decision making by principles of due process, which is required because these actions affect constitutionally protected property rights. As noted above, the legislature has enacted specific voting rules to avoid conflicts of interest that apply in these situations. In addition, quasi-judicial hearings must be conducted consistent with the basic rules for a legal proceeding, including swearing in of witnesses and decisions based exclusively on evidence presented in the proceeding. These types of hearings should be distinguished from those designed to provide open forums for public comment or opinion. Indeed, only those who are qualified as witnesses or who have a stake in the outcome may speak at quasi-judicial hearings.

Remote Participation in Meetings

A board member who is unable to attend a meeting may wish to participate remotely by phone or Internet connection. The question of whether a person must be physically present to count toward a quorum is unclear under the statutes. The open meetings law definition of *official meeting* includes electronic meetings.[41] But the open meetings law applies to all public bodies throughout the state, not just to local government boards, and it does not specifically authorize or even address the use of electronic meetings or individual electronic participation by local government boards. As noted above, the quorum and voting statutes refer to members being "present,"[42] but courts in other states have found that a person may be considered to be present when participating remotely. Until there is more specific guidance from the legislature or the courts, remote participation may create a risk if the remote participant casts a deciding vote or is necessary to create a quorum. On the other hand, there is no legal risk if a member participates in a discussion (no vote being taken) or if there is a sufficient number of board members physically present to constitute a quorum. It is up to the governing board, in any event, to decide whether and under what circumstances to allow remote participation. Local governments may also authorize remote participation for boards they create and appoint. Boards that wish to allow remote participation should establish policies governing when it will be allowed.[43]

Meeting Requirements for Appointed Boards

The preceding section of this chapter focused on rules that apply to county and city governing boards. Appointed boards are, of course, subject to the open meetings law but not to many of the more specific rules described above.

For purposes of understanding meeting requirements for appointed boards, it is helpful to consider them in two categories: those created by statute and those created by local county or city ordinance. Statutory boards include social services, public health, and ABC boards. Statutes establishing these boards include specific procedural and other requirements. Other boards and commissions are created by local ordinance or resolution under the governing

41. G.S. 160A-75.

42. G.S. 153A-44, 160A-74.

43. For a more detailed analysis of the legal aspects of remote participation, along with considerations for local policies, see Frayda S. Bluestein, "Remote Participation in Local Government Board Meetings," *Local Government Law Bulletin* No. 133 (Aug. 2013), http://sogpubs.unc.edu/electronicversions/pdfs/lglb133.pdf.

boards' general authority to organize the local government[44] or under more specific authority, such as that authorizing the creation of boards of adjustment.[45]

Statutes establishing or allowing the creation of specific appointed boards may include membership and procedural requirements that must be met. County and city governing boards establish other local boards by adopting ordinances, which contain the membership, purpose, and procedure under which they are to operate. Two School of Government resources are recommended for the creation and operation of these types of boards: *Suggested Rules of Procedure for Small Local Government Boards*[46] and *Creating and Maintaining Effective Local Government Citizen Advisory Committees*.[47]

Additional Resources

Additional information can be found by searching *Coates' Canons: NC Local Government Law Blog* (http://sogweb.sog.unc.edu/blogs/localgovt) using the keyword "open meetings." Also see David M. Lawrence, *Open Meetings and Local Governments in North Carolina: Some Questions and Answers* (UNC School of Government, 7th ed. 2008).

About the Author

Frayda S. Bluestein is a School of Government faculty member specializing in local government law.

This chapter updates and revises previous chapters authored by David M. Lawrence and Joseph S. Ferrell, whose contributions to the field and to this publication are gratefully acknowledged.

44. G.S. 153A-76 (counties); G.S. 160A-146 (cities).

45. G.S. 153A-345 (counties); G.S. 160A-388 (cities).

46. A. Fleming Bell, II, *Suggested Rules of Procedure for Small Local Government Boards* (UNC School of Government, 2d ed. 1988).

47. Vaughn Mamlin Upshaw, *Creating and Maintaining Effective Local Government Citizen Advisory Committees* (UNC School of Government, 2010).

Chapter 10

Citizen Involvement

Maureen M. Berner and John B. Stephens

In a democratic republic, government gains its legitimacy exclusively from "the people." The most visible way this occurs is through periodic elections of representatives at all levels of government. Citizen influence can be exercised on a more regular basis, however, by communicating to those representatives—and to others in government—opinions, desires, proposals, criticisms, and even demands about what should be done to create a better community, state, and nation. Citizen involvement is a key element of the First Amendment to the U.S. Constitution—"the right of the people peaceably to assemble, and to petition the government for a redress of grievances."

This chapter presents several aspects of citizen involvement[1] in North Carolina local government. First, the tension between the philosophical and practical value of an involved citizenry for North Carolina cities and counties is examined, including the commonly cited weaknesses and problems of citizen involvement at the local level. Next, North Carolina's statutory requirements for citizen involvement are set out.[2] Third, the chapter describes particular ways government officials invite or create involvement. Primary among these are public hearings and appointed citizen boards. Other means of outreach and response, including citizen surveys and newer avenues created by email and Web-based resources and exchange, are also covered. The chapter also notes the growth of proactive education efforts known as citizen academies and citizen police academies and closes with a description of local government employee responsibility for fostering citizen involvement.

1. In this chapter "citizen involvement" in local government refers to involvement by any residents of a city or county. Most forms of involvement other than voting are open to any resident of a community, regardless of U.S. citizenship status.

2. Other chapters, primarily Chapter 8, "Public Records," and Chapter 9, "Open Meetings and Other Legal Requirements for Local Government Boards," discuss the law governing public documents and open meetings and hearings.

A few passages in the state constitution form the basis of political philosophy about the importance of government's responsiveness to its citizens. Article I, Declaration of Rights, Section 2, Sovereignty of the people, of the North Carolina Constitution provides, "All political power is vested in and derived from the people; all government of right originates from the people, is founded upon their will only, and is instituted solely for the good of the whole." Later in the same article, Section 3, Internal government of the State, says, "The people of this State have the inherent, sole, and exclusive right of regulating the internal government and police thereof and of altering or abolishing their Constitution and form of government whenever it may be necessary to their safety and happiness; but every such right shall be exercised in pursuance of law and consistently with the Constitution of the United States." Finally, similar to the U.S. Constitution, Section 12, Right of assembly and petition, declares, "The people have a right to assemble together to consult for their common good, to instruct their representatives, and to apply to the General Assembly for redress of grievances. . . ." Such passages serve as a useful reminder that citizen involvement beyond campaigns and elections is a bedrock principle of governance in North Carolina. These very basic rights raise several questions and concerns about the exercise of those rights and about local government's responsibility to provide informal or day-to-day opportunities for citizen involvement.

Citizen Involvement: Interest, Low Voter Turnout, and Common Reasons for Lack of Engagement

Does interest in local government translate into citizen involvement? For some citizens, public participation in government occurs primarily through the electoral process. For others, campaigns and elections are just the culmination of an ongoing, interactive relationship between government officials and citizens. If voting in elections is the primary measure of public participation, the data are mixed. In a February 2011 general poll of adults in North Carolina, Elon University found that 89 percent of respondents had some interest (44 percent) or a lot of interest (44.6 percent) in the "actions and activities of state and local governments."[3] Similar results came from 2009 and 2010 polls.[4] Some of this interest was translated into seeking out government public documents: 57 percent of respondents had tried to obtain some kind of public document, the most common being crime reports, property tax records, and the names and addresses of registered sex offenders.[5] Finally, in a 2009 statewide Elon poll,[6] 79 percent of respondents agreed with the statement "I am as well-informed about politics and government as most people" and 67 percent agreed that "I consider myself well-qualified to participate in politics."

Since the 2011 statewide survey, the only other relevant information gleaned from polls involved citizens' trust in government and how often they sought government documents. A 2013 Elon poll showed North Carolina residents placing higher trust in local and state government than in the federal government: "Forty-nine percent said they trust their local government to do what is right most of the time or just about always, compared to 26.5% for state government and 14% for the federal government."[7] Thirty-eight percent of respondents said they had attempted to obtain some type of public information, and 87 percent said they were successful in obtaining that information. The most common type of record requested was related to real estate (18 percent), followed by birth certificates (17 percent), and criminal or police records (11 percent).[8]

North Carolina voting statistics, when considered alongside the self-reported "interest in politics" discussed in the survey described above, create an ambiguous picture of citizen engagement with government. According to the state board of elections, in 2008 nearly 88 percent of the voting age population was registered to vote; in 2010, nearly

3. "Elon University Poll," Elon University, www.elon.edu/docs/e-web/elonpoll/031111_PollMethodology.pdf, 6.

4. "Elon University Poll," Elon University, www.elon.edu/docs/e-web/elonpoll/031111_PollMethodology.pdf.

5. *Id.* at 9.

6. "Elon University Poll," Elon University, www.elon.edu/docs/e-web/elonpoll/112309_ElonPollDATA2.pdf, 5–6.

7. Elon University Poll, "Do NC Residents Trust Government?" (Open Government Survey, Nov. 15–18, 2013), www.elon.edu/docs/e-web/elonpoll/120413_ElonPollOpenGovt_ExecSum.pdf, 3.

8. *Id.*, 3–4.

86 percent was registered.[9] The percentage of voters voting in elections, however, is much lower than the percentage of those eligible and registered to vote. General elections including presidential candidates have the highest percentage of voting. Since 1972, presidential-year general elections have had turnouts of registered voters ranging from 59 to 70 percent. Between 1972 and 1992, turnout was fairly consistent, at 62–69 percent. Wider variation has occurred in the last twenty years, with a low of 59 percent in 1996 and 2000 and a high of 70 percent in 2008. Since 1974, turnout in non-presidential-year general elections has typically been 42–47 percent, with a high of 62 percent in 1990 and a low of 37 percent in 2006.[10] For many local government elections—bond and tax issues and candidate races—the turnout can be very low. For example, in November 2009 the statewide turnout for municipal elections was 16.3 percent.[11]

There is no specific data on why North Carolina registered voters do not vote. However, a national survey identified the most common reasons as (1) too busy/conflicting schedule (17.5 percent), (2) illness or disability (14.9 percent), (3) not interested (13.45 percent), and (4) did not like candidates or campaign issues (12.95 percent).[12] Thus, while the vast majority of North Carolina citizens register to vote, only two-thirds or less participate in government through voting in elections.

What can explain this low rate of participation? Low voter turnout in many elections could be due to one or more of four factors: (1) citizens feel disconnected from government, (2) citizens perceive a lack of time, (3) there is a lack of encouragement or support from the government, and (4) the specific issue at hand seems either too complex or long range.

First, citizens may not feel as though they have any connection to government. The sentiments of a significant segment of residents can be characterized as apathy, alienation, or distrust. There are many polls about attitudes toward federal government leaders but far less scientific polling concerning attitudes about North Carolina state and local government officials. The 2009 Elon poll queried respondents about state level government, and only two questions concerned North Carolina elected state and local officials. Seventy-three percent of respondents in this poll thought corruption is common among elected officials, and 65 percent believed that elected officials in North Carolina look out more for their own interests than for the public interest.[13] Perceptions of government can be extremely negative—some citizens, for example, believe government actively discourages citizen involvement and they subsequently adopt an "us-versus-them" mentality. Others might not necessarily believe government is the enemy, but they still feel it is not to be trusted, either because government employees are incompetent or because they are actively biased against individual citizens. Far more common and disturbing is the sense of apathy or antipathy toward government. National political headlines such as those concerning disaffection with the 2010 heath care reform law and the 2011 protests about the power wealthy individuals and companies have over the U.S. Congress might have a trickle-down effect on public participation in North Carolina state and local government.

Citizen apathy regarding government may be an important reason for low voter turnout. Some individuals may feel that a single vote does not matter and others might believe the local, state, or national political situation is simply hopeless. In either case, the perception may exist that voting for one candidate over another will not result in meaningful change. Similar is the view that candidates are all alike, and again, choosing one rather than another won't make a difference.

---

9. *See* ftp://alt.ncsbe.gov/.

10. *See* North Carolina State Board of Elections, www.ncsbe.gov/ncsbe/voter-turnout.

A comparison of North Carolina voting statistics to those from other regions of the country also yields some interesting information. For example, in November 2010 voter turnout in North Carolina was 43.75 percent, compared to 55.4 percent in Minnesota (which often has the highest voter turnout in the country). North Carolina exceeded the nationwide average of 40.4 percent, however. "Official Results," North Carolina State Board of Elections, http://results.enr.clarityelections.com/NC/22580/41687/en/summary.html; "Sabato's Crystal Ball: 2010 by the Numbers," University of Virginia Center for Politics, www.centerforpolitics.org/crystalball/articles/ljs2010111102/.

11. "Official Results," North Carolina State Board of Elections, http://results.enr.clarityelections.com/NC/10950/19547/en/reports.html.

12. Thom File and Sarah Crissey, "Voting and Registration in the Election of November 2008—Population Characteristics," U.S Census Bureau, www.census.gov/prod/2010pubs/p20-562.pdf, 20–56.

13. "Elon University Poll," Elon University, www.elon.edu/docs/e-web/elonpoll/112309_ElonPollDATA2.pdf.

A second reason people may not vote is a perceived lack of time. Lack of time per se, however, may not be the true issue. In some cases, citizens cannot get to polling places when they are open. Policies to extend polling place hours, create multiple polling locations and early voting options, and expand electronic voting and voting by mail have all been put in place to address voting accessibility problems. "Lack of time" may also be a variant of voter apathy—if citizens believe voting in an election has little impact, it is no surprise that waiting in line at a polling place would not feel worth their effort.

Third, the public may not feel that government officials are making an obvious and consistent effort to encourage and support citizen participation. Often, when government employees picture an "involved citizen," they imagine an irate citizen. Anecdotes suggest, for example, that if a citizen makes an appointment with a city manager, it is probably not to compliment the local government on a job well done. Local government officials thus tend to anticipate citizen involvement as if it were a problem to solve. Many citizens are aware of this perception. If citizens feel their involvement is unwelcome, it is not surprising that they will be reluctant to participate in the governing process.

Finally, low voter turnout may be due to the issue being considered. Citizens may feel no connection to or may not understand the issue on the ballot, whether it involves a complex matter, such as municipal water and sewer system management, planning, or rate-setting, or projects seemingly so long-range that voters cannot imagine any foreseeable impact. A proposal to build a big-box retail store may elicit sizable citizen response, positive or negative, because the project's impact is immediate and the decision appears clear-cut. On the other hand, a project such as updating a community's long-term land use plan for stormwater management may be perceived as overly complex and having too remote of an impact and thus may not generate much citizen interest and input.

The four reasons for low voter turnout discussed above concern the citizens themselves. But what about the government's role? Why don't governments seek greater citizen involvement? In various School of Government training sessions conducted with government employees, participants cited reasons they typically do not encourage high levels of citizen participation. Some mirror the reasons associated with individual citizens, as described above, and include the following:

- Encouraging public participation takes significant time and resources but has uncertain payoffs.
- There is a lack of resources with which to provide adequate information and administrative support. Officials mentioned frustration when complex issues are involved; extensive time and effort are required to educate citizens before they can meaningfully participate in decision making.
- Only a small, vocal, and typically oppositional segment participates in the policy process; people who are generally satisfied with government policies and programs do not attend meetings.
- Government officials said they sometimes feared raising expectations that may not be met.
- Encouraging citizen input may mean giving up or losing some control over the decision-making process.

One other hurdle involves a lack of information on practical, efficient, and successful ways to involve citizens in government. A 1998–99 survey asked North Carolina local government officials how they involved citizens in the budget process, since this is one of the most common areas in which citizen participation is required. Of the approximately one-third of cities that responded, less than one-half made any effort to involve citizens beyond the state-mandated public hearing. Slightly over one-half of the counties responded to the survey. Of those, less than a third provided opportunities for involvement other than the mandated public hearing.[14]

Several jurisdictions do create more opportunities for input on city or county budgets. In the past decade, the City of Durham has conducted what it calls "citizen public hearings" in January or February, at the beginning of the normal budget preparation time. A clip-out coupon was offered to allow citizens to list their priorities and mail them to the budget office. Over time, the response to the coupons tapered off, but Durham still holds at least two public hearings on the budget—one early and one later in the process. In 2009 Durham used more informal methods to solicit citizen input, such as "Coffees with Council" in February and March, in which interested groups invited members of the city

14. Maureen M. Berner, "Citizen Participation in Local Government Budgeting," *Popular Government* 66 (Spring 2001): 23–30.

council to meet with citizens and staff attended to answer questions.[15] Other examples of active outreach by various communities in the state are noted in recent research.[16]

Of all the options available for reaching citizens, what are some best practices to incorporate citizen input in a meaningful fashion? A 1998–99 survey of North Carolina local government officials asked what they felt was the *least* effective way to involve citizens. The most common answer, not surprisingly, was public hearings. However, the most common answer to the question of what is the *most* effective way to involve citizens was also public hearings! Obviously something other than a specific method helps make citizen involvement a positive or negative experience. A more recent, but smaller, study examined the perceptions and goals of staff, elected officials, and highly involved citizens in four larger North Carolina cities.[17] When asked what constituted effective participation by citizens on budget issues, each constituency expressed different expectations. For example,

> . . . elected officials tend to define effective public participation by reflection and a lack of citizen complaints. For staff, [effective participation] means providing information to the public and encouraging them to act as macro-level community advocates[,] . . . thus making informed citizens a valuable resource to get other members in the community to understand tough, controversial, or pressing decisions made by local officials. [Staff members] want citizens to be advocates for the organization out in the community as much as they want to hear from citizens what "the community" thinks.
>
> Citizens view effective participation through a different lens. Overall, [they] believe an effective participation system should include two-way communication (between all three stakeholder groups), more opportunity to be heard earlier in the process (not in late May at the budget public hearing), and involvement in honest dialogue with staff and elected officials regarding the budget and [the citizens'] role in the process."[18]

Defining, and then assessing, the costs and benefits of citizen involvement in general, and for particular topics, is very challenging. Beyond staff time, preparation of materials, and other "hard costs" are the important and often amorphous political or civic costs. Informally, officials cite the political and practical dangers in an inadvertent mismatch between citizens' and government officials' priorities. While interest groups may actively participate in the governing process, there remains a "silent majority" of citizens who do not even vote in most elections, let alone attend hearings or other events. This includes those who are satisfied with government services, those unable or unwilling to voice their opinion, and those too discouraged to participate.

For the local governments involved, what are the benefits of participation? First, at a minimum level, participation means sharing information. One of the benefits of public participation cited by local government officials is that citizens will have an increased understanding of problems and thus offer possible solutions. This interchange lays the foundation for better decisions. For example, active communication with citizens can help government officials decide if a particular policy option is feasible.

Is it acceptable to trade efficiency for effectiveness? After all, efforts to more fully involve the public take time and resources. The resulting decision may be more effective, but the process leading to that decision may be difficult and time consuming. From a cost-benefit perspective, however, making better and more popular decisions may outweigh the significant costs involved in increasing citizen participation.

Efficiency and effectiveness are only two values underlying a government decision-making process. As discussed above, citizen participation is a fundamental democratic value in North Carolina, and the response to the question of

15. "Join City Council For Coffee and Conversation," Durham Citizens' Newsletter, Public Affairs Office, City of Durham, N.C., http://durhamnc.gov/ich/pa/Documents/citizens_newsletter0109.pdf. See John B. Stephens, "Creating Effective Citizen Participation in Local Government Budgeting: Practical Tips and Examples for Elected Officials and Budget Administrators," *Public Management Bulletin* No. 6 (June 2011), for other examples of active outreach.

16. John B. Stephens, "Creating Effective Citizen Participation in Local Government Budgeting: Practical Tips and Examples for Elected Officials and Budget Administrators," *Public Management Bulletin* No. 6 (June 2011).

17. Maureen Berner, Justin Amos, and Ricardo Morse, "What Constitutes Effective Citizen Participation? Views from Stakeholders," *Public Administration Quarterly* 35 (Spring 2011).

18. *Id.* at 158–59.

why instigate, continue, or expand efforts to involve the public in local government falls back on assumptions, values, and aspirations that are part of the appropriate relationship between citizens and government in a democratic society.

Legal Requirements

"Participation" is a broad term. By state law, the main requirement relating to participation for local governments is that they provide an opportunity for members of the public to observe the decision-making process in open meetings and to comment on major proposals before the government takes action. The open meetings law, described in Chapter 9, "Open Meetings and Other Legal Requirements for Local Government Boards," covers the responsibilities of government officials to give the public notice of and access to meetings of all public bodies. This law also applies to advisory boards and meetings where no decisions are made. The public records law, discussed in Chapter 8, "Public Records," covers the government's responsibility to make records related to government activities available for public review. Both of these sets of laws focus on the public's access to government information and actions.

On the other hand, what responsibilities does the government have to ascertain the public's view of government decisions? Local governments are required to obtain opinions and feedback from citizens in two ways: (1) in public hearings and (2) in public comment periods held during regular meetings of county commissions or city councils.

Public Comment Periods

In 2005 the North Carolina General Assembly mandated that city councils, boards of county commissioners, and boards of education provide at least one period for public comment per month at a regular board meeting.[19] The history of the act, as well as case law on citizen comment periods as "limited public forums" under the First Amendment, both suggest that the board probably must allow comment on any subject that is within the local government's jurisdiction. A board can, however, adopt reasonable regulations governing the conduct of the public comment period, including but not limited to rules setting time limits for speakers and providing for (1) the designation of spokespersons for groups supporting or opposing the same position, (2) the selection of delegates from groups holding the same position when the meeting hall's capacity is exceeded, and (3) the maintenance of order and decorum in the conduct of the hearing. This authorization of regulations is taken almost verbatim from earlier statutes governing the conduct of public hearings by counties and municipalities, respectively.[20]

Public Hearings

Public hearings are held for many types of activities involving government decision making. Some of these activities are very common, such as city rezonings and annexations and city or county annual budget adoption. Sometimes the laws requiring a public hearing are relatively obscure, as in the case of the adoption of an ordinance to franchise ambulance services[21] or for any changes to the schedule of stormwater charges[22] (although hearings are not required for other enterprises or water/sewer charge changes).

19. N.C Gen. Stat. (hereinafter G.S.) § 153A-52.1 (counties) and G.S. 160A-81.1 (cities).

20. G.S. 153A-52 and G.S. 160A-81.

Guidance on the law concerning public comment periods and discretion in their structure and management is available from the School of Government. *See* John Stephens and A. Fleming Bell, II, "Public Comment at Business Meetings of Local Government Boards, Part One: Guidelines for Good Practices," *Popular Government* 62 (Summer 1997): 2–14; A. Fleming Bell, II, John Stephens, and Christopher Bass, "Public Comment at Business Meetings of Local Government Boards, Part Two: Common Practices and Legal Standards," *Popular Government* 63 (Fall 1997): 27–37; Fleming Bell, "Statutorily Required Public Comment Periods: What Are They and How Do They Work?" *Coates Canons: NC Local Government Blog* (UNC School of Government, May 20, 2010), canons.sog.unc.edu/?p=2459.

21. G.S. 153A-250.

22. G.S. 160A-314(a1)(1) (cities) and G.S. 153A-277(a1)(1) (counties).

Whether a public hearing, or any other type of opportunity for public involvement, is necessary or required depends on the particular issue or action being considered. Local government officials should research the legal requirements for citizen notification and involvement in each case.[23] Nationally, forty states require public hearings for city budgets and forty-two for county budgets. Far fewer must actually make the budget available for review, let alone involve the public in any other way. Public participation is usually encouraged, to a greater or lesser extent, rather than mandated.

Ways to Involve Citizens

Municipal and county government leaders in North Carolina can structure opportunities for citizen input in several ways. The two most common and traditional means are public hearings and appointed citizen boards (also called citizen advisory boards). Other methods with which governments can solicit citizen participation are also described below. These include surveys; community visioning; electronic communication, including email, websites, and social media; television, radio, and print media; and citizen academies.

Public Hearings and Appointed Citizen Boards

Voting is an individual and private action (i.e., by secret ballot), but, taken cumulatively, is the "voice of the people." Citizens also participate in government on an individual basis through contact with representatives, whether by phone or email or in more informal settings, such as in line at the grocery store or in a restaurant or similar venue. This one-on-one contact with public officials, on the one hand, and voting in elections, on the other, represent two ends of the spectrum of types of citizen involvement with government. In the middle of this spectrum lie other types of citizen interaction with government, such as attendance at appointed committee and public hearings, participation in public comment periods, and electronic communications such as blogs and social media. All of these activities are characterized by both government and citizen input in varying degrees.

Figure 10.1 Levels of Participation

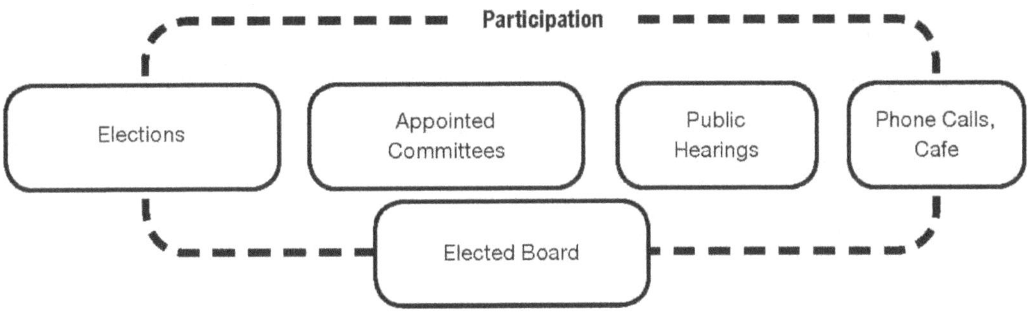

Source: Jeanne Lawson, "Choosing a Format for Public Advisory Groups," *Participation Quarterly* (December 1994).

Figure 10.1 illustrates the part public hearings and citizen advisory boards play within a dynamic interrelationship that is the foundation of effective citizen participation in local government.

23. See David Lawrence, "When Are Public Hearings Required," canons.sog.unc.edu/?p=77, for a summary of the types of local government decision-making activities for which public hearings are required.

Public Hearings

Public hearings are a long-standing way that municipal and county elected boards have formally obtained citizen input. As described above, some local government actions can be taken only after a public hearing is held. However, boards of county commissioners (BOCCs) and city councils (CCs)[24] can convene hearings for any matter they wish (other than for matters that must be discussed in closed meetings). A hearing can occur as a single agenda item among other matters considered at a governing board's regular business meeting, or it can be held as a separate meeting. In a typical public hearing, citizens are asked to address a topic, question, or proposal being considered by an appointed citizen board or by the principal legislative body (i.e., the BOCC or CC). There may already be a draft ordinance or written policy proposal, and citizens' opinions are solicited on those matters. Alternatively, the issue could be a more general matter of current interest. The board typically regulates the topic and how long and the order in which people speak. Otherwise, there are no legal restrictions on how the hearing is conducted.[25]

Public hearings vary widely in terms of length, whether people speak for themselves or for a group, whether the hearing is pro forma with few or no speakers, or whether it draws a large crowd and speakers express strong emotions. As a matter of fairness, equal time (or at least an equal opportunity to speak) is reserved for proponents and opponents of a draft ordinance. Often proponents and opponents will alternate, with all speakers on behalf of one side speaking, followed by all speakers on the other. Frequently, however, opponents outnumber proponents. As mentioned above, a common complaint about public hearings is that a few vocal naysayers attend, and many other citizens who quietly agree with a draft ordinance stay home. This can leave the impression, especially when newspapers or other media report on the hearing, that the majority of a community's citizens oppose a particular issue or ordinance.

Another common approach is to have citizens sign up in advance to speak. Usually a sheet is available in the meeting room, and potential speakers add their names to it shortly before the hearing begins. Again, the structure of hearings varies widely across the state; the formality of a particular hearing often hinges on its size and the prevailing culture in a specific jurisdiction. Using sign-up sheets presents both advantages and disadvantages. A benefit of this practice is that the government may be able to identify active citizens when it is seeking volunteers for citizen positions on boards or commissions. On the other hand, if citizens must record their names, positions, or contact information, they may be inhibited from speaking. Because there are no strictures on the format for many kinds of public hearings, BOCCs and CCs may employ other approaches for receiving citizen input during the hearings. For example, local governments may hold public forum meetings or other special outreach or hearing-like events on particular topics. In this format citizen questions and comments are the centerpiece of the event. The Ocean Isle Beach website provides the following:

> The Board of Commissioners . . . conduct[s] open forum meetings on the second Monday, during the months of February, April, September, and November beginning at 6:00 p.m. The purpose of the open forum meeting is to hear comments and concerns from the citizens of Ocean Isle Beach.[26]

Sidebar 10.1 lists meeting formats that should help meet the goals of any particular hearing. The fundamental objective of any hearing is to provide citizens a fair and equal opportunity, in a public arena, to express their views and have them heard and recorded by the BOCC, CC, or a body that reports to the local elected governing board. What usually distinguishes hearings from other forms of citizen involvement is that the hearing is structured as part of the board's decision-making process where a particular action is pending.

Appointed Citizen Boards

The second most common form of structured citizen involvement is the appointed citizen board (ACB), in which a BOCC or a CC appoints members of the community to a committee, board, or commission. City and county elected

---

24. Municipal governing bodies have different titles, such as board of aldermen or town council. This chapter uses "city council" in reference to all municipal elected boards in North Carolina.

25. However, actions by boards of adjustment must take place in a quasi-judicial public hearing. See Chapter 25, "Community Planning, Land Use, and Development," for details about rules for some public hearings.

26. "Town Council and Boards: Board of Commissioners," Ocean Isle Beach Unchanged, www.oibgov.com/board-of-commissioners.cfm.

Sidebar 10.1 Formats for Meetings That Satisfy Public Hearing Goals

- Comments and/or questions submitted in writing at the meeting, and responses made by local government staff or elected board.
- Polling the room—seeking views based on particular questions, especially if there is more than one proposal being considered, or there are particular changes sought in a draft ordinance/plan/policy.
- Splitting the audience into small groups for "kitchen-table" style discussion, which can allow for more people to speak, in a more informal way, and have give-and-take conversation with local government staff or elected board members.
- Board of county commissioners or city council convenes meetings in different parts of the community—moving away from its regular meeting place—as a way to be more accessible to citizens in certain neighborhoods.

Source: Debra Henzey, John B. Stephens, and Patrick Liedtka, "Listening to Citizens: County Commissioners on the Road," *Popular Government* 64, (Spring 1999): 17–28.

boards have full or partial control over a wide variety of ACBs, whose powers and scope of work vary widely. Many are advisory and have little influence over resources and modest to moderate influence over policies or personnel. Some, however, have oversight of or policy-making power over departments, agencies, or programs, and some make regulatory decisions. Figure 10.2 describes the range of these boards' powers and responsibilities.

Most often, ACBs are formed by and operate at the discretion of a single BOCC or CC. A handful of ACBs must follow state statutory requirements concerning membership and duties; most prominent among these are county social service, health, and county or regional mental health (MH/DD/SA) boards. Occasionally, the federal government can require citizen participation as a condition for receiving federal funds. For example, the Department of Housing and Urban Development requires that recipients of its funds, most notably community development block grants, develop

Figure 10.2 Appointed Citizen Boards—Powers and Responsibilities

Higher-level boards

- Render binding decisions (e.g., board of adjustment)
- Make policies that can be reviewed and changed by elected board (e.g., planning board)
- Review ongoing programs (e.g., social services)
- Hire and fire staff (e.g., social services, mental health)
- Hear appeals

Lower-level boards

- Hear complaints
- Be a sounding board (representing different viewpoints on the board or providing opportunities for citizens to make presentations)
- Make recommendations to address a particular problem (at advisory board's initiative or at the direction of the elected board)

and follow a detailed citizen participation plan.[27] Local governments can satisfy such a requirement with hearings or other activities but will often use an ACB.

Common city-appointed citizen boards include parks and recreation boards, planning boards, and zoning boards of adjustment. In larger communities typical ACBs address greenways and/or open space, alcoholic beverage control, downtown revitalization, and public housing.

The most common county ACBs are health, social service, planning, and jury commission boards and county-level or regional boards responsible for mental health, developmental disabilities, and substance abuse services (the technical

27. 24 C.F.R. § 91.225.

term for these is area authority). A key difference between city and county ACBs is that several county boards are created by statute rather than by an elected board. County human services boards, for example, have statutory obligations, sometimes include elected officials, and may be authorized to actually make law. Thus, some common county boards or committees have distinct powers while at the same time serving in an advisory role on certain matters to the county commission (these types of boards are discussed in other chapters of this publication). Many counties also make appointments to a wide variety of boards. Issues or areas addressed by these boards, commissions, and councils include transportation, airports, adult care homes, juvenile crime prevention, nursing homes, volunteer fire departments or fire districts, community colleges, aging, and tourism and conventions.[28]

Some types of boards include appointments from more than one local government jurisdiction. Economic development boards, for example, are commonly made up of members appointed by separate towns and the county. The Perquimans County Economic Development Commission, for example, includes members appointed by the towns of Winfall and Hertford and by the Perquimans Board of County Commissioners. Other regional boards consist of appointments made from several more widespread jurisdictions. The most common example of these is the LME board, which, except for the most populous areas of the state, typically includes members from several counties. Another example derives from operation of a regional service. The ACB of the Tri-County Animal Shelter, for instance includes members appointed by the boards of county commissioners from Perquimans, Gates, and Chowan counties.

The membership of some ACBs must include appointees with designated skills or training set by law or regulation. Historic preservation or architectural review boards, for example, must reserve one or more seats for architects or others of particular professional expertise. State law mandates that county boards of health have eleven members and include a doctor, a dentist, a veterinarian, a registered nurse, an optometrist, a pharmacist, a professional engineer, a county commissioner, and three members of the general public. The membership must also "reasonably reflect the population make-up of the jurisdiction."[29]

The number of ACBs typically varies in relation to the size of the city or county, but not always. Some North Carolina cities have very few advisory boards. Municipalities with six or fewer ACBs include

- Haw River, 1 (Planning and Zoning/Adjustment)
- Laurinburg, 2 (Board of Adjustments, Planning Board)
- Weaverville, 3 (Planning and Zoning, Zoning Board of Adjustment, Tree Board)
- Garner, 5 (Board of Adjustment, Planning Commission, Parks and Recreation, Senior Citizens, Veterans Advisory Committee)
- Elkin, 6 (Airport, Alcoholic Beverage Control Board, Library, Parks and Recreation, Main Street, Planning Board/Board of Adjustment)

Several of the more populous counties have dozens of ACBs. Examples include

- Mecklenburg County, 38 (33 solely county boards, 10 city and county ACBs, 4 independent)
- Guilford County, 50
- Orange County, 48
- Pitt County, 50

Interestingly, one smaller county, Northampton, has over thirty ACBs.

The number of ACBs is not indicative of the importance of citizen involvement to a particular jurisdiction or reflective of the opportunities for citizens to be involved. Factors influencing the establishment of ACBs include (1) BOCC or

28. Information regarding prevalent types of boards is drawn from the authors' review of North Carolina city and county government websites and consultation with county and city leaders and employees. An initial review was conducted in 1997–98 and updated in 2014.

29. *See* G.S. 130A-35 and 130A-37.

CC interest in addressing issues in depth, (2) capacity to provide staff and other resources to support ACB operations, and (3) the availability of interested and qualified citizens to serve on ACBs.

Local jurisdictions contemplating forming and managing ACBs should consider the following factors that distinguish the nature and types of these boards.

1. *Substance of the work.* The subject matter addressed by the board is usually reflected in its name. The most common areas addressed are social services, planning and zoning, transportation, environmental protection, neighborhood/community development, senior citizen services, parks and recreation, cemeteries, and juries, among others.
2. *Geographic reach.* The city or county jurisdiction of the governing board is typically the geographic area of concern. As noted above, however, some common ACBs address city–county, region, or state government–local government matters.
3. *Powers and responsibilities.* The authority and duties of local government ACBs vary significantly. Almost all ACBs serve as a venue in which citizen concerns, complaints, and suggestions are heard and to which proposals are referred by the governing body for detailed consideration and recommendations for action. As Figure 10.2 indicates, however, some boards possess greater rule-making, executive, and even legislative authority (including hiring, firing, and evaluation of high-level staff members and making binding decisions that can only be reviewed by a court).
4. *Duration and permanence.* BOCCs and CCs are authorized to appoint temporary task forces, study groups, or committees of which citizen involvement is an important part. These single-topic ACBs are intended to be temporary in nature. They are typically created by passage of a motion specifying the focus of the group and a time limit for completing the work and making a recommendation to the governing body. Other ACBs are long-standing or permanent primarily due to the ongoing nature of the matters they address, such as community planning and economic development, parks and recreation, mental health, social services, and the like. These types of committees are often created by local ordinance. Others are established and regulated by state law such that the BOCC or CC cannot abolish them.
5. *Membership.* Most people are eligible to serve on ACBs by simply being an adult resident of the town or county. State law does not, however, restrict appointments to only residents of the jurisdiction, and nonresidents are common on some boards. Membership may be restricted according to other criteria. Youth commissions, for example, are often limited to young adults. Some localities may only appoint people to ACBs who are U.S. citizens or are registered to vote. Members of BOCCs and CCs (and/or other government employees) usually recruit people to fill seats on certain ACBs.

   With the exception of appointees who must fit into particular categories or have specific expertise or training, anyone interested and willing to serve on an ACB is deemed acceptable for membership. Members are typically formally appointed by the BOCC or CC. Often ACBs will recommend people to fill vacancies; these recommendations may include citizens who have previously attended meetings or participated in other ACB activities. In some instances the ACB authorizes local government staff to have a significant role in the selection and management of the board's membership.

Figure 10.3 illustrates four basic types of ACBs and their relative levels of authority and open participation. The first of these, a *sounding board,* solicits views on a topic or proposal. It is not expected to reach consensus or give specific recommendations. Membership is open, and its duration is normally short to medium term. An *advisory committee,* as its name implies, advises decision makers on issues, options, and so forth and serves as a liaison to a neighborhood, constituency, or business group. Members are officially appointed, and its duration can either be medium term or ongoing. A *task force* focuses on an issue-specific recommendation for action or a detailed evaluation of alternatives. Its membership is officially appointed and is often smaller than an advisory committee. Its duration can vary greatly. While normally temporary, a task force could operate short, medium, or long term. Finally, *commissions* or *boards* vary the most in purpose, addressing any of a range of topics and sharing various characteristics with the other three types

Figure 10.3 Levels of Authority

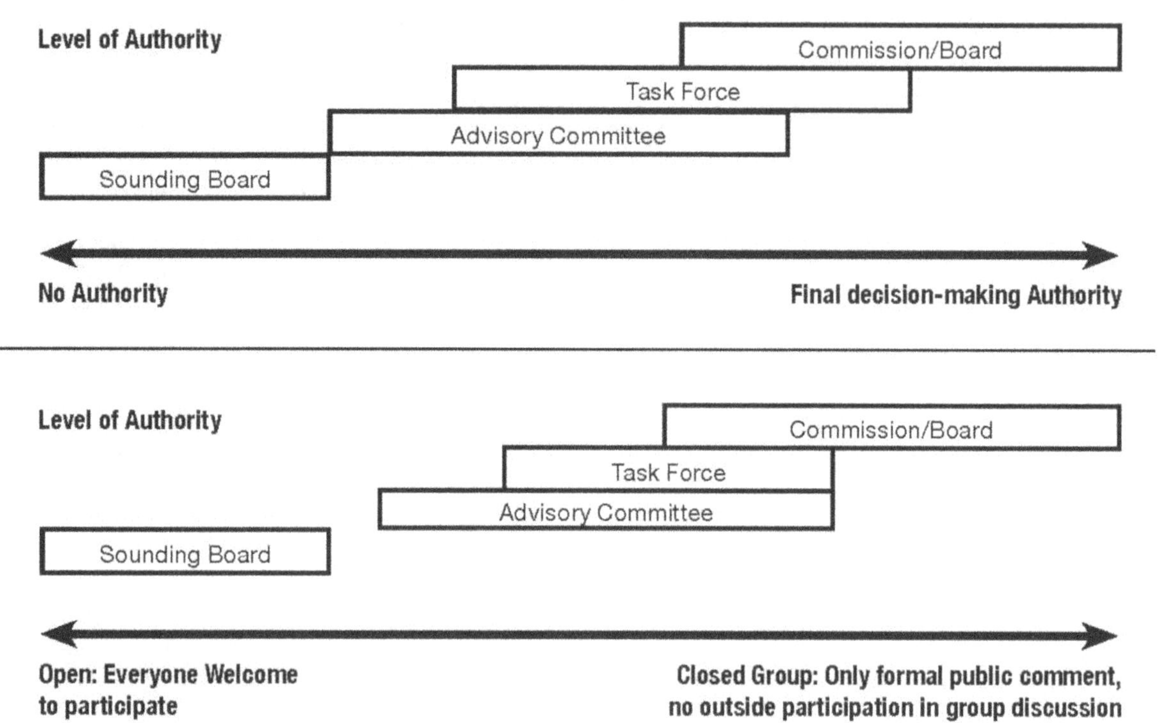

Source: Jeanne Lawson, "Choosing a Format for Public Advisory Groups," *Participation Quarterly* (December 1994).

of ACBs. They are of ongoing duration, and members are officially appointed. In North Carolina they usually have the greatest level of responsibility, some or all of which is spelled out by state law and local ordinance.

Neighborhood councils, a related type of group found in several larger North Carolina cites, often function outside of government and provide a structured opportunity for citizen input. Ranging from homeowner associations to neighborhood nonprofits, these groups provide grassroots ways to solicit feedback from the community and convey it to city officials. Some local governments play sort of an umbrella role for these councils, serving as a connector among all the local groups.[30]

Community Visioning

Community visioning, or strategic planning, is an increasingly common method of soliciting citizen involvement and typically addresses long-term goals of a city, county, or region. Often a task force of six to twelve months' duration will request community input and seek "buy-in" through active citizen participation during the decision process. Participation can involve anything from being an appointed member of a task force and investing many hours in meetings

30. The Raleigh Citizens Advisory Councils are an example of this type of arrangement. *See* "Citizens Advisory Councils," The Official City of Raleigh Portal, Raleigh, N.C., www.raleighnc.gov/neighbors/content/CommServices/Articles/CitizensAdvisoryCouncil.html. Other cities having neighborhood or citizen advisory councils include Asheville ("Coalition of Asheville Neighborhoods," www.ashevillecan.org/), Durham ("Interneighborhood Council of Durham," www.durham-inc.org/), and Greenville ("Community Development: Neighborhood Advisory Board," City of Greenville, N.C., www.greenvillenc.gov/government/city-council/boards-and-commissions/neighborhood-advisory-board.

For more details about the benefits and costs of ACBs, including guidance and policies for the establishment and operation of these groups, see Vaughn M. Upshaw, *Creating and Maintaining Effective Local Government Citizen Advisory Committees* (Chapel Hill, N.C.: UNC School of Government, 2010), available for purchase at http://shopping.netsuite.com/s.nl/c.433425/it.A/id.4284/.f.

Table 10.1 A Comparison of Planning Processes: Roxboro City, Wilkes County, and Wilson County

	Re-Visioning Roxboro	Wilkes Vision 20/20	Wilson 2020 Community Vision
Start	December 2005	Fall 1998	October 2006
Initiators	Public sector City council	Private sector Chamber of commerce	Private and public sectors Cross-sector collaborative group
Governance	City council City manager Management team	Chamber board of directors Steering committee Foundation teams	Management committee Steering committee Action teams
Input	Some outreach to employees (21) and citizens (24)	Large numbers, extensive: town hall meeting (400)	Large numbers, extensive: community forums (630); survey (900); summit (150)
Ongoing Oversight	City of Roxboro City government	Wilkes Vision 20/20 Nonprofit organization	Management committee Cross-sector collaborative group
Follow-through	Ongoing and regular review, integration, implementation, and revisions of plan by council, management team, and employees	Ongoing and regular review, integration, implementation, and revisions of plan by committees Paid staff	Ongoing and regular review, integration, implementation, and revisions of plan by committees Paid staff
Consultants	Public: UNC School of Government[1]	Private: Luke Planning Inc.	Public: UNC School of Government[2]

Throughout this article we provide examples of strategic planning and community visioning projects from the Roxboro, Wilkes, and Wilson communities. Two of these efforts began relatively recently. The third has been under way for nearly a decade. Just as each community is unique, each planning process is distinctive to fit local circumstances. These examples purposely provide variations along a spectrum of options and approaches so that readers can consider what elements might be adapted to their own situations.

1. School of Government staff from the Public Intersection Project, www.publicintersection.unc.edu, consulted on the Roxboro strategic plan.
2. School of Government staff and faculty from the Public Intersection Project and the Community and Economic Development Program, www.sog.unc.edu/programs/cednc, consulted on the Wilson 2020 Community Vision project.
3. This figure includes the cost of initial plan development in 2005–6, work with the management team on incorporating the strategic plan into departmental work plans, and first-year review of the plan in 2007.
4. Henry Luke, of Luke Planning Inc., Jacksonville, Florida (www.lukevision.com), facilitated the process at an initial fee (quoted in 1998) of $44,000 for Phase 1 and provided first-year oversight in Phase 2 for $9,500. Travel and other expenses were additional.
5. This figure represents the cost of the School of Government contract. Significant additional costs were covered by several community organizations, including Barton College, the City of Wilson, and Wilson County. The effort continues to be funded by public and private dollars.

Source: Lydian Altman and Ricardo S. Morse, "Creating Their Own Futures: Community Visioning and North Carolina Local Governments," *Popular Government* 73 (Winter 2008): 26, sogpubs.unc.edu/electronicversions/pg/pgwin08/article2.pdf.

to being interviewed or surveyed for one-time input to the task force. City or county governments may initiate community visioning or may participate in an effort launched by a chamber of commerce or some other business, civic, or nonprofit group.

In 1998 Wilkes County created Wilkes Vision 20/20 to help community leaders and citizens focus on long-term goals (see Sidebar 10.2). Table 10.1 compares Wilkes Vision 20/20 to two other visioning or strategic planning efforts from 2005–07.

Surveys

Surveys are another way local governments actively seek public input. According to a 2009 estimate by the International City/County Management Association (ICMA), three hundred citizen surveys are conducted each year in U.S. cities with a population of over 1,000, an approximate 30 percent increase over an ICMA estimate from 2000.[31] In North Carolina, as of 2014, approximately ten counties and forty cities conduct citizen surveys on a regular basis.[32]

31. Thomas I. Miller, Michelle Miller Kobayashi, and Shannon Elissa Hayden, *Citizen Surveys for Local Government: A Comprehensive Guide to Making Them Matter*, 3rd ed. (Washington, D.C., ICMA, 2009), ix.

32. The authors' estimate is based on information from the North Carolina City and County Communicators Association (NC3C), companies that conduct surveys, and direct contact with city and county employees responsible for conducting surveys.

Sidebar 10.2 Wilkes Vision 20/20

OUR VISION

By 2020, Wilkes will...

- have a comprehensive educational environment that encourages lifelong learning and produces a globally competitive workforce;
- be an environment that attracts new businesses and promotes the growth of existing business by providing a first class workforce & infrastructure;
- have responsible, representative government, that leads our community with *vision* toward excellence;
- be a stimulating, comfortable, open and enjoyable community that enhances the quality of life for each citizen;
- have infrastructure that supports life, growth and development in Wilkes County and serves as a bridge in relationships with surrounding areas;
- have private sector leadership and government that work together to pave a path of prosperity & growth for the future of Wilkes.

Source: "Wilkes Vision 20/20," Wilkes Chamber of Commerce, www.wilkesnc.org/vision.htm.

Surveys can be very useful for gathering information from the public. They offer (1) the ability to gather direct, and often quantifiable, answers to questions; (2) anonymity and thus the possibility of obtaining more responses and more honest responses; and (3) randomness, or the likelihood of obtaining a true cross-section of views from the public. Surveys can have several disadvantages, however. They do not provide an opportunity for citizens to interact directly or expeditiously with government officials. They consist of specific questions and may not offer an opportunity for citizens to provide other relevant input. Finally, due to expense, surveys may be conducted only infrequently. Costs vary significantly, depending on whether a survey is conducted by mail, by phone, through the Internet, or in person. Type and size of sample, survey length, and whether the related work is undertaken in-house or outsourced are other factors affecting cost. A survey of the general public in a mid-sized community, for example, may cost as much as $20,000.

A smaller-scale survey, when combined with other efforts to encourage public involvement, can be a more economical method for obtaining citizen feedback. In 2010 the City of Hickory, for example, used four public meetings and a citizen survey to gauge community sentiments about swimming pools, splash pad preferences, potential pool locations, and costs.[33] Other examples of large- and small-scale local government surveys include the following:

- An annual general community survey[34]
- A comment opportunity that uses a survey device to measure perceived level of service and the quality of citizen interaction with government employees but does not attempt to obtain a representative sample of the community[35]
- A narrowly targeted survey in which citizens are asked to provide feedback about development in a particular area of the jurisdiction[36]

See "Additional Resources" at the end of this chapter for other resources pertaining to local government citizen surveys.

33. The Jackson Group, "Asking, Listening, Learning and Responding: Presentation of Survey Results, City of Hickory Aquatic Survey," PowerPoint presentation, October 2010, available from the authors.

34. 2014 Community Survey, County Manager's Office, Mecklenburg County, N.C., http://charmeck.org/mecklenburg/county/CountyManagersOffice/Pages/Annual-Community-Survey.aspx.

35. "How Are We Doing?" Buncombe County, N.C., www.buncombecounty.org/Staying-Connected/Contact/Doing.aspx.

36. "Community invited to take survey about West Asheville and Haywood Road," City News, Asheville North Carolina, www.ashevillenc.gov/NewsandEvents/CityNews/tabid/662/articleType/ArticleView/articleId/27080/Community-invited-to-take-survey-about-West-Asheville-and-Haywood-Road.aspx.

Information and Outreach via Television, Radio, and Print Media

Print and electronic media provide countless opportunities for local governments to reach and involve citizens and for members of the public to express their views. Whether writing a letter to the editor of a weekly or daily newspaper or observing their representatives in action in public meetings broadcast on television, citizens can take advantage of these opportunities to become more informed and will perhaps move on to other more active forms of engagement with local government. About one-quarter of the one hundred county commissions and many towns with populations of 25,000 or more televise their regular meetings on a government access channel or a shared public access/government access cable channel.[37] Although an admittedly passive form of participation, these television broadcasts provide an excellent way for interested citizens to educate themselves about government processes and activities.

Radio and print media provide other avenues for public participation in government. Although traditional newspapers have been in decline in many parts of North Carolina and the country,[38] a daily, weekly, or community newspaper is published in ninety-six of the one hundred counties.[39] Radio call-in programs offer citizens a way to speak to and question local government officials. In addition, governments advertise or run public service announcements on the radio and in newspapers to announce openings on ACBs and dates and times of public hearings, publicize other opportunities for citizen engagement, and provide information about community issues.

Email and the Internet

As changes in information technology have affected business and home life, so have they affected government and how citizens contact local government officials. Town and county websites are now ubiquitous in North Carolina.[40] From these websites citizens can find phone numbers (for government offices or for home or cell phones) and email addresses for mayors, commission chairmen, and other elected members of various deliberative bodies. Individuals can submit work orders or make general comments.[41] More rarely, some websites employ online polls or "choice exercises."[42]

---

37. County data was provided by Todd McGee, Director of Communications, N.C. Association of County Commissioners, in an email exchange with John Stephens, February 21, 2006. McGee's survey yielded seventy-two responses, twenty-seven of which indicated that the county commission meetings are televised. Municipal data was provided by Beau Mills, Director of Intergovernmental Relations for the N.C. Metropolitan Coalition, N.C. League of Municipalities, in an interview with John Stephens, March 2, 2006. Stephens confirmed and updated data on cable broadcasts in November 2011.

38. A comprehensive analysis of newspaper decline in North Carolina is not available. A sample of ten weeklies and eight dailies of different sizes comparing 1987 and 2007 circulation figures yielded the following statistics:

- Among weeklies: one ceased publication, three had lower circulation, three more had higher circulation but appear to not have kept up with population growth for the town and region, and three had increased circulation ranging from 45 to 92 percent.
- Among dailies, Monday–Saturday: seven of eight papers had lower circulation, most having a decline of 12 to 23 percent and one a decline of 48 percent, not adjusting for population growth.
- Among dailies, Sunday: two communities started Sunday editions between 1987 and 2007, four others had a decline in circulation (ranging from 11 to 35 percent), and two had increased circulation but apparently as the result of the consolidation of two separate papers.

The communities sampled above included the following:

- Weeklies: Farmville, Black Mountain, Wallace, Fairmont, Yadkinville, St. Pauls, Kings Mountain, Randleman, Person County, Manteo–Dare County.
- Dailies, Monday–Saturday: Asheboro, Durham, Eden, Goldsboro, Greensboro, New Bern, Raleigh, Rocky Mount.
- Dailies, Sunday: Asheboro, Durham, Eden, Goldsboro, Greensboro, New Bern, Raleigh, Rocky Mount.

Editor & Publisher International Year Book (New York: Editor & Publisher Company, 1987 and 2007, parts 1–3).

39. North Carolina Press Association database and authors' research.

40. The School of Government maintains a clearinghouse for the home pages of North Carolina counties and cities. *See* "Counties in North Carolina," Knapp Library, UNC School of Government, www.sog.unc.edu/node/724 and "Cities in North Carolina," Knapp Library, UNC School of Government, www.sog.unc.edu/node/723.

41. For example, see the City of Fayetteville website, www.cityoffayetteville.org/contactus.aspx.

42. John B. Stephens, "Creating Effective Citizen Participation in Local Government Budgeting: Practical Tips and Examples for Elected Officials and Budget Administrators," *Public Management Bulletin* No. 6 (June 2011), 16.

Blogs, a more interactive Internet tool, are being utilized with increasing frequency. Blogs—Web logs—are Web pages in which an author posts information and opinions and can allow others to comment on the posts. The use of social media for disseminating information and, to a lesser extent, for engaging citizens is growing in North Carolina localities. As with other innovations, larger cities and counties have been early adopters. An informal 2014 analysis estimates that 166 cities North Carolina cities and about 90 North Carolina counties have some type of social media. Facebook and YouTube are the most popular platforms, with Twitter, RSS feeds, UStream, Flickr, and Pinterest used by only a small number of localities.

Social media appear to have reached many smaller jurisdictions. About half of the North Carolina towns with populations of 2,500 to 5,000 have a social media presence. One incentive for smaller communities to use social media is the importance of tourism and the ability to reach out to visitors and nonresident landowners.

Local governments using blogs, social media, and various other Internet resources should consider several important issues.

- Does a link from a government Web page to one of a private organization or other group indicate an endorsement? What sort of guidelines or policies should be established to help government employees responsible for Web pages determine what links or other material is appropriate for the local government website?
- How should comments and other postings on government social media sites be monitored? Blogs were initially designed for opinions and responses. Are government blogs platforms for free speech? Can rules be set to filter comments before they are posted? How can a local government monitor public input but avoid discriminating among viewpoints expressed in blog comments?
- Facebook and other providers have different levels of transparency and privacy. As interactive media play an increasingly important role in the delivery of key services, governments should consider the possibility that posted material could pass into the ownership of the company operating the social media site. Are local governments willing to take that risk?
- Although governments are focusing more resources on Web and wireless technology and increasing reliance on digital and electronic media to disseminate information and interact with citizens, the fact remains that many people do not have ready access to those avenues of communication. How will local governments deal with these persistent inequities?

Elected officials must decide if and how blogs and other electronic interactive tools encourage citizen involvement. In addition they must consider the legal ramifications of government-owned online platforms for providing information and opportunities for interaction as well as other practical issues.[43]

Formal Civic Education about Local Government Operations

An increasing number of communities are employing citizen academies or citizen police academies to educate and inform citizens about government activities and operations. These academies are a relatively new way of fostering civic engagement, with most having been created only in the last ten years. The academies combine formal instructional sessions with exposure to the work of either law enforcement or other operational departments of cities and counties. The goals of most citizen academies are to

- inform residents about and orient them to the functions of city or county government,
- increase civic engagement and improve the quality of citizen participation in local government, and
- strengthen communication and relationships between citizens and government officials.

Some academies provide opportunities for more interactive engagement on particular issues, needs, or challenges facing the community. The goal of many programs is to increase citizen participation on advisory boards, interest people

43. For more information and guidance on this topic, see "Citizen Participation: Resources," UNC Chapel Hill School of Government, www.sog.unc.edu/node/1509.

in running for local office, or, in the case of police or sheriffs' academies, recruit volunteers to support department operations.

Citizen academy sessions are usually held on evenings or weekends and total between eight and thirty hours. Typically between ten and twenty-five people participate. Citizens pay nothing or up to $40 to enroll. The cost to counties and cities ranges from $300 to $2,000 per class and is primarily due to staff time. Materials, meals, and so forth are often part of this expense.

According to a database of citizen academies in North Carolina and other localities compiled in 2014,[44] forty-five North Carolina counties and cities had citizen academies; an increase from thrity-six listed in 2011.[45] A survey conducted in 2014, with assistance from the N.C. Sheriffs Association and the North Carolina Association of Chiefs of Police, identified twenty municipal police departments and twelve sheriffs' offices having citizen police academies. The number of participants in each academy ranged from six to fifty-seven, with most having between ten and twenty-five participants annually. Since a 2011 survey, three city police departments have suspended their academies. Those departments most often cited staffing changes as the reason for not holding an academy since 2011.[46]

The development of citizen and police or sheriffs' academies reflects a local government's interest in fostering citizen participation and informed involvement through adult education. Typically the cost for direct expenses is relatively small compared to that for staff time, as employees may have to work overtime to plan and present a particular program. It is unclear if efforts have been successful to recruit academy participants who reflect a community's demographics.[47]

Local Government Employee Responsibilities for Citizen Involvement

Interactions with citizens—as property owners, victims or suspects of crime, or community volunteers—are part of many local government employees' work. Many government jobs involve transactions with citizens and businesspeople, such as processing permits, providing direct services (e.g., libraries, schools), and working on road maintenance or other infrastructure projects. Two types of local government positions in particular, however, have duties that pertain specifically to citizens' views and guidance to county or municipal government. These are (1) clerks and (2) public information officers. Cities and counties may also employ existing staff and utilize other strategies in efforts to foster civic engagement and improve the quality of interaction between government and the public.

Clerks to the board of county commissioners and town clerks typically are responsible for monitoring appointed citizen board (ACB) appointments and terms. They inform their respective elected bodies when citizens leave an ACB position or when the term of office in an ACB is about to expire, requiring a new appointment. Clerks' other responsibilities for supporting ACBs vary. Some prepare public notices and manage the minutes of ACBs, but others do not. Since the ACBs are created for the benefit of elected boards, they typically provide reports to the board. Often part of the clerk's work is to assemble and distribute material for all board meetings, and this material would necessarily include any ACB reports.

Public information officers (PIOs)[48] are an increasingly important part of the local government staff. Since the 1970s about forty North Carolina cities and towns and have created this position, and approximately twenty counties have similar positions.[49] Recently a few jurisdictions have created job positions such as community participation

44. "Citizens Academies," UNC Chapel Hill School of Government, www.sog.unc.edu/programs/citizensacademies.

45. Dr. Rick Morse supervised the survey. Most data were self-reported, and Morse believes more academies are active but did not report. The survey did not reach all 500+ North Carolina municipalities. There is, however, high confidence about the accuracy of the data for cities with a population of 25,000 or more.

46. Survey conducted by email and phone October–November 2014.

47. For more information about citizen academies in general, see "Citizens Academies," UNC Chapel Hill School of Government, www.sog.unc.edu/programs/citizensacademies.

48. Other job titles for similar positions include communications manager, communications specialist, and community service or community affairs specialist/manager.

49. The author's estimates for towns and counties are extrapolated from NC3C membership data and assume that one quarter to one third of towns and counties that are not NC3C members staff a similar position. "Member Pages," North Carolina City &

coordinator[50] or public information and social media specialist[51] that are specifically involved with citizen engagement and interaction with the public.

While PIOs primarily focus on disseminating information to help further the work and goals of the elected board, town or county manager, or department heads, they also often conduct and design other activities involving citizen interaction and engagement, including hearings, information meetings, surveys, and other means of citizen input. For example, in 2010 the PIO worked with other staff of the City of Hickory on four public meetings and a citizen survey about swimming pool and splash pad facilities. PIOs are usually involved, in conjunction with information technology staff, in creating social media policies and overseeing city- and county-managed postings to Twitter, Facebook, YouTube, and so forth.

Other local government staff members are also involved in activities focused on citizen input and participation, especially in the areas of land use and transportation planning, historic preservation, elderly services, and health and social services. These employees staff ACBs, arrange for public hearings, solicit input from clients or customers in particular service areas, and have other responsibilities pertaining to citizen interaction and feedback.

Large scale organizational changes or plans to promote or support general citizen input on policy matters have been rare. In 2008 the Mecklenburg County commissioners adopted a 2008–10 strategic business plan to promote citizen involvement. The initiative was called MeckConnect and included a set of outreach activities and mechanisms.[52] The City of Raleigh's Community Services Department 2010–13 Strategic Plan addresses "meaningful civic and community engagement for all of Raleigh's diverse citizenry" as well as supporting volunteer opportunities and quality of life issues for the city's residents.[53]

Conclusion

This chapter addresses the value of and barriers to common and newer forms of citizen involvement in local government. While the North Carolina Constitution and general political culture advocate civic engagement and the responsiveness of elected officials, local governments face several practical challenges when creating and supporting opportunities for citizen involvement. State law mandates some basic requirements pertaining to citizen participation and feedback, but otherwise local governments can and do employ a variety of methods to encourage and facilitate citizen involvement in government. This chapter presented many of these methods and discussed the advantages, disadvantages, benefits, and difficulties associated with each.

Additional Resources

General Resources

"Civic Education." N.C. Civic Education Consortium, UNC School of Government. www.sog.unc.edu/node/989.

Creighton, James L. *The Public Participation Handbook: Making Better Decisions through Citizen Involvement.* San Francisco: Jossey-Bass (John Wiley & Sons), 2005.

Epstein, Paul D., Paul M. Coates, and Lyle D. Wray (with David Swain). *Results that Matter: Improving Communities by Engaging Citizens, Measuring Performance and Getting Things Done.* San Francisco: Jossey-Bass, 2006.

County Communicators, www.nc3c.com/member-profiles/; email inquiry to NC3C, November 18, 2011. The author also directly queried officials from selected medium and large counties and cities, such as New Hanover County and Winston-Salem, for information about PIOs.

50. "Contact Us: Communications and Public Affairs," Town of Chapel Hill, www.ci.chapel-hill.nc.us/index.aspx?page=1374.

51. "Community Relations," Asheville, N.C., www.ashevillenc.gov/Departments/CommunityRelations.aspx.

52. See "Citizen Involvement in Mecklenburg County," County Manager's Office, Mecklenburg County, N.C., http://charmeck.org/mecklenburg/county/PI/MeckConnect/Documents/MeckConnect%20Stategy%20and%20Busines%20Case.pdf.

53. 2010–2013 Strategic Plan, Community Services Department, City of Raleigh, May 2010.

ICMA. "Citizen Academies." http://bookstore.icma.org/Citizen_Academies_e-Document_P693C7.cfm?UserID=7159820&jsessionid=4e3048d58f402e6f3f5e.

International Association for Public Participation. www.iap2.org.

Leighninger, Matt, and Bonnie Mann. *Planning for Stronger Local Democracy: A Field Guide for Local Officials.* Washington, D.C.: National League of Cities, 2011. www.nlc.org/Documents/Find%20City%20Solutions/Research%20Innovation/Governance-Civic/planning-for-stronger-local-democracy-gid-nov11.pdf.

National Coalition for Dialogue & Deliberation (NCDD). www.ncdd.org.

Local Government Citizen Surveys

Berner, Maureen. *Statistics for Public Administration: Practical Uses for Better Decision-Making.* Washington, D.C.: ICMA Press, 2010.

Berner, Maureen, Ashley Bowers, and Laura Heyman. "So You Want to Do a Survey . . ." *Popular Government* 67 (Summer 2002): 23–32. www.sog.unc.edu/sites/www.sog.unc.edu/files/article3_14.pdf.

Miller, Thomas I., Michelle A. Miller, and Shannon Elissa Hayden. *Citizen Surveys for Local Government: A Comprehensive Guide to Making Them Matter.* 3rd ed. Washington, D.C.: ICMA Press, 2009.

UNC School of Government. "Citizen Surveys by Local Governments in North Carolina." www.sog.unc.edu/node/522.

School of Government Publications and Resources

Stephens, John B. "Creating Effective Citizen Participation in Local Government Budgeting: Practical Tips and Examples for Elected Officials and Budget Administrators." *Public Management Bulletin* No. 6, June 2011. Available at http://shopping.netsuite.com/s.nl/c.433425/it.I/id.479/.f.

Stephens, John, Rick Morse, and Kelley O'Brien. *Public Outreach and Participation.* Chapel Hill, N.C.: UNC School of Government, 2011. Available for purchase at http://shopping.netsuite.com/s.nl/c.433425/it.A/id.4226/.f.

UNC School of Government. "Citizen Participation." www.sog.unc.edu/node/66.

_____. "Citizens Academies." www.sog.unc.edu/programs/citizensacademies/.

_____. "Webinar on-Demand: Citizen Participation in Local Government Budgeting." Available for purchase at www.sog.unc.edu/node/1088.

_____. "Webinar on-Demand: Delivering Bad News: How to Help Citizens Understand the Realities of Tough Economic Times." Available for purchase at www.sog.unc.edu/node/290.

_____. "Webinar on-Demand: Social Media for Citizen Participation." Available for purchase at http://shopping.netsuite.com/s.nl/c.433425/it.A/id.2700/.f.

Upshaw, Vaughn M. *Creating and Maintaining Effective Local Government Citizen Advisory Committees.* Chapel Hill, N.C.: UNC School of Government, 2010. Available for purchase at http://shopping.netsuite.com/s.nl/c.433425/it.A/id.4284/.f.

About the Authors

Maureen M. Berner is a School of Government faculty member who specializes in citizen participation and program evaluation. John B. Stephens is a School of Government faculty member who specializes in citizen participation and public policy dispute resolution.

Chapter 11

Interlocal Cooperation, Shared Services, and Regional Councils

Ricardo S. Morse

As local governments seek new and innovative ways to provide public goods and services to their communities, they often find that some facilities and services can be operated more efficiently or effectively through cooperative arrangements with other local governments. North Carolina counties and municipalities have entered into a wide variety of agreements establishing such cooperative arrangements. Regional councils have also been established across the state to deliver some services regionally and to provide forums for discussing cross-jurisdictional issues. Given the fiscal challenges local governments will continue to face in the foreseeable future, alternative service delivery strategies such as shared services are likely to become even more widespread across the state.

Interlocal Cooperation and Shared Services

Local government collaboration with other governments, as well as with citizens and private and nonprofit organizations, has long been an integral aspect of local governance and has become more and more common in recent years. As urbanization spilled beyond municipal limits, for example, municipal and county governments found it useful to cooperate in the provision of urban services to unincorporated neighborhoods. Local governments have long contracted out certain functions to private vendors (see Chapter 23, "Public Contracts, Competitive Bidding Requirements, and Property Disposal") and have successfully partnered with nonprofit organizations to more effectively address public needs (see Chapter 10, "Citizen Involvement"). Citizens have also been involved in various aspects of public decision making and even service delivery for quite some time now (see Chapter 12, "Local Government and Nonprofit Organizations).

However, the combination of reduced state and federal aid, pressures to hold steady or to reduce local taxes, and increasing demands for services is putting pressure on local governments to innovate and change "the way they do business."[1] In some cases, response to fiscal pressures has been in the form of reductions or even elimination of some services. But an alternative approach has been to look to collaborative approaches to accomplishing some local government functions. Other chapters in this book (referenced above) address the ways in which local governments work with the private sector, nonprofits, and citizens to deliver services and otherwise address public issues. This chapter provides an overview of *local governments working with other local governments.*[2] The terms most often used when discussing this topic are "interlocal cooperation" and "shared services."

"Interlocal cooperation" is a broad term that refers to the myriad ways local governments can work together to accomplish public purposes. Cooperation might take the form of information-sharing or coordinated planning, county contributions to municipal services, municipal provision of services to unincorporated areas through contracts with the county, or jointly financed and operated services. In some cases, municipalities and counties have found advantages in merging (i.e., consolidating) parallel functions in order to have just one agency providing a particular service or activity countywide.[3] While the term "shared services" (or "service-sharing" or "joint public services") is often used interchangeably with interlocal cooperation, it can be thought of as a specific form of cooperation, that is, cooperation for the provision of some public service or public good. Cooperation and shared services offer several potential advantages over sole (in-house) production[4] of a particular public good or service:

1. It may be more efficient and/or less expensive to provide a new service through a collaborative approach. As a county or a small town begins to provide fire inspection services, for example, a contract with an existing municipal inspection department utilizes the services of experienced inspectors available immediately, with no administrative overhead. Many municipalities find it more cost-efficient to contract tax collection with their respective counties for similar reasons.
2. Shared services arrangements may also increase *economies of scale,* which occur when the per-unit cost of service provision *decreases* as a result of *increasing* the size of the operation. A municipal or county recreation program might add additional participants from other jurisdictions with negligible additional administrative costs, for example, resulting in lowering the cost per participant. A water utility with excess capacity might add customers from outside its jurisdiction and significantly lower its average unit cost. The reality of such per-unit cost savings is why there are an increasing number of countywide, and even multi-county, regional libraries. While increasing the scale of a particular public service operation does not automatically mean there will be increased economies of scale, there are nevertheless likely numerous opportunities for achieving greater economies of scale for most municipal and county governments.
3. Collaboration often allows for a more effective response to problems that refuse to respect jurisdictional boundaries. For example, air pollution may drift from one county to another and require a regional problem-solving approach. Cooperation around emergency dispatch can lead to shortened response times, as the nearest first responder may not be in the same jurisdiction as the emergency. In other words, service *effectiveness* can be as compelling a reason to cooperate as efficiency.
4. Interlocal cooperation may increase effectiveness by enhancing communication and coordination of interdependent functions that otherwise are carried out independently. Such coordination may be needed, for

1. Cheryl Hilvert and David Swindell, "Collaborative Service Delivery: What Every Local Government Manager Should Know," *State and Local Government Review* 45, no. 4 (2013), 240–54.

2. The related topic of municipal-county consolidation is not discussed here. Information on that topic can be found in Chapter 2 in this publication.

3. Counties also cooperate among themselves in providing services more traditional to county government (e.g., regional health departments).

4. An important distinction can be made here between local government as service *provider* and local government as service *producer.* A community, through its local government, can decide that a particular service should be provided communitywide. This does not mean, however, that the local government necessarily needs to *produce* that service. Rather, the service can be produced by a private or nonprofit vendor, by another local government, or through a partnership of some kind. The local government remains responsible for service provision, but it may choose between producing the service in-house or through some alternative (often collaborative) means.

instance, to provide water and sewer services in areas just beyond city limits. There, counties must often work with cities to establish policies on extensions, supplies, costs, and the like.

5. Local governments are able, through cooperation and shared services, to adjust inequitable situations concerning payment for and use of services. For example, municipalities often provide recreational programs that are utilized by people from throughout their respective counties, so many counties contribute funds to these city-sponsored programs.
6. Cooperation is a flexible concept. It may begin by simple action of the governing boards involved in a given matter and may involve different tasks and parties. A local government may engage in several cooperative ventures, each differing from the others in scope, administrative structure, and financial support. While a cooperative relationship established for one service may provide a model for another, it in no way establishes a mold that must be followed.
7. Cooperation can also lead to more cooperation. As the saying goes, success breeds success, and this is often true with collaborative ventures like shared services and other forms of interlocal and regional cooperation. Many would argue that strong interlocal and regional collaboration is needed to address complex and interconnected public problems like economic development, pollution control, disaster preparedness, or, in many places, maintaining a sustainable water supply.[5]

Types of Interlocal Cooperation and Shared Services

Following what is, as mentioned above, common practice, this chapter will refer to interlocal cooperation and shared services as more-or-less interchangeable terms that describe the variety of ways local governments work together to provide public services to the community or support services for an organization, as opposed to producing those services entirely in-house. It should be noted that shared services may include, in addition to local government actors, not-for-profit or even for-profit entities, making the line between private service contracting and shared services arrangements somewhat fuzzy. Shared services arrangements thus may assume a variety of forms; several are discussed in the text below.

Grants or Contributions

Occasionally a local government will provide a program that benefits the property or citizens of another government without receiving direct financial support from these beneficiaries. In such cases, the government whose citizens are benefitting from the program might contribute funds to the government that is providing it. County financial support for a city recreation program or a municipal contribution to a countywide economic development agency are examples of such contributions.

Resource Sharing

Local governments frequently engage in the sharing of information, personnel, equipment, and other resources. Examples of this practice include two municipalities sharing equipment like street-sweepers or backhoes, or separate local law enforcement agencies sharing personnel in certain situations. Resource sharing is normally an informal process and is based on norms of reciprocity, though it may also be formalized, as in the case of *mutual aid agreements*.[6]

Cooperative Purchasing

Local governments may find it advantageous to jointly purchase materials and equipment. Often, cost savings can be realized through obtaining volume discounts not available to a smaller, single purchaser. Furthermore, cooperative

5. See the following for excellent overviews of the "whys" of interlocal cooperation and shared services: John Ruggini, "Making Local Government More Workable through Shared Services," *Government Finance Review* 22, no.1 (2006), 30–35; William A. Holdsworth, "The Case for Interlocal Cooperation," *Government Finance Review* 23, no. 1 (2007), 40–46.

6. Mutual aid agreements involve two or more governments agreeing to come to one another's aid (if possible) in police or fire emergencies or natural disasters.

purchasing may reduce administrative costs and expand purchasing expertise. Cooperative purchasing can be organized in different ways—with a lead agency as purchaser, for example, or through a third-party contracted program or a regional council program.

Interlocal Service Contracts

A local government may contract with another local government for the provision of a public service or for administrative support services. Examples include small municipalities contracting with their county sheriffs for law enforcement and public safety services or, as happens frequently, municipalities contracting with counties for tax collection. The category of interlocal service contracts includes all agreements in which one government contracts with another to provide a service—either an administrative service to the receiving government itself or a service provided directly to the citizens of that government.

Joint Operations

Sometimes a public service is jointly produced through a partnership between two or more local governments. Examples of such joint operations include recreation programs provided through municipal–county partnerships and jointly operated libraries. The line between joint agreements and interlocal service contracts (discussed immediately above) is often a thin one. In theory, a joint agreement is different in that it involves two or more government units exercising jointly a power that each could exercise individually. Thus, two towns might employ a joint manager or a city and a county might organize a joint planning or inspections department. City–county planning boards fit into this category as well.

Joint Facilities/Assets

Two or more local governments might decide to share a common facility. For example, the Matthews Town Center was a joint venture between the Town of Matthews and Mecklenburg County. It houses both Matthews Town Hall and a branch of the county library. The City of Hickory, the City of Conover, and Catawba County together operate a regional sludge management facility that transforms residuals from the cooperating governments' wastewater plants into compost. On a smaller scale, organizations can share various types of capital assets. For instance, two or more entities can jointly purchase an expensive piece of equipment (e.g., a backhoe) and then establish agreements on how it will be shared.

Transfer of Functions

Sometimes a county and a municipality, each authorized to perform a particular function, will agree that one of them should assume total responsibility for the activity. Such a transfer of responsibility can be thought of as achieving a functional consolidation of the particular service involved across two or more jurisdictions. For example, smaller, neighboring municipalities in eastern Wake County have transferred water and wastewater operations to the City of Raleigh Public Utilities Department. Such transfers of responsibility occur frequently, with counties assuming responsibility for libraries, hospitals, and solid waste disposal. Less frequently, a city might assume countywide responsibility for a particular service or administrative function.

Merged Departments

Local governments may also choose to merge duplicate departments into a single unit that is shared by all partners (though usually administratively located under just one of them). The terms of any such merger agreement are spelled out in formal agreements. Several counties in North Carolina have merged separate municipal and county 911 dispatch operations into single, countywide centers.

New Joint Entities

On occasion, two or more local governments may cooperatively create a new political subdivision or nonprofit organization for the purpose of managing and governing a shared asset and/or service. This form of cooperation is less frequent in North Carolina than in some other states, but examples include some airport authorities, water and sewer authorities, metropolitan water or sewerage districts, regional solid waste management authorities, and regional transportation agencies. Multi-jurisdictional economic development commissions (which are nonprofit organizations) also fit under this category.

Authority for Cooperation

The North Carolina General Assembly, through a series of statutes, has provided ample authority for intergovernmental cooperation among local governments. The critical language, from Chapter 160A, Article 20, Section 461 of the North Carolina General Statutes (hereinafter G.S.), reads as follows:

> *Any* unit of local government in this State and any one or more other units of local government in this State or any other state (to the extent permitted by the laws of the other state) may enter into contracts or agreements with each other in order to execute *any undertaking.* The contracts and agreements shall be of reasonable duration, as determined by the participating units, and shall be ratified by resolution of the governing board of each unit spread upon its minutes (emphasis added).

As the statutory language makes clear, the authorization for interlocal cooperation and shared services is as broad as can be. The General Assembly has also set out additional provisions authorizing interlocal cooperation in various service areas. The principal statutes are listed in Appendix 11.1 at the end of this chapter.

Barriers to Cooperation

It is important to note that there can be barriers to shared services that may be significant enough to stymie interjurisdictional discussions around opportunities for collaboration or prevent discussions from happening in the first place.[7] Some of the more prominent barriers, or potential barriers, to cooperation include the following:

- "Turf" issues having to do with the psychology of community and with natural desires for autonomy and control. Elected officials and managers can be reluctant to explore opportunities for shared services when they perceive that such collaboration may involve a loss of control over the service. Local officials as well as citizens may also feel threatened by the thought of losing something that is viewed as part of their community's identity.
- Lack of, or low levels of, trust among potential partners can stem from historical mistrust (rivalries, even) or from differences in community characteristics (e.g., urban versus rural), but such feelings can also simply be the result of not having a history of working together.
- *Transaction costs* include staff time and money involved in developing and monitoring cooperation agreements. If these costs are viewed as outweighing the potential benefits of working together, then this may represent a significant barrier.
- Similarly, it can be difficult to clearly articulate the "business case" for cooperation—why an affirmative decision is warranted based on an analysis of the costs and benefits. On the other hand, even if the benefits of collaboration are clear, perceived inequities in the distribution of those benefits can pose a challenge.
- Related to all of the issues set out in the bullet points above, *community politics* often play a role in would-be cooperative ventures. Elected officials may be particularly concerned about accountability and control. Staff members may fear change, including the fear of losing jobs held by community members. Community members may fear decreased service quality or customer service. All of these perceived concerns can give rise to what might be viewed as "political" barriers to cooperation and shared services.

The prevalence of these and other barriers to cooperation will vary depending on a variety of factors, including the goods or services in question, financial realities, community history and culture, the nature of interlocal relationships, and the presence of external mandates or incentives.

7. Robert Agranoff, *Collaborating to Manage: A Primer for the Public Sector* (Washington, D.C.: Georgetown University Press 2012).

Overcoming Barriers When Cooperation Is Warranted

Collaboration is difficult. Working effectively *within* an organization is difficult enough. Working *across* organizations presents a host of additional challenges, including many potential barriers or stumbling blocks, some of which were summarized above. However, when the advantages of collaboration in the form of shared services or some other kind of interlocal cooperation are compelling, it is incumbent upon public leaders—elected officials and public managers—to try to knock down those barriers for the greater public good. Leaders can have great impact by

- cultivating relationships of trust with neighboring jurisdictions (potential partners),
- creating a sense of urgency, communicating clearly the "why now" for a would-be cooperative endeavor, and
- communicating honestly and effectively with stakeholders throughout the process (including early on, before decisions have been made).

These strategies can help managers and elected officials overcome inertia and work past barriers to cooperation. Public managers in particular can make a difference by ensuring that appropriate ground-work is done, e.g., ordering feasibility studies, examining financial and cost allocations, and generally just making sure that good data is available.

Another effective strategy for overcoming barriers to collaboration involves networking across jurisdictions and participating in and supporting forums for interjurisdictional dialogue.[8] Two practices in particular stand out. First, regional councils (which are discussed in more detail below) serve as neutral regional forums and can be positive forces for engendering cooperation if member local governments use them as such. Actively participating in regular regional managers' meetings and, in the case of board members, participating in regional council boards, are important capacity-building activities for interlocal cooperation.

Another somewhat common practice, happening mainly at the county level, is for county government officials, along with officials from municipalities within the county, to meet regularly (often quarterly) to encourage relationship-building and discussion of countywide issues. In some cases, the gatherings open with a meal, which is then followed by a business meeting of some sort. These meetings take a wide variety of forms, sometimes including all board members and senior management staff from the county, municipalities, and school district, sometimes including just managers and mayors/chairs, and other times something in between.[9] These opportunities for officials to "break bread" together, or to at least meet and talk to one another, serve an important purpose beyond any specific issue that may be on the agenda. They serve to build relationships and open up lines of communication that can serve as a catalyst for identifying opportunities for interlocal cooperation and shared services. County governments can play a critical convening role for these kinds of meetings.

Provisions of Interlocal Agreements

Some forms of interlocal cooperation happen without any kind of explicit agreement. Information sharing, for example, and even some forms of coordination (such as between law enforcement agencies), can occur simply out of courtesy, tradition, or good management practices. However, shared services arrangements usually involve some form of interlocal agreement, though even here the agreement is sometimes informal—a "handshake" agreement, as occurs in many instances with the sharing of equipment or personnel. Most shared services agreements, however, do involve formal interlocal agreements. Such a formalized arrangement creates the legal basis for the relationship, outlines a method of financing and cost allocations, spells out governance and administration rules (how decisions are made, disputes settled, etc.), and describes any special procedures or provisions of the partnership.

Some types of cooperative arrangements are quite simple. When one government contributes to an ongoing program of another, the contributing government typically does not concern itself with the administration of the program; it simply includes an appropriation for the program in its budget ordinance. The amount of the appropriation may be

8. Kelly LeRoux, Paul W. Brandenburger, and Sanjay K. Pandey, "Interlocal Service Cooperation in U.S. Cities: A Social Network Explanation," *Public Administration Review* 70, no. 2 (2010), 268–78.

9. These standing, multi-jurisdictional bodies are sometimes even formally named, such as the Stokes County League of Governments. It is important to note that these meetings are subject to the requirements of the state open meetings law (see Chapter 9).

negotiated, but the negotiations probably do not extend to other subjects. This same lack of involvement in program administration will probably exist when program functions are transferred. Once such a transfer is made, the function becomes the sole responsibility of the contributing government. Where there is a compelling interest on the part of the recipient government in how the function is administered, however, such as in the case of one municipality providing water and sewer utilities to neighboring municipalities, it is likely in the recipient government's best interest to have interlocal agreements in place spelling out terms of service, input on infrastructure extensions, and so on.[10]

Other sorts of cooperative arrangements can be quite complex, and negotiations can become difficult. Questions may arise concerning financing, operations, administration, property, and many other matters. This chapter cannot suggest "correct" solutions because the needs, administrative structures, traditions, and services involved can differ depending on the type of collaborative arrangement and the government actors. Nor can it even suggest all the questions that should be asked. But it can point out the most common decisions that negotiating governments might face (see Table 11.1, below).

The General Assembly has provided a framework for interlocal agreements, stating in G.S. 160A-464 that "[a]ny contract or agreement establishing an undertaking shall specify:

(1) The purpose or purposes of the contract or agreement;
(2) The duration of the agreement;
(3) If a joint agency is established, its composition, organization, and nature, together with the powers conferred on it;
(4) The manner of appointing the personnel necessary to the execution of the undertaking;
(5) The method of financing the undertaking, including the apportionment of costs and revenues;
(6) The formula for ownership of real property involved in the undertaking, and procedures for the disposition of such property when the contract or agreement expires or is terminated;
(7) Methods for amending the contract or agreement;
(8) Methods for terminating the contract or agreement;
(9) Any other necessary or proper matter."

Two broad considerations need to be explicitly discussed any time local governments are considering entering into a shared services arrangement. The first is the specific *type* of service-sharing arrangement (discussed above) under consideration. The options can be thought of as falling along a continuum of *more consolidated* or *less consolidated*. The second consideration that must be factored into the partnership decision is the extent of *shared governance*. Partners could agree that a service should be fully consolidated (into one entity) across the multiple jurisdictions involved, but the parties must still determine the extent to which they will share in the governance of that entity. A high degree of shared governance might involve the creation of a new special purpose government (e.g., a regional water authority), whereas a low degree of shared governance might involve one jurisdiction being the service provider, with the other jurisdictions simply agreeing to a per capita fee for that service.

Regional Organizations

The conditions that have given rise to cooperative relationships between local governments have also prompted the creation of regional organizations. The development of road systems, the operation of water and sewer facilities, the protection of air quality, and the regulation of land use are examples of activities that, when undertaken by one jurisdiction, will nevertheless affect people and property in neighboring jurisdictions. Sometimes, as noted above, these common interests may be recognized and managed through cooperative relationships. At other times, however, the administration of some joint interests may be accomplished most effectively by creating a joint, regional agency.

10. Such is the case for the several municipalities in Eastern Wake County that transferred their water/sewer services over to the City of Raleigh.

Table 11-1 Common Decisions Facing Negotiating Governments

Function	Questions/Decisions
Administrative	Should the units jointly supervise the function, or should one simply contract with the other to supervise it for both units?
Finances	Are user charges to be levied? Should the agreement establish the schedule of charges? Should the agreement establish the basis of charges? How should charges be modified? Should charges be the province of the operating government alone? On what basis are costs to be divided? What should be included as costs attributable to the activity? What will be the timing and the manner of payment between governments? What budgeting procedures should be established? Are special assessments to be used? If so, on what basis? In capital projects, who will make expenditure decisions?
Operations	What will be the territorial scope of activity? What performance levels will be expected? Can they be modified? If so, how? In capital projects, will the parties mandate specific features? On facilities, what limitations or priorities on use will be necessary?
Personnel	How are personnel to be selected? Whose employees will they be? Should there be special provisions in regard to position classification, pay plan, fringe benefits, etc.?
Property	How will decisions to buy real or major personal property be made? How are sites to be selected? How are specifications to be established? How will the acquisition be made? Who will own the property? Under what circumstances may the property be disposed of?
Miscellaneous	What reports will be required? What records must be retained? What rights of inspection should be allowed? How will potential liabilities be allocated and paid?
Joint Agencies	How will joint agencies be structured? What will the size of the coordinating body be? What will the terms of members be? Who will appoint them? How often will the body meet? What powers and duties will be conferred on/delegated to the body? What provisions should be made for budgeting? What reports and records will be required?
Duration, Termination, and Renewal	How long will the cooperative activity continue? What should the provisions for renewal, modification, and termination say?

Impetus for Regional Organization

By 1960, an increasing number of federal agencies required some form of regional planning and the creation of multi-county organizations to administer categorical programs under their jurisdictions. State agencies likewise have a long history of dividing the state into local administrative regions. In 1961, the General Assembly authorized the creation of regional planning commissions (G.S. 153A-391, -398) and economic development commissions (G.S. 158-8, -15) by general law. These actions built on the successful experience with regional planning and economic development organizations that had been established in previous years by local legislation. Today's most frequently used form of regional organization, the regional councils of government, was authorized by legislation in 1971 (G.S. 160A-470, -478).

The big push for multi-county regional organizations, however, came from the federal government after Congress enacted the Intergovernmental Cooperation Act of 1968. This act encouraged states to establish a uniform system of area-wide planning and development districts. Regional review of local grant and program proposals, as required by *Circular A-95* of the Office of Management and Budget, became standard procedure. In 1969, the General Assembly directed the Department of Administration to cooperate with "the counties, the cities and towns, the federal government, multi-state commissions and private agencies and organizations, to develop a system of multi-county, regional planning districts to cover the entire State."[11] This charge was part of the department's broader role in undertaking and supporting state and regional planning and development.

Regional Councils in North Carolina

In May 1970, Governor Robert Scott designated seventeen multi-county regions by executive order. Following this designation, many state agencies took action to align their regional administrative organizations with the new regional designations. Cities and counties in the designated regions also moved to create a new regional organization or to reshape an existing one to fit the new pattern. In 1971, the state announced a policy of designating a single organization within each region as the *lead regional organization* (LRO). This organization is open to all cities and counties in the region and is the organization through which many state and federal programs are channeled. While a few LROs are planning and economic development commissions and the balance are councils of governments, all of the organizations are today referred to as "regional councils." It is important to note here that regional designations are not static. Boundaries can be changed by constituent governments via a petition to the governor. In the 1990s, Region H was dissolved and constituent counties were reassigned to other regions. Further, on July 1, 2011, the regional councils from regions G and I merged into one (G), called the Piedmont Triad Regional Council. Currently, the number of regions (and regional councils) in North Carolina is sixteen.[12]

The governing bodies of the regional councils comprise representatives from the member governments. Most North Carolina counties and municipalities are members. Because the regional councils are not authorized under law to levy taxes, they must depend on membership dues, earnings from technical assistance, and grants from other governments for their financial support. Traditionally, most support has come from federal sources, with state grants, membership dues, and revenues from local projects and miscellaneous revenues accounting for the remainder.

Programs and activities of regional councils vary. Each engages in economic planning and development, provides intergovernmental review, serves as a data center for the region, and administers programs for the aging in cooperation with state and federal agencies.[13] Most participate in administering community development block grants and the Job Training Partnership Act and provide technical assistance in local solid waste and land use planning, housing, and programs to enhance water quality. For a number of regional councils, transportation services, regional transportation planning, management consulting, and land and water conservation are significant activities. Although these regional organizations focus principally on planning and coordinating activities and technical assistance in the areas within which they work, they are also available to carry out almost any function or activity that their members may require.

11. N.C. Gen. Stat. § 143-341(6)i.

12. See www.ncregions.org for more information on North Carolina's sixteen regional councils.

13. All regional councils administer federal and state aging programs in their regions in collaboration with federal agencies and with the North Carolina Division of Aging and Adult Services.

Beyond the specific programs and services that regional councils provide is their important role as convener of and forum for interlocal and regional discussions on cross-jurisdictional issues in their regions. Regional councils can in this capacity help overcome barriers to cooperation through the provision of time and space for relationship-building and discussion. These organizations also often provide facilitation and technical expertise and thus can be instrumental in fostering interlocal and regional partnerships. Having an organization that can take the lead on collaborative efforts where there is no one in charge is often a key factor in moving projects and partnerships forward.

Planning and Implementing Interlocal Cooperation and Shared Services

The following recommendations from a 2013 report[14] on local government shared services published by the IBM Center for the Business of Government are a good starting point for thinking about the primary steps in planning for and implementing interlocal cooperation or shared services arrangements.

1. Create a team or task force made up of relevant stakeholders to explore shared services opportunities in a transparent manner.
2. Build on the strengths of participating governments. Local governments should consider the relative strengths of potential partner organizations and be open to service delivery alternatives that leverage the different strengths available.
3. Consider pilot projects that can reduce risk and provide an opportunity for "small wins," ultimately contributing to trusting relationships and creating a track record of success that can lead to more cooperation in the future.
4. Clarify and document roles and responsibilities with partners. Have them clearly articulated in a written agreement and regularly review the agreement to ensure that it is sufficient over time.
5. Be flexible and revise agreements as necessary. Circumstances change, and effective partnerships are able to adapt to changes.

It is important to note that interlocal cooperation and shared services should not be viewed as a panacea to all of the problems local governments face. While cost savings may be realized with some shared services arrangements, it is certainly not the case with *all* such arrangements. Thus, opportunities for shared services and interlocal cooperation should be considered as *one of many* potential innovations in service delivery approaches available to local leaders.

At the same time, local government officials in the twenty-first century need to appreciate the highly interconnected nature of the problems their communities face. These complex and interconnected problems point to the increasing relevance of collaborative approaches to local governance, including the use of interlocal cooperation and shared services, to get the public's business done in as efficient, effective, and equitable a way as possible.

About the Author

Ricardo S. Morse is a School of Government faculty member specializing in public management, collaborative governance, and leadership.

The author is indebted to David M. Lawrence and to the late Warren Jake Wicker, authors of chapters on these topics in earlier editions of this publication. This chapter reflects their contributions.

14. Eric Zeemering and Daryl Delabbio, *A County Manager's Guide to Shared Services in Local Government* (Washington, D.C.: IBM Center for the Business of Government, 2013).

Appendix 11.1 N.C. General Statutes Authorizing Cities to Cooperate with Other Local Governments

Function	G.S. Citation
General Powers of Cooperation	
Administrative and governmental powers	160A-460 through -464
Revenue and expenditures for joint undertakings	160A-466
Property transactions	160A-274
Buildings	153A-164
Councils of governments	160A-470 through -478
Consolidation study commissions	153A-401 through -405
Elections	
Registration	163-288
Planning and Regulation of Development	
Transfer of territorial jurisdiction	160A-360
Planning contracts	160A-363
Historic preservation commissions	160A-400.7
Appearance commissions	160A-451 through -455
Inspection services	160A-413
Housing	157-39.5
Community development	160A-456
Planning Boards	153A-321; 160A-361
Regional planning commissions	153A-391 through -398
Regional economic development commissions	158-8 through -15
Regional redevelopment commissions	160A-507
City–county redevelopment commissions	160A-507.1
Redevelopment project financing	160A-515.1
Annexation agreements	160A-58.23 through -58.28
Environmental Matters	
Air pollution control	143-215.112
Sedimentation control	113A-60
Stormwater runoff programs	143-214.7
Water supply financing	139-49(b)
Public Safety	
Law Enforcement	
Training	160A-289
Auxiliary police	160A-283
General cooperation between agencies	160A-288
Local confinement facilities	153A-219
Fire protection	160A-293
County and municipal emergency management	166A-19.15
Ambulance services	153A-250
Animal shelter	160A-493
Hospitals	131E-7
Social Services	
Human relations programs	160A-492
Manpower programs	160A-492
Community action programs	160A-492
Senior citizens	160A-497
Library services	153A-270

Appendix 11.1 N.C. General Statutes Authorizing Cities to Cooperate with Other Local Governments (*continued*)

Social Services (*continued*)

Recreation, generally 160A-355
Regional sports authorities .... 160A-479 through -479.17

Public Enterprises

Airports 63-56; 153A-278
Water services 153A-278
Sewer services 153A-278
Solid waste services 153A-278
Solid waste collection and disposal facilities 153A-292
Utility emergencies 160A-318
Water and sewer authorities .... 162A-1 through -19
Metropolitan water districts .... 162A-31 through -58
Metropolitan sewerage districts .... 162A-64 through -81
Regional natural gas districts .... 160A-660 through -676
Public transportation systems 153A-278
Public transportation authorities .... 160A-575 through -588
Electric power generation .... 159B-4 through -39
Regional public transportation authorities .... 160A-600 through -627
Regional transportation authorities .... 160A-630 through -651
Regional solid waste management authorities .... 153A-421 through -432
Research and production service districts .... 153A-311 through -317.1
Communications services .... 160A-340 through -340.6

Chapter 12

Local Government and Nonprofit Organizations

Margaret Henderson and Tom Kelley

Introduction

In North Carolina today, there are 100 counties, 553 towns and cities,[1] and more than 30,000[2] active 501(c)(3) nonprofits. These entities, together, with our state and federal governments, comprise the public sector in North Carolina, interacting in myriad ways on a daily basis.

The diversity within the nonprofit sector is broad, similar to that of local governments. The largest nonprofits include private universities like Duke and Wake Forest, as well as hospitals and health systems. The nonprofits that local governments are most likely to partner or contract with, however, tend to be much smaller organizations, ranging from volunteer fire departments to literacy councils to economic development partnerships.[3] This chapter will focus on the relationships likely to be formed between local governments and community nonprofit organizations.

1. *See* NC League of Municipalities, Resource Center: NC Cities & Towns, www.nclm.org/resource-center/municipalities/Pages/Default.aspx; www.sog.unc.edu/node/427.

2. In 2013, North Carolina had 43,192 nonprofits, with 29,303 of them being 501(c)3 public charities registered with the IRS, including registered congregations, http://nccsweb.urban.org/PubApps/profile1.php?state=NC. In 2012, the 10,357 reporting public charities alone had over $59 billion in gross receipts, http://nccsweb.urban.org/PubApps/profile1.php?state=NC.

3. According to the National Center for Charitable Statistics, http://nccsdataweb.urban.org/PubApps/profileDrillDown.php?rpt=US-STATE, in 2010, there were a total of 42,806 nonprofits in North Carolina, with 23,143 of those with a purpose and size (more than $50,000 annual gross receipts) that require them to file with the IRS. The NC Center for Nonprofits reports in "Quick Facts: Nonprofits' Impact on North Carolina," www.ncnonprofits.org/sites/default/files/public_resources/NPSectorFacts.pdf, that "Most nonprofits are very small. North Carolina has 10,361 organizations that are 501(c)(3) nonprofits with annual revenues over $50,000."

At the local level, counties, municipalities, and nonprofits share a common interest in encouraging the success of their communities. Their organizational differences are both their strongest collective asset and a frequent source of tensions. Nonprofit–government relationships can be viewed as complementary, supplemental, adversarial—or even all three things at once—depending on the circumstances. A successful public administrator learns how to identify, appreciate, and manage the value of these diverse responsibilities and perspectives within his or her community.

Nonprofits can serve as privately supported supplementary service providers of public goods (by providing more food for the hungry, for example), as complementary partners providing services that differ from what governments provide (for instance, by providing food for those not eligible for government assistance), and as advocates and adversaries for particular groups in the process of forming and implementing public policies (by bringing attention to the unmet food needs of a particular population).[4]

What Are Nonprofit Organizations and How Are They Different from Local Government?

Nonprofit organizations are defined by their legal statuses. In this section, we describe the laws relating to nonprofit corporations. We discuss how a nonprofit's legal status differs from that of a local government in ways that affect its relationships. Then we describe important mission, staffing, and resource differences between local governments and the community nonprofits with which they most often work.

Legal Characteristics

Nonprofit organizations are either corporations, limited liability companies (LLCs), or unincorporated associations. If the nonprofit is a corporation, it is governed by Chapter 55A of the North Carolina General Statutes (hereinafter G.S.). Because the North Carolina laws governing nonprofit corporations are reasonably well settled and predictable, and because the corporate form offers additional advantages discussed in the following paragraphs, most nonprofits choose to incorporate.

If the nonprofit organization is an LLC, it is governed by G.S. Chapter 57C. Until recently, it was unclear whether an LLC formed under the laws of North Carolina (or any other state) would be granted tax-exempt status by the federal government. Although it is now clear that LLCs can be tax-exempt nonprofit organizations, it is still comparatively rare for organizations to choose this form of organizing.

If the nonprofit is an unincorporated association,[5] it is governed by a combination of G.S. Chapter 59B and North Carolina common law. Until recently, unincorporated associations were governed exclusively by common law, which, because of its diffuse nature, made life unpredictable and inconvenient for nonprofit organizations.[6] Chapter 59B, known as the Uniform Unincorporated Nonprofit Association Act, was intended as a means to provide legal predictability and protection to unincorporated nonprofit organizations; however, because it is so new and untested, and because it does not provide guidance on all legal aspects of a nonprofit organization's existence, most nonprofits continue to choose the corporate form.

Due to the uncertainty associated with nonprofit LLCs and unincorporated associations, governments generally prefer to partner with or to fund nonprofit corporations. This section on legal characteristics will focus on nonprofit corporations and will use the term "nonprofit" throughout the discussion.

---

4. Young, Dennis R., "Complementary, Supplementary, or Adversarial? A Theoretical and Historical Examination of Nonprofit-Government Relations in the U.S.," *in Nonprofits & Government: Collaboration and Conflict* (1999), 38.

5. For example, many churches are not incorporated but are, rather, unincorporated associations, as are many neighborhood associations or other similar groups.

6. Common law is judge-made law that evolves on a case-by-case basis and is found in the written opinions that accompany the decisions in cases appealed to the North Carolina Supreme Court and the North Carolina Court of Appeals. Because the legal principles of common law are not codified in a single place as statutes are, the legal status of an unincorporated association in a given matter may be more difficult to determine.

Nonprofit Definition

G.S. 55A-1-40(17) defines a nonprofit corporation as one "intended to have no income or intended to have income none of which is distributable to its members, directors or officers." That definition illustrates two important points about nonprofits. First, a nonprofit is permitted to generate income and to do so in amounts that exceed its expenses. Indeed, if it does not do so, its long-term viability may be in doubt. Second, the use of that surplus income is limited; it may not benefit people who govern the organization but must be used instead to benefit the purposes the organization was created to serve.

Governance Documents

It is relatively simple to organize as a nonprofit corporation. The group forming the organization must file articles of incorporation with the secretary of state's office.[7] Those articles must list the corporate name, the purpose for which the nonprofit is being established, its mailing address, the names and addresses of the persons incorporating the nonprofit, and they may include any other governing rules the organization finds appropriate. Typically, articles of incorporation are broadly written and do not contain detailed governance provisions. Such governing principles are left to the corporate by-laws, which act as operating instructions for the nonprofit organization.[8] Unlike articles of incorporation, by-laws are not filed with the secretary of state, a fact which, among other things, makes amendments simpler. By contrast, when articles of incorporation are amended, the amendments have to be submitted to the secretary of state.

In recent years, the federal government has begun to require additional corporate policies for nonprofits. For example, as a result of corporate governance scandals in the for-profit and nonprofit sectors, nonprofit organizations now must adopt whistle-blower protection and document retention and destruction policies.[9] Also, although the law does not require it, the federal government strongly suggests that all nonprofit organizations adopt written conflict of interest policies.[10]

As this discussion shows, the governance provisions of a nonprofit corporation come from several sources. First are the relevant state and/or federal (primarily tax) statutes. Any mandatory provisions of those statutes control over any conflicting provisions in the nonprofit's articles of incorporation.[11] The articles of incorporation, if they are consistent with the statutes, control over the by-laws and other corporate policies in cases of conflicts. Policies adopted by the nonprofit's board or other governing entity may be applicable, but they must be consistent with statutes, articles, and by-laws.

Tax Status

One common way of classifying nonprofits is by their tax status under the federal Internal Revenue Code (IRC),[12] interpreted and enforced by the Internal Revenue Service (IRS). That code confers special tax status on more than a dozen types of nonprofit organizations, for purposes ranging from labor unions, political parties, or chambers of commerce to country clubs or other social clubs. The section of the code most commonly associated with nonprofit organizations is Section 501(c)(3) (described in more detail below). Other examples of nonprofits that have IRS statuses are IRC Section 501(c)(4) (social welfare organizations and employee associations) or 501(c)(6) (chambers of commerce and business leagues) entities. Other status categories are provided for social clubs (like country clubs) and various

7. N.C. Gen. Stat. (hereinafter G.S.) § 55A-2-01.

8. G.S. 55A-2-06(b) provides that "[t]he bylaws may contain any provision for regulating and managing the affairs of the corporation that is not inconsistent with law or the articles of incorporation."

9. These requirements are contained in the Sarbanes-Oxley Act (15 U.S.C.A. §§ 7201 *et seq.*), adopted by Congress in 2002.

10. The Internal Revenue Service (IRS) recommends written conflict of interest policies as a best practice for nonprofit organizations and asks all nonprofit applicants for Section 501(c)(3) tax-exempt status whether they have adopted such policies. *See* National Council of Nonprofits, "Conflict of Interest," www.councilofnonprofits.org/conflict-of-interest (accessed Oct. 26, 2012).

11. The federal tax statutes are not mandatory. Their violation can alter an organization's tax status but not its status as a state-chartered nonprofit organization.

12. The IRC is found at Title 26 of the United States Code.

political organizations and labor unions. Nonprofits are generally exempt from paying income taxes on the revenues they generate; the exceptions to this rule are complex and well beyond the scope of this publication.

IRC Section 501(c)(3) establishes the tax status for most nonprofit corporations established to engage in "charitable" activities.[13] These nonprofits have a substantial tax advantage not conferred on other nonprofits—donations to them may be taken as a charitable deduction in determining the donor's federal income tax liability.[14] North Carolina's income tax scheme contains a similar deduction from state income tax.[15] Many of these nonprofit organizations are also given some special treatment in the administration of the sales tax law.[16] For example, these nonprofits are exempt from collecting sales taxes relating to certain activities during which they sell goods and some of them are entitled to a refund of the sales taxes they pay on goods and services they purchase.[17] In addition, many activities of nonprofits exempt the corporation from paying property taxes on property they own to support those activities.[18] These state tax laws do not apply to all 501(c)(3) nonprofits, but most, if not all, of the organizations covered by the exemptions are 501(c)(3) organizations.

Limits on Liability

In general, corporations are liable for harm they cause to others in the same way that individuals or for-profit corporations are liable. In keeping with this principle, nonprofit organizations do not enjoy immunity from such liability; in 1967 the General Assembly abolished the common law defense of charitable immunity.[19] But nonprofits may claim the basic protections that come from having corporate status. That status generally means that (1) only corporate assets may be used to satisfy the corporation's liability and (2) the assets of members, officers, or directors are not reachable for that purpose. In limited circumstances, for example, where a corporation has consistently failed to follow proper governance procedures or where an individual has intermingled personal and corporate finances, this "corporate veil" may be pierced and individuals associated with a corporation may be liable for a corporation's liabilities; again, such scenarios are rare. [20]

The volunteers who manage nonprofits nonetheless remain concerned that they will be sued as individuals for actions taken while operating in their capacities as officers or directors. Both state and federal law, in recognition of the need to encourage volunteers to work in nonprofits, provide some immunity to such liability.

One important protection, immunity for service as a member of a nonprofit's board of directors, comes from state law and applies to all nonprofits. Under this provision, directors and officers who are not compensated for their service beyond reimbursement for expenses are, as a general rule, immune from civil liability for money damages (except to

13. 26 U.S.C.A. § 501(c)(3). The kinds of organizations included in this section must be operating solely (1) for charitable, religious, scientific, public safety testing, educational, or literary purposes; (2) to foster amateur sports competition; or (3) for the prevention of cruelty to children or animals. Churches qualify as 501(c)(3) organizations without having to file paperwork with the IRS (although they may do so) and are so treated even if they are not incorporated.

14. *See generally* 26 U.S.C.A. § 170; Department of the Treasury, Internal Revenue Service, Publication 526, Charitable Contributions (Jan. 2012), www.irs.gov/pub/irs-pdf/p526.pdf.

15. For tax years pre-dating January 1, 2012, G.S. 105-134.5 provided that one's taxable income for state income tax purposes was the same as it was for federal income tax purposes, subject to certain exceptions not relevant to this issue. For taxable years starting on or falling after January 1, 2012, "North Carolina taxable income" means "the taxpayer's adjusted gross income as modified in G.S. 105-134.6 [listing specific exemptions and deductions]." G.S. 105-134.5, *as amended by* S.L. 2011-145, sec. 31A.1(b) (June 15, 2011). G.S. 105-151.26 allows a tax credit for "excess charitable deductions" against the personal income tax of certain taxpayers who elect not to itemize their deductions.

16. *See* N.C. Department of Revenue, *Sales and Use Tax Bulletins, Section 17*, www.dor.state.nc.us/practitioner/sales/bulletins/section17.pdf (Jan. 2009).

17. *See, e.g.*, G.S. 105-164.13 (34) and (35) (examples of exemptions from tax-collecting mandate for nonprofits); *id.* § 105-164.14(b) (list of nonprofits entitled to refunds).

18. *See id.* § 105-275 (list of categories of exempt property).

19. *Id.* § 1-539.9.

20. North Carolina's recently adopted Uniform Unincorporated Nonprofit Association Act, G.S. Chapter 59B, purports to extend corporate-like entity liability protections to unincorporated associations. However, as discussed above, this law is new, and it is not yet clear that its liability protections will withstand legal challenge.

the extent they are covered by insurance) for any actions they take in their official capacities.[21] In addition, nonprofit corporations may indemnify (reimburse) directors and officers for their expenses in defending lawsuits, subject to certain limits and exclusions.[22] Specific nonprofit activities may also have special rules limiting the liability attached to them or that of volunteers engaged in said activities.[23]

IRC Section 501(c)(3) nonprofits have even greater protection. Their volunteers (not just the officers and directors) are immunized from liability for their acts of negligence in some circumstances. There are both state and federal statutes on this subject, and in cases of conflict the federal law controls.[24] The federal law generally protects volunteers from liability for harm caused by negligent acts or omissions during volunteer service for a governmental agency or 501(c)(3) nonprofit.[25] The law does not, however, protect volunteers from liability for criminal, intentional, or reckless conduct,[26] nor does it protect them from simple negligence when (1) the action at issue was not in the scope of the volunteer's duties,[27] (2) the situation involved activity for which a license is required,[28] or (3) it involved conduct when the volunteer was under the influence of alcohol or drugs.[29] State law contains a similar rule,[30] but it has fewer exceptions than its federal counterpart. The state statute also provides that "[t]o the extent that any charitable organization or volunteer has liability insurance, that charitable organization or volunteer shall be deemed to have waived the qualified immunity herein to the extent of indemnification by insurance for the negligence by any volunteer."[31]

Legal Rules Applicable to Nonprofits

Nonprofits who deal with governments often have to answer questions about the extent to which they are subject to laws that regulate the governments themselves. In most of these scenarios, the nonprofit's nongovernmental status means that it is not subject to rules applicable only to the government. There are some exceptions to that general rule, however, and there are some laws applicable only to nonprofits (charitable solicitation rules).[32] But the general rule of thumb is that a nonprofit is not subject to a statute that regulates solely governmental activity (most typically "open government"–type rules), absent some unusual circumstances. Further, simply receiving governmental funds, through grants or contracts, will not subject a nonprofit to statutes applicable to governments.

Some examples will illustrate the point. Governments are subject to public records and open meetings laws. Nonprofits, as a rule, are not. But there are statutory exceptions. For example, the nonprofit corporation act makes corporations organized upon request of the state for the sole purpose of financing projects for public use subject to the same rules that are applicable to the state.[33] In some very limited instances, a nonprofit may be so closely aligned

21. G.S. 55A-8-60. The immunity does not apply if the board member was acting beyond the scope of his or her official duties, if the board member was not acting in good faith, if the action in question constituted gross negligence or intentional misconduct, or if the action involved the operation of a motor vehicle (for which the law requires liability insurance). This immunity can be limited by the articles of incorporation. *See id.* § 55A-2-02(b)(4).

22. G.S. 55A-8-50 *et seq.*

23. For example, G.S. 58-82-5 limits liability for volunteer fire departments and their volunteers for damages caused by their simple negligence in fighting a fire; either the organization or its volunteers can still be liable for gross negligence or intentional misconduct, however.

24. The state statute is G.S. 1-539.10, and the federal statute is the Volunteer Protection Act of 1997, codified at 42 U.S.C.A. §§ 14501–14505. *See, in particular,* 42 U.S.C.A. § 14502 (covering federal preemption).

25. 42 U.S.C.A. § 14503(a).

26. *Id.* § 14503(a)(3).

27. *Id.* § 14503(a)(1).

28. *Id.* § 14503(a)(2).

29. *Id.* § 14503(f)(1)(E).

30. *See* G.S. 1-539.10(a).

31. G.S. 1-539.10(b). *See also* Charles E. Daye and Mark W. Morris, *North Carolina Law of Torts* (2d ed., 1999), 406–7; Anita R. Brown-Graham, *A Practical Guide to the Liability of North Carolina Cities and Towns* (Chapel Hill: UNC Institute of Government, 1999), 4-13–14.

32. *See, e.g.,* G.S. Chapter 131F, Articles 2 and 3 (charitable solicitation rules requiring many nonprofits to obtain licenses from the secretary of state).

33. G.S. 55A-3-07(2).

with a governmental unit that it becomes subject to the same disclosure rules that control the government's conduct. This can happen when the nonprofit is (1) organized by a unit of government, (2) operated by a governmental unit, or (3) performing a function so closely associated with the government that it is viewed as part of the government.[34]

And there are some transparency requirements with which certain entities that receive public funds—namely, nonprofit corporations—must comply. Specifically, G.S. 55A-16-24 requires a nonprofit corporation that receives over $5,000 of public funds (from a local government, the state, or the federal government) within a fiscal year in grants, loans, or in-kind contributions, to provide the following information upon written request from any member of the public:

(1) The nonprofit's latest financial statements, including a balance sheet as of the end of the fiscal year and a statement of operations for that year, as well as "details about the amount of public funds received and how those funds were used."

(2) The nonprofit's most recently filed Internal Revenue Service Form 990. This requirement is satisfied if the Form 990 is posted on a website where the public can access it without charge. If the nonprofit does not post the information itself, it should provide a link to the other entity's website (for example, Guidestar.org).

The statute exempts a few entities from disclosing this information because they already are required to report it to the N.C. Medical Care Commission or the Local Government Commission. Certain private colleges are exempt because they report to the state.[35]

Except for these specific situations, nonprofit organizations do not have to open their records to the public. They do have to provide access to their records for members of the organization,[36] though, but most Section 501(c)(3) nonprofits do not have members. Federal tax laws require some disclosures of basic informational documents for most nonprofits other than churches.[37] Also, it is common for governments dealing with nonprofits in a formal way to specify in the legal documents defining the relationship (i.e., contracts or grants) the kinds of disclosures and access to records required of the nonprofit.

Charities that solicit funds, unless exempted by law, need to comply with the state's rules on charitable solicitations. There is an extensive set of statutes that regulate solicitations by many nonprofits.[38] As for other statutes, such as civil rights laws, there are generally no exemptions specifically for nonprofits, but each set of laws should be analyzed on a case-by-case basis. For example, G.S. 159-40 allows a city or county that appropriates at least $1,000 in any fiscal year to a nonprofit entity to require that the nonprofit "have an audit performed for the fiscal year in which the funds are received" and file a copy of that audit with the local government. There are certain entities that are exempt from this requirement, including volunteer fire departments, rescue squads, and ambulance squads. A local government still may require these entities (and all other private entities and individuals that receive public funds) to provide an accounting of how the moneys are spent and to comply with other requirements as a condition of receiving the funds. These requirements should be spelled out clearly in a contractual agreement between the local government and the grantee.

Lobbying

As noted earlier, contributions to Section 501(c)(3) nonprofits are tax-deductible for their donors. That gives those nonprofit organizations an advantage in raising funds. That special status is based on each nonprofit's special mission

34. For a more extensive discussion of this issue, see Frayda Bluestein, "Privatization: Legal Issues for North Carolina Local Governments," *Popular Government* (Winter 1997): 28–40.

35. *See* Kara Millonzi, "Accountability Requirements for Certain Entities that Receive Appropriations from Local Governments," *Coates' Canons: NC Local Government Law Blog* (UNC School of Government, Sept. 7, 2012), http://canons.sog.unc.edu/?p=6837.

36. G.S. 55A-16-02.

37. The annual disclosure form is IRS Form 990. Until recently, many small nonprofit organizations were not required to file annual 990s; now even the smallest nonprofits must file an abbreviated version of the form and can have their exempt status rescinded if they fail to do so. A discussion of the required disclosures is included in Department of the Treasury, Internal Revenue Service, Publication 557, Tax-Exempt Status for Your Organization (Oct. 2011) (hereinafter IRS Publication 557), www.irs.gov/pub/irs-pdf/p557.pdf.

38. G.S. 131F-1 *et seq.*

to benefit its community as a whole. But with that advantage come special responsibilities, including a limited ability to engage in *lobbying* and a prohibition on using the nonprofit's resources for *political expenditures*. Both those terms have specific meaning in the IRS Code. *Lobbying* in this context means any effort aimed at influencing legislation, at any level of government.[39] Thus it does not include advocacy aimed at executive (non-legislative) actions, but it does include *grass roots* and *direct lobbying* aimed at influencing legislative actions.[40] *Political expenditures*, in contrast, are aimed at helping specific candidates or political parties in elections.[41]

For 501(c)(3) organizations, some limited lobbying is allowed. The general rule of thumb is that the amount of resources spent on lobbying may not be a "substantial part" of the organization's activities.[42] Since this is a subjective term, the IRS Code also establishes a "safe harbor," specifying with particularity amounts of money that may be spent on lobbying activities. It all comes down to a formula based on the amount of money an organization spends; for most organizations, the amount allowed is 20 percent of their expenditures to accomplish their stated purposes, plus depreciation.[43] For larger organizations, the percentages go down from 20 percent.[44] Organizations that devote more than a "substantial part" of their activities to lobbying can lose their Section 501(c)(3) status.[45] Organizations that elect to use the "safe harbor" provision can be assessed an excise tax if their level of expenditures exceeds the allowed amounts.[46]

Lobbying in this sense does not include an organization's act of (1) responding to questions posed by legislative bodies, (2) making available results of any nonpartisan studies or research, (3) examining broad social or economic problems, or (4) giving testimony about legislation that directly affects the organization's status or its powers and duties.[47] It also does not include communications by the organization to its members about specific legislation, unless the communication asks the members to take specific action with respect to the legislation; communications with government officials are similarly affected by these rules, though only when they involve legislative advocacy.[48] In sum, the nonprofit rules in this area are relatively complicated, and nonprofit organizations planning to engage in more than occasional lobbying should study them with care.

In contrast to the rules that allow lobbying on a limited basis, the rules on partisan or candidate-specific political expenditures are simple. Such spending is flatly prohibited and can result in both a loss of tax-exempt status and the imposition of excise taxes on the expenditures.[49] Individuals associated with nonprofits may participate as citizens in the political process but may not do so on behalf of their respective nonprofit organizations.

Other non–Section 501(c)(3) organizations that are tax exempt are not regulated as closely as 501(c)(3) entities. Many of those organizations could have elected to organize under IRC Section 501(c)(4), which grants exempt status for civic leagues and social welfare organizations. The rules on lobbying and political expenditures are not as strict for Section 501(c)(4) organizations, and for that reason some entities elect not to seek Section 501(c)(3) status. Similarly, chambers of commerce and other business leagues organize under IRC Section 501(c)(6). They may then engage in

39. IRS Publication 557, at 49.

40. "Grass roots" lobbying is "[a]ny attempt to influence any legislation through an effort to affect the opinions of the general public or any segment thereof," and "direct lobbying" is "[a]ny attempt to influence any legislation through communication with any member or employee of a legislative body or with any government official or employee who may participate in the formulation of legislation." IRS Publication 557, at 49.

41. IRS Publication 557, at 24.

42. IRS Publication 557, at 49.

43. The amount spent on lobbying is included in the organization's expenditures in making this calculation.

44.For a more detailed explanation of these rules, see IRS Publication 557, at 49–51.

45. IRS Publication 557, at 49.

46. IRS Publication 557, at 50.

47. IRS Publication 557, at 49. It is not clear whether an organization's lobbying for its own funding from a legislative body would be included in an exception to the lobbying ban for activities related to legislative matters that affect an organization's status (commonly known as the "self-defense" exception; see IRS Publication 557, at 49). If it is not excluded under the self-defense exception, there is no other exception that would exclude this kind of lobbying for self-funding from these rules, which means that an organization could engage in this activity but the funds used in the activity would be considered in determining if an organization had exceeded its limits.

48. IRS Publication 557, at 49.

49. *See, e.g.*, IRS Revenue Ruling 2007-41, 2007-1 C.B. (*Cumulative Bulletin*) 1421 (2007), www.irs.gov/pub/irs-drop/rr-07-41.pdf (clarifying what does and does not count as prohibited political activity).

lobbying to promote their members' interests, subject to certain rules affecting the members' ability to deduct their dues as business expenses. Each type of organization has rules that apply to it, and it is important to consult the rules applicable to the kind of organization with which one is dealing.

Opportunities and Challenges Presented by Differing Characteristics of Nonprofits and Local Governments

The different structures and purposes of local governments and nonprofits generate other kinds of contrasts in activities, organizational cultures, and guiding philosophies. By mining the opportunities presented by these differences, each sort of entity can complement the other for the betterment of their respective communities. The sections below focus primarily on items unique to nonprofits.

Individual Missions—Narrower, More of a Driving Force for Nonprofits

The mission or purpose of any nonprofit is stated in its organizational charter and provides the basis for its legal status, including its tax classification. The nonprofit's mission also typically attracts and motivates those who support the organization. Its board members, employees, volunteers, and donors are drawn to that mission and want to work toward achieving it.

Because of their dedication to the mission of the nonprofit, those who work and volunteer for it often develop considerable knowledge about the goals of the organization, not to mention a strong attachment to the work necessary to achieve them. Volunteer firefighters learn a lot about fighting fires, for example, and care deeply about performing that organizational purpose well. The same can be said about people who work or volunteer in animal shelters, art museums, and so on.

Attracting Volunteers, Donations—Key for Nonprofits

With a compelling mission, a nonprofit has an enhanced ability to recruit volunteers and solicit contributions. The opportunity for individuals to offer time, money, and other support for causes they believe in has been a distinguishing feature of our culture since before the United States won independence. In this vein, many of the paid employees of nonprofit organizations work at below market rates because of their commitment to the causes their nonprofits seek to serve.

Connection to Communities Served—Strong for Nonprofits

The board members, staff, and volunteers of nonprofits are frequently members of the client community themselves, whether that is defined by geography, shared experience, common interests, or similar personal characteristics. This shared identity serves as another tie between the nonprofit and the community being served, contributing to both mutual trust and insight that external parties might not acquire.

Procedural Restrictions—Generally Fewer in Number for Nonprofits

Nonprofits can act more quickly and with greater flexibility than can local governments to adopt and implement new programs, to hire and fire employees, and to buy and sell property. Nonprofits are private corporations and thus are usually not subject to the requirements for public notice, public hearings, open meetings, or public access to records that apply to local governments. Nonprofits do, however, have to act in accordance with their missions and charters, lest they risk losing their special tax status. Further, all personnel actions and property transactions of the nonprofit corporation are subject to laws that regulate businesses. Nonprofits also have to comply with any terms or expectations set forth in the contractual agreements into which they enter.

Also, some special regulations apply only to nonprofits. Accounting practices and standards for nonprofits differ from both those applicable to businesses and those pertaining to governments. For example, any nonprofit with receipts of more than $25,000 is required to file a Form 990 with the IRS, and any North Carolina nonprofit that solicits contributions is required to get a Charitable Solicitation License from the North Carolina Secretary of State.[50]

Effect of Variation in Size, Sophistication of Nonprofits

Because of a diversity in organizational characteristics among and between nonprofits, local governments will benefit from establishing expectations and practices that can be calibrated to properly align with those of the nonprofit(s) with which they are dealing.

For example, it does not make sense that a small neighborhood association requesting $500 to support a local clean-up day has to fill out the same twenty-page application required of a homeless shelter requesting $50,000 for a particular shelter activity. It does make sense, however, for the neighborhood association to have to clearly explain how it wants to use the money being sought from the local government and then provide verification that it did, in fact, use the funds accordingly, but the form that the request and accountability take can be relatively simple.

Also, consider a small or new nonprofit that is uniquely situated to meet the needs of a population group that the local government wants to serve in new or better ways. The government's interests might best be met by providing one-on-one attention to strengthen the professional capacity of the existing unsophisticated nonprofit, building on the community ties it already holds, instead of trying to build a new program from scratch.

How Nonprofits and Local Governments Work Together

Local governments all across the United States are regularly involved with nonprofit organizations. Many governments face the challenges of having to provide more and better services while being constrained by difficult fiscal limits. To help meet these challenges, many local governments have involved nonprofits in service delivery, drawing on these organizations' volunteers and private financial resources as well as their greater flexibility of action. Some nonprofits have also become skilled advocates for the clients they serve, making persuasive appeals for public funding of their work or otherwise helping shape governments' priorities.

Local governments can work effectively with nonprofits to address public needs by funding the nonprofits, giving them property, sharing training opportunities with them, providing expertise or other types of in-kind assistance to them, or partnering with them to jointly develop and implement public service programs. Government funding of nonprofits—through direct appropriations, grants, or purchase-of-service contracts—is the most common sort of continuing relationship between the two types of organizations.

Why Fund Nonprofits?

North Carolina law provides that public funds are to be spent only for "public purposes."[51] Thus, local governing boards need to understand that funds provided to a nonprofit organization are, like any government expenditure, to be used for purposes for which the local government has authority to spend funds. Local governments may, and do, choose to fund nonprofits to provide for many such "public purposes."

One possible reason for funding nonprofits is to support the work nonprofits do to better the community. For example, a city may want to reach homeless people by helping fund a homeless shelter or a community kitchen

50. Details are available on the N.C. Secretary of State's website, www.secretary.state.nc.us/csl/.

51. N.C. Const. art. V, § 2(1), (7); Hughey v. Cloninger, 37 N.C. App. 107 (1978), *aff'd*, 297 N.C. 86 (1979). The North Carolina General Statutes also specifically authorize local governments to "contract with and appropriate money to any person, association, or corporation, in order to carry out any public purpose that the [local government] is authorized by law to engage in." G.S. 153A-449 (counties), 160A-20.1 (cities).

operated by a nonprofit. A county may want to encourage new employment opportunities by helping fund an economic development corporation or a chamber of commerce.

Or a local government might fund a nonprofit so that the nonprofit can provide specific programs or services. Instead of simply building and staffing a swimming pool, for example, a town might decide to partner with a nonprofit organization and help fund its capital or operating expenditures for the pool. Instead of operating an animal shelter, a county might contract with a nonprofit to run the facility. Rather than funding a broad range of valuable community services, elected officials may decide to tie their expenditures to programs that directly support a specific goal of the jurisdiction's strategic plan. For example, if economic development is a primary goal of a particular county, that county's funding for nonprofits might focus on economic development, literacy, and subsidized child care to enable parents to take jobs. If the county's priority is youth development, it might support nonprofits that provide after-school programs, tutoring, or recreation opportunities. Examples like the ones mentioned above abound.

Finally, local governments might fund nonprofits to increase the impact of public expenditures. Even small nonprofits can multiply the effects of public spending by leveraging other resources. For example, by using volunteers in an efficient and effective manner, a nonprofit can increase the impact of each local government dollar. Many nonprofits also receive donations, grants, sales receipts, or other funds, thus expanding the work supported by local government funding.

Ways to Fund or Support Nonprofits

There are a variety of options available to local governments to fund or support nonprofits. Some are described briefly below.

Purchase of Services

Local governments may purchase services from nonprofit organizations in the same way they do from other entities. These purchases can be made through the government unit's regular processes and may contain the same terms and conditions as those regularly imposed on the unit's other service providers. The North Carolina General Statutes do not require bidding for the purchase of services. In fact, the process used to acquire these services is left to the local government.[52]

Grants

Generally speaking, a grant is a provision of funds in exchange for a promise by the grantee to perform certain prescribed activities or to produce particular results. The process for awarding grants is usually different from the process for purchasing services. Competition is typically structured differently, and in many cases a grant may describe the required services in less detail than a contract for the purchase of services.

Another important difference between grants and the purchase of services is that local government grants often involve "pass-through" funds from the state or federal government. Funds and eligibility standards for these grants originate with the state or federal government, but the funds are awarded to nonprofits by local government. These types of grants may require that the local government comply with reporting, accounting, and other requirements from the granting entity and that the local government use specified procedures for awarding the grants. With other kinds of contracts, the local government has more discretion to include terms and requirements as it deems appropriate.

52. For four specific types of services—architectural, engineering, surveying, and construction-management-at-risk—North Carolina local governments must use a qualifications-based selection process to choose a service provider. G.S. 143-64.31. Even then, local governments may exempt themselves from this process if they do so in writing; they must provide a justification for their selection if the fee for the service involved is $30,000 or more. G.S. 143-64.32.

Sidebar 12.1 Tips for Deciding Whether to Fund Nonprofits

Nonprofits may deliver services more effectively or at less cost than governments. When deciding whether to provide funds to a nonprofit, the local government should ask itself the following:

- Can the nonprofit supplement public funds with contributions of time, expertise, and money from volunteers and other donors?
- Can the nonprofit move more flexibly or quickly than the government to address a community need?
- Is the nonprofit in a position to build a sense of partnership or encourage civic participation by involving volunteers, neighbors, or others known and trusted by a particular community?
- Can the nonprofit provide specialized expertise in community issues or connect with a specific population because of its mission and experience?
- How can the nonprofit augment, complement, or fill gaps in government services?
- What is our local government's experience working with nonprofit organizations?
- What has worked well? What could be improved?
- How is the nonprofit perceived within the community?

Appropriations

Like a grant or service purchase, a direct appropriation may be made to a nonprofit organization to carry out any activity for which the local government is authorized to spend money. Broadly, an appropriation is a budgetary action in which the governing board approves the expenditure of funds for a particular purpose. Although an appropriation may not be accompanied by the same paperwork as a grant or a purchase of services, it really should be treated in the same way. In practice, an appropriation is likely to be less specific than a grant or other contract and may simply take the form of a lump-sum payment by the local government to the nonprofit. However, the local government and the nonprofit must ensure that the funds are used only for purposes the local government has authority to support. Many local governments enter into contracts with nonprofits that specify terms for using these government-appropriated funds.

Other Kinds of Support

Local governments also provide in-kind support to nonprofits by contributing property or personnel assistance to programs provided by those nonprofits. For example, a local government might include nonprofit staff in its training programs or use its purchasing power to purchase goods or services on behalf of the nonprofit for use in programs the local government has authority to fund.[53] Further, a local government may make the expertise of its staff available to the nonprofit as a form of in-kind assistance that might save money for both the local government and the nonprofit. In each case the basic legal limitations on these types of in-kind assistance are the same as those discussed above. If the activity of the nonprofit is one the local government has legal authority to support, that government can provide in-kind assistance in a wide variety of ways.

Designing a Process for Funding Nonprofits

When local governments are deciding whether and how to fund nonprofits, having a streamlined decision-making process in place can make an enormous difference. Government officials are always looking for guidance when making tough funding decisions, especially when those decisions involve controversial, time-consuming, or passionate appeals from community-based nonprofit organizations. What community services do government officials want to support

53. G.S. 160A-279 and 160A-280 give cities and counties the authority to donate property to nonprofits carrying out a public purpose.

Sidebar 12.2 Contracting with Nonprofits

Although local governments and nonprofits work together/interact in many circumstances without contracting, contracts are the most common vehicles for these collaborations. The questions and answers in this sidebar explain the basic principles behind the legal limitations on government contracts with (and other support for) nonprofits.

1. What authority do local governments have to contract with nonprofit organizations and what are the limitations on the exercise of that authority?

   For North Carolina local governments, the authority to contract is directly related to the basic authority to spend funds. A local government may contract for any purpose for which it may spend money. The three key legal limitations on the expenditure of funds by a local government are that (1) the expenditure must be for a public purpose; (2) the activity supported must be one in which the local government has statutory authority to engage; and (3) the expenditure must not be inconsistent with the laws or the constitution of the state or federal government. The next three questions discuss these limitations.

2. What is a public purpose?

   The definition of *public purpose* is difficult to pin down. The North Carolina courts have relied upon two guiding principles in determining whether a particular activity is for a public purpose: (1) whether the activity involves "a reasonable connection with the convenience and necessity of the [local government]" and (2) whether the activity "benefits the public generally, as opposed to special interests or persons."[a] State courts have also offered at least two refinements of the second principle. First, it is not necessary to show that every citizen will benefit from an activity for it to be considered a public purpose. Furthermore, the fact that one or more private individuals benefit does not eliminate the public purpose. In other words, a private individual or business may directly benefit from a contract or an appropriation. This does not extinguish the public purpose as long as the public will benefit and the private benefit does not outweigh the public benefit.

3. Explain the requirement for "statutory authority." Must a statute specifically authorize the contract?

   North Carolina local governments do not have inherent authority. That is, they operate under authority delegated to them by the state legislature through enabling laws. So, in addition to serving a public purpose, a particular action of a local government (including an expenditure or a contract) must be authorized by a state statute.

   This does not necessarily mean that there must be a statute that specifically authorizes the local government to enter into a contract for every activity it might wish to support. The state constitution contains a general authorization for contracts with private entities. Thus, as long as a statute authorizes a particular activity, the local government may carry out the activity itself or contract with a third party to carry out all or part of the activity.

4. Are local governments prohibited from contracting with religious (faith-based) organizations?

   No. Local governments may contract with faith-based nonprofits for services as long as those contracts do not violate the federal or state constitutions or other laws. Generally speaking, a contract with a faith-based group will be deemed lawful if the contract has a neutral purpose and effect both toward and among religions and avoids excessive government entanglement with religion. In other words, the terms of the contract must have the effect of safeguarding (1) the religious freedom of beneficiaries, both those who are willing to receive services from religious organizations and those who object to receiving services from such organizations, and (2) the religious integrity and character of faith-based organizations willing to accept government funds to provide services to the needy.

5. What, if any, limitations *must* a contract involving public funds impose on the activities of a religious/faith-based organization? What limitations *may* the contract impose?

   Notwithstanding widespread thought to the contrary, there are few legal limitations on religious organizations that receive public funding for programs. Although the public funder may impose religion-neutral restrictions, the only

a. Frayda S. Bluestein and Anita R. Brown-Graham, "Local Government Contracts with Nonprofit Organizations: Questions and Answers," *Popular Government* 67, no. 1 (Fall 2001): 32–44, 34 (quoting Madison Cablevision v. City of Morganton, 325 N.C. 634, 646 (1989)).

generally applicable restriction is that public funds not be used to pay for worship services, sectarian instruction, or proselytization.

A common misperception is that the use of public funds in program delivery automatically subjects the faith-based institution to the same standards as the public funder. This is not so. Religious institutions retain their autonomy even when under contract with local governments. So, for example, religious organizations retain their right to use religious criteria in hiring, firing, and disciplining employees, despite the fact that they are involved in a contract with a local government (that is subject to myriad laws in these same areas). Thus, although it would be illegal for local government employers to discriminate in employment on the basis of religion, they may fund a religious group that does so.

6. Do the rules about contracting apply regardless of whether government funding is a purchase of services, a grant, or an appropriation?

   Yes. Both the basic authority for local governments and the limitations discussed above are the same regardless of the form of assistance being provided. Service purchase contracts, grants, appropriations, and in-kind contributions (such as donations of property or land) are all subject to the same limitations.

7. Must a local government determine whether it can provide the service in-house before contracting with a private entity to provide the service?

   No, although some may do so as a matter of local discretion. There is no legal requirement or preference for performing functions or delivering services using public employees rather than doing so through contracts with private entities. However, when bidding requirements apply, the local government must obtain competition from outside the local government.[b] In addition, some units of government have privatization or managed-competition programs in place, in which the units systematically compare the cost and the desirability of using the private sector for service delivery with the cost and the desirability of public delivery. These programs are implemented as a matter of local policy, however, and are not mandated by law.

8. What about conflicts of interest? For example, if a county commissioner also serves on the board of a nonprofit, is the county legally barred from contracting with that nonprofit?

   State law makes it unlawful for a public official to benefit from a contract with the unit he or she represents.[c] For example, a local government generally may not contract with a business owned by one of its board members. A number of exceptions apply, however, including one that allows a limited amount of contracting in small jurisdictions. The conflict-of-interest laws do not apply if the public official does not receive any financial benefit from the contract. Also, a public official is not considered to have an interest in a contract if the official is an employee, rather than an owner, of the entity that contracts with the local government. So it is legal for a local government to contract with or provide other support to a nonprofit when a member of the local government's board is a volunteer (unpaid) member or salaried employee of the nonprofit board.

   The board members and the employees of both a local government and a nonprofit always must consider the nonlegal issues that might arise when a person is involved on both sides of a contract. Negative publicity may stem from this type of transaction, and citizens as well as members of the nonprofit may question whether the board member or other person can adequately execute his or her responsibilities to both organizations, especially if a conflict was to arise over the contract. Thus, even when the law does not prohibit a contract, avoiding it may be advisable if an ethical issue or a perception of conflict of interest might result.

b. Regarding local governments, formal bidding is required by statute for purchases of apparatus, materials, supplies, and equipment costing $90,000 or more and for construction and repair contracts costing $500,000 or more. G.S. 143-129. The informal bidding threshold is $30,000. G.S. 143-131. In addition, North Carolina law requires local governments to solicit competition (using a qualifications-based selection process) for architectural, engineering, surveying, and construction-management-at-risk services, although local governments may exempt themselves from this process. G.S. 143-64.31, -64.32. Local government policies or practices may require bidding for other types of contracts as well.

c. G.S. 14-234(a)(1).

by funding nonprofits? How can government officials decide which nonprofits to fund? How can they determine the appropriate level of funding? These are common questions when it comes to nonprofit funding.

Unfortunately there is no one right answer or practice; a process that works well in one jurisdiction may be ill-suited to another. This chapter does not suggest a single, one-size-fits-all solution for nonprofit funding. Instead, it suggests six steps for local officials to follow (and perhaps modify, as needed) when designing a process for funding nonprofits. (See Sidebar 12.3)

Elected officials and staff may ask, "Isn't there an easier way to do this?" Formulating answers for each step laid out in Sidebar 12.3 may require numerous meetings and discussions and may generate disagreements as decision makers progress toward a single, useful product. However, if key stakeholders, especially elected officials, do not participate in the design of the funding process, it may repeatedly be subject to challenge, circumvention, or revision.

Comparing the relative merits of nonprofit applications for funds can be a challenging endeavor. Decision makers face difficult choices concerning different groups of people in need (such as youth, the working poor, and senior citizens) and competing political interests (for example, the arts, economic development, and human services). Criteria to consider in making determinations on resource allocations include the government's goals and the organizational capacity of individual nonprofits to achieve those goals, plus any specific governmental priorities.

Having to spread what are sometimes limited funds among many worthy recipients is understandably frustrating. Decision makers may be tempted to take out their frustration on nonprofits by not engaging in a fully impartial or well-thought-out evaluation process. The dilemma local government officials face is not that there are too many nonprofits, but, rather, how to allocate scarce public funds among so many worthy efforts. Nonprofits can articulate existing community needs and present innovative opportunities for addressing those needs in a manner that can assist local governments in navigating this difficult and sometimes contentious process.

Any local government that funds nonprofits has at least one "process" for doing so. The steps of that process might be informal, spontaneous, variable, or political rather than strategic, consistent, and objective. Nonprofit advocates will obviously use the process that works for them, whether that means approaching an elected official individually or completing an application and making a presentation at a public hearing, or both. It is up to the local government to set and uphold the standards for its particular funding process.

Accountability

For both local governments and nonprofits, accountability expectations establish performance responsibilities, responsiveness limits, and reporting relationships, as well as the authority for evaluating success and adjusting plans for the future. Sometimes a government creates these expectations and presents them to a nonprofit as conditions for working together. Sometimes mutual negotiations produce accountability expectations. Mutual accountability is particularly appropriate when governments and nonprofits need to learn from each other and from experience how to better serve the public.

Effective accountability within partnerships is multidirectional and multidimensional. Governments and nonprofits can design new accountability patterns together if they are willing to share decision making, take time to deliberate and experiment, and respect the different perspectives of each other's organizational representatives. Using a model of mutual accountability, the challenge for community partners is to move beyond the limited buyer–seller relationship often embodied in government–nonprofit contracts and to move toward real collaboration—ongoing, shared responsibility for improving public services.

Sidebar 12.3 Steps to Consider in Designing a Process for Funding Nonprofits*

Each of the steps below is followed, denoted by bullet points, by common responses from local government officials. Some steps are complementary; others represent either/or choices. The steps listed are intended to stimulate discussion; decision makers should explore their own options with regard to each step.

1. Define the local government's reasons for appropriating funds for nonprofits.
   - To help meet public needs not addressed by local government programs
   - To augment existing local government services
   - To help meet specific local government goals
2. Define the government's objectives for the decision-making process.
   - To create a fair process
   - To include citizen input
   - To maximize accountability
   - To minimize negative consequences
   - To streamline decision making
   - To coordinate decision making with other local funders
   - To fund nonprofits that will achieve the government's objectives
3. Define how the government will assess needs or gather information.
   - Rely on nonprofits to present needs to government in formal proposals
   - Rely on the knowledge of government staff and elected officials
   - Rely on citizens to identify needs and inform the government of them
   - Search for information informally through community contacts
   - Conduct a needs assessment to collect data directly or partner with others doing community needs assessments
4. Decide how to obtain proposals from nonprofits.
   - Let the nonprofits take the initiative
   - Have government staff or elected officials notify particular nonprofits
   - Put out a formal notification, a request for applications, or a request for proposals to all nonprofits or the whole community
5. Evaluate how various processes for making funding decisions support identified goals. Any of the following groups, or various combinations of them, can participate in the review of proposals and recommendations for funding:
   - Local government staff
   - Community volunteers
   - Standing advisory boards
   - Members of the elected body
6. Determine who will make the funding decisions.
   - Do the elected officials want to make the funding decisions themselves?
   - Would they rather defer the funding decisions to staff or volunteers?

* A more complete discussion of these steps is offered in Margaret Henderson et al., *Working with Nonprofit Organizations* (Chapel Hill: UNC School of Government, 2010 (part of the Local Government Board Builders Series)), http://shopping.netsuite.com/s.nl/c.433425/it.A/id.4225/.f.

Sidebar 12.4 Tips for Creating Effective Funding Processes

- Define clearly at the outset how you will make funding decisions. Ensure that the criteria or standards for awarding funds are shared with applicants as well as with decision makers.
- Clearly state all expectations related to due date, format, content, and delivery of the applications.
- Assign staff to manage the logistics of the funding process.
- Use a broad-based, flexible strategic plan that includes goals nonprofits are expected to achieve.
- Avoid personal or professional biases.
- As early as possible, share information regarding the total funding available and the process for application with all nonprofits and the public.
- Use the same application process for all nonprofits seeking funding.
- Provide opportunities for input from citizens who represent the community.
- Coordinate with other local governments, foundations, and other community funders to use the same application form and, if possible, hold consolidated hearings to receive funding requests.[a]
- After the decisions are made, share information publicly about the amounts that nonprofits sought and received.
- Share information about the decision-making process equally and openly within the community.

---

a. Although the government mandates of cities and counties may differ, overlapping goals might make working across organizational boundaries worthwhile. Philanthropies may have similar strategic interests as well. In general, a community is likely to benefit from both procedural efficiencies and strategic focus if all public funders share information and coordinate processes related to the nonprofits.

The general public often equates *accountability* with *fiscal integrity* and focuses on *finances* instead of *fairness* and on *process* rather than *performance*. While financial accountability in relationships with nonprofits is important, a local government's limiting the concept of accountability to finances is inadequate when trying to ensure that the services the community wants and needs are provided effectively. A more service-oriented focus regards accountability goals as multidimensional, addressing three general categories:

- **Fairness.** Standards apply to all people equally, whether a given standard involves hiring practices for staff or eligibility criteria for clients. Fair decisions are made according to impartial standards and not based on favoritism.
- **Performance**. Activities are carried out successfully and produce the intended results.
- **Financial Integrity.** Funds are administered in an honest and responsible manner, commonly in accordance with generally accepted accounting principles.

All three categories are important and should be considered in any comprehensive approach to defining and implementing accountability targets. To ensure that all three goals for accountability are addressed, a local government must express them explicitly. That is, key stakeholders must discuss their expectations about fairness, performance, and finances and build these expectations into the tools used to manage the relationship. Discussions about mutual expectations and the contracts, reports, audits, and one-to-one contacts that reflect those expectations should address all three accountability goals.

Often, the acts of setting accountability expectations and monitoring how well these expectations are met are both accomplished independently by government and nonprofit staffs. Each contingent assesses accountability on its own and decides whether and how it wants to continue the working relationship with the other entity. This unilateral approach limits the ability of governments and nonprofits to learn from each other but may save staff time and effort. If the transaction is a one-time purchase and the government has no reason to develop trust in the vendor, then hierarchical accountability may be appropriate. Collaboration is neither sought nor needed.

Frequently, however, governments and their nonprofit partners are interested in exploring ways to address broad public problems together. If both entities want to refine their expectations of each other and develop more effective ways to serve the public, they may choose to work jointly in revising their accountability expectations. Trusting each other helps sustain effective partnerships.

Sidebar 12.5 Tips for Developing Mutual Accountability

- Determine whether both the local government and the nonprofit are willing to take responsibility for ensuring fairness, performance, and financial integrity.
- Work through the questions in Sidebar 12.6, "Defining Expectations for Mutual Accountability," below. Putting the answers into practice constitutes accountability.
- Recognize that, often, managing accountability is an appropriate role for staff members. Elected local government officials should focus on clarifying their reasons for funding nonprofits and understanding the gains they expect to achieve. The details of managing the accountability process can be delegated to staff.

Mutual accountability can improve public service as key stakeholders review a government–nonprofit relationship and decide whether and how to change it. By reviewing their accountability expectations together, the parties can refine and revise those expectations to fit new circumstances or challenges. This process can be time-consuming and difficult but will be worth the extra effort if government and nonprofit partners learn how to collaboratively address important public needs that neither party could meet alone. Mutual accountability can shift the focus from surveillance to service.

Sidebar 12.6 Defining Expectations for Mutual Accountability

This exercise offers up a process for defining mutual expectations about future interactions in a local government–nonprofit partnership. Discuss the following four questions as they relate to the mutual accountability dimensions of fairness, performance, and financial integrity:

Product. Who is expected to carry out which actions and for whose benefit?

- In relation to fairness
- In relation to performance
- In relation to financial responsibility

Alteration. Who can invoke or alter these expectations?

- In relation to fairness
- In relation to performance
- In relation to financial responsibility

Information. Who should provide what information to whom about how responsibilities are fulfilled?

- In relation to fairness
- In relation to performance
- In relation to financial responsibility

Review. Who is expected to use what information to make decisions about the future of the relationship?

- In relation to fairness
- In relation to performance
- In relation to financial responsibility

Strengthening Relationships between Local Governments and Nonprofits

Local government and nonprofit organizations frequently serve the same clients and address the same community problems and, accordingly, each can often support the other. Although the perspectives of the two sectors frequently differ, they are potentially complementary. The challenge for both entities is to find ways to work together that will permit each to fulfill its unique responsibilities while complementing the other's work.

However, the differences between the two sectors—in organizational structure and culture, for example—can create tension or obstacles. Local governments are subject to laws and regulations concerning financial management and other issues that do not apply to nonprofit/other private corporations. Also, local government officials must solicit and consider the viewpoints of many citizens and balance competing views from throughout their communities in making decisions. Many nonprofit organizations rely largely on volunteers who are, by definition, committed to and unified behind the specific causes their organizations address. Nonprofits can be attractive to local governments as a way to try out new or pilot programs because they can react and implement services quickly. Yet this same characteristic—the ability to move quickly—can be perceived by local governments as a liability because all necessary viewpoints may not be considered before action is taken.

Close collaboration can help strike the balance between nonprofits' focus on a particular set of issues and the need for local governments to consider a broad range of interests and concerns affecting the entire community. Collaboration between nonprofit organizations and local governments is most effective when

- the focus is on one issue,
- the goals are clearly defined,
- representatives of all the stakeholders are involved in the problem-solving process, and
- time and resources are available to support planning.

Because developing and maintaining true collaboration over the long haul is very difficult, both nonprofits and local governments should explore just how closely they truly want—and can afford—to work together. Both can benefit from a joint evaluation of their current connections and a joint decision about how connected they would like to be in relation to what activities and concerning which issues. Furthermore, each type of entity must identify, evaluate, and set limits on the resources it is willing to expend to work more closely with the other.

There is no one "right" relationship between governments and nonprofit organizations. Indeed, within a community the relationship may shift as different issues or events arise. Also, relationships will vary among communities. Each partnership must decide for itself how to achieve the most effective balance of independence and connection. The optimal degree and type of connection will depend on each community's situation.

Local governments and nonprofits trying to build effective partnerships face several obstacles, including (1) different perceptions about the same situations; (2) a lack of understanding of each other's work; (3) the various effects of the economic and cultural base of a community on the style of communication, information sharing, and decision making; and (4) an imbalance of power in relationships. Frequent and accurate communication can help to overcome these potential roadblocks.

Navigating the tensions between nonprofit organizations and local governments can be a tricky proposition for any community. Like any segment of the population, people in the public sector represent a broad diversity of expertise, professional skills, styles of interpersonal communication, and level of passion for their work. This diversity may be viewed either with suspicion and rigidity or with celebration and possibly amusement. By using their differences constructively, people who work in local governments and those in nonprofit organizations can draw on each other's strengths to help compensate for their weaknesses. Together they may be able to serve the public more effectively than either sector could alone.

Conclusion

Local governments may work with nonprofit organizations for a variety of reasons and in a variety of ways. One of the most common kinds of collaborations involves program funding, whether via grants, appropriations, purchase-of-service contracts, or other kinds of assistance. A government must observe legal restrictions when making funding choices but, in general, may fund a nonprofit to provide any services that fulfill a "public purpose." A local government might decide to partner with a nonprofit to take advantage of the nonprofit's expertise, flexibility, capacity, efficiency, or community connections. In designing funding processes, governments should consider their reasons for (1) funding

Sidebar 12.7 Tips for Strengthening Relationships

What Local Governments Can Do

- Minimize the mistrust, frustration, or misunderstanding that nonprofits experience during budget planning by sharing information about funding, including data about the following:
  - The amount of money available
  - Government priorities
  - The application and evaluation process
  - Criteria to be used in reviewing applications
  - The expectations for reporting and accountability
- Coordinate nonprofit organizations' funding applications and presentations to the local government with those to the United Way or other local private-sector grant makers to minimize duplication of effort and to improve communication among local funders.
- View problems or needs as belonging to the whole community, not just to a nonprofit.
  - Recognize that the clients of nonprofit organizations are community members deserving of resources.
  - Express appreciation for the missions of nonprofit organizations.
- Acknowledge nonprofit organizations as serious businesses.
  - Recognize the value that professional, paid employees can bring to an organization.
  - Support nonprofits in their efforts to strengthen internal professionalism.
  - Consider the impact that the payrolls and programs of nonprofit organizations can have on their local economies.

What Nonprofits Can Do

- Inform local governments about their progress throughout the year, not just during the funding application process.
- Pay attention to the workings of the whole community, not just the target client population.
- Be as financially responsible and accountable as possible, and present evidence of accountability to the public.
- Reinforce their organization's trustworthiness by presenting a reliable, professional image.
- Help the community learn how to deal with issues of concern to the nonprofit organization that are overwhelming, unattractive, or frightening to the general public.

What Nonprofits and Local Governments Can Do Together

- Share information, both during and outside of day-to-day working relationships.
  - Sponsor an annual forum that brings government and nonprofit staff, elected officials, and community volunteers together to focus on shared community concerns.
  - Undertake joint strategic planning efforts, especially around specific issues such as homelessness or juvenile delinquency.
  - Collaborate on community needs assessments.
  - Consider locating varied services that serve the same population at the same site.
  - Hold regular meetings among nonprofit organization directors, county department heads, and program staff of both organizations.
- Share resources.
  - Invite staff of the other type of organization to participate in training opportunities.
  - Offer to share expertise by providing training to or by meeting with staff of the other type of organization.
  - Invite program staff from other organizations to meet in your facility.
  - Make it possible for staff to serve on community boards, committees, and task forces.
  - Make second-hand furniture or equipment available for others to use.
- Jointly develop clear, written guidelines about mutual expectations and work to be accomplished together.
- Recognize that each organization can be the other's best support for understanding and handling the stresses associated with working in the public sector. After all, local governments and nonprofits are dealing with similar challenges.

nonprofits and (2) having a formal funding process in place and should establish/implement plans for (a) identifying community needs they can help to address, (b) obtaining funding proposals, and (c) reviewing and making decisions on those proposals. Careful deliberation about these issues takes effort but can help create effective funding procedures.

When governments and nonprofits expect to have an ongoing relationship, they should use a mutual accountability model and work together to craft expectations about how the project or program will be funded, monitored, and evaluated. No single practice, process, or documentation system can, in isolation, adequately ensure good government–nonprofit relationships. Having good practices, processes, and clear documents certainly is important, but it is not sufficient for creating and maintaining effective working relationships. Straightforward communication and mutual trust are also necessary ingredients.

The different perspectives, positions, and cultures of the government and nonprofit sectors can lead to tension and strained relationships. Yet governments and nonprofits are both working to improve their communities and often face similar challenges in doing so. Learning to work together effectively can help both organizations better serve their communities.

Additional Resources

Much of the information in this chapter was taken from the following publications, most of which are available online through the "Publications" link on the School of Government's Public Intersection Project page at www.publicintersection.unc.edu. The seven articles listed here were originally published in *Popular Government*, a publication of the School of Government. They can all be downloaded, free of charge, at http://shopping.netsuite.com/s.nl?c=433425&sc=7&category=-107&search=popular%20government (simply scroll through the listed items and select the issue desired).

Henderson, Margaret, Lydian Altman, Suzanne Julian, Gordon P. Whitaker, and Eileen R. Youens. *Working with Nonprofit Organizations.* Chapel Hill: UNC School of Government, 2010 (part of the Local Government Board Builders Series). http://shopping.netsuite.com/s.nl/c.433425/it.A/id.4225/.f.

Altman-Sauer, Lydian, Margaret Henderson, and Gordon Whitaker. "Building Community Capacity to Meet Public Needs." *Popular Government* 70 (Winter 2005): 28–36.

_____. "Strengthening Relationships between Local Governments and Nonprofits." *Popular Government* 66 (Winter 2001): 33–39.

Bluestein, Frayda S., and Anita R. Brown-Graham. "Local Government Contracts with Nonprofit Organizations: Questions and Answers." *Popular Government* 67 (Fall 2001): 32–44.

Henderson, Margaret, Lydian Altman-Sauer, and Gordon Whitaker. "Deciding to Fund Nonprofits: Key Questions." *Popular Government* 67 (Summer 2002): 33–39.

Henderson, Margaret, Gordon P. Whitaker, and Lydian Altman-Sauer. "Establishing Mutual Accountability in Nonprofit–Government Relationships." *Popular Government* 69 (Fall 2003): 18–29.

Whitaker, Gordon P., and Rosalind Day. "How Local Governments Work with Nonprofit Organizations in North Carolina." *Popular Government* 66 (Winter 2001): 25–32.

Gulati-Partee, Gita. "A Primer on Nonprofit Organizations." *Popular Government* 66 (Summer 2001): 31–36.

About the Authors

Margaret Henderson is a School of Government faculty member and Tom Kelley is a faculty member at the UNC School of Law. This revised chapter, originally written by Gordon P. Whitaker and James C. Drennan, includes work that was originally published elsewhere and which is listed at the end of the chapter. The authors would like to thank School of Government faculty members Kara A. Millonzi and Christopher B. McLaughlin, whose contributions to this chapter made its updating possible.

Part 3

Administration

Chapter 13

Public Employment Law

Diane M. Juffras

The municipal and county employment relationship in North Carolina is a function of the North Carolina General Statutes, federal statutes, the United States Constitution, the North Carolina Constitution, decisions of state and federal courts, and the personnel ordinances and policies adopted by the cities and counties themselves. Public personnel administration encompasses everything concerned with the human resources of city and county government, including classification of positions, recruitment and selection of employees, performance evaluation, pay-and-benefits administration, and discipline. The General Assembly has delegated broad authority for human resources management to cities and counties, essentially reflecting the view that providing a framework within which cities and counties may determine their individual employment policies is better than prescribing numerous specific requirements. This chapter provides an overview of the law governing the relationship between North Carolina cities and counties and their employees.

The Employment-At-Will Rule

When a North Carolina employer hires someone, the legal presumption that governs the working relationship is that the employment is "at will." That is, the employment is at the will of either party, and the employer is free to dismiss the employee at any time without explanation or legal penalty.[1] The employment-at-will presumption applies to both public- and private-sector employment.

For most city and county employees, there is a presumption of employment at will unless the employee proves otherwise. For some city and county employees, however, their status as at-will employees is explicitly stated in the General Statutes (hereinafter G.S.). For example, G.S. 160A-147(a) provides that the city manager serves at the pleasure of the city council, while G.S. 153A-81 provides that the county manager serves at the pleasure of the board of county commissioners. Similarly, G.S. 153A-103(2) provides that sheriff's deputies "serve at the pleasure of the appointing officer."

The existence of the employment-at-will rule does not mean that cities and counties may always discharge employees without worrying about possible legal challenges. In fact, three broad categories of exceptions to the employment-at-will rule have developed: statutory exceptions, common law exceptions, and property right exceptions.

Statutory exceptions represent legislative restrictions, by both Congress and the General Assembly, of an employer's right to discharge employees. Federal statutes that modify the employment-at-will rule include the Civil Rights Act of 1964,[2] which prohibits discharge for discriminatory reasons; the Age Discrimination in Employment Act (ADEA),[3] which prohibits discharge solely on the basis of age; the Americans with Disabilities Act of 1990 (ADA),[4] which bars dismissal of otherwise qualified employees if reasonable accommodation of their disabilities can be made; the Genetic Information Nondiscrimination Act of 2008 (GINA),[5] which prohibits discharge on the basis of an employee's genetic information or on the medical history of an employee's family member; and the Uniformed Services Employment and Reemployment Rights Act (USERRA),[6] which prohibits dismissal on the basis of an employee's military obligations. Similarly, the North Carolina General Statutes modify the employment-at-will rule in several ways.[7]

In addition to statutory exceptions, judicially created exceptions to the employment-at-will rule restrict an employer's right to fire employees. These common law exceptions take the form of breach of contract or the tort of wrongful discharge. They arise when the court finds either that the parties themselves, through their actions, have created a contractual exception to the employment-at-will rule or that the employer's motive in dismissing an employee violates some tenet of public policy.

For example, in *Coman v. Thomas Manufacturing Co.*,[8] the North Carolina Supreme Court heard a claim in which an employee alleged that he had been fired for refusing to drive his truck longer than the time allowed under United States Department of Transportation regulations and for refusing to falsify the logs required to be maintained by the department to ensure compliance with the law. The court held that the employee had stated a cause of action for wrongful discharge, stating "[W]hile there may be a right to terminate a contract at will for no reason, or for an arbitrary or irrational reason, there can be no right to terminate such a contract for an unlawful reason or purpose that contravenes public policy."[9] Other circumstances under which the courts have recognized the tort of wrongful discharge in violation of public policy include terminations based on a deputy sheriff's reporting of perjury and falsification of

---

1. The general statement of the employment-at-will rule in North Carolina is found in *Soles v. City of Raleigh Civil Service Commission*, 345 N.C. 443, 446 (1997); *Harris v. Duke Power Co.*, 319 N.C. 627, 629 (1987); and *Presnell v. Pell*, 298 N.C. 715, 723–24 (1979).
2. Title VII of the act covers discrimination in employment. *See generally* 42 U.S.C. §§ 2000 *et seq.*
3. *See generally* 29 U.S.C. §§ 621 *et seq.*
4. *See generally* 42 U.S.C. §§ 12101 *et seq.*
5. *See generally* 42 U.S.C. §§ 2000ff *et seq.*
6. *See generally* 38 U.S.C. §§ 4301 *et seq.*
7. For example, Article 21 of N.C. Gen. Stat. (hereinafter G.S.) Chapter 95 prohibits dismissal of an employee because the employee has filed or intends to file a complaint or otherwise participates in a proceeding under the Workers' Compensation Act, the Occupational Safety and Health Act, the Wage and Hour Act, or the Mine Safety and Health Act.
8. 325 N.C. 172 (1989).
9. *Id.* at 176 (quoting Sides v. Duke Univ., 74 N.C. App. 331, 342 (1985)).

evidence by another deputy,[10] employees' complaints that their pay was below the state's minimum wage,[11] truthful testimony at an unemployment compensation hearing,[12] an employee's refusal to give in to sexual advances of his or her supervisor,[13] an employee's report of possible patient abuse to the State Bureau of Investigation and State Department of Human Resources,[14] and a nurse's compliance with the state statutes and administrative code provisions regulating the practice of nursing.[15]

A third source of exceptions to the employment-at-will rule is found only in public-sector employment: the vesting of a "property right" to employment. The Fourteenth Amendment's guarantee that no person may be deprived of property without due process has been construed to extend to a property interest in employment.[16] A property interest arises when a public employee can demonstrate a reasonable expectation of continued employment because the employer has established a binding policy that dismissal will occur only for stated reasons. For example, county employees subject to the State Human Resources Act (SHRA) may be fired only for "just cause" (G.S. 126-35).

The effect of this language is to create a property right in employment that may be taken away from the employee only after the constitutional requirements of substantive and procedural due process have been met.[17] Whether a city or county's personnel policies confer a property right in employment depends not only on the wording of the policies but also on the form in which those policies were adopted by the city council or board of county commissioners. In *Pittman v. Wilson County*,[18] the court held that personnel policies adopted by resolution, not by ordinance, by the Board of County Commissioners of Wilson County were not sufficient to vest county employees with a property right. Instead the court held that because the restrictions were set forth only in a resolution, not in an ordinance or a statute, they were not binding. Stated the court:

> [T]he resolution is a part of a manual that describes itself as merely a "WELCOME TO ALL EMPLOYEES OF WILSON COUNTY." . . . The language simply is not typical of that used in an ordinance or statute having the effect of law. Moreover, the subject matter of the personnel resolution is administrative in nature. It supplies internal guidelines to County officials for the administration of the County's employment positions, including the disciplining and discharge of employees.[19]

Having found no basis for the plaintiff's claim that she was other than an at-will employee, the court concluded that she was not entitled to due process in the termination of her employment.

In *Kurtzman v. Applied Analytical Industries, Inc.*,[20] the North Carolina Supreme Court addressed the question of whether an employer's assurances of continued employment made as part of the recruiting process could create an exception to the employment-at-will rule. In the *Kurtzman* case, the plaintiff was recruited to move from Rhode Island to North Carolina to accept a new position with the defendant employer. During negotiations, the plaintiff inquired into the security of his proposed position with the employer and was told: "If you do your job, you'll have a job;" "This is a long-term growth opportunity for you;" "This is a secure position;" and "We're offering you a career position." He took the job but was fired six months later.

The plaintiff argued that the combination of the additional consideration of moving his residence and the defendant's specific assurances of continued employment removed the employment relationship from the traditional at-will presumption and created an employment contract under which he could not be terminated absent cause. The question

10. Hill v. Meford, 357 N.C. 650 (2003).
11. Amos v. Oakdale Knitting Co., 331 N.C. 348 (1992).
12. Williams v. Hillhaven Corp., 91 N.C. App. 35 (1988).
13. Harrison v. Edison Bros. Apparel Stores, 924 F.2d 530 (4th Cir. 1991).
14. Lenzer v. Flaherty, 106 N.C. App. 496 (1992).
15. Deerman v. Beverly Cal. Corp., 135 N.C. App. 1 (1999).
16. *See, e.g.*, Cleveland Bd. of Educ. v. Loudermill, 470 U.S. 532, 541–42 (1985).
17. Faulkner v. N.C. Dep't of Corr., 428 F. Supp. 100 (W.D.N.C. 1977).
18. 839 F.2d 225 (4th Cir. 1988).
19. *Id.* at 229.
20. 347 N.C. 329 (1997).

of first impression for the court was whether it should recognize a "moving residence" exception to the general rule of employment at will. The North Carolina Supreme Court answered in the negative and rejected the plaintiff's claim, stating:

> The employment-at-will doctrine has prevailed in this state for a century. . . . The narrow exceptions to it have been grounded in considerations of public policy designed either to prohibit status-based discrimination or to insure the integrity of the judicial process or the enforcement of the law. The facts here do not present policy concerns of this nature. Rather, they are representative of negotiations and circumstances characteristically associated with traditional at-will employment situations. . . .
>
> The society to which the employment-at-will doctrine currently applies is a highly mobile one in which relocation to accept new employment is common. To remove an employment relationship from the at-will presumption upon an employee's change of residence, coupled with vague assurances of continued employment, would substantially erode the rule and bring considerable instability to an otherwise largely clear area of the law. . . . We thus hold that plaintiff-employee's change of residence in the wake of defendant-employer's statements here does not constitute additional consideration making what is otherwise an at-will employment relationship one that can be terminated by the employer only for cause.[21]

The employment-at-will rule in North Carolina continues to evolve as the courts hear claims from employees asserting that the rule does not apply to them. Continued monitoring of this developing area of the law is essential for those who advise cities and counties on employment matters.

Hiring and Firing Authority in North Carolina Cities

Mayor–Council Form of Government

G.S. 160A-155 states that the council in mayor–council cities shall appoint, suspend, and remove the heads of all city departments and all other city employees. However, the council may delegate to any administrative official or department head the power to appoint, suspend, and remove city employees assigned to his or her department. The mayor has no hiring or firing authority. For cities with a population of 5,000 or more, neither the mayor nor any member of the council may serve as the head of any city department, even on an acting or interim basis (G.S. 160A-158).

Council–Manager Form of Government

G.S. 160A-147 authorizes a city council to appoint a city manager to serve at its pleasure. Irrespective of the size of the city, neither the mayor nor any member of the council may serve as the manager, on a permanent or temporary basis (G.S. 160A-151).[22] For cities with a city manager, the General Statutes delegate the authority to hire employees to the manager. G.S. 160A-148(1) provides that the city manager shall appoint, suspend, and remove all city officers and employees who "are not elected by the people, and whose appointment or removal is not otherwise provided for by law" in accordance with such personnel rules as the council may adopt. Examples of city employees whose appointments are otherwise provided for by law include the city attorney and, in some jurisdictions, the city clerk. The city council appoints the city attorney, who serves at its pleasure (G.S. 160A-173). The General Statutes direct cities to appoint a city clerk but fail to specify who is to appoint the clerk (G.S. 160A-171). Instead, the hiring and firing authority over the city clerk is usually found in the city charter, with some charters providing that the clerk serves at the pleasure of the council and others granting hiring and firing authority to the manager.

21. *Id.* at 333–34, 334, respectively (citations omitted).

22. When a vacancy is created in the office of the city manager, the council is authorized to "designate a qualified person to exercise the powers and perform the duties of manager until the vacancy is filled" (G.S. 160A-150).

Hiring and Firing Authority in North Carolina Counties

G.S. 153A-87 provides that in counties not having a county manager, the board of commissioners shall appoint, suspend, and remove all county officers, employees, and agents except those who are elected by the people or whose appointment is otherwise provided for by law. Counties may choose to adopt the manager plan (and all have), which allows them to hire a county manager to serve at the pleasure of the board of commissioners. Although a city council member may not serve as city manager, the General Statutes permit a member of the board of commissioners to serve as county manager (G.S. 153A-81(2)).

If a manager plan is adopted, the manager is vested with hiring authority. However, the manager's hiring power is subject to the approval of the board of commissioners unless the board passes a resolution permitting the manager to act without first securing the board's approval (G.S. 153A-82(1)).

Dismissal authority is also vested in the county manager but without the requirement that the dismissal action be ratified by the board. There are certain county officers whose appointment and dismissal are required by law to be made by the board of commissioners, even in counties in which the county manager plan has been adopted. The clerk of the board (G.S. 153A-111) and the county attorney (G.S. 153A-114) are appointed by the board and serve at its pleasure. The tax collector is a board appointee who serves for a term determined by the board (G.S. 105-349(a)). The tax collector may be removed only for good cause after written notice and an opportunity for a hearing at a public session, except that no hearing is required if the tax collector is removed for failing to deliver tax receipts properly. The General Statutes also provide for board appointment of deputy tax collectors for specified terms (G.S. 105-349(f)) but do not explicitly state how they are to be removed. Finally, the county assessor is a board appointee who serves a term of not less than two nor more than four years. The assessor may be removed only for good cause after written notice and an opportunity for a hearing at a public session (G.S. 105-294(a)). The county assessor may in turn hire listers, appraisers, and clerical assistants (G.S. 105-296(b)).

Unlike a city council and manager, a board of county commissioners and its manager do not have direct authority over all those who work for the county. The General Statutes have established multiple hiring authorities within county government. Although many positions are under the control of the board of commissioners and the county manager, others are under the control of elected officials; still others are under the control of various county boards subject to the State Human Resources Act (SHRA). This makes human resources administration at the county level more difficult than at the city level.

Officers Elected by the People

Article VII, Section 2, of the North Carolina Constitution provides that each county shall have a sheriff elected by the people for a four-year term, subject to removal for cause as provided by law. G.S. 153A-103(1) states that each sheriff has the exclusive right to hire, discharge, and supervise the employees in the sheriff's office[23] except that the board of commissioners must approve the appointment of a sheriff's relative or of a person convicted of a crime involving moral turpitude. Each sheriff is entitled to at least two deputies who serve at the pleasure of the sheriff.

The register of deeds is also an elected officer, with a four-year term (G.S. 153A-103(2)). As is the case with the sheriff, each register of deeds has the exclusive right to hire, discharge, and supervise the employees in the register of deeds' office, except that the board of commissioners must approve the appointment of a relative of the register of deeds or of a person convicted of a crime involving moral turpitude (G.S. 153A-103(1)). Each register of deeds is entitled to at least two deputies, provided that the register of deeds justifies to the board the necessity of the second deputy. Deputies serve at the pleasure of the register of deeds (G.S. 153A-103(2)).

23. Peele v. Provident Mut. Life Ins. Co., 90 N.C. App. 447 (1988).

Employees Whose Appointments Are Made through or Are Subject to Boards

Requirements of Boards

Certain positions are filled either by designated boards or by the manager (where the manager plan exists) in accordance with the requirements established by the board of commissioners.

Public library employees are appointed either directly by the board of commissioners or, where the commissioners have appointed a library board of trustees and delegated hiring authority to it, through the library board. The board, not to exceed twelve members, is appointed by the board of commissioners for a term set by the county. Library trustees may be removed only for incapacity, unfitness, misconduct, or neglect of duty (G.S. 153A-265). If the commissioners have granted hiring authority to the board, the trustees may appoint a chief librarian or a director of library services. The trustees appoint other library employees upon the advice of the chief librarian or the director of library services (G.S. 153A-266(4)). G.S. 153A-267 states that the employees of a county library system are, for all purposes, employees of the county.

County boards of elections are composed of three members appointed by the State Board of Elections for two-year terms. The board's clerk, assistant clerks, and other employees, including precinct transfer assistants, are appointed and dismissed by the county board of elections (G.S. 163-33(10)). The county director of elections is appointed and dismissed by the Executive Director of the State Board of Elections, upon recommendation by the county board of elections (G.S. 163-35(a)).

Employees Subject to the State Human Resources Act

The State Human Resources Act (G.S. Chapter 126) (SHRA) governs recruitment, selection, and dismissal of four county departments: health, social services, mental health, and emergency management (G.S. 126-5(a)(2)). These departments receive federal funds that require the use of certain recruitment and selection and discipline and discharge procedures as a condition for their receipt. The SHRA incorporates these federal requirements. Rather than requiring each county to adopt a personnel policy consistent with these requirements, the General Assembly has made county health, social services, mental health, and emergency management employees subject to the State Human Resources Act. Local government employees covered by the State Human Resources Act may be dismissed only "for just cause" (G.S. 126-35) and have a property interest in their employment.

Thus, county health department employees are subject to the SHRA. A county board of health is composed of eleven members appointed by the board of commissioners to serve three-year terms (G.S. 130A-35). A district health department including more than one county may be formed instead of county health departments, upon agreement of the county boards of commissioners and local boards of health having jurisdiction over each of the counties involved (G.S. 130A-36). The board of health, in turn, appoints the local health director after consultation with the board(s) of commissioners having jurisdiction over the area served by the health department, subject to the approval of the State Health Director (G.S. 130A-40). The local health director may be dismissed only in accordance with the due process requirements of the SHRA.[24] Similarly, health department employees are appointed and dismissed by the local health director in accordance with the act (G.S. 130A-41(b); G.S. 126-5(a)).

Social services department employees are also SHRA employees. The county board of social services is composed of three or five members, appointed for three-year terms (G.S. 108A-1 through G.S. 108A-5). The county director of social services is appointed and dismissed by the board in accordance with the SHRA (G.S. 108A-9). Social service employees are appointed and dismissed by the county director of social services, also in accordance with the act[25] (G.S. 108A-14(2)).

Employees of a mental health, developmental disabilities, and substance abuse authority constitute the third category of SHRA employees at the county level. An area authority is a local political subdivision of the state except that a single-county area authority is considered a department of the county in which it is located for purposes of G.S. Chapter 159 ("Local Government Finance," G.S. 122C-116). The governing unit of the area authority is the area board, composed of

24. *See* Opinion of Attorney General to Michael S. Kennedy, Esq., 55 Op. N.C. Att'y Gen. 113 (1986).

25. *In re* Brunswick Cnty., 81 N.C. App. 391 (1986) (director has exclusive power to hire and fire department personnel).

eleven to twenty-five members. The area board for a multi-authority area consisting of eight or more counties may have up to thirty members. For a single-county area authority, the area board is appointed by the board of county commissioners. For a multi-county area authority, the board of commissioners for each county making up the multi-county authority appoints one board member. The county-appointed board members appoint the remaining board members, although the governing boards of county commissioners may adopt other methods of selection. (G.S. 122C-118.1(a)). The director of the area mental health, developmental disabilities, and substance abuse authority is appointed by the area board, subject to the approval of the board(s) of commissioners and serves at the pleasure of the area board. The area director is not covered by the SHRA (G.S. 122C-117(a)(7); G.S. 122C-121). Employees of the area authority are appointed and dismissed by the area director in accordance with the SHRA (G.S. 122C-121(c)(1); G.S. 122C-154; G.S. 126-5(a)(2)). Like employees of county health and social services departments, area authority employees have property rights in their employment.

Emergency management employees are the fourth category of county employees subject to the SHRA. G.S. 166A-7(a) states that the governing body of each county is responsible for emergency management within the county and is authorized to establish and maintain an emergency management agency. The governing body of each county that establishes an emergency management agency is to appoint a coordinator, who will have a direct responsibility for the organization, administration, and operation of the county program and will be subject to the direction and the guidance of such governing body (G.S. 166A-7(a)(2)). Although there is no General Statutes provision on the dismissal of the coordinator, dismissal must presumably be made in accordance with the SHRA. The General Statutes do not specify who has the appointing authority over emergency management employees. Given the absence of a provision granting hiring authority to any other person or body, the county manager presumably has the hiring authority. Employees of the emergency management agency are appointed and dismissed in accordance with the personnel act (G.S. 126-5(a))—unlike all of the other county employees over whom the county manager has hiring and firing authority.

"Substantially Equivalent" Personnel Systems

G.S. 126-11 permits the State Human Resources Commission to exempt all county State Human Resources Act (SHRA) employees from portions of the State Human Resources System when the commission finds that the county has a substantially equivalent personnel system for all county employees. The commission may approve as "substantially equivalent" such portions of a local personnel ordinance as the position classification plan, the county's selection procedures, the salary administration plan, and the grievance and dismissal procedures. A relatively small number of counties and area authorities have had all or part of their personnel systems approved as "substantially equivalent."

Consolidated Human Services Agencies

G.S. 153A-77 authorizes each county to consolidate its health, social services, mental health, developmental disabilities, and substance abuse agencies into one county department of human services.[26] A consolidated human services agency is managed by a single human services director, who is appointed and supervised by the county manager with the advice and consent of a human services board appointed by the county commissioners.[27] The human services director then appoints all human services agency employees subject to the approval of the county manager.[28] When a county consolidates its human services agencies pursuant to G.S. 153-77, employees of the consolidated agency lose the protections of the State Human Resources Act (SHRA) and become subject to county personnel policies.[29] To the extent that federal funds administered by consolidated human services agencies require the use of so-called competitive

26. As a practical matter, the current structure of mental health service delivery through multi-county area authorities will preclude the consolidation of mental health services into a single-county consolidated human services agency, except in Mecklenburg County, where mental health was consolidated into a single agency with health and social services in the past. *See* G.S. 153A-76(6) and -77(c)(1a).

27. *See* G.S. 153A-77(b)(1), (e).

28. *See* G.S. 153A-77(e)(1).

29. *See* G.S. 153A-77(d).

recruitment and selection procedures, the board of commissioners will have to adopt such policies for human services employees, if not for all county employees.

Organization of the Human Resources Function

Cities take the authority to determine their organization and establish personnel policies from G.S. Chapter 160A, Article 7. Counties take their authority from G.S. Chapter 153A, Article 5. G.S. 160A-162 authorizes a city council to create, change, abolish, and consolidate city offices and departments and to determine the most efficient organization for the city, with only three limitations. G.S. 153A-76 authorizes boards of county commissioners to do the same for county government, again with three limitations. First, neither the council nor the board may abolish any office or agency established and required by law. For example, a council may not abolish the office of city attorney; G.S. 160A-173 requires a city to have one. Similarly, a board may not abolish the office of county attorney, as G.S. 153A-114 requires a county to have one. Second, neither the council nor the board may combine offices when forbidden by law. For example, G.S. 160A-151 provides that neither the mayor nor any member of the council may serve as the city manager, even on a temporary basis. Third, neither the council nor the board may discontinue or assign elsewhere any functions assigned by law to a particular office. For example, G.S. 160A-171 establishes the office of the city clerk and G.S. 153A-111 establishes the office of the county clerk, and certain duties in both cities and counties may be performed only by the clerk or a deputy clerk. In addition, G.S. 153A-76 prohibits the board from changing the composition or manner of selection of a local board of education, board of health, board of social services, board of elections, or board of alcoholic beverage control.

Personnel Officers in Cities

In mayor–council cities the council must appoint or designate a personnel officer or confer human resources duties on some city administrative officer. The personnel officer is responsible for administering the position classification and pay plan in accordance with general policies and directives adopted by the council (G.S. 160A-162(a)). In both cities and counties, when there is a manager, he or she is responsible for the personnel or human resources functions unless a human resources director has been appointed.

Position Classification

G.S. 160A-162 and G.S. 153A-25, respectively, provide that the city council and board of county commissioners may fix qualifications for any appointive office. A governing board's most important use of this authority is to adopt a position classification plan.

A position classification plan is one of the basic tools of human resource management. By adopting such a plan, the governing board determines the duties and responsibilities of each position in advance and sets the minimum qualifications as to education, training, and experience that will be required of each employee and each applicant for employment. Either the manager, the human resources director and staff, or an outside consultant generally prepares the classification plan for presentation to the board. Plan preparation involves identifying the duties and responsibilities of each position and grouping jobs into classes similar enough in duties and responsibilities that the same job title, the same minimum qualifications, and the same pay range can apply to all positions in that class. An accurate description of duties and responsibilities and minimum qualifications can serve as a basis for or assist in all aspects of city or county administration, including planning, organizing, budgeting, selecting, training, paying, promoting, transferring, demoting, and discharging employees.

Compensation: Wages

In addition to position management, the city council and board of county commissioners have the responsibility to make compensation determinations for all city employees and for all county employees. The council and board may fix the compensation and allowances of the chairperson of their respective boards and of other board members (and the council may fix the compensation of the mayor) by including their compensation and allowances in the annual budget ordinance when it is adopted. If the chair of the board of county commissioners or another board member undertakes the duties of county manager full time, his or her salary or allowances may be adjusted during the fiscal year. Otherwise, the compensation of board members may not be changed until the next budget is adopted. The same is true of the expense allowances of board members (G.S. 160A-64(a); G.S. 153A-92).

Both the city council and the board of county commissioners control compensation by adopting position classification plans and pay plans, adopting personnel rules governing the administration of the pay plan, adopting the budget that appropriates funds to the several departments and establishes expense allowances, and reviewing the reports of the manager and the city's independent auditor.

A pay plan is simply a list of job titles and a schedule of the amount of money to be paid to whomever performs the prescribed duties of each position during a fixed period. The plan establishes pay rates for positions, not persons. Many pay plans are step-based: a salary range is established for each position, and within the minimum and maximum salaries of the range there are specific "steps" pegged to specific salaries or rates. Employees are assigned to a specific step within the range for their position based on some combination of experience, performance, and longevity.

Only the city council and the board of county commissioners have the authority to adopt pay plans. In *Newber v. City of Wilmington*,[30] the North Carolina Court of Appeals interpreted the pay provisions of the statutes to bar the payment of stand-by and on-call time to a police officer when the Wilmington City Council had not previously authorized the payment. Stated the court, "G.S. 160A-148(1) prohibits the city manager from unilateral adoption of a policy establishing the funding for stand-by and on-call duty for any city department. The manager's role is limited to recommending position classification and pay plans to the city council for their ultimate approval."[31]

Restrictions on a County Board's Compensation Authority

There are certain restrictions on a board of county commissioners' authority to set salaries:

- Neither the register of deeds' nor the sheriff's compensation may be reduced during a term of office without the officeholder's approval or unless ordered by the Local Government Commission (G.S. 153A-92). Commissioners must give notice of intent to reduce the compensation for the next term of either office no later than fourteen days before the last day for filing as a candidate for that office. Further, the sheriff or register of deeds must approve any reduction in the salaries of employees assigned to his or her office, unless the board has made a general reduction of all county salaries subject to its control. If the board wants to reduce salaries of one or more employees of the sheriff or register of deeds and the elected officer will not agree, the board may refer the matter to the senior regular resident superior court judge for binding arbitration.
- The salaries paid to county health, social services, mental health, and emergency management agency employees must conform to the pay plan approved for those departments by the State Human Resources Commission (G.S. 126-9(b)).
- All agricultural extension personnel salaries are set jointly by the North Carolina Agricultural Extension Service and the board of county commissioners under a "Memorandum of Understanding"—a contract—entered into by the extension service and the board.

State Human Resources Commission policies allow counties considerable discretion in developing local salary schedules applicable to health, mental health, social services, and emergency management employees in order to conform

30. 83 N.C. App. 327 (1986).
31. *Id.* at 330 (citation to statute omitted).

to local ability to pay and fiscal policy. With the State Human Resources Commission's approval, counties may add to or reduce the number of salary steps in the state's salary schedule and may vary the percentage change between steps. The pay plan adopted by the county for these employees is subject to the commission's approval, and the commission may require a county to provide data and information to justify any deviation from the standard state salary ranges. A county's failure to adhere to the State Human Resources Act (SHRA)'s provisions for compensating county SHRA employees not only makes the county ineligible for certain state and federal funds but also results in an unauthorized expenditure of public money.

Despite these restrictions, the board of county commissioners has an important role in determining the salaries of county SHRA employees. For example, G.S. 108A-13, which authorizes the board of social services to set the social services director's salary, requires that board to obtain the approval of the board of commissioners for the salary paid. Similarly, a local health department has no authority to raise the salaries of health department employees without the board of commissioners' approval, since all county expenditures must be made in accordance with the provisions of the Local Government Budget and Fiscal Control Act (G.S. Ch. 159, Art. 3).

Salary Increases and Longevity Pay

The city council and board of county commissioners may provide for salary increases for all employees or for a class of employees as part of the annual budget. Many local governments in North Carolina have implemented pay systems that have a merit pay component. Others use across-the-board systems that reward all employees equally, regardless of individual performance.

Another widespread practice in North Carolina cities and counties is the use of longevity pay, under which employees receive additional pay increases on the basis of number of years of service. Longevity pay plans are popular among long-term employees, who stress several advantages of such plans:

1. They reward employees who have given the best years of their lives to local government.
2. They help to compensate for the low salaries at which many long-term employees were originally hired.
3. They provide some relief to long-term employees who are "frozen" at the top of their salary range.
4. They reduce turnover and training costs.
5. They do not cost much money.

Critics of longevity pay plans assert in response that the plans are not effective in recruiting desirable or better employees, retaining employees during the early years when turnover is higher, or retaining truly outstanding employees. They charge that the plans encourage marginal employees to stay when they should move on to other jobs.

Minimum Wage and Overtime Requirements

In designing their compensation plans, cities and counties must be aware of the minimum wage and overtime requirements of the federal Fair Labor Standards Act (FLSA).[32] The FLSA is administered and enforced by the United States Department of Labor.

The critical inquiry under the FLSA is whether a given position is *exempt* or *nonexempt* from the minimum wage and overtime requirements of the law. All local government positions are *nonexempt* positions unless (1) the employee is paid a minimum of $455 per week on a salaried basis and (2) the position's duties satisfy the FLSA's executive, administrative, or professional duties test. The FLSA provides that salaried executive, administrative, and professional employees are exempt from its minimum wage and overtime provisions.[33]

---

32. 29 U.S.C. §§ 201–219.

33. *Id.* § 213. Title 29, Section 541.602(a), of the Code of Federal Regulations (C.F.R.) provides that employees are considered paid on a salary basis if they regularly receive each pay period a predetermined amount not subject to reduction because of variations in the quality or the quantity of work performed. Employers may not make deductions from a salaried employee's paycheck without jeopardizing the employee's salaried status unless explicitly authorized by Title 29, Sections 541.602(b) and 541.710, of the C.F.R.

The typical nonexempt employee is entitled to overtime compensation at the rate of one and one-half hours for every hour worked over forty hours in a seven-day workweek. A partial exemption from the FLSA requirements is found at Section 207(k) of the statute, which permits cities and counties to pay overtime for law enforcement personnel[34] only for hours in excess of 171 in a twenty-eight-day cycle and for firefighters[35] only for hours in excess of 212 in a twenty-eight-day cycle. The FLSA also provides a complete overtime exemption for any employee of a local government engaged in law enforcement or fire protection if that local government entity has fewer than five employees during the workweek in either capacity.[36]

For all employees, overtime compensation may be in the form of wages or compensatory time off. Section 207(o) of the FLSA permits government employers to give compensatory time off rather than monetary overtime pay at a rate of not less than one and one-half hours for each hour of employment for which overtime would be required. However, such an arrangement is permitted only when the employees have been given prior notice that the city's or county's policy is to give compensatory time in lieu of wages and have indicated acceptance of that policy.

Equal Pay

All city and county employees, whether exempt or nonexempt, are covered by a 1963 amendment to the FLSA known as the Equal Pay Act.[37] The act states that an employer may not pay an employee of one gender less than it pays an employee of the opposite gender for work that is performed under similar working conditions and that requires equal skill, effort, and responsibility. To be considered equal work under the act, jobs need not be identical, only substantially equal.[38] The Equal Employment Opportunity Commission (EEOC), which has enforcement responsibility for the act, states in its regulations that the question of "what constitutes equal skill, equal effort, or equal responsibility cannot be precisely defined."[39] Each element constitutes a separate requirement, each of which must be met for the equal pay standard to apply. An employer must show substantial differences, not minor ones, to justify pay differences.

Compensation: Benefits

North Carolina cities and counties have almost complete discretion in choosing what type of benefits to offer to employees. The General Statutes permit them to provide benefits to all employees *or* to any *class* of employees and their dependents (G.S. 160A-162(b); 153A-92(d)). Premiums for hospital, medical, or dental insurance may be paid by the employer, the employee, or both. If a government employer pays the entire premium, G.S. 58-58-135 requires that all eligible employees (except those who are deemed unsatisfactory to the insurer) be insured. Similarly, group accident insurance may be provided by the local government employer, and premiums may be paid by the employer, the employees, or both. If any part of the premium is paid by employees, the covered group must be structured on an actuarially sound basis (G.S. 58-51-80).

Local Governmental Employees' Retirement System

A major benefit available to city and county employees is the Local Governmental Employees' Retirement System (LGERS), established at G.S. Chapter 128, Article 3. G.S. 128-23 permits individual cities and counties to elect to have their employees become eligible to participate in the retirement system if a majority of employees vote to do so. The term *employee* is defined at G.S. 128-21(10), and in the implementing regulations, to include all officers and employees in a

34. Defined at 29 C.F.R. § 553.11.
35. Defined at 29 C.F.R. § 553.210.
36. U.S.C. § 213(b)(20). This provision is explained in the Department of Labor regulations at 29 C.F.R. § 553.200.
37. 29 U.S.C. § 206.
38. Corning Glass Works v. Brennan, 417 U.S. 188 (1974); *see also* 29 C.F.R. § 1620.13(a).
39. C.F.R. § 1620.14(a).

regular position that requires not less than 1,000 hours of service per year.[40] The employer must file an application for participation in the retirement system with the LGERS Board of Trustees and agree to meet the terms of membership. A resolution approved by the board of trustees is then passed by the city council or board of county commissioners.

An employee may retire at age sixty with five years of creditable service or at any age with thirty years of creditable service. A firefighter may retire at age fifty-five with five years of creditable service (G.S. 128-27(a)(1)). Law enforcement officers may retire at age fifty with fifteen years of creditable service or at age fifty-five with five years of creditable service (G.S. 128-27(a)(5)).

Upon retirement, members receive a service retirement allowance computed as follows: if retirement is at age sixty-five with five years of service, or at any age after thirty years of service, or after age sixty with twenty-five years of service, the allowance is 1.85 percent of average final compensation (highest four-year average) multiplied by years of service (G.S. 128-27(b21)(2)). A reduced benefit is paid for earlier retirement (G.S. 128-27(b21)(2)(a); G.S. 128-27(b21)(1)(b) for law enforcement officers). Law enforcement officers also receive a service retirement allowance computed as follows: if retirement is at age fifty-five with five years of service, or at any age after thirty years of service, the allowance is 1.85 percent of average final compensation (highest four-year average) multiplied by years of service (G.S. 128-27(b21)(1)).

In addition to the regular retirement benefits paid to employees under LGERS, law enforcement officers are entitled to two other retirement benefits. First, cities and counties make a 5 percent contribution to a Section 401(k) retirement plan for each officer they employ.[41] Second, cities and counties must pay a special separation allowance to retiring law enforcement officers. The allowance is computed as follows: the last salary multiplied by .85 percent, multiplied by the number of years of creditable service. This allowance is payable to all officers who (1) have completed thirty or more years of creditable service or have attained age fifty-five with five or more years of creditable service, (2) have not attained age sixty-two, and (3) have completed at least five years of continuous service as a law enforcement officer immediately before service retirement (G.S. 143-166.42).

Social Security

Another benefit provided to virtually all local government employees is coverage under the Social Security Act.[42] The General Statutes authorize establishment of plans for extending Social Security benefits to state and local government employees (G.S. 135-21 covers state employees, G.S. 135-23 local government employees). The Social Security Act, in turn, provides that states may obtain coverage for political subdivisions by executing agreements with the secretary of the United States Department of Health and Human Services. The initial decision to participate in Social Security, then, is a voluntary one by the government employer. Once having elected to participate in the system, however, government employers may not revoke that election. In 1990, Congress enacted the Omnibus Budget Reconciliation Act,[43] which provides that all employees of state and local governments who are not members of a retirement system are automatically covered by the Social Security Act.[44]

Personnel Rules and Conditions of Employment

Policies

The General Statutes set out a nonexclusive list of personnel policies that a city council or board of county commissioners may adopt by rules, regulations, or ordinances (G.S. 160A-164; G.S. 153A-94). Thus, a council or board may

40. Title 20, Chapter 02C, Section .0802, of the N.C. Administrative Code (hereinafter N.C.A.C.).

41. In *Abeyounis v. Town of Wrightsville Beach*, 102 N.C. App. 341 (1991), the court held that the employer, not the employee, had to fund the 401(k) plan and that a budget ordinance that gave a 1.5 percent raise to town police and a 3.5 percent raise to all other municipal employees, with the 2.0 percent difference being used to fund the Section 401(k) plan, violated G.S. 143-166.50(e).

42. 42 U.S.C. §§ 301–2007.

43. Pub. L. No. 101-508, 104 Stat. 1388 (1990).

44. The regulations implementing this change are found at 29 C.F.R. pt. 31.

choose to adopt personnel policies governing leave, overtime, training, residency, or any other issue. The important point is that the General Assembly has not mandated that North Carolina cities and counties establish any personnel policies other than classification and pay plans.

Vacation and Other Leave

Most cities and counties provide paid leave to employees. Typically, nine to twelve days a year are designated as paid holidays. In addition, employees usually earn sick leave and vacation leave. Some local government employers also grant petty leave (periods of less than a day), court leave, and funeral leave. Under the General Statues, the decision to establish personnel policies allowing various types of leave rests solely with the city or county (G.S. 160A-164; G.S. 153A-94).

Military leave is time off from regular duties to participate in the activities of a reserve component of the United States armed forces. City and county employees are entitled to unpaid leave for this activity under the Uniformed Services Employment and Reemployment Rights Act (USERRA).[45] USERRA applies to any employee serving in the United States Army, Navy, Air Force, Marine Corps, and Coast Guard, as well as in the Army National Guard and Air National Guard, the commissioned corps of the Public Health Service, and "any other category of persons designated by the President in time of war or national emergency," whether such persons are serving on a voluntary or involuntary basis.[46] USERRA applies equally to active duty, active duty for training, initial active duty for training, inactive duty training, full-time National Guard duty, and any period during which an employee is absent either for a medical examination to determine fitness for duty or to perform funeral honors duty.[47] An employee returning from military leave must then be permitted to return to his or her position with the same seniority, status, pay, and vacation as the employee would have had if he or she had not been absent on military leave.[48]

Maternity leave policies adopted by cities and counties must meet the requirements of the Pregnancy Discrimination Act of 1978.[49] That act prohibits disparate treatment in employment of pregnant women. Specifically, the act (1) requires employers to treat pregnancy and childbirth the same as they treat other causes of disability under fringe benefit plans, (2) prohibits terminating or refusing to hire or promote a woman solely because she is pregnant, (3) bars mandatory leaves for pregnant women arbitrarily set at a certain time in their pregnancy and not based on their individual inability to work, and (4) protects the reinstatement rights of women on leave for pregnancy-related reasons. The act also makes it unlawful for an employer to differentiate between pregnancy-related and other disabilities for purposes of fringe benefits, including leave policies. The general rule that emerges from the Pregnancy Discrimination Act is that cities and counties must treat pregnant employees the same way they treat other employees with temporary disabilities.

Recruitment and Selection

The responsibility for adopting specific requirements for recruitment and selection is placed on the individual city and county; it is not mandated by the General Statutes. The decision to advertise positions, to post vacancy announcements, to interview candidates using panels or individual interviews, and to make outreach efforts to improve minority recruitment is one to be freely made by the local government employer. It is not required by federal or state law. Obviously, however, a city's or county's recruitment and selection decisions are less likely to be challenged successfully under federal statutes prohibiting discrimination if they are based on a system that reaches a large applicant pool and gives full and fair consideration to all candidates.

---

45. *See generally* 38 U.S.C. §§ 4301 *et seq.*
46. *Id.* § 4303(16)
47. *Id.* §§ 4303(13), (16).
48. *Id.* § 4316(a).
49. 42 U.S.C. § 2000e(k).

Federal Statutes and the Local Government Employment Relationship

A number of federal statutes limit the discretion of cities and counties in recruitment and selection, promotion, and dismissal of employees. These are briefly summarized in the following sections.

Title VII of the Civil Rights Act of 1964

No single piece of legislation has had greater impact on the employment relationship than Title VII of the Civil Rights Act of 1964,[50] which applies to employers with fifteen or more employees (42 U.S.C. 2000e(b)). Title VII is enforced by the United States Equal Employment Opportunity Commission (EEOC).

Title VII bars employers from hiring, dismissing, or making other decisions with respect to terms and conditions of employment on the basis of race, color, religion, gender, or national origin (42 U.S.C. 2000e-2(a)(1)). The courts have recognized two kinds of violations: those involving disparate treatment and those resulting in disparate impact. In the first category, the employer is found to have intended to discriminate. In the second, what the employer intends does not matter; rather, the court considers only the question of whether the employer's employment practices disproportionately exclude members of a protected class and, if so, if the practices may be justified as job related. Most claims brought under Title VII are disparate treatment claims.

Disparate treatment claims allege intentional discrimination. An employer violates Title VII if it treats some employees or applicants less favorably than it treats others because of race, color, religion, gender, or national origin. Disparate treatment may be shown either by direct evidence or, as is usually the case, by indirect evidence.

The United States Supreme Court has created a straightforward way for an aggrieved employee or applicant to claim that he or she is the victim of unlawful discrimination. In *McDonnell Douglas Corp. v. Green,*[51] the Court ruled that an applicant may create a prima facie case of discrimination in hiring (that is, enough of a case to require the employer to come forward to rebut) by showing the following:

1. The applicant belongs to a protected class.
2. The applicant applied and was qualified for a job for which the employer was seeking applicants.
3. The applicant was rejected, despite the fact that he or she met the qualifications for the job.
4. After the applicant was rejected, the employer continued to seek applicants from persons with the same qualifications as the applicant.

The employer then has the burden of presenting evidence that the applicant was rejected not because of race (or sex or another unlawful basis at issue) but because of a legitimate, nondiscriminatory reason. Such reasons might be, for example, another applicant's superior qualifications or the applicant's poor performance in the employment interview. Finally, once the employer has advanced its legitimate reason for the applicant's rejection, the applicant has an opportunity to show that the employer's proffered reason is just a pretext and that the real reason is discrimination.

Affirmative Action and Use of Race as a Criterion in Government Employment Decisions

The term *affirmative action* refers to the deliberate use of race and gender preferences in selection or promotion.[52] All government decisions are subject to challenge under the Equal Protection Clause of the Fourteenth Amendment to the United States Constitution. As a general rule, it is relatively easy for the government to prevail on such a challenge. If the decision that the government made is rational, the government will prevail. This "rational basis" test is the regular scrutiny that courts apply in ruling on equal protection claims.

Where race plays a role in a government decision, however, the courts do not apply regular scrutiny. They take a much closer look, applying "strict scrutiny." Under strict scrutiny analysis, it is not sufficient that the government's use of race in making a decision has a rational basis. More is required. The use of race must be justified by a *compelling*

50. *See generally* 42 U.S.C. §§ 2000e *et seq.*

51. 411 U.S. 792 (1973).

52. The Equal Employment Opportunity Commission (EEOC) defines *affirmative action* as "actions appropriate to overcome the effects of past or present practices, policies, or other barriers to equal employment opportunity" (29 C.F.R. § 1608.1(c)).

government interest, not just a rational basis. Strict scrutiny is applied regardless of whether the use of race by the government is thought to be aimed at harming a particular racial group or helping one.

What interests can qualify as compelling interests for this purpose? One interest is universally acknowledged as sufficiently compelling: overcoming the present effects of past discrimination by a unit of government itself. This compelling interest is rarely used to justify the use of race in decision making, however, because it would require the government unit to admit its own prior discrimination and to point to ongoing effects of that discrimination.

Outside of overcoming the present effect of past discrimination, it is easier to say what is *not* a compelling interest than it is to say what is. Thus, the United State Supreme Court has rejected as a compelling interest the need for role models in the public schools,[53] the interest in overcoming "general societal discrimination,"[54] a state's interest in avoiding liability under the Voting Rights Act of 1965,[55] and the desire to reduce the historic deficit of minorities in the medical profession and to increase the number of physicians who will practice in underserved minority communities.[56]

In 2003, the Supreme Court opened the door to the possibility that the benefits of diversity could be a compelling interest that justifies the narrowly tailored use of race in government employment decisions. In *Grutter v. Bollinger* and *Gratz v. Bollinger*,[57] two closely related cases, the Court held that a university's desire to achieve "that diversity which has the potential to enrich everyone's education and thus make a . . . class stronger than the sum of its parts"[58] was a compelling government interest. But these cases held that while a university may consider an applicant's race as part of an effort to achieve a critical mass of minority admissions, it can only do so by giving individualized consideration to *all* applicants of *all* races and by using race as no more than a generalized "plus" factor. The Supreme Court expressly found unconstitutional the use of a quota system wherein a certain number or proportion of seats is set aside for minority applicants.

Several courts have since applied the *Grutter* and *Gratz* standard to public employment cases with mixed results. The case *Petit v. Chicago*,[59] for example, involved the City of Chicago's adjustment of test scores for promotion from patrol officer to supervisor in order to make up for the adverse impact that the subjective parts of the test had for African American candidates for promotion. The Seventh Circuit Court of Appeals held that standardizing of scores acted more as a "plus factor" in the promotion scheme than as a quota, and it therefore met the *Grutter* and *Gratz* test. The court found that the practice did not violate the Equal Protection Clause because (1) there was individualized consideration of each and every candidate for promotion; (2) the standardization did not unduly harm members of any racial group in that rather than giving an advantage to minority officers, it eliminated an advantage that white officers had on the test; and (3) the program had ended and was thus not unlimited in time.[60]

In contrast, in the 2006 case *Kohlbek v. City of Omaha*,[61] the affirmative action plan governing promotions within the city fire department was found to violate the Equal Protection Clause because there was no evidence of past discrimination. Under Omaha's plan, whenever the minority representation in a particular position was less than its stated goal (which was based on the minority population in the area and within the fire department ranks), candidates on the promotion-eligible list were promoted out of rank order based on their race. The city contended that the affirmative action plan was developed to remedy past discrimination within the fire department. The Eighth Circuit Court of Appeals held, however, that before a remedial racial classification could be justified, there must be identifiable past discrimination. In this case, there was neither a statistically significant difference between the actual and expected number of minorities in the relevant fire officer ranks nor any other evidence of past or continuing discrimination.

---

53. Wygant v. Jackson Bd. of Educ., 476 U.S. 267 (1986) (employment case).
54. Richmond v. Croson Co., 488 U.S. 469 (1989) (minority-owned business contracting case).
55. Shaw v. Hunt, 517 U.S. 899 (1996) (electoral district case).
56. University of Cal. v. Bakke, 438 U.S. 265 (1978) (medical school admissions case).
57. Grutter v. Bollinger, 539 U.S. 306 (2003); Gratz v. Bollinger, 539 U.S. 244 (2003).
58. *Grutter*, 539 U.S. at 315; *Gratz* references *Grutter* and uses similar language to describe the government's interest.
59. 352 F.3d 1111 (7th Cir. 2003).
60. This section on affirmative action is based on unpublished written material prepared by School of Government faculty member Robert Joyce.
61. 447 F.3d 552 (8th Cir. 2006).

Thus, the plan could not be considered "narrowly tailored to further the goal of remedying past discrimination," as the strict scrutiny test required.[62] At trial, the city had also argued in the alternative that it had a compelling interest in developing and retaining a diverse workforce—an argument that sounds much like the University of Michigan's successful argument in the *Grutter* case, mentioned above—but the trial court did not decide the issue and it was therefore not considered by the Eighth Circuit.[63]

Other Federal Antidiscrimination Acts

In addition to the Civil Rights Act of 1964, federal legislation exists to bar age discrimination, to require accommodation of disabled individuals, to prohibit discrimination on the basis of genetic information, and to preserve the employment rights of persons called to military duty.

The Age Discrimination in Employment Act

The Age Discrimination in Employment Act of 1967 (ADEA) (29 U.S.C. §§ 621 *et seq.*) prohibits discrimination on the basis of age for all persons aged forty and above. The ADEA makes it unlawful for an employer to fail or refuse to hire, to discharge, or to otherwise discriminate against any person with respect to compensation, terms, conditions, or privileges of employment because of the person's age. The ADEA is enforced by the Equal Employment Opportunity Commission (EEOC).

Statutes Prohibiting Discrimination on the Basis of Disability

Title I of the Americans with Disabilities Act (ADA) prohibits employers from discriminating against a qualified individual on the basis of disability in any aspect of employment (42 U.S.C. § 12112). This includes hiring, promotion, dismissal, compensation, and training. Specific prohibitions include (1) limiting or classifying a job applicant or current employee in a way that adversely affects the opportunities or the status of that person because of their disability; (2) using standards or criteria that have the effect of discriminating against the disabled; (3) denying job benefits or opportunities to someone because of his or her association or relationship with a disabled person; (4) using employment tests or selection criteria that screen out the disabled and are not job related; (5) failing to use tests that accurately measure job abilities; and (6) not making reasonable accommodations that would allow an otherwise qualified disabled person successfully to perform a job's essential duties.

Title I of the ADA and the ADA regulations issued by the EEOC (29 C.F.R. Part 1630) cover all state and local government employers with fifteen or more employees.[64] Local government employers with fewer than fifteen employees are covered by regulations issued under the Rehabilitation Act of 1973 (29 U.S.C. §§ 701 *et seq.*), which also prohibits discrimination in employment against disabled persons. The law that governs the treatment of disabled persons by local government employers is not measurably different for those small jurisdictions with fewer than fifteen employees than it is for jurisdictions with fifteen or more employees because the ADA is based on the earlier Rehabilitation Act.

---

62. *Id.* at 555 (footnote omitted); *see generally id.* at 557–58 (discussing the strict scrutiny analysis undertaken by the court). *See also* Lomack v. City of Newark, 463 F.3d 303 (3d Cir. 2006) (race-based transfer and assignment policy in city fire department did not pass strict scrutiny test where racial imbalance in fire houses was not the result of past discrimination).

63. *See Kohlbek*, 447 F.3d at 557–58. *Cf.* Reynolds v. City of Chicago, 296 F.3d 524, 528, 530 (7th Cir. 2002) (jury's finding of past discrimination against African Americans in the Chicago police department was neither erroneous nor unreasonable; remedying past discrimination was a compelling government interest and out-of-rank promotion of African American, female, and Latino officers did not violate the Equal Protection Clause).

64. 42 U.S.C. § 12111(5)(A).

The Genetic Information Nondiscrimination Act

The Genetic Information Nondiscrimination Act of 2008 (GINA) prohibits employers from discriminating on the basis of genetic information and medical history.[65] An employer may never use genetic information to make an employment decision because genetic information is not relevant to an individual's current ability to work. Although the two statutes are related, GINA is distinct from the ADA in that the ADA prohibits discrimination on the basis of manifested conditions that meet the ADA's definition of disability, while GINA prohibits discrimination based on genetic information that may indicate that a condition may manifest itself in the future. For the purposes of the statute, genetic information includes not only the genetic test results of employees and their family members but the manifestation of any disease or disorder in any of the employee's family members.[66] GINA also requires employers to keep any genetic information that they accidentally acquire confidential. GINA applies to employers with fifteen or more employees.[67]

Defense of Employees

G.S. 160A-167 *allows* cities to provide for the legal defense of employees or officers and to pay judgments entered against them but does not *require* cities to do so. However, a city may not simply decide informally whether or not to provide for the legal defense of its employees. G.S. 160A-167(c) requires the city council to adopt uniform standards under which claims may be paid in advance of any agreement to provide a defense or make a payment. These standards must be made available for public inspection.

Similarly, G.S. 160A-167 and G.S. 153A-97 authorize counties, on request, (1) to provide for the defense of any civil or criminal action or proceeding brought against a present or former county employee, officer, or governing board member; member of a volunteer fire department or rescue squad that receives public funds; soil and water conservation employee; and any person providing medical or dental services to inmates of the county jail, on account of that person's conduct in the scope and course of his or her employment and (2) to pay any judgment rendered against them. Again, these statutes are permissive: counties are not required to pay for the defense of or any judgment against a county employee.

Local health department sanitarians are entitled to legal defense by the state attorney general for their actions arising from the enforcement of state public health. In either case, assistance may be provided whether the person is sued or charged as an individual or in his or her official capacity (G.S. 143-300.8).

Workers' Compensation

G.S. Chapter 97, the North Carolina Workers' Compensation Act, is an employer-financed program of benefits to provide for medical coverage, rehabilitation expenses, and loss of income for employees who have job-related injuries or illnesses.[68] All city and county employees are automatically covered by North Carolina's workers' compensation law (G.S. 97-2 and 97-7). Cities and counties may not reject coverage. Under the law, employers are liable only for accidents that arise out of and in the course of employment. They may cover their liability for compensation payments either by purchasing insurance or by self-insuring.

Employees receive full coverage for medical and rehabilitation treatment and two-thirds of their salary for lost time at work. Income benefits begin on the seventh calendar day after the lost time begins; however, if the lost time exceeds

65. 42 U.S.C. §§ 2000ff–2000ff-11. The Equal Employment Opportunity Commission (EEOC)'s GINA regulations are located at 29 C.F.R. Part 1635.

66. *See* 29 C.F.R. § 1635.3(b).

67. 42 U.S.C. § 2000ff(2)(B)(i); 29 C.F.R. § 1635.2(d).

68. The employee must prove that he or she suffered an injury by accident, that the injury arose from employment, and that the injury was sustained in the course of employment. Gallimore v. Marilyn's Shoes, 292 N.C. 399 (1977).

twenty-one days, income benefits are then also paid for the first seven days (G.S. 97-28). Income replacement continues until the employee returns to work or reaches the maximum medical improvement. In the case of permanent and total disability, income replacement is a lifetime benefit, continuing until the employee's condition changes or the employee dies (G.S. 97-29(d)).

When an injury or illness results in permanent partial disability, a lump-sum settlement based on a schedule set out in G.S. 97-31 is paid to the employee. Death benefits are paid to survivors of employees who suffer job-related injuries or illnesses. Survivors of employees who served as law enforcement officers or firefighters receive a higher-level benefit for job-related death (G.S. 97-38).

Employees whose workers' compensation claims are denied have the right to appeal to the North Carolina Industrial Commission and to state court. An award of the Industrial Commission is binding on all questions of fact but may be appealed to the court of appeals on errors of law (G.S. 97-86).

Traditionally, North Carolina courts have held the Workers' Compensation Act to provide the exclusive remedy available to an injured employee, even when the injury has been caused by gross negligence or the willful, wanton, or reckless behavior of the employer (G.S. 97-10.1). In 1991, however, the North Carolina Supreme Court held in the case *Woodson v. Rowland* [69] that the Workers' Compensation Act was not the exclusive remedy for an employee who was killed or injured when the employer engaged in conduct knowing that it was substantially certain to cause serious injury or death. Such misconduct, held the court, was tantamount to an intentional tort, and in such a circumstance a plaintiff might maintain a civil action against the decedent's employer.

Unemployment Compensation

G.S. Chapter 96, Article 2, sets forth an employer-financed program to provide partial income-replacement benefits to employees who lose their jobs or have their work hours reduced to less than 60 percent of their last schedule. The program is administered by the North Carolina Employment Security Commission (ESC) and covers state and local government employers. Public employers may pay contributions on an experience-rating basis or on a reimbursement basis (G.S. 96-9(a)(4); G.S. 96-9(f)).

Individuals are eligible for benefits if they register for work and continue to report at the ESC employment office, make a claim for benefits, and are able and available to work (G.S. 96-13(a)). An individual may be disqualified for benefits if he or she has left work voluntarily and without good cause attributable to the employer (G.S. 96-14(1)). Further, if the ESC determines that an individual was discharged for misconduct connected with the work, then benefits will be denied (G.S. 96-14(2)). The term *misconduct connected with the work* is defined at G.S. 96-14(2) as

> conduct evincing a willful or wanton disregard of the employer's interest as is found in deliberate violations or disregard of standards of behavior which the employer has the right to expect of an employee or has explained orally or in writing to an employee or conduct evincing carelessness or negligence of such degree or recurrence as to manifest an intentional and substantial disregard of the employer's interests or of the employee's duties and obligations to the employer. . . . [The term also includes] [v]iolating the employer's written alcohol or illegal drug policy[;] . . . [r]eporting to work significantly impaired by alcohol or illegal drugs[;] . . . [c]onsuming alcohol or illegal drugs on employer's premises[;] . . . [and] [c]onviction by a court of competent jurisdiction for manufacturing, selling, or distribution of a controlled substance . . . while in the employ of said employer.

69. 329 N.C. 330 (1991). *Woodson* was a wrongful death claim brought by the administratrix of a deceased employee's estate against the employer, a utility subcontractor on a construction site. The employee had been killed when a trench that had not been adequately sloped—in violation of occupational health and safety regulations—caved in on him.

A finding of a voluntary quit or discharge for misconduct by the ESC results in disqualification of the claimant for benefits. A finding of substantial fault results in disqualification for a period of four to thirteen weeks, after which the claimant is eligible for benefits. A claimant may also be disqualified for refusal of a suitable offer of work.

Unionization and Employee Relations

G.S. Chapter 95, Article 12, is a comprehensive ban on collective bargaining by public employees. An earlier statuory provision that has since been repealed prohibited public employees from becoming members of trade or labor unions, but it was held unconstitutional in 1969 in the case *Atkins v. City of Charlotte.*[70] Thus, city and county employees may exercise their First Amendment right of association and speech by belonging to labor unions. But the *Atkins* case also held that G.S. 95-98, which makes contracts between any city and any labor organization "illegal, unlawful, void, and of no effect," is constitutional. As a result, city and county employees may belong to unions, but local governments are prohibited by law from bargaining with those unions over the terms and conditions of their members' employment. Nothing in the statute affects the right of employees and labor organizations to present their views to city councils and officials, however, to the same extent that other citizens may.[71] Finally, G.S. 95-98.1 and 95-98.2 prohibit strikes by public employees, and G.S. 95-99 makes the violation of Chapter 95, Article 12, a misdemeanor. The constitutionality of these latter provisions has never been tested.

Restrictions on Political Activity

North Carolina law makes it a crime to give or promise any political appointment or support for political office in return for political support or influence (G.S. 163-274(9)). Similarly, it is unlawful for any city or county officer or employee to intimidate or oppress any other officer or employee on account of the way that person or any member of his or her family exercises his or her right to vote (G.S. 163-271).

The General Statutes also prohibit certain partisan political activities by city and county employers and employees (G.S. 160A-169; G.S. 153A-99). Employees may not, while on duty or in the workplace, use official authority or influence to interfere with or affect the result of an election or a nomination for political office, or to coerce, solicit, or compel contributions for political or partisan purposes by any other employee. In addition, no employee may be required to contribute funds to political campaigns, and no employee may use local government funds or facilities for partisan political purposes. Several city councils and boards of county commissioners have adopted additional restrictions on political activity by appointive employees, including prohibitions on running for office.

Nevertheless, city and county employees enjoy First Amendment free speech protection that includes the right to engage in political activity, if not to run for office. The courts have limited the circumstances in which political party affiliation may be used as a basis for personnel actions, such as hiring and dismissal of employees, to instances in which it can be shown that "affiliation with the employer's party is essential to the employee's effectiveness in carrying out the responsibilities of the position held."[72]

70. 296 F. Supp. 1068 (W.D.N.C. 1969).

71. Hickory Fire Fighters Ass'n, Local 2653 v. City of Hickory, 656 F.2d 917 (4th Cir. 1981).

72. Jones v. Dodson, 727 F.2d 1329, 1334 (4th Cir. 1984) (citing Branti v. Finkel, 445 U.S. 507 (1980), and Elrod v. Burns, 427 U.S. 347 (1976)). *See also* Rutan v. Republican Party of Ill., 497 U.S. 62 (1990); Joyner v. Lancaster, 815 F.2d 20, 23 (4th Cir. 1987) (upholding discharge of captain in Forsyth County sheriff's department based on his disruption of working relationship).

Discipline, Dismissal, and Grievances

The Fourteenth Amendment to the United States Constitution guarantees that no state shall "deprive any person of life, liberty, or property, without due process of law."[73] The United States Supreme Court has held that this guarantee of due process extends in two distinct circumstances to a public employee's job security. First, when a public employee has a vested property interest in the job (for example, the requirement under G.S. 126-35 that employees subject to the State Human Resources Act (SHRA) may be discharged only for "just cause"), the employee may be removed only after notice, an opportunity to respond, and a demonstration that cause exists.[74] Second, when a public employer dismisses an employee for reasons "that might seriously damage his standing and associations in his community" or that might stigmatize the employee and foreclose "his freedom to take advantage of other employment opportunities,"[75] the public employee has been deprived of his or her liberty interest under the Fourteenth Amendment. If the employer makes public such stigmatizing charges, the employee is entitled to notice and an opportunity for a hearing to clear his or her name.[76]

Cities and counties may create a property interest in employment by enacting personnel ordinances that confer on employees the understanding that they may be disciplined or dismissed only for poor performance or misconduct.[77] For example, in *Howell v. Town of Carolina Beach*,[78] the North Carolina Court of Appeals held that the personnel manual enacted by the town through its ordinance procedure gave rights comparable to those of state employees under the SHRA and that the summary dismissal of an employee had violated his due process rights.

If a city or county creates a property interest in employment, what process is due the public employee under the Fourteenth Amendment? In brief, due process requires that (1) the employee be given notice of the charges against him or her, (2) the employee be given an opportunity to respond to those charges before being dismissed, and (3) the decision of whether or not to uphold the charges be made by an impartial decision maker.[79] This means that the employer must specify the reasons for the proposed dismissal in such a way that the employee clearly understands the basis for the action. It further requires that the employer give the employee a reasonable amount of time to prepare a response to the proposed action. Finally, it requires that the employer conduct a pre-dismissal hearing with an impartial decision maker, at which proceeding the employee may present evidence and arguments against the proposed dismissal—with the assistance of counsel if there is no right of further appeal. The decision maker then decides whether or not to uphold the charges. For cities and counties, the impartial decision maker may be the manager. Impartiality does not mean without any knowledge of the relevant facts and circumstances. The decision maker may have some knowledge of the facts and individuals involved and still be impartial. What is required is that the decision maker not be presumptively biased.[80]

County employees subject to the SHRA (that is, those employed by county health departments, departments of social services, and mental health departments and those engaged in emergency management activities) have a property interest in employment since the SHRA prohibits dismissal of covered employees except for "just cause." The regulations of the State Human Resources Commission governing local government SHRA employees set forth mandatory procedures for dismissal that satisfy the requirement of due process (25 N.C.A.C. 1I, .1700–1I, .2310).

---

73. U.S. Const. amend. XIV, § 1.
74. Cleveland Bd. of Educ. v. Loudermill, 470 U.S. 532, 541–42 (1985).
75. Bd. of Regents v. Roth, 408 U.S. 564, 573 (1972).
76. *Id.* at 573; Bishop v. Wood, 426 U.S. 341, 348–49 (1976); McGhee v. Draper, 564 F.2d 902, 909 (10th Cir. 1977).
77. *Loudermill*, 470 U.S. 532, 541–42; Howell v. Town of Carolina Beach, 106 N.C. App. 410, 418 (1992).
78. *Howell*, 106 N.C. App. 410.
79. *Loudermill*, 470 U.S. 532.
80. Crump v. Bd. of Educ. of the Hickory Admin. Sch. Unit, 326 N.C. 603, 616–17 (1990) (jury could find that bias of one school board member deprived teacher of due process in dismissal proceeding).

Personnel Records

G.S. 160A-168 exempts the personnel files of city employees from the provisions of G.S. 132-6, the statute that requires that public records be made available for inspection and copying, and G.S. 153A-98 exempts the personnel files of county employees from G.S. 132-6. Under both G.S. 160A-168 and G.S. 153A-98, certain information in personnel files is open to the public and other information is not to be disclosed except under special circumstances. Both statutes cover the personnel files of three groups: current employees, former employees, and applicants for employment.

Although G.S. 160A-168 covers city employees and refers to city government and G.S. 153A-98 covers county employees and refers to county government, the two statutes are substantively identical. The term *personnel file* is defined very broadly in subsection (a) of both statutes to include "any information *in any form* gathered by the [employer] . . . relating to [the employee's] application, selection or nonselection, performance, promotions, demotions, transfers, suspension and other disciplinary actions, evaluation forms, leave, salary, and termination of employment" (emphasis added). No matter where or in what form the information maintained on an employee is kept—in the personnel office or elsewhere, in a file folder or as a computer record—the release of it is governed by G.S. 160A-168 or 153A-98, respectively.

Information Permitted to Be Released

Whether a given type of information in an employee's personnel file is open or confidential is determined by the status of the person or the agency requesting the information. The information that may be released to each type of person or agency requesting it is as follows:

The general public. Ten items in an employee's personnel file must be disclosed to the public when requested (G.S. 160A-168(b); G.S. 153A-98(b)):

1. the employee's name;
2. the employee's age;
3. the date of the employee's original employment or appointment;
4. the terms of any employment contract, whether written or oral;
5. the employee's current position, title, and salary;
6. the date and amount of each increase or decrease in the employee's salary (including pay, benefits, incentives, bonuses, and deferred and all other forms of compensation);
7. the date and type of each promotion, demotion, transfer, suspension, separation, or other change in position classification;
8. the date and a general description of the reasons for each promotion;
9. the date and type of each dismissal, suspension, or demotion for disciplinary reasons. If the disciplinary action was a dismissal, a copy of the written notice of the final decision of the city or county setting forth the specific acts or omissions that are the basis of the dismissal; and
10. the office or station to which the employee is currently assigned.

Employees. An employee has the right to have access to any information contained in his or her personnel file "in its entirety," except for letters of reference solicited before the employee was hired. Also exempt from disclosure to the employee is information concerning medical disabilities that a prudent physician would not disclose to a patient (G.S. 160A-168(c)(1); G.S. 153A-98(c)(1)).

Prospective employers. The personnel records acts governing North Carolina local government employees also provide that employees may sign a written release permitting the city or the county to give information about the employee to prospective employers or others (G.S. 160A-168(c)(6); 153A-98(c)(6)).

Applicants, former employees, or their agents. No information about applicants is subject to disclosure, either to the general public or to the applicant himself or herself.[81] A former employee or his or her agent may examine the former employee's personnel file to the same extent that an employee may examine his or her own file.

Government officials. The broadest right of access is afforded to a person having supervisory authority over the employee whose information is being requested. Such supervisory officials may examine all material in the employee's personnel file. This provision allows not only an employee's immediate supervisor, but also others in the chain of command, to have access to the personnel file. Similarly, members of the city council and the council's attorney, and members of the board of county commissioners and the board's attorney, as well as officials of federal or state agencies, have the right to examine a personnel file when the custodian of the personnel records deems it "necessary and essential to the pursuance of a proper function" (G.S. 160A-168(c)(3),(5); G.S. 153A-98(c)(3),(5)). Thus, no council or board member or other official has a right to look at a personnel file merely to satisfy his or her curiosity; rather, some legitimate need must exist to warrant the examination.

Party with a court order. Finally, a party to a judicial or administrative proceeding involving an employee may, on obtaining a proper court order (not a subpoena), inspect and examine a particular portion of an employee's personnel file that otherwise would be confidential.

Exceptions to the Rule of Confidentiality

The General Statutes contain two exceptions to the rule that all matters not specifically listed as open to inspection are confidential. The first exception is found in G.S. 160A-168(c)(7) and G.S. 153A-98(c)(7), which provide that personnel information otherwise confidential may be disclosed by the city manager or county manager if "the release is essential to maintaining public confidence in the administration of [city] [county] services or to maintaining the level and quality of . . . [city] [county] services." In such a case the manager, with the concurrence of the city council or board of county commissioners, may "inform any person or corporation of the employment or nonemployment, promotion, demotion, suspension or other disciplinary action, reinstatement, transfer, or termination of a[n] . . . employee and the reasons for that personnel action" (G.S. 160A-168(c)(7); 153A-98(c)(7)). To illustrate, if a former employee falsely tells a newspaper reporter that he was dismissed for exposing corruption by the local city council or board of county commissioners, the act permits the council or board to correct the record by informing the newspaper of the actual basis for the employee's dismissal. However, if the manager decides to disclose the circumstances of the employee's dismissal, he or she must first propose disclosure to the council or board, which must determine whether release of the information in this case is "essential." If the council or board agrees that disclosure is warranted, the manager must prepare a memorandum stating the circumstances that require disclosure and specifying the information to be disclosed. The memorandum itself then becomes a public record and is maintained in the employee's personnel file. Only after this process is completed may the manager discuss the reasons for the employee's dismissal with the newspaper reporter.

The second exception is found in the open meetings law (G.S. Ch. 143, Art. 33C), which provides that the terms of any settlement of a "claim, judicial action, mediation, arbitration, or administrative procedure" in which a public body is a party or has a substantial interest shall be disclosed (G.S. 143-318.11(a)(3)). Disclosure is required even when the parties to the judicial action agree to keep the terms of the settlement confidential.[82] In addition to the provision of the open meetings law, G.S. Chapter 132, the Public Records Act, provides that the term *public records* includes "all settlement documents in any suit, administrative proceeding, or arbitration instituted against any agency of North Carolina government or its subdivisions" (G.S. 132-1.3(a)).[83] The act further prohibits settlement agreements between government employers and plaintiffs that contain confidentiality clauses.

81. Elkin Tribune v. Yadkin Cnty. Bd. of Cnty. Comm'rs, 331 N.C. 735 (1992).

82. News & Observer Publ'g Co. v. Wake Cnty. Hosp. Sys., 55 N.C. App. 1, 12–13 (1981).

83. The term *settlement documents* is broadly defined at G.S. 132-1.3(c) to include "correspondence, settlement agreements, consent orders, checks, and bank drafts."

A public official who knowingly, willfully, and with malice gives anyone access to information contained in a personnel file, except as the General Statutes permit, is guilty of a misdemeanor. Any unauthorized person who knowingly and willfully examines, removes, or copies any portion of a confidential personnel file also commits a misdemeanor.

Conclusion

North Carolina cities and counties manage their employees under the limits of the General Statutes, federal statutes, and the requirements of the common law. The challenge is to administer personnel policies in a way that is both legally defensible and efficient for all parties concerned.

Additional Resources

Juffras, Diane M. *Employee Benefits Law for North Carolina Local Government Employers* (Chapel Hill: UNC School of Government, 2009).

_____. *Recruitment and Selection Law for Local Government Employers* (Chapel Hill: UNC School of Government, 2013).

About the Author

Diane M. Juffras is a School of Government faculty member who specializes in public employment law.

Chapter 14

The Attorney and the Clerk

A. Fleming Bell, II

The attorney and the clerk are mainstays of the governing board as it attempts to govern wisely and well. Together, city and county attorneys, city clerks, and clerks to the board of county commissioners help to ensure that local government activities are carried out in a legally correct manner. The documents created and maintained by the attorney and the clerk provide the written record needed to ensure that the board is accountable to the city's or county's citizens and to other public and private officials. Ideally, the attorney and the clerk work as partners with the manager and the board—the attorney advising on the legal consequences of board actions, the clerk keeping a record of those actions, and both officials ensuring that proper procedures are followed to enable the corporate entity, the city or county, to "speak" and "act" clearly and effectively.

The Attorney

Every city council and board of county commissioners in North Carolina must appoint an attorney to be its legal adviser,[1] although some very small towns nevertheless do not appoint one. The diversity of arrangements that cities and counties have made for legal representation is notable; it reflects the varied legal needs of the nearly 600 cities and 100 counties in the state. The typical city or county attorney in North Carolina is an independent practitioner or a member of a law firm who works for the city or county on a contractual basis. Larger cities and counties have at least one full-time attorney—the city or county attorney or an assistant or staff attorney—who is an employee of the unit, is

1. N.C. Gen. Stat. (hereinafter G.S.) §153A-114 (counties); G.S. 160A-173 (cities).

paid a salary, and works only on the local government's legal matters. The number of full-time attorneys has increased slowly but steadily in recent decades. This section reviews some of the issues that a city council or board of county commissioners might consider in deciding what sort of legal representation it needs.

Typical Arrangements

The typical city or county attorney[2] is an independent contractor.[3] In some local governments, all legal work is provided on a fee-for-service basis. In many jurisdictions, however, the attorney is paid a yearly retainer to provide agreed-on basic services. The retainer usually covers such services as

- attending all meetings of the city council or board of commissioners;
- being available for routine consultation with board members and department heads;
- drafting and reviewing ordinances and resolutions;
- preparing and reviewing routine legal documents, such as deeds and simple contracts; and
- preparing and reviewing legal advertisements.

In some cities or counties, the retained attorney's performance of agreed-on retainer services is charged against the retainer on a per-hour basis; the retainer then is a minimum annual fee for legal representation. If the attorney exceeds the number of hours covered by the retainer for the established services or does work not included in the retainer arrangement, he or she is reimbursed on a per-hour or other fee basis. As independent contractors, attorneys are responsible for providing their own insurance, retirement, and other benefits. Their retainer and hourly charges also pay for office and administrative expenses.

As noted earlier, some jurisdictions have at least one full-time salaried attorney, with the larger cities and counties having legal staffs of varying sizes. In addition to the attorneys' salaries, the city or county provides fringe benefits, office space and supplies, and administrative and other assistance.

A number of jurisdictions have hybrid arrangements for legal representation. Several, for instance, retain as city or county attorney an individual attorney who is an independent contractor, even though the attorney spends upward of 80 percent of his or her time exclusively on the local government's legal matters. The advantage of this arrangement for attorneys is that quite often they can remain partners in their law firms and thus share in the firms' overall economic success. The advantage to the city or county is that one person brings knowledge, to his or her legal service, having represented the local government's affairs over a period of time, knowing its personalities, issues, and operations, and having developed considerable expertise in the field of local government law.

Still other cities and counties classify their attorney as an employee even though the attorney may devote less than half of his or her time to city or county matters. This arrangement may be advantageous to the attorney in terms of fringe benefits, such as insurance and pension provisions. However, the local government and the attorney should make sure that the local government's insurance, pension, or other benefit programs do in fact apply to the attorney under this type of arrangement. The experience of some attorneys suggests that there is some uncertainty about the extent to which they do.

Some local governments retain a member of a law firm but also employ a full-time staff attorney as an assistant. This arrangement gives the city or county the benefit of a valued legal counselor while maintaining a full-time lawyer on hand for day-to-day legal matters.

Governing boards also need to consider the need for additional, specialized attorneys to work with particular local government officials or departments on a regular basis. For example, counties often have separate attorneys—retained

---

2. In some cities and counties, legal services are provided by a firm of attorneys, even though one attorney in the firm is usually designated as the city or county attorney.

3. See *County Salaries in North Carolina*, compiled by the MAPS Group for the School of Government, for information about each county's arrangements for legal services, including salaries, retainer fees, and departments served. *County Salaries* is an annual survey that is available exclusively online from the School of Government at http://shopping.netsuite.com/s.nl/c.433425/it.I/id.565/.f.

or full-time—for social services work, and both counties and cities frequently have separate attorneys to deal with the unique issues faced by the sheriff's office or the police department.

Considerations in Providing Legal Services

The best way to provide legal services for a particular local government depends on its legal needs. The legal matters affecting even the smallest jurisdictions have become steadily more complex and costly to handle over the last few decades. The proliferation of state and federal laws and programs and their consequent demands on local governments suggest that the trend will not reverse itself in the foreseeable future. City councils and boards of county commissioners should regularly assess what sorts of legal representation will be best for the local government as it changes over the years. They should not be afraid to ask hard questions and to expect clear answers as they conduct this evaluation.

Take the issue of better service, for example. The quality of service a city or county attorney provides depends primarily on his or her professional capability and personality. Whether the attorney is an independent contractor or an employee, the city or county is best served by a capable lawyer who is well versed in a variety of general legal subjects and also familiar with the specific legal principles and laws that apply to local governments. Thus, ideally a city or county attorney should be both a generalist and a specialist. He or she should be knowledgeable in such general legal areas as contracts, civil procedure and litigation, torts, and constitutional law. The attorney should also feel at home with such local government legal matters as governing board procedures, open meetings, public records, purchasing, planning and zoning, taxation, and budget and financial procedures. Familiarity with federal and state civil rights, employment, liability, and environmental laws and regulations is important as well.

A city or county attorney should be able to work and communicate effectively with public officials, local government employees, the press, and the public. Governing boards want to rely on the attorney's judgment and his or her ability to articulate ideas clearly when asked an unanticipated question during a public meeting. Also, the attorney must represent the board effectively even when the board members do not agree among themselves. The attorney must be able to understand the job requirements of administrators and department heads and give them accurate and practical legal advice. The county attorney must develop relationships with separately elected county officials such as the sheriff and the register of deeds. The attorney may also represent other local government boards and must be able to deal with them effectively even when they and the governing board do not see eye to eye. The attorney must be both forthright and discreet in dealing with representatives of the news media, who often assume a watchdog role over the affairs of the city or county. The attorney must maintain credibility while not disclosing his or her client's confidences. Finally, he or she should be able to represent the local government to the public on occasion, even though it is not usually the attorney's role to be a spokesperson for the city or county. All these criteria suggest that an ideal local government attorney should be talented, well-rounded, and experienced.

The question of political affiliation and relationships may also arise when the governing board chooses the city or county attorney. While a board or a dominant faction on the board may feel comfortable with a political ally as the city or county attorney, appointing an attorney mainly on the basis of political qualifications may be unwise. Governing board members may come and go with each election, and the board and the local government are best served by impartial advice that is not unduly influenced by close political affiliation or by fear of partisan retribution.

In addition to its regular attorney, a local government may sometimes employ expert counsel for specialized matters—for example, a title search for a major acquisition of real estate. A city or county may also retain outside counsel for unusually complex litigation. Certain civil rights, tax, or environmental cases might fall into this category. Litigation of this type requires either professional specialization in the field or the full-time attention of the attorney, or both. In addition, many cities and counties have insurance policies to cover lawsuits involving tort matters, and in those cases the insurance company chooses and compensates the attorney who is representing the local government. The city or county attorney, whether retained or full-time, will likely need assistance with complex or unusual litigation if he or she is to continue providing routine and day-to-day legal assistance to the local government in an effective manner. The governing board should be ready and willing to pay for the additional expertise that the city or county may need from time to time.

Retained or Full-Time Attorney

General Factors

Whether hiring a full-time attorney is appropriate for a particular city or county depends on the local government's specific legal needs, its governing board, and other relatively subtle issues, such as what *types* of litigation the city or county anticipates and whether a contract or full-time attorney will be more effective with government officials and personnel. Perhaps the most salient advantages of hiring a full-time attorney are his or her intimate knowledge of the city's or county's day-to-day affairs and the ability to practice preventive law. Because of the economics of legal fees and the social environment within which local government law is practiced, one can expect a steady increase in the number of cities and counties employing full-time attorneys. But not all jurisdictions will need such an attorney—particularly those without continuous, recurring legal needs.

If the local government uses a retained attorney, however, it must be very careful not to be penny-wise and pound-foolish in employing his or her services. Even very small towns and smaller counties comprise complicated public corporations with substantial annual budgets, and it is wise to err on the side of caution, consulting the attorney whenever a legal question is raised. Regardless of the jurisdiction's size, the governing board members owe it to their citizens and themselves to be more concerned with ensuring that competent legal advice is always readily available than with the immediate cost of that advice. The governing board and staff should not only seek the attorney's assistance with complex issues but should also involve him or her in matters that to the layperson may seem routine, such as reviewing contracts, advising on potential agenda items for meetings, and drafting or revising policies. Many cities and counties have avoided significant legal difficulties over the years by obtaining competent advice up front rather than after a costly mistake had already been made.

In practice, most city or county attorneys who are retained as independent contractors place an emphasis on advising the council or board of commissioners and the manager, if any, and on attending their meetings. To minimize their retainer fees, some attorneys provide routine legal service to only those parties or, in many small towns, attend meetings only when specifically asked to do so. However, as noted above, the governing board may want to consider long-term costs and not just immediate expenses in deciding how much time the attorney should devote to the local government's issues.

A full-time city or county attorney, on the other hand, handles the full range of the local government's legal needs. This might be better service in the sense that a full-time attorney is available for consultation and to provide advice to all governmental departments and offices (such as a purchasing or recreation department), to other local boards and commissions (such as a social services board or a board of adjustment), and, in the case of counties, to other elected county officials (such as the sheriff and the register of deeds).

Officials and employees in a city or county with a full-time attorney may also feel that legal consultation is more convenient when the attorney is available full time. Full-time attorneys may be more accessible simply because they have offices close to other local government offices. Or, the officials and employees may not feel the constraint they might experience consulting with an independent-contractor attorney, which may involve escalating legal fees as the consultation becomes more complex or extensive. In a jurisdiction with a full-time attorney, the local government's personnel know that the attorney's client is the city or county and that they will not be interrupting the attorney while he or she is handling matters for other clients. Similarly, on occasion, retained city or county attorneys may not be readily available because they are entirely occupied with a major matter—perhaps a trial—for another client, or there may be a conflict of interest in a particular situation that involves both the local government and another of the attorney's clients, so that the attorney cannot ethically represent either side. A full-time attorney should be in closer touch with developments affecting the local government's business than retained counsel due to his or her day-to-day presence and exposure. Full-time attorneys will not need to be briefed as extensively on certain matters because they are already somewhat familiar with the background. And, of course, because they are full-time salaried employees, no additional charges are associated with legal consultations.

Cost Concerns

Whether having a full-time city or county attorney will save the local government money depends on whether it has full-time legal needs. The answer to this question will in turn depend on at least two important factors.

First, the amount and the type of litigation in which the city or county is engaged are very important. If the city or county is frequently in court, a full-time attorney may be justified. Court cases tend to raise the cost of a local government's legal services sharply, and the amount of litigation is often unpredictable. Local governments have taxing power, which means that they may be viewed by potential litigants as having deep pockets. This can lead to more frequent threatened or actual lawsuits. A full-time attorney ordinarily can handle much of the jurisdiction's recurring litigation, such as zoning disputes, tax foreclosures, and (for counties) social services child support suits. If the council members or commissioners are contemplating a full-time attorney, they should also keep in mind the nature of the city's or county's litigation as they decide what experience and capabilities that attorney should have.

Also very important to the decision about full-time legal representation are the number and complexity of the transactions in which the city or county is involved on a regular basis. For example, a local government with an active development program in which it has partnerships with private developers may need a great deal of legal work, even without litigation. Similarly, if land development is occurring rapidly in the city or county, local planning and zoning officials will frequently need an attorney's advice.

On the other hand, the city or county may incur significant additional costs if it hires a full-time attorney, costs that are ordinarily covered by the fees charged by a retained attorney. Paralegal and administrative support, subscriptions to legal research services, law books, and computer equipment are among the overhead expense items that a local government must plan to absorb if it has full-time legal representation.

Other matters should also be considered. Will city or county departments and commissions need legal consultation frequently enough to keep an attorney busy throughout the year? A great advantage of in-house attorneys is that they can practice preventive law by counseling the local government's personnel regarding appropriate policies and practices, exploring legal considerations before disputes erupt into lawsuits, advising employees regarding courses of action when problems suddenly arise, and so on. The daily presence of an attorney can have an intangible value in avoiding legal expenses that might otherwise be incurred without timely legal advice.

Does the cost of the local government's litigation fluctuate sharply from year to year? If so, having a salaried attorney can give the city or county a more predictable measure of its annual legal expense, assuming that a full-time attorney is justifiable in other respects. Even if complex or time-consuming litigation is routed to specialized counsel, a full-time attorney may be better able to absorb much of the jurisdiction's unforeseen legal requirements without a large corresponding increase in legal fees. The local government can better anticipate and estimate its budget requirements for legal representation if a full-time city or county attorney can handle most of its routine legal affairs. The attorney's and legal support staff's salaries and benefits, other overhead expenses, and a contingency reserve for outside counsel's representation in extraordinary litigation will be a fair measure of the city's or county's annual budget requirement for legal services.

Options for Full-Time Representation

If the local government decides that it needs full-time representation, it has at least three options with varying costs. It can hire a less experienced and less expensive attorney, it can hire a more experienced but more costly attorney, or it can adopt a hybrid arrangement involving a less experienced staff attorney and a more experienced attorney on retainer. Several questions need to be asked concerning each arrangement.

Are the personalities in the local government and its legal needs such that the city or county can hire an unseasoned or inexperienced attorney? Inexperienced attorneys command lower salaries, but to some degree they will be training and acquiring experience on the job. Will the city council or board of county commissioners give due weight to an unseasoned attorney's legal advice? Will they respect his or her judgment and counsel? Will an unseasoned attorney become rattled in a public meeting when suddenly confronted with an unanticipated query? Character and potential should be carefully evaluated for inexperienced candidates as compared to a seasoned attorney with years of experience summarized on a resume.

Other considerations emerge if a city or county decides to hire a more experienced lawyer as its full-time attorney. Since such a person's salary requirements will be substantially more than a less experienced attorney's, yearly cost-of-living adjustments will have more impact because they are being made from a substantially larger base. A policy should be agreed on for merit increases. Pension arrangements may have to be examined closely. The shorter funding period for a more experienced attorney in the Local Government Employees' Retirement System may result in less than optimum retirement payments if an inflationary environment follows retirement. If a more experienced attorney is taking a significant cut in remuneration to become the local government's attorney, the governing board should satisfy itself that he or she will devote an appropriate amount of energy and initiative to continuing employment on a public salary.

Hiring a less experienced full-time staff (or assistant) attorney when the city or county needs more legal services than a retained attorney can provide may be an appropriate arrangement for some jurisdictions. The local government that follows this plan continues to retain an outside attorney, at a reduced retainer. The city's or county's costs rise at first as it picks up the salary for the staff attorney. The retained attorney can devote most of his or her time to private law practice, which is typically more remunerative than representing local government, while still being available to the council or commissioners to counsel them on policy questions. The retained attorney will also be available to the staff attorney when the staff attorney feels that guidance or supervision would be appropriate for certain issues. As the staff attorney gains experience, the governing board, manager, and department heads should come to rely on his or her advice in his or her areas of expertise. It is important for the two attorneys to be able to get along and work well together for this arrangement to be effective.

The position of city or county attorney is a very important and sensitive one. A wide range of factors should be considered as city councils and boards of county commissioners seek to determine what amount of legal representation, at what costs, will best serve the needs of the local government and the city's or county's citizens. The best balance of cost, experience, and service level will vary from jurisdiction to jurisdiction and from year to year. City and county governing boards should review their legal representation on a regular basis, asking questions and making adjustments as needed to ensure that they are getting what they need and what they are paying for from the local government's lawyers.

The Clerk

The position of clerk is one of the oldest in local government, dating at least to biblical times. For example, the book of Acts in the Christian New Testament records that when a conflict arose between the people of Ephesus and the missionary Paul and his companions, the town clerk quieted the crowd and prevented a riot.[4]

The term *clerk* has long been associated with the written word. Indeed, an archaic definition of a clerk is a person who can read or read and write, or a learned person, scholar, or person of letters. Clerk can also mean cleric or clergyman; during the Middle Ages, the clergy were among the few literate people in many European communities.

Those who can read and write can keep records for their fellow citizens; so it is that modern-day clerks are official recordkeepers for their cities and counties. Each city and county in North Carolina must have a clerk,[5] and the most important records maintained by the clerk, such as minutes of governing board meetings, must be kept permanently

4. Acts 19: 23–41.

5. G.S. 153A-111 (clerk to the board of county commissioners); G.S. 160A-171 (city clerk).

for the use of future generations.[6] The city council or board of county commissioners may also provide for a *deputy clerk*, who may exercise any of the powers and perform any of the duties of the clerk that the governing board specifies.[7]

Appointment

The city clerk generally works directly for the city council, keeping the city's records, giving notices of meetings, and performing various other functions as the council requires. In mayor–council cities, the clerk is almost always appointed by the council. In council–manager cities, situations vary. Some city charters in such cities provide for appointment of the clerk by the council, although in recent years some charters have been revised to specify that the clerk is to be appointed by the manager.

In the absence of a charter provision in a council–manager city, the manager will probably appoint the clerk, although the clerk will still perform duties for the council. Section 160A-148(1) of the North Carolina General Statutes (hereinafter G.S.) specifies that the manager is to appoint and suspend or remove, in accordance with any council-adopted general personnel rules, regulations, policies, or ordinances, all non-elected city officers and employees "whose appointment or removal is not otherwise provided for by law, except the city attorney." G.S. 160A-171 states, "There shall be a city clerk," but it does not specify how the clerk is to be appointed, so the provision for appointment by the manager probably applies. However, both G.S. 160A-171 and G.S. 160A-172, which deals with deputy clerks, state that these officials are to perform duties required[8] or specified[9] by the council.

Under G.S. 153A-111, the board of county commissioners appoints or designates the clerk to the board of commissioners, who serves as such at the board's pleasure. The clerk performs any duties required by the board or by law. Although any county officer or employee may be designated as clerk, most counties have created a separate position with these responsibilities.

City and county clerks and their deputies have a variety of duties relating to the creation and maintenance of records and other subjects. These diverse responsibilities of clerks are the focus of this section of the chapter. The detailed legal requirements of the public records law with respect to records retention and access are discussed primarily in Chapter 8.

Record Keeping

Minutes

General Rules and Practices

One of the clerk's most important statutory duties is to prepare the minutes of the governing board and to maintain them in a set of minute books.[10] The legal powers of a city and many of the legal powers of a county are exercised by the city council or board of county commissioners, respectively, and the minutes of a board's meetings are the official record of what it does.

The minutes must be "full and accurate,"[11] for they are the legal evidence of what the governing board has said and done. The board "speaks" only through its minutes, and their contents may not be altered nor their meaning explained by other evidence.[12]

---

6. North Carolina Department of Cultural Resources, Division of Archives and Records, Government Records Section, *Retention Schedules—Local* (Raleigh, N.C.: Government Records Section, various dates). The schedules may be found online at www.ncdcr.gov/archives/ForGovernment/RetentionSchedules/LocalSchedules.aspx#chart.

7. For cities, see G.S. 160A-172; boards of county commissioners may rely on their general authority under G.S. 153A-76 to create offices and positions of county government to create the position of deputy or assistant clerk.

8. G.S. 160A-171.

9. G.S. 160A-172.

10. *See* G.S. 160A-171 (requiring the city clerk "to keep a journal of the proceedings of the council"); G.S. 153A-42 (requiring the clerk to the board of commissioners "to keep full and accurate minutes of the proceedings of the board of commissioners"); and G.S. 143-318.10(e) (part of the open meetings law, requiring public bodies to keep "full and accurate minutes" of their official meetings but allowing the sealing of minutes and "general accounts" of closed sessions in certain instances).

11. G.S. 153A-42; G.S. 160A-72; G.S. 143-318.10(e).

12. *See* Norfolk S. R.R. v. Reid, 187 N.C. 320, 326 (1924) (minutes of county commissioners).

Full and accurate does not generally mean, however, that the clerk must make a verbatim transcript of a meeting's proceedings. Rather, the minutes must record the results of each vote taken by the governing board,[13] and they should also show the existence of any condition that is required before a particular action may validly be taken.[14] The clerk should record the full text of each motion that is introduced, including the full text of all ordinances and resolutions passed by the board. This permanent, unchanging record of board actions can be extremely important in later years to supplement and back up information sources that may be frequently revised, such as ordinance books and codes of ordinances.

Other details are also important. The minutes should state that the meeting was legally convened and at what time. They should list the members in attendance and should show that a quorum was present at all times during the meeting. They should note the late arrival and early departure of members (including whether someone leaving was excused by the remaining members). A list of the members who voted each way on a particular question (the "ayes and noes") must be included if any member so requests.[15]

The minutes should also show that any other legally required conditions for taking action were met—for example, that a properly advertised public hearing was held on a proposed rezoning or that an ordinance received a sufficient number of votes to be adopted finally on first reading. As another example, if the board awards a formally bid construction contract, the minutes should record the fact that the award standard specified in G.S. 143-129(b) was followed.

As noted earlier, minutes generally do not need to include a verbatim transcript or even a summary of the discussion that took place at the council or board of commissioners meeting. Indeed, including a detailed record of comments may well be counterproductive; the governing board may find itself spending an excessive amount of time at its next meeting discussing the details of this record, which could have been omitted altogether.

A verbatim transcript of council or commissioner proceedings may be required in one limited instance. When the governing board is sitting as a quasi-judicial body—for example, when it is considering issuance of a special use permit under a zoning ordinance—it must act somewhat like a court, and a full transcript of the proceedings must be provided if requested by any court to which the decision is appealed.

Council and commissioner meetings need not be audio or video recorded by the city or county. (Persons attending the meeting may make their own recordings if they desire.)[16] If the clerk or another public official does make a tape, it may be disposed of after the minutes of that meeting are approved. Should the city or county attorney or the governing board wish that meeting tapes be retained for a longer period, the board should establish a clear, uniform policy for the clerk's guidance. The city's or county's tape of a meeting is a public record available for public inspection and copying for as long as it exists. Recordings of quasi-judicial proceedings are sometimes retained indefinitely in lieu of a transcript, in case they are needed later by a court or one of the parties involved in the case.

Draft copies of council and commissioner minutes are generally sent by the clerk to the board members several days before the meeting at which they are to be considered for approval. The circulated draft minutes are a public record that must also be made available for public inspection and copying. (Minutes and general accounts of closed sessions that the board intends to seal may be handed out at the meeting and taken up again once they have been approved. See the discussion of the open meetings law in Chapter 9.)

Council members and commissioners should carefully review the minutes and bring their suggested changes and corrections to the meeting for consideration by the full board. Although the clerk records the draft minutes for the council or the board of commissioners, the governing board itself, acting as a body, must finally determine what the minutes will include. The minutes do not become the official record of the board's actions until it approves them.

---

13. G.S. 153A-42; G.S. 160A-72.

14. For a discussion of the meaning of "full and accurate minutes," see *Maready v. City of Winston-Salem*, 342 N.C. 708, 732–34 (1996).

15. G.S. 153A-42; G.S. 160A-72.

16. *See* G.S. 143-318.14.

The governing board may correct minutes that it has already approved if it later finds that they are incorrect.[17] In such a case, the correction should be noted in the minutes of the meeting at which the correction is made, with an appropriate notation and cross-reference at the place in the minutes book where the provision being corrected appears.

Minutes and General Accounts of Closed Sessions

North Carolina's open meetings law, including the rules for closed sessions, is discussed in detail in Chapter 9. The minutes of these sessions, like other minutes, must be "full and accurate."[18] In particular, the open session minutes must record the motion to go into the session and the purpose of the closed session (the open meetings law specifies the purposes for which closed sessions may be held), while the closed session minutes record any actions taken, the existence of the conditions needed to take particular actions, and the motion to return to open session. In addition to the minutes, G.S. 143-318.10(e) requires the board subject to the open meetings law also to keep a "general account of the closed session so that a person not in attendance would have a reasonable understanding of what transpired." The general account may be either a written narrative or audio or video recordings. The minutes and general account "may be withheld from public inspection so long as public inspection would frustrate the purpose of a closed session."[19] If the clerk does not attend the closed session, he or she should designate someone who does attend to record the minutes and general account and should explain to that person the correct procedures for so doing.

Minutes of Meetings of Other Public Bodies

The open meetings law requires that "full and accurate" minutes also be kept of the meetings of the other "public bodies" that are part of city or county government. Included are all boards, committees, and other bodies of the county that perform legislative, policy-making, quasi-judicial, administrative, or advisory functions, including appointed subcommittees of larger bodies, such as the governing board. These public bodies must also keep minutes and general accounts of their closed sessions. The governing board, aided by the clerk, should establish procedures to ensure that the minutes of all public bodies under its direction are properly recorded and maintained, either by the clerk or under the clerk's guidance. The minutes of these various public bodies may be kept either in written form or, at the option of the public body, in the form of sound or video-and-sound recordings.[20] Most minutes of local public bodies are considered permanent public records.

Ordinance Book and Code of Ordinances

Among the other records of the city council's or board of county commissioners' actions maintained by the clerk are the ordinance book[21] and the code of ordinances, if there is one.[22] These books and codes are intended to make the city's or county's laws readily accessible to its citizens. Accordingly, ordinances may not be enforced or admitted into evidence in court unless they are properly filed and indexed or codified. The law presumes, however, that a city or county has followed the proper procedure unless someone proves otherwise.[23] For a description of the ordinance book and code requirements, see Chapter 5, "General Ordinance Authority."

Other Records

The city clerk is the official custodian of all other city records in addition to minutes and ordinances.[24] Similarly, the clerk to the board of county commissioners and the board itself are the custodians of many other county records.[25] Governing board resolutions, contracts, the correspondence of the governing board and the mayor or chair, signed oaths of office, copies of legal and other notices, financial and personnel records, and a variety of miscellaneous documents

17. *Norfolk S. R.R*, 187 N.C. at 326–27.
18. G.S. 143-318.10(e).
19. *Id.*
20. *Id.*
21. G.S. 153A-48; G.S. 160A-78.
22. G.S. 153A-49; G.S. 160A-77.
23. G.S. 153A-50; G.S. 160A-79(d).
24. G.S. 160A-171.
25. See G.S. 132-2, which provides that the person in charge of an office having public records is the custodian of those records.

(for example, board members' travel records and applications from citizens to be appointed to various local government boards) are all to be maintained in the clerk's office or under the clerk's guidance.

The clerk (in the case of cities) or the clerk and the board of commissioners (in the case of counties) have primary responsibility for ensuring that local government records are kept safely, are accessible for use by the public and local officials (except as restricted by law), and are disposed of in accordance with the appropriate schedule for records retention and disposition promulgated by the North Carolina Department of Cultural Resources, Division of Archives and Records.[26] This is the case regardless of whether the records are under the clerk's immediate, day-to-day control or are kept and used in another local government office. As noted earlier, records access and disposition are discussed in detail in Chapter 8, "Public Records."

Notice Giving

The clerk is usually responsible for giving notice of governing board meetings and for a variety of other public notices. Giving notice of all meetings of the city council is a statutory responsibility of the city clerk,[27] and it is a common practice for county clerks to give notice of all commissioners' meetings. In addition, both city and county clerks are statutorily responsible for keeping on file up-to-date regular meeting schedules of all public bodies that are part of city or county government, respectively. By making these schedules available for public reference, the clerk gives the main notice of regular meetings that the open meetings law requires.[28] Both city and county clerks often handle the posting and distribution of special meeting notices for other city or county boards as well. The details of these requirements are discussed in Chapter 9, "Open Meetings and Other Legal Requirements for Local Government Boards." Clerks frequently oversee the legal advertisements required for public hearings, bid solicitations, bond orders, and other matters as well.

Oaths of Office

The clerk is one of the few officials who may administer the oaths of office[29] that are required of elected and appointed city and county officers.[30] The clerk should also take such an oath. Deputy clerks, when discharging the clerk's duties, are also permitted to administer oaths as long as they are themselves sworn officers.[31] The text of the required oath of office is found in Article VI, Section 7, of the state constitution. G.S. 11-7 and 11-11 prescribe oaths to be administered in addition to the constitutional oath. A signed copy of all oaths administered to city or county officials must be filed with the clerk.[32]

Closing-Out Sales (City Clerks)

The city clerk is responsible for enforcing within the city limits the state's law regulating all going-out-of-business and distress sales.[33] The clerk must deal both with the false advertising claims of merchants who are not really going out of business and with the differing statutory rules that apply depending on whether a merchant is holding a "going-out-of-business sale" (the merchant is really closing its doors) or a "distress sale" (going out of business is possible or anticipated or the seller is forced to conduct the sale because of difficult business conditions). Regardless of the type of sale, the clerk must ensure that unhappy failing merchants comply with what they may well regard as intrusive state requirements regarding inventories, length of sales, and the like. The clerk should generally seek the advice and

26. See the online publications cited in note 6.
27. G.S. 160A-171.
28. G.S. 143-318.12(a).
29. G.S. 11-7.1(a).
30. G.S. 153A-26; G.S. 160A- 61.
31. G.S. 11-8.
32. G.S. 153A-26; G.S. 160A-61.
33. G.S. Chapter 66, Article 17.

cooperation of the city attorney, the city police department, and other city officials in performing his or her statutorily mandated duties in this area.[34]

General Assistance to the Governing Board

Research and General Assistance

In addition to the responsibilities previously outlined, clerks must perform other duties "that may be required by law or the [governing board]."[35] Individual board members or the board as a whole frequently call on the clerk to find answers to questions. They may ask the clerk to learn how others have solved a particular problem, to find sample ordinances for the attorney, or to search the minutes for information about the actions of a previous board. Individual members also look to the clerk for help in arranging official appointments and making official travel plans.

The governing board can help the clerk and its other professional staff (the attorney and the manager or administrator) serve it more effectively by remembering the limits of these professionals' roles. For example, the clerk generally performs research and provides information for the benefit of the entire board, just as the attorney serves and provides legal advice for the entire board's benefit. In addition, board members can help their professional staff by remembering the limits of staff members' time and energy when making individual requests.

Agendas and Preparations for Meetings

One of the most important services that the clerk provides to the city council or board of county commissioners is assistance with preparations for meetings. The clerk is usually involved in preparing the tentative agenda for governing board meetings and in compiling background information for the board's agenda packet. He or she may also arrange for the recording of meetings and may set up other audiovisual equipment and the meeting room.

Clear procedures for handling these matters can serve both the governing board and the clerk. The board should establish and enforce a realistic schedule for placing items on the agenda that allows adequate time to compile and duplicate background materials, and it should clearly state any preferences concerning the order of items on the agenda. As part of his or her meeting-preparation and post-meeting procedures, the clerk is required by law to comply promptly with public and press requests for information about upcoming gatherings and for access to minutes (including draft minutes), tapes, and electronic and other records of prior meetings. (For more information, see the discussion of the laws governing access to public records in Chapter 8.

Information Source

The clerk is sometimes described as "the hub of the wheel" in local government because of the central role that he or she plays in the government's communication network.[36] Clerks provide information daily to governing board members, city or county employees, other government officials, citizens, and the press. A clerk in a larger North Carolina county expressed the following thoughts about her role:

> Your description of a clerk as the hub of the wheel is much the way I think of my position here. The clerk is the hub and serves as one of the major sources of information on board actions. I communicate daily with the commissioners, the county manager, and the county attorney. I interact frequently with the planning director, other department heads, other government employees, and the press. The clerk also serves as a link between citizens and government. One of my primary functions is to provide information.[37]

A clerk in a medium-sized North Carolina city had similar thoughts about her position:

> Basically my office is an information office. I am in the center of things because as clerk I am usually more accessible than the mayor, council members, and other city officials. I have immediate access to information

34. G.S. 66-77(a).
35. G.S. 153A-111; G.S. 160A-171.
36. Carolyn Lloyd, "The Hub of the Wheel," *Popular Government* 55 (Spring 1990): 36–43.
37. *Id.* at 38.

> because I am on the front line in the city council meetings. I communicate daily with the mayor, the city manager, and various department heads, depending on what is going on. My office has quite a bit of contact with the newspapers, and we get anywhere from fifteen to twenty calls a day from the general public.[38]

These comments are as true today as they were when they were first made. City and county clerks remain at the hub of the wheel in local government as they respond to an ever-increasing variety of requests for information and assistance on a wide range of topics.

Dealing with such a wide variety of information requests requires tact, judgment, empathy, organizational skills, energy, and a good sense of humor. Although clerks work *for the council* or *for the board of county commissioners*, they truly provide *public* service—helping the press understand the meaning of a complicated motion, assisting a citizen in finding the correct person to help with a complaint, keeping department heads advised of governing board actions, and keeping board members informed of administration proposals. As local government becomes larger and more complicated, the clerk's role as a professional, dispassionate provider of information to citizens, government officials, and the media becomes more and more important.

Combination of the Clerk's Position with Other Responsibilities

Many clerks perform still other tasks. City clerks are often tax collectors, and some serve as purchasing agents. A city or county clerk may also be the human resources or finance officer, manager, assistant manager, or assistant to the manager.[39] In North Carolina's smallest towns, the clerk may be the only administrative official and may have to function in every role, from substitute operator of the waste treatment plant to zoning administrator.

Wearing many hats can be both stressful and invigorating for clerks and other public servants. Governing boards can take three important steps to help ensure that their cities and counties continue to attract highly competent clerks and other employees who can perform the varied duties of their offices well or can blend their primary positions effectively with other roles. First, they can provide employees with adequate authority as well as responsibility. Second, they can offer sufficient financial rewards to make government service an attractive career choice. Third, they can provide ongoing professional continuing education opportunities for their staff members.

Professionalism and Continuing Education

City and county clerks have the opportunity to participate in two of the most active professional associations of public officials in North Carolina, the North Carolina Association of County Clerks to the Boards of County Commissioners and the North Carolina Association of Municipal Clerks. Both organizations are dedicated to improving the professional competency of clerks through regular regional and statewide educational opportunities.[40] In cooperation with the School of Government and the International Institute of Municipal Clerks (IIMC), the associations help to sponsor a nationally recognized, examination-based certification program that culminates in receipt of the designation of Certified Municipal [or County] Clerk. In addition, the county and municipal associations and the School sponsor state certification programs leading to the designations of North Carolina Certified County Clerk and North Carolina Certified Municipal Clerk, respectively. They also provide opportunities for experienced clerks to obtain the continuing professional education needed to remain state-certified or to earn an advanced Master Clerk designation from the IIMC. In addition to conducting educational programs, both associations also directly assist clerks on the job with

---

38. *Id.*

39. *See, e.g.*, A. Fleming Bell, II, "Facts about North Carolina's Clerks," *Popular Government* 55 (Spring 1990): 43; and *County Salaries in North Carolina 2013*, compiled by the MAPS Group for the School of Government. The *Popular Government* article includes information about the percentages of clerks who were performing various other duties at the time that it was written. *County Salaries* is an annual survey that is available exclusively online from the School of Government at http://shopping.netsuite.com/s.nl/c.433425/it.I/id.565/.f. It provides specific information about which county clerks also hold other positions.

40. The home page for the North Carolina Association of County Clerks may be found at www.nccountyclerks.org/AboutUs.aspx. The home page for the North Carolina Association of Municipal Clerks is located at www.ncamc.com.

mentoring programs to provide guidance for new clerks and reference guides and newsletters to assist clerks in their day-to-day work.[41] Clerks also exchange ideas through two very active listservs maintained by the School of Government with the cooperation of the two clerks' groups.[42] Clerks are involved at the state level as well in potential legislation and other matters of interest. City clerks work with other municipal officials through permanent representation on the Board of Directors of the North Carolina League of Municipalities and through service on various committees of that organization and of the North Carolina Association of County Commissioners.

Additional Resources

Lloyd, Carolyn. "The Hub of the Wheel." *Popular Government* 55 (Spring 1990): 36–43. Additional information about the role of county and city clerks may be found in this article, which is based on interviews with several clerks.

MAPS Group for the UNC School of Government. *County Salaries in North Carolina 2014.* Chapel Hill: N.C.: Institute of Government, The University of North Carolina at Chapel Hill, 2014. Available free exclusively online at http://shopping.netsuite.com/s.nl/c.433425/it.I/id.565/.f. This is an excellent source for information about retainer arrangements for county attorneys and the salaries of county attorneys and county clerks.

North Carolina Association of County Clerks to the Boards of County Commissioners. *Job Descriptions: Clerk and Deputy Clerk.* www.nccountyclerks.org/JobDescriptions.aspx. This site provides detailed job descriptions for the positions of county clerk and deputy clerk. The clerk job description has been officially endorsed by the Board of Directors of the North Carolina Association of County Commissioners.

About the Author

A. Fleming Bell, II, is a retired School of Government faculty member who specializes in local government law. He coordinated the School's programs for city clerks, clerks to the boards of county commissioners, regional agency secretaries, and their deputies for more than three decades. During his career, he also worked extensively with a wide variety of other elected and appointed public officials, including local government attorneys.

The portion of this chapter on the attorney has been adapted from Grainger R. Barrett, "County Legal Representation: Retained or Full-Time County Attorney?" *Local Government Law Bulletin* No. 20 (October 1980), published by the Institute of Government. The materials on the clerk are based on A. Fleming Bell, II, "City and County Clerks: What They Do and How They Do It," *Popular Government* 61 (Summer 1996): 21–30.

41. The *Reference Guide and M.O.R.E. Manual (Minutes, Ordinances, Resolutions, Etc.)* of the municipal clerks' association are available online through the "Document Library" link of the municipal clerks' association home page. Please go to www.ncamc.com/nc_document.php.

42. The clerks' listservs are available online through the School of Government's website, at www.sog.unc.edu/node/265. The School also publishes Clerk-Net, which serves as the School's official home page for municipal and county clerks and regional council secretaries, with links and information of interest to clerks in North Carolina. The site's main objective is to facilitate the dissemination of information to North Carolina's county and municipal clerks and regional agency secretaries and their deputies. Clerk-Net's online address is www.sog.unc.edu/node/75.

Chapter 15

Local Government Information Technology

Shannon Howle Tufts

Information technology (hereinafter IT) has fundamentally altered many aspects of daily life, including interactions with the government. The importance of the Internet continues to grow as more citizens use it to find pertinent information, purchase goods and services, and participate in virtual communities. By capitalizing on the Internet revolution, governments can create new channels of communication and new methods for participation via electronic government (e-government).

It is undeniable that the role of IT in the public sector has changed rapidly over the past decade. This fact, coupled with increased citizen and business demands for information and services, should encourage government involvement in e-government initiatives and related uses of information technologies. The computer systems that were once luxury investments for wealthy cities and counties are now supporting almost every function of local government. In virtually all local governments across North Carolina, IT investments are becoming an increasingly important area of attention for elected officials and administrative leadership alike.

Certain key technology changes have emerged over the last several years that have directly impacted local and state government entities. The first involves a transition to a digitally converged world. Almost all aspects of telephony, television, video, audio, and other communication technologies are converging into single-source platforms, as evidenced by the proliferation of smart devices which can do everything from remotely starting your car, to paying your bills, to streaming live video. Such newly converged media require robust, secure infrastructures and mobile applications. For example, local governments can now use basic smart phones to capture video of public meetings and stream the recordings directly to the Internet without any sophisticated interfaces or equipment.

Another important change relates to local governments having to grapple with supporting older, legacy systems (such as applications running on mainframe computers or using outmoded programming language) while migrating to more robust systems. Maintaining legacy systems while planning for their phasing out is critical. However, large-scale investments are required to replace such systems with newer technologies that are scalable for the future.

Computer and telecommunications security is another area that has grown in importance in our ever-evolving technical world. Technological security, both physical and logical, is critical to protecting the data and property collected and maintained by government. Such protection, however, should not limit opportunities for new forms of digital civic or employee engagement.

As the foregoing examples show, the management of and investment in IT has become more critical than ever, and budgetary pressures and media coverage of large-scale technology failures in the public sector further drive this point home. Fortunately, there are many new tools, such as IT governance structures and IT service management, that can help to improve the quality of IT investments.

IT service management, as found in the Information Technology Infrastructure Library (ITIL), a recognized set of best practices, centers on a pervasive service orientation that enables end users to work more efficiently and effectively, while building a knowledge base of all technology assets within a given organization. This repository of knowledge, in turn, has a positive impact on IT investments and effective risk management, as seen in utilizing asset management and GIS[1] to maintain appropriate inventory and rapidly troubleshoot public works issues such as broken water mains.

Additional recent technological changes, while exciting, could prove challenging for local governments. These include the pervasive use of personal technology in the workplace, the "greening" of IT, and cloud computing. Smart phones have become commonplace, with individuals using them to do many things—transact personal business by, for example, engaging in social media interactions and banking and shopping online—in many places, including at the office. These devices are now ubiquitous in the workplace, but too often associated security and information management issues are not fully understood or taken into account. "Green" —or environmentally sustainable—computing has become a popular term in the technology realm. With increased financial pressures on governments due to lackluster economic conditions, organizations are working to improve their energy efficiency by consolidating data centers, moving to virtual platforms, and investing in cloud computing.[2] The use of cloud computing to manage basic applications and data stores is becoming an increasingly useful option for governments. In particular, private cloud computing with limited service access and governmental control and ownership of the service implementation is expected to have positive returns for local jurisdictions.

Information systems are not merely a necessary investment in the overall business planning of government, they are also vital for conducting future governmental affairs. Proper attention placed on governmental and technological trends can provide a foundation and roadmap for examining future technology projects. The State of North Carolina and its cities and counties have received considerable recognition for their efforts in public information technology and e-government. A variety of early activities and key factors at the state and local government levels created a favorable environment for technology investments across the state, including a technology-savvy business and citizen population that adds additional impetus to government investment in technology; strong legislative support of strategic management of IT resources; and an excellent association for government IT professionals, the North Carolina Local Government Information Systems Association (NCLGISA), which allows for knowledge sharing and true collaboration across state and local government entities. All of these pieces—plus the fact that there are many major research universities located throughout the state—make North Carolina quite attractive for technology advancement.

Overview of Trends

A variety of advancements and trends have occurred in the past decade related to IT adoption and implementation in North Carolina's public sector. This section highlights some of the most critical trends, including the continued professionalization of IT staff, particularly the Chief Information Officer (CIO); a move to enterprise-wide technology efforts complete with performance metrics; and the advent and impact of social media. These trends offer significant advantages to citizens, businesses, employees, and visitors. In addition, the trends have been proven to generate cost savings, increase efficiencies, and improve effectiveness in a variety of cases.

Chief Information Officers and Professional Staff

The public sector has made incredible strides in technology over the past decade. Investments in IT have placed many states, counties, and municipalities on equal footing with leading private sector companies across the nation. In virtu-

1. GIS stands for geographic information systems.

2. Stated simply, this involves using remote servers that are hosted on the Internet to store, manage, and process data, as opposed to using local servers to do these things.

ally every governmental jurisdiction, IT is playing a vital role, impacting every department and function within the jurisdiction. In order to help the public sector move beyond the status quo and leverage technology as a means of delivering more efficient and effective services, as well as to help it gain and maintain a competitive economic development advantage, the role of Chief Information Officer (CIO) has emerged as a mechanism for connecting the business units within an organization with the IT staff. In essence, the CIO is the linchpin between these two seemingly disparate, and often contentious, components of an organization.

In the past few decades, CIOs have been revered as supreme organizational aligners. They have also been assailed as over-titled technocrats. Regardless of the hyperbole, one thing is certain: the job of CIO is always demanding and often difficult. The CIO is responsible for reaching out and disseminating critical technology plans to senior executives in order to engender their support, while keeping one foot firmly planted in the realm of current technologies and while keeping an eye on emerging technologies. The CIO must possess both a vision for the future and an ability to remember and honor the historical legacies of the organization. Too often, CIOs are forced to choose between the business units on one side and the information technology department on the other when, in fact, the crux of their role is to build bridges between these organizational silos. The CIO must learn to skillfully navigate the various minefields and bear traps that can blow up and ensnare technology projects.

While the role of the CIO in the public sector is not as established as it is in the private sector, it has been gaining in status over the past few decades.

As early as 1981, the title "Chief Information Officer" emerged in private sector literature as the defined leadership role for IT.[3] Extensive research has been conducted on the attributes and characteristics of successful CIOs in the private sector.[4] Some of the most commonly cited traits include being a generalist, having significant power and authority in the organization, and providing a common vision for the implementation of strategic information technology.

Based on the success of the CIO in providing leadership and status to IT projects in the private sector, the federal public sector followed suit by institutionalizing the position with the passage of the 1996 Clinger-Cohen Act.[5]

Today, as public sector IT investment decisions are, by necessity and as described above, becoming increasingly strategic at the federal, state, and local government levels, the existence of the CIO position and of a strategic planning structure has become critical to facilitating technology implementation. As critical, in fact, in the public sector as in the private realm.

As the lines between traditional functional services and departments begin to blur, public sector CIOs, along with IT directors, are charged with managing the constantly expanding role of IT within government and with providing the leadership and skills necessary to successfully capitalize on technology investments.

CIOs are in unique and challenging positions within their respective organizations and within their peer groups. Increasingly, CIOs and IT professionals are considered central to strategic organizational enhancement and goal attainment. The rate of growth of CIO positions in the public sector in recent years speaks to the importance of the role and, more importantly, to the shift away from traditional operational roles for IT professionals to emerging roles as leaders and strategic value creators. Karahanna and Watson discuss the unique nature of CIO leadership as being a hybrid of operational and technical efficacies balanced by classic business management skills such as relationship, change, and people management. This balancing act is often skewed by organizational culture and situational contingencies.[6]However, the penultimate role for the CIO according to recent studies is to serve effectively in both the strategic and tactical realms of the organization, thereby managing the competing values of being a hands-on

---

3. S.H. Schelin, "Managing the Human Side of Information Technology: A Public-Private Comparison of Chief Information Officers." Dissertation, North Carolina State University, 2004.

4. See, for example, IBM Corp., *The New Voice of the CIO: Insights from the Global Chief Information Officer Study* (Somers, NY, 2009); E. Karahanna and R.T. Watson, "Information Systems Leadership," *IEEE Transactions on Engineering Management* 53, no. 2 (2006): 171–76; L.M. Applegate and J.J. Elam, "New Information Systems Leaders: A Changing Role in a Changing World," *MIS Quarterly* 16, no. 4 (1992): 469–90.

5. 40 U.S.C. §§ 11101 *et seq.*

6. Karahanna and Watson, "Information Systems Leadership," *supra* note 4.

technologist and a visionary leader.[7] Furthermore, in 2009, IBM released a study detailing the competencies of the effective CIO based on a study of more than 2,500 private and public sector CIOs. The findings of the study highlight the need for the CIO to serve in both operational and strategic capacities, with a clear focus on realistic innovation, creating organizational value, and enhancing financial investments.[8] Each of these areas of focus speaks to the need for CIOs to perform higher-level managerial and leadership roles within their departments, as well as within their organizations. In fact, a common theme across the body of CIO leadership research is the need for the CIO to become operationally excellent internally (within the technology realm) and to become politically astute and powerful externally (i.e., across the organization).

Enterprise IT Investments and Performance Metrics

Over the past three decades, the primary role of government IT organizations was to improve the efficiency of business processes. Now, IT has moved beyond its efficiency role to become a significant partner in helping organizations gain a business advantage. Today, CIOs are being asked to show quantifiable value from IT investments. As we advance through the twenty-first century, all government sectors have become interested in using "interoperable" technologies—those that allow various departments to work between systems or products without special efforts on the part of the staff. The need to be able to traverse across all platforms, operating systems, and traditional departmental-focused data stores, also called "stovepipes," has become an increasingly necessary, albeit arduous, requirement.[9] The use of interoperable systems is necessary to achieve a seamless government—one that is citizen-centric, efficient, and effective. By allowing data to be shared between departments and agencies, governments can, among other improvements, begin to view people as individuals and not just case numbers. Implementing new interoperable technologies is a laborious process, however, given problems with connectivity, infrastructure, hardware, and software often seen in government units at all levels.

Despite these challenges, the digital government paradigm, which emphasizes coordinated network-building, external collaboration, and customer service, is slowly replacing the traditional bureaucratic paradigm, with its focus on standardization, hierarchy, departmentalization, and operational cost-efficiency.[10] All of the possibilities and the transformational aspects of IT are now taking root in the public sector. To realize the ideal of digital government, state and local government officials, elected and appointed, must be able to tap into existing capacities and work to expand them.

One of the key concerns of this networked and interconnected bureaucracy involves figuring out the best ways to successfully adopt and implement information technologies. The varying rates of success for IT projects and initiatives has led to the question, What types of factors affect the ability of a governmental entity to capably adopt and implement technologies? State and local governments constantly invest in IT initiatives for advancing the efficiency and effectiveness of service delivery, thereby expanding the need for governors, legislators, chief agency executives, and IT professionals to consider, evaluate, and approve these investments in valid and transparent ways. Given mounting fiscal pressures, there is an even greater need for state and local government decision makers to understand how specific commitments of organizational resources for IT result in improved outputs and outcomes. In reality, many of these investment decisions are made based on the need to maintain existing IT systems, to implement policy initiatives, or to respond to mandates imposed on specific governmental entities. Very often these investments leave administrators and elected officials wondering if the benefits were worth the resources sacrificed.

The realities of a large percentage of IT failures, the fiscal pressures from struggling national and state economies, and the need to align organizational goals with IT investments combine to create an environment at all levels of gov-

7. G. Westerman and P. Weill, *What Are the Key Capabilities of Effective CIOs?* (Center for Information Systems Research, MIT Sloan School of Management, 2004).

8. IBM Corp., *The New Voice of the CIO, supra* note 4.

9. David Landsbergen, Jr., and George Wolken, Jr., "Realizing the Promise: Government Information Systems and the Fourth Generation of Information Technology," *Public Administration Review* 61, no. 2 (2001): 206–20.

10. Alfred TatKei Ho, "Reinventing Local Government and the EGovernment Initiative," *Public Administration Review* 62, no. 4 (2002): 434–44.

ernment that requires a more systematic approach for validating IT investment decisions. One of the more popular approaches to assessing a diverse IT portfolio is through performance measurement and management.

Performance Measurement and Management

Performance measurement is a quantitative way to link the inputs (resources used to provide a service) to the outputs (immediate results) and outcomes (long-term results) of service provision. Performance measurement is often defined as "measurement on a regular basis of the results (outcomes) and efficiency of services or programs."[11] In the public sector, the focus of performance measurement and management has centered on analyzing key aspects of service delivery to determine quantifiable indicators of performance.

Traditional public sector performance metrics include various input, output, activity, productivity, quality, and outcome measures. These metrics are used in a variety of governmental areas. One area lacking clearly defined, repeatable, and comparable measures, however, is the realm of IT. While many state and local government IT departments have implemented some form of performance measurement, these metrics have typically tended to focus on input, output, and process areas. As technology investments become more mission-critical, and as budgetary pressures to reduce governmental expenditures show no signs of letting up, IT professionals must embrace other aspects of performance measurement, such as service quality, outcomes, and financial impact (cost-benefit). These kinds of metrics will provide senior elected and appointed officials with accurate and reliable information about the true value and return on investments associated with IT investments.

One of the primary public sector IT goals is to support the business objectives of government and to facilitate organizational efforts to provide efficient and effective services to citizens, businesses, and visitors. IT has become a strategic partner in governmental efforts to provide high-quality, consistent, and equitable services. The development of an enterprise-wide focus on IT—a focus on the customer and on the use of IT to produce efficient and effective customer service—is part of the driving vision of IT divisions within governments. This vision marks a significant departure from the traditional government "silo" approach, with its individualistic, department- or agency-centric efforts.[12]

Many current technology efforts cross multiple state and local governmental agencies with a single goal of providing services to citizens, businesses, and visitors. In this new environment, technology is used as the basis for communication, interoperability, and data and resource sharing. Furthermore, technology is the vehicle through which cost reductions can occur by increasing the efficiency and effectiveness of services through the use of an enterprise architecture and standards (these concepts are discussed more fully in the section immediately below). Governments throughout the United States are using enterprise approaches to achieve high levels of return on investments, greater customer satisfaction, and increased cost savings. As the role of performance measurement and management increases within state and local governments due to political and economic pressures, the focus on enterprise-based, centralized technology services and solutions is further intensifying.

Enterprise Approaches to IT Investments

The enterprise approach to technology investments is one of the core competencies required for a strong, useful performance measurement and management program. Essentially, this approach involves looking at an organization as a holistic unit instead of as separate, individual, "stovepipe" departments. Too often, technology departments in both the public and private sectors are asked to allocate resources to projects that benefit only one department of their given organizations. For example, it is not uncommon to find more than ten different work-order systems within one governmental department or agency being used to serve citizens. This type of individualistic design, procurement, and deployment leads to highly inefficient, ineffective technology solutions that do not create strategic value. In fact, using these disparate work-order systems actually adds significant costs to an organization's bottom line, given the amount of duplicate data entry and poor customer service that occurs.

11. Harry Hatry, *Performance Measurement: Getting Results* (Washington, DC: Urban Institute Press, 1999).

12. Note, however, that many performance metrics do not echo this newfound focus on service and enterprise thinking.

The enterprise approach allows the governmental CIO, through the use of an IT governance structure, to understand the needs of the various departments and agencies that make up the governmental unit and then create a comprehensive technological solution to serve multiple groups, whenever possible. Essentially, this approach identifies commonalities and applies sound economies of scale principles to investment decisions. It also allows the organization to begin analyzing business processes, operating rules and procedures, and functional work flows in order to identify where cost savings can occur. Through business process mapping, a component of the enterprise approach, unnecessary hand-offs can be eliminated, processes can be streamlined, and automation can be applied to serve the newly created operating environment. The benefits of the enterprise approach also extend into strategic decision making. By creating clear channels of communication and empowering an IT governance structure, the value of specific projects can be weighed in light of other projects, based on enterprise impact, in order to diffuse perceived agency favoritism. Although the enterprise approach concept is not new, its potential for adding significant value to governments and their technology departments is often overlooked.

Traditional Business Case Metrics

Many of the desired effects and outcomes of IT investments are obscured by a lack of uniformity across investments and a tendency to justify investments on a stand-alone basis. Other challenges emerge from a lack of interest and attention from management, as well as from limited controls and evaluation mechanisms. The business case, and related business case analysis, is an analytical concept used by organizations to understand and support decision-making processes under conditions of priority, economic return, benefit enhancement, and fiscal constraint. Given current economic conditions, business case analysis provides a sound, valid mechanism to manage performance, as well as to understand the fiscal impact of technology investments.

Business case analysis, as touted by the federal, state, and local governments, presumes an investment portfolio management strategy for technology endeavors and requires planning which ensures that IT investments are reconciled with the goals and objectives at the organization-wide level (enterprise approach) and at the programmatic level (agency approach).[13] Furthermore, the business case process requires demonstrable congruence between the stated goals and objectives of a government's strategic plan, objectives, goals, or roadmap and the proposed technology project's own plan and requirements. This articulated relationship is based on the establishment of the technical approach, timetable, and resources required to begin to flesh out the performance criteria for the project but, more importantly, it is designed to ensure alignment between IT investments, organizational goals, and, ultimately, to assist in the determination of appropriate performance metrics centered on business value. Typically, these metrics have a classic financial focus and are viewed as benefits and costs.

Classic examples of technology-related business metrics include total cost of ownership, return on investment, and effectiveness of service delivery as a function of technology enhancement. These types of metrics require that governments engender the ability to link technology investments to performance and results related to service delivery or tax dollar expenditures. A renewed focus on demonstrating these linkages has been forged, out of necessity, by the current economic situation and has challenged many government technology organizations to develop new processes to capture such information for dissemination and managerial/public evaluation.

Additional Value-Based Performance Metrics

While the aforementioned business case approach and the associated business metrics are valuable components of a performance measurement and management practice for IT, they do not present a complete picture for performance measurement and management associated with IT investments. Using the business case alone, it is all too common for governments to become mired in a business case metrics mentality, to the exclusion of other critical technology performance measures. Therefore, additional metrics focused on the areas of internal effectiveness and efficiency,

13. L. Douglas Smith, James F. Campbell, Ashok Subramanian, David A. Bird, and Anthony C. Nelson, "Strategic Planning for Municipal Information Systems," *American Review of Public Administration* 31, no. 2 (2000): 139–57.

customer satisfaction, and learning and innovation are needed. These measures provide feedback about other critical functions of IT investments, including user experiences, staff skillsets, and back-office improvements, many of which do not demonstrate a true financial return. The following metrics are not designed to be comprehensive or all-inclusive but, rather, to provide a provocative approach to re-examining IT investments and performance through the eyes of the business units and agencies served by those investments.

Internal Effectiveness and Efficiency Metrics

These types of metrics are becoming increasingly important, as privatization conversations and efforts are taking place across governments. In order to adequately assess the benefit of privatizing IT, governments must have accurate and reliable metrics related to their current operating costs. In addition, utilizing these internal effectiveness and efficiency metrics to benchmark against comparable governments may identify cost savings potential and business process re-engineering opportunities, thereby lowering IT expenditures.

Examples of internal effectiveness and efficiency metrics include the following:

- IT support cost per employee—IT staff salary and fringes divided by the total number of government employees supported
- Comparison of IT support cost per employee to peer governments
- IT maintenance and support cost per employee—use same formula as in first bulleted item above, but add in the total operating/maintenance costs for the government and then divide by the total number of full-time equivalents

Customer Satisfaction and Responsiveness Metrics

Commonly used in the IT arena, these metrics denote the value of technology services to internal customers. Too often, though, these metrics involve discussions of system availability in broad strokes, which provide little value to the IT agency and do not adequately describe the user experience in true business terms. The following customer satisfaction and responsiveness metrics do, however, include assessing business unit impacts and business priority levels as a means of applying the measurement to business outcomes.

- Customer satisfaction surveys—conducted annually or biannually, supplemented with monthly customer satisfaction surveys based on help desk tickets
- System availability by application priority level—
  - measured as a percentage of employees affected by outages, based on application priority level (as established by the IT governance group)
  - measured as a percentage of business hours affected by outages, based on application priority level
  - measured as cost by business unit
- Incident resolution within service level agreement target

Learning and Innovation Metrics

This is an area of IT performance measurement that has enjoyed continued growth and significance in recent years. These metrics are designed to stimulate IT staff creativity by focusing on innovation and organizational engagement. The underlying purpose of these metrics extends beyond innovation for innovation's sake and requires the IT staff to gain deep working knowledge of business units' needs, processes, and goals. Ultimately, these metrics offer a vehicle for creating high levels of employee engagement and involvement, coupled with intrinsic motivation tools, to offset the limited funding and salary increases seen of late due to budget situations.

Learning and innovation metrics include the following:

- Number of innovative ideas generated per IT employee over a given period
- Ratio of innovative ideas implemented to innovative ideas generated
- Cost savings associated with innovative idea implementations
- Training days per employee—mechanism to demonstrate increased skill-sets and knowledge base
- Number of professional certifications per IT employee

The aforementioned performance metrics are offered as a primer for developing a comprehensive performance measurement and management program. However, such a program should be comprehensive, incorporating not only clear business metrics, led by goal alignment between government business needs and technology investments, but also metrics that will ensure organizational competitiveness, satisfaction, and improvement. IT organizations today rely upon a wide variety of performance metrics, but many of these tend to focus too much on classic IT measures, such as broad system availability, minimizing downtime, and website page visits. While these sorts of metrics are useful internally to the IT department, they offer little to the larger business units to help determine if IT investments are having a positive impact on organizational strategy. By contrast, business case metrics, focused on financial returns, coupled with metrics related to business alignment; customer satisfaction; IT responsiveness, efficiency, and effectiveness; and innovation provide a holistic approach to both incentivize IT staff to higher levels of performance and to ensure that the strategic value of IT investments is apparent to the business units.

Social Media Usage in Government: The New E-Government Frontier

Social media, defined as "a group of Internet-based applications that build on the ideological and technological foundations of Web 2.0, and that allow the creation and exchange of user-generated content,"[14] has become a phenomenon of epic proportions. Every day, new social media sites emerge offering end-users a vehicle for technology-based engagement. The hallmark applications found in the social media landscape include Facebook, Twitter, LinkedIn, Flickr, YouTube, and Instagram, among hundreds of others. Facebook is consistently viewed as the leader among social media tools, and recent metrics solidify its utility and importance in the lives of individual and organizational users. Current estimates place the number of "monthly active" Facebook users at roughly 1.23 billion, with more than 51 percent of all U.S. Internet users aged twelve and older having a Facebook account.[15] With more than half of the American population using Facebook, the platform offers governments a unique opportunity to efficiently engage and inform citizens in lean economic times.

There is a perception that social media can bring benefits to areas such as citizen participation, transparency, accountability, and customer service, and this perception is pushing governments to use social media more and more, even making it part of the work expectation for some employees. Many of these perceived benefits are drawn from successful e-government efforts to utilize technology to improve efficiency and effectiveness and to facilitate service delivery. In this vein, a study conducted by Stateline.org indicates that forty-seven of the fifty U.S. governors have a social media presence for official governmental communications, with Facebook pages and Twitter accounts being the most frequently used tools.[16] Even with high usage rates, however, governments are lacking clear guidance on how to effectively use Facebook, Twitter, and other social media vehicles to meaningfully affect citizen engagement and produce positive outcomes for their citizens and their respective organizations.

Further complicating governmental use of social media are issues of employee rights and employee conduct. The issue of employee conduct, both on- and off-duty, is certainly not a new concern, but social media use offers additional twists on old challenges. For example, in Savannah, Georgia, a female firefighter was terminated due to personal photographs posted on her private MySpace page; in response, she brought a lawsuit alleging bias and violation of her constitutional free speech rights. The fire chief contended that the firefighter was using her role as a Savannah firefighter to "promote herself as a model for other personal publicity reasons," which violated departmental policy.[17] The court upheld the termination and denied the firefighter's claims of discrimination and First Amendment protection. In another case, a Staten Island, New York, human resources manager was fired due to falsely claiming to be serving

14. Andreas M. Kaplan and Michael Haenlein, "Users of the World Unite! The Challenges and Opportunities of Social Media," *Business Horizons* 53, no. 1 (2010): 59–68.

15. *See* Facebook, "Facebook Reports Fourth Quarter and Full Year 2013 Results, Full Year 2013 Business Highlights" (Jan. 29, 2014), http://investor.fb.com/releasedetail.cfm?ReleaseID=821954.

16. M. Mahling, "How Many Governors Are Using Social Media?" *Stateline* (July 22, 2011), www.pewstates.org/projects/stateline/headlines/how-many-governors-are-using-social-media-85899376875.

17. Jan Skutch, "Judge: Firefighter Not Victim of Discrimination," *Savannah Morning News* (June 13, 2009), http://savannahnow.com/intown/2009-06-13/judge-firefighter-not-victim-discrimination#.U2pq84FdU05.

jury duty while her Facebook status indicated that she was on vacation in Baltimore. Beyond losing her job, the woman was arrested and charged with jury duty summons forgery and faces up to fourteen years in prison.[18]

The examples above speak to a range of issues, including First Amendment rights, Fourth Amendment rights, conduct policies, and discipline and termination practices. The challenges employees face in managing both their professional/work-related use of social media and their personal/off-duty use of social media are plentiful and add another layer of complexity to the orderly functioning of e-government by moving the focus from the citizen to the employee.

Social media tools, practices, and abuses can create additional challenges within workplaces, particularly in public sector venues, where the constitutional rights of employees differ from the constitutional rights of workers in the private sector. Rosenbloom and Bailey underscore the importance of understanding the legal rights of employees, particularly in light of the personal liability a state or local government manager may take on for infringing on the constitutional rights of an employee.[19] Too often, the IT department is being tasked with managing employee access to and participation in social media endeavors through technical solutions without involvement or consideration of human resources issues and challenges. This decision to utilize technology to attempt to mediate what can involve nontechnical, human resources matters is problematic at best and has the potential to create multiple legal challenges. Therefore, social media policies should be linked to and take direction from the values of the organization around communication and conduct. Communicating on a social media platform is just another means of communication, after all—it just happens to be one that tends to have more immediate and far-reaching impact.

Conclusion

IT can be a useful tool for delivering higher-quality, more cost-efficient services. Wise investments by local government in IT can lead to improved service access, reduced transaction costs, and improved internal efficiencies. As governments strive to be more customer-oriented and to provide effective services, technology investments become essential. But few investments pay off when used in isolation or in less than ideal circumstances. Thus, it is critical to understand that the application of technology to poor or inefficient processes will not produce desired cost savings or effectiveness gains. The administration, policies, and procedures surrounding a given function or process also must be revised and fine-tuned in order to provide the highest quality of service. Benefits are most likely to be seen when technology and business processes work in unison, and therefore it is imperative that all technology projects and investments be tightly integrated with and continually measured against a government unit's articulated business goals and vision.

Several steps can be taken to ensure that government technology investment decisions are wise ones. First, a cost-benefit analysis of all projects should be undertaken, along with a clear, multi-year understanding of the total cost of ownership for individual projects. "Total cost of ownership" includes hardware and software maintenance, ongoing training, support, and operations. It is a measure that allows a government unit to plan expenditures in an appropriate manner without neglecting the funding requirements of a given project in the years to come. Next, because upgrades and replacement plans for existing systems are imperative for local governments, funding for them must be included in the unit's budget. Ideally, the governmental entity should separate its budget requests and funding for ongoing IT infrastructure and maintenance from IT project budget requests and funding (typically focused on user departments).

North Carolina is home to a multitude of successful, technology-friendly local governments and should continue investing in technology to enhance the internal and external services of these entities and of the state at large. Government is focused on growth and on the future, and it is imperative that technology investments keep pace with that

18. John Slattery, "S.I. Woman Allegedly Faked Jury Duty to Take Vacation," CBS New York (Oct. 28, 2010), http://newyork.cbslocal.com/2010/10/28/s-i-woman-allegedly-faked-jury-duty-to-take-vacation/.

19. D.H. Rosenbloom and M. Bailey, "What Every Public Personnel Manager Should Know About the Constitution," in eds. S. W. Hays and R. C. Kearney, *Public Personnel Administration: Problems and Prospects*, 4th ed. (Upper Saddle River, NJ: Prentice Hall, 2003), 20–36.

vision. One potential roadblock to this happening is the outsourcing of critical functions. While strategic, or multisector, sourcing—which involves identifying specific cost centers or lines of business within IT where privatization offers the greatest opportunities for cost savings—can be beneficial, complete privatization or outsourcing of all IT functions has not proved successful in most state and local governments.[20] Cost savings are rarely achieved when privatization occurs, regardless of initial contract assurances, especially given the level of 24/7 service expected by staff and citizens alike.

The State of North Carolina and its counties and municipalities are moving into an exciting period of growth and renewal. It is critical—for both the government and its citizens—that this momentum be sustained. Using technology as a tool for improving efficiency, effectiveness, and responsiveness in government will go a long way toward realizing this goal.

Additional Resources

Friedman, Thomas L. *The World Is Flat: A Brief History of the Twenty-first Century.* New York: Farrar, Straus, and Giroux, 2005.

Garson, G. David. *Public Information Technology and E-Governance: Managing the Virtual State.* Boston: Jones & Bartlett, 2006.

Garson, G. David, ed. *Handbook of Public Information Systems.* 2nd ed. New York: Marcel Dekker, 2005. The second edition has many new articles, and the articles carried over from the first edition are all revised.

Gordon & Glickson, LLC. *Information Technology Outsourcing: A Handbook for Government.* Washington, DC: International City and County Management Association, 2005.

Gottshalk. P. "The Changing Roles of IT Leaders." In *Strategic Information Technology: Opportunities for Competitive Advantage,* edited by R. Papp. Hershey, PA: Idea Group Publishing, 2001, 150–68.

West, Darrell M. *Digital Government: Technology and Public Sector Performance.* Princeton, NJ: Princeton University Press, 2005.

About the Author

Shannon Howle Tufts is a School of Government faculty member whose areas of interest include information technology planning, electronic government, survey methodology, wireless technologies, and business process reengineering.

The Center for Public Technology (CPT), housed within the School of Government, provided assistance in the preparation of this chapter. The CPT was created in 2001 in response to requests from local governments for help developing the capacity to improve services and strengthen their communities through the skillful use of IT.

The CPT focuses on three dimensions: education/teaching, advising, and research and writing. The CPT offers training, assessment and evaluation, and best practices for engaging in e-government, along with a host of other services. One important offering is the Chief Government Information Officers Certification Program (CGCIO), the first local government–specific course in the nation to certify IT professionals as chief information officers. The center also offers specialized training on topics such as security, wireless technologies, IT investment methodologies, performance-based technology contracting, the role of IT in growing populations, and stakeholder evaluation of e-government efforts. The training is integrated with other courses offered by the School of Government and by associations such as the Carolinas Association of Governmental Purchasing, the State of North Carolina, Western Carolina University's Local Government Training Partners, and Public Technology Inc.

20. The rate of success appears to depend upon the size of the government unit. U.S. Government Accountability Office (GAO), Competitive Sourcing: Greater Emphasis Needed on Increasing Efficiency and Improving Performance (Feb. 2004), 6 (discussing GAO's findings regarding competitive sourcing).

The CPT also offers advising services to help address issues, opportunities, and challenges in IT management that are specific to North Carolina local governments. Finally, the center conducts a variety of research and publishes on numerous technology-related topics, including studies of leadership, best practices, legislative updates, and case studies. Additional information on the CPT can be found at www.sog.unc.edu/cpt.

Chapter 16

Performance Measurement: A Tool for Accountability and Performance Improvement

David N. Ammons

Operating in today's environment of limited resources ratchets up the pressure on local government programs to achieve their intended results and to do so efficiently. Citizens depend on county and city services and increasingly are adamant not only that they be produced in sufficient quantity and with adequate timeliness to satisfy public needs but also that they meet reasonable standards of quality.

Those local governments that have been most aggressive in their pursuit of service quality and efficiency tend also to be the counties and cities that have been most interested in measuring their performances. For them, performance measurement is a useful tool that confirms their successes and alerts them to programs in need of greater scrutiny.

Uses of Performance Measures: Accountability and Performance Improvement

A rudimentary set of performance measures reveals how many units of service have been delivered. More sophisticated sets of measures provide this basic information and much more. A good set of performance measures also reveals how efficiently a given service was rendered, at what level of quality it was delivered, and, ideally, what effect it is having on service recipients or on the community as a whole.

Good sets of performance measures have multiple uses. A partial list of these uses includes the following:

- accountability/communication
- support of planning/budgeting efforts
- catalyst for improved operations
- program evaluation
- reallocation of resources
- directing operations
- contract monitoring
- benchmarking

Local governments that are among the leaders in performance measurement rarely limit the application of their measures to a single use. In most cases, their measures support two, three, or even more of the functions noted in the list above. Almost always, one of these uses is accountability.

Citizens like to be reassured that someone in their local government is minding the store. Even if they have little interest in most of the detailed facts and figures of service delivery, citizens rightfully expect that elected and appointed officials will collect and monitor those facts and figures and will ensure that quality service is provided at a fair price.

A good set of performance measures is an important tool for building accountability throughout an organization. By compiling key indicators of performance, supervisors can confirm that work crews are meeting expectations and delivering quality services—in short, they can ensure the accountability of front-line employees. Periodic reporting of selected measures allows supervisors to be accountable to department management for their work, department management to be accountable to central administration, and central administration to be accountable to the governing board. In turn, the periodic publication of key performance measures allows board members to be accountable to the citizenry for local government operations as a whole.

True accountability means more than just assuring the public that revenues are properly collected and reported and that expenditures are made in accordance with prescribed procedures. Accountability includes these important assurances but also entails assurances to the public that government resources are being spent wisely as well as legally and that services of good quality are being produced efficiently. Performance measurement offers a tool for providing such assurances.

The value of performance measurement extends beyond reporting for the sake of accountability, important as that purpose is. Good sets of performance measures also can support a variety of other management purposes. The city manager, for instance, might use performance measures to review with department heads each department's progress on key objectives. The county manager might introduce performance statistics for parks, recreation, and library services as background for a planning retreat of the board of commissioners focusing on leisure services needs. If the local government plans to make major changes in a given program, it might use performance measures to establish a baseline prior to program change and continue monitoring these measures after implementation to see if new strategies are working as intended. Perhaps the government's monitoring system for contracted services relies on performance measures to be sure that contractors are living up to their promises. Some counties and cities compare their own performance to standards or results achieved by other service producers as a step toward improving the quality or efficiency of local services. In each of these examples for all of these governments, performance measurement is an essential tool.

The Importance of Performance Measurement for Management

Good performance measures support a variety of management functions. A good set of measures allows a manager or supervisor to identify operating strengths and weaknesses, target areas for improvement, and recognize improvements when they occur. A good set of measures also helps the manager defend good operations against unwarranted criticism.

Some managers and supervisors operate without good sets of performance measures. They rely instead on general observation and perhaps the comments of service recipients to form their impressions of operating strengths and weaknesses. Often, such impressions are correct and would be borne out by systematic assessments. More frequently than many managers care to admit, however, occasional observations and anecdotes depict a picture that differs from the reality that would be revealed by systematic assessment. Occasionally, strong performers do not look quite so strong when examined in the light of objective evidence, and supposedly weak performers are discovered to be more proficient than previously imagined. With appropriate measurement systems, managers and supervisors can more objectively detect operating deficiencies and target additional attention where it is needed most.

A good measurement system can enhance a talented supervisor's ability to develop the skills of workers, to instruct them in their tasks, to plan and schedule their work, to draw upon the pride and commitment of a work unit, and to motivate greater performance. With the benefit of reliable measures, instructions to subordinates can be more focused, planning more precise, and feedback more objective. In this way, a systematic gauge of program efficiency and effectiveness can augment the value of on-site supervision, with greater value provided not only to upper management but also to the supervisor and the workforce in general.

Receiving customer or citizen feedback is an important responsibility of managers and supervisors, but listening only to intermittent complaints and compliments can produce an incomplete and sometimes inaccurate picture of service quality and efficiency. With systematic performance measurement and reporting, local government programs are less vulnerable to isolated anecdotes that misrepresent the normal state of affairs in service delivery. With good performance measures, a service complaint can be viewed in the context of the norms for that service rather than isolated from such context. Service units with strong performance can more adequately be defended. Weaker units can be identified with greater confidence and targeted for corrective action.

The Value of Performance Measurement to Governing Boards

Even when the governing board hires a manager to handle matters of day-to-day administration, the board retains responsibility for providing general oversight of the local government as a whole and for establishing program priorities. It also retains responsibility for assessing the performance of the manager in directing local government operations. Good performance measures can be helpful in performing these duties. For instance, the governing board might ask the following questions in performing its oversight role:

- Are services being provided efficiently and equitably?
- Do they meet expectations for quality?
- Could better services be provided at a more reasonable cost by contracting out some functions?
- Have deficiencies been identified and are improvements being made where needed?
- Do service results indicate that programs are being properly managed?

Each of these questions can be answered adequately only if reliable data are available.

In recent years, many management experts have advocated more decentralized decision making, allowing field unit supervisors and even front-line employees to make more of the service delivery decisions, as long as their decisions are consistent with a vision or culture established and nurtured by central authorities. Much can be said in favor of a strategy that places greater discretion in the hands of those who know the program best and are closest to the problems. However, without a dependable system for guaranteeing accountability, few governing boards will be willing to increase managerial discretion or encourage managers to permit greater discretion at lower levels of the organization. In the absence of a system for compiling and reporting evidence that programs are being run efficiently and effectively, top officials are more likely to believe that their oversight responsibilities require involvement in or approval of a large portion of the individual decisions made on behalf of the government. Upper management and governing boards are more likely to be receptive if greater supervisory discretion and reductions in administrative red tape are accompanied by clear evidence of favorable program results.

The expense of administering a good performance measurement system is not trivial, but neither are the benefits of a good system. Because of its value to board members, appointed administrators, and the general citizenry, performance measurement has been endorsed by a host of professional associations, including the International City/County Management Association, the Government Finance Officers Association, the Governmental Accounting Standards Board, and the National Academy of Public Administration.

Types of Performance Measures

Performance measures may be divided and categorized in different ways. For the most part, however, the short list below covers the types of measures most relevant to tracking and improving performance in local government:

- output (workload) measures
- efficiency measures
- outcome (effectiveness) measures
- productivity measures[1]

Output (Workload) Measures

When a department reports the number of applications processed, inspections made, or cases handled, it is reporting on its workload or output. These statistics are relatively simple to compile and report, but they are very limited in what they can say about a department or program. They say nothing about the quality or efficiency of the service. They only report how many units of a service were produced or how much of an activity was undertaken.

Although counting and tabulating workload numbers is the most common form of performance reporting in local government, the value of raw output measures for policy and management purposes is extremely limited. This is not to suggest that keeping track of output is unimportant. Comparing output from year to year provides an indication of growing or declining demand for a given service. More importantly, output numbers are often critical ingredients in the calculation of higher-order measures that hold greater value for managerial and policy decisions. Unfortunately, too many local governments depend almost entirely on raw output or workload measures to report their performance. With workload measures alone, the message conveyed by a department or program cannot be "We are efficient" or "We provide quality services." With raw workload measures alone, the only message is "We are busy!"

Efficiency Measures

Measures of efficiency report the relationship between resources used and services produced. Sometimes this relationship is expressed in terms of unit cost—for example, cost per application processed or cost per inspection—or as units of service per $1,000. The relationship between resources and outputs also may be expressed as the ratio of outputs to staff hours—for example, staff hours per license application or curb miles swept per operator hour. When cost accounting systems will not support precise unit cost calculations and the calculation of employee output ratios is impractical, many local governments opt for less precise alternatives by tracking average turnaround time, average daily backlog, or similar operating characteristics.

Outcome (Effectiveness) Measures

Measures of outcome (also known as effectiveness measures) gauge the quality of services and the extent to which a program's objectives are being achieved. Suppose, for instance, that an objective of the solid waste department is to complete at least 95 percent of all refuse collection routes on the scheduled day of collection. If the department compiles statistics showing that 94 percent of the routes were completed as scheduled, this would be an outcome measure, for it measures the extent to which the objective was achieved. Among many other commonly reported types of outcome measures are various measures of responsiveness (for example, average response time to emergencies) and citizen satisfaction (for example, percentage of citizens who are "satisfied" or "very satisfied" with the local recreation program).

1. Readers familiar with the literature on performance measurement will notice that a common category of measurement has been omitted from this list: input measures. Raw input alone, typically in the form of dollars or personnel, does not measure performance. However, when input is measured in relation to output, the result is a measure of efficiency, which does measure an aspect of performance. Hence, efficiency measures are included here, even as inputs alone are excluded.

Productivity Measures

Productivity measures combine efficiency and effectiveness in a single index. These indices are rare in local government, but their absence is of little concern as long as good measures of efficiency and effectiveness are present to guide program efforts.

Examples of productivity indicators include measures produced by calculating unit costs more restrictively than a government calculates its efficiency measures. Rather than dividing program costs by all cases processed, for instance, a productivity measure might divide total program costs by the number of successful cases (that is, only the cases achieving desired results). In essence, a program is penalized in this ratio for poor-quality outputs or unsuccessful results. The ratio reflects both cost and quality.

Developing a Good Set of Performance Measures

Good sets of performance measures include measures that are valid, reliable, understandable, timely, resistant to undesired behavior, sensitive to data collection costs, and focused on important facets of performance.[2] A good set of performance measures reports not only how much service is provided but also how well and how efficiently. Even more important to local governments intent on truly managing their performance, a good set inspires managerial thinking by providing crucial performance data that cannot be ignored. To truly inspire managerial thinking, performance data must focus on important dimensions of service and must be compiled in a manner that either reassures operating officials and program personnel that services are being provided at suitable levels of quality and efficiency or, if not, causes them to investigate possible causes of shortcomings and consider options for improvement.[3] A fundamental test for a set of performance measures, then, is whether it provides data of sufficient importance and in a form that can inspire managerial thinking.

Examples of sets of performance measures for planning and inspection services are provided in Tables 16.1 and 16.2, below. Examples for fire and social services are shown in Table 16.3 and Figure 16.1, below.

Use of Performance Measures in Budgeting

The budget process provides an opportunity to influence program design and priorities among various services. While it is true that the budget itself is a financial document, it is, in fact, much more than that: It is a financial document that reflects program planning and service priorities in financial terms and also, ideally, in terms of performance expectations.

Some public sector budgets retain a strictly line-item format, listing appropriations for each detailed expenditure category. Many governments, however, have adopted formats more conducive to management or policy deliberations. Program budgets, for example, omit most of the object-of-expenditure details that characterize line-item budgets. Instead, they are organized around programs or types of services and report only broader categories of anticipated expenditures. Program budgets often include several measures of performance that reveal past performance and reflect performance expectations for the future.

---

2. C. K. Bens, "Strategies for Implementing Performance Measurement," *ICMA Management Information Service Report* 18 (Nov. 1986): 1–14; C. Broom, M. Jackson, V. Vogelsang Coombs, and J. Harris, *Performance Measurement: Concepts and Techniques* (Washington, DC: American Society for Public Administration, 1998); H. P. Hatry, "Performance Measurement Principles and Techniques," *Public Productivity Review* 4 (Dec. 1980): 312–39; H. P. Hatry, *Performance Measurement: Getting Results* (Washington, DC: The Urban Institute Press, 1999); H. P. Hatry, D. M. Fisk, J. R. Hall Jr., P. S. Schaenman, and L. Snyder, *How Effective Are Your Community Services?* (Washington, DC: Urban Institute and International City/County Management Association and The Urban Institute, 2006), 3.

3. David N. Ammons, "Performance Measurement and Managerial Thinking," *Public Performance and Management Review* 25 (June 2002): 344–47.

Table 16.1 Example of Performance Measures for Planning

	FY10 Actual	FY11 Actual	Target
Encourage participation by a wide cross-section of area residents on advisory boards			
% of neighborhoods with at least one appointee to four standing advisory boards	78%	78%	75%
Integrate green buildings into development projects			
% of projects requiring town board review to incorporate "green" building standards	100%	0%	50%
Provide timely response to complaints and violations			
Average number of business days from receipt of complaint to site inspection	1	1.22	< 5
% of violations brought into voluntary compliance	57%	83%	80%
Provide timely information to applicants			
% of development application submittals reviewed and sent comments within ten business days	79%	100%	90%
Improve departmental coordination through Technical Review Committee (TRC) review of new development			
% of applications for TRC review able to be approved or approved with conditions in the first meeting	75%	100%	75%
Promote professional development through certification			
% of zoning officials certified	25%	33%	33%
% of planners certified	66%	66%	100%
Represent the town on regional committees and efforts			
% of regional meetings attended where town had an appointed seat	67%	88%	80%

Source: Excerpted from Town of Hillsborough, North Carolina, *FY13 Adopted Budget & Financial Plan*, 109.

Another prominent budget format is the performance budget. Once again, many line-item details are omitted from the document itself, and broader categories of expenditure are organized around departments, activities, or programs. In the case of performance budgeting, measures of performance become the central focus of budget deliberations as managers and governing boards discuss performance successes and disappointments, hammer out plans for performance improvement and resource reallocation, and focus on budgetary decisions that will enable operating units to achieve desired performance levels.

A local government's decision to choose a program or performance budget format over a line-item format does not guarantee a change in the focus or nature of budgetary debate. However, it does set the stage for budget deliberations that focus a little less on office supplies, fuel, insurance premiums, and other categories of expenditure, and a lot more on services and program results. Budget formats that incorporate good performance measures—especially efficiency and outcome measures—recognize and advance the planning and managerial opportunities in the budgetary process. They are designed to equip elected and appointed decision makers with the performance facts and figures for a given program, as well as the resource facts and figures, that will help them plan wisely and manage prudently.

Although the Government Finance Officers Association (GFOA) refrains from endorsing one particular budget format over all others, it nevertheless advocates the use of performance measures. Included among the criteria for the GFOA's Distinguished Budget Presentation Award is this guideline: "The document should provide objective measures of progress toward accomplishing the government's mission as well as goals and objectives for specific units and programs."[4]

Echoing the GFOA's assertion that performance measurement is an ingredient of a good budget, the National Advisory Council on State and Local Budgeting considers performance evaluation to be the fourth of the four principles

4. Government Finance Officers Association, *GFOA Detailed Criteria Location Guide: Distinguished Budget Presentation Awards Program* (Chicago: GFOA, 2011).

Table 16.2 Example of Performance Measures for Inspections

Durham City–County Inspections

The City–County Inspections Department is a merged City and County department that administers and enforces the North Carolina State Building Codes and Durham City–County Zoning Ordinances.

	FY11 Actual	FY12 Estimated	FY13 Adopted
Objective: To provide accurate and prompt plan review by reviewing 90% of all residential plans within five working days			
% of residential plans reviewed within five days	99%	95%	90%
% plan errors found in field	0.34%	1%	1%
Number of plans reviewed	2,625	2,324	2,324
Objective: To provide timely response to customer requests by responding to requested inspections within twenty-four hours 90% of the time			
% of inspections performed within twenty-four hours	98.2%	90%	90%
Number of inspections per inspector per day	17.3	17.3	16.0
Number of inspections performed	71,103	73,736	73,736
Objective: To provide for the safety and health of citizens by ensuring that all construction meets the North Carolina State Building Codes by performing two quality control inspections of the work of each inspector per month			
Number of quality control inspections per inspector per month	2.7	2.0	2.0
% inspections found to be accurate	99%	98%	98%
Number of quality control checks	643	523	480

Source: Excerpted from City of Durham, North Carolina, *FY 2012–2013 Adopted Budget*, VIII.4–VIII.6.

of the budget process, following the setting of goals, developing approaches to achieve them, and developing a budget consistent with these approaches.[5]

> Performance measures, including efficiency and effectiveness measures, should be presented in basic budget materials, including the operating budget document, and should be available to stakeholders. . . . At least some of these measures should document progress toward achievement of previously developed goals and objectives. More formal reviews and documentation of those reviews should be carried out as part of the overall planning, decision-making, and budget process.[6]

Despite all the advantages that performance measurement offers and the numerous endorsements it boasts, the act of incorporating performance measures into the budget process will not render the often arduous task of making budget decisions suddenly simple. Performance measures will help identify operational strengths and weaknesses and will gauge changes in efficiency and progress toward meeting objectives, but they can neither formulate the perfect budget nor prescribe remedies for operational deficiencies. Governing boards will still struggle to set priorities—and struggle to stretch resources to fund those priorities. Operating officials must still design program improvement strategies, but performance measures can provide a baseline and a gauge for assessing the success or failure of those strategies.

5. National Advisory Council on State and Local Budgeting, *Recommended Budget Practices: A Framework for Improved State and Local Government Budgeting* (Chicago: GFOA, 1998), 4–5.

6. National Advisory Council on State and Local Budgeting, *Recommended Budget Practices*, cited in full at note 5, above, at 62. Quoted material is drawn from Practice 11.1.

Table 16.3 Example of Performance Measures for Fire Services

	FY10–11 Actual	FY11–12 Estimated	FY12–13 Projected
Effectiveness			
Average response time to fire/medical/rescue calls (target: ≤ 4 minutes)	3.64 min.	3.60 min.	3.60 min.
Average turnout time (target: ≤ 1 minute)	0.85 min.	0.72 min.	0.75 min.
% of fire/medical/rescue calls responded to within 4 minutes	64.6%	65.0%	66.0%
Average response time to hazardous materials (HazMat) incidents (target: ≤ 10 minutes)	10.05 min.	10.5 min.	10.5 min.
% of HazMat incidents responded to within 10 minutes	62%	60%	60%
% of structure fires contained within the room of origin (target: ≥ 70%)	78%	70%	70%
% of fires where cause was determined (target: ≥ 85%)	96%	97%	95%
Fires per 1,000 population (target: ≤ 5)	3.86	5.0	5.0
% of commercial properties inspected annually (target: 100%)	99%	98%	98%
Workload			
Building fires	321	300	310
Medical calls	17,638	18,000	18,000
Hazmat calls	139	150	200
Participants in fire prevention education events	36,902	60,000	60,000
Annual inspections performed by suppression companies	6,211	6,000	6,000
Annual inspections performed by inspectors	3,039	3,200	3,500

Source: Adapted from City of Winston-Salem, North Carolina, *FY 2012–2013 Adopted Budget*, 118.

Rarely will budget decisions be made solely on the strength of performance measures. Well-intentioned strategies of rewarding good performance with budgetary increases and penalizing poor performance with budget reductions inevitably deteriorate when crucial programs, struggling and seemingly losing ground to intractable problems, might be helped by a budgetary boost. When crime statistics are climbing, should the governing board penalize the police department or sheriff's office with a blanket reduction, or should it reinforce law enforcement efforts with a budgetary increase?

Even if performance measures rarely yield clear budgetary direction, they almost always contribute positively to the process. Difficult decisions are best made with clear evidence of program performance and realistic expectations of future impact. Perhaps more important, awareness of downward performance trends often prompts managers to design remedies prior to budget deliberations. These suggested remedies may then be presented in the budget process. Furthermore, meaningful performance measures can enhance communication between governing boards and managers regarding performance expectations and service priorities.

Performance Measurement as a Tool for Productivity Improvement

Local government productivity may be defined as "the efficiency with which resources are consumed in the effective delivery of public services."[7] Not only should the quantity of outputs be considered in assessing productivity, but the quality of outputs should be weighed as well. Productivity improvement occurs when the ratio of outputs to inputs is increased, with output considered in both a quantitative and a qualitative sense.

In other words, a department or program may appropriately claim a gain in productivity when, for a given amount of dollars, it is able to provide services to more citizens without reducing quality, it is able to improve the quality of the ser-

7. Nancy S. Hayward, "The Productivity Challenge," *Public Administration Review* 36 (Sept.–Oct. 1976): 544.

vice without reducing the number of service recipients, or it is able to increase quantity and quality simultaneously. If efficiency gains for a program are produced by cutting corners and damaging service quality, then gains in one aspect of productivity are offset by losses in the other. Furthermore, if gains in quantity or quality are propelled by disproportionately greater amounts of resources (i.e., inputs), the program's productivity—i.e., its ratio of outputs to inputs—is impacted negatively, not positively.

Although productivity improvement strategies do not spring magically from performance measures, it is difficult to imagine effective strategies in the absence of performance measures. A good set of performance measures identifies areas of performance deficiency in which improvement strategies are likely to yield the greatest return. Formal approaches to the design of performance improvements often are guided by benchmarking projects or embedded in larger managing-for-results initiatives—both of which rely on performance measurement. Even less formal approaches, which often rely on someone's hunch that a new approach might work better, can benefit from careful monitoring of the new technique using appropriate performance measures. Such measures will yield feedback that may prompt midcourse corrections in strategies and improve the odds of success. Subsequently, performance measures will help policy makers decide whether a given strategy is working and deserving of additional funding for continuation.

Identifying Strengths and Weaknesses

Often, local government officials have a notion about where the operating strengths and weaknesses lie in their organization, based on personal observation and a history of complaints and compliments. In many cases these notions are correct and can be substantiated by more objective performance measures. In other cases, however, officials' guesses are incorrect. They may be surprised to discover evidence that a favorite program is not as effective as previously thought or that a department once presumed to be wasteful is instead shown to be rather efficient.

Serious productivity improvement efforts are neither simple nor inexpensive. Done properly, they require considerable time, analysis, and careful implementation. It makes sense, then, to direct these substantial efforts toward opportunities most likely to yield

Figure 16.1 Example of Performance Measures for Social Services

1. Percentage of Children Retained in Their Own Homes after Receiving In-Home Prevention and Family Support Services

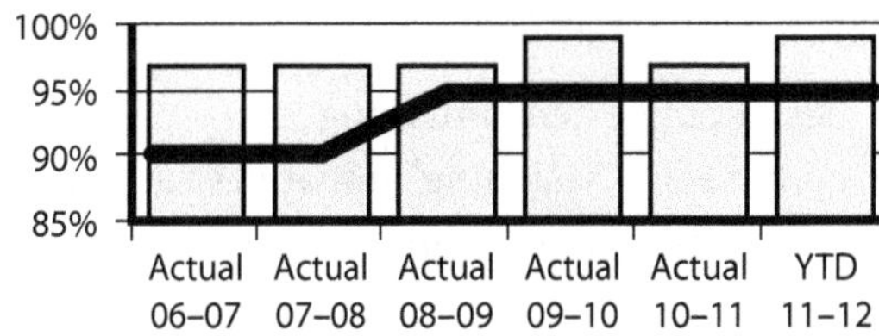

2. Percentage of Adults Retained in Their Own Homes for at Least 12 Months After Initiating Services

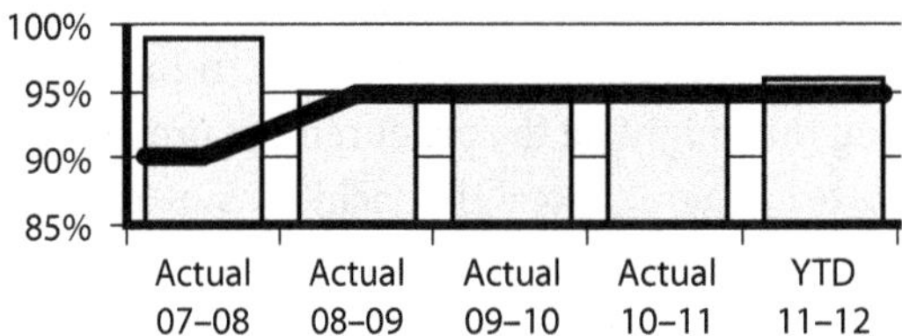

3. Percentage of Applicants Who Received General Assistance Aid

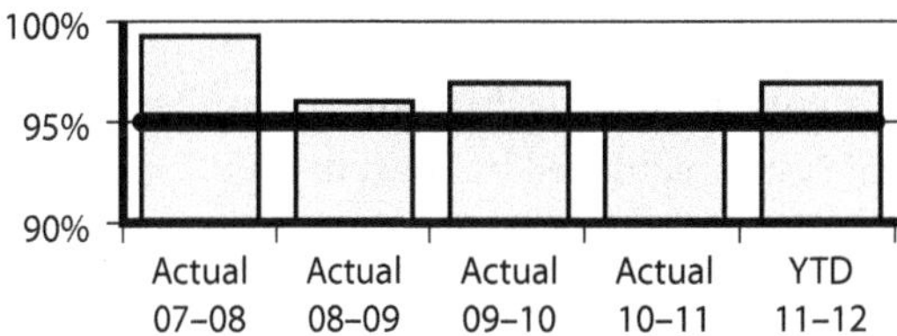

4. Percentage of Applicants Who Received Emergency Assistance Aid

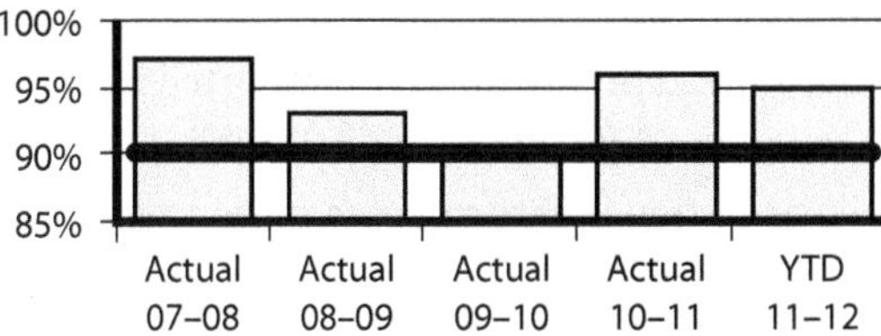

5. Percentage of Applicants Who Received Crisis Intervention Assistance

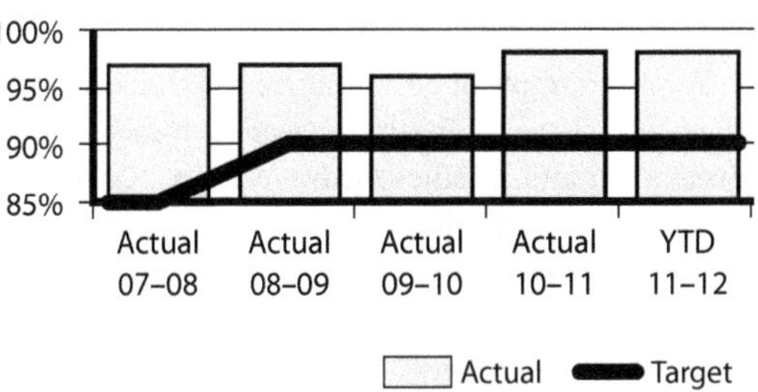

Source: Rockingham County, North Carolina, *Rockingham County Performance Management Program: Comprehensive 2011–2012 Mid-Year Report*, 22, available at www.co.rockingham.nc.us/docview.aspx?docid=28205.

ample returns. In most cases, services with the greatest performance deficiencies offer the greatest opportunity for improvement.

Benchmarking

Benchmarking projects in the public sector have taken one of three forms:

- best practice benchmarking
- community "visioning" initiatives with targets as benchmarks
- comparison of performance statistics as benchmarks[8]

More than a few governments and government agencies have adopted the formal benchmarking model commonly used in the private sector—labeled here as "best practice benchmarking"—and have applied it to public sector programs.[9] This model was popularized by corporate giants such as Xerox, Motorola, and IBM when they pioneered efforts to cooperatively analyze and adopt the procedures of others to improve their own practices. Local governments that follow this best practice benchmarking model focus on a single process in their operation (in a local government setting this might be the procurement process, the process for issuance of permits, or emergency dispatching); identify other organizations that achieve superior results from that process; carefully analyze the process in their own organization and the process in their benchmarking partners; identify factors that contribute to the superior results of their partners; and figure out how to modify their own process to improve their results. Because this approach focuses on processes and identifies performance leaders, it is linked to the search for best practices and carries that label.

A second form of benchmarking sets targets—often societal targets like low rates of illiteracy, unemployment, low-birth-weight babies, and teen pregnancy or high rates of education and volunteerism—and tracks progress toward achieving them. In contrast to best practice benchmarking, which focuses narrowly on key processes, this form of benchmarking focuses broadly on results and community conditions. And while best practice benchmarking uses actual results achieved by "best in class" performers as its benchmarks, the benchmarks in the second form often are set arbitrarily.

The third form of benchmarking is perhaps the most common type used in the public sector. In this form of benchmarking, government units compare their own performance statistics with performance standards or with the performance targets and actual results of other units. For example, a property appraisal unit in one county government might compare its appraisal accuracy, measured as the degree to which appraised values match market prices from actual sales, with the appraisal accuracy of other counties, or it might compare the daily workload of its appraisers with the typical production rates reported by the International Association of Assessing Officers.[10] Occasionally, major projects of considerable scope are developed around this form of benchmarking. Long-standing examples include a multijurisdictional performance measurement project involving local governments across the nation, sponsored by the International City/County Management Association, and a project involving more than a dozen cities and towns in North Carolina, coordinated by the University of North Carolina's School of Government.[11]

---

8. David N. Ammons, *Municipal Benchmarks: Assessing Local Performance and Establishing Community Standards*, 3rd ed. (Armonk, NY: M.E. Sharpe, 2012).

9. For an example of best practice benchmarking by nine North Carolina cities and towns, see David N. Ammons, Ryan A. Davidson, and Ryan M. Ewalt, *Development Review in Local Government: Benchmarking Best Practices* (Chapel Hill: UNC School of Government and Alliance for Innovation, 2009).

10. Richard R. Almy, Robert J. Gloudemans, and Garth E. Thimgan, *Assessment Practices: Self-Evaluation Guide* (Chicago: International Association of Assessing Officers, 1991).

11. Carla Pizzarella, "Achieving Useful Performance and Cost Information in a Comparative Performance Measurement Consortium," *International Journal of Public Administration* 27, nos. 8 & 9 (2004): 631–50; William C. Rivenbark, ed., *A Guide to the North Carolina Local Government Performance Measurement Project* (Chapel Hill: UNC Institute of Government, 2001). For current information on the two projects listed here, see http://icma.org/en/results/center_for_performance_measurement/home and www.sog.unc.edu/programs/perfmeas.

Comparison of performance statistics—the third form of benchmarking—differs from the second form in that the performance statistics here typically focus on government services rather than social indicators or broad quality-of-life measures and benchmarks are more often tied to externally established standards or to the records of leading performers rather than being set arbitrarily. The third benchmarking form differs from best practice benchmarking in two major ways. First, it typically focuses broadly on multiple services or operations rather than narrowly on a single key process. Second, it focuses primarily on results and only secondarily, if at all, on the details of the processes that produce these results.

Local government officials who choose to compare performance statistics rather than to apply best practice benchmarking accept a trade-off. They trade the depth of analysis associated with best practice benchmarking for the breadth of coverage that comes with the comparison of performance statistics across several government operations. Those who make this trade do not necessarily rule out more detailed analysis at a later point. In fact, the broad comparison of performance statistics across several departments may help them identify functions that would benefit most from best practice benchmarking, operations analysis, or the application of managing-for-results strategies.

Managing for Results

Over the past two decades, many governments and government agencies across the nation—local, state, and federal—have been engaged in cost-cutting or performance-enhancing initiatives that they often label "managing for results." A host of management strategies has been adopted by local government proponents of managing for results. Among these strategies are the following:

- performance bonuses for achieving targets
- gainsharing awards, whereby employee efforts that produce savings are rewarded with a share of the savings
- enterprise management in which selected services charge their customers and raise their own revenues
- managed competition, whereby local government departments bid against outside competitors for the right to deliver services
- "bid-to-goal" strategies that simulate market competition without actually seeking outside bids
- policies that allow departments to carry over a portion of end-of-year savings to the next fiscal year, thereby encouraging savings rather than end-of-year spending sprees
- giving department heads and supervisors greater purchasing and personnel management flexibility if they achieve targeted results—that is, greater managerial discretion in exchange for greater accountability for results.[12]

These managing-for-results strategies have one common denominator. Each requires a method of gauging results. Each requires performance measurement.

Various strategies for productivity improvement are promising but hardly fail-safe. Often, operational changes achieve the desired results, but sometimes they do not. Sometimes adjustments are needed. And occasionally new strategies or techniques fail and should be abandoned. The monitoring of performance before, during, and after operational change, therefore, is very important. Performance measurement provides a tool for doing so.

---

12. David Osborne and Peter Hutchinson, *The Price of Government: Getting the Results We Need in an Age of Permanent Fiscal Crisis* (New York: Basic Books, 2004).

Keys to the Successful Use of Performance Measures

Many local governments have undertaken performance measurement with the best of intentions. Some have been pleased with the results, but others have been disappointed. More often than not, disappointments can be attributed to falling short on one or more of the following keys to success:

- *Align performance measures with goals and objectives.* Performance measures should focus on important dimensions of service and should gauge progress on key objectives.
- *Measure efficiency and effectiveness—not just workload.* Output (workload) measures are the most rudimentary form of performance measurement. Simply counting units of service is the local government equivalent of "bean counting." Unfortunately, systems that do nothing more than "count beans" have very limited managerial and policy value. In contrast, systems that also report a department's efficiency, the quality of its services, and the effectiveness of its programs receive a lot more attention from managers—and they deserve to receive it because they are much more valuable.
- *Link the performance measurement system to important policy processes and to other management systems.* High-impact performance measurement systems are linked to important processes and contribute meaningfully to major and minor policy and managerial decisions. The presentation of key performance measures as background for policy retreats held by the governing board, the review of performance measures during managerial or department head performance appraisals, the analysis of performance measures in the formulation of operating strategies and the development of budget requests, and the use of performance measures to diagnose employee training needs are but a few examples of possible applications.
- *Present performance measures in context.* A performance measure reported out of context is "just a number" to all but the best-informed consumers of that information. Is a five-minute average response time to law enforcement emergencies good? What about a library circulation rate of five items per capita? Or a citizen satisfaction rate of 87 percent? When the information is presented out of context, it is difficult to know whether it reflects good performance or not. Last year's numbers are the easiest context to provide for this year's numbers, but a more informative context might be the applicable standards of service quality and efficiency or the performance of other respected units. Presented in context, performance statistics become more valuable—and to a much broader audience, even interesting!

Additional Resources

Ammons, David N., ed. *Leading Performance Management in Local Government.* Washington, DC: ICMA, 2008.

_____. *Municipal Benchmarks: Assessing Local Performance and Establishing Community Standards.* 3rd ed. Armonk, NY: M.E. Sharpe, 2012.

Broom, Cheryle, Marilyn Jackson, Vera Vogelsang Coombs, and Jody Harris. *Performance Measurement: Concepts and Techniques.* Washington, DC: American Society for Public Administration, 1998.

Fountain, James, Wilson Campbell, Terry Patton, Paul Epstein, and Mandi Cohn. *Reporting Performance Information: Suggested Criteria for Effective Communication.* Norwalk, CT: Governmental Accounting Standards Board, 2003.

Hatry, Harry P. *Performance Measurement: Getting Results.* 2nd ed. Washington, DC: The Urban Institute Press, 2006.

Hatry, Harry P., D. M. Fisk, J. R. Hall Jr., P. S. Schaenman, and L. Snyder. *How Effective Are Your Community Services? Procedures for Performance Measurement.* 3rd ed. Washington, DC: Urban Institute and International City/County Management Association and The Urban Institute, 2006.

International City/County Management Association. *From Performance Measurement to Management: FY 2012 Case Studies and Comparative Analysis.* Washington, DC: International City/County Management Association, 2013.

North Carolina Local Government Performance Measurement Project. *Final Report on City Services for Fiscal Year 2012–2013: Performance and Cost Data.* Chapel Hill, N.C.: UNC School of Government, 2014.

Poister, Theodore H. *Measuring Performance in Public and Nonprofit Organizations.* San Francisco: Jossey-Bass, 2003.

About the Author

David N. Ammons is a School of Government faculty member whose work focuses on performance measurement, benchmarking, and productivity improvement in local government.

Part 4

Finance

Chapter 17

Revenues

Kara A. Millonzi

Introduction

One major responsibility for a local governing board is to identify, and generate or obtain, sufficient revenue to cover the costs of the services it wishes to provide for its citizens. Counties legally are required to provide for and/or fund at least a portion of certain state-mandated activities, including public schools, social services programs, mental health programs, emergency medical services (EMS), courts, jail facilities, registers of deeds, and building code enforcement. But counties also are authorized to provide many other services, ranging from zoning and land use planning, to water and sewer utilities, to recreation and cultural activities, to economic development, and beyond. Cities legally are required to provide only a single service—building code enforcement. Like counties, though, cities are authorized to provide a wide array of services. In fact, with a few notable exceptions, counties and cities legally are authorized to provide, and fund, most of the same services. The actual mix of services that any single government chooses to offer, however, varies significantly across the state and depends on a number of factors.

No matter where a unit of government falls on the service-provision spectrum, it is important for local officials to understand the full range of available funding options. As creations of the legislature, counties and cities may impose only the local taxes and fees specifically authorized by the General Assembly. The major types of revenues available to North Carolina counties and cities are local taxes, state-shared taxes and charges, and local user fees and charges. There also are a few miscellaneous revenue sources available to most local governments. Which specific funding mechanism(s) a local government chooses has very different legal implications as to who can be charged and what procedures must be followed. If a local government unit chooses to fund its services through a property tax, for example, then tax-exempt entities, such as religious organizations, state agencies, educational institutions, and federal facilities, typically are not obligated to pay. Furthermore, there may be restrictions on the tax rate and, under certain circumstances, a voter approval requirement. On the other hand, if a user fee approach is employed, usually only those who avail themselves of particular government services or activities pay, and the rate structure must be reasonable and bear some relationship to the service being provided to each individual user. The chart in Appendix 17.1, "Local Revenue Authority and Limitations," briefly outlines the revenue sources available to counties and cities. It specifies whether the revenue source is available to counties, to cities, or to both types of general purpose local government. It also indicates whether the revenue source is authorized under general law or local act and outlines any restrictions on the use of the proceeds. Following the chart is a more detailed description of each revenue source.

Local Taxes

Taxes are compulsory charges that governments levy on persons or property. They need not bear any relation to the benefit from public services received by the taxpaying persons or property. The most important taxes for North Carolina local governments are the property tax and local sales and use taxes. On a statewide average, property taxes constitute about 39 percent of total county revenues and local sales and use taxes constitute about 15 percent. In cities, by contrast, property taxes constitute about 18 percent of total city revenues while local option sales taxes constitute slightly less than 9 percent. The reason for cities' lower reliance on property and sales taxes as a percentage of their total revenues is widespread city operation of utilities, which account for 34 percent of total city revenues.

In addition to the property tax and local sales and use taxes, local governments also are authorized to levy transportation sales and use taxes (levied by counties but shared with cities), animal taxes, rental car gross receipts taxes, heavy equipment rental taxes, and motor vehicle license taxes. A number of local units also levy or share in other local taxes as authorized by local acts of the legislature.

The Property Tax

The property tax is levied against real and personal property within the local unit and ultimately is an obligation of the property, not just its owner(s). The following sections describe the property tax in more detail.

Tax Base

The property tax base consists of real property (land, buildings, and other improvements to land); personal property (business equipment, automobiles, and so forth); and the property of public service companies (electric power companies, telephone companies, railroads, airlines, and certain other companies). Not all property is subject to taxation, though. Government-owned property is exempt under Article V, Sections 2(2) and (3), of the North Carolina Constitution. In addition, the General Assembly may exempt property from taxation or classify property to exclude it from the tax base, give it a reduced valuation, or subject it to a reduced tax rate. It must do so, however, only on a statewide basis.[1] A local government itself may not exempt, classify, or otherwise give a tax preference to property within its jurisdiction.[2]

Tax Rate Limitations and Voter Approval

A local governing board's job is to determine whether or not to levy property taxes each year and at what rate or rates. A governing board may adopt a single tax rate and use the revenue generated from the tax to fund a variety of authorized

1. N.C. Gen. Stat. (hereinafter G.S.) §§ 105-275 through -278.9.
2. The administration of the property tax is discussed in much greater detail in Chapter 19, "The Property Tax."

local government services. Alternatively, a board may adopt a series of tax rates and earmark the proceeds for specific services. A board also has the option of adopting a combination of both methods. Property taxes levied for certain purposes are subject to rate limitations and, in a very few cases, must be approved by the voters. These restrictions are pursuant to Article V, Section 2(5), of the state constitution, which reads as follows:

> General Assembly shall not authorize any county, city or town, special district, or other unit of local government to levy taxes on property except for purposes authorized by general law uniformly applicable throughout the State, unless the tax is approved by a majority of the qualified voters of the unit who vote thereon.

This provision means that unless the General Assembly specifically authorizes the levy of property taxes for a particular purpose and does so on a statewide basis, property taxes may be levied for that purpose only with voter approval.

To implement Article V, Section 2(5), the General Assembly has enacted Section 153A-149 of the North Carolina General Statutes (hereinafter G.S.) for counties and Section 160A-209 for cities. Generally, the total of all property tax rates may not exceed \$1.50 per \$100 assessed valuation. However, there are a few purposes for which property taxes may be levied without limitation on the rate or amount. For cities, the most important of these purposes is to fund debt service on general obligation debt. For counties, the purposes include debt service on general obligation debt along with the most significant state-mandated services: schools and social services. On the flip side, there are a limited number of services or activities that a local government is not authorized to fund with property tax dollars without specific voter approval through a voter referendum.

A unit may seek voter approval to fund with property tax proceeds an activity that is not listed in the property tax statutes but that the local government otherwise has statutory authority to undertake. A local governing board also may hold an advisory referendum on levying a tax for any of the expressly authorized purposes at a certain rate or up to a maximum rate per purpose. Additionally, voters may approve an increase in the overall property tax rate cap of \$1.50 per \$100 assessed valuation.

Uniformity of Taxation and Service Districts

Generally, the property tax rate must be uniform throughout the taxing unit. A governing board may not adopt different tax rates for different types of properties or citizen populations within the unit. There is one significant exception, though. A unit's governing board may define one or more service districts within the local unit for the purposes of providing certain, statutorily specified, services to the properties or property owners within that district to a greater extent than it provides those services in the rest of the unit. The governing board may levy an additional property tax rate on the taxable properties within the district and specifically earmark the proceeds to provide the designated service or services. Counties may establish service districts for beach erosion and flood and hurricane protection, fire protection, recreation, sewage collection and disposal systems, solid waste collection and disposal systems, water supply and distribution systems, ambulance and rescue, watershed improvement projects, drainage projects, water resources development projects, and cemeteries.[3] Counties use service districts most often to fund fire protection services, though.[4] Cities may establish service districts for beach erosion and flood and hurricane protection, downtown revitalization projects, urban area revitalization projects, transit-oriented development projects, drainage projects, sewage collection and disposal systems, off-street parking facilities, watershed improvement projects, and water resources development projects.[5] Like counties, cities use service districts almost entirely for a single purpose: downtown revitalization. Cities have used downtown districts to finance services, such as additional police patrols or more frequent

---

3. G.S. 153A-301. The law allows certain counties to create service districts for a few additional purposes.

4. There is a separate statutorily authorized process to create special taxing districts for fire protection and emergency services. *See* G.S. Ch. 69. This process requires a voter petition and a voter referendum. It also sets a maximum tax rate of either \$0.10 per \$100 valuation or \$0.15 per \$100 valuation. For more information on the two different types of special taxing districts for fire services, see Kara A. Millonzi, "County Funding for Fire Services in North Carolina," *Local Finance Bulletin* No. 43 (May 2011), www.sogpubs.unc.edu/electronicversions/pdfs/lfb43.pdf.

5. G.S. 160A-536.

solid waste collection; for capital improvements, such as sidewalk or street improvements; and to finance downtown promotional programs, such as the Main Street program.

A service district does not have its own governing body separate from the board of county commissioners or city council that established it. Occasionally, though, the governing board will create an advisory board within the district, especially for districts established for fire protection, or it will contract for operation of the district with a nonprofit organization that represents district property owners, especially in downtown districts.

A district is defined by simple action of the governing board. No petition from district residents or property owners is required, although the board could establish a policy of defining districts only when it receives such a petition. A vote need not be held within the district in order to create it. In fact, there is no authority to hold a vote even if the governing board thinks that one is desirable. The board has only to find that the district needs the proposed service or services "to a demonstrably greater extent" than the rest of the county or city. With a few exceptions, a county or city must set the effective date for a new service district at the beginning of a fiscal year. Once the district becomes effective, the unit must "provide, maintain, or let contracts for" the service or services involved within a reasonable time, not to exceed one year.[6]

There is no specific limitation on the service district tax rate. However, the total of all property taxes levied within a district, including the general property tax rate(s) and any service district tax rate(s), may not exceed $1.50 per $100 valuation.

Tax-Levy Formula

The formula for setting the property tax rate and enacting property taxes is relatively simple: the local government determines the amount of property tax revenue that must be collected to balance the budget, considering estimated expenditures and the amount of money that other revenue sources are likely to yield. It should be noted that the full property tax levy—the total dollar value of the tax enacted—is never collected. Most North Carolina local governments collect 95 to 99 percent of the levy; the statewide average is almost 97 percent. In calculating the amount of tax expected to be collected, the government may not use an estimated collection percentage that exceeds the current year's collection percentage.

To illustrate the procedure for determining the tax levy and rate, assume that a county must collect $10,000,000 in property tax revenue to balance its budget and that the unit estimates a collection percentage for the previous fiscal year of 95 percent. The total required levy is determined by dividing the $10,000,000 of required property tax revenue by 0.95, which yields a property tax levy of $10,526,000. Divide the resulting figure by the county's taxable valuation—say, $1.5 billion—which yields $.007017. This figure is multiplied by 100 to produce a tax rate of $.7017 per $100 valuation.

The governing board sets the property tax rate(s) when it adopts its annual budget ordinance, and with very limited exceptions, the rate(s) may not be changed once the budget is adopted. Property taxes are due on September 1, but taxpayers may delay payment until January 5 without incurring a penalty. Thus, local governments typically experience a concentration of property tax collections in the middle of the fiscal year and must rely on fund balances and other revenue sources to finance expenditures during the first part of the fiscal year.

The Local Sales and Use Tax

The local sales and use tax is made up of two separate components—a sales tax on the retail sale or lease of tangible personal property and on the rental of motel and hotel rooms, and an excise tax on the right to use or consume property in North Carolina or elsewhere. The sales tax is imposed on retailers for the privilege of selling the tangible personal property in the state. Currently, most services are exempt from the sales tax. The use tax is imposed on purchasers whenever the sales tax does not apply, such as for goods purchased out of state that will be used in North Carolina.

6. *See* G.S. 153A-302 (counties); G.S. 160A-537 (cities).

Local Sales and Use Tax Authorizations

The local sales and use taxes (local sales taxes) are levied by counties, not cities. Currently, all counties levy 2 percent in local sales tax, which is composed of three different taxes—the Article 30 one cent tax, the Article 40 one-half cent tax, and the Article 42 one-half cent tax. Counties also are authorized to levy an additional 0.25 percent tax (Article 46 tax), pursuant to voter approval.[7]

The local sales tax is added to the state sales and use tax of 4.75 percent for a combined rate of between 6.75 percent and 7 percent, depending on the county. The proceeds of the sales tax component of the local sales tax are collected by retailers and remitted to the North Carolina Department of Revenue (DOR). Of the 2 percent of local sales taxes that all counties levy, the DOR allocates the revenues generated from approximately 1.5 percent to counties on a point-of-origin basis. That basically means that the tax proceeds are returned to the county in which the purchased goods were delivered. This allocation method benefits counties with higher levels of commercial activity. The remaining 0.5 percent of the tax proceeds are pooled and allocated among counties on a per capita basis, based on the relative population of each county. The revenue generated by the additional 0.25 percent tax currently levied only by some counties is returned to the counties in which the goods were delivered.

Distribution of Local Sales and Use Tax Proceeds

Counties must share the tax proceeds generated from 2 percent of local sales taxes with cities within their territorial jurisdictions. County commissioners choose annually one of two different distribution methods. Under the first method, known as the *per capita* method, the funds are distributed among the county and its incorporated cities based on relative populations. Under the second method, referred to as the *ad valorem* method, the proceeds are distributed among the county and its incorporated cities based on relative property tax levies. Counties that levy the additional 0.25 percent tax are neither required nor authorized to share the tax revenue generated by that tax with their cities or other taxing units in the county.

During the 2007 and 2008 legislative sessions, the General Assembly made significant changes to local sales tax authorizations in exchange for assuming the counties' share of Medicaid expenses. Pursuant to this legislation, all counties must hold cities that were incorporated before October 1, 2008, harmless for the revenue that would have been generated from a formerly authorized additional 0.50 percent local sales tax.[8] Each city must receive the equivalent amount of revenue that it would have received if the 0.50 percent tax were still in effect. The hold harmless funds are equivalent to the proceeds a city receives from the Article 40 tax. The hold harmless calculation also must factor in any increase or decrease in municipal revenue due to a change that was made in 2009 to switch the allocation method of the Article 42 proceeds from a per capita to a point-of-origin basis. To calculate the revised hold harmless amount, subtract the amount determined by taking 25 percent of the amount of local sales tax revenue a city receives from the Article 39 tax from the amount determined by taking 50 percent of the amount of local sales tax revenue a city receives from the Article 40 tax. The difference, positive or negative, is added to the hold harmless amount to determine the revised hold harmless amount. The total hold harmless payment is added to the per capita or ad valorem distribution to cities described above.

Also pursuant to the Medicaid funding reform legislation, the state guarantees that all counties will experience an annual financial gain of at least $500,000 as a result of the Medicaid swap (defined as the state's assuming of the counties' Medicaid costs in exchange for the state's repealing a portion of the counties' local sales tax authority). The state must make a supplemental payment to a county for the absolute value of the difference if the amount of a county's Medicaid costs assumed by the state minus $500,000 (county hold harmless threshold) is less than the county's repealed sales tax amount plus its municipal hold harmless amount. A county's repealed sales tax amount is calculated as the amount distributed to the county under Article 40. Added to this figure is the amount, positive or negative, determined

---

7. The articles are in G.S. Ch. 105.

8. For more information on the Medicaid funding reform legislation, see Kara A. Millonzi & William C. Rivenbark, "Phased Implementation of the 2007 and 2008 Medicaid Funding Reform Legislation in North Carolina," *Local Finance Bulletin* No. 38 (Sept. 2008), www.sogpubs.unc.edu/electronicversions/pdfs/lfb38.pdf.

by subtracting 25 percent of the Article 30 tax proceeds distributed to a county from 50 percent of the Article 40 tax proceeds distributed to a county. The municipal hold harmless amount is the amount of a county's Article 30 tax revenue distributed to eligible cities in the county to compensate those cities for their loss in Article 44 tax revenue. If the amount of the county's Medicaid costs assumed by the state minus $500,000 is greater than or equal to the county's repealed sales tax amount plus its municipal hold harmless amount, the county will not receive a supplemental payment from the state.[9]

Cities may use local sales tax proceeds for any public purposes for which they are authorized to expend funds. Counties must earmark a portion of their local sales tax revenue for public school capital outlay or debt service payments associated with school construction projects—60 percent of a county's share of the Article 42 tax proceeds and 30 percent of the Article 40 tax proceeds must be used for this purpose.[10] The remaining funds may be used for any public purpose for which they are authorized to engage.

Transportation Sales and Use Tax

Counties also are authorized to levy an additional sales and use tax to fund public transportation systems. Mecklenburg, Wake, Durham, Orange, Forsyth, and Guilford counties are authorized to adopt a 0.50 percent sales and use tax, the proceeds from which are earmarked for public transportation.[11] All other counties are authorized to levy a 0.25 percent transportation sales and use tax.[12] A governing board may levy the transportation sales and use tax only after receiving specific voter approval in a referendum held on the issue. The proceeds of the transportation sales and use taxes are allocated on a per capita basis among the county and other units of local government in the county that operate public transportation systems. The revenue from these taxes must be used for financing, constructing, operating, and maintaining local public transportation systems.

Other Local Taxes

The general law authorizes both counties and cities to levy a few other taxes: the rental car gross receipts tax, the animal tax, the heavy equipment rental tax, and motor vehicle license taxes. (Units used to have the authority to levy privilege license taxes, but that authority was repealed for tax years beginning on or after July 1, 2015.)[13] In addition, many counties and cities may levy occupancy taxes pursuant to local acts of the General Assembly, and a few local governments may levy prepared food taxes, deed transfer taxes, and motor vehicle taxes, also pursuant to local acts. Although these local taxes are not significant in the overall revenue picture for North Carolina's local governments, they produce hundreds of thousands of dollars for many counties and cities and up to several million dollars for some of the state's largest local governments. Except for the county motor vehicle license taxes and a portion of the municipal motor vehicle license taxes, revenue from the taxes authorized by general law may be spent for any public purpose. Revenue from the taxes permitted by local act is usually earmarked for specific purposes.

---

9. The state supplemental payments are made semiannually. The secretary of revenue estimates the hold harmless amount and sends each county 90 percent of any estimated supplemental payment with the March local sales tax distribution. The secretary of revenue determines the actual amount owed, if any, at the end of the fiscal year and remits the balance to each county by August 15.

10. Counties also must hold their local school administrative units harmless for the loss of any Article 42 tax revenue earmarked for public school capital outlay or debt service on county borrowing for school projects due to the change in allocation method of the Article 42 proceeds from a per capita to a point-of-origin basis in 2009. A county must use 60 percent of the following for public school capital outlay purposes or to retire any indebtedness incurred by the county for public school capital outlay purposes:

The amount of revenue the county receives from the Article 42 tax

If the amount allocated to the county under G.S. 105-486 (Article 40 tax) is greater than the amount allocated to the county under G.S. 105-501(a) (Article 42 tax), the difference between the two amounts

It appears that the legislature intended that the phrase "amount allocated to the county" be interpreted to refer to the amount a county receives from both the Article 40 and Article 42 taxes—after the full amount of the proceeds due to the county from these taxes is distributed among the county and any eligible cities.

11. G.S. Ch. 105, Art. 43, Parts 2, 4, and 5.

12. G.S. Ch. 105, Art. 43, Part 6.

13. *See* S.L. 2014-3.

Rental Car Gross Receipts Tax

In 2001, the General Assembly removed rental cars from the property tax base and instead authorized cities and counties to levy a tax on the gross receipts of car rental companies operating inside the city or county.[14] The maximum rate of tax is 1.5 percent of gross receipts.

Animal Tax

Counties and cities may levy taxes on the privilege of keeping dogs and other pets.[15] These taxes evolved from local dog taxes, and most counties and cities still tax only dogs, although an increasing number of cities tax cats as well. A local government is free to decide which pets to tax and to set the rate of the tax. Rates often are based on the type of animal and whether it has been spayed or neutered, with higher rates—as much as $30 in some local governments—for animals that have not been fixed. The moneys generated by these taxes may be spent for any public purpose. It is no longer legally required (or lawfully authorized, for that matter) to use the proceeds of dog taxes to compensate people for damage done to their livestock by dogs running at-large.

Short-Term Heavy Equipment Rentals Tax

In 2008, the General Assembly removed heavy equipment that is rented or leased on a short-term basis from the property tax base and instead authorized counties and cities to levy a tax on the gross receipts of entities operating within a county or city whose principal business is the short-term lease or rental of heavy equipment at retail. Counties and cities are authorized to adopt resolutions imposing the gross receipts tax—counties are authorized to impose a tax of 1.2 percent of gross receipts if the place of business from which the heavy equipment is delivered is located in the county, and cities may impose a tax of 0.8 percent of gross receipts if the place of business from which the heavy equipment is delivered is located in the city.[16]

Heavy equipment is defined as earthmoving, construction, or industrial equipment that is mobile, weighs at least 1,500 pounds, and is either

1. a self-propelled vehicle that is not designed to be driven on a highway; or
2. industrial lift equipment, industrial handling equipment, industrial electrical generation equipment, or a similar piece of industrial equipment.

The definition includes attachments for heavy equipment, regardless of the weight of the attachments.

Motor Vehicle License Taxes

Cities may levy two motor vehicle license taxes on the privilege of keeping a motor vehicle within the city.[17] The first tax carries no earmark, and for almost all cities the rate may not exceed $5 per vehicle per year. The proceeds of the second tax, also subject to a maximum of $5 per vehicle per year, may be used only to support public transportation systems.

Counties also are authorized to levy a vehicle license tax of up to $7 per year on any vehicle located within the county, but only if the county, or at least one city located within the county, operates a public transportation system.[18] The proceeds of the tax are distributed on a per capita basis among all the units in the county that operate public transportation systems. They must be used to fund the construction, operation, and maintenance of the public transportation system.

Privilege License Tax

A privilege license tax is a tax imposed on the privilege of carrying on a business or engaging in certain occupations, trades, employment, or activities. Cities used to have broad authority to levy privilege license taxes on most businesses

14. G.S. 160A-215.1 and G.S. 153A-156.
15. G.S. 153A-153 and G.S. 160A-212.
16. G.S. 153A-156.1 (counties) and G.S. 160A-215.2 (cities).
17. G.S. 20-97.
18. G.S. 105-570.

and occupations within their territorial jurisdictions.[19] Counties had much more limited authority.[20] In 2014, however, the General Assembly eliminated the authority for both cities and counties to levy most privilege license taxes, effective for taxable years beginning on or after July 1, 2015.[21] The only privilege license taxes that remain as of that date are for the sale of beer or wine.[22]

Cities and counties retain the right to "regulate and license occupations, businesses, trades, professions, and forms of amusement or entertainment and prohibit those that may be inimical to the public health, welfare, safety, order, or convenience."[23] A local unit may charge a reasonable fee to obtain a license. Unlike privilege license taxes, licensing fees may not be used to generate general revenue for the unit.[24] The fees should not exceed the costs of operating the licensing program.

Taxes Permitted by Local Act—Occupancy and Meals Taxes

Local governments in more than seventy counties are permitted by local act to levy occupancy taxes, which are taxes on the occupancy of hotel and motel rooms. Although most of these taxes are levied by county governments, a few are levied by cities, and cities frequently receive a share of the tax even if it is levied by the county. In most cases, the local act authorizing the tax limits the use that the levying government may make of the proceeds, often to travel- or tourism-related programs. In some instances, though, the levying government may use the money for any public purpose. The authorizations are usually for a tax of up to 3 percent of gross receipts, although several permit a rate of up to 6 percent.

A much smaller number of counties are authorized to levy taxes on prepared food (or restaurant meals) and on the transfer of real estate, in both cases at the rate of 1 percent.

Local Fees, Charges, and Assessments

Local governments are increasingly turning to alternative revenue sources to supplement, or in some cases supplant, local taxes. There are a variety of other local revenue sources, but most fall into the following categories: general user fees and charges, regulatory fees, public enterprise fees and charges, franchise fees, special assessments, statutory fees, and impact fees.

General User Fees and Charges

General user fees and charges typically are assessed on individuals who voluntarily avail themselves of certain government services. User fees and charges are feasible for any service that directly benefits individual users, are divisible into service units, and can be collected at a reasonable cost. Most revenue generated from general user fees and charges is placed in a unit's general fund and is available to support any general fund activity or program. User fees and charges typically cover only a portion of the cost of providing the services for which they are assessed.

Local governments must have specific statutory authority to assess general user fees and charges or such authority must be reasonably implied from the underlying authority to provide the service or activity. Common local government services funded at least in part through general user fees and charges are recreation and cultural activities, art

---

19. Cities were authorized to levy privilege license taxes except as specifically restricted or prohibited by law. G.S. 160A-211 (repealed effective for taxable years beginning on or after July 1, 2015).

20. Counties were authorized to levy privilege license taxes only as specifically authorized by law. The authorizations appeared primarily in Article 2, Schedule B, of G.S. Chapter 105. G.S. 153A-152 (repealed as of July 1, 2015).

21. S.L. 2014-3. The legislation also modified the authority to levy privilege license taxes for the 2014–15 fiscal year. For more information on the changes for this interim period, see Christopher McLaughlin, "The Axe Finally Falls on Local Privilege License Taxes," *Coates' Canons: NC Local Government Law Blog* (UNC School of Government, May 30, 2014), canons.sog.unc.edu/?p=7711, and Christopher McLaughlin, "More Questions and Answers about the New Privilege License Law," *Coates' Canons: NC Local Government Law Blog* (UNC School of Government, June 13, 2014), canons.sog.unc.edu/?p=7730.

22. G.S. 105-113.77 (cities) and G.S. 105-113.78 (counties). The privilege license taxes for beer and wine are levied on persons holding certain ABC permits. The amounts are set by statute.

23. G.S. 160A-194 (cities); G.S. 153A-134 (counties).

24. Licensing fees are a type of regulatory fee. See note 25 and accompanying text.

galleries and museums, auditoriums, coliseums, convention centers, EMS, cemeteries, certain public health services, and certain mental health services.

Regulatory Fees

Regulatory fees are assessed to cover the costs of certain regulatory activities performed by counties and cities, such as issuing building permits, performing inspections, evaluating environmental impacts, reviewing development plans, and enforcing other local ordinances. There is no explicit authority to assess regulatory fees, but the North Carolina Supreme Court has held that the authority is implied by the power of the local unit to engage in the regulatory activity.[25] There is one important restriction, though. The regulatory fees must be reasonable and may not exceed the costs of funding the regulatory activity. In other words, a local governing board may not use regulatory fees as a general revenue-raising mechanism. The fees may be used only to cover the (direct and indirect) costs of performing the regulatory activity.

Public Enterprise Fees and Charges

Some activities supported by user charges are set up and operated as public enterprises. A public enterprise is an activity of a commercial nature that could be provided by the private sector. Many public enterprises are self-supporting or largely self-supporting. That means that the revenue generated through fees and charges is sufficient to cover the costs of providing the services. The most common public enterprise services are water supply and distribution systems, sewage collection and treatment, and solid waste collection and disposal utilities. The North Carolina General Statutes also authorize both counties and cities to operate public enterprises for airports, public transportation and off-street parking, and stormwater systems.[26] Cities additionally are authorized to operate enterprises for electric power generation and distribution, gas production and distribution, and cable television. A local unit that provides any of these services may assess a variety of fees and charges, including impact or capacity charges to support capital projects and monthly user fees to support operational expenses.

Franchise Fees

Franchises are special privileges granted by local governments to engage in certain types of businesses within the unit's boundaries. Counties and cities have authority to grant franchises to private entities to engage in a variety of activities. The ability to grant a franchise does not necessarily include the ability to charge a franchise fee. A unit must have specific statutory authority to assess a franchise fee. Counties have authority to grant franchises and charge licensing fees for solid waste collection and disposal.[27] Cities have authority to grant franchises and assess franchise fees without limitation for the following purposes: airports, ambulance companies, off-street parking facilities, and solid waste collection and disposal.[28] Cities also have authority to grant franchises and charge franchise fees with certain limitations for taxicabs.[29] Generally, a unit may use its franchise fee revenue for any authorized public purpose.

Special Assessments

Special assessments are levied against property to pay for public improvements that benefit that property. Like user charges, and unlike property taxes, special assessments are levied in some proportion to the benefit received by the assessed property. Unlike user charges, special assessments are levied against property rather than persons and are typically for public improvements rather than for services.

---

25. *See* Homebuilders Ass'n of Charlotte v. City of Charlotte, 336 N.C. 37 (1994).
26. G.S. 153A-274 (counties); G.S. 160A-311 (cities).
27. G.S. 153A-136.
28. G.S. 160A-319; G.S. 160A-211.
29. G.S. 160A-304; G.S. 20-97.

Currently, there are two different statutory methods of levying special assessments in North Carolina.[30] Under both methods, a governing board defines an area within a unit that includes all properties that will directly benefit from a certain capital project. Under the first special assessment method (Special Assessment Method A), counties may levy assessments to fund the following projects: water systems; sewage collection systems; beach erosion control; certain, limited street improvements; and street light maintenance.[31] Cities may fund streets, sidewalks, water systems, sewage collection systems, storm sewer and drainage systems, and beach erosion control.[32] Special Assessment Method A requires a unit to front the full costs of the project before imposing assessments. Thus, assessment revenue reimburses the government for some or all of the cost of the public improvement. Generally, a local unit may levy special assessments without specific property owner approval. (Counties and cities must receive petitions signed by certain percentages of affected property owners before levying assessments to fund streets and sidewalk projects.) A governing board must follow a detailed procedural process, however, which includes at least two public hearings. The amount of each assessment must bear some relationship to the amount of benefit that accrues to the assessed property. Assessments may be paid (and often are) in up to ten annual installments along with interest on the amount outstanding in any year. Assessment revenue, including the interest portion, generally is not earmarked and may be used for any authorized public purpose. Local improvements are often financed from special-assessment revolving funds. Assessment revenues generated from finished projects are used to finance new improvements.

The second special assessment method (Special Assessment Method B) largely overlaps the first method but differs in a few key respects.[33] First, there is an expanded list of projects for which both counties and cities may levy assessments. Also, assessments may be levied before the projects are completed; a governing board may lock in assessments based on estimated costs and begin collecting assessment revenues before a project even begins. A governing board may authorize assessments to be paid in up to thirty yearly installments. In order to levy an assessment under Special Assessment Method B for any of the authorized projects, though, a local unit must receive a petition signed by a majority of property owners to be assessed, representing at least 66 percent of the total property valuation of all properties to be assessed. The final difference between the two assessment methods is that under Special Assessment Method B, a unit may pledge assessment revenue as security for revenue bonds issued to fund the capital improvement project. Thus, a unit may acquire funds to front the costs, or most of the costs, of a project and use the assessment installments to make its annual debt service payments. The authority for Special Assessment Method B is set to expire on July 1, 2015.

Statutory Fees

Fees of Public Officers

At one time the entire cost of operating the offices of the county sheriff and register of deeds was financed by the statutory fees charged by these officers for the performance of official duties. They collected the fees, hired their own help, paid their own expenses, and kept the remainder as their compensation. Although this financing system has been abolished throughout the state, the statutory fees remain. They are collected by the sheriff or register of deeds and deposited in the county's general fund.

Sheriff

The sheriff collects fees for executing a criminal warrant and for serving any civil process paper. A sheriff who is also the jailer collects a jail fee from individuals held awaiting trial if the person being held is convicted. When conducting a sale of real estate or personal property, the sheriff receives a commission plus reimbursement of associated expenses.[34]

30. For more information on special assessment authority, see Chapter 21, "Financing Capital Projects."

31. G.S. 153A, Art. 9.

32. G.S. 160A, Art. 10.

33. G.S. 153A, Art. 9A (counties); G.S. 160A, Art. 10A (cities).

34. G.S. 7A-304(a)(1), -311, -313.

Register of Deeds

The register of deeds collects fees for virtually every official act performed, ranging from fees for issuing marriage licenses to fees for certifying probate instruments.[35] The largest revenue-producing fee is for recording deeds and other instruments that affect land titles. Fees for recording security interests under the Uniform Commercial Code and for issuing marriage licenses are also major sources of revenue. In many counties, the fees received by the register of deeds exceed the cost of operating the office.

Each county must deposit an amount equal to 1.5 percent of register of deeds fees collected under G.S. 161-10 with the state treasurer. This money is earmarked for a supplemental pension payment for eligible retired registers of deeds. In addition, a portion of the register's fees retained by the county must be used for computer and imaging technology in the register's office. Other portions of the fee revenue must be remitted to various state agencies to support specific programs.[36]

Court Facilities and Related Fees

The state assesses fees against criminal defendants and civil litigants to help offset the costs of operating the court system. As part of these charges, the government employing the officer making an arrest or serving criminal process collects an arrest fee. In addition, the local government unit (usually the county) that provides the courtroom in which judgment in a case is rendered collects a facilities fee.[37]

The proceeds of the facilities fee may be used only for providing courtrooms and related judicial facilities, including jails and law libraries. In most counties the fees barely cover the cost of utilities, insurance, and maintenance of the building(s) occupied by the court system.

State-Shared Revenue

Certain revenues are generated by the state and shared with local governments. The principal advantage of state-shared revenue is that the state is levying the tax or assessing the fee; thus, at least in theory, state officials rather than local officials bear the political burden of raising the revenue. The principal disadvantage of state-shared revenue is that a local governing board lacks control over the revenue sources. The General Assembly may reduce or eliminate the revenue it shares with local governments at any time. State tax and fee revenues that currently are shared with counties are video programming services taxes, beer and wine taxes, the solid waste tipping tax, the real estate transfer tax, disposal taxes, and the 911 charge on voice communication services. State tax and fee revenues that are shared with cities include all of the above except the real estate transfer tax and the disposal taxes. Cities also receive a portion of state electric franchise taxes, telecommunications taxes, the piped natural gas tax, and motor fuels taxes.

Video Programming Services Taxes

In 2007, the General Assembly replaced the local cable franchise system with a statewide video service franchising process, and local governments lost the authority to assess and collect the cable franchise taxes. In lieu of the cable franchise tax revenue, all cities and counties currently receive shares of three state sales tax revenues—7.7 percent of the net proceeds of tax collections on telecommunications services, 23.6 percent of the net proceeds of taxes collected on video programming services, and 37.1 percent of the net proceeds of taxes collected on direct-to-home satellite services.[38]

A portion of the proceeds from these three taxes is distributed to local governments to support local public, educational, or governmental access channels (PEG channels). An eligible unit will receive one-fourth of its proportional

35. G.S. 161-10.
36. G.S. 161-11.1 through -11.6.
37. G.S. 7A-304(a)(2), -305(a)(1), -306(a)(1), and -307(a)(1).
38. G.S. 105-164.44F; G.S. 105-164.44I.

share each quarter. A unit's share is determined by adding $4 million to the amount of any funds returned to the secretary of revenue in the previous fiscal year and then dividing that figure by the number of certified PEG channels. In order to qualify for certification, a PEG channel must meet specified programming requirements.[39] Each unit may certify up to three PEG channels. A local government must equally allocate the supplemental PEG channel support funds for the operation and support of each of its qualifying PEG channels.

The remaining funds are distributed according to each local government's proportionate share. A city's or county's proportionate share is indexed to the share it received in fiscal year 2006–07. In fiscal year 2006–07, each unit's share was calculated by dividing the local government's base amount for that year by the aggregate base amounts of all the cities and counties. The base amount was determined in one of two ways: (1) for cities or counties that did not impose a cable franchise tax before July 1, 2006, the base amount was $2 times the most recent annual population estimate; or (2) for cities or counties that did impose a cable franchise tax before July 1, 2006, the base amount was the total amount of cable franchise tax and subscriber fee revenue the county or city certified to the secretary of state that it imposed during the first six months of the 2006–07 fiscal year. In each subsequent fiscal year, the proportionate share is adjusted for per capita growth.[40]

These funds are partially earmarked. A city or county that imposed subscriber fees during the first six months of the 2006–07 fiscal year must use a portion of the funds distributed to it for the operation and support of PEG channels. The amount of funds that must be used for this purpose is the proportionate share of funds that were used for this purpose in fiscal year 2006–07, which was equal to two times the amount of subscriber fee revenue the county or city certified that it imposed during the first six months of fiscal year 2006–07. Additionally, a county or city that used a part of its franchise tax revenue in fiscal year 2005–06 to support one or more PEG channels or a publicly owned and operated television station must use the remaining funds to continue the same level of support for PEG channels and public stations. The remainder of the distribution may be used for any public purpose.

Beer and Wine Taxes

The state levies a number of taxes on alcoholic beverages. These include license taxes, excise taxes on liquor, and excise taxes on beer and wine.[41] The state shares 20.47 percent of its excise tax on beer, 49.44 percent of its excise tax on unfortified wine, and 18 percent of its excise tax on fortified wine with cities and counties.[42] A city or county is eligible to share in beer or wine excise tax revenues if beer or wine legally may be sold within its boundaries. If only one beverage may be sold, the city or county shares only in the tax for that beverage. General law permits beer and wine to be sold statewide but allows any county to hold a referendum on prohibiting the sale of either beverage (or both) within the county. The statutes also allow a city in a dry county to vote to permit the sale of beer or wine within its boundaries.[43]

Distribution of state beer and wine tax revenue that is shared with local governments is based on the population of eligible cities and counties. Counties are given credit only for their *nonmunicipal* population. The money is distributed annually, around Thanksgiving. Counties and cities may spend state-shared beer and wine tax revenue for any authorized public purpose.

---

39. G.S. 105-164.44J defines a qualifying public, educational, or governmental access channel (PEG channel) as one that operates for at least ninety days during a fiscal year and meets the following programming requirements:

Delivers at least eight hours of scheduled programming a day

Delivers at least six hours and forty-five minutes of scheduled non-character-generated programming a day

Does not repeat more than 15 percent of the programming content on any other PEG channel provided to the same county or city

40. There are additional eligibility requirements for municipalities incorporated after January 1, 2000.

41. North Carolina Department of Revenue, Tax Research Division, *Statistics of Taxation 1980* (Raleigh, N.C.: North Carolina Department of Revenue, 1981), 172.

42. G.S. 105-113.80, -113.81, and -113.82.

43. There are additional eligibility requirements for cities incorporated after January 1, 2000.

Solid Waste Tipping Tax

The state imposes a $2-per-ton statewide excise tax on the following:

- the disposal of municipal solid waste and construction and demolition debris in any landfill permitted under the state's solid waste management program;
- the transfer of municipal solid waste and construction and demolition debris to a transfer station permitted under the state's solid waste management program for disposal outside the state.

Municipal solid waste is defined as any solid waste resulting from the operation of residential, commercial, industrial, governmental, or institutional establishments that would normally be collected, processed, and disposed of through a public or private solid waste management service.

The state shares a portion of the excise tax revenue with counties and cities that provide and pay for solid waste management programs and services or that are served by a regional solid waste management authority. In order to receive a distribution of the excise tax proceeds, a city or county must provide and pay for solid waste management programs and services. State law directs that 37.5 percent of the excise tax proceeds (after certain administrative expenses are subtracted) be distributed to qualifying counties and cities on a per capita basis, with one-half distributed to counties and one-half distributed to cities.[44] For purposes of calculating the per capita amount, the population of a county does not include the population of its incorporated areas. The revenue must be used to fund solid waste management programs and services.

Real Estate Transfer Taxes

The state imposes an excise stamp tax on the conveyance of an interest in real estate. The tax is levied on each recorded deed and is measured by the price paid for the property. The tax rate is $1 for each $500 of the sales price. (There is a local deed transfer tax in effect in a few counties, which is in addition to this statewide tax.) The tax is collected by the county, which must remit one-half of the proceeds to the state (minus up to a 2 percent administrative fee).[45] The county's portion may be used for any authorized public purpose.

Disposal Taxes

The state imposes special sales taxes on the sale of automobile tires and white goods and distributes the major portion of the proceeds of each tax (70 percent of the net tire tax proceeds and 72 percent of the net white goods tax proceeds) to counties on a per capita basis.[46] A county must use the tire tax to fund the disposal of scrap tires or the abatement of a nuisance at a tire collection site. It must use the white goods tax for management of discarded white goods.

911 Charge

In 2008, the General Assembly established a new consolidated system for administering both wireline (landline) and wireless 911 systems. The legislation created the North Carolina 911 Board and authorized it to develop a comprehensive state plan for communicating 911 call information across networks and among local public safety answering points (PSAPs), defined as the local public safety agencies that receive incoming 911 calls and dispatch appropriate public safety agencies to respond to the calls.

Among other powers, the 911 Board is authorized to levy a monthly service charge of 70 cents on each active voice communications service connection, defined as each telephone number assigned to a residential or commercial subscriber. (Local governments are not authorized to levy any charges for 911 services.) The 911 Board must develop a funding formula each year to determine the share of the 911 charge proceeds that is distributed to local governments with eligible PSAPs. To be eligible for a 911 charge distribution, a local government must (1) serve as a primary PSAP,

44. G.S. 105-187.63.
45. G.S. 105-228.28 through -228.37.
46. G.S. 105-187.15 through -187.19; G.S. 105-187.20 through -187.24.

defined as the first point of reception of a 911 call by a PSAP; (2) provide enhanced 911 service; (3) comply with the 911 Board's rules, policies, procedures, and operating standards; and (4) have received distributions from the 911 Board in the 2008–09 fiscal year. In developing the funding formula, the 911 Board must consider a number of statutorily specified factors. A PSAP also must comply with several statutory directives in order to receive a distribution. The 911 Board has some leeway to make additional distributions to some primary PSAPs and to reduce distributions to other primary PSAPs under certain circumstances.[47]

A primary PSAP must use the 911 charge proceeds only for certain limited expenditures associated with operating and maintaining its 911 system. Specifically, the revenue is earmarked to pay for the lease, purchase, or maintenance of the following:

- emergency telephone equipment,
- addressing,
- telecommunicator furniture,
- dispatch equipment located exclusively in a building where a PSAP is located (but not the costs of base station transmitters, towers, microwave links, and antennae used to dispatch emergency call information from the PSAP).

The proceeds also may be used to fund the nonrecurring costs of establishing a 911 system; certain training expenditures for 911 personnel on the maintenance and operation of the 911 system; and charges associated with the service supplier's 911 service and other service supplier recurring charges.

The 911 Board must notify each primary PSAP of its estimated distribution by December 31 of each year and determine the actual distribution for the year by June 1. The PSAP must deposit the funds in a special revenue fund designated as the Emergency Telephone System Fund. A PSAP may carry forward distributions for eligible expenditures for capital outlay, capital improvements, or equipment replacement. If the amount carried forward exceeds 20 percent of the average yearly amount distributed to the PSAP in the prior two years, the 911 Board may reduce the PSAP's distribution.

Electric Taxes

The state used to levy a franchise tax on electric utilities and share a portion of the tax proceeds with cities.[48] The General Assembly enacted major tax reform in 2013, pursuant to which it eliminated the franchise tax on electric utilities as of July 1, 2014.[49] Instead, as of that date, electric utilities are subject to a 7 percent state sales tax rate.[50] To offset the revenue loss to municipalities due to the repeal of the franchise tax, the Department of Revenue must distribute 44 percent of the net proceeds of the sales tax collected on electricity, less the cost to the department of administering the distribution.[51] Each city's share of the tax proceeds is determined according to a statutory formula.[52] According to the formula, on a quarterly basis, each municipality first will be allocated an amount equal to the franchise tax on electricity that it received for the same quarter in FY 2013–14.[53] If the total amount available to be distributed is not sufficient to provide each city with its FY 2013–14 franchise tax amount for the equivalent quarter, then each city's allocation will be reduced by an equal percentage.

If the total amount available for distribution exceeds the amount needed to provide each municipality with its FY 2013–14 franchise tax amount for the equivalent quarter, the remaining funds will be distributed among the cities

47. G.S. 62A-44; G.S. 62A-46.
48. G.S. 105-116.1 (repealed July 1, 2014).
49. *See* S.L. 2013-316. Cities will receive their final distribution of franchise tax revenue in September 2014.
50. G.S. 105-164.4(a)(9).
51. G.S. 105-164.44K.
52. *Id.*
53. G.S. 105-164.44K(b).

that levy a property tax, in proportion to their property tax levy as a share of the total amount of property tax levied by all cities.[54]

Cities will receive their first quarterly distribution of sales tax on electricity in December 2014.

The Telecommunications Tax

The state levies a sales tax on the gross receipts of telecommunications services; the rate is the total of the state's sales tax rate plus the rates of local sales taxes levied in all 100 counties. The state shares a portion of the proceeds from this tax with cities.[55] Each quarter, the state is to distribute to cities 18.7 percent of the proceeds from that quarter, minus $2,620,948.[56] The telecommunications tax was enacted in 2001 and replaced a telephone franchise tax that was identical to the electric franchise tax described above; each city's share of the telecommunications tax is the same percentage of the new tax that the city received from the repealed telephone franchise tax during the last comparable quarter that the earlier tax was still in force. (Cities incorporated after January 1, 2001, receive a per capita share of the tax; distributions to such cities are subtracted from the total amount going to cities before the much larger distribution described just above is made.) Cities may spend telecommunications tax revenue for any public purpose.

Piped Natural Gas Taxes

As with electricity, the state also used to levy a franchise tax on piped natural gas and share a portion of the tax proceeds with cities.[57] The General Assembly eliminated this franchise tax effective July 1, 2014.[58] As of that date, the sale of piped natural gas will be subject to a state sales tax rate of 7 percent. To offset the loss of revenues to cities from the repeal of the franchise tax, the Department of Revenue must distribute 20 percent of the net proceeds of the sales tax collected on piped natural gas, less the cost to the department of administering the distribution.[59] Each city's share of the tax proceeds is determined according to a statutory formula.[60] Specifically, on a quarterly basis, each city is allocated an amount equal to the franchise tax on piped natural gas that it received for the same quarter in FY 2013–14.[61] If the total amount available for distribution is not sufficient to provide each city with its FY 2013–14 franchise tax amount for the equivalent quarter, then each city's allocation is reduced by an equal percentage.

If the total amount available for distribution exceeds the amount needed to provide each municipality with its FY 2013–14 franchise tax amount for the equivalent quarter, the remaining funds will be distributed among the cities that levy a property tax, in proportion to their property tax levy as a share of the total amount of property tax levied by all cities.[62]

Cities will receive their first quarterly distribution of sales tax on piped natural gas in December 2014.

The Motor Fuels Tax (Powell Bill Funds)

North Carolina levies motor fuel taxes pursuant to a formula that increases taxes when the wholesale price of motor fuels increases.[63]

54. G.S. 105-164.44K(c). The amount of ad valorem taxes levied by a city does not include ad valorem taxes levied on behalf of a special taxing district.

55. G.S. 105-164.44F.

56. G.S. 105-164.44(a)(1).

57. G.S. 105-116.1 (repealed July 1, 2014).

58. *See* S.L. 2013-316. Cities will receive their final distribution of franchise tax revenue in September 2014.

59. G.S. 104-164.44L.

60. *Id.*

61. G.S. 105-164.44L(b). Cities that operate a piped natural gas distribution system receive a distribution equal to the amount that they would have received in FY 2013–14 if they had been subject to the piped natural gas franchise tax.

62. G.S. 105-164.44L(c). The amount of ad valorem taxes levied by a city does not include ad valorem taxes levied on behalf of a special taxing district.

63. The motor fuels excise tax is a flat rate of 17.5 cents per gallon or 7 percent of the average wholesale price of motor fuel for the base period, whichever is greater. The tax is capped through June 30, 2015, at 37.5 cents per gallon.

The state distributes a portion of the revenue generated from these taxes among the state's cities.[64] The legislation that first established this distribution is known as the Powell Bill (after its principal sponsor in the North Carolina Senate), and the moneys distributed to the cities often are called Powell Bill funds.

The available funds are distributed according to a two-part formula. Three-quarters of the local proceeds are distributed among cities on a per capita basis, and the remaining proceeds are distributed according to the number of miles of non-state streets in each city.[65] To be eligible to receive Powell Bill funds, a city incorporated after January 1, 1945, must have (1) held the most recent election required by its charter or the general law, (2) levied a property tax for the current fiscal year of at least $0.05 per $100 valuation and collected at least 50 percent of the total property tax levy for the previous fiscal year, (3) adopted a budget ordinance in substantial compliance with general law requirements, and (4) appropriated funds for at least two of a list of eight possible services. A city incorporated after January 1, 2000, must appropriate funds for at least four services. A city incorporated before January 1, 1945, only must demonstrate that it has conducted an election of municipal officers within the preceding four-year period and that it currently imposes a property tax or provides other funds for the general operating expenses of the city.[66]

The funds are distributed to eligible cities twice per year—half on or before October 1 and half on or before January 1. Cities may use motor fuel tax revenue only for maintaining, repairing, and constructing streets or thoroughfares, including bridges, drainage, curbs, gutters, and sidewalks. They may also use the revenue for traffic control devices and signs, debt service on street bonds, and the city's share of special assessments for street improvements. The proceeds may not be used for street lighting, on- or off-street parking, traffic police, or thoroughfare planning. Generally, a city may not accumulate an amount greater than the sum of the past ten distributions (five years' worth).[67]

Other Local Revenues

There are a few miscellaneous revenue sources available to counties and cities, including Alcohol Beverage Control store profits, investment earnings, grants, fines and penalties, and other minor revenue sources.

Alcohol Beverage Control Store Profits

Both counties and cities may establish and operate Alcohol Beverage Control (ABC) stores. About 80 percent of the net profits of these stores are distributed to the units that are authorized to share in the profits.[68] The rest of the profits are kept by the ABC systems as working capital. Under general law, a portion of a local government's distribution must be spent on alcohol or substance abuse research or education programs. The remaining funds may be spent for any authorized public purpose. However, local acts of the General Assembly frequently earmark all or some portion of a system's profits for a particular purpose.

Investment Earnings

Counties and cities are authorized to invest their idle cash.[69] Funds for investment come from capital and operating revenues and fund balances. State law prescribes the authorized types of investments, and the law reflects the dual policy goals of minimizing the risk of investments and maximizing the liquidity of invested funds. The most common investments are certificates of deposit in banks and savings and loan associations, obligations of the U.S. government (called "treasuries"), obligations that mature no later than eighteen months from the date of purchase of certain agen-

64. G.S. 136-41.1.

65. *Id.*

66. G.S. 136-41.2.

67. A small city may apply to the Department of Transportation to be allowed to accumulate up to the sum of the past twenty distributions.

68. G.S. 18B-805.

69. G.S. 159-30.

cies set up under federal law (called "agencies"), and the North Carolina Capital Management Trust, a mutual fund for local government investment. The interest earned on investments must be credited proportionately to the funds from which the moneys that were invested came. The amount of investment income a unit earns fluctuates from year to year because of changes in short-term interest rates.

Grants

Federal, state, and private grants to support specific programs, projects, or activities are another potential source of local government income. The degree to which local governments participate in grant programs varies significantly across jurisdictions and over time. Local governments have used grant revenue to fund educational programs and activities, local housing projects, economic development activities, energy programs, police programs, environmental programs, and infrastructure projects, just to name a few. The expenditure of grant revenue typically is restricted to one or more specific purposes.

Fines and Penalties

Local governments sometimes impose penalties for violations of local ordinances or for delinquent payments for government services. Local units also collect some fines and penalties that are statutorily imposed (such as penalties for failure to list property taxes or failure to pay property taxes on time). The primary purpose of these penalties and fines is to punish violators and deter future violations. The revenue generated from penalties and fines also may serve to compensate a local government for enforcement or collection costs or lost interest income. There are many instances, however, in which a local unit is not allowed to retain the proceeds of locally collected fines and penalties. That is because a constitutional provision directs that the funds be distributed to the public schools.

Article IX, Section 7, of the North Carolina Constitution requires that "the clear proceeds of all penalties and forfeitures and of all fines collected in the several counties for any breach of the penal laws of the state" are to be used for maintaining the public school system. The constitutional provision only applies to penalties and fines (and forfeitures) that are imposed for breaches of the state's penal laws. North Carolina courts, however, have held that certain locally collected penalties and fines are subject to Article IX, Section 7, because they actually are assessed for either (1) a violation of the state's penal law or (2) a violation of a state statute or state regulatory scheme where the penalty or fine is intended to punish the violator.

For example, by statutory default all local government ordinances are criminally enforceable. That means that the violation of any ordinance a local unit adopts constitutes a misdemeanor under state penal law. Because of this, the clear proceeds of any civil penalties collected for violation of a county or city ordinance must be distributed to the public schools. (Note that it is the clear proceeds—that is, gross proceeds minus up to 10 percent in collection costs—of penalties recovered to which the public schools are entitled.) A local governing board may opt out of this criminal enforcement mechanism by specifically so stating in its ordinance. If a unit opts out of criminal enforcement of a particular ordinance, typically the civil penalties collected for violation of the local ordinance are not subject to the constitutional provision and may be retained by the local government.

A couple of other types of locally collected penalties are subject to this constitutional mandate. If a local unit collects a penalty (or fine) that is imposed under state law *and* the penalty is intended to punish the violator, then the clear proceeds of the penalty must be distributed to the local school administrative unit(s) in the county in which the penalty was assessed. Examples of penalties that fall within this category are penalties imposed for the late listing of or failure to list property for ad valorem property taxation,[70] penalties imposed for the submission of a worthless check for payment of ad valorem property taxes,[71] penalties imposed for operating a business without an appropriate privilege license,[72] penalties imposed for failure to file or failure to pay occupancy taxes,[73] penalties imposed for failure to file

70. G.S. 105-312.
71. G.S. 105-357.
72. G.S. 153A-152; G.S. 160A-211; G.S. 105-109; G.S. 105-236.
73. G.S. 153A-155; G.S. 160A-215; G.S. 105-236.

or failure to pay prepared food or meal taxes,[74] and penalties imposed for failure to file or failure to pay motor vehicle and heavy equipment rental gross receipts taxes.[75]

Additionally, if the violation of a local ordinance also constitutes violation of a substantive provision of the state's penal law, the clear proceeds of any civil penalty imposed by the local government for the violation must be distributed to the public schools. An example of this is the use of red light cameras by local governments (to record vehicles that run red traffic lights) for the purpose of imposing a civil penalty on the vehicle's owner. Running red lights also is a violation of the state's traffic laws. Thus, the clear proceeds of any civil penalty collected by a local government for this purpose must be remitted to the public schools.[76]

Minor Revenue Sources

Local governments have numerous minor sources of local revenue. For example, many units receive payments from other local governments for joint or contractual programs. Several units receive funds from the management of their property, such as leasing of government-owned building space or land or sale of surplus equipment. Additionally, counties and cities receive refunds on the state sales taxes that they pay. Many units receive periodic donations of money or property from individuals or entities to fund one or more services or activities. Occasionally, a local government receives a bond forfeiture from a prospective vendor or contractor. Finally, some local governments receive payments from federal or state government entities because such entities are exempt from property taxation. These payments often are referred to as payments in lieu of taxation (PILOTs). There are a handful of PILOTs that are authorized by federal or state law.

About the Author

Kara A. Millonzi is a School of Government faculty member whose interests include the legal aspects of local government finance.

74. G.S. 153A-154.1; G.S. 160A-214.1; G.S. 105-236.

75. G.S. 153A-156; G.S. 153A-156.1; G.S. 160A-215.1; G.S. 160A-215.2; G.S. 105-236.

76. In addition to the penalties and fines that must be distributed to the public schools by operation of Art. IX, § 7, and G.S. 115C-437, the General Assembly also may direct local governments to distribute certain revenues to local school administrative units that are not covered by the constitutional provision. For example, G.S. Ch. 15, Art. 2, prescribes procedures for disposing of personal property that is seized by, confiscated by, or in any way comes into the possession of a local police department or a local sheriff department. A unit is authorized to sell this property at auction after complying with certain notice and waiting period requirements. The net proceeds (after deduction of certain costs and expenses) must be distributed to the local school administrative unit(s) in the county in which the sale is made. This statutory mandate goes beyond what would be required under Art. IX, § 7.

Appendix 17.1 Local Revenue Authority and Limitations

Revenue Source (by category)	Available to Counties, Cities, or Both?[a]	Restriction on Use of Proceeds?
Local Taxes		
Property Tax	Both	Proceeds may be expended only for purposes specified in G.S. 153A-149 (counties) or G.S. 160A-209 (cities) unless voters approve otherwise in referendum.
Local Sales and Use Tax	County only (but certain proceeds must be shared with cities)	A portion of a county's distribution must be used for public school capital outlay. The remaining funds may be expended for any public purpose in which the unit is authorized to engage.
Transportation Sales and Use Tax	County only	Proceeds must be expended to finance, construct, operate, and maintain local public transportation systems.
Rental Car Gross Receipts Tax	Both	Proceeds may be expended for any public purpose in which the unit is authorized to engage.
Short-Term Heavy Equipment Rentals Tax	Both	Proceeds may be expended for any public purpose in which the unit is authorized to engage.
Motor Vehicle License Taxes	Both	Counties must expend proceeds to fund the construction, operation, and maintenance of one or more public transportation systems. Cities may expend proceeds for any public purpose in which the unit is authorized to engage.
Occupancy and Meal Taxes	Authorized by local act only	Local act typically restricts use of proceeds to particular purpose(s).
Local Fees, Charges, and Assessments		
General User Fees and Charges	Both	Proceeds may be expended for any public purpose in which the unit is authorized to engage.
Regulatory Fees	Both	Proceeds must be used to fund direct and indirect costs of performing regulatory activity.
Public Enterprise Fees and Charges	Both	Some proceeds are restricted to use only for the particular public enterprise activity.
Franchise Fees	Both (but county authority very limited)	Proceeds may be expended for any public purpose in which the unit is authorized to engage.
Special Assessments	Both	Proceeds may be expended for any public purpose in which the unit is authorized to engage.
Statutory Fees	Both (mainly county)	Most of the proceeds are restricted to use only for a particular purpose.

(*continued*)

Appendix 17.1 Local Revenue Authority and Limitations (*continued*)

Revenue Source (by category)	Available to Counties, Cities, or Both?[a]	Restriction on Use of Proceeds?
State-Shared Revenue		
Video Programming Services Taxes	Both	Some proceeds must be used to support local public, educational, or governmental access channels. The remaining proceeds may be used for any public purpose in which the unit is authorized to engage.
Beer and Wine Taxes	Both	Proceeds may be expended for any public purpose in which the unit is authorized to engage.
Real Estate Transfer Taxes	County only	Proceeds may be expended for any public purpose in which the unit is authorized to engage.
Disposal Taxes	County only	Proceeds must be used to manage the disposal of tires or white goods.
911 Charge	Both	Proceeds restricted to certain, specified expenditures related to the operation of a 911 system.
Electric Taxes	City only	Proceeds may be expended for any public purpose in which the unit is authorized to engage.
Telecommunications Tax	City only	Proceeds may be expended for any public purpose in which the unit is authorized to engage.
Piped Natural Gas Taxes	City only	Proceeds may be expended for any public purpose in which the unit is authorized to engage.
Motor Fuels Tax (Powell Bill Funds)	City only	Proceeds must be used for maintaining, repairing, and constructing streets or thoroughfares, including bridges, drainage, curbs, gutters, and sidewalks. Proceeds also may be used to fund traffic control devices and signs, debt service on street bonds, and the city's share of special assessments for street improvements.
Other Local Revenues		
Alcohol Beverage Control Store Profits	Both	Some of the proceeds are earmarked for alcohol and substance abuse research and education programs. Under general law, the remaining funds may be expended for any public purpose in which the unit is authorized to engage. Local acts of the General Assembly frequently earmark all or some portion of a system's profits for a particular purpose.
Investment Earnings	Both	Proceeds may be expended for any public purpose in which the unit is authorized to engage.
Grants	Both	Proceeds typically are restricted to a particular purpose.
Fines and Penalties	Both	The clear proceeds of some locally collected fines and penalties must be distributed to the public schools. Other fine and penalty revenue typically may be expended for any public purpose in which the unit is authorized to engage.

a. Note that there may be certain eligibility requirements to qualify for a particular revenue stream or employ a particular revenue-raising mechanism.

Chapter 18

An Introduction to Revenue Forecasting

Whitney B. Afonso

Introduction

Revenue forecasting is the process of estimating future collections of individual or multiple taxes or fees. As described in the local government finance literature:

> Forecasting attempts to identify the relationship between the factors that drive revenues (tax rates, building permits issued, retail sales) and the revenues government collects (property taxes, user fees, sales taxes) . . . . Revenue forecasts can apply to aggregate total revenue or to single revenue sources such as sales tax revenues or property tax revenues. There is no single method for projecting revenues. Rather, different methods tend to work better depending on the type of revenue. Similarly, there is no standard time-frame over which to attempt a forecast.[1]

Forecasting revenues is a critical part of quality financial management in both the short and long term. Budgets are built around forecasted revenues, and their reliability can dramatically alter the direction and scope of government services. In fact, it has been said that "without exception, revenue forecasting is the most important task in budget preparation."[2]

1. Thomas A. Garrett and John C. Leatherman, "An Introduction to State and Local Public Finance," *The Web Book of Regional Science* (Morgantown: Regional Research Institute, West Virginia University, 2000), IV.A, www.rri.wvu.edu/WebBook/Garrett/contents.htm.

2. Robert L. Bland, *A Budgeting Guide for Local Government* (Washington, D.C.: International City/County Management Association, 2007), 35.

Although revenue forecasting is critical, no clear, universal rules or guidelines have been established for the process. There is no best forecast method to follow; indeed, each type of forecast method has both merits and weaknesses.

This chapter explains why revenue forecasting is important for local governments and provides information about how to develop an administrative process for forecasting revenues. The different methods used for forecasting—from expert judgment to methods employing advanced statistics—are discussed. Consideration is then given to choosing the *right* method by highlighting issues of concern as well as best practices.

Reasons for Revenue Forecasting

Revenue forecasting is not only considered a best practice, but for local governments in North Carolina, it is required by law. The Local Government Budget and Fiscal Control Act (LGBFCA) provides that "[e]ach local government and public authority shall operate under an annual balanced budget ordinance . . . . A budget ordinance is balanced when the sum of estimated net revenues and appropriated fund balances is equal to appropriations."[3] The estimated net revenues are the revenue forecasts. The law does not dictate how local governments must estimate those revenues, but it clearly requires them to do so. The law also requires that "[e]stimated revenue shall include only those revenues reasonably expected to be realized in the budget year . . . "[4] This suggests that the estimates or forecasts must be reasonable and reliable and should be justifiable.

Beyond legal mandates, there are at least two universally recognized reasons for local governments to perform revenue forecasting. In addition, there are three types of forecasting. The two reasons to engage in revenue forecasting are (1) it improves financial management by reducing uncertainty, and (2) it helps with strategic planning.

Improved Financial Management

The National Advisory Council on State and Local Budgeting provides recommended practices for financial management and a series of guiding principles and corresponding elements.[5] One principle is that a local government should develop a budget consistent with approaches to achieve goals. An element of this principle is development and evaluation of financial options. A recommended practice associated with this element of the broader principle is the preparation of revenue projections.

By estimating future collections of individual or multiple tax instruments or fees, revenue forecasting reduces uncertainty about the future levels of revenue that a local government can expect. Revenue forecasting is also important to bond rating agencies, which look at short- and long-term plans, assumptions, and reserves.

Strategic Thinking

Within a broader framework of financial forecasting, revenue forecasting allows a local government to consider its long-term fiscal health and ability to balance its budget by projecting long-term fiscal outcomes. It also encourages strategic thinking. Creating a financial forecast provides hypotheticals that can be evaluated based on current policies and assumptions. This is a key aspect of forecasting: forecasts provide a set of likely outcomes and costs for different programs to help decision makers better plan for their long-term goals.

3. N.C. Gen. Stat. (hereinafter G.S.) § 159-8(a).

4. G.S. 159-13(b)(7).

5. National Advisory Council on State and Local Budgeting, *Recommended Budget Practices: A Framework for Improved State and Local Government Budgeting* (1998), www.gfoa.org/sites/default/files/RecommendedBudgetPractices.pdf.

Types of Revenue Forecasts

There are three primary types of revenue forecasts: short term, medium term, and long term. Each type serves a different purpose for both managers and elected officials.

Short-term forecasts estimate revenues for the near future, or less than one year. They are most commonly used by managers to make informed operational choices, such as in-year cash flow.[6] They are used more frequently for forecasting expenditures, use, or attendance than for forecasting revenue. One exception is when short-term forecasts are used to update existing forecasts as the year proceeds.

Medium-term forecasts estimate future revenues for a period of one to three years. They are used in developing budgets and programs. Medium-term forecasts provide important budget constraints and decisions and inform more strategic organizational decisions.[7] They balance ongoing trends while incorporating the effects of economic cycles and other short-term considerations. Medium-term forecasts are the focus of this chapter.

Long-term forecasts estimate revenue over a period of longer than three years, most frequently five years. Long-term forecasts are a critical component of long-term strategic planning and can encourage local governments to consider and assess their current path, where it will likely lead in terms of long-term fiscal health, and how changes implemented now may affect that trajectory.

Recommended Process for Revenue Forecasting

There are many ways in which a local government can structure its process for revenue forecasting. Some of these choices depend on capacity, diversity of the revenue portfolio, and the stability of the local economy. There are four basic steps, all consistent with North Carolina law, for creating and implementing a transparent and easily replicated (internally and externally) forecasting process:

1. Create a revenue manual.
2. Compile estimates for major nondepartmental revenue sources.
3. Compile estimates from revenue-generating entities within the local government.
4. Update all estimates.[8]

Each of these steps is discussed in detail below.

Step 1: Create a Revenue Manual

The first step is to create a revenue manual, which is a complete list of all revenue sources.[9] The list will often include the following information about each revenue source: the statute authorizing the revenue source and any applicable limitations; the current rate, previous rates, and collection rates; the forecast method; what elements in the local economy affect the revenue generated (or the tax base); and the groups that pay the tax or fee. It is also critical to identify who collects the revenue. For example, is it collected by the local government, a public utility, or the state? Ultimately, a revenue manual should contain information on all revenue sources and provide any data that will be helpful in understanding trends (including fluctuations) in revenue generation.

---

6. *Cash flow* refers to the money "flowing" in and out of a business, or in this case, a government—revenues and expenditures. *In-year* simply refers to the time frame, here the current fiscal year.

7. See Kenneth A. Kriz, "Long-Term Forecasting," in *Handbook of Local Government Fiscal Health*, ed. Helisse Levine, Jonathan B. Justice, and Eric A. Scorsone (Burlington, Mass.: Jones and Bartlett, 2013), 130.

8. Adapted from Bland, *A Budgeting Guide for Local Government.*

9. This step is recommended as a best practice by the Government Finance Officers Association (GFOA) in the publication *Recommended Budget Practices: A Framework for Improved State and Local Government Budgeting* (Chicago: GFOA, 1999), 49, www.gfoa.org/services/nacslb.

Many local governments perform individual forecasts only for *major* revenue sources and use an additional combined forecast for all other *minor* revenue sources. Even if a local government creates a unique forecast for only three or four revenue sources, it is considered a best practice to create a revenue manual that includes all of the sources from which the local government collects revenue.

Step 2: Estimate Major Revenue Sources

Before beginning work on a proposed budget, the budget office should create and compile estimates of major revenue sources that are not collected directly by departments.[10] The Local Government Budget and Fiscal Control Act (LGBFCA) allows local governments quite a bit of discretion in the ways in which they present budgets and estimate revenues, but it does state that the budget ordinance "shall make appropriations by department, function, or project and show revenues by major source."[11] Local governments should present forecasts of major revenue sources by department or function separately as a best practice and for legal compliance. These estimates or forecasts should constantly be updated as new information surfaces.[12]

It is important to forecast revenue sources separately because they usually have different tax bases and are affected differently by changes in the economy. Two good examples of this principle are the major revenue sources on which North Carolina local governments rely: sales taxes and property taxes. Sales taxes are often estimated based on recent history but also are weighted by recent trends and anticipated fluctuations to the economic base. They are more reactive to these shifts than are property taxes. Also, sales tax revenue grows more quickly with the economy and decreases more quickly than property tax revenue. Therefore, it is unreasonable to expect that sales and property taxes will change at the same rate for forecasting purposes.[13] In fact, a forecaster will likely choose different forecasting methods for each of these revenue sources.

Step 3: Departmental Revenue Forecasts

The third step is for the budget office to request estimates of projected revenues from revenue-generating departments.[14] Examples of such departments include utilities, libraries, and recreation. In addition, a budget office may ask the various departments to offer estimates under different scenarios. For example, it may be helpful to have the utilities department provide several estimates based on different levels of expected rainfall. The different examples help elected officials consider options, likely outcomes, and the sensitivity of these estimates to various assumptions.

This process is considered a best practice, but it is also required in North Carolina. The LGBFCA dictates that "before April 30 of each fiscal year (or an earlier date fixed by the budget officer), each department head shall transmit to the budget officer the budget requests and revenue estimates for his department for the budget year. . . . The revenue estimate shall be an estimate of all revenues to be realized by department operations during the budget year."[15]

It is important to keep in mind that Steps 2 and 3 are broadly made up of many substeps.

---

10. Step 2 and Step 3 happen in parallel but involve different actors and are discussed here separately. The distinction between the two steps is how the revenue is generated and who forecasts it. In Step 2 the revenue forecast is done by the budget office, whereas Step 3 is concerned with revenue generated by a department and thus the forecast is done by the collecting department.

11. G.S. 159-13(a).

12. Bland, *A Budgeting Guide for Local Government*. This type of new information includes relevant economic and political factors as well as current revenue. It is possible that the new information will reinforce or alter the forecast.

13. John L. Mikesell, "Consumption and Income Taxes," chap. 9 in *Management Policies in Local Government Finance*, ed. John R. Bartle, W. Bartley Hildreth, and Justin Marlowe (Washington, D.C.: International City/County Management Association, 2013).

14. Bland, *A Budgeting Guide for Local Government*.

15. G.S. 159-10. This is another reason that revenue manuals are useful. This information should be housed there, adding to the manual's administrative value.

Step 4: Update Estimates

The quality of the forecasts will improve as more (and more recent) data are collected, so it is critical to update forecasts both before and after the budget is adopted. This includes monitoring actual revenues and comparing those numbers with projections. There are many potential sources of information and data that can aide in this process, including changes in laws and rates, changes to the tax base, changes to the underlying growth factors that drove the forecasts, and actual collection numbers.

This step is especially critical for taxes or fees that generate revenues throughout the year, such as the sales tax, and less critical for taxes or fees that are collected at one time within a specific period, such as the property tax. Actual collections, especially those of a periodic nature, need to be closely monitored and checked against the forecasts. Comparing actual collections to forecasted collections can give budget officers early warning if collections appear to be falling short of budget expectations.[16] This early warning provides time for midyear reductions, if necessary.

A North Carolina local government may amend its budget ordinance any time after the ordinance is adopted.[17] The LGBFCA provides that "[e]xcept as otherwise restricted by law, the governing board may amend the budget ordinance at any time after the ordinance's adoption in any manner, so long as the ordinance, as amended, continues to satisfy the requirements of Sections 159-8 and 159-13 of the North Carolina General Statutes."[18] Although there are more legal restrictions surrounding amendments to the property tax forecasts, the LGBFCA provides for unanticipated events: "[I]f after July 1 the local government receives revenues that are substantially more or less than the amount anticipated, the governing body may, before January 1 following adoption of the budget, amend the budget ordinance to reduce or increase the property tax levy to account for the unanticipated increase or reduction in revenues."[19] Thus, the LGBFCA encourages local governments to carefully monitor their forecasts for accuracy and allows them to make updates throughout the fiscal year.

Forecasting Methods

There are *many* ways to forecast revenues. This chapter discusses the most common methods used by local governments, but it is by no means an exhaustive list:

> [Forecasting methods] range from relatively informal qualitative techniques to highly sophisticated quantitative techniques. In revenue forecasting, more sophisticated does not necessarily mean more accurate. In fact, an experienced finance officer can often "guess" what is likely to happen with a great deal of accuracy.[20]

The following sections provide an introduction to the concepts and explain why certain methods may be preferable.

In determining what method of forecasting is best for a particular local government, there are two broad categories to choose from: qualitative and quantitative. Qualitative methods rely on expert judgment and do not rely heavily on data. Such methods often do not clearly describe how the final forecasted numbers were estimated and what underlying assumptions drove them. Quantitative methods, in contrast, rely heavily on quantifiable data. Ideally, the assumptions that are used to model and categorize the relationships between variables and historical values are clearly identified. Due to their technical nature, estimates using quantitative methods often include information about their level of certainty and reliability.

---

16. Mikesell, "Consumption and Income Taxes."

17. The only exception involves certain aspects of the property tax. "However, except as otherwise provided in this section, no amendment may increase or reduce a property tax levy or in any manner alter a property taxpayer's liability, unless the board is ordered to do so by a court of competent jurisdiction, or by a State agency having the power to compel the levy of taxes by the board." G.S. 159-15.

18. *Id.*

19. *Id.*

20. Garrett and Leatherman, "Introduction to State and Local Public Finance," 1.

Qualitative Methods

Qualitative forecasting relies on the expertise of an individual or a group for forecasting revenue. This may mean that the local government has an internal expert whose judgment is trusted. Often these are budget directors or employees within the agency administering the revenue source (tax or fee). It is also common for the local government to solicit external expertise from academics, economists, business professionals in the community, or other types of consultants. There are two primary types of qualitative forecasting: judgmental and consensus.

Judgmental Forecasting

Judgmental forecasting is the most common form of forecasting used by local governments. Under this method, a single individual estimates likely future conditions. This approach can lead to very good results, especially when the forecaster has experience and the forecaster's expertise, historical trends, the state of the economy, and other factors likely to affect the tax base are considered. According to Garrett and Leatherman, "Judgmental approaches tend to work best when background conditions are changing rapidly. When economic, political or administrative conditions are in flux, quantitative methods may not capture important information about factors that are likely to alter historical patterns."[21]

Consensus Forecasting

Consensus forecasting relies on a panel of experts who provide their input either in a roundtable format or through a survey. Ideally, input should be solicited from experts who understand which factors are important, how those factors have been changing, and how they are likely to change in the future. For a local government, this panel of experts may consist of people who understand the real estate market, economists who study both state and local changes to the relevant sectors of the economy, and officials from local financial institutions.[22] One study found that a survey of experts produced a more accurate long-term forecast than did advanced quantitative methods.[23]

Strengths of Qualitative Forecasting

Qualitative forecasting is attractive to local governments and may be the best method to use for several reasons. First, qualitative forecasts are inexpensive and easy to administer. Second, the actual forecasted revenue numbers are easier to understand than data derived from some quantitative methods, which are often complex and so mathematical that they may be intimidating. (This should not be taken to imply, however, that expert judgments may not be guided by numbers and quantitative models.) Third, qualitative forecasting may be a local government's best choice when there is very little data to input into quantitative models.

Weaknesses of Qualitative Forecasting

While there are many benefits to qualitative forecasting, there are also shortcomings. The final forecasted revenue amount is easy to understand, but it may be very unclear where that revenue projection came from and what considerations and assumptions led the expert to that total. This may limit the unit's ability to analyze the sensitivity and reliability of these forecasts. Additional weaknesses include

1. the presence of anchoring events that might cause a current event to unduly shape perceptions of what the future will bring;[24]

---

21. Garrett and Leatherman, "Introduction to State and Local Public Finance," 3.

22. Garrett and Leatherman, "Introduction to State and Local Public Finance."

23. Reid Dorsey-Palmateer and Gary Smith, "Shrunken Interest Rate Forecasts Are Better Forecasts," *Applied Financial Economics* 17, no. 6 (2007): 425–30.

24. An anchoring event can be many things. Most frequently, it is either something that has happened recently, so that the expectations are built off of it (for example, a stock price is falling, so you expect it to continue to fall), or an event that was dramatic/vivid, that left a strong impression, and that set expectations moving forward.

2. too much emphasis given to the information that is available to the expert;[25]
3. bad assumptions about the causal mechanisms between certain indicators and fiscal outcomes (what is causing or influencing a particular effect);
4. changing methods or strategies over time producing incomparable and inconsistent results (this is especially problematic when the assumptions and tactics are not laid out or well documented);
5. experts allowing their own worldviews to cloud their judgment or, worse, lead them to ignore conflicting data and information;
6. experts letting the outcomes they prefer guide their assumptions and lead them to inaccurately weigh certain numbers and factors;
7. local governments letting "group think" guide choices instead of independently assessing and evaluating the assumptions; and
8. elected officials allowing political pressures to shape assumptions and estimates.[26]

Despite the potential weaknesses of qualitative forecasting, however, there is consensus that expert judgment should be incorporated into quantitative forecasts as well.

Quantitative Methods

There are many quantitative forecasting methods, varying from simple equations and formulas to sophisticated causal models that require technical software and statistical knowledge in addition to high-quality data. Several of these methods are discussed below.

Formula-Based Projections

Formula-based projections are simply mathematical formulas established for estimating future revenues. Once the formulas are created, the forecaster simply plugs in the various values required. If a formula-based projection is used, any additional information about its accuracy, assumptions, and reliability should be included in the revenue manual. The most common formula-based projection for local governments is for property tax forecasts.

Strengths and Weaknesses of Formula-Based Projections

This method works best when the jurisdiction has a great deal of control over the revenue source[27] and it is a stable source, such as property taxes. It is less useful for revenues that fluctuate with the economy, such as sales taxes. Formula-based projections are very transparent and the assumptions are clearly laid out, which makes them easy to understand.

This method's weaknesses include not reflecting changes in assessments, such as when new properties are added or property defaults occur. Fundamentally, formula-based projections are good for property taxes at the local level but not for more dynamic revenues with harder to characterize (and less stable) tax bases.

Trend Analysis

Trend analysis, also referred to as time-series analysis, encompasses a great many methods of forecasting. There are two basic trend analysis models: moving averages and univariate regression.

---

25. All pertinent or desired information is not always available. It is a risk to make forecasts based exclusively on what is available and exclude any missing data as a factor. For example, imagine that the forecaster had only previous property tax revenue available to make forecasts, even though the municipal government had recently annexed a neighborhood for which it did not yet have property tax values. If the forecast were based exclusively on previous revenues, the estimate would be much lower than an estimate based on updated information.

26. These eight additional weaknesses are laid out in S. A. Guajardo and R. A. Miranda, *An Elected Official's Guide to Revenue Forecasting* (Chicago: Government Finance Officers Association of the United States and Canada, 2000).

27. This method also works best when the jurisdiction controls and has detailed information on the tax base. For property taxes, the local government quantifies the property tax base and sets it via assessments.

Figure 18.1 Revenue Forecasting Methods

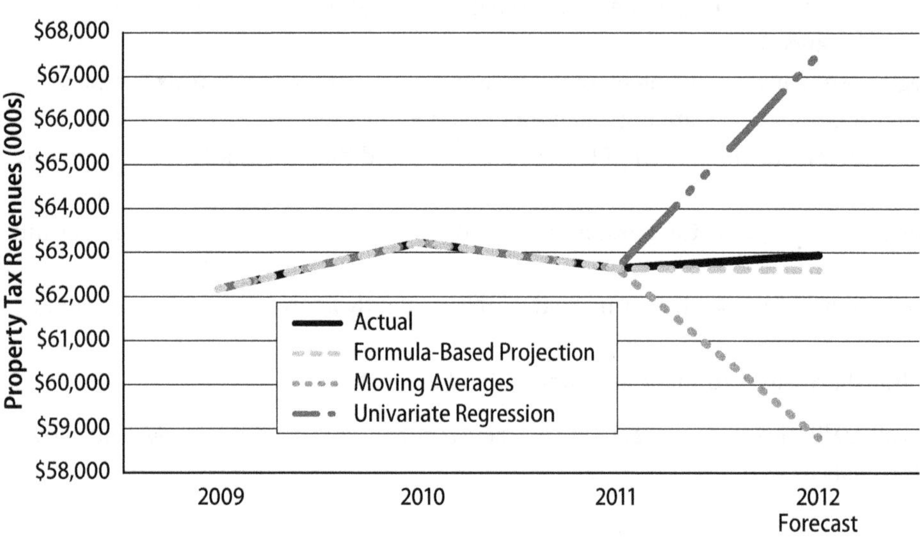

The moving averages model involves many methods of forecasting. One method is simply to project that revenue will increase or decrease by the average amount it has changed over the past five years, giving no additional weight to recent years. Another method is to forecast the revenue as the average of those years. These methods are often based on the assumption that the revenue source is too volatile for a forecaster reasonably to expect a trend to continue upward or downward.[28]

Univariate regression is a simple way to forecast revenues using a statistical model. *Univariate* simply means that only one independent (or control) variable is used to predict the dependent variable. If modeling property taxes, the independent variable would be year, and the dependent variable would be revenue collections. Regression software captures the relationship between the progression of time and revenue collections. Univariate regression analysis can be performed in many statistical packages, including Microsoft Excel.

Using actual property tax collections, Figure 18.1 presents one year of property tax forecasts using the methods above and the actual collections. In the case of the property tax, the formula-based allocation was much more accurate than moving averages or univariate regression.

Strengths and Weaknesses of Trend Analysis

Research suggests that trend analysis is most effective when used in combination with expert judgment.[29] Trend analysis is fundamentally based on the idea that the past can be used as a good predictor of the future. However, if a community has experienced large economic shocks or changes, this will not hold true. Not being able to anticipate coming changes or incorporate known changes into the model results in forecasts that lag behind changes to the economy. Nonetheless, trend analysis is largely accurate for more stable revenue sources. It also requires modest data and is relatively straightforward to implement. For that reason, it is heavily used by smaller local governments.[30]

Causal Modeling

Causal modeling, also referred to as econometric modeling or multiple (multivariate) regression, models the relationship between the revenue source and the economic variables that drive the tax base. In other words, this approach

28. There are several types of moving averages, which are explained in more detail in Kara A. Millonzi, ed., *Introduction to Local Government Financing*, 2nd ed. (Chapel Hill, N.C.: UNC School of Government, 2014), 189–92.

29. Gloria A. Grizzle and William Earle Klay, "Forecasting State Sales Tax Revenues: Comparing the Accuracy of Different Methods," *State and Local Government Review* 26, no. 3 (1994): 142–52.

30. Trend analysis is also often used by larger local governments, especially for their more minor revenue sources.

looks for the causes behind the amount of revenues collected and creates a model of the relationship.[31] Causal modeling recognizes that demographic and economic changes to a community, such as changes in population, median income, inflation, and industry, will affect tax revenues. It allows the forecaster to take data on an individual local government (and its community) and determine how tax revenue is expected to change when a component of the model changes and how that change is expected to affect a revenue source. Causal modeling becomes more valuable as the size and/or complications of the government, its respective economy, and its revenue portfolio grow.[32]

Strengths and Weaknesses of Causal Modeling

Causal models are used less frequently at the local level and can be very complex and challenging to implement. They are also very sensitive to specification and assumptions about the economy, so the forecaster must take particular care in identifying the independent variables to be included.

Forecasters undertake causal modeling because it allows taxes, which are more sensitive to the changing economic environment, to be forecasted based on those changes. This means that causal modeling is more likely to capture shocks and trends. Causal modeling makes it less likely that revenue forecasts will lag behind changes to the tax base in the way they do with trend analysis.

Causal modeling, however, is very difficult to do. Most local governments that use this methodology rely on economists from either a local university or a consulting firm. In addition, data is often incomplete, and "the absence of data on economic and structural variables at the city level" is very restricting.[33] Many of the key variables that are needed, such as personal income and population, are not available annually and potentially are not even collected for a unit of government (some data are collected just for counties and some just for large cities or even Metropolitan Statistical Areas). This makes causal modeling difficult if not impossible to accomplish.

Overall Assessment of Quantitative Methods

In sum, quantitative forecasting methods may more accurately model future revenues than do qualitative methods. When using data, though, it is always important to follow the acronym GIGO: garbage in, garbage out. Reliable data is critical. In addition, evidence suggests that simple, straightforward models perform as well as complicated models. In both the short and medium term, trend analysis models tend to perform better than causal models. Therefore, local governments should not necessarily embark on heroic efforts to perform sophisticated causal models if it is not within their means to do so and if trend analyses have proven reliable for them.

Considerations in Choosing the *Right* Method

There are many factors to consider in determining what method of forecasting is best. This section discusses some of the more universal factors, recognizing, however, that a local government can modify these perspectives in light of its own needs and capacity. Especially with regard to quantitative methods, the capacity of the forecasting staff is a crucial consideration. There is also always the question of the budget and whether or not a local government can afford to hire experts to assist with or conduct qualitative or quantitative analysis. Local governments typically rely heavily on expert judgment (internal and external) and the sophisticated modeling the experts provide.

The forecast method should also be based on the types of revenue sources (taxes, fees, etc.) that are in use within the local government. Typically, a revenue forecast is created for every major revenue source. For the smaller revenue sources, a local government may just look at historical numbers and establish an estimated total for each source. Nonetheless, the same forecast method is most likely not the best choice for all of the revenues to be forecasted.

31. Mikesell, "Consumption and Income Taxes," 210.

32. Bland, *A Budgeting Guide for Local Government.*

33. Mikesell, "Consumption and Income Taxes," 211.

Another important consideration is looking for trends, patterns, and rates of change and determining how stable each revenue source is; that is, how closely the source follows the trend.[34] For example, sales taxes are more unstable than property taxes, making trend analysis more problematic in light of the cyclical nature of the economy. Therefore, a formula-based forecast or a trend analysis may be best suited for property taxes, and a causal model may be best suited for sales taxes revenue forecasts.

Yet another consideration is economic, political, and social influences on the revenue source. It is important to look beyond the data. Is the revenue instrument, or more accurately its base, likely to be affected by a recession? Is citizen demand for this service growing? Considering these types of relationships and assumptions can help a local government choose the appropriate forecasting method.[35]

Best Practices in Forecasting Revenues

There are many best practices when it comes to forecasting. This section focuses on the most successful practices. This is by no means an exhaustive list, however, and not every method is necessarily right for every local government.

First, local governments should create revenue manuals as described in Step 1 of the recommended process for revenue forecasting, discussed above. All local governments should be able to take this action, which is of universal benefit. If a local government does not have a revenue manual in place, the process of creating one may be a multi-year undertaking. The place to start is at the top, with major revenue sources.

Second, forecasters should consider creating hybrid or conditional models that present alternative forecasts of possible revenues, test assumptions in the model, and provide elected officials options if they are considering changing elements of local government policy. A hybrid model that is transparent, with its assumptions clearly laid out, enables forecasters to adjust their forecasts for other scenarios, such as changes in tax rates and the tax base.[36] For example, in a formula-based allocation, adjusting the tax rate is a straightforward process.[37] In fact, one of the common uses of forecasting, beyond establishing one-year revenue projections for the budget, is guiding tax rate adjustments. This is helpful in trying to establish consistent tax policies so that tax rates do not have to be adjusted every year.[38] It is important to remember, however, that forecasts are projections, not predictions. While a hybrid model may be useful for testing assumptions and providing options, and, in some cases, for advising long-run planning, it is not appropriate or acceptable for annual budget forecasts. Revenue numbers must be decided on and used to balance the budget.

Third, local governments should consider factors beyond the revenue forecasts, such as the local government's fund balance. It is clear that revenue projections or forecasts are not going to be completely accurate, and while it is considered best to err slightly on the conservative side of forecasting, it should nonetheless be apparent that this is one of the many reasons for maintaining a fund balance—not just for downturns, but also for years when estimates are on the high end of the spectrum. This is especially important when a local government is less confident in the forecasts. For example, if a local government relies heavily on sales taxes and the amount of sales taxes collected has been unpredictable from year to year, the local government may choose to maintain a larger fund balance reserve.[39]

---

34. Guajardo and Miranda, "An Elected Official's Guide to Revenue Forecasting."

35. *Id.*

36. "The forecast may even be conditional, in the sense that it is prepared with alternative assumptions (high/low scenarios) for certain economic or developmental factors." Mikesell, "Consumption and Income Taxes," 209.

37. Also, if rates have changed over time, it is critical to adjust the data to reflect that. If the forecaster is engaged in causal modeling, the adjustment may be as straightforward as controlling for rate. However, if a more basic trend analysis is being used, it would be crucial to adjust the data to reflect that the rate, and not a change in the economy or the tax base, is driving the change in collections.

38. William C. Rivenbark, "Financial Forecasting for North Carolina Local Governments," *Popular Government* 73, no. 1 (Fall 2007): 6–13.

39. Whitney Afonso, "Diversification toward Stability? The Effect of Local Sales Taxes on Own Source Revenue," *Journal of Public Budgeting, Accounting and Financial Management* 25, no. 4 (2013): 649–74.

Fourth, local governments should consider creating long-term financial plans. The National Advisory Council on State and Local Budgeting encourages local governments to develop such plans by using a strategic process that gives them greater insights into revenues and expenditures and the information needed to establish policies that will lead to long-term fiscal health.[40]

Forecasting Is Not Perfect

It is important to remember that no forecast it is ever completely accurate: the numbers will inevitably be wrong. The goal is to minimize how wrong they are. With that in mind, there are several points to be made about error in forecasting.[41]

The forecaster should always strive to include predicted error with the estimates and should be clear about how confident he or she is that the forecasts are reliable. It should be noted that the farther out in time the forecast extends, the larger the errors are likely to be. As well, forecasts are built on the past, which has two important implications: (1) if the future deviates from the past in a meaningful way, the forecasts will not be accurate; and (2) if key data or trends from the past are ignored, more error will be introduced into the estimates. Finally, forecasting for a period greater than three years will be more reliable if the revenues are more aggregated. While it is useful to forecast individual revenue streams for both the short and medium term, doing so is less valuable for long-term forecasting.

Because errors inevitably do occur, it is advisable to forecast conservatively, but only slightly so. It is not prudent to dramatically underestimate revenues, because budgets do have to be balanced. An unnecessarily conservative forecast could cause the board to make unnecessary cuts to services or to increase taxes unnecessarily. While estimates that are too high can create crises and require expenditure cuts during the execution phase, estimates that are too low can result in needless reductions to programs at the beginning of the fiscal year.[42]

Politics can, unfortunately, hinder the forecasting process. For example, it is often considered a best practice to be slightly conservative and to estimate revenues just below where the forecaster thinks they will be.[43] However, this makes it harder for a local government to balance the budget and may require it to make service cuts or increase taxes, so forecasters sometimes find themselves pressured to be more *optimistic*. It is important for the forecaster to resist these political pressures, however, because "in revenue forecasting, your sins find you out, and they do have a cost."[44]

The cyclical nature of the economy is also a persistent problem in generating reliable forecasts. Historical data reveal periodic dips in growth, and revenues are cyclical and influenced by the *natural* expansions and shrinkages (recessions) of the economy.[45] As local governments reduce their reliance on property taxes and increase their reliance on user fees and sales taxes, awareness of these cycles will become even more critical. Forecasters must keep this in mind, especially in preparing long-term forecasts.

---

40. R. Calia, S. Guajardo, and J. Metzgar, "Putting the NACSLB Recommended Budget Practices into Action: Best Practices in Budgeting,"*Government Finance Review* (April 1998).

41. Adapted from Kriz, "Long-Term Forecasting," 125–58.

42. Robert D. Lee, Ronald W. Johnson, and Philip G. Joyce, *Public Budgeting Systems* (Burlington, Mass.: Jones & Bartlett, 2008).

43. "In both larger and smaller counties, the acceptable overestimation range was lower than the acceptable under-estimation range. These findings confirm the conservative behavior among government revenue forecasters in the presence of uncertainty. And, when the county revenue forecasters were asked how conservative they are in forecasting sales taxes, 90% of the counties responded that their estimation was at least somewhat conservative." D. Kong, "Local Government Revenue Forecasting: The California County Experience," *Journal of Public Budgeting, Accounting & Financial Management* 19, no. 2 (2007): 178–99.

44. Bland, *A Budgeting Guide for Local Government*, 37.

45. Garrett and Leatherman, "An Introduction to State and Local Public Finance."

Conclusion

All local governments perform revenue forecasting. Despite that universality, however, there is a great deal of diversity in the methodologies they employ. Some local governments may simply forecast next year's revenue to equal the previous year's revenue, while others may create sophisticated causal models that attempt to capture the changing nature of the underlying tax base. These potential extremes highlight the need for transparency, both internally and externally. Revenue forecasts should provide not just a number, but also the methodology and assumptions on which a forecast is based. This information should be included in the revenue manual.

In addition, local governments need to be thoughtful when choosing which methods are best for them and should consider employing different methods for different revenue instruments. However, the benefit of having a more advanced forecasting method with *slightly* more accurate forecasts may not outweigh the additional costs of performing it.[46] These costs may be direct, such as paying outside consultants, or indirect, such as staff time and additional training. While expert and trend analyses are the most common methods for forecasting revenues and expenditures in North Carolina, it should not be surprising that there is no standard model or methodology, because each local government develops its own based on its particular needs.[47]

Although revenue forecasting may seem like a challenging undertaking, there are many excellent resources available to local governments in North Carolina.[48] The following organizations provide resources for local government officials and finance officers:

- North Carolina League of Municipalities (NCLM), www.nclm.org
- North Carolina Association of County Commissioners (NCACC), www.ncacc.org
- North Carolina Government Finance Officers Association (NCGFOA) www.ncgfoa.org
- North Carolina Local Government Budget Association (NCLGBA), www.nclgba.org
- UNC School of Government (SOG), www.sog.unc.edu

For an in-depth discussion of revenue forecasting, see Whitney B. Afonso, "Revenue Forecasting," chap. 8 in *Introduction to Local Government Financing*, 2nd ed., ed. Kara A. Millonzi (Chapel Hill, N.C.: UNC School of Government, 2014).

About the Author

Whitney B. Afonso is a School of Government faculty member. Her research interests are in state and local government finance; in particular, how the choice of revenue streams by state and local governments affects government and citizen behavior. She has also written on ways to engage citizens through local budgeting.

46. Kong, "Local Government Revenue Forecasting: The California County Experience."

47. Rivenbark, "Financial Forecasting for North Carolina Local Governments."

48. For example, the North Carolina Association of County Commissioners prepares a report on projections for county revenues every year. While the projections are not specific to individual counties, they can offer insight and direction. For fiscal year 2014, see www.ncacc.org/index.aspx?nid=327.

Similarly, the North Carolina League of Municipalities prepares a memo on municipal revenue projections for the state. For fiscal year 2015, see www.nclm.org/SiteCollectionDocuments/FY%2014-15%20Revenue%20Projections%20Memo.pdf?cm_mid=3292936&cm_crmid={e33f955b-aea5-de11-830f-005056a07b49}&cm_medium=email.

Chapter 19

The Property Tax

Christopher B. McLaughlin

I. Overview

Property taxes are one of the oldest forms of taxation in the United States and have been central among revenue sources in North Carolina since the early days of statehood. Through the 1930s, property taxes were levied by the state as well as by local governments. Now property taxes are levied only by cities, counties, and special districts.

Property taxes are the single largest source of revenue for counties in North Carolina, representing just under 50 percent of county revenues statewide.[1] For municipalities, property taxes represent roughly 20 percent of revenue statewide and are the largest source of revenue other than fees for utility services.[2] However, while revenues generated from utilities such as water and sewer pay only for the service provided, property taxes paid to local governments subsidize all types of government functions and services, from schools to health departments to jails to trash disposal.

Both real property and personal property are subject to taxation in North Carolina. Real property includes land, buildings, and permanent fixtures, as well as rights and privileges pertaining to land, such as mineral or forestry rights. Personal property includes all other property, both tangible and intangible, that is not permanently affixed to land. With the exception of certain software and leasehold interests in real property, only tangible personal property is subject to property taxes in North Carolina.

Property taxes are said to be in rem, from the Latin phrase meaning "on the thing," because they are levied upon the property itself—unlike "in personam" taxes, such as income taxes, which are levied "on the person." Notwithstanding the in rem nature of the property tax, property owners who fail to pay property taxes are personally liable for the delinquent taxes. Tax collectors may satisfy past-due taxes by seizing or attaching personal property of the taxpayer or, for taxes that are liens on real property, by foreclosing upon that real property. Because property taxes are in rem, the lien for property taxes is not extinguished upon transfer of real property to a new owner. This means that if taxes on real property remain unpaid after its transfer, the new owner must pay the taxes or risk having the land foreclosed upon, even if the tax liability was incurred when someone else owned the property. Property taxes on personal property, in contrast, become a lien on personal property only upon seizure by the tax collector. As a result, the liability for taxes on personal property generally does not follow that property from one owner to another.

Constitutional Provisions Governing Taxation

For Public Purposes Only

Article V, Section 2(1), of the North Carolina Constitution permits the power of taxation to be used "for public purposes only," meaning that a city or county wishing to pay for a program, function, or activity with property tax revenues must ensure that the program, function, or activity serves a public purpose. This analysis requires more than simply determining whether the expenditure somehow benefits more than a limited segment of the community.

In 1947 the North Carolina Supreme Court struck down as unconstitutional a local act that permitted the Town of Tarboro to issue bonds and levy taxes to construct a hotel, which the town planned to own and maintain.[3] While recognizing that the proposed hotel would promote business in Tarboro and enhance property values, the court held that such benefits were too incidental to justify the expenditure of public funds for what was essentially a private business. Because the hotel was not a public purpose, the court concluded that the General Assembly exceeded its authority in authorizing the expenditure of tax revenues for its construction. In reaching its conclusion, the court listed many types of expenditures that fell within the definition of *public purpose*, including expenditures for streets, sidewalks, bridges; water, light, and sewerage plants; municipal buildings; auditoriums; hospitals; playgrounds; parks; railroads; armories; fairs; and airports.

---

1. North Carolina Department of State Treasurer, *North Carolina County and Municipal Financial Information for Fiscal 2010*, www.nctreasurer.com/lgc/units/D_E.htm.

2. *Id.* at www.nctreasurer.com/lgc/units/D_AG.htm.

3. Nash v. Town of Tarboro, 227 N.C. 283 (1947).

Consideration of the Town of Tarboro case in the modern era of economic incentive grants raises the question of whether tax revenues may be used for incentive payments to private businesses, which are intended to encourage private businesses to locate or expand in a particular jurisdiction. Are such incentive payments for a public purpose? The state supreme court answered this question affirmatively in a 1996 case resulting from a lawsuit filed by a private citizen, William Maready, against the City of Winston-Salem and Forsyth County.[4] Maready alleged that a state statute authorizing local governments to make economic development incentive grants to private businesses was unconstitutional because it violated the constitutional requirement that the power of taxation be used only for public purposes. Maready challenged twenty-four economic development incentive projects entered into by the city or county at a cost of $13 million, most of which was generated from property taxes. The city and county estimated that those projects resulted in a $240 million increase in the tax base and the creation of 5,500 new jobs.

The state supreme court sided with the city and county after determining that the incentive payments were made to spur economic development, which had long been recognized as a proper governmental function to further the general economic welfare of city and county residents. In distinguishing a 1968 opinion in which it struck down a statute that authorized the issuance of industrial revenue bonds to finance the construction of facilities for private industry, the supreme court explained the incongruity of preventing cities and counties that expend large sums on humanitarian and social programs "from promoting the provision of jobs for the unemployed, an increase in the tax base, and the prevention of economic stagnation."[5]

The Power to Exempt and Classify Property

A provision dating from Article V, Section 2(3), of the 1868 North Carolina Constitution exempts from taxation property belonging to the state, counties, and municipal corporations. The provision further authorizes the General Assembly to exempt from taxation cemeteries; property held for educational, scientific, literary, cultural, charitable, or religious purposes; personal property to a value not exceeding $300; and $1,000 in property held and used as the place of residence of the owner. In 1961 this constitutional provision was amended to require that every such exemption apply statewide and be made by general law uniformly applicable in every county, city, or special district. Only the General Assembly may grant exemptions.

The granting of the power to classify property in 1936, Article V, Section 2(2), of the North Carolina Constitution, rendered largely meaningless the permissible exemptions clause dating from 1868. This is so because the General Assembly may enact a general law designating some type of property as a special class and then exclude that class from taxation. In 1985 the General Assembly did just that with respect to household personal property by designating all nonbusiness personal property (other than motor vehicles, mobile homes, aircraft, watercraft, and watercraft engines) as a special class of property and excluding it from the tax base.[6] Using its classification power, the legislature exempted from taxation far more than the $300 in personal property authorized by the earlier constitutional provision. Similarly, the General Assembly exceeded the $1,000 residence exemption authorized in the permissible exemptions clause when it relied on the classification power to create the elderly or disabled residential homestead exclusion.[7] This classification excludes from taxation the greater of $20,000 or 50 percent of the portion of the residence of a qualifying disabled or elderly person.

Statewide Application of Exemptions and Classifications

The requirement that classifications and exemptions be made by general law uniformly applicable in every county, city, and state bars the General Assembly from passing local acts that exempt certain types of property only in a particular

4. Maready v. City of Winston-Salem, 342 N.C. 708 (1996).
5. *Id.*
6. N.C. Gen. Stat. (hereinafter G.S.) § 105-275(16).
7. G.S. 105-277.1.

tax district. For example, an act exempting cemeteries in a particular county would be unconstitutional. But a law exempting *all* cemeteries in the state from taxation would satisfy the uniformity clause.[8]

The Uniform Rule Requirement and Service Districts

The uniform rule requirement mandates uniformity in the tax rate as well as in the method of assessment. This uniformity must be coextensive with the territory to which it applies. A local tax such as the property tax must be based upon rates and standards of assessment that apply uniformly throughout the city, county, or special or service district in which the tax is levied.[9]

With respect to tax rates, the uniformity requirement means that a local government must adopt a single tax rate for all property—real property, personal property, and registered motor vehicles—within its taxing jurisdiction. A provision added to the state constitution in 1973, however, permits the General Assembly to enact laws authorizing the governing body of a taxing unit to define a territorial area and to levy additional property taxes within that area to provide for additional or greater services, facilities, or functions than those provided elsewhere in the local government.[10] Known as special service districts, these tax districts are statutorily authorized for both counties and municipalities.[11]

With respect to tax assessments, the uniformity requirement has prompted the General Assembly mandate that all property other than certain public service company property and property located in a development financing district be assessed for taxation at its true value or, in the case of certain agricultural, horticultural, or forestland property, at its present-use value.[12] Moreover, the Machinery Act provides that the county assessor's assessment of property applies to all cities and special and service districts within the county.[13]

II. The Machinery Act

Statutes Governing the Administration of Property Taxes

The Machinery Act, codified at Subchapter II of Chapter 105 of the North Carolina General Statutes (hereinafter G.S.), sets forth the procedures for assessing and collecting property taxes. The title of the act dates from the time of a state-levied property tax. Before 1931, the General Assembly passed each session a Revenue Act, which levied the property tax, and a Machinery Act, which set forth the procedures for levying and collecting the tax.[14] A permanent Machinery Act, governing the assessment and collection of local property taxes, was enacted in 1939.[15] The 1939 version of the Machinery Act was overhauled in 1971.[16] The 1971 Machinery Act, as modified by subsequent enactments of the General Assembly, remains in effect today.

The Machinery Act divides property into two general types: *real* and *personal*. Real property is defined in G.S. 105-273(13) of the North Carolina General Statutes (hereinafter G.S.) to include land and improvements, which consist of

8. G.S. 105-278.2 exempts from property taxes cemetery plots not held for sale; in other words, those that are owned by the individuals who intend to make use of the plots.

9. Hajoca Corp. v. Clayton, 277 N.C. 560, 569 (1971).

10. N.C. Const. art. V, § 2(4).

11. G.S. 153A-301 (counties); G.S. 160A-536 (municipalities). *See also* Christopher B. McLaughlin, *Fundamentals of Property Tax Law in North Carolina* (Chapel Hill, N.C.: UNC School of Government, 2012), 311.

12. G.S. 105-284 (uniform assessment standard); G.S. 105-277.4 (present-use value assessment).

13. G.S. 105-284 and -327. An exception applies to property located in a city that straddles two or more counties. The governing board for such a city may appoint a city assessor to appraise and assess city property. G.S. 105-328. Another exception applies to public service company property, which is appraised by the N.C. Department of Revenue. G.S. 105-335.

14. Joseph S. Ferrell, "A Taxpayer's Guide to Property Tax Revaluation," *Popular Government* 47 (Winter 1982): 36.

15. N.C. Pub. Laws 1939, Ch. 310.

16. N.C. Pub. Laws 1971, Ch. 806.

buildings and fixtures that are permanently attached to land, including manufactured homes placed upon land owned by the same person who owns the home. G.S. 105-273 subdivides personal property into tangible property, such as motor vehicles, boats, and machinery, and intangible property, such as bank accounts, stocks, and bonds. All real and personal property is taxable unless specifically exempted or excluded from taxation.[17] Thus, taxation is the rule and exemption or exclusion is the exception. As noted above, very little intangible property is subject to ad valorem taxation today.[18]

All one hundred counties and nearly all cities levy property taxes. In fiscal year 2013–14, the average tax rate was $0.62 per $100.00 in value for counties and $0.41 per $100.00 for cities.[19] County tax rates ranged from $0.28 to $1.03 per $100.00, while municipal tax rates ranged from $0.0165 to $0.82 per $100.00.[20]

Steps in the Taxation of Property

The Machinery Act creates six basic steps in administering the property tax at the local level.

1. Property must be identified as to ownership, location, and whether it is taxable. This step is called *listing.*
2. The tax office must estimate the market value of the listed property. This step is called *appraisal.*
3. The portion of the market value to be taxed must be calculated, and the property must be formally placed on the roll of taxable property. This step is called *assessment.*
4. Once property has been formally assessed for taxation, the taxing authorities must allow time for *review and appeal* of assessments. The owner may want to challenge the valuation placed on the property or whether the taxing jurisdiction has authority to tax it at all, and the governing board may want to correct assessment inequities.
5. Once the review process has concluded, the governing body of the taxing unit sets the *tax rate* for the current tax year, and the tax office begins the *billing* process that notifies each taxpayer how much he or she owes and when and where to pay the tax.
6. The last step is *collection* of the tax levy.

The Administrative Structure

The county assessor and the county and city tax collector stand at the heart of the administrative structure created by the Machinery Act. The county commissioners appoint, pay, assist, and supervise the county assessor and the county tax collector. The city council does the same for the city tax collector. The county assessor also is supervised at the state level by the Department of Revenue and the Property Tax Commission.

Traditionally, the county board of commissioners appointed separate individuals to serve in the role of county assessor and tax collector. The assessor and tax collector headed separate departments and reported to the board of commissioners and related to the county manager independently of each other. Some counties still follow the traditional model, while others have combined the assessing and collecting functions in a single tax department under one department head. Some counties accomplish this by appointing the same person as assessor and tax collector. The Machinery Act permits the office of assessor to be held concurrently with any other appointive or elective office except that of county

17. G.S. 105-274.

18. The only intangible property that is taxable today is private leasehold interests in exempt property (G.S. 105-275(31)) and computer software that is either embedded in computer hardware or purchased/licensed from a third party and capitalized in the financial records of the taxpayer.

19. See note 1 (counties) and note 2 (municipalities), above.

20. N.C. Department of Revenue, *County and Municipal Tax Rates and Year of Most Recent Revaluation*, www.dor.state.nc.us/publications/propertyrates.html.

commissioner.[21] Other counties name a tax administrator who heads a combined tax department. A tax assessor may serve as administrator as well as collector without violating the prohibition on holding more than two appointive or elective offices because the third position—tax administrator—is an administrative and not an appointed or elected position identified in the General Statutes.

The work of the county assessor is subject to review by the county board of equalization and review. The principal function of this board is to hear and decide taxpayer appeals. In many counties the board of equalization and review is composed of the county commissioners, who sit for that purpose for a limited time each year. In other counties special boards of equalization and review are appointed by the county commissioners.

At the state level, over and above the county officials, are the Department of Revenue and the Property Tax Commission. As an administrative agency, the Department of Revenue is charged with supervising the valuation and taxation of property by local units of government and with appraising public service company property for local taxation. The Property Tax Commission is an administrative appeals board that has the power to review and change listing and valuation decisions made by local officials or the Department of Revenue. It hears appeals from county boards of equalization and review.

Terms and Qualifications of the County Assessor

The county assessor[22] is appointed directly by the board of county commissioners rather than by the county manager. The initial term of office is two years, beginning on July 1 of odd-numbered years. An assessor who has completed a two-year term and has been certified by the Department of Revenue may be reappointed for a four-year term at the discretion of the board. The commissioners may remove the assessor at any time for good cause after giving him or her notice in writing and an opportunity to appear and be heard at a public session of the board.

While the term *cause* is not defined by the Machinery Act, in this context it is generally understood to mean substantial misconduct that affects the tax collector's performance of the duties of the office and that directly affects the public interest.[23] For example, misappropriation of funds would be cause for discharge.

Persons appointed as assessors must be certified by the Department of Revenue. Certification requires satisfactory completion of four basic training courses and a comprehensive examination. New appointees have two years to complete these requirements and are not eligible for reappointment if they fail to do so within the time allowed. Assessors also are required to complete at least thirty hours of continuing education instruction every two years to remain eligible for reappointment.

The Property Tax Calendar

Many citizens and local government officials are surprised to learn that property taxes are levied for a *fiscal year* that opens on July 1 and closes on the following June 30. This confusion is likely caused by several factors. First, North Carolina real estate attorneys routinely prorate taxes between buyers and sellers in real estate closings on a calendar year basis. Second, the January 1 date of assessment and the January 6 delinquency date the following year roughly follow a calendar year cycle. In addition, property taxes levied for the 2014–15 year generally are referred to simply as "2014 taxes." Anyone familiar with local government finance and budgeting will recognize, however, that property taxes, which are the bread and butter of local government finance, could be levied on nothing other than a fiscal year

21. G.S. 105-294(f). Similarly, the office of tax collector may be held by an individual also holding any other appointive or elective office except that of membership on the local government's governing board. The tax collector also may not concurrently serve as the local government's treasurer, finance officer, or chief accounting officer without written approval from the Local Government Commission. G.S. 105-349(e). See part V, below.

22. G.S. 105-294.

23. 63C Am. Jur. 2d *Public Officers and Employees* § 181 (2009).

basis. After all, county commissioners and city council members adopt their budgets and set the property tax rate by July 1 of each year. Bills for property taxes, which supply the revenue for budgeted expenditures, are then mailed to taxpayers as soon as possible after July 1. Taxes are due September 1 (a date that is widely ignored by taxpayers in all taxing jurisdictions that do not offer a discount for early payment of taxes) and are payable without interest at any time through the following January 5. Most taxpayers, and all mortgage companies paying on behalf of homeowners, pay property taxes before January 1 so that the amount paid may be deducted from the property owner's income tax return for the current calendar year. Thus, midway through the fiscal year, the local government unit will have received most of its revenues from current fiscal year property taxes.

After the delinquency date (January 6), local tax collectors begin to use enforced collection remedies against those who have not paid on time in the current year. In addition to collecting delinquent taxes for the current year after January 6, the tax collector continues efforts to collect delinquent taxes from prior years.

To tax property according to value in the correct taxing jurisdiction and bill the taxes to the proper owner, the taxing authorities must know where the property is located (situs), its value, who owns the property, and whether it is subject to taxation. Situs, taxability, and ownership of real and personal property (other than registered motor vehicles) are determined annually as of the January 1 that precedes the fiscal year for which taxes are to be levied. Situs, taxability, and ownership of registered motor vehicles are determined as of the date of vehicle registration. The value of real property is determined as of January 1 of the year in which property is revalued. Counties must conduct a countywide revaluation at least every eight years. Personal property other than registered motor vehicles is valued annually as of January 1. Registered motor vehicles are valued as of January 1 of the year in which the taxes become due.

The information needed to determine situs, taxability, ownership, and value is compiled each year during the listing period, which begins in January and normally runs for about thirty days. During this time, taxpayers must submit to the county assessor a list of their taxable personal property and any improvements they have made to their real property. While taxpayers were formerly required to list real as well as personal property, every county now has a permanent listing system for real property that requires the assessor to list all real property. The form on which taxable property is declared is called the *abstract*. The listing period also is the time for property owners who want to claim the benefit of exemption or other special tax treatment to submit their applications.

After the listing period closes, the county assessor determines the appraised and assessed value of each taxable item and compiles the *scroll*, which is a tentative list of taxable property showing the owner's name and address and the aggregate assessed value of his or her taxable property. The scroll is then submitted to the board of equalization and review for approval. Most counties begin this process on the first Monday in May. The Machinery Act contemplates that the board of equalization and review will remain in session for three weeks, but in any event not later than July 1. In reality, most boards of equalization and review now meet for several months after July 1, though they do so only to hear appeals filed before July 1. While the board is authorized to make any changes in the scroll needed to bring the listing and assessments into conformity with legal requirements, in practice virtually all of the changes it makes result from appeals by property owners.

After the board of equalization and review has completed its work and the tax rate has been set, the tax office computes the precise amount of taxes due from each person entered on the scroll, which is now more properly called the *tax list and assessment roll* because it has been finalized for the current year. The list of taxpayers with the amount of taxes due from each is called the *tax book*. In the modern era of electronic recordkeeping, many of the Machinery Act titles for records have lost much of their earlier significance. For example, in many counties, the data formerly reflected in a printed tax book and tax list and assessment roll are combined in a computerized database.

Tax receipts prepared from information in the tax book double as billing notices to the taxpayers. Once the tax has been paid, the tax receipt serves as legal evidence that the tax lien has been discharged.

Figure 19.1 lists the important dates in the annual property tax cycle. Note that taxpayer deadlines falling on a holiday or weekend are moved to the following business day. The School of Government issues a more detailed tax calendar for the coming year each December.[24]

24. For a link to the most recent calendar, see http://shopping.netsuite.com/s.nl/c.433425/sc.7/category.59/.f.

Figure 19.1 Important Dates in the Annual Property Tax Cycle

January

1	Value, ownership, taxable status, and situs of real and personal property determined for the new fiscal year.[a]
	Liens for taxes from the new fiscal year attach to all real property in the taxing unit. These liens include taxes on the real property itself plus taxes on all personal property owned by the same taxpayer in the taxing unit.[b]
5	Last day to pay taxes from the current fiscal year without interest (in other words, at par).[c]
6	2 percent interest accrues on unpaid real and personal property taxes from the current fiscal year.[d]
	Unpaid taxes on real and personal property from the current fiscal year become delinquent and enforced collections remedies (foreclosure, attachment, levy) may begin.[e]
31	Last day of listing period for the new fiscal year. Unless this date is extended by the governing board, taxpayers must list all taxable personal property and improvements to real property by this date.[f]
	Last day for taxpayers to submit timely applications for exemptions and exclusions other than the three residential property tax relief exclusions (elderly and disabled, circuit breaker, and disabled veterans) for the new fiscal year. This application deadline is extended automatically if the listing period is extended.[g] Upon a showing of good cause by a taxpayer, a late application may be approved by the governing board.[h]

February

1st Monday	County tax collector must report to the county commissioners all delinquent taxes from the current fiscal year that are liens on real property.[i]
2nd Monday	Municipal tax collector must report to the governing board all delinquent taxes from the current fiscal year that are liens on real property.[j]

March

1	Tax collector must advertise delinquent taxes from the current fiscal year that are liens on real property between March 1 and June 30.[k]
2	Last date to which the listing period may be extended in a nonreappraisal year.[l]

April

1	Last date to which the listing period may be extended in a reappraisal year.[m]
1st Monday	Earliest date for first meeting of board of equalization and review to hear valuation, ownership, taxable status, and situs appeals for the new fiscal year. Assessor must publish three notices of this meeting at least ten days prior.[n]

May

1st Monday	Latest date for first meeting of board of equalization and review to hear valuation, ownership, taxable status, and situs appeals for the new fiscal year. Assessor must publish three notices of this meeting at least ten days prior.[o]

a. G.S. 105-285.
b. G.S. 105-355(a).
c. G.S. 105-360(a).
d. *Id.*
e. G.S. 105-365.1(a).
f. G.S. 105-307(a).
g. G.S. 105-282.1(a).
h. G.S. 105-282.1(a1).
i. G.S. 105-369(a).
j. *Id.*
k. G.S. 105-369(c).
l. G.S. 105-307(b)(1).
m. G.S. 105-307(b)(2).
n. G.S. 105-322(e).
o. *Id.*

June

1 Budget officer must file with the governing board the proposed budget including the property tax rate for the new fiscal year by today.[p] Until that occurs, the tax collector is not required to accept prepayments of taxes from the new fiscal year.[q]

Last day to submit timely applications for the three residential property tax relief exclusions (elderly and disabled, circuit breaker, and disabled veterans) for the new fiscal year.[r] Upon a showing of good cause by a taxpayer, a late application may be approved by the governing board.[s]

30 Current fiscal year ends.[t]

July

1 New fiscal year begins.[u]

Governing board should adopt final budget and property tax rate for new fiscal year by today.[v]

Last day for county board of equalization and review to adjourn in a nonreappraisal year. Taxpayers must submit appeals of current year's tax assessments before the board adjourns.[w]

After July 1 and before being charged with taxes for the new fiscal year, the tax collector must make a sworn report to the governing board showing a list of unpaid taxes on real and personal property for the prior fiscal year. The tax collector must also make settlement for the taxes from the prior fiscal year before being charged with taxes for the new fiscal year.[x]

August

31 Last day to pay property taxes from the new fiscal year with a discount adopted by the governing board under G.S. 105-360(c).

September

1 Property taxes from the new fiscal year become due.[y]

Last day to initiate enforced collection remedies (foreclosure, attachment, levy) for taxes that were originally due on this date ten years prior.[z]

On or before today, tax receipts for the new fiscal year shall be delivered to the tax collector. Before tax receipts are delivered, the collector shall have delivered duplicate receipts for prepaid taxes to the finance officer, provided a collector's bond for the new fiscal year approved by the governing body, and made annual settlement for taxes from the prior fiscal year.[aa]

December

1 Last day for county board of equalization and review to adjourn in a reappraisal year. Taxpayers must submit appeals of current year's tax assessments before the board adjourns.[bb]

31 Last day for taxpayers to submit late applications for exemptions or exclusions for the new fiscal year.[cc] Upon a showing of good cause by a taxpayer, a late application may be approved by the governing board.[dd]

p. G.S. 159-11(b).
q. G.S. 105-359(b).
r. G.S. 105-277.1(c).
s. G.S. 105-282.1(a1).
t. G.S. 159-8(b).
u. *Id.*
v. G.S. 159-139(a).
w. G.S. 105-322(e) (adjournment date) and G.S. 105-322(g)(2)(a) (appeal deadline).
x. G.S. 105-373(a).
y. G.S. 105-360(a).
z. G.S. 105-378(a). For example, September 1, 2010, was the last day on which enforced collection remedies could begin for taxes from the 2000–01 fiscal year that were originally due on September 1, 2000.
aa. G.S. 105-352.
bb. G.S. 105-322(e) (adjournment date) and G.S. 105-322(g)(2)(a) (appeal deadline).
cc. G.S. 105-282.1(a1).
dd. *Id.*

Real Estate Transfers, Prorations, and Annexation

In nearly every real estate transfer, property taxes are prorated between the buyer and seller. A portion of the property taxes attributable to the period of the seller's ownership is deducted from the seller's proceeds and credited to the buyer. Many property owners mistakenly believe that this balance sheet deduction and credit at a real estate closing satisfies any liability for property taxes for the year in which the transfer takes place. Yet, unless the transfer occurs after property tax bills have been issued in late July or early August, the general practice is that the property taxes are not paid from the proceeds at closing. For many years, the nonpayment of taxes at closing led to several problems. First, the owner of record of property as of the assessment date traditionally was defined as the "taxpayer," and that person's name appeared on the tax receipt and in any advertisement of tax liens published in the newspaper. He or she was also the person against whom enforced collection remedies were authorized if the taxes were not paid. It is not difficult to imagine a seller's surprise upon having his or her wages garnished for property he or she sold in the previous calendar year. And the proration of taxes at closing was no defense to an enforced collection action, because the prorating was merely a private agreement between the parties and did not result in the actual payment of taxes at closing.

The General Assembly in 2006 addressed this problem by redefining the term "taxpayer," for purposes of enforced collection of delinquent property taxes assessed on real property, as the owner of record on the date the taxes become delinquent and any subsequent owner of record of the property if conveyed after that date.[25] Thus, beginning with property taxes imposed for the 2006–07 fiscal year, payment of delinquent property taxes assessed on real property transferred after January 1 may be secured by attaching or levying upon personal property of the owner as of the date of delinquency or any subsequent owner, but not the owner of the property as of January 1.

The nonpayment of taxes at closing also presents potential problems for purchasers of property, who often do not receive the bill for property taxes because the former owner's name appears on the tax receipt, which doubles as the bill. If a new owner does not receive the tax bill, he or she may neglect to pay the taxes before they become delinquent. This is less of an issue if the property is subject to a mortgage, in which case the mortgage company usually maintains an escrow account from which the taxes are paid even if the new owner does not receive the tax bill.

Finally, the proration of taxes upon the transfer of real property leads to confusion because of the manner in which such prorations are calculated. Although property taxes are levied on a fiscal year basis, real estate attorneys generally prorate them based upon a calendar year. Indeed, the General Assembly specifically endorsed this method of proration in 2006 by enacting new G.S. 39-60, which states that the calendar-year basis is the presumptive manner of prorating property taxes upon the sale of real property. Pursuant to the calendar year method of proration, if property is sold on July 1, 2014, one-half of the 2014 property taxes is deducted from the seller's proceeds—even though the seller did not own the property during the period for which the 2014 taxes were levied, July 1, 2014, through June 30, 2015.

Taxpayers often fail to understand that the proration agreement between the buyer and seller has no effect on the tax office's obligation and right to collect the taxes that were subject to the proration agreement. As discussed above, the owner as of the delinquency date and all subsequent owners are personally responsible for the delinquent taxes, regardless of what type of proration agreement was involved with the sale of the property in question.

III. Listing and Appraisal of Property

The Listing Process

A taxing unit must, of course, know what property is subject to its jurisdiction before it can levy a tax on such property. The process of listing property with the county and municipal assessor, which dates from the era of the township list taker, accomplishes this objective.

25. G.S. 105-273(17).

One significant characteristic of the modern listing process is the permanent listing of all real property by the county assessor. By 2004, every county had implemented a permanent listing system that charged the county assessor with listing all real property in the name of the owner of record. Taxpayers are no longer required to list real property with the county, but they are required to provide the assessor with information regarding improvements made to the property since the time of the last reappraisal; any ownership of separate rights, such as mineral or timber rights in the property; and separate ownership of improvements to the property.

Who is responsible for listing property? Generally speaking, the listing taxpayer is the record owner of real property and the owner of personal property (for which there often is no formal record) as of January 1. The person in whose name property is listed becomes important for purposes of carrying out enforced collection remedies in the event the taxes become delinquent. Taxpayers list property and apply for exemptions or exclusions of property with the county tax assessor, although municipalities retain the right to affirm or deny an exemption or exclusion application notwithstanding the county's determination. The listing period generally is the month of January, but individual listing extensions that permit a taxpayer to file his or her listing as late as April 15 may be granted during the regular listing period.

Determining the tax situs of real property is a relatively easy task given the permanent and immobile character of such property. Except in the case of real property situated on or near a jurisdictional boundary, few disputes arise over the tax situs of real property. Determining the tax situs of personal property, which may travel through several taxing units in and out of state during a given year, is a more complicated task. The Machinery Act provides that personal property generally is taxable at the residence of its owner. An individual's residence is the place where he or she dwelt for the longest period of time during the preceding calendar year. A corporation's residence is its principal place of business in North Carolina. Property commonly used at some other premises is, however, excepted from the general rule of taxation at the place of residence. Tangible personal property commonly used at a seasonal dwelling is taxable at the place of the seasonal dwelling. Tangible personal property used in connection with the owner's business is taxable at the business premises. Tangible personal property used or stored at premises other than the owner's residence pursuant to a business agreement is taxable at the place where the property is located. Thus, a boat owned by a Wake County resident but stored in a Craven County marina for a monthly fee is taxable in Craven County rather than in Wake County.

Property that is not listed and thereby escapes taxation, or that is listed at a substantial understatement in value, is subject to discovery by the taxing unit. Penalties apply in the amount of 10 percent per elapsed listing period for the taxpayer's failure to list. Property may be discovered for the current tax year and for up to five previous years.

The taxpayer lists and values personal property on an abstract form submitted to the assessor—a vestige of self-assessment. Many counties now permit these forms to be submitted electronically. Unlike in the days of the list taker, however, many counties now have aggressive auditing procedures in place as a check on the abuses inherent in the self-reporting and self-valuation of property. The abstract for personal property must include any city in which the listed property is taxable. Given the exclusion of household personal property from taxation, most personal property abstracts list business property. Some individual personal property abstracts remain, however, as individuals are required to list boats, manufactured homes, and unregistered motor vehicles on annual abstracts.

Role of the City in the Listing Process

Cities may copy listings from the county records or may require that property be separately listed with the city. Most cities copy the county's listings. These cities remain responsible for deciding for themselves whether specific property should be listed for taxation or be granted an exemption or exclusion. This responsibility is independent of county decisions about the same property. If a county and a city differ on whether certain property is entitled to exemption or other preferential treatment, the owner may appeal to the Property Tax Commission for resolution of the dispute.

Although a city may elect to do its own listing, it must accept the property valuations fixed by the county authorities unless the city lies in more than one county. In that case, G.S. 105-328 grants special appraisal authority to the city to appoint its own assessor. However, no eligible cities have taken advantage of this authority to date.

Property Not Subject to Taxation: Requests for Tax Relief

Under G.S. 105-282.1, exempt and excluded property is not required to be listed, but owners of such property have the burden of demonstrating to tax authorities that it qualifies for this preferential treatment by filing a request for tax relief. This is normally done during the regular listing period. (No request need be made for government-owned and certain other types of property.)

For most of the property currently granted tax immunity or other preferential treatment by the Machinery Act, requests for relief must be made only once, then revised when improvements or additions are made or a change in use occurs. However, for some types of exempt and classified property (primarily business-related property), annual requests for relief must be made.

As the requests are made or revised, tax officials must review them to ensure that the property in question qualifies for the relief requested. Personal property that is not listed and for which no exemption or exclusion application is filed is subject to discovery.

For example, consider the elderly and disabled homestead exclusion. This popular exclusion provides partial property tax relief for elderly or disabled low-income people who own their own homes. An individual who is sixty-five or older or who is permanently and totally disabled and who had income below a certain level in the preceding calendar year may exclude from property taxes the greater of $25,000 or 50 percent of the tax value of his or her permanent residence. For example, if Tom Taxpayer owns a home with a tax value of $200,000 and he qualifies for the exclusion, his home will be taxed at a value of $100,000.

The income limitation for this exclusion was $28,600 for the 2014–15 tax year. It is indexed to the annual change in federal Social Security benefits. All income other than gifts or bequests from direct relatives is included when determining eligibility for the elderly and disabled homestead exclusion. As a result, the determination includes nontaxable income such as Social Security benefits.

Homeowners must apply for the benefit of this exclusion, but once an application is approved it remains valid for succeeding tax years if there is no change in circumstances that affects eligibility.

Appraisal

Statutory Elements of Value

Market-Value Standard

The Machinery Act requires that all property not singled out for special tax treatment be assessed at its true value as determined under G.S. 105-283 or at its use value as determined under G.S. 105-277.6. *True value* is defined in G.S. 105-283 as "market value, that is, the price . . . at which the property would change hands between a willing and financially able buyer and a willing seller, neither being under any compulsion to buy or to sell and both having reasonable knowledge of all the uses to which the property is adapted and for which it is capable of being used." Thus, property not qualifying for assessment based on its use value is said to be valued at its highest and best use rather than its current use.

Taxability of All Rights in Land

Several entities or people may have ownership rights in the same parcel of land. Notwithstanding a division of ownership interests, the entire value of the property, including the interests of all owners, is assessed for taxation. Property is thus taxed as though one person has complete ownership of all interests in the property.

The classic example of property interests divided among several people is the *life estate*. Here, one owner, the *life tenant*, has the right of current possession and the right to all of the rents and profits from the land for his or her lifetime but does not have the right to sell the land or dispose of it by will. The remaining interest in the property belongs to persons known as *remaindermen*. Upon the death of the life tenant, all of the interest in the property will belong to the remaindermen, who only then become full owners of the property. North Carolina taxes the entire value of all interests in this form of ownership. The property is appraised as if both the life tenant and all the remaindermen were willing to sell their respective interests at the same time to the same buyer. That is, the property is assigned one value for tax purposes. There is no apportionment of the value among the separate ownership interests of the life tenant and remaindermen.

Rental property subject to long-term leases provides a similar example. Here, the right of possession of the property has been leased to another for a specific term of years, often at a fixed monthly or annual rent that cannot be adjusted for inflation or other changes in market conditions. The landlord can sell his or her underlying ownership of the property but cannot evict the tenants until the lease expires. A purchaser will take the building subject to the outstanding leases. If the rent being paid under the leases is less than the current market demands for similar space, the value of the landlord's ownership interest can be adversely affected. The difference will depend on the gap between market rent and rent under the leases and on how long the leases have to run. Conversely, the value of the leasehold interests held by the tenants will be enhanced. This kind of property is taxed as if the owner had all of the interest in the property; that is, as though the property was leased at the current market rate.[26]

Use-Value Appraisal of Farmlands

In 1973 the General Assembly classified land used for agricultural, horticultural, or forestry purposes that meets certain ownership and size requirements as a special class of property eligible for taxation on the basis of its value in its present use, even though it may have a greater market value for other uses.[27] G.S. 105-277.2 defines *present-use value* as "the value of land in its current use as agricultural land, horticultural land, or forestland, based solely on its ability to produce income and assuming an average level of management."

Market value still plays an important part in the taxation of farmland and forestland, however. If the land ceases to be used for agricultural, horticultural, or forestry purposes, or if title passes to a disqualifying owner, a deferred tax must be paid. The amount of this tax is the difference between the taxes paid based on the use value and the taxes that would have been paid based on the market value for the preceding three years.

Personal Property

Personal property, which typically changes in value more rapidly than real property, must be appraised each year when it is listed for taxation. This annual appraisal may be a relatively simple process, as in determining the value of an automobile, or it may be highly complex, as in selecting an appropriate depreciation rate for unusual industrial machinery.

Real Property

The Machinery Act requires that real property be reappraised at least once every eight years. About half of the counties have shortened the reappraisal cycle to terms ranging from four to seven years. A county that shortens its reappraisal cycle is not bound to adhere to the shorter term in perpetuity but may elect to revert to an eight-year cycle. The timing of countywide reappraisals has become increasingly controversial in recent years due to the lingering effects of the 2008 recession.

Appraisal Techniques

In appraising personal property, the appraiser must consider replacement cost, sale price of similar property, age, physical condition, productivity, remaining life, obsolescence, economic utility (that is, usability and adaptability for industrial, commercial, or other purposes), and any other factor that may affect the value of the property.

County appraisers have developed many techniques for estimating the market value of various types of personal property. Industry pricing guides are available for motor vehicles, mobile homes, boats, and aircraft. For machinery and equipment, the current value may be estimated by depreciating the original cost to acquire the item according to a standard depreciation schedule. This technique is further refined in many counties by factoring or "trending" the original cost to current market levels before applying the standard depreciation factor.

26. *In re* Greensboro Office P'ship, 72 N.C. App. 635, *cert. denied*, 313 N.C. 602 (1985).
27. G.S. 105-277.2 through -277.6.

Mass Appraisal of Real Property

A countywide reappraisal of real property is a big undertaking. The typical county has more than 40,000 parcels of land that must be appraised. The process must begin early enough to have the results ready in time for tax billing in the revaluation year but not so early that the value estimates will be out of date by the time they take effect. Also, the cost of the revaluation must be reasonable. A person who is borrowing money from a lending institution to buy a new house can expect to pay about $350 for an appraisal of the house and the lot. A tax appraisal must cost much less than that. Most counties estimate about $20 per parcel. Obviously, to accomplish a job of such magnitude at reasonable cost requires specialized appraisal techniques that rapidly, efficiently, and economically yield a high degree of accuracy.

Development of an Appraisal Manual for Establishing Market Value

G.S. 105-317 lays out the essential elements of a modern mass appraisal system. The foundation of the system is the assessor's appraisal manual or, as the statute describes it, "uniform schedules of values, standards, and rules to be used in appraising real property." The manual is formulated from two basic sources: the local real estate market and national data on the cost of building construction, adjusted to reflect local building costs. The manual identifies characteristics exhibited by real property in the county and indicates the ranges for dollar amounts that each characteristic can normally be expected to contribute to the value of a given parcel of land or a given building according to an appropriate unit of measure. For example, the appraisal manual contains a land schedule. For rural land the appropriate unit of measure is usually the acre, whereas urban land is typically measured by square footage, front footage (the number of feet of a lot that front on a street), or standard-sized lot (such as the 100- by 200-foot lot often found in newer subdivisions). Buildings are usually measured by square footage.

The value increments attributed to the various units of measurement vary considerably. Some land may be worth $100,000 or more per acre, other land only $1,000 per acre. Buildings of top-quality construction may be priced at $150 or more per square foot, lower-quality buildings at $100 per square foot. Other characteristics may increase or reduce the value indicated by the basic unit of measurement. Agricultural land may be decreased in value by poor soil or topography. The value of an urban residential lot may be adversely affected by other development in the neighborhood. The value of buildings is always adjusted to reflect accrued depreciation. Values may increase or decrease based on the grade of construction.

The characteristics mentioned above are but the tip of the iceberg; a well-conceived appraisal manual will identify many more. The manual is a comprehensive, complex document designed to enable the assessor to estimate the value of thousands of parcels and buildings accurately, efficiently, and rapidly by means of a manageable number of characteristics that influence value.

Developing the appraisal manual is the single most important step in a revaluation. The manual's designation of the property characteristics to be examined and the value increment to be attributed to each determines the accuracy with which the assessor can estimate the fair market value of real property in the county. If the manual sets values too high, most properties will be appraised higher than market value. If the manual sets values too low, most properties will be underappraised. If too few characteristics are used, the accuracy of appraisals will vary widely from parcel to parcel. If too many characteristics are used, the assessor may not be able to complete the job on time.

Development of a Present-Use Value Schedule

Similarly, the assessor establishes a special schedule for appraising eligible agricultural land, horticultural land, and forestland at its present-use value. The assessor may use a statewide valuation manual prepared by the Department of Revenue with the assistance of the Use-Value Advisory Board, which is composed of representatives of the Agricultural Extension Service, the state Department of Agriculture, and the state Division of Forest Resources. This manual is based upon the rental value of land used for agricultural and horticultural purposes and the net income earned for forestland. Use of the Department of Revenue's manual is not mandatory, but it carries great authority.

Approval of the Manuals

After the manuals on market value and present-use value have been prepared and a public hearing has been held, the board of county commissioners adopts them and places a newspaper notice stating that it has done so. Property owners then have thirty days to challenge the manuals by appeal to the state Property Tax Commission on grounds that the manuals do not adhere to the appropriate statutory valuation standard (that is, that they will produce values that are too high, too low, or inconsistent). The commission has the power to order the board of county commissioners to revise the manuals if they do not adhere to the statutory valuation standard, although such revisions are seldom deemed necessary or ordered. The commission's decision regarding a challenge to an appraisal manual may be appealed to the North Carolina Court of Appeals.

Preparation of Record Cards

After the manuals are adopted, the assessor prepares a record card for each parcel of land in the county. On this card the assessor notes all the characteristics of the parcel that will be considered in making the appraisal. Although the land and the buildings on it are appraised separately, data for both appear on the same property record card. The Machinery Act specifically directs the assessor to show on the card all characteristics considered in appraising the parcel, points out that they must be consistent with the appraisal manual, and requires that the data be accurate.

Collecting data about property characteristics is called *listing* the property. For buildings, this process consists of measuring their outside perimeter, showing special features such as air conditioning and the number of bathrooms, and recording such crucial factors as depreciation and quality or grade of construction. For agricultural land and forestland, the process is similar but simpler. Characteristics of such land usually include the number of acres in the tract, its road frontage if the manual identifies this as a relevant characteristic, its fertility or productivity grade, and any crop allotments. Much of this information can be gathered by persons who are not trained appraisers; for example, no advanced training is needed to measure a house or compute the number of acres in a tract of land from the tax map. Other computations, such as estimating depreciation, require trained and experienced personnel.

Appraisal of Property

After the basic data have been gathered and recorded on the property record card, the parcel is appraised. G.S. 105-317 requires that a competent appraiser do this for each parcel individually. The first step is usually carried out mechanically. The property characteristics gathered by the listers are used to compute a preliminary value estimate according to the value increments set out in the manual for those characteristics. This value is tentatively recorded on the property record card. The appraiser then takes the cards into the field and revisits each property. This procedure, known as the *review*, is the critical fine-tuning step in which the training, experience, and judgment of the appraiser play a large part. Recognizing the crucial importance of appraising property on the basis of accurate data, G.S. 105-317 gives each property owner the right to have the assessor (or one of the assessor's agents or employees) actually visit and observe the property to verify the accuracy of characteristics on record for it.

Notice to Property Owners

The Machinery Act requires that when the final review has been completed, the assessor send each property owner a written notice of the appraised value on each parcel owned by that person. At this point nearly all assessors allow for a period of informal appeals that is not required by law. Typically, the value notice sent to taxpayers states that they may contact the assessor for an appointment to review the appraisal if they believe it to be in error. Most counties engage the services of a professional appraisal company to assist in the revaluation, although the legal responsibility remains entirely in the hands of the assessor appointed by the county commissioners. If professional appraisers have helped in the revaluation, taxpayers may obtain an appointment with the company appraiser, at which time they may be able to persuade the appraiser that a mistake was made in measurement, calculation, or judgment. The time allowed for these informal appeals is within the discretion of the assessor.

Formal Appraisal and Assessment

When the informal appeal process is over, the assessor formally appraises and assesses each parcel. Ideally, the appraisals are adopted before January 1 of the revaluation year. This may not always be possible because the appraisal may take more time than was planned or there may be more informal appeals than were expected. In any event, after the assessor has adopted the appraisals, the taxpayer may appeal directly to the assessor at any time before the county board of equalization and review convenes.

Appeal and Review

Valuation Appeals

G.S. 105-322 governs listing and valuation appeals. The county board of equalization and review is the local body charged with hearing property tax appeals. It also has the power to correct the tax lists and to increase or reduce values on its own motion. As explained earlier, in some counties the board of equalization and review is the board of county commissioners sitting in another capacity. In other counties, however, the board of commissioners has created a special board to hear appeals. In still others, a special board has been created by local act of the General Assembly. In all counties, the primary work of the board of equalization and review is essentially the same: to hear and decide valuation appeals. The board convenes no earlier than the first Monday in April and no later than the first Monday in May. It sits for at least three weeks and may meet longer if needed. It may not sit later than July 1 except to decide appeals filed before that date.

The Property Tax Commission hears taxpayer appeals from the county boards of equalization and review across the state. If the taxpayer prevails at the board of equalization and review, the county may not appeal the board's decision. An appellant taxpayer who believes that the Property Tax Commission made an error of law in reaching its decision on his or her property may appeal further to the North Carolina Court of Appeals. Normally this is the court of last resort. The state supreme court will hear a property tax appeal only if the court of appeals was not unanimous in its decision or if the supreme court believes that a major issue of law in the case warrants its attention.

Adjustment of Real Property Values in Nonreappraisal Years

The Machinery Act provides for annual appraisals of personal property and reappraisals of real property at least every eight years. Yet for the sake of equity and uniformity, some parcels of real property may need reappraisal in a year in which general revaluation of real property is not undertaken. G.S. 105-287 directs the assessor in a nonreappraisal year to reappraise specific parcels in order to correct clerical or mathematical errors in the former appraisal; correct appraisal errors resulting from misapplication of the county's appraisal manual; or recognize an increase or a decrease in value resulting from some factor other than normal depreciation, economic changes affecting property in general, or certain improvements such as repainting and landscaping. Reappraisals made under the authority of G.S. 105-287 must conform to the appraisal manual adopted in the last revaluation year so that they will represent market or present-use value as of January 1 of the revaluation year rather than current value. Also, these appraisals take effect as of January 1 of the year in which they are made and do not affect previous tax years.

The most important consequence of G.S. 105-287 is that real property tax values may not be adjusted in between reappraisals for general changes in market value. For example, assume that Tina Taxpayer owns a home that was appraised by Carolina County at $300,000 in 2011. Carolina County is on an eight-year reappraisal cycle. In 2013 Tina's next-door neighbor sells his house, which is identical to Tina's, for $200,000. Neither Tina's tax value nor her neighbor's tax value should be adjusted to account for the changes in market value until the county's next reappraisal in 2019, a situation that the taxpayers may find hard to accept.

Discovered Property

To *discover* property, as the expression is used in the tax statutes, means to find that an item of taxable property has not been listed for taxation during the annual listing period established by law or has been listed at a substantial understatement of value, quantity, or other measurement. Under G.S. 105-312 it is the duty of the assessor to see that all property not properly listed during the regular listing period is accurately listed, assessed, and taxed. The assessor is also required to file reports of such discoveries with the governing boards of all taxing units affected by the discovery at such times and in such form as those boards may require.

When unlisted real or personal property has been identified, the county assessor must first sign an abstract listing it and then make a tentative appraisal of it, in accordance with the best information available. The assessor must then mail a notice to the person in whose name it has been listed.

When property is found not to be listed for a given year, it has often not been listed for a number of years or perhaps has never been listed. Accordingly, there is a statutory presumption that it should have been listed by the same taxpayer for the preceding five years. The taxpayer can overcome this presumption by showing that the property was not in existence, that it was actually listed for taxation, or that it was not his or her duty to list the property during all or some of the years in question.

The penalty for failing to list property for taxes is an amount equal to 10 percent of the tax for each listing period that has elapsed since the failure to list occurred. For example, if a taxpayer failed to list his or her property for 2009 taxes and was subjected to discovery procedures in September 2014, the penalty for the 2009 failure to list would be 60 percent of the tax (10 percent for each year from 2009 through 2014). If the taxpayer had failed to list the same item of property for each of the intervening years, the penalty rates would be 50 percent for 2010, 40 percent for 2011, and so on down to 10 percent for 2014. In addition to the penalty, the taxpayer also is, of course, liable for the principal amount of the taxes for each year of the discovery.

Special cases may arise in which the county commissioners feel that the statutory provisions place an undue burden on the property owner. In such situations the board is empowered to reduce the penalty (or even the principal amount of the tax) to what it finds to be equitable. This authority does not arise until the discovery procedures have been completed, and it may be exercised only on written petition of the taxpayer. The assessor has no authority to waive any part of the penalty or the tax, and the board may not delegate such authority to him or her.

IV. Special Classes of Property

As noted earlier, the General Assembly may classify property for special tax treatment so long as the classifications apply on a statewide basis. While the General Assembly has exercised this authority with respect to numerous types of property, there are three types of classifications that result in property receiving substantially different treatment under the Machinery Act. These classifications apply to qualifying agricultural, horticultural, and forestry property (also known as present-use value classification); registered motor vehicles; and property owned by public service companies. The assessment of present-use value property was discussed in part III of this chapter. An overview of the taxation of registered motor vehicles and public service company property follows.

Registered Motor Vehicles

The collection rate for taxes on registered motor vehicles (RMVs) has long been substantially lower than the rate for all other types of property. In fiscal 2012–13 the difference for county property tax collections was more than 10 percent in favor of non-RMV taxes.[28] Certainly the mobility of motor vehicles is problematic from the standpoint of the assessment and collection of taxes, but this alone does not explain the difficulties associated with motor vehicle taxation. After all, nearly all personal property is mobile. Likewise, the value associated with motor vehicle taxes explains only one component of the focus on motor vehicle collections since in some urban counties, taxes imposed upon business personal property equal the taxes imposed on registered motor vehicles. The issues associated with motor vehicle taxation instead result from the combined effect of mobility, frequent transfers, and significant value under individual, rather than business, ownership. Mobility, transfers between owners, and the large number of vehicles make routine levies difficult, and individuals, unlike businesses, often lack other personal property that the tax collector may seize to secure payment of delinquent motor vehicle taxes. In addition, individuals may sell a vehicle or move out of the county in which the vehicle is assessed without giving a thought to resolving any outstanding property taxes.

Recognizing the need for improvement in this area, in 2005 the General Assembly mandated dramatic changes in the process for taxing RMVs.[29] Known as House Bill 1779, this law took effect on September 1, 2013.

The "Old" Process

For twenty years, counties billed taxes on registered motor vehicles roughly two months after the taxpayer applied for a new registration or renewed an existing registration. The Division of Motor Vehicles (DMV) did not require payment of any property taxes at the time of registration or renewal. Taxes on the registered motor vehicle were not due until four months later, after the DMV informed the relevant county of the registration or renewal and the county prepared a property tax bill for that vehicle.

If the taxpayer failed to pay the property taxes on a registered motor vehicle, then the taxing county could ask the DMV to place a registration block on that vehicle. The block prevented the taxpayer from renewing the registration on the vehicle until the delinquent taxes were satisfied. Then the process would begin again, with the DMV alerting the county of the renewal and the county preparing a tax bill for the new tax year.

Besides registration blocks, county collectors could employ wage and bank account attachments or levy and sale of personal property to collect delinquent taxes on registered motor vehicles. But taxes on registered motor vehicles were not liens on real property, meaning foreclosure was never a collection remedy for these taxes.

The "New" Process

With the implementation of House Bill 1779 in late 2013, there is no longer a lag between the registration of a vehicle and the collection of property taxes on that vehicle. The DMV is now responsible for collecting property taxes for the coming tax year at the time the vehicle receives a new registration or a renewal of an existing registration. If the taxpayer refuses to pay the property taxes, the DMV will refuse to register the vehicle.

The only exception to this requirement is for purchasers of new automobiles from car dealers. Those taxpayers have the option of receiving limited two-month registrations without paying any property taxes. The DMV will issue a full twelve-month registration for a new car after the owner pays the property taxes on that car.

Counties no longer have any responsibility or authority to collect taxes on registered motor vehicles. The only collection remedy for taxes on registered motor vehicles under the new process is the requirement that taxes be paid before registering a vehicle.

But as before, unregistered vehicles must be listed and taxed by the county as personal property. Counties also have responsibility for issuing prorated "gap" bills for vehicles that move from registered to unregistered status and then back again to registered.

---

28. See note 1, above.
29. S.L. 2005-294 (H 1779).

Public Service Company Property

Real and personal property owned or leased by a public service company, such as a railroad, pipeline, gas, power, or telephone company or an airline or motor freight carrier, is appraised and assessed at the state rather than the county level.[30] Public service companies are required to list property with the Department of Revenue. The department allocates public service company property values among the counties pursuant to statutory rules and certifies values to counties. The counties must tax the assessed valuations at the rate of tax levied against other property in the county or city.

While real and personal property generally is assessed at 100 percent of its appraised value, this is not always the case for public service company property. Pursuant to G.S. 105-284, the Department of Revenue must assess only a percentage of the appraised value of public service company property if the property is taxable in a county in which real property on average is taxed at less than 90 percent of its market value in certain years. The department determines the assessment level for real property in every county on an annual basis by comparing assessed values to arm's-length sales of property. By April 15 of each year, the department determines each county's sales assessment ratio for real property from the previous calendar year. In the year of revaluation, sales assessment ratios typically equal 100 percent. Given that property values generally rise in the ensuing years before the revaluation, the sales assessment ratio typically drops below 100 percent in those years.

The Department of Revenue examines each county's sales assessment ratio for real property in the fourth and seventh years after revaluation. If the ratio is below 90 percent in those years, public service company property in the county is taxed at that percentage of its appraised value until the department's next review of ratios. Thus, if a county's sales assessment ratio drops to 80 percent four years after a revaluation, public service company property in the county will be assessed at 80 percent of its appraised value until at least three years later when the department studies ratios seven years after the revaluation. Counties that revalue property every four years have little to be concerned about with respect to the sales-ratio study since each year of study will be a revaluation year in which appraised values should equal 100 percent of market value established by sales.

V. The Collection of Property Taxes

Office of Tax Collector

In the absence of special legislation, the governing body of each city and county must appoint a tax collector, for a term to be determined by the appointing body, to collect the taxes it levies.[31] Many if not most municipalities contract with their county tax offices to collect their taxes. By entering into a contract with the county for the collection of its taxes, a city effectively appoints the county collector as the city's collector. Ordinarily, collectors are named early enough in the fiscal year to prepare themselves to take over the new taxes when the time comes for collection.

Often persons charged with tax collection also have other duties. As noted earlier, it is increasingly common for the same person to serve as both assessor and tax collector. The Machinery Act declares the office of tax collector to be "an office that may be held concurrently with any appointive or elective office other than those hereinafter designated, and the governing body may appoint as tax collector any appointive or elective officer who meets the personal and bonding requirements" (discussed under the next section). Only two restrictions are placed on double-office-holding by collectors, but they are important:

> A member of the governing body of a taxing unit may not be appointed tax collector, nor may the duties of the office be conferred upon him. A person appointed or elected as treasurer or chief accounting officer of a

30. G.S. 105-335.
31. G.S. 105-349.

> taxing unit may not be appointed tax collector, nor may the duties of the office of tax collector be conferred upon him except with the written permission of the secretary of the Local Government Commission who, before giving his permission, shall satisfy himself that the unit's internal control procedures are sufficient to prevent improper handling of public funds.[32]

Most cities and counties pay their tax collectors' salaries. Some also pay a travel allowance. A few collectors who are specially appointed to collect delinquent taxes unpaid at the close of the fiscal year for which levied are paid wholly or in part from commissions on collections. The Machinery Act provides simply that "[t]he compensation and expense allowances of the tax collector shall be fixed by the governing body" of the taxing unit.[33]

Qualification as Tax Collector

The Machinery Act does not create certification requirements for tax collectors as it does for assessors.[34] However, many local governments now expect their tax collectors to obtain and retain certification by the North Carolina Tax Collectors' Association. This nonstatutory certification process requires successful completion of several tax collection courses and ten hours of continuing education annually.[35]

Governing boards and councils may only assign collection responsibility for a tax year to an individual who satisfies the statutory requirements set forth in G.S. 105-352. First, the tax collector must turn over to the finance officer the receipts issued for prepayment of taxes not yet charged to the collector. The collector must also demonstrate that the funds associated with these receipts have been deposited. Finally, the collector must settle for all taxes currently in his or her hands for collection and provide satisfactory bond for taxes for the current year and all prior years in his or her hands for collection.

The courts have not defined *satisfactory bond* for a local tax collector. A useful test might be a reasonable approximation of the maximum amount of money that the collector will have in his or her hands at any one time, plus a reasonable allowance for cumulative losses.

By law, any member of a governing body who votes to deliver the tax receipts to the tax collector before the collector has met the requirements just listed is individually liable for the amount of taxes charged against the tax collector for which he or she has not made satisfactory settlement. Any member who so votes is also guilty of a misdemeanor punishable by fine or imprisonment, or both, at the discretion of the court.

Removal of the Tax Collector

Collectors who cannot meet the bonding and settlement requirements outlined in the preceding section are not entitled to serve and may be removed from office or simply not permitted to collect taxes. In addition, cases may arise in which a collector who meets the statutory prerequisites and conditions should not be permitted to remain in office. The Machinery Act gives the governing body express authority to remove the tax collector from office during the tax collector's term for good cause after giving notice in writing and an opportunity to appear and be heard at a public session of the governing body. As discussed previously, the term "good cause" is not defined by the Machinery Act but generally is interpreted to mean substantial misconduct related to the tax collector's professional duties that directly affects the public interest.

Deputy Tax Collectors

Governing boards and councils have discretion over whether to appoint deputy tax collectors. The governing body of a taxing unit also sets the term and the pay of each appointed deputy collector as well as the amount of his or her

---

32. G.S. 105-349(e).
33. G.S. 105-349(d).
34. *Id.*
35. The complete certification requirements are listed on the N.C. Tax Collectors' Association website at www.nctca.org/content/certification-requirements.

bond. Unless the governing body specifically limits the scope of the deputy's authority, he or she has the authority to perform, under the direction of the tax collector, any act that the tax collector may perform.

Necessary Collection Records

Apart from the tax records, which include the scroll and tax book described earlier, the most important document in the collection process is the *tax receipt*. The tax receipt furnishes the taxpayer with evidence of payment and provides the tax collector with the payment information necessary to support a credit in the settlement.

The Machinery Act does not require that tax collectors send a bill for property taxes unless they are specifically ordered to do so by their governing board. Moreover, the Machinery Act provides that all persons with an interest in real property are charged with notice that the property should be listed for taxation, that taxes may become a lien on the property, and that action may be taken to enforce the lien.[36] Thus, while all taxing units, as a practical matter, bill for property taxes owed, the failure of a particular taxpayer to receive a bill for property taxes is not a defense to nonpayment of taxes.

Reports of Progress in Collection

The tax collector must keep adequate records of all collections[37] and must submit at each regular meeting of the governing body a report showing the amount collected on each year's taxes, the amount remaining uncollected, and the steps being taken to encourage or enforce payment.[38] These reports enable the governing body to evaluate the tax collector's collection activities and to compare collection activities from current years to the taxing unit's present position.

Tax Due Dates: Periods Covered

As pointed out earlier, property taxes are due and payable on the first day of September of the fiscal year for which they are levied.[39] The tax collector may use enforced collection remedies to collect the taxes for a period of ten years measured from the September 1 due date.[40]

Order of Collection

Once the tax collector enters a settlement for the previous year's taxes and provides satisfactory bond, the governing body must adopt an order to be entered in its minutes directing the tax collector to collect taxes for the current fiscal year.[41] The board must then deliver the current year's tax receipts to the collector.[42] The order to collect must be entered and the receipts turned over by September 1. The wording of the order to collect is prescribed by statute.[43]

---

36. G.S. 105-348.
37. G.S. 105-350(4).
38. G.S. 105-350(7).
39. G.S. 105-360(a).
40. G.S. 105-378.
41. G.S. 105-321.
42. G.S. 105-352(a).
43. G.S. 105-321(b).

The order has the force and effect of a judgment and execution against the taxpayers' real and personal property, which affords the tax collector the authority to seize and attach personal property of a taxpayer without a court order.[44] While the issuance of the order is a critical step in the collection process, G.S. 105-321(b) contains a safety-net clause, which provides that a governing body's failure to deliver the order does not affect a tax collector's use of enforced collection remedies.

The Property Tax Lien

The North Carolina Supreme Court has defined a *lien* as "the right to have a demand satisfied out of the property of another."[45] This right runs against the property rather than against the owner. As used in the property tax laws of this state, the lien for taxes runs in favor of the local government unit and may be enforced against the property of the taxpayer.

A taxing unit acquires a lien against all real property that each taxpayer owns within its jurisdiction on January 1.[46] As of the date the lien attaches, the amount of taxes it represents is indeterminate, as the governing body will not set the tax rate until the following June or July. Moreover, the tax collector may take no action to enforce this lien until the taxes become delinquent on January 6 of the next year. The lien against real property includes not only the taxes levied on the real property itself but also the taxes levied on all the taxpayer's personal property (other than registered motor vehicles) by the taxing unit. Property taxes levied on other parcels of real property do not, however, become a lien on any real property other than that for which they were levied. In addition, all penalties, interest, and costs allowed by law are added to the amount of the lien for the principal amount of the taxes.[47]

The taxing unit does not acquire an automatic lien against personal property each January 1. Instead, a lien for property taxes against personal property only attaches upon the tax collector's seizure of the property, either through levy or attachment.[48] Once attached, the lien against personal property includes all taxes due the county, not merely those levied on the particular item seized nor merely those levied on the personal property of the taxpayer.[49]

Ordinarily the tax lien on real and personal property continues until the principal amount of the taxes and penalties, interest, and costs are fully paid.[50] Nevertheless, the tax collector's issuance of a full payment receipt may release the lien even if it is erroneously issued before taxes are paid in full. Because the lien is the taxing unit's security interest, tax collectors must exercise care in issuing such receipts.

The lien for property taxes against real property is superior to all other liens and rights except previously recorded liens for state taxes, regardless of whether the other liens were acquired before the lien for taxes.[51] Furthermore, once the lien has attached to real property, its priority is not affected by transfer of title, by death, or by receivership of the property owner.[52]

As already pointed out, taxes, interest, penalties, and costs become a lien on personal property from and after levy or attachment. The priority of the lien depends upon whether the lien is for taxes on the particular item seized or whether it is for other taxes. The portion of the lien that is for taxes levied on the specific personal property levied upon or attached is superior to all other liens and rights.[53] The portion that is for taxes levied on property other than the specific personal property levied upon or attached is inferior to prior valid liens and perfected security interests but superior to all subsequent liens and security interests.[54]

---

44. G.S. 105-321.
45. Thigpen v. Leigh, 93 N.C. 47, 49 (1885).
46. G.S. 105-355(a).
47. G.S. 105-355(b).
48. *Id.*
49. *Id.*
50. G.S. 105-362(a).
51. G.S. 105-356(a)(1), (2).
52. G.S. 105-356(a)(3).
53. G.S. 105-356(b)(1).
54. G.S. 105-356(b)(2).

Payment of Taxes

Taxes may always be paid in cash, and the Machinery Act permits tax collectors to also accept—at their own risk—checks and electronic payments.[55] Taxing units are permitted to pass along to the taxpayers the cost of accepting credit cards and other electronic payments. Tax collectors may issue receipts immediately upon payment by check or may withhold the receipt until the check is collected.[56] When a collector has taken a check in payment of taxes, has issued a receipt, and has had the check returned unpaid, the taxes are treated as being unpaid. In such a case the collector has the same remedies for collection that he or she would have had if the receipt had not been issued (as well as the right to bring a civil suit on the check), provided that the collector has not been negligent in presenting the check for payment.

Buyers and sellers of property and their representatives frequently ask tax collectors for information on whether an individual owes taxes or the amount of taxes owed on a given parcel of real property. Sometimes the requests are for an oral statement of taxes owed, and other times they are for a written statement, called a *certificate*. The Machinery Act requires the tax collector to provide a certificate of the taxes that constitute a lien on specified real property when requested to do so by the following people:[57]

- an owner of the property
- an occupant of the property
- a person having a lien on the property
- a person having a legal interest or estate in the property
- a person or a firm having a contract to purchase or lease the property
- a person or a firm having a contract to make a loan secured by the property
- the authorized agent or attorney of anyone in one of the first six categories

Before furnishing a certificate, the collector should require the requester to identify the person in whose name the property was listed for each year for which tax information is desired. When a qualified person obtains a certificate of taxes owed and relies on it by (1) paying the amount of taxes certified as a lien on the property, (2) purchasing or leasing the property, or (3) lending money secured by the property, then a lien will exist against the property in relation to that person only to the extent that taxes and special assessments are stated to be due in the certificate. An understatement of the tax liability in the certificate causes the lien to be released in the amount of the understatement. Although the taxing unit retains the ability to proceed against personal property of the taxpayer for unpaid taxes omitted from the certificate, an erroneous certificate may surrender the county's security for payment.

Tax collectors are liable on their bond for any loss that the county suffers as the result of an erroneous certificate.[58] Unlike a certificate, an oral statement made by the tax collector about the amount of taxes, penalties, interest, and costs due binds neither the tax collector nor the taxing unit.[59]

Discounts

If the governing board chooses to provide discounts for payments made before September 1, it may do so by adopting a resolution or an ordinance not later than the first day of May preceding the due date of the taxes to which the resolution or the ordinance first applies, specifying the amounts of the discounts and the periods during which they are to be applicable.[60] The resolution or the ordinance must be approved by the Department of Revenue, and the discount schedule must be published at least once in some newspaper that has a general circulation in the taxing unit.[61] The

55. G.S. 105-357(a).
56. G.S. 105-357(b).
57. G.S. 105-361(a).
58. G.S. 105-361(b).
59. G.S. 105-361(d).
60. G.S. 105-360(c)(1).
61. G.S. 105-360(c)(3).

Department of Revenue will not approve a discount schedule if in its opinion the rates are excessive or the discount period is unreasonable.[62] Most commonly discounts range from 1 to 2 percent.

Interest for Late Payment of Taxes

If taxes are not paid before January 6 of the fiscal year in which they are levied, interest accrues at a rate of 2 percent for the first month and 0.75 percent for every subsequent month the taxes remain unpaid.[63] Interest is not compounded. For example, if a delinquent 2014 tax of $1,000 is not paid until May 1, 2015, the taxpayer would owe a total of $1,050—$1,000 in principal taxes and $50 in interest (2 percent for January, 3 percent for February through May).

Report of Delinquent Taxes and Lien Advertisements

Report of Delinquent Taxes Constituting Liens on Realty

In February of each year the tax collector is required to report to the governing body of the taxing unit "the total amount of unpaid taxes for the current fiscal year that are liens on real property."[64] When it receives this report, the governing body must order that the liens be advertised.[65]

Time and Place of Lien Advertisement

The governing body may choose any date from March 1 through June 30 on which to advertise the liens. The liens must be advertised at least once by (1) posting a notice at the county courthouse in the case of unpaid county taxes or at the city hall for delinquent city taxes and (2) publishing a notice in a newspaper of general circulation.[66] If the county tax collector collects taxes for a city, the taxes of the county and city must be advertised separately unless the county and city have agreed to joint advertisement.

Enforced Collection of Property Taxes

The Machinery Act supplies the tax collector with several effective means of enforced collection: foreclosure on real property, attachment and garnishment of funds owed to the delinquent taxpayer, and levy and sale of the taxpayer's personal property. An additional remedy found outside of the Machinery Act is *set-off debt collection*, the process of attaching state income tax refunds and lottery winnings owed to the taxpayer.

As a general rule, enforced collection actions cannot begin until after the tax has become delinquent; that is, not until after January 5 following the September 1 due date. The right to use these remedies continues until the expiration of the ten-year statute of limitations.[67] Actions against personal property must terminate once a foreclosure action is initiated.[68]

Foreclosure

Foreclosure of real property is often the collection remedy of last resort because it is complex and expensive and requires the forced public sale of private property. Before proceeding with this remedy, the governing body must decide which of the two available foreclosure methods it will employ. One foreclosure method is characterized as being "in

62. G.S. 105-360(c).
63. G.S. 105-360(a).
64. G.S. 105-369(a).
65. *Id.*
66. G.S. 105-369(c).
67. G.S. 105-378(a).
68. G.S. 105-366(b).

the nature of an action to foreclose a mortgage,"[69] and the other is described as an action in rem.[70] The first method is a civil lawsuit that requires the services of an attorney. The second is a summary procedure that in most instances can be handled by the tax collector or a paralegal, with occasional advice from an attorney. Both methods require a title examination to determine the persons who are entitled to receive notice of the foreclosure action. The in rem procedure can usually be concluded more expeditiously and less expensively than the mortgage-style foreclosure. Some counties use one method exclusively; other counties sometimes use the mortgage-style foreclosure and sometimes use the in rem method, depending on circumstances relating to the property being foreclosed.

After the foreclosure sale, the proceeds are used to reimburse the taxing unit for its costs and then to satisfy the liens on the property. In most situations, the local property tax lien will have priority and will be paid first. Surplus proceeds remaining after all liens have been satisfied should be submitted to the court for distribution to the taxpayer. The property is sold to the buyer free and clear of all tax liens other than taxes that could not be calculated at the time of sale.

Enforcement against Personal Property: Levy and Sale

Any tangible personal property owned by the taxpayer may be levied upon and sold to satisfy delinquent taxes.[71] The property levied upon need not be the property that generated the delinquent taxes. To initiate a levy and sale, the tax collector (or a law enforcement officer) must actually seize the property. Once seized and secured, the property should be sold at public auction to the highest bidder, with the proceeds being used to pay the cost of the levy and all liens on the property in their order of priority. Local tax liens generally have the highest priority if the property being sold is the property that generated the delinquent taxes. Otherwise, pre-existing liens on the property must be paid before the delinquent taxes. Any remaining funds after the payment of costs and liens are returned to the taxpayer.

Enforcement against Personal Property: Attachment and Garnishment

Perhaps the most commonly used enforced collection remedy is the attachment and garnishment of intangible personal property (money) owed to the taxpayer.[72] This property could be a bank account, wages, rents, or any other money that would otherwise be payable to the taxpayer. The process is initiated by providing notice to both the taxpayer and to the party holding the funds owed to the taxpayer—usually a bank or employer. If the party holding the funds neglects to satisfy the attachment and garnishment notice, that party can be held responsible for the delinquent taxes. When wages are attached, the employer must remit to the tax collector 10 percent of the employee's gross wages. For bank accounts and other funds, the party holding the funds must remit all funds held in the taxpayer's name up to the amount of delinquent taxes.

Reduction, Release, and Refund of Property Taxes

The tax collector has no authority to reduce, release, or refund taxes, including accrued interest, penalties, and costs. To the extent there is any authority to release taxes, it rests with the governing body. A strong public policy supports the stability of sources of government revenue. As previously noted, property taxes are the largest source of general fund revenue for both counties and cities. For this reason, governing bodies are given only limited authority to release or refund property taxes and are strictly prohibited from compromising taxes for any other reason not expressly authorized.[73] Lest any governing body ignore this admonition, the Machinery Act provides that any member of a governing body who votes for the unlawful release, refund, or compromise of taxes may be held personally liable for the

69. G.S. 105-374(a).
70. G.S. 105-375(a).
71. G.S. 105-367.
72. G.S. 105-368.
73. G.S. 105-380.

amount of the taxes forgiven.[74] The governing body of a taxing unit may release or refund only those taxes that were (1) imposed through clerical error, (2) illegal, or (3) levied for illegal purposes.[75]

Clerical Error Defined

Just what sorts of errors are clerical? The North Carolina Court of Appeals provided some guidance on that point in *Ammons v. Wake County*.[76] The taxpayer acquired forestland from a family corporation and inquired of the Wake County assessor whether the property would qualify for reduced taxation based upon present-use value. The county assessor stated that the property would not qualify for taxation based on present-use value because it did not meet the ownership requirements. Thus, the taxpayer did not apply for present-use taxation. The next year, notwithstanding the assessor's previous advice, the taxpayer applied for taxation at present-use value, which the assessor predictably denied. The taxpayer appealed to the board of equalization and review, and the board determined that the property was eligible for present-use taxation based on a recent ruling from the state court of appeals. The taxpayer then requested a refund from the board of county commissioners for the years during which the property was taxed at market, rather than present-use, value. The board denied the taxpayer's request for a refund, and the taxpayer filed suit. The case reached the court of appeals, which determined that the taxes were not "imposed through clerical error" and that the taxpayer was not entitled to a refund. The court of appeals held that the term "clerical error" applied only to transcription errors; that is, mistakes in writing or copying that were ordinarily apparent on the face of the document. The court noted that the error in *Ammons* was not apparent on the face of the assessor's statement but only by reference to a subsequent court decision. Moreover, the court noted that a clerical error must produce an unintended assessment. In other words, judgment errors—such as the assessor's incorrect judgment that the taxpayer's property would not qualify for present-use value taxation—do not constitute clerical errors and do not justify a refund or release.

What Is an Illegal Tax?

If the assessed valuation of the property taxed has been reduced under proper exercise of legal authority, a reduction in the tax bill follows as a matter of course. Otherwise, the tax would be illegal. If the property has been listed and taxed twice—that is, if it has been *double-listed*—one of the duplicate claims should be released on the basis that it is an illegal tax. If the property concerned is not taxable by the unit—that is, if the property is legally entitled to exemption or if it does not fall within the unit's jurisdiction—a release of the claim also is justified under the illegal tax basis. One of the most common occurrences of illegal taxes is when a city mistakenly taxes property that lies outside its boundaries. When the mistake is later discovered, usually after a more accurate survey is made, the taxes levied by the city should be released or refunded under G.S. 105-381.

When Is a Tax Imposed for an Illegal Purpose?

A tax refund or release is warranted pursuant to the illegal purpose defense if the tax is levied for something other than a "public purpose," if it is levied without a vote of the people in a situation in which such a vote is required by law, or if it is for an amount greater than that authorized by the state constitution, the statutes, or a vote of the people. Few taxes fall into this category.

Time Limitation on Refunds and Releases

Refunds are limited to five years from the original due date of the taxes being released, usually September 1 of the fiscal year in which they were levied.[77] Releases are not subject to any time limitation, which means that a taxpayer can submit a request to release an unpaid tax at any time.

---

74. *Id.*
75. G.S. 105-381.
76. 127 N.C. App. 426 (1997).
77. G.S. 105-381(a).

To claim a right to release or refund of taxes, the taxpayer must submit a written statement of his or her demand to the governing body of the taxing unit. Upon receiving the taxpayer's request, the governing board must decide within ninety days whether legal grounds for the release or refund exist.

The board of commissioners may delegate authority to make refunds and releases of less than $100 to the county attorney, finance officer, or manager. The officer to whom this authority is delegated must make a monthly report to the board of all releases and refunds granted.

Settlements

Settlement refers to the tax collector's annual report to the board of commissioners concerning his or her tax-collection efforts throughout the preceding fiscal year along with an accounting of the funds collected. In addition to reporting collection efforts and funds collected for taxes for the preceding fiscal year, the tax collector or other person charged with the collection of delinquent taxes from prior years must settle with the governing body for sums received in payment of delinquent taxes. While this annual settlement must occur after July 1 and before the tax collector is charged with taxes for the current fiscal year, settlement must also take place at the end of a tax collector's term of office and at any other time required by the governing body.[78]

Governing boards and councils must adhere to the requirement that the tax collector settle for the prior fiscal year before being charged with current-year taxes. Not only does the settlement statute provide that it is a misdemeanor for a member of a governing body to fail to perform duties assigned under the statute, but a member of the governing body who votes to deliver the tax receipts to the tax collector before the collector has settled for the prior year and met other statutory requirements is individually liable for the amount of taxes for which the collector has not made satisfactory settlement.[79]

Insolvents

The governing body of a taxing unit must evaluate the collector's report at settlement to determine whether the collector has utilized all available legal remedies to attach and garnish property of taxpayers whose taxes are delinquent.[80] It is particularly important that the governing body closely review the efforts of the collector to collect taxes that are not secured by a lien on real property. Taxpayers who owe personal property taxes but own no real property comprise a separate list in the collector's report at settlement. The collector is required to append to this list a sworn statement that he or she has been diligent in using levy and attachment and garnishment to collect the taxes; has attempted to work out payment schedules for taxpayers; has used all the procedures available in collecting from estates, receivers, and bankrupts; and, in appropriate circumstances, has called on collectors of other taxing units to assist in collecting the sums owed. Finally, the collector must report any other information that may be of interest to the governing body.

The governing body must review the report for purposes of rendering the insolvents list to be credited to the tax collector in his or her settlement. The governing body may reject the name of any taxpayer if, in its opinion or knowledge, the taxpayer is not insolvent. In the event of a rejection, the governing body may hold the collector liable on his or her bond for the uncollected tax. Having reviewed the list submitted by the collector and having come to a conclusion about the collector's justification in asking that he or she be allowed credit in the settlement for the uncollected items on the ground of the taxpayers' insolvency, the governing body must enter in its minutes the names of the taxpayers found to be insolvent and designate them as the insolvent list "to be credited to the tax collector in his settlement."[81]

The governing board can relieve the tax collector of the responsibility of collecting taxes that are on the insolvent list and are at least five years past due.[82]

---

78. G.S. 105-373.
79. G.S. 105-352(d)(1).
80. G.S. 105-373(a)(2) and (g).
81. G.S. 105-373(a)(2).
82. G.S. 105-373(g).

Form of Settlement

The Machinery Act specifies the items that must be charged against the collector and the items that must be allowed as credits. In summary, they include the following:

Charges

1. The total amount of all taxes placed in the collector's hands for collection, including taxes on discoveries, increased assessments, and values certified by the Property Tax Commission
2. All late-listing penalties collected by the tax collector
3. All interest on taxes collected by the tax collector
4. Any other sums collected or received by the tax collector, including, for example, fees allowed in levy and attachment and garnishment
5. Any fees that the tax collector may have taken for making collections for other taxing units

Credits

1. All sums deposited by the collector to the credit of the taxing unit or for which the proper official has given receipts
2. Releases allowed by the governing body, including refunds and reductions in value
3. Discounts allowed for prepayments, if the principal amounts of such accounts were collected after the books were placed in the collector's hands
4. The principal amount of unpaid taxes constituting liens against real property
5. The principal amount of taxes found by the county commissioners to be uncollectible in the current year because the taxpayers who owe them are insolvent
6. Any commissions to which the collector is entitled

The charges and the credits should balance. The collector is liable on his or her bond for any deficiency and is subject to criminal penalties for failure to perform any duty imposed by the settlement statute. Importantly, the governing body's approval of a collector's settlement does not relieve the collector of liability for any shortage that existed at the time of the settlement but is only later discovered.

Additional Resources

McLaughlin, Christopher B. *Fundamentals of Property Tax Collection Law in North Carolina.* Chapel Hill, N.C.: UNC School of Government, 2012. Available for purchase at www.sog.unc.edu/pubs.

About the Author

Christopher B. McLaughlin is a School of Government faculty member who specializes in the legal aspects of local taxation.

This chapter updates and revises the previous chapter authored by Shea Riggsbee Denning, whose contributions to the field and to this publication are gratefully acknowledged.

Chapter 20

Budgeting for Operating and Capital Expenditures

Kara A. Millonzi and William C. Rivenbark

Introduction

North Carolina counties, municipalities, and public authorities (collectively, local units) are required to budget and spend money in accordance with the Local Government Budget and Fiscal Control Act (LGBFCA), codified as Article 3 of Chapter 159 of the North Carolina General Statutes (hereinafter G.S.). In fact, a local unit may not expend any funds, regardless of their source, unless the money has been properly budgeted through the annual budget ordinance, a project ordinance, or a financial plan adopted by the unit's governing board.[1] Revenues and expenditures for the provision of general government services are authorized in the annual budget ordinance.[2] Revenues and expenditures for capital projects or for projects financed with grant proceeds are authorized in the annual budget ordinance or in a project ordinance.[3] Revenues and expenditures accounted for in an internal service fund are authorized in the annual budget ordinance or in a financial plan.[4]

This chpater describes the legal requirements to budget for operating and capital expenditures. It also presents common budget tools and techniques for both the annual (operating) and capital budgeting processes. The chapter is divided into three sections. Part I discusses how to prepare, adopt, and amend a unit's annual budget ordinance and presents various tools available to aid local officials during the budgeting process. Part II focuses on adopting a project ordinance for capital projects and expenditures. It also discusses common strategies for capital planning. Finally, part III briefly details the requirements for adopting and implementing a financial plan.

I. Annual Budget Ordinance

The annual budget ordinance is the legal document that recognizes revenues, authorizes expenditures, and levies taxes for the local unit for a single fiscal year. (Each unit's fiscal year runs from July 1 through June 30.)[5] It must be adopted by the unit's governing board. At its core, the budget ordinance reflects the governing board's policy preferences and provides a roadmap for implementing the board's vision for the unit. The Local Government Budget and Fiscal Control Act (LGBFCA), however, requires the board to include certain items in the budget ordinance and to follow a detailed procedure for adopting the budget ordinance.

---

1. There is an exception to this inclusiveness requirement. The Local Government Budget and Fiscal Control Act (LGBFCA) permits the revenues of certain local government trust and agency funds to be spent or disbursed without being budgeted. N.C. Gen. Stat. (hereinafter G.S.) § 159-13(a)(3). Many counties and cities set aside and manage moneys in a pension trust fund, for example, to finance special separation allowances for law enforcement officers. The employees and retirees for whom the local government is managing these moneys have ownership rights to them. Although a county or city must budget its initial contributions on behalf of employees into the pension trust fund, once the moneys are in the fund, earnings on the assets, payments to retirees, and other receipts and disbursements of the funds should not be included in the local government's budget.

Another example is when a county or city collects certain revenue for another governmental unit and records this revenue in an agency fund. Although the moneys are held temporarily by the county or the city, they belong to the other unit. The collections, therefore, are not revenues of the county or city collecting them and should not be included in its budget.

2. G.S. 159-13.

3. G.S. 159-13.1.

4. G.S. 159-13.2.

5. G.S. 159-8(b). The Local Government Commission (LGC) may authorize an authority to have a different fiscal year if it facilitates the authority's operations.

Substantive Budget Ordinance Requirements and Restrictions

Although counties and municipalities, and to a lesser extent public authorities, enjoy broad legal discretion over what programs they choose to provide, and at what levels, there are limits on this discretion. The LGBFCA imposes certain substantive requirements and limitations.

Balanced Budget

Perhaps the most important statutory requirement is that the budget ordinance be balanced. A budget ordinance is balanced when "the sum of estimated net revenues and appropriated fund balances is equal to appropriations."[6] The law requires an exact balance; it permits neither a deficit nor a surplus. Furthermore, each of the accounting funds that make up the annual budget ordinance (e.g., general fund, enterprise fund, etc.) also must be balanced.

Estimated net revenues is the first variable in the balanced-budget equation; it comprises the revenues the unit expects to actually receive during the fiscal year, including amounts to be realized from collections of taxes or fees levied in prior fiscal years. (Typically debt proceeds are not considered a form of revenue, but for budgetary purposes debt proceeds that are or will become available during the fiscal year are included in estimated net revenues.) The LGBFCA requires that the unit make reasonable estimates as to the amount of revenue it expects to receive.[7] And, it places a specific limitation on property tax estimates. The estimated percentage of property tax collection budgeted for the coming fiscal year cannot exceed the percentage of collection realized in cash as of June 30 during the fiscal year preceding the budget year.[8]

Revenues must be budgeted by "major source."[9] This includes, at a minimum, property taxes, sales and use taxes, licenses and permits, intergovernmental revenues, charges for services, and other taxes and revenues. A unit is free to group revenues in more specific categories.

The second variable in the balanced-budget equation is *appropriated fund balance.* Legally available fund balance is money remaining at the end of one fiscal year that may be appropriated to finance expenditures in the next year's budget. The LGBFCA defines appropriated fund balance as "the sum of cash and investments minus the sum of liabilities, encumbrances, and deferred revenues arising from cash receipts, as those figures stand at the close of the fiscal year next preceding the budget year."[10] Legally available fund balance is different from fund balance for financial reporting purposes as presented on the balance sheet of a local government's annual financial report. It includes only cash and investments. It does not include any receivables or other current assets. The calculation starts with an estimate of cash and investments at the end of the current year and subtracts from them estimated liabilities, encumbrances, and deferred revenues from cash receipts at the end of the current year. All these figures are estimates because the calculation is being made for budget purposes before the end of the current year. If the estimate of available fund balance is for the general fund, typical liabilities are payroll owed for a payroll period that will carry forward from the current year into the budget year and accounts payable representing unpaid vendor accounts for goods and services provided to the local government toward the end of the current year. Encumbrances arise from purchase orders and other unfulfilled contractual obligations for goods and services that are outstanding at the end of a fiscal year. They reduce legally available fund balance because cash and investments will be needed to pay for the goods and services on order. Deferred revenue from a cash receipt is revenue that is received in cash in the current year, even though it is not owed to the local government until the coming budget year. Such prepaid revenues are primarily property taxes.

---

6. G.S. 159-8(a).
7. G.S. 159-13(b)(7).
8. G.S. 159-13(b)(6). The statute provides for a different calculation when budgeting for property taxes on registered motor vehicles. The percentage of collection is based on the nine-month levy ending March 31 of the fiscal year preceding the budget year, and the collections realized in cash with respect to this levy are based on the twelve-month period ending June 30 of the fiscal year preceding the budget year.
9. G.S. 159-13(a).
10. G.S. 159-13(b)(16).

They should be included among revenues for the coming year's budget rather than carried forward as available fund balance from the current to the coming year.

Legally available fund balance results when any of the following occur: unbudgeted fund balance carries forward from prior years, actual revenues exceed estimated revenues in the current fiscal year, actual expenditures are less than appropriations in the current fiscal year, or actual revenues exceed actual expenditures in the current fiscal year.

Note that the formula references appropriated fund balance. Not all legally available fund balance must be appropriated by a unit in the annual budget ordinance, only that which is required, when added to estimated net revenues, to equal the budgeted appropriations for the fiscal year. The remaining money serves as cash reserves of the unit, to be used to aid in cash flow during the fiscal year. A unit also may use unappropriated fund balance to save money to meet emergency or unforeseen needs and to be able to take advantage of unexpected opportunities requiring the expenditure of money. And some units accumulate fund balance as a savings account for anticipated future capital projects.

The third variable in the balanced-budget equation is *appropriations for expenditures.* An appropriation is a legal authorization to make an expenditure. Only the governing board may authorize appropriations. The LGBFCA allows a governing board to make appropriations in the budget ordinance by department, function, or project.[11] A governing board may not make appropriations by line item or by individual object of expenditure in the budget ordinance itself. It is a summary document that aggregates expenditures for ease of exposition. Many governing boards require submittal of more detailed line-item budgets by each department to justify the requested expenditures. A board may require that the manager or each department head follow the more detailed budgets ("working budgets") during the fiscal year. The budget ordinance represents the legal appropriations of the unit, though.[12]

Required Budget Ordinance Appropriations

In addition to the balanced-budget requirement, the LGBFCA directs a governing board to include certain appropriations in its budget ordinance.[13]

Debt Service

A governing board must appropriate the full amount estimated by the local government's finance officer to be required for debt service during the fiscal year.[14] During the spring the Local Government Commission (LGC) notifies each finance officer of that local government's debt service obligation on existing debt for the coming year. If a county or municipality does not appropriate enough money for the payment of principal and interest on its debt, the LGC may order the unit to make the necessary appropriation; if the unit ignores this order, the LGC may itself levy the local tax for debt service purposes.[15]

Continuing Contracts

A governing board must make appropriations to cover any obligations that will come due during the fiscal year under continuing contracts.[16] Continuing contracts are those that extend for more than one fiscal year.

---

11. G.S. 159-13(a).

12. This distinction is significant. For example, the statute governing disbursements of public funds requires that the finance officer or a deputy finance officer verify that there is an appropriation authorizing a particular expenditure before an obligation may be incurred by a unit. G.S. 159-28(a). The statute refers to an appropriation in the budget ordinance, not in more detailed, working budgets.

13. Note that the budget ordinance requirements discussed in this chapter generally are limited to those imposed by the LGBFCA. Units must be mindful that other statutory provisions may place additional requirements or restrictions on the budget ordinance.

14. G.S. 159-13(b)(1).

15. G.S. 159-36. Note that the LGC may not require a unit to make appropriations for repayment of installment financing debt incurred under G.S. 160A-20. The provision also does not apply to contractual obligations undertaken by a local government in a debt instrument issued pursuant to G.S. Chapter 159G unless the debt instrument is secured by a pledge of the full faith and credit of the unit.

16. G.S. 159-13(b)(15).

Fund Deficits

A governing board must make appropriations to cover any deficits within a fund. If a unit follows the provisions on expenditure control in the LGBFCA, a deficit should not occur. However, should a deficit occur, a governing board must appropriate sufficient moneys in the next fiscal year's budget to eliminate that deficit.

Property Taxes

If a local unit levies property taxes (which it is not required to do), the governing board must do so in the budget ordinance.[17] The property tax levy is stated in terms of rate of cents per $100 of taxable value.

Limits on Appropriations

Other LGBFCA provisions place upper or lower limits on certain appropriations in the budget ordinance.

Contingency Appropriations

In each fund a governing board may include a contingency appropriation; that is, an appropriation that is not designated to a specific department, function, or project. The contingency appropriation may not exceed 5 percent of the total of all other appropriations in the fund, though.[18]

Tax Levy Limits

If a unit levies property taxes, the proceeds must be used only for statutorily authorized purposes. A governing board may not include an appropriation of property tax revenue that is not authorized by law. Furthermore, there is a $1.50 per $100 property valuation aggregate property tax rate cap.[19]

Limits on Interfund Transfers

The annual budget ordinance often makes appropriations to transfer money from one fund to another. The LGBFCA generally permits appropriations for interfund transfers, but it sets some restrictions on them, each designed to maintain the basic integrity of a fund in light of the purposes for which the fund was established. In addition, the LGBFCA prohibits certain interfund transfers of moneys that are earmarked for a specific service.

Each of the limitations on interfund transfers discussed below is subject to the modification that any fund may be charged for general administrative and overhead costs properly allocated to its activities as well as for the costs of levying and collecting its revenues.[20] A transfer of money to reimburse one fund for administrative or overhead services that it provides to other funds should be budgeted and accounted for as a reimbursement of expenditures rather than as a revenue source or as "other financing sources" in the fund receiving the reimbursement. Alternatively the appropriations for departments that serve other funds as well as their own fund may be budgeted or allocated initially between the respective funds.

17. G.S. 159-13(a).

18. G.S. 159-13(b)(3).

19. G.S. 159-13(b)(4). Note that G.S. 160A-209 and G.S. 153A-149 authorize a municipality and a county, respectively, to seek voter approval to levy property taxes for purposes not authorized under general law. If a unit receives voter approval to expend property tax proceeds for another purpose, the total of all appropriations for that purpose may not exceed the total of all other unrestricted revenues and property taxes levied for the specific purpose. G.S. 159-13(b)(5). Voters also vote on levying tax rates for one or more purposes such that the combined total rate exceeds the $1.50 per $100 valuation cap.

20. G.S. 159-13(b).

Voted Property Tax Funds

Proceeds from a voted property tax may be used only for the purpose approved by the voters. Such proceeds must be budgeted and accounted for in a special revenue fund and generally may not be transferred to another fund,[21] except to a capital reserve fund[22] (if appropriate).

Agency Funds for Special Districts

Some units collect moneys on behalf of a special district. (A special district is a unit of local government, other than a county or municipality, "created for the performance of limited governmental functions or for the operation of a particular utility or public service enterprises.")[23] These moneys must be budgeted and accounted for in an agency fund and may not be transferred to another fund of the collecting unit.[24]

Enterprise Funds

A governing board may transfer moneys from an enterprise fund to another fund only if other appropriations in the enterprise fund are sufficient to meet operating expenses, capital outlays, and debt service for the enterprise.[25] This limitation reflects the policy that enterprise revenues must first meet the expenditures and the obligations related to the enterprise. (Note that other statutory provisions further restrict or prohibit a unit from transferring moneys associated with certain public enterprises.)

Service District Funds

A service district is a special taxing district of a county or municipality. Although a service district is not a separate local government unit, the proceeds of a service district tax and other revenues appropriated to the district belong to the district. Therefore no appropriation may be made to transfer moneys from a service district fund except for the purposes for which the district was established.[26]

Reappraisal Reserve Fund

A reappraisal reserve is established to accumulate money to finance the county's next real property revaluation, which must occur at least once every eight years. Appropriations may not be made from a reappraisal reserve fund for any other purpose.[27]

Optional Budget Ordinance Provisions

The budget ordinance must contain revenue estimates, appropriations for expenditures, and, if applicable, the property tax levy. The ordinance must show revenues and expenditures by fund and demonstrate a balance in each fund. A governing board, however, is free to include other sections or provisions in the budget ordinance. For example, it might include instructions on its administration. If the ordinance makes appropriations very broadly, it might direct that expenditures comply not only with the ordinance but also with the more detailed working budgets on which the ordinance is based. If a fund contains earmarked revenues and general revenues or supports a function for which property taxes may not be used, the ordinance might specify the use of the earmarked funds or direct which non-property-tax revenues are to support the function in question. The ordinance also may authorize and limit certain transfers among departmental or functional appropriations within the same fund, place certain restrictions on interfund loans within the year, and set rates or fees for public enterprises or other governmental services.

---

21. G.S. 159-13(b)(10).

22. A unit may establish and maintain a capital reserve fund to save moneys over time to fund certain designated capital expenditures. G.S. 159-18.

23. G.S. 159-7(b)(13).

24. G.S. 159-14(b).

25. G.S. 159-13(b)(14).

26. G.S. 159-13(b)(18).

27. G.S. 159-13(b)(17).

Adoption of Budget Ordinance

In addition to imposing certain substantive requirements related to the budget ordinance, the LGBFCA also prescribes a detailed process for adopting the budget ordinance.

Role of Budget Officer

Before discussing the specifics of the budget process, it is important to understand the role of the budget officer. The governing board of each unit must appoint a budget officer.[28] In a county or municipality having the manager form of government, the manager is the statutory budget officer. Counties that do not have the manager form of government may impose the duties of budget officer on the finance officer or any other county officer or employee except the sheriff, or in counties having a population of more than 7,500, the register of deeds. Municipalities not having the manager form of government may impose the duties of budget officer on any municipal officer or employee, including the mayor if he or she consents. A public authority or special district may impose the duties on the chairman or any member of its governing board or any other officer or employee.

The LGBFCA assigns to the budget officer the responsibility of preparing and submitting a proposed budget to the governing board each year. Having one official who is responsible for budget preparation focuses responsibility for timely preparation of the budget, permits a technical review of departmental estimates to ensure completeness and accuracy, and allows for administrative analysis of departmental priorities in the context of a local unit's overall priorities. In many units, the statutory budget officer often delegates many of the duties associated with budget preparation to another official or employee; for example, the finance officer or a separate budget director or administrator. This is strictly an administrative arrangement, with the official or employee performing these duties under the direction of the statutory budget officer. Under the law, the budget officer retains full responsibility for budget preparation.

Once the budget ordinance is adopted, the budget officer is charged with overseeing its enactment. As discussed below, the governing board also may authorize the budget officer to make certain limited modifications to the budget ordinance during the fiscal year.

Budgeting Process

Before the budgeting process begins, the budget officer, often with guidance from the governing board, establishes an administrative calendar for budget preparations and prescribes forms and procedures for departments to use in formulating requests. Budget officers often include fiscal or program policies to guide departmental officials in formulating their budget requests. The LGBFCA specifies certain target dates for the key stages in the budgeting process, which should be incorporated into the budget officer's plan.

A budget officer's calendar often includes other steps that, although not statutorily required, are integral to an effective budgeting process. For example, many units kick off the annual budget process with one or more budget retreats or workshops for governing board members, department heads, and others. This allows governing board members to set policy for the coming year and provide directives to the budget officer and department heads about budget requests at the outset of the budget process.

Sometimes a budget officer will need to include other boards, organizations, or citizens in the budgeting process. Counties must provide funding for several functions that are (or may be) governed by other boards, such as public schools, community colleges, elections, social services, mental health, and public health. These boards have their own processes for formulating proposed budgets and requesting funds from the county. (The specific processes and requirements are discussed in the chapters pertaining to each of these function areas.) And both counties and municipalities routinely receive requests from private organizations or citizens for appropriations to support certain community activities and projects. The budget officer often serves as the liaison between these other boards, private entities, and citizen groups and the governing board. The budget officer should work with the governing board to establish an organized process for the board to receive and evaluate these various requests.

---

28. G.S. 159-9.

Budget Calendar

By April 30: Departmental Requests Must Be Submitted to the Budget Officer

The LGBFCA directs that each department head submit to the budget officer the revenue estimates and budget requests for his or her department for the budget year. Each department, or the unit's finance officer, also must submit information about current year revenues and expenditures. The budget officer should specify the format for, and detail of, these submissions.

By June 1: Proposed Budget Must Be Presented to the Governing Board

The budget officer must compile each department head's revenue estimates and budget requests and submit a proposed budget for consideration by the governing board.[29] Generally the proposed budget must comply with all of the substantive requirements previously discussed. A governing board, however, may request that the budget officer submit a budget containing recommended appropriations that are greater than estimated revenues.[30] This affords the board a ready opportunity to discuss different expenditure options.

When the budget officer submits the proposed budget to the governing board, he or she must include a budget message.[31] The message must contain a summary explanation of the unit's goals for the budget year. It also should detail important activities funded in the budget and point out any changes from the previous fiscal year in program goals, appropriation levels, and fiscal policy.

If a revaluation of real taxable property in the unit occurs in the year preceding the budget year, the budget officer must include in the proposed budget a statement of the revenue-neutral tax rate, "the rate that is estimated to produce revenue for the next fiscal year equal to the revenue that would have been produced for the next fiscal year by the current tax rate if no reappraisal had occurred."[32] The rate is calculated as follows:

1. Determine a rate that would produce revenues equal to those produced for the current fiscal year.
2. Increase the rate by a growth factor equal to the average annual percentage increase in the tax base due to improvements since the last general reappraisal.
3. Adjust the rate to account for any annexation, de-annexation, merger, or similar events.

After Proposed Budget Presented to Governing Board but before Its Adoption: Notice and Public Hearing

When the budget officer submits the proposed budget to the governing board, he or she also must file a copy in the office of the clerk to the board, where it remains for public inspection until the governing board adopts the budget ordinance.[33] The clerk must publish a statement that the proposed budget has been submitted to the governing board and is available for public inspection.[34] The clerk also must make a copy of the proposed budget available to all news media in the county. It may be helpful, although it is not legally mandated, for a unit to also post the proposed budget to its website.

The governing board is required to wait at least ten days after the budget officer submits the proposed budget to it before adopting the budget ordinance. This is true even if the board makes no changes to the proposed budget. This interim period affords citizens time to review the proposed budget and voice their opinions or objections to governing board members.

The governing board must hold at least one public hearing on the proposed budget before adopting the budget ordinance. During the public hearing any person who wishes to be heard on the budget must be allowed time to speak. The board should set the time and place for the public hearing when it receives the proposed budget, if not before. And this information must be included in the notice published by the clerk. Sometimes a board holds a series of budget review meetings and briefings on each of the major budget categories. These do not satisfy the statutory requirement. The law requires that at least one public hearing be held on the entire budget. The statute requires no specific minimum

---

29. G.S. 159-11(a).
30. G.S. 159-11(c).
31. G.S. 159-11(b).
32. G.S. 159-11(e).
33. G.S. 159-12(a).
34. *Id.* The notice also must specify the date and time of the public hearing to be held on the budget.

number of days between the date on which the notice appears and the date on which the hearing is held; however, the notice should be timely enough to allow for full public participation at the hearing.

By July 1: Governing Board Must Adopt Budget Ordinance

After the governing board receives the proposed budget from the budget officer, it is free to make changes to the budget before adopting the budget ordinance. In fact, based on citizen input, as well as that from other boards and department heads, the governing board often makes adjustments to the proposed budget before finalizing and adopting the budget ordinance. Questions often arise when a board makes changes to the proposed budget about whether and to what extent it must make the changes known to the public before adopting the budget ordinance. The statute only requires that the budget officer's proposed budget be made available for public inspection and that one public hearing be held after the proposed budget is submitted to the board. A unit is under no legal obligation to keep the public informed of modifications to the proposed budget during the budgeting process.

The LGBFCA allows a budget ordinance to be adopted at any regular or special meeting, at which a quorum is present, by a simple majority of those present and voting.[35] The board must provide sufficient notice of the regular or special meeting, according to the provisions in the applicable open meetings law.[36] The budget ordinance must be entered in the board's minutes, and within five days after it is adopted copies must be filed with the budget officer, the finance officer, and the clerk to the board.[37]

Interim Appropriations

Missing the April 30 or June 1 deadline does not invalidate the budgetary process or budget ordinance. There are some consequences to missing the July 1 deadline, though. A unit has no authority to make expenditures (including to pay staff salaries) under the prior year's budget after June 30. If a board does not adopt the budget ordinance by July 1 and needs to make expenditures, it must adopt an interim budget, making "interim appropriations for the purpose of paying salaries, debt service payments, and the usual ordinary expenses" of the unit until the budget ordinance is adopted.[38] This is a stopgap measure. An interim budget should not include appropriations for salary and wage increases, capital items, and program or service expansion. It may not levy property taxes, nor should it change or increase other tax or user fee rates. The purpose of an interim budget is to temporarily keep operations going at current levels. An interim budget need not include revenues to balance the appropriations. All expenditures made under an interim budget must be charged against the comparable appropriations in the annual budget ordinance once it is adopted. In other words, the interim expenditures eventually are funded with revenues included in the budget ordinance.

LGC Action for Failure to Adopt a Budget Ordinance

At some point if a local unit's governing board refuses or is unable to adopt its budget ordinance, the LGC may take action. State law empowers the LGC to "assume full control" of a unit's financial affairs if the unit "persists, after notice and warning from the [LGC], in willfully or negligently failing or refusing to comply with the provisions" of the LGBFCA. If the LGC takes this action, it becomes vested "with all of the powers of the governing board as to the levy of taxes, expenditure of money, adoption of budgets, and all other financial powers conferred upon the governing board by law."[39] LGC takeover will only occur in extreme cases, though. Most of the time, a unit's governing board is left to work out any differences and adopt its budget ordinance.

---

35. G.S. 159-17. Adoption of the budget ordinance is not subject to the normal ordinance-adoption requirements of G.S. 153A-45 for counties and G.S. 160A-75 for municipalities.

36. *See* G.S. 143-318.12. However, G.S. 159-17 specifies that

> no provision of law concerning the call of special meetings applies during [the period beginning with the submission of the proposed budget and ending with the adoption of the budget ordinance] so long as (i) each member of the board has actual notice of each special meeting called for the purpose of considering the budget, and (ii) no business other than consideration of the budget is taken up.

37. G.S. 159-13(d).

38. G.S. 159-16.

39. G.S. 159-181.

Budgetary Accounting

The LGBFCA requires local units to maintain an accounting system with applicable funds as defined by generally accepted accounting principles (GAAP).[40] Local units enter their adopted budgets into their accounting systems at the beginning of the fiscal year, which allows them to accurately track the difference between an appropriation and the accumulated expenditures and encumbrances applied against that appropriation. Budgetary accounting is considered a best practice for several reasons. It provides the foundation for budget-to-actual variance reports, providing critical information to departments for remaining within their budgets and to elected officials who possess the ultimate fiduciary responsibility of the organization. It provides the information needed for managing budget amendments and for complying with the preaudit requirement.[41] Finally, it provides the needed information for following GAAP when local units issue their annual financial statements.

Amending the Budget Ordinance

The adopted budget ordinance is the legal authority to make all expenditures during the fiscal year. Before a unit may incur an obligation (order goods or enter into service contracts), the finance officer or a deputy finance officer must ensure that there is an appropriation authorizing the expenditure and that sufficient moneys remain in the appropriation to cover the expenditure.[42] Events during a fiscal year may cause greater or less spending than anticipated for some activities, or needs may arise for which there is no appropriation or for which the existing one is exhausted. To meet these situations the local unit may need to amend the budget ordinance.

The budget ordinance may be amended at any time after its adoption.[43] A governing board may modify appropriations for expenditures or appropriate fund balance to cover new expenditures. As amended, however, the budget ordinance must continue to be balanced and comply with the other substantive requirements previously discussed. There is an additional restriction on changing the property tax levy.[44] Although not legally required to do so, a governing board also may amend the budget ordinance to reflect changes in revenue estimates during the fiscal year.

A budget ordinance may be amended by action of a simple majority of governing board members as long as a quorum is present. There are no notice or public hearing requirements. A governing board may delegate certain authority to make changes to the budget officer. This authority is limited to (1) transfers of moneys from one appropriation to another within the same fund or (2) allocation of contingency appropriations to certain expenditures within the same fund. All other changes to the budget ordinance, including any revenue changes, must be made by the governing board.

Changing the Property Tax Levy

There is a legal limitation on changing the property tax levy or otherwise altering a property taxpayer's liability once the budget ordinance has been adopted. A board may alter the property tax levy only if (1) it is ordered to do so by a court, (2) it is ordered to do so by the LGC, or (3) the unit receives revenues that are substantially more or less than the amount anticipated when the budget ordinance was adopted. A board may change the tax levy under the third exception only if it does so between July 1 and December 31.

40. G.S. 159-26.

41. See G.S. 159-15 for budget amendments. See G.S. 159-28 for the preaudit requirement.

42. *See* G.S. 159-28(a).

43. Sometimes a board adopts the budget ordinance before July 1. The budget ordinance is not effective until July 1; however, it may be amended at any time after its adoption subject to the limitations set forth in G.S. 159-15.

44. There also are a few additional restrictions on amending the budget ordinance imposed by other laws. For example, a board may not change its own compensation or benefits once the budget ordinance is adopted. *See* Kara A. Millonzi, "Altering Local Elected Officials' Compensation During the Fiscal Year," *Coates' Canons: NC Local Government Law Blog* (UNC School of Government, Dec. 9, 2010), http://canons.sog.unc.edu/?p=3653.

Common Budgeting Tools and Techniques

Local units may adopt any budgeting process that facilitates effective decision making for adopting a balanced budget ordinance as long as they comply with the legal requirements of the LGBFCA. Local units, historically, have approached the budget process as a financial exercise, focusing primarily on the financial inputs and outputs of the organization. Today, however, local units often take a broader perspective of the budgeting process and include information derived from their strategic plans and performance measurement systems to help guide budgetary decision making. The goal, as articulated by the reinventing government movement of the early 1990s, is for local units to make decisions that enable them to steer the boat rather than just row it.[45]

Line-Item Budgeting

Line-item budgeting places the focus of decision making on revenue estimates by each revenue category and on appropriations by each expenditure account. This form of budgeting is often criticized for its incremental approach to decision making, resulting in an adopted budget for the forthcoming fiscal year that simply reflects the current year's budget with slight adjustments, the assumption being that the collection of services contained in the current year's budget should continue for the following fiscal year. While line-item budgeting is often criticized for this reason, it nonetheless provides the foundation of budgetary accounting. Local units prepare line-item budgets to accurately appropriate the necessary resources for each expenditure account contained in the categories of personnel, operations, and capital outlay; to record the line-item budgets in the local unit's financial management system to track budget-to-actual variances over the course of the fiscal year; and ultimately to document budgetary compliance as required by the LGBFCA.[46]

Strategic Budgeting

A management tool that is often used by local units to embrace long-term decision making is the creation and adoption of a strategic plan. As previously mentioned, local units often begin their budgetary processes with budget retreats or workshops for elective officials. These retreats and workshops commonly focus on how the forthcoming budget will help advance the long-term goals contained in the local unit's strategic plan. For example, a local unit may focus on infrastructure during the annual budget process because economic development is a long-term goal of the community. An advantage of broadening the budget process to include the organization's strategic plan is shifting the focus of the local unit's leadership from individual line-item accounts to long-term strategic goals that impact the direction of the community.

Performance Budgeting

Another common management tool used by local units to track service efficiency and effectiveness is performance measurement, where individual programs adopt mission statements, goals, objectives, and performance measures to demonstrate the outputs, efficiencies, and outcomes of service delivery. For example, a major output for public safety is the number of service calls. A major outcome is the timeliness of these service calls as tracked by response time. An advantage of performance budgeting, or the incorporation of performance measurement information in the budget, is that it enables the local government unit to use efficiency and effectiveness measures in making resource allocation decisions.[47] Returning to the public safety example, performance budgeting represents the process of deciding whether or not to add an additional officer based on the objective of responding to 95 percent of service calls within four minutes rather than solely on the local unit's ability to afford an additional position.

Zero-Based Budgeting

A technique that is commonly cited for its advantage of eliminating or reducing incremental budget decisions is zero-based budgeting. This budgeting technique, in theory, requires that every line item be reviewed and justified from a

45. David Osborne and Ted Gaebler, *Reinventing Government* (New York: Penguin, 1992).

46. G.S. 159-26(a).

47. Janet M. Kelly and William C. Rivenbark, *Performance Budgeting for State and Local Government*, 2nd ed. (Armonk, N.Y.: M. E. Sharpe, 2011).

base budget of zero rather than from the current year budget. Zero-based budgeting, in practice, requires each department to submit three budget packages for review: its current year budget, a reduced budget, and an expansion budget.[48] Departments are ranked based on the priorities of the organization and, based on that ranking, assigned one of the three budget packages, thereby reducing the probability that all departmental budgets reflect current year budgets with slight adjustments. However, there are mixed reviews on the effectiveness of zero-based budgeting for eliminating or reducing incremental decision making.

Balanced Scorecard

The balanced scorecard is specifically designed to help a local unit translate its mission and strategy into tangible objectives and outcomes.[49] Originally designed for the private sector, the balanced scorecard was adopted in the public sector as part of administrative reform and is now used as a management tool that helps local units broaden their budgeting processes during the preparation, implementation, and evaluation stages. The balanced scorecard requires a local unit to track a collection of metrics within the four quadrants of citizens, operations, financial resources, and employees, providing local units with a broader and balanced context when making budgetary decisions.

II. Capital Budgeting

In North Carolina, local units may budget revenues and expenditures for the construction or acquisition of capital assets (capital projects) or for projects that are financed in whole or in part with federal or state grants (grant projects) either in the annual budget ordinance or in one or more project ordinances. A project ordinance appropriates revenues and expenditures for however long it takes to complete the project rather than for a single fiscal year.[50]

Capital Projects

The Local Government Budget and Fiscal Control Act (LGBFCA) defines a capital project as a project (1) that is financed at least in part by bonds, notes, or debt instruments or (2) that involves the construction or acquisition of a capital asset. Although a capital project ordinance may be used to recognize revenues and appropriate expenditures for any capital project or asset, it typically is used for capital improvements or acquisitions that are large relative to the annual resources of the unit, that take more than one year to build or acquire, or that recur irregularly. Expenditures for capital assets that are not expensive relative to a unit's annual budget or that happen annually usually can be handled effectively in the budget ordinance.

Grant Projects

A grant project ordinance may be used to budget revenues and expenditures for operating or capital purposes in a project financed wholly or partly by a grant from the federal or state government. However, a grant project ordinance should not be used to appropriate state-shared taxes or other federal or state revenue or aid that is provided on a continuing basis to a unit. Such revenue or aid, even if it is earmarked for a specific purpose, should be budgeted in the annual budget ordinance.

---

48. Robert L. Bland, *A Budgeting Guide for Local Government*, 2nd ed. (Washington, D.C.: International City/County Management Association, 2007).
49. F. Stevens Redburn, Robert J. Shea, and Terry F. Buss, *Performance Management and Budgeting* (Armonk, N.Y.: M. E. Sharpe, 2008).
50. G.S. 159-13.2.

Creating a Project Ordinance

A governing board may adopt a project ordinance at any regular or special meeting by a simple majority of board members as long as a quorum is present. And it can be done at any time during the year. The ordinance must (1) clearly identify the project and authorize its undertaking, (2) identify the revenues that will finance the project, and (3) make the appropriations necessary to complete the project.

Each project ordinance must be entered in the board's minutes, and within five days after its adoption copies of the ordinance must be filed with the finance officer, the budget officer, and the clerk to the board.

The budget officer also must provide certain information about project ordinances in the proposed annual budget that he or she submits to the governing board each year. Specifically, the budget officer must include information on any project ordinances that the unit anticipates adopting during the budget year. The proposed budget also should include details about previously adopted project ordinances that likely will have appropriations available for expenditure during the budget year.[51] This is purely informational. The board need take no action to reauthorize a project ordinance once it is adopted.

Balanced Project Ordinance Requirement

The LGBFCA requires a capital or grant project ordinance to be balanced for the life of the project. A project ordinance is balanced when "revenues estimated to be available for the project equal appropriations for the project."[52]

Estimated revenues for a project ordinance may include bond or other debt proceeds, federal or state grants, revenues from special assessments or impact fees, other special revenues, and annually recurring revenues. If property tax revenue is used to finance a project ordinance it must be levied initially in the annual budget ordinance and then transferred to the project ordinance. Other annually recurring revenues may be budgeted in the annual budget ordinance and transferred to a project ordinance or appropriated directly in a project ordinance.

Appropriations for expenditures in a project ordinance may be general or detailed. A project ordinance may make a single, lump-sum appropriation for the project authorized by the ordinance, or it may make appropriations by line-item, function, or other appropriate categories within the project. If a capital project ordinance includes more than one project, the revenues and appropriations should be listed separately and balanced for each project.

The key characteristic of a project ordinance is that it has a project life, which means that the balancing requirement for such an ordinance is not bound by or related to any fiscal year or period. Estimated revenues and appropriations in a project ordinance must be balanced for the life of the project but do not have to be balanced for any fiscal year or period that the ordinance should happen to span.

Amending a Project Ordinance

A project ordinance may be amended at any time after its adoption, but only by the governing board. If expenditures for a project exceed the ordinance's appropriation, in total or for any expenditure category for which an appropriation was made, an amendment to the ordinance is necessary to increase the appropriation and identify additional revenues to keep the project ordinance balanced. A board also may amend a project ordinance to change the nature or scope of the project(s) being funded.

51. G.S. 159-13.2(f).
52. G.S. 159-13.2(c).

Closing Out a Project Ordinance

Unlike the annual budget ordinance, a project ordinance does not have an end date. It remains in effect until the project is finished or abandoned. There are no formal procedures for closing out a project ordinance when a project is done. Projects sometimes are completed with appropriated revenues remaining unspent. Practically speaking, such excess revenues are equivalent to a project fund balance. The remaining moneys should be transferred to another appropriate project, fund, or purpose at the project's completion. Annual revenues budgeted in a project ordinance that remain after a project is finished may be transferred back to the general fund or another fund included in the annual budget ordinance. Bond proceeds remaining after a project is finished should be transferred to the appropriate fund for other projects authorized by the bond order or to pay debt service on the bonds. Note that any earmarked revenues in a project ordinance retain the earmark when transferred to another project or fund.

Justification for Capital Budget

The National Advisory Council on State and Local Government Budgeting encourages the adoption of a comprehensive policy to successfully implement and manage the various aspects of capital budgeting.[53] A common question in local government is why local officials need to manage two budgeting processes, one for the operating budget and another for the capital budget. There are several reasons for implementing and managing a separate capital budgeting process.[54]

The first reason involves the lasting impact of decisions. For example, a decision to expand bus routes during the operating budget process can be changed during the operating budget process for the following fiscal year. A decision to expand the police station, however, is more permanent in nature, requiring a level of review beyond incremental adjustments to the operating budget.

A second reason, which builds on the first, is that debt financing is often used to acquire capital assets. The issuing of debt has a long-term impact on the county or city because the law requires that debt service payments be appropriated as part of the budget ordinance.[55] The processes and procedures for capital budgeting can provide a more structured review for a critical decision such as issuing debt, where additional debt service payments may impact the organization's financial condition and possibly reduce future operating budget flexibility.

A third reason for implementing and managing a separate capital budgeting process can be traced back to state law. The budget ordinance adopted by counties and cities in North Carolina covers a single fiscal year beginning July 1 and ending June 30.[56] The acquisition of major capital assets or the completion of infrastructure projects often extends over multiple fiscal years from approval to completion. State law allows local units to adopt their capital budgets with a capital project ordinance, which authorizes all appropriations necessary for project completion and prevents project proceeds from having to be readopted in subsequent fiscal years.

A final reason is the variation in assets and costs as compared to the operating budget, where decisions are often incremental from one fiscal year to the next. In any given fiscal year during the capital budgeting process, local officials may be faced with using cash reserves for anything from purchasing a new fire truck for $750,000 to issuing $20 million of debt for infrastructure improvements. Capital budgeting allows for the use of specific techniques for evaluating and prioritizing capital requests in terms of organizational need, capacity for acquisition, and community impact.

53. National Advisory Council on State and Local Government Budgeting, *Recommended Budget Practices* (Chicago: Government Finance Officers Association, 2003).

54. Robert L. Bland, *A Budgeting Guide for Local Government*, 2nd ed. (Washington, D.C.: International City/County Management Association, 2007).

55. G.S. 159-13(b)(1).

56. G.S. 159-8(b).

Capitalization and Capital Budget Thresholds

An important policy decision for local units is establishing a capitalization threshold, which dictates how the costs associated with the acquisition of capital assets are reported in the annual financial statements as required by G.S. 159-25(a)(1). The Government Finance Officers Association (GFOA) defines *capital assets* as tangible items (e.g., land, buildings, building improvements, vehicles, equipment, and infrastructure) or intangible items (e.g., easements and technology) with useful lives that extend beyond a single reporting period.[57] The GFOA recommends that local governments adopt a capitalization threshold of no less than $5,000 for any individual item, which means that capital assets that cost $5,000 or less are reported as expenditures or expenses in the period in which they are acquired. Capital assets that cost more than $5,000 are reported on the balance sheet and depreciated based on their estimated useful lives.

It is a professional practice for counties and cities also to establish a financial threshold to determine what capital requests are considered part of the operating budget process and what capital requests are considered part of the capital budget process. This threshold is often based on the size of the local government. For example, a smaller local government with a population of approximately 20,000 might establish a financial threshold of $50,000, meaning that capital assets that cost $50,000 or less would be part of the operating budget process and capital assets that cost more than $50,000 would be part of the capital budget process. An additional criterion often used in determining this threshold is the estimated useful life of the capital asset, because capital assets with longer estimated useful lives are more appropriate for the capital budget rather than the operating budget. A reason for applying this additional criterion is that debt is often used to finance capital assets, and debt payments should never exceed the estimated useful life of the asset.

Common Capital Budgeting Tools and Techniques

As with the annual budgeting process, a local unit may adopt any capital budgeting process that facilitates effective decision making as long as it complies with the legal requirements of the LGBFCA. An essential component of any well-designed capital budgeting process is planning. Many units have adopted a formalized capital improvement program (CIP) to facilitate the planning process. And increasingly units are relying on more sophisticated analysis relating to the financial condition of the unit to make accurate budget forecasts.

Capital Improvement Program

A CIP is a forecast of capital assets and funding sources over a selected period of time. While local officials often refer to the capital budget and CIP as one and the same, they are separate management tools. The capital budget covers one fiscal year and is adopted by ordinance. The CIP, which commonly contains five years of proposed capital assets and funding sources beyond the capital budget, is approved as a long-term plan that local officials update on an annual basis.

There are numerous reasons why local officials prepare and approve a CIP in conjunction with their capital budget. It provides a schedule for the replacement and rehabilitation of existing capital assets, which is fundamental to all capital improvement programs. It allows time for project design and for exploring financing options, both of which are critical to evaluating the merits of a capital asset from a cost-benefit perspective. It is also the primary vehicle for providing the necessary infrastructure to support economic and community development in a coordinated manner, which is fundamental to land use and master plans. As well, a CIP has the potential to help a local government maintain or improve its bond rating due to the premium that bond rating agencies place on planning.

Table 20.1 provides an example of a capital budget for a local government. The capital budget of $900,000 is adopted by ordinance for fiscal year 2014, appropriating the necessary financing sources to fund the capital assets aggregated by functional area. The major capital project for fiscal year 2014 is the expansion of the public safety building, which is

57. Government Finance Officers Association, *Establishing Appropriate Capitalization Thresholds for Capital Assets*, approved by the GFOA executive board on February 24, 2006.

Table 20.1 Capital Budget and Capital Improvement Program (CIP)

	Capital Budget	Capital Improvement Program				
Item	**FY 2014**	**FY 2015**	**FY 2016**	**FY 2017**	**FY 2018**	**FY 2019**
Capital Assets by Function						
Public safety	500,000	50,000	50,000	50,000	50,000	50,000
Environmental services			250,000			250,000
Streets and transportation	200,000			400,000		
Parks and recreation			100,000			
Water and sewer	200,000	50,000			200,000	
Total	900,000	100,000	400,000	450,000	250,000	300,000
Financing Courses						
Operating revenue	100,000	50,000	50,000	50,000	50,000	50,000
Capital reserve fund		50,000	250,000			250,000
Grants			100,000			
General obligation bonds	600,000			400,000		
Revenue bonds	200,000				200,000	
Total	900,000	100,000	400,000	450,000	250,000	300,000

funded by $100,000 from annual operating revenue and $400,000 from general obligation (GO) bonds. The $200,000 of asphalt maintenance (streets and transportation) is funded from the remaining GO bonds, and revenue bonds will be used to fund an expansion of the water and sewer system.

Table 20.1 also provides an example of a five-year CIP for the local government, beginning with fiscal year 2015. While the CIP represents a plan and is updated on an annual basis as new requests are considered, it gives local officials time to prepare for future events. In fiscal year 2016, for example, $100,000 is allocated for a new park, giving local officials the time required to negotiate with multiple land owners to secure the necessary property. And in fiscal year 2017, $400,000 is allocated for GO bonds, giving local officials time to prepare for a bond referendum. These two examples highlight another critical reason that local officials prepare CIPs: doing so allows them to anticipate how the funding of capital assets will impact future operating budgets. Once the park is functional, adequate proceeds must be appropriated in the annual operating budget for additional park maintenance. The operating budget must also appropriate the debt service payments for the issuance of the GO bonds as required by G.S. 159-13(b)(1). Preparing CIPs enables departments to consider the impact of proposed capital assets on their operating budgets when evaluating and submitting capital improvement requests.

Financial Condition and Forecasting

The CIP is a management tool that facilitates long-term planning for the acquisition of capital assets in local government. There are two additional management tools—financial condition analysis and financial forecasting—that support the capital budgeting process from a financial perspective. This is critical given the ways in which the acquisition of capital assets can impact the organization's current financial condition and future operating budget flexibility.

Financial Condition Analysis

The first of these additional management tools, financial condition analysis, allows local officials to move beyond reporting on the financial position of the organization with an unqualified audit opinion of its annual financial statements to actually analyzing and interpreting the financial statements in order to determine and report on the financial condition of the organization. The reason financial condition analysis is so important to capital budgeting and finance is that acquiring and financing capital assets has the potential to drastically change the financial condition of a county or city; therefore, it is imperative to monitor these changes on an annual basis for the financial sustainability of the local government.

Fortunately, local officials have access to two Web-based dashboards that provide key financial ratios for analyzing the financial condition of any county or city in North Carolina. The fiscal analysis tool dashboard, which is located on the North Carolina Department of State Treasurer's website (www.nctreasurer.com), provides selected financial ratios for the governmental activities, the general fund, the water and sewer fund, and the electric fund. The tool calculates the ratios over a five-year period and benchmarks them against other local governments. The North Carolina water and wastewater rates dashboard, which is located on the Environmental Finance Center's website at the School of Government (www.efc.sog.unc.edu), provides selected operations, debt service, and liquidity financial ratios for water and wastewater activities.

While the details of financial condition analysis are beyond the scope of this chapter, two financial ratios associated with the general fund and two financial ratios associated with an enterprise fund are discussed below to highlight the critical connection between acquiring financial capital assets and the financial condition of a local government.[58]

General Fund Financial Ratios

A financial ratio from the general fund's statement of revenues, expenditures, and changes in fund balance is the *debt service ratio*, which is calculated by dividing principle and interest by total expenditures. This ratio provides feedback on the percentage of annual expenditures being committed to annual debt service, which impacts service flexibility. The International City/County Management Association cautions local governments not to exceed 10 percent;[59] however, counties in North Carolina often exceed this percentage because of school financing. This ratio plays an important role when local officials are making the decision to issue additional debt for capital assets. Another financial ratio from the general fund's balance sheet is *fund balance as percentage of expenditures*. This ratio provides feedback on the solvency of the general fund, which is extremely important to monitor as cash reserves often are used to finance capital assets.

Enterprise Fund Financial Ratios

Two critical ratios calculated from the financial statements of an enterprise fund are the *debt coverage ratio* and the *capital-assets-condition ratio*. The enterprise fund's debt service ratio is calculated by dividing net income of the enterprise by annual debt service—for example, a ratio of 1.25 means that net income exceeded debt service by 25 percent. This ratio is an important indicator of the financial condition of an enterprise fund. It is also important to creditors and bond rating agencies, particularly when local officials seek to issue revenue bonds. The capital-assets-condition ratio provides feedback on the accumulated depreciation of the capital assets assigned to an enterprise fund (the ratio is 1.0—accumulated depreciation divided by capital assets being depreciated). A high ratio provides evidence that the county or city is investing in its capital assets, while a low ratio suggests that a local unit needs to review its annual investment in capital assets.

Financial Forecasting

Financial condition analysis provides extremely important information about capital budgeting and finance; however, financial ratios are typically calculated from audited financial statements (historical data). The second management tool, which is more aligned with the CIP, is financial forecasting—a projection of revenues and expenditures (expenses) over a selected period of time to show the future operating results of a fund on the basis of an agreed-upon set of assumptions.[60] Research has shown that a five-year model is standard in local government, which reconciles with the typical CIP.[61] The implementation of a capital budget and CIP, as previously discussed, addresses the operating results

58. For more information on financial condition analysis, see William C. Rivenbark, Dale J. Roenigk, and Gregory S. Allison, "Communicating Financial Condition to Elected Officials in North Carolina," *Popular Government* 75 (Fall, 2009): 4–13.

59. International City/County Management Association, *Evaluating Financial Condition*, 4th ed. (Washington, D.C.: International City/County Management Association, 2003).

60. Larry Schroeder, "Local Government Multiyear Budgetary Forecasting: Some Administrative and Political Issues," *Public Administration Review* 42, no. 2 (1982): 121–27.

61. William C. Rivenbark, "Financial Forecasting for North Carolina Local Governments," *Popular Government* 73 (2007): 6–13.

of the respective funds based on additional debt service payments, changes in positions and operating expenses, and additional revenue. Financial forecasting provides local officials with a methodology to estimate how the acquisition of capital assets contained in the CIP will affect the relationship between the inflow and outflow of resources in a fund over the selected forecast period.

Table 20.2 presents an example of a five-year financial forecast for the general fund. The forecast of all revenues and expenditures is based on a 2 percent growth rate, with the exception of property taxes and debt service. The forecast for property taxes is based on a 3 percent growth rate, and the forecast for debt service is based on amortization schedules. The current fiscal year (CFY) balance, as noted, is an estimate based on nine months of annualized data; however, the estimate shows that revenues are expected to exceed expenditures by $5,449 for the CFY, increasing fund balance by that amount. The forecast shows that estimated revenues are expected to exceed estimated expenditures for the following two fiscal years, increasing fund balance to $134,947 at the end of fiscal year 2016. The forecast then shows that estimated expenditures are expected to exceed estimated revenues for the remaining three fiscal years, reducing fund balance to $79,935 at the end of fiscal year 2019. The reason for the reverse in trend is that the local government expects to double its debt service payment from $50,000 to $100,000 in fiscal year 2017 due to the implementation of its CIP.

The five-year financial forecast shown in Figure 20.2 gives local officials time to begin discussing how the county or city can afford the additional debt service payment schedule for fiscal year 2017. Changes can be made to operating revenues and expenditures, for example, or changes can be made to the capital budget and CIP to reduce the impact of taking on more debt. Local officials need information on the different ways in which counties and cities in North Carolina can use pay-as-you-go strategies to acquire capital assets and on how they can issue and structure debt to accommodate the needs of the organization and community.

III. Financial Plans for Internal Service Funds

An internal service fund may be established to account for a service provided by one department or program to other departments in the same local unit and, in some cases, to other local governments. If a local unit uses an internal service fund, the fund's revenues and expenditures may be included either in the annual budget ordinance or in a separate financial plan adopted specifically for the fund.[62]

Adopting a Financial Plan

The governing board must approve any financial plan adopted for an internal service fund, with such approval occurring at the same time that the board enacts the annual budget ordinance.[63] The financial plan also must follow the same July 1 to June 30 fiscal year as the budget ordinance. An approved financial plan is entered into the board's minutes, and within five days after its approval copies of the plan must be filed with the finance officer, budget officer, and clerk to the board.

62. G.S. 159-8(a); 159-13.1.

63. At the same time that he or she submits the proposed budget to the governing board, the budget officer also must submit a proposed financial plan for each intragovernmental service fund that will be in operation during the budget year.

Table 20.2 Five-Year Financial Forecast for General Fund

	*CFY	Forecast				
Item	**FY 2014**	**FY 2015**	**FY 2016**	**FY 2017**	**FY 2018**	**FY 2019**
Fund balance, beginning	$100,000	$105,449	$117,006	$134,947	$109,551	$91,112
Revenues						
Property taxes	500,140	515,144	530,598	546,516	562,911	579,799
Local option sales taxes	101,985	104,024	106,105	108,227	110,391	112,600
Permits and fees	52,444	53,492	54,562	55,653	56,767	57,902
Intergovernmental	50,000	51,000	52,020	53,060	54,121	55,204
Sanitation fees	74,785	76,280	77,806	79,362	80,949	82,568
Total	779,354	799,940	821,091	842,818	865,139	888,073
Expenditures						
Administration	100,691	102,705	104,759	106,854	108,991	111,171
Public safety	246,123	251,045	256,066	261,188	266,411	271,740
Environmental services	182,654	186,307	190,033	193,834	197,711	201,665
Transportation	98,585	100,557	102,568	104,619	106,712	108,846
Parks and recreation	95,852	97,769	99,724	101,719	103,753	105,828
Debt service	50,000	50,000	50,000	100,000	100,000	100,000
Total	773,905	788,383	803,150	868,214	883,578	899,250
Difference	5,449	11,557	17,941	(25,396)	(18,439)	(11,177)
Fund balance, ending	$105,449	$117,006	$134,947	$109,551	$91,112	$79,935

*Current fiscal year (CFY) balance is an estimate based on nine months of annualized data.

Balanced Financial Plan Requirement

A financial plan must be balanced. This is accomplished when estimated expenditures equal estimated revenues of the fund.[64]

Internal service fund revenues are principally charges to county, municipality, or authority departments that use the services of an internal service fund. These charges are financed by appropriated expenditures of the using departments in the annual budget ordinance. Internal service fund revenues or other resources also may include an appropriated subsidy or transfer unrelated to specific internal service fund services, which would come from the general fund or some other fund to be shown as a transfer-in rather than revenue for the internal service fund.

64. G.S. 159-13.1.

Expenditures for an internal service fund are typically for items necessary to provide fund services, including salaries and wages; other operating outlays; lease, rental, or debt service payments; and depreciation charges on equipment or facilities used by the fund.

In adopting the annual financial plan for an internal service fund, a governing board must decide what to do with any available balance or reserves remaining from any previous year's financial plan. The law permits fund balance or reserves to be used to help finance fund operations in the next year, or if the balance is substantial, to fund long-term capital needs of the fund. Alternatively, fund balance may be allowed to continue accumulating for the purpose of financing major capital needs of the fund in the future, or it may be transferred to the general fund or another fund for an appropriate use. A unit should avoid amassing in its financial plans large fund balances that are unrelated to the specific needs of the internal service fund.

Amending a Financial Plan

A financial plan may be modified during the fiscal year, but any change must be approved by the governing board.[65] Any amendments to a financial plan must be reflected in the board's minutes, with copies filed with the finance officer, budget officer, and clerk to the board.

Summary

Local units in North Carolina are required to budget and spend money in accordance with the Local Government Budget and Fiscal Control Act (LGBFCA), which provides a comprehensive legal framework for preparing, adopting, and amending the annual budget ordinance, project ordinances, and financial plans. The majority of this chapter, as a result, focused on interpreting the numerous statutes in the LGBFCA, including the definition of a balanced budget ordinance, the limits on appropriations and interfund transfers, the adoption and amending of the budget ordinance, and the use of project ordinances and financial plans. After a brief overview of budgetary accounting, the chapter presented management tools and processes used by local government to make budgetary decisions within the broader context of the organization.

About the Authors

Kara A. Millonzi is a School of Government faculty member who specializes in local government and public school finance law. William C. Rivenbark is a School of Government faculty member who specializes in local government administration.

65. G.S. 159-13.1(d).

Chapter 21

Financing Capital Projects

Kara A. Millonzi

Introduction

Constructing, acquiring, and maintaining the facilities, equipment, and other capital infrastructure needed to perform public services (collectively, capital projects) are important responsibilities of county and city officials. Capital projects also present unique challenges. A capital asset is an asset that is of significant value and has a useful life of more than a single year. This broad definition covers everything from the acquisition of office furniture to the construction of a water treatment facility or a new high school. Thus, in any given year, the capital projects a unit undertakes may vary substantially in number, cost, complexity, and timing. Local governments therefore need different tools to budget and finance capital assets than to budget and finance current assets or operating expenses.

This chapter explores the different tools available to North Carolina local governments to finance capital projects. It focuses on funding public infrastructure—that is, capital outlay used for (or primarily for) governmental purposes. (Chapter 20, "Budgeting for Operating and Capital Expenditures," discusses the capital budgeting process.) The financing mechanisms can be broken into roughly five categories—current revenues, savings, special levies, borrowing money, and grants and partnerships. Table 21.1 lists the authorized funding mechanisms within each category. The remainder of this chapter discusses the funding mechanisms in the first four categories,[1] detailing the authority to use each method as well as its procedural requirements and limitations.

1. Several of the mechanisms in the fifth category are discussed in other chapters. For information on leases, see Chapter 23, "Public Contracts, Compeititive Bidding Requirements, and Property Disposal." For information on reimbursement agreements,

Table 21.1 Authorized Capital Financing Mechanisms in North Carolina

Current Revenues	Savings	Special Levies	Borrowing Money	Grants and Partnerships
• General fund revenues • Enterprise fund revenues	• Fund balance • Capital reserve fund	• Special taxing (service) districts • Special assessments • Impact fees • Development exactions[a]	• General obligation bonds • Installment financings • Revenue bonds • Special obligation bonds • Project development financings	• Leases • Reimbursement agreements • Redevelopment areas • Grants • Gifts/donations/ crowd-funding[b] • State direct appropriations

a. Development exactions are not discussed in this chapter. See Chapter 25, "Community Planning, Land Use, and Development."

b. Crowd-funding involves the use of online platforms to raise private money to fund public infrastructure projects. At its core, crowd-funding simply provides a newer mechanism to accept private donations for specific public improvement projects.

Current Revenues

Current revenues are revenues collected by the local unit each fiscal year. The largest source of current revenue in the general fund is property taxes, followed by sales and use taxes. Current revenues in an enterprise fund typically encompass user fees and other specialty charges. Current revenues are used primarily by a local unit to fund government programs and activities and cover annual operational expenses, including salaries, utilities, and supplies. Most units, however, also use a portion of their current revenues to fund capital projects each year.

Two categories of capital projects are typically funded with current revenues. The first includes capital expenditures that fall below a certain dollar amount. Some units actually set a capital budget threshold amount in the annual budget ordinance, using current revenues to fund any capital outlay that costs less than that amount. The second category includes capital expenditures that recur on a regular basis. These expenditures may or may not fall below the capital budget threshold but are nevertheless funded in the annual budget ordinance with current revenues. Common examples of the first category are regular maintenance and repair expenditures on existing capital assets and computer hardware and software upgrades and replacements. The second category varies depending on the size of the unit and the budget year, but most units use current revenues, for example, to fund the purchase of some vehicles that are on a regular replacement schedule.

Savings

Often a unit must save current revenues over a period of time to fund a capital expenditure. North Carolina local governments can do this in two ways. One is to allow money to accumulate in fund balance. The other is to allocate revenue to a capital reserve fund.

Fund Balance

Local governments use fund accounting to track assets and liabilities. An accounting fund is a separate fiscal and accounting entity, with its own set of self-balancing accounts. Thus, a fund has its own assets, liabilities, equity, revenues,

see Chapter 25, "Community Planning, Land Use, and Development." Chapter 26, "Community Development and Affordable Housing," and Chapter 27, "Economic Development," provide information on redevelopment.

and expenses. There are eleven types of funds, the most common being the general fund, which accounts for most general government revenues and expenditures. The equity associated with a fund is referred to as "fund balance." In the simplest terms, fund balance is an accumulation of revenues minus expenditures.

Fund balance generally serves three purposes. The primary purpose is to provide the unit with cash flow. A local government's fiscal year begins on July 1. Most units, though, do not receive the majority of their operating revenue (in the form of property tax proceeds) until late December or early January. Because of this delay, a local government typically must rely on cash reserves from the prior fiscal year to cover up to several months of expenditures.

The second purpose of fund balance is to provide a unit with an emergency fund, often referred to as a rainy day fund. It is difficult for a local government to raise additional money quickly during the fiscal year. Fund balance can provide a unit available cash to cover unexpected operating or capital expenses.

Some units use fund balance for a third purpose—to facilitate saving money over time for anticipated capital expenditures. If a unit knows, for example, that it needs to engage in a capital project in the next several years, it might allow its fund balance to grow each year and then appropriate the accumulated moneys to finance the project.

The Local Government Commission (a state agency with oversight responsibility for local government financial management practices) has set a minimum fund balance target for counties and municipalities at 8 percent of general fund expenditures, or roughly one month's operating expenditures. Many counties and municipalities maintain fund balances well in excess of this level, though, to provide needed cash flow and to save moneys for future expenditures—both unexpected and expected.

The benefit of using fund balance to save money for future capital projects is that it provides a local governing board a great deal of flexibility. A governing board may use the accumulated moneys to fund either operating or capital expenditures; it is not locked in to spending its unrestricted fund balance on a particular project or asset. (Fund balance, however, often includes some moneys that are restricted to certain purposes.)[2] For example, assume that a county board of commissioners wishes to expand its solid waste disposal facility in approximately five years. The board begins to purposefully accumulate fund balance toward this goal. In year three, a major economic recession hits the county. The county board may divert the accumulated fund balance to pay for operating expenses or more pressing capital expenses. The only exception is if a portion of the fund balance includes earmarked moneys (by grant or state statute) such that they may be used for only the solid waste disposal facility expansion.

To expend fund balance, a governing board must amend its budget ordinance or a project ordinance to appropriate the fund balance and authorize its expenditure for one or more projects.

Using fund balance as a savings account for future capital expenditures is controversial in some units. Citizens may question why a local unit continues to raise revenue (through taxes and fees) when the unit has significant cash reserves. They may not trust that the governing board ultimately will spend the accumulated fund balance appropriately.

Capital Reserve Funds

Instead of accumulating fund balance, a unit's governing board may establish a capital reserve fund and periodically appropriate money to it. A local government may establish and maintain a capital reserve fund for any purpose for which the unit may issue bonds.[3] And a unit may issue bonds for any capital project in which it is authorized to engage.[4]

To establish a capital reserve fund, a unit's governing board must adopt an ordinance or resolution that states the following:

1. The purposes for which the fund is being created. A board may accumulate moneys for multiple capital projects within a single capital reserve fund, but it must list each project separately.
2. The approximate periods of time during which the moneys will be accumulated and expended for each capital project.

---

2. For a detailed description of the components of fund balance, see Chapter 22, "Accounting, Fiscal Control, and Cash Management."

3. N.C. Gen. Stat. (hereinafter G.S.) § 159-18.

4. G.S. 159-48.

3. The approximate amounts to be accumulated for each capital project.
4. The sources from which moneys for each purpose will be derived. A board must indicate the revenue sources it intends to allocate to the capital reserve fund to finance each project (for example, property tax proceeds, utility fees, local sales and use tax proceeds, grant proceeds, and so forth).

Establishing a capital reserve fund affords a unit's governing board a more formalized mechanism to save moneys for future capital expenditures than using fund balance. Arguably it is more transparent because the governing board must specify the capital projects for which it is accumulating funds. However, appropriating money to a capital reserve fund is a less flexible savings option. Once moneys are appropriated to a capital reserve fund, they must be used for capital expenditures. The moneys may not be used to fund operating expenses, even in an emergency situation.

A governing board must list specific capital projects in the capital reserve fund. It may not simply establish the fund to raise money for general capital expenditures. A governing board, however, may amend its capital reserve fund at any time to add new capital projects, delete capital projects, or change the nature of the capital projects.[5] The board is not required to expend the accumulated moneys for the capital projects initially identified in the reserve fund. For example, assume that a city is growing fairly rapidly. The governing board anticipates needing a water system expansion within the next eight to ten years to accommodate new growth. The board establishes a capital reserve fund and allocates moneys to the fund each year for the water system expansion project. Five years later a major recession hits the city. Growth slows significantly. It now appears that a water system expansion will not be necessary. The governing board could amend the capital reserve fund to delete the water system expansion project and substitute one or more new capital projects, such as road improvements, building maintenance, vehicle acquisition, or a new recreation building. The board, however, could not divert the accumulated revenues in the fund to cover operating expenses.

Special Levies

Local units derive most of their current revenue and savings from general fund revenue sources. The largest source of general fund revenue for both counties and municipalities is the property tax. And the hallmark of property taxation is that all property owners (except those whose property is statutorily exempt) pay the tax, regardless of whether they directly benefit from the projects or services funded with the tax proceeds. Citizens trust their local elected leaders to expend the proceeds for the general benefit of the community. Local elected leaders, however, often feel pressure to provide and fund an ever-increasing number of projects and services while maintaining or reducing the property tax levy. Thus, units have come to rely on targeted revenue generation mechanisms, such as user charges, that are paid only by the citizens or property owners who most directly benefit from specific services or projects. For example, in the past many municipalities funded solid waste services, including disposal facilities, convenience centers, and even curbside pickup, with property tax proceeds. Now these units typically assess user charges to cover some or all of the costs associated with these services. Other common user charges levied by counties and municipalities are for water and wastewater utilities services, recreational and cultural activities, health and mental health services, ambulance services, parking, public transportation, stormwater, cemeteries, and airports. Units also rely on fee revenue to fund certain regulatory activities such as inspections and plan reviews. Generally user charges are feasible for any service that directly benefits individual "users" and can be divided into service units and when the charges can be collected at a reasonable cost.

What about funding capital projects or acquisitions with user charges? Although dividing capital projects or assets into divisible units with defined beneficiaries can be difficult, some units attempt to apportion some of the capital costs associated with a particular service among the users of that service. For example, a unit's water or sewer customer is assessed a monthly or bi-monthly charge for the utility service. The charge typically consists of two components—a usage charge, which varies based on actual usage, and a fixed overhead charge. The fixed charge covers both operating overhead and at least some capital outlay expenses.

5. G.S. 159-19.

In addition to user fees, the law allows for targeted revenue generation through three different types of special levies—special assessments, special taxing districts, and, to a limited extent, impact fees—to fund capital projects.

Special Assessments

A special assessment is a charge levied against property to pay for public improvements that benefit that property. It is neither a user fee nor a tax but it has characteristics of both. Like a user fee, a special assessment is levied in some proportion to the benefit received by the assessed property. However, like a property tax, it is levied against property rather than persons and is a lien on each parcel of real property that is assessed. The lien may be foreclosed in the same manner as property tax liens.[6]

Special assessment authority provides local units a potentially important tool for funding capital projects. The ability to recoup some or all of the costs of a particular project from those property owners who most directly benefit from the project makes sense both financially and politically, at least in some instances. Levying assessments also allows a local government to collect revenue from property owners who benefit from the capital projects but whose properties are exempt from property taxation.[7] And using special assessments as a part of its revenue mix allows a governing board to direct property tax proceeds and other general fund revenues to services or capital projects that benefit a broader subset of the unit's citizens.

Currently, there are two different statutory methods for levying special assessments in North Carolina. Under both methods, a governing board defines an area within a unit that includes all properties that will directly benefit from a certain capital project. And under both methods a unit must follow a detailed statutory process to determine and impose the assessments.[8]

Traditional Special Assessment Method

The traditional special assessment method has not been widely used by North Carolina local governments due to a number of factors. The authority to levy assessments is limited to only a few categories of projects.[9] And the process to levy the assessments is fairly onerous. A local unit must front all of the costs of the project, which can be high. Only after a project is complete may a unit levy the assessments, and assessments often are paid in installments over a number of years (up to ten). Some local units have set up special assessment revolving funds, using yearly special assessment payments from former projects to fund new projects. Establishing a sufficient revolving fund, however, often takes several years.

For most projects, a unit's governing board may levy assessments within its own discretion. Street and sidewalk projects first require that the unit receive a petition signed by a certain percentage of affected property owners.[10] The amount of each assessment must bear some relationship to the amount of benefit that accrues to the assessed property.

---

6. For more information on enforcing property tax liens, see Chapter 19, "The Property Tax."

7. A unit may not levy assessments on state or federal government property, however, without the consent of the property owner.

8. For a detailed exposition of the authority, procedures, and limitations of each method, see Kara A. Millonzi, "An Overview of Special Assessment Bond Authority in North Carolina," *Local Finance Bulletin* No. 40 (Nov. 2009), http://sogpubs.unc.edu/electronicversions/pdfs/lfb40.pdf; see also Kara Millonzi, "Special Assessments for Economic Development Projects," *Coates' Canons: NC Local Government Law Blog* (UNC School of Goverment, Oct. 31, 2013), http://canons.sog.unc.edu/?p=7392.

9. Counties may levy assessments to fund water systems, sewage collection and disposal, beach erosion control and flood and hurricane protection, watershed improvement, drainage, water resources development projects, local costs of Department of Transportation improvements to subdivision and residential streets outside municipalities, and streetlight maintenance. G.S. 153A-185. Municipalities may levy assessments to finance public improvements involving streets, sidewalks, water systems, sewage collection and disposal systems, storm sewer and drainage systems, and beach erosion control and flood and hurricane protection. G.S. 160A-216.

10. Before a county may fund street improvements, it must first receive a petition signed by at least 75 percent of the owners of property to be assessed, who represent at least 75 percent of the lineal feet of frontage of the lands abutting on the street or portion of the street to be improved. G.S. 153A-205. Similarly, for street and sidewalk improvements, a city must receive a petition signed by a majority of the owners of property to be assessed, who represent at least a majority of all the lineal feet of frontage of the lands abutting on the street or portion of the street to be improved. G.S. 160A-217.

The most common basis of assessment is front footage: each property is assessed on a uniform rate per foot of property that abuts on the project. Other common bases include the size of the area benefitted and the value added to the property because of the improvement. A unit also may set up benefit zones—setting different assessment rates in each zone according to the degree of benefit to the properties in the zone.

Newer Assessment Method

During the 2008 and 2009 legislative sessions, the General Assembly temporarily bestowed the newer special assessment authority—entitled special assessments for critical infrastructure needs—on counties and municipalities to fund a wide range of capital projects.[11] (The legislature recently extended the authority for the newer assessment method to July 2015.)

The purpose of the newer authority, modeled on legislation from other states, is to help local units fund public infrastructure projects that benefit new private development. It allows a unit to impose assessments, with payments spread out over a period of years, with the expectation that all or at least a majority of the assessments will be paid by the eventual property owners (instead of the developer or the local government). As with traditional assessments, the unit can front the costs of the project and recoup its investment over time with the yearly assessment payments. Alternatively, under the newer assessment method the unit may be able to borrow money, pledging the assessment revenue as security, and use the yearly assessment payments to meet its debt service obligations.

Conceptually, the newer special assessment authority functions much like an impact fee. An impact fee is imposed on new development to pay for infrastructure costs necessitated by the new development. The fees usually are assessed on developers upon the issuance of a building permit. Special assessments also may be used to fund infrastructure projects necessitated by new development. Unlike an impact fee, the newer assessment method imposes little to no costs on the developer. Most of the payments are collected once the development is completed (assuming, of course, the development occurs as expected).

A much broader array of public infrastructure projects may be funded through the newer special assessment method than through the traditional method. The authorized projects are almost exclusively government infrastructure projects, ranging from constructing and maintaining public roads to building public schools. The list includes most capital projects in which a unit is authorized to engage.[12] Before imposing any assessments under the newer method, however, a unit must receive a petition signed by a majority of owners of property to be assessed, representing at least 66 percent of the value of the property to be assessed.[13]

A potential benefit of the newer assessment method is that it allows a unit to borrow money to front the costs of a project. The unit pledges the assessment revenue as security for the loan and uses the revenue to make its yearly debt service payments (special assessment–backed revenue bonds). Thus, the unit can avoid committing any of its funds to the project.

Of course, there is a risk that the unit will not be able to collect all of the assessment revenue needed to meet the debt service obligations. The assessments are a lien on the properties assessed, and a unit has the same remedies available to collect delinquent assessments as it does delinquent property taxes. (The bonds likely will include a covenant requiring the unit to use all available collection remedies in the case of nonpayment by a property owner. This may pose some cost to the unit.) Despite the robust collection authority, the debt is relatively risky for investors. And the riskier the debt is, the more expensive the borrowing. Thus, special assessment–backed revenue bonds often carry a very high rate of interest.

---

11. *See* S.L. 2008-165; S.L. 2009-525.

12. *See* G.S. 153A-210.2 (counties); G.S. 160A-239.2 (cities). For a list of authorized capital projects for counties and cities, see Kara A. Millonzi, "An Overview of Special Assessment Bond Authority in North Carolina," *Local Finance Bulletin* No. 40 (Nov. 2009), http://sogpubs.unc.edu/electronicversions/pdfs/lfb40.pdf.

13. G.S. 160A-239.3 (cities); G.S. 153A-210.3 (counties).

Special Taxing Districts

Another targeted revenue generation mechanism available to a local unit to fund capital projects is to establish one or more special taxing districts. With one exception the state constitution requires that a local government's property tax rates be uniform throughout the jurisdiction. The constitution, however, authorizes the General Assembly to allow a local government to carve out one or more areas within the unit as service districts. The unit may levy a property tax in each district additional to the countywide or municipalwide property taxes and use the proceeds to provide services or fund capital projects in each district.

County and Municipal Service Districts

The General Assembly has authorized counties and cities to establish service districts,[14] which are defined areas in the unit in which additional property tax rates can be imposed to fund certain services and capital projects. Counties are authorized to define a service district for the following functions:[15]

- Beach erosion and flood and hurricane protection
- Fire protection
- Recreation
- Sewage collection and disposal
- Solid waste collection and disposal
- Water supply and distribution
- Ambulance and rescue services
- Watershed improvement, drainage, and water resources development
- Cemeteries

And municipalities may establish a service district for any of the following functions:[16]

- Beach erosion and flood and hurricane protection
- Downtown revitalization projects
- Urban area revitalization projects
- Transit-oriented development projects
- Drainage projects
- Sewage collection and disposal systems
- Off-street parking facilities
- Watershed improvement, drainage, and water resources development projects

Counties typically use service districts to fund the capital and operational expenses of fire and rescue services.[17] Cities most often use service districts to fund projects and programs in their central downtown areas.[18]

Taxing Authority in Service District

A service district is in no way a separate unit of government. It is simply a geographic designation—a defined part of a county or municipality in which the government levies an extra property tax and provides extra services or undertakes capital projects that more directly benefit the properties within the district. Service district taxes are subject to the same exemptions and exclusions as the general property taxes (that is, property that is exempt from property taxes also is exempt from service district taxes).

---

14. G.S. 160A, Art. 23 (cities); G.S. 153A, Art. 16 (counties).

15. G.S. 153A-301.

16. G.S. 160A-536.

17. For more information on taxing districts for fire services, see Kara A. Millonzi, "County Funding for Fire Services in North Carolina," *Local Finance Bulletin* No. 43 (May 2011), http://sogpubs.unc.edu/electronicversions/pdfs/lfb43.pdf.

18. For more information on taxing districts for downtown revitalization, see Kara Millonzi, "A Guide to Business Improvement Districts in North Carolina," *Coates' Canons: NC Local Government Law Blog* (UNC School of Government, Apr. 1, 2010), http://canons.sog.unc.edu/?p=2146.

A unit's governing board sets the service district tax rate each year in its annual budget ordinance. The rate, combined with the unit's general property tax rate, may not exceed $1.50 per $100 assessed valuation of property in the district, unless the unit's voters have approved a higher maximum rate.

All of the revenue generated by the service district tax must be used to provide the services or undertake the capital projects in the district. A unit also may supplement the district tax revenue with other unrestricted revenues. The district tax proceeds and any other moneys allocated to the district may not be diverted to other purposes.

Process for Establishing a Service District

A service district is defined by simple action of the governing board. No petition or voter referendum is required to create it, although the governing board must hold a public hearing. The board, however, must find that the district needs the proposed services or projects to a demonstrably greater extent than the rest of the unit. A district generally must become effective at the beginning of a fiscal year, and the unit must "provide, maintain, or let contracts for" the services or projects within a reasonable time, not to exceed one year after the service district tax is levied.[19]

Additional Special Taxing Districts

In addition to the service district authority, counties also are allowed to set up special taxing districts for rural fire protection services,[20] public schools,[21] and water and sewer services.[22] These taxing districts provide counties an additional mechanism to fund both capital and operating expenses associated with the specified functions.

Impact Fees

As discussed above, impact fees are charges assessed on new development to pay for public infrastructure projects necessary to support the new development. North Carolina local governments do not have authority under general law to impose impact fees. A handful of units have received authority through local legislation.

Borrowing Money

The most common method to finance large or costly capital projects is to borrow money. Neither current revenues nor savings nor even special levies are likely to generate sufficient revenues to finance a significant construction project or capital acquisition without borrowed funds. Borrowing money allows a local government to leverage future revenue streams—providing the unit cash in the short term that is repaid over time.

When a local unit borrows money, it has a contract with its lenders. The contract typically is referred to as a debt instrument or a debt security. Under that contract, the local unit agrees to pay the principal and the interest on the loan as they come due and to honor any other promises it has made as part of the loan transaction. This contract is enforceable by a lender should the local government breach any obligation.

The traditional debt instrument through which a local government borrows money is the issuance of bonds. A bond itself is simply an evidence of a debt. Although bonds remain a common loan form, North Carolina local governments also are authorized to borrow money through a variety of transactional structures. In fact, five legally authorized methods are available to local units to borrow money for most capital projects: general obligation bonds, revenue bonds, special obligation bonds, project development financings, and installment financings.

19. G.S. 160A-540(a) (cities); G.S. 153A-305(a) (counties).

20. G.S. Ch. 69.

21. G.S. Ch. 115C, Art. 36.

22. G.S. Ch. 162A, Art. 6.

Table 21.2 Authorized Securities for Borrowing Transactions

	General Obligation Bonds	Revenue Bonds	Special Obligation Bonds	Project Development Financing Bonds	Installment Financings
Primary Security	• Full faith and credit (taxing power)	• Revenues generated by revenue-generating asset or system	• Any unrestricted revenues other than unit-levied taxes	• Incremental increase in property tax revenue within defined area due to new private development	• Asset or part of asset being financed
Authorized Secondary Securities	• Revenues generated by revenue-generating asset or system	• Asset or part of asset being financed	• Asset or part of asset being financed	• Asset or part of asset being financed • Any unrestricted revenues other than unit-levied taxes • Special assessments	

Security

The major distinguishing feature among the different methods is the nature of primary security pledged by the unit. The most fundamental promise made when a local unit borrows money is to pay the money back. Closely associated with and reinforcing this promise is the pledge or the designation of one or more forms of security. The security for a debt is defined by reference to the contractual rights of the lender—what the lender can require the borrowing government to do, or to give up, should it fail to repay the loan. If the government does not repay its loan, the lender may look to the security to compel repayment or otherwise protect itself.

The security for a borrowing affects what form the loan transaction takes, whether voter approval is required, whether Local Government Commission (LGC) approval is required, and how the bond will be marketed and at what cost.

Each of the five authorized borrowing methods involves a distinct primary security pledge. For most of the borrowings, however, state law allows secondary security pledges. Pledging additional security may be necessary to satisfy lenders and make the borrowing feasible, or more affordable, for the unit. Table 21.2 lists the primary security and additional authorized securities that may be pledged by a unit for each of the authorized debt structures.

The primary securities for each borrowing transaction are discussed in more detail below.

Entities Involved

When a unit borrows money, it typically requires the assistance of a variety of outside entities, including bond counsel, financial advisors, underwriters, and rating agencies. And most local government borrowings are subject to approval by the state's LGC. Not all borrowings involve these entities, however; local governments complete many simple, lower dollar borrowings without any outside guidance or oversight.

Bond Counsel

Bond counsel is a lawyer hired by the local unit to assist in many debt authorization and issuance processes. Bond counsel is one of the key participants involved with issuing debt and is usually selected in the very early stages of the process. The essential role of bond counsel is to issue a legal opinion as to the validity of the bond offering. A typical opinion letter will describe the bond issue in detail. It will then state that in the bond counsel's judgment the bonds are valid and binding obligations of the borrowing unit. The opinion will describe the nature of the security behind the debt. Finally, the opinion indicates the status under the federal tax laws of interest being paid on the debt by the local government and may also indicate other aspects of the taxability of the debt securities or any income derived from holding the securities.

Bond counsel often also performs other functions in relation to the issuance, including preparing bond documents and shepherding the government through the myriad process requirements involved in the issuance.

Anytime a unit is issuing bonds—general obligation bonds, special obligation bonds, revenue bonds, or project development bonds—bond counsel will necessarily be involved. Bond counsel also often is involved in more complicated installment financings.

Financial Advisor

A financial advisor advocates for the borrowing government and provides its officials the information necessary to make informed decisions. A financial advisor often advises the unit on how to structure the financing to get the best interest rate and may coordinate the bond issuance process. In North Carolina the LGC often functions as the financial advisor for local units.

Underwriter

A bond underwriter is a financial institution that purchases a new issue of municipal securities for resale. The underwriter may acquire the bonds either by negotiation with the borrowing unit or by award on the basis of a competitive bidding. The underwriter essentially functions as a middleman in the borrowing transaction, bringing together the borrowing government and the investors who ultimately purchase the government's bonds or certificates of participation. General obligation bond sales typically are conducted competitively, with underwriting firms submitting sealed bids to buy the bonds. In a public sale the underwriter is the formal lender or buyer of the securities; the title to the securities passes to that entity. The underwriter bears the risk of finding a sufficient number of investors to whom to sell the securities. Other bond sales (revenue bonds, special obligation bonds, project development bonds) and certificates of participation generally are sold by negotiation. The unit selects one or more underwriters at the beginning of the process and negotiates the structure of the financing and the sales price with the underwriters.

Rating Agencies

When a unit sells bonds publicly, it is subject to considerably more extensive disclosure requirements than a private placement requires. Additionally, as a practical matter, securities that are publicly sold must be rated. Bond ratings play a crucial role in the marketing of bonds. Many investors, particularly individuals, cannot personally investigate the creditworthiness of a government's securities. Bond ratings are an accepted indication of the creditworthiness of a particular issuance. The bond rating often is the single most important factor affecting the interest cost on bonds.

Three national agencies rate local government bonds and certificates of participation for the national market—Moody's Investors Service, Standard & Poor's, and Fitch Ratings. Additionally, a private North Carolina agency, the North Carolina Municipal Council, rates each general obligation issue of local governments in the state. Each agency uses a slightly different formula for determining its ratings. All of the agencies assess the following factors—the economy; the particular debt structure; the unit's financial condition; the unit's demographic factors; the management practices of the governing body and administration; and, if applicable, the user charges supporting the issuance and any covenants and other protections offered by the bond documents.

Local Government Commission

The Local Government Commission is a nine-member body responsible for fiscal oversight of local governments and public authorities in North Carolina.[23] Additionally, the LGC approves most local government borrowings and sells bonds on a unit's behalf. All general obligation bonds, revenue bonds, special obligation bonds, and project development bonds must be approved by the LGC. The same is true of some installment financings, certain leases, and other financial

23. *See* G.S. 159-3.

agreements.[24] A unit must determine if LGC approval is mandated by statute for its proposed borrowing transaction because if approval is required and a unit fails to obtain it, the entire borrowing transaction is void.

In reviewing proposed issuances, the LGC must consider statutory criteria, which vary somewhat depending on the type of borrowing. Generally, however, the LGC must determine if the amount being borrowed, when added to the existing debt of the unit and at the rate of interest the unit probably will have to pay, is an amount the unit can afford.

LGC staff members will work with a unit from the outset of the borrowing process to help local officials determine the best borrowing method for the particular project being funded. The staff also will identify any deficiencies in the unit's financials or management practices that might prevent the unit from receiving commission approval. Thus, local officials should contact LGC staff very early in the unit's internal process—preferably immediately after the scope of the capital project is determined and preliminary engineering studies are completed.

Joint Legislative Committee on Local Government

In 2011 the General Assembly created the Joint Legislative Committee on Local Government as a standing interim legislative study committee.[25] The purpose of the committee, among other things, is to review and monitor local government capital projects that both require approval by the LGC and that debt exceeding $1 million be issued. The committee's directive does not apply to capital projects related to schools, jails, courthouses, and administrative buildings. It also does not apply to the re-funding of existing debt. Furthermore, the committee's authority is limited to reviewing and monitoring the capital projects and debt issuances within its purview; it is not authorized to approve or reject a capital project or financing.

The committee has promulgated guidelines to carry out its statutory responsibility.[26] A local unit seeking approval from the LGC to borrow money for a capital project subject to the committee's oversight must submit a letter to the committee at least forty-five days prior to the unit's formal presentation before the LGC. The letter must include (1) a description of the project, (2) the debt requirements of the project, (3) the means of financing the project, and (4) the source or sources of repayment for project costs.

The committee may meet at the discretion of its chairs to review a proposed capital project. It may send a letter of objection or support to the LGC for a particular project and it may ask to speak at an LGC meeting on a particular project. The committee also may make periodic reports and recommendations to the General Assembly for proposed new legislation related to local government debt authority.

Types of Authorized Debt

The five debt mechanisms available to local governments are general obligation bonds, revenue bonds, special obligation bonds, project development financings, and installment financings. (A unit has some limited additional borrowing authority under certain circumstances.) The following provides a brief summary of each debt mechanism, including the primary security, the projects which may be funded, and any significant limitations.

General Obligation Bonds

Security and Authority

The strongest form of security a county or city can pledge for debt is the unit's full faith and credit, making the debt a general obligation of the borrowing unit. All of the resources of that government stand behind such a pledge, but

24. For more information on the types of financial agreements subject to LGC approval, see Kara Millonzi, "Local Government Commission (LGC) Approval of Contracts, Leases, and Other (Non-Debt) Financing Agreements," *Coates' Canons: NC Local Government Law Blog* (UNC School of Government, Aug. 9, 2012), http://canons.sog.unc.edu/?p=6786.

25. S.L. 2011-291.

26. Copies of the guidelines and letters submitted to the committee by local governments are available at www.ncleg.net/gascripts/DocumentSites/browseDocSite.asp?nID=159&sFolderName=\12-09-2013.

specifically, a full-faith-and-credit pledge of a North Carolina county or city is a promise to levy whatever amount of property tax is necessary to repay the debt.[27]

The primary authority to incur a general obligation debt is the Local Government Bond Act,[28] which authorizes the issuance of general obligation (GO) bonds. State law specifies the types of capital projects a county or city may fund with GO bonds, which includes most, if not all, capital projects in which a unit is authorized to engage.[29]

Requirements and Limitations

The legal authority to issue GO bonds is very broad. Practically it is much more limited, as the North Carolina Constitution generally requires that a unit hold a successful voter referendum before pledging its full faith and credit.[30] State law also places a limit on the amount of outstanding GO debt a unit may have at any one time, referred to as the net debt limit. Finally, all GO borrowings must be approved by the LGC.

Voter Approval Requirement

The voter approval requirement can be a significant hurdle to issuing GO bonds. Voters, for example, are unlikely to vote for controversial or less popular projects such as jails or landfills. Referenda for even popular projects, such as schools or parks, sometimes fail. Thus, although issuing GO bonds is the simplest form of borrowing, and generally the cheapest, local units often look to one of the other authorized borrowing mechanisms to avoid the voter approval requirement. (The state constitution does not require voter approval if any other form of security is used, and therefore voter approval is never necessary for loans secured by the other authorized borrowing methods.)

Voter approval is not always necessary for GO bonds. The constitution carves out a few exceptions, the most significant of which are re-funding bonds and two-thirds bonds.[31]

Net Debt Limitation

The other restriction on issuing GO bonds is the net debt limitation. A proposed GO borrowing (as well as a proposed installment financing) contract must satisfy this requirement. The limitation recognizes that both GO bonds and installment financings are retired with property tax proceeds, and it therefore restricts the net debt of a unit to 8 percent of the appraised value of property subject to taxation by the unit. Net debt is calculated by taking gross GO and installment financing debt and then deducting the amount of this debt that in most units is repaid from sources other than the property tax. There is a fairly complicated statutory formula for both calculating gross debt and determining the appropriate deductions.[32]

For most local units, the net debt limitation is more of a theoretical than an actual limitation. The net debt of any unit rarely exceeds 2 percent.

State Approval

All GO bond issuances must be approved by the LGC. Typically commission staff will meet with unit representatives to aid in structuring the deal and advise the unit on the likelihood of commission approval. When reviewing a GO bond issuance, the commission considers a number of factors to help it determine if the unit will be able to repay the debt. Such factors include the unit's outstanding debt, its debt and financial management practices, its tax base and the projected tax rates needed to repay the debt, and the proposed interest rates and total cost of the borrowing.[33]

---

27. By law, a general obligation pledge is not subject to the $1.50 per $100 valuation property tax rate limitation. G.S. 153A-149(b)(2) (counties); G.S. 160A-209(b)(1) (cities). Thus, a general obligation pledge is a pledge of the unlimited taxing power.

28. G.S. Ch. 159, Art. 4.

29. *See* G.S. 159-48.

30. N.C. Const. art. V, § 4(2).

31. For a list of all the purposes for which a local government may issue GO bonds without voter approval, see N.C. Const. art. V, § 4(2), and G.S. 159-49.

32. G.S. 159-55.

33. G.S. 159-52.

Revenue Bonds

Security and Authority

The primary security for a revenue bond is the revenue generated by the financed asset or the system of which the financed asset becomes a part. By law such a pledge creates a lien on the pledged revenues in favor of the bondholders, and normally the bondholders have the contractual right to demand an increase in the user charges generating the revenues if those revenues prove inadequate to service the debt. If the revenue pledge is the only security, however, the bondholders have no right to demand payment from any other source, or to require an increase in taxes, if facility or system revenues remain inadequate even after charges are increased. Although typically a security pledge represents the rights of a lender or investor in the event of a default by the borrowing unit, state law restricts the funds a unit may use to meet its revenue bond debt service payments to the pledged security.[34] Thus, a unit may make its principal and interest payments from only the revenues pledged as security for the loan.

A variety of statutes permit counties to borrow money and secure the loan by a pledge of the asset- or system-generated revenues. The principal statute is the State and Local Government Revenue Bond Act,[35] which authorizes the issuance of revenue bonds. Revenue bonds are most commonly issued to fund water and sewer utility projects, although they may legally fund a variety of other revenue-generating capital assets, including gas facilities, solid waste facilities, parking, marine facilities, auditoriums, convention centers, economic development, electric facilities, public transportation, airports, hospitals, stadiums, recreation facilities, and stormwater drainage.[36] As discussed above, a unit also may pledge special assessments levied under the newer special assessment authority as security for revenue bonds used to finance specially assessed projects.

Requirements and Limitations

A vote of the people is not required to issue revenue bonds.[37] However, other requirements effectively limit the types of projects revenue bonds may be issued to fund. The requirements are reflected in covenants. Revenue bonds also are subject to LGC approval.

Covenants

Because the security for the debt is revenue from the debt-financed asset, or the system of which it is a part, lenders are naturally concerned about the construction, operation, and continued health of the financed asset or system. This concern is expressed through a series of covenants, or promises, the borrowing government makes to the lenders as part of the loan transaction. The most fundamental of these is the rate covenant, under which the unit promises to set and maintain the rates, fees, and charges of the revenue-producing facility or system so that net revenues will exceed annual debt service requirements by some fixed amount or percentage. For example, a common requirement is that the rate structure generate annual net revenues at some specified level—usually between 120 and 150 percent—of either the current year's debt service requirements or the maximum annual debt service requirements during the life of the loan. This margin of safety required by the rate covenant is referred to as times-coverage of the loan. The times-coverage requirement serves as a practical limitation on the types of projects that may be funded with this loan structure.

Because prospective investors typically will want independent verification that revenues will be adequate to service the bonds, a borrowing government normally is expected to commission a feasibility study by a consulting engineer or another independent professional. The professional will evaluate the demand for the services the financed facility or system will provide, look at likely operating costs, and suggest the net revenue stream likely to result.

Other common covenants require the unit to maintain a debt service reserve fund and to have borrowed funds maintained by an independent trustee who must authorize any disbursements.[38]

---

34. G.S. 159-94.

35. G.S. Ch. 159, Art. 5. G.S. 159-61 permits any government authorized to issue revenue bonds to also issue revenue bond anticipation notes.

36. *See* G.S. 159-83.

37. If a unit covenants or otherwise agrees to effectively pledge its taxing power as additional security for a revenue bond, the unit must first hold a voter referendum. *See* G.S. 159-97.

38. G.S. 159-89 lists authorized covenants.

State Approval

All revenue bonds must be approved by the LGC. As with GO bonds, the commission will consider the feasibility of the bond issuance and the likely ability of the unit to repay the loan.

Special Obligation Bonds

Security and Authority

A special obligation is secured by a pledge of any revenue source or asset available to the borrowing government, except the unit's taxing power. In a broad sense a revenue bond is a type of special obligation bond. The term special obligation, as used in North Carolina, however, refers to debts secured by something other than (or in addition to) revenues from the asset or system being financed. For example, a county might pledge proceeds from fees charged for building rentals or from special assessments. A county could not pledge local sales tax, animal tax, privilege license tax, or property tax proceeds because these are locally levied taxes.

The authority to issue special obligation (SO) bonds is very limited. Section 159I-30 of the North Carolina General Statutes (hereinafter G.S.) permits a county or city to issue SO bonds for solid waste projects, water projects, and wastewater projects.[39] The statute also allows a city to issue SO bonds for any project for which a city is authorized to create a municipal service district.[40]

Requirements and Limitations

As with revenue bonds, there is no statutory process for issuing SO bonds. Because the debt market perceives the security for special obligation debt as weaker than that for general obligation debt, the market normally demands of special obligation debt some of the same safeguards demanded of revenue bonds. And the process for issuing SO bonds is similar to that for issuing revenue bonds.

The LGC must approve all SO bond issuances. The commission may consider the same criteria as it does for a GO bond issuance, a revenue bond issuance, or both.[41]

Project Development Financings

Security and Authority

The newest form of borrowing available to North Carolina counties and cities is project development financing.[42] Project development financing is structurally equivalent to a type of borrowing prevalent in other states known as tax increment financing, or TIF. In fact, this form of borrowing is often referred to as TIF or TIF bonds by practitioners in this state.

Project development financing is a method of increasing the overall property value in a currently blighted, depressed, or underdeveloped area within a county or city. A unit borrows money to fund public improvements within the designated area (development district) with the goal of attracting private investment. The debt incurred by funding the improvements is secured and repaid by tax increment revenue—the additional property taxes resulting from the district's new development. The Project Development Financing Act[43] permits counties and cities to issue project development financing bonds and to use the proceeds for many, but not all, of the purposes for which either taxing unit

39. G.S. 159I-13 also permits a local unit that borrows money from the state's Solid Waste Management Loan Fund to secure the loan, among other ways, from "any available source or sources of revenue" as long as the pledge "does not constitute a pledge of the [borrowing] unit's taxing power."

40. See note 16 and accompanying text for a list of municipal service district purposes.

41. G.S. 159I-30.

42. For more detailed information on project development financings, see William C. Rivenbark, Shea Riggsbee Denning, and Kara A. Millonzi, "2007 Legislation Expands Scope of Project Development Financing in North Carolina," *Local Finance Bulletin* No. 36 (Nov. 2007), http://sogpubs.unc.edu/electronicversions/pdfs/lfb36.pdf.

43. G.S. Ch. 159, Art. 6.

may issue GO bonds.[44] The act also allows local governments to use the proceeds for any service or facility authorized to be provided in a municipal service district, although no district actually need be created.

Requirements and Limitations

There are detailed procedure requirements for issuing project development bonds. A unit must define a financing district, adopt a financing plan, and secure various approvals from governmental entities.

Financing District

At the outset of a project development financing project, a county or city must establish a development financing district. The total land area within this district may not exceed 5 percent of the total land area of the taxing unit.[45] Counties also are specifically prohibited from including in a development financing district land located within a city at the time the district is created, although a county and city may jointly agree to create such a district.[46] In the absence of such an agreement, any land included in a development financing district established by a city that issues debt instruments to be repaid from the incremental valuation does not count against the 5 percent of unincorporated land in that county that may be included in a development financing district.[47] If a county and city jointly create a development financing district, with each unit pledging its incremental tax revenue in support thereof, the area included within the district likely counts against the 5 percent limit for both the county and the city.

Financing Plan and County Approval

Once it identifies the development financing district, a unit must adopt a financing plan. Among other things, the plan must describe the proposed public and private development, the costs of the public projects, and the projected increase in the assessed valuation in the district due to the private development.[48]

The unit must hold a public hearing on the proposed financing plan.[49] After the public hearing, a county board may approve the plan, with or without amendment, unless the plan has been disapproved by the secretary of the Department of Environment and Natural Resources (DENR). A city board has an additional procedural requirement. It must provide notice to the governing board of each county in which the proposed district is located.[50] The county governing boards have twenty-eight days to disapprove the plan. If the plan is not disapproved by the county boards, the city board may proceed to adopt it.

State Approval

The plan and district do not become effective until the LGC approves the issuance of project development financing bonds for the district.

Two other state agencies must approve some project development financings. If a development financing plan involves the construction and operation of a new manufacturing facility, the plan must be submitted to the secretary of DENR. The secretary's review will determine whether the facility will have a materially adverse effect on the environment and whether the company that will operate the facility has previously complied with federal and state environmental laws and regulations.[51]

The plan also must be submitted to the secretary of Commerce. The secretary must certify that the average weekly manufacturing wage required by the plan to be paid to the employees of the initial users of the proposed new manufacturing facility is either above the average weekly manufacturing wage in the county in which the district is located

---

44. G.S. 159-103. For a list of authorized projects, see UNC School of Government, "Tax Increment Financing in North Carolina: Frequently Asked Questions," www.sog.unc.edu/node/1100.

45. G.S. 158-7.3(c); G.S. 160A-515.1(b).

46. G.S. 158-7.3(c); G.S. 159-107(e).

47. Conversely, land in a county district subsequently annexed by a city does not count against the city's 5 percent limit unless the county and city have entered into an increment agreement; in such an agreement, the city agrees that city taxes collected on part or all of the incremental valuation in the district will be paid into the reserve increment fund for the district. G.S. 159-107(e).

48. G.S. 158-7.3(d); G.S. 160A-515.1(c).

49. The unit must publish notice of the public hearing in a newspaper of general circulation and mail notice to all affected property owners in the proposed district.

50. G.S. 160A-515.1(e).

51. G.S. 158-7.3(g); G.S. 160A-515.1(f).

or not less than 10 percent above the average weekly manufacturing wage paid in the state.[52] The secretary may exempt a facility if certain criteria are met.

Bond Anticipation Notes

Sometimes a local unit will authorize a bond issue (for GO, revenue, SO, or project development bonds) but will not wish to borrow the full sum at one time. Alternatively, if the local government plans to sell the bonds to USDA Rural Development, the bond sale will not occur until the project is close to fully constructed. In either case the government might decide to borrow, pursuant to the bond authorization, on a short-term basis. If it does so, it will issue bond anticipation notes (BANs).[53] These are short-term notes, usually maturing in a year's time, that are primarily secured by the proceeds of the eventual bond issue itself. Because such notes are issued in anticipation of the eventual issuance of bonds, there is no separate authorization process for the notes. The county or city must, however, receive the approval of the LGC before the notes are issued, and the commission will sell the notes on the government's behalf.[54]

Installment Financings

Security and Authority

The final borrowing method, installment financing, is the borrowing structure most commonly used by North Carolina local governments. It differs from the other mechanisms in that it often does not involve the issuance of bonds. Both counties and municipalities (along with several other local entities) are authorized to borrow money by entering into installment financing agreements.[55] An installment finance agreement is a loan transaction in which a local government borrows money to finance or refinance the purchase of a capital asset (real or personal property) or the construction or repair of fixtures or improvements on real property owned by the local unit.[56]

The unit of local government must grant a security interest in the asset that is being purchased or in the real property or fixtures and improvements to that real property (or both) being financed with the borrowed funds. A unit of local government may not grant a security interest in real or personal property that is not part of the financing transaction. To illustrate, take a routine construction project of a maintenance garage that will be located on property owned by a county or municipality. The government may borrow money to finance the cost of constructing the maintenance garage and may pledge as security the garage structure itself or the real property on which the garage is built (or both). The unit may not pledge as security any other property it owns, however, such as the city hall or county library. There are no specific limitations on what revenue may be used to make the installment payments. A local government is free to use any unrestricted funds to repay the debt.

The authority for this type of borrowing transaction, as well as the procedural requirements and limitations, is found in a single statute—G.S. 160A-20. Thus, installment financings often are referred to as 160A-20s.

Under a proper installment financing contract, a unit must take legal title to the property or the fixture or improvement at the outset of the contract. The vendor, bank, or other entity that provides the financing for the project may

---

52. G.S. 158-7.3; G.S. 160A-515.1.

53. G.S. Chapter 159, Art. 9, Part I, authorizes a unit to issue GO bond anticipation notes, and G.S. 159G-18 authorizes GO debt instruments. However, a unit must follow the procedures and meet the requirements of the Local Government Bond Act before it issues either GO bond anticipation notes or GO debt instruments.

54. G.S. 159-165.

55. G.S. 160A-20. G.S. 160A-20(h) lists the local entities (including cities, counties, water and sewer authorities, sanitary districts, local airport authorities, area mental health authorities, and regional transportation authorities) authorized to enter into installment-purchase contracts (collectively referred to as "unit of local government"). Additionally, G.S. 115C-528 provides (more limited) authority for local school administrative units to enter into installment-purchase agreements for certain purposes.

56. Specifically, G.S. 160A-20 allows a unit of local government to "purchase, or finance or refinance the purchase of, real or personal property by installment contracts that create in some or all of the property purchased a security interest to secure payment of the purchase price . . . ." The statute also allows an authorized entity to "finance or refinance the construction or repair of fixtures or improvements on real property by contracts that create in some or all of the fixtures or improvements, or in all or some portion of the property on which the fixtures or improvements are located, or in both, a security interest to secure repayment of moneys advanced or made available for the construction or repair."

not take title to the asset at the time of purchase and keep the title until the loan is repaid. For example, if a county or municipality purchases a vehicle and procures vendor financing over a five-year term, the unit of government must take title to the vehicle when it takes possession of the vehicle. If the vendor owns the car until the end of the five-year term (when the loan is repaid), the financing agreement is not an authorized installment financing under G.S. 160A-20. Similarly, an option to purchase at the end of a lease term is not sufficient to satisfy the requirements of G.S. 160A-20.

Forms of Installment Financings

Vendor Financing

Installment finance contracts generally take one of three basic forms. The simplest form is commonly referred to as vendor financing. The parties enter into a contract under which the vendor conveys the equipment or property to the local government and the local government promises to pay for the equipment or property through a series of installment payments. The contract gives the vendor a lien on the equipment or a deed of trust on the property to secure the government's payment obligations under the contract. If the government defaults under the contract, the vendor may repossess the equipment or foreclose on the property.

Lending Institution Contracts

A more common form of an installment finance contract transaction involves two different contracts—one between the unit of government and the vendor or contractor and one between the unit of local government and the lending institution. The government enters into a purchase contract with a vendor or contractor, who is paid in full upon delivery of the asset or completion of the construction project. The government enters into a separate installment finance contract with a financial institution; under this contract the institution provides the moneys to pay the vendor or the contractor and the local government agrees to repay those moneys in installments with interest. The financial institution takes a security interest in the asset being purchased or constructed (or the land on which it is constructed) to secure the government's payment obligations under the installment finance contract.

Bond Market Financing

Most installment finance contracts are arranged with a single bank or financial institution. If the project is particularly large or if the local government has borrowed a significant amount of money during the current calendar year, however, a single institution usually is unwilling to make the loan and retain it within its loan portfolio. This is because of certain federal tax advantages for a financial institution that loans money to a government that borrows less than $10 million within a calendar year. Governments that fall below this borrowing threshold (and meet certain other criteria) are classified as bank qualified. If a local government is not bank qualified, it typically turns to the bond market—the installment financing is publicly sold. That is, rather than the government borrowing the money from a single bank or vendor, the loan is sold to individual investors through the issuance of limited obligation bonds (LOBs) (formerly certificates of participation (COPs)). The actual form of the installment finance transaction is very complicated.

Requirements and Limitations

A local government must satisfy some constitutional and statutory requirements before entering into an installment financing contract. These requirements apply no matter what form the installment finance transaction takes (simple installment financing COPs, or LOBs).

Non-appropriation Clause

An installment purchase contract must include a non-appropriation clause. The clause makes all loan repayment obligations subject to yearly appropriation decisions by the unit's governing board. The non-appropriation clause is necessary to avoid an inadvertent pledge of the unit's taxing power. Such a pledge, even a limited pledge, likely would violate the North Carolina Constitution's prohibition against contracting debts secured by a pledge of a unit's faith and credit without obtaining voter approval.[57] G.S. 160A-20 further provides that "no deficiency judgment may be rendered against any unit of local government in any action for breach" of an installment finance contract.

57. *See generally* Wayne Cnty. Citizens Ass'n v. Wayne Cnty. Bd. of Comm'rs, 328 N.C. 24 (1991).

Figure 21.1 Installment Financings Subject to LGC Approval

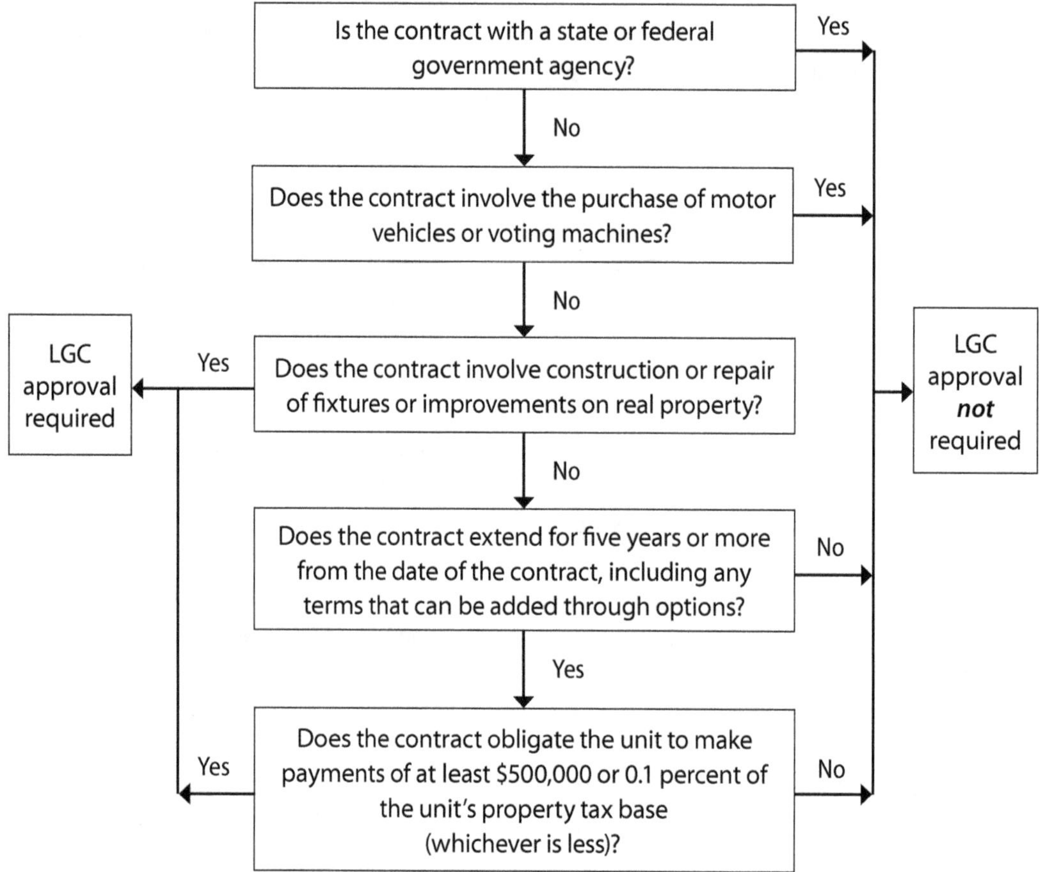

Non-substitution Clause

An installment finance contract may not include a non-substitution clause. Specifically, the contract may not "restrict the right of the local government to continue to provide a service or activity" or "replace or provide a substitute for any fixture, improvement, project or property financed, refinanced, or purchased pursuant to the contract."[58]

Public Hearing

A unit of government entering into an installment purchase contract that "involves real property" must hold a public hearing on the contract.[59] No public hearing is required, however, for acquiring personal property.

State Approval

Some, but not all, installment financings are subject to LGC approval.[60] To determine if a particular installment finance contract must be approved by the LGC, the unit should ask (and answer) the following questions according to the flowchart in Figure 21.1. If LGC approval is required, the commission considers the same factors as it does for a GO debt issuance.

Synthetic Project Development Financings

Because of the risk to investors, project development financing often is the most expensive way for a unit to borrow money to fund public infrastructure. What makes the financing attractive to units, and particularly to governing

58. G.S. 160A-20(d).
59. G.S. 160A-20(g).
60. G.S. 160A-20(e); G.S. 159-148.

boards, however, is that a unit does not pledge or obligate any of its current revenues. Instead, it pledges future revenue streams generated by new development.

A synthetic project development financing occurs when a local government determines that the projected increment revenue from proposed new private development in the unit justifies issuing debt to fund a public infrastructure project that will benefit or incentivize the new private development. The unit does not issue project development bonds, however. It uses another form of financing, usually an installment financing—whereby the unit pledges the financed asset as security for the loan—to fund the public improvement. If the private development occurs according to projections, the unit is able to use the new revenue generated to repay the loan. Because local governments in North Carolina can get relatively good bond ratings on installment financing debt, synthetic project development financing is often a cheaper, and thus more attractive, alternative to a formal project development financing.

Conclusion

Local governments face unique challenges when funding capital projects. The projects are often very expensive. They also typically last for many years, raising equity issues as to whether current or future citizens should bear the costs. Operating and maintaining capital assets also imposes costs that a unit must anticipate and account for as ongoing operating expenses. Local officials have an array of financing tools available to help fund the initial (and some recurring maintenance) costs of a capital project. A unit must choose the appropriate mix of funding mechanisms based on its community goals, needs, and current and future financial capacity.

About the Author

Kara A. Millonzi is a School of Government faculty member who specializes in local government and public school finance law.

Chapter 22

Accounting, Fiscal Control, and Cash Management

Gregory S. Allison

Public confidence in government depends on proper stewardship of public moneys. The North Carolina Local Government Budget and Fiscal Control Act (LGBFCA) sets forth requirements for fiscal control that provide a framework for ensuring accountability in a local government's budgetary and financial operations. This chapter focuses on these requirements, which are generally equally applicable both to county governments and city governments. They pertain to the appointment and the role of the finance officer, the accounting system, control of expenditures, cash management and investments, the annual audit, and audits of federal and state financial assistance.

A short discussion of the role of the North Carolina Local Government Commission and its relationship to North Carolina local government entities will facilitate understanding of references that occur throughout this chapter. The Local Government Commission, often referred to as simply the LGC, is briefly mentioned in Chapter 21, "Financing Capital Projects," of this volume.

The LGC, established by Section 159-3 of the North Carolina General Statutes (hereinafter G.S.), operates as a division of the Department of State Treasurer. The commission itself consists of nine members. The state treasurer, the state auditor, the secretary of state, and the secretary of revenue serve as ex officio members; the remaining five members are appointed by the governor (three members) and the General Assembly (two members). The commission's primary responsibility is to provide fiscal and debt-management oversight to local government entities in North Carolina. The commission's policy directives are carried out on a day-to-day basis by the staff of the LGC, who are employees of the Department of State Treasurer.

The LGC's oversight of the counties and cities in North Carolina is extensive. A local government's financial condition, cash management practices, and audit procurement procedures are all subject to LGC review and approval. As a general rule, counties and cities are not allowed to enter into most types of indebtedness without the express permission of the LGC. Counties and cities in North Carolina have benefited extensively from this level of oversight: their financial condition and reputation in the national debt markets are among the best in the nation.

The Finance Officer

G.S. 159-24 requires that each county and city government have a finance officer who is legally responsible for establishing the accounting system, controlling expenditures, managing cash and other assets, and preparing financial reports. The Local Government Budget and Fiscal Control Act (LGBFCA) does not specify who is to appoint this official, leaving the decision to each jurisdiction. In many counties and cities, the manager appoints the finance officer.[1] In counties and cities that do not have a manager, the governing body typically makes the appointment. According to G.S. 159-24, the finance officer serves at the pleasure of the appointing board or official.

In most counties, the official exercising the statutory duties of finance officer carries that title; in most cities, the official exercising these same duties carries the title of finance director. In some of the larger counties and cities, the title of chief financial officer (CFO) is used. Other titles, such as accountant or treasurer, may be used by some jurisdictions, but this is less common. There are also other derivations in some smaller counties. For example, the county manager may also be the legally designated finance officer, or the finance officer may also serve as an assistant county manager. The LGBFCA permits the duties of the budget officer and finance officer to be conferred on one person. In contrast, G.S. 105-349(e) specifies that the duties of tax collector and those of the "treasurer or chief accounting officer," which should be understood to mean the finance officer, may not be conferred on the same person except with the written permission of the secretary of the North Carolina Local Government Commission (LGC). This limitation recognizes both the hazards to internal control of one person holding the two offices and the fact that some local government entities are too small to make any other arrangement. While it is currently very rare for one person to serve as both the finance officer and the tax collector in a county, the commission has allowed a number of cities to operate under this arrangement. However, these approvals have typically been made with restrictions, such as suggesting that the city contract with the county for property tax billing and collection.

The finance officer's duties are summarized in G.S. 159-25(a): establish and maintain the accounting records, disburse moneys, make financial reports, manage the receipt and deposit of moneys, manage the county's or the city's debt service obligations, supervise investments, and perform any other assigned duties.

Official Bonds

The finance officer must give "a true accounting and faithful performance bond" of no less than $50,000; the amount is to be fixed by the governing board.[2] The bond must be given on the individual, not the position. The usual public official's bond covers faithful performance as well as true accounting. In determining the amount of the bond, the board should seek protection against both a large single loss and cumulative smaller ones. The bond insures the county or the city for losses that it suffers as a result of the actions or negligence of the finance officer; it offers no insurance or protection to the officer. The county or the city must pay the bond's premium.

G.S. 159-29 also requires that each "officer, employee, or agent . . . who handles or has in his custody more than one hundred dollars . . . at any time, or who handles or has access to the inventories" be bonded for faithful performance. If separate bonds for individuals are purchased, the $100 minimum should be understood to mean that the bonding

1. N.C. Gen. Stat. (hereinafter G.S.) § 153A-82 (counties); G.S. 160A-148 (cities).

2. G.S. 159-29.

requirement applies only to those persons who frequently or regularly handle that amount or more. The governing board fixes the amount of each such bond, and the county or city may (and normally does) pay the premium.

In lieu of requiring a separate bond for each employee, a county or city may purchase a "blanket" faithful-performance bond, and nearly all counties and cities do (primarily for cost reasons, as blanket bonds are more economical than the total cost of separate bonds). The blanket bond does not substitute for the separate bond required for the finance officer or other county officials (tax collector, sheriff, and register of deeds) or city officials (tax collector), who must still be bonded individually and separately.

The Accounting System

An accounting system exists to supply information. It provides the manager and other officials with the data needed to ascertain financial performance and to plan and budget for future activities with projected resources. The accounting system is also an essential part of internal control procedures.

The governing board depends on accounting information in making its budgetary and program decisions and in determining whether or not they have been carried out. This kind of information is also valuable to outside organizations. The investment community and bond-rating agencies rely on it as they assess a county's or a city's financial condition. Also, in counties and cities where bonds have recently been issued, the local government is often required to provide various types of annual financial information to meet continuing disclosure requirements. State regulatory agencies such as the Local Government Commission (LGC) review data generated by the accounting systems to determine whether counties and cities have complied with the legal requirements regulating accounting and finance. Federal and state grantor agencies use the information to monitor compliance with the requirements of the financial assistance programs that they administer. The media and the public depend on the information to evaluate a local government's activities.

County and city accounting practices are formed in response to the general statutory requirements set forth in G.S. 159-26, which are generally accepted accounting principles (GAAP) promulgated nationally by the Governmental Accounting Standards Board (GASB) and other organizations. In North Carolina, the rules and regulations of the LGC as well as the local government's own needs and capabilities directly impact its accounting practices.

Statutory Requirements

G.S. 159-26 requires that each county and city maintain an accounting system, which must do the following:

1. *Show in detail its assets, liabilities, equities, revenues, and expenditures.*
2. *Record budgeted as well as actual expenditures and budgeted or estimated revenues as well as their collection.*
3. *Establish accounting funds as required by G.S. 159-26(b).* A *fund* is a separate fiscal and accounting entity having its own assets, liabilities, equity or fund balance, revenues, and expenditures. Government activities are grouped into funds to isolate information for legal and management purposes. The types of funds that are set forth in G.S. 159-26(b) for use by counties and cities are discussed later in this chapter.
4. *Use the modified accrual basis of accounting. Basis of accounting* refers to criteria for determining when revenues and expenditures should be recorded in the accounting system.[3] The *modified accrual basis* requires

3. Although the Local Government Budget and Fiscal Control Act (LGBFCA) requires the use of the modified accrual basis of accounting, it also requires that financial reporting be in conformity with generally accepted accounting principles (GAAP). Enterprise, internal service, and certain trust funds primarily follow accrual accounting standards for reporting in accordance with GAAP, similar to the commercial sector. A county's annual financial report must both demonstrate compliance with legal requirements (i.e., the LGBFCA) and report on operations in conformity with GAAP. Therefore, enterprise funds should be reported on both the modified accrual and accrual basis in a county's financial statements, and internal service and certain trust funds should also be reported on the accrual basis in the annual financial report.

that expenditures be recorded when a liability is incurred (time of receipt) for a good or service provided to the local government. The expenditure should be recorded then, usually before the funds are disbursed. This type of accounting also requires that revenues be recorded when the revenues are measurable and available. *Measurable* means that they can be reasonably estimated, and *available* means that they will be received within the current fiscal year or soon enough thereafter to be able to pay liabilities of the current fiscal year. In actual practice, for various reasons some revenues are recorded when they are received in cash. For example, in North Carolina, property tax revenues are generally recorded on the cash basis because taxes receivable are not considered to be collectible soon enough after the year's end to meet the availability criterion. Permits and fees are also recorded on the cash basis because they are not considered to be measurable at the year's end. However, certain revenues collected after the fiscal year end but soon enough thereafter to pay liabilities outstanding as of June 30 would be reflected as revenue for the year ending June 30 because they would be considered measurable and available. For example, the monthly sales tax payments received by counties and cities in July, August, and September are recorded by most local governments as revenue for the year ending June 30 because the payments can be measured; they are directly related to sales that occurred during the previous fiscal year (i.e., the July distribution is related to the previous April's sales, the August distribution is related to the previous May's sales, and the September distribution is related to the previous June's sales); and they are received soon enough after June 30 to be able to pay liabilities at the fiscal year's end.

The modified accrual basis of accounting helps keep financial practices on a prudent footing: expenditures are recorded as soon as the liabilities for them are incurred, and some revenues are not recorded until they have actually been received in cash. In addition, the modified accrual basis enhances the comparability of financial reporting for counties and reduces the opportunity for manipulation of financial information.

5. *Record encumbrances represented by outstanding purchase orders and contractual obligations that are chargeable against budgeted appropriations.* An *encumbrance* is created when a contract that will require a county or a city to pay money is entered into or when a purchase order is issued.

   Although the Local Government Budget and Fiscal Control Act (LGBFCA) does not explicitly mention any exceptions, in practice, expenditures for salaries and wages, fringe benefits, and utilities are usually not encumbered. Salaries, wages, and fringe benefits are not encumbered because they are generally budgeted at the full amounts expected for all positions, and this significantly reduces the risk of over-expenditure. Utilities expenditures are normally not encumbered because the amounts are generally not known in advance.

   An encumbrance exists as long as the contractor or supplier has not delivered the goods or the services and the contract or purchase order is outstanding. While this is the case, the local government is not yet liable to pay for the goods or the services and has not yet incurred an expenditure for it. G.S. 159-26(d) requires that a county's or a city's accounting system record encumbrances as well as expenditures. This recognizes that the encumbrance is a potential liability, and once the purchase order is filled or the contract fulfilled, liability for payment is created and an expenditure is incurred. Although this requirement applies only to counties with more than 50,000 citizens or cities with more than 10,000 citizens, nearly all counties and cities record encumbrances in their accounting systems.

Generally Accepted Accounting Principles for Governments

Governmental accounting, as a branch of general accounting practice, shares basic concepts and conventions with commercial accounting. However, because of major differences in the governmental environment, a distinct set of national accounting and financial reporting principles has evolved in this field. They are promulgated by the GASB. Established in 1984, the GASB is responsible for the establishment of GAAP for county and city governments as well as state governments. The GASB succeeded the National Council on Governmental Accounting (NCGA), which had formerly established GAAP for government entities. Although the GASB at its creation accepted the existing NCGA pronouncements, it has actively set forth standards in areas of accounting and finance that the NCGA did not formally consider. Likewise, it has updated and modified much of the guidance that it initially accepted.

The LGC plays a key role in defining and interpreting accounting standards and procedures for local governments in North Carolina. It issues rules and regulations that interpret state statutes as well as national professional standards, and it provides advice about requirements and improvements in accounting and financial reporting practices. The commission's staff has focused much attention in recent years on annual financial reports, working closely with local officials and the state's public accounting profession to keep local government accounting systems up to date with the increasingly more rigorous reporting and disclosure standards being promulgated by the GASB.

Counties' and Cities' Own Needs and Capabilities

Counties' and cities' own needs and capabilities also shape their accounting and financial reporting systems. For example, a growing number of counties and cities have improved their annual financial reports to the point that they have earned the Certificate of Achievement for Excellence in Financial Reporting, awarded by the Government Finance Officers Association (GFOA) of the United States and Canada to recognize outstanding achievement in governmental financial reporting. While all North Carolina local governments issue professionally acceptable annual financial reports, those winning the Certificate of Achievement provide full disclosure above and beyond the minimum standards set by GAAP and relate current financial conditions and performance to past financial trends. Approximately four thousand local governments in the United States participate in the Certificate of Achievement program, which offers a tremendous resource to help local governments continually improve their financial reporting.

Nationwide, capital asset accounting and reporting continues to be one of the more significant challenges in state and local government accounting. In recent years, the LGC and the independent public accountants auditing local governments, as well as the aforementioned GFOA, have placed increased emphasis on capital asset records. If they are inadequate, the annual auditor's opinion may be qualified, and this may adversely affect a county's or a city's bond rating. Also, a qualified audit opinion may affect a county's or a city's ability to obtain approval from the LGC for debt issuance. In addition, an adequate capital asset accounting system can provide significant advantages. It places responsibility for the safekeeping of such assets with management, thereby improving internal control. It also serves as a basis for establishing maintenance and replacement schedules for equipment and for determining the level of fire and hazard insurance that should be carried on buildings and other capital assets.

It should be noted that the capitalization threshold that management establishes for financial reporting purposes should *not* be presumed to be directly correlated to adequate internal control of government property. For years, there has often been the misconception that the lower the capitalization threshold, the less likely it is that the capital asset will be lost, misplaced, or misused. However, low capitalization thresholds simply clutter the internal capital asset records with immaterial items and actually make them less useful. The external financial statements should focus on material items, and there is a significant internal cost to maintaining unusually low capitalization thresholds. For North Carolina governments, it is recommended that capital asset thresholds be no less than $1,000, and thresholds up to $5,000 are preferable. The threshold is only used to determine *where* on the external financial statements capital assets will be reported. The threshold does *not* mitigate the need for management at the departmental level to maintain adequate internal controls and records to safeguard *all* government property. Also, it should be noted that, as a general rule, capitalization thresholds for financial reporting purposes are a management responsibility and there is no required official action by governing boards to establish or modify them.

Control of Expenditures

Preauditing Obligations

Through the annual budget ordinance and any project ordinances (see Chapter 20, "Budget Preparation, Adoption, and Amendment," and Chapter 21, "Financing Capital Projects," in this volume), the governing board authorizes county and city managers and other officials to undertake programs and projects and to spend moneys. Except for trust and agency funds and internal service funds, which may be excluded from the budget ordinance, G.S. 159-8 directs that no county or city "may expend any moneys . . . except in accordance with a budget ordinance or project ordinance."

The proper functioning of the budgeting process depends on adherence to the terms of these two types of ordinances. For example, budget and project ordinances are required by law to be balanced. If they are complied with, deficit spending should not occur. Just as important, these ordinances embody the county's or the city's policies and priorities, which are carried out if the ordinances are followed.

The preauditing of obligations, required by G.S. 159-28(a), is a principal legal mechanism for assuring compliance with the budget ordinance and each project ordinance. The preaudit rule provides that no obligation may be incurred in an activity accounted for in a fund included in the budget ordinance or for a project authorized by a project ordinance unless two requirements are met. First, the obligation must be authorized; that is, one of the ordinances must contain an appropriation to cover it. Second, the authorization must not be exhausted; sufficient unspent and unencumbered funds must remain in the appropriation to meet the obligation when it comes due. Only if both requirements are met is the obligation validly incurred.

The Meaning of Appropriation

The *appropriations* that may not be overspent without violating the law are the figures that *actually appear* in the annual budget ordinance or a project ordinance. For example, the annual budget ordinance may make appropriations by department. If $2,200,000 is appropriated to the recreation department and the ordinance contains no further breakdown of that amount, the $2,200,000 is the maximum that the recreation department may spend, and all its expenditures are charged against that figure. Various line items or *objects of expenditure* within the overall departmental appropriation could be overspent without violating the budget ordinance or the Local Government Budget and Fiscal Control Act (LGBFCA) as long as total departmental expenditures do not exceed $2,200,000.

In counties and cities where the governing board makes appropriations by department in the annual budget ordinance, the budget officer, sometimes at the board's direction, typically imposes a further requirement that each operating department stay within the object of expenditure amounts set out in its budget. Usually, the budget officer's or finance officer's permission is needed to exceed these line-item limits. However, such a requirement is administrative rather than legal in nature because the legally binding appropriations in the budget ordinance are made only by department, not by line item.

Encumbrances

To find out whether a particular contract or purchase will cause an appropriation to be overspent, it is not enough to know the unexpended balance of the appropriation. The preauditor must also ascertain whether contracts or purchase orders are outstanding and chargeable against the appropriation. As already mentioned, an encumbrance is created when a county or a city enters into a contract that will require it to pay moneys, or when it issues a purchase order. This encumbered portion of an appropriation is unavailable for a proposed expenditure as if the funds had already been expended; once the contract is completed or the purchase order is filled, the encumbrance is replaced by an expenditure. To make the required preaudit, one must know the *unexpended* and *unencumbered balance* (which is often referred to simply as the unencumbered balance) of the proper appropriation.

The Preaudit Certificate

An obligation is invalid if incurred without meeting the preaudit requirements.[4] For this reason, those who deal with a local government entity—vendors, contractors, consultants, and others—understandably want to be told whether the purchase order they have received or the contract they have been offered is a valid obligation. This information is provided by the *preaudit certificate.* G.S. 159-28(a) requires that any contract or agreement requiring the payment of moneys and any purchase order for supplies or materials include on its face "a certificate stating that the [contract, agreement, or purchase order] has been pre-audited to assure compliance" with the preaudit requirements—namely, that the budget includes an appropriation for the contract or the agreement and that unspent and unencumbered moneys remain in the appropriation to cover payments in the current year for the contract or the agreement. The certificate,

4. G.S. 159-28(a).

which may be printed or stamped, should read substantially as follows: "This instrument has been preaudited in the manner required by the Local Government Budget and Fiscal Control Act." It must be signed by the finance officer or by a deputy finance officer approved for this purpose by the governing board.

Besides providing some assurance to a vendor, the certificate emphasizes to the person who signs it the importance of the preaudit to the entire budget and fiscal control system. Any finance officer or deputy finance officer giving a false certificate is personally liable for any sums illegally committed or disbursed thereby.[5]

Disbursements

Two Stages of Review

G.S. 159-28(b) outlines a two-stage procedure for approving payment of any "bill, invoice, or claim" (these include any item for which an expenditure may be made). First—and this stage applies to transactions involving moneys in any of the local government's funds—the finance officer must determine that the amount claimed is owed to the claimant. Second—and this stage applies only to transactions authorized by the annual budget ordinance or a project ordinance—the finance officer must ascertain that the expenditure is authorized and that either an encumbrance exists for it or a sufficient unencumbered balance remains in the appropriation to pay the claim. Only if the finance officer has made both determinations may the disbursement be made.

The Finance Officer's Certificate

Completion of the two-stage review is evidenced by placing the *finance officer's certificate* on the face of the check or draft used for payment. The certificate, which may be printed or stamped on the check, must follow substantially the following form: "This disbursement has been approved as required by the Local Government Budget and Fiscal Control Act." Normally the certificate is signed by the finance officer or by a deputy finance officer approved for this purpose by the governing board.[6] Having a deputy finance officer authorized to sign checks is especially important. The absence of the finance officer could delay their issuance if that officer were the only one authorized to sign the certificate. While not a common practice in cities, in some counties the board of commissioners designates a deputy finance officer in the county finance department or another county department to regularly sign checks on a limited basis to make certain that specific payments, such as monthly benefit payments to public assistance recipients, are proper and correct. Such delegation of the payment function should occur only with the approval of the county finance officer and only if adequate internal controls are built into the payment procedures that are used.

Governing Board Approval of Bills, Invoices, or Claims

The LGBFCA authorizes the governing board to approve by formal resolution a bill, an invoice, or another claim that has been disapproved by the finance officer. The governing board may do this only for a valid claim for which an encumbrance exists or an unencumbered appropriation remains in the budget ordinance or a project ordinance, and only by following certain specified procedures. Governing board members approving invalid payments under this statute may be held personally liable for the payments. These procedures are rarely, if ever, used.

Form of Payment

Payment of obligations by cash is not allowed. G.S. 159-28(d) directs that all bills, invoices, salaries, or other claims be paid by check or draft on an official depository, bank wire transfer from an official depository, or electronic payment or electronic funds transfer originated by the local government through an official depository. Wire transfers are used, for example, to transmit the money periodically required for debt service on bonds or other debt to a paying agent, who in turn makes the payments to individual bondholders. Automated Clearing House (ACH) transactions are used by local governments to make retirement system contributions to the state, to make payroll payments, and to make

5. G.S. 159-28(e).
6. G.S. 159-28(d).

certain other payments. The state has extended the use of the ACH system to most transfers of moneys between the state and local governments that are related to grant programs and state-shared revenues.

G.S. 159-25(b) requires each check or draft to "be signed by the finance officer or a properly designated deputy finance officer and countersigned by another official . . . designated for this purpose by the governing board." The finance officer's signature attests to completion of review and accompanies the certificate described above. The second signature may be by the chair of the board of commissioners, the mayor of the city, or some other official. (If the governing board does not expressly designate the countersigner, G.S. 159-25(b) directs that for counties it should be the chair or the county's chief executive officer (i.e., the county manager) and for cities it should be the mayor.)

The purpose of requiring two signatures is internal control. The law intends that the finance officer review the documentation of the claim before signing the certificate and check. The second person can independently review the documentation before signing and issuing the check. The fact that two persons must separately be satisfied with the documentation should significantly reduce the opportunities for fraud.

In many local government entities, however, the second signer does not exercise this independent review, perhaps relying on other procedures for the desired internal control. Recognizing this, G.S. 159-25(b) permits the governing board to waive the two-signature requirement (thus requiring only the finance officer's signature or a properly designated deputy finance officer's signature on the check) "if the board determines that the internal control procedures of the unit or authority will be satisfactory in the absence of dual signatures."

As an alternative to manual signatures, G.S. 159-28.1 permits the use of signature machines, signature stamps, or similar devices for signing checks or drafts. In practice, these are widely used in counties and cities all across North Carolina. The governing board must approve the use of such signature devices through a formal resolution or ordinance, which should designate who is to have custody of the devices. For internal control purposes, it is essential that this equipment be properly secured. The finance officer or another official given custody of the facsimile signature device(s) by the governing board is personally liable under the statute for illegal, improper, or unauthorized use of the device(s).

Cash Management

Daily Deposits

G.S. 159-32 generally requires that "all taxes and other moneys collected or received by an officer or employee of a local government" be deposited daily, either with the finance officer or in an official depository. (Deposits made under the second alternative must immediately be reported to the finance officer.) If an agency is part of a county or a city for purposes of budget adoption and control, it and its officers and employees are also part of the county or the city for purposes of the daily deposit requirement.

In many counties and cities, the daily deposit to an official depository is made before the cutoff time (e.g., 2:00 p.m.) set by the depository for crediting interest earnings on deposits made that day. A deposit should be made intact; all moneys collected up to the deposit time should be included. There need be only one deposit per day, although in some local governments a second one is made toward the end of the day if substantial moneys are received after the first deposit. It is more common, however, for entities to place funds collected after the daily deposit has been made into a locked vault for inclusion in the following day's deposit.

There is a potential exception to the requirement for daily deposit. If the governing board approves, an officer or employee need make deposits only when moneys on hand amount to $250 or more, although a deposit must always be made on the last business day of each month. Note that only the governing board may approve the use of this exception. Managers, finance officers, other officers, or advisory boards or commissions may not authorize it.

Official Depository

All moneys belonging to a county or a city (including those transmitted to a fiscal agent for payment of debt service) must be deposited in an official depository.[7] The governing board designates which banks or financial institutions are to serve as the official depositories. It also decides how many of them there will be. It may so designate any bank, savings institution, or trust company in the state. With the permission of the secretary of the Local Government Commission (LGC), the governing board may also designate a nationally chartered bank located in another state to serve as an official depository. For a number of reasons, the secretary to the LGC will approve the use of out-of-state depositories only in rare circumstances, such as when authorizing a governing board to designate a nationally or state-chartered out-of-state bank as a depository or fiscal agent for payment of debt service.

G.S. 14-234 generally forbids governing board members and other officials involved in the contracting process to make contracts for the local governments in which they have an interest. An exception exists, however, for transacting business with "banks or banking institutions." Therefore, a county or a city may designate as a depository a bank or a savings institution in which a governing board member, for example, is an officer, owner, or stockholder.

Depository accounts may be non-interest-bearing accounts with unlimited check writing privileges; interest-bearing accounts with unlimited check writing privileges (NOW or super-NOW accounts); interest-bearing money market accounts for which check writing privileges are restricted; or certificates of deposit (CDs) that have no check writing privileges. Generally, the use of interest-bearing accounts is recommended.

Both counties and cities follow a variety of methods in selecting or designating official depositories. Some name each bank and savings institution with an office located within their jurisdiction as a depository and place an account in each. Others maintain just one account, rotating it among the local financial institutions that are qualified to serve as official depositories and changing it according to a predetermined schedule (commonly every one to three years). Although these methods demonstrate a local government's support of local banks and financial institutions, they can complicate the government's cash-management procedures, hinder its investment program, and cause it to pay more than it would otherwise for banking services. For these reasons, the majority of counties and cities statewide follow a third method—selecting the bank or financial institution to serve as the depository through a request for proposals process. This method is currently recommended by the LGC staff. It awards the business to the institution that offers the most services for the fees charged or the most services for the lowest compensating balance that the county or the city must maintain at the bank or financial institution.

Insurance and Collateralization of Deposits

G.S. 159-31(b) requires that funds on deposit in an official depository (except funds deposited with a fiscal agent for the purpose of making debt service payments to bondholders) be fully secured. This is accomplished through a combination of methods. First, government funds on deposit with a bank or savings institution or invested in a CD issued by such an institution are insured by the Federal Deposit Insurance Corporation (FDIC). If the funds that a county or a city has on deposit or invested in a CD do not exceed the maximum amount of FDIC insurance—currently $250,000 per official custodian for interest-bearing accounts and an additional $250,000 per official custodian for non-interest-bearing accounts—no further security is required. For purposes of FDIC regulation, the finance officer is always the official custodian.

Uninsured county or city funds in a bank or savings institution may be secured through a collateral security arrangement. Under one type of arrangement, the institution places securities with a market value equal to or greater than the local government's uninsured moneys on deposit or invested in CDs into an escrow account with a separate, unrelated third-party institution (usually the trust department of another bank, the Federal Reserve, or the Federal Home Loan Bank). The escrow agreement provides that if the depository bank or savings institution defaults on its obligations to the local government, the county or the city is entitled to the escrowed securities in the amount of the default less the amount of FDIC insurance coverage. Under this method, the local government must execute certain

7. G.S. 159-31(a).

forms and take certain actions to ensure that deposits are adequately collateralized. Responsibility for assuring that the deposits are adequately secured under this method rests with the finance officer, who should closely supervise the collateral-security arrangement.

Alternatively, a bank or savings institution may choose to participate in a pool of bank- and savings institution–owned securities sponsored and regulated by the state treasurer to collateralize state and local government moneys on deposit or invested in CDs with these institutions. A third-party institution, chosen by the various pooling-method banks, holds the securities in the pool. Participating depository banks and savings institutions are responsible for maintaining adequate collateral securities in the pool, although each financial institution's collateral balances are monitored by the state treasurer. In the unlikely event of defaults or similar financial troubles, the state treasurer would be considered the beneficiary of reclaimed deposits and collateral. Certain standards of financial soundness are required by the state treasurer before a financial institution is allowed to participate in this system.

Investments

Local governments cannot afford to let significant amounts of cash lie idle in non-interest-bearing depository accounts. Investment income can amount to the equivalent of several cents or more on the property tax rate. G.S. 159-30 makes the finance officer responsible for managing investments, subject to policy directions and restrictions that the governing board may impose. Because of the expanded opportunities and risks associated with the investments that North Carolina counties and cities may legally make, both national investment authorities and the LGC recommend that governing boards establish general investment policies and restrictions for their finance officers to follow.

Such board-adopted policies could, for example, limit the maximum maturities for investments of general fund moneys; require the use of informal competitive bidding for the purchase of securities; authorize the finance officer to invest in the cash and/or term portfolios of the North Carolina Capital Management Trust (discussed below); and make clear that safety and liquidity should take precedence over yield in the county's or the city's investment program. In a growing number of local governmental entities, governing boards are adopting such investment policies.

In conducting their investment programs, finance officers must forecast cash resources and needs, thus determining how much is available for investment and for how long. They must also investigate what types of investment securities are authorized by law and by their own internal investment policies and decide which ones to purchase. If an investment security is to be sold before maturity, the finance officer must make that decision.

Custody of Investment Securities

G.S. 159-30(d) states: "Securities and deposit certificates shall be in the custody of the finance officer who shall be responsible for their safekeeping." Investment securities come in two forms: *certificated* and *noncertificated*. Ownership of certificated investments is represented by an actual physical security. Some CDs and certain other securities are issued in certificated form. To obtain proper custody of certificated securities, the finance officer should hold the securities or the certificates in the county's or the city's vault or its safe deposit box at a local bank or trust company. Alternatively, certificated securities may be delivered to and held by the local government's third-party safekeeping agent, which can be the trust department of a North Carolina bank.

Many investment securities—United States Treasury bills, notes, and bonds; federal agency instruments; some commercial paper; and other types of securities—are not certificated. Ownership of them is evidenced by electronic book-entry records that are maintained by the Federal Reserve System for banks and certain other financial institutions and by the financial institutions themselves. Additionally, for certain other securities, the Depository Trust Company in New York maintains the electronic records of ownership. When a county or a city buys noncertificated securities from a bank or a securities dealer, the record of ownership is transferred electronically from the seller or the seller's bank to the local government's custodial agent. To obtain proper custody of book-entry securities, a local government should have a signed custodial agreement in place with the financial institution that serves as its custodial agent. The financial institution agent should be a member of the Federal Reserve System authorized to conduct trust business in North Carolina. Counties and cities may not use securities brokers and dealers or the *operating divisions* of banks and savings institutions as custodial agents for their investment securities. Generally, the trust department of a bank or financial institution that sells securities to a county or a city may act as the custodial agent for the securities, as long as the trust department itself did not sell the securities to the local government and provided that the institution is licensed to do trust business in North Carolina and is a member of the Federal Reserve. It is essential that a county or a city or its applicable custodial agent obtain custody of all investments. Major losses from investments suffered by local governments in other states have been due to the failure of those governments to obtain proper custody of their investments.

Authorized Investments

Among the securities and instruments in which both counties and cities invest are CDs or other forms of time deposit approved by the LGC that are offered by banks, savings institutions, and trust companies located in North Carolina.[8] Certificates of deposit issued by banks in the state have traditionally been the most widely used investment instrument, especially by small- and medium-sized local governments. Other investments authorized by G.S. 159-30(c) include the following:

1. *United States Treasury obligations (bills, notes, and bonds)—called Treasuries—and United States agency obligations that are fully guaranteed by the United States government.* Because these obligations are full-faith-and-credit obligations of the United States, they carry the least credit risk—that is, risk of default—of any investment available to either counties or cities. As a result, short-term Treasuries are usually lower yielding than alternative investment securities. Long-term Treasuries and Government National Mortgage Association securities (fully guaranteed by the United States government) can experience significant price variations. This is characteristic of long-term securities in general; therefore such securities should be carefully evaluated and should be considered only for investing certain, limited funds such as capital reserve moneys that will not be needed for many years.
2. *Direct obligations of certain agencies that are established and/or sponsored by the United States government but whose obligations are not guaranteed by it.* Examples are the Federal Home Loan Bank Board, the Federal National Mortgage Association, and the Federal Farm Credit System. Direct debt issued by these agencies generally carries very low credit risk, although economic conditions adverse to an economic sector the agency finances (e.g., housing) can create some risk for local governments or others who invest in its securities. Some securities of these agencies are not their direct debt and are therefore not eligible investments for either North Carolina counties or cities. Moreover, even though longer-term direct debt of these agencies carries low credit risk, it can experience significant price fluctuations before maturity.
3. *Obligations of the State of North Carolina or bonds and notes of any of its local governments or public authorities, with investments in such obligations subject to restrictions of the secretary of the LGC.* Because the interest paid to investors on these obligations, bonds, and notes is typically exempt from federal and state income taxes, they generally carry lower yields than alternative investment instruments available to counties and cities. However, should the state and local governments in North Carolina begin to issue significant amounts of securities on which the interest paid is subject to federal income taxes, those securities would carry higher interest rates than tax exempt state and local government obligations. This could make the taxable obligations attractive as investment instruments to both counties and cities.
4. *Top-rated United States commercial paper issued by domestic United States corporations.* Commercial paper is issued by industrial and commercial corporations to finance inventories and other short-term needs. Such paper is an unsecured corporate promissory note that is available in maturities of up to 270 days, although maturities from 30 to 90 days are most common. For any local government to invest in commercial paper, the paper must be rated by at least one national rating organization and earn its top commercial paper rating. If the paper is rated by more than one such organization, it must have the highest rating given by each.

---

8. G.S. 159-30(b), (c)(5).

Historically, commercial paper has been relatively high yielding, and many counties and cities have invested heavily in it over the years. In economic recessions, some commercial paper issuers are downgraded. This means that their commercial paper is no longer eligible for investment by North Carolina local governments. Occasionally the downgrade occurs after the investment is purchased but before it matures. In this situation, it is most common for the entity to continue to hold the investment to maturity as the risk of loss is typically low. As long as a commercial paper issuer is top rated and the finance officer closely monitors its ratings, the risk for this type of investment is small. Officials should understand, however, that eligible commercial paper issued by banks is not a deposit and consequently is not covered by insurance and collateralization.

5. *Bankers' acceptances issued by North Carolina banks or by any top-rated United States bank.* Bankers' acceptances are bills of exchange or time drafts that are drawn on and guaranteed by banks. They are usually issued to finance international trade or a firm's short-term credit needs and are usually secured by the credit of the issuing firm as well as by the general credit of the accepting bank. Most bankers' acceptances have maturity terms of 30 to 180 days. Both counties and cities may invest in bankers' acceptances issued by any North Carolina bank. Only the largest banks in the state issue them, and they are not as common as they once were. For a local government to invest in bankers' acceptances of non–North Carolina U.S. banks, the institution must have outstanding publicly held obligations that carry the highest long-term credit rating from at least one national rating organization. If the bank's credit obligations are rated by more than one national organization, it must have the highest rating given by each.
6. *Participating shares in one of the portfolios of the North Carolina Capital Management Trust.* This trust is a mutual fund established specifically for investments by North Carolina local governments and public authorities. It is certified and regulated by the LGC, and unlike other state-sponsored investment pools for public entity investments, it is registered with the United States Securities and Exchange Commission, which imposes extensive reporting and other requirements that ensure the safety of moneys invested in the trust. The trust manages two separate investment portfolios. One is the money market portfolio, which was started in 1982 and is intended for the investment of short-term or operating cash balances. The principal value of moneys invested in a share in this portfolio remains fixed at $1. The term *portfolio,* which was established in 1987, is intended for capital reserve funds and other moneys that are not subject to immediate need. The principal value of investments in this portfolio fluctuates with changes in market interest rates. Because of this, the term portfolio should primarily be used for the investment of funds that will not be needed immediately or in the short term.

   Either portfolio permits the return of funds invested with it within one day of notice; however, the managers of the portfolios do request that local governments provide longer advance notice if large withdrawals will be made. The trust's portfolios may invest only in securities in which local governments may invest under G.S. 159-30(c).
7. *Repurchase agreements.* A *repurchase agreement* is a purchase by an investor of a security with the stipulation that the seller will buy it back at the original purchase price plus agreed-upon interest at the maturity date. These agreements were once popular for short-term or overnight investments by North Carolina local governments. Unfortunately, some local governments in other states suffered substantial losses by buying repurchase agreements from unscrupulous securities dealers. As a result, strict laws and requirements for the safe use of these agreements have been enacted, both in North Carolina and across the country. G.S. 159-30(c) authorizes local governments to invest in repurchase agreements, but only under very limiting conditions.[9] These conditions have greatly reduced the cost-effectiveness of local government

9. The following restrictions apply to local government investments in repurchase agreements: (1) The underlying security acquired with a repurchase agreement must be a direct obligation of the United States or fully guaranteed by the United States. (2) The repurchase agreement must be sold by a broker or a dealer that is recognized as a primary dealer by a Federal Reserve Bank or be sold by a commercial bank, a trust company, or a national bank whose deposits are insured by the Federal Deposit Insurance Corporation (FDIC). (3) The security underlying the agreement must be delivered in physical or in electronic book-entry form to

investments in repurchase agreements, and such agreements are no longer used to any significant degree by either counties or cities.

8. *Evidences of ownership of, or fractional undivided interests in, future principal and interest payments of stripped or zero-coupon instruments issued directly or guaranteed by the United States government.* These instruments were first authorized as a local government investment in 1987. They are sold at discount from face or par value and pay no interest until maturity. At maturity the investor receives the face value, with the difference between that value and the discounted purchase price of the security representing the effective interest earned. Stripped or zero-coupon securities may be a useful investment vehicle for certain limited moneys, such as those held in a Capital Reserve Fund that will not be needed until after the instrument matures. However, because most strips or zero-coupon securities have long maturities, they are subject to considerable price fluctuations before maturity and should not be used for the investment of general county funds. If investments are made in these securities and market interest rates later rise substantially (as they did in 1994), a county that has to cash in the investment before maturity may lose a significant portion of the principal invested in the securities.
9. *Certain mutual funds for moneys held by either a county or a city that are subject to the arbitrage and rebate provisions of the Internal Revenue Code.* The LGBFCA authorizes unspent proceeds from bonds or other financings subject to the Internal Revenue Code's arbitrage and rebate provisions to be invested in tax-exempt and taxable mutual funds under strict procedures. Operating moneys and proceeds from financings that are not subject to the arbitrage and rebate provisions may not be invested in these mutual funds. Because of the complexity of the federal tax code and the wide variety of available mutual funds, a local government entity should consult with its bond counsel before placing moneys in this type of investment.
10. *Derivatives issued directly by one of the federal agencies listed in G.S. 159-30(c)(2) or guaranteed by the United States government.* Derivatives are not specifically mentioned in the law, but they may be eligible investments if they are otherwise authorized in G.S. 159-30(c). The term *derivatives* refers to a broad range of investment securities that can vary in market price, yield, and/or cash flow depending on the value of the underlying securities or assets or changes in one or more interest-rate indices. Derivatives commonly include mortgage pass-through instruments issued by federal agencies, mortgage obligations guaranteed by federal agencies (but not by the United States government), callable step-up notes, floaters, inverse floaters, and still other securities that go by even more interesting names. It is beyond the scope of this chapter to explain these different types of derivatives. It shall suffice to say that derivatives are generally complex instruments, and many of them are subject to rapid and major changes in value as market interest rates change. Some local governments in other states have lost vast amounts of moneys by investing in derivatives. The volume of derivatives available to investors has grown dramatically, and investment brokers and dealers often try to sell various types of derivatives to county, city, and other local government finance officers. Many derivatives are not legal investment instruments for North Carolina's local governments. Those that are direct debt (i.e., a balance sheet liability) of the federal agencies listed in G.S. 159-30(c)(2) or guaranteed by the United States government are usually legal investments. However, many if not most of these are inappropriate as investment vehicles for counties or cities except in very special circumstances. Even though legal, many of them are subject to extreme price and cash-flow volatility. A finance officer considering investing the county's or the city's moneys in one or more derivatives should do so only pursuant to a governing board investment policy that explicitly authorizes such an investment, only if the finance officer understands the nature of the security and the risks associated with it, and only for a short maturity.

---

the county or its third-party agent. (4) The value of the underlying security must be determined daily and must be maintained, at least, at 100 percent of the repurchase price. (5) The county must have a valid and perfected first security interest in the underlying security. This can be achieved through delivery of the security to the county or its third-party safekeeping agent under a written agreement. (7) The underlying security acquired in the repurchase agreement must be free of a lien or third-party claim.

Guidelines for Investing Public Funds

Because of great changes and technological innovation in financial markets, the challenges presented to these markets by international events, and the availability of many new types of investment instruments, the investment and general management of public moneys have become very complex. North Carolina counties and cities can avoid many of the problems that have harmed local governments in other states by adhering to the following guidelines in conducting their investment programs:

1. *The investment program should put safety and liquidity before yield.* A local government should not put its investment funds at risk of loss in the interest of obtaining higher investment earnings. The substantial, highly publicized losses of several local governmental entities across the nation in 1994 and 1995 underscore the potential problems of risky investments. The temptation to sacrifice safety for yield is particularly great when interest rates are falling and local government officials are attempting to maintain investment earnings and revenues. Any local government should always have funds available to meet payment obligations when they come due. This requires maintaining adequate liquidity in an investment portfolio and limiting most investments to securities with short-term maturities.
2. *A local government entity should invest only in securities that the finance officer understands.* Many investment vehicles, including most derivatives, are extremely complex. Before purchasing a security, a finance officer should thoroughly understand all of its components—especially how its value is likely to increase or decrease with changes in market interest rates. Whenever the finance officer is considering investing in a type of security that has not been used before, the finance officer should obtain and study the prospectus or equivalent information for the security and talk to LGC staff and other informed, disinterested parties about the nature and risks of the security.
3. *The finance officer and other officials involved in investing a local government entity's funds should know the financial institutions, the brokers, and the dealers from which the government buys investment securities.* Investment transactions are made by phone, and investment funds and securities are often electronically transferred in seconds. Funds and securities can be lost or "misplaced" quickly in such an environment. To protect the local government, the officials conducting the investment program must be sure that they deal only with reputable and reliable institutions, brokers, and dealers. In fact, the authoritative literature that establishes generally accepted accounting principles (GAAP) also refers to the importance of knowing one's brokers or dealers. The finance officer should obtain a list of the North Carolina local government clients of any firm or person attempting to sell investment securities and obtain references from officials in these other governments. The finance officer should also obtain and evaluate current financial statements from any institution, broker, or dealer that sells or wishes to sell securities to the local government entity. Local governments in other states have lost invested funds because they placed moneys with firms that later went bankrupt and were unable to return the funds. A discussion of how to analyze the financial position of banks and similar financial institutions can be found in the North Carolina Department of State Treasurer's *Policies Manual.*[10] A county should also enter into an investment trading agreement with any firm or person from which it buys investments. Model investment trading agreements are used by and are available from several of North Carolina's large counties.
4. *The finance officer should ensure that the county or the city adequately insures or collateralizes all investments in CDs (as well as other deposits in banks) and that it has proper custody of all investment securities.* Insurance and collateralization must be in accordance with the statutory requirements.
5. *The local government's investment program should be conducted pursuant to the cash management and investment policy approved by the governing board.* Such a policy should be based on G.S. 159-30 and related statutes. It should set forth the governing board's directions and expectations about which investments will

10. North Carolina Department of State Treasurer (NCDST), *Policies Manual* (Raleigh, N.C.: NCDST, May 2010).

be made and how they will be made and should establish general parameters for the receipt, disbursement, and management of moneys.

6. *The finance officer should report periodically to the governing board on the status of the government's investment program.* Such a report should be made at least semiannually and preferably quarterly or monthly and should show the securities in the local government's investment portfolio, the terms or the maturities for investments, and their yields. If possible, average investment maturity and yield should be calculated and also shown in this report.
7. *The local government should understand that the use of investment managers does not relieve the finance officer of the responsibility for the safety of public funds.* A few counties and cities in North Carolina have considered the engagement of outside professional investment managers to administer their routine investment functions. Obviously, there are advantages and disadvantages to this arrangement. The most obvious disadvantage is the inability of the finance officer to have direct control of the investments even though the responsibility for them remains with the finance officer. Also, because of the legal restrictions on the investments that local governments can make, the return that an investment manager can earn once management fees have been deducted may be lower than the return the unit can earn on its own. It should be noted that local legislation may be required for an entity to engage an outside investment manager. If it is determined that an outside investment manager would be beneficial, a written agreement should be executed outlining permissible investments, safekeeping arrangements, diversification requirements, maturity limitations, the liability to be assumed by both parties, and the fees of the contract.

The Annual Audit

Contents of the Comprehensive Annual Financial Report

G.S. 159-34 requires local governments to have their accounts audited by independent auditors after the close of each fiscal year. The auditor's opinion is set out in an annual financial report, which must include "the [county's/city's] financial statements prepared in accordance with generally accepted accounting principles, all disclosures in the public interest required by law, and the auditor's opinion and comments relating to [the] financial statements."

Preparation of the report's financial statements and their accompanying notes is the responsibility of management. Finance officers and their staff should prepare the annual financial statements, though it is not uncommon for the independent auditors to assist with their preparation. It should be noted that it is obviously less costly if the finance department staff prepare as much of the annual financial statements as is possible.

More and more local governmental entities are preparing a comprehensive annual financial report (CAFR). Comprehensive annual financial reports are not required by generally accepted accounting principles (GAAP) or by state statute, but they are very useful to external users of a government's financial statements. These reports go above and beyond the minimum external reporting requirements and provide useful financial and nonfinancial data about a local government. Comprehensive annual financial reports contain three primary sections: introductory, financial, and statistical. A fourth section consisting of the compliance or single audit reports and schedules may be included, but this is not required. Table 22.1 summarizes the contents of the CAFR. If a local government does not prepare a CAFR, only the financial section, including financial statements and notes, will be found in the annual financial report.

Introductory Section

The introductory section of a CAFR includes the transmittal letter, which is primarily an overview of the report, a brief introduction of the government, and the official transmission of the report to external users; an organization chart; and a list of principal elected and nonelected officials. The transmittal letter should provide useful information to members of the public and the business community who may not be aware of all the government's functions and services.

Table 22.1 Contents of a Comprehensive Annual Financial Report

SECTION	DESCRIPTION
Introductory Section	
Letter of transmittal	Overview of the unit's operations and financial statistics
Organizational chart	Diagram of the unit's organizational structure
List of principal officials	List of elected and appointed officials
Financial Section	
Auditor's opinion	Independent auditor's opinion on the financial statements
Management's discussion and analysis	Overview of the government-wide and fund financial statements and the changes in the financial condition of the local government unit during the reporting year
Government-wide financial statements	Statement of net assets and statement of activities for the unit's governmental activities and its business-type activities
Fund financial statements	Information on a unit's fund activity (e.g., General, Special Revenue, Enterprise), with a focus on the major funds
Notes to the financial statements	Explanations of accounting policies and statutory violations and detailed explanations of financial statement items (e.g., cash and investments, capital assets, receivables, long-term liabilities)
Combining statements	Detailed information supporting columns reported in the fund financial statements that include more than one fund
Individual fund statements	Detailed information about individual funds (e.g., prior year amounts, budgeted amounts, actual amounts)
Required supplementary information	Trend data for funding of pension trust funds
Statistical Section	
Statistical tables	Tables, usually on multi-year basis (e.g., ten years), showing information on financial trends, revenue capacity, debt capacity, demographic and economic information, and operating information of the reporting unit
Compliance Section (optional)	
Single audit reports	Reports from independent auditor on compliance and internal control
Schedule of findings and questioned costs	Listing of grant findings and questioned costs
Schedule of expenditures of federal and state awards	Listing of federal and state financial assistance programs

Financial Section

The financial section of a CAFR contains financial statements, which present information in various formats and levels of detail. The financial section includes the financial statements required by GAAP—known as the Basic Financial Statements—as well as financial presentations in greater levels of detail that are often used to exhibit budgetary compliance or to provide opportunities for more detailed analysis.

The first presentation in the financial section is the Management's Discussion and Analysis (MD&A). The MD&A is a written summary and overview of the government's financial condition and the ways in which its financial condition has changed during the year. Governmental entities are required to prepare an MD&A even if they are not preparing a CAFR.

The Basic Financial Statements are presented after the MD&A. As noted earlier, these statements represent the minimum information required in the external financial statements for them to be in accordance with GAAP. The Basic Financial Statements are broken down into two main sections—the government-wide financial statements and the fund financial statements. A comprehensive set of note disclosures supports each section. The government-wide financial statements, which include a statement of net assets and a statement of activities, focus on the two broad *activities* of a local government—the governmental activities and the business-type activities. The fund financial statements, however, focus on the *funds* that are reported by and are unique to local governments. The three main categories of funds—governmental, proprietary, and fiduciary—include numerous fund types. The fund types most common to counties and cities in North Carolina include the General Fund, Special Revenue Funds, Capital Projects Funds, Enterprise Funds (e.g., utility funds), and Pension Trust Funds.

The notes to the financial statements immediately follow the government-wide and fund financial statements and are considered an integral part of the Basic Financial Statements. The content and form of the notes are prescribed by GAAP. Through written advisory memoranda and illustrative financial statements interpreting GAAP, the Local Government Commission (LGC) provides guidance to local officials and their independent auditors on the content of the note disclosures. These disclosures contain significant information for anyone attempting to interpret the financial statements and understand the finances of a local government entity. While all disclosures are important for a good understanding of information presented in the financial statements, the note disclosures related to the definition of the reporting entity, statutory violations (if any), the collateralization of deposits and investments, capital assets, and types and terms of long-term liabilities should be of particular interest to users of the financial statements.

Statistical Section

The statistical section follows the financial section. It includes multi-year information on financial trends of a government, its revenue and debt capacity, relative demographic and economic information, and various operating information. The statistical section is considered an invaluable tool for bond-rating agencies and potential investors and creditors. As a general rule, the statistical tables include ten years' worth of comparative data. In a few cases, the comparisons are not for a complete ten years but are comparisons of the current year with nine years prior, thus exhibiting a ten-year spread.

The Auditor's Opinion

The auditor's task is to render an independent opinion on the accuracy and reliability of the Basic Financial Statements and the related note disclosures, as well as on their conformity with GAAP. The auditor opines not that the financial statements and disclosures are always exact but that they are reliable enough for a knowledgeable reader to use them to make informed judgments about a local government entity's financial position and operations.

The auditor's opinion most commonly takes one of two forms. First, it may be *unmodified* (previously referred to as an *unqualified* and frequently referred to as a "clean" opinion). With an unmodified audit opinion, the auditor is opining that the financial statements present fairly the unit of government's financial position at the close of the fiscal year, in conformity with GAAP. Thus, there is no *modification* placed on the opinion (i.e., there are no exceptions noted). All North Carolina local governments should strive for an unmodified opinion.

A *modified* opinion is a second possibility (previously referred to as a *qualified* opinion). If in some way a local government's practices vary from GAAP, the opinion may state that the statements fairly present the local government's financial position except for any such deviation. For example, the most common type of problem that may result in a modified audit opinion is inadequate records supporting the valuation of a government's capital assets in its financial statements. An opinion modification also may be due to a *scope limitation*. This occurs when the independent auditor is unable to perform certain tests that are an essential part of the audit. For example, a county's or a city's accounting system may fail to provide adequate documentation for some revenue and expenditure transactions, in which case the auditor's ability to test such transactions would be limited.

The auditor normally suggests improvements to the government entity's internal control procedures in a *management letter* that accompanies the audit report. This letter is a public document addressed to the governing board and typically makes various specific suggestions for improving internal control and financial procedures. These suggestions normally arise from the audit, and the letter is delivered at the same time as the audited financial statements. Often the suggestions have been informally made earlier, and some may already have been addressed at the time of the formal presentation. Significant weaknesses in internal controls will also be addressed by the independent auditor in the internal control reports that are required as part of the single audit on federal and state financial assistance programs. These are discussed in the next section.

In addition to providing the management letter, the independent auditor can often be an excellent source of advice on accounting system design, internal control procedures, and finance in general.

Selection of an Independent Auditor

G.S. 159-34 establishes certain requirements and procedures regarding contracting for the annual audit. First, the auditor must be selected by and report to the governing board. The auditor should not report to the manager, the budget officer, or the finance officer.

Second, the governing board may choose any North Carolina certified public accountant (CPA) or any accountant certified by the LGC as qualified to audit local government accounts. In practice, no non-CPA accountants have requested certification or met the requirements for certification to perform local government audits in recent years. Board members should assure themselves that the person or firm selected is familiar with the particular features of government accounting and auditing. Auditors should be engaged early in the fiscal year so that they can become familiar with the government's procedures and can complete some of the necessary testing before the fiscal year's end. This also ensures that the auditor can plan the audit engagement and complete it in a timely manner.

Many counties and cities select the auditor through a *request for proposals* (RFP) process. Although this is not required by state statute, using an RFP is recommended by the LGC staff to secure the best audit proposal. Also, selecting an independent auditor through a competitive procurement process is often required by federal regulations in many grant agreements where audit costs are chargeable to the grant. It is most common for audit agreements procured through an RFP process to range from three- to five-year terms. The RFP should cover both the technical qualifications of a potential audit firm and the firm's cost proposals. Local officials should give more weight to an auditor's technical skills than to the firm's proposed audit fees. References from other local government clients should be requested from an auditor. These references should be contacted so that local government officials may obtain information on other local governments' experiences with a potential auditor.

Contrary to popular belief, government entities are not required to rotate auditors periodically. As mentioned earlier, the LGC recommends that governments issue an RFP process at least every three to five years. This does not preclude, however, current auditors from retaining the engagement if they continue to meet the service and price requirements established in the RFP. Many government entities have retained the same audit firm for years. Some benefits of these established relationships are the auditor's familiarity with the government's environment and the government's avoidance of costs (particularly in staff time) incurred in changing auditors. On the other hand, some governing boards choose to contract with different auditors to provide a fresh look or to allocate the work to other qualified auditors in the region. Both approaches have merit, and the LGC has not encouraged or endorsed either method. It should again be noted that rotation is not statutorily required but is a policy left to the discretion of each entity's governing board.

Finally, a local government's contract with an auditor must be approved by the LGC. Payment may not be made for any audit services until the secretary of the commission has approved the billing.

Audits of Federal and State Grants

Federal and state grants and other financial assistance programs provide moneys to support county and city programs. In the past, individual federal and state agencies providing these moneys audited the recipient government's expenditure of them to verify that the moneys were spent for the purposes intended and in accordance with prescribed procedures. Since the mid-1980s, however, the federal government has required local governments to procure a *combined financial and compliance audit*, or single audit, of all federal financial assistance programs that meet certain expenditure thresholds.

To build on the federal single audit, the 1987 General Assembly, with the support of local officials, passed a law requiring state financial assistance programs to be included with federal programs in a combined single audit. In North Carolina, this combined single audit is performed in conjunction with the annual financial audit by the local government's independent auditor. Federal and state agencies are allowed to build on the single audit and perform monitoring work on the programs they administer. However, they should not duplicate the work performed by the independent auditor.

The independent auditor issues a number of compliance and internal control reports to disclose findings from the single audit. These reports usually are included in the last section of the annual financial report or in a fourth section of the comprehensive annual financial report (CAFR). The most significant items for local officials in these reports are the internal control weaknesses, findings, and questioned costs identified by the auditor. Internal control weaknesses are usually significant deficiencies and should be corrected unless corrective actions would not be cost-effective. For example, an internal control weakness commonly cited is the lack of proper segregation of duties. However, especially for small governments, complete correction of the problem could involve additional hirings, the costs of which could outweigh the benefits. In these situations, mitigating controls can be put into place to lessen the risks and weaknesses involved. Otherwise, findings and questioned costs almost always require corrective action, which may necessitate the repayment of grant funds. County and city officials' formal responses to findings and questioned costs and material internal control weaknesses are included in the single audit reports.

The Local Government Commission (LGC) monitors the single audit of grant funds as part of its review of the annual financial report. If the commission determines that the single audit reports and schedules are not prepared according to the applicable standards, the independent auditor may be required to revise them before the annual financial report can be accepted. If the commission finds that the single audit is satisfactory, then all state grantor agencies must accept the audit. If the commission determines subsequent to its approval of the annual financial report that the single audit is not reliable, it may revoke its approval. This opens a county or a city to individual federal and state agency audits.

Additional Resources

Government Finance Officers Association (GFOA). *Governmental Accounting, Auditing and Financial Reporting.* 2013 ed. Chicago, Ill.: GFOA, 2013.

Governmental Accounting Standards Board (GASB). *Codification of Governmental Accounting and Financial Reporting Standards as of June 30, 2013.* Norwalk, Conn.: GASB, 2013.

Larson, Corinne, ed. *A Public Investor's Guide to Money Market Instruments.* Chicago, Ill.: GFOA, 1998.

Millonzi, Kara A. *Introduction to Local Government Finance.* 2nd ed. Chapel Hill, N.C.: UNC School of Government, 2014.

About the Author

Gregory S. Allison is a School of Government faculty member who specializes in governmental accounting and financial reporting for state and local governmental entities.

This chapter updates and revises a previous chapter authored by K. Lee Carter Jr. and A. John Vogt, whose contributions to the field and to this publication are gratefully acknowledged.

Part 5

Contracting and Property Transactions

Chapter 23

Public Contracts, Competitive Bidding Requirements, and Property Disposal

Norma R. Houston

Obtaining the goods and services for the operation of counties and cities is a major administrative responsibility. In a legal sense, this responsibility involves questions of proper authority, adequate authorization for the expenditure of funds, and the making of contracts in accordance with statutory requirements. Administratively, the organizational arrangements should be both efficient and legally sufficient. Contracting procedures must also be designed to avoid violation of state conflict-of-interest laws, to promote fairness and objectivity, and to avoid the appearance of impropriety in contracting decisions.

Similar legal and administrative considerations apply when disposing of surplus property, which must be done according to statutory requirements intended to recoup taxpayer dollars expended to purchase the property.

I. General Public Contract Requirements

Contracting Authority/Authorized Purposes

The statutes that delegate to counties and cities broad corporate powers necessary to govern and to conduct basic activities include a delegation of authority to contract.[1] Other statutes authorize counties and cities to perform particular functions and contain specific contracting powers.[2] These specific authorizations do not limit the general authority to contract. Indeed, parallel statutes for counties and cities authorize each form of local government to contract with a private entity to perform any activity in which the county or city has authority to engage.[3]

An important legal requirement for local government contracts is that the person or persons who make the contract must have authority to contract on behalf of the entity that will be bound by the contract. A local government is not bound by a contract entered into by an individual who does not have authority to contract on its behalf. North Carolina law provides that the governing board of a county or city is the body that has authority to act for the local government, and this includes the authority to contract.[4] The governing board may delegate its authority to others within the organization, unless a statute specifically requires action to be taken by the governing board or by another named official. For example, the state competitive bidding laws require the governing board to award construction or repair contracts that are subject to the formal bidding requirements[5] and to approve a contract under certain exceptions to the bidding requirements,[6] so the board is not permitted to delegate authority to award these contracts. Similarly, most methods of surplus property disposal require governing board action.[7] For contracts that are not subject to these types of limitations, however, the county or city governing board has discretion to delegate its contracting authority.

A delegation of authority to contract may be either explicit or implicit. An example of explicit delegation might be found in a city charter, a local act of the General Assembly, or a county or city policy adopted by the governing board delegating to the manager or some other official the authority to enter into contracts on behalf of the local government. A governing board might also adopt a resolution explicitly delegating authority for awarding purchase contracts, as permitted under the formal bidding statute, or in other circumstances, including the awarding of informal contracts where the statutes do not require the governing board to award contracts. In addition, a job description or personnel policy could constitute an explicit delegation of contracting authority if it has been approved by the governing

1. N.C. Gen. Stat. (hereinafter G.S.) § 153A-11; G.S. 160A-11.

2. For example, G.S. 153A-275 and 160A-312 authorize counties and cities, respectively, to contract for the operation of public enterprises.

3. G.S. 153A-449 (counties); 160A-20.1 (cities).

4. G.S. 153A-12; 160A-12.

5. G.S. 143-129(b). G.S. 143-129(a) authorizes the board to delegate the authority to award purchase contracts in the formal range.

6. G.S. 143-129(e)(6) (sole sources); 143-129(g) (previously bid contracts/“piggybacking”).

7. See part IV in this chapter for a discussion of property disposal procedural requirements.

board. Thus, a purchasing agent or department head may have authority to contract if doing so is part of his or her job responsibilities as defined by the board. Implicit authority might be found in cases where employees regularly make contracts with the knowledge and tacit approval of the board but without a formalized policy. Many local government contracts are made by local employees with implicit authority based on historical patterns of activity and consistent with assigned job responsibilities.

The extent to which contracting is delegated within a county or city is a function of local policy, management philosophy, and administrative organization. Responsibility for contracting should be allocated in a manner that best balances the need for efficiency and flexibility with the need to comply with legal contracting and fiscal internal control requirements. Centralization of contracting for items that require bidding or that involve commonly used items helps to ensure compliance with legal requirements and can provide better value through economies of scale and consistency in administration.

Multi-Year Contracts

Counties and cities have specific authority to enter into contracts that extend beyond the current fiscal year.[8] The statutes allow the unit to enter into continuing contracts and require the board to appropriate the amount due in each subsequent year for the duration of the contract.

Contracts generally continue to bind the unit despite changes in board membership or philosophy. Courts have held that this rule does not apply, however, to any contract that limits essential governmental discretion, such as a contract that promises not to annex property or a contract in which the unit promises not to raise taxes.[9] Most county and city contracts, however, involve basic commercial transactions and, assuming all other requirements for a valid contract are met, will be enforceable against the unit for the duration of the contract.

Because multi-year contracts impose an ongoing fiscal obligation on the unit for the duration of the contract, units may include a non-appropriation clause that makes the continuation of the contract in subsequent years contingent on the governing board's appropriation of funds for that contract. A non-appropriation clause is required for all installment financings.[10] It also may be required on any other contract, agreement, or lease that could be construed as a borrowing by the unit. Whether a non-appropriation clause should be included in a contract is a matter of policy and is subject to negotiation with, and agreement by, the contractor or vendor concerned.

Expenditures Supported by Appropriations/Preaudit Certifications

State laws governing local government finance require counties and cities to establish internal procedures designed to ensure that sufficient appropriated funds are available to pay contractual obligations. Contracts involving the expenditure of funds that are included in the budget ordinance must be "preaudited" to ensure that they are being spent in accordance with a budget appropriation and that sufficient funds remain available in the appropriation to pay the obligation created by the contract. All written contracts must contain a certification by the finance officer, as specified in Section 159-28(a) of the North Carolina General Statutes (hereinafter G.S.), stating that the instrument has been "preaudited in the manner required by the Local Government Budget and Fiscal Control Act." Under that statute, a

8. G.S. 153A-13 (counties); 160A-17 (cities).

9. *See* David M. Lawrence, "Contracts that Bind the Discretion of Governing Boards," *Popular Government* 56 (Summer 1990): 38–42.

10. *See* Wayne Cnty. Citizens Ass'n v. Wayne Cnty. Bd. of Comm'rs, 328 N.C. 24 (1991).

person who incurs an obligation or pays out funds in violation of the statute is personally liable for the funds committed or disbursed.[11] Obligations incurred in violation of this requirement are void and are not enforceable against the unit.[12]

Most local governments use computerized financial systems that automatically conduct the preaudit procedure. These programs keep track of appropriated funds by category or account and encumber obligations as they are created by removing them from the pool of available funds. With the increasing use of automated contracting systems, counties and cities should be aware that the law requires governing board approval for the use of a "facsimile signature" for the preaudit certification.[13]

Contract Execution

As noted above, counties and cities have broad authority in allocating responsibility for contract approval. It is very important to distinguish, however, between the authority to approve a contract and the authority to execute (sign) a contract. Execution of the contract is a formality that is used to prove assent. Contracts are sometimes executed at the same time that they are approved. In other cases, the contract is executed after approval, such as when the board approves a contract that is later executed by the manager. Even if a contract is properly executed, it is not enforceable against the unit if it was not approved or authorized by someone with authority to contract on behalf of the unit. The fact that someone has authority to execute a contract does not necessarily mean that he or she also has authority to approve a contract, although it may constitute evidence of implicit authority if there is no explicit delegation. Except for the preaudit certification by the finance officer, state laws do not dictate who must sign county and city contracts, so this is left to local discretion.

Form of Contracts/Electronic Contracts

In addition to the specific rules that apply to public contracts, all contracts must be enforceable under general common law and state statutory requirements. Most importantly, contracts must be supported by adequate consideration,[14] and there must be evidence to support any claim that the county or city actually agreed to be bound by the terms of an alleged contractual commitment. While there is no general statutory requirement that all contracts must be in writing, the North Carolina Court of Appeals has held invalid due to the lack of a preaudit certificate (see discussion above) oral contracts that involve the expenditure of public funds.[15] Because a preaudit certificate must be affixed to a written document, all contracts involving the expenditure of public funds in the current fiscal year necessarily must be in writing. In addition, statutory writing requirements apply to certain types of contracts.

A state statute requires that all contracts made by or on behalf of cities must be in writing.[16] A city contract that is not in writing is void, but the governing board can cure this defect by expressly ratifying the written contract. The North Carolina Supreme Court has held that the board's actions as recorded in the minutes do not satisfy a statutory requirement that a contract be in writing.[17] There is no parallel statute that requires county contracts to be in writing. The formal bidding statute, G.S. 143-129, however, requires all local government contracts that are within its scope to be in writing. (See Appendix 23.1, "Dollar Thresholds in North Carolina Public Contracting Statutes," for information on which contracts are subject to formal bidding.)

11. G.S. 159-28(e).

12. G.S. 159-28(a); *see also* L & S Leasing, Inc. v. City of Winston-Salem, 122 N.C. App. 619 (1996).

13. G.S. 159-28.1.

14. That is, by something of value on each side of the contract.

15. Exec. Med. Transp., Inc. v. Jones Cnty. Dep't of Soc. Servs., ___ N.C. App. ___, 735 S.E.2d 352 (2012).

16. G.S. 160A-16.

17. Wade v. City of New Bern, 77 N.C. 460 (1877). In addition, board minutes would not satisfy the preaudit certificate requirement under G.S. 159-28(a).

Another important writing requirement is contained in the Uniform Commercial Code (UCC). The UCC was developed to modernize and standardize the law governing commercial transactions, eliminating variations from state to state and removing many of the technicalities in the common law of contracts. In North Carolina, the UCC has been adopted as G.S. Chapter 25. The provisions governing contracts for the sale of goods are contained in Article 2, beginning at G.S. 25-2-101. Article 2 requires that all contracts (not just local government contracts) for the sale of goods exceeding $500 must be in writing.[18] In addition, while the common law requires that a contract specify all of the essential terms of the agreement, the UCC modifies common law contract requirements relating to the contents of a writing and the formalities for a valid signature.[19]

Other writing requirements are found in G.S. Chapter 22. Of greatest significance to local governments is the requirement of a writing for any contract or deed evidencing the sale of land or for any interest in land, including an easement; for any sale or lease of mining rights; and for any other lease of more than three years in length.[20]

A writing serves important purposes, even when it is not required by statute or when the agreement at issue does not involve the expenditure of public funds (such as a lease of government property for a term of less than three years), the most significant being the clear expression of the agreement between the parties. In addition, for local governments the written document, usually a purchase order, incorporates the fiscal and departmental approvals required by statute and by local policy, and it provides documentation for the annual audit.

State and federal laws address the acceptability of electronic contracts, providing broad authority for the use of electronic transactions in general and in governmental contracting.[21] These laws generally provide that a contract may not be denied legal effect or enforceability solely because it has been created as an electronic document or has been affixed with an electronic signature. It is up to the county or city to determine whether it wishes to use or accept electronic contracts and to develop systems for assuring their authenticity and enforceability.

II. General Competitive Bidding Requirements

Contracts Covered by Bidding Laws

State law requires local governments to obtain competitive bids before awarding certain types of contracts. The competitive bidding process is designed to prevent collusion and favoritism in the award of contracts and to generate favorable pricing to conserve public funds. As discussed later, the law does not always require that contracts be awarded to the lowest bidder, and the bidding requirements are best viewed as requiring prudent investment of public dollars. This means that quality and value can be as important as initial price in evaluating products and contractors in competitively bid contracts.

The two key bidding statutes, G.S. 143-129 (formal bidding) and 143-131 (informal bidding), apply to two categories of contracts: (1) contracts for the purchase or lease-purchase of "apparatus, supplies, materials, or equipment" (hereinafter purchase contracts) and (2) contracts for construction or repair work. As discussed in the next section, many contracts do not fall within either of these categories and thus are not subject to any mandatory competitive bidding requirements. Bidding requirements are triggered when expenditures of public funds for the two specified

18. G.S. 25-2-201(1).

19. G.S. 25-1-201(b)(37) (a contract can be signed "using any symbol executed or adopted with present intention to adopt or accept a writing.").

20. G.S. 22-2.

21. At the federal level, see the Electronic Signatures in Global and National Commerce Act (E-SIGN), 15 U.S.C. § 7001; at the state level, see the Uniform Electronic Transactions Act (UETA), G.S. Chapter 66, Article 40 (G.S. 66-311 through -330), and the Electronic Commerce in Government Act, G.S. Chapter 66, Article 11A (G.S. 66-58.1 through -58.12).

categories of contracts occur at the dollar thresholds specified in the statutes. The current dollar thresholds are set forth in Appendix 23.1.

The competitive bidding requirements described here apply to counties, cities, local school units, and other local government agencies. With respect to purchase contracts, state agencies, including universities and community colleges, are governed by Article 3 of G.S. Chapter 143 and by the rules and policies of the State Department of Administration, Division of Purchase and Contract. With respect to contracts for construction or repair work, state agencies, including universities and community colleges, are governed by the statutes described here, along with rules and policies of the State Construction Office.

Private entities, whether nonprofit or for-profit, that contract with counties or cities are generally not required to comply with bidding statutes, even when they are spending funds they have obtained from counties or cities. The funds are no longer considered public once they are received by the private entity under a contract or grant from a public agency. A local government contracting with a private entity may, however, require compliance with bidding requirements. In addition, federal or state agencies administering grant programs may require as a condition of the grant that private subgrantees use competitive bidding procedures when expending grant funds.

Contracts Not Covered by Bidding Requirements/Optional Procedures

Contracts for services, such as janitorial, grounds maintenance, and solid waste collection, as well as contracts for professional services, such as those with consultants, attorneys, and auditors, fall outside the scope of the competitive bidding statutes. (As discussed later, special rules apply to contracts for architectural, engineering, surveying, and alternative construction delivery services.) Contracts for the purchase of real property and contracts for the lease (rental) of real or personal property also fall outside the scope of the laws that require competitive bidding. It is important to note that contracts for the lease-purchase of personal property, the installment-purchase of personal property, or the lease with option to purchase of personal property are subject to competitive bidding.[22] Purchase contracts and contracts for construction or repair work that fall below the informal bidding threshold are not subject to competitive bidding, though many local policies require bidding even at these lower levels.

In this vein and more broadly, it is common for counties and cities to seek competitive bids on contracts even when state law does not require it, such as by issuing a request for proposals (RFP) for solid waste services. This is a good practice whenever there is competition for a particular service or product. Counties and cities often use the statutory procedures when seeking competition voluntarily, but this is not required. It is important for the unit to specify what procedures and standards it will use for awarding contracts in solicitations that are not subject to state statutes, especially if the procedures will be different from those set forth in the statutes. The unit is legally bound to adhere to the procedures it opts to use when bidding is not required by statute, or it may terminate the procedure and contract using some other procedure if it deems this to be in its best interest. The decision to competitively bid a contract when it is not statutorily required does not obligate the unit to use bidding in the future for that contract or for that type of contract.

Exceptions to Bidding Requirements

The state bidding laws contain a number of exceptions. County and city officials should be cautious when contracting without bidding to make sure that the contract falls within an exception. Courts have recognized the importance of the public policy underlying the bidding requirements and have strictly scrutinized local government justifications for claiming an exemption from bidding. Except as identified below, no specific procedures apply to contracts made under these exceptions. The exceptions to the competitive bidding requirements are as follows:

22. G.S. 160A-19.

- Purchases from other governments—G.S. 143-129(e)(1). Local governments may purchase directly from any other unit of government or from a government agency (federal, state, or local) and may purchase at government surplus sales.
- Emergencies—G.S. 143-129(e)(2). An exception applies in "cases of special emergency involving the health and safety of the people or their property." The only North Carolina case interpreting the emergency exception indicates that it is very limited, applicable only when the emergency is immediate, unforeseeable, and cannot be resolved within the minimum time required to comply with the bidding procedures.[23]
- Competitive group purchasing programs—G.S. 143-129(e)(3). A group purchasing program is sometimes created by a separate organization on behalf of public agencies, or by a group of public agencies, in order to take advantage of economies of scale for commonly purchased items. Local governments may purchase without bidding items available under contracts that have been established using a competitive process undertaken as part of a group purchasing program.
- Change order work—G.S. 143-129(e)(4). For construction or repair work, competitive bidding is not required for work undertaken "during the progress" of a construction or repair project initially begun pursuant to the formal bidding statute. Change order work that is not within the scope of the original project could be challenged as an unlawful evasion of the bidding requirements.
- Gasoline, fuel, or oil—G.S. 143-129(e)(5). Purchases of gasoline, diesel fuel, alcohol fuel, motor oil, fuel oil, or natural gas are exempt from the formal bidding procedures but must be carried out using the informal procedures under G.S. 143-131.
- Sole sources—G.S. 143-129(e)(6). This exception applies to purchase contracts only, when performance or price competition is not available, when a needed product is available from only one source of supply, or when standardization or compatibility is the overriding consideration. Note that this exception applies when there is only one source for the item; simply being available from one manufacturer does not necessarily qualify the purchase under this exception, as that item may be available from more than one vendor or retailer. The governing board must approve each contract entered into under this exception, even if the board has delegated authority to award purchase contracts under G.S. 143-129(a).
- State and federal contract purchases—G.S. 143-129(e)(9), (e)(9a). Local governments may purchase items from contracts awarded by any North Carolina state agency or federal agency if the contractor is willing to extend to the local unit the same or more favorable prices, terms, and conditions as established in the state or federal contract. This includes purchases of information technology from contracts established by the State Office of Information Technology Services (G.S. 143-129(e)(7)).
- Used apparatus, supplies, materials, or equipment—G.S. 143-129(e)(10). Competitive bidding is not required for the purchase of used items. The exception does not define what constitutes a used item, but it specifically excludes items that are remanufactured, refabricated, or "demo" items.
- Previously bid contracts ("piggybacking")—G.S. 143-129(g). Local governments may purchase from a contractor who has entered into a competitively bid contract with any other unit of government or with a government agency (federal, state, or local), anywhere in the country, within the past twelve months. The contractor must be willing to extend to the local government the same or more favorable prices and terms as are contained in the previously bid contract. This exception applies to purchase contracts in the formal bidding range only. The North Carolina local government's governing board must approve each contract entered into under this exception at a regular board meeting on ten days' public notice, even if the board has delegated authority to award purchase contracts under G.S. 143-129(a).
- Force account work—G.S. 143-135. For construction or repair work, bidding is not required for projects to be completed using the local government unit's own employees. This exception actually operates as a limitation on the amount of work that may be done by local government employees. The exception limits such work to

23. Raynor v. Comm'rs of Louisburg, 220 N.C. 348 (1941).

projects estimated to cost no more than $125,000 including the cost of labor and materials, or to projects on which the cost of labor does not exceed $50,000. The competitive bidding statutes still apply to materials to be used on such force account projects. Some have argued that the exception to the bidding requirements does not limit the use of the unit's own forces as long as the local unit itself submits a bid. There does not appear to be any authority in the statutes for a local government to submit a bid to itself as a way of complying with bidding requirements and avoiding application of the force account limits.

- School food services—G.S. 115C-264. Local boards of education may purchase without competitive bidding supplies and food for school food services programs.
- Voting systems—G.S. 163-165.8. Counties may purchase without competitive bidding voting systems that have been approved by the State Board of Elections.
- Alternative procedures—Requests for Proposals. Several types of contracts that involve a combination of goods and services may be entered into using alternative—usually more flexible—competitive procedures. A more flexible "request for proposals" (RFP) procedure is authorized for contracts for information technology goods and services, including computer software, hardware, and related services (G.S. 143-129.8); guaranteed energy savings contracts (G.S. 143-129(e)(8)); and contracts involving solid waste and sludge management facilities (G.S. 143-129.2). Unless specifically authorized under an exception, local governments do not have authority to use an RFP procedure for contracts that are subject to the competitive bidding statutes.

Specifications

While competitive specifications are an essential element of a bidding process, there are no statutory procedures governing the preparation of specifications for purchases. Local officials may develop specifications that are most appropriate for their respective units. They cannot, however, intentionally or unjustifiably eliminate competition by using overly restrictive specifications. If only one brand of product is suitable, the specification can be limited to that brand, although the unit may be called upon by competitors to consider products alleged to be comparable or to justify the elimination of other products from consideration. A brand-specific specification is not necessarily a sole-source purchase since there may be more than one supplier of a particular brand.

G.S. 133-3 imposes specific limitations on the development of specifications for construction or repair projects. The statute requires that specifications for materials included in construction projects be described in terms of performance characteristics and allows brands to be specified only when performance specification is not possible. In such cases, at least three brands must be specified unless it is impossible to do so, in which case the specifications must include as many brands as possible. The unit must specifically approve in advance of the bid opening preferred products that are to be listed as alternates in specifications for construction projects.

Contracts for the construction or repair of buildings are subject to additional statutory requirements for specifications. Depending on the cost, some project specifications must be drawn by a licensed architect or engineer.[24] If the building project is estimated to cost $300,000 or more, separate specifications must be prepared for heating, plumbing, and electrical work as well as general construction work.[25]

Trade-Ins

G.S. 143-129.7 authorizes local governments to include in bid specifications for a purchase an allowance for the trade-in of surplus property, and to consider the price offered, including the trade-in allowance, when awarding a contract for

24. G.S. 133-1.1(a).
25. G.S. 143-128(a).

the purchase. This statute effects an exemption from otherwise applicable procedures for disposing of surplus property. See part IV of this chapter for a full description of procedures for disposing of property.

III. Summary of Bidding Procedures

Informal Bidding

Informal bidding under G.S. 143-131 is required for contracts for construction or repair work and for the purchase of apparatus, supplies, materials, or equipment costing between the minimum informal bid threshold and the formal bidding limit (see Appendix 23.1 for current threshold amounts). No advertisement is required, and the statute does not specify a minimum number of bids that must be received. Informal bids can take the form of telephone quotes, faxed bids, or other electronic or written bids. The statute requires that the county or city maintain a record of informal bids received and specifies that such records are subject to public inspection after the contract is awarded. This prevents bidders from having access to bids already submitted when preparing their bids, a situation not present in formal bidding because bids are sealed until the bid opening. The standard for awarding contracts in the informal range is the same as the standard for formal bids—the lowest responsive responsible bidder—and is discussed later in this chapter.

As noted below, for building construction or repair contracts in the informal range, the informal bidding statute requires counties and cities to solicit bids from minority firms and to report to the state Department of Administration on bids solicited and obtained for contracts in this dollar range.

Formal Bidding

Advertisement

The formal bidding statute, G.S. 143-129, requires counties and cities to advertise opportunities to bid on contracts for construction or repair, or for the purchase of apparatus, supplies, materials, and equipment, within the formal bid thresholds as described in Appendix 23.1. The minimum time period for advertisement under the statute requires that a full seven days pass between the day of the advertisement and the day of the bid opening. It is common practice to place the advertisement more than once or for a longer period of time prior to the bid opening in order to provide sufficient opportunity for response. The advertisement must list the date, time, and location of the bid opening, identify where specifications may be obtained, and contain a statement that the board reserves the right to reject any or all bids. For construction projects, the advertisement may also contain information about contractor licensing requirements that apply to the project.

The formal bidding statute requires the advertisement to be published in a newspaper of general circulation within the given county or city. The statute also authorizes the governing board to approve the use of electronic advertisement of bidding opportunities instead of published notice. The board may authorize electronic advertisement of bids for particular contracts or for contracts in general. Action to approve electronic notice of bidding must be taken by the county or city governing board at a regular meeting. No specific action is required to provide electronic notice in addition to published notice.

Sealed Bids

Bids must be sealed and submitted prior to the time of the bid opening. Bids must be opened in public and cannot be opened prior to the advertised time of the bid opening without the permission of the bidder. Under the "dual-bidding" method of construction contracting (discussed later), separate-prime bids must be received (but not opened) one hour before the single-prime bids. Staff generally conduct bid openings, but contracts must be awarded by the governing board, except for purchase contracts in jurisdictions where the board has delegated the authority to award these contracts as authorized in G.S. 143-129(a).

Once formal bids are opened they become public records and are subject to public inspection. The only exception to this rule is contained in G.S. 132-1.2, which allows a bidder to identify trade secrets that are contained in a bid and protects that information from public disclosure.[26]

Electronic Bids

Counties and cities have several alternatives to receiving paper, sealed bids for purchase contracts in the formal bidding range. Under G.S. 143-129.9, formal bids for purchase contracts may be received electronically[27] or through the use of a "reverse-auction" process.[28] Under a reverse-auction procedure, bidders compete to provide goods at the lowest selling price in an open and interactive electronic auction process. An electronic bid or reverse-auction process can be conducted by the unit itself or by a third party under contract with the unit. The statute does not allow the use of reverse auctions for the purchase of construction aggregates, including crushed stone, sand, and gravel, nor does it authorize the use of electronic bids or reverse auctions for construction contracts in the formal bidding range.

Number of Bids

According to G.S. 143-132, three bids are required for construction or repair contracts that are subject to the formal bidding procedures. If three bids are not received after the first advertisement, the project must be readvertised for at least the minimum time period listed under the formal bidding statute (seven days, not including the day of advertisement and the day of the bid opening) before the next bid opening. Following the second advertisement, a contract can be awarded even if fewer than three bids are received.

Note that the statute only applies to contracts for construction or repair work in the formal bidding range. This means that three bids are not required for purchase contracts in the formal range or for any contracts in the informal range. Some counties or cities may have local policies that require three bids for all contracts, but this is not required by state law.

Bid, Performance, and Payment Bonds

Bonds or statutorily authorized bond substitutes are required for construction or repair contracts in the formal bid range. A bid for construction or repair work submitted in the formal process must be accompanied by a bid deposit or bid bond of at least 5 percent of the bid amount. The bid bond or deposit guarantees that the bidder to whom a contract is awarded will execute the contract and provide performance and payment bonds when they are required. The statute specifies the forms in which the bid security may be submitted: a bid bond, a bid deposit in cash, a cashier's check, or a certified check.

Specific procedures are set forth in G.S. 143-129.1 for the withdrawal of a bid. A bid may be withdrawn under those procedures without forfeiting the bid bond only if the bidder can demonstrate that he or she has made an unintentional and substantial error, as opposed to an error in judgment. The law does not allow a bidder to correct a mistake, only to withdraw a bid if proof of an unintentional error is shown.

The formal bidding statute also requires that counties and cities obtain performance and payment bonds from the successful bidder on major construction or repair projects. A performance bond guarantees performance of the contract and provides the county or city with security in the event that the contractor defaults and cannot complete the contract. The payment bond is obtained for the benefit of subcontractors who supply labor or materials to the project and provides a source of payment to those contractors in the event that they are not paid by the general contractor. Performance and payment bonds are required on construction or repair projects that meet or exceed the dollar thresh-

26. A "trade secret" is defined under G.S. 66-152(3). For further discussion of when bid documents become open to public inspection, see Eileen Youens, "When Are Bids and Proposals Subject to Public Inspection?" *Local Government Law Bulletin* No. 119 (Feb. 2009).

27. G.S. 143-129.9(a)(1).

28. G.S.143-129.9(a)(2).

olds set forth in Appendix 23.1. The statute authorizes counties and cities to accept deposits of cash, certified checks, or government securities in lieu of bonds.[29]

Evaluation of Bids/Responsiveness

Once received, bids must be evaluated to determine whether they meet the specifications and are eligible for award—that is, whether they are responsive bids. The bid evaluation process is important to maintaining the integrity of the bidding process. If a county or city accepts bids that contain significant deviations from the specifications, the other bidders may object. Indeed, courts have recognized that a governmental unit receiving bids does not have unlimited discretion in waiving deviations from specifications. Courts have held that the unit must reject a bid that contains a "material variance" from the specifications, defined as a variance that gives the bidder "an advantage or benefit which is not enjoyed by other bidders."[30] Even though specifications may reserve to the unit the ability to "waive minor irregularities," the unit's assessment of what constitutes a minor irregularity must be based upon the legal standard established by the courts. Thus, if the low bid omits a required feature that the unit feels it can live without, the unit must reject the defective bid. The unit then has the option of accepting the next-lowest responsive, responsible bid or rejecting all the bids, revising or clarifying the specifications, if necessary, and rebidding the contract.

A bid must also be rejected as nonresponsive if it fails to satisfy a statutory requirement applicable to the particular contract. For example, a bid in the formal range that is submitted after the advertised bid deadline, or a formal bid for a construction project that is submitted without the required bid bond, must be rejected. While the unit has the discretion to waive minor irregularities, it does not have the authority to waive statutory requirements.

Standard for Awarding Contracts

Both the formal and informal bid statutes require that contracts be awarded to the "lowest responsible bidder, taking into consideration quality, performance, and the time specified in the proposals for the performance of the contract."[31] Although this standard probably creates a presumption in favor of the bidder who submits the lowest dollar bid, it clearly does not require an award to the lowest bidder in all cases. The North Carolina Court of Appeals has held that the formal bid statute authorizes the board to request information from the bidders about their experience and financial strength and to consider this information in determining whether the low bidder is responsible.[32] The court found that the term "responsibility" refers to the bidder's capacity to perform the contract and that the statute authorizes the board to evaluate the bidder's experience, training and quality of personnel, financial strength, and any other factors that bear on the bidder's ability to perform the work.

It is somewhat less clear whether this standard of award allows the county or city to award a contract for the purchase of apparatus, supplies, materials, or equipment to a bidder who proposes a more expensive, higher-quality piece of equipment than the lowest bidder. Assuming all of the items proposed are within the scope of the specifications, it seems reasonable to interpret the statute as allowing the board to choose a higher-quality item if doing so is the best investment of public funds.

The unit must carefully document the factual basis for any award to a bidder who did not submit the lowest bid and be diligent in investigating the facts to make sure that the information it relies upon is accurate and reliable. The

29. The performance and payment bonds required under the formal bidding statute are governed by Article 3 of G.S. Chapter 44A.

30. Prof'l Food Servs. Mgmt. v. N.C. Dep't of Admin., 109 N.C. App. 265, 269 (1993) (internal quotation marks, citation omitted). *See also* Frayda Bluestein, "Understanding the Responsiveness Requirement in Competitive Bidding," *Local Government Law Bulletin* No. 102 (May 2002).

31. *See* G.S. 143-29((b) and 143-131(a).

32. Kinsey Contracting Co., Inc. v. City of Fayetteville, 106 N.C. App. 383, 386 (1992).

county or city does not necessarily have to demonstrate that a contractor is not responsible generally, only that the contractor does not have the skills, experience, or financial capacity for the contract in question.

Construction or repair contracts that are subject to the formal bidding requirements must be awarded by the governing body. For purchase contracts, G.S. 143-129(a) authorizes the board to delegate to the manager or chief purchasing official the authority to award contracts or to reject bids and readvertise the contract and opportunity to bid. The informal bidding statute does not dictate who must award contracts. This responsibility is usually delegated to the purchasing agent or to other employees responsible for handling informal contracts.

Local governments also have broad authority to reject any or all bids for any reason that is not inconsistent with the purposes of the bidding laws.[33]

Local Preferences

Local governments in North Carolina do not have specific statutory authority to establish preferences in awarding contracts, such as preferences for local or minority contractors. A local preference would conflict with the legal requirement in both the formal and informal bidding range that contracts be awarded to the lowest responsible bidder. Although some may think it economically or politically desirable, it is not legal to assume that a local contractor is more responsible than others under this standard for awarding contracts. Preferences or targeted contracting efforts for local government may be permissible, however, for contracts that are not subject to the competitive bidding requirements, such as service contracts or contracts below the minimum bid threshold (see Appendix 23.1). Counties and cities can also establish procedures to identify local and minority contractors and notify them of contracting opportunities.

Special Rules for Building Contracts

Bidding and Construction Methods

In addition to the bidding requirements for contracts involving construction or repair work described above, there are several special requirements for construction and repair contracts involving buildings. First, state law limits the bidding and construction methods counties and cities may use for major building construction. For building construction projects that are above the dollar threshold contained in G.S. 143-128 (see Appendix 23.1), local governments may use any of the following contracting methods: separate prime,[34] single prime,[35] construction management at risk,[36] design-build,[37] design-build bridging,[38] or public–private partnership.[39]

Under traditional construction delivery methods (separate prime and single prime), the prime contract is the contract directly between the owner (the unit of government) and the contractor. In a single-prime contract, the general contractor has the prime contract with the owner and all other contracts are subcontracts with the general contractor. Under the separate-prime (also called multiple-prime) system, contractors in the major trades (general contracting, plumbing, electrical, heating, ventilating, and air conditioning) submit separate bids to and contract directly with the owner. Bids may also be received on a "dual-bidding" basis, under which both separate-prime and single-prime bids are solicited. Under dual bidding, the unit may consider cost of construction oversight, time for completion, and other factors it deems appropriate in determining whether to award a contract on a single-prime or separate-prime basis, and it may award to the lowest responsive, responsible bidder under either category.

33. G.S. 143-129(a).
34. G.S. 143-128(b).
35. G.S. 143-128(d).
36. G.S. 143-128.1.
37. G.S. 143-128.1A.
38. G.S. 143-128.1B.
39. G.S. 143-128.1C.

The procurement process for alternative construction delivery methods (construction management at risk, design-build, design-build bridging, and public–private partnership) is substantially different from that for traditional construction delivery methods. Generally, contracts for alternative construction delivery methods are procured using the qualification-based process that applies to design and related services (described below). The construction manager at risk contracts to oversee and manage construction and to deliver the completed project at a negotiated guaranteed minimum price. The construction manager is required to solicit bids and award contracts for all of the actual construction work (including general contracting work) to prequalified subcontractors. Under the design-build method, the unit enters into one contract with a team comprised of design professionals and contractors (design-build team) to both design and build the project. The design-build bridging method involves a two-contract process under which the unit first contracts with a design professional to design 35 percent of the project and then contracts with a design-build team to complete the design and perform the construction. While the contract with the design professional is procured using the qualification-based selection method, the contract with the design-build team is awarded under the lowest responsive, responsible bidder standard. A public–private partnership contract involves one contract between the unit and a private developer in which the developer finances at least 50 percent of the project and where the roles and responsibilities of the unit and the developer are delineated in a negotiated development contract.

Other construction methods not specifically authorized by statute may be used only for projects below the threshold set out in the statute or with special approval from the State Building Commission or by authority of local legislation enacted by the General Assembly.[40]

Historically Underutilized Business Participation

Public agencies, including counties and cities, are required under G.S. 143-128.2 to establish a percentage goal for participation by historically underutilized business (HUB) contractors in major building construction or repair projects, to make efforts to include these contractors in these projects, and to require prime contractors to either meet or make good-faith efforts to attain the established HUB participation goal.[41] The current dollar thresholds for HUB participation requirements are set forth in Appendix 23.1. The law does not establish or authorize a set-aside of particular contracts for HUB contractors or a preference for HUB contractors in awarding contracts. Failure to make the statutorily mandated minimum good-faith efforts is grounds for rejection of a bid.[42] The statute specifically states, however, that contracts must be awarded to the lowest responsible, responsive bidder and prohibits consideration of race, sex, religion, national origin, or handicapping condition in awarding contracts. Counties and cities are required to establish a minority business participation outreach plan and to report data regarding minority outreach and participation on specific projects to the State Department of Administration.

Counties and cities also have authority under G.S. 160A-17.1 to comply with minority/women business enterprise program requirements that may be imposed as a condition of receiving federal or state grants and loans.

Requirements for Design and Related Services

State law specifies when plans and specifications for public building projects must be prepared by a registered or licensed architect or engineer.[43] The statutory thresholds, set forth in Appendix 23.1, apply based on whether the project involves new construction or renovation that calls for foundation or structural work or that affects life safety

40. For a comparison of various construction methods, see Valerie Rose Riecke, "Public Construction Contracting: Choosing the Right Project-Delivery Method," *Popular Government* 70, no. 1 (Fall 2004): 22–31.

41. G.S. 143-128.2(a), (b). *See also* Norma R. Houston and Jessica Jansepar Ross, "HUB Participation in Building Construction Contracting by N.C. Local Governments: Statutory Requirements and Constitutional Limitations," *Local Government Law Bulletin* No. 131 (Feb. 2013).

42. G.S. 143-128.2(c).

43. G.S. 133-1.1(a).

systems. This requirement applies even if the work is to be done by the unit's own forces, subject to the force account limits discussed earlier.

Another statute, G.S. 143-64.31, requires that public agencies select architects, engineers, surveyors, and alternative construction delivery methods (construction manager at risk, design-build, design-build bridging, and public–private partnership) based on qualifications instead of bid prices. The statute prohibits counties and cities from asking for pricing information, other than unit prices (understood to mean hourly rates), until after the best qualified person or firm is identified. Fees are then negotiated to develop a final contract. Local government units that do not wish to use the qualification-based process required under the statute have the ability under G.S. 143-64.32 to approve an exemption for any particular project where the design fee is less than $50,000. While governing board approval is not required, the statute does require the unit to exempt itself in writing. Once exempt, the board can either negotiate a contract or conduct a competitive bidding or other process to select the design professional for services in these categories.

Protests and Legal Challenges

Unlike the laws governing state and federal contracting, North Carolina laws governing local government contracting do not establish bid protest procedures. North Carolina courts have held that if a contract is subject to the statutory competitive bidding procedures and those procedures are not followed, the contract is void.[44] If a bidder is dissatisfied with a decision of the county or city—for example, to award a contract to the second-lowest bidder or to accept a bid that does not meet specifications—the bidder can register his or her complaint with the local official responsible for the contract or register it directly with the governing board. As a practical matter, it is best for the unit to attempt to resolve the matter, but there is no legal requirement for a hearing or other formal disposition of the complaint. If the matter is not resolved administratively, the only legal option is for the aggrieved party to sue the unit of government, typically for an injunction to prevent the unit from going forward with an illegal contract.[45] It is not unusual for protests to be lodged with local government officials or with governing boards, although legal challenges are rare.

IV. Property Disposal

County and city governments generally dispose of both real and personal property in accordance with the procedures set forth in G.S. Chapter 160A, Article 12 (G.S. 160A-265 through -280), although there are a few other disposition procedures set out in other statutes, applicable to special situations.[46] These various statutes authorize several methods for selling or disposing of property and set forth the procedures for each one. Before examining these methods, it is useful to discuss one introductory matter: the need for consideration when disposing of local government property.

Consideration

Under the North Carolina Constitution, it is generally unconstitutional for a local government to dispose of property for less than its fair market value.[47] A gift of property or a sale at well below market value constitutes the granting of an "exclusive privilege or emolument" to the person receiving the property, which is prohibited by Article 1, Section 32,

44. Raynor v. Comm'rs of Louisburg, 220 N.C. 348, 353 (1941).

45. *See* Frayda S. Bluestein, "Disappointed Bidder Claims Against North Carolina Local Governments," *Local Government Law Bulletin* No. 98 (May 2001).

46. G.S. 153A-176 requires counties to comply with the procedures for property disposal in Article 12 of G.S. Chapter 160A.

47. Redevelopment Comm'n v. Security Nat'l Bank, 252 N.C. 595 (1960).

of the state constitution. Most of the procedures by which a local government is permitted to sell or otherwise dispose of property are competitive, and the North Carolina Supreme Court has indicated that the price resulting from an open and competitive procedure will be accepted as the market value.[48] If a sale is privately negotiated, the price will normally be considered appropriate unless strong evidence indicates that it is so significantly below market value as to show an abuse of discretion.[49]

It is not always constitutionally necessary that a local government receive monetary consideration when it conveys property. If the party receiving the property agrees to put it to some public use, that promise constitutes sufficient consideration for the conveyance.[50] (The recipient in this case is often, but not always, another government unit.) The General Statutes expressly permit the following such conveyances: those made to the state and to local governments within North Carolina (G.S. 160A-274); those made to volunteer fire departments and rescue squads (G.S. 160A-277); conveyances to nonprofit preservation or conservation organizations (G.S. 160A-266(b)); to nonprofit agencies to which the county or city is authorized to appropriate money (G.S. 160A-279); and to governmental units within the United States, nonprofits, charter schools, and sister cities (G.S. 160A-280).

Disposal Methods

G.S. Chapter 160A, Article 12, sets out three competitive methods of sale, each of which is appropriate in any circumstance for disposing of both real and personal property: sealed bid, negotiated offer and upset bid, and public auction. Article 12 also permits privately negotiated exchanges of property in any circumstance (so long as equal value changes hands) and privately negotiated sales or other dispositions of property in a number of limited circumstances. In addition, a few other statutes permit privately negotiated sales or other dispositions of property, again in limited circumstances. These various methods of disposition are summarized in the following sections. In undertaking any of them a local government must remember that the statutory procedure must be exactly followed or the transaction may be invalidated by a court.[51]

Sealed Bids

A local government may sell any real or personal property by sealed bid (G.S. 160A-268). The procedure is based on that set forth in G.S. 143-129 for entering into purchase contracts in the formal bidding range, with one modification for real property. An advertisement for sealed bids must be published in a newspaper that has general circulation in the county (for a county government) or in the county in which the city is located (for a city government). Publication must occur seven full days (not counting the day of publication or the day of opening) before the bids are opened if personal property is being sold and thirty days before the bids are opened if real property is being sold. The advertisement should generally describe the property; tell where it can be examined and when and where the bids will be opened; state whether a bid deposit is required and, if so, how much it is and the circumstances under which it will be retained; and reserve the governing board's right to reject any and all bids. Bids must be opened in public, and the award is made to the highest responsible bidder.

The sealed bid procedure appears to be designed to obtain wide competition by providing public notice and good opportunity for bidders to examine the property being sold. Invitations to bid may be mailed to prospective buyers, just as they are typically sent to prospective bidders in the formal purchasing procedures for personal property.

---

48. *Id.*

49. Painter v. Wake Cnty. Bd. of Educ., 288 N.C. 165 (1975).

50. Brumley v. Baxter, 225 N.C. 691 (1945). However, see *infra* note 53 regarding the limitation on disposal of local school property.

51. Bagwell v. Town of Brevard, 267 N.C. 604 (1966). Some government boards routinely declare as surplus any property that is to be sold. No statute requires such a declaration, however, and it does not appear to be necessary. A city or county evidences its conclusion that property is surplus by selling it.

Negotiated Offer and Upset Bids

A local government may sell any real or personal property by negotiated offer and upset bid (G.S. 160A-269). The procedure begins when the local government receives and proposes to accept an offer to purchase specified government property. The offer may be either solicited by the local government or made directly by a prospective buyer on his or her own initiative. The governing board then requires the offeror to deposit a 5 percent bid deposit with its clerk and causes a notice of the offer to be published. The notice must describe the property; specify the amount and terms of the offer; and give notice that the bid may be raised by not less than 10 percent of the first $1,000 originally bid, plus 5 percent of any amount above $1,000 of the original bid. Upset bids must also be accompanied by a 5 percent bid deposit. Prospective bidders have ten days from the date on which the notice is published to offer an upset bid. This procedure is repeated until ten days have elapsed without the local government receiving a qualifying upset bid. After that time the board may sell the property to the final offeror. At any time in the process, it may reject any and all offers and decide not to sell the property.

Public Auctions

A local government may sell any real or personal property by public auction under G.S. 160A-270. The statute sets out separate procedures for the auctioning of real and personal property and authorizes electronic auctions. For real property, the governing board must adopt a resolution that authorizes the sale; describes the property; specifies the date, time, place, and terms of the sale; and states that the board must accept and confirm the successful bid. The board may require a bid deposit. A notice containing the information set out in the resolution must be published at least once and not less than thirty days before the auction. The highest bid is reported to the governing board, which then has thirty days to accept or reject it.

For personal property, the same procedure is followed except that (1) the board may in the resolution authorize an appropriate official to complete the sale at the auction and (2) the notice must be published not less than ten days before the auction.

G.S. 160A-270(c) permits a local government to sell either real or personal property electronically. The governing board must follow the same procedures as set out above, but in addition the notice must specify the electronic address where information about the property to be sold can be found and the electronic address at which electronic bids may be posted. In recent years, electronic auctions through sites such as GovDeals[52] have largely replaced public auctions and have become the most common method of competitive sale disposal for personal property.

Exchange of Property

A local government may exchange any real or personal property for other real or personal property if it receives full and fair consideration for the property (G.S. 160A-271). After the terms of the exchange agreement are developed by private negotiations, the governing board will authorize the exchange at a regular meeting. A notice of intent to make the exchange must be published at least ten days before it occurs. The notice must describe the properties involved; give the value of each, as well as the value of other consideration changing hands; and cite the date of the regular meeting at which the board proposes to confirm the exchange. The exchange procedure is probably most useful in connection with a trade of real property when boundaries must be adjusted or when an individual who owns land needed by the county or city wants some other tract of government land.

Trade-In

A local government may convey surplus property as a "trade-in" as part of a purchase contract (G.S. 143-129.7). The local government must include a description of the surplus property in its bid specifications, and the amount offered by bidders for the surplus property is taken into account when evaluating bids. The unit awards one contract to the winning bidder for both the sale of the surplus property and the purchase of the new property. While the purchase

52. *See* www.govdeals.com/.

contract must comply with the applicable competitive bidding requirements, the transaction need not comply with the disposal procedures of G.S. 160A-271 (exchange of property).

Private Negotiation and Sale: Personal Property

A local government may use private negotiation and sale to dispose of personal property valued at less than $30,000 for any one item or any group of similar items (G.S. 160A-266, -267). Note that this procedure may not be used to dispose of real property. Under G.S. 160A-266(b) and -267, the governing board, by resolution adopted at a regular meeting, may authorize an appropriate official to dispose of identified property by private sale. The board may set a minimum price but is not required to do so. The resolution must be published at least ten days before the sale.

Alternatively, G.S. 160A-266(c) authorizes a governing board to establish procedures under which county or city officials may dispose of personal property valued at less than $30,000 for any one item or any group of similar items without further board action and without published notice. The procedures must be designed to secure fair market value for the property disposed of and to accomplish the disposal efficiently and economically. The procedures may permit one or more officials to declare qualifying property to be surplus, to set its market value, and to sell it by public or private sale. The board may require the official to use one of the statutory methods, including an electronic auction, or may permit other sorts of procedures, such as a consignment agent or a surplus property warehouse. The statute requires the selling official to maintain a record of property sold under any such procedures.

Private Negotiation and Conveyance to Other Governments

G.S. 160A-274 authorizes any governmental unit in the state, on terms and conditions it "deems wise," to sell to, purchase from, exchange with, lease to, or lease from any other governmental unit in North Carolina any interest in real or personal property that one or the other unit may own. "Governmental unit" is defined to include cities, counties, the state, school units, and other state and local agencies. The only limitations on this broad authority are that before a local board of education may lease real property that it owns, it must determine that the property is unnecessary or undesirable for school purposes, and it may not lease the property for less than $1 per year.[53] While governing board approval is required, bids or published notices are not. Thus, when reaching agreements on property with another governmental unit, a unit's governing board has full discretion concerning procedure.

Other Negotiated Conveyances: Real and Personal Property

A city or county may, in limited circumstances, convey real and personal property by private negotiation and sale, and sometimes without monetary consideration.

Economic Development

G.S. 158-7.1(d) permits a county or city (but no other form of local government) to convey interests in property suitable for economic development by private sale. Before making such a conveyance, the governing board must hold a public hearing with at least ten days' published notice of the hearing. The notice must describe the interest to be conveyed; the value of the interest; the proposed consideration the government will receive; and the board's intention to approve the conveyance. In addition, before making the conveyance the board must determine the probable average wage that will be paid to workers at the business to be located on the property.

The statute requires the governing board to determine the fair market value of the property and prohibits the board from conveying the property for less than that value. The county or city, in arriving at the amount of consideration it will receive, may count prospective tax revenues for the next ten years from improvements added to the property after

53. Although in general local governments may transfer property among themselves without monetary consideration, the North Carolina Supreme Court has held that a local school board must receive fair consideration whenever it conveys property for some nonschool use, including some other governmental use. Boney v. Bd. of Trs., 229 N.C. 136 (1948). The $1 requirement for leases of school property presumably is a legislative determination that this amount is adequate consideration when title to the property remains with the school administrative unit.

the conveyance; prospective sales tax revenues generated by the business located on the property during that period; and any other income coming to the government during the ten years as a result of the conveyance.

Community Development

G.S. 160A-457 permits a city (but not a county or any other sort of local government) to convey interests in property by private sale when such property is within a community development project area. The property must be sold subject to covenants that restrict its eventual use to those consistent with the community development plan for the project area. The statute requires that the property be appraised before it is sold and prohibits the city from selling it for less than the appraised value.

Once a city has reached agreement on a conveyance pursuant to this statute, it must publish notice of a public hearing on the transaction for the two weeks running up to the hearing. The notice should describe the property, disclose the terms of the transaction, and give notice of the city's intention to convey the property. At the hearing itself, the city must disclose the appraised value of the property.

Nonprofit Agencies

G.S. 160A-279 permits a county or city to convey real or personal property to any nonprofit agency to which it is authorized by law to appropriate funds. (Property acquired through condemnation may not be so conveyed.) The same procedures must be followed as are required by G.S. 160A-267 for other private sales. In making a conveyance under this statute, a county or city may accept as consideration the nonprofit agency's promise to put the property to some public use. G.S. 160A-280 authorizes conveyances of personal property to nonprofits and governmental entities outside of the state.

Property for Affordable Housing

Both counties and cities may convey property by private sale in order to provide affordable housing (i.e., housing for persons of low or moderate income), but they do so under separate statutes that have somewhat different provisions. G.S. 153A-378 includes two provisions that permit a county to make two sorts of conveyances. First, a county may convey residential property directly to persons of low or moderate income. If it does so, it must follow the same procedures as are required by G.S. 160A-267 for other private sales. Second, a county may convey property to a public or private entity that provides affordable housing for others. The statute imposes no procedural requirements for such a conveyance.

A complicated series of statutes permits cities to convey property to nonprofit entities that will construct affordable housing. First, G.S. 160A-456(b) permits a city council to exercise any power granted by law to a housing authority. Second, G.S. 157-9 authorizes a housing authority to provide "housing projects," a term defined in G.S. 157-3 to include programs that assist developers and owners of affordable housing. Third, G.S. 160A-20.1 permits a city to appropriate money to a private organization to do anything a city is authorized to do, including providing affordable housing. And fourth, G.S. 160A-279, summarized in the subsection just above, authorizes a city to convey property to any nonprofit agency to which it may appropriate money.

Fire or Rescue Services

G.S. 160A-277 permits counties and cities to lease or convey to volunteer fire departments or rescue squads serving their jurisdictions land to be used for constructing or expanding fire or rescue facilities. The governing board must approve the transaction by adoption of a resolution at a regular meeting after ten days' published notice. The notice should describe the property, state its value, set out the proposed monetary consideration or the lack thereof, and declare the board's intention to approve the transaction. (Almost all fire or rescue organizations are nonprofit in nature, so a local government may also use G.S. 160A-279 to convey property to them, including personal property; G.S. 160A-280 also provides authority for donating personal property to these nonprofit organizations.)

Architectural and Cultural Property

G.S. 160A-266(b) permits a county or city to convey, after private negotiation, real or personal property that is significant for its archaeological, architectural, artistic, cultural, or historic associations; for its association with such property; or for its natural, scenic, or open condition. The conveyance must be to a nonprofit corporation or trust whose purposes include the preservation or the conservation of such property, and the deed must include covenants and other restrictions securing and promoting the property's protection.[54] A local government making a conveyance under this provision must follow the same procedures as noted earlier for the private sale of real or personal property under G.S. 160A-267.

Open Space

G.S. 160A-403 permits a local government to conserve open space by acquiring title to property, then conveying it to the original owner or to a new owner, in each case subject to covenants that require the property to be maintained as open space. If the conveyance is back to the original owner, the statute permits it to be made by private sale. If the conveyance is to an appropriate entity, it may be made by private sale pursuant to G.S. 160A-266(b), discussed in a preceding paragraph. Otherwise, however, the government must use one of the competitive sale methods.

Other Private Conveyances

A number of other statutes permit private sales of property in narrow circumstances; only one of these statutes includes any required procedures.

1. G.S. 160A-321 permits the private sale of any entire city enterprise. Unless the enterprise is conveyed to another government, however, the statute requires the city's voters to approve the conveyance for the following kinds of enterprises: electric power distribution; water supply and distribution; wastewater collection, treatment, and disposal; natural gas distribution; public transportation; cable television; and stormwater management.
2. G.S. 105-376(c) permits a government that has acquired property through a tax foreclosure to convey the property back to the original owner or to any other person or entity that had an interest in the property (such as a deed of trust).
3. G.S. 153A-163 permits a government that has acquired property through a loan foreclosure to sell the property by private sale, so long as it receives at least as much as it paid for the property.
4. G.S. 153A-176 permits a government that has been given property for a specified purpose to give the property back to the donor if it will not use the property for the specified purpose.
5. G.S. 40A-70 permits a government that has acquired property through eminent domain which it no longer needs to convey the property back to the condemnee, so long as the government receives in return its original purchase price, the cost of any improvements, and interest.
6. G.S. 160A-342 permits a city that operates a cemetery to convey it to a private operator of cemeteries.

Lease of Property

A county or city may lease any real or personal property it owns that the governing board finds will not be needed during the term of the lease—in essence, the city is permitted to make a temporary disposal of the property since the lease agreement gives exclusive use of the property to the lessee (G.S. 160A-272). The procedure to be followed depends on the length of the lease. The board may, by resolution at any meeting, make leases for one year or less. It may also authorize the manager or some other administrative officer to take similar action concerning government property for the same period.

The governing board may lease government-owned property for periods longer than one year and for up to ten years by a resolution adopted at a regular meeting after ten days' published notice of its intention to do so. The notice

54. These deed restrictions must be in the form of a preservation agreement or conservation agreement as defined in G.S. 121-35.

must also specify the annual lease payment and give the date of the meeting at which the board proposes to approve the action.

A lease for longer than ten years, including renewal periods, must be treated, for procedural purposes, as if it were a sale of property. It may be executed by following any procedure authorized for selling real property.

Grant of Easements

A county or city may grant easements over, through, under, or across any of its property (G.S. 160A-273). The authorization should be by resolution of the governing board at a regular meeting. No special published notice is required, nor is the grant subject to competition.

Sale of Stocks, Bonds, and Other Securities

A county or city that owns stocks, bonds, or other securities that are traded on the national stock exchanges or over the counter by brokers and securities dealers may sell them in the same way and under the same conditions as a private owner would (G.S. 160A-276).

Warranty Deeds

G.S. 160A-275 authorizes a city council or board of county commissioners to execute and deliver deeds to any governmentally owned real property with full covenants of warranty when the council or board determines that it is in the unit's best interest to do so. Council/board members are relieved of any personal liability arising from the issuance of warranty deeds if their actions are undertaken in good faith.

Additional Resources

Bluestein, Frayda S. *A Legal Guide to Purchasing and Contracting for North Carolina Local Governments.* 2nd ed. Chapel Hill, N.C.: UNC Institute of Government, 2004.

Houston, Norma R. *A Legal Guide to Construction Contracting with North Carolina Local Governments.* 5th ed. Chapel Hill, N.C.: UNC School of Government, forthcoming 2015.

______. *North Carolina Local Government Contracting: Quick Reference and Related Statutes.* Chapel Hill, N.C.: UNC School of Government, 2014.

Lawrence, David M. *Local Government Property Transactions in North Carolina.* 2nd ed. Chapel Hill, N.C.: UNC Institute of Government, 2000.

School of Government Web materials on purchasing and construction contracting, available at www.ncpurchasing.unc.edu.

About the Author

Norma R. Houston is a faculty member at the School of Government whose areas of interest include public contracting and bidding.

The author wishes to express her appreciation to Frayda S. Bluestein, David M. Lawrence, and the late Warren Jake Wicker, whose work in public purchasing and authorship of this chapter in the previous editions of this book are reflected in this edition's chapter.

Appendix 23.1

Dollar Thresholds in North Carolina Public Contracting Statutes

Dollar limits and statutory authority current as of September 1, 2013

Requirement	Threshold	Statute
Formal bidding	*(estimated cost of contract)*	
Construction or repair contracts	$500,000 *and above*	G.S. 143-129
Purchase of apparatus, supplies, materials, and equipment	$90,000 *and above*	G.S. 143-129
Informal bidding	*(actual cost of contract)*	
Construction or repair contracts	$30,000 to formal limit	G.S. 143-131
Purchase of apparatus, supplies, materials, and equipment	$30,000 to formal limit	G.S. 143-131
Construction methods authorized for building projects	*Over* $300,000	G.S. 143-128(a1)
Separate Prime	*(estimated cost of project)*	
Single Prime		
Dual Bidding		
Construction Management at Risk *(G.S. 143-128.1)*		
Design-Build and Design-Build Bridging *(G.S. 143-128.1A; G.S. 143-128.1B)*		
Public-Private Partnership (P3) *(G.S. 143-128.1C)*		
Historically Underutilized Business (HUB) requirements		
Building construction or repair projects		
– Projects with state funding *(verifiable 10% goal required)*	$100,000 *or more*	G.S. 143-128.2(a)
– Locally funded projects *(formal HUB requirements)*	$300,000 *or more*	G.S. 143-128.2(j)
– Projects in informal bidding range *(informal HUB requirements)*	$30,000 to $500,000*	G.S. 143-131(b)
**Note: Formal HUB requirements should be used for informally bid projects costing between $300,000 and $500,000*		
Limit on use of own forces (force account work)	*(not to exceed)*	G.S. 143-135
Construction or repair projects	$125,000 *(total project cost)* or $50,000 *(labor only cost)*	
Bid bond or deposit		
Construction or repair contracts *(at least 5% of bid amount)*	Formal bids *($500,000 and above)*	G.S. 143-129(b)
Purchase contracts	Not required	
Performance/Payment bonds		
Construction or repair contracts *(100% of contract amount)*	Each contract *over* $50,000 of project costing *over* $300,000	G.S. 143-129(c); G.S. 44A-26
Purchase contracts	Not required	
General contractor's license required	$30,000 *and above*	G.S. 87-1
Exemption	Force account work *(see above)*	
Owner-builder affidavit required	Force account work *(see above)*	G.S. 87-14(a)(1)
Use of licensed architect or engineer required		
Nonstructural work	$300,000 *and above*	G.S. 133-1.1(a)
Structural repair, additions, or new construction	$135,000 *and above*	
Repair work affecting life safety systems	$100,000 *and above*	
Selection of architect, engineer, surveyor, construction manager at risk, or design-build contractor		
"Qualification-Based Selection" procedure (QBS)	All contracts unless exempted	G.S. 143-64.31
Exemption authorized	Only projects where estimated fee is *less than* $50,000	G.S. 143-64.32

From *A Legal Guide to Purchasing and Contracting for North Carolina Local Governments*, 2nd ed., by Frayda S. Bluestein,

Chapter 24

Eminent Domain

Charles Szypszak

The United States Constitution forbids government from taking private property "for public use without just compensation" or "without due process of law."[1] The North Carolina Constitution guaranties that no person may be deprived of property "but by the law of the land."[2] The North Carolina Constitution does not expressly give government bodies a right to take private property, but the state's courts have deemed such a power of eminent domain to be inherent in the power to govern and to be essential to the government's ability to provide for the public welfare.

Whenever counties and cities exercise their powers of eminent domain, they must abide by the constitutional requirements of taking property only for public uses and benefits and paying the owners just compensation for the property taken. No power of eminent domain exists unless the legislature has invoked the authority by legislation. The authority of counties and cities to take private property by eminent domain is expressed in Chapter 40A of the North Carolina General Statutes (hereinafter G.S.), which identifies the allowed public purposes for a taking and the procedure for exercising it.[3] Other statutes describe additional public purposes and benefits for which certain districts, authorities, and organizations may take private property.

Compliance with the statutory requirements is important to avoid objections and complications, so any county or city that is taking property by eminent domain should review the current version of the statutes to confirm the existence of authority for the action and to ensure compliance with procedural requirements.

1. U.S. Const. amend. V.
2. N.C. Const. art. I, § 19.
3. Section 40A-1 of the North Carolina General Statutes (hereinafter G.S.).

Public and Private Condemnors

The governing body of a county or city is a "public condemnor," as are certain other authorities such as sanitary district boards, hospital and housing authorities, community college boards of trustees, and regional transportation authorities, among others.[4] "Private condemnors" that have a statutory power of eminent domain include railroads, utilities, private educational institutions for water supply purposes, and union bus station companies.[5]

Authorized Public Uses and Benefits

The condemnation statute identifies a number of purposes for which public condemnors may use the power of eminent domain, including

- roads, streets, alleys, and sidewalks;
- systems for water supply and distribution, wastewater, septic, solid waste, and stormwater management;
- airports;
- parking;
- public transportation;
- electric and gas power generation, transmission, and distribution under defined circumstances (cities only);
- parks, playgrounds, and other recreational facilities;
- storm sewer and drainage systems;
- hospital facilities, cemeteries, and libraries;
- city halls, fire stations, office buildings, jails, and other buildings for use by any department, board, commission, or agency;
- drainage programs and programs to prevent obstruction to the natural flow of streams or to improve drainage facilities;
- acquisition of designated historical properties;
- public wharves;
- beach erosion control and flood and hurricane protection and for public trust beaches and related parking areas (certain coastal counties and cities).[6]

Local government condemnation authority extends to land outside the local government's boundaries for these authorized purposes.[7] The statutes require most, but not all, local governments and authorities seeking to use eminent domain to acquire land in another county to obtain the consent of the other county's board of commissioners.[8] Other recognized public purposes are identified in statutes creating public bodies or establishing public programs: for example, G.S. 160A-515 allows urban redevelopment commissions to take blighted parcels of property, while G.S. 115C-517 allows local boards of education to acquire suitable sites for schoolhouses or other school facilities.

Counties and cities may not condemn property owned by the State of North Carolina unless the state consents to the taking. The state's consent is given by the Council of State or by the Secretary of Administration if the council delegates that authority to the secretary. When state property is taken, the only issue is the compensation to be paid.[9] Except as otherwise provided by statute, public condemnors may take private condemnors' property if the property is not in actual public use or is not necessary to the operation of the owner's business. A public condemnor may condemn

4. G.S. 40A-3(b), (c).
5. G.S. 40A-3(a).
6. G.S. 40A-3(b).
7. *Id.*
8. G.S. 153A-15.
9. G.S. 40A-5.

another public condemnor's property if the property is not being used or held for future use for any governmental or proprietary purpose.[10]

Just Compensation

The owner is entitled to be paid "just compensation" for the property taken, which must reflect the property's fair market value as of the date immediately before the county or city files a complaint.[11] Fair market value is based on the highest and best uses available for the property, not just the actual uses to which the property has been put. The analysis assumes a ready and able buyer who is willing but not compelled to buy.[12] The usual approach is market comparison based on recent sales data for properties similarly configured, with adjustments for material differences. If only part of a tract is taken, the measure of compensation is the greater of two calculations. The first is diminution in value, which is the amount by which the fair market value of the entire tract immediately before the taking exceeded the fair market value of the remainder immediately after the taking. The second is the fair market value of the part of the property that was taken.[13] In the case of an easement, the assessment of diminution in value, if any, will include consideration of the impact on the value of the property outside the easement area. The compensation will not include changes in value before the date of valuation that were caused by the proposed improvement or project for which the property is taken.[14] Possible future loss of profits for a business operating on the property affected by the taking is not an element of compensable loss, although the anticipated income stream for income-producing property is sometimes an appropriate element of appraisal of the real estate value.

The condemnor may allow the owner to remove timber, buildings, fixtures, and improvements that are not needed for the intended condemnation use. If the compensation award deducted the value of these materials and the owner does not remove them within a reasonable time, the removal and storage cost is chargeable to the owner and secured by a lien on any remaining part of the owner's property.[15]

Condemnation Procedure

In many cases, the condemning authority and the property owner will be able to reach an agreement on the taking and the amount of compensation for it, usually based on appraisal reports. When such an agreement cannot be reached, any dispute about the legitimacy of the public purpose for which the property is being taken will be determined by a superior court, and disagreements about the amount of compensation will be determined by the court or by commissioners appointed by the superior court clerk.

Negotiations and Right of Entry

The public condemnor may negotiate with an owner about acquiring the property without impairing its power to take the property by eminent domain. The statute provides that the power to acquire property by condemnation does not depend on any prior effort to acquire the same property by gift or purchase, nor is the power to negotiate for the gift or the purchase of property impaired by initiation of a condemnation proceeding.[16] A condemnor who seeks to

10. G.S. 40A-5(b).
11. G.S. 40A-63.
12. Barnes v. Highway Comm'n, 250 N.C. 378, 387–88 (1958).
13. G.S. 40A-64.
14. G.S. 40A-65.
15. G.S. 40A-9.
16. G.S. 40A-4.

acquire property by purchase or gift must give the owner a written notice of the owner's right to reimbursement of taxes allocable to the period before the taking.[17]

With thirty days' advance notice to the landowner, a condemnor may enter on private land, but not structures, to make surveys, borings, examinations, or appraisals without filing a complaint, making a deposit, or taking any other formal action. The condemnor must reimburse the owner for any damages resulting from these activities.[18]

Notice

At least thirty days before filing a complaint for condemnation, the condemnor must give written notice to the owner of the condemnor's intent to institute such an action.[19] This notice must contain information prescribed by G.S. 40A-40, including a description of the property to be taken and the condemnor's estimate of the just compensation, the purpose for which the property is being taken, and the date the condemnor intends to file a complaint.[20] Additional notice requirements apply to condemnation actions in which title will vest upon the filing of the complaint and deposit—the so-called quick take procedure, described below.[21]

Complaint, Registry Memorandum, and Deposit

A public condemnor institutes an eminent domain action by filing a complaint in the superior court of the county in which the land is located, with a declaration of taking. The complaint must include a statement of the authority under which the taking is occurring, a description of the property, the purpose of the condemnation, information about the owner's identity, the estimated just compensation, a statement about whether any improvements may be removed by the owner, a description of any known liens, and a request for a determination of just compensation.[22] The condemnor must deposit the amount of estimated compensation with the court when the complaint is filed.[23] This means that condemning authorities must already have the funds for the estimated compensation at the time the eminent domain procedure is begun. At the same time, the condemnor also must give third parties constructive notice of the pending condemnation by recording a memorandum of action with the register of deeds in any county where involved land is located.[24]

The summons, together with a copy of the complaint and a notice of the deposit, is served on the named parties.[25]

If an owner's property is taken by a county or city that did not commence a condemnation proceeding, the owner may begin an action for compensation within twenty-four months of the date of the taking or the completion of the public project, whichever occurs later. The procedure in such cases is similar to that in cases in which the action is begun by the condemnor.[26]

Disbursement of Deposit

When there is no dispute about title, the persons named in the complaint may apply to the court for disbursement of all or part of the deposit, without prejudice to the owner's challenge to the sufficiency of the compensation. The condemnor is not entitled to notice of a hearing on the owner's request for disbursement of the deposit.[27]

---

17. G.S. 40A-4; G.S. 40A-6.
18. G.S. 40A-11.
19. G.S. 40A-40.
20. G.S. 40A-40(a).
21. G.S. 40A-40(b).
22. G.S. 40A-41.
23. *Id.*
24. G.S. 40A-43.
25. G.S. 40A-41.
26. G.S. 40A-51.
27. G.S. 40A-44.

Transfer of Title

The point at which the condemnor becomes owner of the property depends on the condemnation's purpose. When a county or city condemns property for certain listed purposes, the title to the property and the right to immediate possession vest when the complaint is filed and the deposit is made. This is known as the "quick take" procedure. It applies to such uses as roads, water and wastewater systems, solid waste collection and disposal, and city systems for electricity, gas, cable, storm sewer and drainage. It also applies to certain beachfront communities for beach erosion control and flood and hurricane protection and for public trust beaches and related parking areas. The quick take procedure does not apply to property to be taken for public transportation systems, off-street parking facilities, airports, and certain other purposes.[28]

When title does not transfer upon the filing of the complaint, the timing of the transfer depends on the course of the condemnation proceeding. If the owner does not dispute the taking but only the amount of compensation, title vests when the owner files the answer stating this to be so. If the owner fails to file an answer within 120 days, title vests when the deadline passes. Title also vests upon disbursement of the deposit at the owner's request. The owner may seek an injunction to prevent title from vesting.[29]

Answer and Reply

The owner has 120 days to file an answer admitting or denying the allegations of the complaint and stating any affirmative defenses. No answer is filed to the declaration of taking and notice of deposit. The condemnor may file a reply within thirty days of receipt of the answer.[30] If an owner does not file an answer as required, the owner is deemed to have admitted that the amount deposited is just compensation. In such a case, the judge enters final judgment and orders disbursement of the deposited money.[31]

Within ninety days after receipt of the answer, but no sooner than six months after filing the complaint, the condemnor must file a plat of the property taken and of such other areas as are necessary for a determination of the compensation, and this plat is mailed to the parties or counsel.[32]

The court will appoint an attorney to represent any party in interest who is unknown or cannot be found, as may occur when the current holder of an interest in property cannot be determined based on the available public records. In addition, the court will appoint a guardian ad litem to represent those who do not have the legal capacity to defend themselves, such as children or those under a legal disability.[33]

Challenge to Taking

Challenges to the sufficiency of the public purpose for the taking, the condemnor's authority, the area taken, the presence of necessary parties, or any other matters besides the amount of just compensation will be heard and decided by a judge. Either party may raise these issues by motion to the court with ten days' notice.[34]

Appointment and Duties of Commissioners

If the owner disputes the condemnor's just compensation amount, either the owner or the condemnor may, within sixty days after the answer has been filed, request the clerk of superior court to appoint commissioners. The clerk then appoints three competent, disinterested persons who reside in the county to serve as commissioners. The commissioners have the power to inspect the property, hold hearings, swear witnesses, and take evidence as they deem necessary. When they have completed these tasks, they must file with the court a report on a statutorily prescribed form reciting

28. G.S. 40A-42(a).
29. G.S. 40A-42.
30. G.S. 40A-45; G.S. 40A-46.
31. G.S. 40A-46.
32. G.S. 40A-45(c).
33. G.S. 40A-50.
34. G.S. 40A-47.

the formalities of the process and stating the amount of compensation. The clerk mails a copy to the parties or their counsel.[35]

If no request is made for commissioners, the case is placed on the court's civil docket for trial to determine the amount of compensation.[36]

Challenge to the Commissioners' Determination

Either party has thirty days after the commissioners' report is mailed to challenge the commissioners' determination and demand a trial on the issue of compensation. The trial will be by jury unless both parties waive the right. The issue of compensation is newly determined by the jury or court based on evidence presented at the trial; the amount of the deposit and the commissioners' determination are not considered. If no exception is filed, the judge still reviews the commissioners' award to determine if it is just, and if it is so determined, the award is entered as a final judgment. If the judge decides the award is not just, the amount is set aside and the matter is set for a trial.[37]

Costs and Interest

An owner is entitled to interest on the award at the rate of 6 percent from the date of taking to the date of judgment, but not on the deposit amount for the period after it was made.[38] The court has the power to order a condemnor to pay an owner's court costs.[39] The court has discretion to order the condemnor to pay the owner's costs of appraisers, engineers, and plats used as evidence in the procedure,[40] and courts typically do order such reimbursement in eminent domain cases. If the condemnor abandons the condemnation after filing a complaint or is determined not to have had authority for the taking, the court may award the owner compensation for costs, disbursements, expenses, and loss suffered as a result of not being able to transfer title during the proceeding.[41] Owners are also entitled to such compensation if they were forced to bring an action to recover compensation for a taking not instituted by the condemnor.[42]

About the Author

Charles Szypszak is a School of Government faculty member. He specializes in real estate matters and since 2005 has advised North Carolina registers of deeds in their daily operations and their initiatives for legislative and regulatory reforms. He has drafted or contributed to the composition of many of the current laws and regulations that govern the registers and teaches certification and continuing education programs. Previously he was a practicing attorney for nineteen years with a focus on real estate transactions and real estate litigation.

35. G.S. 40A-48.
36. G.S. 40A-49.
37. G.S. 40A-48(d).
38. G.S. 40A-53.
39. G.S. 40A-13.
40. G.S. 40A-8(a).
41. G.S. 40A-8(b).
42. G.S. 40A-8(c).

Part 6

Planning, Development Regulation, Community and Economic Development

Chapter 25

Community Planning, Land Use, and Development

Richard D. Ducker

As far as most North Carolina communities are concerned, growth, development, and change are desirable and probably essential. And for many North Carolina communities some form of growth, development, and change is inevitable. Will such changes be haphazard and unpredictable or organized and purposeful? The effectiveness of a community's local planning program will determine the answer. Community planning is based on the premise that the community as a whole has a substantial stake in determining how, when, and where it should grow. Community planning is concerned about capturing the benefits of growth and avoiding its pitfalls. North Carolina local governments have a number of tools to use in influencing growth. However these tools are used, effective planning also means cooperating intelligently with the inevitable.

For most North Carolina local governments, city or county planning means *land use and development planning.* Land use and development planning involves the application of the planning process to all public and private activities that affect the physical use and development of land, which in turn affect the growth and the character of a community. Some jurisdictions view land use planning as simply an aspect of *community development,* emphasizing that the economic and social development of the community is closely related to its physical development. Many cities and some counties consider growth management to be an especially important aspect of community planning. For others the task is simply one of managing to grow. No matter the terminology used, influencing the use and development of land is a crucial function of local government.

One feature of land use planning that distinguishes it from many other types of public planning is its concern with private sector activities as well as those of the public sector. Some local governments view their function in this regard as simply accommodating or responding to the growth that private development generates and providing public services wherever and whenever they are needed. It is also undeniable, however, that the location of a new highway, the extension of utilities, or the standards of a zoning ordinance may strongly influence the location, type, and timing of private development. This interplay between public and private activities creates the need for community planning.

A city or county may influence development by (1) establishing clear plans and policies providing direction to citizens, businesses, the development community, and other units of government in matters of growth and development; (2) constructing and maintaining public facilities (streets, utilities, parks, schools, and so forth) and providing services in connection with them; (3) regulating the use, development, and maintenance of private and public property (for example, through zoning and subdivision regulations, a minimum housing code, and so forth); and (4) extending subsidies, loans, and financial incentives to induce private parties to act consistently with municipal objectives. Table 25.1 lists an array of these measures.

Since community planning involves so much coordination and facilitation, these approaches are often combined. For example, in a community development block grant area, a local government may install drainage facilities and make street improvements while offering subsidized housing rehabilitation loans to property owners in the affected area. Planners concerned about revitalizing a central business district may suggest landscaping plans or building facade designs for downtown merchants who wish to upgrade the area. At the same time the zoning ordinance may establish sign standards and height limits in the same area.

Ironically, much of the de facto planning a local government carries out does not primarily involve local staff planners. Street design standards are established in public works departments, and community public reinvestment programs are handled by community development. Utility extension planning may implicate a joint utility provider, and the North Carolina Department of Transportation makes critical road network decisions. Working together to achieve community policy can be both conceptually and practically difficult, but it also illustrates that planning may be too important to be left solely to planners.

Table 25.1 Methods Used by Cities for Influencing Land Use and Development

1. Providing Public Facilities

- Estimating needs, selecting sites, and determining sequence and timing of capital improvements (for example, streets and roads)
- Influencing pattern of development
- Extending utilities to manage growth
- Protecting future roadway corridors
- Acquiring land and public improvements
- Purchasing sites in advance
- Encouraging donations of land
- Requiring compulsory dedication of land and improvements in new developments (for example, parkland, streets, and utilities)
- Requiring compulsory reservation of land
- Imposing impact fees to pay for capital improvements required to serve new growth

2. Regulating Land Use and Development

- Regulating division of land and construction of community or public improvements
- Enforcing land subdivision ordinances
- Adopting utility-extension policies
- Adopting special assessment and cost reimbursement policies for public facilities
- Regulating water supply and wastewater disposal systems
- Establishing standards for designing, constructing, and accepting subdivision streets
- Enforcing driveway permit regulations
- Regulating use and development of land
- Enforcing zoning ordinances
- Adopting watershed protection regulations
- Regulating soil erosion and sedimentation control
- Establishing development standards for flood hazard areas
- Adopting special zoning restrictions around airports
- Designating historic landmarks and establishing historic districts
- Adopting special-purpose police-power ordinances (such as those regulating mobile home parks, outdoor advertising, and junkyards)
- Requiring local environmental impact statements
- Adopting roadway corridor official map ordinances
- Enforcing the State Building Code
- Establishing property maintenance and public health and safety standards
- Adopting minimum housing code
- Condemning abandoned or unsafe structures
- Establishing junked-car program
- Controlling weeds and litter
- Abating public nuisances

3. Providing Direction and Leadership

- Adopting comprehensive plan and publicizing it
- Providing assistance to property owners, neighborhood groups, environmental groups, and other nonprofit organizations
- Establishing voluntary design guidelines
- Establishing capital improvement programs (CIPs) to link budgeting to comprehensive land use planning

4. Providing Financial Incentives

- Providing rehabilitation grants and loans for housing
- Providing housing rental subsidies
- Providing loans and grants for historic preservation
- Acting as economic entrepreneur
- Constructing and leasing shell buildings
- Making site improvements on privately owned property
- Making cash grants

Growth North Carolina Style

Between 2000 and 2010 North Carolina's population grew by more than 1.5 million to reach a total of about 9.54 million residents by the end of the decade.[1] This increase represents a growth rate of 18.5 percent, nearly double the national growth rate of 9.7 percent. North Carolina was the sixth fastest growing state in the country during that decade. However, one-third of that population increase occurred in only two counties, Wake and Mecklenburg. Metropolitan areas throughout the state, particularly Wake County, Mecklenburg County, and the suburbanizing counties that ring them had high population growth rates while certain northeastern and central coast counties experienced slow growth or population declines. Only seven North Carolina counties actually lost population in the last decade, but thirty-eight counties are projected to see a decline between 2010 and 2020 as their population ages.[2]

1. U.S. Department of Commerce, U.S. Census Bureau, "State and County Quick Facts: North Carolina," rev. Jan. 6, 2014, http://quickfacts.census.gov/qfd/states/37000.html.

2. Rebecca Tippett, "Population Growth and Population Aging in North Carolina Counties," Carolina Demography, UNC Population Center, October 14, 2013, http://demography.cpc.unc.edu/2013/10/14population-growth-population-aging-in-north-carolina-counties/.

Job growth has been tied to population growth. Since 2010 the state's three largest metropolitan areas (the Triangle, the Piedmont Triad, and the Charlotte region) have created jobs at a rate of 7 percent, some 40 percent faster than the national and state rates. The three areas have accounted for 70 percent of all job growth in the state.[3] Job growth since 2010 in all other parts of the state has expanded at a rate of about 3 percent. The number of North Carolinians living in urban areas (as defined by the U.S. Census) grew from 50 percent in 2000 to 66 percent in 2010. Urban transportation needs are growing even faster. The North Carolina Department of Transportation now estimates that the amount of surface vehicular traffic, measured in vehicle miles traveled, is increasing at about 1.4 times the population growth rate statewide.[4] The amount of land converted into urban use may be growing still faster. Between 1970 and 1990 eleven communities in North Carolina, all municipalities, met the census definition for an urbanized area. In every case the physical size of the urbanized area grew faster than the rate of the corresponding population increase. In Charlotte the urbanized area grew twice as fast; in Wilmington, 2.4 times faster. In Winston-Salem the size of the urbanized area grew 2.8 times faster than the growth rate of the population in the corresponding area.

The picture these statistics paint is not simply one of growth, but of an increasingly dispersed form of land development concentrated in urban and metropolitan regions. This form of growth appears to be highly correlated with dependency on the automobile and is sometimes known as urban (or more precisely, suburban) sprawl.

Critics of this form of development have reacted. Planners, designers, and even some developers have lamented the decline of downtowns and urban life, the development of strip commercial projects with "big box" or franchised design, and the decline of the social cohesiveness that makes diverse neighborhoods and communities attractive. They have pointed to decreasing reinvestment in existing urban infrastructure and a continuing emphasis on new public investment in the urban fringe. They have criticized the form of development that fosters dependency on the automobile. Sprawl, they contend, tends to result in conversion of open space and agricultural land to urban development and makes preservation of the environmental features of the countryside more difficult as the distinction between urban and rural areas becomes increasingly blurry. As development disperses, it encourages North Carolina cities to "chase" new projects and the property tax revenues they represent by trying to annex them.

What kind of growth is responsible and attainable and how can a local government help ensure that it occurs? To some planners "smart growth" and the emphasis on new urbanism are vindication of the principles they have been advocating for years. For some developers this form of local planning emphasizes that urban residents and municipalities must be prepared to accept higher-density development projects and change in existing neighborhoods. Property rights advocates see it as a further unwarranted attempt to limit the free hand of the local land development market.

In any event certain planning and development principles are central to city and county planning. Not all of them, however, will likely be put into practice.

One key planning principle is associated with compact development. It encourages the more efficient use of vacant or underused parcels of land within existing urban areas. If land already served by streets, utilities, schools, and other facilities is used for development, the need for investment in major infrastructure on the urban fringe is reduced. Adaptive reuse involves making existing buildings suitable for new activities; urban infill suggests that passed-over undeveloped or underutilized land parcels can be productively used. Adaptive reuse (one form of which is historic preservation) and urban infill can revive older neighborhoods and provide increased access to jobs in older, established employment centers. Opposition comes from real estate developers and owners of land in outlying areas who might be precluded from developing on the urban fringe and in rural areas where land is less expensive. Thus the goal of making productive use of pre-established infrastructure and underutilized land in urban areas is unlikely to be achieved in many areas of the state.

Revitalizing older existing neighborhoods is typically a goal of local governments. Yet critics claim that such programs focus on issues of interest to the more affluent, such as traffic congestion, urban sprawl, the design of new

3. Michael Walden, "N.C. Recovery Difficult as Urban-Rural Divide Deepens," NC SPIN, July 12, 2013, www.ncspin.com/2013/07/12/nc-recovery-difficult-as-urban-rural-divide-deepens/.

4. Blue Ribbon Commission to Study North Carolina's Urban Transportation Needs: Final Report to the 2006 Session of the 2005 General Assembly of North Carolina, 9.

development, and environmental protection, and pay insufficient attention to issues of interest to those who remain in cities, such as housing, crime, and employment. Revitalizing older areas can be disruptive, resulting in more traffic and higher property values, property taxes, and rents, and, in some cases, can dramatically change the neighborhood's character. The likelihood of the success of these programs often depends on the influence of neighborhood organizations and the strength of the market for renovated or redeveloped properties.

Ensuring a range of housing choices has long been a bedrock planning goal for most communities, but it may be inconsistent with certain other development policies. Making development generally more compact and dense and protecting rural open space and environmentally sensitive areas from development often result in higher prices for urban property. Well-financed commercial developers that prefer urban areas, environmentalists, and owners of potential urban sites may favor the idea. Residential property owners enjoy an advantage if existing property values rise, but renters and those who do not own a home but wish to buy suffer a disadvantage. One strategy for overcoming higher land and housing prices is to increase housing densities in and near existing residential neighborhoods. But residents who live near areas where higher density is proposed often intensely oppose it and are likely to argue "not in my back yard" (NIMBY). As a result, increasing residential densities in existing neighborhoods is difficult except in certain special areas in large cities. An alternative is to encourage more compact development in newly developing "greenfield" areas.

Another planning principle concerns mixing land uses and developing pedestrian-friendly projects. These ideas also involve urban form and design. In this context planners, architects, and developers refer to "new urbanism," "traditional neighborhood design," "pedestrian-friendly development," and "transit-oriented development." Such projects require a richer mix of land uses (residential, office, and commercial) than traditional zoning ordinances tend to promote. One concept associated with traditional neighborhood design involves construction of a town square or a village center surrounded by smaller shops, restaurants, theaters, and the like, with apartments and single-family houses all within walking distance. Well-designed developments incorporating these features have generally been popular with consumers. Land development regulations that incorporate these concepts tend to be accepted by the development community if these regulations are offered as options to those applicable to conventional development.

Another important planning concept emphasizes the reduction of traffic congestion and the availability of transportation alternatives. Suburban-style development skews toward a street system hierarchy with higher-capacity streets designed to move traffic as quickly as possible with relatively little consideration given to pedestrians and bikers. Traditional neighborhood designs (and the development regulations that enable them) favor a system of narrow roads with on-street parking allowed on residential streets. Street connectivity is improved so that the streets in one neighborhood are connected to those in another, and a driver need not drive out to a more congested collector street or thoroughfare to go anywhere. Street-design standards, applied through land subdivision regulations, can significantly influence the character of residential development. Making a community "walkable" means also providing sidewalks, pedestrian ways, and bike paths that connect different types of buildings and diverse land uses. These features can be incorporated into development regulations fairly easily and with relatively little opposition. Improving public transit to provide transportation alternatives is often a costly proposition and typically necessitates making operating subsidies available to transit service providers. However, opposition to pedestrian, bicycle, and public transit programs is often not potent because auto users do not typically feel disadvantaged if others shift to transportation alternatives.

Recent planning innovations, particularly those associated with the "new urbanism," also address building design. Design issues tend to concern the relationship between the "built environment" (typically private buildings) and the "public realm" (including streets, sidewalks, plazas, and open spaces). Proponents argue that neighborhood design should favor buildings and the pedestrians that use them, not automobiles and trucks. To accomplish this, new development in urban areas is brought forward to the street right-of-way (to a "build-to" line), sidewalks are furnished, on-street parking is allowed, and off-street parking is situated to the rear of buildings or in courtyard areas. Close attention should therefore be paid to building configuration, bulk, and density. Increasing emphasis on building design often results in land development regulations that focus more on building form and less on the ways buildings are actually used. In urban areas whether portions of a several-story building are used for commercial, office, or residential purposes may not be so important. Form-based codes do not dispense with land use restrictions, but, similar to historic preservation design standards, they emphasize the form of buildings and how they fit into their surroundings. (See the section entitled "Form-Based Codes" below.) Design review and regulation of appearance are thus integral parts of smart growth. These changes are occurring because opposition from the development community is fading.

Improvements in project design can also support environmental concerns. Clustering of new development so that substantial areas are left as open space can protect environmentally sensitive land, and vegetated buffers can limit the impacts of stormwater runoff and help preserve wetland habitats. Landscaping and tree protection practices can preserve or restore vegetation as development occurs. Improved street design not only improves traffic circulation; it facilitates stormwater management as well.

Matters concerning urban form and development patterns, transportation, housing, and environmental quality routinely transcend the boundaries of individual local governments. Effective planning, at least as described above, is unlikely to occur without strong cooperation among local governments and state agencies. Cities will likely find it very difficult to rein in urban sprawl or achieve more compact development without at least some cooperation from counties. Indeed, a commitment to compact development might mean that more development is encouraged within municipal boundaries or within a municipality's planning jurisdiction and less in areas located within a county's planning jurisdiction. North Carolina counties that depend on new development outside of cities to generate tax revenues or that are particularly responsive to the interests of entities in unincorporated areas may not be inclined to support these efforts. Utility extension policies illustrate this dilemma. Many North Carolina cities own and operate their own water supply and sewage disposal systems. Historically most utility systems have been expected to serve customers and, it is hoped, generate a surplus of revenues, not necessarily to shape growth and development. But cities, the local governments most likely to provide water and sewer services in urban areas, are generally authorized to do so outside as well as inside city limits and may be the only public providers of utility service in the urban fringe. Some utility providers have defined an *urban service area* as a geographic area within which urban services are provided or will be provided within a certain planning period and outside of which such services will not be extended.[5] Using an urban service boundary saves money because serving areas close to an existing network of lines costs less than extending the network into peripheral areas. Urban service boundaries are also consistent with policies promoting compact development. Increasingly, however, counties are becoming involved in providing water and sewer service. Some have their own systems. Some provide financial assistance to cities that choose to extend their systems. Some have entered into more elaborate agreements with cities concerning the financing, construction, ownership, and maintenance of public systems. The increasing involvement of counties in public utility extension policy allows cities and counties to fashion joint utility arrangements that will shape development in a large region. Ironically, however, since many county governments are relatively indifferent to or oppose municipal policies promoting compact development, improved intergovernmental cooperation does not necessarily result in the kind of development that some planning proponents would like to see.

General Comprehensive Plan (Land Use Plan)

The centerpiece of a local planning program has traditionally been a *general comprehensive plan*. This plan provides a community with an overview of its current physical development and serves as a guide for its future development policy.[6] Typically the plan includes a sketch of the city's or county's historical development and statistical information about the community; discusses urban development issues and problems; and presents a series of maps, charts, illustrations, and photos displaying both current information and future projections. However, the primary function of the plan document is to outline in writing the policy the community intends to pursue with respect to growth and

5. *See* Richard D. Ducker and David W. Owens, "A Smart Growth Toolbox for Local Government," *Popular Government* 66 (Fall 2000): 29–42.

6. The national-award-winning "Legacy 2030" plan adopted by the city of Winston-Salem and Forsyth County is available at http://www.legacy2030.com/.

development and to help determine the steps necessary to put this policy into effect. For this reason the process by which the community establishes its development goals and objectives and the extent to which it develops a consensus about the proper role local government can play in influencing development are critical. The comprehensive plan as a document can be only as effective as the process that has shaped it.

Except for cities and counties subject to the Coastal Area Management Act (CAMA) (see below), local governments are not required by state law to adopt or use a comprehensive plan or land use plan. As a general rule, the state's planning legislation does not mandate the adoption of a plan, spell out or suggest what such a plan might consist of, or indicate the process for its formulation and adoption. As a result, the nature of plans and how they are used vary widely among North Carolina local governments. However, amendments in 2005 to the state zoning statutes requiring cities and counties to adopt statements analyzing the consistency of proposed zoning amendments with locally adopted plans (see below) provide additional recognition of comprehensive plans.

The process for developing a comprehensive plan is an important one. Certain parties with interests that will be affected by the plan (land developers and realtors, business owners, chambers of commerce and merchant associations, economic development proponents, members of the farming community, housing and environmental organizations, utility providers, neighborhood groups, and other local governments and state agencies) are typically involved. It is often difficult for local governments to generate enthusiasm about plan-making from citizens at large. But the Internet affords new options for doing so. Web pages provide easy access to graphics that allow laypeople to better understand the nature of growth and development and planning proposals. Email, listservs, and even chat rooms support media for discussions that are more responsive and easier to use than were formerly possible. Some communities have devised online surveys to gauge citizen preferences. Of course, there may be no complete substitute for face-to-face meetings. Planners can use small focus groups to test new ideas. Neighborhood community meetings are a staple of bringing proposals to people where they live. Some local governments have experimented with charrettes. A *charrette* is an intense design exercise in which decision makers, supported by a cadre of information, staff resources, and drafting supplies, literally sketch out a proposal for the future of a downtown, a street corridor, a neighborhood, or some other small area. Such an exercise certainly encourages participants to buy into the ideas the charrette generates and reduces planning abstractions to practical applications.

A pivotal component of a general comprehensive plan is the *land use plan*. Land use plans are based on projections of population growth and land development patterns that have implications for public facilities, transportation, and economic development as well as housing, cultural and natural resource protection, and community appearance. In fact, many local governments use the terms *general comprehensive plan* and *land use plan* interchangeably.

Land use plans must be prepared for cities and counties in the twenty coastal counties subject to CAMA. These plans must be consistent with guidelines adopted by the Coastal Resources Commission. Local governments elsewhere in the state are under no similar legal obligation.

Certain rudimentary assumptions about land use must also be made if a city engages in transportation planning. Section 136-66.2 of the North Carolina General Statutes (hereinafter G.S.) directs each North Carolina municipality outside a metropolitan area, with the cooperation of the North Carolina Department of Transportation (NCDOT), to prepare a comprehensive transportation plan, which typically includes a local thoroughfare and street plan. Counties are authorized, but not compelled, to join in the process. By law, NCDOT may participate in the plan development only if all of the cities and counties within the area subject to the plan are in the process of developing a land development plan or all of those governments have adopted such a plan within the past five years. In metropolitan areas metropolitan transportation planning organizations made up of member governments prepare and adopt regional plans of the same type.

Increasingly cities and counties are preparing and adopting small-area development plans. Such plans may apply to downtowns, older inner-city neighborhoods, major growth corridors, or areas whose development may have implications for other jurisdictions. Small-area plans are typically prepared primarily to assist local governments in determining appropriate development policies. In addition, various state and federal aid programs require local government applicants to prepare a plan (often with land use and development implications) to qualify for financial assistance.

The Comprehensive Plan and Zoning Amendments

A comprehensive plan is generally intended to provide guidance to local governments when they make important development-related decisions. One prominent use of the plan has resulted from the changes made in 2005 to the zoning statutes. These changes provide that prior to adopting or rejecting any zoning amendment proposal, a city or county governing board must adopt a statement "describing whether its action is consistent with an adopted comprehensive plan and explaining why the board considers the action taken to be reasonable and in the public interest."[7] Similarly, the planning board is directed to comment on "whether the proposed amendment is consistent with any comprehensive plan that has been adopted and any other officially adopted plan."[8] Determining whether a project is consistent with the comprehensive plan or officially adopted plans may also be a requirement in certain other land development permitting decisions.[9]

Strategic Planning

A model that serves as an alternative to comprehensive planning is *strategic planning*. Strategic planning focuses on a few critical issues important to the community's future rather than trying to deal with everything at once. It involves looking outward at trends that may affect a community's destiny but that are beyond the community's control. Strategic planning is designed to be action-oriented, setting out what steps must be taken to achieve goals, who must take them, how much planned changes will cost, and who will pay. It is well adapted to the resolution of economic development and housing issues involving a number of players (government units, businesses, private individuals, and nonprofit organizations) when a distribution of responsibility is necessary and the ability to respond to opportunities is important. Strategic planning is particularly useful for making spending decisions. Also, its focus on setting achievable goals and timetables for action make it valuable in resolving regulatory issues. Although comprehensive planning is still the primary model used in land use and development planning, it has been substantially influenced by the principles of strategic planning.

Organization for City or County Planning

Local planning programs involve a number of functions, departments, and local boards. The organizational arrangements often differ from one jurisdiction to another. The most important elements of a local planning program are listed below.

Governing Board

The key to the success of any local land use and development planning program is the governing board. The council or board of county commissioners exercises a number of powers affecting a land use planning program. It approves the budget and the financing for capital projects to be undertaken in the current fiscal year. (It may also approve a five- or six-year capital improvement program as an advisory measure.) The board allocates funds for boards, agencies, and departments that carry out planning-related responsibilities. It approves the location and design of public buildings and other public facilities. In its legislative capacity, the board adopts and amends various land use and development-related ordinances. It may retain for itself authority to assume any responsibility of the zoning board of adjustment (for example, granting conditional use permits for certain land uses outlined in the zoning ordinance)[10] and to approve subdivision plats. The governing board also affects the planning program by the quality of the appointments it makes

---

7. N.C. Gen. Stat. (hereinafter G.S.) § 160A-383; G.S. 153A-341.

8. *Id.*

9. Although not required by state law, a local government may bind itself in its zoning ordinance to grant a special use permit or to rezone property only if the proposal is consistent with the unit's own land development plan. In addition, a subdivision ordinance may require that the dedication of land and the construction of improvements be consistent with the public facilities element of a comprehensive plan.

10. G.S. 160A-388(a).

to the planning board, the zoning board of adjustment, and other planning-related commissions and agencies. Finally, it has ultimate authority to enforce local ordinances, and it approves any judicial action taken against violators of the various land use and development-related ordinances.

Planning Board

One of the primary citizen boards critical to a local planning program is the *planning board* (also called the *planning commission*). Most North Carolina cities and counties have established a planning board made up of lay members appointed by the governing board. Many of the planning board's duties and responsibilities are advisory. The planning board is generally responsible for supervising the development of the comprehensive plan. It may arrange for and supervise the preparation of special studies, land use plans and policies, and drafts of ordinances. It may adopt plans and policies, advise the governing board on them, and recommend ordinances and methods of carrying out plans. In addition, the planning board generally has specific duties related to the zoning ordinance. As described above, the planning board must provide a written recommendation to the governing board concerning whether a proposed zoning amendment is consistent with the comprehensive plan or any other officially adopted plan and any other matters deemed appropriate by the planning board. City and county planning boards must be granted a thirty-day opportunity in which to make a recommendation concerning any proposed amendment before the governing board may adopt the proposal.

In addition to having advisory responsibilities, a planning board may be delegated the authority to review certain development proposals. In particular, the planning board may be delegated the authority to approve subdivision plats.[11] The planning board's potential versatility is indicated by the fact that it can take on the duties of certain other agencies, if the governing board so desires. For example, the governing board may assign to a planning board any or all of the duties of the zoning board of adjustment (such as approval of zoning variances, issuance of conditional use permits, and hearing of appeals from decisions of the zoning official).[12] In addition, if at least two planning board members have demonstrated special interest, experience, or education in history or architecture, the planning board may be designated the historic preservation commission.[13]

North Carolina local governments may also establish a joint planning board representing two or more local units of government. The Winston-Salem/Forsyth City-County Planning Board and the Charlotte-Mecklenburg Planning Commission are two of the better-known examples of such joint agencies.

Zoning Board of Adjustment

The zoning board of adjustment may be assigned four major responsibilities under North Carolina law.[14] First, it hears appeals of interpretations of the zoning ordinance. Generally this involves hearing appeals from decisions of the zoning enforcement official when an applicant for a permit or another aggrieved party claims that the zoning official has misinterpreted the ordinance. Second, the board of adjustment often grants variances to the zoning ordinance. Third, it may be authorized by the governing board to grant conditional use or special use permits for certain land uses and types of development outlined in the ordinance. Fourth, it also may hear appeals from decisions of the historic preservation commission. Although commonly a board of adjustment will be charged with some combination of these duties, any of these responsibilities may be delegated by the governing board to the planning board or retained by the governing board for itself.[15] In fact, many smaller municipalities have chosen to merge their planning boards and boards of adjustment.

Changes made to the board of adjustment statute (Section 160A-388 of the North Carolina General Statutes) in 2013 provide that certain board of adjustment decisions (whether to grant a conditional or special use permit or whether to reverse a decision of the zoning enforcement officer) must be made with the concurring vote of a majority of its

11. G.S. 160A-373; 153A-332.
12. G.S. 160A-388(a); 153A-345(a).
13. G.S. 160A-400.7.
14. G.S. 160A-388; 160A-400.9(e).
15. G.S. 160A-388(a); 153A-345(a).

members. However, the law still requires that a zoning variance may be granted only with the concurring vote of four-fifths of the board's membership.

Board of adjustment decisions may not be appealed to the governing board; rather, judicial review of such decisions may be had in county superior court.

Historic Preservation Commission

To initiate special review of development in a historic district or to designate a property as a historic landmark, a city or county must appoint a local historic preservation commission (see the section entitled "Historic Districts and Landmarks," below). The governing board may assign the functions of a historic preservation commission to a planning agency or to a community appearance commission (see the next section).

Community Appearance Commission

To focus attention on the entire community's aesthetic condition, a city or county may appoint a community appearance commission[16] and may also participate in forming a joint city–county appearance commission. The commission generally has no permit-granting or mandatory-approval authority; its powers are thus persuasive and advisory in nature.[17]

Economic Development Commission

To promote local economic development, a city or county governing board may establish an economic development commission.[18] The commission, with the help of any staff it hires, may engage in community promotion and business recruitment; provide advice, analysis, and assistance concerning economic and business development matters; and help form nonprofit corporations that develop industrial park sites and shell buildings for relocating businesses. (See Chapter 27, "Economic Development.")

City or County Manager

The manager generally plays an unrecognized role in any land use planning program. In small cities or counties, the manager may make recommendations on matters affecting the city's development, enforce planning-related ordinances, and supervise plan preparation. In large cities that have a staff planner, the manager may be less directly involved in planning affairs. Still, he or she may coordinate the capital improvement program; administer the housing, community development, transportation, parks and recreation, and inspection programs; make recommendations on annexation and utility-extension plans, downtown revitalization plans, and economic development proposals; and coordinate the interdepartmental staff review of major development proposals that come before the council.

Planning Staff

A local government land use planning program generally needs some professional planning help, which may be provided in any of the following ways:

1. The city or county may hire staff. Most cities with a population over 10,000 employ at least one staff planner to help execute a land use planning program. Usually planning personnel are hired by and are ultimately responsible to the manager but serve as staff to the planning board and other appointed boards with planning-related responsibilities.
2. The planning board itself may hire staff. The governing body that creates the planning board may authorize it to hire its own full-time staff with funds allocated for this purpose.[19] Except by joint planning boards that represent more than one jurisdiction, however, this authority has not been used.

16. G.S. 160A-451.
17. G.S. 160A-452.
18. G.S. 158-8.
19. G.S. 160A-363; 153A-322.

3. A city or county may contract for technical planning services provided by some other local unit of government.[20]
4. Several local government units may share staff, each jurisdiction retaining its own planning board. Arrangements may be established through an interlocal agreement.[21]
5. A joint planning board created by two or more local governments may hire staff.[22] Some of the state's large planning agencies are city–county boards with their own staff. The interlocal agreement establishing the joint planning board determines the financial contributions of each jurisdiction, the manner of appointment of board members, personnel practices affecting staff members, and the way in which work is assigned and supervised.
6. A private consultant may furnish technical assistance. Private planning consultants have been particularly active in preparing municipal zoning ordinances, economic development plans, and plans for downtown revitalization.
7. A substate regional organization may furnish technical assistance. North Carolina is divided into eighteen regions, each represented by a *lead regional organization* (LRO). LROs in North Carolina take one of three forms: a regional planning commission,[23] a regional planning and economic development commission,[24] or a regional council of governments.[25] Most LROs provide at least some local government planning and related technical assistance.
8. The Division of Community Development (DCD) of the North Carolina Department of Commerce may furnish technical assistance. This agency provides a broad range of planning and managerial assistance through six field offices. It and its predecessor agencies have prepared a number of land use plans and zoning and subdivision ordinances for communities throughout the state. The DCD also provides help with annexation studies, grant proposals, and a variety of other planning tasks.

Zoning Enforcement Official

In a large city, enforcement of the zoning ordinance may be the sole responsibility of the zoning enforcement official. In small cities and many counties the official may also be a building inspector, a city manager or clerk, or a police chief and may enforce other local ordinances as well.

Inspection Department

The inspection department is the primary enforcement agency for a variety of development-related ordinances and codes. It typically enforces the State Building Code and sometimes also the minimum housing code. In many cities, both large and small, it also enforces the zoning ordinance.

Community Development Department

In recent years the Community Development Block Grant (CDBG) program has become a key short- and mid-range program for carrying out a city's housing and development objectives in low- and moderate-income neighborhoods. Many cities and some counties have established a new, separate community development department or office to administer the program. In others the CDBG coordinator may report to the planning director. In some large cities the CDBG program may be administered within a community development division of an umbrella development or planning department. (See Chapter 26, "Community Development and Affordable Housing.")

---

20. *Id.*
21. G.S. Ch. 160A, art. 20, part 1.
22. G.S. 160A-363; 153A-322.
23. G.S. 153A-395.
24. G.S. 153A-398.
25. G.S. 160A-475.

Extraterritorial Jurisdiction for Land Use Planning

In North Carolina, as in many other states, a city may exercise jurisdiction in some planning-related matters over areas located outside its boundaries.[26] Extraterritorial jurisdiction is justified on several grounds. North Carolina annexation laws have encouraged cities to annex nearby unincorporated urban areas (this justification, however, has been undercut by changes in the annexation laws in 2011 and 2012 that curtail substantially the authority of cities to annex territory unilaterally (without the consent of the owners of the property annexed)). It is in a city's interest to ensure that areas that may ultimately be annexed into the city are (1) developed in a manner consistent with the city's development standards and land use planning objectives and (2) served by appropriate public facilities. Otherwise, unplanned growth and substandard development may thwart whatever municipal annexation may occur. Even when a city has no annexation ambitions, unplanned growth and substandard development on the urban fringe may have detrimental effects on nearby city areas.

In general, a city of any size may establish planning jurisdiction for one mile outside its boundaries. However, North Carolina law permits a city to exercise such extraterritorial jurisdiction unilaterally only if there is evidence that the county has not adopted a full-blown land use regulatory program in the affected area. Specifically a city may assume authority outside its limits without the consent of the county only if the county is not already enforcing three major types of development regulations in the target area: (1) zoning, (2) subdivision regulations, and (3) the State Building Code.[27]

Where local governments work cooperatively, other jurisdictional arrangements are also possible. With the approval of the board of county commissioners, a city with a population of 10,000 to 25,000 may extend its jurisdiction up to two miles outside city limits, and a city with a population of over 25,000, up to three miles.[28] Alternatively, at the city council's request, the county may exercise any of the various land use regulatory powers within the city's extraterritorial jurisdiction or even within the city limits.[29] Under a third arrangement a city may not exercise extraterritorial jurisdiction unilaterally, but it and the county may agree on the area in which each will exercise the various powers.[30]

The land use planning–related powers that may be exercised outside municipal boundaries include (1) zoning, (2) subdivision regulation, (3) enforcement of the State Building Code, (4) minimum housing code regulation, (5) historic district regulation, (6) historic properties designation and regulation, (7) community development projects, (8) jurisdiction of the community appearance commission, (9) acquisition of open space, (10) floodway regulation, and (11) soil erosion and sedimentation control regulation. No city may exercise in its extraterritorial area any power it does not exercise within its city limits. Also, the boundaries of a city's extraterritorial jurisdiction are the same for all powers.

If a city intends to enforce zoning or subdivision regulations in its extraterritorial area, it must provide some means by which residents of the extraterritorial area may influence the decision making of both the planning agency and the zoning board of adjustment.[31] A city is directed to ask the county commissioners to appoint some outside members to both the planning board and the zoning board of adjustment. The number of such appointees and their voting power are determined by the city, but the number of extraterritorial appointees on each board relative to the number of appointees who are municipal residents must reflect the population of the extraterritorial area relative to the municipality's population. If the board of county commissioners does not make these appointments within ninety days after it receives the request, the city council may make them instead.

---

26. G.S. 160A-360. *See* Richard Ducker, "The Territorial Jurisdiction of Cities and Counties in Planning and Regulating Development" (prepared for the North Carolina House Committee on Property Owner Protection and Rights, North Carolina General Assembly, Raleigh, March 3, 2014); David Owens, *The North Carolina Experience with Municipal Extraterritorial Planning Jurisdiction*, Special Series No. 20 (Chapel Hill, N.C.: School of Government, University of North Carolina at Chapel Hill 2006).

27. G.S. 160A-360(e).

28. G.S. 160A-360(a).

29. G.S. 160A-360(d).

30. G.S. 160A-360(e).

31. G.S. 160A-362.

In 2011 the General Assembly adopted a significant change affecting the application of these powers. It added G.S. 160A-360(k) to exempt property located in a municipality's extraterritorial planning jurisdiction (ETPJ) that is used for bona fide farm purposes[32] from the exercise of any and all powers the city may exercise in its ETPJ area. When the 2011 statutory amendment first became effective, municipal planning and development powers were rendered inapplicable to these properties if the agricultural lands were located within the boundaries of a city's ETPJ. A 2014 amendment takes a different tack. It makes farm properties within a city's ETPJ subject to county flood hazard regulations (apparently the regulations of the county within which the city is located) without affecting the scope of ETPJ in other respects or the applicability of other development powers. This change was intended to preserve the continuity and integrity of North Carolina's flood hazard prevention program and to allow the state to continue to qualify for federal flood hazard assistance.

Permits and Permit Extensions

Most of the land use and development regulations promulgated by cities and counties are enforced through permits and approvals designed to ensure compliance. These take the form of building permits, zoning permits, preliminary subdivision plat and final plat approvals, grading permits, flood hazard permits, and other types of permits and approvals. Some permits require that specified forms of development progress must occur within certain windows of time or the permit will expire. For example, Section 160A-418 of the North Carolina General Statutes (hereinafter G.S.) (cities) and G.S. 153A-358 (counties) provide that building permits expire if work authorized by the permit has not been initiated within six months (local governments may shorten the period) or if the work is discontinued for twelve months after it has initially begun. Similarly, local ordinances or permit conditions may provide that zoning permits may expire if a building permit is not obtained within a certain period of time after the zoning permit is issued. Likewise, approvals of preliminary subdivision plats often expire after a year or two if final plat approvals have not been obtained.

In 2009, as North Carolina development activity was sinking into recession, the General Assembly took action[33] to suspend the expiration of land use and environmental permits issued and approvals granted by both local and state government agencies during the period from January 1, 2008, through December 31, 2010. The purpose of this legislation was to save permit holders the money and time involved in renewing or reapplying for permits that had expired because of poor economic conditions. In 2010 the duration of this permit extension period was itself extended for one more year through December 31, 2011.[34] Once these permit extension laws expired, the ordinary expiration periods applicable to particular permits resumed. By the spring of 2014, however, most of these older permits and approvals had either expired for good because of lack of development progress, or the development they represented had weathered the recession and resumed.

Subdivision Regulation

The word "subdivision"[35] usually calls to mind a relatively large residential development of single-family homes. For regulatory purposes, however, subdivision may best be thought of as a process by which a tract of land is split into smaller parcels, lots, or building sites so that the lots or parcels may eventually be sold, developed, or both.

---

32. See the discussion of the definition of a bona fide farm under "Special Treatment of Certain Activities," below.

33. S.L. 2009-406.

34. S.L. 2010-117. This 2010 law, however, provided that a city or county (but not state agencies) was authorized to "opt out" of the one-year extension by adopting a resolution to that effect.

35. *See* Richard Ducker, "Subdivision Ordinances: What's Regulated, What's Not," *Coates' Canons: NC Local Government Law Blog* (UNC School of Goverment, April 21, 2011), http://canons.sog.unc.edu/?p=4400.

Most subdivision ordinances are based on the premise that the division of land generally signals that the land will soon be developed and used more intensively than it was before subdivision. As a result, those who purchase the subdivided tracts or lots will make more demands for community facilities and services. The platting and recording of a subdivision map offer a city the opportunity not only to review the design of the resulting lots but also to ensure that the subdivider provides streets, utilities, and other public improvements required to serve the needs of those who purchase the subdivided land.

Subdivision Design

The most fundamental subdivision design considerations involve the arrangement of lots and streets. Ordinance provisions commonly specify minimum lot sizes and lot widths or require lots to front on a dedicated street for a certain distance. Standards for street design may include width specifications for rights-of-way and pavements and maximum lengths for blocks and cul-de-sacs; these provisions ensure that emergency vehicles can easily reach any lot and that traffic is not overly concentrated at a particular intersection. One design factor that can cause some controversy is the balance between adequate access to lots and lot owners' privacy. Although developers and lot purchasers generally value cul-de-sacs for the isolation from traffic that they afford, they may be inappropriate if they make travel especially circuitous; put an excessive burden on existing through streets; or make garbage collection, emergency vehicle response, and street and lot drainage substantially more difficult.

Subdivision Review Process

In North Carolina, final approval of subdivision plats may be granted by (1) the governing board, (2) the governing board on recommendation of a designated body such as the planning board, (3) a planning board, (4) a technical review committee, or (5) a designated body or staff person. Most cities and counties also review a preliminary or tentative plat. Local units have many choices in organizing the review process.

Pre-application Procedures

Some communities encourage developers first to submit a sketch plan or design plan to the planning staff or the plat approval agency. The purpose of these plans is to bring representatives of local government and the subdivider together so that the local unit can learn what the subdivider has planned and the subdivider can better understand the unit's requirements for approving the subdivision.

Review and Approval of the Preliminary Plat

Normally the next important step in the review process is submission and approval of a preliminary plat. To call a subdivision map submitted at this stage "preliminary" may be misleading because the plat will, in large measure, fix the nature, design, and scope of the subdividing activity to follow. Furthermore, it serves as a general blueprint for the installation of whatever improvements or community facilities the developer is to provide. Comments and recommendations from various city and county departments and agencies outside local government made before formal action is taken on the preliminary plat are an important aspect of preliminary plat review.

Review and Approval of the Final Plat

Generally, the final plat is submitted for approval and reviewed by various agencies in much the same manner as the preliminary plat. The final plat must be approved if it is consistent with the approval given the preliminary plat. If the developer plans to install improvements after final plat approval, the approval of construction plans may be delayed until the final plat approval stage. In some circumstances a city or county may require no preliminary plat at all; only the final plat is reviewed. Many local governments classify subdivisions as major or minor on the basis of the number and size of the lots involved. Major subdivisions are typically subject to the two-stage review process described earlier; minor subdivisions (those that do not involve the installation of public improvements and do not have a significant impact on the community) are often reviewed just once—at the final plat stage.

Once the final plat is approved, the plat must be recorded in the county register of deeds' office before lots may be sold. The register of deeds may not record a plat of a subdivision subject to regulation unless the chair or the head of the plat approval agency has indicated on the face of the plat that it has been approved and a plat review officer (typically a county tax mapper) has certified that various other state law requirements for the recording of plat maps have been met.

Guarantee of Developer Performance

In general, a developer may not begin to construct subdivision improvements until the preliminary plat is approved. Once that approval is granted, the developer is obliged to arrange for certain dedications to be made and improvements to be installed or constructed before the final plat may be approved. One way to ensure that streets are properly constructed, and utilities and drainage facilities properly installed, is to withhold final plat approval until these improvements are completed, inspected, and, if appropriate, accepted by the city or another government unit. A much more common practice is to allow final plat approval if the subdivider has provided adequate financial assurance to the local government that improvements will be completed after the final plat is approved. If these performance guarantees are required, the ordinance must provide a range of options from which a developer may choose. Common forms of guarantees include letters of credit, bonds, and securities held in escrow.

In addition, a city or county may withhold the building permit for a lot that has been illegally subdivided.[36]

Exactions and the Financing of Subdivision Improvements

The questions of who will finance subdivision improvements and community facilities and how they will be maintained are fundamental to subdivision regulation. Many local governments now expect subdividers to provide certain public improvements at their own expense. These exactions may take the form of requirements for (1) construction or installation of infrastructural improvements, (2) dedication of land, (3) payment of fees in lieu, or (4) payment of impact fees.[37] Table 25.2 details the authority of cities and counties to exact various types of facilities by the different means at their disposal.

Forms of Exactions

Construction or Installation of Infrastructural Improvements

Virtually all subdivision regulations require the subdivider to construct or install certain subdivision improvements. The subdivision enabling statutes (G.S. 160A-372, G.S. 153A-331) allow cities and counties to require the "construction of community service facilities in accordance with (municipal) (county) policies and standards. . . ." *Community service facilities* defies exact definition, but the most commonly required subdivision improvements include streets, curbs and gutters, drainage swales or storm sewers, sidewalks, and water or sewer lines or both.

Subdivision development sometimes provides an excellent opportunity to arrange for streets, utility lines, or stormwater drainage improvements designed not only for a particular subdivision but also for future development. If a sewer line is extended from the end of a sewerage network to a tract being subdivided, the owners of land along the line may wish to connect to it at some future time. A 6-inch water line might adequately serve the particular subdivision, yet it might be wise to lay a 12-inch main that could eventually serve expected development on the far side of the subdivision. Several approaches are used to allocate costs. If a developer is the first to demand service in a newly developing area, the developer may be required to furnish the line. However, the local government may impose acreage fees or other charges on later developers who use the facility and pay over some of these funds to the original developer in partial reimbursement for all the extra costs the original developer assumed. Alternatively, if a city or county requires a subdivider to provide capacity exceeding that necessary to serve the subdivision, then the local unit may pay for the extra capacity from its general funds on the theory that the oversized facilities will benefit the community generally.

36. G.S. 160A-375; 153A-334.

37. For discussion of development exactions generally, see Richard Ducker, "Development Exactions: An Introduction" (prepared for the North Carolina Legislative Research Commission Study Committee on Property Owner Protection and Rights, North Carolina General Assembly, March 3, 2014).

Table 25.2 Local Government Authority to Impose Exactions as a Condition of Subdivision Plat Approval under the General Statutes

	Type of Community Facility				
Type of Exaction	**Parks**	**Utilities**	**Streets**	**Schools**	**Fire Stations**
Construction or installation of improvements	Yes	Yes	Yes	Probably not	Probably not
Dedication of land	Yes	Yes, for utility easements	Yes	No	No
Payment of fees in lieu	Yes	No express authority	Yes, to construct streets	No	No
Payment of impact fees	No	Probably	No	No	No

Dedication of Land

Sometimes improvements are required on lands or within easements the developer does not own or control (for example, the extension of a water line within an existing public utility easement). More commonly, however, improvements will be made on site. If the improvements are to be available for public use or are to be connected to a public system, the city or county will require the dedication of the land so improved and will accept the dedication only after the improvement has been completed and inspected. For purposes of development approval, then, a dedication is a form of exaction requiring that the developer donate to the public some interest in land for certain public uses. North Carolina law allows both cities and counties, as a condition of subdivision plat approval, to require the dedication of sites and easements for streets, utilities, and recreation areas.

Compulsory dedication is based on the assumption that generally a public agency should own, control, and maintain the improvements, facilities, and open space in a new subdivision. In many instances, however, such government control and maintenance is neither possible nor practical. Local governments must give careful thought as to whether common facilities are made public or are allowed to remain private.

Payment of Fees in Lieu

An alternative to compulsory dedication and improvement is to require or allow a subdivider to pay a fee that represents the value of the site or improvement that would otherwise have been dedicated or provided. Fees in lieu can be an attractive option when the developer's contribution must be prorated if the exaction is to be fair and legal. Both city and county ordinances may provide for fees in lieu of the dedication of recreation areas and for fees in lieu of road improvements. Because of the administrative burdens of accounting for these funds, relatively few North Carolina jurisdictions allow fees in lieu.

Payment of Impact Fees

In contrast to the forms of exactions just listed, the use of impact fees by North Carolina cities and counties is not expressly authorized by general statute. A small number of municipalities and several counties are subject to local acts authorizing the use of impact fees, which are also known as facility or project fees. In addition, express enabling legislation authorizing impact fees may not be necessary if the facilities are part of a public enterprise such as providing a public water supply, disposing and treating sewage, or carrying out a stormwater control system.[38] However, express enabling authority is required to use impact fees for governmental functions such as providing streets, parks, or schools. Some counties have been interested in impact fees to supplement funds for public school construction. In

38. The statutes allowing North Carolina cities to finance public enterprises and fix rates, fees, and charges for services furnished by a public enterprise (G.S. 160A-313, 160A-314) have been held to authorize implicitly the use of impact fees to fund capital improvements to water and sewer systems. South Shell Investment v. Town of Wrightsville Beach, 703 F. Supp. 1192 (E.D.N.C. 1988), *aff'd*, 900 F.2d 255 (4th Cir. 1990) (unpublished). *See also* Town of Spring Hope v. Bissette, 53 N.C. App. 210 (1981), *aff'd*, 305 N.C. 248 (1982).

Durham Land Owners Association v. County of Durham,[39] however, the North Carolina Court of Appeals ruled that the general statutes did not provide counties with express or implied enabling authority to adopt impact fees for public school construction. (See the discussion of adequate public facilities ordinances, below.)

Impact fees are similar to fees in lieu but generally are established as part of a comprehensive attempt to allocate the costs of a wide range of community facilities to new development. Impact fees can be applied to multi-family residential, commercial, and even office and industrial development; they are rarely restricted in application to new subdivisions. They are generally collected when building permits are issued, usually just before the development creating the need for new services actually begins, rather than at the time of plat approval.

The validity of a system of impact fees depends on the system's analytical basis. The steps that follow highlight the elements of a plan for the application of impact fees:

1. An estimate is made of the cost of acquiring land for and constructing each new public facility within the local government's jurisdiction that must be provided during the planning period (for example, twenty to twenty-five years) and that will be funded with impact fees. These estimates usually extend far beyond the time horizons used in a typical five- or seven-year capital improvement program.
2. The appropriate distribution of costs is determined on the basis of the costs of each facility that are attributable to and should be equitably borne by both new and existing developments in each zone, service area, or planning district. Such a distribution assumes that the community at large is obliged to provide public facilities such as roads and drainage improvements to serve existing residents at appropriate service standards. These costs are then allocated among the various development sectors—residential, commercial, and industrial.
3. A series of formulas or factors is used to allocate the appropriate portion of costs to each development project. For example, in the case of street improvements, the impact fee may be based on the number of trips generated by the land uses in the proposed development.
4. Once collected, these fees must be placed into trust funds or capital improvement funds, where they are earmarked by both type of facility and zone, service area, or planning district to be served.
5. When the funds reach appropriate levels, they are expended on the facilities for which they were collected so that residents of the new development actually benefit from the facilities. The fees may have to be refunded if they are not spent and facilities are not constructed within a reasonable time.

Exactions and the Constitution

Unless exactions are flexibly applied, they can amount to an unconstitutional taking of private property for public use without just compensation. Exactions must be properly and fairly related to the need for the new public facilities generated by a new development.

Several decisions by the United States Supreme Court provide guidance. The Court first held in *Nollan v. California Coastal Commission*[40] that if a government unit conditions approval of a development permit, the condition must have an "essential nexus" to an allowable purpose of the regulation. In *Dolan v. City of Tigard,*[41] the Court also ruled that the U.S. Constitution requires "rough proportionality" between the impact of the development and the nature and extent of the exaction. Although precise mathematical calculation is not required, some sort of individualized determination must be made to justify an exaction requirement as it is applied in a particular case. The Court also held that a local government bears the burden of proving that an exaction is constitutional.

Suppose, however, that a development approval is denied because an applicant refuses to comply with an unreasonable and illegal government demand for property or the payment fees. May the applicant be legally vindicated and recover damages? In the more recent case of *Koontz v. St. Johns River Water Management District,*[42] the U.S. Supreme

39. 177 N.C. App. 629, *cert. denied,* 360 N.C. 532 (2006).
40. 483 U.S. 825 (1987).
41. 512 U.S. 374 (1994).
42. 133 S. Ct. 2586 (2013).

Court held that the Nollan and Dolan standards apply to these circumstances as well.[43] The tests apply to demands for the conveyance of property, the installation of improvements, or the payment of fees made prior to permit approval. The impermissible demands need not necessarily be formal conditions attached to an approved permit. In each case they are illegal and give rise to damage claims.

Adequate Public Facilities Regulations

Adequate public facility ordinances (APFOs) are based on the principle of concurrency—that is, development approval should not be granted unless and until the public facilities necessary to serve that development are available for use when the development is occupied.[44] Under some programs if area streets, parks, or schools are already at or near capacity, a developer may be expected to postpone development plans, scale back plans to better fit facility capacity, or "mitigate" the capacity deficiency. Mitigation has sometimes been equated with the dedication of property or the payment of fees to help finance the improvement.

For many years local governments have taken into account public facility capacity when considering conditional use permit applications, rezoning petitions, and the like. In the last several decades a small number of key rapidly growing counties in metropolitan areas (including Franklin, Lincoln, Currituck, Union, Cabarrus, and Stanly) adopted APFOs with respect to public school capacity as a part of their subdivision ordinances or unified development ordinances. Many of these counties also began to allow or encourage developers to make payments to the county to help it fund needed school construction.

The legal challenges that have resulted have not necessarily been based on claims that mitigation measures are unconstitutional forms of developer exactions. Instead the challenges have alleged inadequate statutory authority to administer such programs in the first place. In 2006 Durham County's school impact fee ordinance was invalidated by the North Carolina Court of Appeals on grounds the county lacked enabling authority to adopt such an ordinance (see above). That case emboldened developers to challenge the Union County adequate public facility program, which applied primarily to schools and was largely characterized as an impact fee program in disguise. In 2009 Union County's APFO program was invalidated by the court of appeals in *Union Land Owners Association v. County of Union*.[45] The court held that neither the county's land subdivision plat approval authority, its zoning authority, nor its general police power authority provided an adequate legislative basis for the county's APFO. According to the court, the county's land subdivision control authority was inadequate in spite of language in G.S. 153A-331 allowing ordinances to provide "for the distribution of population and traffic in a manner that will avoid congestion and overcrowding and will create conditions that substantially promote public health, safety, and the general welfare." More recently the North Carolina Supreme Court in *Lanvale Properties v. County of Cabarrus*[46] invalidated the APFO provisions adopted by Cabarrus County because of inadequate legislative authority. (See the further discussion of the *Lanvale Properties* case below.)

Zoning

Of all the programs, tools, and techniques associated with land use planning, zoning is perhaps the best known. It may be used to achieve a variety of purposes. First, it can ensure that the community's land uses are properly situated in relation to one another so that one use does not become a nuisance for its neighbors. Second, zoning can ensure that adequate land and space are available for various types of development. Third, it can ensure that the location and density

43. *See* Adam Lovelady, "The *Koontz* Decision and Implications for Development Exactions," *Coates' Canons: NC Local Government Law Blog* (UNC School of Government, July 1, 2013), http://canons.sog.unc.edu/?p=7191.

44. *See* Richard Ducker, "Are Adequate Public Facilities Ordinances Adequate?" *Coates' Canons: NC Local Government Law Blog* (UNC School of Government, Dec. 16, 2009), http://canons.sog.unc.edu/?p=1519; David Owens, "School Impact Fees and Development Regulations: Another Round," *Coates' Canons: NC Local Government Law Blog* (UNC School of Government, Oct. 16, 2012), http://canons.sog.unc.edu/?p=6882.

45. 201 N.C. App. 374 (2009).

46. 366 N.C. 142 (2012).

of development are consistent with the government's ability to provide the area with streets, utilities, fire protection, and recreation services. Finally, it can set minimum design standards so that new development reflects aesthetic values, is of appropriate scale, and helps protect privacy.

Zoning involves the exercise of the state's police power to regulate private property in order to promote the public health, the public safety, and the general welfare. It may legitimately be used to protect property values. Zoning can foster economic development and expansion. However, it can also restrict competition among commercial activities because the land available for certain uses may be limited. Promotion of the general welfare is a sufficiently elastic purpose to allow the adoption of standards justified solely in terms of aesthetics. Because zoning is concerned with the use of property and not its ownership, the identity of owners is irrelevant from a legal perspective. Zoning permits, approvals, and requirements "run with the land" and apply to future owners as well as present ones. Similarly, zoning distinctions based on whether property is owner- or renter-occupied are unenforceable. Although zoning may legitimately be used to protect property values, requirements that new developments meet minimum-floor-area standards or cost a certain amount may well be legally indefensible. The obligation of North Carolina local governments to accommodate low- and moderate-income housing through zoning remains unclear; nonetheless, zoning may not be used to discriminate on the basis of race or national origin.

Although zoning is primarily a tool for influencing the use of private property, in North Carolina it is also applicable to the construction and use of buildings by the state and its political subdivisions.[47] Zoning is prospective in nature: only land uses begun after the ordinance's effective date must comply with all the regulations. However, existing buildings and lots with characteristics that do not comply with the regulations are said to be *nonconforming* (see the section entitled "Nonconformities and Amortization," below), and a special section of the ordinance deals with them.

Zoning regulations are distinct from most other types of land use regulations because they differ from district to district rather than being uniform throughout a city. This feature permits the tailoring of zoning to address development problems but also means that local governing bodies may be tempted to abuse the power by treating certain property owners in arbitrary or discriminatory ways.

Basic Elements

A *zoning ordinance* consists of a text and a map (or series of maps). The text includes the substantive standards applicable to each district on the map and the procedures that govern proposals for changes in both the text and the map. The zoning ordinance divides the land within a city's jurisdiction into a number of zoning districts. The land in each district is governed by several types of regulations: (1) use regulations; (2) dimensional requirements, including setback and density standards; and (3) other miscellaneous requirements dealing with matters such as off-street parking, landscaping and screening, property access, required public improvements, and signs.

Uses Permitted by Right

If a use is permitted by right, the zoning standards for that use are typically spelled out in specific terms, and the zoning enforcement official grants the applicant routine permission to proceed. In some cases an applicant for a zoning permit must hire a design professional (for example, an engineer, a landscape architect, or an architect) to prepare a site plan for a use authorized by right. Such a site plan may have to be reviewed by various departments, outside agencies, or a technical review committee made up of representatives of those departments or agencies. In some cities the city council or the planning board approves such a site plan. As a general rule, however, these site plans must be approved as submitted if they meet local standards.

Uses Permitted by Conditional Use Permits

Many jurisdictions include a variety of uses that merit closer scrutiny because of their scale and effect or their potential for creating a nuisance. These conditional uses may be permissible in a particular district but only at particular locations

47. G.S. 160A-392; 153A-347.

and then only under particular conditions. *Conditional use permits* (also known as *special use permits*) may be issued by the council, the zoning board of adjustment, or the planning board. Regardless of which body issues the permit, the decision to grant or deny it must be based on evidence supplied at a quasi-judicial hearing. The zoning ordinance must explicitly list the requirements the applicant must meet and the findings the issuing body must make in order for the permit to be issued. If these requirements are met, the board may not refuse to issue the permit. However, the board may impose additional conditions and requirements on the permit that are not specifically mentioned in the ordinance. Such conditions may include specifications on the particular use to be made of the property; sign, parking, or landscaping requirements; requirements that the property owner dedicate land for and construct certain public improvements such as streets, utilities, and parks; and specifications dealing with the timing of development. Conditional use permits may be used to deal with small-scale land uses such as electric substations and day care centers or with large-scale developments such as shopping centers and group housing developments. Permission to develop or use land in accordance with a conditional use permit runs with the land and applies with equal force to future owners of the property.

Types of Zoning Districts

Most zoning ordinances include three basic types of zoning districts—residential, commercial, and industrial—and a variety of more specialized zones—office and institutional, flood hazard, mobile home park, agricultural, and perhaps planned unit development. There may be a number of residential districts, each based on different permissible dwelling types and required lot sizes (or densities).

Zoning districts may also be classified as *general use districts, conditional use districts* (also known as *special use districts*), or *conditional districts.* All zoning ordinances include at least some general use districts. Various uses or activities are permitted to locate and operate in a general use district either (1) by right or (2) subject to a conditional use (or special use) permit. Generally, any use not specifically listed as permitted is, by implication, prohibited.

The zoning ordinances of some North Carolina cities and counties also provide for conditional use districts. Any use of land in a conditional use district is subject to a conditional use permit; no uses are permitted by right. Thus all development in a conditional use district is subject to discretionary review. In cities and counties that rely on conditional use districts, the governing board will customarily grant the conditional use permit. Thus, the governing board can consider the application for a conditional use permit at the same time it considers a petition for the rezoning of land to the conditional use district that authorizes such a permit.

A third type of zoning district authorized for cities and counties is the conditional district. Each conditional district is unique. The text of the zoning amendment adopting the zoning map change incorporates a series of conditions, stipulations, and requirements agreed to by both the property owner and the local government and typically includes a site development plan detailing just how and when the property will be developed. No conditional or special use permit is involved.

Form-Based Codes

In the last twenty years, an increasing number of towns and cities have adopted zoning and other development regulations that differ from traditional zoning. One of the more prominent alternative forms of zoning involves form-based codes.[48] Form-based codes emphasize predictable results by using physical form rather than the separation of uses as the organizing principle for the code. They also focus on the relationship between buildings and the "public realm," the form and mass of structures, and the scale and types of streets and blocks. At the heart of form-based codes is a "regulating plan" that classifies sites according to street, block, and district characteristics and includes illustrations of build-to lines, projected building footprints, location of public spaces, and allowable building types for each site. Any

48. For a comparative analysis of form-based codes used in North Carolina, see Matthew Boyer, "Form or Fluff?: Assessing the Proposed Advantages of Form-Based Codes for Municipalities," Paper submitted to School of Government, University of North Carolina at Chapel Hill for Master's in Public Administration degree, March 2010, www.mpa.unc.edu/sites/www.mpa.unc.edu/files/MatthewBoyer.pdf.

site is viewed as part of a larger unified design. Building envelope standards are intended to ensure that development fits the desired character of the zone by regulating building height, placement, and orientation.[49] Architectural standards may, but need not necessarily, be a part of the ordinance. Form-based codes also may include street standards that apply to landscape materials as well as "hardscape materials" like sidewalks, pavers, and street materials. They also may specify tree species.

Form-based codes can apply to specific areas of a community with common characteristics. Or they can be used as an alternative to conventional zoning regulations for specific areas. They can also be combined with conventional zoning to form a hybrid, with form-based coding regulating physical form and conventional regulations applying to land use. Belmont, Huntersville,[50] Cornelius, Davidson, Salisbury, Brevard, and Knightdate[51] are among North Carolina cities with form-based regulations.

Government Roles in Zoning

In most cities and counties, zoning involves the governing board, a planning board, the zoning board of adjustment, and planning and zoning staff. Collectively these groups carry out the legislative, quasi-judicial, advisory, and administrative functions of a local zoning program. The legislative and quasi-judicial roles of citizen boards in local zoning are a source of some confusion.

Legislative Role

The board of county commissioners or city council acts in its legislative role when it adopts or amends the zoning ordinance. When it makes the law, such a board has substantial discretion to make decisions as it sees fit. The governing board must hold a public hearing before it adopts or amends the ordinance. It need not explain its decision or make written findings of fact, but it must adopt a statement indicating that a proposed zoning amendment is consistent with any adopted plan and in the public interest. The hearing required for legislative action is relatively free of formality. Speakers need not make sworn statements or restrict their statements to standards or topics set forth in the ordinance. City council members or county commissioners may be subject to lobbying efforts before or after the hearing.

Quasi-judicial Role

Public hearings are also required when three other important zoning actions are taken: (1) issuance of variances, (2) issuance of conditional use permits, and (3) appeal of decisions of a zoning official. Each of these proceedings, however, must occur in a quasi-judicial hearing. The decision must be based on the criteria in the ordinance, witnesses must be sworn and offer testimony according to certain rules of evidence, board members may not discuss the case with any of the parties outside the hearing, and the board must justify its decision. Thus, quasi-judicial hearings (sometimes known as *evidentiary hearings*) are more formal than legislative hearings and more demanding on those who participate in them. The types of zoning actions just identified are often heard by the zoning board of adjustment, but if any of them are heard instead by the planning board or governing board, then that board must also follow quasi-judicial procedures when it hears the case.

The zoning board of adjustment statute (G.S. 160A-388) was amended in 2013 to require the board to prepare and adopt a written decision in each case it hears and to deliver it to the parties and anyone who requests a copy of it before it is filed. The new amendments also elaborate the manner in which the board may issue subpoenas to secure both witnesses and documents.

---

49. *See* City of Locust, North Carolina, Code of Ordinances, art. 4, Building and Lot Types, www.amlegal.com/nxt/gateway.dll/North%20Carolina/locust_nc/cityoflocustnorthcarolinacodeofordinance?f=templates$fn=default.htm$3.0$vid=amlegal:locust_nc.

50. *See* Town of Huntersville Planning Department, Design Guidebook: Town of Huntersville, North Carolina (Summer 2008), www.huntersville.org/Portals/0/Planning/Design%20Guidebook%20for%20web.pdf.

51. *See* Knightdale Unified Development Ordinance § 2.2, Form-Based Standards by Zoning District, www.knightdalenc.gov/Modules/ShowDocument.aspx?documentid=1989.

Variances

Because a zoning ordinance cannot anticipate every land use or development situation that will arise, it must include a procedure for varying or waiving its requirements when unnecessary hardships would result from its strict enforcement. The permission granted by this procedure is known as a *variance*. In most North Carolina local governments, granting a variance is the responsibility of the zoning board of adjustment.

Even though zoning regulations may be burdensome on individual property owners, the board of adjustment's authority to grant variances is limited under the law. The board of adjustment lacks the wide legislative discretion the governing board has. Often, matters that come before it could be better handled by the planning board and the governing board as proposals to amend the zoning ordinance.

Changes made to the zoning board of adjustment statute (G.S. 160A-388) in 2013 affect the circumstances in which a variance may be granted.[52] In order to grant a variance the board must now find that unless a variance is granted, the property owner will undergo unnecessary hardships. (For decades the standard was "practical difficulties or unnecessary hardships.") More specifically, to grant a variance the board must conclude all of the following:

1. If the property owner complies with ordinance provisions, the owner will undergo unnecessary hardship. (Prior to this 2013 change, the law apparently required a board to determine that the owner could neither make any reasonable return from the property nor any reasonable use of it.)
2. The hardship affecting the property results from the application of the ordinance (not from market conditions or the existence of private restrictive covenants).
3. The hardship is suffered by the applicant's property. (The applicant's personal, social, or economic circumstances are irrelevant.)
4. The hardship does not result from the applicant's own actions. (Purchasing a site with knowledge that development plans may necessitate a variance does not qualify as a "self-imposed" hardship.)
5. The hardship is peculiar to the applicant's property and does not affect other properties in the same neighborhood. (If a number of properties suffer the same problem, the governing board should consider amending the zoning ordinance.)
6. The variance is in harmony with the general purpose and intent of the zoning ordinance and preserves its spirit. Use variances, which purport to authorize land uses not otherwise authorized in the district, are prohibited by statute.[53]
7. By granting the variance, the board will ensure the public safety and welfare and promote substantial justice.

Special Treatment of Certain Activities

Zoning applies to virtually all uses of property. However, one major exemption is important for both counties and municipalities: bona fide farms and agricultural activity. Many other activities are noteworthy because special state legislation affects how zoning requirements apply.

Bona Fide Farms

Bona fide farms are exempt from county zoning[54] and, as mentioned above, are exempt from any of the powers that a municipality may enforce in its extraterritorial planning jurisdiction, including zoning. Bona fide farms involve activities relating to the production of crops, fruits, vegetables, ornamental and flowering plants, dairy, poultry, and livestock. But the exemptions do not include large-scale swine farms, as long as they are not excluded entirely from the jurisdiction. The general bona fide farm exemption also includes timber harvesting, the care and training of livestock, aquaculture, agritourism, and various packing, storage, treating, and processing functions, including the storage of

---

52. For a summary of the 2013 changes, see David Owens, "BOA Changes Are Coming," *Coates' Canons: NC Local Government Law Blog* (UNC School of Government, June 12, 2013), http://canons.sog.unc.edu/?p=7155.

53. G.S. 160A-388(d).

54. G.S. 153A-340.

grain in elevators.[55] In addition, if a property is located in a voluntary agricultural district and is subject to a conservation agreement, up to 25 percent of the receipts generated by the property may come from the sale of nonfarm products without the farmer losing the bona fide farm exemption.[56]

Manufactured Housing

Manufactured home is the term used in state and federal law for what used to be called a *mobile home.* These units must be built to special construction standards adopted by the United States Department of Housing and Urban Development. The zoning of manufactured homes is subject to legislation adopted by the General Assembly in 1987 designed both to counter the exclusionary tendencies of many local zoning ordinances and to clarify that some special treatment of such units is permitted. G.S. 160A-383.1 and G.S. 153A-341.1 prohibit cities and counties from adopting zoning regulations that have the effect of excluding manufactured homes from all city and county zoning jurisdictions. However, cities and counties are expressly authorized to adopt special requirements affecting the appearance and dimensions of manufactured homes that do not also apply to site-built homes. (The law recognizes prior case law holding that a municipality need not allow manufactured homes in every district in which it allows site-built residences.)

This legislation does not affect *modular homes.* Modular homes are built in a factory but meet the construction standards of the State Building Code. For zoning purposes they are typically treated the same as site-built residences.

Establishments Selling Alcohol

The sale and consumption of alcohol are activities beyond the scope of zoning. The sale, consumption, and transportation of alcohol are subject to a uniform system of state regulation administered by the North Carolina Alcoholic Beverage Control (ABC) Commission, which controls the issuance of permits for these activities and preempts local zoning. State law provides that the ABC Commission "shall consider" local zoning requirements in determining whether a permit should be issued for an establishment at a particular location. However, a local government may not use zoning requirements to prohibit the sale or consumption of alcohol at a particular establishment if the ABC Commission has issued a permit for that activity.

Historic Districts and Landmarks

In its zoning text and on its zoning map, a city or a county may establish a historic district. Before doing so, it must establish a historic preservation commission; undertake an investigation; and create a report describing the buildings, sites, and features that give the proposed district historical, prehistoric, or architectural significance. Once a district is established, no exterior portion of a building or a structure may be erected, altered, relocated, or demolished unless the historic preservation commission issues a certificate of appropriateness for the change based on the design guidelines and the ordinance criteria adopted for the district. The commission is also authorized to delay the effective date of a certificate of appropriateness for the demolition of a building in a historic district for up to one year after its approval. During this period the commission and those interested in historic preservation may try to negotiate with the owner to save the building.

The historic preservation commission may also regulate the alteration and demolition of individual buildings or sites designated as historic landmarks. These landmarks may or may not be located within a historic district. Their demolition or relocation may be delayed for up to one year as well.

Signs and Billboards

The erection and display of signs and billboards (outdoor advertising displays) have long been subject to local government zoning. Certain commercial off-premise signs located along particular major federal highways are also subject to requirements imposed by the North Carolina Outdoor Advertising Control Act, which is administered by the North Carolina Department of Transportation. Where both sets of regulations apply, local sign standards for newly erected

55. The agricultural activities set forth in G.S. 106-581.1 are incorporated into the exemption by reference.
56. G.S. 106-743.4(a).

signs are typically more restrictive and demanding than those adopted by the state and take precedence. However, as described in the subsection "Nonconformities and Amortization," below, local governments are prohibited from amortizing nonconforming signs subject to the Outdoor Advertising Control Act without paying "just compensation."[57]

Watershed Protection and Stormwater Runoff Standards

North Carolina's watershed protection legislation, initially adopted in 1989, has important implications for cities and counties whose planning and zoning jurisdiction includes land within the watershed of a public drinking water supply. This program is designed to protect water supplies from the impurities in the runoff from land within a watershed (nonpoint sources of pollution). The North Carolina Environmental Management Commission has classified over two hundred such watersheds into five water supply categories: WS-I, WS-II, WS-III, WS-IV, and WS-V. It has also established statewide minimum watershed protection requirements that apply to the use and development of land in both the *critical area* of such watersheds and the remainder of the watershed. State law requires affected local governments to incorporate the appropriate land development standards into local zoning, land subdivision, and special purpose watershed protection ordinances. Perhaps the two primary standards established by state law are the *minimum lot size* for single-family residential lots and the *built-upon-area ratios* for multi-family and nonresidential development. For example, the minimum residential lot size in the critical area of a WS-III watershed is 1 acre. In such a watershed the portion of the lot that is built upon (that is, the area with impervious surface) may not exceed 36 percent of the total lot area. The regulations also allow a local government to choose a *high-density option*, which permits a property owner to develop a lot more intensively if certain engineering measures are taken to control stormwater.

In addition, North Carolina cities and counties are increasingly being expected to enforce similar development standards in order to comply with federal stormwater requirements under the Clean Water Act.

Solar Energy Facilities

The rise of alternative energy has led local governments to reassess how they treat energy facilities. Solar collectors and systems gather solar radiation as a substitute for traditional energy sources for water heating, active space heating and cooling, passive heating, or generating electricity. Solar energy systems are becoming increasingly common in North Carolina.[58] They can serve as accessory uses (and structures) by primarily producing power for the benefit of a principal use. They can be roof-mounted or ground-mounted. G.S. 160A-201, adopted in 2007, prohibits a city ordinance from effectively prohibiting collectors used for detached single-family residences. Ordinances may, however, include certain siting standards.

Solar generation of electricity for sale serves as the principal use for solar farms. Common siting issues, which tend to be aesthetic in nature, concern the height and site location of the equipment, appropriate screening and fencing, and the difficult problem of potential glare.

Scope of the Zoning Power

As local governments devise new zoning techniques and the reach of zoning broadens, questions arise about the scope of the zoning power. G.S. 153A-341 and G.S. 160A-383, some portions of which have remained essentially unchanged for over seventy-five years, outline the public purposes county and city zoning regulations may address. They declare that

> [z]oning regulations shall be designed to promote the public health, safety, and general welfare. To that end, the regulations may address, among other things, the following public purposes: to provide adequate light and air; to prevent the overcrowding of land; to avoid undue concentration of population; to lessen congestion in the streets; to secure safety from fire, panic, and dangers; and to facilitate the efficient and

57. G.S. 136-131.1.

58. *See* Adam Lovelady, Planning and Zoning for Solar in North Carolina (UNC School of Government, 2014), http://sogpubs.unc.edu/electronicversions/pdfs/pandzsolar2014.pdf.

> adequate provision of transportation, water, sewerage, schools, parks, and other public requirements. The regulations shall be made with reasonable consideration as to, among other things, the character of the district and its peculiar suitability for particular uses, and with a view to conserving the value of buildings and encouraging the most appropriate use of land throughout the county. In addition, the regulations shall be made with reasonable consideration to expansion and development of any cities within the county, so as to provide for their orderly growth and development.

G.S. 153A-340(a) and G.S. 160A-381(a) provide for the particular means used to achieve these purposes by authorizing local governments to

> regulate and restrict the height, number of stories and size of buildings and other structures, the percentage of lots that may be occupied, the size of yards, courts and other open spaces, the density of population, and the location and use of buildings, structures, and land for trade, industry, residence, or other purposes.

Although this language is general in nature, it is not without limitation. In *Lanvale Properties, LLC v. County of Cabarrus*,[59] developers challenged a county's adequate public facility ordinance, which effectively conditioned approval of new residential construction projects on developers paying fees to subsidize new school construction. The North Carolina Supreme Court held that the statutory parameters set forth above did not provide the county with sufficient implied zoning authority to adopt and enforce such requirements. Even the language of G.S. 153A-4,[60] which declares that the county enabling statutes "shall be broadly construed and grants of power shall be construed to include any powers that are reasonably expedient to the exercise of the power," was insufficient to change the result. Thus, whether local governments are prohibited from taking steps under their zoning ordinances or any other ordinances to link the timing of development approval to the availability of public facilities needed to serve that development remains unclear.

Another issue affecting the scope of the zoning power concerns the circumstances in which local governments may regulate the design elements of buildings and structures. The law already expressly authorizes regulation of the design features of structures located in historic districts and landmarks. Similarly, local governments may adopt appearance standards for manufactured housing and enforce design elements integral to the State Building Code and the flood hazard regulations associated with the federal flood insurance program. May design and appearance standards be imposed in other situations where no specific enabling legislation applies? The answer remains unclear in light of *Lanvale Properties*. Note that zoning regulations are to be made "with reasonable consideration as to, among other things, the character of the district . . . and with a view to conserving the value of buildings. . ."[61] The answer is important because design elements are prominent in the development and approval of traditional neighborhood developments, new urbanism projects, and similar proposals. The legislature has considered restrictions on design regulations, but to date none have been enacted.

A third example that tests the legal reach of the zoning power concerns proposals to require residential developers to reserve a certain portion of the dwelling units they build for low- and moderate-income housing. Arrangements guaranteeing that a certain number of rental or for-sale units will be rent- or price-restricted can be imposed as conditions when property owners and developers receive state and local community development and housing funds. Imposing restrictions such as these in the context of zoning, however, is another matter. The zoning statutes provide no express authority for local governments to mandate low- and moderate-income unit set-asides. However, some

---

59. 366 N.C. 142 (2012).

60. G.S. 160A-4, the parallel statute for cities, provides:

> It is the policy of the General Assembly that the cities of this State should have adequate authority to execute the powers, duties, privileges, and immunities conferred upon them by law. To this end, the provisions of this Chapter and of city charters shall be broadly construed and grants of power shall be construed to include any additional and supplementary powers that are reasonably necessary or expedient to carry them into execution and effect: Provided, that the exercise of such additional or supplementary powers shall not be contrary to State or federal law or to the public policy of this State.

61. G.S. 160A-383; 153A-341.

cities and counties look more favorably upon rezoning proposals that include plans for affordable housing. Other local governments have experimented with density bonuses when developers voluntarily designate residential units for below-market pricing. Courts in North Carolina have not had the occasion to rule on the legal defensibility of zoning set-asides for low- and moderate-income housing.

Nonconformities and Amortization

When land is zoned or rezoned, certain legally existing uses and structures may not conform to the new set of zoning regulations. These nonconformities may take a variety of forms: nonconforming uses, nonconforming buildings (as to height, setback, and so forth), and nonconforming lots (as to width, frontage, or area). In addition, a property could be nonconforming with respect to its provisions for off-street parking, its landscaping and buffering, or the position or size of advertising signs on it.

It is widely assumed that the policy of zoning is to discourage the perpetuation of nonconformities. However, a close look at many ordinances reveals that most communities take a rather passive approach to elimination of nonconformities. Most ordinance provisions allow nonconforming uses or structures to continue. There are, of course, restrictions on their expansion or extension. Nonconforming structures may generally not be structurally altered or replaced. Nonconforming uses may generally not be converted to other nonconforming uses, and uses once abandoned may not be reopened. Nonetheless, nonconformities have been very resistant to attempts to get rid of them.

A quite different method of treating nonconforming situations involves *amortization*. Amortization is based on the assumption that the owner of a nonconforming property may be required to come into full compliance with new development standards if the ordinance provides a time period within which the owner may recover the investment made while relying on the former rules. Amortization may require either the removal or the upgrading of a nonconforming use or structure. Amortization provisions are most often applied to nonconforming signs and certain outdoor land uses (such as junkyards), which can be moved to other locations and do not involve entrepreneurial investments of great magnitude. These regulations have been upheld both in principle and application by the North Carolina courts, overcoming challenges that they violate the landowner's due process rights or amount to an unconstitutional taking of private property without just compensation.[62]

Commercial off-premises (outdoor advertising) signs are nonconforming uses that constitute a major exception to rules allowing amortization. For many years the amortization of outdoor advertising signs along interstates and certain federal- and state-numbered highways has been effectively prohibited by a statutory requirement providing that if a sign owner is forced to remove such a sign, some governmental unit must pay the owner "just compensation."[63] (The U.S. Department of Transportation has required such a statute as a condition for a state to receive a full allocation of federal highway money.) In 2004 the amortization of off-premises outdoor advertising signs was also prohibited with respect to signs located anywhere in a city or county.[64] The legislation provides for certain exceptions, however, if the sign owner and local government agree to relocate the nonconforming sign.

Ironically, nonconforming on-premises commercial signs, often thought to be smaller and less objectionable than nonconforming outdoor advertising displays, may still be made subject to amortization.

Vested Rights

Generally speaking, a project that fails to comply with new ordinance standards may be accorded nonconforming status only if it has already begun when the new standards become effective. A major issue in zoning law involves how new standards affect construction projects that are begun but not yet completed. If the project is largely a figment of the property owner's imagination, then the project when built will be required to comply with the new standards. If the

62. *See, e.g.,* State v. Joyner, 286 N.C. 366, *appeal dismissed*, 422 U.S. 1002 (1975) (validating the amortization of salvage yards and junkyards over three years); Naegele Outdoor Advertising v. City of Durham, 803 F. Supp. 1068 (M.D.N.C. 1992), *aff'd*, 19 F.3d 11 (1994) (validating the amortization of commercial off-premise signs over five and one-half years).

63. G.S. 136-131.1.

64. G.S. 160A-199; 153A-143.

law allows the owner to complete the project without complying with the new requirements (the project thus becomes nonconforming), the owner has established a *vested right.*[65]

Under North Carolina zoning law, a property owner can qualify for protection in one of five ways.[66] The first is to establish a *common law vested right.* A common law vested right is established if an owner has made substantial expenditures to carry out a project in good faith reliance on a valid project approval. Actual on-site construction is not required. Expenditures of money and binding contracts to purchase land, construction materials, inventory, and equipment qualify. So do expenditures of time, labor, and energy. However, proceeding in good faith requires that the owner not work at an extraordinary pace to beat a potential rezoning. In addition, the expenditures must be made in reliance on a valid project approval. A valid zoning or building permit will normally suffice.

The second method was established in 1985 by the General Assembly to provide an alternative form of protection to the property owner that is far easier to apply than the common law vested rights doctrine. G.S. 160A-385(b) and G.S. 153A-345(b) simply provide that no zoning ordinance amendment may be applied to property without the owner's consent if a valid building permit for the property was issued before the adoption of the amendment and the permit remains outstanding. This statute does not apply, however, when the adoption of an initial zoning ordinance is involved.

The third method was established in 1990 to allow property owners to establish a vested right still earlier in the development process. The General Assembly directed local governments to provide for a vested right when a property owner obtained approval of a *site-specific development plan*, a plan for a particular use of land as proposed for a particular site, or a *phased development plan*, a general plan for a large-scale project staged over a long period. G.S. 160A-385.1 and G.S. 153A-345.1 provide that approval of a site-specific development plan establishes a vested right for between two and five years, as determined by the city or county. Approval of such a plan protects against zoning amendments affecting the type and intensity of property use, with certain exceptions. The law also authorizes but does not compel a local government to provide for the approval of a phased development plan establishing a vested right for up to five years. However, this statute also does not offer protection from adoption of an initial zoning ordinance.

Fourth, a zoning ordinance may, without reference to the law just described, define the extent to which it applies prospectively, if it is less restrictive than state law. For example, an ordinance may provide that projects for which development applications are received or lots recorded before the effective date of newly adopted amendments need not meet their terms.

Finally, a developer may negotiate the right to complete a project under pre-existing development standards as part of a development agreement between the developer and the local government (see below).

Development Agreements

Recently North Carolina has seen development projects far larger in scope and built over longer periods of time than ever before. Local governments have recognized that the off-site impacts and public facility implications of such projects outstrip the capacity of their regulatory tools to manage them. Developers have major concerns of their own, particularly in regard to the risk involved in committing substantial funds to projects without adequate assurance that local development standards will not become more demanding as the full extent of the project takes form. Legislation adopted in 2005 allowing cities (G.S. 160A-400.20 to G.S. 160A-400.32) and counties (G.S. 153A-379.1 to G.S. 153A-379.13) to enter into so-called development agreements provides a new way to address these issues.

---

65. Technically the term *vested right* applies to a constitutionally protected property right to complete the project. However, for purposes of this discussion the term is used to apply also to the rights of property owners to complete a project based on provisions in state statutes or local ordinances that grandfather projects and that are more liberal than required by the U.S. Constitution.

66. Legislative changes made in 2014 added a sixth method of vesting that applies to all development permits issued by state agencies or local governments, other than zoning permits. The version of a rule or regulation that applies to an application sometimes changes between the time the permit application is submitted and the time a decision on the application is made. In such circumstances, G.S. 153A-320.1 (counties) and G.S. 160A-360.1 (cities) allow a local government permit applicant to choose which version of the regulation or ordinance will apply to the application. This method of vesting does not apply to zoning permits and changes made to zoning ordinances.

These development agreements are limited in scope. Under such an agreement, a local government may not impose a tax or a fee or exercise any authority not otherwise allowed by law. Unless the agreement specifically provides for the application of subsequently enacted laws, the laws applicable to development of the property are those in force at the time of the execution of the agreement. (Thus, the time of the execution of the agreement may be viewed as the point at which "vesting" may occur.) Cities and counties are not necessarily authorized to commit their legislative authority in advance. For example, cities may not make enforceable promises to refrain from annexing the subject property, using their taxing authority in a particular way, or even rezoning affected lands at some future time. The agreement may require the developer to furnish certain public facilities, but it must also provide that the delivery date of these facilities is tied to the developer's successful completion of the private portion of the development. (This stipulation is designed to protect developers from having to complete public facilities in circumstances where progress in build-out may not generate the need for the facilities.) The ordinances in effect when the agreement is executed remain in effect for the life of the agreement, but the development is not immune from changes in state and federal law. A development agreement may require the project to be commenced or completed within a certain period of time. It must provide a development schedule and include commencement dates and interim completion dates for intervals of no greater than five years.[67]

The property subject to a development agreement must be at least 25 acres in size. Agreements may last no more than twenty years. To be valid, the agreements must be adopted by ordinance of the governing board. The same public hearing requirements that apply before a zoning text amendment may be adopted also apply before a development agreement may be adopted. Once executed by both parties, the agreement must be recorded, and it binds subsequent owners of affected land as well as the current owner.

Moratoria

Despite their best efforts to plan, local governments must often react quickly to new development issues or projects that are large, unusual, or impact the community in ways current land development regulations do not address. This fast pace of change sometimes motivates a local government to adopt a development moratorium of some sort to preserve the status quo while the unit makes plans, formulates development strategies, and revises ordinances. Often a moratorium takes the form of a rather stringent development restriction adopted for a fixed period of time until a more permanent solution to a particular problem can be devised.

Legislation adopted in 2005 provides express authority for cities and counties to adopt moratoria but also sets up restrictions for their use. The statute allows temporary moratoria to be placed on city or county development approvals (such as zoning permits, plat approvals, building permits, or any other development approval required by local ordinance).[68] However, it requires local governments, at the time of the adoption of the moratorium, to set forth the rationale for the moratorium, its scope and duration, and what actions the city or county plans to take to address the issues that initially led to the moratorium and a schedule for completing those actions. In particular, the ordinance must set a clear date for the termination of the moratorium and explain why the time period is reasonably necessary to address the problems.

The statute also establishes procedures a city or county must follow in adopting a moratorium ordinance. If the moratorium will last longer than sixty days, a public hearing must first be held with the same type of newspaper notices provided that are required for the adoption or amendment of other land use regulations.

Development projects on which certain types of progress have been made may not be subject to a moratorium. In the absence of an imminent threat to public health or safety, moratoria do not apply to projects with legally established vested rights—that is, projects for which a valid outstanding building permit has been issued, a site-specific or phased development plan has been approved, or substantial expenditures have been made in good faith reliance on prior administrative or quasi-judicial permission. The law also provides a special benefit to property owners and developers

---

67. See the 2009 draft development agreement between the Town of Chapel Hill and the University of North Carolina at Chapel Hill concerning the satellite campus area known as "Carolina North" at www.ci.chapel-hill.nc.us/Modules/ShowDocument.aspx?documentid=4284.

68. G.S. 160A-381(e); 153A-340(h).

by providing that moratoria do not apply to projects for which a special use or conditional use permit application or a preliminary or final plat approval application has been accepted by the city or county before the call for the public hearing to adopt the moratorium. Thus, where a moratorium is concerned, special protection is accorded to projects in the pipeline that otherwise would be expected to conform to new regulations.

Amendment of the Zoning Ordinance

Zoning Amendment Process

Unlike many local government ordinances, local zoning ordinances are amended fairly often. Most zoning ordinance amendments are map amendments that change the zoning district classification of particular properties and are known as *rezonings*. However, important alterations may also be made in the ordinance text.

When a local governing board amends the zoning ordinance, it acts in its legislative capacity. Proposals to amend the zoning ordinance may typically be submitted by anyone—a planning board member, a governing board member, a local government agency or commission, or a person in the community whether or not he or she is a property owner. State law stipulates that before the governing board may consider a proposed amendment, the planning board must have an opportunity to make recommendations on it. In some communities a zoning amendment petition is reviewed by the planning staff to ensure that the petition is complete before the council decides whether to set a date for a public hearing to consider the proposal. In other communities the governing board refers the petition to the planning board and holds a public hearing on virtually every such petition submitted. State law requires the council to hold a public hearing before it adopts any zoning ordinance amendment. Notice of this hearing must be published several times in a local newspaper. In addition, in rezoning cases notice must be posted on the property involved and additional notice must be made to neighbors.

Substantive Limitations on Zoning Map Amendments

Rezoning is easily one of the most controversial aspects of zoning. Rezoning procedures do not always conform to the expectations that property owners and neighbors have about how zoning should work. Part of the problem is that property owners, neighbors, and local government board members are interested in discussing the nature of the particular use that will be made of land proposed for rezoning. However, most conventional zoning districts provide for a range of permissible uses. North Carolina zoning case law has made it rather difficult for those who participate in rezoning hearings to focus on the specific plans of the petitioner or to have any assurance about the specific way in which the property will be used if the land is rezoned. The use of conditional use districts and conditional districts may be viewed as legitimate means of circumventing restrictions placed on rezonings involving traditional zoning districts. In this regard several important legal principles have been established by North Carolina state courts:

1. To be rezoned to a general use district, land must meet the *general suitability* criterion, which requires that the property be suitable for any use permitted in that district. Any rezoning to a general use district that cannot be justified in terms of all the possible uses permitted in the new district is arbitrary and capricious and may be invalidated. Just how demanding this principle can be is illustrated when a petitioner suggests to the governing board that if the land is rezoned, it will be developed in a particular way. A series of North Carolina court rulings demonstrate that a petitioning developer does so at its peril.[69]
2. Ad hoc conditions may not be attached to a zoning amendment involving a general use district. When rezoning a particular property, many governing boards have been tempted to include, in the amending ordinance, conditions on the manner of development that apply to the petitioner's land but not other lands zoned the same way. In doing so, however, boards run afoul of the zoning statute (G.S. 160A-382; G.S. 153A-342) that requires regulations to be uniform with respect to all properties within a general use district. Under North Carolina case law, special requirements not spelled out in the ordinance that are added as conditions to a

69. Allred v. City of Raleigh, 277 N.C. 530 (1971); Blades v. City of Raleigh, 280 N.C. 531 (1972); Hall v. City of Durham, 323 N.C. 293, *reh'g denied*, 323 N.C. 629 (1988).

rezoning are invalid and hence unenforceable.[70] The rezoning itself is not necessarily invalid, but the city or county does not gain the control that it expected over the land of the petitioning property owner.

3. A local government may not engage in *contract zoning*. Contract zoning involves a transaction in which both the landowner who seeks a rezoning and the governing board itself undertake reciprocal obligations in the form of a bilateral contract.[71] For example, a landowner might agree to subject his property to deed restrictions or make certain road improvements to enhance access to the land if the city council would agree to rezone the land when the landowner took these steps. Contract zoning of this type is illegal because by agreeing to exercise its legislative power in a particular way at a future date, a city abandons its duty to exercise independent judgment in making future legislative zoning decisions.[72]

Special Rezoning Methods and Issues

Conditional Use Districts

The relatively conservative legal doctrines just outlined have motivated North Carolina cities and counties to find more flexible ways of rezoning land. One such technique combines the discretion offered by the rezoning process with the condition-adding power of the conditional use permit. *Conditional use districts* were first expressly authorized by legislation in 1985 (codified primarily at G.S. 160A-382 and G.S. 153A-342), but several cities and counties were using the technique in the early 1970s.[73] In ordinances that provide for conditional use districts, each such district commonly corresponds to or "parallels" a conventional general use district. For example, an ordinance that provides for a highway business district (a general use district) may also authorize a conditional use highway business district. The list of uses that may be approved for a conditional use district typically corresponds to the list of uses allowed in the particular general use district that is its parallel. In sharp contrast to a general use district, however, a conditional use district allows no uses by right. Instead, every use allowed in it requires a conditional use permit granted by the governing board. Because of this feature, the statutes prohibit the rezoning of land to a conditional use district unless all the owners of land to be rezoned consent to the proposal. The key feature of the conditional use district as a zoning technique is that the petition for the rezoning to such a district and the application for the conditional use permit required for any development in such a district are generally considered together. The public hearing for the rezoning and the public hearing for the conditional use permit are consolidated into a single quasi-judicial proceeding.[74] Some cities amend the zoning map and grant the permit with the same vote.[75] Most importantly, the petitioner or the applicant is encouraged to submit a development plan that indicates the proposed use of the land. If the city council is not pleased with the development proposal, it may choose not to rezone the property. If it is generally pleased with the proposal, it may restrict the use of the land (generally to that proposed by the developer) or mitigate the expected adverse impacts of the development by adding conditions to the conditional use permit, which is granted contemporaneously with the rezoning.

---

70. In *Decker v. Coleman*, 6 N.C. App. 102 (1969), the city council rezoned a property bordering a residential area to permit a shopping center but made the rezoning subject to a proviso that the developer leave a buffer strip around the development and not cut any access road through this strip into residential neighborhoods. The regulations for the particular commercial zoning district made no mention of such requirements. When the developer ignored these conditions, affected neighbors sought compliance in court. The court held that the conditions were unenforceable because they applied only to this property and not to other land with the same zoning district designation.

71. Chrismon v. Guilford County, 322 N.C. 611, 635 (1988).

72. North Carolina courts have not had the occasion to rule on the validity of such a contract. However, *Chrismon* strongly implies that such contracts are void and unenforceable. Id. at 635.

73. In *Chrismon*, the North Carolina Supreme Court approved the use of these districts even though the controversy in that case predated the adoption by the North Carolina General Assembly of express enabling legislation for all local governments.

74. It stands to reason that if a legislative hearing and a quasi-judicial hearing are combined, the more demanding requirements of quasi-judicial hearings have to be observed. Most, but not all, cities treat such hearings as quasi-judicial.

75. The grant of a special use or conditional use permit by a city council, board of county commissioners, or planning board requires only a majority vote. G.S. 160A-381; 153A-340.

Conditional Districts

Conditional districts are a variation on the theme of conditional use districts. Conditional districts, used for many years by the City of Charlotte and Mecklenburg County, were found to be authorized implicitly by North Carolina's zoning enabling legislation in the case of *Massey v. City of Charlotte.*[76] In 2005 this legislation was amended to explicitly authorize the use of these districts. Each conditional district is unique, the result of a process of bargaining by interested parties, including, of course, the local government staff, planning board, and governing board. Most such districts, however, incorporate certain use restrictions and development standards. In addition, the text of the zoning amendment adopting the zoning map change incorporates a series of conditions, stipulations, and requirements agreed to by both the property owner and the local government. The amendment also incorporates a site development plan that shows in some detail just how and when the property will be developed. Since no conditional use permit or special use permit is involved, the process is purely legislative. The formalities of quasi-judicial evidentiary hearings do not apply.

Protest Petitions

The North Carolina municipal statutes provide an important procedure that allows neighboring property owners to protest rezoning proposals that affect nearby land. A zoning map amendment requires a super-majority vote (three-fourths of all city council members) if enough affected property owners formally protest the proposed rezoning.[77] The three-fourths vote is required if a protest petition is submitted by the owners of at least 5 percent of the land encompassed in a 100-foot perimeter around the area to be rezoned. A super-majority vote may also be triggered if the owner or owners of at least 20 percent of the area proposed for rezoning file a timely protest. This latter possibility allows some protection for the property owner in case neighbors propose that his or her property be down-zoned. In any event an eligible petition must be submitted to the city clerk at least two working days prior to the public hearing date. However, anyone who signs the protest petition may withdraw from the petition at any time up to the vote on the rezoning.

Municipal zoning protest petitions have now become a relatively common and effective tool for neighbors who oppose a particular rezoning to use. The protest petition procedure is apparently unavailable in the context of county zoning. Advocates of protest petitions weathered an attempt in 2013 to repeal the statutory authority that allows their use.

Spot Zoning

Another legal doctrine that limits a governing board's discretion in rezoning property involves *spot zoning.* The North Carolina Supreme Court defines spot zoning as

> [a] zoning ordinance or amendment which singles out and reclassifies a relatively small tract owned by a single person and surrounded by a much larger area uniformly zoned, so as to impose upon the small tract greater restrictions than those imposed upon the larger area, or so as to relieve the small tract from restrictions to which the rest of the area is subjected. . . .[78]

Zoning decisions that result in this spot zoning pattern are not necessarily invalid and illegal, however, unless there is no reasonable basis for treating the singled-out property differently from adjacent land. Whether there is good reason for the distinction depends, for example, on (1) the size of the tract; (2) the compatibility of the disputed zoning action with an existing comprehensive zoning plan; (3) the benefits and detriments of the rezoning for the petitioning property owner, the neighbors, and the surrounding community; and (4) the relationship between the uses envisioned under the new zoning and the uses of adjacent land.[79] Whether a specific instance of spot zoning is illegal thus depends to a substantial degree on the particular facts and circumstances of the case. In any case the evolving doctrine of spot zoning is consistent with the notion that any rezoning that smacks of favoritism or lacks proper justification risks invalidation.

---

76. 145 N.C. App. 345, *rev. denied*, 354 N.C. 219 (2001).
77. G.S. 160A-385.
78. Blades v. City of Raleigh, 280 N.C. 531, 549 (1972).
79. Chrismon v. Guilford Cnty., 322 N.C. 611, 628 (1988).

Confiscatory Zoning

Because zoning is a potent form of land use regulation, zoning requirements may have a drastic impact on a particular property. The constitutional doctrine that comes into play most frequently in this context is the provision of the Fifth Amendment to the U.S. Constitution that prohibits the taking of private property for public use without the payment of just compensation. It has long been true that a law restricting the use of property can have such a confiscatory effect as to constitute a regulatory taking. However, it was 1987 before the U.S. Supreme Court clarified that if a property owner proves such a taking, the remedy is not merely the invalidation of the regulation; the offending government may be held liable in damages for losses suffered by the property owner during the period when the unconstitutional regulation was in effect.[80]

Determining whether an unconstitutional taking has occurred typically depends on a balancing of the interests of the regulating government and the interests of the property owner. Two rules of thumb are clear. If a regulation prevents a use or development of land that would create a common law nuisance (for example, if a rule prevents the construction of new residences in a floodway), it is not a taking, regardless of its effect on property value. In contrast, if a regulation does not prevent a nuisance but does prevent an owner from making any practical use of a property or enjoying any reasonable return from it, the regulation amounts to a taking.[81]

Exclusionary Zoning

In general, the term *exclusionary zoning* describes zoning efforts designed to prohibit certain types of land uses within a jurisdiction. Some communities have tried to completely exclude certain less popular land uses such as junkyards, massage parlors, hazardous waste storage facilities, billboards, mobile homes and other types of low- and moderate-income housing, pawnshops, and nightclubs. Although the courts have not addressed constitutional challenges to exclusionary zoning, at least one North Carolina case suggests that important housing types and land use activities that are otherwise legal and do not constitute nuisances per se cannot normally be excluded from a jurisdiction where they would otherwise locate or operate.[82]

Other Regulatory Tools and Techniques

Thoroughfare Planning

In 1987 the General Assembly adopted a series of legislative measures to enhance the ability of both cities and the North Carolina Department of Transportation to acquire or protect rights-of-way for proposed new streets and highways. These measures give cities the power to (1) establish setback requirements for structures based on proposed rather than actual rights-of-way,[83] (2) require fees in lieu of road improvements as a condition of subdivision plat approval,[84] (3) require the construction of road improvements as a condition of obtaining a municipal driveway permit,[85] (4) approve transfers of density to other portions of a development site in order to obtain the dedication of the full right-of-way for a thoroughfare,[86] and (5) adopt a roadway corridor official map to reserve a right-of-way for a proposed road.[87]

---

80. First English Evangelical Lutheran Church of Glendale v. Cnty. of Los Angeles, 482 U.S. 304 (1987).

81. Lucas v. South Carolina Coastal Council, 505 U.S. 1003 (1992). *See also* Finch v. City of Durham, 325 N.C. 352, *reh'g denied,* 325 N.C. 714 (1989).

82. Town of Conover v. Jolly, 277 N.C. 439 (1971) (invalidating special "trailer" ordinance prohibiting mobile homes used as permanent residences anywhere within city limits).

83. G.S. 160A-306.

84. G.S. 160A-372.

85. G.S. 160A-307.

86. G.S. 136-66.10; 136-66.11.

87. G.S. 136-44.50 through 136-44.53.

Currently perhaps the most frequently used of these tools is the one related to municipal driveway permits. Cities may require an applicant for a driveway permit for a city street to provide medians, acceleration or deceleration lanes or both, and turning lanes if necessary to serve driveway traffic generated by a development.

Another potent tool is the roadway corridor official map.[88] A city may adopt an official map ordinance for a road shown on the city's comprehensive street plan or included in the city's capital improvement program. (The North Carolina Board of Transportation may also adopt an official map designation; the board's action must apply to a portion of the existing or proposed State Highway System included in the state's Transportation Improvement Program). Once an official map is adopted and recorded, no building permit may be issued for land within the corridor, and no land within the corridor may be subdivided for up to three years after the application for development permission is submitted. A city may adopt an official map for a corridor located either inside its city limits or within its extraterritorial planning jurisdiction. If the county consents, a city may even adopt an official map for a route located outside its extraterritorial planning jurisdiction. A city is also authorized to acquire the right-of-way for a road shown on an official map even though the road is located outside city limits.

Because North Carolina counties are not generally authorized to acquire rights-of-way for or maintain public streets and roads, their role in thoroughfare planning through the use of right-of-way protection is much less prominent than that of cities.

Building Code Enforcement

The North Carolina State Building Code, adopted by the North Carolina Building Code Council, applies throughout the state. However, each city and county is responsible for enforcing the code within its jurisdiction. The code generally applies to new construction, but it includes a fire code volume that applies to the use of existing buildings and other provisions governing existing buildings and their rehabilitation. The code also provides for the issuance of building permits and certificates of occupancy. These approvals are particularly important in the development and construction processes because they signify not only consistency of plans and work with the requirements of the State Building Code but also compliance with other applicable state and local regulations.

The North Carolina State Building Code is based on a model international building code that has been adapted with amendments exclusive to North Carolina. The code applies to all types of new buildings, structures, and systems except farm buildings outside city building code enforcement jurisdiction and several other minor classes of property. Generally, a city or county may not modify or amend the code as it applies locally. However, proposed local amendments to the fire prevention volume of the code found to be more stringent than the state code must be approved by the North Carolina Building Code Council.[89] To arrange for local code enforcement services, a city may (1) create its own inspection department; (2) form a joint inspection department with another local unit; (3) hire an inspector from another unit on a part-time basis, with the approval of the other unit's governing board; (4) contract with another unit for the second unit to furnish inspection services to the first; (5) request the county of which it is a part to provide inspection services throughout the city's jurisdiction without any contract between the two; or (6) contract with a certified code enforcement official who is not a local government employee. A county may make similar arrangements.

Since 1979 no person may enforce the State Building Code without a certificate from the North Carolina Code Officials Qualification Board. Each inspector must hold a certificate for one of several levels of competency.[90] All inspectors must complete certain training and continuing education courses to obtain and retain their respective certifications. In addition to supervising code official training and certification, the Code Officials Qualification Board may revoke an inspector's certificate for various reasons, including gross negligence.[91]

---

88. *See* G.S. 136-44.50 through 136-44.54.

89. G.S. 143-138(e).

90. G.S. 143-151.13.

91. In a limited number of instances, the owners of new residences have been successful in convincing the board that an inspector's certificate should be revoked because of the inspector's failure to inspect adequately a house they bought or to detect and have corrected construction mistakes made by contractors.

Minimum Housing Code Enforcement

A local government is authorized to adopt its own minimum housing ordinance establishing the standards any dwelling unit must meet to be fit for human habitation.[92] The standards may deal with structural dilapidation and defects, disrepair, light and sanitary facilities, fire hazards, ventilation, general cleanliness, and other conditions that may render dwellings unsafe and unsanitary. Most units try to use this authority to encourage the rehabilitation of substandard housing. If a housing inspector finds after a formal hearing that a dwelling is unfit for human habitation but can be rehabilitated, the inspector may issue an order requiring the building to be repaired, improved, or vacated and closed. If the dwelling cannot be rehabilitated, the inspector may issue an order requiring it to be removed or demolished. If the property owner fails to comply with such an order after having every reasonable opportunity to do so, the inspector may carry out the order directly. No demolition order may be executed unless the governing board (typically the city council) enacts an ordinance to that effect for each property to be demolished.

Additional Resources

Ducker, Richard D. "Adequate Public Facility Criteria: Linking Growth to School Capacity." *School Law Bulletin* 34 (Winter 2003): 1–12.

_____. *Dedicating and Reserving Land to Provide Access to North Carolina Beaches.* Chapel Hill, N.C.: Institute of Government, University of North Carolina at Chapel Hill, 1982.

_____. *Subdivision Regulations in North Carolina: An Introduction.* Chapel Hill, N.C.: Institute of Government, University of North Carolina at Chapel Hill, 1980.

_____. "'Taking' Found for Beach Access Dedication Requirement: *Nollan v. California Coastal Commission.*" *Local Government Law Bulletin* 30 (August 1987).

_____. "Using Impact Fees for Public Schools: The Orange County Experiment." *School Law Bulletin* 26 (Spring 1994): 1–13.

Ducker, Richard D., and George K. Cobb. "Protecting Rights-of-Way for Future Streets and Highways. *Popular Government* 58 (Fall 1992): 32–40.

Ducker, Richard D., and David W. Owens. "A Smart Growth Toolbox for Local Government." *Popular Government* 66 (Fall 2000): 29–42.

Lovelady, Adam. *Planning and Zoning for Solar in North Carolina.* Chapel Hill, N.C.: School of Government, University of North Carolina at Chapel Hill, 2014.

Mulligan, Tyler, and James Joyce. *Inclusionary Zoning: A Guide to Ordinances and the Law.* Chapel Hill, N.C.: School of Government, University of North Carolina at Chapel Hill, 2010.

Owens, David W. *Introduction to Zoning and Development Regulation.* 4th ed. Chapel Hill, N.C.: School of Government, University of North Carolina at Chapel Hill, 2013.

_____. *Land Use Law in North Carolina.* 2nd ed. Chapel Hill, N.C.: School of Government, University of North Carolina at Chapel Hill, 2011.

_____. *The North Carolina Experience with Municipal Extraterritorial Planning Jurisdiction.* Special Series No. 20. Chapel Hill, N.C.: Institute of Government, University of North Carolina at Chapel Hill, January 2006.

_____. *The Use of Development Agreements to Manage Large-Scale Development: The Law and Practice in North Carolina.* Special Series No. 25. Chapel Hill, N.C.: School of Government, University of North Carolina at Chapel Hill, October 2009.

92. G.S. 160A-441.

Owens, David W., and Adam Bruggemann. *A Summary of Experience with Zoning Variances.* Special Series No. 18. Chapel Hill, N.C.: Institute of Government, University of North Carolina at Chapel Hill, Feb. 2004.

Owens, David, and Andrew Stevenson. *An Overview of Zoning Districts, Design Standards, and Traditional Neighborhood Design in North Carolina Zoning Ordinances.* Special Series No. 23. Chapel Hill, N.C.: School of Government, University of North Carolina at Chapel Hill, 2007.

Selected Blogs from Coates' Canons: NC Local Government Law

Ducker, Richard. "Are Adequate-Public-Facility Ordinances Adequate?" December 16, 2009. http://canons.sog.unc.edu/?p=1519.

_____. "Demolition and Code Enforcement Involving Historic Districts and Landmarks." November 14, 2013. http://canons.sog.unc.edu/?p=7407.

_____. "Land Subdivision Ordinances: The Regulatory Exceptions." May 31, 2011. http://canons.sog.unc.edu/?p=4606.

_____. "Local Governments and the Special Status of Bona Fide Farms." August 17, 2011. http://canons.sog.unc.edu/?p=5237.

_____. "Zoning Variances: Is It Better to Ask for Forgiveness than Permission?" December 21, 2010. http://canons.sog.unc.edu/?p=3724.

Lovelady, Adam. "Determining and Distinguishing Land Uses." May 31, 2013. http://canons.sog.unc.edu/?p=7143.

_____. "The *Koontz* Decision and Implications for Development Exactions." July 1, 2013. http://canons.sog.unc.edu/?p=7191.

_____. "Relinquishing Extraterritorial Planning Jurisdiction." November 26, 2013. http://canons.sog.unc.edu/?p=7434.

_____. "Subdivision Performance Guarantees." February 7, 2014. http://canons.sog.unc.edu/?p=7521.

_____. "Who Says I Can't Rezone My Rezoning? November 14, 2012. http://canons.sog.unc.edu/?p=6920.

Owens, David. "BOA Changes Are Coming." June 12, 2013. http://canons.sog.unc.edu/?p=7155.

_____. "A Conditional What?: Clarifying Some Confusing Zoning Terminology." November 13, 2012. http://canons.sog.unc.edu/?p=6916.

_____. "Does Zoning Have to Provide a Place for Everything?" May 10, 2010. http://canons.sog.unc.edu/?p=2397.

_____. "School Impact Fees and Development Regulations: Another Round." October 16, 2012. http://canons.sog.unc.edu/?p=6882.

_____. "What If a Proposed Rezoning Is Inconsistent With Our Plan?" September 13, 2011. http://canons.sog.unc.edu/?p=5398.

About the Author

Richard D. Ducker is a retired School of Government faculty member whose interests include land use controls, planning, transportation, and code enforcement.

Chapter 26

Community Development and Affordable Housing

C. Tyler Mulligan

Community development refers to an expansive set of activities designed to address the plight of economically distressed communities. Individual community development programs undertaken by North Carolina local governments include efforts such as improving the appearance of neglected neighborhoods or commercial areas, constructing housing that is affordable to low-income wage workers, providing financial counseling and services, fostering local leadership, strengthening civic organizations, conducting visioning and community planning exercises, and alleviating problems associated with unemployment and underemployment. Community development programs are typically instituted under the direction of or in partnership with citizens in the affected community. The goal of such programs is to enhance the built, financial, environmental, and social conditions of disadvantaged communities in a way that benefits all members of that community.

The approach to community development that has attracted the most attention from scholars and practitioners is described as asset-based development. This approach starts by identifying the assets available in a particular community—the gifts, skills, and capacities of its residents, associations, and institutions—rather than focusing on what is absent, or what is problematic, or what the community needs.[1] The next step, sometimes referred to as building community capacity, seeks to use or leverage existing assets to create or enhance other built, financial, human, social,

1. John P. Kretzmann and John L. McKnight, *Building Communities from the Inside Out: A Path toward Finding and Mobilizing a Community's Assets* (Evanston, Ill.: Institute for Policy Research, Northwestern University, 1993), 1–11.

and institutional assets within the community.[2] Outside help may be sought, but in recognition of the scarcity of resources available to assist distressed communities, the focus is more internal than external.

It should be noted at the outset that North Carolina local governments possess no inherent powers to engage in community development. Whatever powers they possess must be granted to them by the state, even when all of the funds to support an activity come from the federal government. Any action taken without authority is considered to be *ultra vires*, that is, outside the scope of the powers delegated by the state. It is important, therefore, to consider the specific grants of authority for community development efforts.

This chapter loosely categorizes the wide range of community development activities undertaken by local governments according to the community capitals framework, which is a framework for assessing a community's assets or community capital. Community development activities are therefore categorized herein according to the community assets—built, financial, human, social, and others—that such activities seek to build upon or utilize.[3] Affordable housing receives special attention due to its traditional association with community development efforts. The chapter then considers the statutory authority granted to local governments for community development activities, including a description of some of the more often used statutes, and explains the different ways in which local governments organize delivery of community development programs. Finally, the chapter describes two of the major federal funding sources for community development.

Built Assets: Buildings, Housing, and Infrastructure

In the context of community development, the built environment refers to buildings (houses, retail stores, factories) and infrastructure (roads, water and sewer, telecommunications). These built assets are essential to attracting private investment to a community, and the implications of absent or inadequate built assets can be far-reaching. Water and sewer infrastructure is almost always a prerequisite for economic development.[4] Access to broadband contributes to both economic development and access to education and health care.[5] A well-maintained historic downtown—even in a rural area—confers benefits on the wider community.[6] In addition, there is evidence of a link between the built environment in a community and public health outcomes, because residents who live in a "walkable" neighborhood or have convenient access to full-service grocers are more likely to engage in greater physical activity and consume a healthier diet.[7] By contrast, a built environment permeated by liquor stores and fast food restaurants with few venues for exercise and recreation tends to facilitate negative and unhealthy lifestyles.

---

2. C. Tyler Mulligan and Lisa F. Stifler, *Building Assets for the Rural Future: A Guide to Promising Asset-Building Programs for Communities and Individuals on the Economic Margin* (Web guide featuring asset-building approaches for distressed rural communities according to the asset being leveraged or developed), www.sog.unc.edu/node/1804.

3. Gary Paul Green and Anna Haines, *Asset Building and Community Development*, 2nd ed. (Thousand Oaks, Calif.: Sage, 2008).

4. Faqir S. Bagi, "Economic Impact of Water/Sewer Facilities on Rural and Urban Communities," *Rural America* 17 (Winter 2002): 44, 45–46.

5. Peter Stenberg and Sarah Low, eds., *Rural Broadband at a Glance, 2009 Edition*, Economic Information Bulletin No. 47 (Washington, D.C.: Economic Research Service, U.S. Department of Agriculture, Feb. 2009), www.ers.usda.gov/publications/eib-economic-information-bulletin/eib47.aspx; Peter Stenberg, Mitchell Morehart, Stephen Vogel, John Cromartie, Vince Breneman, and Dennis Brown, *Broadband Internet's Value for Rural America*, Economic Research Report No. 78 (Washington, D.C.: Economic Research Service, U.S. Department of Agriculture, Aug. 2009), www.ers.usda.gov/publications/err-economic-research-report/err78.aspx. North Carolina's efforts are led by the e-NC Authority. *See* e-NC, *Capturing the Promise: A 10-Year Action Plan Using Broadband Internet to Increase North Carolina's Competitiveness and Sustainability in the Global Economy* (Jan. 2009), www.ncbroadband.gov/broadband-101/e-nc-publications.

6. Dagney Faulk, "The Process and Practice of Downtown Revitalization," *Review of Policy Research* 23 (March 2006): 625, 629.

7. The Prevention Institute has profiled eleven examples of predominantly low-income communities that have been transformed by changes in the built environment, particularly in terms of health outcomes. *See* Manal J. Aboelata, *The Built Environment and Health: Eleven Profiles of Neighborhood Transformation* (Oakland, Calif: Prevention Institute, July 2004), www.preventioninstitute.org/builtenv.html.

Preservation, Revitalization, and Redevelopment

Where possible, local governments typically seek to preserve existing built assets, such as historic buildings and neighborhoods.[8] In some cases, preservation of existing housing is the key to maintaining sufficient affordable housing stock for residents. However, lower income communities are often characterized by distressed or blighted built environments, so revitalization also has been a traditional focus of community development activities. Indeed, beginning in 1949, many states, including North Carolina, created a redevelopment process for blighted areas.[9] Blighted areas typically exhibit such characteristics as

- high crime;
- vacant buildings;
- unsafe structures;
- aging, deteriorating, and poorly maintained buildings; and
- inadequate infrastructure to support development (i.e., utilities, storm drainage, sewers, street lighting).

Under redevelopment programs, local governments seek to revitalize blighted areas through the acquisition, clearance, rehabilitation, or rebuilding of areas for residential, recreational, commercial, industrial, or other purposes. North Carolina's urban redevelopment law[10] grants authority to both counties and municipalities to engage in programs of blight eradication and redevelopment.

Infrastructure programs commonly used to support community development involve sidewalk and street repairs, water and sewer projects, and open space improvements. Local governments have also established public enterprises for the provision of broadband to low-income citizens who are not well served by the private market. However, the traditional focus of local government community development programs has been affordable housing.

Affordable Housing

Community development activity often occurs in neighborhoods that have been largely ignored by homebuilders, realtors, lending institutions, and home insurers. Thus, public and private sector community developers regularly aim to create new and preserve existing affordable housing options in areas underserved by private markets.

The term *affordable housing* is often a source of confusion in public debate. Affordable housing refers to decent housing for those who, without some special intervention by a government or other provider of housing, could not afford to pay the minimal rent or mortgage that ordinarily would be available in the private marketplace. The term involves judgments about the proportion of income that a family should pay for housing. These judgments are expressed in a federal housing affordability standard, which defines affordable units as those for which a family would pay no more than 30 percent of their income.[11] This standard for affordability has changed over time. In 1969, the federal government set the housing affordability standard at 25 percent of income. It raised the standard to 30 percent in 1981. The federal government considers households paying more than 50 percent of their incomes for housing costs to be experiencing severe affordability problems. More recently, advocates have argued that commuting costs should also be considered in the affordability standard.

Even higher income persons may struggle to afford the housing they desire.[12] However, as used in this chapter, affordable housing programs are those that typically are targeted to low- and moderate-income households. Low-income

8. Historic preservation is also discussed in Chapter 25, "Community Planning, Land Use, and Development."

9. *See* William H. Simon, *The Community Economic Development Movement: Law, Business, and the New Social Policy* (Durham, N.C.: Duke University Press, 2001).

10. N.C. Gen. Stat. (hereinafter G.S.) §§ 160A-500 through -526 (Urban Redevelopment Law). G.S. 160A-456 (cities) and G.S. 153A-376 (counties) authorize local governments to exercise directly the powers of a redevelopment commission.

11. According to the U.S. Department of Housing and Urban Development (HUD), housing is affordable when all housing costs (rent or mortgage, utilities, property taxes, and insurance) do not exceed 30 percent of total household income. This standard applies to any person or household regardless of the source or level of income. HUD, "Affordable Housing," www.hud.gov/offices/cpd/affordablehousing.

12. *See* Charles G. Field, "Building Consensus for Affordable Housing," *Housing Policy Debate* 8, no. 4 (1997): 802–807.

households are defined by the U.S. Department of Housing and Urban Development (HUD) as those with incomes that are less than 80 percent of the local area's median income. The North Carolina Housing Authorities Law, by contrast, defines low-income households as those earning less than 60 percent of the area median. Moderate-income households are defined as those earning as much as 120 percent of the area median under some federal programs,[13] while North Carolina law allows the income limit to fluctuate based on local housing costs and conditions.[14]

Many of North Carolina's local governments are actively engaged in creating housing opportunities for families facing affordable housing challenges. These families live in diverse circumstances that require diverse solutions. In some fast-growing communities, teachers, firefighters, and young families may lack the income or savings to buy, or sometimes even to rent, a home. These families often need only one-time or short-term housing subsidies. Other lower-income households require longer-term subsidy assistance to supplement their inadequate incomes. In some localities, families might need a broad range of housing choices, including manufactured housing. For other families, the eradication of discrimination in the private market would make available a host of housing opportunities.

Cost is only one dimension of the housing problem. In 2010, hundreds of thousands of households in North Carolina were suffering from some kind of housing problem, whether physical inadequacy, overcrowding, or cost burden.[15] Local governments have therefore attempted to address all of these dimensions. Each will be discussed in turn.

Affordability Concerns for Renters

The affordable housing squeeze has led to a significant increase in housing cost for many renters. This problem has become even more acute as a result of the drop in homeownership rates that resulted from the recession that began in 2008. From 2010 to 2013, the median rent and utility costs for renter households in North Carolina rose from $731 a month to $778 a month, despite the fact that the economy was in the midst of a recession and wages remained stagnant during that period. Rising housing costs have forced many renters to spend a large percentage of their income on housing. Some 42.3 percent of all North Carolina renters—over 509,000 households—spent at least 30 percent of their income on rent and utilities in 2011. The statistics are starker when one considers just those renters that HUD defines as low income. It is estimated that some 64.3 percent of these poorer renters in North Carolina—or more than 477,000 households—spent at least 30 percent of their income on housing.

Local governments have sought to ease the burdens on renters by employing either or both of two broad strategies: demand-side strategies and supply-side strategies. Demand-side strategies typically consist of rent subsidies for low-income persons, with funds for these subsidies coming from federal or local sources. Supply-side strategies undertaken by local governments involve increasing the supply of rental housing for low- and moderate-income households. These strategies range from owning and operating rental housing units through a public housing authority to establishing inclusionary housing programs that encourage private developers to build affordable rental units.[16]

Housing Cost Burdens for Homeowners

Homeownership has long been a cherished part of the American dream. Additionally, owning a home has been shown to confer benefits on household members. Compared to renting, homeownership is linked to greater life satisfaction, expanded social networks, greater neighborhood satisfaction, and greater participation in voluntary organizations.[17]

13. Households earning as much as 120 percent of the area median income qualified for participation in certain aspects of the Neighborhood Stabilization Program (NSP) first enacted under Title III of the Housing and Economic Recovery Act of 2008.

14. Compare the definitions of low and moderate incomes in G.S. 157-3(15a) and (15b), respectively.

15. 2013 American Community Survey, available from the U.S. Census Bureau website at www.census.gov/acs. The data on the extent of affordable housing problems cited in this section come from the decennial census, the American Community Survey, the American Housing Survey, and Comprehensive Housing Affordability Strategy (CHAS) data.

16. C. Tyler Mulligan and James L. Joyce, *Inclusionary Zoning: A Guide to Ordinances and the Law* (Chapel Hill: UNC School of Government, 2010).

17. William M. Rohe, Roberto G. Quercia, and Shannon Van Zandt, "The Social-Psychological Effects of Affordable Homeownership," in *Chasing the American Dream: New Perspectives on Affordable Homeownership*, ed. William M. Rohe and Harry L. Watson (Ithaca, N.Y.: Cornell University Press, 2007), 215–232.

Ownership by low-income persons has been shown to lead to greater household wealth, improved health of household members, greater workforce participation, and higher educational attainment by children.[18] In North Carolina in 2010, 67.2 percent of all occupied housing units were owned by their residents. This is lower than the 2000 ownership rate of 69.4 percent but higher than the national rate of 66.7 percent.

Even when potential homeowners can afford the monthly mortgage payment, the down payment and other financing requirements to secure a loan nonetheless pose insurmountable barriers to home ownership. Local governments have used both federal and local funds to help overcome these barriers for low-income households. Some jurisdictions offer down payment assistance or specialized loan products to low-income, first-time homebuyers. For low-income persons who already own a home, local governments have provided direct assistance to enable them to weatherize and rehabilitate their homes, including manufactured housing.[19]

One innovative model for placing home ownership within reach of low-income persons is a hybrid form of home ownership known as a community land trust (CLT).[20] Under the typical CLT model, a nonprofit land trust purchases land and constructs housing on that land. The land trust retains ownership of the land and sells only the built improvements to a qualified low-income buyer. By selling only the improvements, the cost of land is essentially removed from the sale price, in theory making it affordable to a low-income person. The improvements are sold subject to a ground lease that dictates the terms of any future sale, usually requiring that the improvements be sold only to another qualified low-income buyer at a price that is affordable to that buyer at the time of sale. The sale price restriction is typically designed to permit the seller to make a small return on the sale (provided incomes have risen over time), but the price is pegged to prevailing incomes so that it remains affordable to the next low-income buyer. This arrangement is designed to ensure that the community's initial investment in affordable housing in the CLT is not lost—the housing ideally remains affordable over the long term over the course of many transfers of ownership. In 2009, the General Assembly enacted legislation to clarify that CLT property is to be assessed for property tax purposes based on the restricted sale price, not on the (presumably higher) prevailing market price of similar housing in the community.[21]

Physical Inadequacy

As defined by the U.S. Census Bureau, a housing unit has a complete kitchen facility if it has all of the following: (1) a sink with piped water, (2) a range or cook top and an oven, and (3) a refrigerator. Estimates in the Bureau's 2013 American Community Survey indicate that almost twenty-two thousand units of *occupied* housing in North Carolina do not contain a complete kitchen facility. To be counted as having complete plumbing facilities, a housing unit must have (1) hot and cold piped water, (2) a flush toilet, and (3) a bathtub or shower. More than eleven thousand *occupied* housing units in North Carolina failed to meet this standard in 2013.

In addition to inadequate kitchen and plumbing facilities, other conditions might make a home inadequate, such as exposed electrical wiring or inadequate heating equipment. Local governments can respond to physical inadequacy by requiring owners to comply with minimum housing codes and providing funds to subsidize the cost of improving the housing.[22] The most dilapidated housing may be subject to demolition.

In recent years energy efficiency has become an important component of affordable housing. This is especially true for manufactured housing units (or mobile homes), which make up the lion's share of the state's privately owned

---

18. Michal Grinstein-Weiss, Jung-Sook Lee, Johanna K. P. Greeson, Chang-Keun Han, Yeong H. Yeo, and Kate Irish, "Fostering Low-Income Homeownership through Individual Development Accounts: A Longitudinal, Randomized Experiment," *Housing Policy Debate* 19, no. 4 (2006): 711, 712 (reviewing benefits of homeownership).

19. The North Carolina Weatherization Assistance Program is administered through the Division of Energy, Mineral, and Land Resources in the N.C. Department of Environment and Natural Resources.

20. Variations of the community land trust model are located in Durham and Orange County. See Durham Community Land Trustees, www.dclt.org/index.cfm; Community Home Trust, www.communityhometrust.org. More information on the community land trust model is available from the National Community Land Trust Network, www.cltnetwork.org.

21. S.L. 2009-481 (H.B. 1586, community land trust property taxation).

22. C. Tyler Mulligan and Jennifer L. Ma, *Housing Codes for Repair and Maintenance: Using the General Police Power and Minimum Housing Statutes to Prevent Dwelling Deterioration* (Chapel Hill: UNC School of Government, 2011).

affordable housing stock. Some community organizations offer programs for the removal and replacement of old manufactured housing units with new, energy-efficient units at essentially the same monthly cost to the occupant.[23]

Overcrowding

An overcrowded unit can be thought of as one that contains more than one person per room. According to HUD's more technical definition, overcrowding occurs in a unit that has more than 1.01 persons per room, whereas severe overcrowding occurs when more than 1.51 persons per room reside in a unit. In 1980, 4.5 percent of all occupied housing units in the state were overcrowded. By 1990, this figure had dropped to 2.9 percent. By 2010, an estimated 2.0 percent of households in North Carolina were overcrowded. Among units occupied by low-income households, more than 3.2 percent are overcrowded. While overcrowding rates are dropping across the state, the rates have been known to rise in some urban areas. Orange County, for example, experienced a 398 percent increase in overcrowded units between 1990 and 2000. Local governments respond directly to overcrowding issues by establishing occupancy standards that limit the number of people who can live in a unit. Recognizing that overcrowding is often symptomatic of a tight affordable housing market, local governments may also seek to respond to the issue by increasing the supply of affordable housing.

Accessibility

As used in this chapter, accessibility refers to the access that individuals have to the full range of available housing choices. The term covers (1) efforts to make housing physically accessible to the disabled; (2) activities to eradicate illegal discrimination in the housing markets based on race, national origin, religion, gender, familial status, and disability; and (3) efforts to affirmatively expand housing opportunities for groups that have traditionally been discriminated against. The best statewide source of information on barriers to housing access is the North Carolina Human Relations Commission (NCHRC), which was created in 1963 to promote civil rights and equal opportunities for the residents of North Carolina. In addition to other functions, the NCHRC enforces the State Fair Housing Act by receiving and investigating housing discrimination complaints. During the ten-year period beginning July 1, 2000, more than one thousand housing discrimination complaints were received by NCHRC for investigation, averaging over 105 per year. In fiscal year 2011 alone, NCHRC received 167 complaints. More than 40 percent of the complaints pertained to racial discrimination, and over one-third pertained to discrimination against disabled persons. After race and disability, the next most frequently cited complaint basis was familial status.

In addition to complaints addressed at the state level by NCHRC, a number of complaints are handled locally by human relations commissions established by local governments. These local commissions, in cities such as Charlotte and Winston-Salem, handle all complaints within their respective jurisdictions independently of NCHRC. A local commission is entitled to investigate and adjudicate fair housing complaints locally provided it possesses all of the same powers and authority of NCHRC.[24]

At the national level, HUD also handles fair housing complaints. HUD is permitted to refer complaints to a local agency only when the agency's procedures and powers are certified to be "substantially equivalent" to HUD's.[25] NCHRC has been certified by HUD for this purpose.

Financial Assets

Affordable credit, basic financial services, and investment of capital are critical to the health of communities. Unfortunately, private capital markets and traditional financial services often do not adequately meet the needs of low-income

23. Mulligan and Stifler, *Building Assets for the Rural Future*, *supra* note 2, at § 5.b (Increase the Asset-Building Potential of Manufactured Housing).

24. G.S. 41A-7.

25. 42 U.S.C. § 3610.

people, minorities, and small firms in distressed urban and rural areas. As a result, these persons and firms rely on nonbanking transactions, such as check-cashing services for which exorbitant fees are charged, making it even more difficult for low-income persons to save for the future. The Federal Deposit Insurance Corporation (FDIC) estimated in 2013 that 8.4 percent of North Carolina's households are unbanked and another 21.5 percent are underbanked; both percentages are worse than the national average.[26] The reasons for this are varied and include discrimination, suburbanization, and consolidation of the banking industry.[27] As a responsive strategy, community development focuses on creating access to capital to purchase homes, start businesses, obtain schooling, and provide community amenities in economically distressed places. There are two basic approaches to increasing access to capital. The first forces the existing private market to make financial capital available in these communities. The second creates alternatives to the private market to serve the specific needs of community residents.

The primary regulatory approach for increasing access to financial capital in underserved communities is implemented through the federal Community Reinvestment Act (CRA). The CRA was enacted in 1977 to prevent banks from engaging in the practice of redlining; that is, refusing to make loans in low-income and/or minority areas. Local governments have no direct oversight of CRA activity.

Most public sector activity in the creation of financial capital involves tools that either provide incentives for private financing or create new sources of capital outside the private market. These mechanisms include special tax credits, the creation of community development financial institutions (CDFIs), microloan programs, financial literacy, and individual development accounts (IDAs). Local governments either engage directly in these strategies or partner with organizations that do.

The U.S. Congress passed the New Markets Tax Credit (NMTC) as part of the federal Community Renewal Tax Relief Act of 2000. Designed to stimulate billions of dollars of new investment in low-income areas, the NMTC allows taxpayers to receive a credit against their federal income taxes for investing in commercial and economic activities that will benefit low-income communities. There are other related federal tax credit programs, such as the Low-Income Housing Tax Credit and the Historic Tax Credit. In addition, North Carolina has developed tax credits at the state level that aim to stimulate private investment of distressed places. For example, North Carolina offers its own tax credit for investments in historic rehabilitation projects. Local governments are usually active partners in seeking to have qualified areas of their communities designated for special tax treatment.

The Community Development Financial Institutions (CDFI) Fund was established in 1994 and is administered by the U.S. Treasury Department.[28] CDFIs, some of which existed before the fund was established, have the primary mission of improving economic conditions for low-income individuals and communities. These entities provide a range of financial products and services that often are not available from more mainstream lenders and financiers. One of the largest CDFIs in the nation, the Self-Help Credit Union, is headquartered in Durham, North Carolina.

Microenterprise lending originated in Bangladesh, India, in the late 1970s when the Grameen Bank began making loans to groups of poor women villagers to finance small enterprises and self-employment ventures.[29] Variants of microenterprise development have subsequently emerged in the United States, and research suggests that program participants realize noneconomic benefits that often outweigh tangible economic outcomes, such as increased pride,

---

26. Federal Deposit Insurance Corp., *2013 FDIC National Survey of Unbanked and Underbanked Households* (Oct. 2014), 116, www.fdic.gov/householdsurvey/2013. Nationally, it is reported that 7.7 percent of households are unbanked and another 20 percent are underbanked.

27. Lehn Benjamin, Julia Rubin, and Sean Zielenbach, "Community Development Financial Institutions: Current Issues and Future Prospects," *Journal of Urban Affairs* 26 (Apr. 2004): 177–78. *See also* Melvin Oliver and Thomas Shapiro, *Black Wealth/White Wealth* (New York: Routledge, 1995); Michael Stegman, *Savings for the Poor: The Hidden Benefits of Electronic Banking* (Washington, D.C.: Brookings Institution Press, 1999).

28. *See* Benjamin, Rubin, and Zielenbach, "Community Development Financial Institutions," *supra* note 27.

29. *See* David Bornstein, *The Price of a Dream: The Story of the Grameen Bank and the Idea That Is Helping the Poor Change Their Lives* (Chicago: University of Chicago Press, 1997).

self-esteem, and a sense of ownership.[30] Although providing microcredit is an important part of the U.S. approach to making credit available in low-income communities, economic literacy training is becoming equally important.[31]

Financial literacy levels among high school students and working-age adults are low and have been decreasing over time, but levels are particularly low among the poor, the less educated, and certain minority populations.[32] Some local governments have therefore supported financial literacy programs in distressed communities.[33] Some of the more innovative programs include personal financial coaching for low-income persons by specially trained financial social workers.[34]

Individual Development Accounts (IDAs) are another asset-building strategy designed to increase access to financial capital and expand economic opportunities for low-income people. In contrast to income maintenance programs, IDAs provide a mechanism for poor people to save cash to use for buying a home, starting a business, or obtaining higher education and job training.[35] The public sector is often the source of funds used to match the agreed-upon savings goals of program participants using a ratio of 1:1 up to 1:8, and the matched funds are released only when the participant makes a qualified investment, such as buying a home or paying for college.[36] North Carolina has one of the leading statewide networks of IDA programs. By year end 2012, the North Carolina Department of Labor reported that it hosted twenty-three IDA sites serving forty-six counties and that 620 participants had graduated from its program.[37]

Human Assets

Beyond access to capital, community developers recognize that their work must include a focus on linking residents to jobs. This focus is often called "workforce development." Education and formal training, on-the-job training, and family and nonfamily mentoring are all sources of workforce development that must be made available to community residents if they are to be competitive applicants for jobs in the new economy.

Two federal laws have raised the significance of workforce development. The first law, the 1996 Personal Responsibility and Work Opportunity Reconciliation Act (PRWORA), made job training and placement efforts for low-income people particularly important as federal welfare reform sought to eliminate long-term eligibility for welfare benefits of employable applicants. People being moved from welfare to work require opportunities to develop needed skills.

The second law, the Workforce Investment Act (WIA), passed in 1998, reflects the need to train people for jobs. Under the WIA, workforce investment boards made up of private sector businesses and employer representatives must work in concert with public sector representatives to design effective workforce development services for both job seekers and employers. The WIA addresses three types of job seekers: adults, dislocated workers, and young people,

---

30. Margaret S. Sherraden, Cynthia K. Sanders, and Michael W. Sherraden, *Kitchen Capitalism: Microenterprise in Low-Income Households* (Albany: State University of New York Press, 2004).

31. Margaret A. Johnson, "An Overview of Basic Issues Facing Microenterprises in the United States," *Journal of Developmental Entrepreneurship* 3 (1998): 5–21.

32. Lewis Mandell, *The Financial Literacy of Young American Adults: Results of the 2008 National Jump$tart Coalition Survey of High School Seniors and College Students* (Washington, D.C.: Jump$tart Coalition for Personal Financial Literacy, 2009), www.jumpstart.org/assets/files/2008SurveyBook.pdf; Marianne A. Hilgert, Jeanne M. Hogarth, and Sondra G. Beverly, "Household Financial Management: The Connection between Knowledge and Behavior," *Federal Reserve Bulletin* (July 2003): 309, 311, www.federalreserve.gov/pubs/bulletin/2003/0703lead.pdf.

33. Sandra Braunstein and Carolyn Welch, "Financial Literacy: An Overview of Practice, Research, and Policy," *Federal Reserve Bulletin* (Nov. 2002), www.federalreserve.gov/pubs/bulletin/2002/1102lead.pdf.

34. Mulligan and Stifler, *Building Assets for the Rural Future, supra* note 2, at § 1.c (Provide Financial Education, Counseling & Coaching).

35. *See* Michael Sherraden, *Assets and the Poor: A New American Welfare Policy* (Armonk, N.Y.: M. E. Sharpe, 1991); Thomas Shapiro and Edward Wolff, eds., *Assets for the Poor: The Benefits of Spreading Asset Ownership* (New York: Russell Sage Foundation, 2001).

36. William Rohe, Lucy Gorham, and Roberto Garcia, "Individual Development Accounts: Participants' Characteristics and Success," *Journal of Urban Affairs* 27 (Dec. 2005): 505.

37. N.C. Department of Labor, "Individual Development Accounts Program," www.nclabor.com/ida/IDA_Annual_Report.pdf.

providing each with basic support services. Services include job search assistance, assessment and case management, and job training provided by local one-stop job centers. Although the WIA focuses on a broader population than that of welfare reform, the two laws overlap in practice. One requires job training for poor people, many of whom live in economically distressed communities, and the other provides strategic direction to job training programs.

Social and Civic Assets

In order to harness a community's capacity and focus its efforts toward a common goal, two interrelated community assets must be present. The first consists of the community's social networks and connectedness—the bonds that tie talented residents to each other, to the community, and to resources outside of the community.[38] The second is its civic organizations—those organizations that actively participate in the community, provide examples of leadership, and are capable of organizing talented individuals to accomplish community goals.[39] Local governments are often at the core of each of these assets, but private organizations, such as fraternal, religious, and charitable groups, are just as important to the social and civic health of a community.

Community development corporations (CDCs) are among the most active private institutional actors in efforts to build the social and civic fabric of communities while enhancing other community assets. Incorporated as private non-profit corporations, they typically have broad community betterment missions and engage in a wide variety of activities. These internal institutions often reflect the community's attitude toward change, experimentation, entrepreneurship, and success. They are often formed by neighborhood residents and typically have residents on their boards and in their membership. As such, they are considered to be credible voices for and accountable to the communities they serve.

CDCs have grown in numbers, variety, and sophistication in recent decades. In 1967, the first CDC was born in the Bedford-Stuyvesant neighborhood of Brooklyn, New York.[40] A national survey of CDCs indicated that about forty-six hundred of these organizations operated in communities across the nation in 2005.[41] In comparison, in the mid-1970s, the estimated number of CDCs was two hundred.[42] Today, dozens of CDCs operate in North Carolina alone. For the majority of CDCs, housing production is the primary activity. However, it is important to note that, in addition to housing, CDCs engage in business enterprise development, commercial and industrial real estate development, and an impressive array of social programs. Indeed, very few CDCs engage solely in activities to improve the built or financial infrastructure of communities without also offering complementary social programs.

The increased prominence of CDCs presents challenging issues for local governments, which are being asked by the public to evaluate their own records on making low- and moderate-income communities better places to live. In answering the call for evaluation, many local governments have concluded that governments, acting alone, cannot revitalize these communities. While governments can provide the brick and mortar, they are sometimes unable to build communities in the comprehensive way that is the trademark of CDCs. Recognizing this limitation, many local governments have entered into successful joint ventures with CDCs.[43]

---

38. Cornelia Butler Flora and Jan L. Flora, "Social Capital," in *Challenges for Rural America in the Twenty-First Century*, ed. David L. Brown and Louis E. Swanson (University Park: Pennsylvania State University Press, 2003), 214, 222; Robert D. Putnam, *Bowling Alone: The Collapse and Revival of American Community* (New York: Simon & Schuster, 2000), 19.

39. Green and Haines, *Asset Building and Community Development, supra* note 3, at 197.

40. David Holtzman, "The Emergence of the CDC Network," *Shelterforce*, November/December 2005, www.nhi.org/online/issues/144/cdcnetworks.html.

41. National Congress for Community Economic Development (NCCED), *Reaching New Heights: Trends and Achievements of Community-Based Development Organizations* (Washington D.C.: NCCED, 2005).

42. Rachel G. Bratt and William M. Rohe, "Organizational Changes among CDCs: Assessing the Impacts and Navigating the Challenges," *Journal of Urban Affairs* 26 (Apr. 2004): 197.

43. Anita R. Brown-Graham, "Thinking Globally, Acting Locally: Community-Based Development Organizations and Local Governments Transform Troubled Neighborhoods," *Popular Government* 61 (Winter/Spring 1996): 2–18.

Statutory Authority for Community Development Activities

There is considerable statutory authority for local governments to engage in community development activities, including development of affordable housing. Because these statutes were enacted at different times and in response to different programmatic needs, a local government's authority to undertake various activities under the rubric of housing and community development is not laid out neatly in one place.

Community Development and Redevelopment

The General Assembly passed the Housing Authorities Law in 1935 to enable communities to take advantage of federal grants for public housing. This law, as amended, appears as Chapter 157, Article 1, of the North Carolina General Statutes (hereinafter G.S.). In 1951, responding to the broader purposes of blight eradication in the federal Housing Act of 1949, the General Assembly passed the Urban Redevelopment Law, which, as amended, appears as G.S. Chapter 160A, Article 22. Finally, in response to the Housing and Community Development Act of 1974, the General Assembly passed and later amended G.S. 153A-376 and G.S. 153A-377 (counties) and G.S. 160A-456 and 160A-457 (cities) to permit local governments to engage in Community Development Block Grant (CDBG) activities authorized by the federal act, subject to the provisions of other state laws. These statutes authorize all counties and cities to engage in programs designed to assist persons of low and moderate incomes, from "employment" to "economic development," using either federal and state grants or local funds.

Minimum Housing Codes and Nuisance Ordinances

North Carolina local governments often use housing codes, also known as minimum housing ordinances, to combat blight in existing neighborhoods. The tool authorizes a local government to require that a property owner rehabilitate his or her property without the benefit of any public financing.[44]

In order to enact a local housing code, a city or county must rely upon the authority granted to it by G.S. Chapter 160A, Article 19, Part 6, which authorizes cities and counties to adopt ordinances that establish the minimum standards a dwelling must meet in order to be judged fit for human habitation. Enforcement options under the statute vary according to the classification and size of the city or county and the extent of structural disrepair of the property in question.

Minimum housing ordinances may address issues relating to

- structural dilapidation and defects,
- general disrepair,
- lighting,
- sanitary facilities,
- fire hazards,
- ventilation, and
- general cleanliness.

Minimum housing procedures may also be employed against nonresidential structures when those structures are abandoned. Other nonresidential buildings in disrepair are subject to procedures outlined in G.S. 160A-439.

Many local governments have nuisance ordinances that prevent one person's use of land from harming neighbors. For example, nuisance lot ordinances typically set minimum standards to prevent lots from becoming overgrown or becoming repositories for unsightly and unhealthy collections of refuse. These nuisance standards are an exercise of a local government's police powers.

44. Mulligan and Ma, *Housing Codes for Repair and Maintenance*, *supra* note 22.

Relocation Assistance

Finally, local governments are authorized to deal with displacement problems that might be created by their community development activities. When extensive rehabilitation is under way or when a house that is beyond repair is to be demolished, residents may have to be relocated either temporarily or permanently. G.S. 133-5 through -18, originally enacted in 1971 in accord with the federal Uniform Relocation Assistance and Real Property Acquisition Act, allows the local government to help relocated residents with moving expenses, temporary or permanent rental payments, a down payment on the purchase of a house, or a lump sum to buy another house if the permanently displaced family owns the house to be demolished. The law also contains procedural requirements that give reasonable protection to a person or family displaced by a government program.

Organizing Local Governments for Delivery of Community Development Programs

Whether a local community development program consists of only federally funded and directed activities or a broad range of federal, local, and private activities, it requires effective coordination and management. Meeting legal requirements as well as community needs and expectations to conduct an effective program necessitates widespread community involvement, on the one hand, and concentrated executive control of a complex set of activities on the other. Neither the federal government nor the General Statutes mandates any specific form of organization to carry out a community development strategy. Each local government, then, must use the options available in the General Statutes to accomplish its community development objectives in a way that satisfactorily balances community involvement and executive control and that best suits its local program and circumstances.

Board of County Commissioners/City or Town Council

The organizational starting point for community development must be the board of county commissioners and the city or town council. Each has the authority either to undertake directly or to appoint an appropriate body to undertake on its behalf all of the local-government community development activities discussed in the earlier sections of this chapter.

Public Housing Authorities

In North Carolina, the General Assembly set out the requirements by which cities with populations greater than five hundred and counties may create traditional housing authorities. Under G.S. 157-4 and 157-33, any twenty-five residents of a county or twenty-five residents of a city (or its environs within ten miles) may file a petition with the clerk to the governing board declaring that there is a need for a housing authority. The clerk will then give notice of the time, place, and purposes of a public hearing at which the governing board will determine the need for the authority. At the hearing, the governing board must determine whether people in the jurisdiction are living in unsanitary or unsafe homes or whether there is a lack of safe or sanitary dwellings in the community.[45] If the board determines that either is true, a housing authority may be duly organized. Thereafter, the mayor will appoint the members of the board for a city's housing authority, and the board of county commissioners will appoint the members of the board for a county's housing authority. A regional housing authority can be created under G.S. 157-35 by two or more contiguous counties with an aggregate population of at least sixty thousand.

Alternatives to the Traditional Housing Authority

Across the country, public housing authorities (PHAs) have been at the center of significant controversy. More recently, under the weight of long waiting lists and fiscal limitations on the construction of new units, public housing has lost

45. In making these determinations, the governing board must take into consideration the physical age and condition of the buildings, the degree of overcrowding, the percentage of land coverage, the light and air available to the inhabitants, the size and arrangement of rooms in these dwellings, the sanitary conditions, and the extent to which conditions in the dwellings pose a threat to life or property by fire or other causes (G.S. 157-4 and -33).

favor even among some former supporters. As a result of public displeasure, some public housing authorities have attempted to reform themselves, and some have been abolished by their local governments.

Most local housing authorities have traditionally operated quite independently of the local government. With most of their funding coming from the federal government (except for some rental income), PHAs operate primarily under federal rules and policies. In recent years, however, especially as federal support for housing programs has decreased, a number of local governments, primarily cities, have taken a more assertive role in the operation of their housing authorities. There are two main reasons for this change. First, some local governments have inserted themselves into PHA operations in an effort to streamline PHA bureaucracy. Second, PHAs have been charged recently with operating complicated and comprehensive programs that require more active participation with local governments. For example, HUD's HOPE VI program and its successor, the Choice Neighborhoods program, were developed to respond to the criticism that PHAs were warehousing poor people in massive high-rise projects. These programs require significant involvement by the local government in order to demolish and rebuild new public housing units in a way that avoids overconcentration of low-income persons.

G.S. 157-4.1 and -4.2 offer several alternative organizational arrangements to the traditional independent housing authority. First, under G.S. 157-4.2, a local government may retain a separate housing authority but integrate that authority's budgeting and financial administration activities into its own. Under this arrangement, the housing authority remains a separate organization with personnel and operating responsibilities under the control of the appointed housing authority board and is treated like a local government department only for purposes of budgeting, accounting, and expenditure control.

Two organizational alternatives eliminate the housing authority altogether: the governing board may assign the powers of the housing authority to a redevelopment commission, or it may exercise those powers directly.[46] Any designation of the governing board as the housing authority should be done by passing a resolution adopted in accordance with the procedures set out in G.S. 157-4 or -33 as appropriate. In the event that an action of the housing authority requires recommendation or approval by both the housing authority and the governing board, then under the new arrangement, action by the governing board will be deemed sufficient.

Redevelopment Commissions

A city or county is authorized to create a redevelopment commission by resolution when the governing board finds that blighted areas exist in the jurisdiction and that the redevelopment of such areas is necessary for its residents. Alternatives to the standard redevelopment commission are available. G.S. 160A-505 allows a governing board to eliminate the redevelopment commission and designate itself or a housing authority as a redevelopment commission. G.S. 160A-505.1 allows a jurisdiction to retain a separate redevelopment commission but integrate the commission's budgeting and financial administration activities into its own, similar to the arrangement described above for PHAs. G.S. 160A-507 and -507.1 permit the creation of a regional commission or a joint county–city commission.

Professional Staff: Coordinators, Departments, and Task Forces

Local governments with professional community development staff have organized themselves using one of three major approaches: a coordinator, a department, or a task force.

Communities that need few specialized staff may use a coordinator. This one person is responsible for initiating, negotiating, monitoring, and evaluating the planning and execution of development activities by several departments—usually planning, public works, and inspection departments and sometimes the rehabilitation staff of a redevelopment authority. Where the coordinator is placed within the administration can be an important consideration. If the person is a member of the planning staff, he or she can certainly integrate the community development program with other planning activities but might have little influence on operating departments that carry out the program. If the person

46. G.S. 157-4.1, -33. *See also* G.S. 153A-376(b) and G.S. 160A-476(b).

is a member of the chief administrator's staff, he or she has more potential clout but usually only as much as the chief administrator chooses to support.

A city or county can form a community development department with status equal to that of the more traditional departments that might have a part in the program: public works, inspection, recreation, and so on. Such an arrangement may originate in a community's decision to abolish its separate redevelopment authority or housing authority and to bring the staff into its administration. The multifunctional department might be formed from an existing planning department and from existing building inspection staff, housing inspection staff, engineering staff, housing and redevelopment staffs, economic development staff, or various combinations of all of these. Obviously, the more functions that the department includes the more powerful the community development director's influence will be over the performance of tasks that are critical to the program.

A community that takes the broadest possible view of community development—as an endeavor involving many local agencies as well as, from time to time, private sector organizations—might adopt a task force approach to planning and managing its programs. Often, primary responsibility for the program goes to a deputy or assistant manager who, by his or her position, clearly and often acts with the full authority of the manager. This person organizes and supervises department and agency heads who will be responsible for various aspects of program planning and implementation and serves as a critical link to organizations outside the government. The composition of task forces might change over time as the community development program goes through different stages or changes its character. This process tends to be most successful when the manager delegates effectively and department heads and other staff are comfortable and competent in using team-management techniques.

Citizen Boards, Commissions, and Committees

Although the governing board holds most of the ultimate authority for community development activities, it can make efficient use of citizen interest and expertise by appointing a variety of citizen boards, commissions, and committees for advice or for implementation of program mandates. In fact, to help in planning and administering activity funded by the federal Community Development Block Grant program, the board is required to have a citizen advisory body through which to channel public opinion.

Many local governments find these bodies to be helpful. First, such a body can focus its full attention on the community development strategy, whereas the board has many other responsibilities. Second, the board can effectively delegate to the advisory group the time-consuming task of gaining widespread citizen participation in planning. Third, the professional staff can secure from this body a fairly continuous flow of informal comment and information during planning. Fourth, consultants and councils of governments working with the local government will look to this body to provide a meaningful frame of reference on the community to be served. Finally, the advisory body can supplement professional staff advice with a lay point of view when a program is recommended to the governing board. Other agencies also may play a role. For example, the local government's planning board and its housing authority, if the latter exists, are usually prepared to offer advice on community development activities, so the governing board should consider what role (if any) it expects these agencies to play in planning and executing community development programs. It can be effective to integrate community development programs with the planning board's work on comprehensive planning and capital improvement planning. The governing board should also consider whether to seek advice from other boards and commissions, such as parks and recreation, streets, and public works.

Contracting with Others

The state constitution contains a general authorization for government contracts with private entities. In addition, parallel statutes for cities and counties authorize them to contract with any private entity to carry out any public purpose in which they have statutory authority to engage. For North Carolina local governments, the authority to contract is directly related to the basic authority to spend money. A local government may contract for any purpose for which it may spend money if the expenditure is for a public purpose, the activity to be supported is one in which the local government has statutory authority to engage, and the expenditure is not inconsistent with the laws of the state or federal government.[47]

Councils of Governments

Regional councils of governments often assist local governments in the preparation and administration of federal or state grants when there is no local government staff to carry out these functions. For more information about regional councils of government, see Chapter 11, "Interlocal Cooperation, Shared Services, and Regional Councils."

Consultants

Many local governments delegate responsibility to private, for-profit consultants for completing applications for and administering state grants. A consultant typically works closely with a member of the local government (usually the manager, mayor, or clerk to the board) and the citizen advisory body to develop and implement the project. The board should be kept informed of important policy decisions, such as program amendments, because it retains ultimate responsibility for the grant.

A primary advantage of using consultants is that the community does not have to provide gap funding for personnel costs between grants. A disadvantage may be that consultants are less familiar with aspects of the community that may bear on a project.

Nonprofits

Nonprofit organizations have long worked with governments to respond to community needs. The resulting partnerships have been powerful, combining the flexibility and service-delivery capabilities of the nonprofit sector with the financial and direction-setting capabilities of the for-profit sector. They have resulted in improved local services in many areas, including community development.

Local governments may support nonprofit community development efforts in a number of ways beyond the provision of direct funding and tax exemptions.[48] For example, a local unit might include nonprofit staff in its training programs or use its purchasing power to purchase goods or services on behalf of the nonprofit for use in programs that the local government has authority to fund. Further, a local government may make the expertise of its staff available to a nonprofit as a form of in-kind assistance that can save money for both the local government and the nonprofit. In each case, subject to requirements of public purpose and statutory authority, local governments may provide in-kind support of whatever nature they choose. Although the state constitution generally prohibits a local government from giving public money or property to a private person or entity, North Carolina court cases have recognized that a promise to use property for a public purpose is legally sufficient consideration to support its conveyance. This means that as long as the proposed use is one for which the local government has authority to spend money, the local government may provide in-kind support as an outright donation in lieu of or in addition to a cash appropriation.

Faith-Based Organizations

Faith-based nonprofit organizations have been involved in community development on behalf of lower income persons since the eighteenth century, and local government agencies have long funded religiously affiliated organizations, such as Catholic Charities, Lutheran Family Services, the Salvation Army, and others. Recent laws and federal policies go beyond this, however, mandating that local governments must make their federally funded programs available to religious organizations, even those programs with a primary purpose of providing religious instruction and spiritual

47. For a detailed analysis of conflict-of-interest laws and of codes of ethics for public officials, see A. Fleming Bell, II, *Ethics, Conflicts, and Offices: A Guide for Local Officials*, 2nd ed. (Chapel Hill, N.C.: UNC School of Government, 2010).

48. For more information, see Chapter 12, "Local Government and Nonprofit Organizations," and Margaret Henderson et al., *Working with Nonprofit Organizations* (Chapel Hill, N.C.: UNC School of Government, 2010).

support to their members rather than social services to clients.[49] Such laws and policies (including HUD policies) make clear that

- faith-based organizations are eligible for federal funding on an equal basis with other organizations;
- faith-based organizations may retain authority over their internal governance, may retain religious terms in their names, and may select board members and employees on a religious basis;
- faith-based organizations that receive public funding remain independent in matters relating to governance and expression of beliefs;
- direct federal funds may not be used to support inherently religious activities, such as worship, religious instruction, or proselytization;
- federal provisions apply to state or local funds in cases where a state or local government commingles its own funds with the federal funds covered by the regulations.

Federal Funding for Housing and Community Development

The primary sources of direct funding for community development activities in North Carolina are the Community Development Block Grant (CDBG) and HOME programs.

Community Development Block Grants

The CDBG program is the largest and most flexible source of federal community development funds. Created in 1974 as an offshoot of several different existing community development programs, the CDBG program operates in furtherance of three objectives: (1) benefit low- and moderate-income persons, (2) help to prevent or eliminate slums or blight, and (3) meet urgent needs.

With the participation of their citizens, communities have devoted CDBG funds to a wide range of activities, including the creation of affordable housing, improvements in infrastructure, the expansion of economic opportunities, and the enhancement of community facilities and services. Notwithstanding the program's flexibility—that is, the wide range of activities that are deemed appropriate under it—Congress and HUD have mandated that, at a minimum, no less than 70 percent of all CDBG funds must be used for activities that directly benefit low- and moderate-income persons.

The formulas for distributing federal CDBG funds to states and local governments are based primarily on the local government's housing problems and the number of persons in that community who have incomes below the poverty level.

The CDBG program is divided into two sections, the Entitlement Program (for large cities and urban counties) and the Small Cities Program (for small cities and rural areas). Communities that are eligible for Entitlement Program CDBG funds are generally municipalities that have fifty thousand or more residents and urban counties (generally those with populations of two hundred thousand or more, excluding any entitlement cities contained within the county). In North Carolina, twenty-three municipalities and three counties participate in the CDBG Entitlement Program. The entitlement counties are Cumberland, Mecklenburg, and Wake; the entitlement cities are Asheville, Burlington, Cary, Chapel Hill, Charlotte, Concord, Durham, Fayetteville, Gastonia, Goldsboro, Greensboro, Greenville, Hickory, High Point, Jacksonville, Kannapolis, Lenoir, Morganton, Raleigh, Rocky Mount, Salisbury, Wilmington, and Winston-Salem. Together, all North Carolina entitlement communities received a total of $26 million in 2013, down from more than $28 million in 2010.

The other CDBG section, the Small Cities Program, provides North Carolina and most other states with annual direct grants, which the states in turn award to local governments in small communities and rural areas. States receive CDBG funds as an annual block grant, and then the states develop a method of distributing funds to eligible local governments. To ensure that Small Cities Program funds are used appropriately and distributed in amounts that are

49. 24 C.F.R. § 5.109 and 24 C.F.R. § 570.200.

large enough to have an impact, most states (and North Carolina) hold annual funding competitions for nonentitlement communities. States may reflect statewide priorities by earmarking funds for specific activities (e.g., economic development). States also may keep a small percentage to cover administrative costs and to provide technical assistance to local governments and nonprofit organizations. North Carolina received over $43 million in CDBG funds for the Small Cities Program in 2013, down from almost $49 million in 2010. In addition, other funds are often made available to the state's Small Cities program from additional HUD allocations; recapture, reversion, or carryover of prior year funds; and program income.

The HOME Investment Partnerships Program

HOME is a federal program designed to increase the supply of housing for low-income persons.

HOME provides funds to states and local governments to implement local housing strategies, which may include tenant-based rental assistance, assistance to homebuyers, property acquisition, new construction, rehabilitation, site improvements, demolition, relocation, and administrative costs. After certain mandated set-asides, the balance of HOME funds is allocated by formula between qualified cities, urban counties, and consortia (contiguous units of local government) and states. In North Carolina, the state portion is then reallocated to remaining jurisdictions by the North Carolina Housing Finance Agency. In 2013, the federal government allocated $12 million in HOME funds to qualified local jurisdictions (down from $19 million in 2010). Another $12 million (down from $21 million in 2010) went to the Housing Finance Agency for use statewide. The statewide funds are allocated regionally within the state based on each region's housing needs and are available through both competitive and open funding cycles.

About the Author

C. Tyler Mulligan is a School of Government faculty member whose interests include community development, economic development, development finance, redevelopment, and affordable housing.

This chapter updates and revises chapters authored by Anita R. Brown-Graham, Kurt Jenne, and David M. Lawrence, whose contributions to the field and to this publication are gratefully acknowledged.

Chapter 27

Economic Development

Jonathan Q. Morgan and C. Tyler Mulligan

Economic development is the process whereby cities and counties attempt to support and influence private investment decisions in an effort to increase employment, expand the tax base, and raise the standard of living. As North Carolina confronts the challenges of globalization, industrial restructuring, and fiscal pressures, local officials have become more concerned about economic development. However, local governments are not the only, and often are not the primary, entities involved in economic development. Various agencies at the federal, state, regional, and local levels spanning the public, private, and nonprofit sectors work to promote economic development. Thus, it is helpful to understand how local government programs relate to the activities of this broader set of organizational players.

This chapter begins by describing four fundamental approaches to economic development and how their use in North Carolina has evolved over time in response to a changing economy. The following section highlights the key factors that businesses consider in deciding where to make new investments and identifies those factors for which local governments have some responsibility. The chapter then reviews relevant federal, state, and regional programs prior to discussing the specific legal authority allowing local governments to engage in various economic development activities and the organizational options available to them in doing so. The chapter concludes with a set of critical challenges that local governments face in the pursuit of economic development.

Basic Approaches to Economic Development

In order to understand the role of local government in the development process, it is useful to review four basic approaches to economic development and consider what cities and counties typically do with respect to other organizations. The four broad approaches to economic development are

- business recruitment,
- business retention and expansion,
- business creation and entrepreneurship, and
- place-based development.

Historically, industrial recruitment has been the primary focus of economic development programs. For years North Carolina enjoyed a degree of success in luring large branch plant manufacturing facilities by marketing and promoting the state's relatively cheap labor, lower cost of living, and good quality of life. Over time, incentives became an important, albeit controversial, recruitment tool at both the state and local levels. The upside of the industrial recruitment approach is that it produced large numbers of low- to mid-skill jobs for people with limited education. The downside is that the jobs were mostly concentrated in labor-intensive industries that proved to be extremely vulnerable to global competition. The recruitment of branch plant manufacturing worked well for North Carolina until it became cheaper to produce certain types of goods—furniture, textiles, and apparel—in foreign countries, such as China, India, and Mexico. At the same time, manufacturing industries utilize automation and technology such that they can produce more with fewer workers. As a result the state has lost thousands of jobs in traditional manufacturing sectors.

The strategy of recruiting large manufacturing facilities has not benefited communities evenly across the state. Some communities and regions are better suited than others for traditional industrial recruitment because of their location, workforce, and other advantages. In addition, while the number of large industry recruitment projects has declined over time, the use of incentives to lure them has increased. It is estimated that, in a given year, on average, some 15,000 communities vie for roughly 1,500 major industrial development projects available nationally.[1] This creates an intensively competitive and often costly situation in which the odds of success are low. North Carolina now takes a more targeted approach to industrial recruitment by attempting to attract particular types of economic activity and providing inducements for investment to locate in certain areas within the state. Two examples of major recruitment projects are the location of Dell Computers to Winston-Salem in 2005 and Google's decision to build a data center in Caldwell County, which opened in 2008.[2]

Although industrial recruitment remains central to state and local economic development efforts, business retention and expansion and entrepreneurship are garnering more attention. This is not surprising given the limitations of the recruitment approach. In addition, some studies suggest that anywhere from 60 to 80 percent of new jobs come from existing industry expansions and small start-up firms.[3] Retaining companies that already exist in a jurisdiction and helping them grow is considered a less risky and more cost-effective approach to economic development because it (1) builds the local economy from within and (2) strengthens a company's ties to the local community. A typical business retention and expansion program seeks to build relationships with local companies in order to identify critical needs and facilitate access to resources and assistance that will help firms become more competitive.

Similarly, small business development and entrepreneurship programs provide support to smaller firms and encourage the start-up of new enterprises in order to stimulate economic development. Local governments usually defer to

---

1. Timothy J. Bartik, "Economic Development," in *Management Policies in Local Government Finance*, 5th ed., ed. J. Richard Aronson and Eli Schwartz (Washington, D.C.: International City/County Management Association, 2004), 364; Ted Levine, "Six Revolutions in Economic Development Marketing," *Economic Development Journal* 1, no. 1 (2002): 5–12.

2. The Dell facility in Winston-Salem ceased operations and officially closed in November of 2010. This experience shows how important it is for local governments to include repayment provisions in their contractual agreements with companies receiving incentives in the event that a company fails to meet performance targets or shuts down. For a detailed discussion of the Dell and Google deals, see Jonathan Q. Morgan, "Using Economic Development Incentives: For Better or for Worse," *Popular Government* 74 (Winter 2009): 16–29.

3. *See* David Birch, *Job Creation in America* (New York: Free Press, 1987).

other entities, such as state agencies, community colleges, universities, chambers of commerce, and local nonprofits, to take the lead on small business development. However, several North Carolina counties and cities help fund and facilitate certain development activities, including business incubators and revolving loan funds for small firms.

Many communities support place-based development strategies, such as downtown revitalization, promotion of tourism, and retiree attraction, often to complement their business recruitment, retention, and entrepreneurship efforts. These strategies focus on improving the physical environment and leveraging the natural attributes, cultural heritage, and distinctive character of a place in order to encourage investment and growth.[4] (They are related to the activities discussed in Chapter 26, "Community Development and Affordable Housing.") Small towns and rural communities are finding that place-based strategies can be promising methods of utilizing local assets for economic development. The work of Handmade in America in western North Carolina demonstrates the potential of place-based development, in this case, building upon local crafts and the region's cultural heritage.[5]

Some economic development projects represent a combination of approaches. The luring of the NASCAR Hall of Fame to Charlotte in 2006 is an example of how a major recruitment effort involving substantial state and local incentives can be tied to place-based development. Public officials who supported the incentives hoped that the hall of fame would become a major tourist attraction because it plays on the region's historical connection to stock car racing and motor sports. Moreover, its location in downtown Charlotte was expected to provide a boost to downtown revitalization efforts. Many small towns pursue development in ways that link entrepreneurship and place-based strategies in order to generate greater economic activity from the creative talent represented in local arts and crafts traditions.[6]

The Process of Economic Development

A primary purpose of economic development is to affect private investment decisions about where to locate, expand, or start up a business enterprise. If new private investment is what triggers the job creation, tax base expansion, and income growth that local officials desire for their jurisdictions, then it is important to know what factors influence the investment decision. Most often private investment decisions are driven by issues related to the inputs in the production process: land, labor, and capital.

Recent surveys indicate that the following are among the most important factors that companies weigh when choosing a location for a new facility or an expansion of an existing facility:[7]

- labor costs,
- availability of skilled workers,
- highway accessibility,
- state and local incentives,
- energy availability and costs,
- corporate tax rates,
- high-speed Internet access,
- construction and occupancy costs,
- quality of life.

---

4. *See* William Lambe and C. Tyler Mulligan, introduction to "Local Innovation in Community and Economic Development: Stories from Asheville, Edenton, Kannapolis, Wilson and Winston-Salem," *Carolina Planning* 34 (2009): 17–38.

5. Jay Fields for HandMade in America, *Crafting Large Successes in Small Towns: HandMade in America Small Town Program; The First Fifteen Years, 1996–2010* (Asheville, N.C.: HandMade in America, n.d.), s3.amazonaws.com/hia_user_files/files/32/original.pdf?1297952464.

6. *See* Jonathan Q. Morgan and William Lambe, "Find a Way or Make One: Lessons Learned from Case Studies of Small Town Development," *IEDC Economic Development Journal* 8, no. 3 (2009): 5–13. Also available at www.nclm.org/SiteCollectionDocuments/Resource/IEDC_EDJ_Morgan%20Lambe.pdf.

7. *See Area Development Online*'s annual corporate survey at www.areadevelopment.com.

This list is not exhaustive and numerous other factors, including some that are beyond the control of individual counties and cities, can shape private investment decisions. Labor and workforce concerns are paramount to most any type of company. Firms in knowledge-based, technology industries, in particular, rely on highly educated and skilled employees in order to compete and grow. County governments play a crucial role in workforce development through their funding of public schools and support for community colleges. Another area that is increasingly important to knowledge-based technology companies is quality of life. Local governments are perhaps most directly responsible for ensuring that their communities are good places to live, work, and play. There is good reason to believe that quality of life issues will take on greater relevance in the new economy.

The level of local government involvement in economic development varies considerably from place to place, and there are differing viewpoints regarding the extent to which localities should intervene. Some argue that the most effective role for local government is to help create an overall business climate that is conducive to economic growth by maintaining competitive local tax and utility rates and streamlining regulations. From this perspective, counties and cities can best support economic development by operating efficiently, providing quality services, and making long-term public investments in infrastructure, education, and local amenities. Others argue that local government should more actively stimulate private investment by providing incentives and other types of direct assistance to businesses, such as those discussed later in this chapter. Counties and cities enjoy broad statutory and constitutional authority to engage in economic development activities and can organize these activities in a number of ways. Before describing local government authority and organizational choices, however, it is first useful to set the context by summarizing federal, state, and regional programs in economic development.

Federal Programs

The federal government does not get directly involved in state and local economic development efforts. However, it can be a source of funding for certain types of projects. While several federal agencies administer programs related to economic development, two are most relevant for counties and cities. The first is the Economic Development Administration (EDA), which is a part of the U.S. Department of Commerce. EDA provides funding for local governments to engage in economic development planning and to implement projects. EDA targets its funding to economically distressed communities and regions by making grants for projects focusing on (1) public works (infrastructure), (2) technical assistance, (3) economic and trade adjustment assistance, and (4) planning.

The second major federal program is the U.S. Department of Housing and Urban Development's Community Development Block Grant (CDBG). As discussed in Chapter 26 ("Community Development and Affordable Housing"), CDBG is designed to assist low-income persons and distressed communities, and as part of that effort, it also funds economic development activities. The N.C. Department of Commerce administers the economic development component of CDBG (discussed in the next section). In addition to these two programs, other federal agencies administer and fund various types of loan guarantees for private lenders and support revolving loan programs. These agencies include the Small Business Administration, the U.S. Department of Agriculture, and the U.S. Treasury Department.

State Programs

The state's economic development activities are centered in the Department of Commerce. As the lead agency for statewide economic development efforts, the Department of Commerce is often the initial point of contact for prospective businesses. The department employs a number of professionals who work with companies interested in North Carolina to help them identify a suitable industrial or commercial site and to bring their executives together with local officials to discuss local incentives that might be offered to the companies. In recent years, the Department of Commerce has become more involved in assisting existing businesses with expansion projects and in supporting small businesses. The department has existing industry specialists located within regional field offices across the state. In addition, the department administers a number of grant and loan programs to encourage the location and the expansion of companies in the state, including some of those discussed below. The department currently houses the Office of the Commissioner for Small Business and a small business ombudsman.

Starting in 2014, North Carolina joins the ranks of several other states that have formed public–private partnerships to use in carrying out certain economic development functions. To facilitate this reorganization of the state's economic development efforts, S.L. 2014-8 (H.B. 1031) authorizes the N.C. Department of Commerce to contract with a nonprofit corporation to assist with job creation, retention, business development, marketing, international trade, and tourism activities.

Approval for Industrial Revenue Bonds

Industrial Revenue Bonds (IRBs) are a potential source of financing that businesses can use for land, building, and equipment purchases as well as for facility construction. The interest paid to bondholders is exempt from federal and state income taxes, which makes it possible to offer loans to firms at below-market rates. Only manufacturing companies are eligible to receive IRB funds, and the maximum issuance for a single company in a jurisdiction is $10 million. IRB issues must be backed by a letter of credit from a bank, so most IRB transactions are completed in partnership with a bank that issues the letter of credit and places the bonds. The county industrial facilities and pollution control financing authority in which the project will be located issues the bonds after approval has been obtained from the county, the secretary of the North Carolina Department of Commerce, and the Local Government Commission. Although government approvals are part of the process, no government guarantees the bonds. The bonds are secured only by the credit of the company. The approval process for IRBs entails additional transactional costs, so the N.C. Department of Commerce advises that in order to be cost-effective, issuances should be for at least $1.5 million.[8]

Community Development Block Grants

The North Carolina Department of Commerce administers the economic development portion of the Community Development Block Grant (CDBG) program, which is a federal grant program managed by the U.S. Department of Housing and Urban Development (HUD). Units of local government (city or county, except HUD entitlement cities and designated urban counties) may apply for these funds on behalf of a business that will create or retain jobs. Eligible projects must benefit low- or moderate-income individuals as designated by CDBG policy guidelines. Grant funds can be used to pay for the public infrastructure required to meet business needs. The local government applicant typically must provide a partial cash match unless it is located in one of the state's most distressed counties as designated by the N.C. Department of Commerce. In conjunction with a participating bank, the Department of Commerce can also provide funds to make loans to businesses to assist with machinery and equipment purchases or construction costs. Loans for the construction of publicly owned industrial shell buildings also are available, but a cash match by the local government is required in most circumstances.

Job Development Investment Grants

The General Assembly created the Job Development Investment Grant (JDIG) in 2002. The JDIG program provides discretionary grants directly to new and expanding companies that increase employment in the state. The grant amount ranges from 10 to 75 percent of withholding taxes paid for each eligible position created over a period of time. Grant payments are disbursed annually for up to twelve years. The terms of the grant are specified in an agreement that requires the company to comply with certain standards regarding employee health insurance, workplace safety, and wages paid. The grant agreement must include a clawback provision to recapture funds in the event that the company relocates or closes before a specified period of time.

8. North Carolina has an industrial revenue composite bond program for smaller projects.

Tax Credits and Exemptions

The state has, at various times, supported tax credits and various exemptions for companies that create jobs and invest in facilities and equipment in the state. Benefits and credit amounts under state programs are often based on the relative distress of the county in which the project is located, as signified by a county tier designation assigned by the Department of Commerce. For example, the tier designation system employed in 2013 assigned the forty most-distressed counties as tier one, the next forty as tier two, and the twenty least-distressed counties as tier three. The most generous benefits and tax credits are reserved for projects located in tier one counties, with lower benefit amounts offered in higher tiers.

Industrial Development Fund

The Industrial Development Fund (IDF) helps local governments in the most economically distressed counties provide incentives to new and expanding companies that create jobs. A county or city government may receive grants to make public infrastructure improvements or use funds to offer loans for building renovation and equipment purchases. IDF funds cannot be used to acquire land or buildings or for the construction of new facilities. The exact amount of funding is tied to the number of new, full-time jobs created or retained by the company. Eligible public infrastructure projects include construction or improvement of water, sewer, gas, telecommunications, high-speed broadband, electrical utility facilities, or transportation infrastructure.

One North Carolina Fund

The governor awards a limited number of cash grants from the One North Carolina Fund annually. The General Assembly funds this grant program through nonrecurring appropriations, and the amount available each year varies. Each grant is awarded to a local government to secure a commitment from private companies to locate or expand within the local government's jurisdiction. Companies must use the grants to install or purchase new equipment; make structural repairs, improvements, or renovations of existing buildings in order to expand operations; construct or improve existing water, sewer, gas or electric utility distribution lines; or equip buildings. Applications for the grants are submitted according to guidelines promulgated by the Department of Commerce, with grants being awarded on the basis of the strategic importance of the industry, the quality of jobs to be created, and the quality of the particular project. The local government must provide matching funds to assist the company.

Workforce Training, Small Business Services, Industrial Extension, and Transportation

Along with the programs administered by the Commerce Department, additional critical services are provided by other agencies. The N.C. Community College System participates in economic development by providing customized training for the employees of new and expanding industries.[9] The community college system also coordinates a network of small business centers located on its campuses that assist new and existing small firms.[10] The N.C. Commission on Workforce Development coordinates and guides implementation of the federal Workforce Investment Act of 1998/ Workforce Innovation and Opportunity Act of 2014, which includes the state's network of local employment/career (JobLink) centers. North Carolina State University administers the state's Industrial Extension Service through regional field offices, providing training and technical assistance to businesses and industries to help them stay competitive. Finally, the Department of Transportation makes road and highway improvements that encourage both industrial and commercial development. In an effort to enhance planning and cooperation between state agencies and local officials in each region of the state, the General Assembly has directed the departments of Commerce, Environment and Natural Resources, and Transportation to locate staff in the same physical office in each of eight regions of the state called

9. *See* www.nccommunitycolleges.edu.

10. *See* the N.C. Small Business Center Network (SBCN) website at www.sbcn.nc.gov.

"Collaboration for Prosperity Zones."[11] The community college system must also designate a representative to serve as a liaison in each zone.[12]

Programs Administered by State-Funded Nonprofits

The North Carolina General Assembly appropriates funds from time to time to support the work of nonprofit economic development organizations that operate statewide. For example, the General Assembly funded the N.C. Rural Economic Development Center (Rural Center) and the Institute of Minority Economic Development (NCIMED) for many years. The Rural Center provides grants and runs programs in the state's rural communities for leadership training, workforce development, and support for entrepreneurs. NCIMED promotes economic development in low-wealth, underrepresented communities by providing financial and technical assistance to minority- and women-owned businesses. Another example is the N.C. Biotechnology Center, which receives state appropriations to support the development of the biotechnology sector.

North Carolina created the Golden Leaf Foundation in 1999 to receive a portion of the state's tobacco settlement funds to be used to assist tobacco-dependent and economically distressed counties. The foundation provides grants on a competitive basis to eligible applicants, including local units of government. Golden Leaf grants have funded infrastructure for economic development, workforce training, business incubators, and other economic development priorities.

In 2014, the Department of Commerce was authorized to enter into a contract with a private nonprofit in order to deliver certain economic development services.[13] Members of the board of directors of the nonprofit are appointed by the governor, the President Pro Tempore of the Senate, and the Speaker of the House of Representatives. The nonprofit is intended to assist the Department of Commerce with many of the department's marketing and business recruiting functions. The nonprofit is not permitted to exercise any authority over state-administered grant and incentive programs.

Regional Economic Development Programs

Various organizations work to support and implement regional approaches to economic development within North Carolina. For our purposes here, three are pertinent. The first set of organizations is the Regional Economic Development Partnerships that market and promote seven multi-county regions and support local development efforts. The regional partnership organizations, which at one time received state appropriations, are now structured as public–private entities.

The second set of regional organizations involved in economic development is the Councils of Government (COGs). In North Carolina, seventeen COGs or regional councils serve multi-county regions by assisting local governments with planning and development issues. COGs provide technical assistance to local governments and help coordinate access to state and federal programs. Some COGs are more directly engaged in economic development activities than others, with activities ranging from administering a revolving loan fund to operating a regional business incubator to staffing a nonprofit economic development commission.

A third set of regional entities related to economic development is the Workforce Development Boards. These boards coordinate with the state's Commission on Workforce Development and oversee and coordinate federal workforce programs at the local level. Some Workforce Development Boards serve single counties, but many serve multi-county regions and are based within COGs. Local elected officials appoint board members, most of whom must be business representatives.

---

11. N.C. Gen. Stat. (hereinafter G.S.) § 143B-28.1.
12. S.L. 2014-18 (H.B. 1031).
13. *Id.*

Traditional Local Government Authority for Economic Development

Local governments engage in a number of traditional activities to encourage economic development and about which there is little philosophical dispute. These include employing agents to meet and negotiate with and assist companies interested in locating or expanding in the community, undertaking surveys to identify community strengths and weaknesses, developing strategic plans for economic development, and advertising the community in industrial development publications and elsewhere. Counties and cities also provide public services and facilities to attract new development and to stimulate economic growth, such as by extending (or assisting in the extension of) utility lines, expanding water supply and treatment facilities and sewage treatment facilities, and constructing road improvements.

Industrial Revenue Bond Financing

Chapter 159C of the North Carolina General Statutes (hereinafter G.S.) permits counties (but not cities) to create special authorities that issue industrial revenue bonds, subject to approval by the Department of Commerce and the Local Government Commission, as discussed above under "State Programs." These bonds finance the construction of factories and other industrial facilities and debt service is paid by the companies using the facilities. Use of an authority permits issuance of the bonds in tax-exempt form, thereby reducing the capital costs paid by the benefiting company. The bonds are secured only by the credit of the benefiting company. The local government acts merely as a conduit for the bond issuance and carries no obligation for payment.

Direct Incentives

For a number of years there were serious questions about the constitutionality of local governments providing direct incentives to specific industrial and commercial prospects, but those questions were resolved in favor of constitutionality in the 1996 case of *Maready v. City of Winston-Salem*.[14] The issue in that case was whether direct incentives benefited the public at large or only the companies receiving the incentives. The North Carolina Supreme Court decided it was the former: the predominant benefit from incentive programs is public, extending to the citizens, who, as a consequence of the programs, have greater employment opportunities, and to the governments through stronger revenue bases. In explaining its rationale, the court noted the importance of competing with other states' incentives, and it expressed confidence that the strict procedural requirements of the authorizing statute would prevent abuse by public officials. Direct incentives can therefore serve a public purpose under the right circumstances. The basic authorization to provide incentives is found in G.S. 158-7.1. When a North Carolina local government turns funds over to a private entity for expenditure (through an incentive payment), the local government must give prior approval to how the funds will be expended by the private entity and "all such expenditures shall be accounted for" at the end of the fiscal year.[15] Subsection (b) specifically permits a number of industrial and commercial assistance activities, including developing industrial parks, assembling other potential industrial sites, constructing and leasing or selling shell buildings, helping extend public and private utility lines to private facilities, and preparing sites for industrial facilities. Subsection (d2) permits a local government to convey real property to a private company that promises to create a substantial number of jobs, accepting as consideration for the conveyance the increased property and sales tax revenues that will accrue to the government over the succeeding ten years as a result of improvements by the company to the property. Finally, subsection (a), which has been in the statutes since 1925, grants broad authority to "make appropriations for the purposes of aiding and encouraging the location of manufacturing enterprises." Local governments have relied on this last provision as support for specific incentives not included in subsections (b) or (d2), especially the making of direct cash grants to companies that provide a public benefit as described in the *Maready* decision.

G.S. 158-7.1(c) requires any local government that makes appropriations for activities specifically listed in subsection (b) to first hold a public hearing on the expenditure in question. Although the statute does not specifically require

14. 342 N.C. 708 (1996).

15. G.S. 158-7.2. *See also* Kara Millonzi, "Ensuring Appropriate Expenditures by Private Entities," *Coates' Canons: NC Local Government Law Blog* (UNC School of Government, June 17, 2010); updated August 2013, http://canons.sog.unc.edu/?p=2632.

it, most local governments also hold a public hearing if the statutory authority for the incentive is subsection (a). In the *Maready* decision, the court clearly encouraged public hearings in that latter circumstance. If a local government intends to convey property to a private company, whether for monetary consideration or pursuant to subsection (d2), it must hold an additional public hearing on the conveyance. Finally, subsections (f) and (h) place limits on local government authority by imposing a cap on the total investment of a single local government in certain economic development programs and by requiring that incentive agreements contain provisions to recapture incentive grants from companies that fail to maintain promised levels of job creation, investment, and operations.[16]

Tax Abatements and Cash Incentive Policies

One form of industrial or commercial development and recruitment often used in other states is not directly available in North Carolina: offering special property tax breaks to new industries or businesses. Under Article V, Section 2, of the state constitution, property tax exemptions and classifications may be made only by the General Assembly and then only on a statewide basis. A local government may not constitutionally offer a special classification to a property owner if it is not available statewide. The legislature has not enacted any special classifications for new industrial or commercial development; therefore, none can be offered by local economic development officials.

In recent years, however, a number of counties (and the cities in those counties) have developed a cash grant incentive policy that very much resembles tax abatements. These policies follow a common pattern: the local government offers to make annual cash grants over a number of years (typically five) to industrial companies that make investments of certain minimum amounts in the county or city. (The investment might be either a new facility or the expansion of an existing facility.) The amount of the cash grant is specifically tied to the amount of property taxes paid by the company. For example, a company that made an investment of at least $5 million might be eligible for a cash grant in an amount up to 50 percent of the property taxes it paid on the resulting facility; larger investments would make the company eligible for a grant that represented a larger percentage of the property taxes paid. These policies closely approach tax abatements, with one important difference: the company receiving the cash incentives has paid its property taxes. No court has directly addressed whether this sort of policy is an unconstitutional attempt to grant a tax abatement or whether it is simply a constitutionally permitted cash incentive. There is no question, however, that an increasing number of local governments have adopted such policies.

Open Meetings and Public Records

Both the open meetings and the public records laws permit a good bit of confidentiality while a local government is negotiating incentives with a company. The open meetings law permits a public body—board of county commissioners, city council, economic development commission—to hold closed sessions to "discuss matters relating to the location or expansion of industries or other businesses in the area served by the public body, including agreement on a tentative list of economic development incentives that may be offered by the public body" (G.S. 143-318.11(a)(4)). The statute requires, however, that any action approving the signing of an incentives contract or authorizing paying an incentive be taken in open session. (In addition, as noted above, G.S. 158-7.1(c) requires a public hearing before certain incentives can be approved.)

G.S. 132-6(d) permits denying public access to otherwise public records "relating to the proposed expansion or location of specific business or industrial projects . . . so long as their inspection, examination or copying would frustrate the purpose for which such public records were created." Once the company has committed to locate or expand in the community, however, or has decided not to locate or expand, the statute requires that the records be made public. Occasionally, a local government will rely upon elaborate economic modeling and impact analysis to assess the value of a company's decision to locate in the jurisdiction. These analyses typically attempt to estimate the fiscal and economic impact in a community of promised capital investment, jobs, and operations. Whenever a public agency performs such analysis, G.S. 132-1.11 requires that the agency "describe in detail the assumptions and methodologies used in

16. For more detail on analyzing the legal validity of economic development incentives, see C. Tyler Mulligan, "Economic Development Incentives and North Carolina Local Governments: A Framework for Analysis," 91 N.C. L. Rev. 2021 (2013).

completing the analysis or assessment." This description becomes a public record and must be included in the release of all public records pertaining to a company's location decision.

The open meetings and the public records statutes are discussed at length in Chapter 8, "Public Records," and Chapter 9, "Open Meetings and Other Legal Requirements for Local Government Boards."

Downtown Development Authority

Much of the legal authority discussed above can be applied to projects within a city's downtown as well as in other parts of the community. There are two statutes, however, that are particularly useful for economic development programs and projects in a downtown area.

Business improvement districts (BIDs) are a popular tool for downtown or commercial development throughout the United States. Such a district draws a line around some or all of a downtown area or other urban area, raises extra revenue from property owners or businesses in the enclosed area, and uses those revenues to undertake a potentially wide variety of activities intended to increase the economic vitality of the defined area. While North Carolina does not have a specific BID statute, cities can create such a district under the Municipal Service District Act (G.S. 160A-535 through -544). Specifically, a city can create a municipal service district for the purpose of downtown revitalization or urban area revitalization. Such a district is created by action of the city council after a public hearing, and it is funded by levy of an additional ad valorem property tax on all property within the district. Because the district is funded by property tax levies, the city council retains ultimate control over expenditures within the district. Many cities, however, establish advisory boards of property owners within the district and give strong weight to the program recommendations of the board.

The second statute is G.S. 160A-458.3, which provides special authority for a city to cooperate with one or more private parties in the construction and operation of new capital projects in the downtown area. The statute is intended to allow a city to participate with one or more private partners in projects that mix public facilities, such as parking decks or city offices, with private commercial facilities. The statute offers two specific advantages to cities entering into such projects. First, it permits the city to delegate construction of the entire project, including the city-owned portion, to the private participants, so long as no more than 50 percent of the total cost is paid for with city funds. Second, it permits the city to contract with a private party for operation of the entire project, including the city-owned portions. Note that a recently enacted statute, G.S. 143-128.1C, authorizes local governments to enter into similar arrangements as part of a public–private partnership construction contract without regard to a project's location in a downtown area.

Other Authority to Assist in Economic Development

A local government has considerable authority to attract business development by facilitating the location, preparation, and transfer of a suitable site in the community. In addition to the authority for industrial and commercial development activities under G.S. 158-7.1, a local government may acquire land with or without buildings for commercial or industrial development and for public facilities to serve a major private development under two sources of authority: the Urban Redevelopment Law (G.S. 160A-500 through -526; -512 contains authority to acquire land) and general redevelopment authority (G.S. 153A-377, for counties, and G.S. 160A-457, for cities). A local government may dispose of property acquired under each of the cited statutes to a private developer either directly or after clearing, refurbishing, or adding public improvements to make the site more attractive for development. If the property was acquired under the redevelopment law, any disposition must be done by competitive procedures. In addition, a county that acquires property pursuant to G.S. 153A-377 must also dispose of it by competitive procedures; but a city that acquires property under the parallel statute, G.S. 160A-457, has authority under that statute to convey the property by private sale as well as competitively. In addition to acquiring and developing property, authority is provided under redevelopment law for programs of assistance and financing, including the making of loans, for acquisition, rehabilitation, or construction of residential units and commercial facilities in a redevelopment area (G.S. 160A-503).

The redevelopment law allows a county or city to condemn property, if necessary, in order to acquire property for any of the purposes identified in the preceding paragraph (G.S. 160A-512(6), -515). There is no other general authority to condemn property for economic development projects.

Land acquisition and public improvements undertaken for economic development purposes may be financed by federal funds or by appropriation of local tax revenues without special voter approval. General obligation bonds may be used to finance any improvement authorized by G.S. 159-48 but generally only with voter approval before issuance. Revenue bonds may be used to finance such public service enterprise improvements as sewer or water facilities built in conjunction with an economic development project. No vote is required for such bonds, but the facility must yield adequate revenue from operations to retire the debt. Finally, in certain circumstances some capital projects that are useful for economic development may be financed by project development (or tax increment) bonds, for which the primary security is tax proceeds on new private development generated because of the public investment financed by the bonds. All these forms of debt financing are detailed in Chapter 21, "Financing Capital Projects."

Interlocal Cooperation on Economic Development

Smaller, rural jurisdictions often find it difficult to develop large-scale projects like industrial parks alone. When cities and counties collaborate on such ventures, they can enjoy economies of scale and pursue projects that otherwise might not be feasible. The General Assembly enacted G.S. 158-7.4 to facilitate interlocal cooperation on economic development. The statute authorizes two or more units of local government to enter into a contract or agreement to share financing, expenditures, and revenues related to joint development projects. It specifically authorizes the sharing of property tax revenues generated from a joint industrial/commercial park or site.

An example illustrates how cities and counties might utilize this provision. The Triangle North network of business and industrial parks is a joint effort of Franklin, Granville, Vance, and Warren counties.[17] Officials from each of the participating counties signed an interlocal agreement to share the costs of developing four distinctive business and industrial parks—one in each county—that will benefit all four counties. The interlocal agreement provides for equal representation on the board of the Kerr-Tar Regional Economic Development Corporation, the nonprofit created to develop and manage the network of business parks. Additionally, the agreement stipulates how the counties will share costs and allocate revenues created by the industrial parks. The Kerr-Tar Regional Council of Government played a central role in facilitating this collaborative effort.

Organization for Economic Development

A local economic development program requires effective coordination and management. Conducting an effective program requires widespread community involvement on the one hand and concentrated executive control of a complex set of activities on the other. There is no single administrative structure in common use; rather counties and cities have turned to a variety of structures, either singly or collectively.

The starting point for organizing economic development activities is the unit's governing board, which has the authority either to undertake directly or to appoint one or more appropriate bodies to undertake on its behalf the various activities discussed earlier. Some larger cities have economic development units and staff within the manager's office. Although a local government can rely on the governing board and in-house staff for large-scale and long-term economic development efforts, most counties and many cities rely on an appointed commission to do the work on their behalf.

G.S. Chapter 158, Article 2, allows the governing board to appoint an economic development commission. Such a commission is a public agency, but once it is created and members are appointed, it may act with some independence from the government that created it. Advantages of such a commission include the opportunity to ensure that local business leaders have an active role on the commission through their membership and the possibility of setting such a commission up cooperatively with other jurisdictions to coordinate efforts in one body. One disadvantage is that an

17. *See* Crystal Morphis and Ernest Pearson, "Creating Economic Opportunity: Multi-Jurisdictional Parks as a Product Development Tool," *IEDC Economic Development Journal* 10 (Spring 2011): 28–35.

Table 27.1 Characteristics of Organizational Structures for Economic Development

Characteristics	Line Development	Economic Commission	Dependent Nonprofit	Independent Nonprofit
Organizational Powers				
Own property	Yes	No	Yes	Yes
Develop industrial park	Yes	No	Yes	Yes
Construct shell building	Yes	No	Yes	Yes
Borrow money	Yes	No	Yes	Yes
Guarantee private loans	No	No	Probably no	Yes
Finance and Taxation				
Subject to Budget/ Fiscal Control Act	Yes	Yes	No	No
Income tax status	Exempt	Exempt	Exempt	Exempt
Contributions deductible	Yes	Yes	If 501(c)(3)	If 501(c)(3)
Property tax status	Exempt	Exempt	Taxable	Taxable
Procedural Issues				
Subject to open meetings/ public records laws	Yes	Yes	Yes	No
Follow G.S.158.7.1	Yes	N/A	No	No
Policy Coordination/Control				
Policy coordination	High	Medium	Medium	Low
Financial control	Appropriation	Appropriation	Contract	Contract
Employee Benefits	Public	Public	Private	Private
Private Sector Involvement	Low	Medium	Medium	High

Source: Adapted from David M. Lawrence, *Economic Development Law for North Carolina Local Governments* (Chapel Hill: UNC School of Government, 2000).

economic development commission does not enjoy any authority to own real property and therefore cannot directly undertake some of the incentive programs authorized to cities and counties by G.S. 158-7.1(b).

Some counties and cities delegate their economic development activities to chambers of commerce, committees of 100, or other private nonprofit corporations, limiting the direct role of the public body to one of providing funding in some measure (and, in some cases, appointing some of the members of the nonprofit's board of directors). For example, the Alamance County Area Chamber of Commerce is the lead agency responsible for economic development in that county. Similarly, Durham County contracts with the Greater Durham Chamber of Commerce to implement economic development for the county. The Greater Raleigh Chamber of Commerce administers the Wake County Economic Development program on behalf of twelve municipalities in the county. Onslow County, the City of Jacksonville, and the local Committee of 100 provide funding to the Jacksonville–Onslow Office of Economic Development to carry out development activities for both the city and county. The Carteret Economic Development Council is a nonprofit membership organization that receives most of its funds from Carteret County to engage in economic development activities. The Catawba County Economic Development Corporation is chartered as a nonprofit, 501(c)(3) organization that receives local government funding but also generates substantial revenue from private sources, including the local Committee of 100. A last example is the City of High Point, which relies on the nonprofit High Point Economic Development Corporation to run its economic development program.

These private groups share the benefits of an economic development commission in that they permit the involvement of the local business community and facilitate cooperation among several local governments. They also bear two advantages not characteristic of economic development commissions. First, there is no bar to their owning real property; thus, they can act directly as developers of industrial parks or shell buildings or can hold industrial sites for conveyance to newly locating companies. Second, because they are private organizations, they can raise private funds within the community and spend those funds without concern for the possible constitutional or statutory limitations placed on public funds. (Any public moneys appropriated to these organizations, however, retain their public character and remain subject to such limitations.) A possible disadvantage of using these private organizations, depending on how their governing boards are selected, is that they may have considerable independence from local government, and therefore might sometimes pursue goals and strategies inconsistent with the wishes of local government officials.

Over time, some counties and cities will adopt a different structural arrangement for implementing economic development activities in order to better coordinate resources and promote greater efficiency and effectiveness (see Table 27.1). For example, Wayne County decided in 2006 to replace its Economic Development Commission, which had been in existence since 1966, with a new, nonprofit, public–private organization to conduct economic development for the entire county. This entity called the Wayne County Development Alliance represents a formal partnership between the Wayne County Board of Commissioners, the Goldsboro Committee of 100, and the Mount Olive Committee of 100. A second example is the Carolinas Gateway Partnership, which was formed in 1995 to merge the economic development activities of two counties, Edgecombe and Nash, into one nonprofit organization.

Conclusion: Challenges for Local Government

Economic development is a long-term process that involves numerous organizational players and a variety of tools and strategies. Much of what happens in the global, new economy appears beyond the control of individual local governments. Yet local officials will do what they can to help their communities adapt, respond, and prosper in the midst of changing economic conditions and fiscal uncertainty. Counties and cities face several challenges as they seek to stimulate private investment, promote job creation, and expand the tax base in their jurisdictions:

1. *Strategic visioning, organization, and the role of local government.* More communities recognize the need to be proactive and deliberate in their economic development efforts. This is evident in the increase in strategic visioning and planning efforts taking place across the state. These planning efforts help communities be more systematic in choosing the right mix of strategies and tools. They also connect a community's goals and objectives to what is actually done in economic development. A good strategic plan for economic development specifies which organizations will be responsible for different action steps and delineates the role of local government in the process.
2. *Taking a long-term view.* There are no quick fixes or silver bullets in economic development. An effective approach includes a mix of strategies and tools that are consistent with a community's long-term vision and goals. Immediate results are more the exception than the norm. Counties and cities that make strategic public investments over time and implement a program that looks beyond the next election cycle are better positioned to withstand the ups and downs of the new economy.
3. *Using incentives as a public investment.* Though widely used, incentives are considered by most to be a necessary evil to compete for investment and jobs. Very few jurisdictions are willing to take the risk of losing a potential project on account of not offering an incentive package to match that of rival communities. The challenge for those counties and cities that choose to use incentives is how to do so as an investment of public dollars for the greater good rather than as a mere subsidy of private business activities. To achieve this, some communities target incentives at certain types of industries that are expected to produce higher rates of return on the public investment and tie incentives to specific job creation and investment levels. Other

mechanisms to protect the public investment include payback guidelines, performance agreements, clawback provisions, and cost-benefit analysis of incentive projects.

4. *Balancing the tax base.* Several counties and cities in North Carolina have experienced rapid population growth and have seen an increase in residential development as a result. Indeed many "bedroom" communities are taking shape across the state. Local governments must figure out how to pay for the additional public services that growth requires. The problem is that residential development does not tend to generate sufficient tax revenue to fund expanded public services. By contrast, industrial and commercial development usually more than pays for itself in terms of the ratio of tax revenues to the cost of public services. Therefore, as communities grow, they should pay attention to diversification, or the lack thereof, in the tax base.
5. *Ensuring that the benefits of economic development are widely shared.* Using public funds for economic development assumes that doing so serves a larger public interest. Local governments face a challenge in ensuring that public economic development activities extend beyond narrow private interests to benefit the community in a broader sense. More specifically, local governments often intervene in the process to steer growth and development to disadvantaged areas and residents. Indeed, providing jobs for dislocated workers was specifically mentioned in the *Maready* decision as one of the public benefits that justified making direct incentives to private companies.
6. *Measuring and evaluating success.* So much is done in economic development without ever knowing what difference it has made in communities. A comprehensive approach to gauging success in economic development will focus on a broad set of performance measures. Systematic evaluation of economic development programs can shed light on what is working and where resources should be focused.
7. *Knowing when to collaborate and when to compete.* Although economic development is an inherently competitive process that often pits one jurisdiction against another, there is increasing recognition that regional collaboration makes sense in certain instances. Regional solutions to infrastructure, workforce development, and incentives are difficult to initiate and implement. Yet, the reality is that economies tend to be regional in nature and cut across political boundaries. A major question that arises is how to reconcile the fact that taxation, land use, and infrastructure decisions are tied to local political jurisdictions but regional economies are not.

Additional Resources

Publications

Ammons, David, and Jonathan Morgan. "State-of-the-Art Measures in Economic Development." *Public Management* 93 (June 2011): 6–10.

Austrian, Ziona, and Jill Norton. *Strategies and Tools in Economic Development Practice.* Cleveland: Center for Economic Development, Cleveland State University, 2002. http://urban.csuohio.edu/economicdevelopment/knight/index.htm.

Blakely, Edward J., and Ted K. Bradshaw. *Planning Local Economic Development: Theory and Practice.* 3rd ed. Thousand Oaks, Calif.: Sage, 2002.

Forman, Maury, and Jim Mooney. *Learning to Lead: A Primer on Economic Development Strategies.* Dubuque, Iowa: Kendall/Hunt, 1999.

Koven, Steven G., and Thomas S. Lyons. *Economic Development: Strategies for State and Local Practice.* 2nd ed. Washington, D.C.: International City/County Management Association, 2010.

Lambe, William. *Small Towns, Big Ideas: Case Studies in Small Town Community Economic Development.* Chapel Hill and Raleigh: Community and Economic Development Program, UNC School of Government, and N.C. Rural Economic Development Center, 2008. www.cednc.unc.edu/stbi.

Lawrence, David M. *Economic Development Law for North Carolina Local Governments.* Chapel Hill: UNC Institute of Government, 2000.

Malizia, Emil, and Edward Feser. *Understanding Local Economic Development.* New Brunswick, N.J.: Center for Urban Policy Research, 1999.

Morgan, Jonathan Q. "Clusters and Competitive Advantage: Finding a Niche in the New Economy." *Popular Government* 69 (Fall 2004): 43–54.

______. *Economic Development Handbook.* 3rd ed. Raleigh and Chapel Hill: N.C. Economic Developers Association and UNC School of Government, 2009.

______. *The Role of Local Government in Economic Development: Survey Findings from North Carolina.* Chapel Hill: UNC School of Government, 2009.

______. "Using Economic Development Incentives: For Better or for Worse." *Popular Government* 74 (Winter 2009): 16–29.

______. "Analyzing the Benefits and Costs of Economic Development Projects." *Community and Economic Development Bulletin* No. 7 (Apr. 2010).

Mulligan, C. Tyler. "Incentives for Infill Development on Main Street." In *Coates' Canons: Local Government Law Blog, 2009–2010.* Chapel Hill: UNC School of Government, 2010.

______. "Public Hearings for Economic Development Incentives: An Unwritten Rule?" In *Coates' Canons: Local Government Law Blog, 2009–2010.* Chapel Hill: UNC School of Government, 2010.

______. "Valid Cash Incentive or Illegal Tax Rebate?" In *Coates' Canons: Local Government Law Blog, 2009–2010.* Chapel Hill: UNC School of Government, 2010.

______. "Is Interstate Competition Required for Economic Development Incentives?" In *Coates' Canons: Local Government Law Blog, January–June 2011.* Chapel Hill: UNC School of Government, 2011.

______. "Economic Development Incentives and North Carolina Local Governments: A Framework for Analysis," 91 N.C. L. Rev. 2021 (2013).

Rivenbark, William C., Shea Riggsbee Denning, and Kara A. Millonzi. "2007 Legislation Expands Scope of Project Development Financing in North Carolina." *Local Finance Bulletin* No. 36 (Nov. 2007).

Seidman, Karl F. *Economic Development Finance.* Thousand Oaks, Calif.: Sage, 2004.

Shively, Robert W. *Economic Development for Small Communities: A Handbook for Economic Development Practitioners and Community Leaders.* Washington, D.C.: National Center for Small Communities, 2004.

Organizations (listed in order of relevance)

State-Level

North Carolina Department of Commerce, Commerce Finance Center: www.nccommerce.com/finance

North Carolina Community College System: www.nccommunitycolleges.edu

North Carolina Commission on Workforce Development: www.nccommerce.com/workforce

N.C. Regional Councils (N.C.'s Association of Regional Councils of Government): www.ncregions.org

N.C. Economic Developers Association: www.nceda.org

N.C. Industrial Extension Service: www.ies.ncsu.edu

Federal/National

U.S. Economic Development Administration (U.S. Department of Commerce): www.eda.gov

U.S. Small Business Administration: www.sba.gov

International Economic Development Council: www.iedconline.org

About the Authors

Jonathan Q. Morgan is a School of Government faculty member who specializes in economic development. C. Tyler Mulligan is a School of Government faculty member whose interests include economic development law and finance.

Part 7

Local Government Services and Enterprises

Chapter 28

Law Enforcement

Robert L. Farb

This chapter discusses law enforcement agencies and their authority to enforce criminal laws and includes a brief summary of a sheriff's civil duties.[1]

City and County Law Enforcement Agencies

City Law Enforcement Agencies

Law enforcement powers are conferred on cities by Chapter 160A, Article 13, of the North Carolina General Statutes (hereinafter G.S.). North Carolina law is simple and specific in authorizing a city to create a police department. G.S. 160A-281 empowers a city "to appoint a chief of police and to employ other police officers who may reside outside the corporate limits of the city unless the council provides otherwise." The law also allows a city to authorize voluntary auxiliary police officers.[2]

1. For information about a law enforcement officer's authority to search and seize people and property, execute search warrants, and conduct interrogations and lineups, see Robert L. Farb, *Arrest, Search, and Investigation in North Carolina*, 4th ed. (Chapel Hill, N.C.: UNC School of Government, 2011).
2. N.C. Gen. Stat. (hereinafter G.S.) § 160A-282.

Sheriffs' Offices

The office of sheriff is established by the North Carolina Constitution. The sheriff, elected directly by the county's voters, operates the sheriff's office independently of the board of county commissioners, except that the commissioners receive and pass on the sheriff's budget and appropriate funds for operating the sheriff's office. All 100 counties have a sheriff's office.

The North Carolina Constitution does not specify the sheriff's duties. G.S. Chapter 162 defines a sheriff's civil duties (discussed below) but does not specify the sheriff's law enforcement functions. Nor does any other statute specify that the sheriff's duty is to enforce criminal laws. However, the sheriff's office has common law responsibilities to provide law enforcement protection.

Other sheriff's functions broadly related to law enforcement include transporting inmates and prisoners to and from jails, prisons, and courts; maintaining local confinement facilities; serving as bailiffs or court officers; and transporting people who may be involuntarily committed to mental health facilities.[3]

The sheriff's civil duties include serving civil process. Civil process includes the service of pleadings, motions, orders, subpoenas, and other papers on parties in civil cases and the service of orders to enforce judgments entered by courts.[4] In North Carolina, process service is a mandated responsibility of the sheriff's office, and, for the most part, only the sheriff and the sheriff's deputies may perform civil process duties. Other law enforcement officers are not given that authority, and only in limited situations are private process servers allowed to serve civil process. Serving civil process requires a significant commitment of time and resources on the part of the sheriff's office. Each order must be carried out in strict compliance with the law; otherwise, a deputy sheriff subjects the sheriff to liability. Another civil duty of a sheriff is to serve orders (called "writs") commanding the sheriff to enforce judgments entered in North Carolina civil courts. Most writs are enforced after a judgment is entered, but sometimes enforcement is ordered before the judgment is entered, and these writs are called "prejudgment remedies."

County Police Departments

A county police department may be created by an act of the North Carolina General Assembly. Gaston County currently has a county police department, which assumes much of the general responsibility for enforcing criminal law traditionally associated with the sheriff's office. (Mecklenburg County had a county police department until it merged with the Charlotte Police Department to create the Charlotte–Mecklenburg Police Department.) In a county that establishes a county police department, responsibility for executing court-issued civil process remains with the sheriff.

Other Law Enforcement Agencies and Officers

State Highway Patrol

The North Carolina State Highway Patrol is located in the state Department of Public Safety. It primarily enforces the laws and regulations involving travel and use of vehicles on state highways.

State Bureau of Investigation

The State Bureau of Investigation (SBI) is located within the Department of Public Safety. The SBI responds to requests for assistance in criminal investigations from local law enforcement agencies and others. It also has the authority to investigate on its own (that is, without a request) drug, arson, and election law offenses; theft and misuse of state property; child sexual abuse in day care centers; and computer crimes against children.

Wildlife Enforcement Officers

Wildlife enforcement officers in the Enforcement Division of the state Wildlife Resources Commission primarily enforce game, fish, trapping, and boating laws.

---

3. *See* G.S. Ch. 162, Art. 3.

4. G.S. 162-13, -14.

Marine Patrol Officers

Marine Patrol officers in the Division of Marine Fisheries of the state Department of Environment and Natural Resources primarily enforce state laws and regulations involving marine and estuarine fisheries.

State Alcohol Law Enforcement Agents

Alcohol law enforcement (ALE) agents of the state Department of Public Safety primarily enforce alcohol beverage laws, as well as lottery and drug laws.

Local Alcohol Beverage Control Officers

Local alcohol beverage control (ABC) officers, who are employed by county or city ABC boards, primarily enforce ABC and drug laws.

License and Theft Bureau Agents

Agents of the License and Theft Bureau of the state Division of Motor Vehicles primarily enforce laws concerning vehicle theft, document fraud, driver's license fraud, vehicle inspection fraud, and odometer rollbacks.

Other Agencies and Officers

Other agencies and officers, in addition to those discussed above, include company police officers, University of North Carolina campus law enforcement officers, community college law enforcement officers, and private nonprofit campus law enforcement officers.

Criminal Justice Commissions

Criminal Justice Education and Training Standards Commission

The Criminal Justice Education and Training Standards Commission is established under G.S. Chapter 17C. It promulgates rules and regulations and establishes the minimum education and training standards required for all entry-level employment as a criminal justice officer (with the exception of sheriffs' personnel, as described below). It certifies officer candidates as qualified under the law and establishes minimum standards for certifying criminal justice training schools. It advises in such areas as (1) identifying the types of criminal justice positions that require advanced or specialized training and education and (2) establishing standards for certifying candidates for these positions based on specified education, training, and experience.

Sheriffs' Education and Training Standards Commission

The Sheriffs' Education and Training Standards Commission is the sheriff's counterpart to the Criminal Justice Education and Training Standards Commission described above. The sheriffs' commission similarly promulgates rules and establishes minimum education and training standards for deputy sheriffs, detention officers, telecommunicators, and other sheriff's personnel regulated under G.S. Chapter 17E.

Governor's Crime Commission

The Governor's Crime Commission is the state's criminal justice planning entity and is housed in the Department of Public Safety. The commission's role has evolved over many years in response to federal mandates, the needs of the criminal justice system, and state priorities. G.S. 143B-1101(a)(2) delineates seven major goals of the criminal justice system that form the basis of the commission's planning: (1) to reduce crime, (2) to protect individual rights, (3) to achieve justice, (4) to increase efficiency in the criminal justice system, (5) to promote public safety, (6) to provide for the administration of a fair and humane system that offers reasonable opportunities for adjudicated offenders to develop progressively responsible behavior, and (7) to increase professional skills. The commission also disburses federal funds.

Jurisdiction of City Officers, Sheriffs and Deputies, and County Police Officers

Officers may use their law enforcement authority over a person only within certain geographical areas and only with certain kinds of offenses. These limitations are called the officers' *jurisdiction.* Officers must have both *territorial* (geographical) and *subject-matter* (offense) jurisdiction to exercise their law enforcement powers lawfully.

Limits on Territorial Jurisdiction

Except in cases of hot pursuit, discussed below, state and local law enforcement officers in North Carolina may not use their arrest powers outside the boundaries of the state. Within North Carolina, the officers' jurisdiction depends on their employing agency.

Sheriffs, Deputy Sheriffs, and County Police Officers

Sheriffs and their regularly employed deputies, county police, and officers of consolidated county–city law enforcement agencies may arrest anywhere in the state for felonies committed in their county and on any property and rights-of-way owned by the county outside its limits.[5] They may make other arrests only within their own county or on property or rights-of-way owned by the county outside its limits.[6] In addition, sheriffs and their deputies may arrest with a warrant on any river, bay, or creek adjoining their county.[7] Sheriffs have arrest jurisdiction in cities within their county as well as in the area outside the city, although as a matter of policy, they tend to exercise routine arrest authority only in those parts of the county not served by local police departments.

City Law Enforcement Officers

City law enforcement officers may arrest in the city where they serve, in the property and rights-of-way that the city owns or leases outside its limits, and in the area within one mile of the city limits.[8] It would appear that officers may exercise arrest authority even when the extension of one mile from their city's limits would place them within an adjoining city, as the one-mile extension applies without limitation in the statutory language granting that authority.[9]

City law enforcement officers should check with their city attorneys to determine whether they have any arrest jurisdiction beyond these limits; sometimes a special legislative act expands a particular city's limits beyond a mile.

City law enforcement officers are authorized to transport a person in custody to or from any place in North Carolina so that the person can attend a criminal court proceeding. Officers also are authorized to arrest that person for any offense he or she commits while being transported.[10]

---

5. G.S. 15A-402(e).

6. G.S. 15A-402(b).

7. G.S. 162-14. Of course, a sheriff's territorial authority to arrest with or without a warrant extends to that part of a waterway that is included within the county. See also G.S. 15-129, which places the venue of an offense committed on any water or watercourse (or its sides or shores) that divides counties in either of the two counties nearest to the place where the offense was committed.

8. G.S. 15A-402(b) and (c); G.S. 160A-286. G.S.160A-286 authorizes a city law enforcement officer to exercise all the powers of a law enforcement officer, not just arrest authority, within one mile of the city's corporate limits and on all property "owned by or leased" to the city, wherever located. G.S. 15A-402(b) speaks of arrest authority on property "owned" by the city outside the city's limits. Therefore, G.S. 160A-286 broadens an officer's arrest authority, beyond the provisions of G.S. 15A-402(b), to include property leased by the city that is outside the city's limits.

9. G.S. 15A-402(c); G.S. 160A-286. It would also appear that officers can exercise their authority within one mile of all property owned by or leased to the city, wherever located. Because the one-mile provision is designed in part to relieve officers from having to determine the precise location of a property line or else face potential legal liability for their actions, it is reasonable to interpret the legislature's intent that the provision applies to this property as well.

10. G.S. 15A-402(c).

Expanded Territorial Jurisdiction for DWI-Related Offenses

Officers with subject matter jurisdiction, discussed below, who are investigating DWI-related offenses or vehicle crashes that occurred in their jurisdiction have expanded territorial jurisdiction.[11] For these offenses,[12] officers may investigate and seek evidence of the driver's impairment anywhere inside or outside the state and may make arrests anywhere in the state. Officers may take the arrested person to any place in the state (1) for one or more chemical analyses at the request of any law enforcement officer, medical professional, or other person to determine the extent or cause of the person's impairment; (2) to have the person identified; (3) to complete a crash report; and (4) for any other lawful purpose.[13]

Arrest after Continuous Flight (Hot Pursuit)

Law enforcement officers may arrest outside their territorial jurisdiction when in hot pursuit.

Hot Pursuit within the State

Local law enforcement officers, who normally are restricted to arresting within the limits of the unit that employs them, may arrest outside that territory when the offender has committed a criminal offense within the territory and the arrest is made during hot pursuit while the offender is making an immediate and continuous flight from that territory.[14] Officers may pursue the offender throughout the state, but if they are to retain their authority to arrest, they must continue the pursuit and not stop to do something else. They need not keep the offender in sight at all times, however, so long as the offender remains in continuous flight. Officers also may await the arrival of assistance if they would be endangered by making the arrest without additional assistance.[15]

Hot Pursuit outside the State

Although normally North Carolina law enforcement officers may not arrest once they leave the state, they may arrest outside the state when they pursue a person who has committed an offense in North Carolina and is fleeing into an adjoining state whose laws permit an arrest to be made under these circumstances.[16] All four border states—Georgia,[17] South Carolina,[18] Tennessee,[19] and Virginia[20]—permit such arrests, but only for felonies (and certain impaired driving misdemeanors mentioned in the accompanying note for pursuit into Georgia and South Carolina).[21]

---

11. G.S. 20-38.2.

12. Included among the offenses are G.S.20-138.1 (impaired driving); G.S. 20-138.2 (impaired driving in commercial vehicle); G.S. 20-138.2A (operating commercial vehicle after consuming alcohol); G.S. 20-138.2B (operating school bus, school activity bus, or child care vehicle after consuming alcohol); G.S. 20-138.3 (driving by person under twenty-one years old after consuming alcohol or drugs); G.S. 20-138.5 (habitual impaired driving); G.S. 20-138.7 (transporting open container of alcoholic beverage); G.S. 20-141.4 (felony death by vehicle, felony serious injury by vehicle, and other offenses involving impaired driving); G.S. 20-12.1 (impaired supervision or instruction); G.S. 20-179.3(j) (violation of limited driving privilege by consuming alcohol); G.S. 14-17 (first-degree and second-degree murder) and G.S. 14-18 (involuntary manslaughter) when impaired driving is involved.

13. G.S. 20-38.3.

14. G.S. 15A-402(d).

15. State v. Melvin, 53 N.C. App. 421 (1981).

16. See notes 17–20.

17. Ga. Code Ann. § 35-1-15 (2010) (pursuit limited to offenses punishable in other states by death or imprisonment in excess of one year). This statute thereby limits the offenses to felonies under North Carolina sentencing laws, except that misdemeanor impaired driving (G.S. 20-138.1) and commercial impaired driving (G.S. 20-138.2) may also be included because they are punishable by up to two years' imprisonment under G.S. 20-179.

18. S.C. Code Ann. § 17-13-47 (2010) (pursuit limited to offenses punishable in other states by death or imprisonment in excess of one year). This statute thereby limits the offenses to felonies under North Carolina sentencing laws, except that misdemeanor impaired driving (G.S. 20-138.1) and commercial impaired driving (G.S. 20-138.2) may also be included because they are punishable by up to two years' imprisonment under G.S. 20-179.

19. Tenn. Code Ann. § 40-7-203 (2011) (pursuit limited to felonies).

20. Va. Code Ann. § 19.2-79 (2011) (pursuit limited to felonies).

21. G.S. 15A-403 permits officers from other states to enter North Carolina to arrest a person fleeing from the other state only to the extent that the other state authorizes a North Carolina officer to enter that state. Because Georgia, South Carolina, Tennessee, and Virginia permit entry into those states only in hot pursuit to arrest for felonies (with the additional misdemeanors of impaired driving and commercial impaired driving for pursuit into Georgia and South Carolina, as discussed in notes 17 and

When officers pursue a person into another state and arrest the person there, they may not simply bring the arrestee back to North Carolina. Instead, they must take the arrestee to a judicial official in that state and follow that state's procedures on completing custody.

Subject-Matter Jurisdiction

Some law enforcement officers, such as State Highway Patrol officers, may arrest only for certain kinds of offenses. However, city law enforcement officers may arrest for any criminal offense.[22] And sheriffs, deputy sheriffs, and county police officers also may arrest for any criminal offense.[23]

Special Jurisdiction Issues

Violations of Federal Laws

State and local law enforcement officers are authorized to arrest for violations of federal laws.[24] When officers make an arrest for a federal offense, they should follow the same rules of arrest that they would follow when arresting for a violation of state law. Although they may take the arrestee before a state magistrate,[25] they normally should take the arrestee before a federal judicial official such as a United States magistrate. Despite this formal authority to arrest for violations of federal laws, it is often advisable to leave arrests for federal offenses to federal officials, as they are more familiar with federal laws and arrest procedures.

Immigration Enforcement by North Carolina Law Enforcement Officers

North Carolina law provides that, when authorized by federal law, a state or local law enforcement agency may authorize its officers to perform functions of an officer under 8 U.S.C. § 1357(g) (immigration officer functions performed by state officers and employees) if the agency has a memorandum of agreement or memorandum of understanding for that purpose with a federal agency.[26] State and local law enforcement officers are authorized to hold any office or position with the applicable federal agency required to perform the functions.

Desertion and AWOL

State and local law enforcement officers may arrest a person who has deserted from the armed forces[27] and either deliver the person to armed forces personnel authorized to receive deserters or take the person before a state or federal

---

18, above), officers from these states may enter North Carolina only in hot pursuit to arrest for felonies (and the impaired driving misdemeanors previously mentioned for Georgia and South Carolina officers) committed in their respective states. *See generally* United States v. Goings, 573 F.3d 1141 (11th Cir. 2009) (irrelevant under Fourth Amendment if Georgia officers' arrest of defendant in Florida after pursuit violated state law; only issue under Fourth Amendment is whether probable cause existed to arrest defendant).

22. G.S. 160A-285.

23. Sheriffs and their deputies derive their authority to arrest for any crime from common law. County police agencies derive their authority from local legislative acts. *See, e.g.*, 1929 N.C. Public–Local Laws, Ch. 93 (Gaston County police).

24. In the absence of a federal statute setting out the authority of a state officer to arrest for a federal offense, the law of the state where an arrest occurs determines the arrest's validity. United States v. DiRe, 332 U.S. 581 (1948); United States v. Swarovski, 557 F.2d 40 (2d Cir. 1977); United States v. Santana-Garcia, 264 F.3d 1188 (10th Cir. 2001) (court found that Utah state law, which authorizes law enforcement officer to arrest for "any public offense," authorized state law enforcement officer to arrest for federal immigration law violation; state law need not affirmatively authorize arrest for federal immigration law violation); United States v. Villa-Velazquez, 282 F.3d 553 (8th Cir. 2002) (similar ruling). Because there is no federal statute and state law authorizes arrests for felonies and misdemeanors without limiting them to state crimes, North Carolina law enforcement officers may arrest for federal offenses. Other pertinent cases include *United States v. Bowdach*, 561 F.2d 1160 (5th Cir. 1977) (state law enforcement officer had authority to arrest defendant based on knowledge of outstanding federal arrest warrant) and *United States v. Haskin*, 228 F.3d 151 (2d Cir. 2000) (Vermont state police officer had authority to seize firearms for violation of federal firearms laws).

25. 18 U.S.C. § 3041.

26. G.S. 128-1.1.

27. 10 U.S.C. § 808 (Art. 8, Uniform Code of Military Justice).

magistrate so that the arrestee may be committed to a detention facility to await the arrival of military authorities.[28] Officers may arrest a person who is AWOL (away without leave) from the armed forces, although it is unclear whether their authority to arrest for being AWOL depends on a request to arrest by military authorities.[29]

Offenses That Occur in Other States (Extradition)[30]

North Carolina law enforcement officers may arrest a person who flees to North Carolina after the person has committed a misdemeanor or felony in another state if the officers obtain a fugitive warrant for the person's arrest from a North Carolina judicial official.[31] To obtain a fugitive warrant, officers must show either (1) probable cause to believe that the person committed a crime in another state (the same standard for obtaining an arrest warrant for a crime committed in North Carolina) or (2) that the person has been charged in another state with committing a crime. A fugitive warrant also may be issued to arrest a person who has come from another state after escaping from imprisonment or violating conditions of probation or parole.[32]

If the fugitive warrant is issued because the person has been charged with a crime in another state, it must be supported by an affidavit to that effect, based on information from someone in the other state. A Division of Criminal Information (DCI) message or other reliable hearsay is sufficient to support a fugitive warrant.[33] A certified copy of the warrant or indictment from the other state should be attached to the fugitive warrant when it arrives, but its absence should not delay execution of the warrant. If a question exists about either the continuing validity of the charge in the other state or the other state's interest in having the person arrested, the officer should check with the appropriate authorities in that state before seeking a fugitive warrant. Verification of DCI messages in such instances is often advisable. Although the authority to arrest fugitives is not limited to felonies, most states normally will not extradite a misdemeanant.

Officers in North Carolina may arrest a fugitive from another state without a fugitive warrant if the person has been charged in the other state with a crime that is punishable there by more than one year's imprisonment.[34] Although the law does not require such an action, it is advisable to obtain a fugitive warrant in all cases unless taking the time to obtain the warrant would jeopardize the officer's ability to apprehend the fugitive.

A fugitive also may be arrested if the governor of North Carolina has issued a Governor's Warrant[35] for the fugitive's arrest. This warrant is usually issued after a person is already in custody in North Carolina; it is based on a formal request for extradition from the governor of the requesting state to the governor of North Carolina.

---

28. Military deserters may be confined in local detention facilities. G.S. 162-34; 45 N.C. Att'y Gen. Rep. 169 (1975). A military deserter has no right to bail. Huff v. Watson, 99 S.E. 307 (Ga. 1919).

29. Bledsoe v. Garcia, 742 F.2d 1237 (10th Cir. 1984); Myers v. United States, 415 F.2d 318 (10th Cir. 1969).

30. For a more complete discussion of extradition, see Robert L. Farb, *State of North Carolina Extradition Manual* (Chapel Hill, N.C.: UNC School of Government, 2013).

31. Broadly defined, a person is a *fugitive from justice* when he or she commits a crime within a state and then leaves the state. It is unnecessary that the prosecution show that the person was charged before leaving the state or that the person fled to avoid prosecution. *In re* Sultan, 115 N.C. 57 (1894); Gee v. State of Kansas, 912 F.2d 414 (10th Cir. 1990); Dunn v. Hindman, 836 F. Supp. 750 (D. Kan. 1993). There is common law authority to arrest a person for a felony committed in another state even when a charge has not been brought against the person there. State v. Klein, 130 N.W.2d 816 (Wis. 1964); Desjarlais v. State, 243 N.W.2d 453 (Wis. 1976).

32. G.S. 15A-733.

33. 45 N.C. Att'y Gen. Rep. 236 (1976). An officer's telephone conversation with a knowledgeable person in the other state that provided information about the fugitive also could be used in the officer's affidavit to justify issuing a fugitive warrant.

34. G.S. 15A-734.

35. G.S. 15A-727. The majority view is that a person arrested pursuant to a Governor's Warrant has no right to bail, and judges have no common law or inherent authority to grant release on bail. See the cases cited in Farb, *supra* note 30, at 57. No right to bail exists when a fugitive waives the issuance of a Governor's Warrant and all other extradition proceedings and consents to return to the demanding state. 50 N.C. Att'y Gen. Rep. 40 (1980).

When a fugitive is arrested by other than a Governor's Warrant, a magistrate or judge may set bail by bond, with sufficient sureties, before service of the Governor's Warrant unless the charged offense is punishable by death or life imprisonment under the laws of the state where it was committed. G.S. 15A-736.

Expanded Jurisdiction through Cooperating Law Enforcement Agencies (Mutual Aid Agreements)

Several statutes authorize the head of one law enforcement agency to provide temporary assistance to another agency upon its written request.[36] If this assistance includes officers' working temporarily with the other agency, the officers have the jurisdiction and authority of both the requesting agency and their own agency. Thus, a Raleigh police officer who was working for the Greensboro Police Department would have the jurisdiction and authority of both departments.[37]

A question that arises under these statutes is whether a standing written request may be made for specific types of temporary assistance or whether the requesting agency's head must make a written request for each individual situation. The attorney general has issued an opinion that a city or county governing body can adopt guidelines that enable the head of a law enforcement agency to make a standing written request for temporary assistance that will be valid for a specific period of time for specific types of assistance; the head of the requested agency can then furnish assistance within the guidelines without needing an individual written request each time.[38] Although long-term undercover work would require an individual written request, guidelines could provide for a standing written request for temporary assistance in making arrests, executing search warrants, and the like.

Expanded Jurisdiction through Emergency Management Assistance Compact

The Emergency Management Assistance Compact provides for mutual assistance between states that are party to the compact in managing emergencies or disasters that are declared by the governor of the affected state or states.[39] The compact applies only to requests for assistance made by and to authorized representatives of each state. Law enforcement officers in one state who are sent to another state do not have the power to arrest in the other state unless specifically authorized by the other state.[40] All fifty states are members of the compact, as well as the District of Columbia, Puerto Rico, and the U.S. Virgin Islands.

About the Author

Robert L. Farb is a retired School of Government faculty member. He continues as an adjunct professor of public law and government to work on occasional special projects in criminal law and procedure, a field in which he is widely published.

36. G.S. 90-95.2 (temporary assistance among law enforcement agencies in enforcing drug laws); G.S. 153A-212 (authorizing county cooperation in law enforcement matters as set out in other statutes); G.S. 160A-288 (authorizing mutual aid agreements among city police, sheriff's office, or county police); G.S. 160A-288.2 (authorizing city or county to provide assistance to state law enforcement agency). *See also* G.S. 18B-501(e) (local ABC officer may assist federal or state agency). For a discussion of mutual aid agreements between law enforcement agencies, including sample resolutions and mutual assistance agreement forms, see Michael F. Easley and Jeffrey P. Gray, *Mutual Aid Agreements Between Law Enforcement Agencies in North Carolina* (North Carolina Department of Justice, March 1996).

37. In *State v. Locklear*, 136 N.C. App. 716 (2000), a Robeson County deputy sheriff called for assistance in responding to a stabbing at a home three to four miles outside the Red Springs city limits. A Red Springs law enforcement officer responded to the call and was later assaulted by the defendant there. The defendant argued that the officer was outside his territorial jurisdiction (one mile beyond the city limits) when the assault occurred, and thus he could not be convicted of assault with a firearm on a law enforcement officer because he was not acting as an officer then. The court ruled that a mutual aid agreement between the Robeson County Sheriff's Department and the Red Springs Police Department permitted the officer to respond to the request for assistance, based on the agreement's permitting an oral request to be made for an "emergency." The court ruled that an emergency existed: the deputy sheriff was transporting a prisoner when he received the order to investigate the stabbing, and he was the only deputy in the vicinity of the residence.

38. 47 N.C. Att'y Gen. Rep. 181 (1978). The opinion specifically discussed G.S. 160A-288, but the other statutes cited in note 36 are similar.

39. G.S. Ch. 166A, Art. 4.

40. G.S. 166A-44(b).

Chapter 29

Fire Services

Kara A. Millonzi

Introduction

Local governments are not required to furnish (or fund) fire protection services for their citizens, but many provide, or contract for the provision of, these services within their units. In fact, fire protection has been considered a core municipal service since the nineteenth century, when a few of the larger cities in the state boasted firefighting companies with hand and horse-drawn steam-powered fire pumpers. Fire protection was important in cities, where compact development with largely wooden buildings posed a constant danger of communitywide conflagration. Up until the mid-1900s, fire protection in rural, unincorporated areas was regarded as a matter of concern for individual property owners. Yet, as urban development spread to formerly rural areas and citizen expectation for fire protection in such areas increased, county governments and, to a limited extent, sanitary districts, also assumed a greater role in providing these services. Most areas in the state today are afforded some level of fire protection. And, typically, that fire protection extends beyond basic fire prevention and suppression services to include, among other things, emergency dispatch services, medical and other response services, and state building fire code enforcement.

The types and level of fire services that cities, counties, and sanitary districts (collectively, local units) provide and fund often vary across their territorial boundaries. There is no duty of equal service to all properties or citizens within a unit. A local governing board may choose to provide fire services in some areas within its jurisdiction and not in others, or it may choose to provide a higher level of fire services in some areas than in others. Because of the unique nature of fire protection services, units need flexibility in both service provision and funding. This chapter discusses the options available to local units in North Carolina. It begins by identifying the various legal structures available to local units for providing fire services. It then analyzes the local revenue options available to these entities for this purpose. Finally, it describes fire insurance districts and the insurance rating system and discusses the relationship between fire insurance districts and fire tax districts.

Fire Services Provided by Local Governments

There are three local governmental entities—cities, counties, and sanitary districts—that are authorized under general law to provide fire protection services. Each local unit may establish a fire department to provide fire protection and rescue services. Alternatively, each unit also is authorized to contract with external entities—municipal fire departments or corporate fire departments—to carry out these duties. Some units use a combination of these structures. The most common arrangements are described below.

Municipal, County, or Sanitary District Fire Department

One option available to a local unit is to establish and maintain its own fire department. Many local units have a fire department, but the size and scope of duties of the departments varies widely across the jurisdictions. Some departmental fire departments provide full-fledged fire protection and rescue services. Other departments provide a more limited array of services, relying on contracts with other governmental or private entities to fulfill most fire suppression and rescue duties.

Municipal Fire Department

A city is authorized to "establish, organize, equip, and maintain a fire department."[1] Many cities provide fire protection services through a municipal fire department, which typically encompasses multiple fire stations. Under this structure, a city's governing board sets all policies related to the fire services. The fire department's assets, including fire stations, fire trucks, and all related equipment, are titled to the city. Fire personnel are city employees. (A city has the option to staff its department with volunteer or paid firefighters and other staff members.)[2]

The primary function of most municipal fire departments is to provide fire suppression services. Many fire departments also support rescue squads, ambulances, and other emergency management services. In addition to these response activities, a municipal fire department often undertakes fire prevention activities, such as community outreach programs and fire safety demonstrations, to inform and educate the public about preventing and extinguishing fires. Fire departments commonly sponsor installation and battery-replacement programs for residential smoke alarms and carbon monoxide detectors. This is just one example of the myriad of community programs and services typically provided by a municipal fire department. Another function that most municipal fire departments serve is to perform inspections to enforce the state fire code. Since 1991, a fire prevention code has been included in the North Carolina State Building Code (hereinafter State Building Code). Counties and cities are responsible for enforcing the State Building Code within their jurisdictions.[3]

May a municipal fire department provide services outside the municipality? The answer is yes. A municipal fire department may contract with other units of government to provide services. A municipal fire department also may enter into mutual aid agreements with other fire departments and may send "firemen and apparatus beyond the territorial limits which it normally serves."[4] The most common arrangements are described below.

---

1. N.C. Gen. Stat. (hereinafter G.S.) § 160A-291.

2. If a unit employs five or more full-time paid firefighters and other full-time paid staff, special rules apply to calculating overtime pay and trade time. *See* G.S. 160A, Art. 14A.

3. The fire prevention chapters of the 2012 North Carolina State Building Code (hereinafter State Building Code) are available at http://ecodes.biz/ecodes_support/free_resources/2012NorthCarolina/Fire/12NC_Fire.html (last visited March 28, 2014). For more information on the State Building Code, see Chapter 25, "Community Planning, Land Use, and Development."

4. G.S. 58-83-1.

The city's general fund is the primary source of funds for capital expenditures, equipment, and salaries. Thus, the city council's ability and willingness to appropriate funds to the fire department largely controls the level and breadth of service it is able to provide. Courts have ruled that failure to provide adequate facilities or to control a fire does not constitute a liability against a city. Nevertheless, people expect the fire department to be reasonably competent in controlling fire—taking into consideration, of course, the adequacy of equipment, personnel, and water supply; the nature of the fire; and its headway when discovered.

Fire Chiefs

Regardless of whether a city establishes a municipal fire department or contracts with one or more private or municipal fire departments to provide fire services, a city may appoint a fire chief. Fire chiefs are charged with directing firefighting and training activities, maintaining equipment, correcting fire hazards, and, where appropriate, making annual reports to the city council concerning department activities.[5] A fire chief also often is charged with conducting inspections to enforce the fire prevention sections of the State Building Code.[6]

County Fire Department

A county may "establish, organize, equip, support, and maintain a fire department; may prescribe the duties of the fire department . . . ."[7] A county fire department is authorized to provide the same fire suppression and prevention services as a municipal fire department, both within and outside the county's territorial jurisdiction. It also may support rescue squads, ambulances, and other emergency management services. And, like a city, a county is responsible for enforcing the fire prevention provisions in the State Building Code. Unlike cities, however, most counties do not maintain full-fledged fire departments. Serving geographically disparate and often rural areas generally proves cost prohibitive. Instead, counties typically contract with incorporated fire departments or municipal fire departments to provide fire protection and rescue services within their unincorporated territories (discussed below). To delineate the different service areas, a county's governing board may divide its unincorporated territory into multiple fire response zones, each of which is served by one or more fire departments. The response zones often correspond to fire insurance districts (discussed below).

Fire Marshal

Most counties, even those that do not maintain a county fire department, appoint a fire marshal or assign the duties of a fire marshal on another employee or official. By statute, a fire marshal is charged with the following:

1. Advising the board on improvements in the firefighting or fire prevention activities under the county's supervision or control
2. Coordinating firefighting and training activities under the county's supervision or control
3. Coordinating fire prevention activities under the county's supervision or control
4. Assisting incorporated volunteer fire departments in developing and improving their firefighting or fire prevention capabilities
5. Making fire prevention inspections, including the periodic inspections and reports of school buildings required by Chapter 115 of the North Carolina General Statutes (hereinafter G.S.) and the inspections of child care facilities required by G.S. Chapter 110[8]

A county board may prescribe other duties to the fire marshal as warranted. For counties that contract with multiple incorporated fire departments or municipal fire departments, the fire marshal performs an important coordination role, often serving as a liaison between the county and the various fire departments. The fire marshal advises the county board about budgetary requests from fire departments, monitors contract compliance, oversees training of firefighting

5. G.S. 160A-291.
6. *Id.* The fire chief must be certified in accordance with G.S. 143-151.13.
7. G.S. 153A-233.
8. G.S. 153A-234.

personnel, conducts public outreach programs and services, and aids the county in drawing and amending fire service areas and fire tax districts.

Sanitary District Fire Department

A sanitary district is a regional unit of local government that is created by the Commission for Public Health.[9] The primary function of a sanitary district is to provide water and sewer services within its territorial boundaries. The boundaries of a sanitary district often include territory in two or more cities or even two or more counties. In addition to water and sewer services, a sanitary district is authorized to provide fire protection services. Specifically, G.S. 130A-55(12) allows a sanitary district to "provide or contract for rescue service, ambulance service, rescue squad or other emergency medical services for use in the district." These services must be provided within the territorial boundaries of the district.

A sanitary district that maintains its own department performs many of the same duties as a municipal or county fire department, with the exception of State Building Code inspections. A sanitary district will rely on the counties and/or cities in which it is located to enforce the building code.

Contracting with Incorporated Fire Departments or Other Governmental Fire Departments

As an alternative to (or in addition to) maintaining a fire department, a local unit may contract with one or more municipal fire departments or, more commonly, with one or more incorporated fire departments to deliver fire protection and rescue services. Additionally, some municipalities allow the county or counties in which they are located to contract for and fund the fire services within the municipal territory.

There is broad authority for local units to enter into contractual arrangements whereby the unit appropriates revenues to a corporate or municipal fire department to pay for both the capital and operating costs associated with fire suppression and prevention throughout all or a portion of the unit.[10] Cities and counties have equally broad authority to contract with and appropriate funds to "rescue squads or teams to enable them to purchase and maintain rescue equipment and to finance the operation of the rescue squad either within or outside the boundaries of the city or county."[11]

Contracting with Municipal Fire Departments

Some counties, sanitary districts, and even other cities contract with municipal fire departments to provide fire protection services. The structure of these contractual arrangements varies significantly. Some units rely entirely on the municipal fire department to procure the necessary equipment, supplies, and personnel and to provide the necessary training to carry out the contracted fire protection services. A municipal fire department is authorized to install and maintain water mains and hydrants, as well as buildings and equipment, outside its territorial limits.[12] In addition, personnel and equipment may be dispatched to protect unincorporated areas pursuant to an agreement between a city and another government entity or between a city and the owner of property to be protected.

Other units purchase some or all of the needed real property or equipment and donate or lease it to the municipal fire departments that serve the unit. A county, sanitary district, or city has authority to lease, sell, or convey land, with or without consideration, and to donate personal property, to a municipal fire department.[13]

---

9. G.S. Ch. 130A, Art. 2, Part 2. The process is initiated by a petition by 51 percent of the freeholders in the proposed district. G.S. 130A-48. No municipal territory may be included in a sanitary district unless approved by the municipality's governing board. G.S. 130A-47.

10. *See* G.S. 160A-11 and G.S. 160A-461 (authority for cities to contract with other entities for fire and rescue services); G.S. 153A-11 and G.S. 153A-233 (authority for counties to contract with other entities for fire and rescue services); G.S. 130A-55 (authority for sanitary districts to contract with other entities for fire protection services).

11. G.S. 160A-487.

12. G.S. 160A-293.

13. G.S. 160A-274; G.S. 160A-280.

Neither a city nor its employees may be held liable for failure to answer or delay in answering a fire call outside the corporate limits.[14] Moreover, cities (but not individual firefighters) are immune from civil suit for acts committed in rendering fire protection outside their city limits.[15] Employees of city fire departments, while performing services outside the city on the orders of the fire chief or the city council, have the same jurisdiction, authority, rights, privileges, and immunities as they enjoy within the city.[16] One important privilege conferred by this provision is coverage under the North Carolina Workers' Compensation Act.

Contracting with Incorporated Fire Departments

An incorporated fire department is a nonprofit corporation, established in accordance with G.S. Chapter 55A. Corporate status allows the fire department to raise funds, purchase equipment and real property, set up bank accounts, conduct fundraisers, receive grants, qualify for special state and federal tax breaks, and negotiate contractual agreements. An incorporated fire department is not a government entity, even if it receives most or all of its revenue from a local unit. Incorporated fire departments are often referred to as nonprofit fire departments. Incorporated fire departments that are composed entirely or mainly of volunteer personnel are volunteer fire departments (VFDs). And incorporated fire departments that serve rural areas typically are called rural fire departments.

A local unit may contract with one or more incorporated fire departments to provide the full range of fire protection and rescue services. Similar to contracts with municipal fire departments, these contractual arrangements are structured in a variety of ways. Some units enter into yearly contracts with the incorporated fire department that commit the unit to paying the department a certain sum of money in exchange for the department providing a certain level of service within a defined area and maintaining a certain fire insurance rating.[17] Other local units enter into multi-year service contracts and set a fixed appropriation each year. Still others enter into multi-year contracts but renegotiate the budgeted amounts annually.

With respect to capital outlay, a local unit may appropriate money to the fire department to cover the costs of purchasing or leasing real and personal property. Alternatively, a unit may choose to purchase real property or equipment and sell, lease, or otherwise convey it to the fire department. State law allows a local unit to "lease, sell, or convey to a volunteer fire department or to a volunteer rescue squad any land or interest in land, for the purpose of constructing or expanding fire department or rescue squad facilities, if the volunteer fire department or volunteer rescue squad provides fire protection or rescue services to the [unit]."[18] The statute does not define "volunteer fire department." It likely includes incorporated fire departments that are staffed exclusively or at least primarily with volunteers. A city or county (but not a sanitary district) also may convey real or personal property to an incorporated fire department by private sale as long as the property is used for a public purpose.[19]

In addition to providing capital resources to a corporate fire department, a local unit sometimes employs some or all of the department's firefighters or other staff members. Being classified as employees of the local unit may afford the staff members additional benefits, such as retirement plans and health insurance.

County Contracts for Service in Municipality

Another common arrangement for providing fire services is for counties to contract for, and pay for, the provision of fire protection services in one or more of their municipalities (with the permission of the affected municipal boards). This arrangement derives from the fact that counties have authority to set up special taxing districts to fund fire services

14. G.S. 160A-293(b).

15. *Id.*

16. G.S. 160A-293(c).

17. For more information on fire insurance ratings, see notes 108–110 and accompanying text.

18. G.S. 160A-277.

19. G.S. 160A-279. For more information on disposal of property procedures, see Chapter 23, "Public Contracts, Competitive Bidding Requirements, and Property Disposal."

and to include municipal territories within these districts.[20] Counties typically contract with one or more incorporated fire departments to provide the fire protection services in the municipal territory.

Funding Fire Services

Local units have broad authority to levy property taxes to fund fire services.[21] Sanitary districts also have authority to assess fire fees. With few exceptions, cities and counties do not have authority to charge fees for fire and rescue services. Most fire services must be funded with tax revenues.

Property Taxation

Authority to Levy Property Taxes

The property tax is levied against real and personal property within the local unit and ultimately is an obligation of the property, not just its owner(s). The property tax base consists of real property (land, buildings, and other improvements to land); personal property (business equipment, automobiles, and so forth); and the property of public service companies. Not all property is subject to taxation, though. Government-owned property is exempt under Article V, Sections 2(2) and (3), of the North Carolina Constitution. In addition, the General Assembly may exempt property from taxation or classify property to exclude it from the tax base, give it a reduced valuation, or subject it to a reduced tax rate. It must do so, however, only on a statewide basis.[22] A local government itself may not exempt, classify, or otherwise give a tax preference to property within its jurisdiction.[23]

A unit's governing board determines whether or not to levy property taxes each year and at what rate or rates. The board may adopt a single tax rate, the revenue generated from which is used to fund a variety of authorized local government services. As an example, a city may adopt a general property tax rate of $0.63 per $100 in assessed valuation of taxable property in the unit to fund its general administration, public safety, fire services, recreation services, zoning services, and solid waste services. In its annual budget ordinance, the city's governing board may divvy up the revenue generated by the general property tax rate to fund these services in any manner it chooses. And, with few exceptions, the board may, at any time after the budget is adopted, amend the budget ordinance to change its appropriations.[24]

Alternatively, a board may adopt a series of property tax rates, the proceeds from which are earmarked for specific services. For example, it may adopt a $0.15 per $100 valuation for general administration, a $.06 per $100 valuation for recreation services, a $0.20 per $100 valuation for law enforcement, a $0.13 per $100 valuation for fire services, and so forth. If a governing board adopts its property tax rates in this manner, it provides greater transparency as to how particular services and activities are funded. However, even if a governing board adopts separate property tax rates for each service or activity, it likely retains discretionary authority to amend the budget ordinance in order to divert the property tax revenue for different purposes during the fiscal year.[25]

Finally, a governing board may take a hybrid approach, adopting a general property tax rate to cover most general fund activities and adopting one or more additional property tax rates (listed separately in the budget ordinance)

20. For more information on special tax districts for fire services, see notes 31–97 and accompanying text.

21. G.S. 160A-209 (cities); G.S. 153A-149 (counties); G.S. 130A-55(3) (sanitary districts).

22. G.S. 105-275 through -278.9.

23. The administration of the property tax is discussed in much greater detail in Chapter 19, "The Property Tax."

24. *See* G.S. 159-15.

25. *See* Long v. Comm'rs of Richmond Cnty., 76 N.C. 273, 280 (1877) ("We know of no statute nor any rule of law or of public policy which prevents County Commissioners from applying a tax raised professedly for one purpose; to any other legitimate purpose."); *see also* Parker v. Comm'rs of Johnston Cnty., 178 N.C. 92 (1919). Note that a city's or county's governing board may hold a referendum to get voter approval to expend property tax dollars on any expenditure item that is specifically authorized by the property tax statute. G.S. 153A-149 (county); G.S. 160A-209 (city). A unit also may seek voter approval to fund with property tax proceeds an item that is not listed in the property tax statutes but is an activity that the local government otherwise has statutory authority to undertake. If the voters specifically approve a tax levy for a specific purpose, the governing board likely is prohibited from using the tax proceeds for a different purpose.

the proceeds of which are earmarked for particular purposes, such as to fund fire protection services. At least a few local governments have taken this approach because it allows governing boards to justify a property tax increase if it is to support what is deemed by the public to be an essential (or at least very important) service. Again, however, the governing board likely retains discretionary authority to amend the budget ordinance to divert the property tax revenue for different purposes during the fiscal year.[26]

Legal Restrictions on General Property Tax Rates

For cities and counties, the total of all property tax rates may not exceed $1.50 per $100 assessed valuation of property in the unit.[27] A governing board may hold a referendum to increase the $1.50 limit or to specifically approve a dedicated property tax rate for a particular purpose, such that it does not count against the $1.50 limit. For example, a city's governing board could put to the unit's voters the question of whether or not to levy a dedicated property tax, at a specific rate, to fund fire services.[28] There is no statutory limit on a sanitary district's tax rate.

Use of General Property Tax Revenue to Fund Fire Services

If a local unit uses its general property tax revenue to fund fire services, the governing board determines how much to allocate yearly to providing these services as well as what specific programs or activities are to be funded. The board may use the money to fund a fire chief or marshal and to fund inspection, training, and education programs that are furnished unit-wide. The revenue also may be used to fund fire prevention or suppression services in specific areas within the unit. Services may be provided by the unit's personnel or through contracts with one or more volunteer or municipal fire departments. The benefit of funding fire services in this manner is that the property tax provides a relatively stable stream of revenue, and a local unit's governing board has a good deal of flexibility in allocating this revenue to provide different types and levels of services in different response areas.

Limitations of the General Property Tax

The difficulty with this funding mechanism is that the tax is levied on all (nonexempted or nonexcluded) properties within the unit. A fundamental tenet of property taxation in North Carolina is that a local government's property tax rate(s) must be applied uniformly to all taxable properties within a unit's jurisdiction.[29] That means that, unlike some local taxes and fees, property taxes generally may not be assessed only on property owners that directly benefit from particular services provided by the local government. Fire services are not required to be provided equally across a unit's territorial boundaries, though. In fact, differences in topography and development densities throughout a county often necessitate different types of service and equipment. The result is that some taxpayers pay for fire services they do not receive.[30]

County Special Taxing Districts

The North Carolina Constitution carves out an exception to the general rule of uniform taxation, however, allowing the General Assembly to "enact general laws authorizing the governing body of any county, city, or town to define territorial

---

26. *See* note 25.

27. *See* G.S. 153A-149(c) (counties) and G.S. 160A-209(d) (municipalities). There are a few purposes for which property taxes may be levied without limitation on the rate or amount. For municipalities, the most important of these purposes is to fund debt service on general obligation debt. For counties, the purposes include debt service on general obligation debt as well as the most significant state-mandated services: schools and social services. On the flip side, there are some (very limited) services or activities that a local government is not authorized to fund with property tax dollars without specific approval through a voter referendum.

28. If the voters approve a dedicated property tax, at a specific rate, for a particular purpose, the governing board may not divert the proceeds to a different purpose.

29. This limitation stems from Article V, Section 2, of the North Carolina Constitution, which provides that "[n]o class of property shall be taxed except by uniform rule, and every classification shall be made by general law uniformly applicable in every county, city and town, and other unit of local government."

30. For example, a county's general property tax is levied on all (nonexempted or nonexcluded) properties located in incorporated municipalities. Counties typically do not provide any fire services within municipal territory, though.

areas and to levy taxes within those areas, in addition to those levied throughout the county, city, or town, in order to finance, provide, or maintain services, facilities, and functions in addition to or to a greater extent than those financed, provided, or maintained for the entire county, city, or town."[31] Recognizing the disparate needs for fire protection throughout a county, in particular, fire services are among the handful of purposes for which the General Assembly has authorized counties to establish special tax districts to fund.[32] (Cities and sanitary districts are not authorized to establish special taxing districts for this purpose.) Thus, instead of appropriating its general property tax revenue to fund its fire services, a county may establish one or more special tax districts to fund different types and levels of fire services in different parts of the county. There are actually two different types of tax districts—rural fire protection districts and fire service tax districts. The major difference between the two is how the districts are formed and how they can be altered or abolished, but there are a few other distinctions. Each type of taxing district will be discussed in turn.[33] Additionally, a chart summarizing the major differences between the districts is presented in Appendix 29.1.[34]

Rural Fire Protection Districts

One of the methods that a county may employ to raise revenue only from those citizens who directly benefit (or most directly benefit) from fire services provided by the county is to establish one or more rural fire protection districts and levy an additional ad valorem tax on all taxable real and personal properties within each of the districts, the revenue from which is earmarked specifically to fund the fire services provided within the districts. The General Assembly bestowed this authority on counties in the early 1950s in recognition of the fact that rural areas were increasingly becoming subject to urban-type development, resulting in pressure on county governments to provide and fund fire protection services in these areas.

Establishing a Rural Fire Protection District

A county's governing board may not simply establish a rural fire protection district. It first must receive a petition signed by at least 35 percent of the resident freeholders living within the proposed district. The proposed district must encompass only territory outside the corporate limits of any municipality,[35] but it may include territory that lies in more than one county. (If the proposed district falls within more than one county, the petition must be submitted to the boards of county commissioners of all the counties in which the area lies.) The county tax office must verify the freeholder status and confirm the location of the property owned by the petitioners.

Once a county board of commissioners receives a valid petition, it must call an election within the proposed district on the question of whether or not the county may levy a special property tax to fund fire services within the district.[36] The statute sets the maximum tax rate at $0.15 per $100 assessed valuation of taxable property. A county is not required to accept a petition that calls for a different maximum rate limit, even if it is lower than $0.15 per $100 valuation.[37] In fact, the statutorily prescribed ballot language allows citizens to vote only to approve or not approve the levy by the county commissioners of the statutory maximum rate of $0.15 per $100 valuation.[38] It does not authorize the county to hold an election on any tax rate that differs from the statutory maximum rate. Thus, for example, a county board of

---

31. N.C. Const. art. V, § 2(4).

32. Under general law, neither municipalities nor sanitary districts are authorized to establish special tax districts to fund fire services.

33. For a more detailed explanation of how to establish, maintain, modify, and abolish a special tax district for fire services, see Kara A. Millonzi, "County Funding for Fire Services in North Carolina," *Local Finance Bulletin* No. 43 (May 2011), sogpubs.unc.edu/electronicversions/pdfs/lfb43.pdf.

34. Note that the authority, procedures, and limitations of special tax districts discussed in this chapter are those prescribed by general law. *See* G.S. Chapter 69, Article 3A; G.S. Chapter 153A, Article 16. A number of special tax districts have been created by local act of the General Assembly to fund fire services, and a handful of local modifications to the general law authority apply to individual counties. Local officials should determine and follow the applicable laws in their jurisdictions.

35. As discussed below, municipal territory may be added to an existing rural fire protection district after the district is established. G.S. 69-25.11(5).

36. G.S. 69-25.1.

37. *Id.*; *see* Op. N.C. Att'y Gen. July 8, 1969 (on file with author).

38. G.S. 69-25.3.

commissioners may not propose a maximum rate of $0.12 per $100 valuation on the ballot, even if it receives a petition signed by at least 35 percent of the resident freeholders in the proposed district requesting the $0.12 maximum tax rate.[39]

All qualified voters in the proposed district may vote in the election.[40] The county board of commissioners, after consulting with the county board of elections, must adopt a resolution setting the date for the election.[41] The election is conducted by the county board of elections, with the cost borne by the county.[42] If a district ultimately is established, the county may recoup the costs of the election from tax revenue generated by the district tax. (If the proposed district lies within multiple counties, each board of county commissioners must call for an election and the election must be conducted jointly by the counties' boards of elections, with the cost shared equally by all counties.)[43]

If a majority of the voters voting in the election approve the ballot issue to allow the county to impose a special property tax to fund fire services within the district (rural district tax), the county board(s) of commissioners must establish the district.[44] The district is a municipal corporation, a separate legal entity from the county or counties in which it lies. As a municipal corporation, a rural fire protection district's governing board is authorized to enter into contractual agreements to purchase property or procure fire protection services.

Governing a Rural Fire Protection District

There are three possible governing structures for a district. If the district lies within a single county, the county's board of commissioners may serve as the district's governing board. If the district lies in more than one county, the boards of commissioners of those counties may jointly govern the district. And whether the district lies in a single county or in multiple counties, the board or boards of county commissioners may appoint a three-member fire protection district commission (fire commission) to govern the district. Members of the fire commission must be qualified voters who reside in the district. The fire commission serves "at the discretion of and under the supervision of the board[s] of county commissioners."[45] Although technically the governing board of the district, the fire commission legally functions more like an advisory board to the county board(s) of commissioners. In fact, even if a fire commission is appointed, it is the board(s) of county commissioners that must determine the district tax rate each year. The county board(s) may not delegate this responsibility to the fire commission or to any of the fire departments with contracts to provide services within the district.[46] The county commissioners also are statutorily responsible for determining the methods of providing fire services in the district (discussed below), though this function likely may be delegated

---

39. A more difficult issue is whether a county may call for a referendum if it receives a petition that specifies a tax rate that differs from the statutory rate of $0.15 per $100 valuation. The safest approach is for a county board to reject the petition and not call an election unless and until a proper petition is presented. If the board chooses to proceed with the referendum despite receiving a petition that specifies a different maximum tax rate, the referendum may not specify a maximum tax rate that is different from that provided in the statute. Thus, for example, even if the petition calls for a maximum tax rate of $0.12 per $100 valuation, if the county holds a referendum on establishing the rural fire protection district and the referendum is successful, the maximum authorized tax rate is $0.15 per $100 valuation. It is possible, however, that the levy of the rural district tax subsequently could be challenged as invalid because the petition calling for the referendum did not satisfy the statutory requirements. As of this writing, there is no case law addressing this issue.

40. *See* G.S. Chapter 163, Article 6, for voter qualification requirements.

41. G.S. 69-25.2. Note that the board of county commissioners likely may not proceed to call for an election if, before the board takes action, one or more resident freeholders withdraws his or her signature from the petition, thereby keeping the 35 percent threshold from being met. *Cf.* Idol v. Hanes, 219 N.C. 723 (1941).

42. The county board of elections must advertise and conduct the election in accordance with the applicable provisions in G.S. Chapter 163.

43. G.S. 69-25.9.

44. If the ballot issue fails, the issue may not be put to the voters again for at least two years. G.S. 69-25.1.

45. G.S. 69-25.7.

46. *See* G.S. 69-25.4. The fire protection district commission may advise the county commissioners as to whether or not to levy a district tax each year and at what rate, but the county commissioners likely must retain the discretionary authority to determine the tax rate each year. *See* Plant Food Co. v. City of Charlotte, 214 N.C. 518 (1938). *See generally* David M. Lawrence, "Contracts That Bind the Discretion of Governing Boards," *Popular Government* 56 (Summer 1990): 38–42.

to the fire commission.[47] In fact, the fire commission typically enters into the actual contractual agreements with the volunteer or municipal fire department(s) on behalf of the district.

Levying the Rural Fire Protection District Tax

The county commissioners levy the rural district tax each fiscal year at a rate not to exceed $0.15 per $100 valuation. (If the district was formed before June 9, 1959, the maximum tax rate is $0.10 per $100 valuation, unless the district's voters have approved an increase to $0.15 per $100 valuation.)[48] With one exception, the rural district tax applies to all real and personal property subject to the county's ad valorem property tax.[49] Property owners in the district may not opt out of paying the rural district tax even if the property owners procure their own fire protection. Commissioners are not required to levy the tax—instead, the board is instructed to "levy and collect [the district tax] *in such amount as it may deem necessary*."[50] Commissioners determine whether or not to levy the district tax, and at what rate, each year during budget time. The tax typically is adopted in the county's budget ordinance.[51]

If the district lies in more than one county, each county board of commissioners may adopt a yearly rural district tax rate for the portion of the district that lies within its county.[52] The tax rate adopted in each county need not be the same as that adopted in the other counties that comprise the district, though the boards of county commissioners may agree in any given year to adopt the same rate. No county may adopt a tax rate that exceeds the maximum rate approved by the voters.[53] Also, the rate adopted in each county must apply uniformly to all taxable properties that lie within that county's portion of the rural fire protection district.[54]

Providing Services within a Rural Fire Protection District

In administering the fund, the district's governing board may expend district tax proceeds to finance any fire suppression or prevention programs or activities in the district.[55] Additionally, district tax revenue may be used for "furnishing emergency medical, rescue, and ambulance services to protect persons within the district from injury or death."[56] Service provision does not need to be provided uniformly throughout the district.

A rural district's board has much discretion in allocating funds in any manner it chooses—splitting the funds among multiple fire and rescue departments or even appropriating a portion of the funds to support the county's fire marshal—to procure the desired fire services in the district.[57] That said, many district boards contract with a single incorporated fire department or municipal fire department to serve an entire rural fire protection district. There often is confusion as to who controls the district—the district's governing board, the county board(s) of commissioners, or the fire department's governing board. The practical answer is that all three have some degree of control. The county board(s) of commissioners must set the tax rate and determine how services will be provided in the district. The district's governing board (which often is the county board(s) of commissioners) enters into contractual agreements with the fire department to procure services for the district. The fire department is a contracting agent of the district. As such, its degree of control over service provision is dictated by the contract's terms.

---

47. *See* G.S. 69-25.5.

48. G.S. 69-25.1.

49. If the rural fire protection district was established after May 1, 1971, the district tax does not apply to any electric generating plant that provides electricity to the public.

50. G.S. 69-25.4 (emphasis added).

51. Once the tax is adopted, it likely may not be altered during the fiscal year unless it satisfies one of the criteria set forth in G.S. 159-15.

52. G.S. 69-25.9.

53. Although the statutes specifically allow for the formation of a rural fire protection district that crosses county boundary lines, for purposes of adopting the district tax rate, each county controls the revenue generation for the portion of the district that lies within its territory.

54. *See* N.C. Const. art. 5, § 2(2).

55. A rural district's governing board may not expend the tax proceeds to procure services or finance projects outside the district's boundaries.

56. G.S. 69-25.4(b). A rural fire protection district that provides ambulance services is subject to the provisions in G.S. 153A-250.

57. Thus, although rural district tax revenue must be used to fund services in the district, there is no requirement that the funds be used to support a single fire department.

A district governing board may enter into multi-year contractual arrangements with fire departments to procure fire services. These contracts can take many different forms. They may provide for specified types and levels of services in exchange for specified reimbursement each year.[58] Alternatively, they may set forth a general agreement that a fire department will serve a particular area but leave the specific service and pay provisions to be negotiated each year. If a district has valid contractual agreements with one or more fire departments, it must abide by the provisions in those contracts or face liability for breach of the agreements.[59] However, subject to any existing contractual agreements, a district's governing board may change service providers or the nature of the services that are being provided at any time.[60] An incorporated or municipal fire department does not have a statutory right to continue to serve a particular district, even if the fire department has incurred significant expense (or even borrowed money) to fund operating or capital expenses to serve the district.[61]

Funding Capital Projects in a Rural Fire Protection District

In addition to being used for the provision of services in the district, district tax proceeds may be used to fund capital projects. A question sometimes arises as to which entity owns the real or personal property funded with the rural district tax revenue. The answer to this question depends, at least in part, on which entity purchased the capital assets or engaged in the construction project. If a municipal or volunteer fire department that serves a rural district purchases land, vehicles, or other equipment or constructs or makes capital improvements to a fire station or substation, it is the fire department (not the district or the county) that owns the property. This is true even if the district's governing board appropriated district tax moneys to fund all or a portion of the capital outlay. On the other hand, if the district's governing board purchases the capital assets or engages in the construction project itself, the real or personal property belongs to the district. The district may convey the property to a fire department, though. Or it may otherwise allow a fire department to use the property as part of a service contract. A county also has the option to fund capital projects related to the provision of fire services in a rural district with general fund moneys.

What if the fire department, district, or county needs to borrow money to fund the capital projects? A rural fire protection district has no authority to borrow money. The fire department that serves a rural district may borrow money to fund capital equipment or projects necessary to furnish the appropriate level of fire protection services. If an incorporated or municipal fire department borrows the money, neither the district nor the county (or counties) in which the district lies legally is responsible for the debt service payments. As a practical matter, the fire department likely will use some of its appropriated district tax moneys to repay the loan.

The county or counties in which a rural district lies also may borrow money to fund certain capital expenses related to the provision of fire services within the district. According to G.S. 159-48(b)(6), a county may issue general obligation debt to provide "facilities for fire fighting and prevention, including without limitation headquarters buildings, station buildings, training facilities, hydrants, alarm systems, and communications systems." By issuing general obligation debt, the county pledges its general taxing power as security for the debt. That means that if the county failed to meet its debt service payments, the bondholders could force the county to raise its general property tax rate (not its district tax rate) to a sufficient amount to cover the payments. A county also could finance the purchase of real or personal property (or improvements made to real property) by borrowing funds and pledging the property as security for repayment of the loan.[62] If the county borrows money to fund a capital project related to the provision of fire service in a rural district, it may use rural district tax revenue to meet its debt service obligations.

---

58. Note that a county board of commissioners likely may not contract away its legal authority to determine the rural district tax rate each year.

59. *See, e.g.*, Knotville Volunteer Fire Dep't, Inc. v. Wilkes Cnty., 85 N.C. App. 598 (1987), *other proceeding*, 94 N.C. App. 377 (1989).

60. *See Knotville*, 85 N.C. App. 598.

61. With the exception of some limited protections when a municipal annexation occurs (see G.S. 160A-37.1 and G.S. 160A-49.1), a rural volunteer fire department's only legal protection is pursuant to the contractual arrangements it enters into with the district.

62. *See* G.S. 160A-20.

Altering a Rural Fire Protection District

From time to time a county, or citizens residing in a county, may wish to alter an existing rural fire protection district to, for example, increase the maximum tax rate, add territory, or remove territory. Changes are also necessitated when property included in a rural fire protection district becomes part of an incorporated municipality (through incorporation or annexation). Each of these actions requires fairly detailed, statutorily prescribed processes.[63]

It is important to note that although it may be difficult to officially alter a rural fire protection tax district's boundaries or increase its maximum allowable tax rate, a county has much discretion to change the nature of the fire services provided within a district and to change who provides those services. Rural fire protection districts are simply taxing districts. Counties are in no way impeded from establishing fire protection response areas or insurance districts that cut across one or more rural fire protection districts. Thus, in many instances a county board of commissioners may make the desired changes to its fire protection services without resorting to officially altering rural fire protection district boundaries.

Abolishing a Rural Fire Protection District

In order to abolish a rural fire protection district altogether, a board of county commissioners (or the joint boards of county commissioners if the district lies in more than one county) must receive a petition with the signatures of at least 15 percent of the resident freeholders within the district requesting that it be abolished.[64] Upon receiving a valid petition, the board(s) of county commissioners must call for an election on the issue in the district, to be conducted by the county board of elections.[65] If a majority of voters voting in the election approve of abolishing the district, then the board(s) of county commissioners must cease collecting the rural district tax. County commissioners are not required to cease providing fire services to properties or citizens located in the district, though. As discussed above, counties are free to provide and fund fire protection services with general property tax proceeds or other unrestricted general fund revenues. Any unused district tax funds that remain after the district is abolished revert to the county's (or counties') general fund(s) to be used for any public purpose.[66] And any district property may be used or disposed of by the board(s) of county commissioners.[67]

Instead of abolishing the district, which requires both a petition and a voter referendum, could the commissioners allow the district to remain but treat it as if it had been abolished by not levying a rural district tax? The answer is yes. County commissioners have full discretion to choose whether or not to levy a district tax in any given year. If the commissioners wish to cease providing fire services within the district, or to fund the fire services in a different manner,[68] they may simply cease levying the district tax. Unless the district is officially abolished, though, any unused district tax proceeds must be used to provide fire protection services within the district.

County Fire and Rescue Service Districts

The second type of special tax district that a county may establish to fund fire protection and rescue services is a county service district.[69] A county is authorized to define one or more areas within the county to establish a service district to "finance, provide, or maintain" one or more of a specific list of authorized services, facilities or functions "in addition to or to a greater extent than those financed, provided or maintained for the entire county."[70] This authority stems

63. For detailed explanations of the required processes to alter a rural district, see Kara A. Millonzi, "County Funding for Fire Services in North Carolina," *Local Finance Bulletin* No. 43 (May 2011), http://sogpubs.unc.edu/electronicversions/pdfs/lfb43.pdf. Note that district boundaries also may be altered or districts may be abolished by local act of the General Assembly.

64. G.S. 69-25.10.

65. The election must be conducted according to the procedures prescribed by G.S. 69-25.2.

66. G.S. 69-25.10.

67. *Id.*

68. As discussed below, county commissioners effectively may convert a rural fire protection district to a county fire service district (authorized by G.S. Chapter 153A, Article 16) without actually abolishing the rural fire protection district by ceasing to levy a rural fire protection district tax and establishing a county fire service district and imposing a county fire service district tax instead.

69. County service districts are governed by G.S. Chapter 153A, Article 16.

70. G.S. 153A-301.

from an effort by the General Assembly in the mid-1970s to make municipal-type services more widely available to county residents. Among the authorized services for which service districts may be created are "fire protection" and "ambulance and rescue" services.[71] Unlike a rural fire protection district, a county service district is not a municipal corporation and has no independent authority. It is established and maintained by the county and is under the control of the county board of commissioners.

Establishing a Fire or Rescue Service District

It is much easier to establish a fire or rescue service district than to create a rural fire protection district. A county board of commissioners may create one or more fire service districts or one or more rescue service districts (collectively, service districts) without receiving a petition from affected property owners and without holding a voter referendum. (There is no provision for multiple counties to establish fire or rescue service districts that cross county borders.) The board simply must find that

1. there is a demonstrable need for providing one or more of the services in the district,
2. it is impossible or impracticable to provide the services on a countywide basis,
3. it is economically feasible to provide the proposed services in the district without unreasonable or burdensome annual tax levies, and
4. there is a demonstrable demand for the proposed services by persons residing in the proposed district.[72]

In making its determination, the board must consider a number of factors, including the resident or seasonal population and population density in the proposed district, the appraised value of property subject to taxation in the proposed district, the present tax rates of the county and any municipalities or other special districts in which the proposed district is located, and the ability of the proposed district to sustain the additional taxes necessary to support the proposed district.[73] Although a county board does not need to solicit formal citizen approval to create a district because it must establish "demonstrable demand" for the services that will be provided in the district, it likely may not create a county service district if there is strong opposition to the county providing the fire protection services in the proposed district by the current residents.

Once the board makes the appropriate findings, it must hold a public hearing on the proposed creation of the service district. At least four weeks before the public hearing, the board (or staff) must prepare and make available for public inspection in the office of the clerk to the board a report that contains a map of the proposed district, a statement that the proposed district meets the required standards, and a plan for providing the fire or rescue services (or both) to the district.[74] After it holds the public hearing, the county board may adopt a resolution establishing the district. The district must take effect at the beginning of a fiscal year.[75]

A county may include municipal territory in a newly established district, but only if the municipality's governing board adopts a resolution agreeing to the inclusion.[76] If municipal property becomes part of a county fire service or rescue district, the county board of commissioners controls the tax levy and service provision (to the extent funded by the service district tax) in the municipality. The municipality's governing board has no authority to determine the amount of the service district tax or how its proceeds are expended. A municipality is free to supplement the fire services provided to municipal property in the district with municipal revenue.

71. G.S. 153A-301(a)(2) and (7).

72. G.S. 153A-302(a1).

73. G.S. 153A-302(a)(1)–(4).

74. G.S. 153A-302(b) and (c). Notice of the public hearing must state "the date, hour, and place of the hearing and its subject, and [must] include a map of the proposed district and a statement that the report . . . is available for public inspection in the office of the clerk to the board." G.S. 153A-302(c). The notice must be published at least one week before the date of the hearing and mailed at least four weeks before the date of the hearing to the owners of all property located within the proposed district. *Id.*

75. G.S. 153A-302(d).

76. G.S. 153A-302(a1). Similarly, if territory to be included in the proposed district lies within a sanitary district, the sanitary district's governing board must consent to its inclusion. *Id.*

Levying a Fire or Rescue Service District Tax

Once a service district is created, the county board of commissioners may levy an annual property tax within the service district in addition to the property tax or taxes it levies throughout the county (service district tax), but it is not required to do so. The service district tax applies to all real and personal property that is subject to the county's ad valorem property tax(es). As with rural fire protection districts, property owners in a county service district may not opt out of paying the tax, even if they procure their own fire protection. The board typically adopts the service district tax rate in its annual budget ordinance. Once the rate is adopted, the board generally may not alter it during the fiscal year.[77] County commissioners may adopt a new tax rate each year to reflect the estimated costs of servicing the district. Unlike rural fire protection districts, service districts generally have no specific maximum tax rate. Such taxes are subject to the general aggregate property tax limit of $1.50 on each $100 valuation. That means that the district tax rate, when combined with the county's general ad valorem property tax rate(s), may not exceed $1.50, unless the portion of the rate in excess of the limitation is submitted to and approved by a majority of the qualified voters in the district.[78]

Under certain circumstances, a county board of commissioners is restricted to a lower maximum allowable service district tax rate. With respect to a fire protection service district, if within ninety days before holding the public hearing on the proposed district (and before the first publication of notice of the public hearing) the board of commissioners adopts a resolution that states that property taxes within the fire protection service district may not exceed $0.15 per $100 valuation, then the yearly service district tax may not exceed this maximum rate.[79]

Similarly, with respect to an ambulance and rescue district, if within ninety days before holding the public hearing on the proposed district (and before the first publication of notice of the public hearing) the board of commissioners adopts a resolution stating that property taxes within the ambulance and rescue service district may not exceed $0.05 per $100 valuation, then the yearly service district tax may not exceed this maximum rate.[80]

Revenue generated from the service district tax is specifically earmarked to finance the fire or rescue services to be provided in the district.[81] Service district tax proceeds may not be diverted to any other purpose, even if a service district is abolished. In addition to the service district tax revenue, a county may allocate to a service district any other unrestricted revenues.[82] Once these revenues are allocated to the service district they also are specifically earmarked to be used only to fund the fire or rescue services provided within the district.

Providing Services within a Fire or Rescue Service District

The service district tax revenue must be used to furnish fire or rescue services "in addition to or to a greater extent than those financed, provided or maintained for the entire county."[83] That means that a county may create a service district to provide fire or rescue services that it is not providing at all in other areas of the county or that it is not providing at the same level in other areas of the county. Service provision need not be uniform throughout the district. A county also may establish multiple service districts to provide fire or rescue services in different areas of the county. Each district may have the same tax rate and support the same level of services, or each may have different rates to fund different types or amounts of services. In addition, multiple authorized services may be provided within the same district.

---

77. *See* G.S. 159-15.

78. G.S. 153A-307.

79. G.S. 153A-309.2. The notice requirements for the public hearing are different if the county commissioners adopt a resolution restricting the maximum tax rate for the district. Notice must be published at least twice, with one publication not less than two weeks before the hearing and the other publication on a different day that is also not less than two weeks before the hearing. *Id.*

Note that there also are special rate limitations for industrial facility property that meets certain requirements and that is removed from an existing fire protection service district and simultaneously placed within a new fire protection service district. *See* G.S. 153A-309.3.

80. G.S. 153A-310. The notice requirements for the public hearing are different if the county commissioners adopt a resolution restricting the maximum tax rate for the district. Notice must be published at least twice, with one publication not less than two weeks before the hearing and the other publication on a different day that is also not less than two weeks before the hearing. *Id.*

81. G.S. 153A-307.

82. *Id.*

83. *Id.*

For example, fire protection services and ambulance and rescue services may be provided within the same district.[84] Alternatively, a county may establish co-extensive service districts to provide different services. For example, a county may establish a fire service district and an ambulance and rescue service district with the exact same boundaries.

A county must "provide, maintain, or let contracts for the services for which the residents of the district are being taxed within a reasonable time, not to exceed one year, after the effective date of the definition of the district."[85] The statutes are silent, though, as to how services may be provided within the district. Counties generally are authorized to contract with any private entity to "carry out any public purpose that the county is authorized by law to engage in."[86] So, as with rural fire protection districts, a county is free to establish and maintain a county fire, ambulance, or rescue department to provide the services within its service districts, or it may contract with one or more municipal or volunteer fire departments to furnish these services. (Many adopt some combination of both.) The county has a good deal of flexibility in how it allocates the service district tax revenue to procure services for the district.

As with rural fire protection districts, the relationship between counties and municipal or volunteer fire departments is of a contractual nature. The county board of commissioners retains legal control over setting the service district tax rate each year, and the county board of commissioners determines what fire services are provided within the district and by whom. That means that, subject to any existing contractual agreements, a board of county commissioners may change service providers or the nature of the services that are being provided at any time. A volunteer or municipal fire department does not have a statutory right to continue to serve a particular district, even if the fire department has incurred significant expense (or even borrowed money) to fund operating or capital expenses to serve the district.

Single County Fire or Rescue Service District

In recent years several counties have explored ways to increase their flexibility in allocating resources among the various fire or rescue service areas. One option that is gaining popularity is to create a single county fire or rescue service district that encompasses the entire unincorporated area of the county. Under this approach, a county levies a single tax rate across the entire service district and allocates the proceeds among the various fire and rescue departments that service each response zone according to their individual budgetary needs. This approach provides a county board with the same flexibility as using its general property tax proceeds, with the added advantage that the tax is not levied in municipal territories. And creating a single county fire or service district that comprises the county's unincorporated area satisfies the statutory requirements for creating a service district: the district tax proceeds are used to provide services "in addition to or to a greater extent than those financed, provided or maintained for the entire county"[87] because services are not being provided in the incorporated areas.

Funding Capital Projects in a County Fire or Rescue Service District

District tax proceeds also may be used to fund capital projects. As with rural fire protection districts, a question sometimes arises as to which entity owns the real or personal property funded with the rural district tax revenue. The answer is the same as for rural districts: it depends, at least in part, on which entity purchased the capital assets or engaged in the construction project. If a municipal or volunteer fire department that serves a fire or rescue service district purchases land, vehicles, or other equipment or constructs or makes capital improvements to a fire station or substation, it is the fire department (not the county) that owns the property. This is true even if the county's governing board appropriated service district tax moneys to fund all or a portion of the capital outlay. On the other hand, if the county's governing board purchases the capital assets or engages in the construction project itself, the real or personal property belongs to the district. A county may use district tax proceeds or county general fund revenue to fund the

---

84. Generally, in order to provide multiple services within a single district, the services need to have been identified in the report generated on the proposed district and adopted in the governing board's resolution establishing the district. G.S. 153A-309 provides an exception to this process. If a service district initially was established for fire protection purposes only, the board of county commissioners may adopt a resolution to permit the service district to provide emergency medical, rescue, and ambulance services and to use service district tax proceeds to fund these services. The resolution must take effect at the beginning of a fiscal year.

85. G.S. 153A-305.

86. G.S. 153A-449.

87. G.S. 153A-307.

capital project. And, the county may convey the property to a fire department, or it may otherwise allow a fire department to use the property as part of a service contract.

What if the fire department or county needs to borrow money to fund the capital projects? A county fire or rescue service district is not an independent legal entity and has no authority to borrow money. The fire department that serves a service district may borrow money to fund capital equipment or projects necessary to furnish the appropriate level of fire protection services. If an incorporated or municipal fire department borrows the money, the county is not legally responsible for the debt service payments. As a practical matter, the fire department likely will use some of the appropriated district tax moneys to repay the loan, though.

The county in which a service district lies also may borrow money to fund certain capital expenses related to the provision of fire services within the district. According to G.S. 159-48(b)(6), a county may issue general obligation debt to provide "facilities for fire fighting and prevention, including without limitation headquarters buildings, station buildings, training facilities, hydrants, alarm systems, and communications systems." By issuing general obligation debt, the county pledges its general taxing power as security for the debt. That means that if the county failed to meet its debt service payments, the bondholders could force the county to raise its general property tax rate (not its district tax rate) to a sufficient amount to cover the payments. A county may also finance the purchase of real or personal property (or improvements made to real property) by borrowing funds and pledging the property as security for repayment of the loan.[88] If the county borrows money to fund a capital project related to the provision of fire service in a rural district, it may use rural district tax revenue to meet its debt service obligations.

Note that before a county may issue general obligation debt, it must first receive specific voter approval through a referendum process. And, G.S. 153A-308 stipulates that if general obligation bond proceeds will be used to fund a capital project within a county service district and will be repaid with district tax proceeds, "the proposed bond issue must be approved concurrently by a majority of those voting throughout the entire county and by a majority of the total of those voting in all of the affected or to-be-affected service districts."[89] There is no statutory counterpart to this provision applicable to rural fire protection districts.

Altering a Fire or Rescue Service District

Once a county establishes a service district, it may alter it by adding additional territory to the district, consolidating it with one or more other service districts, relocating the boundaries with an adjoining service district, or (under certain circumstances) removing territory from the service district. It also may abolish the district. A county board of commissioners must follow the appropriate statutory procedures for accomplishing each of these actions.

As with rural fire protection districts, it is important to note that a county has much discretion to change the nature of the fire services provided within a district and to change who provides those services without actually altering the district's boundaries. County fire or rescue service districts are simply taxing districts. Counties are in no way impeded from establishing fire protection response areas or insurance districts that cut across one or more service districts. Thus, in many instances a county board of commissioners may make the desired changes to its fire protection services without resorting to officially altering service district boundaries.

Abolishing a Fire or Rescue Service District

If the board of county commissioners determines that a fire or rescue service district tax is no longer needed to fund the fire or rescue services provided in the district, it has two options. The first option is to adopt a resolution abolishing the district.[90] The board may not abolish a district, however, if the county has any "outstanding bonds or notes issued to finance projects in the district."[91] That means that if the county issued general obligation debt to purchase capital equipment or fund infrastructure projects associated with fire or rescue protection, it may not abolish the district until the debt is repaid.[92] The board must hold a public hearing before abolishing a district, and the abolition must take effect

---

88. *See* G.S. 160A-20.

89. This requirement is imposed because district tax proceeds likely will be used to make debt service payments.

90. G.S. 153A-306.

91. *Id.*

92. The restriction does not apply if a volunteer fire department or municipal fire department that serves the district borrows money to fund capital purchases or projects. The restriction also technically may not apply if the county has entered into

at the end of a fiscal year.[93] Any service district tax funds remaining after a district is abolished must continue to be used to provide fire services to properties that were in the district. The moneys may not be diverted for a different purpose.

The second option is to keep the district but simply not levy a service district tax.[94] The county board could levy the district tax again in future fiscal years without having to re-establish the district. Even if the county does not levy the service district tax, it may continue to provide fire and rescue services in the district, funded through alternative means.

Relationship between Rural Fire Protection Districts and County Fire or Rescue Service Districts

It is not uncommon for a county to have a mix of rural fire protection districts and county fire and rescue service districts within its territorial boundaries. As described above, there are various procedural processes (some more onerous than others) to modify the boundary lines of the two different types of districts. But, what if a county wishes to replace one type of district with another or modify boundary lines between the two different types of districts? Both types of districts serve largely the same purpose—namely, they both provide a mechanism to target a county's taxing power on those property owners who most directly benefit from the expenditure of the tax proceeds. Despite this, there is not an easy process to convert one type of taxing district into another type of taxing district or to modify the boundary lines between the different types of taxing districts.

Converting a Rural Fire Protection District to a County Fire Service District

Most often, counties wish to convert a rural fire protection district to a county fire service district (or transfer property from a rural fire protection district to a county fire service district), because the latter has fewer statutory restrictions. Territory in a rural fire protection district may not be transferred directly into a county fire service district. There are two methods to accomplish this result indirectly, though. The first is to abolish the rural fire protection district according to the relevant statutory procedures and then establish one or more county fire service districts, again according to the relevant statutory procedures. The second is to overlay one or more county fire service districts over a rural fire protection district.

Under the latter option, a county's board of commissioners could continue to levy the rural fire protection district tax and also levy the county service district tax on real and personal properties located in both districts.[95] Alternatively, the governing board could cease levying the rural fire protection district tax and rely only on the service district tax to fund fire services in the area that is encompassed by both districts. Several counties have taken advantage of this second option in recent years. They have stopped levying taxes in some or all of their existing rural fire protection districts (without actually abolishing the districts) and they have established one or more county fire or rescue service districts in their place. The county service districts often have the same boundaries as the rural fire protection districts, but the new service district boundaries need not be c-extensive with the existing rural district boundaries.[96] Even if a county service district has the same boundaries as an existing rural fire protection district, the county establishes, maintains, and modifies the county service district according to the provisions set forth in G.S. Chapter 153A, Article 16 (not the provisions in G.S. Chapter 69, Article 3A). The county board, for example, is not limited to the statutory maximum tax rate (of $0.15 or $0.10 per $100 valuation) imposed on rural fire protection districts.

Converting a County Fire Service District to a Rural Fire Protection District

A county may overlay a county service district over an existing rural fire protection district, but it may not overlay a rural fire protection district over an existing county service district. G.S. 153A-304.2 provides that all or any portion of a fire service district that is annexed by a rural fire protection district immediately ceases to be a county fire

installment purchase contracts, pursuant to G.S. 160A-20, to fund the projects in the district. Although installment financing is a form of borrowing, a county does not always issue bonds or notes when it enters into such financing agreements.

93. G.S. 153A-306. Notice of the public hearing must state the "date, hour and place of the hearing, and its subject." It must be published at least one week before the hearing. *Id.*

94. G.S. 153A-307 allows a county's governing board to determine whether or not to levy the service district tax, and at what rate, each fiscal year.

95. Note that a county service district may not contain territory in more than one county.

96. As discussed above, at least a few counties have created a single county fire service district that encompasses the entire unincorporated territory in the county.

service district or a part of a county fire service district. Although the statute is not entirely clear, it likely applies if an existing rural fire protection district annexes territory in a county fire service district according to the provisions in G.S. 69-25.11 and if a new rural fire protection district is created pursuant to G.S. 69-25.1 that encompasses territory in a county fire service district. Once the territory becomes part of a rural fire protection district, the county no longer has authority to levy a service district tax on the properties within the annexed territory. The properties in the annexed territory are subject instead to the rural fire district tax.[97]

Fees and Charges

Under general law, cities and counties do not have authority to impose fees on citizens or property owners to fund most fire protection services. Local units also do not have authority to assess fees on motor vehicle owners, drivers, or insurance companies to recoup the costs of responding to, and cleaning up after, accidents or other incidents. There are some limited exceptions, though. For example, local units have authority to charge fees to recoup costs associated with responding to and mitigating a hazardous materials emergency.[98] Cities and counties also have authority to impose reasonable fees and charges to fund their fire code inspection services. The North Carolina Supreme Court has held that local governments have inherent authority to recoup the costs of performing a regulatory function as long as the amounts collected are reasonable and do not exceed the aggregate (direct and indirect) expenses of performing the regulatory activity.[99] Counties are authorized to franchise ambulance operators and adopt a schedule of rates, fees, and charges to be imposed by those ambulance operators for emergency rescue services.[100]

Sanitary districts, on the other hand, have explicit authority to "apply service charges and rates based upon the exact benefits derived."[101] A sanitary district board may charge fees for responding to fires or providing other fire protection or rescue services. A district also may charge fees for some services and use property tax revenue to cover other fire protection costs.

Grant Funding

Although fire departments typically receive the majority of their funding from the local units where they provide services, most departments engage in additional fundraising efforts. They also routinely seek out grants to support projects, programs, and services. The state provides aid to volunteer fire departments and volunteer rescue and emergency medical services (EMS) units.

State Grant Programs

Volunteer Fire Department Fund

The General Assembly created the Volunteer Fire Department Fund, which authorizes the state's Insurance Commissioner to make grants to eligible fire departments.[102] To be eligible for a grant, a fire department must serve a response area of 12,000 or less in population, have no more than six paid members, and be certified as serving a rated fire district by the North Carolina Department of Insurance (DOI). A department may receive up to one $30,000 grant per fiscal year and must match the grant on a dollar-for-dollar basis. Grants are awarded in May each year.

---

97. The transfer of territory from a county fire service district to a rural fire protection district does not present much difficulty if it occurs at the beginning of a fiscal year. If the annexation occurs at a time other than the beginning of a fiscal year, however, the property owners in the affected territory likely will end up paying both the county fire district tax and the rural fire protection district tax for the fiscal year in which the annexation occurs. That is because, according to G.S. 153A-304.2(b), once the county board of commissioners levies the fire service district tax, property owners within the fire service district are responsible for paying the tax even if the property is subsequently annexed into a rural fire protection district. And, pursuant to G.S. 69-25.12, property owners whose properties are annexed into a rural fire protection district are responsible for paying the rural fire protection district tax as if the properties had been part of the district at the time the tax was levied.

98. *See* G.S. 166A-27.

99. *See* Homebuilders Ass'n of Charlotte v. City of Charlotte, 336 N.C. 37 (1994).

100. *See* G.S. 153A-250.

101. G.S. 130A-64.

102. *See* G.S. 58-87-1.

Volunteer Rescue/EMS Fund

The General Assembly also has established the Volunteer Rescue/EMS Fund, authorizing the state's Insurance Commissioner to make grants to eligible rescue or rescue/EMS units.[103] There are two types of grants—a matching grant of up to $25,000[104] and a nonmatching grant of up to $3,000. The grants may be used only for equipment purchases or other capital expenditures. To be eligible, a unit must have no more than ten full- or part-time paid positions, must be recognized by the Office of the State Fire Marshal and the county board as a unit that provides rescue or EMS (or both) services in a particular district, and must be recognized by the DOI as having met the requirements of the North Carolina Association of Rescue Squads and EMS, Inc. Grants are awarded in December each year.

State Fire Protection Grant Fund

The purpose of the State Fire Protection Grant Fund is to compensate local fire departments for providing local fire protection to state-owned buildings and other state-owned property. The fund is administered by the DOI.[105]

Other Aid to Fire Departments

The state also supplies targeted aid to fire and rescue personnel.[106] As well, there are numerous federal government and private grant opportunities for incorporated fire departments, particularly those that are staffed entirely or mainly with volunteers.[107]

Insurance Districts and Ratings

Generally there are two types of fire protection that are available to a property owner. The first is private fire protection, such as automatic sprinklers, automatic fire detection systems, and automatic extinguishing systems like those found in commercial property and other particularly hazardous areas. The second is normally referred to as public fire protection, which consists of a publicly supported fire department, a public water system, and a building inspection function. The availability of both private and public fire protection services to a real property parcel affects the ability of the property owner to procure property insurance and the cost of that insurance.

Counties are authorized to establish fire insurance districts within their unincorporated territories, with the approval of the Office of the State Fire Marshal of the North Carolina Department of Insurance.[108] The primary purpose of insurance districts, as their name suggests, is to delineate the fire protection coverage afforded to particular properties for purposes of determining whether those properties may be covered by fire insurance and at what cost.

The North Carolina commissioner of insurance and the state fire marshal are responsible for rating departments that serve areas with populations of 100,000 or less.[109] A private corporation, the Insurance Services Office, Inc. (ISO), rates departments that serve more populous areas.[110] Insurance ratings are based on the staffing levels and apparatus of

---

103. *See* G.S. 58-87-5.

104. If an applicant has $1,000 or less in liquid assets, it is not required to provide matching funds.

105. G.S. Ch. 58, Art. 85A.

106. *See, e.g.,* G.S. Ch. 58, Art. 84 (Firefighters' Relief Fund); G.S. Ch. 58, Art. 86 (North Carolina Firefighters' and Rescue Squad Workers' Pension Fund); G.S. Ch. 58, Art. 88 (Rescue Squad Workers' Relief Fund); G.S. Ch. 58, Art. 87 (Volunteer Safety Workers Assistance); G.S. 58-87-10 (Workers' Compensation Fund for the benefit of volunteer safety workers).

107. The North Carolina Firefighters Association provides a list of grant opportunities at http://ncfma.com/grants___information (last visited March 28, 2014).

108. G.S. 153A-233. The statute authorizes a county to "designate fire districts or parts of existing districts and prescribe the boundaries thereof for insurance grading purposes." There is no mention of approval by the state fire marshal. However, the North Carolina Department of Insurance requires that proposed insurance boundaries be submitted to the state fire marshal for approval. *See* North Carolina Fire Service Reference Manual (2011), http://www.ncafc.com/files/ncafc_resources/fire_service_reference_manual_2011.pdf (last visited March 28, 2014).

109. *See* G.S. 58-36-10(3); G.S. 58-40-25(4).

110. Additional information on ISO's rating systems is available at www.isomitigation.com/ppc/0000/ppc0001.html (last visited March 28, 2014).

the fire department itself as well as on the applicable emergency response communication system and available water supply. A fire department that serves the properties within an insurance district is rated on a scale of 1 to 10, with 10 effectively constituting no fire protection for purposes of setting insurance rates. Thus, the minimum insurance grade for departments rated by the commissioner of insurance is 9S. In order to qualify for a 9S rating, the boundaries of a county insurance district may be no more than six road miles from the fire station and the fire station that serves those properties must meet certain requirements. Some fire departments receive a split rating—providing a lower (better) insurance rating to properties in the insurance district that are located within 1,000 feet of a fire hydrant.

A secondary (and related) purpose of fire insurance districts is to delineate fire response areas for particular fire departments. Fire insurance district boundaries often are co-extensive with fire tax district boundaries. This allows for ease of administration by identifying a particular funding source for a particular set of services provided in a particular area by a particular service provider. Fire insurance districts are legally distinct from fire tax districts, though, and they do not have to have the same boundaries. There may be times when a county alters its insurance districts to account for new growth and development or new service providers, but it is not practical for it to change its existing tax districts. As a result of the change, an insurance district may cut across two or more tax districts. If properties in the insurance district are served by a single fire department, the county's (or rural district's) governing board may appropriate moneys from each of the tax districts to the fire department to provide services across the insurance district. A change in insurance district boundaries also may result in a tax district that comprises properties in two or more insurance districts. In this case, the county's (or rural district's) governing board may divvy up the district's tax proceeds and allocate them among the various fire departments that serve the tax district.

As described above, in recent years a handful of counties have officially (or unofficially) abolished their rural fire protection tax districts and established a single county fire service tax district that encompasses all of the unincorporated territory in the county. These counties maintained their insurance districts, and they contract with multiple fire departments to serve the different insurance districts. The counties' governing boards appropriate the service district tax revenue among the various fire departments according to their yearly budgetary needs.

Conclusion

Although no local unit is required to provide fire services to its citizens, fire protection has become one of the core local government services. Local governments in North Carolina have a variety of options for providing the array of fire protection and rescue services within their units. Most of the services are paid for with property tax proceeds—derived either from the general property tax or, increasingly, from special taxing districts.

About the Author

Kara A. Millonzi is a School of Government faculty member who specializes in local government and public school finance law.

Appendix 29.1 Summary Comparison of Rural Fire Protection Districts and County Fire and Rescue Service Districts

	Rural Fire Protection District	County Fire or Rescue Service District
Creating District	County board(s) of commissioners receives petition signed by at least 35 percent of resident freeholders in proposed district and holds successful referendum of qualified voters in proposed district Municipal territory may not be included	County board of commissioners makes certain statutory findings and holds public hearing Municipal territory may be included with consent of municipality's governing board
Maximum Tax Rate	\$0.15 per \$100 valuation (\$0.10 per \$100 valuation if district established before June 1959, unless voters have approved increase to \$0.15 per \$100 valuation maximum)	No maximum district tax rate, but district tax, combined with county's general ad valorem property tax rate(s), may not exceed \$1.50 per \$100 valuation, unless the portion of the rate in excess of the limitation is approved by the district's voters County board of commissioners may impose maximum tax rates (of \$0.15 per \$100 valuation in fire district, or \$0.05 per \$100 valuation in rescue district) if board follows certain procedures in establishing district
Governing Structure	County board of commissioners *or* Joint county board(s) of commissioners if district lies in more than one county *or* Three-member appointed fire commission under supervision of the county board(s) of commissioners	County board of commissioners
Authorized Services and Projects	Any fire suppression or prevention programs including, but not limited to, inspections; training and educational activities; emergency medical, rescue, and ambulance services; and any capital projects related to the provision of these services	*Fire Service District* Any fire suppression or prevention programs including, but not limited to, inspections; training and educational activities; emergency medical, rescue, and ambulance services; and any capital projects related to the provision of these services *Rescue Service District* Emergency medical, rescue, and ambulance services and any capital projects related to the provision of these services

Appendix 29.1 Summary Comparison of Rural Fire Protection Districts and County Fire and Rescue Service Districts (*continued*)

	Rural Fire Protection District	County Fire or Rescue Service District
Modifying Tax Rate	County board(s) of commissioners sets district tax rate each year up to maximum authorized by voters If district established before June 1959, maximum tax rate may be increased from \$0.10 per \$100 valuation to \$0.15 per \$100 valuation if county board(s) of commissioners receives petition signed by at least 35 percent of the resident freeholders in the district and the increase is approved by a majority of qualified voters voting in referendum on the increase	County board of commissioners sets district tax rate each year
Adding Territory to District	*Unincorporated Territory* District's governing board must receive a petition from owner of a single adjoining parcel or from two-thirds majority of the owners of adjoining territory Petition must be approved by fire commission (if created), majority of the board(s) of directors of any fire departments servicing the district, and the majority of the county board(s) of commissioners of the county (or counties) in which the district lies County board(s) of commissioners must hold public hearing *Incorporated Territory* Municipal governing board and county board(s) of commissioners adopt resolutions approving inclusion of municipal territory in district	Area to be added is contiguous to district, with at least one-eighth of the area's aggregate external boundary coincident with the district's boundary and county board of commissioner determines that area needs services provided in district *or* county board of commissioners receives petition signed by 100 percent of real property owners in area to be added County board of commissioners must make certain statutory findings and hold public hearing (If the area to be added is in a municipality, the municipality's governing board must adopt a resolution consenting to the inclusion)

Appendix 29.1 Summary Comparison of Rural Fire Protection Districts and County Fire and Rescue Service Districts (*continued*)

	Rural Fire Protection District	County Fire or Rescue Service District
Changing Boundaries between Districts	*Districts with Same Tax Rate* County board(s) of commissioners receives petition from fire commission (if appointed) and the board(s) of directors of any fire or rescue departments providing fire services in the district County board(s) of commissioners must hold public hearing *Districts with Different Tax Rates* County board(s) of commissioners receives petition signed by at least two-thirds of the owners in the territory County board(s) of commissioners receives favorable recommendation from fire commission (if appointed) and the board(s) of directors of any fire or rescue department providing services in the district County board(s) of commissioners must hold public hearing	If two districts were established for "substantially similar purposes," the county board of commissioners may alter the boundary lines on its own accord or after receiving a petition from affected property owners County board of commissioners must make certain statutory findings and hold public hearing
Removing Territory from District	Property owner applies to county board(s) of commissioners County board(s) of commissioners receives unanimous written consent from fire commission (if appointed) and approval of the majority of members of the board(s) of directors of any fire or rescue departments servicing the district If property in a district is annexed by municipality that provides fire services, the property ceases being part of the district	No statutory authority to remove territory from district unless property in district is annexed by rural fire protection district or by municipality that provides fire services If territory in district is annexed to existing or new rural fire protection district it ceases to be part of the service district If territory in district is annexed by municipality that provides fire services it ceases to be part of the service district
Abolishing District	County board(s) of commissioners receives petition signed by at least 15 percent of the resident freeholders in the district and holds successful referendum of qualified voters in the district	Board of county commissioners adopts resolution abolishing the district (District may not be abolished if the county has any "outstanding bonds or notes issued to finance projects in the district")

Chapter 30

Public Enterprises

Kara A. Millonzi

Introduction

North Carolina counties and municipalities are authorized to engage in certain public enterprise activities. A *public enterprise* is an activity of a commercial nature that could be provided by the private sector. When a local government owns or operates a public enterprise it acts in a proprietary capacity, and it has more flexibility to treat the enterprise like a private business venture than it does with its traditional government functions. The majority of public enterprises are funded with user charges and are self-supporting (or predominantly self-supporting). That means that the local government generates enough income from the user charges to support the operating and capital expenses of the enterprise each year.

A local government is not required to provide any public enterprise services. Further, if a local government chooses to provide one or more of the authorized public enterprises, it need not make them available to all citizens or property owners within the unit. There is no duty of equal service. Generally, as long as it is not unlawfully discriminating against a protected class of citizens, a local government can choose where, and under what circumstances, it will provide the services. If, however, a municipality involuntarily annexes property into its jurisdiction, the annexation triggers special statutory requirements regarding the provision of water and sewer services. Under certain circumstances, a municipality may be required to provide these services to newly annexed properties.[1]

1. For more information on these requirements see Chapter 2, "Incorporation, Annexation, and City–County Consolidation."

Authorized Types of Public Enterprise Services

The most common types of public enterprises are water and sewer utility services, but the general statutes authorize both counties and municipalities to operate public enterprises for all of the following purposes:

- Water supply and distribution
- Sewage collection and treatment
- Solid waste collection and disposal
- Airports
- Public transportation
- Off-street parking
- Stormwater management programs and structural and natural stormwater and drainage systems[2]

Municipalities additionally are authorized to operate enterprises for the following purposes:

- Cable television (and broadband)[3]
- Electric power generation and distribution
- Gas production and distribution[4]

Scope of Authority

Local government authority to operate public enterprises is broad—the statutes allow a county or municipality to "acquire, lease as lessor or lessee, construct, establish, enlarge, improve, extend, maintain, own, operate, and contract for the operation of" the above listed functions.[5] A municipality may provide the enterprise services both inside and outside its territorial boundaries. A county may provide the services in its unincorporated areas and, with the permission of the relevant municipal boards, within its incorporated areas as well.[6]

The authority is not absolute, though. Governments must be careful not to exceed the scope of an authorized enterprise function. In *Smith Chapel Baptist Church v. City of Durham*,[7] the City of Durham had established a stormwater enterprise and assessed a fee on all properties within the unit. The fee revenue funded, among other things, educational programs and other outreach efforts associated with the city's comprehensive stormwater management program. The city established the program to satisfy state and federal regulatory requirements. The North Carolina Supreme Court held that the city had exceeded its public enterprise authority when it used revenue generated from the stormwater fee to fund the stormwater quality management program, because the relevant statute at the time specified that a unit could establish a public enterprise only to fund structural and natural stormwater and drainage systems.[8]

---

2. *See* N.C. Gen. Stat. (hereinafter G.S.) § 153A-274 (counties); G.S. 160A-311 (municipalities). Note that counties also are authorized to establish county water and sewer districts to provide water supply and distribution and sewage collection and treatment services. G.S. 162A, Art. 6. A county that establishes a water or sewer district also may use its public enterprise authority under G.S. 153A, Art. 15, to regulate the services and set user fees. *See* McNeill v. Harnett Cnty., 97 N.C. App. 41 (1990).

3. In *BellSouth Telecommunications, Inc. v. City of Laurinburg*, 168 N.C. App. 75 (2005), the North Carolina Court of Appeals held that the authority to provide cable television services included the authority to provide broadband services. The General Assembly significantly limited the authority for cities to provide cable television and broadband services in 2011. *See* S.L. 2011-84.

Counties have limited authority to provide grants to certain unaffiliated high-speed Internet providers to expand service in unserved areas for economic development. *See* S.L. 2012-86.

4. *See* G.S. 160A-311.

5. *See* G.S. 153A-275(a) (counties); G.S. 160A-312(a).

6. Note that a county does not need a municipality's governing board's permission to construct utility lines or other infrastructure within the municipal boundaries. The county may negotiate with private property owners to obtain the necessary easements and other property rights. A county, however, may not actually provide a public enterprise service within a municipality unless consented to by the municipal board.

7. 350 N.C. 805 (1999).

8. Note that the statute subsequently was revised to allow a unit to establish an enterprise to fund a comprehensive stormwater quality management program. *See* G.S. 160A-311 (municipalities); G.S. 153A-274 (counties).

Recently the General Assembly has imposed additional limitations on two other enterprise activities—solid waste collection and cable television. A unit of local government may not "displace" a private company that is providing collection services for solid waste or recycled materials without providing appropriate notice and waiting at least fifteen months or providing due compensation to the displaced company.[9] Displacement of a private provider occurs when a local government either (1) takes any formal action to prohibit a private company from providing all or a portion of the collection services that the company is providing in the affected area or (2) uses availability fee or tax revenue to fund competing collection services. There are even more significant limitations on the provision of cable television services by a municipality, which effectively may prohibit a municipality that is not currently providing cable television services from establishing this enterprise activity.[10]

Interlocal Cooperation to Provide Enterprise Services

Counties and municipalities have largely co-extensive authority to provide most of the public enterprise services. Because of that, two or more local governments may enter into interlocal agreements authorizing one unit to provide services to citizens in the other unit or authorizing the units to jointly engage in the provision of services.[11] An interlocal agreement is a contract that sets forth the terms or conditions of service and payment and, as long as it does not conflict with state or federal law, governs the parties' relationship. State law limits a municipality to a forty-year contract for the supply of water and a thirty-year contract for the supply of other public enterprise services.[12] A county is not subject to the same term limits. Use of interlocal agreements to contract for water and sewer services between and among local governments is common practice. For example, Forsyth County and Winston-Salem have used this authority to create a joint agency, the City/County Utility Commission, to provide water, sewer, and solid waste services within their territories.[13] And the City/County Utility Commission has entered into interlocal agreements to provide these services in other area municipalities.

The authority to enter into interlocal agreements, however, only applies to the services that all parties to an agreement are allowed to provide. For example, a county could enter into an interlocal agreement to provide solid waste services to one or more other counties or municipalities, but it could not enter into an interlocal agreement to provide cable television (broadband) services.

Franchise Agreements

In addition to the interlocal agreement authority, a municipality also may enter into one or more franchise agreements with another government entity or a private entity[14] to provide any of the public enterprise services (except cable television and broadband).[15] A county may enter into franchise agreements only for solid waste collection and disposal.[16] The franchise authority includes the ability to prohibit any government or private provider from furnishing a public enterprise service within a unit's territorial boundaries without a franchise. A municipal or county board may use a franchise agreement to impose reasonable terms of service on a provider, and, except for solid waste, an agreement may authorize the operation of the franchised activity for up to sixty years.[17] (A solid waste franchise agreement

9. *See* G.S. 160A-327.

10. *See* G.S. Ch. 160A, Art. 16A.

11. *See* G.S. 160A, Art. 20. Note that counties and municipalities only may enter into interlocal agreements to provide services that both entities have statutory authority to provide.

12. G.S. 160A-322.

13. More information on the City/County Utilities Commission is available at www.cityofws.org/Home/Departments/Utilities/Articles/Utilities.

14. A privately owned public utility corporation may petition the state's Public Utilities Commission to provide services in a designated area. *See* G.S. Ch. 62, Art. 6.

15. G.S. 160A-319.

16. G.S. 153A-136.

17. Note that if a municipality is providing the services to another municipality under a franchise agreement, it is subject to G.S. 160A-322, which limits the time periods for contracts for the provision of water services to forty years and the provision of other public enterprise utility services to thirty years.

may not exceed thirty years.)[18] A municipality may assess franchise fees or taxes as part of its franchise agreements for airports,[19] off-street parking facilities,[20] and solid waste collection and disposal services.[21] There are no statutory limits on the amounts of the fees or taxes, but generally they must be reasonable and not unlawfully discriminatory. A municipality may not charge franchise fees or taxes for water,[22] sewer,[23] electric,[24] natural gas,[25] cable television,[26] and certain public transportation[27] services. A county likely may set a reasonable franchise fee or tax on solid waste collection or disposal providers.[28]

Other Public Enterprise Service Providers

Counties and municipalities are not the only authorized government providers of public enterprises. There are a number of limited-purpose government entities that can provide one or more of the public enterprise services. These other government entities often are created to serve regional populations that cut across municipal or county boundaries. For example, there are several government entities that are authorized to provide water and sewer services: (1) counties or two or more political subdivisions (such as municipalities or sanitary districts) can organize water and sewer authorities;[29] (2) any two or more political subdivisions in a county can petition the board of commissioners to create a metropolitan water or sewer district;[30] and (3) the Commission for Health Services can create a sanitary district to operate sewage collection, treatment, and disposal systems and water supply systems for the purpose of preserving and promoting public health and welfare, without regard for county or municipal boundary lines.[31] (Sanitary districts also may provide solid waste collection, fire protection, and rescue services.) There also are parking authorities,[32] public transportation authorities,[33] regional natural gas districts,[34] regional solid waste management authorities,[35] and various airport authorities and commissions.[36] The authorities, districts, and commissions may serve customers within a county or municipality directly or may contract with the unit of local government to furnish the utilities.

Regulating Public Enterprises

General Regulatory Authority

When public enterprise services are provided by counties and municipalities, they are *not* subject to regulation by the state's Public Utilities Commission. The Public Utilities Commission only has jurisdiction over privately owned utility companies. The General Assembly has accorded a county or municipal board "full authority to protect and regulate any public enterprise system belonging to or operated by it by adequate and reasonable rules."[37] The rules must be adopted

---

18. G.S. 160A-319; G.S. 153A-136.
19. G.S. 160A-211.
20. *Id.*
21. *Id.*
22. G.S. 105-116 (repealed July 1, 2014).
23. *Id.*
24. G.S. 105-116(e1).
25. G.S. 160A-211.
26. *Id.*
27. G.S. 20-97.
28. G.S. 153A-136.
29. *See* G.S. 162A, Art. 1.
30. *See* G.S. 162A, Arts. 4 and 5.
31. *See* G.S. 130A, Art. 2, Pt. 2.
32. *See* G.S. 160A, Art. 24.
33. *See* G.S. 160A, Arts. 25, 26, and 27.
34. *See* G.S. 160A, Art. 28.
35. *See* G.S. 153A, Art. 22.
36. *See* G.S. 63-4.
37. G.S. 160A-312(b); *see also* G.S. 153A-275(b).

by ordinance and must apply throughout the area in which the public enterprise service is provided. The legislature has bestowed on the state's Local Government Commission some oversight authority over the financial management of a county's or municipality's water or sewer system.

A local governing board may impose reasonable restrictions on who may connect to its public enterprise systems and how those connections are made. Furthermore, a unit may specify terms of continued service and may discontinue service to any customer if the conditions are not met. All of the regulations must be adopted by ordinance, and because most public enterprise services are provided under contract with a customer, regulations, restrictions, and other terms of service should be memorialized in a written contract as well. In fact, the more detailed the provisions in an enterprise service contract, the more protection afforded to a local government to deal with a customer who fails to live up to the terms of service.

Mandating Participation in Public Enterprise Services

Participation by a unit's citizens or others in public enterprise services generally is voluntary. A local government may, however, mandate use of the enterprises under certain circumstances. A municipality may require an owner of developed property (which includes one or more residential or commercial units) located both within its municipal boundaries and within a reasonable distance of any water line or sewer collection line owned or operated by the municipality to connect to the municipal system.[38] A municipality also may mandate participation in a stormwater enterprise[39] and in a municipal solid waste collection service if a property owner has not otherwise contracted with a private hauler.[40]

A county may require the owner of developed property (which includes one or more residential or commercial units) located within a reasonable distance of any water line or sewer collection line owned or operated by the county to connect to its system.[41] A county also may mandate participation in its stormwater enterprise.[42] Unlike a municipality, a county may not compel participation in a curbside solid waste or recycling collection program.

Using Public Enterprise Authority to Enforce Other Laws and Regulations

Questions often arise about whether a local unit may use its relationship with public enterprise customers to enforce other state or local rules or requirements. For example, if a unit provides water services to a customer who has not paid her property taxes, may the local government discontinue the water services until the property taxes are satisfied? Or, may a unit refuse to provide sewer services to a business that is operating without a required privilege license or to one that is not in compliance with the fire code? The answer to all of these questions is no. That is because when a local government owns, operates, or contracts for the provision of public enterprise services, it is acting in a proprietary capacity (as opposed to a governmental capacity).[43] The North Carolina Supreme Court has distinguished between the two functions as follows:

> Any activity . . . which is discretionary, political, legislative or public in nature and performed for the public good in behalf of the State, rather than to itself, comes within the class of governmental functions. When, however, the activity is commercial or chiefly for the private advantage of the compact community, it is private or proprietary.[44]

---

38. G.S. 160A-317(a). As discussed below, in lieu of requiring connection, the unit may impose a periodic availability fee on the property owner, not to exceed the minimum periodic service or administrative charge assessed on properties that are connected.

39. G.S. 160A-314.

40. G.S. 160A-317(b).

41. G.S. 153A-284.

42. G.S. 153A-277.

43. This distinction has two significant meanings. The first is that it allows a government more flexibility to operate a public enterprise like a private business entity. A local government still must operate within the confines of statutory authority, but that authority often is much broader in the public enterprise context, affording a unit much discretion in setting service terms. The second distinction is that it may have liability consequences for local governments. When a unit acts in a governmental capacity, it generally is immune from civil liability for torts arising out of the negligence of the unit's employees when acting within the scope of their employment. The state does not afford a local government immunity when it acts in a proprietary capacity.

44. Millar v. Town of Wilson, 222 N.C. 340 (1942).

The North Carolina Court of Appeals has held that a local government must not comingle its proprietary and governmental functions. Specifically, in *Dale v. City of Morganton*,[45] the court specified that the city's right to refuse a service it renders in its capacity as a public enterprise utility provider must be determined separately from the functions it performs in its role as a unit of local government. In that case, the city had supplied electricity and water to a certain house in a newly annexed area but later inspected the dwelling and found it unfit for human habitation. It subsequently cut off the electricity supply to the house and refused to reconnect the service. In its review of a challenge to the city's actions, the court concluded that a city could not deprive an inhabitant "otherwise entitled thereto, of light, water or other utility service as a means of compelling obedience to its police regulations, however valid and otherwise enforceable those regulations may be."[46]

Local Government Commission Oversight

The Local Government Commission (LGC) is a nine-member state body in the Department of State Treasurer.[47] The LGC approves most local government borrowing transactions and issues bonds on behalf of local units. The commission monitors the fiscal health of local units in the state. The General Assembly has empowered the commission to "issue rules and regulations having the force of law governing procedures for the receipt, deposit, investment, transfer, and disbursement of money and other assets [by local units] . . . ."[48] The LGC also may "inquire into and investigate the internal control procedures" and issue warnings to local units of any internal control deficiencies or violations of the LGBFCA."[49]

Under certain circumstances, the LGC is empowered to take more drastic action, including assuming "full control over a [local unit's] financial affairs . . . ."[50] The LGC becomes "vested with all the powers of the governing board as to the levy of taxes, expenditure of money, adoption of budgets, and all other financial powers conferred upon the governing board by law."[51]

In 2013, the General Assembly clarified and arguably expanded this authority in relation to a local unit's operation of water and sewer systems. The commission may assume full control of a unit's water or sewer system and assume all powers of the governing board as to the operation of the public enterprise if the system, for three consecutive fiscal years, experiences negative working capital, has a quick ratio of less than 1.0, or experiences a net loss of revenue.[52] Working capital is defined as "current assets, such as cash, inventory, and accounts receivable, less current liabilities. . . ."[53] A quick ratio of less than 1.0 "means that the ratio of liquid assets, cash and receivables, to current liabilities is less than 1.0."[54]

Funding Public Enterprises

User Fee Authority

As stated above, public enterprises tend to be funded mainly with user fees. Both counties and municipalities have parallel authority to impose "schedules of rents, rates, fees, charges, and penalties for the use of or the services furnished by any public enterprise . . . ." This authority is very broad. A local government unit may include in such rates and charges the capital costs associated with actual or anticipated growth, as well as operating expenses and depreciation.

45. 270 N.C. 567 (1967).
46. *Id.* at 573.
47. G.S. Ch. 159, Art. 2
48. G.S. 159-25(c).
49. *Id.*
50. G.S. 159-181(c).
51. *Id.*
52. S.L. 2013-150.
53. *Id.*
54. *Id.*

And the fees may be assessed on all users of the enterprise services, regardless of their property status. Unlike with property taxes, there are no statutory exemptions from paying user fees for government property or property used for educational, charitable, or religious purposes.[55]

With all this flexibility, local government officials face difficult decisions about who should pay and how much. County and municipal officials tend to adopt policies that relate elements of a system cost to particular revenue measures. Units almost always assess periodic (monthly or bimonthly) user charges on public enterprise service customers to fund operational elements of an enterprise system, and they often impose impact fees,[56] special assessments,[57] or other one-time fees for capital improvements or expansions. Many local governments also have implemented various block-rate fee structures—either charging increased (increasing-block) or decreased (decreasing-block) rates based on additional units of usage of an enterprise service. Finally, most local governments have categorized consumers into various classes for purposes of setting rate schedules that closely track the costs of providing the enterprise services.

User fee schedules are influenced by the policy prerogatives of a local government's governing board. Consequently, the numbers and types of classifications vary greatly among North Carolina's counties and municipalities. A local government that wishes to promote conservation may impose a different rate structure than one hoping to foster commercial or industrial development. Municipalities also may configure rates so as to encourage or discourage annexation of extraterritorial property.

Although local governments have broad discretion to accomplish these and other goals, there are some constraints on their power to set public enterprise rates. A unit may establish service classifications for purposes of charging different rates to different customer groups.[58] These classifications are subject to the common law of utilities, though.[59]

Under the common law, different rate classifications may reflect differences in the costs of providing services to certain customer groups. Additionally, rate classifications may be "based upon such factors as . . . the purpose for which the service or the product is received, the quantity or the amount received, the different character of the service furnished, the time of its use or any other matter which presents a substantial ground of distinction."[60] In other words, courts have upheld classifications for purposes of assessing different utility rates when there is a utility-based reason for the differentiation. However, classifications based on the type—or status—of the customer, or customer group, that do not relate to one of the above-listed purposes are not valid. For example, a local unit may assess a different rate for water used for irrigation purposes than for household or other commercial purposes (classification based on the purpose for

---

55. Note that a local government may have difficulty collecting stormwater fees from certain state entities. That is because unlike other enterprises, a unit need not have a contractual agreement with a "customer" before imposing a stormwater fee. The fee may be imposed on all real properties within the unit. Several state agencies have argued that they are shielded from paying the stormwater fee under the doctrine of sovereign immunity in the absence of a written contractual agreement with the local government.

56. An *impact fee* is a charge assessed on new development to fund capital improvements or services that are necessitated by the new development.

57. A *special assessment* is a charge levied against a subset of properties within a local government unit to fund a capital project that directly benefits those properties.

58. G.S. 160A-314; G.S. 153A-277.

59. For more information on utility ratemaking, see "Lawful Discrimination in Utility Ratemaking, Part 2: Classifying Extraterritorial Customers," *Local Finance Bulletin* No. 34 (Oct. 2006); "Lawful Discrimination in Utility Ratemaking, Part 1: Classifying Customers within Territorial Boundaries," *Local Finance Bulletin* No. 33 (Oct. 2006).

Note that the General Assembly has placed the following additional statutory restrictions on setting fees for stormwater services:

> Schedules of rates, fees, charges, and penalties for providing stormwater management programs and structural and natural stormwater and drainage system service may vary according to whether the property served is residential, commercial, or industrial property, the property's use, the size of the property, the area of impervious surfaces on the property, the quantity and quality of the runoff from the property, the characteristics of the watershed into which stormwater from the property drains, and other factors that affect the stormwater drainage system.

G.S. 160A-314; G.S. 153A-277.

60. *See* Wall v. City of Durham, 41 N.C. App. 649 (1979).

which the water is used), but it cannot charge a different rate to all farmers (classification based on status). A unit may vary its sewer rates based on the size of the house or the number of bathrooms (proxies for different costs or capacity demands), but it may not charge a different rate based on customer income levels (classification based on status). A unit may charge a different solid waste collection fee rate to all commercial customers than it does to residential customers (proxy for different capacity demands), but it may not charge a different rate to all churches or all nonprofit organizations (classification based on status.) Or, a unit may assess a different rate to customers who request service after a certain date (again, proxies for different costs or capacity demands), but it may not set rates based on the age of its customers (classification based on status).

One further statutorily sanctioned rate differentiation is between customers located within a unit's territorial boundaries and customers residing outside these boundaries. This authority applies to all public enterprise activities, although it is mainly used for water and sewer services. Counties and municipalities typically assess higher fees on extraterritorial customers. For municipalities, the rate differential often serves as an incentive for voluntary incorporation by customers in surrounding unincorporated communities.

General Fund Subsidies for Certain Utility Customers

Note that there are methods by which a local government may accomplish a purpose similar to discounting public enteprise rates, at least for certain customer groups. First, counties and municipalities are to "undertake programs for the assistance and care of [their] senior citizens" (defined as citizens who are least sixty years of age).[61] Under this authority, a county or municipality may establish a utility rate subsidy program for its senior citizens. The program must be established in the unit's General Fund (not its Enterprise Fund) but can be structured in a number of different ways. For example, the program may authorize a unit to transfer moneys from the General Fund to the Enterprise Fund to pay all or a portion of a qualifying senior citizen's utility bill. It also may set up a reimbursement system for utility customers from the General Fund. Additionally, a county or municipality may apply a rate subsidy program to all of its senior citizens, or it may limit the program to senior citizens at or below a certain income level or senior citizens who are disabled.

Second, counties and municipalities may undertake community development programs "concerned with . . . welfare needs of persons of low and moderate income."[62] Under this authority, a local unit likely may establish a utility rate subsidy program similar to the one described above but for low- or moderate-income citizens. Again, the unit must use General Fund moneys, not Enterprise Fund proceeds, to fund the subsidy program. The statutes do not define low or moderate income. However, local officials may wish to consult the Section 8 income limits established by the federal Department of Housing and Urban Development for guidance in determining qualifying income limits.

Process for Adopting Public Enterprise User Fees

Generally, the process for adopting public enterprise fees is simple. The governing board sets the fees in its annual budget ordinance or in a separate ordinance or resolution. With a few exceptions, there are no notice, public hearing, or other formal public comment requirements. The governing board also is free to change the fees at any time during the fiscal year.

There are additional procedural requirements to adopt a stormwater fee. The governing board must hold a public hearing and provide sufficient notice of that hearing.[63] There also are added procedural requirements for water and sewer charges that apply to new subdivision development. Unless the applicable fees are adopted in the unit's annual budget ordinance, the unit must give notice of the fees and provide an opportunity for public comment.[64]

61. G.S. 160A-497.

62. G.S. 153A-376; G.S. 160A-456.

63. G.S. 160A-314; G.S. 153A-277.

64. G.S. 160A-4.1; G.S. 153A-102.1.

Additional Financing Sources

In addition to imposing user fees, a local government is authorized to finance the cost of any public enterprise "by levying taxes, borrowing money, and appropriating any other revenues therefor, and by accepting and administering gifts and grants from any source on behalf thereof."[65] For accounting purposes, enterprise services often are accounted for in an Enterprise Fund, whereas general government activities and revenues are accounted for in the General Fund. Local governments are free to transfer any property tax proceeds or unrestricted revenues from the General Fund to an Enterprise Fund to finance the capital or operating costs of an enterprise activity.

Transferring Moneys from an Enterprise Fund to the General Fund

What about transferring moneys the other way—may a unit transfer funds from an Enterprise Fund to the General Fund? The answer is a little more complicated. There are two types of transfers. The first is a transfer of funds from the Enterprise Fund to the General Fund to reimburse the General Fund for administrative overhead expenses to support a public enterprise activity, such as covering a portion of the manager's and finance officer's salaries (which are paid out of the General Fund). A reimbursement is allowed to the extent that it represents actual expenses incurred (or reasonable approximations thereof) on behalf of the public enterprise.

The second type of transfer involves using revenue generated by a public enterprise activity to support other general government programs and functions. As to this type of transfer, state law specifies that

> [n]o appropriation may be made from a utility or public service enterprise fund to any other fund than the appropriate debt service fund unless the total of all other appropriations in the fund equal or exceed the amount that will be required during the fiscal year, as shown by the budget ordinance, to meet operating expenses, capital outlay, and debt service on outstanding utility or enterprise bonds or notes.[66]

Although the statute is written as a prohibition, it actually allows a local government to transfer moneys from an Enterprise Fund to the General Fund to support general government functions as long as all of the enterprise activity expenses that will come due during the fiscal year are covered. In essence, it allows a unit to transfer profits generated by the enterprise activity to the General Fund to supplement other General Fund revenue sources. There are some further restrictions on moneys generated by some enterprise activities, though. For example, certain solid waste fee revenue and all stormwater fee revenue collected by counties and municipalities may not exceed the costs of providing the actual enterprise services.[67] This restriction effectively prohibits a local government from transferring most solid waste proceeds and all stormwater proceeds from an Enterprise Fund to the General Fund.

Collection Methods for Public Enterprise Revenues

Because most public enterprise services are voluntary, they often are governed by an express or implied contract between the government and each enterprise customer. And it is the contracting party that the government must look to for payment for enterprise services. Sometimes payment is collected before services are rendered. In many cases, however, and particularly for utility services, customers are billed after the services are received. What happens when a customer fails to pay? The following collection remedies are at a local unit's disposal.

65. G.S. 160A-313; *see also* G.S. 153A-276.
66. G.S. 159-13(b)(14).
67. *See* G.S. 160A-314; G.S. 160A-314.1; G.S. 153A-277; G.S. 153A-292.

Disconnecting Services

A local unit generally may disconnect public enterprise services at the property or premises where the delinquency occurred.[68] A county- or municipal-owned or operated enterprise must wait ten days from the date the account becomes delinquent to suspend service. If a government operates more than one public enterprise and includes the fees for multiple public enterprises on the same bill, the governing board may adopt an ordinance ordering partial payments. That means that if a customer does not satisfy the bill in full for all enterprise services, the governing board determines what fees are paid first, and a unit may disconnect any services that remain unpaid (after the ten-day waiting period). Typically a unit orders the payments such that water service is paid for last because it is more essential than other public enterprise services.

Civil Suit

A local unit may institute a civil suit against the contracting party to recover the amounts owed. The statute of limitations for collecting delinquent water, electric, and natural gas payments is four years.[69] The statute of limitations for collecting delinquent sewer, cable television, stormwater, and solid waste payments is three years.[70] The statute of limitations is the time period in which the unit must institute suit in order to collect on the debt.

Debt Set-Off

Another collection option is to submit the claim to the state's debt set-off program for recovery against the contracting party's state income tax return or state lottery winnings, if any.[71] The amount owed must exceed $50 to be eligible for debt set-off, and the unit must follow the detailed statutory procedural requirements to participate in the program.

Prohibited Collection Methods

There are some collection actions that a local utility provider is legally prohibited from taking. A local government may not place a lien on the property where enterprise services are provided. It also may not hold anyone other than the contracting party liable for the enterprise debts.[72] If, for example, a tenant establishes an account for water service with the local government, the tenant is the contracting party. That means that if the tenant defaults on his or her water payments, the local government may enforce collection only against the tenant. It may not proceed against the property owner. The unit also may not refuse service to a new tenant at the property where the delinquency occurred. This action would be akin to holding the new tenant liable for the former occupant's debt.

Finally, a local government generally may not refuse service to a delinquent former customer at a new property or premises. Although there is very little case law addressing this issue, a unit may be able to refuse future service if it has adopted a detailed written policy stating that the public enterprise service is conditioned on satisfaction of all previously owed (and still legally collectible) debts to the government.

---

68. G.S. 153A-277(b); G.S. 160A-314(b). Note that if a customer has filed for bankruptcy, a utility provider may not disconnect service, at least for a period of time. *See* 11 U.S.C. 366.

69. *See* G.S. 25-2-725.

70. *See* G.S. 1-52. State law allows solid waste fees to be billed on the property tax bill. *See* G.S. 153A-293; G.S. 160A-314.1. If a unit chooses this billing method, the unit may use the same collection remedies available to collect delinquent property taxes, and the statute of limitations for civil suits is ten years.

71. *See* G.S. 105A.

72. Under very limited circumstances, a local government may add the amount owed by the delinquent former customer to the bill for services provided at a new property (and disconnect services at the new property for nonpayment) if the former customer resides at the new property receiving the services, even if the former customer is not the contracting party for services at the new property. *See* G.S. 160A-314; G.S. 153A-277.

Discontinuing a Public Enterprise Service Altogether

As stated above, a local government is not required to provide any public enterprise services. If, however, a municipality chooses to furnish one or more of the services, there are some restrictions on discontinuing the services altogether. State law prohibits a municipality from selling, leasing, or discontinuing an electric power generation, transmission, or distribution system; a gas production, storage, transmission, or distribution system; or a public transportation system unless the proposed transaction is first approved in a voter referendum.[73] A municipality may, but is not required to, hold a referendum on a sale, lease, or discontinuance of a water treatment or distribution system or a wastewater collection or treatment system.[74] A voter referendum is not required (or authorized) before the sale, lease, or discontinuation of airports, off-street parking systems, solid waste collection or disposal systems, or cable television.[75] A county is free to sell, lease, or discontinue any of its public enterprise functions without voter approval.[76]

About the Author

Kara A. Millonzi is a School of Government faculty member specializing in the areas of municipal and county finance law, special assessments, utility finance law, solid waste finance law, and public school finance law.

73. G.S. 160A-321(a).
74. G.S. 160A-321(b).
75. *See* G.S. 160A-321; G.S. 160A-340.1(b).
76. *Cf.* G.S. 153A-283 ("In no case may a county be held liable for damages for failure to furnish water or sewer services.").

Chapter 31

Solid Waste Services

Richard B. Whisnant

History

Solid waste collection and disposal (once called *garbage collection and disposal*)[1] are services that citizens have come to expect from North Carolina local governments. Over much of the state's history, these services would be more accurately described as "collection and removal"; there was no disposal in the manner now considered essential. Removal was frequently to open dumps, sometimes with burning to reduce the accumulation of waste. Many of these historical open dumps have contaminated groundwater on which people rely for drinking water, and their cleanup remains a major policy problem for the state. Solid waste collection and disposal are now much more automated, capital intensive, and highly regulated than they were historically.

The *Municipal Year Book* for 1902[2] provided brief descriptions of garbage services for the state's twenty-four largest cities. A sample of the entries indicates the range of practices at that time:

> Concord: "Collected by contract; used as fertilizer."
> Durham: "Collected by day-labor; dumped."
> Goldsboro: "Collected by day-labor; hauled out of city."
> Greensboro: "Collected by day-labor; cremated."
> Raleigh: "Collected by day-labor; hauled to city farm and burned."
> Winston and Salem: "Collected by contract and day-labor; burned."

The state first offered significant technical assistance regarding solid waste to local governments in the 1930s, through the State Board of Health's Sanitary Engineering Division.[3] Government paid increased attention to waste disposal after World War II, starting with moves to replace open dumps with sanitary landfills—landfills in which clean dirt

---

1. For an excellent early history of American public solid waste services, see Martin V. Melosi, *The Sanitary City: Urban Infrastructure in America from Colonial Times to the Present* (Baltimore, Md.: Johns Hopkins University Press, 2000), 175–204.

2. M. N. Baker, ed., *The Municipal Year Book, 1902* (New York: Engineering News Publishing Co., 1902), 128–32.

3. North Carolina Department of Environment, Health, and Natural Resources (NCDEHNR), *North Carolina Recycling and Solid Waste Management Plan: Volume II, State Strategy* (Raleigh: NCDEHNR, Feb. 1992), 1–1.

or other cover was used on top of layers of garbage. The environmental movement, which may roughly be dated as starting with the publication of Rachel Carson's *Silent Spring* in 1962, increased attention to solid waste. A decade later the energy crisis arrived with the Middle East oil embargo, bringing increased public attention to conservation of all natural resources and underscoring the value of waste reduction and recycling.

Efforts to improve the management of wastes continued throughout the 1960s and 1970s, but progress was slow. A survey in 1968 found North Carolina local governments operating 479 disposal sites. Of these, only 23 were determined to operate in a manner that provided reasonable protection of the public health. State and local efforts were directed mostly at improving landfill operations. By the mid-1970s most of the open dumps had been abandoned or consolidated into 160 sanitary landfills.[4]

The Resource Conservation and Recovery Act (RCRA), passed by Congress in 1976, brought more attention to and increased restriction on waste disposal.[5] The major step affecting municipal landfills, however, came with the 1984 amendments to RCRA.[6] This legislation required states to implement permit programs to ensure that municipal solid waste landfills complied with federal criteria for such landfills, creating the "Subtitle D" or "lined landfill" that is now the norm for municipal solid waste.[7] The Environmental Protection Agency (EPA) has responsibility for determining whether state programs are adequate. North Carolina developed a permitting plan that EPA determined to be adequate on October 7, 1993.[8]

By October 1993, twenty lined, Subtitle D landfills (meeting the rules relating to siting, design, operation, financial assurance, closure, and postclosure care) had been permitted, and the applications of an additional nine landfills meeting the same standards were under review.[9] Of the twenty-nine entities involved as owners, one was a city, seven were private corporations, and twenty-one were county governments.[10] Throughout the 1990s North Carolina moved aggressively to close all nonlined municipal solid waste landfills and convert them to lined landfills. By fiscal year 1998–99, all municipal solid waste[11] disposed of in North Carolina was disposed of in lined landfills.[12]

Who Provides Solid Waste Services?

Since 1965 a major change in local responsibility for solid waste disposal has occurred. Before that time, most medium- and large-sized cities owned and maintained their own landfills or other disposal sites. State and federal programs to improve solid waste disposal encouraged a shift to fewer landfills that met higher environmental standards. As of 2011, the state had forty permitted municipal solid waste landfills.[13] Although the proportion of landfills that are owned and operated by private firms is increasing, most are still owned by counties. However, as of 2006, the percentage of

4. Warren Jake Wicker, "Other Enterprises: Solid Waste, Electricity, Gas, Airports, Public Transportation, and Stormwater," *Municipal Government in North Carolina* (Chapel Hill: Institute of Government, University of North Carolina at Chapel Hill, 1996), chap. 25.

5. U.S.C. §§ 6901–6992 (1995).

6. *Id.*

7. 40 C.F.R. § 258 (1995).

8. 58 Fed. Reg. 52,305 (Oct. 7, 1993).

9. Report of Dexter R. Matthews, chief, Solid Waste Section, Division of Solid Waste Management, to the Environmental Management Commission, Oct. 28, 1993.

10. *Id.*

11. The statute defines "municipal solid waste" as "any solid waste resulting from the operation of residential, commercial, industrial, governmental, or institutional establishments that would normally be collected, processed, and disposed of through a public or private solid waste management service. Municipal solid waste does not include hazardous waste, sludge, industrial waste managed in a solid waste management facility owned and operated by the generator of the industrial waste for management of that waste, or solid waste from mining or agricultural operations." Section 130A-290(a)(18a) of the North Carolina General Statutes (hereinafter G.S.).

12. NCDENR, *North Carolina Solid Waste Management: Annual Report, July 1, 1998–June 30, 1999* (Raleigh: NCDENR, 2000).

13. NCDENR, *North Carolina Solid Waste and Materials Management Report FY 2010–2011* (Raleigh: NCDENR, Jan. 2012), http://portal.ncdenr.org/web/wm/sw (retrieved Apr. 24, 2012).

permitted landfill *capacity* in the state represented by private landfills had reached or exceeded 50 percent. As discussed further below, in addition to municipal solid waste landfills, several other important types of solid waste facilities operate within the state: facilities for industrial waste, construction and demolition waste, land-clearing waste, scrap tires, medical waste, compost, and septage as well as transfer stations permitted to receive and redistribute waste to its ultimate disposal location.

Private parties must obtain a franchise (not necessarily an exclusive franchise) from local governments with jurisdiction over proposed landfill sites to be owned by the private party.[14] The process for cities and counties to enter into franchises for landfills and to approve proposed landfill sites has grown more complicated with the passage of several statutes in the 1990s and 2000s as well as with the overall change in the private market for waste. In general, cities and counties can award franchises, exclusive or nonexclusive, of up to thirty years for waste collection and/or disposal.[15] Local governments with jurisdiction over landfill sites have the power to give or withhold local government approval for the sites, based on local concerns, such as land use planning consistency. Under a Department of Environmental and Natural Resources (DENR) rule, a public meeting to give details about the proposed site is required before that approval is given.[16] The waste management statutes provide only a few details that must be included in franchise agreements, such as the population to be served, a description of the volume and characteristics of the waste stream, and a projection of the useful life of the landfill.[17] Passage of S.L. 2006-193 established much more complex requirements for a local government that wants to "displace" an existing franchisee or waste collection service prior to the end of a franchise term.[18]

Typically each landfill serves several cities as well as unincorporated areas of a county. Many serve more than one county, and the newer, large private landfills serve several counties and cities as well as waste generators outside the state.[19] Some of the county-owned landfills are operated by the county, a few by a city, and some by private firms under contract with a county or with two or more cities and counties jointly. Usually each local unit makes some payment to meet its share of the cost. The payments may be based on population, the quantity of waste, or a negotiated share. In a few counties the landfill is county-operated and financed, and no charge is made to either cities or private haulers that use it.

Regulation of Solid Waste and Its Market

The North Carolina requirements for landfills are a major part of the state's solid waste program. The basis for the program is found in Chapter 130A, Article 9, of the North Carolina General Statutes (hereinafter G.S.), originally enacted in 1989 but the subject of numerous amendments since then. Rules covering the collection and the disposal of solid wastes, prepared by the Division of Solid Waste Management within DENR, may be found in Title 15A, Subchapter 13B, of the North Carolina Administrative Code. Landfills for municipal solid waste are, however, by no means the only important type of solid waste facility used or regulated by state and local government in North Carolina.

As the municipal waste market has grown more regional and national in scope, with waste traveling much farther to its eventual disposal site, the "transfer station" has become an important part of the waste handling system for many

14. G.S. 130A-294(b1)(3).

15. G.S. 153A-136(a)(3) (counties); 160A-319 (cities).

16. N.C. Admin. Code tit. 15, ch. 13B, § .1618.

17. G.S. 130A-294(b1)(4).

18. S.L. 2006-193, codified inter alia at G.S. 160A-37.3 and 160A-327.

19. In a series of decisions construing the "dormant" Commerce Clause of the U.S. Constitution, the Supreme Court established that solid waste is an article of commerce and cannot be unduly discriminated within its flow across state and county boundaries. *See, e.g.,* C&A Carbone, Inc. v. Town of Clarkstown, 511 U.S. 383 (1994); Fort Gratiot Sanitary Landfill, Inc. v. Michigan Dep't of Natural Res., 504 U.S. 353 (1992); City of Philadelphia v. New Jersey, 437 U.S. 617 (1978). However, in *United Haulers Ass'n, Inc. v. Oneida–Herkimer Solid Waste Management Authority,* 550 U.S. 330 (2007), the Court greatly narrowed the *Carbone* decision by allowing states and local governments to control and direct the flow of solid waste to public facilities.

communities. A transfer station is a facility for moving waste from local collection trucks or containers to longer-haul trucks, trains, or barges. "Land-clearing" and "inert" debris is solid waste generated by land clearing that is virtually inert; such debris does not have to be disposed of in Subtitle D landfills. Similarly, much construction and demolition waste is disposed of in special facilities or cells of Subtitle D landfills with less rigorous regulatory requirements. However, some construction debris (for example, asbestos-containing material or lead paint residue) is itself hazardous and subject to special, stringent regulatory requirements. Medical waste began to be separately regulated in the 1990s given the concern for infectious disease transmission. Several types of recycling facilities, such as oil reclaiming and battery handling facilities, are provided for under the regulations. In the 1980s and 1990s the state went through difficult and ultimately unproductive attempts to site disposal facilities for low-level radioactive and hazardous waste. The broader world of solid waste collection and disposal in North Carolina includes all these categories, but the principal source of local government attention continues to be residential and commercial municipal solid waste.

North Carolina has historically been fairly aggressive in creating bans on the landfilling of waste streams that are usually suitable for recycling; current bans include used oil, yard trash (except in special facilities), white goods, antifreeze, aluminum cans, scrap tires, lead-acid batteries, motor vehicle oil filters, recyclable rigid plastic containers, wooden pallets, and oyster shells. Legislation in 2012 allowed a city or county to petition not to prohibit the last four of these waste categories in landfills based on economic hardship.[20] North Carolina has special programs for disposal of white goods and scrap tires, involving fees paid on purchase of new merchandise and special funds set up to handle these waste streams.

Solid waste legislation in 1989 and 1991 put in place a state and local planning and reporting system that was intended to reduce waste generated in the state.[21] Many elements of that system remain, even though the targeted waste reduction objective for the ten-year period ending in 2001 was missed by a wide margin. The legislation created a solid waste management hierarchy (from most to least desirable) as follows:

1. waste reduction at the source,
2. recycling and reuse,
3. composting,
4. incineration with energy production,
5. incineration for volume reduction,
6. disposal in landfills.

The numeric goal for the reduction of waste going into landfills was set at 40 percent for the period from July 1991 to July 2001. Each county, along with cities that were not working cooperatively with a county, was required to submit a solid waste management plan showing how it would achieve this 40 percent reduction. At the end of the ten-year period, only Allegheny, Cleveland, Martin, and Orange counties had attained the goal, and per capita solid waste generation had in fact increased significantly statewide.

The state began preparing a solid waste management plan and updating it every three years. Counties were to prepare a plan consistent with the state plan. Cities were to cooperate in the preparation of county plans or to prepare one of their own. In 2013, however, the legislature removed the requirement for local solid waste plans.[22] Counties and cities still must report to the state on their solid waste management activities by year end. For fiscal year 2010–11, 100 counties and 544 cities submitted annual reports. A status report on solid waste management in North Carolina is prepared each year by the Department of Environment and Natural Resources, Division of Waste Management, as required by G.S. 130A-309.06, and this annual report is a very useful summary of solid waste practices.

The legislature made other changes to solid waste laws in 2013 as part of its regulatory reform efforts. Local governments lost authority to regulate storage, retention, and use of non-hazardous materials like asphalt pavement and shingles unless those materials were within two hundred yards of residential districts. The state scaled back its efforts

20. G.S. 130A-309.10. Petitions to allow certain waste streams to be landfilled due to economic hardship are authorized at G.S. 130A-309.10(f2).

21. *See* S.L. 1989-784, S.L. 1991-621.

22. S.L. 2013-409.

to review proposed new solid waste disposal facilities for their environmental justice impacts. Several technical siting and operational requirements for landfills were reduced. The legislature eased an existing requirement that solid waste collection equipment had to be "leak proof," instead mandating only that it be "leak resistant."[23] The political specter of leaking trash trucks prompted the governor to respond to this last regulatory reform by issuing an executive order asserting that law enforcement would continue to cite leaking trucks despite the new legislation.[24] In 2014, the legislative Environmental Review Commission proposed legislation to "terminate" this executive order, setting up a potential constitutional and political struggle over the power to regulate solid waste in North Carolina.[25]

Trends in Solid Waste Services

A comparison of the 1992,[26] 2002,[27] and 2012[28] reports on the status of solid waste management in North Carolina gives a good picture of trends in solid waste management in the state:

- Some 6.8 million tons of municipal solid waste were generated in North Carolina in 1992. This was approximately one ton per capita per year. By 2002, total tons of waste had risen to 10.2 million, approximately 1.23 tons per capita per year. As of 2012, the total tonnage had dropped to 9.4 million tons, with per capita disposal dropping below 1 ton. However, this drop was driven both by the severe economic slump from 2008 through 2011 as well as by changes in waste generation in the state.
- Sixty local governments—twenty-two counties and thirty-eight cities—had source reduction programs under way in fiscal year 1992. One hundred twelve had programs in 2002, but the state reported that interest in and commitment to source reduction had "stagnated." By 2012, the number of source reduction programs was 108.
- In fiscal year 1992, local governments reported recycling 433,695 tons of materials. By fiscal year 2002, total recycled tonnage had increased to 1,173,082, but the state reported that several local governments had ceased their recycling operations and that total tonnage and the recovery ratio (recycling:disposal) had flattened out. By 2012, however, the number of curbside recycling programs reached a record high of 28, serving more than 1.68 million households across the state. Tonnage increased to 1,324,716 tons, and the recovery ratio was at an all-time high.
- At the end of fiscal year 1992 there were 110 municipal solid waste landfills, 150 land-clearing and inert debris landfills, 9 incinerators, 14 yard-waste composting facilities, 11 mixed-waste processing facilities, and 94 scrap tire collection sites with permits in North Carolina. In 2002, there were only 40 operational municipal solid waste landfills. The state did not report that year on the total numbers of other permitted facilities, but in general, the numbers of land-clearing and inert debris, composting, mixed-waste processing, and yard-waste composting facilities have increased over time, as municipal solid waste landfills and incinerators have decreased (and the remaining municipal solid waste landfills have become much larger). By 2012, 40 municipal solid waste landfills were still operational.

---

23. S.L. 2013-434 (H.B. 74), secs. 50, 59, 59.1, and 59.2. See also S.L. 2013-25 for eased restrictions on construction and demolition landfill siting and S.L. 2013-55 for special rules on demolition waste for energy generating facilities.

24. N.C. Exec. Order 22 (Aug. 22, 2013).

25. See http://www.ncleg.net/gascripts/DocumentSites/browseDocSite.asp?nID=12&sFolderName=\2013-2014%20ERC%20 Documents\Commission%20Meetings\6%20-%20April%209%202014\Handouts%20and%20Presentations (accessed April 15, 2014) for draft bill entitled "Terminate Certain Executive Orders."

26. NCDEHNR, *North Carolina Solid Waste Management: Annual Report, July 1, 1991–June 30, 1992* (Raleigh: NCDEHNR, Dec. 12, 1993).

27. NCDENR, *North Carolina Solid Waste Management: Annual Report, July 1, 2002–June 30, 2003* (Raleigh: NCDENR, Dec. 12, 2004).

28. NCDENR, *N.C. Solid Waste and Materials Management Report FY 2010–2011* (Raleigh: NCDENR, 2012), http://portal.ncdenr.org/web/wm/sw (retrieved Apr. 24, 2012).

- In 1992 there were 17 permitted transfer facilities in the state. As of February 2002 there were 77 permitted transfer facilities, the 353 percent increase from 1992 showing clearly the direction that solid waste handling has gone. The state did not report on the number of transfer facilities in its FY 2010–11 annual report.

Although cities have broad authority to provide solid waste services both inside and outside their boundaries, only a few have provided service outside. Those few have usually done so only within a limited area near their boundaries. North Carolina cities historically provided the collection service with city employees. But a 1993 survey by the North Carolina League of Municipalities (NCLM) found that an increasing number of cities were contracting with private firms to provide collection services.[29] As of the 2005 NCLM survey, of 259 responding cities, 55 percent used a city-paid contractor for residential solid waste, while only 41 percent used city employees.[30] Some small cities provide no collection service; citizens and businesses are served under individual agreements with private collectors.

Collection frequency for residential areas varies from one to three times per week. At one time, most cities collected twice a week. The 1993 NCLM survey found over 60 percent of the cities collecting household wastes once a week. By the time of the 2005 NCLM survey, 81 percent had gone to once a week collection.

At one time most cities collected solid waste from the rear of the house in residential areas, but the 1993 NCLM survey found that over two-thirds of the cities were collecting from the curb. As of 2005, the percentage of responding cities with curbside collection had risen to 80 percent. The advent of large-capacity roll-out containers made the switch feasible (but not always without political fallout). Curb collection costs the city less than collection from the backyard because the resident helps to move the waste. Of sixteen cities participating in the School of Government's benchmarking project in 2005, which included most of the larger cities in the state, only two provided backyard service, and their average cost per ton for residential refuse collection was $138. The average cost for curbside cities was $85 per ton.[31] Most cities with curb collection make special provisions for people who are physically unable to move their waste to the curb.

Similar differences also prevail with respect to collection from commercial and industrial establishments and collection of leaves, household furnishings, recyclables, and other special items. Cities whose citizens have agreed to separate their own recyclables before they are collected have generally lower costs than cities where recyclables are all lumped and centrally sorted, although the technology for these central materials recovery facilities (MURFs) continues to improve, and citizens are more willing to recycle if they do not have to keep materials separated.[32] Large cities usually require commercial establishments, apartment units, and other places with lots of waste to use central containers (dumpsters) that can be handled with special transport equipment, and most cities do not collect wastes from manufacturing facilities or from construction sites or clearings, leaving this service to private firms or collectors. Most cities do remove dead animals. A local government's policies, practices, and regulations relating to collection, storage, and control of solid wastes are usually set forth in an ordinance. The ordinance typically establishes the various classes of service; defines the minimum standards for containers and prescribes their placement; proscribes placement of leaves, refuse, and other banned materials into the landfill-bound waste stream; specifies charges and penalties; and defines the wastes to be collected.

In the past, the role of counties in the collection of solid waste was to do nothing, to license or franchise private haulers in areas not served by municipal collectors, or to provide collection sites at various locations around the county

29. Lee M. Mandell and David S. Kaplan, *What Are We Doing with Garbage: 1993?* (Raleigh: North Carolina League of Municipalities, 1994). The survey covered some 75 percent of cities with populations above 2,500 and about 30 percent of cities below that population level.

30. Lee M. Mandell and Owen Franklin, *What Are We Doing with Garbage—2005?* (Raleigh: North Carolina League of Municipalities, Dec. 2005). The survey covered 62 percent of cities with solid waste operations.

31. Calculated by the author from North Carolina Benchmarking Project, *Final Report on City Services for Fiscal Year 2004–2005: Performance and Cost Data* (Chapel Hill: School of Government, University of North Carolina at Chapel Hill, 2006).

32. For cost figures, see *Final Report on City Services for Fiscal Year 2004–2005: Performance and Cost Data* (Chapel Hill: School of Government, University of North Carolina at Chapel Hill, 2006). Two cities in the group of sixteen participating in the project in fiscal year 2004–05 had commingled recycled pickup; their cost per ton averaged $248 compared to the other fourteen cities' average of $178 per ton.

(sometimes called the "green box" system after the green dumpsters used to receive the waste). Most counties have moved away from the green box system and have instead chosen to have fewer, staffed, collection centers. At these centers, containers are provided for recyclable materials as well as for waste that is to be buried or burned. Under the current state planning and waste reduction requirements, doing nothing is rarely an option. As noted above, counties have ample legal authority to license or franchise private haulers, including authority to grant exclusive franchises and set the fees to be charged by private haulers. They may also require the separation of recyclable materials and participation in recycling programs.[33]

Just as the collection of solid waste has traditionally been a municipal function, waste disposal has historically been a county function. At one time, most counties operated a county-owned landfill. This is no longer the typical pattern for two reasons: (1) it has become more and more difficult to site a landfill for political and environmental reasons and (2) the federal requirements for Subtitle D landfills have made the construction and operation of landfills more difficult (from an engineering standpoint) and much more expensive. As a consequence, there is a trend for counties to dispose of waste in large, privately owned and operated landfills that serve several cities and counties or for several counties to operate jointly a landfill either through contractual arrangements or by creating a regional authority. S.L. 2007-550, the Solid Waste Management Act of 2007, added further procedural and technical requirements for new landfills, further raising the cost of new facilities and thus increasing the value of existing landfill capacity.

Financing of Solid Waste Services and Programs

Solid waste management activities are public enterprises within the meaning of G.S. Chapter 153A, Article 15, and G.S. Chapter 160A, Article 16. Therefore, local governments may finance solid waste services, including recycling programs, by levying property taxes, borrowing money, accepting grants, imposing fees and charges, or by any combination of these financing arrangements. More extensive discussion of financing solid waste enterprises is contained in Chapter 30, "Public Enterprises."

About the Author

Richard B. Whisnant is a School of Government faculty member. The author wishes to thank William A. Campbell and the late Warren Jake Wicker, the authors of this chapter in earlier editions, whose work is reflected in the current version, as well as Jeffrey A. Hughes, director of the UNC Environmental Finance Center, for his suggestions on this chapter.

33. G.S. 153A-136.

Chapter 32

Transportation: Streets, Parking, Public Transportation, and Airports

Richard D. Ducker and David M. Lawrence

Streets

The development of roads and streets has a long history in North Carolina.[1] Many years before the arrival of the first European settlers, Native Americans had developed a system of trails throughout much of the state. The settlers brought with them a well-developed appreciation of the importance of roads in the advancement of any society. Despite this appreciation and increasing attention to road building, some 300 years passed before North Carolina could lay claim to being the Good Roads State.

In 1715 the colonial legislature adopted a comprehensive plan for laying out roads, constructing bridges, and establishing and maintaining ferries. Responsibility for the development of the plan was placed with local governments—

1. The information in this section is drawn from Hugh Talmage Lefler and Albert Ray Newsome, *North Carolina, The History of a Southern State*, 3rd ed. (Chapel Hill: The University of North Carolina Press, 1973); Capus Waynick, *North Carolina Roads and Their Builders*, vol. 1 (Raleigh, N.C.: Superior Stone Company, 1952); and Albert Coates's history of North Carolina roads and streets in "Report of the State-Municipal Road Commission," *Popular Government* 17 (Dec. 1950/Jan. 1951): 10–13.

counties and cities—where it remained for more than 200 years. The opening of the twentieth century brought the automobile and increased demand for better roads. (The first cross-country trip by automobile was made in the summer of 1903—in seventy days. North Carolina first imposed license fees for autos in 1909.) Inspired by the good macadam roads built by George Vanderbilt on his Biltmore estate, the Good Roads Association of Asheville and Buncombe County was organized. Later, it expanded into a statewide organization. The association's efforts were initially directed at improving roads at the county level. Increased auto travel and the prospect of federal aid (which started in 1916) resulted in the creation of the State Highway Commission in 1915 with an appropriation of $10,000. It was charged with appointing a state highway engineer who advised counties on their road-building responsibilities.

In 1921 the state assumed responsibility from the counties for the roads connecting the 100 county seats and running through all other cities and towns with a population of 3,000 or more.[2] This first statewide system, which totaled 5,500 miles, was financed by a combination of license fees and a gasoline tax of 1 cent per gallon.

Between 1921 and 1927 the state issued $115 million in road bonds to build and improve the system. The Great Depression found counties heavily in debt for roads and schools. In 1931, under the leadership of Governor O. Max Gardner, the state took over the remaining county roads—some 45,000 miles.[3]

The 1931 action relieved counties of all road responsibilities except for retirement of their road debt, which was to take another twenty-five years for some counties to eradicate. The move did nothing for cities and towns, however. They remained responsible for all the roads and streets within their boundaries.

City officials started working for state aid for city streets. The North Carolina General Assembly responded in 1935 with an appropriation of $500,000 to assist cities in maintaining city streets carrying state highways. Over the years the appropriations increased, reaching $2.5 million in 1949.

The 1949 General Assembly, the first of Governor Kerr Scott's administration, took two major actions to improve highways. First, it authorized (and the voters approved) the issuance of $200 million in road bonds to improve rural ("farm-to-market") roads, as promoted by Governor Scott.[4] The proceeds financed the paving of 12,000 miles of rural roads and the stabilizing of another 15,000 miles. Second, it created the State-Municipal Road Commission. The commission's recommendations led in 1951 to allocation of a part of the state's gasoline tax to municipalities for use on local streets that were to remain municipal responsibilities.[5] The same legislation transferred to the state full responsibility for the construction and the maintenance of some 2,300 miles of roads and streets *within* cities that were part of the state highway system but were being constructed and maintained by cities.

Another major highway action came in 1989 during Governor James Martin's administration with the establishment of the North Carolina Highway Trust Fund.[6] This legislation increased motor fuel and other vehicle taxes and fees to finance a multibillion-dollar highway improvement program from the fund's current receipts. The program funded improvements that would place more than 90 percent of the state's population within ten miles of a four-lane highway, build urban loops, and add funds for rural secondary roads and municipal street aid. However, the legislation also favored rural projects over urban projects and encouraged legislative involvement in project selection.

North Carolina's Streets and Highways

To understand how cities manage their municipal street systems, it is necessary to understand the state's role in managing its own system. (As was noted earlier, counties have no responsibility for maintaining streets under North Carolina's transportation system.) The state system may be defined in terms of the roads that are maintained by the North Carolina Department of Transportation (NCDOT). The system, thus, includes five types of routes: (1) Interstate routes, (2) Interstate business routes, (3) U.S. routes, (4) "N.C. routes," and (5) "state secondary routes." The order of

2. 1921 Pub. Law ch. 2.
3. 1931 Pub. Law ch. 145.
4. 1949 N.C. Sess. Laws ch. 1250.
5. 1951 N.C. Sess. Laws ch. 260. This is the so-called Powell Bill.
6. 1989 N.C. Sess. Laws ch. 292, sec. 1.1, codified as N.C. Gen. Stat. (hereinafter G.S.) §§ 136-175 to -185, partially repealed by S.L. 2013-183 (H 817).

this list also suggests in a rough way the significance of the various categories of routes in handling traffic. The federal government provides the most substantial portion of the funding for the construction and maintenance of highways in the first three categories, although in each case the state provides some support. The first three categories, along with certain key state routes, comprise the National Highway System. The construction and maintenance of N.C. routes (which generally are state primary routes) and state secondary routes are funded by the state. The first three categories of routes and many of the N.C. routes, that is, both federal and state routes, comprise the state's primary highway system. Such a route may extend into and through a municipality as it connects certain municipalities with others, one area of the state with another, and one portion of the country with another. In contrast, most of the state's secondary road system is located outside municipal limits. Virtually all municipalities include at least one road or highway that is a N.C. route. Within the boundaries of larger North Carolina cities, it is often possible to find Interstate routes, Interstate business routes, U.S. routes, and N.C. routes. If a road or highway is one of these four types of routes, then the state (or the federal government) takes primary responsibility for the maintenance, improvement, and construction of such a route, wherever it is located. Municipalities, in turn, share responsibility with the state for state-maintained roads inside city limits and take full responsibility for the remaining public streets within town limits. Streets and highways, both inside and outside cities, are financed primarily from state and municipal shares of vehicle-related revenues. Each motorist, whether driving inside or outside cities in North Carolina, is contributing to the operation of the road or the street on which he or she drives through motor fuel and other taxes.

State, Metropolitan, and Municipal Transportation Planning

The financial and operational responsibility for public highways and streets in North Carolina is shared among the federal government, the state, and the state's municipalities. However, regional transportation planning organizations play a significant role in local transportation planning. Metropolitan planning organizations (MPOs) in North Carolina have been established in response to federal highway legislation,[7] which recognizes their role in urban areas. MPOs date to 1962 when the U.S. Congress initiated a requirement that a continuing, cooperative, and comprehensive transportation planning process had to be established for all urban areas with a population of over 50,000 in order to qualify for federal transportation funds. Each MPO is created by a memorandum of understanding among the affected local governments. There are seventeen MPOs in North Carolina ranging in size from the Goldsboro MPO to the Mecklenburg-Union MPO. An MPO typically includes not only territory within municipal limits but unincorporated urban areas, as well. Although MPO boards are typically composed primarily of local elected officials (known as transportation advisory committees), it is not uncommon for the staff of such organizations to come from the largest central city represented in the MPO.

Each MPO is expected to develop a comprehensive transportation plan that will serve present and anticipated travel demand in and around urban areas.[8] These comprehensive plans are multimodal in nature and include not only a highway or thoroughfare element but also transit and bicycle or pedestrian elements. Once completed, the plan must be adopted by the MPO and NCDOT so that it can serve as the basis for future improvements within the MPO. The plan also serves as the basis for determining which roads and streets will be part of the state highway system and which streets will be part of municipal street systems. Once the MPO plan is adopted, any municipality within the MPO yields its transportation planning and programming interests to the MPO. In other words, the MPO represents the interests of its municipalities to the NCDOT.

In addition, each municipality that is not a part of an MPO is also directed by statute to develop a comprehensive transportation plan using similar procedures. In the past five to ten years, a growing number of counties have participated in the transportation planning process, and more and more transportation plans include multiple local governments. Those cities and counties that are not part of an MPO are organized into rural planning organizations (RPOs).

A significant link has been forged between the development of transportation plans and the adoption of land development plans. Since 2001, NCDOT has been authorized to contribute to the development and adoption or amendment

7. 23 U.S.C. § 134.
8. G.S. 136-66.2(a).

of a transportation plan only if all of the local governments that will be party to the plan have adopted land development plans within the previous five years or are in the process of developing one. Similarly, NCDOT may not adopt or update a transportation plan until a local land development plan has been adopted.

Street and Highway Improvement Programming

In addition to developing transportation plans, MPOs also play in role in establishing funding priorities. MPOs typically submit regional project priority lists to NCDOT in advance of the state's development of its six-year State Transportation Improvement Program (STIP). Once adopted as part of the STIP, projects for each MPO are then incorporated into its Metropolitan Transportation Improvement Program (MTIP). The MTIP reflects the priorities, scheduling, and source of funding for improvement projects on state system roads in the metropolitan area. It may also reflect projects involving municipal streets.

The state takes primary responsibility for construction and maintenance of state thoroughfares located inside municipal limits. However, municipalities, particularly larger ones, sometimes contract with NCDOT to perform various maintenance tasks on these routes, including repair work and some reconstruction and widening projects. They may also contract to maintain highway signs, traffic control devices, and traffic signals on these state highways. NCDOT reimburses cities for this more routine work.

In other instances, however, a city may wish to improve a state thoroughfare running through it in a manner that suits the interests of the municipality but is unnecessary for the route to serve an interregional function. For example, a city may be interested in adding curbs and gutters, constructing sidewalks, adding lanes for parking, or making intersection improvements to integrate the thoroughfare better into the urban area. For a municipality to undertake these improvements, it must obtain the approval of NCDOT, but the cost must be borne entirely by the municipality. In addition, a city may agree with NCDOT to reimburse the costs for either improvement costs or the cost of additional rights-of-way for a STIP project if those features would not normally be included in the project by NCDOT.

In 1989 state law was changed to limit the ability of cities to contribute or share in the cost of improvements to the state highway system, except to the limited extent described above. Section 136-66.3 of the North Carolina General Statutes (hereinafter G.S.) reflected the view that large cities should not be able to influence the priority and funding of state projects shown on the STIP by offering to share the cost with the state. However, in 2000 North Carolina reversed course and began to allow cities fully to "participate" in the costs of a state project, but with the caveat that NCDOT may not allow such a practice to "cause any disadvantage" to a project elsewhere. In the case of a road in a new location, a city may share in the project cost by acquiring the right-of-way for a particular project or by contributing to the cost of construction. Equally important, because many state highway projects affecting municipalities are, when built, outside city limits, G.S. 136-66.3(c) provides clear authority for a municipality to "participate" in the costs of projects located outside as well as those located inside current municipal limits. What's more, counties may also participate in NCDOT improvement projects to the extent that the improvements are in addition to those that NCDOT would normally make.[9]

The Strategic Mobility Formula divides projects into three categories: statewide, regional, and division level. Projects of statewide significance compete for 40 percent of the available revenue. The selection process for this money depends entirely upon factors such as traffic volumes, accident statistics, effect on economic competitiveness, and freight movement. Regional projects compete for 30 percent of the available revenue, which is divided among seven regions on the basis of population. Each region is composed of two of the fourteen transportation divisions. Some 70 percent of the regional project rating is based on transportation and related data factors; 30 percent of the rating is based on project rankings developed by area transportation planning organizations and NCDOT transportation division personnel. Finally, S.L. 2013-187 calls for the remaining 30 percent to be shared among all fourteen divisions equally. Half of these ranking are based on data concerning safety, congestion, connectivity, and the like, and half are based on more subjective local rankings.

9. G.S. 136-66.3(e).

Once a project is included in the STIP, the environmental review and route selection processes begin. The Transportation Corridor Official Map Act is an important tool in protecting potential transportation corridors from being compromised by future development.[10] It allows any of several governmental entities (including the North Carolina Board of Transportation, as well as cities and counties that are party to a local transportation plan) to adopt and record an "official map" for a corridor for which functional plans have been completed and to "reserve" land for future acquisition. Once adopted, no building permit may be issued nor a subdivision plat approval granted for land encompassed within the protected corridor for a period of three years from the time a valid application for one of these permissions is submitted by an owner whose land is included within the corridor of land. In order for the corridor map reservation to remain valid, work on an environmental impact statement or preliminary engineering must be begun within one year after the map's adoption. The adoption of an official map gives the adopting entity the power to acquire land in advance of a determination of the specific route of the facility. The example of the southeastern segment of the Triangle Expressway that follows illustrates the difficulties highway planners have in protecting road corridors and evaluating the advantages and disadvantages of different routes.

Possible future locations for the southeastern segment were protected in the 1990s by NCDOT through the adoption of roadway corridor official maps. However, one primary corridor protected in the mid-90s involved certain environmental and transportation planning problems, so highway planners refocused their attention on two alternative routes for this portion of the expressway. A route alternative more to the north (the "red route") would cut through a relatively developed, populated area of southern Garner. Presentation of this red route to the public resulted in significant local opposition. As a result, in 2011 the General Assembly amended G.S. 136-89.183(a)(2)a. to prohibit consideration of that alternative. However, federal highway authorities determined that the environmental impacts of the red route should be formally considered as an alternative, even if a third route (the "orange route") was ultimately chosen as most appropriate. With the southeastern portion of the Triangle Expressway thus in limbo, the General Assembly in 2013 added sections 5.7 and 5.6 to S.L. 2013-183 (H.B. 817) to delete the 2011 language prohibiting the location of the expressway in the "red" corridor. This change will enable the federal environmental impact statement process to proceed for the southeastern segment of the Triangle Expressway and for the process to be expedited.

The North Carolina Turnpike Authority

The North Carolina Turnpike Authority is an important state transportation entity whose role is likely to grow. Established in 2002, the authority is empowered to construct state highway projects that are financed at least in part with tolls. The General Assembly has designated nine projects to be built by the authority. Remarkably, the identity of some of the projects has changed as the political complexion of the state has changed in the past several years. G.S. 136-89.183, which names the projects, was changed in 2013. It retains five projects: the Triangle Expressway (consisting of four individual segment projects) and the Monroe Connector. Three turnpike projects previously authorized in the statute, the Cape Fear Skyway, mid-Currituck bridge, and Garden Parkway (Gaston County), were specifically deleted along with the specific gap funding for the latter two. The four remaining projects, to be selected later, must meet a variety of requirements, be included in the STIP and appropriate local transportation plan, and be approved by affected MPOs and RPOs.

North Carolina toll projects must be authorized by the General Assembly prior to construction. No tolls may be charged on existing roads. Each toll project must be associated with an alternate route that is not subject to a toll. Tolls must be removed once any debt is repaid.

Municipal Street System Components

Streets

An ideal street network accommodates growth, is part of a system of transportation choices, and serves to define the physical characteristics of a city in a fundamental way. Streets play an important role in establishing a community's

10. G.S. 136-44.50 to -44.54.

image and serving as the framework for future land development. In this regard streets demonstrate how the community expects and prefers to grow. Streets reflect choices about whether the community is trying to become more compact and focused on growth. Streets reflect whether travelers enjoy a range of travel choices. Streets reflect the extent to which a city tries to encourage infill and revitalize older areas. Streets reflect how sensitive the community is to environmental protection values.

Many cities have systems for classifying streets and for establishing street design standards that aid in planning. A street classification system provides the framework, allowing a city to determine street capacity and manage traffic on the existing street grid and to plan the streets that will serve the community in the future. The street design standards established for various types of streets govern the terms under which a city will accept the dedication of a new street offered by a developer and the standards that a city commits to meeting in those instances when a city contracts to build a street itself.

One design issue concerns the street cross-section. Street rights-of-way typically accommodate more than just the paved area for vehicular travel. Where and how will various utility lines located within the right-of-way (or behind the right-of-way) be accommodated? Will the street be designed with curbs and gutters and a conventional storm sewer system or with a system of shoulders and swales? Will on-street parking be allowed? Is the traveled portion of the street designed to accommodate bicycles and scooters? Will sidewalks and crosswalks be provided to make the street pedestrian friendly? Will the right-of-way be landscaped? These concepts are embodied in the concept of "complete streets." NCDOT adopted a complete streets policy in 2009, which directs the department to consider and incorporate several modes of transportation when building new projects or making improvements to existing infrastructure.[11]

Another emerging issue is whether the street system promotes connectivity. Connectivity refers to the extent to which a system of streets provides multiple routes and connections between origins and destinations. Areas with high connectivity have multiple access points around the perimeters and a dense system of parallel routes and cross connectors within the area. A system of streets with high connectivity generally results in less traffic congestion, more convenient travel routes, and greater safety and often results in reduced travel time. High connectivity is associated with multiple connecting streets that carry moderate levels of traffic and directly serve adjacent land uses. Low connectivity systems are associated with a hierarchy of streets ranging from cul-de-sacs to freeways with each roadway serving a more specialized function. Such systems allow more privacy to owners of property served by more minor streets, as North Carolinians who live on a residential cul-de-sac know. Many of the state's small towns rely on a grid system of streets that still promotes high connectivity. However, the suburban form of development that has predominated in many urban areas since the 1970s has resulted in less connectivity and more circuitous travel. More recently the pendulum has swung back to simpler street systems that are designed with more connections.

A good local street system integrates the transportation system with the pattern of existing and expected pattern of land uses. Local streets provide access to residential, industrial, or commercial districts and probably represent the majority of the land-miles of a city's street network. Speeds and motor vehicle traffic volumes on these streets are low, providing a safe environment for pedestrians and cyclists. Most new local streets are built by developers.

Collector streets (sometimes classified as avenues) are the most common nonlocal street type. They link neighborhoods to commercial areas, connect intercity destinations, and, in some cases, traverse residential neighborhoods. In larger cities collector streets are often quite versatile. They may carry significant auto traffic while providing bike lanes, accommodating transit, and serving pedestrians. In metropolitan transportation plans collector streets are often classified as minor thoroughfares.

Arterials are intended to carry a considerable volume of through traffic and to allow minor access to smaller streets, land, and buildings. These thoroughfares are typically multilane, and access to them is often restricted in some way. Arterials with substantial landscaped medians are commonly referred to as boulevards. Four-lane urban thoroughfares require 90–120 feet of right-of-way and are built in a variety of divided or undivided forms.

---

11. *See* North Carolina Department of Transportation, "Complete Streets Planning and Design Guidelines," July 2012, www.completestreetsnc.org/wp-content/themes/CompleteStreets_Custom/pdfs/NCDOT-Complete-Streets-Planning-Design-Guidelines.pdf.

Sidewalks and Bikeways

In the past half century transportation systems have focused on promoting the safety and convenience of the motor vehicle, particularly the private automobile and the commercial truck. However, designing and building roads has become more complex. Transportation engineers now have to consider accessibility, utilities, landscaping, historic and community preservation, wetland mitigation, and other matters when designing roads. The result has been less space and fewer resources with which to work at a time when traffic volumes have been growing steadily. Proposals for bicycle and pedestrian facilities have been rejected because of these space and funding limitations and the perceived lack of demand. More recently, however, federal transportation legislation (e.g., the 1998 Transportation Equity Act for the 21st Century) has begun to recognize multiple modes of travel and encourage the fuller integration of bicycle facilities and pedestrian walkways into the construction of transportation projects of various types.

In North Carolina Powell Bill funds have been a primary source of municipal funding for bicycle facilities and pedestrian walkways. Municipalities have been authorized to use these funds for bikeways located within public street and highway rights-of-way since 1977, but for sidewalks only since 1994. More recently bicycle and pedestrian facilities have become part of transportation planning as well. In 2000 the North Carolina Board of Transportation adopted implementing policies that, among other things, encourage municipalities throughout the state to make bicycle and pedestrian improvements an integral part of local transportation planning. A year later, these policies were reflected in changes to G.S. 136-66.2. Prior to 2001, the statute required that a comprehensive thoroughfare plan be prepared and approved for each municipal and metropolitan area in North Carolina. Amendments adopted in 2001 require a comprehensive transportation plan be prepared and adopted, and now bicycle and pedestrian elements must also be included. Changes made in 2013[12] allow Powell Bill funds to be used by cities for greenways, as well as bikeways and sidewalks, and to be used for these facilities regardless of whether they are located within the public street right-of-way. Cities may also use funds for independent bicycle and pedestrian improvement projects inside town limits or within the area of the applicable MPO or RPO.

In the downtown area and in older residential parts of many cities, sidewalks have traditionally functioned as an integral part of the transportation system. Today the areas that are most likely to benefit from sidewalk improvements are higher-density residential and commercial areas, areas that are served by or are expected to be served by public transportation, mixed-use development, and school and recreational facilities. Sidewalks perform several functions. First, they provide safety by separating pedestrians from motor vehicle traffic. This is especially important where there are many pedestrians and vehicles, vehicle speeds are high, and lighting or visibility is poor. Second, sidewalks are a convenience to people who choose to walk wherever they want to go. Third, well-maintained sidewalks can improve the appearance of a community.

There are three major categories of bikeways: bike paths, bike lanes, and bike routes. A *bike path* is a paved way set aside for bicycles only and prohibited to motor vehicles. Bike paths are often inside the street right-of-way but are almost always clearly separated from the motor vehicle pavement by grade separations, plantings, or other barriers. They should also be separated from sidewalks. *Bike lanes* are usually part of the street pavement, but are separated from motor vehicle lanes by striping, small curbs, or other markings or barriers. *Bike routes* usually appear in areas of very light traffic and consist merely of signs to notify motorists that bicycles use the roadway.

Some of the most notable North Carolina projects that accommodate both the pedestrian and the cyclist are greenway projects. Many mid-sized and larger cities have developed greenways (i.e., liner parks along creeks or streams) that include shared-use paths that serve pedestrians, skaters, joggers, cyclists, and users of other nonmotorized vehicles. Most greenway projects, however, are located outside of public street and highway rights-of-way.

Measures for Financing Street and Sidewalk Improvements

North Carolina's cities use a variety of sources of funds in the construction and maintenance of streets and improvements within the street right-of-way. State aid that is earmarked for municipal streets is the primary source of moneys

12. S.L. 2013-183, sec. 3.1.

Table 32.1 Distribution of Powell Bill Funds to Cities

Year	Amount per Capita	Amount per Mile
1951	$ 1.51	$ 435.71
1961	1.92	453.12
1971	2.87	612.42
1982	12.69	845.67
1987	16.28	1,141.76
1990	19.09	1,368.88
1994	22.17	1,547.58
2005	23.20	1,709.23
2007	25.12	1,886.91
2009	19.57	1,589.20
2011	20.02	1,570.78
2013	20.62	1,632.91

Source: North Carolina Department of Transportation, Office of Inspector General, *2013 North Carolina State Street-Aid Allocations to Municipalities* (Raleigh, N.C.: NCDOT, 2014), 2.

for most municipal street programs. In addition, local property tax revenues and general revenues account for a modest portion of city expenditures. Special assessments, a third source, are important in street paving and reconstruction projects. A fourth measure for financing the construction of streets is through the use of developer exactions and contributions that a municipality procures through the land development regulatory process. Streets of this sort are built by developers and accepted by cities when complete. These transactions typically do not appear in the city budget since the municipality typically spends no money on such projects until they become part of the city street system. Counties may also use special assessments for NCDOT secondary roads and development exactions, as well.

General Local Taxes

All cities may levy taxes to finance street and sidewalk improvements.[13] The property tax is the chief local tax, although receipts from a city's auto licenses, privilege license taxes, and dog taxes may be used, as may revenues received from other governments, including community development grants and shared taxes, such as sales, franchise, and beer and wine taxes. All the local taxing measures are levied on the ability-to-pay principle. They are related to property ownership, an indicia that tends to represent financial capacity.

Powell Bill Funds

Ever since 1951 the state has shared part of its gasoline tax receipts with cities for use on city streets.[14] These moneys are called "Powell Bill funds" and are named after the sponsor of the bill in the General Assembly that established the revenue-sharing program. Table 32.1 charts the growth of Powell Bill distributions over the history of the legislation. Until 2013 these funds and some funds from the Highway Trust Fund that were distributed the same way constituted the primary source of revenue for municipal street construction and maintenance. Powell Bill funds were calculated as follows: A portion of the state gasoline tax equal to 1.75 cents per gallon was earmarked for annual distribution to cities in 1986. In addition, after certain adjustments were made, 6.5 percent of the funds in the Highway Trust Fund, launched in 1989, were also made available for municipal use. In 2013, however, the General Assembly changed the way state aid for municipal streets was distributed. The amount of Highway Fund revenues allocated to cities was

13. G.S. Ch. 160A, Art. 9.
14. G.S. 136-41.1.

changed from 1 3/4 cents per gallon subject to the motor fuels tax to 10.4 percent of the net amount generated by the fund during the prior fiscal year. Sponsors of the legislation claimed that these allocations were intended to ensure that municipalities received as much Powell Bill funding over the five years following 2013 as they would have received under prior formulas.

Powell Bill funding reached a high-water mark in 2007. In fiscal 2007–08, for example, adjusted available Powell Bill funds totaling about $93.0 million and Highway Trust Fund distributions totaling about $63.6 million, or a grand total of about $157.7 million, were disbursed to cities on October 1, 2007. Of that grant total, 75 percent of the money was distributed to a city on the basis of its population relative to others and 25 percent on the basis of the municipality's qualifying street mileage. Thus, in October 2007, about $118.2 million was distributed among 512 cities that collectively had a population of 4,709,218, resulting in a rate of $25.12 per city resident. An additional $39.4 million was distributed on the basis of the roughly 20,894 miles of qualifying city streets that were located in those 503 municipalities, resulting in a rate of about $1,886 per mile.

Tax collections and municipal distributions began to decline in 2008, reaching a bottom in 2010. By 2013 they still had not reached the levels of 2007–08. In 2013 the adjusted Powell Bill funds totaled $145,610,105. In October 2013 about $109.2 million was distributed among 507 municipalities with a collective population of 5,295,551, or $20.62 per resident. The 25 percent of the funds divided on the basis of mileage (22,293 miles of qualifying streets) resulted in a per mile rate of $1,632. Whether the new funding formula will result in growing future distributions remains to be seen.

Powell Bill funds are available for a wide range of purposes related to the construction, repair, and maintenance of municipal streets. However, the funds may also be used for a variety of improvements, including the construction and maintenance of landscaping, curbs and gutters, stormwater facilities, sidewalks, and bicycle facilities located within municipal street rights-of-way. Legislation adopted in 2013 broadens the permissible uses of funds to include greenways, as well as bikeways and sidewalks, and allows them to be used for these facilities regardless of whether they are located within public street rights-of-way. In addition, cities may use the funds for independent bicycle and pedestrian improvements inside town limits or within any area that is within the applicable MPO or RPO. Similarly, the funds may be used for traffic control devices, traffic signs and street markings, and speed bumps. Furthermore, the funds may be used for the costs of labor, engineering, equipment and supplies, and certain legal expenses associated with municipal street projects. Certain important limitations on the use of Powell Bill funds, however, include that they may not be used for municipal street lighting, parking meters, street name signs, the installation or removal of underground or overhead utility lines, the collection of garbage or refuse, or the preparation of thoroughfare plans.

Some small cities can finance almost all their street expenditures from these Powell Bill distributions, particularly if their streets lack curbs and gutters and are built to the less-demanding standards that the state uses for its secondary road system. Large cities are far less likely to be able to finance all of their street expenditures from this source, particularly where streets are designed to accommodate paved parking areas along the curb and where traffic control and right-of-way improvements are substantial.

Special Assessments

Special assessments constitute an old tool that allows the assignment of at least some of the costs of public street improvements to the owners of property that stand to benefit from the work. An assessment can be a particularly useful tool for improvement projects on existing streets that are geographically confined. Because they can be procedurally a bit complex to administer, assessments are more popular among large cities than mid-sized and smaller ones. The increasing use of land development ordinance exaction requirements has also lessened the extent to which special assessments are used, because assignment of costs to a developer in advance of development can often be an effective substitute for assessing costs against benefiting properties after they are developed.

G.S. Ch. 160A-217 allows a municipality to assess the costs of street or sidewalk improvements if the city receives a petition signed by the owners of a majority of the lineal feet of frontage of the lands abutting the street. Unless the petition provides otherwise, no more than 50 percent of the costs may be assessed. However, a number of city charters (perhaps over fifty) include provisions that allow cities to use special assessment in the absence of a property owner petition and to assess more than 50 percent of the cost. Special assessments may be apportioned against benefited property in proportion to front footage, land area, or value added by the improvement; on a per-lot basis; or on a combination of these bases. Assessments may be paid as soon as their amount is known or in installments over a period of up to ten years, as the city council determines.

Counties also may play a role in upgrading NCDOT secondary roads through the use of special assessments. G.S. 153A-205 allows a county to finance the local share of the cost of improving residential subdivision streets in unincorporated areas that are already on the NCDOT secondary system. That local share is then assessed against benefitting property. The remainder of the cost is paid by NCDOT, if funds are available. The same approach may also be used to bring streets that have been offered for dedication but not (yet) accepted up to NCDOT's current design and construction standards so they may be accepted. The entire cost of these latter projects is assigned to the affected property owners. Counties also have the authority to use special assessments to pay for street lighting to serve residential subdivisions in unincorporated areas.[15]

Developer Exactions

In the past three decades it has become common for municipalities to expect developers of land to provide the public streets associated with a new development project. In the typical case a developer will be required to set aside land for new streets and construct streets to city standards. The developer will then offer the streets to the city for its acceptance. In other instances when a street is on the perimeter of a development, a developer may be expected to dedicate additional street rights-of-way but make no improvements. Occasionally a developer will be required to construct an acceleration or deceleration lane on an existing street if the land being developed adjacent to the street is, for example, a shopping center or other major commercial development. In each case the extent to which a local government may require a developer to provide right-of-way or traffic improvements as a condition of development approval must be related to the traffic generated by the development project itself, if the requirement is to avoid being an unconstitutional taking of land. A city or county may require the dedication of street right-of-way and various roadway improvements as a condition of land subdivision plat approval[16] or as a condition of the grant of a zoning special-use or conditional-use permit. Cities (but not counties) may require dedications of right-of-way or street improvements to be made as a condition of a municipal driveway permit[17] or may accept these as a voluntary offer by the developer to induce the governing board to rezone land to a conditional zoning district. In some cities much of the mileage added to the city street system consists of streets built by developers and turned over to cities for maintenance.

In some instances it may make more practical sense for a city to accept funds from a developer rather than insisting upon in-kind contributions. G.S. 160A-372 allows a city to accept "fees-in-lieu" of street construction as a condition of subdivision plat approval. Fees such as these can be pooled for a later, more comprehensive road construction or right-of-way purchase. A city may use such funds for land acquisition, design, and construction of streets and roads that serve more than one subdivision or development. Counties may do the same,[18] but all funds collected must be transferred to and expended by a municipality.

Impact fees represent an even more comprehensive approach to collecting fees from property developers than accepting the right-of-way or improvements themselves. In such a system developers of land pay a charge that represents a portion of the prorated cost of the transportation facilities for the entire community made necessary by new growth. North Carolina cities lack express enabling authority to impose such fees, but a small number of cities (Raleigh, Durham, and Cary among them) have obtained local authorizing legislation and have adopted impact fee systems to finance new streets and roads.

15. G.S. 153A-206.
16. G.S. 160A-372; 153A-331.
17. G.S. 160A-307.
18. G.S. 153A-331(c).

The Mix of Funding Options

Powell Bill funds and related forms of state-shared gasoline tax revenues make up the largest and most critical component of the revenues used to support street construction and maintenance. Larger and more rapidly growing cities are also likely to rely on developer exactions and contributions to help fund an expanding street system. Similarly, cities that look to developers for funding help are also more likely to try to use special assessments to fund street improvements; both are based on the principle that the benefiting property owner should pay. But these cities are also much more likely to have capital improvement needs for the construction of major new arterial streets and thoroughfares, traffic control devices, and relative improvements that developers cannot be expected to fund and are unsuitable for special assessment. If a road such as this will become part of the state's system upon completion, then state construction funds may be available. Nonetheless, some of the state's largest cities find it desirable to float bonds to finance the construction of major new streets. In contrast, small and more slow-growing towns and cities are likely to rely more heavily on state aid and on general tax revenues to finance street system improvements. A greater portion of the expenditures will be for existing streets rather than streets on new alignment. Contributions from developers and property owners tend to be relatively less important in overall street funding.

Some Legal Topics Related to Streets

Definition of Street

Highway is the generic term for all ways of passage that are open to the public at large and maintained by public authorities, for both those who are on foot and those who are using vehicles. *Street* is normally used to refer to highways that are found within urban areas. A city's streets include not only *roadways*—the portions of a street used by vehicles—but also sidewalks, public alleys, bikeways, and downtown malls.[19] The city's basic authority to open and maintain streets, found in G.S. 160A-296, includes all these forms of streets.

Street can occasionally bear a narrower meaning, however, depending on the context. This possibility is best illustrated by the use of the word with respect to state street aid to cities.[20] Part of the state's aid is distributed to cities on the basis of the number of miles of streets maintained by the respective cities. G.S. 136-41.1, however, permits a city to count within its mileage only streets with an average width of at least 16 feet. Thus, some city-maintained alleys may not qualify as streets for this purpose.

Street Property Transactions

Acquisition of Streets

A city may acquire control to a street in one of four ways: purchase (or other voluntary conveyance), condemnation, dedication, or prescription. Purchase and condemnation are no different for a street than for a site for a city hall, an easement for a sewer line, or a watershed for the city's water supply, so there is nothing particular to note with regard to these two methods beyond the discussion of them in Chapter 24. The other two methods, however, deserve fuller comment.

Dedication

Dedication consists of an offer by an owner of property to devote (or dedicate) that property to a public use and the acceptance of that offer by the public. Both elements, the offer and the acceptance, are necessary for a dedication to be complete.

By far the most common procedure for offering a dedication is through subdivision plat approval. Most local subdivision ordinances require the developer to offer to dedicate streets, utility easements, and other public spaces to the public; the recorded plat for a regulated subdivision typically expressly states the required offer on its face. In areas of the state not subject to local subdivision regulation, the common law reaches a comparable result. Under common law the preparation of a subdivision plat showing rights-of-way for streets (and other public uses) and the subsequent sale of at least one lot by reference to that plat constitutes an offer of dedication.

---

19. Parsons v. Wright, 223 N.C. 520 (1943).

20. The uses to which state street aid may be put are listed in the discussion of the Powell Bill, above.

Inclusion of an express dedication on the face of a subdivision plat, or, in a common law context, the sale of a lot by reference to the plat, constitutes an offer of dedication, but neither constitutes acceptance of the dedication by the public. For that, the acceptance by proper authorities is necessary.[21] One method of public acceptance is formal action by a public body, such as a city council or the State Board of Transportation, or by its delegate, such as the city manager or public works director. This formal method is preferable to others because it indicates an official decision by the appropriate government to accept the dedication, and it provides a record, such as through the minutes of the public body, of the acceptance.

A city may also, however, indicate acceptance of the dedication simply by beginning to maintain the street.[22] Because the city has no responsibility for maintenance until it accepts the offer of dedication, its undertaking to maintain the street has been held to imply the necessary acceptance.

A third method of acceptance is possible in some states: acceptance through use of the street by the public over a number of years. North Carolina case law, however, indicates that the method, called *public user*, is not possible in this state.[23]

An owner of property who has made an offer of dedication may withdraw the offer before the public has accepted it—and sometimes even after. One way to do this, available when the offer has come through recordation of a subdivision plat, is by subsequently selling lots without reference to the plat.[24] G.S. 136-96 permits a second method. Under this statute, if the public does not open a dedicated street within fifteen years after the offer is made (even if the offer has been accepted), the dedicator may file a notice of withdrawal in the office of the register of deeds. Until that notice is filed, however, the public (city or state) retains the right to accept the offer and open the street, even if more than fifteen years have passed since the offer was made.

A city is the appropriate agency to accept a dedication for a street inside its borders or within its subdivision regulation jurisdiction. Acceptance of a street outside the city does not obligate the city to maintain it.[25] In most cases such an acceptance will probably serve for a temporary period, until the street is accepted by the state for maintenance or becomes part of the city by annexation. The appropriate body to accept a dedication beyond these borders is the State Board of Transportation.

Prescription

Although not often used anymore, one final method of acquisition is by prescription. *Prescription* differs from dedication in that the owner of the property does not intend to offer it for public use. Rather, the public simply uses the property as a street over an extended period—at least twenty years—in a way that is adverse to the interests of the owner, but also known to him or her. The use must be of a specific, definite right-of-way, which must be maintained by the public. If all these elements are met, then acquisition by prescription is possible. In practice this method is rarely used except to confirm title to old streets for which the original title documents are lost.

Closing of Public Streets

Once a city has acquired the right-of-way to a street, it may eventually want to close that street. The street may never have been opened, and closing may be necessary to clear neighboring titles. The city also may wish to relocate the street. Whatever the reason, the city may close a street under the procedure set out in G.S. 160A-299. Similarly, counties enjoy authority to close streets under procedures set out in G.S. 153A-241. In practice, counties most often use this authority to close formerly state-maintained roads that have been abandoned by NCDOT. The two statutes create very similar procedures.

The statutes require the governing board first to hold a public hearing after it has published notice, mailed notice to owners of abutting property, and posted notice on the street itself. After the hearing, the board must find that the clos-

21. Owens v. Elliott, 258 N.C. 314 (1962).

22. Foster v. Atwater, 226 N.C. 472 (1946).

23. *Owens*, 258 N.C. 314; Bumgarner v. Reneak, 105 N.C. App. 362 (1992).

24. Rowe v. Durham, 235 N.C. 158 (1952).

25. G.S. 160A-374.

ing is not contrary to the public interest and would not deprive any person of "reasonable means of ingress and egress to his property." The North Carolina courts have held that although owners are entitled access to the street from their property, they have no right to have traffic pass directly by their property. Thus cutting off access to a street at one end, making that end in effect a cul-de-sac, does not deny reasonable means of ingress or egress to a property owner along the street.[26] When a street is closed in this fashion, the legal effect is that title to the land involved is divided along the middle of the street, among owners of the abutting land.

Other Uses of a Street Right-of-Way

G.S. 160A-273 permits a city to grant easements "over, through, under, or across . . . the right-of-way of any public street or alley that is not a part of the State highway system" as long as the easement will not "substantially impair or hinder the use of the street or alley as a way of passage." (Because counties do not own streets, this statute does not apply to them.) Thus, a city is authorized to permit a utility company to lay pipes or erect poles and string wires in the right-of-way of a street or to permit the owners of property that abuts a street to join their properties by a bridge across the street. If the city's title to the street is itself but an easement for street purposes (rather than full title in fee simple), however, the city's authority to permit other uses of the right-of-way, such as for laying pipes or erecting wires, is subject to the continuing property rights of the owner of the underlying title. The North Carolina Supreme Court has held that utility pipes or poles constitute an additional burden on a street right-of-way, and the owner of the underlying title is entitled to additional compensation, however small that may be. Payment of that compensation, though, is the responsibility of whoever lays the pipes or erects the poles, not the city.[27]

City Liability for Streets

Once a city has assumed control of a street—whether by purchase, condemnation, acceptance of a dedication, or prescription—it becomes responsible for the maintenance and repair of the right-of-way. This responsibility extends to all portions of the right-of-way, including the roadway, any sidewalk, and any other parts that contain conditions that might be a hazard to the normal use of the roadway or the sidewalk. The city's basic duty is to maintain the street in a "reasonably safe condition" so that it may be used for the purpose for which it is intended.[28] If the city fails to meet this responsibility, by failing to correct or warn against a street condition that renders the street unsafe, it may be held liable to any person injured by the condition. For example, if a street is under excavation, a city generally must set up barriers and lights sufficient to keep a careful traveler from falling into the excavation. Furthermore, the city must keep its streets and sidewalks free from obstructions whether permanent, such as a private fire hydrant extending from a building, or temporary, such as a pile of bricks being used by a contractor, that present a hazard to vehicles or pedestrians. Although a very large body of case law details the sorts of conditions that might lead to city liability, much of it is old, with recent cases relatively infrequent. This fact suggests that cities are, by and large, meeting their standard of care in maintaining and repairing streets.

Street Names and Numbers

Inherent in the city's "general authority and control" over city streets is the authority to name streets and establish a system for numbering houses and other buildings along streets. Counties, by contrast, enjoy authority to name and number streets in unincorporated areas under a specific statute, G.S. 153A-239.1. Most current naming of streets goes on in new subdivisions, and the typical subdivision ordinance gives attention to street names within the subdivision. This ordinance often requires that any new street that is a clear continuation of an existing street bear the same name as that street, and it prohibits new names that duplicate or sound very much like the names of existing streets. If these conditions are met, the names of the new streets are left to the subdivider. The power to name streets is legislative in nature, however, and, therefore, the city or county may change the name of a street at any time.

---

26. Wofford v. North Carolina State Highway Comm'n, 263 N.C. 677 (1965).
27. Van Leuven v. Akers Motor Lines, 261 N.C. 539 (1964).
28. Fitzgerald v. Concord, 140 N.C. 110 (1905).

As noted, cities and counties also have statutory authority to establish a system of house numbers for city or rural streets. In a city, such a system usually begins with *reference streets* that divide the city into quarters: north, south, east, and west. The house numbers then proceed from the reference streets to the city's outer boundaries. Any ordinance that sets up a numbering system must establish frontage intervals so that a new number is given each succeeding interval. Intervals are commonly in the range of 20–30 feet, although shorter intervals may be necessary in downtown areas. In addition, the ordinance should also maintain even numbers on one side of the street and odd numbers on the other in a manner that is consistent throughout the city. (The preferred practice is for the even numbers to be on the right side—low to high—and the odd numbers on the left side, going away from the reference streets.) It is also very desirable to establish the numbers so that the building numbers on parallel streets are comparable. Counties number lots or tracts under similar principles, although the lower population densities usual in unincorporated areas often lead to larger numbering intervals than is true of cities.

When cities exercise their power to name or number streets, there is no statutory procedure they must follow. A county's power to do so, however, is conditioned upon the board of commissioners first holding a public hearing after both publishing and posting notice of the hearing.

Franchises

Cities are authorized by G.S. 160A-319 to grant franchises for up to sixty years for the operation of electric, telephone, gas, water, and sewer utilities, and bus lines and other mass transit facilities. Because the historical basis and much of the current justification of the power to franchise lie in local control of streets, the franchising power needs some discussion. A *franchise* is a special privilege, such as the right to erect poles and string wires in a street right-of-way or to operate a bus line, that is granted by a city or county and that may not be exercised in the absence of a franchise.[29] Once granted, the franchise is a contract between its holder and the city or county and may not be revoked by the government except according to the terms of the franchise.[30]

Historically, the first extensive governmental regulation of public utilities was by cities, through their franchising power. In the past half century, however, state regulation through agencies, such as the North Carolina Utilities Commission, has displaced much of the municipal power to regulate. A main continuing justification for city franchising of utilities is the regulation of the franchise holder's activities within the rights-of-way of city streets. For example, the franchise may make clear that any excavation or tree cutting is subject to city regulation and inspection; require the franchise holder to repair fully any street or sidewalk pavement that is removed during an excavation; and make clear the city's right to require removal or relocation of utility structures in the right-of-way, at no cost to the city. However, because of the utilities commission's dominant role in regulating most activities subject to franchise (cable television is not subject to utilities commission regulation but is subject to considerable federal regulation), a city's bargaining power is not nearly as strong as it once was.

In addition to franchises, a city may use an encroachment agreement to regulate its street rights-of-way. A city may require private property owners to enter into such an agreement to erect or bury structures within the right-of-way or to engage in various activities within the right-of-way. So, too, may NCDOT require an encroachment agreement for private use of the right-of-way of NCDOT streets and highways within municipal limits. In 2013 the General Assembly recognized the right of restaurants to offer dining (and in some cases drinking) on sidewalks within the right-of-way of NCDOT streets within city boundaries.[31]

29. Shaw v. City of Asheville, 269 N.C. 90 (1967).

30. Boyce v. City of Gastonia, 227 N.C. 139 (1942).

31. *See* the discussion in Richard Ducker, "Sidewalk Dining: Some Questions and Answers," *Coates Canons: Local Government Law Blog* (UNC School of Government, Sept. 13, 2013), http://canons.sog.unc.edu/?p=7305.

Parking

An integral component of a local transportation system is vehicular parking. Parking opportunities are important in accommodating residents where they live (particularly in multi-family residential areas), promoting the accessibility of commercial land uses for customers, and allowing employees ready access to their places of work. As the amount of automobile travel has increased, so too has the need for parking spaces at various locations. The same travel origin-destination surveys that allow the estimation of trips and routes taken provide critical information about the demand for parking for autos and, to a much lesser extent, trucks, bicycles, scooters, and other means of travel. Just as travel volumes exhibit peaks and valleys, so too does the demand for parking. In larger cities significant public transportation use can diminish slightly the need for parking. Occasionally a community will limit the amount of parking with an eye to encouraging automobile drivers to carpool or use another mode of transportation. However, in the mind of most citizens, the easier it is to park a car near one's destination, the better.

On-Street Parking

On-street parking refers to parking spaces made available along the curb or shoulder of a street or road that are designed to accommodate vehicles. If a city provides on-street parking, particularly in commercial areas, it makes a conscious choice to provide better access to adjacent land uses at the expense of more efficiently moving traffic. The use of streets for parking affects their use for traffic movement in three ways. First, curbside parking significantly reduces a street's capacity. At an intersection with a signal, parking on both sides of both streets usually cuts the intersection's—and, therefore, the street's—capacity roughly in half. Second, curbside parking reduces safety. Vehicles leaving the curb, doors opening into traffic, and pedestrians walking between parked cars are all dangerous concomitants of parking on the street. Third, curbside parking increases service conflict. Curbside space must accommodate not only private cars but also delivery vehicles that need convenient loading zones, buses that need safe and convenient stops, and emergency vehicles that need quick access to buildings and fire hydrants. Furthermore, the alleys that give access to the interior of the block and the crosswalks that permit safe pedestrian crossing of the street all take their slice of curbside space. Virtually all on-street parking involves parallel parking; that is, the car is parked parallel to the curb. Most on-street parking areas outside of single-family residential neighborhoods are restricted, metered, or both.

Off-Street Parking

Most demand for parking, however, is met with off-street parking. Off-street parking spaces may be found in spaces next to buildings, large surface lots, parking decks, garages that serve larger areas, and even underground garages that serve single buildings or entire areas. The number, location, and design of off-street parking areas reflect the interests of both the owners of properties that will benefit from the parking and the city.

Most zoning ordinances include off-street parking requirements for the various categories of land use allowed. These requirements are usually based on some combination of nationally developed standards, rules of thumb on the number of customer and employee spaces that are likely to be needed for each kind of use, and the community's assessment of its own circumstances. More recently emphasis has shifted from the sheer number of spaces to requirements to ensure that lots are appropriately landscaped, stormwater is managed effectively, and the circulation of vehicles within the lot and entrance and exit points are arranged to minimize the effect of drivers entering and leaving parking areas on street traffic.

Off-street parking is closely related to managing how accessible properties are from the adjacent street. North Carolina cities are authorized to undertake access management by adopting an ordinance regulating the design and location of driveways that tie into adjacent streets.[32] Mid-sized and larger cities may require driveway permits, particularly if the adjacent use of land is nonresidential. Driveway regulations often set spacing standards between driveways to ensure that autos and trucks entering or exiting from a street will not cause traffic congestion or cause unsafe driving

32. G.S. 160A-307.

conditions. However, driveway standards can best be enforced if the adjacent street is curbed so that access points are available only at designated locations.[33]

Privately Owned Public Parking

Public parking may be privately owned. This type of parking consists of lots, decks, and garages developed by private parties to provide off-street parking for a fee to customers or workers in an area. Off-street parking is also commonly provided in association with many shopping centers and other commercial enterprises, without charge. A developer or a private lessee may operate these facilities, or a city may operate them under lease. Parking fees, when imposed, are charged to cover operating costs and profit to the investor.

Publicly Owned Public Parking

These facilities are similar to private off-street facilities, but are either developed, or purchased after development, by a public body (the city or a special authority). Parking fees are charged to cover operating costs and retirement of any public debt used to develop the facilities. These facilities may also take the form of lots, decks, or garages. However, municipalities today are less likely to undertake the construction of large-scale parking facilities, particularly parking garages, than they were in the past, because of the financial risk inherent in building and operating facilities requiring large investments over an extended period of time.

Public Financing of Parking

A variety of means are used to finance public parking that is developed or operated by a public body. On-street parking usually involves no significant improvement expense, unless curb and guttering is added. It normally uses existing public rights-of-way and existing street pavement. Beyond the small cost of marking spaces, the only costs that a community is likely to incur for curbside parking are for enforcement by city personnel, parking meters, or both. Parking meters are the most common means of enforcing time limits for curbside spaces. They also provide a source of revenue to help meet the costs of maintenance and enforcement associated with on-street parking.

Off-street parking is usually a much more costly venture for a city. The city might have to acquire land and construct a lot or a deck. Once the facility is in operation, the city has to control parking and maintain the facility separately from routine street maintenance. Usually the large initial outlays for off-street facilities are covered by bonds, either revenue or general obligation, or by installment financing agreements, depending on a variety of factors. Regardless of the type of debt financing used, before the project is undertaken, a city should try to ensure that demand—and, therefore, use—will provide enough revenue to cover the total cost of developing and operating the facility. Meters may be used on off-street facilities, but attended lots (monitored by persons or machines) are more common as a measure to control turnover and to ensure enough revenue to meet obligations.

Public Transportation Systems

The North Carolina Department of Transportation (NCDOT) reported in 2012 that there were ninety-nine public transportation systems operating in North Carolina.[34] Their purpose, size, funding sources, services, and capabilities vary considerably. These transportation systems can be grouped into four different types of systems: community (human service) transportation, regional community transportation, urban transportation, and regional urban transportation.[35]

---

33. Richard Ducker, "What You Need to Know about Driveway Permits and Road Access: Part I," *Coates Canons: Local Government Law Blog* (UNC School of Government, Jan. 16, 2014), http://canons.sog.unc.edu/?p=7484.

34. Public Transportation Division, North Carolina Department of Transportation, "Statewide Regionalization Study: Final Report," May 1, 2012, I-3.

35. Much of the information in this section is drawn from the website of the Public Transportation Division of the North Carolina Department of Transportation at www.ncdot.gov/nctransit/download/transsystems.pdf and the "Statewide Regionalization Study: Final Report."

Community Transportation

Community transportation systems typically are combination systems organized by a single county. They work with local human services agencies to transport agency clients to allow them to take advantage of congregate meals, adult and child day care, medical and recreation services, education and training, and senior and volunteer activities. But they also offer services to the general public. These systems are required to offer public services as a condition of receiving federal support for their operations. Community systems cater particularly to residents of rural areas that are unserved by other forms of public transportation. Rather than the fixed-route systems offered by urban transit operators, single-county community transit systems usually operate by subscription or a "first-come, first served" basis. Rides can be prearranged by individuals, agencies, or groups who may be able to make use of dial-a-ride arrangements.

Administrative arrangements for community transportation systems vary widely. In some counties administrative responsibility may be centered in a single agency, such as aging or social services. Others are organized as transportation authorities or administered through county departments. In others administrative responsibility may be contracted to a private nonprofit agency. Examples include the Avery County Transportation Authority, Martin County, the Onslow United Transit Systems, Inc., and the Hyde County Non-Profit Private Transportation Corp.[36]

Community systems generally rely on undedicated sources of funds from the county, state agencies (including the Public Transportation Division of NCDOT), and the federal government.

NCDOT reports that there are sixty-eight single-county community transportation systems operating in North Carolina.

Regional Community Transportation

Regional community systems are community systems that are composed of two or more contiguous counties providing either coordinated or consolidated service. There are eight regional multi-county community systems in North Carolina serving a rural population. More than a quarter of North Carolina's 100 counties are served by such a system. They represent a mix of authorities, programs that operate as services of multi-service agencies, and private nonprofits. Examples include the Choanoke Public Transportation Authority,[37] serving Bertie, Halifax, Hertford, and Northampton counties, and the Kerr Area Rural Transportation System, serving Franklin, Granville, Vance, and Warren counties.

Urban Transportation

Urban Transit Generally

Urban transit in North Carolina began over a century ago with privately owned horse-drawn coaches. These gave way to electric trolleys, which in turn were replaced by motor buses. The electric trolleys were often operated by power companies; in several cities the power companies, as a part of their franchises, continued to provide transit services after the switch to buses. This era ended in 1991, when Durham and Greensboro assumed ownership of the bus systems in their cities from Duke Power Company.

Today there are seventeen transit systems in North Carolina that primarily provide fixed-route urban service. Most are owned by a municipality or transportation authority. They include Asheville Transit, Boone (ApplCART), Cary C-Tran, Chapel Hill Transit, the Charlotte Area Transit System (CATS), Concord Kannapolis Area Transit (Rider), Durham Area Transit Authority (DATA), Fayetteville Area Systems of Transit (FAST), Gastonia Transit, Greensboro Transit Authority, Greenville Area Transit, High Point HiTran, Jacksonville Transit, Raleigh (Capital Area Transit (CAT)), Salisbury Transit, Wilson Transit, and the Winston-Salem Transit Authority.

Each of these urban systems supports its operations from a combination of revenues: fare-box receipts, appropriations from the local governments that support the system, and federal and state grants. Fare-box receipts are typically quite inadequate to meet the operating costs of an urban transit system. Estimates are that statewide, local revenues

36. For a complete listing of all of these systems see "Statewide Regionalization Study: Final Report," 3-5–3-8.

37. G.S. 160A-588 of the Public Transportation Authorities Act (G.S. 160A-575 to -588, first adopted in 1977) allows for creation of such an authority by resolution of one or more local governments.

(fare-box receipts and general fund appropriations) account for about 55 percent of capital and operating costs, with the rest of the funds coming from federal and state grants.

Urban and community transit systems, and the local governments that support them, can take advantage of several dedicated funding sources for which they may be eligible. First, a municipality that operates a public transportation system may levy a motor vehicle tax of not more than $5.00 for each vehicle with a tax situs in the community.[38] Proceeds may be used for financing, constructing, operating, and maintaining local public transportation systems. Proceeds, however, must supplement and not supplant existing funds used for public transportation purposes. Second, a county may levy a county vehicle registration tax of $7.00 per year for each vehicle with a tax situs there.[39] To qualify, the county or a municipality within that county must operate or contract for the operation of a public transportation system. Proceeds of the tax are distributed on a per-capita basis among the county (as representative of the residents of unincorporated areas) and the municipalities of the county. If the county or a municipality within the county neither operates nor contracts for operation of a public transportation system, that local government is excluded from the distribution of funds. A third potential source of dedicated revenue for public transportation is from a sales and use tax.[40] Counties other than Durham, Forsyth, Guilford, Mecklenburg, Orange, and Wake may levy a sales and use tax of one-quarter percent (1/4 percent) for public transportation purposes. To qualify, the county or a municipality within the county must operate a public transportation system. Such operation includes operation of such a system by another local government by contract or interlocal agreement, by a local or regional transportation authority, or by contract with a private entity. The tax may be adopted by the board of county commissioners only if county voters first approve the proposal in an advisory referendum. Proceeds are distributed on the same per-capita basis as applies to dedicated vehicle registration tax proceeds, as described above. It is worth noting that this enabling authority applies to a number of counties that are already part of regional and regional public transportation authorities (e.g., TT and PART). (See below.)

The Charlotte Area Transit System

One not so typical example of an urban transit system is CATS. Technically, it is not organized as a regional transit system because it is not organized on a multi-county basis. Mecklenburg is the only county that provides financial support for the system. Instead it is based upon an interlocal agreement among Charlotte, Mecklenburg County, and the other municipalities of Mecklenburg County. It provides service primarily to Mecklenburg County, but also to adjacent North Carolina counties and the city of Rock Hill, South Carolina. It is governed by the city council of Charlotte and the Metropolitan Transit Commission, which includes representatives of Mecklenburg County, the seven municipalities in the county, and a representative of NCDOT. A primary source of local funding comes from a one-half cent sales tax earmarked for public transportation that was approved by Mecklenburg County voters in 1998, pursuant to some special Mecklenburg County provisions in the Local Government Public Transportation Sales Tax Act.[41] Long-term development planning of CATS as a regional system is based on "2025 Integrated Transit/Land-Use Plan for Charlotte-Mecklenburg," first adopted in July, 1998. A "Transit Governance Interlocal Agreement" was adopted by the six municipalities and the county in 1999 to define the relationships and mechanisms guiding the planning, financing, and implementation of the 2025 Transit/Land-Use Plan and updates to that plan.

CATS is also notable because it includes the state's first light-rail line. The 10-mile Lynx line between uptown Charlotte and Pineville began operation in 2007. Construction of a second 9.3-mile extension, to connect uptown Charlotte and UNC Charlotte began in the spring of 2014. This $1.2 billion rail line project is scheduled to begin operation in 2017. The federal government will provide roughly half of the construction cost of this Blue Line extension. The rest will be split evenly between the state and the local governments.

38. G.S. 20-97.
39. G.S. 105-570.
40. G.S. 105-511 to -511.4.
41. G.S. 105-507 to -507.4.

Regional Urban Transit

Triangle Transit

The Research Triangle Regional Transit Authority, which operates as Triangle Transit (TT), operates fixed-route bus service within the Research Triangle metropolitan area. It connects Raleigh, Durham, Cary, Chapel Hill, and surrounding areas with the Research Triangle Park and Raleigh-Durham International Airport. Triangle Transit was established under the Regional Public Transportation Authority Act[42] and remains the only transportation authority established under that act. The act specifies that the authority is comprised of three counties; TT operates within Wake, Durham, and Orange counties. Triangle Transit is authorized to impose and has in fact imposed three taxes: a $5.00 vehicle registration fee,[43] a 5 percent tax on vehicle rentals,[44] and a one-half percent (1/2 percent) sales and use tax to support its programs. The authority may establish a special tax district including one or more counties in which the vehicle registration tax or the sales and use tax may be levied. The board of commissioners of the affected county must consent before either of these taxes is adopted. A sales tax must also be approved by voters in an advisory referendum. In addition, the taxes must be approved by a special tax board made up of two commissioners from the boards of Durham, Wake, and Orange counties. A proposal to establish a special tax district comprised of just Durham and Orange counties and to increase the vehicle registration tax from $5.00 to $8.00 was under consideration in the spring of 2014.

Such a special tax district including Durham and Orange was used for another purpose in 2012 when voters in these counties approved a one-half percent (1/2 percent) sales and use tax[45] for public transportation. In the spring of 2013, Durham and Orange counties began collecting the half-cent sales tax to help pay for a light rail line and for enhanced bus service. In the spring of 2014, the Federal Transit Administration approved plans for the 17-mile light-rail line to connect UNC Chapel Hill and east Durham. State and federal funding will be needed to cover most of the cost of the light-rail line, estimated at $1.34 billion. Wake County has yet to schedule a vote on a sales tax levy to support rail line extensions in that county.

Piedmont Authority for Regional Transportation

The Piedmont Authority for Regional Transportation (PART) provides extensive vanpool and express bus service surrounding the core cities of Greensboro, Winston-Salem, and High Point. It was established under the Regional Transportation Authority Act,[46] an act tailored to fit the Piedmont Triad area. According to the act, the jurisdictional area includes any metropolitan planning organization (MPO) that consists of all or part of five contiguous counties, two of which must have a population over 250,000 and the other three of which have a population of 100,000 or more. A regional transportation authority may be expanded to include contiguous areas with the consent of the affected county board of commissioners, but the geographic scope of the authority may not exceed part or all of twelve counties. The Piedmont Authority Regional Transportation now includes ten counties: Guilford, Forsyth, Davidson, Randolph, Alamance, Davie, Surry, Stokes, Yadkin, and Rockingham counties.

The Piedmont Authority Regional Transportation sees its mission as broader than transit. In addition to several transit projects, PART offers vanpool, carpooling, and ride matching services, and it is constructing regional park-n-ride lots to serve carpooling and transit commuters. The system is also presently conducting an "Airport Area Transportation Study" and two separate rail feasibility projects related to a regional rail major investment study and regional intercity rail service.

The authority is authorized to levy three types of taxes: a vehicle registration tax[47] not to exceed $8.00, a vehicle rental tax[48] not to exceed 5 percent, and a sales and use tax of one-half percent (1/2 percent).[49] Under the Regional

42. G.S. 160A, art. 26.
43. G.S. 105-560 to -564.
44. *See* G.S. 105-550 to -555.
45. *See* G.S. 105-509 to -509.1.
46. G.S. 160A Art. 27.
47. G.S. 105-560 to -564.
48. G.S. 105-550 to -555.
49. G.S. 105-510 to -510.1.

Transportation Authority Act the authority may establish a special tax district including one or more counties in which the vehicle registration tax or the sales and use tax may be levied. The board of commissioners of the affected county must consent before any of these taxes are adopted. A sales tax must be approved by voters in an advisory referendum. A 5 percent motor vehicle rental tax now applies in Davidson, Davie, Forsyth, Guilford, Stokes, and Surry counties. Efforts by PART to gain support from these counties for an amendment to G.S. 105-551 that would raise the cap to 8 percent have been unsuccessful. In addition, the Piedmont Authority for Public Transportation receives the proceeds of a 1 percent motor vehicle registration tax that is levied in Randolph County. No sales and use tax for public transportation has been adopted in the PART region. Indeed, the statute does not permit a county other than Guilford and Forsyth to be included in any proposed special tax district for purposes of a sales tax.[50]

Regionalization

The NCDOT's Public Transit Division still administers programs that involve some 99 separate transit systems throughout the state. Regionalization, both at the county level and at the multi-county level, has come slowly despite various regionalization incentives provided by the division and state lawmakers. The administrative burden of complying with federal requirements in order to secure federal funding has been costly for small transit systems. So far, the state has avoided compulsory consolidation of providers. Some regionalization and consolidation of public transportation services in the future seems likely. Just how that might occur in the decades to come remains a key issue.

Airports

Although the exact number of airports and airstrips in North Carolina is not known, the North Carolina Department of Transportation (NCDOT) has estimated that there are nearly 300 privately owned airports and airstrips, the majority of which are personal-use air strips in rural areas. There are some 74 publicly owned airports in North Carolina that are open to general public use.[51] Ten airports have regularly scheduled domestic airline service: Wilmington International Airport, Charlotte-Douglas International Airport, Piedmont Triad International Airport, Raleigh-Durham International Airport, Asheville Regional Airport, Concord Regional Airport, Fayetteville Regional Airport, Pitt-Greenville Airport, Coastal Carolina Regional Airport (New Bern), and Albert J. Ellis Airport (Jacksonville). The first four of these provide international service as well.[52]

The North Carolina airports that are open to general public use are administered in a variety of ways. A significant minority of them are operated by an airport authority or commission; most of these are the creations of two or more local governments. Most of the remainder are operated directly by a city or, more often, a county; most of these, however, have some sort of advisory board or committee. They may also create subordinate boards or commissions to manage airport operations or lease the airports to be operated privately. A few other arrangements have been authorized. For example, the Raleigh-Durham airport is operated by an authority created by special act, with authority members appointed by the four participating governments, Raleigh, Durham, Wake County, and Durham County. These organizational arrangements, however, can be controversial. The Charlotte airport for many years was owned and operated by the City of Charlotte as a city department. In 2013 the General Assembly adopted an act[53] that would have transferred airport ownership and control to a newly created regional airport authority. Bowing to opposition from the city, the General Assembly soon thereafter adopted a second act[54] repealing the first. The second act established an airport commission as an agency of city government. However, the new airport commission includes representation from Mecklenburg, Gaston, Lincoln, Union, Cabarrus, and Iredell counties and is authorized to operate existing and

50. G.S. 105-510(a) (2009).

51. *See* Aviation Division, North Carolina Department of Transportation, "Frequently Asked Questions," www.ncdot.gov/aviation/download/faq.pdf.

52. *See* Aviation Division, North Carolina Department of Transportation, "Airport Locations," www.ncdot.gov/travel/airports/.

53. S.L. 2013-272.

54. S.L. 2013-358, repealing S.L. 2013-272.

future public airports in those counties with the consent of the governing boards of these airports. The legislation also establishes an oversight committee to monitor the commission's progress toward achieving certain goals. A majority of the members of the oversight committee are state appointees, appointed by either the governor, the speaker of the house, or the president pro tem of the senate.

Funding

In 1929, just over twenty-five years after the Wright Brothers made their first flights in Kitty Hawk, North Carolina's cities and counties were authorized to own and operate airports.[55] Their initial powers were broad and have since been enlarged. Counties and cities may levy taxes for airports, issue bonds to finance facilities, condemn land for airport facilities, and join with other cities or counties in supporting and operating airports.

The Federal Aviation Act, passed by Congress in 1958, created the Federal Aviation Agency and provided federal funding for airport development. However, the federal government placed its emphasis on large airports. Since North Carolina was the beneficiary of relatively little federal money during the first decade of the program, the General Assembly established a funding program of its own. In 1967 North Carolina adopted its first State Aid to Airports Program with an appropriation of $250,000. State money was originally available only to airports without airline service. But in 1974 funds for general aviation airports were increased to $1 million per annum, and funds were first made available to airline service airports in an equal amount. In 1975 the distinction between types of airports was eliminated. Today only airports that are owned by a governmental unit are eligible for state financial assistance.[56] Grants of state and federal funds are available through the Division of Aviation for planning, land acquisition, and construction of runways, taxiways, and aprons. Local matching shares of 10–50 percent of the total cost are required, the share depending upon the type of project.

Perhaps the most significant change affecting state aviation funding occurred in 2013 with the strategic prioritization legislation. Now aviation projects must compete for funding with other transportation projects, regardless of mode. Most aviation projects will compete in the "division" tier, with 50 percent of a project's rating coming from the Division of Aviation's project prioritization, 25 percent from the NCDOT division engineer, and 25 percent from the local metropolitan planning organization or rural planning organization. Only the airports served by major airlines are fully self-supporting for both operations and capital improvements. In fact, most of the airports operated by local governments do not generate enough revenues to meet even their operating expenses. Rather, they rely on local appropriations and state and federal aid to meet their remaining capital needs and operating expenses. The smaller airports, though, have only modest needs. Their annual operating costs are often restricted to utilities, grass cutting, and limited pavement and building maintenance. They usually contract for actual operation by one or more private companies, usually known as fixed-base operators.

NCDOT does not provide funding for private airports. However, such airports are eligible to receive technical guidance and assistance from the state.

Additional Resources

Brookings Institution. *Report on a Survey of the Organization and Administration of County Government in North Carolina.* Washington, D.C.: The Institution, 1930.

Ducker, Richard D. "Adequate Public Facility Criteria: Linking Growth to School Capacity." *School Law Bulletin* 34 (Winter 2003): 1–12.

_____. *Dedicating and Reserving Land to Provide Access to North Carolina Beaches.* Chapel Hill, N.C.: Institute of Government, University of North Carolina at Chapel Hill, 1982.

55. G.S. Ch. 63.

56. *See* Aviation Division, North Carolina Department of Transportation, "State Aid to Airports and State Block Grant Program," https://connect.ncdot.gov/municipalities/State-Airport-Aid/Pages/default.aspx.

Ducker, Richard, Adam Lovelady, and David W. Owens, "2013 North Carolina Legislation Related to Planning and Development Regulation." *Planning and Zoning Bulletin* No. 22, October 2013.

Ducker, Richard D., and David W. Owens. "A Smart Growth Toolbox for Local Government." *Popular Government* 66 (Fall 2000): 29–42.

Ducker, Richard D., and George K. Cobb. "Protecting Rights-of-Way for Future Streets and Highways." *Popular Government* 58 (Fall 1992): 32–40.

Ferrell, Joseph S. *Tort Liability of North Carolina Cities and Towns for Street Defects.* Chapel Hill, N.C.: Institute of Government, University of North Carolina at Chapel Hill, 1965.

Lawrence, David M. *Property Interests in North Carolina City Streets.* Chapel Hill, N.C.: Institute of Government, University of North Carolina at Chapel Hill, 1985.

McMahon, John Alexander. "Roads and Streets in North Carolina: A Report to the State-Municipal Road Commission." *Popular Government* 17 (September 1950): Entire issue.

North Carolina Department of Transportation, Division of Highways, Planning and Environmental Branch. *Summary of Municipal Local Road and Street Finance Report, June 30, 1990.* Raleigh, N.C.: NCDOT, April 1991.

Owens, David W. *Land Use Law in North Carolina.* 2nd ed. Chapel Hill, N.C.: UNC School of Government, 2011.

"Report of the State-Municipal Road Commission." *Popular Government* 17 (December 1950/January 1951): 10–13.

Wager, Paul W. *County Government in North Carolina.* Chapel Hill: University of North Carolina Press, 1982.

Selected Posts from Coates' Canons: NC Local Government Law Blog

Ducker, Richard. "What You Need to Know about Driveway Permits and Road Access: Part I." January 16, 2014, http://canons.sog.unc.edu/?p=7484.

_____. "Sidewalk Dining: Some Questions and Answers." September 13, 2013, http://canons.sog.unc.edu/?p=7305.

_____. "Snakes with Too Much for Dinner: Conforming to the Transportation Plan." January 20, 2011, http://canons.sog.unc.edu/?p=3824.

Lovelady, Adam. "The Koontz Decision and Implications for Development Exactions." July 1, 2013, http://canons.sog.unc.edu/?p=7191.

About the Authors

Richard D. Ducker is a retired School of Government faculty member interested in, among other things, land use control and zoning. David M. Lawrence is a retired School of Government faculty member whose interests include legal aspects of economic development.

Chapter 33

Animal Control

Aimee N. Wall

North Carolina local governments take the lead in managing traditional animal control activities. Much of the work is discretionary, but state law does impose some mandates related to rabies and dangerous dogs. Many local governments, however, have elected to offer more comprehensive animal control programs as a general public service. Counties and municipalities often handle their respective animal control activities separately. As a result, North Carolina local governments have developed many different animal control programs and ordinances over the years.

State law addresses several important areas of animal control, including rabies, dangerous dogs, and animal cruelty. Animal control activities, however, are largely governed by local ordinances and customs.

Administrative Responsibility

Various local government agencies, offices, and departments assume responsibility for providing animal control services. County animal control programs are often housed in county health departments because health directors have several statutorily mandated duties related to rabies control. Some local governments have elected to make animal control a function of law enforcement or public safety. Having law enforcement officers available to enforce animal control law can be advantageous when it becomes necessary to conduct a search or to make an arrest. Other local governments place animal control responsibilities directly in the manager's office or within a separate department. Finally, some contract with private nonprofit agencies to manage some functions of animal control.

Primary responsibility for enforcing animal control laws and running related programs typically rests with animal control officers, though, as noted, in some jurisdictions law enforcement officers take the lead. In the past, many counties relied on dog wardens, officials who were authorized to enforce laws related to dogs.[1] Some counties have entertained the idea of appointing dog wardens because the statute appears to grant wardens the power of arrest. It is important to remember, however, that wardens would still need to be sworn law enforcement officers in order to exercise the power of arrest.[2]

1. N.C. Gen. Stat. (hereinafter G.S.) § 67-31.
2. G.S. 17C-11 (prohibiting persons from making arrests if they fail to satisfy the standards and requirements established by the North Carolina Criminal Justice Education and Training Standards Commission).

Services

Local government animal control programs and services vary among jurisdictions. The key areas that many programs address are rabies, dangerous dogs, animal cruelty, stray and nuisance animals, and shelter management. The rest of this chapter focuses on the laws governing each of these primary animal control functions. It also briefly discusses several other functions of interest to only some jurisdictions, such as exotic animal regulation. Note that hunting, fishing, and other activities involving wildlife fall under the jurisdiction of the state Wildlife Resources Commission, and for the most part, its officers enforce statewide laws. Farm and other animals raised to be commercially processed as food fall under the jurisdiction of the North Carolina Department of Agriculture and Consumer Services.

Rabies Control

Rabies is a communicable disease that is transmitted to humans most often through the bite of a raccoon, bat, or dog. If left untreated, the disease is almost always fatal for humans; therefore, the public health system has a significant interest in ensuring that the disease, whenever present, does not spread. North Carolina, like most other states, has adopted a series of state laws governing the control of rabies. The statutes can be found in the public health chapter of the North Carolina General Statutes (hereinafter G.S.), Chapter 130A, Article 6, Part 6.

The cornerstone requirement of the rabies control laws relates to pet vaccination. Every owner of a dog, cat, or ferret over four months of age is required to have the animal vaccinated against rabies. At the time of vaccination, the owner is given a copy of a vaccination certificate (G.S. 130A-189) and a rabies tag (G.S. 130A-190). State law requires that dogs wear their rabies tags at all times. Cats and ferrets must wear their rabies tags at all times unless exempted from the tag requirement by a local ordinance (G.S. 130A-190).

Vaccinations may be administered by a licensed veterinarian, a registered veterinary technician (under the supervision of a veterinarian), or a person who has been designated as a certified rabies vaccinator (G.S. 130A-185). Certified rabies vaccinators are persons appointed by a local health director and trained and certified by the state public health veterinarian (G.S. 130A-186). Pet owners may take their animals to a private veterinarian to be vaccinated. Alternatively, they may be able to take their pets to a public rabies clinic. Local health departments are required to organize (or assist other county departments in organizing) at least one public vaccination clinic per year (G.S. 130A-187). Boards of county commissioners are required to establish their clinics' vaccination fee, which is limited by statute to the actual cost of the vaccine, the certificate, and the tag plus an administrative fee not to exceed ten dollars. Often the county coordinates these public clinics with private veterinarians in the area. The county's role may be to organize and advertise the clinic with the veterinarians participating at selected locations or, at times, in their own offices.

Local government animal control officers are required to canvass their jurisdictions to find animals not wearing rabies tags (G.S. 130A-192). If an officer finds a dog or cat without a tag, the officer has the authority to take action, which may include impounding the animal. If the officer knows who owns the animal, he or she must notify the owner in writing about the vaccination requirements. The owner must produce a copy of the animal's vaccination certificate within three days of receiving the notification. If the owner fails to do so, he or she may be charged with a Class 1 misdemeanor.

If the officer does not know who owns an animal, he or she may impound it. Note that the officer is not *required* to impound the animal; state law provides local governments with the authority to seize animals, but it but does not require them to impound all dogs and cats found without rabies tags. If the officer does seize the animal, the officer is required to make a reasonable effort to locate its owner. The local government is required to hold the animal for a time period established by the board of county commissioners, which must be at least seventy-two hours. Many cities and counties hold animals for periods longer than seventy-two hours.

If the owner of an impounded animal does not claim the animal within the established time period, the local government may allow another person to adopt the animal or it may euthanize it. If an animal is to be euthanized, state law currently allows local governments to employ any method approved by the American Veterinary Medical Association (AVMA), the Humane Society of the United States (HSUS), or the American Humane Association (AHA).[3] Most local

3. All three organizations have historically approved of euthanasia by injection, subject to certain limitations. *See* AHA Animal Protection Position Statement on Euthanasia (2009) (on file with author); HSUS Condemns Use of Carbon Monoxide

government animal shelters euthanize animals by either injecting them with sodium pentobarbital or having them inhale carbon monoxide gas.[4]

Local governments play an important role in ensuring that animals are vaccinated, but they also get involved when an animal bites a person, has rabies, or is suspected of having rabies. If a person is bitten by any dog, cat, or ferret—regardless of whether the animal has or is suspected of having rabies—the victim and the pet's owner (or person possessing or in control of the pet) are required to notify the local health director immediately. This law applies to all dogs, cats, and ferrets—not just those suspected of having rabies. The offending animal is then supposed to be confined for ten days in a place designated by the local health director, which may be the owner's property. If an owner fails to confine the animal as directed, he or she may be guilty of a Class 2 misdemeanor. Physicians treating persons bitten by an animal known to be a potential carrier of rabies also must notify the local health director (G.S. 130A-196).

If a dog, cat, or ferret has been bitten (or otherwise exposed to rabies) by a rabid animal or an animal suspected of having rabies and the bitten animal has not had the required vaccinations (including a booster shot within three days of being bitten), the bitten animal must either be destroyed immediately or, at the discretion of the local health director, quarantined for up to six months (G.S. 130A-197). If a dog, cat, or ferret is *suspected* of having rabies, the owner must notify the local health director and confine the animal for ten days at a place designated by the health director (G.S. 130A-98). If an animal other than a dog, cat, or ferret is suspected of having rabies, the state public health veterinarian may order that the animal be destroyed. If an animal is *diagnosed* as having rabies, it must be destroyed and its head sent to the State Public Health Laboratory (G.S. 130A-199). The county typically assumes responsibility for shipping the animal's head to the state laboratory.

If a local government or the state finds that a geographical area has a particularly high number of rabies cases, a local health director may quarantine dogs, cats, and ferrets in the area (G.S. 130A-194; 130A-195). While quarantined, the animals must stay on their owners' premises, in a veterinary hospital, or on a leash (or otherwise under the owners' control). If a wild animal (other than a bat) has rabies, the local health director in that jurisdiction may petition the state to declare a rabies emergency. In such an emergency, the Wildlife Resources Commission will likely become involved in order to minimize the threat to humans and domestic animals.

While state laws governing rabies control are fairly comprehensive, quite a few local governments have chosen to adopt local ordinances or board of health rules addressing rabies. Local governments do not have specific authority to regulate in this area but can rely instead on their general ordinance-making power (G.S. 153A-121; 160A-174) or board of health rulemaking authority (G.S. 130A-39). A rabies ordinance should not duplicate or contradict state law, but it can be useful if the local government wants to supplement state law.

---

for Euthanasia of Animals in Shelters (Aug. 2, 2012), http://www.animalsheltering.org/resources/policies_guidelines/carbon-monoxide-co-for-euthanasia-of-animals-in-shelters-1.html (last accessed Nov. 20, 2014); AVMA Guidelines for the Euthanasia of Animals (2013 edition), www.avma.org/issues/animal_welfare/euthanasia.pdf (last accessed Nov. 20, 2014) (hereinafter AVMA Guidelines).

Both HSUS and AHA have historically disapproved of the use of the carbon monoxide gas method of euthanasia for shelter animals, but for many years the AVMA Guidelines allowed it subject to certain limitations. *See* AVMA Guidelines on Euthanasia (June 2007) (on file with author). When the AVMA Guidelines were revised in 2013, the position on the use of carbon monoxide for the euthanasia of companion animals in shelters changed. The document now states that the method "is not recommended for routine euthanasia of cats and dogs. It may be considered in unusual or rare circumstances, such as natural disasters and large-scale disease outbreaks. Alternate methods with fewer conditions and disadvantages are recommended for companion animals where feasible." AVMA Guidelines, at 45. While this language strongly suggests that shelters should not use this method, the clause "where feasible" may provide North Carolina jurisdictions with some flexibility to continue using the method of euthanasia as long as it complies with all of the safety restrictions outlined in the AVMA Guidelines and the applicable provisions of state law. *See* AVMA Guidelines, at 22-23; G.S. 19A-24(a)(5); 2 N.C.A.C. 52J .0601- .0609.

4. At one point, the board of agriculture considered draft regulations that eventually would have prohibited the use of carbon monoxide gas as a form of euthanasia. In the final regulations, the board authorizes the use of gas but establishes strict guidelines governing its use. N.C. Admin. Code tit. 02, ch. 52J, §§ .0601 to .0609.

Dangerous Dogs

Every local government has probably faced the issue of a dog that is threatening or dangerous to its citizens or to other animals. State law provides a ready framework for handling dangerous dog situations, but local governments need not rely only on the state law (G.S. 67-4.1 through 4.5). They have the option of adopting their own programs for handling such animals. Many local ordinances impose additional procedural requirements, restrictions on dogs, and penalties. Some local governments have even considered (but not pursued) banning the ownership or possession of a specific breed, such as pit bulls.[5]

Under state law, the owner of a dog that is considered dangerous must comply with a series of restrictions on the freedom of that dog. For example, it must be muzzled and securely restrained when it is off its owner's property. Also, if the owner of the dog transfers its ownership or possession to another person, he or she must notify the new owner of the animal's status as a dangerous dog.

A dog is considered dangerous if it

- without provocation killed or inflicted severe injury on a person;
- is owned, kept, or trained for the purpose of dog fighting; or
- is determined by the local government to be "potentially dangerous."

The local government's responsibility under this law is to appoint a person or create a board responsible for determining whether a dog is potentially dangerous according to the definition provided in the state law (or possibly one provided in a local ordinance). In addition, the local government must appoint a separate board charged with hearing appeals from citizens whose dogs have been declared potentially dangerous. There are no requirements or limitations regarding the size or membership of either the designation or the appeals board. For example, some local governments have elected to have an animal control officer or supervisor be responsible for making the initial designation of "potentially dangerous" and identified an existing board (such as the board of health or the board of county commissioners) or a subset of an existing board to hear appeals over such designations. An owner has the right to appeal the decision of the appeals board to superior court.[6]

An owner who violates the restrictions established in state law may be subject to criminal penalties. In addition, an owner will be strictly liable for any injuries or property damage inflicted by his or her dog. Strict liability means that if a property owner or individual files a civil lawsuit against a dog owner for money damages, the court will not require proof that the dog owner was negligent in caring for or restraining the dog.

In addition to the dangerous dog laws, two other options are available to local governments in addressing problems related to dangerous animals of any kind, including dogs. Local governments have the general authority to regulate, restrict, or prohibit the possession or harboring of animals that are dangerous to persons or property (G.S. 153A-131; 160A-187).[7] In addition, local health directors have the authority to declare an animal vicious and a menace to the public's health and require the owner to confine the animal to his or her property (G.S. 130A-200). This vicious animal authority is limited to animals that attacked a person causing bodily harm.

In rare cases the misdeeds of a dog can result in serious criminal charges. In *State v. Powell*,[8] the owner of two Rottweilers was convicted of involuntary manslaughter after his unattended dogs attacked and killed a jogger. In another case, a man was convicted of assault with a deadly weapon on a government official after he directed a dog to attack a police officer and the dog obeyed.[9]

---

5. State law would likely permit a local government to adopt an ordinance banning ownership or possession of pit bulls or other breeds. For more information and recommendations regarding such an ordinance, see Jeannette Cox, "Ordinances Targeting Pit Bulls Must Be Drafted Carefully," *Local Government Law Bulletin* No. 106 (Nov. 2004), http://sogpubs.unc.edu/electronicversions/pdfs/lglb106.pdf.

6. Caswell Cnty. v. Hanks, 120 N.C. App. 489 (1995) (upholding the constitutionality of the dangerous dog law and recognizing that the appeal to superior court must be held de novo).

7. As noted above, primary jurisdiction with respect to wildlife is vested in the North Carolina Wildlife Resources Commission, and for the most part, its officers enforce statewide laws.

8. 336 N.C. 762 (1994).

9. State v. Cook, 164 N.C. App. 139, *aff'd*, 359 N.C. 185 (2004).

Animal Cruelty

Local government animal control officials are usually the first people called when someone discovers a starving animal or suspects that a person is abusing his or her pets. While local governments are not required to take action on a complaint involving animal cruelty, they often feel obliged to do so. There are both civil and criminal remedies available for addressing suspected animal cruelty.

Any citizen, including animal control officers, can seek an injunction in civil court allowing the removal of the animal from the defendant and termination of his or her right of ownership or possession (G.S. 19A-1 through -4). This type of civil action does not require the plaintiff to have "standing" to bring the case, which is unusual. In other words, any person can go to court and ask a judge for injunctive relief.

One can pursue criminal remedies for animal cruelty available under state law (G.S. 14-360 through -363.2). Remedies are available for various types of cruelty, including killing, starving, overloading, tormenting, and abandoning animals. Animal fighting, which includes being a spectator at an animal fight, also is subject to criminal penalties that vary depending on the type of animal and activity involved.

County officials may want to leverage the resources of nonprofit animal rights advocacy organizations in their communities to assist them in responding to cruelty complaints and conducting investigations. They may do so by appointing individuals to serve as animal cruelty investigators (G.S. 19A-45 through -49). These individuals are appointed by the board of county commissioners for one-year terms and serve without compensation or benefits (though they can be reimbursed for expenses). Typically, they are concerned individuals or advocates, not county employees. These investigators also rely on the civil remedies (i.e., injunction) available to resolve cruelty cases, but they have the unique authority to obtain a magistrate's order authorizing them to seize an animal prior to filing a civil complaint in district court. Absent exigent circumstances, animal control officers do not have the authority to seize animals until a court has so ordered.

In addition to the state laws governing cruelty described above, local governments also have the authority to adopt their own ordinances related to animal abuse (G.S. 153A-127; 160A-182). The term *abuse* is not defined in the law but probably is comparable to the term *cruelty*, which is defined broadly in the context of the state's civil remedies to include "every act, omission, or neglect whereby unjustifiable physical pain, suffering, or death is caused or permitted" (G.S. 19A-1).[10] A similar definition is used in the criminal cruelty laws (G.S. 14-360). Some local governments have relied on this authority to outlaw specific types of abuse or cruelty that are illegal, such as leaving an animal inside an unattended vehicle. Others have adopted procedural requirements related to the role of animal control officers when responding to a complaint.

Stray Animals

There are three state laws that address animals running at-large, but they are quite limited in scope. The laws apply to dogs running at-large at night, female dogs in heat, and dogs in wildlife management areas (G.S. 67.2; 67-12; 67-14.1). While the state does not have a statewide leash law, it does authorize animal control officers to impound unidentified animals that are not wearing rabies tags, as discussed above (G.S. 130A-192). Local governments regularly rely on this authority in the rabies law to impound stray animals, but some have found that a local leash law is necessary as well. Cities have specific authority to adopt a law regulating animals running at-large (G.S. 160A-186). Under that statute, cities may adopt ordinances that allow animals running at-large to be seized and, after reasonable efforts to notify their owners, either sold (which likely includes adoption) or destroyed. Counties, however, do not have specific authority but rather must rely on their general ordinance-making power to define, regulate, prohibit, or abate acts, omissions, or conditions detrimental to the health, safety, or welfare of their citizens as well as to define and abate nuisances (G.S. 153A-121).

10. *See* William A. Reppy Jr., "Citizen Standing to Enforce Anti-Cruelty Laws by Obtaining Injunctions: The North Carolina Experience," 11 Animal L. 39, 46–49 (2005) (arguing that the term *cruelty* as used in the state's civil remedies laws should also include mental suffering and that the term *unjustifiable* inappropriately limits the scope of the definition).

Shelter Management

Local governments are allowed to own or operate an animal shelter, but they are not required to do so (G.S. 153A-442; 160A-493). Many have chosen to establish public shelters within their jurisdictions while others have elected to pool resources with other localities to operate a regional shelter. Quite a few have entered into agreements with local humane societies or other nonprofit organizations that allow the local government to house animals at private shelters or, in the case of large animals such as horses, on private farms or boarding facilities.

Providing room and board as well as veterinary care to impounded animals can be expensive. In some situations, the shelter may be able to recover some of its costs, such as when a stray animal is retrieved or an animal is adopted. Also, when a shelter houses an animal seized in the course of a civil or criminal cruelty case, an animal fighting case, or a dangerous dog case, the shelter may ask a court to order the defendant to pay for the care of the animal or to make other arrangements for the animal's care until the case is resolved (G.S. 19A-70). In most cases, however, the local government and its nonprofit partners absorb the costs of sheltering and caring for impounded animals.

Shelters must comply with the state's Animal Welfare Act, which is enforced by the Animal Welfare Section of the Veterinary Division of the Department of Agriculture and Consumer Services (Department of Agriculture) (G.S. Chapter 19A, Article 3). The law addresses the physical condition of shelters, minimum holding periods for animals, public inspection of animals, animal care, euthanasia practices, and training of euthanasia technicians.

Licensing

Local governments have the authority to require pet owners to pay an annual license tax (G.S. 153A-153; 160A-212). Some local governments have generated significant income streams from these taxes. The licensing and taxing authority not only generates revenue, but it can serve two other purposes. First, it can provide local governments with an additional mechanism for addressing stray animals within the jurisdiction. A local government, for example, could have an ordinance authorizing animal control to impound any animal found without a license. Second, a jurisdiction that adopts a program of differential licensing (i.e., higher license taxes for animals that have not been spayed or neutered) can help reduce the population of stray and unwanted animals. Some jurisdictions have concluded, however, that the administrative burden of collecting such a tax outweighs its potential benefits.

Spay/Neuter Assistance Program

The state operates a program that allocates funding to local governments to reimburse them for the direct costs of spay/neuter surgeries for cats and dogs owned by low-income individuals (G.S. 19A-60 through -65). In 2010, the funding stream for the program changed, and administration of the program shifted from the Veterinary Public Health Program in the Department of Health and Human Services to the Animal Welfare Section of the Veterinary Division of the Department of Agriculture and Consumer Services. In 2012, the state reimbursed twenty-eight local governments more than $500,000 for almost 10,000 surgeries.[11]

Exotic Animals

North Carolina does not have a general statewide law regulating the ownership or possession of exotic animals. The Wildlife Resources Commission exercises jurisdiction over native North Carolina wildlife, but it does not have author-

11. More information about the spay/neuter program is available from the Veterinary Division of the North Carolina Department of Agriculture and Consumer Services, www.ncagr.gov/vet/aws/Fix/index.htm (last visited Sept. 13, 2013).

ity to regulate nonnative animals, such as tigers and elephants. The General Assembly has considered establishing a more comprehensive statewide law on the subject but has yet to do so.

In the absence of a statewide law, many local governments have adopted local exotic animal ordinances. Local governments have specific authority under state law to regulate any animals that are deemed dangerous to persons or property (G.S. 153A-131; 160A-187). This authority is clearly applicable to animals that may injure a person (e.g., tigers) but could also be interpreted to extend to the regulation of animals that could transmit diseases to persons or domestic animals. In the absence of a local ordinance, a county health director may place restrictions on any "vicious" animal that has attacked a person without being provoked (G.S. 130A-200).

About the Author

Aimee N. Wall is a School of Government faculty member with an interest in social services law, animal control law, and legislative education.

Chapter 34

Emergency Management

Norma R. Houston

Cities and counties are vested with both the authority and the responsibility to prepare for, respond to, recover from, and mitigate the impact of natural and man-made disasters. These functions are carried out through local emergency management agencies. Growing out of World War II–era civil defense organizations, today's emergency management agencies are expected to prepare for and to respond to a wide array of disasters ranging from floods, tornadoes, and hurricanes to terrorist attacks and pandemic disease outbreaks. As a result, the skills, training, and resources necessary to respond effectively to these threats have become increasingly specialized and complex. In today's post-9/11 world, there is greater public concern about threats both natural and man-made. In today's post-Katrina world, there is also increased public scrutiny of the government's responsiveness to these threats. Regardless of their magnitude or scope, all disasters are, at their core, local events, requiring local governments to act as first responders in protecting public health, safety, and welfare.

What Is Emergency Management?

Protecting the public health, safety, and welfare is a basic function of government at all levels. When a disaster strikes, this function is carried out under what is generally referred to as "emergency management," which is collectively "those measures taken by the populace and government at federal, state, and local levels to minimize the adverse effect of any type emergency."[1] Examples of such measures include evacuation, sheltering, search and rescue, emergency medical care, and debris removal.

1. N.C. Gen. Stat. (hereinafter G.S.) Ch. 166A, § 19.3(8).

Emergency management is, however, more encompassing than the obvious and necessary activities that occur during and immediately after a disaster event. It is a "never-ending preparedness cycle of prevention, response, recovery, mitigation, warning, movement, shelter, emergency assistance, and recovery."[2] Emergency managers typically refer to the following activities as the four phases of emergency management: preparedness, response, recovery, and mitigation. Under federal law, local governments are encouraged to develop comprehensive disaster preparedness and assistance plans, threat analyses, and community risk assessments, as well as hazard mitigation measures to reduce losses from disasters (including developing land use and construction regulations).[3] Under state law, counties are in fact required to develop emergency management plans.[4] Ideally, emergency management plans address not only initial post-disaster first response and subsequent recovery activities, but also prevention and mitigation measures, all of which, when taken together, result in effective and efficient management of disasters in which injury and loss of life and property are minimized.

Sources of Authority

Emergency management programs and authorities are governed by both state and federal law. North Carolina law also authorizes the adoption of local emergency management ordinances that are required for local governments to exercise certain emergency powers .

At the federal level, emergency management activities are governed by statutes, regulations, policies, and guidance documents. The Robert T. Stafford Disaster Relief and Emergency Assistance Act (commonly referred to as "the Stafford Act")[5] is the statute enacted by Congress empowering the federal government to support a state's response in times of crisis. It authorizes the president to issue disaster declarations and establishes the programs and processes the federal government uses to provide emergency and major disaster assistance to states, local governments, and other eligible recipients of federal disaster aid, including individual citizens. Various parts of Title 44 of the Code of Federal Regulations (Emergency Management and Assistance) further define this assistance. Administrative policies and guidance documents adopted by various federal agencies (including the U.S. Department of Homeland Security and the Federal Emergency Management Agency) provide detailed instructions for administering federal disaster assistance programs.

In North Carolina, the legal authority for emergency management activities by state and local governments is found in North Carolina General Statutes (hereinafter G.S.) Chapter 166A (the North Carolina Emergency Management Act of 1977).[6] Article 1A of Chapter 166A outlines the powers of and the relationships between state and local governments for disaster planning and response activities and authorizes both state and local governments to issue disaster declarations. Article 36A of G.S. Chapter 14 (Riots, Civil Disorders, and Emergencies) imposes criminal penalties for certain activities undertaken during riots and emergency situations.

Disaster declarations at the federal, state, and local levels trigger a wide array of governmental powers as well as disaster relief assistance. These declarations, and their significance, are discussed more fully in this chapter.

2. G.S. 166A-19.3(8). *See also* Ward v. Long Beach Volunteer Rescue Squad, 151 N.C. App. 717 (2002).

3. 42 U.S.C. § 5121(b); 44 C.F.R. § 206.3(b).

4. G.S. 166A-19.15(a).

5. Pub. L. No. 93-288, 88 Stat. 143 (May 22, 1974), *codified as amended at* 42 U.S.C. §§ 5121–5206. Enacted by Congress in 1988, the Stafford Act, Pub. L. 100-707, 102 Stat. 4689 (Nov. 23, 1988), amended the Disaster Relief Act of 1974.

6. Enacted in 1977, G.S. Chapter 166A is a rewrite of the former G.S. Chapter 166, the Civil Defense Preparedness Act. Article 1 of Chapter 166A was repealed and recodified as Chapter 1A in 2012.

What Is the Difference Between a "Disaster" and an "Emergency"?

In North Carolina, the word "disaster" often conjures up images of major hurricanes, such as Hugo, Fran, Floyd, Isabel, Ophelia, Ivan, Frances, and Irene, or of severe ice storms accompanied by prolonged power outages. In recent years, tornadoes have struck a number of North Carolina communities with devastating effects. While these examples are certainly disasters in every sense of the word, the meaning of the word "disaster" in North Carolina law refers only to the declaration issued by the governor based on the impact of an "emergency."

State law defines an "emergency" as "an occurrence or imminent threat of widespread or severe damage, injury, or loss of life or property resulting from any natural or man-made accidental, military, paramilitary, weather related, or riot related cause."[7] Federal law, through the Stafford Act, defines a "major disaster" as "any natural catastrophe or, regardless of cause, any fire, flood, or explosion in any part of the United States, which in the determination of the President causes damage of sufficient severity and magnitude to warrant major disaster assistance under this Act to supplement the efforts and available resources of states, local governments, and disaster relief organizations in alleviating the damage, loss, hardship, or suffering caused thereby."[8] The Stafford Act defines an "emergency" as "any occasion for which, in the determination of the President, Federal Assistance is needed to supplement state and local efforts and capabilities to save lives and to protect property and public health and safety, or to lessen or avert the threat of a catastrophe in any part of the United States."[9]

Two points regarding these definitions are worth noting. First, North Carolina's definition of emergency and the federal definition of disaster both include natural and man-made occurrences. Thus, local governments should plan for a broad array of potential threats (not just hurricanes or ice storms). Second, under the Stafford Act, federal assistance is supplemental to the resources of state and local governments, which bear responsibility for the initial disaster response. Indeed, the primary responder in any disaster is, first and foremost, the local government in whose jurisdiction the emergency has occurred.

Roles and Responsibilities—Federal and State

Federal Government

Emergency management operations in any major disaster necessarily involve coordination and cooperation between a myriad of federal, state, and local government agencies and personnel, as well as private disaster relief organizations such as the Red Cross and the Salvation Army. This coordinated effort is led at the federal level by the Federal Emergency Management Agency (FEMA).

FEMA was formally authorized in 1979 in an executive order issued by President Jimmy Carter.[10] Its mission is to lead the national effort to prepare for all hazards and to effectively manage federal response and recovery efforts following any national incident. FEMA also initiates proactive mitigation activities, trains first responders and other emergency management personnel, and manages the National Flood Insurance Program. FEMA operated for more than twenty years as an independent federal agency, with its director appointed by and reporting directly to the president. In March 2003, however, FEMA joined twenty-two other federal agencies, programs, and offices to form the U.S. Department of Homeland Security. Now the director of FEMA serves under the Secretary of Homeland Security, though he or she still retains responsibility for the agency's core mission. Functionally, FEMA is not a *direct* response agency (i.e., FEMA officials are not first responders), but it is a *support* agency, coordinating federal resources and assets to supplement those of state and local governments. In major disasters, this effort can involve numerous federal, state, and local agencies and private disaster relief organizations from across the country.

---

7. G.S. 166A-19.3(6).
8. 42 U.S.C. § 5122(2); *see also* 44 C.F.R. § 206.2(a)(17).
9. 42 U.S.C. § 5122(1); *see also* 44 C.F.R. § 206.2(a)(9).
10. Federal emergency response efforts had actually existed since the early 1800s but had been handled in a fragmented manner by multiple and sometimes overlapping agencies without overall coordination at the federal level.

To better facilitate communication and coordination between multiple governmental agencies across multi-jurisdictional lines in domestic disaster response situations, President George W. Bush directed the Department of Homeland Security to develop and administer a National Incident Management System (NIMS).[11] Under NIMS, federal, state, and local governments are expected to utilize standardized terminology and organizational structures, interoperable (technically compatible) communications, consolidated action plans, unified command structures, and other similar measures designed to facilitate consistent, efficient, and effective incident management.[12] These unified efforts are to be employed in all disaster situations whether natural or man-made (the "all-hazards" approach). By proclamation, Governor Mike Easley established NIMS as the standard for incident management in North Carolina in May 2005 and directed all counties to adopt and apply NIMS for management of all incidents. Similarly, federal directives also require local governments to adopt and utilize NIMS and to train local personnel "directly involved" in emergency management operations on NIMS procedures and protocols.[13] Local governments were required to meet this compliance requirement by October 1, 2006 (corresponding with the beginning of federal fiscal year 2006), in order to be eligible for federal preparedness assistance funds (which include first responder grants, emergency management planning grants, and hazardous materials program grants). Federal disaster relief funds administered under the Stafford Act are not considered "preparedness funds," so local governments not in compliance with NIMS are still eligible for federal aid in a federally declared disaster.

State Government

In North Carolina, the governor has general direction and control of the state's emergency management program and is vested with broad powers to act when necessary in a disaster situation.[14] Under the governor, the Secretary of the Department of Public Safety oversees state emergency management activities. Within the public safety department, the Division of Emergency Management (NCDEM) has direct responsibility for day-to-day operations and primary responsibility in coordinating the state's disaster response efforts. To fulfill this responsibility, NCDEM oversees the State Emergency Response Team (SERT), a group of state agency personnel designated to carry out emergency management support functions and to coordinate "the activities of all agencies for emergency management within the State, including planning, organizing, staffing, equipping, training, testing, and the activation of emergency management programs."[15] NCDEM also administers the state's hazard mitigation program and flood plain mapping program and is authorized to promulgate standards for local emergency management plans and programs and to provide technical assistance to local governments.[16] Other responsibilities of NCDEM include maintaining the State Emergency Operations Center, planning for emergencies at nuclear power plants, and managing mutual aid.

The state coordinates with local emergency management agencies through a regional structure reflecting the state's geography—three branch offices (eastern, central, and western) and fifteen areas within the three branches.[17] During disaster response and recovery operations, local governments communicate damage assessments and requests for assistance through this administrative structure, and deployment of assets and resources are coordinated at the state level. Similarly, in a major disaster involving federal agencies, local needs not met at the state level are communicated

---

11. Homeland Security Presidential Directive/HSPD-5—Management of Domestic Incidents (Feb. 28, 2003) (hereinafter HSPD-5), www.fas.org/irp/offdocs/nspd/hspd-5.html.

12. A key component of NIMS is the Incident Command System (ICS) used by major firefighting agencies for almost thirty years. ICS is a standardized on-scene system used by all emergency responders that allows for coordinated use of equipment and personnel with standardized processes for response to all sizes and types of incidents. ICS is used at the local, state, and federal levels and by private sectors involved in emergency management activities. Information about ICS, including available training courses, is available at www.training.fema.gov/EMIWeb/IS/ICSResource/index.htm.

13. HSPD-5, § (20).

14. G.S. 166A-19.10(b).

15. G.S. 166A-19.12 (1).

16. G.S. 166A-19.12(5).

17. To determine where a particular county is assigned within the area and branch structure, see www.ncdps.gov/imgs/EM/EMGraphics/NCEMareas-August2013.png.

by NCDEM to FEMA. Through its branch and area structure, NCDEM also delivers training programs and planning assistance for local emergency management agencies.

Roles and Responsibilities—Local Government

Emergency management response activities are initiated at the local level, augmented by state resources where local resources are insufficient, and, in major emergencies, augmented by federal resources at the request of the state. Local governments clearly play a critical role in the "never-ending preparedness cycle" of emergency management operations.

Legal Authority

Under the North Carolina Emergency Management Act, the governing body of the county is specifically charged with the responsibility for coordinating all emergency management efforts at the local level, including those of *cities within the county*.[18] To accomplish these functions, counties are authorized to

- establish local emergency management agencies;
- appoint an emergency management coordinator;
- appropriate and expend local funds;
- make contracts;
- obtain and distribute equipment, materials, and supplies;
- develop emergency management plans;
- establish voluntary registries of functionally and medically fragile persons; and
- provide for the health and safety of persons and property.

Counties are also authorized to adopt ordinances imposing restrictions and prohibitions during a declared state of emergency.[19] While cities are similarly authorized,[20] their agencies and activities are still subject to coordination by the county.[21]

Organizational Structure

Each county is required to designate an emergency management coordinator (or director; the terms are used interchangeably herein), and many cities have similarly designated personnel. Roughly, only a quarter of the counties in the state employ full-time emergency management coordinators; the majority designate an employee or department head who performs other duties generally related to emergency management and first responder activities (such as EMS director, fire marshal, or 911 supervisor). The emergency management coordinator maintains and implements the jurisdiction's emergency management plan and oversees other administrative and operational functions. His or her duties include coordinating the activities of other local departments involved in disaster response and recovery operations, such as public information, public works, EMS, fire and rescue, law enforcement, finance, social services, and public health, as well as coordinating local efforts with those of state and federal agencies and private relief organizations. The number of additional staff assigned to local emergency management agencies varies from jurisdiction to jurisdiction and traditionally has been small. Employees of local emergency management agencies receiving federal grant-in-aid funds are covered under the State Personnel Act[22] and are subject to certain statutory requirements as conditions of employment.[23]

18. G.S. 166A-19.15(a).
19. G.S. 166A-19.22.
20. G.S. 166A-19.31.
21. G.S. 166A-19.15(c).
22. G.S. 126-5(a)(2)(d). For more information about the State Personnel Act and its application to local government employees, see Chapter 13, "Public Employment Law."
23. G.S. 166A-19.75.

As with federal and state emergency management agencies, local agencies serve a coordinating role in emergency events; they are not ordinance-enforcing agencies. Some emergencies, by their nature, require other agencies to take certain actions and even assume lead roles, such as public health agencies in pandemic flu outbreaks or law enforcement agencies in terrorism events. Whatever the specific nature of the emergency, however, the local emergency management director is still responsible for coordinating response and recovery efforts and for communicating the local government's needs to state and federal agencies. An effective emergency management director is not only well-prepared and well-trained, but he or she also fully understands the state and federal emergency management systems and has developed within the state the contacts necessary to effectively and efficiently secure the resources his or her local government and community need in times of crisis.

Planning

One of the most important ongoing responsibilities of the local emergency management director is developing and maintaining the local government's emergency management plan. Local plans must be consistent with federal NIMS requirements and are subject to state and federal approval. The county or local emergency operation plan (EOP) may be a single or a multi-jurisdictional (watershed) plan.[24] Taking the federal "all-hazards" approach to incident management, local plans should identify all potential risks and hazards to the community and outline procedures for responding to and recovering from those threats. Plans delineate the roles and responsibilities of agencies and resources at the local level (including volunteer organizations) and set out the chain of command through which decisions are made and communicated. Plans must be updated every five years to be eligible for FEMA hazard mitigation grant funding.[25] Ideally, local jurisdictions conduct exercises and drills of their plans and operations to maintain readiness. Some jurisdictions containing certain high-risk facilities, such as nuclear power plants, have additional planning and exercise requirements mandated by both state and federal law. If properly developed, exercised, and implemented, the local plan can effectively guide the jurisdiction's response and recovery operations in a disaster event and can also serve as the basis for determining whether local resources are sufficient to meet the community's needs. If not, local jurisdictions can seek emergency aid and assistance from other units of government.

State and local governments must also adopt hazard mitigation plans in which mitigation strategies are identified for hazards that threaten the particular jurisdiction.[26] The FEMA plan assessment tool may be used to assist local departments and elected officials involved in implementing the local mitigation plan.[27] Regulations require documentation that all stakeholders, including "agencies that have authority to regulate development including . . . elected officials[,]" had an opportunity to be involved in plan development.[28] Local emergency managers are encouraged to solicit public participation in maintaining the plan through presentations to elected officials and community groups.[29]

24. 44 C.F.R. § 201.6(a)(4). Multi-jurisdictional hazard mitigation plans are prepared jointly by more than one jurisdiction and may include counties, municipalities, cities, towns, townships, school districts or other special districts, councils of government or other regional organizations, or unincorporated areas. These plans may contemplate cost-saving through sharing resources and personnel in large-scale events. For more information about multi-jurisdictional mitigation planning, see FEMA, *Multi-Jurisdictional Mitigation Planning, State and Local Mitigation Planning How-To Guide Number Eight* (Aug. 2006), www.fema.gov/media-library-data/20130726-1523-20490-0509/howto8_092006.pdf.

25. 44 C.F.R. § 201.6(d)(3).

26. The requirements and procedures for state, tribal, and local mitigation plans are set out in 44 C.F.R. Part 201. *See generally* FEMA, "Mitigation Planning Laws, Regulations, & Guidance," www.fema.gov/mitigation-planning-laws-regulations-guidance.

27. FEMA, *Local Mitigation Plan Review Guide* (Oct. 1, 2011) (hereinafter *Plan Review Guide*), www.fema.gov/media-library-data/20130726-1809-25045-7498/plan_review_guide_final_9_30_11.pdf.

28. 44 C.F.R. § 201.6(b)(2).

29. 44 C.F.R. § 6(c)(4)(iii); *see also Plan Review Guide*, p. 17.

Intergovernmental Cooperation

Disasters rarely impact an area conveniently located within just one government's jurisdiction and can exceed the response capabilities of local and even state governments. Recognizing the need for coordinated responses and emergency assistance across jurisdictional lines, North Carolina law authorizes three main forms of interlocal cooperation with other units of government. First, for cooperation with other jurisdictions *outside North Carolina*, the General Assembly enacted the Emergency Management Assistance Compact (EMAC), under which North Carolina and other EMAC member states provide reciprocal emergency assistance when a state of emergency has been declared in an affected state.[30] The governor is authorized to enter into mutual aid agreements with other states and with the federal government for disaster assistance and relief, and local governments in North Carolina are authorized to enter into mutual aid agreements with units of local government in other states (subject to the governor's approval).[31] Operating under mutual aid agreements allows for effective and efficient cooperation among units of government, addresses liability and insurance issues (personnel operating under a mutual aid agreement enjoy the same liability protections as employees of the unit of government to whom the assistance is rendered), and can expedite federal reimbursement in a federally declared disaster. Local personnel providing disaster assistance to out-of-state jurisdictions are advised to do so either under the direction of the state through EMAC or through a mutual aid agreement entered into directly with the jurisdiction they are assisting.

Second, for cooperation between local jurisdictions *within North Carolina*, local governments are authorized to enter into mutual aid agreements with one another for reciprocal emergency management aid and assistance.[32] This assistance includes furnishing or exchanging supplies, equipment, personnel, and services on a temporary basis during an emergency event. A common example of mutual aid is law enforcement personnel from other cities and counties deploying to the affected jurisdiction to assist in enforcing curfews, traffic control, and re-entry checkpoints.

Third, to facilitate coordination *between North Carolina counties and the cities within those counties*, state law authorizes counties and cities within those counties to form joint local emergency management agencies.[33] Typically, each unit of local government participating in the joint agency assigns a representative to serve on that unit's behalf in the command structure of the joint agency, and all units agree to coordinate emergency management functions under a unified set of standard operating procedures. Local governments may also enter into interlocal agreements under Article 20 of G.S. Chapter 160A to cooperatively undertake any function they are authorized to carry out. Under such interlocal agreements, units of local government may agree to perform specific services or functions (such as debris removal) jointly or on behalf of one another instead of forming a joint agency.

Disaster and Emergency Declarations—Federal and State

Federal Declarations

The declaration of a state of disaster (or, in the case of state and local governments, a state of emergency) is issued when the declaring authority has determined that a disaster (or emergency) or the threat thereof exists. At the federal level, a disaster declaration is issued by the president, upon request of the governor of the affected state (after a state declaration has been issued), when the president finds that the disaster is of such severity and magnitude that effective response is beyond the capabilities of the state and the affected local governments and that federal assistance is necessary.[34] The severity and magnitude of the disaster is initially evaluated through preliminary damage assessments that gauge the scope of the damage, estimated repair costs, the combined capabilities of state and local governments to respond, and

30. G.S. Ch. 166A, Art. 4.
31. G.S. 166A-19.72.
32. G.S. 166A-19.72(c).
33. G.S. 166A-19.15(d).
34. 42 U.S.C. § 5170.

unmet needs for which supplemental federal assistance is required.[35] In evaluating the state's request and preliminary damage assessment reports, consideration is given to such factors as

- the amount and type of damage;
- the impact of that damage on state and local governments and individual citizens;
- the level of resources available to affected states, local governments, and their citizens;
- the extent and type of insurance in place to cover losses;
- the existence of imminent threats to public health and safety; and
- any other factors relevant to determining whether federal assistance is needed.

If FEMA recommends and the president finds that the situation is of sufficient severity and magnitude to warrant federal assistance, a presidential major disaster declaration is issued identifying the affected geographic areas covered under the declaration and authorizing federal assistance under various individual and public assistance programs.[36]

State Declarations

At the state level, a state of emergency can be declared by either the governor or the General Assembly upon a finding that an emergency exists.[37] A state of emergency declaration activates the state's emergency operations plan. Once the emergency has passed, the severity and magnitude of the event is determined by preliminary damage assessments. Based on those assessments, the governor is authorized to issue a disaster declaration.[38] Depending on the level of damage and losses, along with additional criteria set out in the statute, one of three types of state disaster declarations can be issued, in ascending order of severity: Type I, Type II, or Type III.[39] The declaration describes the affected geographic area covered under the declaration and authorizes state assistance programs. The length of time that a disaster declaration remains in effect depends on its type, ranging from sixty days to twenty-four months. A state disaster declaration may be extended by either the governor or the General Assembly.

A state disaster declaration triggers a broad array of gubernatorial powers (some of which require concurrence by the Council of State), including the power to direct or compel evacuations; restrict movement of people and vehicular traffic; deploy resources and assets of the state for relief efforts and to maintain public order and safety; establish a system of economic controls over critical resources (such as rationing or price freezing); and condemn, seize, or otherwise take property.[40] The governor also has the authority to declare the existence of an "abnormal market disruption" to the production, distribution, or sale of goods and services resulting from a natural or man-made disaster in this state as well as in other states where a federal declaration has been issued (an example would be the threat of disruption to fuel supplies in North Carolina following Hurricane Katrina and the resulting spiraling increase in gas prices). If the governor finds and declares that an abnormal market disruption exists, then excessive pricing practices prohibitions are triggered and remain in effect for forty-five days unless extended by the governor.[41]

State of Emergency Declarations—Local

At the local government level, only cities and counties are authorized to issue local state of emergency declarations.[42] Such declarations activate local plans, mutual aid and interlocal agreements and compacts, and local ordinances

35. 44 C.F.R. § 206.36.
36. 44 C.F.R. §§ 206.37, .38.
37. G.S. 166A-19.20.
38. G.S. 166A-19.21.
39. *Id.* (describing the three types of declarations in more detail).
40. G.S. 166A-19.30.
41. G.S. 75-38.
42. G.S. 166A-19.22.

authorizing certain restrictions, prohibitions, and other measures taken to protect public health, safety, and welfare during the period of the emergency declaration in the affected areas covered by the declaration.

Through local state of emergency declarations, local officials may put in place temporary restrictions and other measures necessary to preserve public order and protect public safety and welfare during an emergency. When properly authorized by local ordinance, law enforcement personnel (including those from other jurisdictions assisting under mutual aid agreements) can aid in emergency response efforts by fully enforcing locally imposed restrictions and prohibitions. Local declarations are also, in most instances, a prerequisite to receiving financial assistance through state and federal disaster relief programs. This assistance is critical to a local government's response and recovery efforts; it can also help mitigate the fiscal disaster that can follow a natural or man-made disaster.

Who Can Issue a Declaration?

State law authorizes the city or county governing board to issue a local state of emergency declaration. By local ordinance, the board may delegate its declaration authority to the board chair or mayor.[43] State law does not require the governing board to ratify a local official's declaration. The state of emergency remains in effect until terminated by the official or governing body that declared it.

Where Do Local Declarations Apply?

A state of emergency may apply to all or part of the declaring jurisdiction's geographic area. This allows local officials to impose restrictions only on the affected areas of their jurisdictions. If the declaration does not specify a particular geographic area, it applies throughout the entire jurisdiction.[44]

Declarations issued in an individual local jurisdiction are not applicable to neighboring jurisdictions except by consent. Thus, the ordinances adopted by a county imposing the kinds of restrictions and prohibitions discussed above do not apply in a city within that county unless consented to by the mayor or city council. Similarly, a city can only enforce its emergency ordinance within its own corporate jurisdiction. However, the chair of a county board of commissioners may extend to some or all parts of the county emergency restrictions imposed within a city by a mayor if so requested, even if the emergency has not occurred directly within the county itself.[45] Such an extension of city-imposed measures may be necessary to assist the city in responding to an emergency. In major events, it is common for state of emergency declarations to be issued jointly or cooperatively by the county and cities within the county imposing county-wide uniform prohibitions and restrictions.

The authority granted independently to cities and counties to declare emergencies and impose restrictions does not override the management structure set out in G.S. Chapter 166A, where the county is designated as the primary coordinator of emergency management activities at the local level. Cities, while vested with independent authority to declare states of emergency within their jurisdictions,[46] must still coordinate emergency management plans, activities, and operations with and under the direction of the county.[47] While these two statutory provisions may at first appear to be in conflict, taken together, they properly distinguish between the legal authority to impose restrictions and take other such measures necessary in times of emergency and the operational planning and implementation of such plans necessary to respond to emergencies in an efficient and coordinated manner.

---

43. G.S. 166A-19.22(a); 166A-19.15(f)(4). In the case of absence or disability by the board chair or mayor, the person authorized to act in that official's stead may act. G.S. 166A-19.3(2), (11).

44. G.S. 166A-19.22(b)(1).

45. G.S. 166A-19.22(b)(3).

46. G.S. 166A-19.22.

47. G.S. 166A-19.15.

What Restrictions Can Be Imposed?

Local governments may adopt ordinances that are then triggered by local state of emergency declarations.[48] If authorized in the local ordinance, a local governing board or official (if operating under delegated authority) may impose during the state of emergency the following restrictions and prohibitions, alone or in combination depending on the circumstances and severity of the emergency:

- restrictions/prohibitions on the movement of people in public places, including imposing curfews; directing and compelling the voluntary or mandatory evacuation of all or part of the population from any stricken or threatened area within the governing body's jurisdiction; prescribing routes, modes of transportation, and destinations in connection with evacuation; and controlling ingress and egress of an emergency area and the movement of persons within the area;
- restrictions/prohibitions on the operation of businesses and other places to or from which people may travel or congregate;
- restrictions/prohibitions on the possession, transportation, sale, purchase, and consumption of alcoholic beverages;
- restrictions/prohibitions on the possession, transportation, sale, purchase, storage, and use of dangerous weapons and substances and gasoline, except that restrictions on dangerous weapons cannot be imposed on lawfully possessed firearms (handguns, shotguns, and rifles) and ammunition; and/or
- restrictions/prohibitions on any other activity or condition the control of which may be reasonably necessary to maintain order and protect lives or property during a state of emergency.

A local government is not *required* to impose these measures when it declares a local state of emergency; it may elect to impose only those measures it determines are required to effectively respond to that particular emergency. In order to be legally effective, however, these measures *must* be authorized by local ordinance; measures not authorized cannot be triggered under a state of emergency declaration. Nor can such measures be enforced by law enforcement officials without having been authorized by the local ordinance. For example, if a local government restricts or prohibits general public access to a particularly devastated area within its jurisdiction because of public safety concerns (washed-out roads, sinkholes, environmental contamination, unstable and falling buildings, etc.), law enforcement personnel will have difficulty enforcing this restriction, and prosecutors will have difficulty prosecuting violators of it, without proper legal authority for imposing the restriction in the first place. Violations of any such measures or other emergency ordinance provisions are punishable as Class 2 misdemeanors.[49]

Emergency restrictions and prohibitions may remain in effect for the duration of the emergency event, or they may be modified and rescinded as the unit progresses through response and recovery after the event. For example, a mayor might impose a curfew city-wide immediately after a tornado strikes, and then lift the curfew in unaffected areas of the city after damage assessments have been completed. Modifications to emergency declarations are issued in the same manner as the original declaration.

Other Restrictions and Prohibitions

In addition to the restrictions that may be imposed through local ordinance during a state of emergency, Article 36A of G.S. Chapter 14 directly prescribes other restrictions on public conduct in times of emergency. Among these are prohibitions against rioting (G.S. 14-288.2), looting, and trespassing during an emergency (G.S. 14-288.6); manufacturing or possessing weapons of mass destruction (G.S. 14-288.8); and assaulting emergency personnel (G.S. 14-288.9). Addition-

48. G.S. 166A-19.31. The constitutionality of these restrictions and prohibitions has been upheld as a proper delegation of the state's police powers to local governments. State v. Dobbins, 277 N.C. 484 (1971); United States v. Chalk, 441 F.2d 1277 (4th Cir. 1971), *cert. denied*, 202 U.S. 943 (1971).

49. G.S. 14-288.20A.

ally, law enforcement officers are authorized to frisk persons who are violating an emergency curfew (G.S. 14-288.10) and to inspect vehicles entering or approaching a city in which a state of emergency has been declared (G.S. 14-288.11).

A local state of emergency declaration also triggers protections for consumers against price gouging, which, unfortunately, often follows soon after a major disaster.[50] G.S. 75-38 prohibits excessive pricing practices during a state of emergency by a seller of goods or services consumed or used as a direct result of an emergency or which are consumed or used to preserve, protect, or sustain life, health, safety, or economic well-being. This prohibition applies not only to the seller, but to all parties in the chain of distribution of the good or services (such as the manufacturer, wholesaler, or distributor). A state disaster declaration also triggers these consumer protection measures.

Paying for Disasters—Who Bears the Costs?

Local Funding

The regular operational costs for most local emergency management agencies are funded through local General Fund appropriations. All counties receive federal emergency management planning grant (EMPG) funds to support local emergency management operations and are eligible for other federal grant funds for one-time expenses (equipment, training, etc.). Some local governments (typically those in high-risk areas of the state) have established reserve funds to pay for expenses incurred during emergencies. Normal local funding levels are often inadequate to cover the costs of emergency response and recovery operations, however, especially in major disasters. In these instances, federal and state disaster declarations authorize various assistance programs through which eligible local governments can receive supplemental funding.

Federal Assistance Programs

Under a federal disaster declaration, three main categories of assistance can be authorized: *public assistance* (PA), which is assistance to public entities such as cities, counties, school systems, and other units of government; *individual assistance* (IA), which is assistance to private individuals; and *hazard mitigation*, which is available to both public entities and private individuals. Examples of PA include reimbursement for costs incurred for repair to public infrastructure, debris removal, and emergency protective measures. Examples of IA include temporary housing assistance, home repair funds, unemployment benefits, food coupons, legal services, crisis counseling, and small business loans. Examples of hazard mitigation include funding for building elevation and flood control measures.

The guidelines for PA are described in 44 C.F.R. Part 206. PA programs operate primarily on a cost-sharing reimbursement basis—the local government incurs an eligible cost directly associated with a declared disaster and applies to the federal government for reimbursement. Federal reimbursement is provided at a rate of at least 75 percent of the eligible cost[51] and may be extended to cover as much as 100 percent of the eligible costs in severe disasters. The nonfederal share of these costs is traditionally funded by the state, but local governments could be required to assume some portion of the nonfederal share if that share is not fully covered by state funds.

Local governments can seek cost reimbursement for three main categories of disaster-related work expenses: debris removal, emergency protective measures, and permanent restoration (such as repair of public infrastructure). While there are specific eligibility criteria for each category of work, all work performed and all costs incurred must be as a direct result of a declared emergency and must occur within an area covered under an emergency declaration, and the work must be the legal responsibility of the local government. Federal reimbursement is not available for costs that are covered by another source (such as insurance) or for "losses" (as opposed to costs), such as lost tax revenues.

---

50. G.S. 166A-19.23.

51. 42 U.S.C. § 5170b(b); 44 C.F.R. § 206.65. In extraordinary circumstances, the president may authorize direct federal assistance under which the federal government itself performs the emergency work and bears 100 percent of the costs.

There are seven specific categories of disaster-related work for which local governments may seek PA reimbursement:[52]

1. *Debris removal*—generally limited to the removal of debris from public property; debris that presents an imminent threat to public health or safety or to property; or debris removal necessary for the economic recovery of the community.
2. *Emergency protective measures*—includes activities such as Emergency Operations Center activation; search and rescue; emergency medical care; sheltering; distribution of food, water, and other essential supplies; and security measures.
3. *Roads and bridges*—covers repairs to transportation infrastructure not covered under other federal programs such as the Federal Highways Administration (FHWA).
4. *Water control facilities*—covers repairs to dams, reservoirs, levees, irrigation facilities, and pumping stations.
5. *Building and equipment* —covers repairs to public buildings and repairs or replacement of damaged contents such as furnishings and equipment.
6. *Utilities*—covers repairs to water treatment plants, power generation and distribution facilities, and sewage systems.
7. *Parks, recreational, and other*—covers repairs to publicly owned recreational facilities such as playgrounds, boat docks and piers, golf courses, and so on.

When a local government requests reimbursement for an eligible cost, that request is reviewed and processed by FEMA in conjunction with state emergency management personnel and, if granted, funding is awarded. The complexity of this review process depends on the size, scope, and cost of the project. If a reimbursement request is denied, the local government may appeal that decision within FEMA. If the reimbursement request is granted, the local government must manage the federal funds consistent with federal regulations and guidelines governing most federal grant-in-aid programs; individuals who mismanage FEMA PA funds are subject to civil fines and criminal penalties.[53] When all funding requests have been fully processed (including appeals if necessary) and all federal funds have been obligated, the local government's receipt and expenditure of federal PA funds is audited (or reconciled).[54]

IA programs provide assistance directly to eligible individuals and are administered by federal agencies. Local governments might be called upon to help facilitate the delivery of IA assistance to eligible members of their communities through efforts such as publicizing information about the availability of federal assistance or providing temporary office space for federal program counselors.

The Stafford Act also authorizes post-disaster assistance designed to stimulate hazard mitigation efforts at the state and local levels.[55] Hazard mitigation involves measures that are cost-effective and that substantially reduce the risk of future damage and loss, especially where there is evidence of repetitive loss in past disaster events. A typical example of hazard mitigation is property acquisition and relocation assistance for homeowners in flood hazard areas who have suffered repeated flood damage. Other examples include structural hazard controls and retrofitting of facilities. The amount of funding made available for hazard mitigation projects equals either 7.5 or 20 percent (depending on the state's hazard mitigation plan) of the total PA and IA federal funds awarded following a major disaster. The federal funding available for each individual hazard mitigation project may be up to 75 percent of the total project cost. Although federally funded, hazard mitigation programs may be administered at the state level. In order to receive

52. For more information about PA programs and eligibility criteria, see the following FEMA publications: *Public Assistance Policy Digest*, FEMA-321 (Jan. 2008), www.fema.gov/pdf/government/grant/pa/pdigest08.pdf; *Public Assistance Guide*, FEMA-322 (March 2012), www.fema.gov/media-library-data/20130726-1826-25045-1802/fema_publication_322_public_assistance_guide_6_1_07.pdf; *Public Assistance Applicant Handbook*, FEMA P-323 (March 2010), www.fema.gov/pdf/government/grant/pa/fema323_app_handbk.pdf; *Public Assistance Debris Management Guide*, FEMA-325 (July 2007), www.fema.gov/pdf/government/grant/pa/demagde.pdf; and *Public Assistance Debris Monitoring Guide*, FEMA-327 (Oct. 2010), www.fema.gov/pdf/government/grant/pa/fema_327_debris_monitoring.pdf.

53. *See generally* 44 C.F.R. Part 13.

54. 42 U.S.C. § 5161(c).

55. 42 U.S.C. § 5170c; 44 C.F.R. § 206 & Subpart N.

hazard mitigation funding, both the state and the local government applicant must have adopted federally approved hazard mitigation plans, and each hazard mitigation project must be consistent with the jurisdiction's plan.

State Assistance Programs

The state also provides a number of disaster assistance programs that are triggered by a state disaster declaration issued by the governor.[56] State disaster assistance can be made available in certain circumstances regardless of whether a federal declaration is issued, but it does require that a local state of emergency declaration be issued. Mirroring the structure of federal programs (and intended to supplement federal programs where federal assistance is either not available or not adequate), the scope and number of state programs available depends on the type of disaster declaration issued. For Type I disasters (the least severe in terms of damage), both state IA and PA programs are authorized. State IA programs include assistance for temporary housing and home repair, relocation, replacement of personal property and vehicles, medical and dental expenses, and funeral or burial expenses. State PA programs include assistance to local governments for costs incurred in disaster activities such as debris removal, emergency protective measures, road and bridge repair, crisis counseling, and public transportation needs.

In order to be eligible for Type I PA assistance, the unit of local government must meet four criteria: (1) it must have suffered at least $10,000 in uninsurable losses; (2) those uninsurable losses must equal or exceed 1 percent of the unit's annual operating budget; (3) it must have an approved hazard mitigation plan; and (4) for flood damage, it must participate in the National Flood Insurance Program. If the local government meets these criteria, it becomes eligible to receive reimbursement for 75 percent of eligible costs; the local government must absorb the remaining 25 percent of the costs. No PA programs are authorized for Type II and Type III disasters, and only a limited number of IA programs are authorized for these two types of disasters (for which, presumably, greater federal assistance is available).

Contracting and Other Requirements for Reimbursement

It should be noted that compliance with all applicable federal regulations and guidelines is a condition of any federal grant award. Where federal guidelines specify conditions or restrictions not found in state law, those conditions or restrictions still must be followed by the local governments. Local governments should seek the advice of counsel about applicable federal requirements that may not exist within state law and yet could present a barrier to funding awards if not followed. For example, debris-removal contracts are considered service contracts under state law and, as such, are not subject to North Carolina bidding laws. However, federal law requires that certain competitive bidding procedures be followed in the award of service contracts for which federal funds are spent.[57] A local government may, in good faith, award a debris-removal contract without utilizing a competitive bidding process and act entirely consistent with state law, yet not be in compliance with federal law. This is also the case with "piggybacking" onto another local government's existing debris-removal (or other service) contract. While not prohibited under state law, this practice violates federal procurement procedures.

Similarly, North Carolina law allows waivers of competitive bidding requirements "in cases of special emergency involving the health and safety of the people and their property."[58] Again, in a disaster situation, a local government may choose to enter into a contract without following competitive bidding requirements under this emergency exemption. However, no similar exemption exists in 44 C.F.R. Part 13, so a local government would still be required to follow competitive bidding requirements in a federally declared disaster situation if that local government sought federal funding assistance to pay for the costs incurred under that contract.[59]

Another example of a conflict between state/local and federal law that can be a barrier to reimbursement involves personnel costs. Generally, overtime pay for *nonexempt* employees is eligible for federal reimbursement in a federally

56. G.S. 166A-19.41.

57. 44 C.F.R. § 13.36(c).

58. G.S. 143-129(e)(2).

59. For more information on North Carolina purchasing and contracting requirements, see Frayda S. Bluestein, *A Legal Guide to Purchasing and Contracting for North Carolina Local Governments*, 2nd ed. (UNC School of Government, 2004).

declared disaster. Some local governments will authorize, by local ordinance or in their personnel policies, the award of overtime compensation for *exempt* employees in disaster situations, and they will leave the decision to award the overtime compensation in any particular disaster to the discretion of the board or manager; others will award overtime compensation only if a federal disaster declaration has been issued. Such policies are not prohibited under state law. Under federal regulations, however, compensation for personnel costs is contingent on the local government having an "established policy that is consistently applied to both Federal and non-Federal activities."[60] Thus, if the award of overtime pay for exempt employees is not in a written policy and is either discretionary or dependent on a federal disaster declaration, it is not considered "consistently applied to both federal and non-federal activities" and is not eligible for federal reimbursement.

Infrastructure

One of the primary concerns of all local officials is how to expedite the recovery process as much as possible to reinstate private services and begin economic and budgetary recovery. Building and inspections is one area in which local governments may implement extraordinary procedures, such as modifying local ordinances or employing additional inspectors and personnel to expedite recovery. Several inspections and assessments take place in the days following an event. Local building officials may initially conduct safety and habitability inspections of damaged buildings to assess whether each structure is safe to enter, has limited access, or is condemned. Local floodplain management and permitting officials may also inspect structures to assess zoning or floodplain status and obtain information on the property owner's rebuilding plan and compliance with state and local regulations. Under state law, every inspector or code enforcement official must hold a valid certification of qualification issued by the North Carolina Code Officials Qualification Board for building, electrical, mechanical, plumbing, or fire code enforcement.[61] The Board may issue probationary or temporary certificates to any newly employed Code enforcer who lacks prerequisite qualifications for a standard certificate for one to three years.[62] The Board may designate specialty levels with special conditions relating to the place of employment, supervision, or other matters necessary to protect public health and safety.[63] The Board may also issue standard certificates following a short course to any person licensed under state law as an architect, general contractor, plumbing or heating contractor, electrical contractor, or professional engineer.[64]

Under state law, ambulatory surgical centers[65] and hospitals[66] are required to develop "master fire and disaster plan[s]" with input from local emergency management officials. Such disaster plans must "fit the needs of the facility's geographic location."[67] Under Title 10A, Chapter 13B, Section .4110 of the North Carolina Administrative Code, all hospitals in the state are required to describe services available during an external disaster, the role of their emergency department in a disaster, procedures for an internal disaster, and connections to public agencies and emergency suppliers such as the Red Cross.[68] All hospital plans must also provide for evacuation and transfer of all inpatients in case of internal disaster and for mutual agreements with area providers.[69] If local hospitals are damaged or overwhelmed during a given disaster incident, this may greatly affect the availability of emergency transportation and recovery.

60. Office of Management and Budget, *OMB Circular A-87 Revised* (May 2004), Attachment B, www.whitehouse.gov/omb/circulars_a087_2004#attb; *see also* 44 C.F.R. 13.22.

61. G.S. 143-151.13(a), (b).

62. G.S. 143-151.13(d).

63. *Id.*

64. G.S. 143-151.13(f).

65. Title 10A, Chapter 13C, Section .1408(2)(E) of the North Carolina Administrative Code (hereinafter N.C.A.C.).

66. 10A N.C.A.C. 13B, § .6101.

67. 10A N.C.A.C. 13C, § .1408(2)(E).

68. 10A N.C.A.C. 13B, § .4110(a).

69. 10A N.C.A.C. 13B, §§ .4110(c)(5), (6).

The North Carolina Division of Coastal Management has its own natural disaster mitigation and recovery policies that may provide some assistance and resources to coastal counties.[70]

Continuity of Government in the Event of Enemy Attack

In the cold-war era of the late 1950s, the General Assembly enacted not only the Civil Preparedness Act (G.S. Chapter 166, the forerunner to Chapter 166A), but also G.S. Chapter 162B, establishing measures to ensure continuity of local governments in the event of an enemy attack on the state. These statutes, which are triggered only when the governor and Council of State declare the state to be subject to impending or actual hostile attack, authorize local governments to identify alternate sites within and outside of their jurisdictions to serve as emergency locations from which the local governments might operate and to meet and transact public business at these emergency locations.[71] A governing body may even waive compliance with "legally prescribed procedural requirements relating to the conduct of meetings and transaction of business" if the situation makes compliance with such requirements impossible.[72] Local governments are also authorized to enact ordinances providing for emergency interim succession to local offices in the event that local officials are unavailable.[73] In cases where the legally empowered official is unavailable, the successor may exercise the powers and discharge the duties of that office until the vacancy is filled according to statute or the official returns.[74] An interim successor may exercise the powers of the office he or she assumes only in the event of an attack on the state,[75] and his or her status as an interim successor may be terminated by the local governing body at any time.[76]

At the federal level, continuity of government and operations is not limited to enemy attack. The National Continuity Policy Implementation Plan[77] and National Security Presidential Directive 51 (NSPD-51)/Homeland Security Presidential Directive 20 (HSPD-20)[78] define "Continuity of Operations Plans (COOPs)" as plans to ensure that "Primary Mission Essential Functions" continue during an emergency, including natural, man-made, and technological incidents.[79] While requirements for state and local government continuity are left to state law and local ordinance, FEMA encourages the establishment of complete COOPs, incorporating all scenarios. In July 2013, FEMA updated its *Continuity Guidance Circular (CGC 1), Continuity Guidance for Non-Federal Governments (States, Territories, Tribes, and Local Government Jurisdictions).*[80] In July 2010, it issued the *Continuity Guidance Circular 2 (CGC 2), Continuity Guidance for Non-Federal Entities: Mission Essential Functions Identification Process (States, Territories,*

70. Response provisions include streamlining permitting for reconstruction, assisting in damage assessment, participating in the disaster assistance center, and including disaster planning in local land use plans. Mitigation provisions include guidelines for local governments in reconstruction plans to include relocation for development, relocation of roads and utilities, public acquisition of hazardous areas, inventory of structures in hazardous areas, notifications to property owners of potential damage, coordination with FEMA, coordination between city and county plans, advice on easements and rebuilding of rights-of-way in proximity to shorelines, and safe coastal engineering practices. 15A N.C.A.C. 07M, § .0503(b).

71. G.S. 162B-1, -2.

72. G.S. 162B-3.

73. G.S. 162B-6.

74. G.S. 162B-9.

75. Attacks may be accomplished by "sabotage or by use of bombs, missiles, shellfire, or atomic, radiological, chemical bacteriological, or biological means or other weapons or processes." G.S. 162B-7.

76. G.S. 162B-11.

77. *See* Homeland Security Council, *National Continuity Policy Implementation Plan* (Aug. 2007), www.fema.gov/media-library-data/1384886826028-729844d3fd23ff85d94d52186c85748f/NCPIP.pdf.

78. *See* www.fas.org/irp/offdocs/nspd/nspd-51.htm (May 2007).

79. NSPD-51/HSPD 20, at § (2)(d).

80. *See* www.fema.gov/media-library-data/1386609058803-b084a7230663249ab1d6da4b6472e691/CGC-1-Signed-July-2013.pdf. The first (January 2009) version of this document was titled *Continuity Guidance for Non-Federal Entities (States, Territories, Tribal, and Local Government Jurisdictions and Private Sector Organizations). See* www.fema.gov/pdf/about/org/ncp/cont_guidance1.pdf.

Tribes, and Local Government Jurisdictions),[81] and in October 2013, the agency issued the *Continuity Guidance Circular 2 (CGC 2), Continuity Guidance for Non-Federal Governments: Mission Essential Functions Identification Process (States, Territories, Tribes, and Local Government Jurisdictions),* FEMA P-789, an update to the 2010 *CGC 2*.[82]

Immunity and Liability

Broad immunity is granted for emergency management functions. G.S. 166A-19.60 exempts from liability the state, any political subdivision of the state, and any emergency management worker who is, in good faith,[83] complying or attempting to comply with any order, rule, regulation, or ordinance relating to any emergency management measures. This immunity includes situations resulting in death or injury to persons or in damage to property and applies wherever the emergency management worker is engaged in emergency management activities or services, whether inside or outside of the worker's own jurisdiction. Moreover, any professional work or service that would normally require a license under North Carolina law can be performed without a license by an emergency management worker during a declared state of disaster.

Under this statute, an "emergency management worker" is broadly defined as a full- or part-time paid, volunteer, or auxiliary employee of the federal government, the state, political subdivisions of the state, or any agency or organization performing emergency management services in any place in the state, so long as he or she is subject to the order or control of, or is working at the request of, state or local government.[84] The definition also includes state medical assistance teams and emergency healthcare workers. While this definition is very broad, it does not extend to private vendors and contractors working for hire under contract with state or local governments in a disaster situation, although it does include private vendors and contractors working without compensation under a state of emergency declaration. Even though the unit of government itself is granted immunity (and is presumably protected even if its vendors and contractors are not), local governments would be well-served by requiring liability indemnification and hold-harmless clauses in all contracts with private companies, vendors, and individuals for any and all claims arising out of the performance of the contracts.[85]

About the Author

Norma R. Houston is a School of Government faculty member whose areas of interest include emergency management law.

The revised version of this chapter was prepared with the invaluable assistance of Samantha Surles, UNC JD candidate 2014; David Goldberg, UNC MPA-JD candidate 2015; and Timothy Reavis, UNC MPA 2013.

The author wishes to thank the following officials for their assistance in the preparation of the original edition of this chapter: Holly Hollingsworth, Public Assistance Specialist, Region IV, FEMA; David Humphrey, Area I Coordinator, NCDEM; and Sandy Sanderson, Emergency Management Director, Dare County.

81. *See* www.fema.gov/pdf/about/org/ncp/coop/cont_guidance2.pdf.

82. *See* www.fema.gov/media-library-data/1384435934615-7eeac7d0b4f189839f396a3c64eeac7a/Continuity+Guidance+Circular+2.pdf.

83. The immunity under G.S. 166A-19.60 does not extend to cases of willful misconduct, gross negligence, or bad faith.

84. G.S. 166A-19.60(e).

85. The Stafford Act requires indemnification of the federal government in all contracts involving private property debris removal. 42 U.S.C. § 5173(b).

Chapter 35

Public Library Services

Alex Hess

The public library is an educational institution whose objective is to assist people of all ages and interests in continuing to learn. Its purpose is to help individuals educate themselves, keep better informed about public affairs, and enjoy the pleasure of reading. A public library accomplishes this by acquiring, assembling, organizing, and making freely available the resources in its collection and by providing access to remote information sources. The public library plays an important role in the development of a democratic society by giving individuals access to a wide and varied range of knowledge, ideas, and opinions. Automation of local public library operations, creation of systems of shared resources, and advancements in technology that provide access to international networks of information and databases have combined to allow a tremendous increase in the speed and breadth of service delivery to library users.[1]

Library Establishment and Operation

Statutory Authority

The public library—whether city, county, or multi-county (regional)—traditionally has been primarily the responsibility of local government. The legislature may grant authority to a local unit of government to establish library services by a general enabling law or by a special local act. Although most public libraries in the state have been established and are supported by local governments under the general law (Chapter 153A, Article 14, of the North Carolina General

1. See, for example, Christie Koontz and Barbara Gubbin, "The Mission and Purposes of the Public Library," in *IFLA Public Library Service Guidelines*, ed. Koontz and Gubbin, IFLA Publications Series 147 (Berlin/Munich: De Gruyter Saur, 2010), 1–20; Gordon Conable, "Public Libraries and Intellectual Freedom," in *Intellectual Freedom Manual*, 8th ed. (Chicago: Office for Intellectual Freedom, American Library Association (ALA), 2010), www.ifmanual.org/plif.

Statutes (hereinafter G.S.)), some operate under local acts with provisions different from the statewide statutes. The law also authorizes counties and cities to appropriate funds to support libraries that provide free services to all (G.S. 153A-263(6); 153A-264). The local governing body should be familiar with all the laws that created and govern its library.

Library Board of Trustees

The governing body of a city or county (board of county commissioners or city council) may appoint a library board of trustees (G.S. 153A-265). Appointments to the board are made at the discretion of the local governing body, which is authorized to determine the number of trustees (not to exceed twelve), their terms of office, rules for their removal from office, and any compensation they might receive. Powers that may be delegated to a library board by a governing body are listed in G.S. 153A-266. The board is required to make an annual report on library operations to the local governing body and also to the Department of Cultural Resources as required by G.S. 125-5. (If a board of trustees has not been established, the local governing board itself would have to submit the report.)

Library Employees

G.S. 153A-267 requires that the chief administrator of any public library system in North Carolina have a professional librarian certificate issued by the secretary of cultural resources, pursuant to G.S. 125-9 and 125-10 under regulations for certification established by the Public Librarian Certification Commission (G.S. 143B-67; N.C. Admin. Code (hereinafter N.C.A.C.) tit. 7, ch. 2J). All employees of a public library are "for all purposes" bona fide employees of the county or city that supports it (G.S. 153A-267). They are covered by workers' compensation insurance and are eligible for membership in the local retirement system and other fringe benefits. G.S. 160A-463 provides that employees of regional libraries (established under G.S. 153A-270) are entitled to the same rights and privileges as employees of the individual governments that participate in these libraries.

Area Served by the Library

The earliest public libraries in the state were city libraries, serving the immediate community. Local initiative and interest were instrumental in their organization and support. By the mid-1920s, however, the county library had been recognized as a more efficient unit of library service. Primarily for this reason, more libraries that provide countywide rather than citywide service have been established. Also partly accounting for the preponderance of this type is the fact that, until 1979, state aid was given only to libraries that served entire counties.[2]

Both the American Library Association (ALA) and the International Federation of Library Associations (IFLA) have stressed the importance of cooperation and joint action among libraries and between libraries and other entities to sustain and enhance services. Public libraries that are bound together formally or informally in systems and those that establish links with other local organizations are better able to provide needed resources, materials, and access to remote networks of information to meet the full needs of their clientele. The trend toward such broader-based library systems has proved practical not only because the per capita cost is less if the library serves a large area but also because the quality and number of services and resources is improved through cooperation.[3]

The position of the North Carolina Library Association has also been to encourage public libraries to share resources and services. In 1987, it stated as follows:

> Since on a per capita basis it takes more to run a small library than a large one, many communities cannot raise sufficient tax funds to support public libraries that will meet . . . minimum standards. Whenever inadequate support makes it impossible to meet these standards, libraries should find an alternative method of providing library service, either by combining [libraries in] small localities into a large library unit or by

2. In 1979, G.S. 125-7(c) was amended to allow city and regional libraries to share in state-provided library equalization funds.

3. Standards Committee, Public Library Association (PLA), *Minimum Standards for Public Library Systems, 1966* (Chicago: ALA, 1967), 10–11; Koontz and Gubbin, *IFLA Public Library Service Guidelines*, 52–54.

contracting for local services with an existing, strong library unit. In this way, effective library services can be made available to any community, no matter how small.[4]

Toward this end, the law enables two or more units of local government to operate libraries and other undertakings jointly (G.S. Chapter 160A, Article 20, Part 1; 7 N.C.A.C. 2I .0300 (Apr. 2011)) and to acquire or construct public buildings together (G.S. 153A-164). The units may acquire the necessary land for such purposes, or they may use land already belonging to one of the participating governments. In 2011, fifty-three counties and ten cities maintained their own individual units, while forty-six counties had formed fourteen regional library systems, making larger book collections and more varied services possible.[5] These systems are defined as "public authorities" and are subject to the Local Government Budget and Fiscal Control Act (LGBFCA).[6]

The examination of local needs in determining the best way to provide library services has now become the standard criteria. In 1980, the Public Library Association (PLA), a division of the ALA, first recommended that national standards for library performance be abandoned in favor of formulating local goals and objectives based on the needs of particular communities. In *A Planning Process for Public Libraries*,[7] a report of the recommendations from a study commissioned by the association, the importance of such differences between communities was explicitly recognized. The report emphasized the needs of individual citizens as the basis for analyzing the area to be served, and it urged libraries to seek active participation from every segment of the locality in conducting a community survey. As currently formulated, excellence in providing library services must be defined locally and results only when services match community needs, interests, and priorities. In addition, excellence in the provision of services is considered a moving target, and its maintenance requires constant monitoring and planning.[8]

Following the ALA's recommendation, community analyses were conducted by most of the public library systems in North Carolina, and now, as a requirement for eligibility to receive state aid, each library has to be prepared to submit an assessment of a community's library needs if requested by the State Library. Each library also must submit annually a current long-range plan of service (covering at least five years) to the State Library.[9]

Financing the Public Library

Local Financial Support

Since library service to the general public has been considered chiefly a function of local government, financial backing has come predominantly from the locality served. Both counties and cities have authority to support libraries from any available source of funds (G.S. 153A-263(6); 153A-268), including, most importantly, the property tax (G.S. 153A-149(c)(19), for counties; 160A-209(c)(20), for cities). Since both types of governments may finance libraries, cities may contribute to the operation of county or regional libraries. Also, counties may make appropriations to city libraries that are used by county residents who live outside the city. In a few places, libraries are legally entitled to share

4. Standards and Measures Committee, Public Libraries Section, N.C. Library Association, *Standards for North Carolina Public Libraries* (Raleigh: State Library of North Carolina, 1987), 7.

5. Library Development Section, State Library of North Carolina, comp., *Directory of North Carolina Libraries, 2011* (Raleigh: N.C. Department of Cultural Resources, 2012), 1–42; two regional libraries (Hyconeechee and Gaston–Lincoln) composed of all or part of five counties (Caswell, Orange, Person, Gaston, and Lincoln) were set to dissolve in July 2012.

6. Letter from Harlan Boyles, secretary, N.C. Local Government Commission, to Elaine von Oesen, assistant state librarian, Oct. 2, 1973; *see also* N.C. Admin. Code (hereinafter N.C.A.C.) tit. 7, ch. 2I, sec. .0306; and G.S. 159-7(b)(10).

7. Vernon E. Palmour, Marcia C. Bellassai, and Nancy V. DeWath, *A Planning Process for Public Libraries* (Chicago: PLA/ALA, 1980), xi–xii.

8. Sandra Nelson, *The New Planning for Results: A Streamlined Approach* (Chicago: ALA, 2001), 1–2, and *Strategic Planning for Results* (Chicago: ALA, 2008), 4, 7, 35–42.

9. 7 N.C.A.C. 2I .0201(10); G.S. 125-7; *see also* 125-5.

in the profits of the local alcoholic beverage control (ABC) system,[10] and some libraries have their own endowment funds. (See Tables 35.1 and 35.2, below.)

State Aid

History

State financial aid to county and regional public libraries usually takes the form of cash grants and/or services. The state aid fund for public libraries was established in 1941. The first appropriation of $100,000 per annum for "payment to counties" was increased during each successive session of the General Assembly until 1957, when the figure reached $425,000. It remained at that level until an increase was approved in 1965.[11]

In 1964, the Governor's Commission on Library Resources was appointed to study the overall status of libraries in the state and to suggest ways to meet steadily increasing needs for educational and informational materials as well as services. The commission recommended that "continued study be given to the development of a plan for joint local-state-federal responsibility for public library financing."[12]

In 1967, by joint resolution, the General Assembly created the Commission to Study Library Support in the State of North Carolina. Concluding that sources of public revenue for local governments are more limited than other sources of public revenue, this commission recommended that the state gradually assume equal responsibility with local government for public library support. It proposed that this goal be accomplished over a period of several years, during which time annual increases in state grants to public libraries would amount to approximately twenty cents per capita.[13]

The Present System

State funds are intended to stimulate the improvement and expansion of public library services. They are allocated among qualifying library systems on the basis of the rules and regulations formulated by the secretary of the Department of Cultural Resources in accordance with G.S. 125-7 (7 N.C.A.C. 2I .0200).

The present formula for distributing state aid for public libraries was adopted in 1983 after a four-year study of the financial needs of library systems. Under this formula, 50 percent of the state aid appropriation is distributed among qualifying county and regional libraries in equal block grants. Regional libraries receive one overall grant in addition to the ones that are received for each county in the region. The remaining 50 percent of the appropriation is awarded as per capita income equalization grants. Each eligible county, regional, and city library system receives a per capita grant that is inversely proportional to the per capita income of the area served. In the most affluent system the local per capita income is approximately twice that of the least affluent. The per capita equalization grant, therefore, results in the poorest system receiving about twice as much per capita as the richest. The formula thus directs more aid to the counties and cities that are less able to support libraries from local treasuries.[14]

General Assembly appropriations for the state aid fund for public libraries increased rapidly from 1983 to 1987, with the annual total moving from $4.8 million in fiscal year 1982–83 to $11.3 million in fiscal year 1987–88. The annual appropriation declined to below $11 million from 1990 to 1996 but started rising again in the late 1990s to a peak of $16.9 million for fiscal year 1998–99. The appropriation remained in the $14–16 million range through fiscal year

10. *See, e.g.,* 1947 N.C. Sess. Laws ch. 835 for a specific grant of 5 percent of net ABC profits to the Public Library of Charlotte and Mecklenburg County.

11. Financial records on file in the N.C. Department of Cultural Resources, State Library of North Carolina, Raleigh.

12. North Carolina Governor's Commission on Library Resources, *Resources of North Carolina Libraries,* ed. Robert B. Downs (Raleigh, N.C.: The Commission, 1965).

13. North Carolina Legislative Commission to Study Library Support in the State of North Carolina, *Report,* Aug. 1968.

14. "Keeping Up," *North Carolina Libraries* 41 (Fall 1983): 162; State Library of North Carolina, *State Aid to Public Libraries* (Raleigh: N.C. Department of Cultural Resources, n.d.), www.statelibrary.ncdcr.gov/ld/grants/stateaid.html, Cal Shepard, *State Aid in North Carolina,* presented at the NC PLDA, March 25, 1999, www.statelibrary.ncdcr.gov/ld/grants/stateaid/StateAidPresentation1999.pdf.

20110–11 (the only exception was the $12.7 million for fiscal year 2001–02.) For fiscal years 2011–12 through 2013–14, the appropriation has fallen to about $13.5 million.[15]

The rules for the allocation of state aid to public libraries, compiled by the Department of Cultural Resources, specify application procedures for receiving this type of assistance (7 N.C.A.C. 2I .0201). State aid is designed to supplement local funds rather than to replace them (7 N.C.A.C. 2I .0201(4)). Thus, if an appropriation a library system receives from local government sources is less than that of the previous year, a state grant will not be terminated but instead reduced in proportion to the decrease. (See Tables 35.1 and 35.2, below.)

Federal Aid

The Library Services and Construction Act

Federal aid began when Congress passed the Library Services Act[16] in 1956 to help states improve and extend public library services in rural areas. This act was replaced in 1964 by the Library Services and Construction Act (LSCA),[17] which broadened and increased federal assistance to the states for public library services and specified that urban areas could share in those funds on the same basis as rural areas. The 1964 act extended the use of federal allocations to library construction and gave the library agency of each state (the State Library of North Carolina in this state) full authority to plan for the use of LSCA funds.

The act was divided into titles to achieve its objectives. The three main titles to be administered by the State Library of North Carolina were established in the first two years of the LSCA's existence: Title I for Library Services, Title II for construction and improvements, and Title III to encourage interlibrary cooperation.[18] Further titles were added over the next thirty years to extend the use of funding to include development of foreign language materials, literacy programs, services for Indian tribes, library learning centers, evaluation and assessment, and aid for the physically handicapped.[19]

In addition to Title II construction funds, LSCA funding was distributed in the form of direct grants for the enrichment of collections and services, the automation of library services, and the establishment of Internet and local area network services.[20] The LSCA was reauthorized and modified several times between 1964 and 1996, and the State Library of North Carolina continued to submit annual plans and reports to the U.S. Department of Education, the federal oversight agency for funds awarded under provisions of the act.

The Library Services and Technology Act

In 1996 Congress enacted the Library Services and Technology Act (LSTA).[21] It continued the LSCA approach of using a state agency (still the North Carolina State Library in our state) as the conduit for federal funds to local libraries but transferred federal oversight from the U.S. Department of Education to the Institute of Museum and Library Services and expanded the definition of which libraries were to be funded. The LSTA serves as a successor to the library programs found in the Higher Education Act (HEA) as well as those of the LSCA and includes appropriations for programs for library education and academic libraries as well as for local public libraries.[22] The act focused on two key priorities:

---

15. Library Development Section, State Library of North Carolina, *Public Library Statistics; Directory of North Carolina Public Libraries, 1981–1982* through *1999–2000*; and *State Aid to Public Libraries, 2000–2001* through *2013–2014* (Raleigh: N.C. Department of Cultural Services, n.d.), www.statelibrary.ncdcr.gov/ld/grants/stateaid.html.

16. Pub. L. No. 84-597, 70 Stat. 293 (1956).

17. Pub. L. No. 88-269, 78 Stat. 11 (1964). Before its repeal in 1996, the LSCA was codified at 20 U.S.C. § 351 *et seq.*

18. *Id.*; Pub. L. No. 89-511, 80 Stat. 313 (1966).

19. Pub. L. No. 98-480, 98 Stat. 2236 (1984) (Titles IV, V, VI); Pub. L. No. 101-254, 104 Stat. 107 (1990) (Titles VII, VIII); Pub. L. No. 91-600, 84 Stat. 1660 (1970).

20. State Library of North Carolina, *North Carolina Public Library Services Grant Awards, 1996–97* (Raleigh: N.C. Department of Cultural Resources, Nov. 15, 1996; last updated Apr. 24, 1997), www.statelibrary.ncdcr.gov/ld/pubaward.htm, and *LSCA Title I Public Library Services Grants FY 1997–98* (Raleigh: N.C. Department of Cultural Services, n.d.; last updated Sept. 19, 1997), both no longer available on website; copies on file with the author.

21. Pub. L. No. 104-208, 110 Stat. 3009 (1996). The LSTA is codified at 20 U.S.C. § 9121 *et seq.*

22. State Library of North Carolina, *Discussion Paper: Implementing the Library Services & Technology Act in North Carolina, June 1997* (Raleigh: N.C. Department of Cultural Resources; last updated June 23, 1997), copy on file with the author.

(1) activities using technology for information sharing among libraries and between libraries and other community services and (2) programs that make library services more accessible to urban and rural communities, to low-income people, and to others who have difficulty using traditional library services.[23] Specifically, as reauthorized in 2003 and 2010, the act requires that 96 percent of the funds provided to a state library administrative agency be expended either directly to support statewide initiatives and services or indirectly, through subgrants and cooperative agreements, for the following purposes:

1. expanding services for learning and access to information and educational resources in a variety of formats, in all types of libraries, for individuals of all ages in order to support such individuals' needs for education, lifelong learning, workforce development, and digital literacy skills;
2. establishing or enhancing electronic and other linkages and improved coordination among and between libraries and entities, as described in section 9134(b)(6) of this title, for the purpose of improving the quality of and access to library and information services;
3. (A) providing training and professional development, including continuing education, to enhance the skills of the current library workforce and leadership, and advance the delivery of library and information services; and (B) enhancing efforts to recruit future professionals to the field of library and information sciences;
4. developing public and private partnerships with other agencies and community-based organizations;
5. targeting library services to individuals of diverse geographic, cultural, and socioeconomic backgrounds, to individuals with disabilities, and to individuals with limited functional literacy or information skills;
6. targeting library and information services to persons having difficulty using a library and to underserved urban and rural communities, including children (from birth through age 17) from families with incomes below the poverty line (as defined by the Office of Management and Budget and revised annually in accordance with section 9902(2) of Title 42) applicable to a family of the size involved; and
7. developing library services that provide all users access to information through local, State, regional, national, and international electronic networks;
8. carrying out other activities consistent with the purposes set forth in section 9121 of this title, as described in the State library administrative agency's plan (20 U.S.C. § 9141).[24]

The LSTA provided greater flexibility and reduced the administrative burden on the state administering agency. There were no separate titles with individual purposes and no provision for a continuation of the old LSCA Title II construction and facilities funds. Continuity lay instead with the old Title I and III allocations for library services and cooperation, with an emphasis on technological innovation. The LSTA also required the state library agency to file a five-year implementation plan and included strong requirements for increased accountability and evaluation, including an independent evaluation prior to the end of the five-year plan.[25]

The 2003 reauthorization changed the requirement of submitting an initial five-year implementation plan to one requiring a plan to be submitted to the director of the Institute of Museum and Library Services once every five years. The State Library had already prepared an implementation plan in August 2002 that covered the next five-year span (2003–2007). The plan included criteria for eligibility and policies for evaluating proposals in the grant-awarding process established for future fund distribution to public, academic, school, special libraries, state agency libraries, and the State Library of North Carolina itself. Other eligible entities included library cooperative organizations, library-related

23. State Library of North Carolina, *Library Services & Technology Act: Plan for Implementation in North Carolina—2003–2007* (Raleigh: N.C. Department of Cultural Services, Aug. 2002), www.statelibrary.ncdcr.gov/ld/grants/lsta/Plan2003-07.pdf.

24. 20 U.S.C. § 9132(a) allows up to 4 percent of the funds provided to a state library administrative agency to be expended for administrative costs.

25. The description in this paragraph is based on that found in State Library of North Carolina, *Library Services and Technology Act: Plan for Implementation in North Carolina August 1997 [Revised February 1999 and January 2000]* (Raleigh: N.C. Department of Cultural Services, n.d.; this version no longer available on website; printed copy on file with the author).

organizations, state and local professional library associations, library/media center administrative units, graduate library educational programs, and national or regional library organizations.[26]

In summary, the chief goals were to (1) achieve equity in library service for all North Carolinians, (2) create a climate for innovation and change in response to changing needs, opportunities, and environments, (3) have libraries and librarians lead in support of learning and discovery for children and teens, and (4) enable the State Library to serve as a leader in library and information services.[27]

In 2007 the required evaluation of the plan found that these goals had been accomplished and that without the programs and activities of the State Library, "the overall extent and quality of library and information services in North Carolina would have been diminished."[28] Since then, the State Library has operated under two further LSTA five-year plans covering 2008–2012 and 2013–2017 that seek to address the needs of a state undergoing rapid economic and demographic change. Eligibility criteria for aid have remained the same, while new goals were developed to meet the state's requirements. Intended to advance excellence and equity in North Carolina's libraries and to encourage creativity and innovation, the current plan's goals emphasize (1) partnerships and collaboration, (2) continuing education, (3) literacy and lifelong learning, and (4) access, digitization, and preservation.[29]

To achieve these goals, the State Library is awarding a number of different types of grants. As part of the LSTA planning process, the grants are under constant review and are subject to modification depending on their impact for positive change in meeting the goals of the program. Currently, most competitive grants fall under two general categories: EZ Grants and Project Grants.

EZ Grants have a simplified application process, do not require a letter of intent, and are limited to requests for $5,000 to $50,000. Applications are reviewed and evaluated by State Library staff, and funding decisions are made by State Library senior management (applicants have the opportunity to appeal these decisions, and awards are not final until the appeals process is complete).[30] Details and application packages are available at the LSTA Grants section of the State Library website (http://statelibrary.ncdcr.gov/ld/grants/lsta.html).

Project Grants are awarded for more complex projects, require submission of a Letter of Intent Form that explains the proposed project, and provide $50,000 to $100,000 in funding. Letters of Intent are reviewed by State Library staff, the LSTA Advisory Committee, and, in some cases, by peer reviewers. The LSTA Advisory Committee recommends which libraries are approved to submit a full application. Full applications are reviewed and evaluated by the staff and outside peer reviewers, after which the LSTA Advisory Committee makes funding recommendations to the state librarian. No appeal is available since the Project Grants have already been reviewed by all the entities that would consider an appeal.[31] As with EZ Grants, further information on Project Grants is available at the LSTA Grants section of the State Library website (http://statelibrary.ncdcr.gov/ld/grants/lsta.html).

A third category, called Statewide Leadership Grants, makes funds available for initiatives with a broad impact for libraries across the state and is managed directly by the State Library of North Carolina. For examples of this type of

26. State Library of North Carolina, *Library Services & Technology Act Plan for Implementation in North Carolina—2003–2007*, esp. III-3 and III-4.

27. State Library of North Carolina, *Library Services & Technology Act Plan for Implementation in North Carolina—2003–2007*, II-3 and II-4 for full text and context.

28. Jeffrey Pomerantz, Carolyn Hank, and Charles R. McClure, *Program Evaluation of the Library Services and Technology Act Plan for Implementation in North Carolina, 2003–2007* (Raleigh: N.C. Department of Cultural Resources, Division of the State Library, Mar. 2007), ii–iii, www.statelibrary.ncdcr.gov/ld/grants/lsta/LSTA_Eval_Report_2007.pdf.

29. North Carolina State Library, *Library Services and Technology Act Five-Year Plan, 2008–2012* (Raleigh: N.C. Department of Cultural Resources, Aug. 2007), 3–4, http://statelibrary.ncdcr.gov/ld/grants/lsta/plan2008-12.pdf; and North Carolina State Library, *Library Services and Technology Act Five-Year Plan, 2013–2017* (Raleigh: N.C. Department of Cultural Resources, June 2012), 3, http://statelibrary.ncdcr.gov/ld/grants/lsta/plan2013-17.pdf.

30. This description of EZ Grants is based on information provided at the LSTA section of the State Library website, www.statelibrary.ncdcr.gov/ld/grants/lsta.html; see the Anual Program Plan hyperlink for the latest grant cycle.

31. This description of Project Grants is based on information provided at the LSTA section of the State Library website, www.statelibrary.ncdcr.gov/ld/grants/lsta.html; see the Annual Program Plan hyperlink for the latest grant cycle.

Table 35.1 Sources of Income for Public Library Services (in Dollars)

Year	Municipal Funds	County Funds	State Aid*	Federal Aid**	Other Income ***	Total
1942–1943	194,741	201,377	95,380	—	120,168	611,666
1952–1953	612,138	717,319	350,000	—	214,868	1,894,325
1956–1957	822,816	1,019,072	390,000	14,301	266,184	2,512,373
1966–1967	1,649,781	3,041,989	686,250	717,713	550,587	6,646,320
1976–1977	4,454,919	10,859,461	3,514,635	1,262,289	1,969,069	22,060,373
1986–1987	8,026,586	36,347,438	10,789,462	1,335,700	4,911,091	61,410,277
1996–1997	14,828,375	77,065,067	13,910,516	2,534,943	7,783,003	116,121,904
2006–2007	21,790,080	144,971,608	17,226,909	1,157,718	13,709,991	198,856,306
2007–2008	22,899,349	153,593,718	16,920,382	1,419,558	15,058,012	209,891,019
2008–2009	23,140,788	154,772,050	15,844,888	1,635,317	13,827,172	209,220,215
2009–2010	23,152,245	152,400,189	15,776,220	1,633,388	13,883,287	206,845,329
2010–2011	24,624,751	146,453,343	15,876,985	1,436,147	11,182,470	199,573,696
2011–2012	22,911,594	150,739,709	14,174,305	1,420,010	10,876,480	200,122,098
2012–2013	23,433,091	153,773,303	14,040,630	1,675,778	13,237,483	206,160,285

Note. Capital expenditures are not shown in this table.

Sources. Biennial reports of the State Library of North Carolina (1942–1943 through 1966–1967); Library Development Section, State Library of North Carolina, *Public Library Statistics; Directory of North Carolina Public Libraries, 1981–1982* through *1999–2000*, and North Carolina State Library, *Statistical Report of North Carolina Public Libraries, 2006–2007* through *2012–2013* (Raleigh: N.C. Department of Cultural Resources, n.d.), Table 4—Operating Income, www.statelibrary.ncdcr.gov/ld/aboutlibraries/statistics.html.

* Includes Aid to Public Libraries Fund.

** Includes LSCA and LSTA.

*** Private donations, etc.

grant, see the award pages at the LSTA section of the State Library website.[32] Included is funding for the N.C. Cardinal consortium, a public library shared catalog and statewide library card project. N.C. Cardinal Grants made available fiscal year 2014–15 will aid eligible public libraries to join the consortium. For details, see N.C. Cardinal—Guidelines and Application at the N.C. Cardinal information page.[33]

Public libraries are required also to comply with the provisions of the Children's Internet Protection Act (CIPA) in order to receive LSTA funds that are to be used in conjunction with Internet access.[34] Required actions include a policy of Internet safety for minors that includes the operation of a technology protection measure with respect to any computers with Internet access. Further measures are required if the library also receives Universal Service (E-Rate) discounts for Internet access or internal connections. A detailed explanation of what is necessary for CIPA compliance

32. For 2013–2014 (June 11, 2013): www.statelibrary.ncdcr.gov/ld/grants/lsta/2013-2014Awards.htm; for 2012–2013 (June 12, 2012): www.statelibrary.ncdcr.gov/ld/grants/lsta/2012-2013Awards.htm.

33. See State Library of North Carolina, "N.C. Cardinal," www.statelibrary.ncdcr.gov/ld/services/nccardinal.html.

34. This brief description of CIPA certification requirements is based on information provided at the LSTA section of the State Library website, www.statelibrary.ncdcr.gov/ld/grants/lsta.html; see the Related Materials for Applications hyperlink for the latest grant cycle.

Table 35.2 Percentage Contribution and Per Capital Income for Libraries by Source, 1966–2011

Year	County and Municipal Funds Contribution / Per Capita	State Aid Contribution / Per Capita*	Federal Aid Contribution / Per Capita**	Other Support Contribution / Per Capita***	Population July 1
1966–1967	71% / $0.96	10% / $0.14	11% / $0.15	8% / $0.11	4,896,000
1976–1977	69% / $2.73	16% / $0.63	6% / $0.23	9% / $0.35	5,607,964
1986–1987	72% / $7.02	18% / $1.71	2% / $0.21	8% / $0.78	6,321,578
1996–1997	79% / $12.25	12% / $1.85	2% / $0.34	7% / $1.04	7,500,670
2006–2007	84% / $18.70	9% / $1.93	1% / $0.13	7% / $1.54	8,917,270
2007–2008	84% / $19.37	8% / $1.86	1% / $0.16	7% / $1.65	9,113,037
2010–2011	86% / $17.89	8% / $1.66	1% / $0.15	6% / $1.17	9,561,558
2012–2013	86% / $18.17	7% / $1.44	1% / $0.17	6% / $1.36	9,752,073

Sources. Biennial reports of the State Library of North Carolina (1966–1967); Library Development Section, State Library of North Carolina, *Public Library Statistics; Directory of North Carolina Public Libraries, 1981–1982* through *1999–2000,* and North Carolina State Library, *Statistical Report of North Carolina Public Libraries, 2006–2007* through *2012–2013* (Raleigh: N.C. Department of Cultural Resources, n.d.), Table 4—Operating Income, www.statelibrary.ncdcr.gov/ld/aboutlibraries/statistics.html; U.S. Census Population Annual Estimates for States, at www.census.gov/popest/index.html.

* Includes Aid to Public Libraries Fund.

** Includes LSCA and LSTA.

*** Private donations, etc.

can be found at the LSTA section of the State Library website in the Related Materials portion of the current grant program year.[35]

Other Federal Aid

Public libraries continue to apply for and receive funding from a variety of federal grant programs, such as those of the National Endowment for the Humanities (NEH) or the Institute of Museum and Library Services (IMLS), in which the funds are distributed directly to the libraries or through state entities, such as the North Carolina Humanities Council or the North Carolina Arts Council. Naturally, the amount varies from year to year, but these funds can have a considerable impact. For the state as a whole, $295,708 was received for the 2011–2012 reporting period and $442,060 for 2012–2013—a sizable amount of funding for potential projects.[36]

For several years, the Buncombe County Library System has been receiving over $35,000 per year to help pay for Internet access and telecommunications needs from the Schools and Libraries Program (commonly referred to as E-rate) of the Federal Communications Commission (FCC). The program is paid for through a competitive bidding process with money from the Universal Service Fund administered by the Universal Service Administration Company (both created by the FCC).[37]

---

35. See LSTA CIPA Compliance Information at the LSTA section of the State Library website, www.statelibrary.ncdcr.gov/ld/grants/lsta/cipa/compliance12.pdf.

36. North Carolina State Library, *Statistical Report of North Carolina Public Libraries, 2011–2012* and *2012–2013* (Raleigh: N.C. Department of Cultural Resources, n.d.), Table 4—Operating Income, www.statelibrary.ncdcr.gov/ld/aboutlibraries/statistics.html.

37. North Carolina State Library, *Statistical Report of North Carolina Public Libraries, 2005–2006* through *2012–2013* (Raleigh: N.C. Department of Cultural Resources, n.d.), Table 4—Operating Income, www.statelibrary.ncdcr.gov/ld/aboutlibraries/statistics.html; and conversation with Buncombe County Library System personnel on May 21, 2012.

The State Library

General Information

The reorganization of state government enacted by the General Assembly in 1971 brought the State Library under the new Department of Art, Culture, and History (1971 N.C. Sess. Laws ch. 864, § 19). The Executive Organization Act of 1973 renamed the latter the Department of Cultural Resources and assigned the Division of State Library to it (1973 N.C. Sess. Laws ch. 476, § 31).

G.S. 125-2(8) and 125-2(10) authorize the State Library to give assistance to all libraries in the state as to the best means of administering and managing such libraries, to plan and balance cooperative programs between the various types of libraries within the state of North Carolina, and to coordinate state development with regional and national cooperative library programs. In carrying out this mandate, the State Library develops and promotes strategies and initiatives focusing on support for current and emerging technologies in delivering library services, access to digital collections, effective library partnerships and resource sharing, the encouragement of reading and lifelong learning, and the provision of equitable library service for all North Carolinians.[38]

The State Library consults with public libraries on management and intellectual freedom issues, provides training for library trustees and directors, and coordinates statewide programs providing library services for children and teens. It promotes education for digital preservation and is home to the Digital Information Management Program (DIMP), which identifies and promotes solutions to ensure long-term preservation and ready and permanent public access to born-digital and digitized information produced by (or on behalf of) North Carolina state government. The DIMP administers the Access to State Government Initiative, an LSTA grant-funded project to investigate and test technologies and tools to acquire, manage, and preserve state government publications.[39]

In addition to administering state and federal financial aid programs, the State Library provides a program of reference assistance through the Government and Heritage Library, which embraces the range of services traditionally available to users of the State Library's physical and electronic collections. It provides information and reference services concerning North Carolina and federal publications to state and local government officials, members of the General Assembly, state employees, and the general public. The Government and Heritage Library serves as the State Library's resource for population, housing, business, and government statistics about North Carolina, including data from the U.S. Census Bureau, North Carolina state agencies, and other state and federal sources, and is a coordinating agency of the North Carolina State Data Center. The State Data Center is a consortium of agencies cooperating with the U.S. Census Bureau to provide the public with data about the state and its component geographic areas.[40]

The State Library, in promoting better public libraries, has sought to establish standards and guidelines to help them attain their greatest potential in service to their communities. It seeks to serve as the catalyst for exceptional library services and thus ensure that all North Carolinians have access to the information resources they need to achieve their personal, educational, and professional goals. The continued development and implementation of cost-effective

---

38. State Library of North Carolina, "Strategic Framework," in *Strategic Plan 2008–2012* (Raleigh: N.C. Department of Cultural Resources, n.d.), 4, www.statelibrary.ncdcr.gov/strategicPlan_0608.pdf.

39. *See* Library Development Staff section of the State Library website, www.statelibrary.ncdcr.gov/ld/staff.html (last visited Dec. 8, 2014); the Digital Information Management section of the State Library's website, www.statelibrary.ncdcr.gov/dimp/index.html, archived at wayback.archive-it.org/194/20110915004257/http://statelibrary.ncdcr.gov/dimp/index.html (last visited Dec. 8, 2014); and the Digital Repository Collection Guidelines [Draft—updated Apr. 10, 2008], www.digital.ncdcr.gov/ui/custom/default/collection/default/resources/custompages/about/dr_collection_development_guidelines.pdf..

40. This description is based on information at the Government and Heritage Library section of the State Library website, www.statelibrary.ncdcr.gov/ghl/index.html (last visited Dec. 8, 2014); the North Carolina State Publications Clearinghouse, Handbook for State Agencies (Raleigh: N.C. Department of Cultural Resources, Division of State Library, Apr. 20, 2010; updated July 2012), www.statelibrary.ncdcr.gov/ghl/handouts/Agency Handbook.pdf (last visited Dec. 8, 2014); and the State Data Center website, www.osbm.state.nc.us/ncosbm/facts_and_figures/state_data_center.shtm.

services and modern technology for sharing knowledge have become even more essential in the current environment of rapidly changing methods for compiling, sending, and receiving information.[41]

State Documents Depository System and North Carolina State Publications Clearinghouse

In 1987, the General Assembly enacted the Documents Depository Act to improve public access to publications of state agencies and to provide a better system for preserving them (G.S. Chapter 125, Article 1A). The law named the State Library as the official depository of all these publications and created the State Publications Clearinghouse in the Department of Cultural Resources to receive and distribute publications to depository libraries. Taking into account regional distribution patterns and persons served so that the publications will be conveniently accessible to all residents of the state, the State Library may designate at least one library in each congressional district to serve as a depository. The State Library is responsible for formulating standards of operation and rules under which the depository system will be administered.

In addition, the Government and Heritage Library is mandated to serve as the official permanent depository for all state publications. Clearinghouse staff and depository librarians work together to facilitate access to current and historic agency publications by all North Carolinians. In response to the shift in publishing practices from print to digital publishing, the Clearinghouse is now collecting, cataloging, and adding digital publications to the State Publications Collection of the State Library and adding records for these items to WorldCat. The repository provides a unique, stable URL for each publication. These "permanent" URLs may be used by libraries in library catalog records and on Web pages. The Digital Information Management Program manages digital preservation for all items in the repository.[42]

Interlibrary Cooperation

Besides formal organizations, such as regional libraries, other cooperative efforts are being made to help libraries meet increasing demands for a variety of services and materials. On a broad scale, G.S. 125-12, the Interstate Library Compact, authorizes local and state library agencies of those states that are parties to the agreement (North Carolina is one) to engage in joint and cooperative library programs and services.

NC LIVE (North Carolina Libraries and Virtual Education) is a statewide electronic information project serving nearly two hundred member libraries and dedicated to providing North Carolinians with online library and information resources that support education, enhance statewide economic development, and increase their quality of life. Since its inception in 1997, NC LIVE has grown into a huge information gateway and now offers the citizens of North Carolina online access to a diverse collection of electronic resources, including thousands of eBooks; full-text journals, magazines, and newspapers; videos; images and maps; and interactive tests and tools. NC LIVE is available free of charge to library patrons, students, and educators of NC LIVE–affiliated libraries in North Carolina—public libraries, community colleges, the state's university system, and independent colleges and universities. Continuous access is available from any Internet connection through the websites of local (public, college, university) libraries or through www.nclive.org with the patron's library's password.[43]

Another cooperative endeavor is the Triangle Research Libraries Network (TRLN). Consisting of Duke University, the University of North Carolina at Chapel Hill, North Carolina Central University, and North Carolina State University, TRLN seeks to marshal the financial, human, and information resources of their research libraries to create a knowledge environment that furthers the universities' teaching, research, and service missions.

41. State Library of North Carolina, "Vision" and "Mission" headings of "Strategic Framework," in *Strategic Plan 2008-2012* (Raleigh: N.C. Department of Cultural Resources, n.d.), 4, www.statelibrary.ncdcr.gov/strategicPlan_0608.pdf.

42. Description based on information at the N.C. State Government Publications Clearinghouse section of the State Library website, www.statelibrary.ncdcr.gov/ghl/services/clearinghouse.html.

43. "About NC Live," NClive.org, www.nclive.org/about, and NC Live Factsheet, www.nclive.org/newsroom/factsheet (last visited Dec. 8, 2014).

TRLN goals include extending the scope of information resources available to users through libraries and campus networks, creating new library and information services, and making information accessible to users in a convenient, timely, and equitable manner. TRLN hopes to develop strategic partnerships that enhance the delivery of information and services, provide a forum for discussing cooperative library and information issues, seek external funding in support of its goals, and maintain a leadership role among universities in the provision of collaborative research library services.[44]

The new effort by the North Carolina State Library to create the NC Cardinal consortium to share catalog resources and create a statewide library card for public libraries (see above under discussion of the Library Services and Technology Act) is yet another example of innovative efforts at sharing technology and funding.

Additional Resources

Becker, Samantha, Michael D. Crandall, Karen E. Fisher, Bo Kinney, Carol Landry, and Anita Rocha. *Opportunity for All: How the American Public Benefits from Internet Access at U.S. Libraries.* Washington, D.C.: Institute of Museum and Library Services, 2010.

Bertot, John Carlo, Paul T. Jaeger, and Charles R. McClure, eds. *Public Libraries and the Internet: Roles, Perspectives, and Implications.* Santa Barbara, Calif.: Libraries Unlimited, 2011.

Berube, Linda. *Do You Web 2.0? Public Libraries and Social Networking.* Chandos Internet Series. Oxford: Chandos Publishing, 2011.

Fasick, Adele M. *From Boardbook to Facebook: Children's Services in an Interactive Age.* Santa Barbara, Calif.: Libraries Unlimited, 2011.

Fisher, Patricia H., and Marseille M. Pride, with Ellen G. Miller. *Blueprint for Your Library Marketing Plan: A Guide to Help You Survive and Thrive.* Chicago: ALA, 2006.

Hernon, Peter, and Joseph R. Matthews. *Listening to the Customer.* Santa Barbara, Calif.: Libraries Unlimited, 2011.

Huber, John J. *Lean Library Management: Eleven Strategies for Reducing Costs and Improving Customer Services.* New York: Neal-Schuman Publishers, 2011.

Matthews, Joseph R. *The Evaluation and Measurement of Library Services.* Westport, Conn.: Libraries Unlimited, 2007.

Moore, Mary Y. *The Successful Library Trustee Handbook.* 2nd ed. Chicago: ALA, 2010.

Polanka, Sue, ed. *No Shelf Required 2: Use and Management of Electronic Books.* Chicago: ALA, 2012.

Walter, Virginia A. *Twenty-First-Century Kids, Twenty-First-Century Librarians.* Chicago: ALA, 2010.

About the Author

Alex Hess is the School of Government's librarian.

44. Memorandum of Understanding concerning the Triangle Research Libraries Network (TRLN) (originally signed Aug. 29, 1989; last modified Jan. 10, 2012), www.trln.org/about/mou.htm.

Chapter 36

Parks and Recreation

Candace Goode Vick and Paul H. Armstrong

Parks and recreation are essential public services that contribute to the economic and environmental well-being of communities, helping to ensure the health of families and individuals and establish and maintain a better quality of life. According to the National Recreation and Park Association, "There are no communities that pride themselves on their quality of life, promote themselves as a desirable location for businesses to relocate, or maintain that they are environmental stewards of their natural resources, without such communities having a robust, active system of parks and recreation programs for public use and enjoyment."[1] The economic value provided by parks and recreation ranges from increased property values for private property adjacent to a park to revenue generated by regional sporting and special events. Recreation programs, greenways, and open spaces provide services and places where children, youth, and adults can get healthy and stay fit. The environmental benefits of parks and open spaces include improved water quality, flood prevention, improved air quality, and wildlife protection.

The North Carolina General Assembly "declares that the public good and the general welfare of the citizens of this State require adequate recreation programs, that the creation, establishment, and operation of parks and recreation programs is a proper governmental function, and that it is the policy of North Carolina to forever encourage, foster, and provide these facilities for all its citizens."[2] The development of public parks and recreation activities as a local government function in the United States stems from the public park and playground movement that began in large cities such as Boston and Chicago in the 1890s. Since the early days of settlement houses, the provision of parks and recreation services has generally been regarded as a municipal responsibility. The first municipal park and recreation department in North Carolina was established in 1925 in Durham.[3] Growth of parks and recreation services in North Carolina and throughout the nation has been such that even most small towns and cities now provide some measure of financial support for these services. In 2010 full-time parks and recreation services were offered by 159 cities across the

1. National Recreation and Park Association, *Why Parks and Recreation Are Essential Public Services (*Ashburn, Va.: National Recreation and Park Association, 2011).

2. Recreation Enabling Act of 1945, codified as N.C. Gen. Stat. (hereinafter G.S.) § 160A-351.

3. Paul l. Gaskill, *Introduction to Leisure Services in North Carolina* (Dubuque, Iowa: Kendall Hunt Publishing Co., 2006).

state. However, parks and recreation did not become an accepted county function in North Carolina until the 1960s, with the establishment of the Person County Parks and Recreation Department in 1961. Acceptance of public parks and recreation as a county function in the state was slow: in the late 1960s there were only thirteen such departments in North Carolina. By 1974 the number had grown to twenty-seven. Today, seventy-three counties provide sufficient appropriations to fund a full-time department that is professionally directed. There are also eight joint city–county departments, bringing the total number of full-time local parks and recreation departments in North Carolina to 241.[4] Many other counties and cities provide financial support of varying degrees but less than the amount required for full-time, year-round operation.

Generally, cities that have parks and recreation programs tend to spend more on them per capita than do counties that have such programs. In 2013 the average per capita expenditure by cities and counties with parks and recreation programs was $55.29, based on a total statewide outlay of approximately $540 million.[5] In the nation and in North Carolina, local governments spend more for parks and recreation than state governments do. In the nation in 2011, local governments accounted for 87.5 percent of state and local government expenditures for parks and recreation. In North Carolina the local government share was lower at 79.2 percent.[6]

The size and scope of local recreation programs vary greatly across North Carolina. Raleigh and Mecklenburg County, two of the largest communities, operate a wide range of programs and have full-time staffs of 443 and 267, respectively. Smaller communities, however, often provide parks and recreation services with one to three full-time employees and seasonal or volunteer staff. Some local governments are responsible for managing both parks and recreation programs, while others only provide recreation programs. In some cases, municipal departments are being asked to expand their programs to provide some level of recreation services to nonresidents.

Local parks and recreation services are not uniform in either type of activity or level of service. Some are primarily oriented toward team league sports, while others offer a variety of arts, crafts, music, dance, aquatics, drama, boating, environmental education, adventure, and wellness programs for all ages. Many departments have a system of ball fields, tennis courts, golf courses, community centers, greenways, and aquatic facilities. A number of new types of facilities, such as dog parks, disc golf courses, equestrian arenas, and outdoor adventure areas are being built. Others may provide only one or more park sites with limited facilities. Under the Community Schools Act of 1977,[7] some communities have also opened up schools for a variety of recreational uses. Many local parks and recreation departments are expanding their offerings to include nontraditional services such as child daycare, afterschool child care programs, literacy programs, and child care for parents participating in recreation programs. Others have taken over the operation of historic sites, museums, cultural resources, and convention centers, and some departments' services include the maintenance of public buildings, road rights-of-way, and cemeteries. Although each department is unique, all recreation departments share the goal of improving the quality of life for their residents.

Authority to Provide Parks and Recreation Services

The North Carolina Recreation Enabling Act, Chapter 160A, Article 18, of the North Carolina General Statutes (hereinafter G.S.), authorizes local governments to provide parks and recreation services to their citizens. The statute defines *recreation* broadly for purposes of the enabling act: "Recreation" means activities that are diversionary in character and

4. Paul H. Armstrong, ed., *Directory of North Carolina Park and Recreation Agencies* (Raleigh, N.C.: North Carolina State University, Recreation Resources Service, 2014).

5. Matt Whitlow, *Municipal and County Parks and Recreation Services Study* (Raleigh, N.C.: North Carolina State University, Recreation Resources Service, 2014).

6. U.S. Census Bureau, *State and Local Government Finances: 2011* (November 17, 2014), www.census.gov//govs/local/historical_data.html.

7. G.S. 115C, Art. 13.

aid in promoting entertainment, pleasure, relaxation, instruction, and other physical, mental, and cultural development and leisure time experiences.[8]

This legislation specifically authorizes local governments to do the following:[9]

1. Establish and conduct a system of supervised recreation;
2. Set apart lands and buildings for parks, playgrounds, recreational centers, and other recreational programs and facilities;
3. Acquire real property, either within or without the corporate limits of the city or the boundaries of the county, including water and air rights, for parks and recreation programs and facilities by gifts, grant, purchase, lease, and exercise of the power of eminent domain or any other lawful method;
4. Provide, acquire, construct, equip, operate, and maintain parks, playgrounds, recreation centers, and recreation facilities, including all buildings, structures, and equipment necessary or useful in connection therewith;
5. Appropriate funds to carry out the provisions of the Article;
6. Accept any gift, grant, lease, loan, bequest, or devise of real or personal property for parks and recreation programs. Devises, bequests, and gifts may be accepted and held subject to such terms and conditions as may be imposed by the grantor or trustee, except that no county or city may accept or administer any terms that require it to discriminate among its citizens on the basis of race, sex, or religion.

The law provides for local governments to operate a parks and recreation system as a line department or to create a policy-making parks and recreation commission.[10] They may also join with other units of local government to operate a single system of parks and recreation.[11] Cities and counties are permitted to contract with and appropriate money to private entities to provide recreational services as long as they are provided in a nondiscriminatory fashion appropriate for a public activity and the private organization properly accounts to the local government for its expenditures.[12]

Legislation

The funding and operation of parks and recreation departments is being affected more and more by legislation on the state and national level. On the national level, in 1965, Congress authorized the Land and Water Conservation Fund (LWCF) to "preserve, develop and assure accessibility to outdoor recreation resources in order to strengthen the health and vitality of the citizens of the United States."[13] For a number of years, the LWCF was one of the most important sources of funding for parks and recreation agencies. In recent years, however, funding for the LWCF has decreased. Efforts continue by the National Park and Recreation Association and other conservation groups to obtain full funding for the LWCF. The LWCF is authorized to accumulate $900 million annually from designated sources, with most of the money derived from oil and gas leasing in the Outer Continental Shelf. Congress determines the level of appropriations each year, and yearly appropriations have fluctuated widely since the origin of the program. Of the total revenues that have accrued throughout the history of the program ($32.6 billion), less than half have been appropriated ($15.5 billion). Fiscal year 2001 marked the highest funding ever, with appropriations exceeding the authorized level by reaching nearly $1 billion. For 2013, the most recent fiscal year, the appropriation was $305.5 million. Only 13 percent of the funds are available for use by the states.

---

8. G.S. 160A-352.
9. G.S. 160A-353.
10. G.S. 160A-354.
11. G.S. 160A-355.
12. G.S. 153A-449 and G.S. 160A-20.1 authorize counties and cities, respectively, to contract with and appropriate money to any person, association, or corporation in order to carry out any public purpose that the county or city is authorized by law to engage in.
13. Land and Water Conservation Fund Act of 1965, Pub. L. No. 88-578, 16 U.S.C. §§ 4601–04.

The Americans with Disabilities Act (ADA), which was first authorized in 1990, provided suggested guidelines to follow in accommodating citizens with special needs; these are now legally mandated requirements. The Revised Final Title II Rule: A Compilation of Regulatory Provisions and Guidance–Nondiscrimination on the Basis of Disability in State and Local Government Services became effective on March 15, 2011. Compliance with the 2010 Standards for Accessible Design has been required since March 15, 2012. Chapter 10 of the ADA Accessibility Guidelines specifically addresses recreation facilities.

Volunteers in parks and recreation programs are protected by the Volunteer Protection Act (VPA) of 1997. In broad terms, the VPA protects volunteers serving governmental entities and nonprofit organizations from liability for harm caused by negligent acts or omissions during their volunteer service.

More recent federal legislation with an impact on parks and recreation includes the reauthorization of funds for the Community Development Block Grant Program and the Safe, Accountable, Flexible, Efficient Transportation Equity Act: A Legacy for Users. In addition, though not directly addressed in legislation, there are consumer product safety guidelines for the construction and maintenance of playgrounds.

On the state level, other legislation permits both counties and cities to finance public parks and recreation and provides ways to acquire land, lease facilities, and fund the development of recreation facilities. For example, enabling statutes for subdivision regulations permit counties or cities to require that developers reserve or dedicate recreation areas to serve the residents in new subdivisions.[14] The requirement may be imposed only as part of a subdivision ordinance adopted by the city or county to guide and regulate subdivision development. The rationale is that each developed subdivision both increases the demand for recreation and open space and removes open space through land development. The subdivider is thus required to furnish such space for the local government in relation to the need the subdivider creates. The subdivider ordinarily passes the economic cost on to purchasers of subdivision lots. Once the land is dedicated, the cost of maintaining it falls on the city or county. A subdivision ordinance that requires dedication or reservation of land should indicate the amount of land per subdivision that must be dedicated (for example, 5 percent of the total area); the location of the land to be dedicated; and some standard relating to the degree of improvement required. The ordinance should include some provisions to ensure that the land is well suited and properly located for recreation purposes. Local governments also may require developers to provide funds in lieu of land so that additional recreation lands may be acquired to serve the new developments.

The General Statutes contain another authority for local governments to acquire open space: G.S. Chapter 160A, Article 19, Part 4. *Open space* is an area (1) that is characterized by great natural scenic beauty or (2) whose openness, natural condition, and present state of use, if retained, would enhance the present or potential value of abutting or surrounding urban development or would enhance or maintain the conservation of natural or scenic resources.[15] Open space includes undeveloped land in an urban area that has value for (1) parks and recreation purposes, (2) conservation of land or other natural resources, or (3) historic or scenic purposes.[16]

The law authorizes local governments to preserve for public access or enjoyment open areas of significant scenic or aesthetic value that might otherwise be lost because of rapid urban growth and development, and it expressly declares the acquisition and the preservation of open space to be a public purpose of local governments.[17] Cities and counties can acquire open space by purchase, gift, grant, bequest, lease, and through the expenditure of public funds.[18] Local governments may acquire outright ownership of open space or any lesser interest, such as a conservation easement. A local unit may acquire a conservation easement for open space such as farmland, preserving the scenic characteristics of the property for public enjoyment without opening it to public access or granting public access.[19]

---

14. G.S. 153A-331 and G.S. 160A-372.
15. G.S. 160A-407(a).
16. G.S. 160A-407(b).
17. G.S. 160A-402.
18. G.S. 160A-401.
19. *See* www.ncadfp.org/FarmlandPreservation.htm.

Local governments are also authorized to exchange, lease, sell, or purchase property with, to, or from other government units.[20] In general, such arrangements may include whatever terms and conditions the units involved deem wise. This authority has permitted boards of county commissioners and school boards, for example, to work cooperatively to transfer surplus school lands and structures to parks and recreation uses.

The only significant constraint on such transfers is found in Article IX, Section 7, of the North Carolina Constitution, which prevents school systems from giving away school property. As long as the school system receives value in return, however, a transfer to another government unit is permissible. Under G.S. 115C-518(a), the school board must give the board of commissioners the first opportunity to purchase whenever it disposes of real property that is no longer suitable or necessary for public school purposes.

The 1977 Community Schools Act[21] has also benefited recreation programs. It opens schools for a variety of community uses, including recreation. A city or county can agree with a school board to use school gyms, playgrounds, and fields for its recreation programs and thus avoid having to construct or acquire expensive capital facilities in areas where facilities already exist.

In 1994 the North Carolina General Assembly established the Parks and Recreation Trust Fund (PARTF).[22] Other than the Recreation Enabling Act, PARTF has had the most significant impact on parks and recreation agencies in North Carolina. Since its beginning, PARTF has funded 677 grants (approximately $137 million) for improvements to local parks and recreation departments across the state. In 2013 the North Carolina Legislature replaced dedicated funding source with annual appropriations. Grants have been awarded in all 100 of North Carolina's counties. Under this fund, a matching-grant program was established for local parks and recreation purposes. Annually, 30 percent of the funds appropriated to the Department of Environment and Natural Resources from PARTF are allocated to local governments for the following purposes:[23]

1. Fee-simple acquisition of real property for preservation of natural areas and future recreation development
2. Projects for construction, expansion, and renovation or repair of both outdoor and indoor recreation facilities
3. Construction of support facilities and improvements that support primary recreation facilities

To obtain information about how to apply for funds, call the Recreation Resources Service or the N.C. Division of Parks and Recreation or visit the PARTF website. The current phone numbers and website can be found in Appendix 36.1, "Contact Information."

In 1995 the North Carolina General Assembly passed the North Carolina Recreational Use Statute limiting the liability of landowners who make their land and water areas available to the public at no cost for educational and recreational purposes.[24] In 2003 the legislature passed the Hazardous Recreation Parks Safety and Liability Act to encourage governmental owners or lessees of property to make land available to a governmental entity for skateboarding, inline skating, or freestyle bicycling.[25]

In 2011 the North Carolina General Assembly approved S.L. 2011-268 (H.B. 650), which allows concealed gun permit holders to carry guns in parks and recreation facilities. The law does allow local governments to limit weapons by passing local ordinances that prohibit the carrying of concealed handguns in designated buildings and appurtenant premises and at listed and defined recreational facilities. Nothing in the ordinance precludes the holder of a concealed handgun permit from securing a handgun in a locked vehicle within the trunk, glove box, or other enclosed compartment or area within or on the motor vehicle at the recreational facilities.

20. G.S. 160A-274.
21. G.S. Ch. 115C, Art. 13.
22. G.S. 113-44.15.
23. 15A N.C. Admin. Code 12K .0108.
24. G.S. Ch. 38A.
25. G.S. Ch. 99E, Art. 3.

Financing

Before the 1973 revision of Article V of the North Carolina Constitution, recreation was not considered a necessary expense and could not be financed by property tax revenues without a vote of the people. Under the revised constitution and enabling legislation enacted pursuant to it in 1973, public parks and recreation are among the purposes for which counties and cities may levy property taxes without a vote, subject to an overall limitation of $1.50 on the property tax rate. Local governments also may allocate to parks and recreation any other revenues whose use is not restricted by law.

Although local parks and recreation departments are primarily funded through property tax revenues, they do receive operating and capital improvement moneys from other sources. The local departments participating in the 2012 *Municipal and County Parks and Recreation Services Study*[26] reported that they received 71.8 percent of their operating funds from local taxes, 19 percent from fees and charges, 3.1 percent from grants, and 6.1 percent from other sources.

Because of limited federal, state, and even local funding for parks and recreation, local departments are exploring innovative alternative sources of funding for facilities and programs. There is an increased reliance on user fees, use of hotel occupancy tax revenues for recreation facilities as part of tourism development programs, publication of gift catalogs to allow donors to give particular needed items to parks and recreation programs, partnerships between local governments and private businesses to build recreation facilities, and establishment of local foundations and trust funds. A survey by Recreation Resources Service indicated that at least twenty-three communities in North Carolina have parks and recreation supporting foundations,[27] one-third of which are aligned with the North Carolina Community Foundation. Some recreation facilities and programs are developed and operated using enterprise funds. These facilities and programs are built, operated, and maintained without tax revenues. They are supported through revenues generated by the facility.

Additional Funding Sources

In addition to the Parks and Recreation Trust Fund, local governments can use the following funding sources to finance program development and open space, trails, and park land acquisition and development:

1. The North Carolina Trails Program is administered by the North Carolina Division of Parks and Recreation and includes two programs: the Adopt-A-Trail Grant and the Recreational Trail Program. The Adopt-A-Trail Grant awards funding of approximately $110,000 annually to governmental agencies, nonprofit organizations, and private trail groups for building trails, trail signage and facilities, trail maintenance, and trail information brochures and maps. The Recreational Trails Program is a $1.8 million trail grant program funded by Congress with money from the federal gas taxes paid on fuel used by off-highway vehicles. Its intent is to meet the trail and trail-related recreational needs identified by the Statewide Comprehensive Outdoor Recreation Plan (SCORP). The grant applicants must be able to contribute 20 percent of the project cost with cash or in-kind contributions. Applications for both programs can be obtained by calling the State Trails Program or going to the website (see Appendix 36.1, "Contact Information").
2. The Clear Water Management Trust Fund (CWMTF) awards grants to local governments, state agencies, and nonprofit conservation groups to help protect and restore surface water quality. The CWMTF will fund projects that enhance or restore degraded water, protect unpolluted waters, and/or contribute toward a network of riparian buffers and greenways for environmental, educational, and recreational benefits. For more information about the fund, go to the website (see Appendix 36.1, "Contact Information").
3. The North Carolina Department of Transportation Enhancements Fund (DTEF) has twelve funding categories, including bicycle and pedestrian facilities, bicycle and pedestrian safety, historic preservation, and pres-

26. Matt Whitlow, *Municipal and County Parks and Recreation Services Study* (Raleigh, N.C.: North Carolina State University, Recreation Resources Service, 2014).

27. *Id.*

ervation of abandoned railroad corridors. For additional information, go to the website (see Appendix 36.1, "Contact Information").

4. The Urban and Community Forestry Grant Program is a federally funded program that awards matching funds to enhance and promote the urban forest. This program is coordinated by the North Carolina Division of Forest Resources, and information about this program can be found on its website (see Appendix 36.1, "Contact Information").
5. Development and programming funds are available through a number of private and public companies, including the Blue Cross/Blue Shield of North Carolina Foundation, the Hershey Company, Lowes Home Improvement, Major League Baseball, the National Football League, and United States Soccer. A list of corporate funding sources is available from the National Parks and Recreation Association. More than half the counties in North Carolina have private foundations that may support parks and recreation initiatives.

Organization

A local government may provide parks and recreation services through one of three alternatives: (1) a line department within local government, (2) a policy-making parks and recreation commission, or (3) a joint agreement with another city or with a county.

A Line Department

The most common organizational method used in North Carolina is to organize parks and recreation as a line department within a city or county. Under this approach, the parks and recreation department is usually administered by an executive who reports to the city/county manager or the city council or county commissioners. When a department is established, its mission and scope of services determine the title of the department. The most commonly used titles are Parks Department, Recreation Department, or Parks and Recreation Department. There is ongoing discussion regarding making the titles of departments more indicative of the services and benefits they provide (for example, Cary Parks, Recreation, and Cultural Resources Department; Town of Leland Department of Parks, Recreation, and Environmental Programs; Wake County Parks, Recreation, and Open Space). More departments likely will be working to redefine themselves through their titles. In times of budget cuts and "right-sizing," some park maintenance divisions have been moved from parks and recreation to public works. While on paper this seems a viable alternative, caution should be used when consolidating all maintenance under one department. The public works staff must understand the demands for maintenance created by the scope of recreation services and facilities. Recreation facilities are often open seven days a week and operate beyond the traditional hours of many local government services. Maintenance services must be provided when programs are scheduled and facilities are open. Also, participants' demands for quality facilities often dictate the need for a higher standard of maintenance for recreation facilities in order for these facilities to remain competitive with facilities in surrounding communities.

When the line-departmental approach is used, it is beneficial to establish a parks and recreation advisory committee. Appointed by the local governing body, this committee interprets the needs of citizens, works closely with paid professional staff, and assists in providing direction for the department. The advisory group, ideally made up of seven to nine members, has no policy-making authority but can provide a critical link between citizens, department staff, the city/county manager, and local government. Members of the advisory board should be appointed to staggered three-year terms, with all members limited to two consecutive terms. Ideally, the committee membership will be representative of the population based on race, gender, community interests, and geography. Training for advisory committees is imperative to ensure an effective group and is available from Recreation Resources Service.

A Policy-Making Parks and Recreation Commission

A local government may establish a parks and recreation department and appoint a policy-making parks and recreation commission to oversee departmental operations. This commission then has responsibility for the department's organization, personnel, fiscal matters, areas and facilities, programs, and other functions. The commission members report directly to the local government officials. The commission may be established by an ordinance, which ordinarily spells out the commission's general powers and duties, including its relationships to the local government and its finances. This organizational option is not frequently used in North Carolina.

A Joint Agreement with Another City or with a County

A local government may elect to enter into a joint agreement with another city or with a county to provide parks and recreation services for its residents. This type of arrangement is authorized by G.S. 160A-335. The future is likely to bring more joint agreements between cities and counties due to their common purposes and their desire to provide services as efficiently as possible.

The authority of a local government to enter into joint agreements with other governmental entities or agencies to provide parks and recreation services is an important right. These arrangements are authorized by G.S. 160A-355 and G.S. Chapter 160A, Article 20, Interlocal Cooperation. A city or county that does not wish to hire and maintain its own staff may contract with another city or with the county for the use of certain parks and recreation facilities by its residents or for professional staff support from the other unit, or it may agree to set up a joint parks and recreation agency with the other unit. Contracting for support personnel or services is a satisfactory arrangement when one or two units of government are in effect buying the use of park facilities for their residents or seeking professional staff support from another unit's program and when a second full-time staff person is not feasible or a second policy-making body is not needed. Certain contents of the contract are specified in G.S. Chapter 160A, Article 20. The contract must state its purpose and duration and the arrangement for handling the ownership of real property. It should also provide for its own amendment and termination.

A joint agency with its own staff also may be established under G.S. Chapter 160A, Article 20. This approach can provide services that would be impossible or too expensive for any one local unit to provide with its own resources. It can take advantage of the wider population and tax base of several units. Administrative costs can generally be reduced, making more money available for programs and services. The professional staff can be appointed either by one unit or jointly by all participating units. The agency is funded by appropriations from participating units. Title to real property can be held jointly or can continue to be held by the individual participating units. As when services are provided by contract, the contract establishing the joint agency should specify the agency's purpose, duration, organization, appointment of personnel, financing, amendment, and termination. Examples of this type of arrangement include Elizabeth City/Pasquotank County Parks and Recreation Department, Kinston-Lenoir Parks and Recreation, and Henderson-Vance Parks and Recreation.

A Joint Agreement Involving Several Units

A county or city that chooses not to hire and maintain its own staff may find some advantages in arranging for professional services or for the use of certain parks and recreation facilities through contractual agreements with a town or city in the same county or with another county. These joint arrangements could be for a temporary summer program or a year-round program. Several cities and counties have found that this approach has economic value and is a fair way to provide leisure services for county residents who live in the fringe or suburban areas of larger cities and towns. Such a relatively simple contractual arrangement is most likely to prove satisfactory in those situations where one or two units of government are in effect buying the use of parks and recreation facilities and professional staff services from an existing program and when a second full-time staff person is not feasible or a second policy-making body is not needed.

If, instead, a large number of local governments are involved—as might be the case when several counties (including perhaps the smaller towns within each county) band together to provide a regional parks and recreation system or facilities—a more appropriate form of organization may be an independent, jointly financed parks and recreation commission with its own staff. This latter approach is allowed by both the general wording of G.S. 160A-355 and the legislation authorizing interlocal cooperation found in G.S. Chapter 160A, Article 20.

Agency Accreditation

No matter how an agency is organized, consideration should be given to national certification. The National Recreation and Park Association has established the Commission for Accreditation of Park and Recreation Agencies (CAPRA), which provides quality assurance and quality improvement of accredited park and recreation agencies throughout the United States. CAPRA is the only national accreditation for park and recreation agencies, and it is a valuable measure of an agency's overall quality of operation, management, and service to the community. While it is not possible for every agency to achieve this level of certification, the accreditation standards are an excellent model for local governments to follow in establishing their parks and recreation agencies. Topics include staff qualifications, planning, fiscal management, and programs and services management. Currently, seven cities and one joint city–county department are accredited in North Carolina. Additional information is available from the National Recreation and Park Association.

Professional Staff

Professional leadership is probably the most essential ingredient for a successful parks and recreation program. The administrator's major job responsibilities are to organize the department, train and supervise staff, select appropriate program activities, coordinate planning, manage the budget, acquire needed parklands, develop sustainable revenue streams, and construct a variety of recreational facilities. Additionally, the administrator must address safety and liability issues for both staff and participants.

The administrator will also need to hire a number of supervisors, based on the scope of the department's services. Highly competent parks and recreation professionals are available in North Carolina and county and city officials should hire educated and experienced personnel to administer the department and its programs. Volunteers may provide some supplemental assistance, but experience indicates that they should be used to enrich the program and not as a substitute for paid professional leadership.

Many parks and recreation professionals participate in the National Recreation and Park Association Certification for the Park and Recreation Professional Program. Parks and recreation professionals can voluntarily become credentialed as Certified Park and Recreation Professionals and Certified Park and Recreation Executives, verifying that they have met the minimal requirements to practice as parks and recreation professionals. They can also keep up-to-date by joining the North Carolina Recreation and Park Association and the National Recreation and Park Association. In 1986 the General Assembly enacted G.S. Chapter 90C, the Therapeutic Recreation Personnel Certification Act, to credential therapeutic recreation specialists. Other certifications available to professionals include Certified Playground Safety Inspector and Aquatic Facility Operator.

North Carolina is fortunate to have more than twenty colleges and universities that grant bachelor's degrees in parks and recreation. Four state universities confer master's degrees: North Carolina State University, East Carolina University, the University of North Carolina at Greensboro, and the University of North Carolina at Wilmington. North Carolina State University offers a doctor of philosophy degree in Parks, Recreation, and Tourism Management.

Parks and Recreation Planning

Parks and recreation services and facilities must be carefully planned if they are to operate efficiently and economically and provide an appropriate level of service. The parks and recreation program should be a part of the countywide comprehensive strategic plan.

The parks and recreation department should have a system-wide master plan as well as site-specific plans for its facilities. These plans often are a prerequisite for receiving grants to assist with development and programming, such as those offered by the North Carolina Parks and Recreation Trust Fund. All plans should be developed with active citizen input and updated every five to ten years. The facilities must be built with the users' requirements in mind.

Proper location is important, as is acquisition of property before land values have risen to the point that the designation of land for park purposes is no longer feasible. Sites and buildings should be neither too large nor too small for their intended long-term use or for the size of the geographical area to be served. Ideally, parcels of land should be of sufficient size to permit later expansion and the addition of more facilities in an environmentally sensitive manner. The adoption and enforcement of a county zoning ordinance is often required to protect major recreational facilities from possibly adverse uses of nearby property. As noted earlier, subdivision regulations may be helpful in acquiring public parks and recreational areas as large tracts are subdivided for residential purposes.

Whenever possible, planning should occur on a regional basis in order to provide the most efficient and effective recreation opportunities. The Mountains to Sea Trail, the Carolina Thread Trail, and the Overmountain Victory Trail are good examples of regional planning for trails in North Carolina. Planning with local boards of education can also be beneficial: recreation areas can sometimes be jointly financed, constructed, maintained, and operated. As mentioned earlier, the Community Schools Act[28] has encouraged the cooperative planning and use of schools for a multitude of community purposes. Public recreational use of schools has been growing rapidly since the act's passage in 1977.

Parks and recreation planning should include the design of all areas and facilities for use by the disabled and elderly. Local governments must be certain that project designers are aware of and follow pertinent statutes and regulations pertaining to use by the elderly, handicapped access, and safety.

Planning for parks and recreation facilities and services is a cooperative effort. A well-run planning program involves close coordination among the parks and recreation department, its planning department, the local school board(s), user groups, stakeholders, and other interested boards and departments. A number of resources are available to assist agencies with planning, including Recreation Resources Service, regional Councils of Government, regional Resource Conservation and Development Councils, and private consulting agencies.

Trends in Public Recreation

Changes in the state's population patterns, economic growth, and political arena and the emergence of new social issues continue to have a major influence on the provision and management of public parks and recreation. In response to community concern over issues such as at-risk youth, homelessness, violent behavior, the increase in obesity and other health issues among young people, and other social issues, local recreation departments are beginning to organize nontraditional recreation programs such as afterschool child care, daycare for older adults, literacy programs, teen adventure programs, and a variety of self-help classes for children and adults. Local parks and recreation departments are being recognized as viable partners to address communitywide issues and needs. Hospitals, corporations, fitness centers, local health departments, police departments, libraries, the Cooperative Extension Service, and a variety of nonprofit agencies are just a few of the potential partners for local parks and recreation departments. Public recreation programs, facilities, and parks are an important asset that can be used to encourage people to engage in active, healthy lifestyles, to improve the livability of communities, and to help stimulate economic growth.

As the population ages, the demand for recreation programs and services for older adults will increase. North Carolina is affected not only by the aging of the baby boomers but also by an influx of older adults retiring to the state. This older population will demand recreation programs and services to meet their needs and will influence the types of recreation facilities built and the programs offered. The aging population will also present several challenges. On one end of the continuum, the baby boomers who are retiring early and remaining healthy will expect a full range of recreation opportunities beyond the traditional senior programs. At the other end of the continuum, as people live longer and the need for daycare for older adults increases, the public will turn to parks and recreation agencies for assistance.

Public parks and recreation professionals also have to cope with increased government regulations. Constraints on hazardous waste disposal, rules governing pesticide application, Occupational Safety and Health Administration

28. G.S. 115C, Art. 13.

standards, guidelines for playground safety, and the Americans with Disabilities Act are just a few of the regulations, guidelines, and laws that affect service delivery. New regulations are having an impact not only on program delivery and staffing but also on facility design. The challenge facing parks and recreation professionals is how to implement or comply with many of the new regulations without additional financial resources.

As our nation addresses the issues of pollution, limited natural resources, lack of open space, and global warming, parks and recreation departments are often called to lead their communities in conservation efforts. Through recycling efforts at parks and recreation facilities, preservation of open space, limiting carbon footprints, and construction of energy-efficient buildings, parks and recreation departments have the opportunity to lead the way for an environmentally responsible community. Agencies also have opportunities through many of their programs to teach both children and adults environmental responsibility.

The same holds true as communities strive to address obesity and other health issues. Parks and recreation departments have many opportunities to help citizens change their sedentary lifestyles. Through programs that promote physical activity and staff education, agencies can begin to address these very important issues.

Another trend in recreation is the emphasis on risk management. In an era of increasing concern about litigation, parks and recreation departments are being forced to address the issues of liability and safety.[29] Departments must be concerned with the safety of employees—particularly those who work with toxic chemicals—and the safety of participants. More professional staff and volunteers will be trained and certified as part of an overall effort to improve the quality of services. Background checks are now commonplace for volunteers, especially those who work directly with children. Operational safety policies regarding severe weather, bullying, accidents, and injuries to participants—especially children—have to be a top priority. These policies should be reflected in a number of documented plans developed by agencies, including severe weather plans, physical conditioning plans for youth athletes, accident and injury protocol plans, and risk management plans. Some larger departments have their own risk management staffs.

The organizational structure of local parks and recreation systems will continue to evolve. In counties with both municipal and county parks and recreation departments, the opportunity to merge exists. Consideration must be given to regional planning.

The scope of recreation facilities continues to broaden to include facilities such as indoor climbing walls, dog parks, skateboard parks, sand volleyball courts, fitness centers, outdoor splash pools, and large athletic complexes. In order to offer more inclusive recreation services, departments are beginning to design programs that meet the needs of local ethnic groups or other underrepresented populations. A number of cities and regions, including High Point, Cary, Franklin County, and Wilmington, are developing or have developed Miracle Leagues to provide disabled children with the opportunity to play baseball. Outdoor adventure programming has also become very popular in many communities.[30] With the increase in the Hispanic population, a number of adult soccer programs have been developed across the state, which in turn increases the demand for soccer fields. With an increased emphasis on travel and tourism opportunities, many cities and counties are developing large athletic complexes not only to serve local residents but also to host local, regional, and national tournaments. When departments develop these facilities, parks and recreation professionals may be asked to serve in challenging new roles—for example, as project manager during construction and as marketing director once a facility is complete.

The type of person employed by parks and recreation departments is expanding to include not only traditional parks and recreation majors but also employees with majors in early childhood development, nutrition, fitness, computer science, Spanish, and gerontology. These changes will allow parks and recreation departments to provide important services to a greater number of citizens in their communities.

29. Chapter 6, "Civil Liability of the Local Government and Its Officials and Employees," for a discussion of the civil liability of local governments.

30. These programs can often be offered with very little expense to an agency with an aggressive system of fees and charges.

Additional Assistance

Since 1945, the state of North Carolina has provided park and recreation technical and advisory services to local governments. Today, Recreation Resources Service continues to be the primary source of assistance for local governments that provide local parks and recreation services or are contemplating the establishment of a parks and recreation department.

Recreation Resources Service is a division of the Parks, Recreation, and Tourism Management Department at North Carolina State University and is funded through an agreement with the Division of Parks and Recreation, North Carolina Department of Environment and Natural Resources. It provides a wide range of technical assistance to local parks and recreation agencies, including educational workshops on topics such as playground safety, the Americans with Disabilities Act, and athletic field maintenance; training of parks and recreation advisory board members; publication of technical assistance manuals, directories, and a monthly job bulletin; applied research; evaluative studies of parks and recreation agencies; production of park conceptual maps; and provision of individual technical assistance.

The North Carolina League of Municipalities, the North Carolina Association of County Commissioners, and the UNC School of Government can also help with legal, budgetary, and financial aspects of parks and recreation services.

Additional Resources

Edginton, C. R., S. D. Hudson, and S. V. Lankford. *Managing Recreation, Parks and Leisure Services: An Introduction.* Champaign, Ill.: Sagamore Publishing, 2001.

Gaskill, P., ed. *Introduction to Leisure Services in North Carolina.* Dubuque, Iowa: Kendall/Hunt Publishing Co., 2006.

About the Authors

Candace Goode Vick is a faculty member of North Carolina State University and former director of Recreation Resources Service. She specializes in the management of local park recreation agencies. Paul H. "Pete" Armstrong is the Director of Recreation Resources Service.

This chapter updates and revises the previous chapter authored by J. Harold Moses and John C. Poole, whose contributions to the field and to this publication are gratefully acknowledged.

Appendix 36.1 Contact Information

Funding Sources

Recreation Resources Service: 919.515.7118
N.C. Division of Parks and Recreation: 919.715.2661
Parks and Recreation Trust Fund (PARTF): www.ncparks.gov/About/grants/partf_main.php
North Carolina Trails Program: 919.846.9991, www.ncparks.gov/About/trails_grants.php
Clean Water Management Trust Fund: www.cwmtf.net
N.C. DOT Enhancements Fund (TEA21): www.dot.state.nc.us./planning/development/enhancement
Urban and Community Forestry Grant Program: http://ncforestservice.gov/Urban/urban_grant_overview.htm

Other Resources

Recreation Resources Service
North Carolina State University
Campus Box 8004
3024 Biltmore Hall
2820 Faucette Drive
Raleigh, NC 27606
Phone: 919.515.7118
Website: http://rrs.cnr.ncsu.edu

North Carolina Community Foundation
4601 Six Forks Road, Suite 524
Raleigh, NC 27609
Email: info@nccommunityfoundation.org
Phone: 919.828.4387; 800.201.9533
Fax: 919.828.5495
Website: www.nccommunityfoundation.org

North Carolina Recreation and Park Association (NCRPA)
883 Washington St. # A
Raleigh, NC 27605-3251
Phone: 919.832.5868
Email: info@ncrpa.net
Website: www.ncrpa.net

National Recreation and Park Association (NRPA)
22377 Belmont Ridge Road
Ashburn, Va 20148-4501
Phone: 800.626.NRPA (6772)
Email: customerservice@nrpa.org
Website: www.nrpa.org

Chapter 37

Alcoholic Beverage Control

Michael Crowell

North Carolina long has had a conservative approach to the sale of alcohol. The state was dry well before national Prohibition and waited longer than many other states to open up sales after alcohol became legal again. Ever since the end of Prohibition, hard liquor has been available in North Carolina only through government alcoholic beverage control (ABC) stores, and it was not until 1978 that the state became the next to last state to allow the sale of mixed drinks. Today North Carolina still has fewer outlets for alcohol than most other states, but those sales generate more revenue per capita than in most other jurisdictions.

The basic scheme of alcohol regulation in effect today was established in the 1930s after the repeal of Prohibition. Hard liquor is sold through ABC stores operated by local boards whose members are appointed by counties and cities after approval of stores by the voters.[1] All ABC store inventory comes through a state warehouse run by the state Alcoholic Beverage Control (ABC) Commission. Taxes on hard liquor generate hundreds of millions of dollars for the state each year, and local governments reap profits from their ABC stores.

Beer and wine are sold by private retailers—grocery stores, convenience stores, restaurants, bars—in communities where voters have approved such sales. All retailers must have permits from the ABC Commission, which also has authority to suspend or revoke the permission to sell. The ABC Commission will listen to local governments' concerns about permits, but final decisions are made at the state level. Local governments that operate convention centers,

1. North Carolina is one of seventeen states in which liquor sales go through government wholesalers or retailers.

ballparks, and theaters may themselves get in the business of selling alcohol. The state and local governments share revenue from beer and wine taxes.

While the basic structure of the ABC system has remained the same for eighty years, there have been changes on the edges. In recent years in particular it has become more common for the General Assembly to allow sales of alcohol, including mixed drinks, in certain specified communities or particular kinds of businesses, without the need for a local election. As will be discussed below, many of these legislative acts are legally suspect, but they continue to flourish.

Kinds of Alcohol

The state alcoholic beverage control (ABC) laws are found in Chapter 18B of the North Carolina General Statutes (hereinafter G.S.), which was rewritten most recently in 1981. The law's catchall term for all kinds of alcohol is "alcoholic beverage."[2] The term "spirituous liquor" refers to distilled spirits such as whiskey, rum, vodka, brandy, and gin, all of which typically are around 40 percent (80 proof) alcohol, plus liqueurs. "Hard liquor" is used here to mean the same thing.

"Malt beverages," which include beer, lager, porter, ale, and other fermented beverages, range from half a percent of alcohol to about 15 percent, but most are around 5 percent. This chapter uses "beer" as synonymous with malt beverage. The sale of beer with more than 6 percent alcohol was authorized only in recent years. Most of those products are expensive specialty beers, and their labels have to say that they are more than 6 percent alcohol.

"Unfortified wine" refers to wine produced by natural fermentation from grapes, fruits, berries, rice, or honey, and it is not more than 16 percent alcohol. When brandy is added to boost the alcohol content, the result is "fortified wine," which ranges from 16 to 24 percent alcohol. Wine labels indicate the alcohol percentage.

As a general rule, spirituous liquor and fortified wine may be possessed and consumed only where state law specifies.[3] Beer and unfortified wine, on the other hand, may be possessed and consumed anywhere, unless specifically prohibited by the statutes.[4] No alcohol may be sold except with a permit from the ABC Commission. Depending on what kinds of sales have been approved for a given community, some permits may allow sale for consumption at a business ("on-premises" permits) and some may allow only take-out sales ("off-premises" permits). The kinds of places that can get permits, and the kinds of permits allowed, are discussed below.

State Administration

The state Alcoholic Beverage Control (ABC) Commission is made up of three members who are appointed by and serve at the pleasure of the governor.[5] The appointments usually but not always are based on political connections. The chair is paid a full-time salary, while the other two members are paid on a per diem basis. Commission members are subject to the State Government Ethics Act.[6]

The ABC Commission operates the state warehouse and distributes liquor to local ABC boards.[7] It decides what brands of liquor, beer, and wine may be sold in the state and issues all permits to wineries, breweries, distilleries, wholesalers, restaurants, hotels, grocery stores, and so on. The commission also may revoke and suspend permits and levy fines against permit holders for selling to minors, staying open after legal hours, allowing fights on premises, and

2. The definitions of the different kinds of alcohol are found in Section 18B-101 of the North Carolina General Statutes (hereinafter G.S.).

3. G.S. 18B-102, -301.

4. G.S. 18B-300.

5. G.S. 18B-200.

6. The act is codified at G.S. Chapter 138A.

7. The commission's duties and powers are described in Article 2 of G.S. Chapter 18B.

other violations of the ABC statutes and regulations. To investigate complaints the commission relies on state Alcohol Law Enforcement (ALE) officers and on local ABC officers. Commission lawyers handle hearings on violations of the law by permit holders.

Although the commission does not appoint local ABC board members or employees, it has general supervisory authority over all local ABC systems. It also issues regulations that local boards must follow, conducts mandatory training for local board members, audits local boards' finances and general operations, and in some circumstances may remove local board members and employees. The location of all ABC stores has to be approved by the commission. When a local ABC system is losing money, the commission may step in and close stores or require the system to merge with another to maintain solvency.

Local ABC Systems

Alcoholic beverage control (ABC) stores sell only hard liquor and fortified wine.[8] They are operated by units of local governments, not by private businesses, and provide significant revenue to those governments. When a referendum passes to establish ABC stores, the operation of the ABC system is turned over to a local ABC board. The ABC board operates independently of the given county or city, but the relationship is close and interactive.

Elections

Any county may hold a referendum on whether to establish a local ABC system to operate ABC stores.[9] A city may hold an ABC store election only if it has at least 1,000 registered voters and the county does not already have an ABC system.[10]

A referendum may be called by the board of county commissioners or the city council.[11] If the governing body does not want to call a referendum, the ABC system election may be forced by a petition submitted to the county board of elections by 35 percent of the registered voters in the jurisdiction. Petitioners have ninety days from the time they register the petition with the board of elections to get the required signatures. Elections officials then have thirty days to verify the signatures.

Whether the election is called by the local government or by petition, the actual date for voting is set by the board of elections. All ABC elections must be held at the same time as the state and county general election in even-numbered years or at the time of the spring primary preceding that election, or at the same time as a city general election in odd-numbered years.[12] The election procedures are the same as for any other election.[13] A county or city may not hold an election on ABC stores within three years of a previous election on the same issue.[14] Other alcohol issues, such as the approval of mixed drinks, may be voted upon at the same time as the referendum on ABC stores.

All elections are conducted by the county board of elections. A city is required to reimburse the county for the cost of a municipal ABC election.[15]

8. G.S. 18B-800.

9. G.S. 18B-600.

10. G.S. 18B-600(d). When a county approves ABC stores after a city has already established its own ABC system, the city continues to operate its separate stores. There may be pressure to merge the two systems, however.

11. G.S. 18B-601.

12. G.S. 18B-601(f) and G.S. 163-287.

13. For example, just as with any other municipal election, the use of absentee ballots has to be approved by the city council. G.S. 163-302(a). Once approved, the use of absentee ballots remains in effect until rescinded by the city.

14. A city could hold an election on off-premises sale of beer one year, for example, and then vote on on-premises sale of beer and wine the next year, but it could not have another referendum on off-premises beer for three years.

15. G.S. 163-284.

Number of Local ABC Systems

In 2014 there were 168 active local ABC systems in North Carolina, operating more than 420 stores. About half of the counties, mostly in the eastern part of the state, have county ABC systems; municipal systems operate in the other counties. In only one county, Graham, was there no ABC system at all.

The number of ABC systems in the state proliferated after the enactment of liquor-by-the-drink in the late 1970s. To be eligible to have a mixed drink election, a community had to have its own ABC stores to sell the liquor to permit holders, prompting a number of places to approve ABC stores so that a few local restaurants could serve mixed drinks. As a consequence, the number of small ABC systems grew, and some of them had difficulty making money. It was not unusual for new, small municipal systems to take business from neighboring towns, putting their long-term profitability into question. In 2010 the legislature rewrote the ABC laws to increase the population required to have a city ABC store election and, more importantly, to eliminate the requirement that a municipality have ABC stores before it can approve mixed drinks.

Board Size, Members[16]

A county ABC system is governed by an ABC board appointed by the county commissioners; a city ABC board is appointed by the city council. Under state law the board may have either three or five members. Members serve staggered, three-year terms. The size of the board is set by the appointing authority—the county commissioners or city council—when the ABC system is established. If an existing board has three members, the appointing authority may increase it to five by adding two new members with three-year terms. If the commissioners or council want to reduce the ABC board from five to three members, they can do so only when terms expire and only with the agreement of the state ABC Commission. The appointing authority designates one ABC board member to be the chair.

State law says that ABC board members should be appointed on the basis of their "interest in public affairs, good judgment, knowledge, ability, and good moral character."[17] Otherwise, there are no specific qualifications for the job, although conviction of a felony or a violation of the ABC law disqualifies a person from serving on or being employed by an ABC board for three years from the time of conviction.[18] The law does not require that an ABC board member be a resident of the community, but counties and cities usually will not appoint nonresidents.

Occasionally, a board of county commissioners or city council will appoint one or more of its own members to the ABC board, usually in response to troubles in the ABC system. Such appointments are allowed, and the ABC board position does not count as a separate office for purposes of the state dual office-holding law.[19] The commissioners or council might even appoint their manager, attorney, or finance officer. The ABC board is intended to be an independent entity, however, and typically those appointments last only until the ABC board's problems are straightened out.

Duties

The ABC board is responsible for running the local ABC system. The board hires and fires employees and selects one employee to be the manager of the system. The board also designates someone other than this general manager as the system's finance officer, or it may use the finance officer of its county or city appointing authority.[20] The board is required by the state ABC Commission to establish personnel policies and is encouraged to model these after the policies and procedures of the county or city in which the ABC board operates.[21] The ABC board sets employees' salaries but may not pay the general manager more than the salary set by the legislature for the county clerk of court, unless

16. G.S. 18B-700.

17. G.S. 18B-700(d).

18. G.S. 18B-202.

19. *See* G.S. 128-1.2. "Except when the resolution of appointment provides otherwise, whenever the governing body of a county or city appoints one of its own members or officials to another board or commission, the individual so appointed is considered to be serving on the other board or commission as a part of the individual's duties of office and shall not be considered to be serving in a separate office."

20. G.S. 18B-702(j).

21. Title 4, Subchapter 2R, Section .1009(b), of the North Carolina Administrative Code (hereinafter N.C.A.C.).

the board of county commissioners or city council which appointed the ABC board agrees to the higher salary.[22] The general manager may not be given any benefits not offered to all other employees, and no other employee may be paid more than the general manager.

The ABC board decides what products to buy for its ABC stores; buys and leases property as necessary to operate the ABC system; decides where to locate ABC stores (with the approval of the ABC Commission); and oversees the finances of the system. Retail prices for products sold in ABC stores are set by distillers using a statutory markup formula[23] that is to be uniform throughout the state. The local ABC board may dispose of surplus property the same as a city council.[24]

All local ABC board members, general managers, and finance officers are required to complete a training course offered by the state ABC Commission within the first year of being appointed or employed.[25] Board members, the general manager, and the finance officer also are required to be bonded for at least $50,000.[26] The county commissioners or city council may increase the required bond for any member or employee handling ABC board funds.

Compensation

Compensation to local ABC board members is limited to $150 per meeting, unless a different amount is approved by the appointing board of commissioners or city council.[27] Any higher amount has to be reported to the ABC Commission. Travel reimbursement is to be at the same rate as for state government generally, unless the appointing authority has a different policy and the ABC board adopts that policy, with the approval of the board of commissioners or city council.[28] Expenses not covered by the travel policy may be paid only with the written authorization of the county or city's finance officer, and the authorization has to be copied to the ABC Commission.

Ethics

Like other local government officials, local ABC board members are not subject to the financial disclosure laws and other provisions of the State Government Ethics Act,[29] but the ABC statutes regulate the ethical conduct of local board members and subject them to several other important general state laws concerning ethics.[30] The ABC statutes restrict the employment of relatives; require board members to report and refrain from participating in decisions that may benefit certain relatives financially; prohibit board members from using their position to financially benefit themselves or family members; and subject board members to general state law provisions about self-dealing and acceptance of gifts. Board members are obligated to disclose in writing any conflict or potential conflict of interest that might affect their participation in a board action. Each local ABC board is to adopt a code of ethics, which can mirror the model ethics policy prepared by the ABC Commission, and members must complete ethics training within a year of appointment or reappointment.[31]

Removal of Board Members

Local ABC board members serve set terms of three years but may be removed from office sooner under some circumstances. For instance, any board member or employee may be removed from office or discharged from board employment by a judge upon the person's conviction of a felony or any violation of the ABC laws.[32] The board of county commissioners or city council that appointed an ABC board member may remove the member "for cause," but the

22. G.S. 18B-700(g1).
23. G.S. 18B-804; *see also* 4 N.C.A.C. 2R, § .1502.
24. G.S. 18B-701(a)(12). The statutes on disposal of property are found in Article 12 of G.S. Chapter 160A, §§ 160A-265 *et seq.*
25. 4 N.C.A.C. 2R, § .2001.
26. G.S. 18B-700(i).
27. G.S. 18B-700(g).
28. G.S. 18B-700(g2).
29. *See* G.S. Chapter 138A.
30. *See, in particular,* G.S. 18B-201 & -700(h), (k).
31. G.S. 18B-706.
32. G.S. 18B-202.

statute does not specify what "cause" means.[33] A more useful statute allows either the appointing authority or the ABC Commission to remove a local ABC board member or employee for any violation of the ABC laws, for failing to complete any training required by law or by the commission (e.g., ethics training), and for "any conduct constituting moral turpitude or which brings the local board or the ABC system into disrepute."[34] G.S. 18B-704 sets out a specific procedure for removal, including notice in writing of the grounds for removal and a hearing before the commission. The statute also says that the ABC Commission's decision on removal is final, but it allows an appeal to the North Carolina Court of Appeals.

Open Meetings and Public Records

Local ABC boards are governmental bodies subject to the state open meetings and public records laws.[35] Like all other governmental bodies, ABC boards must give notice of each meeting to be held; may call special meetings only on forty-eight hours' notice, unless there is an emergency; may go into closed session only for one of the reasons listed in the open meetings law; must specify the reason for the closed session; must keep minutes of the closed session; and must make its records available to the public. Local ABC boards that have only three members must remember that any meeting of a majority of the board to discuss board business is a meeting requiring notice and public access. Thus, two members of a three-member board may not talk on the telephone about ABC business without taking all of the steps required of an official board meeting.

Mergers and Dissolution of Local Systems

A board of county commissioners or city council may merge its ABC system with that of any other neighboring county or city, with the approval of the state ABC Commission.[36] The appointing authorities have to agree on a joint ABC board and on the distribution of profits.

County commissioners and city councils with ABC systems also may agree to have one of those governmental unit's ABC board operate a store or stores for the other.[37] Again, such an agreement has to be approved by the ABC Commission.

A local ABC system may be shut down if it is not operating profitably. The local ABC board may apply to the state ABC Commission to close the system; the commission may investigate; and if the commission finds that the system cannot be operated profitably, it may order it closed.[38] When that happens, the ABC Commission schedules a phase-out of the system's business and from that point on represents the local board in negotiations with creditors and other interested parties.

Another circumstance in which a local ABC system may be closed or merged is when it fails to meet the performance standards that the ABC Commission sets for all local ABC systems. When this happens, the commission may require the board of commissioners or city council operating the failing system to develop and implement an improvement plan.[39] The plan developed by the commissioners or city council is to set a deadline of not more than twelve months for the specified improvement; the deadline may be extended six months. If at that time the ABC Commission determines that the performance standards cannot be met, the commission may close stores, shut down the system, or merge it with another local ABC system. As part of that process, the ABC Commission may seize the assets of the local ABC board and liquidate any assets to satisfy debt.

---

33. G.S. 18B-700(f).
34. G.S. 18B-704(c).
35. *See generally* G.S. Chapter 143, Article 33C, and G.S. Chapter 132.
36. G.S. 18B-703.
37. G.S. 18B-703(h).
38. G.S. 18B-801(d).
39. G.S. 18B-705.

ABC Finances

Alcohol is taxed heavily by both the federal and state governments. Hard liquor is the source for most of the alcohol revenue that goes to state and local governments. The state receives the excise tax proceeds from the sale of liquor in alcoholic beverage control (ABC) stores; a markup in the price is designed to cover the operating expenses of the stores; and local governments receive the stores' profits. Beer and wine wholesalers collect and pay to the state the excise taxes on beer and wine, and a portion of those moneys is shared with counties and cities where the beer and wine are sold. The state also receives some revenue from the fees charged for ABC permits, and local governments collect license fees from the permit holders located in their communities.

State Revenue

North Carolina law requires uniform pricing for liquor sold in ABC stores throughout the state. Distillers set the price for their products according to a formula set by state law, with various taxes and markups added to the distiller's base price.[40] The statutory formula includes a 30 percent excise tax to be collected by local ABC boards and paid to the state.[41] In the fiscal year that ended June 30, 2013, the excise tax was worth nearly $180 million to the state. When added to sales tax collections of about $46 million and mixed beverage taxes of $14 million, the total tax revenue to the state from hard liquor was nearly $240 million.

There also are state excise taxes of different amounts on beer and wine.[42] Those taxes are collected by the wholesalers who distribute the beer and wine to retail accountholders,[43] and they amount to about $140 million a year. The majority of the beer and wine excise tax proceeds are kept by the state, but a portion is paid to the counties and cities where those products are sold, as explained further below.

The ABC Commission also collects and pays to the state general fund fees for all of the permits it issues; these fees generated more than $15 million in fiscal year 2013. As of early 2014 the fees ranged from $50 for a vendor representative to $1,000 for a mixed drink permit.[44] Most ABC permit fees, including those for the sale of beer and wine and the fees for breweries, wineries, and wholesalers, are one-time fees, but beer and wine permit holders still have to pay an annual registration and inspection fee of $200.[45] A mixed drink permit is only good for one year, and a renewal fee has to be paid annually.

Calculating the Price of Liquor

In addition to the excise tax described above, and the markups for local governments described below, the markup formula for liquor sold in ABC stores includes several other charges that provide revenue to both the state and local governments. For example, there is a penny charge on each bottle of 50 milliliters or less, and a nickel on each larger bottle (a fifth of alcohol is 750 milliliters); a second bottle charge of the same amount; and a $20 charge on each four liters sold to a mixed drink permit holder.[46] The revenue from the first bottle charge goes to the county commissioners to be used for alcoholism programs, while the revenue from the second bottle charge becomes part of the profit to be distributed by the local ABC board to its county or city.[47] Half the revenue from the $20 charge to mixed drink permit holders goes to the state general fund, 5 percent to the state Department of Health and Human Services for alcoholism programs, and the remainder to the local government.[48]

40. G.S. 18B-804; 4 N.C.A.C. 2R, § .1502.
41. G.S. 105-113.80, -113.83(a).
42. G.S. 105-113.80.
43. G.S. 105-113.83(b).
44. G.S. 18B-902(d).
45. G.S. 18B-903.
46. G.S. 18B-804(b).
47. G.S. 18B-805(b)(4), (c)(1).
48. G.S. 18B-805(b)(2), (3).

Local Revenue

A local ABC system pays its profits to the county or city that appoints its board. In the fiscal year ending June 30, 2013, the profits paid to local governments totaled more than $55 million statewide. The price on liquor sold in ABC stores includes markups to go to the local ABC board. The general markup, set at the discretion of the ABC Commission, becomes part of the ABC board's revenue to be mixed into its gross receipts; a second markup of 3.5 percent is earmarked for the local government that appoints the ABC board[49] (along with other profit as discussed below). Counties and cities where beer and wine are sold also share in the excise tax on those products collected by the state.[50] The amount shared currently is slightly more than 20 percent of the excise tax on beer, nearly 50 percent of the excise tax on unfortified wine, and 18 percent of the fortified wine excise tax. Those tax proceeds are allocated to counties and cities based on population.

Counties and cities also collect and keep modest annual ABC license fees set by state law.[51] The fees apply to beer and wine permit holders operating in the county or city and to wholesalers with business locations in cities. Local governments may not charge fees to ABC permit holders other than those specified in state law.[52] Local school systems receive the fines levied by the ABC Commission on permit holders who have violated ABC laws and regulations. In fiscal year 2012, those fines amounted to more than $830,000.

Allocation of ABC Profits

General state law requires a local ABC board to allocate certain portions of its revenue for specified purposes; the remaining profit typically goes to the county or city for which the ABC system is operated.

By law, 5 percent of gross receipts are to be spent on law enforcement, either for the board's own officers or through contract with local law enforcement agencies or with the Alcohol Law Enforcement division of the state Department of Public Safety.[53] Another 7 percent are for alcoholism programs, unless the ABC board is subject to a local act of the legislature setting a different allocation.[54] After those distributions, the remaining profits are to go to the county or city unless, again, there is a local act setting a different distribution.[55] Such acts are not as common today as they used to be, but a number of boards still are subject to local acts specifying that a certain percentage of profits must go to schools, parks, or other particular activities. Those local acts for county ABC systems sometimes specify that a certain percentage of profits are to go to each municipality within the county as well as the portion that is to go to the county itself. In those situations, the affected cities and the county may alter the distribution by mutual agreement.[56]

Local Fiscal Control

Although local ABC boards are not subject to the Local Government Budget and Fiscal Control Act,[57] as are boards of county commissioners and city councils, they are subject to statutes with essentially the same provisions.[58] Under the ABC statutes, for example, the local ABC board's general manager serves as the board's budget officer, with responsibility for preparing and presenting a budget to the board in the same manner as a county or city manager does.[59] The budget year is from July 1 to June 30, the same as for other governmental entities in North Carolina, and the budget process is much the same as for counties and cities. The budget officer—i.e., the general manager—is to submit the proposed budget and a budget message to the board by June 1, and there must be a public hearing where anyone

---

49. G.S. 18B-804(b)(3), (5), & -805(c)(1).
50. G.S. 105-113.82.
51. G.S. 105-113.77, -113.78, -113.79.
52. G.S. 105-113.70(d).
53. G.S. 18B-805(c)(2).
54. G.S. 18B-805(c)(3).
55. G.S. 18B-805(e).
56. *Id.*
57. *See generally* G.S. Chapter 159, Article 3.
58. *See* G.S. 18B-702.
59. G.S. 18B-702.

wishing to be heard on the budget is permitted to appear. The ABC law specifies the form of the budget and requires a balanced budget.

In addition to the budget officer, the local ABC board must appoint a finance officer. The board may designate one of its employees for that role or may use the finance officer of the county or city in which the ABC system operates, with the approval of that other board. The local board may appoint the general manager as the finance officer only with the approval of the state ABC Commission, and the commission is to allow such an appointment only for good cause. The fact that the local board operates no more than two stores is considered good cause.[60]

The finance officer keeps the board's books, receives and deposits all moneys, disburses funds, maintains debt records, supervises the investment of idle funds, and otherwise sees that the board follows its budget and the rules of the ABC Commission. Payment of any bill generally requires the approval of the finance officer, but the board may override the finance officer and pay a bill itself if there is an appropriation in the budget for that purpose. The override has to be by adoption of a resolution, and the board members approving the payment can be individually liable if the payment turns out to break the law.[61]

The statutes allow a local ABC board to set aside a portion of its profits as working capital to operate the system, subject to the rules of the ABC Commission.[62] The current commission rule provides that working capital is to be not less than two weeks' average gross sales nor more than two to four months' average, the maximum being tiered according to the boards' gross sales.[63] With the approval of its board of county commissioners or city council, the local ABC board also may set aside funds for special capital improvement projects.[64] The local board may deposit its money in savings accounts or certificates of deposit and may invest its cash balances in the same kinds of funds as allowed for counties and cities or may deposit the moneys with the State Treasurer for investment.[65]

A local ABC board may borrow money only to buy land, buildings, equipment, or stock needed to operate the ABC system.[66] The board may pledge as security its interest in any of its real or personal property other than the alcohol.

The county or city appointing the ABC board is not responsible for the board's debts.[67]

Each local ABC board is required to have an annual independent audit following a chart of accounts prescribed by the ABC Commission.[68] The audit report is to be provided to the appointing authority and the ABC Commission, either one of which may require additional audits.

Mixed Drink Elections

Mixed drinks are sold in qualified hotels, restaurants, clubs, and other locations. Whether such sales are allowed in a community usually, but not always, is decided in a local referendum.

Standard Election Provisions

To hold a mixed drink election, a county must either already operate alcoholic beverage control (ABC) stores or have an ABC store election at the same time;[69] there has to be a store for mixed drink permit holders to get their liquor. Any city with at least 500 registered voters is eligible to have a mixed drink election; if the city does not have ABC stores, the permit holders may buy their liquor from a store located elsewhere that has been approved by the ABC Commission.

60. G.S. 18B-702(j).
61. G.S. 18B-702(o).
62. G.S. 18B-702(g)(3), -805(d).
63. 4 NCAC 2R, § .0902.
64. G.S. 18B-805(d).
65. G.S. 18B-702(t).
66. G.S. 18B-702(r).
67. *Id.*
68. G.S. 18B-702(s).
69. G.S. 600.

If the county or city governing body does not want to call a mixed drink election, it can be required to do so by a petition from 35 percent of the registered voters.[70]

As with elections for ABC stores, a mixed drink election is conducted by the county board of elections using the same rules that apply for all other elections.[71] See the discussion above about the conduct of ABC store elections; the same rules apply to mixed drink elections. A county or city may not hold a mixed drink referendum within three years of an earlier referendum on the same issue.[72]

Special Provisions on Elections

In addition to the general provisions on mixed drink elections discussed immediately above, the ABC statutes have a number of carefully written sections that describe other kinds of places that may have mixed drink elections. The reason for these provisions is the state constitution's prohibition on local acts regulating trade.[73] Under the constitution, the General Assembly could not enact a bill allowing mixed drink sales in, say, Caldwell and Iredell counties because the sale of mixed drinks is the regulation of trade, and the limitation of the act to specifically named counties makes it a local act. One way around that constitutional restriction is to enact a law applicable to a defined category of counties or cities rather than to specific named locations. An example would be an act allowing mixed drink sales in all counties and cities with populations of 200,000 or more.

The use of such classifications to avoid the unconstitutional local act problem has become a staple of the ABC law, especially with respect to mixed drinks. The categories are crafted to sound like something other than local acts while being limited to a very few targeted communities. One provision, for example, allows mixed drink elections in all cities with at least 300 registered voters located in a county with at least one other city that has approved mixed drinks.[74] Another more egregious example allows any kind of alcohol election in a township (a geographical subdivision of a county that serves no other governmental purpose) that meets all of the following requirements: The county in which the township is located has already approved ABC stores; a third of the employment in the county is travel-related; travel spending exceeds $400 million per year; the entirety of two townships consists of a single island; the island has a population of at least 4,000; and one side of the island faces the ocean and the other side faces a sound.[75]

These categories do not really fool anyone, and it is obvious that they are simply another way of limiting a provision to a specific community without saying its name out loud. If challenged in court they would be found to be invalid local acts, but generally they have not been questioned and have served as a convenient fiction to allow the legislature to extend mixed drink elections to a number of additional localities.

Beer and Wine Elections

Beer and wine are sold both for consumption on-premises and on a take-out basis. Off-premises sales occur in commercial retail outlets like grocery stores and convenience stores, not in alcoholic beverage control (ABC) stores. On-premises sales take place in restaurants, hotels, bars, movie theaters, cafes, and a host of other places. For the most part, the decision on whether to allow on- or off-premises sale of beer or wine is made in a local referendum.

Beer and Wine Election Choices

Counties and cities may vote on a variety of options for the local sale of beer and wine. They may vote for either on-premises (sale and consumption at the location) or off-premises (carry-out) sales of beer, wine, or both. Once a category

70. G.S. 18B-601(b)(2).

71. For example, just as with any other municipal election, absentee ballots may not be used in an ABC referendum unless approved by the city council. G.S. 163-320(a). Once the use of absentee ballots is authorized, it remains in effect until rescinded by the city council.

72. G.S. 18B-604(a).

73. N.C. Const. art. II, § 24(j).

74. G.S. 18B-600(e1).

75. G.S. 18B-600(f).

of sales is approved, state law dictates the kinds of places that may obtain permits. In an on-premises beer election, for example, the local government can choose to limit sales to Class A hotels, motels, and restaurants only.[76]

Any county may hold a beer or wine election.[77] A city may by law have such an election only if the last county election was against such sales—that is, the kind of sales the city wants to put on the ballot are not already legal in the county—and the city either has a population of 500 or more or it operates an ABC store. As discussed above in connection with mixed drink elections, there are various, narrowly drawn provisions of the ABC statutes that allow particular local governments to have ABC elections even though they would not qualify under these general requirements for county and city elections. Those other provisions typically are written to allow mixed drink elections, but some also authorize beer and wine elections. Thus, for example, certain seasonal ski resorts can qualify to conduct beer and wine elections based on the weekly average number of skiers, though they otherwise would not be eligible for an election.[78] The section on mixed drinks, above, explains the reasons for such provisions.

As with ABC store and mixed drink elections, a beer or wine referendum may be called by a board of county commissioners or city council or by a petition submitted by 35 percent of the registered voters in the county or city.[79] The same rules apply as for all other elections, as discussed earlier. Thus, a county or city may not hold a beer or wine election within three years of the same kind of election in the same jurisdiction.

The Fallout Effect of Some Elections

Some elections for particular kinds of alcohol affect the sale of other products. The approval of ABC stores, for example, automatically results in the lawfulness of on- and off-premises wine sales in that jurisdiction, regardless of any separate election on wine.[80] Similarly, if mixed drinks are approved in a referendum, the establishments eligible for permits to serve them automatically qualify also for beer and wine permits, even if those sales have not been separately approved.[81] The reasoning is that once the sale of a more potent form of alcohol has been approved, the community also should have access to products with a lower percentage of alcohol.

Mixed Drink, Beer, and Wine Sales Allowed Without an Election

In an increasing number of situations, the legislature has allowed the sale of beer, wine, and mixed drinks in localities without voter approval at an election. Some of these provisions are applicable statewide, authorizing the issuance of permits to particular kinds of establishments regardless of whether alcohol sales have been approved in that community, while other provisions target specific localities using the same kind of thinly disguised local acts described above for mixed drink elections.

Covered by the first category of provisions are, for example, "tourism resorts," which are eligible for all alcoholic beverage control (ABC) permits even if located in a county or city that has not approved sales.[82] A tourism resort is a restaurant and lodging facility with a golf course and two tennis courts or a restaurant with an equestrian center and two tennis courts.[83] "Sports clubs" receive similar treatment under the ABC laws. A sports club is any 18-hole golf

76. G.S. 18B-602(a)(4). The ABC Commission refers to these as "modified plan" permits and requires that a restaurant have inside seating for at least thirty-six people to qualify for such a permit. *See* 4 N.C.A.C. 2S, §§ .0101(3), .0105(a).

77. G.S. 18B-600.

78. G.S. 18B-600(e2).

79. G.S. 18B-601.

80. G.S. 18B-603(c)(2).

81. G.S. 18B-603(d)(2).

82. G.S. 18B-603(f)(8).

83. G.S. 18B-101(14b).

course and any facility with two or more tennis courts, whether public or private,[84] and it may receive beer, wine, and mixed drink permits regardless of the outcome of any local election on such sales.[85]

Examples falling under the second category of provisions include "historic ABC establishments" and "tourism ABC establishments," each of which qualifies for permits regardless of local elections.[86] A historic ABC establishment, it turns out, is a restaurant or hotel that is on the National Register of Historic Places or within a state historic district; is located on a state highway within 1.5 miles of a designated North Carolina scenic byway and within 15 miles of a national scenic highway; and is in a county in which at least two cities have approved on-premises sale of beer or wine.[87] A tourism ABC establishment has to be within 1.5 miles of an entrance or exit ramp for a national scenic parkway between the North Carolina state line and milepost 460.[88]

Just as with the statutes that authorize elections in certain narrowly defined categories of communities rather than coming right out and naming the city or county, the only purpose of these provisions is to avoid the constitutional prohibition on local acts regulating trade (discussed above). If they were challenged in court they would be tossed out, but until then they serve as a means for the legislature to extend alcohol sales to certain small pockets within larger communities that may not be favorably disposed to beer, wine, and mixed drinks.

As a consequence of these various local provisions, it is not correct to say that the sale of beer, wine, and mixed drinks is allowed only in areas in which they have been approved in a local referendum. There are numerous exceptions to that rule and one needs a scorecard to figure out where sales really are allowed.

Retail Permits

Once sales of beer, wine, or mixed drinks become lawful in a community, either through an election or a provision of the law allowing sales without voter approval, the kinds of establishments that may receive permits is set by state law. And it is the state ABC Commission in Raleigh that issues all permits. Local governments generally have little influence over the issuance of permits. Statewide there are about 18,000 retail outlets with permits to sell some kind of alcohol on or off the premises. Only one county, Graham, remains dry.

Establishments Eligible for Permits

Generally speaking, almost any kind of retail business is eligible for a permit to sell beer on its premises. Such sales are not limited to just restaurants, hotels, and convention centers—movie theaters, snack bars, and even shoe stores and hardware stores could sell beer if they wanted to.[89] Wine permits are only slightly more restricted, requiring at least some minimal sale of food on the premises. Most off-premises sales of beer and wine are in grocery stores and convenience stores, but restaurants and hotels can get such permits as well, as can other kinds of retail businesses.

Fewer places qualify for permits to sell mixed drinks or fortified wine. A restaurant must seat thirty-six and do at least 30 percent of its business from food and nonalcoholic beverages to be eligible.[90] Hotels, private clubs, convention centers, and community theaters also may get permits, as may some nonprofit and political organizations.[91]

---

84. G.S. 18B-1000(f).
85. G.S. 18B-1006(k).
86. G.S. 18B-603(f)(7), (9).
87. G.S. 18B-101(7b).
88. G.S. 18B-101(14a).
89. If, however, a county or city beer referendum is being held on the proposition of limiting beer sales to "Class A hotels, motels, and restaurants," permits are limited to that kind of establishment, mainly meaning that a restaurant must seat at least thirty-six to be eligible for a permit. *See* G.S. 18B-602(a).
90. G.S. 18B-1000(6).
91. *See* G.S. 18B-1000.

Special Permits

Some places that do not have regular ABC permits may get permits for particular events. For example, a restaurant, hotel, diner, club, or convention center may get a "special occasion permit" that allows the host of a party or reception, with the permission of the owner of the business that holds the permit, to bring alcohol onto the premises to serve—not sell—to guests.[92] A "limited special occasion permit" is a slightly different version of the same type of permit; it is obtained by the host of the event, not the establishment, and allows the host to bring liquor in to serve to guests.[93] These permits tend to be used for wedding receptions, anniversary parties, and similar events where the host wants to serve guests but is not in the business of selling drinks.

There also are permits that allow businesses that already have wine and beer permits, usually wine shops or grocery stores, to have wine and beer tastings on the premises. Likewise, a distillery may have liquor tastings.[94] These are promotional events in which small samples are given to customers, not sold.

Additionally, there are special permits that allow particular kinds of organizations to sell or serve alcohol at one-time events.[95] A one-time permit may be issued, for example, to a nonprofit organization to sell beer, wine, or mixed drinks at a fund-raising event, or to a local government or political organization to serve alcohol at a fund-raiser to which patrons must buy tickets.

Local Government Involvement

All ABC permits are issued by the state ABC Commission according to the requirements of state law. The commission also may suspend or revoke permits or fine permit holders for violations of the ABC law and other offenses.[96] Before approving one of the regular on- or off-premises permits, the ABC Commission notifies the city or county where the establishment seeking the permit is located and asks the local government to complete a couple of forms. One is a zoning and compliance form simply to verify that the premises meet local zoning and building and fire codes. The other form allows the local government to object to the issuance of the permit.[97]

If the establishment is in an area zoned for that type of business, say a retail business zone that allows restaurants, and is not otherwise disqualified under state law, the ABC Commission will issue the permit even though local officials would prefer not to have restaurants that serve alcohol in that part of town. In other words, local officials may not exclude businesses from an area based solely on the fact that they sell alcohol, if other businesses of the same nature are allowed there.

The statutes list a number of different factors the ABC Commission is to consider in deciding whether to issue a permit, but no one of those factors by itself explicitly disqualifies an application.[98] The factors include the character of the applicant, the number of establishments with ABC permits already in the area, parking and traffic conditions, proximity to churches and schools, and prior problems with ABC permits in the area. The commission is highly conscious of trying to be uniform in application of the permit requirements throughout the state and rarely will deny a permit application if it meets the minimum standards of state law. The commission will be more sympathetic and helpful to local governments when problems arise at a permitted location, and will suspend or revoke permits when the owner is unable to control the premises properly, but is not likely to pre-judge a location by denying the permit application in the first instance.

As discussed above, under "Local Revenue," state law provides for annual county and city license fees for beer and wine permit holders, but local governments are specifically prohibited from charging any other local license fees.[99]

92. G.S. 18B-1001(8).
93. G.S. 18B-1001(9).
94. G.S. 18B-1001(15) (wine tastings), (18) (beer tastings), (19) (liquor tastings).
95. G.S. 18B-1002.
96. *See generally* G.S. 18B-203, -901.
97. G.S. 18B-901(b), (c).
98. G.S. 18B-901(c).
99. G.S. 105-113.70(d).

Brown-Bagging

While "brown-bagging" used to be common in North Carolina, it now is mostly a thing of the past. Brown-bagging is the practice of bringing one's own bottle of alcohol to a club or restaurant, having it stored in a locker, and then consuming it or serving it to one's guests. It was a popular means of social drinking before mixed drinks became legal. The law still provides for various kinds of establishments to obtain brown-bagging permits so their patrons can bring in their own liquor. Fewer and fewer businesses and clubs are interested in doing so, however. There are no separate elections on whether to allow brown-bagging in a county or city; brown-bagging follows automatically when a community approves ABC stores.[100] If a city or county votes in mixed drinks, brown-bagging may continue for private clubs and veterans organizations but no longer is available for restaurants, hotels, and other businesses that are eligible for mixed drink permits.[101] Brown-bagging permits are issued by the ABC Commission, just like all other ABC permits.

Local Governments as Permit Holders

Local governments may own and operate some of the establishments that are eligible for ABC permits. Convention centers are eligible for beer, wine, and mixed drink permits, for example, and ballparks, snack bars, and other establishments may sell beer and wine.[102] If a local government operates a hotel, it would be eligible for ABC permits as well. Additionally, local governments may rent facilities to organizations or individuals who may want special occasion permits to serve alcohol to guests. A local government itself is eligible for a one-time permit to serve alcohol at a ticketed fund-raising event at which it will serve beer, wine, or hard liquor.

Under general state law, beer and wine may be possessed and consumed anywhere except where prohibited by law.[103] Accordingly, there is nothing unlawful about having beer and wine, and serving it without charge, in county or city buildings or grounds. It is lawful, therefore, to serve beer and wine at a reception, retirement celebration, or other event at city hall. Only if beer or wine is going to be sold is a permit necessary.

For spirituous liquor, the general rule is just the opposite. Spirituous liquor may be possessed and consumed only in those places specifically authorized by law.[104] Consequently, a permit such as a special occasion permit is required to even serve hard liquor at a local government event.

The ABC statutes specifically prohibit the issuance of a permit to sell beer or wine on the property of a public school or college.[105] There are exceptions, however. Beer and wine are allowed, for example, at school and college functions and at campus hotels with mixed drink permits and at college performing arts centers and golf courses.

Local Control of Alcohol Rules

The ABC statutes give local governments limited control over the possession, consumption, and sale of alcohol. A county or city may adopt an ordinance prohibiting possession of open containers and public consumption of beer and wine on county or city property and also prohibiting possession on streets and parking lots closed for special events.[106] A county or city may also by ordinance prohibit Sunday sales of alcohol except in places that have mixed drink or brown-bagging permits.[107]

Other than those local controls, the rules on consumption, possession, and sale of alcohol are governed by state law.

---

100. G.S. 18B-603(c)(3).

101. G.S. 18B-603(d)(4).

102. *See* G.S. 18B-1001.

103. G.S. 18B-300(a).

104. *See* G.S. 18B-102(a), -301(f).

105. G.S. 18B-1006(a).

106. G.S. 18B-300(c). Local ordinances are not needed for public possession and consumption of hard liquor because state law makes such conduct unlawful except where specifically authorized by law. *See* G.S. 18B-301.

107. G.S. 18B-1004(d). State law prohibits alcohol sales before noon on Sunday. The requirement in G.S. 160A-191 that a city have a public hearing before adopting a Sunday closing ordinance does not apply to ordinances to stop Sunday alcohol sales.

Breweries, Wineries, and Distilleries

North Carolina has a number of breweries, wineries, and distilleries. Almost all the breweries are brew-pubs or craft breweries, and almost all the distilleries are small craft operations as well. The requirements for ABC permits are the same, though, regardless of the size of the operation. These kinds of commercial facilities can be located anywhere in the state; they do not depend on local approval at a referendum. In addition to producing their product and selling it to wholesalers for distribution to retail accounts, breweries and wineries also may sell their beers and wines directly to customers at their facilities and at several other locations in the state if they get the regular on-premise permits. They also may hold tastings.[108]

The Three-Tier System of Distribution[109]

Like almost all other states, North Carolina law mandates a three-tier system of distribution of beer and wine. Generally, a brewery or winery, no matter where located, that wants to sell its products in North Carolina may sell only to a wholesaler in the state; the wholesaler may sell only to a retail business like a grocery store or restaurant; a retailer may buy beer or wine only from a wholesaler; and producers and wholesalers may not own retail businesses. This system of regulation was introduced after Prohibition to guard against the abuses of any one entity having too much control over the distribution and sale of alcohol. The three-tier system, for example, prevents a brewery from pressuring a restaurant to carry only its products.[110]

To help enforce the three-tier system and assure that larger commercial businesses cannot exercise undue influence over the smaller fish, the ABC statutes and ABC Commission's rules include detailed instructions on the kinds of goods, favors, and services breweries and wineries and wholesalers can provide to retailers. The rules limit, for instance, the value of neon lights and clocks and other displays a wholesaler may provide to a bar or restaurant with a particular brand name on them.[111]

Smaller breweries and wineries may distribute their products directly to retail accounts without going through a wholesaler. When their production passes a specified level, however, they must use a wholesaler.[112]

The rise of the Internet has increased the interest in direct sales of alcohol to customers. State law allows wineries, whether located in North Carolina or elsewhere, to ship a very limited number of cases directly to customers in the state. The winery must obtain a permit from the ABC Commission and is restricted in both the number of cases that may be sent to any one individual and the total number of cases that may be shipped directly to customers in North Carolina.[113] Those limitations mean that this kind of purchase tends to be used only by wine connoisseurs. It does provide a means for a North Carolinian who has enjoyed a particular wine at a California or other out-of-state winery to have a case shipped home.

Law Enforcement

Many violations of the alcoholic beverage control (ABC) law, such as serving to a minor or to someone who is already intoxicated, are criminal and may be investigated by city police or sheriffs' deputies. Additionally, local ABC boards are required to spend a certain portion of their revenue on law enforcement, either through their own officers or contracting

108. *See* G.S. 18B-1001.
109. *See generally* G.S. Chapter 18B, Articles 11, 12, 13.
110. G.S. 18B-1116(a)(1).
111. *See, e.g.*, 4 N.C.A.C. 2T, § .0713.
112. *See, e.g.*, G.S. 18B-1114.3(b).
113. G.S. 18B-1001.1.

with other agencies,[114] and there is a state agency also charged with alcohol law enforcement. Unlike regular police, those local and state alcohol officers also look for violations of the ABC Commission's rules.[115]

The Law to Be Enforced

Chapter 18B of the General Statutes contains almost all of the state's regulations pertaining to alcohol. Other parts of the General Statutes address alcohol taxation, drunken behavior and driving, minimum ages for employees in establishments that sell alcohol, and a variety of ancillary matters, but all the essential regulatory provisions—who may get permits, hours of sale, approval of brands, etc.—are in Chapter 18B. Those laws are the principal enforcement priority for local and state alcohol enforcement officers. Some violations are criminal and may be prosecuted in court; many others are regulatory and form the bases for actions by the ABC Commission to deny, suspend, or revoke permits or to assess fines against permit holders.

Alcohol enforcement officers also apply the extensive rules of the ABC Commission. Those rules describe in considerable detail how permit holders may conduct their businesses. There are rules governing advertising, storage of bottles, approval of new labels, promotions, gifts from suppliers, recordkeeping, consumer contests, and a host of other issues for the breweries, wineries, distilleries, importers, wholesalers, hotels, restaurants, grocery stores, convenience stores, theaters, ballparks, and numerous other businesses that hold ABC permits. Local and state alcohol officers have authority regular police do not have, namely, the authority to enter licensed premises to inspect for compliance with the many regulatory provisions found in Chapter 18B.[116] That kind of regulatory enforcement takes up much of the officers' time.

State Alcohol Law Enforcement Section

The Alcohol Law Enforcement (ALE) section is within the state Department of Public Safety as is the ABC Commission, but they are separate agancies. While ALE agents' primary mission is enforcement of the ABC laws, they also concentrate on drug, tobacco, and lottery-related offenses.[117] The 100+ agents, operating out of regional offices, have performed background checks for ABC permit applications, conducted educational programs for permit holders, routinely inspected ABC premises, and investigated violations of both the ABC laws and the ABC Commission's rules. Although ALE agents work closely with the ABC Commission and initiate many of their investigations at the request of the commission, they are not employees of nor supervised by the commission.

Local ABC Enforcement

Each local ABC board is required to itself employ one or more law enforcement officers or to contract with a city police department, sheriff's office, or ALE for the enforcement of ABC laws in its jurisdiction.[118] Some counties, including several of the larger ones, still have their own enforcement officers, while most ABC systems contract with the city police or sheriff. A separate statute requires each board to set aside at least 5 percent of its gross receipts for enforcement and says that the local ABC board may contract with ALE for that purpose.[119]

Local ABC officers are authorized to, and often do, assist other law enforcement agencies.[120] Before that can happen, the local ABC board has to adopt a resolution authorizing such assistance and there then has to be a specific written request, acknowledged in the board's minutes. The local board continues to be responsible for any assisting officer's salary, benefits, and workers' compensation while the officer is helping the other agency, unless a different arrangement is agreed upon. Local ABC boards also may work out interlocal agreements with other boards or with cities or counties

114. *See* G.S. 18B-501, -805(c)(2).
115. *See* G.S. 18B-500.
116. G.S. 18B-502.
117. G.S. 18B-500(b).
118. G.S. 18B-501.
119. G.S. 18B-805(c)(2).
120. G.S. 18B-501(e).

for mutual assistance in law enforcement.[121] Because of potential liability for actions taken by its enforcement officers while they are working for another agency, a local ABC board needs to review any proposed assistance or mutual aid agreement carefully and consider whether those liability issues should be explicitly addressed in the agreement.

Local ABC officers have the same inspection authority that ALE agents have.[122] That is, they may enter licensed premises at any time to check for compliance with the ABC statutes and the ABC Commission rules. When a local ABC board contracts with city police or the sheriff for ABC law enforcement, the police officers or deputies assigned to that duty acquire the inspection authority of an ABC officer.[123] As regular law enforcement officers they would have no right to enter and look around a restaurant or bar if the owner did not want them there, but as ABC enforcement officers they are authorized to do so. For that reason, city police departments and sheriffs like to contract with their local ABC boards; the inspection authority gives them easier access to troublesome locations than they would otherwise have. To prevent abuse of the inspection authority, the law allows no more than five city police officers or sheriffs' deputies to be designated as having that power.[124]

To ensure that city police officers and sheriffs' deputies are actually performing the ABC enforcement duties for which the local board has contracted, the respective agencies must submit a monthly report to the local board of the number of (1) ABC arrests in locations with permits and elsewhere and (2) ABC educational programs conducted.[125] The board then shares the report with its appointing authority and with the state ABC Commission.

Seizures and Forfeitures

The ABC statutes include detailed provisions on the disposition of alcohol seized due to violations of the law.[126] Generally, in such cases the alcohol is held until trial and then, depending on the outcome of the trial, is returned to the owner or destroyed or sold. Vehicles, boats, and airplanes used to transport nontaxpaid alcohol (typically bootleg whiskey) and equipment used to unlawfully manufacture alcohol are subject to forfeiture, and again, the statutes set out detailed procedures for seizing and holding such property and then disposing of it following the resolution of the criminal charges.[127]

About the Author

Michael Crowell is a School of Government faculty member with extensive experience in ABC law.

121. G.S. 18B-501(d).
122. G.S. 18B-502.
123. G.S. 18B-501(f).
124. *Id.*
125. G.S. 18B-501(f1).
126. G.S. 18B-503.
127. G.S. 18B-504.

Part 8

Human Services and Other County Functions

Chapter 38

Public Health

Jill D. Moore

In 1988, The Institute of Medicine defined public health as "what we, as a society, do collectively to ensure the conditions in which people can be healthy."[1] The emphasis this definition places on collective action and the conditions that promote good health reflects a distinction between public health and medicine: public health is concerned with the health of populations, not just the health status or condition of particular individuals.

The oldest and most traditional concerns of public health systems—sanitation and disease control—reflect this focus. Practices such as isolation of the ill and proper food handling are described in the Old Testament book of Leviticus, a book that is viewed by public health scholars as the first written public health code. The focus on collective action and population-based activities is also the reason public health has long been a function of government.

In North Carolina, state law has provided the authority and defined the infrastructure for governmental public health since the early eighteenth century, when the territory that is now North Carolina enacted a maritime quarantine law. Today, a full chapter of the North Carolina General Statutes (hereinafter G.S.), Chapter 130A, is devoted to the laws that address the authority and roles of the state and local agencies that constitute North Carolina's public health system and prescribe many of the methods and programs through which public health activities are carried out.

Today, the public health system continues to carry out the traditional functions of ensuring sanitation and controlling infectious diseases, but its focus has expanded to include other duties and embrace other roles. Among other things, the public health system today systematically monitors the health status of the state's residents, serves as a

1. Institute of Medicine, *The Future of Public Health* (Washington, D.C.: National Academy Press, 1988), at 1. The Institute of Medicine expressed its continued support for this definition in its 2002 report, *The Future of the Public's Health in the 21st Century* (Washington, D.C.: National Academy Press, 2002), at 28.

provider of health care services, and engages in a number of community-based activities designed to promote health and prevent chronic disease or injury.

Responsibility for Public Health in North Carolina

The General Assembly has declared that the purpose of the state's public health system is "to ensure that all citizens in the State have equal access to essential public health services," and the system's mission is to promote and contribute to the highest level of health possible for the people of North Carolina by

- identifying and preventing or reducing community health risks;
- detecting, investigating, and preventing the spread of disease;
- promoting healthy lifestyles and a safe and healthful environment;
- promoting the accessibility and availability of quality health care services in the private sector; and
- providing health care services when they are not otherwise available.[2]

In order to satisfy this mission and purpose, the law assigns to local health departments the responsibility for ensuring that ten essential public health services are available and accessible to the residents of each county served by the department.[3]

North Carolina thus has a decentralized public health system, in which the state and county governments share legal authority to act to protect and promote public health as well as the responsibility for assuring that public health services are available to all of the state's residents. However, most public health service delivery occurs at the local level, through various forms of local health departments.[4]

Public Health at the State Level

Statewide public health activities and programs are carried out by officials and agencies within the North Carolina Department of Health and Human Services (DHHS). The officials with primary responsibility for public health are the secretary of DHHS and the state health director. The principal agencies are the Commission for Public Health, the Division of Public Health (within DHHS), and the North Carolina Local Health Department Accreditation Board. Together, these individuals and agencies

- make and enforce statewide rules for public health programs,
- administer statewide public health programs and provide some direct services,
- oversee and provide technical assistance for local public health programs,
- distribute federal and state funds to local public health agencies,
- assure that local public health agencies meet state law requirements for accreditation, and
- coordinate North Carolina's public health activities with other state and federal agencies.

State Officials: Secretary of Health and Human Services, State Health Director

The North Carolina Secretary of Health and Human Services is appointed by the governor and oversees all the department's activities.[5] A state statute gives the general responsibility for administering and enforcing most of the state's

2. N.C. Gen. Stat. (hereinafter G.S.) § 130A-1.1.

3. *Id.* The ten essential public health services are described later in this chapter in the section on local public health services.

4. The term *local health department* encompasses county health departments, district health departments, public health authorities, and the public health components of consolidated human services agencies. *See* G.S. 130A-2(5); 130A-43.

5. At this writing, DHHS has thirty divisions and offices, including early childhood programs; services for the deaf and blind; aging services; health care facilities regulation; public health, social services, and mental health; developmental disabilities; and substance abuse services. The department is also responsible for fourteen state facilities, including psychiatric hospitals, substance abuse treatment centers, and developmental centers for individuals with developmental disabilities.

public health laws to the secretary of DHHS,[6] but in practice many duties are carried out by the state health director, who is appointed by the secretary.[7] In addition, a few state laws give powers and duties directly to the state health director. For example, the communicable disease laws give the director the power to issue temporary orders requiring health care providers to report certain health conditions,[8] the authority to inspect medical records in an outbreak,[9] and the authority to impose isolation or quarantine.[10]

Commission for Public Health

The Commission for Public Health is the primary rulemaking body for public health in North Carolina. A state statute gives the commission the general authority to adopt rules to protect and promote the public health, including rules that are necessary to implement statewide public health programs.[11] In addition, numerous provisions throughout G.S. Chapter 130A direct the commission to adopt rules regarding specific public health activities or programs, ranging from communicable disease control, to the inspection and grading of restaurants, to the decontamination of properties used for the manufacture of methamphetamine.[12] It also has the authority to create metropolitan water districts, sanitary districts, and mosquito control districts. The commission's rules are codified in the North Carolina Administrative Code.[13]

The commission has thirteen members, four of whom are elected by the North Carolina Medical Society. The remaining nine are appointed by the governor and must include a pharmacist, a soil scientist or engineer experienced in sanitary engineering, a veterinarian, an optometrist, a dentist, and a registered nurse. The members serve four-year, staggered terms.

Division of Public Health

The Division of Public Health (DPH) is the agency with primary responsibility for carrying out the public health system's statutory mission: "to promote and contribute to the highest level of health possible for the people of North Carolina."[14] DPH is divided into sections and offices that are responsible for a wide variety of public health services and programs, including chronic disease and injury prevention, environmental health, minority health and health disparities, and

---

6. G.S. 130A-4(a). The secretary of Environment and Natural Resources has responsibility for administering public health laws related to solid waste management and the N.C. Drinking Water Act. G.S. 130A-4(c).

7. G.S. 130A-3.

8. G.S. 130A-141.1.

9. G.S. 130A-144(b).

10. G.S. 130A-145. Local health directors have some of the same powers and duties as the state health director. For example, local health directors may exercise many of the state health director's communicable disease powers, including the authority to order isolation or quarantine. G.S. 130A-145(a). But some powers are given to the state health director alone. For example, the public health bioterrorism laws authorize the state health director to close property or to order examinations of individuals during a suspected bioterrorism event. G.S. 130A-475(a). Local health directors do not share that authority.

11. G.S. 130A-29.

12. *See, e.g.,* G.S. 130A-144 (communicable disease control); 130A-248 (sanitation of food and lodging establishments); 130A-284 (decontamination standards for methamphetamine sites). These are examples only and not a complete list of statutes authorizing the commission to adopt rules. The N.C. Environmental Management Commission also has some rulemaking authority in the area of public health. It makes statewide rules regarding water sources, including rules governing local health departments' inspection and permitting of private drinking water wells. G.S. 87-97; *see also* G.S. 143B-282 (creating the Environmental Management Commission and setting forth its rulemaking authority).

13. The rules for environmental health programs are in Title 15A, Chapter 18, of the North Carolina Administrative Code (hereinafter N.C.A.C.). The rules for all other public health programs are in Title 10A, Chapters 39–48.

14. G.S. 130A-1.1. There are other divisions within DHHS that are relevant to the provision of public health services in North Carolina. These include the Office of Rural Health and Community Care, which operates low-cost rural health centers and places health care providers in underserved communities; the Division of Medical Assistance, which administers the Medicaid program; the Division of Health Service Regulation, which is responsible for licensure and certification of health care facilities; and the Division of Mental Health, Developmental Disabilities, and Substance Abuse Services. The mental health, developmental disabilities, and substance abuse services system is described in Chapter 40.

women's and children's health.[15] It also operates several statewide public health programs, including the medical examiner program that conducts postmortem investigations, the state laboratory for public health, the state vital records program, and the state center for health statistics.

The Division of Public Health has general responsibility for oversight of local health department programs. It monitors local services, conducts periodic reviews of local health departments, and assists local health departments by providing training and technical assistance and conducting quality assurance activities. It also ensures local compliance with state public health program standards through its process for distributing state and federal funds to local agencies. DHHS receives federal and state money for public health programs and determines local public health agencies' allocations. To receive certain funds, the local health department must enter into a contract with DHHS, called the *consolidated agreement*.[16] The consolidated agreement requires local public health agencies to comply with all public health laws and rules and specifies how funds must be managed. This contract has a significant effect on how local public health agencies operate, because noncompliance with its terms can result in loss of state and federal funds. It is renewed annually.

Both the state and local public health officials have the authority to enforce public health laws and rules, but most of the enforcement is carried out by the directors and employees of local health departments. State agencies monitor these local enforcement activities and have the authority to intervene if they determine that it is necessary.

DPH maintains relationships and coordinates its work with federal public health agencies, including the Centers for Disease Control and Prevention (CDC). It also works with other state agencies that have responsibilities relating to public health. The North Carolina Department of Agriculture operates the Grade A milk sanitation program and the sleep products sanitation program,[17] and it shares responsibility with public health for the safety of some foods that are served to the public for pay. It also monitors certain diseases in livestock animals, including some diseases that could spread to humans. The state Department of Environment and Natural Resources' responsibilities include the sanitation of public water supplies, shellfish sanitation, and recreational water quality. The Department of Labor is responsible for occupational health and safety. The North Carolina Department of Public Safety leads the state's emergency management operations, including response to natural disasters and other events that affect the public health.

North Carolina Local Health Department Accreditation Board

Every agency functioning as a local health department in North Carolina must obtain and maintain accreditation from the North Carolina Local Health Department Accreditation Board.[18] The board is responsible for developing a schedule by which local health departments must apply for accreditation, reviewing each department's application for accreditation, and assigning an accreditation status as follows:

- *Accredited* means that the department has satisfied the standards for accreditation. Accreditation expires after four years and the department must apply for re-accreditation.

---

15. At present, the Division of Public Health is composed of eleven sections and offices. *See* http://publichealth.nc.gov/aboutus.htm.

16. The contract is signed by the local health director, the finance director, and, in county health departments, the chair of the board of county commissioners. The chair's signature is required by DHHS; although the health director has authority to enter contracts on behalf of the department, that contracting authority may not be construed to abrogate the authority of the county commissioners (G.S. 130A-41(13)). In district health departments and public health authorities, only the health director and finance director sign the contract.

17. The Grade A milk sanitation program and the sleep products program were transferred from the N.C. Department of Environment and Natural Resources (DENR) to the Department of Agriculture in 2011. S.L. 2011-145. This legislation eliminated the Division of Environmental Health within DENR. Many of the Division of Environmental Health's programs were transferred to the Division of Public Health, but others were transferred to other agencies or abolished.

18. G.S. 130A-34.1. The statutory definition of "local health department" includes a county health department, a district health department, or a public health authority. G.S. 130A-2(5). Although the definition does not mention consolidated human services agencies that include public health, a separate law states that such agencies "shall have the responsibility to carry out the duties of a local health department." G.S. 130A-43(a). Obtaining and maintaining accreditation is one such duty.

- *Conditionally accredited* means that the department has failed to meet the standards for accreditation but has been granted short-term accreditation status that is subject to conditions set by the board. This status is good for two years. By the end of that time, the department must have satisfied the board's conditions and met the criteria for accreditation, or it will become unaccredited.
- *Unaccredited* means that the department has continued to fail to meet the standards after a period of conditional accreditation.

The Commission for Public Health adopts rules and standards for the accreditation process that provide for local health department self-assessments, site visits by the accreditation board, and informal review of board decisions.[19] Effective July 1, 2014, local public health agencies must be accredited by the North Carolina board in order to continue to receive state and federal funding.[20]

When the local health department accreditation requirement was initially imposed, state appropriations provided the funds for the accreditation board to carry out its activities. Those funds were reduced in 2010 and 2011 and completely eliminated in 2012.[21] At present, the program continues to operate through a contract with the North Carolina Association of Local Health Directors. Local health departments voluntarily contribute to the association to pay the cost of the contract.

The accreditation board is composed of seventeen members appointed by the secretary of Health and Human Services. The membership includes representatives of boards of county commissioners, local boards of health, local health directors, and staff members of the state divisions of public and environmental health.

Public Health at the Regional Level

North Carolina law does not contain a formal regional structure for public health services. However, in practice, there are several regional entities that carry out either state or local public health responsibilities.

The state public health agencies hire employees, usually called consultants, who are assigned to serve local health departments in designated regions. Consultants work in different disciplines or service areas. For example, there are administrative consultants, nurse consultants working in areas such as child health or school health, and regional environmental health specialists.

The state is divided into four regions for purposes of public health preparedness and response.[22] Each region has a field office and staff, including planning consultants, training facilitators, industrial hygienists, pharmacists, and program support specialists. Regional staff members are employed by the state and work with local public health officials. Regional public health preparedness and response staff monitor public health conditions in the regions they serve. They are also responsible for a number of public health preparedness activities, including training the public health workforce and developing public health emergency response plans in collaboration with local and regional entities that work with emergency response or disaster management. Finally, many local health departments participate voluntarily in regional partnerships called *public health incubator collaboratives*—voluntary collaborations designed to "hatch"

---

19. The rules are codified in Chapter 48 of Title 10A of the North Carolina Administrative Code.

20. G.S. 130A-34.4.

21. The legislative conference committee report on the 2012 state budget included the reduction and noted that there is a national program that accredits local health departments. North Carolina General Assembly, The Joint Conference Committee Report on the Continuation, Expansion, and Capital Budgets (corrected version, Aug. 31, 2012), at G-9, www.ncleg.net/sessions/2011/budget/2012/Revised_Joint_Conference_Committee_Report_2012_08_31.pdf. The national Public Health Accreditation Board (PHAB) is a voluntary program that local health departments may participate in if they choose; however, state law requires North Carolina local health departments to be accredited through the North Carolina–specific program. G.S. 130A-34.1 (creating the North Carolina program and requiring local health departments to obtain and maintain accreditation through it); 130A-34.4 (requiring health departments to obtain and maintain state accreditation as a condition of receiving state and federal funds, effective July 1, 2014).

22. The public health preparedness and response (PHP&R) teams replaced the seven public health regional surveillance teams (PHRSTs) that were described in the 2007 version of this chapter. A map showing the counties served by each PHP&R team is available at http://epi.publichealth.nc.gov/phpr/regions.html.

new ideas and practices to improve public health. Participation in incubator collaboratives is voluntary, and the incubators themselves do not have specific duties or authorities under North Carolina's public health laws.[23]

Public Health at the Local Level

Local Health Departments

Each county in North Carolina is required by law to provide public health services.[24] A county may satisfy this duty by operating a county health department, participating in a multi-county district health department, forming or joining a public health authority, establishing a consolidated human services agency that includes public health, or contracting with the state to provide public health services. Each type of agency is captured in the generic term *local health department*.[25] Each type of agency has a governing board, which may be called a *board of health, a public health authority board*, or a *consolidated human services board*. For purposes of this chapter, the term *board of health* is used to refer to all of those.[26] A board of health may be an independent board appointed by the county commissioners, or the commissioners may elect to serve as the board of health themselves by adopting a resolution abolishing the board and conferring its powers and duties upon the board of commissioners.[27]

In June 2012, significant new legislation began to change the landscape for local public health agencies in North Carolina. Before that date, the law that established the option of providing public health services through a consolidated human services agency was limited to counties with populations of 425,000 or more. The option for county commissioners to assume the powers and duties of a local board of health was subject to the same population threshold. By 2012, only three North Carolina counties—Guilford, Mecklenburg, and Wake—had populations that large, and only two had exercised the options.[28] The new legislation removed the population threshold and extended the option of creating a consolidated human services agency to any county with a county–manager form of government. It also extended the option of abolishing the local board of health and transferring its powers and duties to the board of commissioners to all counties.[29] As of May 30, 2014, eighteen North Carolina counties had used their new authority under the law to change their local health department, their local board of health, or both. Several other counties were in the process of considering or planning for changes. Figures 38.1 and 38.2 demonstrate the changes that occurred during the law's first two years. An up-to-date map of local health departments in North Carolina is maintained on the School of Government's website.[30]

---

23. For more information about North Carolina's public health incubator collaboratives, see http://nciph.sph.unc.edu/incubator/.

24. G.S. 130A-34.

25. G.S. 130A-2(5) (defining "local health department" as "a district health department or a public health authority or a county health department"); 130A-43 (giving consolidated human services agencies the responsibility to carry out the duties of a local health department); 153A-77(b) (authorizing boards of county commissioners to create consolidated human services agencies that include public health). Cabarrus County provides public health services pursuant to an uncodified state law that authorizes a hospital authority to provide local public health services. S.L. 1997-502, sec. 12. The Cabarrus Health Alliance exercises the legal powers and duties of a local health department.

26. G.S. 130A-2(4) (defining "local board of health" as "a district board of health or a public health authority board or a county board of health"); 153A-77(d) (providing that a consolidated human services board acquires the powers and duties of a local board of health).

27. G.S. 153A-77(a) authorizes commissioners to directly assume the powers and duties of a board of health or a consolidated human services board. It requires the board of commissioners to give thirty days' notice of a public hearing and hold the public hearing before adopting a resolution to abolish the appointed board.

28. Wake County has provided public health services through a consolidated human services agency governed by a consolidated human services board since the mid-1990s. Mecklenburg County was the first in the state to abolish its local board of health and transfer the board's powers and duties to the county commissioners. In 2008, Mecklenburg created a consolidated human services agency but did not appoint a consolidated board, choosing instead to maintain direct governance by the commissioners. Once it reached the population threshold imposed under prior law, Guilford County initially studied its options and elected to continue to operate a county health department governed by an appointed board of health. However, after the 2012 legislation, it revisited the issue and created a consolidated human services agency governed directly by the county commissioners in 2014.

29. S.L. 2012-126.

30. The map is available at www.sog.unc.edu/node/1035, under the heading "Local Public Health Agencies."

Figure 38.1 Local Public Health Agencies and Boards in North Carolina, FY2011–2012

County health department with county board of health

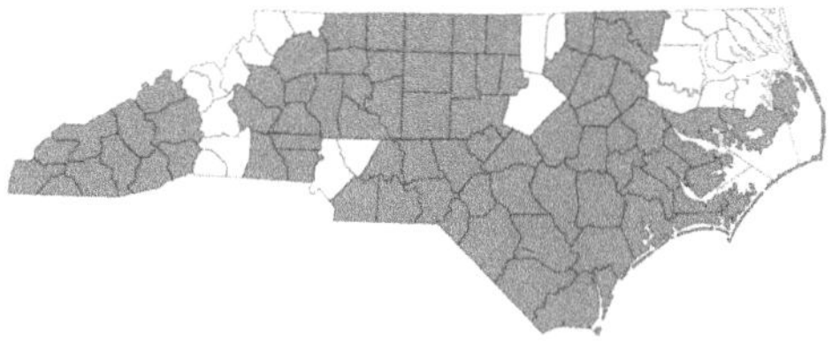

District health department with district board of health (6 districts)

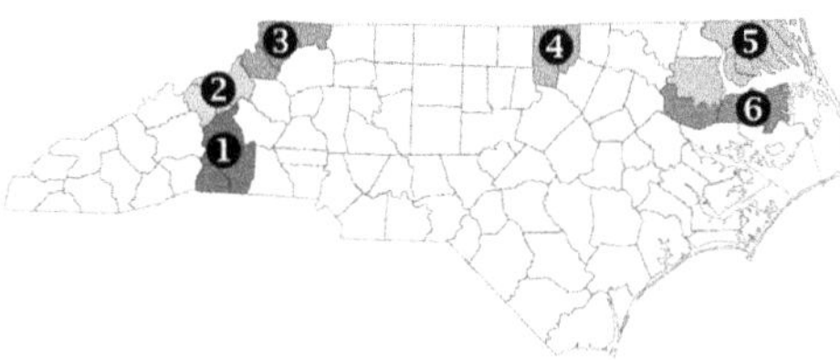

Consolidated human services agency governed by board of county commissioners

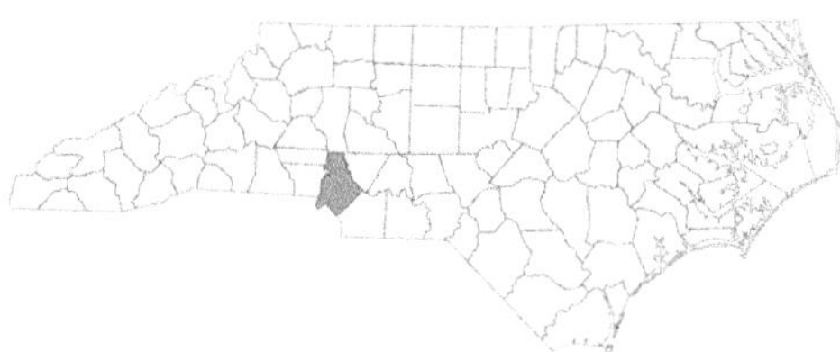

Consolidated human services agency with consolidated human services board

Public health authority with public health authority board

Public hospital authority with hospital board authorized to act as board of health

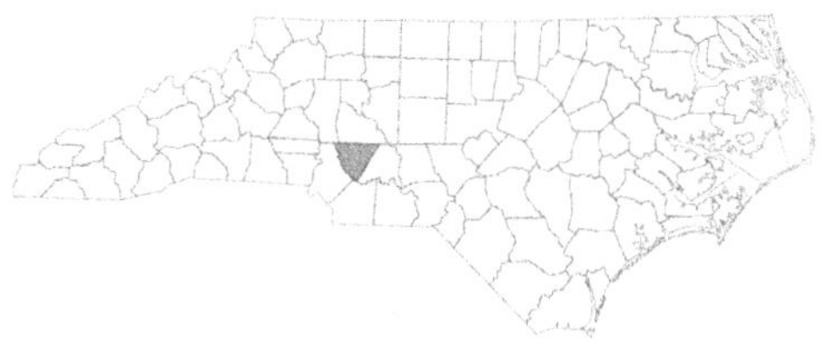

Figure 38.2 Local Public Health Agencies and Boards in North Carolina, May 30, 2014

County health department

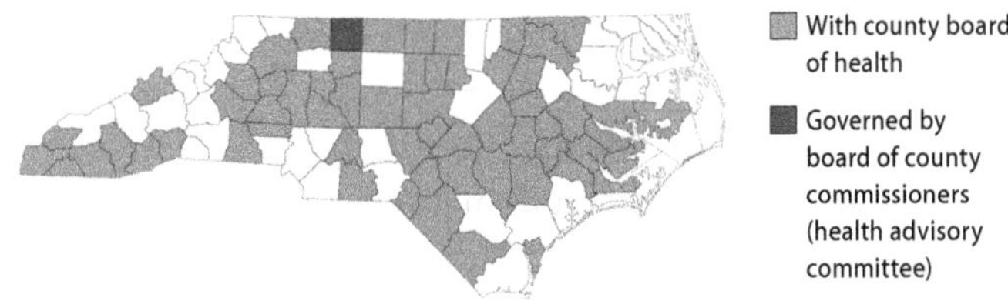

District health department with district board of health (6 districts)

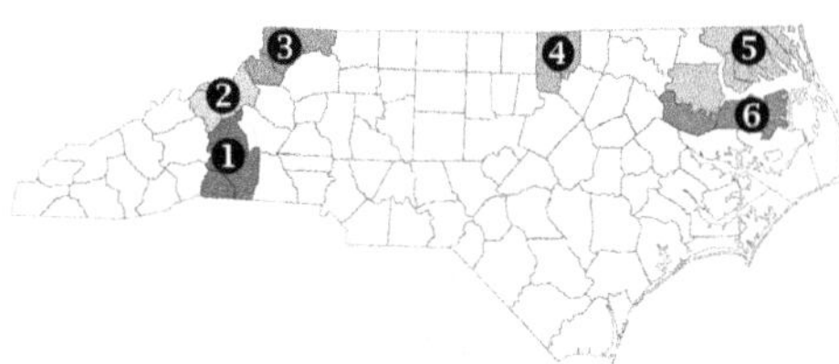

Consolidated human services agency governed by board of county commissioners (health advisory committee)

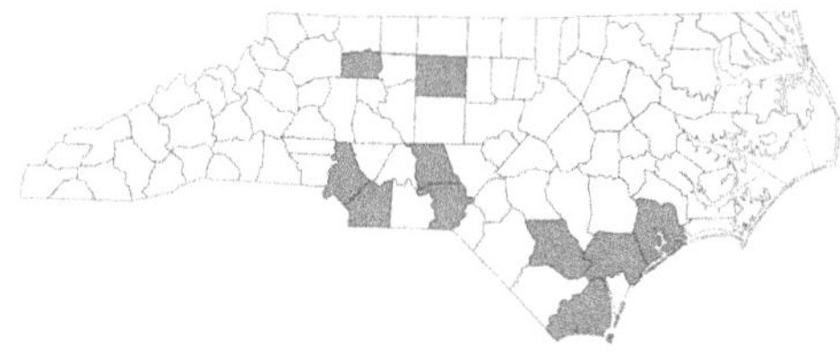

Consolidated human services agency with consolidated human services board

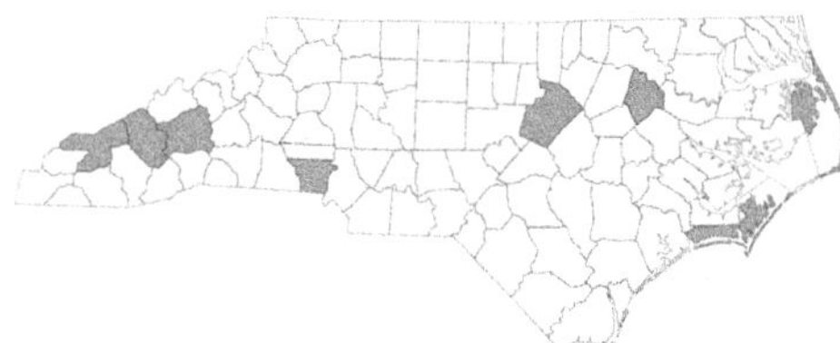

Public health authority with public health authority board

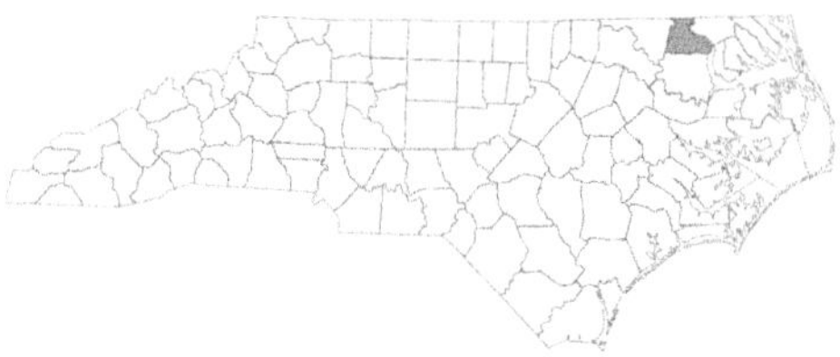

Public hospital authority with hospital board authorized to act as board of health

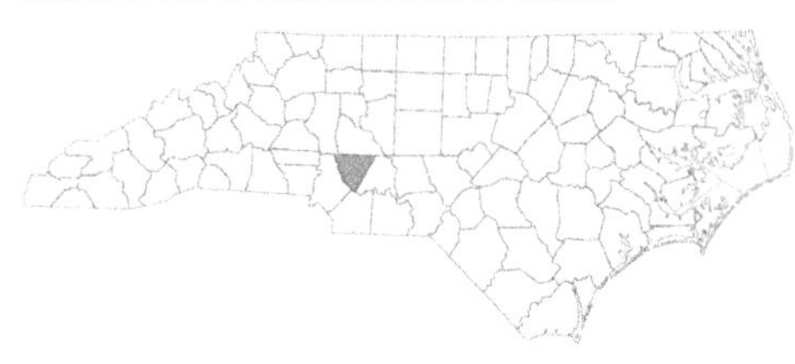

County Health Departments

A county health department is a single-county agency that provides local public health services. It is created by the county commissioners and typically is governed by a board of health appointed by the commissioners.[31] The board of health appoints a local health director after consultation with the county commissioners.[32] The county health director must meet minimum education and experience requirements and has a number of legal powers and duties, which are described in greater detail in the section on local health directors later in this chapter.

District Health Departments

A district health department (sometimes called a regional health department) is a multi-county agency that provides local public health services for all the counties in the district. A district health department may be formed upon agreement of the boards of county commissioners and the boards of health of two or more counties.[33] A county may join an existing district health department upon a similar agreement entered by each affected county. A district health department may have health department offices in each component county, but it is governed by one board of health and administered by one health director.

The governing board is called a *district board of health*. Each county in the district appoints one county commissioner to serve on the board, and those commissioners appoint the remaining members.[34] If a county joins or withdraws from an existing district health department, the district board of health is dissolved and a new board is appointed. After consultation with the board of commissioners of each county in the district, the board of health appoints a district health director.[35] The district health director must meet the same minimum education and experience requirements as a county health director and has the same legal powers and duties.

Any county may withdraw from a district health department when a majority of its county commissioners determines that the district is not operating in the best interests of health in that county. The district may be dissolved upon a similar decision by the boards of commissioners of all the counties in the district. Withdrawal or dissolution may take place only after written notice is given to DHHS and only at the end of the fiscal year. A certified public accountant or an auditor certified by the Local Government Commission distributes surplus funds to the counties according to the percentage each county contributed. When an entire district dissolves or when a county withdraws, any rules adopted by the district board of health remain in effect in the county or counties involved until amended or repealed by the new board or boards governing the affected counties.[36]

Public Health Authorities

A county may meet its obligation to provide public health services by creating a public health authority. A public health authority may be formed by a single county or by two or more counties jointly. To form a single-county public health authority, the board of commissioners and the county board of health must jointly adopt a resolution finding that it is in the interest of the public health and welfare in the county to create a public health authority and provide public health services through it. In the case of a multi-county authority, the resolution must be adopted jointly by the board of commissioners and board of health governing each affected county. A county may join an existing public health authority upon joint resolution of the board of commissioners and board of health of each county involved. Before adopting any such resolution, the county commissioners must give notice to the public and hold a public hearing.[37]

After the resolution has been adopted, a public health authority board is appointed. The board of a single-county public health authority is appointed by the county commissioners of the county. For a multi-county public health authority, the chair of the board of commissioners of each participating county appoints one county commissioner (or designee) to the board, and those members appoint the remaining members.[38] The board replaces the prior local

31. G.S. 130A-35.
32. G.S. 130A-40.
33. G.S. 130A-36.
34. G.S. 130A-37.
35. G.S. 130A-40.
36. G.S. 130A-38.
37. G.S. 130A-45.02.
38. G.S. 130A-45.1.

board of health and becomes the rulemaking, policy-making, and adjudicatory body for the authority. The public health authority board appoints a public health authority director after consultation with the appropriate county commissioners.[39] The public health authority director must meet the same minimum education and experience requirements as a county health director and has similar legal powers and duties.

Once created, a public health authority operates more independently of the board (or boards) of county commissioners than a traditional county health department. For example, a public health authority is not required to submit its budget to the county commissioners. While it may request funding from county commissioners, the authority acts on its own to develop its budget in accordance with state financial management laws. It also may acquire or sell real property without going through the county commissioners.[40]

A board of county commissioners may dissolve a public health authority (or withdraw from a multi-county authority) upon a finding that the authority is not operating in the best health interests of the county. Dissolution may occur only after written notification to DHHS and only at the end of a fiscal year. If the authority was a multi-county authority, a certified public accountant or an auditor certified by the Local Government Commission distributes surplus funds to the counties according to the percentage each county contributed. All rules adopted by the authority board continue in effect until amended or repealed by the new authority board or local board of health.[41]

Consolidated Human Services Agencies

A board of commissioners in a county with a county manager appointed under G.S. 153A-81 may elect to establish a consolidated human services agency (CHSA). G.S. 153A-77(b) authorizes such counties to create a CHSA to "carry out the functions of any combination of commissions, boards, or agencies appointed by the board of county commissioners or acting under and pursuant to the authority of the board of county commissioners." It specifies that a CHSA may include public health, but it does not require public health to be included.[42]

A consolidated human services agency typically is governed by a consolidated human services board. If the CHSA includes public health, the consolidated human services board acquires the powers and duties of a local board of health, with one exception: the board is not authorized to appoint the agency's director. Instead, the director is appointed by the county manager with the advice and consent of the board. The consolidated board also has its own powers and duties set forth in the CHSA statute (G.S. 153A-77(d)).

A consolidated human services agency is administered by a consolidated human services director. If the CHSA includes public health, the director must appoint a person who meets the education and experience requirements for a local health director set out in G.S. 130A-40.[43] The consolidated human services director acquires most of the legal powers and duties of a local health director, with two provisos: (1) the director may serve as the CHSA's executive officer only to the extent and in the manner authorized by the county manager, and (2) the director may appoint CHSA staff

---

39. G.S. 130A-45.5.

40. Other ways in which a public health authority differs from conventional county or district health departments are explored in more detail at www.sog.unc.edu/node/2358.

41. G.S. 130A-45.2.

42. The state law governing CHSAs was changed significantly by legislation enacted in June 2012. S.L. 2012-126 (amending G.S. 153A-77). Under prior law, the only counties that could create CHSAs were those with populations exceeding 425,000. Further, CHSAs were required to include public health, social services, and mental health, developmental disabilities, and substance abuse services. The 2012 legislation removed the population threshold and amended the language describing a CHSA, with the result that counties have a great deal of flexibility in determining which services will be provided. On March 1, 2013, there were nine CHSAs in North Carolina, and all of them provided public health services, but it is possible that at a later date the state may have counties with CHSAs that do not provide public health services.

There are some limitations on what may be included in a CHSA. Among other things, G.S. 153A-76 prohibits county commissioners from including a public health authority in a CHSA. However, a separate law permits commissioners to dissolve or withdraw from a public health authority at the end of a fiscal year. A county that is part of a public health authority could therefore create a CHSA including public health, but the commissioners would have to take the additional step of dissolving or withdrawing from the authority first. Similarly, a county that is presently part of a multi-county district health department could not include public health in a CHSA without first withdrawing from the district at the end of a fiscal year.

43. G.S. 153A-77(e)(9). The county manager must approve the appointment. If the CHSA director meets the statutory requirements for a local health director, there is no need for a separate individual to be appointed.

only with the approval of the county manager.[44] The director may exercise those powers and duties directly or delegate them to the appointee with local health director qualifications or other appropriate persons.[45]

Governance: Local Boards of Health

Each local public health agency in North Carolina has a governing board that is responsible for public health within its jurisdiction. What the board is called varies by agency: a county health department has a county board of health, a district health department has a district board of health, a public health authority has a public health authority board, and a consolidated human services agency has a consolidated human services board. The generic term *local board of health* embraces all of these types of boards when they are carrying out public health duties.[46] A board of health may be an independent board appointed by the county commissioners, or the commissioners may elect to serve as the board of health themselves by adopting a resolution abolishing the board and conferring its powers and duties upon the board of commissioners.[47]

The composition of the different types of boards varies, as illustrated in Table 38.1. In general, board members are county commissioners, professionals with expertise in health care or public health (including physicians, pharmacists, veterinarians, and professional engineers, among others), and the general public. The powers and duties of each type of board also vary somewhat, but each is charged with protecting and promoting the public health and with serving as the policy-making, rulemaking, and adjudicatory body for public health in the county or counties in its jurisdiction. Each board has limited authority to set fees for public health services. Each board also influences the day-to-day administration of the local health department, public health authority, or consolidated human services agency.

Board Membership Qualifications and Terms

The statutes authorizing county boards of health, district boards of health, and consolidated human services boards all require that board members be residents of the county or district. For county and district boards, if there is no resident available to serve in one of the licensed professional positions, a member of the general public must be appointed instead.[48] There is no similar provision for consolidated human services boards, suggesting that a licensed professional position on such a board would simply remain vacant if there were no resident available to serve. Members of public health authority boards are not required to be residents of the county or multi-county area served by the authority.

County and district board of health members are appointed to three-year terms and may serve a maximum of three consecutive three-year terms. There are a couple of exceptions to this general rule. First, if the member is the only county or district resident who is a member of one of the licensed professions that must be represented on the board, the member may serve more than three consecutive three-year terms.[49] Second, if a member of a district board of health is serving in his or her capacity as a county commissioner, the North Carolina Attorney General has advised that the member may serve for as long as he or she remains a commissioner, even if that time exceeds three consecutive three-year terms.[50] Consolidated human services board members are appointed to four-year terms and may serve a maximum of two consecutive four-year terms. There is no exception for a situation in which a member is the only county resident who is a member of a licensed profession that must be represented on the board.[51] The county com-

44. G.S. 130A-43(c).

45. G.S. 130A-6 authorizes an official with authority granted by Chapter 130A to delegate that authority to another person.

46. This is consistent with statutory definitions and usage. G.S. 130A-2(4) defines "local board of health" to mean "a district board of health or a public health authority or a county board of health." G.S. 153A-77(d) gives consolidated human services boards the powers and duties of local boards of health, except when the statutes specifically provide otherwise.

47. G.S. 153A-77(a) authorizes commissioners to directly assume the powers and duties of a county board of health or a consolidated human services board. It requires the board of commissioners to give thirty days' notice of a public hearing and hold the public hearing before adopting a resolution to abolish the appointed board.

48. There is an exception for the member of a *county* board of health who serves in the licensed optometrist spot. G.S. 130A-35(b). If a licensed optometrist who is a county resident is not available for appointment, the county commissioners may fill the position with either (1) a licensed optometrist who resides in another county, or (2) a member of the general public who is a county resident. This provision does not apply to a *district* board of health.

49. G.S. 130A-35(c) (county board of health); 130A-37(c) (district board of health).

50. Attorney General Advisory Opinion to Hal G. Harrison, Mitchell County Attorney, 1998 WL 856356 (Oct. 8, 1998).

51. G.S. 153A-77(c).

Table 38.1 Board Membership Requirements by Type of Local Public Health Agency Board*

	County Board of Health	District Board of Health	Single-County Public Health Authority Board	Multi-County Public Health Authority Board	Consolidated Human Services Board
Number of members	11	15 to 18	7 to 9	7 to 11	Up to 25
Members of the public or consumers	3	✔	✔	✔	4 or more [c]
County commissioner	✔	✔ [a]	✔	✔ [b]	✔
Physician	✔	✔	✔	✔	✔ [d]
Psychiatrist					✔
Psychologist					✔
Social worker					✔
Hospital administrator			✔	✔	
Dentist	✔	✔	✔	✔	✔
Optometrist	✔	✔	✔	✔	✔
Veterinarian	✔	✔	✔	✔	✔
Registered nurse	✔	✔	✔	✔	✔
Pharmacist	✔	✔	✔	✔	✔
Engineer	✔	✔	✔	✔	✔
Accountant			✔	✔	

Shaded area: Two professionals representing the following fields must serve on the board: optometry, veterinary science, nursing, pharmacy, engineering, or accounting. In other words, not *all* of these professions will necessarily be represented.

* These requirements do not apply if the county commissioners serve as the board for a county health department or a consolidated human services agency including public health.

a. One commissioner from each county involved.
b. One commissioner from each county involved. The commissioners may designate someone other than a commissioner to serve in this position.
c. At least four members must be consumers of human services.
d. Two licensed physicians must serve on the board, one of whom must be a psychiatrist.

missioner member of the board may serve only as long as he or she remains a county commissioner. Public health authority board members are appointed to three-year terms, and there is no limit on the number of terms they may serve.[52] If the county commissioners are serving as the board of health, a person's service as a board of health member ends when his or her service as a county commissioner ends.

An appointed board of health member may be removed from office if there is cause for removal under state law. The laws for county and district boards of health, consolidated human services boards, and public health authority boards all state that a member may be removed for any of the following reasons:[53]

- Commission of a felony or other crime involving moral turpitude
- Violation of a state law governing conflict of interest

52. G.S. 130A-45.1.

53. G.S. 130A-35(g) (county board of health); 130A-37(h) (district board of health); 130A-45.1(j) (public health authority board); 153A-77(c) (consolidated human services board). If the board of commissioners is serving as the board of health, these sections do not apply.

- Violation of a written policy adopted by the county commissioners (or all of the applicable boards of commissioners, if it is a multi-county board)
- Habitual failure to attend meetings
- Conduct that tends to bring the office into disrepute
- Failure to maintain qualifications for appointment (for example, professional licensure, residency in the county, and so forth)

Rulemaking

A local board of health has the duty to protect and promote the public health and the authority to adopt rules necessary to those purposes.[54] A board of health rule is valid throughout the county or counties in the board's jurisdiction, including within any municipalities served by the board.[55]

There are several limitations to the board's rulemaking authority that are set out in statutes:

- A board may not adopt rules concerning the issuing of grades and permits to food and lodging facilities or the operation of those facilities (G.S. 130A-39(b)).
- A board may issue its own regulations regarding on-site wastewater management only with the approval of DHHS, which must find that the proposed rules are at least as stringent as state rules and are necessary and sufficient to safeguard the public health (G.S. 130A-39(b); 130A-335(c)).[56]
- A board of health rule regulating smoking in public places must abide by statutory restrictions on this authority and must be approved by the applicable board(s) of county commissioners (G.S. 130A-498).

Additional limitations on the rulemaking authority have been imposed by state courts. The North Carolina Supreme Court has held that a local board of health rule may be preempted by state law if the state has already provided a complete and integrated regulatory scheme in the area addressed by the local rule. However, state law expressly permits a board to adopt a more stringent local rule even in the presence of statewide rules on the same issue if a more stringent rule is required to protect the public health.[57] The supreme court has interpreted this to mean that a board adopting a more stringent rule must provide a rationale for local standards that exceed the statewide standards. To do this, the board likely needs to be able to demonstrate that conditions in the board's jurisdiction are different from the rest of the state in a way that warrants higher standards.[58]

In addition, the North Carolina Court of Appeals has enunciated a five-part test that a local board of health rule must satisfy to be valid. The rule must

1. be related to the promotion or protection of health,
2. be reasonable in light of the health risk addressed,
3. not violate any law or constitutional provision,

---

54. G.S. 130A-39.

55. G.S. 130A-39(c) ("The rules of a local board of health shall apply to all municipalities within the local board's jurisdiction.")

56. If a local board of health adopts rules governing wastewater collection, treatment, and disposal, then it must also adopt rules for imposing administrative penalties when the local wastewater rules are violated (G.S. 130A-22(h)).

57. G.S. 130A-39(b).

58. *See* Craig v. Cnty. of Chatham, 356 N.C. 40 (2002). The *Craig* court considered two local actions regulating swine farms: an ordinance adopted by the Chatham County Board of Commissioners and a rule adopted by the Chatham County Board of Health. The court held that both the ordinance and the rule were preempted by state statutes that amounted to a complete and integrated regulatory scheme for swine farms. *Id.* at 50. However, the court acknowledged that local boards of health may regulate an area already subject to a comprehensive statewide regulatory scheme in some circumstances. G.S. 130A-39 specifically authorizes local boards of health to adopt more stringent rules in areas that are already subject to statewide regulation by the Commission for Health Services or the Environmental Management Commission, but only when a more stringent local rule is necessary to protect the public health. The court concluded that this statute does not authorize a local board of health to "superimpose additional regulations without specific reasons clearly applicable to a local health need." *Id.* at 51–52. The court noted that the board of health had not provided "any rationale or basis for making the restrictions in Chatham County more rigorous than those applicable to and followed by the rest of the state, and it invalidated the rule on that basis. *Id.* at 52.

4. not be discriminatory, and
5. not make distinctions based upon policy concerns traditionally reserved for legislative bodies.[59]

Before adopting, amending, or repealing any local rule, the board of health must give the public notice of its intent and offer the public an opportunity to inspect its proposed action. Ten days before the proposed action is to occur, notice of the proposal must be published in a local newspaper with general circulation. The notice must contain a statement of the substance of the proposed rule or a description of the subjects and issues involved, the proposed effective date, and a statement that copies of the proposed rule are available at the local health department. At the same time, the board must make the text of the proposed rule, amendment, or rule to be repealed available for inspection by placing it in the office of each county clerk within the board's jurisdiction.

Imposing Fees

A local board of health may impose a fee for many services rendered by the health department.[60] County and district boards of health and consolidated human services boards must base their fees on a plan proposed by the local health director, and any fees adopted by the board must be approved by the county commissioners (in the case of a district health department, all applicable boards of county commissioners). Public health authority boards may establish fee schedules and are not required to obtain commissioner approval.

There are some limitations to a board's fee-setting authority. First, a board may not charge fees for services rendered by a health department employee acting as an agent of the state. This covers most environmental health programs, but there are exceptions: cost-related fees may be charged for services provided under the on-site wastewater treatment program, the public swimming pools program, the tattooing regulation program, and the local program for inspecting and permitting drinking water wells.[61]

Second, while local health departments may charge fees for some of their clinical services, the local board of health has limited discretion in determining the amount of the fee. Fees may reflect Medicaid reimbursement rates established by the state Division of Medical Assistance or fees set by a state or federal program that provides funds for a particular service. Also, local health departments are specifically prohibited by state law from charging health department clients for the following services:[62]

- Testing and counseling for sickle cell syndrome[63]
- Examination for and treatment of tuberculosis[64]
- Examination for and treatment of certain sexually transmitted diseases[65]
- Testing and counseling for HIV[66]

Additionally, immunizations that are required by law and supplied by the state must be provided at no cost to uninsured or underinsured patients with family incomes below 200 percent of the federal poverty level.[67]

Sometimes federal laws affect a local health department's ability to set fees or charge clients for services. For example, Title VI of the federal Civil Rights Act of 1964 prohibits recipients of federal financial assistance from charging their

59. City of Roanoke Rapids v. Peedin, 124 N.C. App. 578 (1996).
60. G.S. 130A-39(g); 130A-45.3(a)(5); 153A-77(d)(1).
61. G.S. 130A-39(g).
62. Sometimes a third-party payer such as Medicaid provides reimbursement for one of the listed services. A local health department may bill a third-party payer for the services, but it may not bill the client.
63. G.S. 130A-130.
64. G.S. 130A-144(e).
65. *Id.*
66. 10A N.C.A.C. 41A .0202(9).
67. G.S. 130A-153(a).

limited-English proficient clients for interpretation services.[68] Similarly, the federal HIPAA medical privacy rule limits the fees that may be charged for copies of medical records.[69]

Adjudicating Disputes

In some circumstances, a local board of health acts as an adjudicatory body.[70] When a person is aggrieved by the local health department's interpretation or enforcement of a local board of health rule, or the local imposition of administrative penalties, the person may appeal the department's decision to the board of health. The board hears the case and issues a written decision either upholding or overturning the department's decision. The rules of evidence that are enforced in courtrooms do not apply at the board hearing, but the board's decision must be supported by adequate evidence. The board must put its decision in writing and state the factual findings upon which it is based. If the person is not satisfied with the board of health's decision, he or she may appeal to district court. The procedures and time frames for actions are set out in G.S. 130A-24(b) through (d).

When a person is aggrieved by the local health department's enforcement of state rules, such as the food and lodging rules, the local board of health is not authorized to hear the appeal. Those cases go to the state Office of Administrative Hearings.[71]

Local Health Department Administration

The administrative functions within local health departments include managing operations and programs; providing in-service training for staff; preparing the budget; explaining the department's activities to the board of health, local elected officials, and the public; informing the public of health laws and rules as well as enforcing them; suggesting new rules and services; and purchasing equipment and supplies. These duties generally are the local health director's responsibility, but the management of particular functions may differ from county to county.

Local Health Directors

The local health director is essentially the chief executive officer of the local public health agency—he or she administers the department and exercises specific powers and duties that are prescribed by law. The term *local health director* includes the director of a county health department, a district health department, or a public health authority, as well as the director of a consolidated human services agency or his or her designee.[72] A director of a county or district health department or a public health authority must meet minimum education and experience requirements.[73] In general, the director must have education and experience in medicine, public health, or public administration related to health.[74] A consolidated human services director is not required by statute to meet particular education or experience requirements. However, a consolidated human services director who does not satisfy the statutory qualifications

---

68. *See* Voluntary Compliance Agreement between the Office for Civil Rights, U.S. Department of Health and Human Services, and N.C. Department of Health and Human Services, www.sog.unc.edu/sites/www.sog.unc.edu/files/2004DHHSTitle6VCA.pdf.

69. 45 C.F.R. § 164.524(c)(4).

70. G.S. 130A-24.

71. G.S. 130A-24(a).

72. The term "local health director" is defined by statute to mean "the administrative head of a local health department appointed pursuant to this Chapter." The same statute defines "local health department" as "a district health department or a public health authority or a county health department." G.S. 130A-2. Although these definitions do not capture consolidated human services agencies and directors, a separate statute assigns local public health roles to the agency by (1) giving the agency "the responsibility to carry out the duties of a local health department"; (2) providing that the consolidated human services board "shall have all the powers and duties of a local board of health" except for appointing the director and transmitting or presenting the budget for local health services; and (3) stating that "a human services director shall have all the powers and duties of a local health director provided under G.S. 130A-41," except that the human services director's activities in managing the department are subject to the oversight of the county manager and the human services director may appoint agency staff only with the county manager's approval.

73. G.S. 130A-40(a); 130A-45.4.

74. Another law provides for a limited pilot program (one county only) to allow a person with education and experience in public health nursing to serve as a local health director, as long as the appointment is approved by the N.C. Secretary of Health and Human Services. G.S. 130A-40.1.

for a local health director must appoint a person who does.[75] In addition, North Carolina's standards for local public health agency accreditation specify that the agency's governing board must appoint a local health director who meets the requirements of the law that applies to county and district health directors.[76]

The appointment of the local health director varies by type of local public health agency. For a county or district health department, the local health director is appointed by the local board of health after consultation with all applicable boards of county commissioners. Although the board must consult with the commissioners, the commissioners are not required to approve the appointment.[77] The same procedure is followed by a public health authority board when it appoints the public health authority director.[78] A consolidated human services agency director is appointed by the county manager with the advice and consent of the consolidated human services board.[79] If the county commissioners have abolished the board of health and assumed direct control of the health department pursuant to G.S. 153A-77(a), then the commissioners have all the powers and duties of the local board of health, including the power to appoint the local health director. This is the only circumstance in which the county commissioners may directly appoint the local health director.

All local health directors have powers and duties that come from multiple sources of law.[80] A local health director's powers and duties fall into five general categories:

1. **Administration.** The local health director administers programs under the direction of the board of health. All types of local health directors have the authority to employ and dismiss health department staff, but the employment decisions of a director of a consolidated human services agency must be approved by the county manager. In addition, the director of a county health department, a district health department, or a consolidated human services agency may enter contracts on behalf of the department, but the law that gives local health directors this authority also states that it shall not "be construed to abrogate the authority of the county commissioners."[81] Thus, it is a common practice to have county managers involved in the approval or execution of health department contracts.
2. **Remedies.** The local health director is responsible for enforcing public health laws within his or her jurisdiction and may employ a number of legal remedies when public health laws are violated. The director may
   - initiate civil or criminal proceedings against a public health law violator,[82]
   - abate public health nuisances or imminent hazards,[83]

75. G.S. 153A-77(e).

76. See 10A N.C.A.C. 48B .1304; *see also* 10A N.C.A.C 48B .0901(b)(1) (requiring the agency to have, or be recruiting, a local health director who meets legal requirements for the position).

77. G.S. 130A-40.

78. G.S. 130A-45.4.

79. G.S. 153A-77(e).

80. The main statutes setting forth the powers and duties of local health directors are G.S. 130A-41 (county and district health directors); 153A-77(e) (consolidated human services directors); and 130A-45.5(c) (public health authority directors). However, other powers and duties appear in several other statutes in G.S. Chapter 130A. Except as otherwise noted, the powers and duties discussed in this section of the chapter either originate in or are cross-referenced in G.S. 130A-41.

81. G.S. 130A-41(b)(13). A public health authority director does not have the power to enter contracts. Instead, the public health authority board holds that power. The board could, however, delegate contracting authority to the director or another agent or employee. G.S. 130A-45.3(a)(9) (allowing the public health authority board to "delegate to its agents or employees any powers or duties as it may deem appropriate").

82. G.S. 130A-18 authorizes the local health director to institute an action for injunctive relief in superior court. G.S. 130A-25 makes violation of most state and local public health laws or rules a class 1 misdemeanor (see also G.S. 14-3, providing for the classification of misdemeanors). However, violations of laws and rules pertaining to smoking in public places may not be prosecuted as misdemeanors. G.S. 130A-497(d). Further, in counties in which the county commissioners have assumed the role of the local board of health, the commissioners are authorized to enforce local rules through civil penalties—an option that is not available in counties with other forms of public health governance. G.S. 153A-77(a). However, if the commissioners exercise the option to impose a civil penalty, violation of the local rule subject to the penalty is *not* a misdemeanor unless the rule specifically states that it is.

83. G.S. 130A-19 (public health nuisance); 130A-20 (imminent hazard).

- impose administrative penalties (fines) for violations of state or local laws regulating smoking in public places,[84]
- embargo food or drink in some circumstances,[85]
- impose administrative penalties for violations of local on-site wastewater rules, or conditions imposed on permits issued under such rules.[86]

The local health director may also play a role in actions taken by local public health employees to suspend or revoke permits, such as a permit to operate a restaurant.[87]

3. **Communicable disease control.** The local health director must investigate cases and outbreaks of communicable diseases and ensure that communicable disease control measures are given.[88] The director may order isolation or quarantine if the legal conditions for exercising the isolation or quarantine authority are met.[89] The local health director also has the duty to enforce the North Carolina laws requiring the immunization of children.
4. **Other disease control.** The local health director must examine, investigate, and control rabies in accordance with state public health laws. The director must also investigate the causes of other diseases in the jurisdiction, whether or not they are communicable.
5. **Educate and advise.** The local health director must disseminate public health information, promote the benefits of good health, and advise local officials about public health matters.

This list is not exhaustive. Local health directors are responsible for the overall operation of the local public health agency, which makes the director ultimately accountable for administrative activities associated with the agency's performance of local public health services and functions. A consolidated human services director also has duties that go beyond those of a traditional local health director, largely reflecting the consolidated human services director's role as the chief administrator for human services programs other than public health.

Most of the powers and duties of a local health director may be delegated to another person. However, the director's authority to embargo food and drink in some circumstances may not be delegated.[90]

Local Health Department Personnel

In addition to a director, each type of local public health agency must have certain other staff members. A state regulation that addresses minimum staffing requires each local health department to employ a health director, a public health nurse, an environmental health specialist, and a secretary.[91] In general, these staff members must be full-time employees, but there is an exception that allows an agency to share a health director with another agency. The local health department accreditation rules also address staffing both directly and indirectly. One of the accreditation standards requires a local agency to employ or contract with one or more licensed physicians to serve as medical director.[92] Portions of the accreditation rules refer to other categories of staff members or to specific expertise that the agency

---

84. G.S. 130A-22(h1).

85. G.S. 130A-21.

86. G.S. 130A-22(h). Most North Carolina counties do not have local on-site wastewater rules. Rather, the state rules apply within the county and different remedies are available.

87. See G.S. 130A-23, authorizing the secretary of Health and Human Services to revoke or suspend permits upon finding a violation of state environmental health laws. Although the power to exercise this remedy is given to a state official, in practice violations are discovered and permit actions are taken by local environmental health specialists acting under the supervision of the local health director.

88. G.S. 130A-144.

89. G.S. 130A-145.

90. G.S. 130A-6; 130A-21(a).

91. 10A N.C.A.C. 46 .0301(a).

92. 10A N.C.A.C. 48B .0901(b)(3). It is possible for an agency to be accredited without satisfying every standard. The accreditation rules establish benchmarks and specify how many benchmarks must be met in each of three areas: agency core functions and essential services, facilities and administrative services, and board of health. 10A N.C.A.C. 48B .0103. The medical director provision falls under agency core functions and essential services. An agency could skip the medical director provision and still be accredited if it met enough of the other benchmarks in that area.

must possess or have access to, but they do not explicitly require the agency to have staff positions for those categories or expertise.[93]

There are no other requirements in law for specific numbers or types of staff, but local health departments need sufficient personnel to provide public health services and to perform all the activities and functions associated with other duties of the health department (such as assuring compliance with state and federal laws). Many departments employ or contract with a number of health care providers and environmental health specialists, as well as health educators, social workers, medical records specialists, epidemiologists or statisticians, and administrative staff.

The employees of county and district health departments ordinarily are subject to the North Carolina State Human Resources Act (SHRA) (G.S. 126-5(a)(2)).[94] Public health authorities are exempt from the SHRA and establish their own personnel policies and salary plans.[95] The employees of consolidated human services agencies are subject to county personnel policies or ordinances, unless the board of county commissioners elects to make the CHSA employees subject to the SHRA.[96] When the agency employees are covered by the SHRA, their qualifications and terms of employment are governed by the rules of the State Human Resources Commission.

The hiring authority for local health department employees varies by agency type. The director of a county or district health department is authorized to employ or dismiss department employees in accordance with the SHRA.[97] The director of a public health authority is authorized to employ, discipline, and dismiss employees of the authority.[98] The director of a consolidated human services agency may appoint employees, but the appointments must be approved by the county manager.[99]

Financing of Local Public Health Services

Public health activities in North Carolina are financed at the state level through federal funds, state funds, private grants, and fees. The precise mix of funds to support local public health services varies by locality.

Federal and State Funds

Local health departments receive federal funds both directly and indirectly. Indirect federal support comes from federal funds that are paid to the state and then channeled by the state to the local agencies. Federal categorical funds support maternal and child health services, family planning, the WIC (special supplemental nutrition for women, infants, and children) program, and several other services and programs. The major source of direct support is the state Medicaid program, which in fiscal year 2012 was composed of about 65 percent federal funds and 35 percent state funds.[100] Medicaid provides direct reimbursement for services to Medicaid-eligible clients, as well as an annual cost settlement. Some local health departments also receive federal funds in the form of Medicare reimbursement for services such as home health or diabetes care.

The state provides general aid-to-county funds, which are distributed to local public health agencies by DHHS. Funds are allocated based on population and utilization of allocated funds.[101] The state health director may allocate special

93. *See, e.g.*, 10A N.C.A.C. 48B .0203 (directing agency to assure staff have expertise in data management); 48B .0301 (requiring access to and consultation with an epidemiologist); 48B .0701 (referring to unit directors for communicable disease, nursing, and environmental health).

94. Local health department employees may be removed from SHRA coverage if the State Human Resources Commission determines that the local personnel system is substantially equivalent to the SHRA. G.S. 126-11(a).

95. G.S. 130A-45.12; 130A-45.3(a)(7).

96. G.S. 153A-77(d).

97. G.S. 130A-41(b)(12).

98. G.S. 130A-45.5(c)(12).

99. G.S. 153A-77(e)(1); 130A-43(c)(2).

100. Source: Kaiser Family Foundation, Federal and State Share of Medicaid Spending, kff.org/medicaid/state-indicator/federalstate-share-of-spending/. The match rate varies from state to state and may vary from year to year.

101. 10A N.C.A.C. 46 .0101.

needs funds to local health departments that demonstrate a critical public health need, unique to the department's service area, that cannot be met through other funding mechanisms.[102] Additional support comes from categorical grants, which may include a combination of federal and state funds. The state also awards other grant or contract funds for special projects. Finally, the state reimburses some services on a fee-for-service basis.

To receive state funds and federal funds that the state distributes, a local health department must sign a contract with DHHS called the *consolidated agreement*. The consolidated agreement contains a number of general provisions governing how local health departments must use and account for money flowing from the state, as well as provisions that set out special requirements for the use of certain funds. If a department fails to comply with the terms of the contract, the state may take steps to cut off state funding for the program that is out of compliance. The state first notifies the department that it has sixty days to comply. If the problem is not corrected to the satisfaction of the state within that period, the state may temporarily suspend funding for the program that is out of compliance. If the deficiency remains uncorrected thirty days after the temporary suspension, program funds may be permanently suspended until the department provides evidence that the deficiencies have been corrected. After all other reasonable administrative remedies have been exhausted, the state may cancel, terminate, or suspend the contract in whole or in part and the department may be declared ineligible for further state contracts or agreements. Alternatively, the state can enforce the contract by suing the county. Neither of these actions has ever been taken by the state against a county; nevertheless, the ability to withhold funds gives the state some leverage to require certain levels of service by local public health agencies.

Local Sources of Revenue

County Appropriations

Local boards of health have no power to tax, so a board and its department must depend on other sources for funds. Boards of county commissioners are authorized to appropriate funds from property tax levies and to allocate other revenues whose use is not otherwise restricted by law for the local health department's use.

For county health departments, county commissioners approve the health department budget as a regular part of their responsibility for county finance. For consolidated human services agencies, the budget for public health is a part of the budget planned by the consolidated human services director, recommended by the consolidated human services board, and approved by the county commissioners. Public health authorities and district health departments prepare and approve their own budgets and need not obtain county commissioners' approval. These agencies seek county appropriations, however, and the county commissioners must approve those expenditures.

In the past, there was no minimum level of local funding that county commissioners were required to provide for public health. Local health departments worked with county governments to try to ensure that funding was sufficient to support the services and functions that the health department performed, and the amount appropriated for public health services varied widely from county to county.[103] Legislation adopted in 2012 imposed a maintenance-of-effort requirement for local public health.[104] Effective July 1, 2014, in order to receive state and federal funding for local public health, a county government must maintain its operating appropriations to its local health department from local ad valorem tax receipts at levels equal to amounts appropriated in state fiscal year 2010–11.[105] Two additional non-supplantation provisions in the statutes prohibit reductions of county appropriations when state money increases in certain circumstances. G.S. 130A-4.2 requires the state DHHS to ensure that local health departments do not reduce county appropriations for health promotion services because of state appropriations. G.S. 130A-4.1 places the same requirement on maternal and child health services.

102. 10A N.C.A.C. 46 .0102.

103. A study conducted by the School of Government in 2012 examined funding for local health departments in greater detail and found wide variations in the proportion of local health department budgets that were from county appropriations versus other sources. *See Comparing North Carolina's Local Public Health Agencies: The Legal Landscape, the Perspectives, and the Numbers* (May 2012), at 39–45, www.sog.unc.edu/sites/www.sog.unc.edu/files/REPORT%20Comparing%20North%20Carolina%20Local%20Public%20Health%20Agencies_0.pdf.

104. S.L. 2012-126, sec. 3.

105. G.S. 130A-34.4(a)(2).

Grants

Local health departments may receive grants from government agencies or from private entities, such as foundations. These grants are essentially contracts between the local health department and the granting agency and usually are provided to enable the department to develop a particular project or provide a specific service.

Local Fees

Public health agencies may charge and collect fees, as described earlier in this chapter. Revenues from fees imposed by local boards of health must be used for public health purposes.

Management of Local Funds

All funds received or spent at the local level must be budgeted, disbursed, and accounted for in accordance with the Local Government Budget and Fiscal Control Act (G.S. Ch. 159, Art. 3). The budgeting, disbursing, and accounting for a county health department or consolidated human services agency is done by the county's budget officer and finance officer. District health departments and public health authorities (both single-county and multi-county) are responsible for performing these functions themselves.

Local Public Health Services

Local public health agencies provide services at both the community and individual level. While there is no single law describing the minimum services that a local agency must provide, there are three primary state laws that affect the scope and range of local service provision.

The first of these is a law that describes the public health services that the General Assembly has determined are essential to promoting and contributing to the highest levels of health and that should be available to everyone in the state.[106] This law incorporates the "ten essential public health services," a nationally recognized set of services that was adopted in 1994 by a national committee charged with providing a framework for effective public health systems,[107] and directs local health departments to ensure that the services are available and accessible to the population served by the department. The ten essential public health services fall into three categories: assessment of community health status and health problems; policy development to educate the community about health, solve community health problems, support individual and community health, and protect health and ensure safety; and assurance of quality public health and public and private health care services within the community. Table 38.2 identifies the specific services in each category.

Another law requires each local public health agency in the state to be accredited by the North Carolina Local Health Department Accreditation Board.[108] To be accredited, a local agency must satisfy accreditation standards that address the agency's capacity to provide the ten essential public health services, as well as several additional duties imposed by state law.[109] The accreditation standards are divided into three categories: agency core functions and essential services, facilities and administrative services, and local boards of health. The accreditation board assesses a local health department's performance of 148 specific activities. A health department must satisfactorily perform about 90 percent of the activities in order to obtain or maintain accreditation.[110]

---

106. G.S. 130A-1.1.

107. *See* www.cdc.gov/nphpsp/essentialServices.html.

108. G.S. 130A-34.1.

109. 10A N.C.A.C. Ch. 48.

110. The accreditation rules specify the exact number of activities that must be satisfied in each category for the department to be accredited. 10A N.C.A.C. 48B .0103(a).

Table 38.2 Essential Public Health Services (G.S. 130A-1.1)

Category	Services
Assessment	Monitoring health status to identify community health problems
	Diagnosing and investigating health hazards in the community
Policy development	Informing, educating, and empowering people about health issues
	Mobilizing community partnerships to identify and solve health problems
	Developing policies and plans that support individual and community health efforts
Assurance of services	Enforcing laws and regulations that protect health and ensure safety
	Linking people to needed personal health care services and ensuring the provision of health care when otherwise unavailable
	Ensuring a competent public health workforce and personal health care workforce
	Evaluating effectiveness, accessibility, and quality of personal and population-based health services
	Conducting research

A third statute authorizes the North Carolina Commission for Public Health to establish standards for the nature and scope of local public health services.[111] The commission has adopted rules, known as the *mandated services rules*, which specify some of the public health services that local public health agencies must guarantee.[112] The mandated services rules address thirteen types of services that fall into one of two categories: (1) services that the local agency must provide under the direction of the local health director and the supervision of the local board of health or (2) services that a county may provide through the local agency, contract with another entity to provide, or not provide at all if the local agency can certify to the state's satisfaction that the services are available in the county from other providers. Each of the mandated services has its own rule that identifies more specifically which services must be provided or assured. Figure 38.3 identifies the mandated services.

These laws provide a starting point for understanding local public health services, but they do not paint the complete picture. Local public health agencies also must provide services or perform activities to comply with other laws. For example, in order to comply with the federal HIPAA medical privacy rule, local health departments must develop and maintain numerous forms, notices, and policies and procedures for keeping health information confidential and secure and honoring individuals' rights regarding their health information.[113]

The North Carolina Department of Health and Human Services conducts a biennial survey of services that are provided by local public health agencies in North Carolina, which provides additional insight into the range of local public health services that are provided by the state's local agencies. The services that are typically included in the survey cover a wide range of activities, from epidemic investigations, to school nursing services, to childhood lead poisoning prevention, to chronic disease control, to name just a few.[114]

111. G.S. 130A-9.

112. 10A N.C.A.C. 46 .0201–.0216.

113. 45 C.F.R. Parts 160, 163, and 164.

114. A list of the 127 specific services that were included in DHHS's survey for fiscal year 2011 is available at www.sog.unc.edu/sites/www.sog.unc.edu/files/Comparing%20North%20Carolina%20Local%20Public%20Health%20Agencies%20AppB_0.pdf.

Figure 38.3 Mandated Public Health Services in North Carolina (10A N.C.A.C. 46 .0201–.0216)

Local health department must provide

- Food, lodging, and institutional sanitation
- Individual on-site water supply
- Sanitary sewage collection, treatment, and disposal
- Communicable disease control
- Vital records registration

Local health department must provide, contract for, or certify available

- Adult health
- Home health
- Dental public health
- Grade A milk certification*
- Maternal health
- Child health
- Family planning
- Public health laboratory

*In 2011, responsibility for milk sanitation at the state level was transferred from the former Division of Environmental Health, Department of Environment and Natural Resources, to the Food and Drug Protection Division of the Department of Agriculture and Community Services. S.L. 2011-145, sec. 13.3.(b).

Other Statewide Public Health Programs with Local Components

The focus of this chapter has been on the state and local system for carrying out the core public health functions that are reflected in the statute setting forth the mission and purpose of the state's public health system.[115] The bulk of the state's public health laws and structure are focused on those functions and the duties that accompany them. However, the North Carolina public health code also addresses a number of other governmental functions and duties related to the protection of the public health. Two statewide programs that have significant local involvement are the medical examiner system and the vital records program.

Medical Examiner System

North Carolina has a centralized, state-administered medical examiner system for postmortem investigations.[116] The system is composed of a chief medical examiner (CME), a central staff of professionals, and a network of county medical examiners. Its purpose is to investigate and determine the cause and manner of deaths that are unattended, in order to ensure that appropriate medico-legal follow-up occurs when a death is suspicious or unnatural.

The chief medical examiner is appointed by the state secretary of health and human services. By statute, the CME must be a forensic pathologist who is certified by the American Board of Pathology and licensed to practice medicine.[117] The CME has a staff that includes pathologists, toxicologists, and other professionals who assist with autopsies and forensic investigations. Although county medical examiners are responsible for investigating deaths within their jurisdictions, the CME has oversight of all cases and may assume jurisdiction over any case or reassign a case to another

115. G.S. 130A-1.1.; see also note 2 and accompanying text.

116. G.S. Ch. 130A, Art. 16; 10A N.C.A.C. 44; *see also* North Carolina Office of the Chief Medical Examiner (OCME) Guidelines (available at www.ocme.dhhs.nc.gov/rules/guidelines.shtml).

117. G.S. 130A-378.

local medical examiner. The CME or a member of his or her staff reviews each case investigated by a county medical examiner and is authorized to amend death certificates filed by the local examiners.[118]

For each county, the CME appoints one or more individuals to serve three-year terms as county medical examiners. In making appointments, the CME must give preference to licensed physicians, but he or she may also appoint licensed physician assistants, nurse practitioners, nurses, coroners, or emergency medical technician paramedics.[119] Deaths within the medical examiner's jurisdiction include those that

- result from violence, poisoning, accident, suicide, or homicide;
- occur suddenly when the deceased had been in apparent good health or when unattended by a physician;
- occur in a jail, prison, or correctional institution or in police custody;
- occur in state-operated psychiatric hospitals, substance abuse facilities, and certain other state facilities that provide services to individuals with developmental disabilities;
- are the result of an execution carried out under the state's death penalty laws; or
- occur under any suspicious, unusual or unnatural circumstance.

Such deaths are typically reported to the county medical examiner by health care providers or law enforcement, but the law requires anyone who suspects that a death may fall in one of the above categories to report it.[120] The county medical examiner's duty to investigate is triggered by the receipt of the report. Each county must provide or contract for a facility for the examination and storage of bodies subject to medical examiner jurisdiction.[121]

To facilitate death investigations, state laws authorize county medical examiners to inspect physical evidence and documents, including confidential medical records. The medical examiner may seek an administrative search warrant or issue subpoenas for information as the case requires.[122] A medical examiner may order an autopsy if he or she determines that it would be "advisable and in the public interest."[123] A district attorney or a superior court judge may also authorize an autopsy in a medical examiner case.[124] If a question about a death arises after the body has been buried, the CME may authorize an investigation of the death. In such a case, the district attorney petitions a superior court judge to order the body exhumed and turned over to the CME for investigation.[125]

Upon completion of an investigation, the county medical examiner must complete a certificate of death that states the cause and manner of death. The cause of death is the illness or injury that resulted in death, while the manner of death refers to the medical examiner's conclusion about whether the cause was natural, an accident, suicide, homicide, or undetermined. The county medical examiner must make a full report of the investigation to the CME.[126] The county medical examiner receives a fee of $100 for each completed investigation and report. If the deceased was a resident of the county in which the investigation occurred, the fee is paid by the county; otherwise, the state pays the fee.[127]

---

118. G.S. 130A-382.

119. *Id.* In the past, nonphysician medical examiners were called "acting medical examiners," but this term was deleted from the statute by S.L. 2014-100 (Appropriations Act), sec. 126E.6(a).

120. G.S. 130A-383. In addition, a person who discovers a deceased body or anatomical material that may be part of a human body must report the discovery to the county medical examiner.

121. G.S. 130A-381.

122. G.S. 130A-385 (authority to inspect physical evidence and records and to seek an administrative search warrant); 130A-386 (authority to issue subpoenas for the appearance of persons or production of documents).

123. G.S. 130A-389.

124. *Id.* The North Carolina OCME guidelines specify the types of deaths that require autopsy. There is a fee of $1,250 for each autopsy. If the deceased was a resident of the county in which the investigation occurred, the fee is paid by the county; otherwise, the state pays the fee. If the medical examiner determines that an autopsy is not necessary but the deceased's next of kin requests it, the CME or a designated pathologist may perform an autopsy and the fee is paid by the next of kin.

125. G.S. 130A-390. The cost of the exhumation, autopsy, transportation, and disposition of the body is paid by the county if the deceased was a resident of the county in which the death or fatal injury occurred; otherwise, the state pays those costs.

126. G.S. 130A-385 (investigation reports); 130A-389 (autopsy reports).

127. G.S. 130A-387.

Some North Carolina counties retain the elected office of county coroner, whose duty is to conduct inquests and preliminary hearings into deaths that may have resulted from criminal acts or omissions.[128] In counties with coroners, the county medical examiner must notify the coroner of deaths within the medical examiner's jurisdiction, and the coroner must hold an inquest and file a report with the district attorney and the county medical examiner. However, the medical examiner retains custody and control of the body. He or she also retains the ultimate duty and authority to conduct the medico-legal examination of deaths and file the reports required by law.[129]

Vital Records Program

The North Carolina Vital Records Program is responsible for registering vital events that occur in North Carolina. The vital events registered through the program are births, deaths, fetal deaths, marriages, and divorces. The state program is administered by the North Carolina Department of Health and Human Services, Division of Public Health.[130] At the local level, county registers of deeds and local health departments have extensive duties related to vital records, and clerks of court have a role in the system as well. Private individuals and entities also play a significant role in the vital records system. For example, hospitals and other birthing facilities file birth certificates with local registrars, and funeral directors file death certificates.

The state secretary of health and human services appoints a state registrar to lead the state program.[131] Each county has a local registrar of vital records and a deputy registrar. Some counties also have sub-registrars.

The state registrar's ultimate duty is to ensure that records of vital events are completed accurately and registered. To that end, the state registrar's statutory duties include examining vital records received from local registrars to ensure their satisfactory completion, preserving vital records permanently and in a systematic fashion, and enforcing the state's vital records laws and rules. The state registrar also supervises local registrars, deputy registrars, and sub-registrars.[132]

By law, the local health director serves as the local registrar for each county within the local health department's jurisdiction.[133] He or she must designate in writing a deputy registrar to assist with the local registrar's duties and to act as local registrar in the event of the health director's absence, illness or disability, or removal from office. The local registrar may also appoint one or more sub-registrars with the approval of the state registrar. Sub-registrars are authorized to receive certificates and issue burial-transit permits and are supervised by the state registrar.[134]

The local registrar's duties include

- registering vital events that occur in the county,
- furnishing certificate forms provided by the state registrar to persons who require them and examining certificates that are submitted to assure their satisfactory completion,
- transmitting a copy of each birth or death certificate to the county register of deeds within seven days of receipt,
- sending original certificates to the state registrar, and
- maintaining records and making reports as required by the state registrar.[135]

The county is responsible for ensuring that the local health department has sufficient staff, funds, and other resources necessary to administer the vital records program.[136]

---

128. G.S. Chapter 152 creates the office of county coroner and prescribes the duties of the office.

129. G.S. 130A-394.

130. G.S. 130A-90, 10A N.C.A.C. 41H .0101. The statute requires the state to maintain a vital statistics program. Regulatory definitions clarify that the terms "vital statistics" and "vital records" mean the same thing: "'Vital statistics' or 'vital records' means records of birth, death, fetal death, marriage, divorce, and data related thereto." 10A N.C.A.C. 41H .0102.

131. G.S. 130A-91.

132. G.S. 130A-92.

133. G.S. 130A-94.

134. G.S. 130A-96.

135. G.S. 130A-97.

136. G.S. 130A-98.

County registers of deeds are a significant component of the vital record system and have numerous legal duties associated with it, including

- filing and preserving copies of birth and death certificates furnished by the local registrar,
- making and keeping an index of certificates,
- keeping certificates open to inspection and examination, and
- providing copies or abstracts to persons who request them. [137]

Clerks of court play an important role in the vital records program as well. The clerk of court with jurisdiction must report divorces and annulments of marriages to the state registrar[138] and must notify the state registrar of judgments determining the paternity of a child.[139] The clerk of superior court also has a role in establishing the fact of birth by persons without birth certificates.[140]

The vital records program activity that is most visible to the public is the provision of certificates that prove the occurrence of vital events. Certificates of vital events may be obtained from either the state vital records office[141] or a local official. Locally, county registers of deeds provide certificates of births, deaths, or marriages.[142] (However, birth certificates for an adopted child must be obtained from the state office.) Certificates of divorce may be obtained from the clerk of court in the county where the divorce was filed.

References

Institute of Medicine. *The Future of Public Health* (Washington, D.C.: National Academy Press, 1988).

Institute of Medicine. *The Future of the Public's Health in the 21st Century* (Washington, D.C.: National Academy Press, 2002).

North Carolina General Assembly Program Evaluation Division. *The Division of Public Health Should Remain in the Department of Health and Human Services: Final Report to the Joint Legislative Program Evaluation Oversight Committee* (Report No. 2013-01, Jan. 14, 2013). www.ncleg.net/PED/Reports/documents/PH/PH_Report.pdf.

North Carolina Public Health Task Force. *2008 Final Report: Public Health Improvement Plan.* http://publichealth.nc.gov/taskforce/.

UNC School of Government. *Comparing North Carolina's Local Public Health Agencies: The Legal Landscape, the Perspectives, and the Numbers* (May 2013). www.sog.unc.edu/node/3551.

---

137. G.S. 130A-99. Under this statute, copies of certificates maintained by registers of deeds must be open to inspection and *uncertified* copies or abstracts of the certificates must be provided to any person on request. However, the provision of *certified* copies of vital records is restricted. G.S. 130A-93(c). For more information about obtaining certified copies of vital records, see http://vitalrecords.nc.gov/faqs.htm or contact the county register of deeds. While the copies of certificates that are available in the offices of registers of deeds are open to inspection, only the state registrar may have access to original vital records. G.S. 130A-93. In addition, birth certificates filed with a local health department contain additional medical information that is not open to inspection. G.S. 130A-102.

138. G.S. 130A-111.

139. G.S. 130A-119.

140. G.S. 130A-106.

141. *See* http://vitalrecords.nc.gov/.

142. In Mecklenburg County, certificates of births or deaths that occurred in the county are obtained from the local health department. *See* http://charmeck.org/MECKLENBURG/COUNTY/HEALTHDEPARTMENT/Pages/Default.aspx.

Additional Resources

Websites

School of Government, North Carolina Public Health Systems Research: www.sog.unc.edu/node/2115.
School of Government, North Carolina Public Health Law: www.sog.unc.edu/programs/ncphl.
North Carolina Division of Public Health: http://publichealth.nc.gov/.
North Carolina Local Health Department Accreditation: http://nciph.sph.unc.edu/accred/.
North Carolina Public Health Incubator Collaboratives: http://nciph.sph.unc.edu/incubator/.

Reports, Articles, and Journals

School of Government, Health Law Bulletin Series. http://shopping.netsuite.com/s.nl/c.433425/sc.7/category.49/.f.
UNC School of Government, *Popular Government* Special Issue *Challenges and Successes of Public Health in North Carolina* 71 (Fall 2005). http://shopping.netsuite.com/s.nl/c.433425/it.I/id.122/.f?sc=7&category=5689.

About the Author

Jill D. Moore is a School of Government faculty member who works in the area of public health law.

Chapter 39

Social Services

Aimee N. Wall

The term "social services" refers to a diverse mix of programs and services intended to help individuals in need. Social services may address either personal needs, by providing protection to a child or adult who has been abused, for example, or financial needs, by connecting low-income individuals and families with programs that can help them buy food or pay for heat in the winter. Some of these services and programs are offered by local public agencies, including county departments of social services and programs or agencies serving senior citizens or veterans. In addition, private organizations, including nonprofits and churches, offer many social services programs. This chapter will focus primarily on the services and programs traditionally administered by county departments of social services.

Counties are required to provide certain services within their jurisdictions. Many also offer additional services tailored to community needs. The county services and programs can be divided into two primary categories: economic services and social work services. The first of these, also referred to as public assistance, assists eligible people through money payments and other economic supports such as food and child care subsidies and employment services. Eligibility for most of these programs is determined on the basis of a person's or family's income and resources. The second category, social work services, assists individuals, including many who are at risk of abuse or neglect, in a variety of ways and often without regard to income.

History of Social Services in North Carolina

Today's complex web of programs and services has its roots in the English Poor Laws. The North Carolina Constitution of 1776 did not address care of the poor. Nevertheless, the General Assembly passed laws calling for locally elected overseers of the poor, providing for wardens of the poor to be elected by county courts and authorizing counties to build almshouses or poorhouses to house and provide employment for the poor. Slowly but steadily the use of public tax funds to provide some care for needy citizens became accepted as an important and legitimate function of county government.

The North Carolina Constitution of 1868 established, for the first time, a role for state government with respect to social services:

> Beneficent provision for the poor, the unfortunate and orphan[s] being one of the first duties of a civilized and a Christian state, the General Assembly shall, at its first session, appoint and define the duties of a Board of Public Charities, to whom shall be entrusted the supervision of all charitable and penal State institutions, and who shall annually report to the Governor upon their condition, with suggestions for their improvement.[1]

Statewide public welfare laws, enacted in 1917 and supplemented in 1919, provided for a state Board of Charities and Public Welfare, a state Commissioner of Public Welfare, three-member local boards of charity and public welfare, and county superintendents of public welfare. The enactment in 1923 of a Mother's Aid law provided financial assistance to indigent mothers with children under the age of fourteen. County participation was optional, and the program costs were split between the state and participating counties. Into the 1930s the state's role in social services increased, but both the funding and administration of social services remained primarily county responsibilities.

The Social Security Act of 1935 became, and remains, the "cornerstone of the American welfare state."[2] It included public assistance or "relief" programs for low-income people in specified categories, including children in single-parent families. It marked the beginning of a drastic redefinition of the role of government in the social services field. Needy persons who did not qualify for these categorical programs remained dependent on completely county-funded programs or nongovernmental charitable institutions for assistance. North Carolina enacted laws establishing the new federal programs in the state, requiring all counties to participate, designating a single state agency to supervise administration of the programs, and assigning to counties primary responsibility for the nonfederal share of the programs' costs.

The Federal Government's Role

Congress

Significant parts of the social services system in North Carolina still reflect the programs created by the Social Security Act in 1935, and the system has evolved based largely on changes in the Social Security Act. Federal law does not require any state to operate particular programs. Rather, Congress enacts laws that establish a variety of programs and appropriates funds available to states that agree to operate the programs in accordance with applicable federal laws and regulations. The level of federal financial participation varies from program to program, and within programs it often differs for administrative versus direct benefits costs. In recent years, for example, the federal government has paid over 65 percent of the cost of Medicaid services provided in North Carolina—costs that dwarf those of all other programs combined.[3] With respect to Medicaid administrative costs and all costs of other programs that involve federal or state

1. N.C. Const. of 1868 art. XI, § 7.

2. Edward D. Berkowitz, *America's Welfare State from Roosevelt to Reagan* (Baltimore: Johns Hopkins University Press, 1991), 13.

3. For fiscal year 2014, the federal government's share of the cost of Medicaid services in the state is estimated to be more than $7.5 billion and the state's share is estimated to be almost $4 billion. North Carolina Department of Health and Human Services,

financial participation or both—that is, excluding those funded only by counties—the state Department of Health and Human Services (DHHS) estimates that for state fiscal year 2014 federal funds will provide

- over 90 percent of public assistance payments (those paid to or for clients);
- over 50 percent of associated administrative costs (staff, overhead, and other expenses); and
- almost 60 percent of the costs of service programs.[4]

Thus for states that want to provide certain kinds of financial assistance and services for their citizens, there are significant financial incentives to participate in the federally supported programs.

Federal Agencies

The federal executive agency with primary responsibility for overseeing most social services programs is the federal Department of Health and Human Services. The federal Department of Agriculture oversees the food and nutrition programs. These agencies promulgate regulations to carry out the federal laws, issue policies to the states, and monitor state compliance with federal requirements. They can impose financial sanctions on states for failing to meet these requirements.

Federal laws and regulations define basic characteristics of federally supported public assistance programs but leave a number of decisions to the states. In the Medicaid program, for example, federal law defines categories of people who may be eligible for assistance, while states have leeway to determine which medical services are covered, how much the providers are paid, and what the income limits are for eligibility.

The State Government's Role

In most states, the state, rather than local government, administers social services programs.[5] In North Carolina, however, most social services programs are administered by counties under the state's supervision. State direction and supervision come from the General Assembly, the state Department of Health and Human Services (DHHS), and the appointed rulemaking commissions.

The General Assembly

Since enacting laws in 1937 to enable North Carolina to participate in federally funded welfare programs, the General Assembly has amended or rewritten those laws many times to establish new programs, conform state law to federal changes, modify program features that federal law leaves to the state to determine, and establish or modify programs based solely on state law. Chapter 108A of the North Carolina General Statutes (hereinafter G.S.) contains most of the state's social services legislation, including specific authority for the state DHHS to accept all grants-in-aid for social services programs that may be available under the Social Security Act, other federal laws or regulations, and nonfederal sources. Chapter 108A also addresses confidentiality, appeal rights, and other subjects to ensure the state's compliance with federal requirements. It also reflects state policy regarding social services matters not determined by federal law. Many program details do not appear in the General Statutes. Some are addressed by administrative rules and policies pursuant to authority the General Assembly has delegated to DHHS and the state Social Services Commission

---

Division of Medical Assistance, *SFY 2014 Projected Medicaid Program Services Expenditures*, www.ncdhhs.gov/dss/budget/estimates.htm.

4. North Carolina Department of Health and Human Services, *County Budget Estimates—State Fiscal Year 2013–2014*, www.ncdhhs.gov/dss/budget/estimates.htm.

5. "North Carolina is one of 11 states that provide social services programs through a state-supervised and county-administered system. . . . Most other states operate a state-administered social services system, and counties have little or no role in administering or financing state and federal social services programs." N.C. General Assembly Program Evaluation Division, *Statutory Changes Will Promote County Flexibility in Social Services Administration, Final Report to the Joint Legislative Program Evaluation Oversight Committee, Rep. No. 2011-03 (May 2011)*, www.ncleg.net/PED/Reports/documents/DSS/DSS_Report.pdf.

(described later in the chapter). Others are decided by the legislature when it appropriates funds for public assistance and social services programs.[6]

The General Assembly determines how the state and the counties will share responsibility for the nonfederal portion of the cost of federally supported programs. For example, for many years the state and counties shared responsibility for paying for the nonfederal share of the cost of Medicaid services: the state would pay 85 percent and the counties would pay 15 percent.[7] In 2007 the General Assembly enacted legislation that ultimately phased out the county's share for Medicaid services but still requires counties to help pay for costs of administering the program.[8] Another example is found in G.S. 108A-49.1, which provides that the nonfederal share of foster care and adoption assistance payments will be divided equally between the state and county.[9]

In addition to appropriating state funds to pay the state's share of the cost of certain social services programs, the legislature allocates lump-sum federal funds the state receives under federal block grants for social services programs and approves plans for the expenditure of these funds.[10] The General Assembly also decides issues that federal law leaves to the states' discretion, such as income eligibility limits and the designation of covered medical services for Medicaid. It determines what other nonfederally based public assistance and service programs counties must provide; decides whether to provide state funding for services for which federal funds are not available; and defines counties' responsibilities in relation to programs such as child protective services, adoptions, and guardianship.

Commissions

Three state commissions play a significant role in the state's social services programs: the Social Services Commission, the Child Care Commission, and the State Human Resources Commission. These commissions adopt regulations, which have the force and effect of law, and oversee administration of various programs and services.

- **Social Services Commission.** This commission has broad authority to adopt rules that govern most of the state's social services programs.[11] The commission is also authorized to establish standards for inspecting and licensing maternity homes, adult care homes for aged or disabled persons, and residential child care facilities. The commission may authorize investigations of social problems, subpoena witnesses, and compel the production of documents. In counties having a board of social services (see further discussion below), the commission appoints either one or two members (depending on whether the county has a three- or five-member board). It also may assign responsibilities to county social services boards and directors. The governor appoints the commission's thirteen members, one from each congressional district, for four-year terms.
- **Child Care Commission.** This commission adopts standards and rules for the licensing and operation of child care facilities. It also is charged with making rules for responding to child abuse or neglect in child care facilities.[12] The commission has seventeen members—seven appointed by the governor and ten by the General Assembly—that serve for two-year terms.[13]

---

6. These provisions appear in session laws but are not codified as part of the General Statutes. *See, e.g.*, S.L. 2011-145, § 10.27 (requiring the Division of Medical Assistance to prepare a fiscal analysis before implementing certain changes to medical policy for the N.C. Health Choice program).

7. *See* S.L. 2005-276, § 10.11(b).

8. S.L. 2007-323, § 31; S.L. 2007-345, § 14. For a detailed discussion of this legislative change, see Kara A. Millonzi and William C. Rivenbark, "Phased Implementation of the 2007 and 2008 Medicaid Funding Reform Legislation in North Carolina," *Local Finance Bulletin* No. 38 (Sept. 2008), http://sogpubs.unc.edu/electronicversions/pdfs/lfb38.pdf.

9. N.C. Gen. Stat. (hereinafter G.S.) § 108A-49.1(d) (added by S.L. 2011-145, § 10.51).

10. *See, e.g.*, Social Services Block Grant (42 U.S.C. §§ 1397 through 1397(h)) (providing flexible funding to states to enable them to offer a range of social services).

11. *See* G.S. Ch. 143B, Art. 3, Part 6. The secretary of the Department of Health and Human Services (DHHS), rather than the Social Services Commission, has rulemaking authority for the Medicaid program.

12. G.S. 110-88.

13. G.S. 143B-168.4.

- **Human Resources Commission.** This commission, in conjunction with the Office of State Human Resources, regulates and administers the state personnel system, including the merit system under which many county social services personnel are appointed.[14]

Department of Health and Human Services

The state Department of Health and Human Services (DHHS) is the state agency responsible for most public human services programs. The secretary of DHHS, who is appointed by the governor, appoints the directors of various departmental divisions that issue policies and program manuals for use by county departments of social services in interpreting and implementing the various laws and regulations.[15] DHHS divisions that supervise programs administered by the counties or with which county departments must interact regularly include those described in Table 39.1, below.[16]

The County's Role

As mentioned above, North Carolina is somewhat unusual because most social services programs are not administered directly by the state but rather by counties under the state's supervision. North Carolina's county-administered, state-supervised social services system reflects the state's long history of local (county) responsibility for public social services, the strength of county government in the state, and the role of North Carolina's counties as the primary vehicle for the delivery of basic services to citizens.

County Organization and Governance

Since 2012 the organization and governance of North Carolina's local social services agencies has been changing rather quickly. Until then almost all of the counties had a county department of social services that was governed by a county board of social services.[17] Legislation enacted in 2012 authorized boards of county commissioners to adopt different approaches to organization and governance of human services programs, including social services.[18] Boards of county commissioners must determine what type of organization or agency will be responsible for delivering social services within the county. In addition, they must choose the type of governing board that will oversee the agency.

Organization

Counties have three options available for organizing the agency that delivers social services within the county. They may

- operate a county department of social services,
- establish a consolidated human services agency that includes social services, or
- establish a multi-county department of social services.

---

14. G.S. Ch. 126. Prior to 2013, the agency was named the Office of State Personnel and the commission was named the State Personnel Commission. S.L. 2013-382. Even though the director and staff of county social services departments are county employees, their employment is governed by the State Personnel Act unless (1) the county's personnel system, or a portion of it, has been approved by the State Human Resources Commission (or the former State Personnel Commission) as being "substantially equivalent" to that of the state or (2) the county has incorporated the social services department into a consolidated human services agency and elected to remove the employees of that agency from the State Human Resources Act (or former State Personnel Act).

15. The manuals are available at http://info.dhhs.state.nc.us/olm/manuals/default.aspx.

16. A complete list of DHHS divisions and fuller descriptions of their functions are available at www.ncdhhs.gov/contacts/division.htm.

17. Wake and Mecklenburg counties were the exceptions. Both counties have operated consolidated human services agencies rather than independent departments of social services for several years. Prior to 2012 G.S. 153A-77 allowed a county to establish this type of consolidated agency if its population was greater than 425,000. Wake County's agency is governed by an appointed consolidated human services board and Mecklenburg County's agency is governed by the board of county commissioners.

18. S.L. 2012-126.

Table 39.1 Divisions within the N.C. Department of Health and Human Services Involved with Oversight and Administration of Social Services Programs (as of November 2014)

Division of Social Services	• Oversees county administration of various public assistance programs, including the Work First program, the Supplemental Food and Nutrition program, and State–County Special Assistance. Does not oversee the Medicaid or Health Choice programs. • Oversees county administration of various social services programs, including child protective services, child support enforcement,[a] foster care services, adoption services, child protective services, and family preservation services. • Develops policy, conducts some training for county staff, provides technical assistance to counties, and monitors county performance.
Division of Medical Assistance	• Oversees the Medicaid and Health Choice programs. • Supervises county social services departments' administration of eligibility determination and establishes policies and procedures. • Oversees the payment of medical providers—such as hospitals, physicians, and nursing homes—that deliver services to eligible clients.
Division of Aging and Adult Services	• Oversees county administration of various programs serving disabled and older adults, including adult protective services, guardianship, State–County Special Assistance, adult placement, at-risk case management, and adult care home case management. • Oversees operation of aging programs that focus on providing home and community services to older adults and certifies adult day care programs, adult day health programs, and senior centers. • Administers federal programs focused on elder rights, including the Long Term Care Ombudsman Program. • Develops the State Aging Services Plan, as required by the federal Older Americans Act, and supports Area Agencies on Aging as they implement their area plans.
Division of Child Development and Early Education	• Licenses and monitors most child care programs, enforces regulations that apply to those programs, works with local councils to assure appropriate services for children with disabilities, and assists providers of services under the federal Head Start program. • Administers funds to help low-income families pay for child care and prekindergarten programs. • Provides teacher education and licensure support and services to prekindergarten teachers who work in nonpublic schools. • Offers other services and programs to improve the quality and increase the availability of child care and related services for children and families.
Division of Health Service Regulation	• Licenses and regulates a variety of medical, mental health, and residential child care facilities. • Conducts on-site inspection and monitoring in collaboration with the staff of the county departments of social services and the Division of Social Services.

a. Prior to July 1, 2010, the state directly administered child support enforcement programs in approximately one-third of the counties. The law was amended to require all counties to administer their own programs. G.S. 110-141 (as amended by S.L. 2009-451, § 10.46A).

In November 2014, the vast majority of counties (eighty) still operated a single-county department of social services. Twenty counties had established a consolidated human services agency that includes social services.[19] No counties to date have elected to establish a multi-county department.

19. The twenty counties with consolidated human services agencies that provide social services as of November 2014 are Bladen, Brunswick, Buncombe, Cabarrus, Carteret, Dare, Edgecombe, Gaston, Guilford, Haywood, Mecklenburg, Montgomery, Onslow, Pender, Richmond, Rockingham, Swain, Union, Wake, and Yadkin.

Table 39.2 Organization and Governance of County Agencies Providing Social Services (as of November 2014)

	Appointed board as agency governing board	Board of commissioners as agency governing board
Single-county department of social services (80)	76	4
Consolidated human services agency (20)	9	11

Governance

State law requires that the organization providing social services in the county have some type of governing board in place. The governing board may be an appointed board of social services, a consolidated human services board, or the board of county commissioners.

If the organization is a single-county department of social services, the governing board may be either an appointed board of social services or the board of county commissioners. If the county chooses the latter, the board of county commissioners must abolish the county board of social services and assume its powers and duties. In November 2013, of the eighty-four counties that have a single-county department of social services, eighty are governed by an appointed board and four by the board of county commissioners.

Appointed boards of social services may have either three or five members (as determined by the board of county commissioners). Most counties have five-member boards. For a five-member board, two members are appointed by the board of county commissioners, two by the state's Social Services Commission, and the final member by a majority of the other board members.[20] Members must be county residents. A county board of commissioners may select one of its members as an appointee to the social services board, and many boards of commissioners do so to enhance communication between the two bodies. Subject to some exceptions, board members may not serve more than two consecutive terms.[21]

Social services board members do not serve at the pleasure of the appointing authority and cannot be removed from office for political reasons. Moving out of the county in which the member was appointed almost certainly is grounds for removing a board member, and one would expect a member who moves out of the county to resign from the board. Aside from these narrow circumstances, a social services board member probably can be removed only "for cause." Such a removal can be effected only by the appointing authority and only through procedures that protect the board member's due process rights.[22]

If the organization delivering social services is a consolidated human services agency, the governing board may be either a consolidated human services board or the board of county commissioners. Again, in order for the board of county commissioners to serve as the agency's governing board, the board of county commissioners must abolish the consolidated human services board and assume its powers and duties. As of November 2014, of the twenty counties that have a consolidated human services agency, nine are governed by an appointed consolidated human services board and eleven by the board of county commissioners. See Table 39.2, above, for a summary of organization and governance arrangements.

---

20. If a majority do not agree on a fifth member (or if the two appointed members of a three-member board do not agree on a third member), the senior regular resident superior court judge of the county makes the selection. G.S. 108A-3(b).

21. This limitation does not apply to members who were county commissioners at any time during the first two consecutive terms and are serving in that capacity at the time of reappointment. In addition, if a person is appointed during a term to fill a vacancy, service on the board for the remainder of the former member's term does not count as a term for purposes of determining whether the member has served two consecutive terms.

22. For further discussion of removal of board members, see John L. Saxon, *Handbook for County Social Services Boards* (Chapel Hill: UNC School of Government, 2009), 44–45.

Table 39.3 Comparison of Key Features of Appointed Social Services Governing Boards

	Board of Social Services	Consolidated Human Services Board
Size	3 or 5	Up to 25
Appointments	Board of commissioners (1 or 2) State Social Services Commission (1 or 2) Majority of other members (or a judge)	Board of county commissioners from nominees presented by the consolidated human services board
Terms	3 years	4 years
Qualifications	County resident	County resident Board must include representation from several groups and professions • 4 consumers of human services • 10 professionals: a psychologist, pharmacist, engineer, dentist, optometrist, veterinarian, social worker, registered nurse, psychiatrist, and physician • 1 county commissioner • Others, including members of general public Members may serve in more than one role at the same time
Regular meetings	Monthly	Quarterly
Additional meetings	At the call of the chair	At the call of the chair or three members
Compensation	May receive per diem, subsistence, and travel in accordance with county policy	May receive per diem, subsistence, and travel in accordance with county policy

Appointed consolidated human services boards may have up to twenty-five members. All members are appointed by the board of county commissioners from a list of nominees presented by the consolidated board.[23] Unlike the law related to boards of social services, the law related to consolidated human services agencies outlines several specific reasons for which the commissioners may remove a board member, including commission of a felony, violation of a state law governing conflicts of interest, and habitual failure to attend meetings. Some key differences between boards of social services and consolidated human services boards are illustrated in Table 39.3.

If the county enters into an agreement with one or more other counties to create a multi-county social services agency, each county must still appoint a board of social services and those boards must coordinate on governance of the single agency. While an interlocal agreement provides a means to create a multi-county agency, there is no authority in the law for the counties to create a multi-county social services governing board.[24] This approach to governance would likely be cumbersome, which may be one of the reasons that counties have not elected to create these multi-county departments.

23. When a consolidated human services agency is first established, the initial members of the board must be appointed based on the recommendation of a nominating committee comprising members of the governing boards of the agencies that were consolidated. If the new consolidated human services agency includes both public health and social services, a nominating committee drawn from the governing boards in place prior to consolidation would be charged with identifying the preliminary slate of nominees. G.S. 153A-77(c).

24. In contrast, state public health laws permit counties to join multi-county district health departments or public health authorities with a single multi-county governing board. See Chapter 38, "Public Health," for further discussion.

Role of the Governing Boards

All of the different types of social services governing boards have several powers and duties in common, most of which are primarily advisory in nature. Consolidated human services boards have slightly more expansive responsibilities.

The governing board's most significant responsibility relates to the agency director. A county board of social services has the exclusive authority to recruit and select the department director. Implicit in the board's authority to select the director are the authority to discipline or dismiss a director if necessary, in accordance with state personnel rules, and a responsibility to evaluate the director's performance. The social services board determines the director's initial salary and any salary changes in accordance with the State Human Resources Commission's (or, in some cases, the county's) pay and classification plan, subject to the approval of the board of commissioners. In a county with a consolidated human services agency, the county manager is responsible for selecting the agency director, but the manager must seek and obtain the "advice and consent" of the consolidated human services board or, if the consolidated board has been abolished, the board of commissioners.

Another responsibility of the governing board is advising county and municipal authorities regarding policies and plans to improve the community's social conditions. This broad advisory authority indicates that the county social services board has a legitimate function that extends beyond the programs and activities of the county department of social services. Some social services boards are represented on local human services advisory committees or similar bodies that address social problems and conditions in the community. The law requires that the board be represented on the county's Work First planning committee, which is appointed by the board of commissioners to identify the needs of the population to be served by the Work First program and to review and assist in developing the county plan to respond to those needs.

Some other key responsibilities of the governing board include the following:

- *Consulting with the county social services director about problems relating to the director's office.*
- *Assisting the director in planning department budgets.* The extent to which social services boards are actively involved in planning and presenting the department's budget varies from county to county. County social services directors consult with the county social services board on budget matters, and some directors submit the department's proposed budget to the social services board for a formal vote of approval. Some boards actively help the director develop and advocate for the budget. A consolidated human services board is required to play a more proactive role. It must "plan and recommend" the agency's budget.
- *Establishing policies for programs established by G.S. Chapter 108A.* While the law specifically grants this authority to the governing board, the programs are so heavily regulated by federal and state policy already that there is little room for county boards to engage in programmatic policy making.
- *Providing services for a fee.* Under G.S. 108A-10, boards may enter into contracts to provide services for a fee. The fees may not exceed the cost of furnishing the services and must be based on a plan recommended by the county social services director and approved by both the social services governing board and the board of commissioners. A number of counties have adopted fee policies with respect to the social services department's preparation of home studies for the district court's use in child custody disputes between private parties.
- *Carrying out any other duties and responsibilities the General Assembly, the Department of Health and Human Services (DHHS), the state Social Services Commission, or the board of commissioners assigns to the board.* For example, the state Social Services Commission, through its rules, has given social services boards responsibility for reviewing cases involving suspected public assistance fraud. The boards may either review each case individually or adopt a fraud policy and delegate its enforcement to the county social services director and staff.[25]

25. *See, e.g.,* N.C. Admin. Code tit. 10A, ch. 71W, § .0606, which addresses client fraud and intentional program violations in the Work First program.

The duties and authority discussed above apply to the governing board acting as a board, not to its individual members. Another law, G.S. 108A-11, gives board members the right to inspect confidential social services records relating to public assistance and social services. The statute prohibits members from disclosing or making public any information they acquire from the records. Obviously, individuals should exercise this authority only for purposes related to their responsibilities as board members, not for personal reasons.

Role of the Board of County Commissioners

A primary role of the board of commissioners in relation to social services is ensuring the adequacy of funds for social services programs in the county budget. That role is discussed in the section "Financing County Social Services Programs," later in this chapter. The commissioners' other powers and responsibilities include the following:

- *Determining the type of organization that will provide social services in the county.* As discussed above, the county may have a county department of social services or a consolidated human services agency or it may coordinate with other counties to establish a multi-county department.
- *Determining the type of governing board for the organization.* Depending upon the type of organization chosen to provide social services in the county, the governing board may be a county board of social services, a consolidated human services board, or the board of commissioners.
- *In a county that has a board of social services, determining whether the county should have a three- or five-member board, and appointing one or two, respectively, of the members.*[26] Many boards of commissioners appoint one of their own members to serve on the social services board to foster communication and understanding between the two bodies. The board of county commissioners may change the size of the county social services board from three to five members or from five to three members.
- *Establishing per diem rates and policies for subsistence and travel reimbursement for governing board members.*[27] The commissioners should also include funds in the budget to cover these expenses.
- *Approving, along with the county social services board, fees to cover the cost of certain nonmandated services the social services board contracts to provide.*[28] The board of commissioners should receive an annual report from the social services board concerning the receipt of such fees.
- *In a county that has a board of social services, approving the county social services director's salary.*[29] The social services board appoints the director and determines the director's salary based on the State Human Resources Commission's pay classification plan, but the salary must be approved by the board of commissioners. Although the two boards should make every effort to reach agreement, the commissioners, having control over the budget, have the final say in accepting or rejecting the social services board's recommendation.
- *Appointing, with the approval of the governing board, a special attorney for social services matters and determining the attorney's compensation.*[30] A county is not required to have an attorney designated under this section as a special county attorney for social services. If it does, the attorney's duties include serving as legal adviser to and performing duties assigned by the board of commissioners, the director of social services, and the governing board.
- *Determining whether financial assistance for certain disabled persons will be provided under the State–County Special Assistance for Adults program.*[31] State law requires counties to operate this state- and county-funded program, which is designed primarily to subsidize needy aged or disabled persons who live in residential care facilities. The board of commissioners has the option of including in the program certain needy disabled persons who live in their own homes.

26. G.S. 108A-2, -3.
27. G.S. 108A-8.
28. G.S. 108A-10.
29. G.S. 108A-13.
30. G.S. 108A-16 through -18.
31. G.S. 108A-45.

- *Deciding which nonmandated public assistance programs or services the county will provide.*[32] State law requires counties to participate in a number of social services programs but also authorizes counties to "undertake, sponsor, organize, engage in, and support other social services programs intended to further the health, welfare, education, safety, comfort, and convenience of its citizens."[33] Many counties, for example, provide some form of general assistance to help address emergency needs of people not eligible for other benefits.
- *Determining which agency or entity will operate the Child Support Enforcement program in the county.*[34] Counties must administer a Child Support Enforcement program in the county.[35] Most county child support enforcement programs are operated by the county department of social services. The board of commissioners has the option, though, of creating an independent county department for child support enforcement, locating the program in another county department or office, or contracting with a private entity or another county to operate the program.
- *Planning for, or both planning for and administering, the Work First program in the county.* State law allows each board of county commissioners to indicate to the legislature whether the county wants to be a "standard" or "electing" county for purposes of the Work First program. A board's request to be an electing county must be supported by a three-fifths vote by the commissioners. The legislature designates the electing counties. In an electing county, the board of county commissioners is responsible for the development, administration, and implementation of the Work First program. In a standard county, the state retains more control over the program, which is administered by the county department of social services. State law requires each board of county commissioners, regardless of the county's designation, to appoint a committee to identify the needs of the population to be served by Work First and to review and assist in developing a county plan to respond to those needs. The board of commissioners in electing counties assumes many more direct responsibilities related to oversight and administration of the program.[36]

Role of the Social Services Director

Regardless of the type of organization that administers social services programs in a county, someone must be appointed to serve in the role of director of social services. The director administers the public assistance and service programs directly and through the social services staff. In a county with a department of social services, the governing board must appoint a social services director for the department. In a county with a consolidated human services agency, the county manager must appoint a consolidated human services director who in turn assumes all of the powers and duties of a social services director. The consolidated human services director may delegate some or all of these powers and duties to another person, but the consolidated director retains the ultimate responsibility for ensuring that all obligations and functions involving social services programs and policies are carried out.

The person serving in the role of social services director has overarching administrative responsibilities related to running the agency, many of which are found in G.S. 108A-14. In addition, the director has several specific program-related duties that are the subject of other, more detailed, statutes. Two of the director's most significant responsibilities

---

32. G.S. 153A-255.

33. *Id.*

34. G.S. 110-141.

35. Until 2010 about one-third of the counties chose to have the state operate their Child Support Enforcement program. That option was eliminated and now all counties must have their own programs. S.L. 2009-451, § 10.46A(a).

36. In an electing county, the board of county commissioners is responsible for establishing outcome and performance goals, establishing eligibility criteria, making eligibility determinations, entering into mutual responsibility agreements with Work First recipients, ensuring that services and resources are available to help participants comply with the agreements and monitoring compliance with those agreements, ensuring that participants engage in the required hours of work activities, developing and submitting to DHHS a biennial county Work First plan, and developing and implementing an appeals process for the county's Work First program. A board of commissioners may delegate most of these responsibilities to other public or private entities; however, the board remains accountable for all of them. G.S. 108A-27.3(b).

are administering public assistance and social services programs and appointing and supervising department staff. While program administration is the director's responsibility and the director is statutorily identified as the agent of the state with respect to these programs, much of the work is accomplished through delegation of duties to and supervision of the staff. With respect to personnel-related duties, the director has the exclusive authority to hire, supervise, discipline, and dismiss social services employees, but those duties must be carried out in a manner consistent with applicable federal, state, and local personnel laws and policies.[37]

Another general responsibility is the director's role with respect to the governing board. In a county with an appointed board of social services, the director serves as the executive officer of the board and acts as its secretary. The director must provide clerical services to the board and, as its executive officer, implement its policies and decisions. The director is not a member of the board, however, and may attend closed sessions of board meetings only at the board's invitation.

Some of the more specific, programmatic duties are described below.

- *Investigating and responding to reports of child abuse and neglect.* The state Juvenile Code (G.S. Ch. 7B) includes the child abuse reporting law, which requires anyone who suspects that a child is abused, neglected, or dependent, or has died as a result of maltreatment, to make a report to the county director of social services. The law requires the director to make a prompt and thorough assessment of each report, to evaluate the level of risk to the child or to other children in the home, and to take appropriate protective action.
- *Arranging and supervising children's placements in foster care.* Under the Juvenile Code, a district court judge may place abused, neglected, dependent, undisciplined, or delinquent children in the custody of the county department of social services. Many of these children are placed in state-licensed foster homes. County social services departments also may place and supervise children in foster care pursuant to voluntary placement agreements with parents or following the parents' relinquishment of a child for adoption.
- *Investigating adoption cases and supervising adoptive placements.* Under the state adoption law (G.S. Ch. 48), county departments of social services have many responsibilities in relation to the adoption of children. They arrange for and supervise adoptive placements; recruit, screen, and supervise adoptive parents; and evaluate and report to the court on adoption cases.
- *Receiving and responding to reports of abuse, neglect, or exploitation of disabled adults.* Under G.S. Chapter 108A, Article 6, anyone with reasonable cause to believe that a disabled adult needs protective services must make a report to the county director of social services, who must evaluate each report promptly and thoroughly and respond appropriately.
- *Supervising adult care homes for aged or disabled persons.* Under G.S. Chapter 131D, adult care homes must be licensed by DHHS. The county social services director's responsibilities include monitoring implementation of the Adult Care Home Residents' Bill of Rights (G.S. Ch. 131D, Art. 3) and investigating complaints relating to violations of these rights.
- *Serving as guardian for individuals adjudicated incompetent when appointed by the clerk of superior court to do so.*[38]

This list is not exhaustive. Other statutes address the county social services director's duties or authority in such areas as issuing youth employment certificates for individuals under age eighteen,[39] working with the Department of

37. In a county with a department of social services, the employees are subject to the State Human Resources Act as well as any supplemental county personnel policies. In a county with a consolidated human services agency, the board of commissioners may elect to remove the employees from the State Human Resources Act. G.S. 153A-77(d). If it does so, any applicable county personnel ordinances or policies must comply with federal merit personnel standards. 5 C.F.R. Part 900, Subpart F. State and local governments must adhere to the federal standards if they receive certain categories of federal funding, such as funding for the Food and Nutrition Services program.

38. G.S. 35A-1202(4), -1213(d).

39. G.S. 95-25.5.

Correction on certain issues related to prisoners,[40] arranging for the burial or cremation of unclaimed dead bodies,[41] and performing functions specified under local emergency management plans.[42]

Financing County Social Services Programs

More than any other area of local government finance, social services financing is complicated by intricate patterns of federal, state, and county funding. Since the 1930s the federal government has assumed a major role in financing many social services programs. Those programs contribute many federal and state dollars to local economies; they also require the expenditure of substantial county funds. Some county expenditures are required by the General Assembly's assignment to the counties of responsibility for a portion of the nonfederal cost of certain programs. Some are required as a condition of receiving other federal and state funds for social services. Others are required to provide needed, and sometimes mandated, services and programs for which state and federal funds are either unavailable or insufficient.

Some federally funded public assistance programs, such as Food and Nutrition Services (FNS) and Medicaid, are entitlement programs, meaning that benefits must be provided to every person who applies and meets the program's eligibility requirements. The federal government's financial obligation is open-ended. Regardless of how many people qualify for benefits, the federal government must provide funds sufficient to pay the federal share of benefits for everyone entitled to assistance. In FNS, the federal government pays the full cost of the benefits (but only part of the administrative costs). In the Medicaid program, the state's financial obligation also is open-ended, as the state must provide funds sufficient to pay the nonfederal share of the cost of the benefits.

In other programs, such as Work First, the Low-Income Energy Assistance Program, and most service programs, the amount of federal funding is capped. Federal appropriations provide a fixed amount of funding, often called a *block grant.* State or local funds must provide either a specified percentage match or an amount representing a "maintenance of effort" tied to amounts expended or budgeted for the program in a designated prior period. The state must develop comprehensive plans, such as the Work First plan and the Social Services Block Grant plan, describing the proposed use of the federal block grant funds and related state and local funds. The General Assembly is responsible for approving the distribution of federal block grant funds to counties.

If the federal funds and the required state and local contributions are insufficient to provide benefits or services to everyone who is eligible, the state or local government must limit the number of people served by the program, limit the amount of benefits or the level of services provided, or provide additional state or local funding for the program.

Under G.S. 108A-87 the General Assembly has the authority to decide whether and how to divide the nonfederal share of costs for social services programs between the state and counties. North Carolina generally requires counties to pay the bulk of the nonfederal share of administrative costs as well as a significant portion of the cost of social services provided to county residents.

G.S. 108A-90 requires all boards of county commissioners to levy and collect taxes sufficient to meet the county's share of social services expenses. If a county does not pay or arrange for payment of its full share of the costs, the governor is authorized under G.S. 108A-93 to withhold from it any state appropriations for public assistance and related administrative costs or to direct the secretary of revenue and the state treasurer to withhold specified tax revenues owed to the county. Before withholding funds, the governor must notify the chairman of the board of commissioners of the proposed action. While the commissioners must provide funds sufficient to pay a county's formula-determined share of the cost of mandated programs, they have total discretion as to what, if any, county money to budget for non-mandated social services programs.

G.S. 108A-88 requires the state Department of Health and Human Services, by February 15 of each year, to notify the county social services director, the county manager, and the board of county commissioners of the amount of

40. G.S. 148-33.1(f); G.S. 148-4(7).
41. G.S. 130A-415.
42. G.S. 166A-7.

state and federal funds estimated to be available to the county for public assistance and social services programs and related administrative costs for the next fiscal year. The notice states the percentage of county financial participation expected to be required for each program. Periodically, the state revises these estimates to reflect new state budget figures and actions taken by the General Assembly, Congress, and federal agencies. The budget process in the counties must proceed with some uncertainty as to the exact amount of county funds that will be required to fund the counties' share of the cost of mandated programs.

Every county's social services budget contains more than the amounts indicated in the state's estimates. In the services area, for example, federal and state funds available to the county, along with any county match indicated in the state's estimates, may be insufficient to hire the number of social workers necessary to carry out the county's legal responsibility to provide protective services to abused and neglected children. Some state mandates, such as the requirement that a county social services director serve as guardian for incompetent adults when appointed by the court to do so, are not accompanied by state funding. In addition, to meet local needs, counties may operate programs and provide services that are not mandated and that are funded with only county funds.

Programs and Services

Counties are involved in providing a wide range of public assistance programs and social services in their communities. Some of the most significant programs, in terms of funding and individuals served, are described below, but this summary is not exhaustive. Counties are involved with many other programs, services, and populations and, if they identify a particular need in their communities, are authorized to develop and fund additional programs.[43]

Work First

The federal Temporary Assistance to Needy Families (TANF) program is called Work First in North Carolina. Through TANF the federal government provides a set amount of funding (that is, a "block grant") to each state to implement programs intended to support individuals and families who are in need.[44] Work First is both a public assistance program and a social services program. It provides cash assistance as well as assistance with child care, transportation, job searches, and job training. A program participant must sign a personal responsibility contract that describes his or her plan for moving off of the program. Other requirements and restrictions apply, and participants who do not meet their Work First obligations may be subject to sanctions. In October 2014 the state estimated that there were approximately 19,500 active cases in this program, providing assistance to approximately 30,000 individuals.[45]

Every county must administer a Work First program consistent with federal and state requirements.[46] The General Assembly designates each county either a "standard" county or an "electing" county. An electing county has more authority to set eligibility criteria, payment levels, and other program features that the state sets for other (standard) counties. Both electing and standard counties must develop biennial Work First plans and submit them to the Department of Health and Human Services for approval.

Food and Nutrition Services

State law requires every county to operate the federally funded Food and Nutrition Services program (FNS), previously called the "Food Stamp" program. Through this program, the counties are able to issue electronic benefit transfer (debit)

43. This is not an exhaustive list of public assistance and social services programs. For a more detailed discussion of services and programs, see John L. Saxon, *Social Services in North Carolina* (Chapel Hill: UNC School of Government, 2008), 161–201.

44. North Carolina law states that the purpose of the program "is to provide eligible families with short-term assistance to facilitate their movement to self-sufficiency through gainful employment. . . ." G.S. 108A-27.

45. The North Carolina Division of Social Services now captures and reports this data by month. *See Work First Program Evaluation, Work First Active Cases by Month* and *Work First Individuals by Month (Individuals on Active Cases)*, www.ncdhhs.gov/dss/stats/wf.htm.

46. G.S. 108A-25; G.S. Ch. 108A, Part 2.

cards to eligible recipients for the purchase of food products.[47] Basic policies for eligibility are based on income and resource guidelines issued by the U.S. Department of Agriculture. The federal government pays the full cost of food stamp benefits. The federal government pays half of the administrative costs; the counties pay most of the other half. In October 2014 the state reported that there were over 813,000 active cases in this program, providing assistance to more than 1.7 million people.[48]

Medicaid and Health Choice

Medicaid is a public assistance program that covers most of the cost of medical care and services for several categories of people who cannot afford these costs.[49] Those who may receive Medicaid include low-income aged, disabled, or blind persons; needy children and pregnant women; individuals who receive federal Supplemental Security Income (SSI) benefits; and other low-income people who meet eligibility requirements. The federal government pays for approximately 70 percent of the costs of services as well as 50 percent or more of the costs of program administration. North Carolina Health Choice for Children is a public assistance program that provides free or reduced price health care for children in families whose incomes are too high to qualify for Medicaid but are still below 200 percent of the federal poverty guidelines.[50] In December 2013 the state reported that almost 1.6 million individuals were eligible for Medicaid[51] and approximately 150,000 individuals were eligible for Health Choice.[52]

Other Public Assistance Programs

The four programs described above are perhaps the most recognizable public assistance programs in the state. Social services departments are also involved with administering and counties assist in funding several others, such as the

- Child Care Subsidy Program,
- Low-Income Home Energy Assistance Block Grant Programs,
- State-County Special Assistance for Adults Program,
- Foster Care and Adoption Assistance Programs, and
- Refugee Assistance Program.

The legal framework for these and other public assistance programs varies. Some programs are based on federal law, some on state law, and others on a combination of federal and state law.

Child Support Enforcement Program

The Child Support Enforcement program[53] helps locate absent parents for the purpose of obtaining child support and assists in establishing paternity and establishing and enforcing child support obligations.[54] In most counties the program is administered by the county social services department, but in some it is administered by another department of county government or by a contracted provider. Child support agencies are authorized to use a variety of methods, including the interception of state or federal tax refunds, to collect child support. They must seek support on behalf of children

---

47. G.S. 108A-51 through -53.

48. *See* North Carolina Division of Social Services, *FNS Caseload Statistics, Number of Active Cases by Month* and *Number of Individuals on Active Cases by Month*, www.ncdhhs.gov/dss/stats/fsp.htm.

49. G.S. 108A-54 through -70.16.

50. Under the 2014 guidelines, children in a family of four may be eligible if the family earns up to $47,700 annually (200 percent of the federal poverty guidelines for a family of four). The federal poverty guidelines are re-evaluated each year and published in the Federal Register. 79 Fed. Reg. 3593 (Jan. 24, 2014).

51. North Carolina Division of Medical Assistance, *Statistics and Reports, Title XIX Authorized Medicaid Eligibles*, www.ncdhhs.gov/dma/elig/index.htm.

52. North Carolina Division of Medical Assistance, *Statistics and Reports, North Carolina Health Choice for Children*, www.ncdhhs.gov/dma/elig/index.htm.

53. The Child Support Enforcement program is often referred to as the "IV-D" program because it is based on Title IV-D of the Social Security Act.

54. G.S. Ch. 110, Art. 9.

who receive public assistance and also must provide services to anyone else who applies and pays a modest application fee. According to the Division of Social Services, the state program collected $700 million in fiscal year 2013.[55]

Protective Services for Children

State law requires that cases of suspected child abuse, neglect, dependency, and death from maltreatment be reported to the county department of social services. The North Carolina Juvenile Code, which includes the child abuse, neglect, and dependency reporting law, is designed to protect children under age eighteen from neglect and abuse by parents or other caretakers.[56] The Juvenile Code also requires that protective services be provided for any child who either has no parent or caretaker or whose parent is unable to care for the child or make suitable alternative arrangements. When a county department of social services receives a report, it must conduct a prompt assessment and take appropriate action to protect the child. In these cases, the department provides a wide range of treatment and supportive services to children and their families, often while the children remain at home, since one purpose of the law is to keep families intact unless the risk of harm to a child requires the child's removal from the home. Under the Juvenile Code, the department may file a petition in district court seeking either legal custody of a child or some other court order to protect the child.

Permanency Planning Services

Social services policies emphasize the prevention of unnecessary or unduly long foster care placements, viewing them as costly in terms of both money and children's well-being. A permanency planning program that operates in every county aims to provide all children permanent homes, preferably with their own parents, as early as possible. While the emphasis is on keeping children in or returning them to their own homes, there is a complementary emphasis on moving children into long-term plans like adoption or guardianship if returning them to their homes is unlikely. County departments provide preventive services to help families deal with their problems so that children can remain in their own homes as well as reunification services aimed at reuniting children with their families as soon as possible if removal is necessary.

Adoptions

Every county department of social services has an adoption program that includes accepting children for placement, recruiting and screening adoptive parents, and arranging and supervising placements. State adoption law requires that either the county department of social services or a licensed child-placing agency conduct a preplacement assessment of every prospective adoptive home and report to the court on almost every adoptive placement.[57] The state Division of Social Services supervises county adoption programs. State support includes guidelines for services to biological parents, children in need of adoption, and adoptive parents; a central registry for indexing and filing adoption proceedings and protecting adoption records; and an adoption resource exchange.

Protective Services for Adults

If a person has a reasonable cause to believe that a disabled adult may be abused, neglected, or exploited, the person must submit a report to the county department of social services. This reporting law, which is part of the Protection of the Abused, Neglected, or Exploited Disabled Adult Act,[58] is meant to protect persons who are age eighteen or older; physically or mentally incapacitated; and vulnerable to abuse, neglect, or exploitation. When a county department of social services receives a report, it must conduct a prompt assessment and take appropriate action to protect the adult. The state reported that in 2011 almost 20,000 reports were made and almost 9,000 cases required county intervention.

---

55. *See* North Carolina Division of Social Services, *Child Support Services Statistics*, www.ncdhhs.gov/dss/cse/statistics.htm.

56. G.S. Ch. 7B, Subch. I.

57. G.S. Ch. 48. Some exceptions to the requirement for a preplacement assessment exist for relative and stepparent adoptions.

58. G.S. Ch. 108A, Art. 6. See also G.S. Ch. 108A, Art. 6A, Protection of Older and Disabled Adults from Financial Exploitation, added by S.L. 2013-337.

Services to Aged or Disabled Adults

In addition to, and sometimes in conjunction with, the protective services described above, county departments of social services provide a number of services to aged and disabled adults that range from those furnished in the client's own home, to community-based services, to institutional care. Some of these services are required and some are optional; some are supported by federal or state funding or both, but some may be funded entirely by the county.[59] An example of a mandated service is the duty of county departments of social services to conduct regular inspections of adult care homes to ensure their compliance with state licensing requirements and other state laws and regulations concerning the care and treatment of elderly or disabled residents. An example of an optional service is the operation of a senior center that may be partly supported by federal or state funding.[60] While some services and programs are provided by the county department of social services, some jurisdictions have created separate departments of aging or offer services through another department, such as parks and recreation.

Conclusion

Unlike most states, North Carolina continues to call on counties to be the primary deliverers of public social services. North Carolina's arrangement of county administration and state supervision, and the intergovernmental cooperation it requires, generates some special frustrations and problems. But it also results in a statewide social services system that combines general uniformity with some measure of local flexibility and control.

Given the extent of federal involvement in establishing, regulating, and funding social services programs, the system is perhaps the most complex example of federal-state-county interaction. Social services programs in North Carolina will continue to be greatly influenced by changes at the federal level and by federal funding conditions for the many programs for which federal funding is critical. Even apart from federal influences, however, the state and counties must address serious issues regarding how best to meet the needs of children, families, and disadvantaged adults within the limited resources available.

Additional Resources

Mason, Janet. *Reporting Child Abuse and Neglect in North Carolina.* 3rd ed. Chapel Hill: UNC School of Government, 2013.

Saxon, John L. *Handbook for County Social Services Boards.* Chapel Hill: UNC School of Government, 2009.

_____. *Social Services in North Carolina.* Chapel Hill: UNC School of Government, 2008.

---

59. Local governments, both cities and counties, have the authority to "undertake programs for the assistance and care of senior citizens" but they are not required to do so. G.S. 160A-497.

60. The federal Older Americans Act (OAA), enacted in 1965, provides funding to states for a wide range of services for older Americans (aged sixty years or older), including information and referral, case management, transportation, in-home services, home-delivered meals, congregate meals, senior centers, adult day care, nursing home ombudsman and elder abuse programs, legal services, and other home- and community-based supportive services. In order to receive federal funding, a state must designate one or more aging planning and service areas and identify an area agency on aging (AAA) for each service area. While no North Carolina cities or counties are designated as AAAs, many local governments do receive federal OAA funding to provide congregate or home-delivered meals, in-home services, transportation, or other social or supportive services to senior citizens. A list of the state's AAAs and the counties served by each is available at www.ncdhhs.gov/aging/aaafile.htm#A.

About the Author

Aimee N. Wall is a School of Government faculty member who specializes in social services law, animal control law, and legislative education.

This chapter updates and revises previous chapters authored by Janet Mason and John Saxon, whose contributions to the field and to this publication are gratefully acknowledged.

Chapter 40

Mental Health Services

Mark F. Botts

In North Carolina, public mental health, developmental disabilities, and substance abuse services are a shared responsibility of state and local government in partnership with private enterprise. State and local government play very distinct roles. State government appropriates the vast majority of funds spent on public services from state and federal revenue and, consequently, is the primary policymaker, determining what kinds of services are to be provided and how they will be delivered. But, while the state operates some regionally based mental health, developmental disabilities, and substance abuse (MH/DD/SA) facilities, public services are delivered primarily on the community level through private service providers contracting with local government *area authorities* (the short term used for area mental health, developmental disabilities, and substance abuse authorities). Using the state and federal resources appropriated to them by state government, area authorities authorize, pay for, manage, and monitor services provided by their network of private contractors.

County governments also provide an important but relatively small amount of funding and play a role in establishing area authorities and appointing their governing boards. The area authority is the governance and administrative structure available to counties for carrying out their legal responsibility to provide publicly funded mental health, developmental disabilities, and substance abuse services to their citizens. This chapter discusses the functions of area authorities, their governing structure, and their relationship to county and state government. It also describes the populations served by area authorities and the primary sources of revenue used to pay for services.

Historical Perspective

Development and Evolution of the Public Role

Only in the last half century has local government in North Carolina adopted a significant treatment role in mental health care. In the eighteenth and nineteenth centuries, county governments sometimes confined persons with mental disabilities in poorhouses or jails, but this was solely a custodial function undertaken to protect property or public safety from the dangers, real or perceived, posed by persons believed to be possessed by demons. Confinement for curative or treatment purposes did not begin until 1856, when the General Assembly, concerned about the abuse and neglect endured by persons indefinitely confined in local facilities and influenced by the emerging belief that mental disabilities could be cured if treated in the right environment, opened Dorothea Dix Hospital in Raleigh, the first "State Hospital for the Insane." By 1914, North Carolina had opened two more state hospitals and a state facility for persons with "mental retardation." Due to the limited capacity of state institutions, however, many people with mental disabilities languished in local poorhouses and jails.

During the first half of the twentieth century, state government continued to take primary responsibility for mental health services. Nevertheless, there was growing interest in the development of local mental health care facilities that could intervene with preventive treatment before confinement in a state institution was necessary. Charlotte and Winston-Salem, in the forefront of this movement, each established a local mental health clinic in the 1930s. But most counties did not have the financial resources or substantive expertise to develop mental health clinics. Federal funding spurred further development of community-based services when Congress passed the National Mental Health Act in 1946.[1] By 1959, North Carolina had utilized this funding to establish eleven community mental health clinics and psychiatric services in eight county departments of health.

Despite the federal incentives to develop community-based mental health care, North Carolina continued to focus on state-operated institutions, spending money to improve existing state facilities and adding a fourth mental hospital in 1947 and three more "mental retardation centers" between 1958 and 1963.[2] Ironically, this expansion occurred during a period of increasing dissatisfaction—both in North Carolina and in the rest of the nation—with the institutional model of care, which relied on prolonged or permanent confinement of persons with mental illness or developmental disability in huge, crowded institutions. Revelations of inhumane treatment at some state institutions, advocacy for community-based services by parents of children with developmental disabilities, and new drug therapies for mental illness contributed to a national movement to reduce the traditional emphasis on state institutions in favor of community-based services intended to fulfill the institutional functions of treatment, rehabilitation, medical care, nutrition, recreation, social contact, and social control, without excessive restrictions on personal liberty.

The watershed event in the movement to reform mental health care came in 1963, when President Kennedy proposed[3] and Congress passed the Community Mental Health Centers Act (CMHCA),[4] which authorized federal funding for the construction of community mental health clinics. The level of funding available provided a powerful incentive to states to implement federal mental health policy, a policy that emphasized the responsibility of communities and local governments. The North Carolina General Assembly responded immediately by authorizing local communities to establish and operate mental health clinics as a joint undertaking with state government in which the state would develop a plan for establishing community outpatient clinics, administer federal grants, set standards for clinic operations, and appropriate state funds for community services.[5]

---

1. Pub. L. No. 487, 60 Stat. 421 (1946).

2. Formerly called "mental retardation centers," North Carolina's three state-operated "developmental centers" serve people who have a diagnosis of intellectual or developmental disability.

3. John F. Kennedy, *President's Messages: Mental Illness and Mental Retardation*, H.R. Doc. No. 58, at 1468 (1963). 109 Cong. Rec. 1744.

4. Title II of Pub. L. No. 88-164 (1963).

5. 1963 N.C. Sess. Laws ch. 1166; former Sections 122-35.1 through -35.12 of the North Carolina General Statues (hereinafter G.S.).

Table 40.1 Number and Percentage of Persons Served by Community Mental Health Programs and State Institutions in North Carolina, Fiscal Years 1960–61 to 2012–13

	Persons Receiving Institutional Care		Persons Receiving Community-Based Care		Total Persons Served
Fiscal Year	Number	Percentage of total	Number	Percentage of total	Number
1960–61	23,327	74	8,196	26	31,523
1970–71	30,019	32	63,791	68	93,810
1980–81	25,658	13	171,712	87	197,370
1993–94	21,825	9	225,167	91	246,992
2004–05	24,840	7	330,083	93	354,923
2012–13	10,638	3	333,214	97	343,852

Note: The figures for state-operated institutions include psychiatric hospitals, developmental centers, alcohol and drug abuse centers, specialized nursing facilities, and residential programs for children. The 2004–05 figure for community-based care is an unduplicated headcount, whereas that year's figure for institutional care is a "duplicated headcount," meaning that it includes people who were counted more than once if they had more than one distinct admission event. The duplicated headcount for community services is 337,676 in 2004–05.

Sources: Data for fiscal years 1960-61, 1970-71, and 1980-81 derived from the *Strategic Plan 1983–1989*, Vol. I, Quality Assurance Section, N.C. Division of Mental Health, Mental Retardation, and Substance Abuse Services (Raleigh, N.C.: NCDMHMRSAS, 1981), 39. Fiscal year 1993-94 figures from Deborah Merrill, Data Support Branch, N.C. Division of Mental Health, Developmental Disabilities, and Substance Abuse Services, memorandum to author, 8 December 1994. Data for fiscal year 2004-05 from *Transformation: A Commitment to Make a Difference*, Annual Report for the North Carolina Division of Mental Health, Developmental Disabilities, and Substance Abuse Services (Raleigh, N.C.: NCDMHDDSAS, 2005). Data for fiscal year 2012–13 from North Carolina Local Management Entity, Annual Statistics and Admission Report, Fiscal Year 2013, www.ncdhhs.gov/mhddsas/statspublications/Reports/Financialandstatisticalreports/Statisticalreports/areaprograms/2013lme-annualreport.pdf.

In the two decades that followed the passage of the CMHCA, Congress enacted a series of laws that expanded federal support to include funding for clinic staff and operations, ensuring that federal appropriations would continue to influence the development of mental health care at the state and local level. In North Carolina, as in other states, federal policy achieved the dual goal of reducing the proportion of mental health patients receiving treatment in state hospitals while expanding the number of persons receiving mental health services in the community. By 1980, 740 federally funded community mental health centers were serving areas comprising roughly one-half of the nation, and approximately 3 million persons received services annually. The number of inpatients in state mental hospitals across the nation, which had peaked at 560,000 in 1955, decreased to 160,000 in 1977 and to about 120,000 in 1986, a decline of almost 80 percent since 1955.[6]

North Carolina's experience matched the national trend, as the percentage of public-sector MH/DD/SA clients served by state institutions declined dramatically between 1961 and 1981, from 74 to 13 percent of the total persons served. By fiscal year 2004–05, state-operated psychiatric hospitals, developmental centers, alcohol and drug treatment centers, and other institutions accounted for only 7 percent of admissions to the public-sector system, with the remainder of admissions, 93 percent, occurring at community-based facilities (see Table 40.1). During this period, the relative decline in institutional care, however, appears related more to the dramatic increase in the number of persons served by community programs—from 8,196 in 1961 to 330,083 in 2005—than to any decrease in the actual number of persons served at state institutions, as state institutional admissions held steady with 24,840 persons served in 2005 compared to 23,327 in 1961. The greatest legacy of the development of community-based services, therefore, is not so

6. Rebecca T. Craig and Barbara Wright, *Mental Health Financing and Programming* (National Conference of State Legislatures, 1988): 7. Other factors contributing to the deinstitutionalization included legal decisions restricting the involuntary commitment of persons to psychiatric hospitals and federal funding policies that motivated the transfer of some patients to Medicaid-supported nursing homes.

much the deinstitutionalization of disabled individuals as it is the expansion of services to populations not previously served.

Since 2005, however, there has been an actual decline in the number of persons served by all of the state-operated institutions combined, from 24,840 persons served in 2005 to 10,638 persons receiving institutional care in 2013.[7] This decrease in institutional care is largely due to a deliberate policy decision of state government to decrease inpatient psychiatric services at the three state-operated hospitals since 2004. As a consequence, the total number of persons served at the state-operated psychiatric hospitals decreased 77 percent, from 16,987 in fiscal year 2004 to 3,964 in fiscal year 2013. Because the number of people receiving community-based care increased only slightly during this period, from 330,083 to 333,214, the more significant decrease in institutional care meant a drop in the total number of persons receiving care, from 354,923 to 343,852.

Although the federal government repealed the CMHCA in 1981,[8] the current structure of North Carolina's public MH/DD/SA service system—local governmental entities created specifically for the purpose of ensuring the coordination and delivery of community-based services pursuant to state policy, oversight, and financial support—is founded upon a vision of the community as the locus of care, the original goal of the CMHCA and its legislative progeny. One feature of the system—the central role of local government—remains unaltered since the 1977 General Assembly required counties to establish, either singly or jointly with other counties, local government agencies (area authorities) responsible for managing community-based services and accountable to a locally appointed governing board.[9]

Mental Health Reform

Although area authorities continue to be responsible for the delivery of publicly funded, community-based services, the functions of these governments changed significantly with the 2001 Act to Phase In Implementation of Mental Health System Reform at the State and Local Level.[10] Before this legislative enactment, area authorities were permitted to provide services directly to clients using their own staff, or they could contract with other persons, organizations, or agencies to provide services to clients. Every area authority utilized both means of service provision, and most area authorities employed a large number of personnel with either clinical or case management skills who were devoted to providing services directly to clients. The 2001 mental health system reform act barred area authorities from directly providing services to those in need and, instead, required area authorities to use contracted providers. Services were privatized, and the area authority became responsible for assessing the needs of its geographic *catchment area* (the geographic area served), developing a provider network that could meet those needs through the provision of an array of services, creating a system for clients to access those services, authorizing and paying for services, and monitoring service quality and effectiveness.

To mark this change in function and organizational identity—from a service provider in direct contact with clients to a manager, monitor, and, sometimes, payer of services provided by others—most people affiliated with the public system at the time, including policy makers and administrators, began to use *local management entity* (LME) to refer to an area authority. This term, and the functions it denotes, remained uncodified until the 2006 General Assembly enacted S.L. 2006-142 (H 2077),[11] which defined "local management entity"[12] and described the local management

7. The use of the term "institutional care" when discussing these figures includes only those receiving services in state-operated institutions. For example, many public MH/DD/SA clients receive inpatient psychiatric care from other public and private hospitals. Those admissions are not included in these figures and, therefore, these figures do not include that institutional care.

8. The Omnibus Budget and Reconciliation Act of 1981, Pub. L. No. 97-35, Title IX § 901, 42 U.S.C. § 300x.

9. 1977 N.C. Sess. Laws ch. 568; former G.S. 122-35.35 through -35.57.

10. S.L. 2001-437.

11. This same legislation directed the North Carolina Department of Health and Human Services to develop performance measures for LME functions related to service access, consumer outcomes, individualized service planning, promotion of best practices, system efficiency and effectiveness, quality management, and prevention and early intervention. In some ways, these performance measures foreshadowed today's more extensive data collection and reporting requirements under the state's Medicaid managed care waiver.

12. G.S. 122C-3(20b).

entity functions that area authorities must perform.[13] These functions are a feature of today's service system and are discussed in more detail below in the section entitled "Today's Area Authority."

The 2001 mental health system reform act also did a number of other things. It required the consolidation of the thirty-nine existing area authorities into twenty authorities by January 1, 2007. In an attempt to solicit greater involvement of county government in area authority affairs, the law required the counties served by an area authority to jointly develop, review, and approve an "LME business plan" for the management and delivery of mental health, developmental disabilities, and substance abuse services.[14] The 2001 mental health system reform act also expanded the kinds of administrative units or structures that counties could create to carry out local government functions related to MH/DD/SA services, granting counties the authority to create units of local government that were alternatives to the area authority. Finally, with policy initiated in tandem with mental health reform but not codified until 2006, the state required area authorities to involve consumers and family members of consumers in the governance and management of the public system by establishing consumer and family advisory committees (CFACs) to advise the area authority boards.[15]

Some of the reforms discussed above have gone by the wayside, and some continue to trend forward beyond their original goals. Today, the area authority functions associated with managing care have grown to include substantial new responsibilities; the consolidation of area authorities into fewer entities covering larger geographic areas continues (see Figure 40.1); many of the legislative mechanisms that provided for greater county involvement have been deleted from the statutory law; the organizational alternatives to area authorities have all been eliminated; and consumer and family involvement has grown beyond CFACs to include representation by consumers and family members on the governing body. Most of these recent developments can be attributed to another major step in the evolution, or ongoing reform, of North Carolina's MH/DD/SA service system—one that embraces the concept of "managed care."

It should be noted for purposes of understanding the movement to managed care that area authorities initially did not have the authority to implement all LME functions with respect to most services. Under mental health reform, area authorities were required to perform these functions with respect to services paid for with state appropriations from state revenue sources (non-Medicaid state appropriations), but they did not have the authority to fully perform these functions with respect to Medicaid-funded services because Medicaid funds did not pass through the LME. While LMEs were required to contract with providers for Medicaid-paid MH/DD/SA services, those providers dealt directly with the Department of Health and Human Services' Division of Medical Assistance, or its contracted vendor, to obtain authorization to provide services, submit claims for reimbursement, and receive payment for the services provided. Because state government was the fiscal agent for Medicaid funds and LMEs did not have the authority to approve or deny the expenditure of Medicaid money for those services, LMEs could not adequately exercise the LME functions of utilization management and review,[16] care coordination,[17] and financial management and accountability.[18] The movement to managed care, described below, involves moving responsibility for managing the quality and cost of care for all services, including those paid for with Medicaid funds, from state government to the area authorities.

---

13. G.S. 122C-115.4.

14. *See* G.S. 122C-115.2. The 2001 legislation and some of the factors precipitating its adoption are described in greater detail in Mark F. Botts, "2001 Legislation Affecting Mental Health, Developmental Disabilities, and Substance Abuse Services," *Mental Health Law Bulletin* No. 7 (March 2002).

15. The terms "consumer" and "client" are used interchangeably throughout this chapter, as they are in the General Statutes, to refer to a person receiving services through an area authority.

16. Utilization management and review involves approving a service plan and periodically reviewing it to determine that the level and intensity of services is appropriate to meet the need.

17. Care coordination involves monitoring the effectiveness of services to determine that neither too little nor too much service is being provided to achieve the desired results.

18. Financial management and accountability involves controlling costs by limiting the expenditure of public funds to those services that the provider has demonstrated, through the LME's utilization management and care coordination, to have a sound clinical basis.

Figure 40.1 Area Mental Health, Developmental Disabilities, and Substance Abuse Authorities in North Carolina (Local Management Entities/Managed Care Organizations)

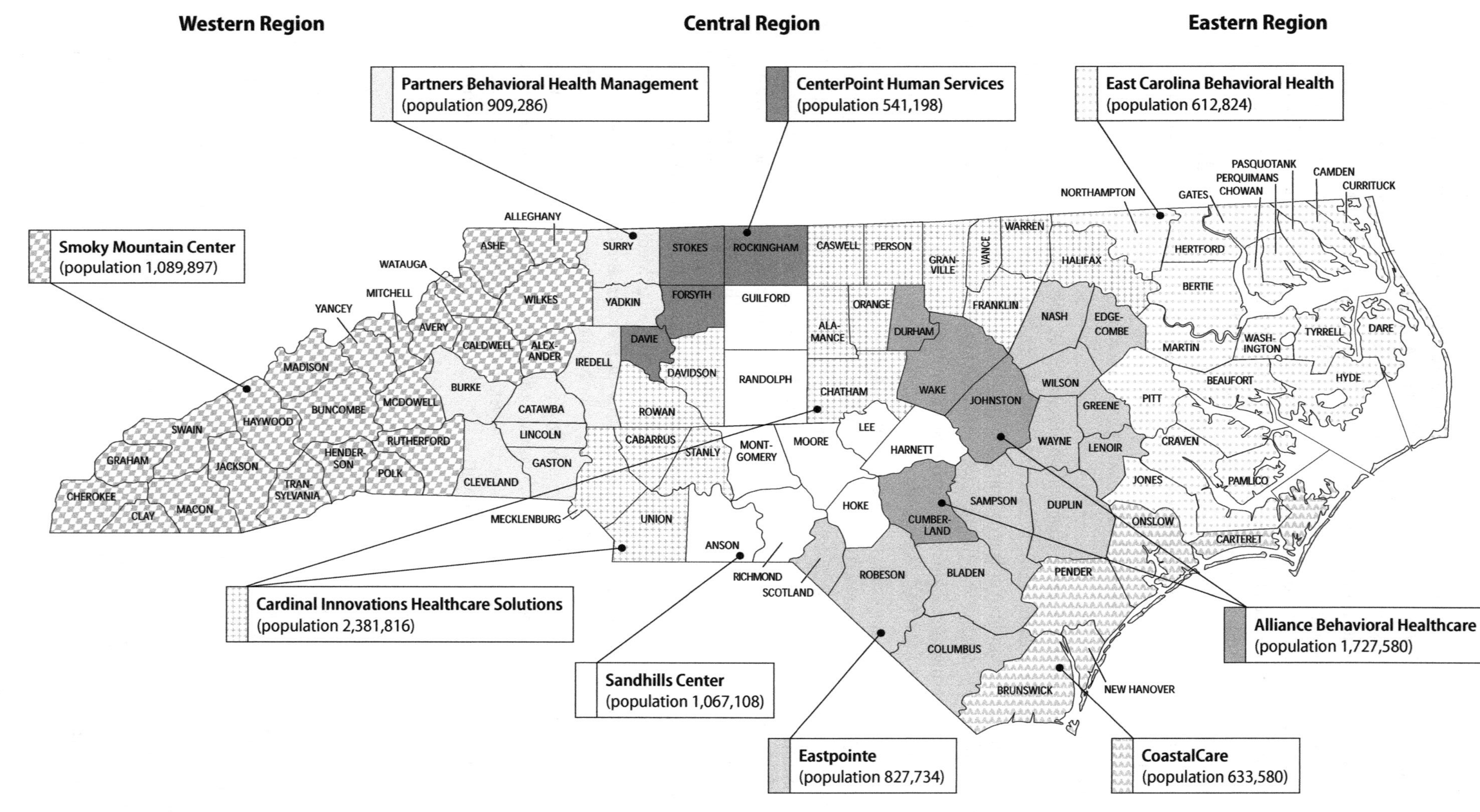

Figure 40.2 LME Revenue Trends

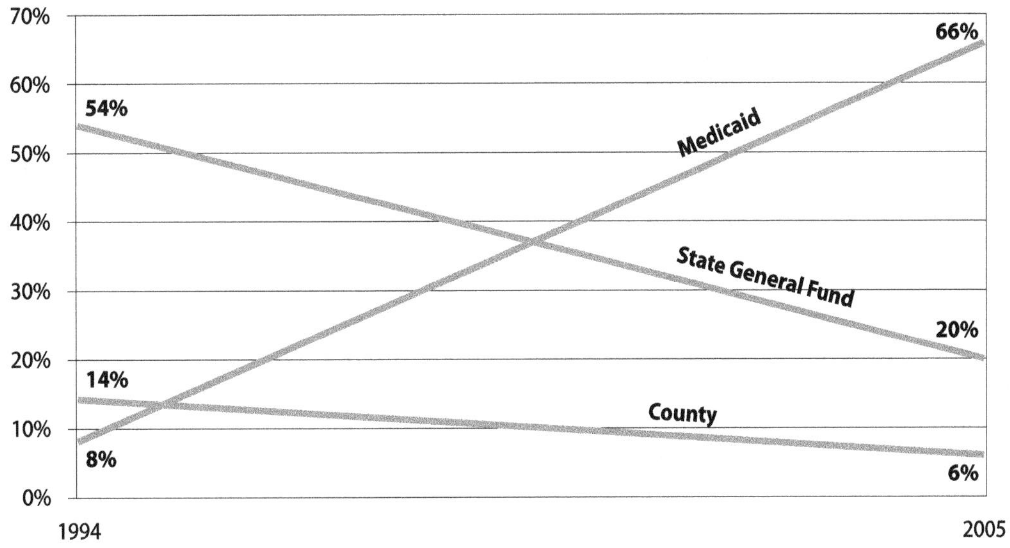

Medicaid Managed Care

The movement to managed care for MH/DD/SA services was precipitated by the confluence of at least three factors. One was the mental health reform act of 2001, which charged area authorities with service management functions that were, in essence, a nascent form of managed care for services funded by non-Medicaid state appropriations.

A second factor has been the rising cost of Medicaid programs nationally and a desire by state legislatures, including the North Carolina General Assembly, to control escalating costs.[19] In 1986, Medicaid ranked lower nationally than state and local governments, private insurance, and patients as payers for mental health care. Today, Medicaid is the largest payer of mental health care, more than any other private or public source of funding. In North Carolina, Medicaid, which was the smallest source of area authority revenue twenty years ago, is now the largest (see Figure 40.2). Because Medicaid is the largest single source of revenue for community-based MH/DD/SA services, policymakers who seek to deal with the rising cost of care look to Medicaid policy.

States have a variety of tools at their disposal to control Medicaid costs, including reducing provider reimbursement rates, changing the eligibility criteria for Medicaid services, and limiting the services paid for by Medicaid. Another tool is managed care, which is really a set of processes and techniques used by an entity responsible for care to control or influence the quality, accessibility, utilization, costs, or outcomes of services provided to a defined enrollee population.

A third factor is a North Carolina demonstration project in managed care that the state was able to look to for a possible statewide model for controlling the quality and costs of care. In 2005, the federal Centers for Medicaid and Medicare Services (CMS) granted the Piedmont Behavioral Healthcare (PBH) area authority, through the state's Department of Health and Human Services (DHHS), the authority to administer and manage a "1915 (b)/(c) Medicaid Waiver"[20] as a pilot project for the delivery of publicly funded MH/DD/SA services. At the time, PBH, now Cardinal Innovations, served Cabarrus, Davidson, Rowan, Stanly, and Union counties, and the demonstration project applied to those five counties.

---

19. A major driver of increasing Medicaid expenditures is long-term care for the elderly in nursing homes. For more information on the escalating cost of Medicaid nationally and in North Carolina, see Christine Kushner, "Medicaid and North Carolina's Aging Population, *North Carolina Insight* 23, no. 2 (N.C. Center for Public Policy Research, Raleigh, N.C., January, 2010).

20. The term "1915 (b)/(c) Medicaid Waiver" refers to two sections of the Social Security Act that allow states to apply for waivers from certain federal Medicaid regulations. The "(b) Waiver" allows Medicaid beneficiaries to enroll in managed care plans and allows the state to limit the provider network based upon the needs of recipients. The "(c) Waiver" permits a state to furnish an array of home and community-based services that assist Medicaid beneficiaries in continuing to live in the community and avoiding institutionalization.

The term "waiver" refers to the federal government waiving, at the state's request, certain federal rules that normally apply to Medicaid so that the state can implement a Medicaid system with certain features that would not be allowed under the regular Medicaid rules. For example, under the PBH demonstration project, all Medicaid-eligible beneficiaries who sought MH/DD/SA services had to use PBH-contracted providers and did not have the freedom to choose providers outside of the PBH network. This was permissible only because the normal patient freedom of choice rule was waived.

In addition, in order for PBH to control the quality and cost of care—in order to fully perform the *managed care* functions of service authorization, utilization management and review, care coordination, and financial management and accountability—all Medicaid funds for MH/DD/SA services in the PBH catchment area were appropriated directly to PBH. Providers looked to PBH, not the state, for service approval and payment, and PBH was required to manage care and funding so that the allocated funds would be sufficient to meet the needs of its catchment area. PBH had the authority to review applications for care and determine whether it would authorize the expenditure of Medicaid funds for the services sought, and if services were authorized, PBH would review the appropriateness and effectiveness of services over time to ensure that Medicaid money was being expended for services that were effective at achieving identified client outcomes. This contrasted with the fee-for-service system that other area authorities were operating under, where providers of services to area authority clients would seek service authorization from, and submit claims for reimbursement directly to, the state's Division of Medical Assistance (DMA).

The waiver of Medicaid rules for the PBH area authority allowed the state to test whether an area authority, if it controlled the funding for care and was permitted a certain level of control over provider behavior and patient choice through managed care techniques, could control both the quality and cost of care. Within a few years, PBH had begun to do so. In 2010 and 2011, it served a greater proportion of those in need, exceeding the state average for percentage of persons served, and it did so in every age and disability category.[21] And beginning in 2008, there was a substantial difference in the average expenditures for care, with expenditures remaining relatively stable at PBH while expenditures soared across the rest of the state.[22]

Based on the success of the PBH program at holding down Medicaid costs compared to other area authorities, in 2009, DHHS recommended that its Division of Medical Assistance and its Division of Mental Health, Developmental Disabilities, and Substance Abuse Services develop a 1915 (b)/(c) Medicaid Wavier application, similar to PBH's, for submission to CMS that would permit North Carolina to expand the PBH model to other parts of the state.[23] The state's proposed model would allow for managed care contracts between DMA and each area authority that would place responsibility for containing costs and improving quality and efficiency on the area authorities, which would be financially at risk if they failed to adequately achieve contract performance goals through the application of a host of managed care functions.

North Carolina was granted authority to expand its Medicaid Waiver in 2010, and at first, the state permitted area authorities to voluntarily choose to apply for DHHS approval to operate under the waiver. That changed in 2011, when the General Assembly enacted a law requiring all area authorities to implement the "1915(b)/(c) Managed Care Waiver" by July 1, 2013.[24] The 2011 law seeks to establish a system that is capable of managing all public resources available

---

21. *See* N.C. Division of Mental Health, Developmental Disabilities and Substance Abuse Services, *The PBH Managed Care Experience: A Comparison to Non-Managed Care Local Managed Entities* (December 1, 2011), www.ncdhhs.gov/mhddsas/statspublications/Reports/DivisionInitiativeReports/LME-MCOPerfReports/PBHExperience2011-12.pdf.

22. The rise of expenses in the rest of the state was due primarily to expenses associated with Community Support Services. PBH reports that it was able to manage and limit these services using managed care tools that other LMEs did not have because they were not operating under the Medicaid managed care waiver.

23. This Wavier Amendment was submitted to CMS on December 16, 2009.

24. S.L. 2011-264. North Carolina's managed care waiver, authorized by § 1915(b) of the Social Security Act, is called the North Carolina Mental Health, Intellectual and Developmental Disabilities and Substance Abuse Services Health Plan. North Carolina's Medicaid Home and Community-Based Services (HCBS) waiver program is authorized in § 1915(c) of the Social Security Act. This program is called North Carolina Innovations, or the Innovations waiver. The North Carolina Innovations waiver targets individuals who meet the ICF-IID eligibility criteria as defined in the State Medicaid Agency's Clinical Coverage Policy, which is located on the DHHS Division of Medical Assistance website at www.ncdhhs.gov/dma/.

for mental health, intellectual and other developmental disabilities, and substance abuse services, including federal block grant funds, federal funding for Medicaid and Health Choice, and all other public funding sources. Through the 2011 law and succeeding legislation, the General Assembly has required North Carolina's area authorities to operate as *managed care organizations* for publicly funded, community-based MH/DD/SA services under the direction and supervision of DHHS.

The State's Role in Community Services

The primary state government actors in the mental health, developmental disabilities, and substance abuse (MH/DD/SA) services arena are the North Carolina Department of Health and Human Services (DHHS); the North Carolina General Assembly; and the Commission for Mental Health, Developmental Disabilities, and Substance Abuse Services, a rulemaking body of DHHS. In general, the General Assembly makes policy by enacting legislation, and the executive branch of state government—in this case, DHHS—implements and administers the legislative policy. But DHHS and the commission also make policy by adopting rules that have the force and effect of law. The General Assembly has authorized the secretary of DHHS and the commission to adopt rules governing numerous matters relating to the delivery of MH/DD/SA services[25] and has charged the secretary with enforcing the rules and legislation governing community-based, publicly funded mental health, developmental disabilities, and substance abuse services.

Policymaking

In 2011, the North Carolina General Assembly directed DHHS to expand the PBH Medicaid Waiver demonstration program to all area authorities by July 1, 2013.[26] Among other things, the General Assembly directed DHHS to establish a system for managing all public funds for MH/DD/SA services that used managed care strategies, such as care coordination and utilization review, to reduce the trend of escalating costs in the state Medicaid program and to ensure easy access to medically necessary care provided at a level of intensity appropriate to a client's assessed need. Significantly, the General Assembly directed DHHS to vest these responsibilities in the state's area authorities—public entities that were uniquely positioned, if not adequately prepared, to carry out these functions. (The local management entity (LME) functions that area authorities were already performing were similar to, if not as complex as, Medicaid managed care functions.) Accordingly, the General Assembly directed DHHS to require all LMEs to operate a 1915(b)/(c) Medicaid Waiver or merge with an LME that was approved by DHHS to operate the Medicaid Waiver.

The kinds of bodies utilized by the General Assembly to develop MH/DD/SA policy have varied over the years. In 2000, the General Assembly created the Joint Legislative Oversight Committee (LOC) on Mental Health, Developmental Disabilities, and Substance Abuse Services and charged it with developing a plan to reorganize the public system of mental health, developmental disabilities, and substance abuse services based on recommendations of the state auditor.[27] After much study and deliberation by its subcommittees, the LOC on MH/DD/SA services introduced a mental health reform bill that addressed, among other things, such issues as the governance of the local service systems, the quality of services, and consumer and family involvement in oversight of the system. The bill ultimately adopted by the General Assembly is known as the mental health system reform act of 2001.[28] In 2006, the LOC recommended and the General Assembly adopted legislation modifying the 2001 act, including changes to clarify the respective powers and duties of state and local government with regard to public services.

In 2011, the General Assembly restructured legislative committees and consolidated the duties of the Joint LOC on MH/DD/SA Services, the North Carolina Study Commission on Aging, the Joint Legislative Health Care Oversight Committee, and the Public Health Study Commission into one body, the Joint Legislative Oversight Committee on

25. G.S. 122C-112.1; G.S. 143B-147 through -150; G.S. 122C-114.
26. S.L. 2011-264.
27. S.L. 2000-83.
28. S.L. 2001-437.

Health and Human Services.[29] This body, composed of eleven members appointed by the Senate and eleven by the House of Representatives, is charged with examining on a continuing basis statewide issues affecting the development, budgeting, financing, administration, and delivery of health and human services. In 2012, the General Assembly directed this body to appoint a Subcommittee on Mental Health to examine the state's delivery of mental health, developmental disabilities, and substance abuse services.[30] This is the current legislative body where most policy review and development related to MH/DD/SA services is initiated, and it is this body, through the Joint Legislative Oversight Committee on Health and Human Services, that makes legislative recommendations to the General Assembly.

Administration

The Department of Health and Human Services, through its Division of MH/DD/SA Services and its Division of Medical Assistance (DMA), is the state agency responsible for administering and enforcing state statutes and regulations governing the funding and operation of area authorities.[31] DHHS allocates federal and state funds appropriated by the General Assembly for community services, enforces requirements for federal aid, and adopts and enforces rules governing the expenditure of area authority funds.

DHHS administers state and federal funding for community services through the application of two contracts that incorporate statutory and regulatory law and add other requirements. One, a contract between each area authority and the Division of MH/DD/SA Services (the DMHDDSAS contract), governs the expenditure of non-Medicaid state appropriations from the state general fund and federal block grants. Another, a contract between each area authority and DMA (the DMA contract), governs the expenditure of state Medicaid funds and is the primary means used by DHHS to restructure area authority "management responsibilities" through "the 1915(b)/(c) Medicaid Waiver."[32] Each of these contracts addresses numerous and specific "management functions"[33] that area authorities must perform to receive funding. These functions include the collecting and reporting of data relating to the functions themselves so that the area authority and the state can determine whether the area authority is meeting the state's "performance expectations."[34]

Pursuant to the DMA and DMHDDSAS contracts, area authorities are required to collect and report to DHHS specified data intended to measure the effectiveness of care, access to and availability of services, patient and provider satisfaction, use of services, treatment prevalence (the percentage of persons estimated to be in need of services who actually receive services), timely initiation and continued engagement in services, the extent of follow-up care after patient discharge from inpatient facilities, and the utilization of crisis and inpatient services.[35] Some of this data, both in the aggregate for a statewide view and separated by area authority for purposes of assessing each area authority's individual performance, is published and available to the public.[36] Pursuant to the area authority's contracts with DHHS, the state must use the foregoing data to evaluate the performance of each of the area authority's management functions. (These functions are discussed under "Agency Functions" in the section of this chapter entitled "Today's Area Authority.")

In 2013, the General Assembly enhanced the DHHS secretary's enforcement authority by requiring the secretary to certify, every six months, that each area authority has met certain contract performance expectations.[37] If the secretary

29. S.L. 2011-191.

30. S.L. 2012-142, sec. 10.11, as amended by S.L. 2012-145, sec. 3.4.

31. G.S. Ch. 143B; G.S. 122C-111 and -112.1.

32. S.L. 2011-264.

33. Generally, the DMHDDSAS contract governs local management entity functions and the DMA contract governs managed care organization functions.

34. *See* DMA and DMHDDSAS contracts and G.S. 122C-124.2.

35. These reporting requirements are set forth in the *North Carolina LME/MCO Performance Measurement and Reporting Guide*, DMA and DMHDDSAS, September 17, 2013.

36. See *MH/DD/SAS Community Systems Progress Report*, prepared quarterly by the Quality Management Team, Community Policy Section, Division of Mental Health, Developmental Disabilities, and Substance Abuse Services, available on the DMHDDSAS website at www.ncdhhs.gov/mhddsas/statspublications/Reports/DivisionInitiativeReports/communitysystems/index.htm.

37. S.L. 2013-85.

does not certify that an area authority has made (1) adequate provision against the risk of insolvency with respect to funding for Medicaid enrollees,[38] (2) timely provider payments,[39] and (3) an adequate exchange of information (billing, payment, and other transaction data) with DHHS and the area authority's contracted providers, then DHHS must reassign the area authority's DMA contract responsibilities to another area authority and move to dissolve the noncompliant area authority. If at any time an area authority is not in compliance with other DHHS contract requirements, then the secretary must notify the area authority in writing, allow the area authority thirty days to demonstrate compliance, and reconsider its initial determination. If the area authority remains out of compliance, the secretary must allow the area authority thirty days to negotiate a merger with another area authority and, if such negotiations are not successful, the secretary must assign the area authority's contract responsibilities, and oversee the transfer of its operations, to another area authority.

Finally, for some inpatient and residential services, area authorities rely upon regionally based facilities operated by the DHHS Division of State Operated Healthcare Facilities. The division operates three alcohol and drug treatment centers, three psychiatric hospitals, three developmental centers for persons with intellectual and developmental disabilities, two residential programs for children with serious emotional and behavioral disorders, and three neuro-medical centers for people with mental illness or developmental disabilities who have significant or long-term medical conditions.

Rulemaking

The Commission for Mental Health, Developmental Disabilities, and Substance Abuse Services is a state body authorized to adopt, amend, and repeal rules governing the delivery of mental health, developmental disabilities, and substance abuse services.[40] Appointed by the governor and the General Assembly, the thirty-two-member commission is made up of persons with knowledge and expertise in these services, including professionals in the field and consumers or immediate family members of consumers of services. Commission rules govern the operation of area authorities and their contract agencies, the admission of individuals to state-operated facilities, and the licensing of public and private facilities that provide mental health, developmental disabilities, and substance abuse services. The commission has the authority to adopt rules establishing a process for non-Medicaid eligible clients to appeal area authority decisions affecting their care and to generally advise the secretary of DHHS on mental health, developmental disabilities, and substance abuse services. Finally, statutory law specifically requires the commission to adopt rules governing the development of a process for screening, triage, and referral of clients to LME providers; the LME monitoring of providers of services; the LME provision of technical assistance to providers; and the requirements of "qualified public or private providers" as those terms are used in Section 122C-141 of the North Carolina General Statutes (hereinafter G.S.).

Financing Community Services

Revenue to support community services comes from a variety of sources, including the state general fund, federal block grants, special purpose grants from the federal government and private foundations, county appropriations, client fees,

38. "Adequate provision" includes submitting financial records and reports to DHHS as required by the DMA contract; having no consecutive three-month periods during which the LME/MCO's ratio of current assets to current liabilities is less than 1.0, based on a monthly review of the LME/MCO's balance sheets for each month of the three-month period; and having an intradepartmental monitoring team designated by the secretary determine that the LME/MCO has made adequate provisions against the risk of insolvency based on a quarterly review of the financial reports submitted to DHHS. G.S. 122C-124.2.

39. The secretary must certify that an LME/MCO is making timely provider payments if there are no consecutive three-month periods during which the LME/MCO paid less than 90 percent of "clean claims" for covered services within the thirty-day period following the LME/MCO's receipt of these claims during that three-month period. A clean claim is a claim that can be processed without obtaining additional information from the provider of the service or from a third party. The term includes a claim with errors originating in the LME/MCO's claims system. The term does not include a claim from a provider who is under investigation by a governmental agency for fraud or abuse or a claim under review for medical necessity. G.S. 122C-124.2.

40. G.S. 143B-147 through -150; G.S. 122C-114.

and federal Medicaid funding. When looking at the sources of revenue for community services, two things become clear. First, the system serves primarily, though not exclusively, individuals who are eligible for Medicaid, as Medicaid funding is the largest single source of revenue for community-based services. Thus, it should come as no surprise that Medicaid policy, both state and federal, drives North Carolina policy governing public mental health, developmental disabilities, and substance abuse (MH/DD/SA) services. Second, the largest source of revenue for providing services to individuals who are not eligible for Medicaid and who have no third-party insurance coverage is the state general fund.

A couple of sample area authority budgets illustrate the funding picture. The Cardinal Innovations area authority, covering fifteen counties in 2013, reported $356 million in budgeted revenues for fiscal year 2012–13, 80 percent of which came from Medicaid (see Figures 40.3 and 40.4).[41] CenterPoint Human Services, an area authority serving four counties, reported that 62 percent of its budgeted revenue came from Medicaid.[42]

Medicaid pays for medically necessary, covered services for eligible people. In other words, to receive services paid for with Medicaid funds, an individual, due to disability or membership in a low-income family, must be eligible for and enrolled in the Medicaid program, must be applying for a service covered by the State Medicaid Plan, and must have a condition that makes the service medically necessary as determined by a clinician conducting an assessment under state clinical guidelines.

Under North Carolina's Medicaid managed care waiver, the state pays area authorities Medicaid funds on a per member/per month capitated model. This means that, based on a calculation of the historical Medicaid spending on MH/DD/SA services in the area authority's catchment area under the former fee-for-service model, the state determines the total annual Medicaid funding that should be needed to meet the MH/DD/SA service needs in the pending fiscal year and disburses that money to the area authority in twelve monthly installments. The funding is "capitated," meaning that the area authority receives the funds up front and is expected to meet the MH/DD/SA service needs of all Medicaid enrollees in its catchment area without any additional funding. This differs from the former fee-for-service model where, from the state's perspective, Medicaid costs were unpredictable: the more services providers provided and billed for in a given year, the greater the amount of Medicaid money spent. Under the capitated funding model, state government shifts the financial risk to the area authority, which accepts full risk for the cost of care and attempts to manage both the cost and quality of care using the managed care techniques described more fully below in "Agency Functions" under the section of this chapter entitled "Today's Area Authority." To enhance the area authority's ability to manage the financial risk, all Medicaid-eligible individuals seeking or receiving MH/DD/SA services must enroll with an area authority so that the area authority can manage their care. And, all providers of these services must enroll in the area authority's provider network—which the area authority can limit—where they are subject to the area authority's performance expectations related to the cost and quality of care.

Non-Medicaid state appropriations—appropriations from the state general fund and federal block grants—represented 29 percent of CenterPoint Human Services' revenues and 18 percent of Cardinal Innovations' revenues in fiscal year 2012–13 (see Figures 40.3 and 40.4). This funding is used by area authorities to provide services to indigent and disabled clients who are not eligible for Medicaid services because their impairment is not severe enough or their income not low enough for them to qualify. To receive services paid for with this state funding, an individual must meet "target population criteria," which are eligibility criteria set by the state to target funds to those with the most serious or severe unmet needs.[43] Area authorities also sometimes use state funding to pay for licensed professional services not covered by Medicaid.

41. In 2014, Mecklenburg County joined Cardinal Innovations, bringing the catchment area to sixteen counties and increasing the size of Cardinal's budget.

42. Medicaid is funded jointly by the state and federal governments, with the federal government contributing about 65 percent and about 35 percent coming from the state. Until the county share was phased out on July 1, 2009, counties contributed 2.7 percent.

43. This source of revenue is commonly referred to as Integrated Payment and Reimbursement System (IPRS) funding. For more about the state's target populations, see "The Populations and Disabilities Served."

Figure 40.3 Who Pays for Services? (CenterPoint Human Services)

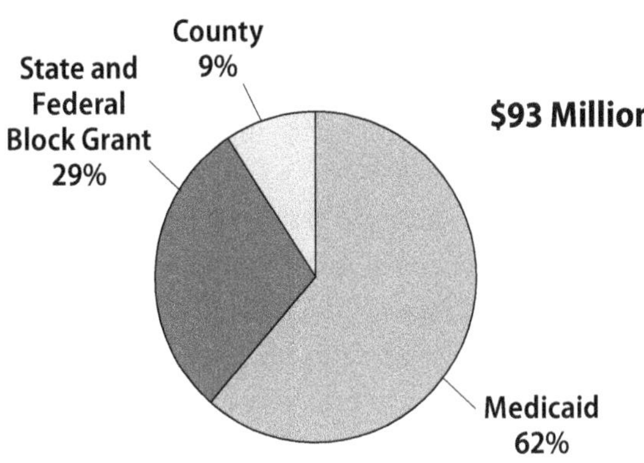

CenterPoint Human Services
FY 2012–13 Budgeted Revenues by Source

Figure 40.4 Who Pays for Services? (Cardinal Innovations)

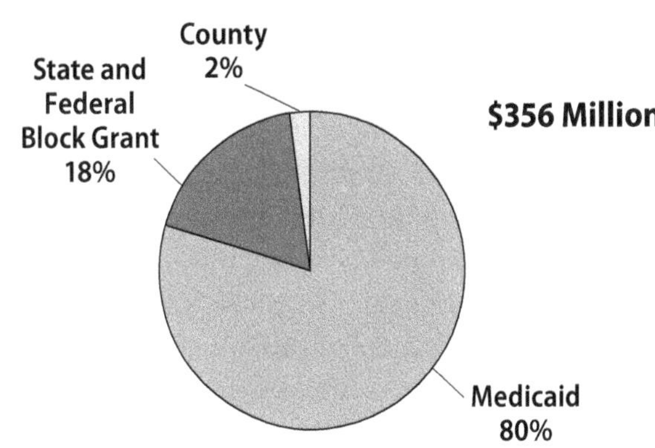

Cardinal Innovations
FY 2012–13 Budgeted Revenues by Source

Counties must, and cities may, appropriate funds to support the LME serving their catchment area.[44] In addition, G.S. 122C-2 provides that the furnishing of services through a public system centered in area authorities "requires the cooperation and financial assistance of counties, the State, and the federal government." Nevertheless, county appropriations comprise a very small percentage of total revenues. County appropriations funded through property tax proceeds or other local revenues comprised 9 percent of the total revenue available to CenterPoint Human Services and 2 percent of the revenue available to Cardinal Innovations in 2012–13

Because area authorities do not have the power to levy taxes, their ability to generate revenue is limited. Client co-payments may provide some revenue, but this is limited, as most area authority clients are indigent and uninsured, and no person may be refused services because of an inability to pay.[45] Any revenue generated by an area authority or its providers through the collection of client co-payments must be used to provide services to individuals who meet the state's target population criteria; it may not be used as a justification for reducing or replacing the budgeted commitment of county tax revenue.[46]

The Populations and Disabilities Served

Area authorities arrange and monitor care and treatment for mental illness, intellectual and developmental disabilities, and substance abuse. As noted earlier, individuals who meet specific *target population* criteria or who are *Medicaid eligible* may qualify for publicly funded mental health, developmental disabilities, and substance abuse (MH/DD/SA) services.

In North Carolina, there are 1.37 million people in need of mental health, developmental disabilities, and substance abuse services—almost 14 percent of the state population.[47] Of these, the state estimates that 609,087 people need

44. G.S. 122C-115(b).

45. G.S. 122C-146. An indigent person can, however, be denied services for not meeting Medicaid or state target population criteria.

46. G.S. 122C-146.

47. Aisander Duda and Mebane Rash, "Mental Health, Developmental Disabilities, and Substance Abuse Service in North Carolina: A Look at the System and Who It Serves," *North Carolina Insight* 23, no. 4/24, no. 1 (N.C. Center for Public Policy Research,

mental health services, 122,813 need developmental disability services, and 639,512 need substance abuse services. Within these figures, children comprise 313,910 of those who need services.[48]

Mental illness[49] covers a group of illnesses, including both emotional and cognitive disorders, characterized by alterations in thinking, mood, or behavior associated with stress or impaired functioning, or both. Examples include major depression, a mood disturbance that interferes with the ability to work, eat, sleep, study, and enjoy life, and attention deficit hyperactivity disorder, manifested by difficulty controlling behavior, staying focused, and paying attention. Other examples include bipolar disorder, characterized by mood swings between mania and depression, and post-traumatic stress disorder, a type of anxiety disorder that may occur as a result of seeing or experiencing a threat of injury or death.

Evidence of mental illness may include perceptual difficulties, delusions, visual and auditory hallucinations, and impairments in personal, social, and occupational functioning. Schizophrenia and related illnesses, affecting a small percentage of the population, are considered the most debilitating of the mental illnesses and the most difficult and expensive to treat. Depression, on the other hand, is more common; a major cause of suicide, it frequently goes unrecognized and untreated, particularly in elderly populations.

Developmental disability is a severe, chronic disability attributable to mental or physical impairment (or a combination of mental and physical impairments) that appears before age twenty-two (unless caused by traumatic head injury), is likely to continue for life, and produces substantial functional limitations in three or more of the following major areas of life activities: self-care, learning, mobility, language, capacity for independent living, self-direction, and economic self-sufficiency.[50] These impairments reflect the individual's need for a combination and sequence of special, interdisciplinary, or generic services, individualized supports, or other forms of assistance that are lifelong or extended in duration and individually planned and coordinated. Depending on severity, the term "developmental disability" includes intellectual disabilities, epilepsy, autism, and cerebral palsy. The term also includes delayed cognitive, physical, or communication and social-emotional development in children.

Intellectual disability is described by the American Association on Intellectual and Developmental Disabilities as one of several developmental disabilities that can occur in an individual's developmental period before the age of eighteen.[51] It is a disability characterized by significant limitations in both intellectual functioning and adaptive behavior. Intellectual functioning—also called intelligence—refers to general mental capacity, such as learning, reasoning, and problem solving, and is sometimes measured by an IQ test. A score of 75 or below can indicate a limitation in intellectual functioning. Adaptive behavior refers to a collection of conceptual, social, and practical skills performed by people in their everyday lives. Conceptual skills include language, literacy, and an understanding of money, time, and numbers. Social skills refer to interpersonal skills, social responsibility, self-esteem, gullibility, naïveté, social problem solving, and the ability to follow rules, obey laws, and avoid being victimized. Practical skills involve activities of daily living such as personal care, occupational skills, health care, transportation, routines, safety, and the use of money and the telephone.

Substance abuse is the use of drugs or alcohol in a dangerous, self-defeating, or destructive way and to a degree that produces impaired personal, social, or occupational functioning. An individual who engages in substance abuse has difficulty controlling his or her use, even though the use may be sporadic. Persons engaging in substance abuse who might receive community-based services include injecting drug users, substance abusing women with children, those convicted of driving while impaired, persons involved in the criminal justice and juvenile justice systems, those under

---

Raleigh, N.C., December 2012): 29, citing N.C. Department of Health and Human Services, Division of Mental Health, Developmental Disabilities, and Substance Abuse Services, "Semi-Annual Report to the Joint Legislative Oversight Committee on Health and Human Services," Statewide System Performance Report, SFY 2011–12, Spring Report, Raleigh, N.C. (April 1, 2012): Tables 1.1.a and 1.1.b.

48. *Id.*

49. Historically, the common term for children is "emotional disturbance."

50. 42 U.S.C. § 15002(8); G.S. 122C-3(12a).

51. The term for the condition we know today as *intellectual disability* has changed over time and most recently was known as *mental retardation.* See the American Association on Intellectual and Developmental Disabilities website, http://aaidd.org/intellectual-disability/definition.

investigation or supervision by child protective services, and those whose substance abuse involves recurring episodes of habitual use requiring assisted detoxification.

Simply suffering from mental illness, substance abuse, or a developmental disability does not qualify an individual for receiving publicly funded, community-based MH/DD/SA services. Due to limited public resources, the primary focus of the publicly funded system, particularly since the redesign that began in 2001, is to provide services to individuals with the most severe disabilities. The goal is to use public resources to allow people with the most severe disabilities to function and receive services in their community and to reduce as much as possible the public system's reliance on expensive institutional care.[52] To meet this goal, the Department of Health and Human Services has established target populations defined by specific diagnostic and functional criteria along with unique individual circumstances. These include several specific sets of criteria for each of the major age and disability categories: children with mental illness, adults with mental illness, adults suffering from addictive disorders, substance abusing youth or those at risk of engaging in substance abuse, and adults and children with developmental disabilities.

Generally, to receive community-based services paid for by appropriations from the state general fund, an individual must fall within the target population for his or her age and disability category. For example, while many children may suffer from mild mental illness, the state's target population criteria generally focus on children with *serious emotional disturbance* (SED).[53] Children with SED—which may include anxiety disorders, disruptive behavior disorders, depression, substance abuse, or eating disorders—are seriously affected in their ability to develop and function normally at school, at home, or with peers, and they typically require mental health and other services during childhood and in many cases throughout their lives.[54] Often these children require placement out of the home or are at risk of out-of-home placement, and without treatment and support, children with SED are more likely to be expelled from school, drop out of school, become pregnant during adolescence, commit suicide, or be convicted of a crime.[55]

Those individuals eligible for Medicaid and with a condition that meets "medical necessity" for a particular service as defined by the federal Centers for Medicare and Medicaid Services are entitled to receive services whether or not they meet the state's target population criteria for receiving state-funded services. Since the majority of funding to support publicly funded, community based MH/DD/SA services comes from the state Medicaid program (see Figures 40.3 and 40.4, above), the state's federally approved service definitions for Medicaid-reimbursable MH/DD/SA services largely determine who receives services and the kinds of services they receive. In comparison, the limited state funding available to address the needs of individuals who are not Medicaid eligible and who have no third-party insurance coverage leads to a state policy that targets state funds to the most severely disabled.

52. Legal developments also contributed to renewed emphasis on this goal. The most recent example is *Olmstead v. L.C.*, 527 U.S. 581 (1999), where the U.S. Supreme Court held that the unnecessary segregation of individuals with mental disabilities in institutions could constitute discrimination based on disability, in violation of the Americans with Disabilities Act. After the ruling, states believed they risked litigation if they did not develop a comprehensive plan for moving qualified persons from psychiatric hospitals to less restrictive settings at a reasonable pace. North Carolina developed its *Olmstead Plan* for individuals institutionalized for sixty or more days in state psychiatric institutions, developmental disabilities centers, and community-based intermediate care facilities for persons with mental retardation. The plan includes a process for assessing individuals to determine the services and support needed to return them to the community and discharging them from institutional care where appropriate.

53. National estimates indicate that 20 to 28 percent of children in the United States suffer from a mild mental health disorder, and 5 to 6 percent suffer from a serious emotional disturbance. *Child Mental Health Plan*, North Carolina Department of Health and Human Services, Division of Mental Health, Developmental Disabilities, and Substance Abuse Services (updated March 2004).

54. *Children's Mental Health: Strategies for Providing High Quality and Cost-Effective Care*, North Carolina Family Impact Seminar (Center for Child and Family Policy, Duke University, Durham, N.C., May 17, 2006): 10.

55. *Id.*

Today's Area Authority

Every county must provide mental health, developmental disabilities, and substance abuse (MH/DD/SA) services through an area authority.[56] A board of county commissioners for a single county or the boards of county commissioners for two or more counties must establish an area authority with the approval of the secretary of the Department of Health and Human Services (DHHS).[57] Thus, an area authority may serve either a single county or multiple counties, with the size of the catchment area (geographic area served) determined by how many counties join together to establish an area authority.

Historically, there has been no requirement relating to the size of an area authority or the number of counties it serves. Beginning on July 1, 2013, however, the catchment area served by an area authority had to meet a 500,000 population threshold to ensure that the area authority has a sufficiently large number of Medicaid enrollees to achieve the administrative efficiencies deemed necessary to effectively implement the Medicaid managed care waiver described above.[58] Thus, the single-county area authority is all but theoretical, and the population requirement led several area authorities to consolidate with each other, resulting in fewer authorities covering larger geographic areas. Today, North Carolina is served by nine multi-county area authorities (see Figure 40.1, above).[59]

As noted earlier, the evolution in area authority functions—through the 2001 law assigning local management entity functions and the 2011 law assigning managed care functions with respect to Medicaid and other public funding—has led area authorities to be called *local management entities* or LMEs and *managed care organizations* or MCOs. As a result of a 2013 legislative enactment, area authorities are also called "LME/MCOs."[60] For the purposes of this chapter, these terms are used interchangeably to refer to the same entity unless otherwise indicated.

Agency Functions

Area authorities are responsible for the management and oversight of the public system of MH/DD/SA services at the community level. As LME/MCOs, area authorities must plan, develop, implement, and monitor services within their catchment area to ensure expected outcomes for consumers of services within available resources.[61] This broad management and oversight responsibility includes many functions, some specified by statute[62] and some set forth in the area authority's Division of Medical Assistance (DMA) and Division of MH/DD/SA Services (DMHDDSAS) contracts.[63]

---

56. G.S. 122C-115(a).

57. G.S. 122C-115(c).

58. S.L. 2011-264, sec. 2 (amending G.S. 122C-115).

59. The 2014 appropriations act cuts funding for LME/MCO administration based on the assumption that the nine LME/MCOs will consolidate to seven or fewer LME/MCOs by June 30, 2015. S.L. 2014-100 (S 744) and Joint Conference Committee Report on the Continuation, Expansion, and Capital Budgets, July 30, 2014.

60. The General Assembly amended G.S. 122C-3 to say that a "local management entity/managed care organization" or "LME/MCO" means a local management entity (area authority) that is under contract with DHHS to operate the combined Medicaid Waiver program authorized under Sections 1915(b) and 1915(c) of the Social Security Act. S.L. 2013-85.

61. G.S. 122C-115.4.

62. G.S. 122C-115.2 and -115.4.

63. The multiple and inconsistent ways that area authority functions are categorized and described across multiple sources of law, including legal obligations not codified in statute or rule, make it challenging to consistently and coherently identify and describe agency functions while maintaining fidelity to the law. The General Statutes enumerate "local management entity functions" (G.S. 122C-115.4) and "core administrative functions" (G.S. 122C-115.2). These are essentially the same functions, although the two lists depart slightly from each other. "Managed care organization functions" are not treated in any comprehensive fashion by the General Statues, and the state chooses to identify and require these functions primarily through the DMA contract that every area authority must enter into to receive and manage Medicaid funds.

In spite of the complexity of the relevant statutory law and contractual obligations that area authorities must carry out, three themes emerge from a review of agency functions: (1) many LME functions are the same as many MCO functions, although they may vary in application because they arise from different contracts that govern two different sources of revenue, each with its own rules on what services and activities are reimbursable; (2) the advent of MCO functions has required area authorities to meet more rigorous financial accountability standards and more intensive information management, analysis, and reporting demands; and (3) some LME functions, such as community collaboration, involve interagency planning and coordination with other public agencies

The primary functions include the following:

1. *Planning.* The area authority must determine the service needs of consumers in its catchment area, assess the quality and availability of services, identify service gaps and methods for filling those gaps, and ensure the availability of an array of services based on consumer needs. Local service planning must address the equitable delivery of services among member counties and the most efficient and effective use of funds. Local planning must be an open process involving key stakeholders. The area authority must annually assess its progress toward implementing its service plans and achieving its goals and outcomes, and it must develop and submit to the secretary of DHHS a business plan that addresses how the area authority will carry out most of the functions described below.[64]
2. *Access.* The LME/MCO must implement a system for citizens to access services and, in particular, for the LME/MCO to respond to the need for emergency or crisis services. This system must include a telephonic access and customer call center that provides a screening, triage, and referral (STR) process available twenty-four hours a day, seven days a week. STR serves as a portal of entry to community services for individuals who are eligible for Medicaid or who meet the state's target population criteria for non-Medicaid state funding. Individuals experiencing an emergency must receive face-to-face service within two hours. Urgent situations, defined as involving a moderate risk or incapacity, require a response within forty-eight hours, and routine situations, those involving mild risk or incapacity, require a referral to a provider capable of delivering face-to-face services within fourteen calendar days.[65]
3. *Provider development and management.* For citizens to access services, providers of services must be available. In light of the assessed service need for its catchment area, the LME/MCO must assess the availability of providers to meet those needs and the qualifications and competencies of available providers. It must contract with qualified[66] public or private agencies or institutions for the provision of services, maintain a stable and high quality network of providers, and provide technical assistance to providers. The area authority must monitor provider performance and service outcomes in accordance with state standards and, to enable the authority to carry out this responsibility, the standard provider contract[67] requires service providers to make timely reports regarding the clients served, the services provided, and the resulting outcomes.[68]
4. *Service management.* This function is designed, in part, to ensure that public dollars are spent on eligible individuals and for services that are at an appropriate level and intensity given the severity of an individual's illness or disability. The LME/MCO must approve specific services to individual consumers (service authorization); evaluate the medical necessity, clinical appropriateness, and effectiveness of services using established guidelines and criteria (utilization management); and monitor individual care decisions at critical treatment junctures to assure effective care is received when needed (care coordination).[69]

(e.g., social services, juvenile justice, schools, and health) that go well beyond the functions of a typical managed care organization and that evince a public role absent in a system where Medicaid funds are managed by private MCOs. For the foregoing reasons, the newer LME/MCO designation for area authorities may more appropriately denote the full scope of area authority functions and more fully recognize the unique role of a public managed care organization.

64. G.S. 122C-117; G.S. 122C-115.2.

65. G.S. 122C-117; G.S. 122C-115.4; G.S. 122C-115.2.

66. A provider is qualified to contract with an area authority if it meets the provider qualifications set forth in rules adopted by the secretary. S.L. 2007-504 amended subsections (d) and (e) of G.S. 122C-141 to replace references to the secretary with references to the Commission for MH/DD/SA Services as the rulemaking entity responsible for promulgating rules defining provider qualifications. S.L. 2007-504 also amended G.S. 122C-114 to add to the powers and duties of the rulemaking commission the duty to adopt rules establishing the qualifications necessary to be a qualified provider. Nevertheless, S.L. 2007-504 left intact the language in G.S. 122C-141(a) that says provider qualifications are defined by the secretary.

67. A standard contract, adopted by the secretary of DHHS, must be used when contracting with qualified providers for the provision of MH/DD/SA services.

68. G.S. 122C-115.2; G.S. 122C-115.4; G.S. 122C-141; G.S. 122C-142.

69. G.S. 122C-115.4; G.S. 122C-115.2.

- *Utilization management.* The area authority's utilization management program must comply with federal Medicaid regulations and include a written utilization management plan that addresses the procedures used to review and approve requests for services, identifies the clinical criteria used to evaluate the medical necessity of the service being requested, and describes the mechanism used to detect underutilization or overutilization of services.[70] Even after services are authorized and paid for, the LME/MCO must conduct post-payment reviews to ensure that authorized services were clinically appropriate and provided in accordance with state standards. The LME also must authorize the utilization of state psychiatric hospitals and other state facilities and prioritize the needs of individuals waiting to participate in the NC Innovations Waiver.
- *Care coordination.* The LME is responsible for individual care decisions at critical treatment junctures (discharge from inpatient facilities, admission to hospital emergency departments, court order to outpatient treatment, transfer from one service to another, movement from a state developmental center to community placement) to assure that client care is coordinated, received when needed, likely to produce good outcomes, and is neither too little nor too much service to achieve the desired results. Care coordination must be provided by clinically trained professionals with the authority and skills necessary to determine appropriate diagnosis and treatment, approve treatment and service plans, link clients to higher levels of care when necessary, resolve disagreements between providers and clinicians, and consult with clinicians, providers, case managers, and utilization reviewers. Specific care coordination activities are required for high-risk/high-cost consumers and consumers of services with unstable medical and MH/DD/SA diagnoses.[71]

5. *Quality management.* The area authority must develop procedures for monitoring and evaluating the quality of services.[72] Consistent with this requirement, the DMHDDSAS contract requires the area authority to establish a quality management (QM) committee to identify and address opportunities to improve LME/MCO operations and the local service system, with input from providers, consumers of services, family members of consumers, and other stakeholders. The LME/MCO must implement a process for the timely identification, response, reporting, and follow-up to consumer incidents and stakeholder complaints about service access or quality. This and other data are available for the QM committee's review, as the LME/MCO must also produce reports that summarize and analyze patterns and trends related to consumers (outcomes, services used, and critical incidents); providers (quality, access by population group, underserved populations, service capacity, barriers to care, system performance); and LME/MCO operations (volume and costs of services, STR processes, management of funds, complaint response). Pursuant to federal regulations, the DMA contract requires the area authority to submit to an annual external quality review by an independent quality review organization hired by DMA.[73]
6. *Community collaboration.* The LME/MCO must collaborate with other local service systems and other area authorities and state facilities to ensure access to and coordination of services at the local level.[74] This includes establishing and maintaining effective collaborative working relationships with departments of social services, local health departments, community hospitals, housing and homeless services agencies, vocational rehabilitation and employment agencies, domestic violence agencies, jails, detention centers, training schools, prisons, public schools, colleges, universities, law enforcement agencies, courts, corrections agencies, juvenile court counselors, Community Care Networks, and other public agencies and health care providers. In addition, the LME/MCO must engage in local service planning to ensure the efficient and effec-

70. 42 C.F.R. § 456 and 42 C.F.R. § 438, Subpart D; DMA Contract, Section 7.4.
71. G.S. 122C-115.4. *See also* DMA Contract, Section 6.13.
72. G.S. 122C-191; G.S. 122C-115.2(b)(1)f.
73. 42 C.F.R. §§ 438.310 through 438.370; DMA Contract, Section 7.
74. G.S. 122C-115.2.

tive use of all funds for targeted services, a planning process that must be open to key stakeholders.[75] Specifically, the area authority is charged with coordinating with Treatment Accountability for Safer Communities the provision of services to criminal justice clients and coordinating and providing services to juveniles in the custody of the Division of Adult Corrections and Juvenile Justice of the Department of Public Safety.[76]

7. *Consumer affairs.* The LME/MCO must establish a client rights committee for protecting consumer rights and a consumer complaint and appeals process.[77] The area authority must adopt and implement grievance and appeals procedures for Medicaid enrollees that meet federal and state requirements[78] and are approved in writing by DMA.[79] These procedures permit Medicaid enrollees to appeal the denial or reduction of services. The LME/MCO must establish and support an effective consumer and family advisory committee (advisory to the governing board) and conduct community outreach and education.[80] For more on the consumer and family advisory committee, see the section entitled "The Role of Consumers and Families."
8. *Financial management and accountability.* The LME/MCO must carry out business functions in an efficient and effective manner and manage resources dedicated to public services—and information related to the delivery of services—in a manner that is accountable to state and local government funding sources.[81] The area authority must review provider reimbursement claims for proper documentation and pay claims promptly according to state requirements. (This *claims processing* function is listed separately from *financial management* in the DMHDDSAS contract.) To minimize the risk associated with operating under an at-risk, capitated Medicaid funding model, the area authority must maintain a restricted reserve account equal to 15 percent of the annualized cost of the DMA contract so that it may meet any cost overruns related to program services covered by the DMA contract. Every six months, the area authority must demonstrate to DHHS that it has made (1) adequate provision against the risk of insolvency with respect to funding for Medicaid enrollees,[82] (2) timely provider payments,[83] and (3) an adequate exchange of information (billing, payment, and other transaction data). For information on the local government finance laws applicable to area authorities, see "Area Board Powers and Duties" in the section entitled "The Governing Board."
9. *Information management analysis and reporting.* The LME/MCO is required to collect and manage information relating to the delivery of publicly funded services.[84] The DMHDDSAS contract requires the area authority to maintain an information technology (IT) infrastructure that complies with federal laws governing the privacy and security of electronic health records and that includes accurate and up-to-date consumer information and eligibility records. The LME/MCO must submit to DHHS, and ensure that providers submit to the LME/MCO, timely consumer information, including information regarding screening, admission, discharge, and eligibility determinations. In addition, the area authority must maintain a website that includes current and accurate information on how consumers and families may access services. The DMA contract also imposes numerous data requirements concerning the collection and reporting of provider claims and clinical information as well as requirements governing the capabilities of the area authority's IT infrastructure.

75. G.S. 122C-115.2; G.S. 122C-115.4.
76. G.S. 122C-117.
77. G.S. 122C-64; G.S. 122C-115.4.
78. 42 C.F.R. § 438, Subpart F; G.S. Ch. 108D.
79. G.S. Ch. 108D.
80. G.S. 122C-115.4; G.S. 122C-64; G.S. 122C-170.
81. G.S. 122C-115.2; G.S. 122C-115.4; G.S. 122C-124.2.
82. G.S. 122C-124.2. See note 38.
83. G.S. 122C-124.2. See note 39.
84. G.S. 122C-115.4.

The Governing Board

The area authority is governed by an area board whose members are appointed by the board or boards of county commissioners for the county or counties participating in the area authority.[85] Each board of county commissioners within an area authority must adopt an area authority business plan that, among other things, describes the area board composition, selection and appointment process, and procedure for notifying each board of county commissioners of all appointments made to the area authority board.[86]

Area Board Appointment and Composition

An area board must have no fewer than eleven and no more than twenty-one voting members, plus two nonvoting members. The board of county commissioners for a county served by a single-county area authority appoints the members of the area board. The boards of county commissioners for the counties participating in a multi-county area authority have the authority to appoint the members of the multi-county area board. The statute is silent on the manner of appointment other than to say that the process for appointing multi-county area board members must ensure participation from each of the constituent counties of the area authority, leaving counties that participate in a multi-county area authority the discretion to devise and agree to a selection and appointment process.[87]

The boards of county commissioners within a multi-county area authority with a population of at least 1,250,000 have the option to appoint members of the area board "in a manner and with a composition other than as required" by G.S. 122C-118.1. To exercise this option, each county participating in the area authority must adopt a resolution to that affect, and the secretary of DHHS must grant approval in writing. Unless such a waiver of the statutory requirements is granted, the area board must include the following:

1. At least one member who is a current county commissioner.
2. The chair of the area authority's Consumer and Family Advisory Committee (CFAC) or the chair's designee.
3. At least one family member of the CFAC, as recommended by the CFAC, representing the interests of individuals with mental illness, individuals with intellectual or other developmental disabilities, and individuals in recovery from addiction.
4. At least one openly declared consumer member of the CFAC, as recommended by the CFAC, representing the interests of individuals with mental illness, individuals with intellectual or other developmental disabilities, and individuals in recovery from addiction. (Categories 2 through 4 must be used to appoint one member who represents individuals with mental illness, one who represents individuals with intellectual or other developmental disabilities, and one who represents individuals in recovery from addiction.)
5. An individual with health care expertise and experience in the fields of mental health, intellectual or other developmental disabilities, or substance abuse services.
6. An individual with health care administration expertise consistent with the scale and nature of the managed care organization.
7. An individual with financial expertise consistent with the scale and nature of the managed care organization.
8. An individual with insurance expertise consistent with the scale and nature of the managed care organization.
9. An individual with social services expertise and experience in the fields of mental health, intellectual or other developmental disabilities, or substance abuse services.
10. An attorney with health care expertise.
11. A member appointed by the secretary of Health and Human Services who represents the general public and who is not employed by or affiliated with the Department of Health and Human Services.

85. G.S. 122C-118.1.
86. G.S. 122C-115.2(b)(2) and -117(a)(8).
87. G.S. 122C-118.1.

12. The president of the area authority's Provider Council or the president's designee to serve as a nonvoting member and who shall participate only in meetings open to the public.
13. An administrator of a hospital providing mental health, developmental disabilities, and substance abuse emergency services to serve as a nonvoting member and who shall participate only in meetings open to the public.

While the board must include representation from all of the categories identified above, county commissioners may elect to appoint a member of the area board to fill concurrently two categories of membership if the member has the qualifications and attributes of the two categories of membership.[88] If the boards of county commissioners responsible for board appointments do not comply with the compositional requirements, or have not utilized the waiver that may be granted for catchment areas containing 1.25 million or more people, the secretary of Health and Human Services must appoint the unrepresented categories.

Except for the two nonvoting members, an individual who contracts with the area authority to provide mental health, developmental disabilities, and substance abuse services may not serve on the area board for the period during which the contract for services is in effect. No person registered as a lobbyist under Chapter 120C of the General Statutes may be appointed to serve on an area board.

Area Board Terms, Officers, and Meetings

Commissioner members on the area board serve in an ex officio capacity at the pleasure of the initial appointing authority for a term not to exceed three years or the member's service as a county commissioner, whichever is earlier. County manager members on the area board serve at the pleasure of the initial appointing authority for a term not to exceed three years or the member's employment as a county manager, whichever is earlier. Other area board members serve three-year terms, except that upon initial formation of an area board to bring it into compliance with the 2012 legislation[89] that set forth the compositional requirements discussed above, one-third of the board members must be appointed for one year, one-third for two years, and all remaining members for three years. No member may serve more than three consecutive terms.

Area board members may be removed with or without cause by the person or group authorized to initially appoint the member. The area board may declare vacant the office of an appointed member who fails to attend three consecutive scheduled meetings without justifiable excuse. If a vacancy occurs on the area board before the end of the term, the person or group who initially filled the seat must choose a replacement before the end of the term of the vacated seat or within ninety days of the vacancy, whichever occurs first, and the appointment must be for the remainder of the unexpired term.

Area board members elect the area board chair, who may be a commissioner member of the area board, to serve a one-year term.[90] The area board must meet at least six times per year. Meetings are called either by the board chair or by three or more members who have given written notice to the chair.

Area Board Finance Committee

The area board must establish a finance committee that meets at least six times per year to review the financial strength of the area authority.[91] This committee must have at least three members, two of whom have expertise in budgeting and fiscal control. The area board member who is the individual with financial expertise, or any county finance officer serving on the board, must serve on the finance committee as an ex officio member. All other finance officers of the counties participating in a multi-county area authority may serve on the finance committee as ex officio members. If the area board so chooses, the entire area board may function as the finance committee, but its meetings as a finance committee must be distinct from its meetings as an area board.

---

88. G.S. 122C-118.1(c).
89. S.L. 2012-151.
90. G.S. 122C-119.
91. *Id.*

Area Board Training

All area board members must receive initial orientation on area board member responsibilities and annual training provided by DHHS that includes training on fiscal management, budget development, and fiscal accountability.[92] A member's refusal to be trained is grounds for removal. The DMHDDSAS contract also requires that the LME/MCO provide annual training, information, or support to ensure that the board actively reviews regular reports on finances, system performance, unmet service needs, provider capacity, and provider compliance with service requirements, and trends in service utilization, consumer health and safety, customer service, and complaints and appeals.

Area Board Powers and Duties

The area board exercises specific powers and duties set forth in the North Carolina General Statutes and the North Carolina Administrative Code. In addition, the DMA and DMHDDSAS contracts that the area authority enters into with DHHS for Medicaid and non-Medicaid funding have additional, often more detailed, requirements related to the implementation of these duties.

Some statutory duties, expressed in broad general terms, can be viewed as encompassing many of the more discrete duties listed below. For example, the board is legally responsible for ensuring, within available resources, the provision of mental health, developmental disabilities, and substance abuse services to citizens in the area authority's catchment area.[93] So that the board may carry out this broad charge, statutory law also requires the board to assess community needs, contract for services, and evaluate service quality.

In another broadly stated charge, statutory law requires the area board to "[e]ngage in comprehensive planning, budgeting, implementing, and monitoring of community-based" services.[94] One particular responsibility related to this general charge is the duty to adopt an annual budget. Another is the duty to develop an *LME business plan* for the management, delivery, and oversight of community services.[95] This plan must be in effect for at least three years and must address how the area authority will carry out the management functions described above under "Agency Functions." The LME business plan must be submitted for approval to the board or boards of county commissioners participating in the area authority before being submitted to the secretary of DHHS for approval.

Because the area board is composed of individuals volunteering their time and expertise at board meetings that may occur at the statutory-minimum frequency of six times per year, the board must rely on the area director and staff to carry out many of the tasks associated with these legal responsibilities; thus, the level of direct board involvement in the operation of the area authority is limited. Nevertheless, some legal responsibilities listed below, including the adoption of certain policies mandated by law, require direct action by the board. For example, the area board must appoint and annually evaluate the area director, develop an LME business plan, adopt an annual budget, and establish a finance committee.

Services. The board's statutory responsibilities related to service provision include the power and duty to do the following:

- Determine the needs of the area authority's clients and annually assess the area authority's ability to meet those needs.[96]
- Enter into contracts for the provision of services.[97]
- Assure that services meet state standards and comply with federal requirements as a condition of receipt of federal grants.[98]

---

92. G.S. 122C-119.1.
93. G.S. 122C-2; G.S. 122C-117; G.S. 122C-115.4.
94. G.S. 122C-117; G.S. 122C-115.4.
95. G.S. 122C-117; G.S. 122C-115.2.
96. G.S. 122C-117.
97. G.S. 122C-141.
98. G.S. 122C-117.

- Develop procedures for monitoring and evaluating the quality of services and assure that services provided are of the highest possible quality within available resources.[99]
- Perform public relations and community advocacy functions.[100]
- Submit to DHHS and the boards of county commissioners quarterly service delivery reports that assess the quality and availability of services within the area authority's catchment area and an annual report that assesses progress toward implementing service plans and achieving service goals and outcomes.[101]
- Recommend to the board of county commissioners the creation of local program services.[102]

In addition, the General Statutes point the board's attention to specific service areas by requiring a crisis response service that includes triage and referral of clients within one hour of notification to appropriate face-to-face crisis providers, coordination with the Treatment Accountability for Safer Communities program, provision of services to criminal justice clients, and coordination and provision of services to juveniles in the custody of the Division of Adult Corrections and Juvenile Justice of the Department of Public Safety.[103]

Client rights and consumer affairs. The area board has the power and duty to do the following:

- Establish a local consumer and family advisory committee to advise the area authority on its planning and management of community services.[104]
- Establish a client rights committee that monitors services for compliance with client rights, reports annually to the area board, and establishes review procedures for client grievances.[105]
- Adopt and implement for Medicaid enrollees grievance and appeals procedures that meet federal and state requirements[106] and are approved in writing by DMA.[107]

Budget and finance. In the area of budget and fiscal control, the area board must do the following:

- Establish a finance committee that meets at least six times a year to review the financial strength of the area authority.[108]
- Develop and maintain an annual budget as required by the Local Government Budget and Fiscal Control Act.[109]
- Submit the area authority budget to the participating boards of county commissioners and county managers for informational purposes.[110]
- Submit quarterly reports on the financial status of the area authority to the county finance officer for each participating county, who in turn submits the reports to the board of county commissioners at its next regularly scheduled meeting.[111]
- Prepare annual financial statements that set out the financial position of the area authority as of the end of the fiscal year and the financial results of operations during the course of the year.[112]
- Appoint a budget officer to serve at the pleasure of the area board.[113]

---

99. G.S. 122C-191.
100. G.S. 122C-117.
101. *Id.*
102. *Id.*
103. *Id.*
104. G.S. 122C-170.
105. G.S. 122C-64.
106. 42 C.F.R. § 438, Subpart F; G.S. Ch. 108D.
107. G.S. Ch. 108D.
108. G.S. 122C-119.
109. G.S. 122C-117; G.S. 122C-144.1.
110. G.S. 122C-117.
111. *Id.*
112. G.S. 159-34.
113. G.S. 159-9. G.S. 122C-121 charges the area director with developing the area authority budget for review by the area board. Because this is a budget officer responsibility under G.S. 159-11, one might conclude that the area director, by virtue of holding

- Appoint a finance officer unless the area director appoints the finance officer. The finance officer may be appointed by either the area board or the area director to serve at the pleasure of the appointing board or director.[114]
- Hire an independent certified public accountant to complete an annual audit for submission to the Local Government Commission in conformance with the Local Government Budget and Fiscal Control Act.[115]
- Submit to each board of county commissioners of participating counties a copy of the area authority's annual audit.[116]
- Enter into a memorandum of agreement (DMHDDSAS contract) with the secretary of DHHS for the purpose of ensuring that state funds are used in accordance with priorities expressed in the area authority's business plan.[117]
- Maintain a restricted risk reserve account equal to 15 percent of the annualized cost of the DMA contract to meet any outstanding obligations, such as cost overruns, related to services covered by the contract.
- Implement for the area authority and its contract providers the family income co-payment schedule adopted by the secretary of DHHS under G.S. 122C-112.1(a)(34). An LME and its contract provider agencies must make every reasonable effort to collect appropriate reimbursement for the costs of services from individuals or entities able to pay, including insurance and third parties who cover the cost of care.[118]

Human Resources. Statutory duties related to human resources require the area board to do the following:

- Appoint an area director to serve at the pleasure of the area board.[119]
- Evaluate annually the area director for performance based on criteria established by the area board and the secretary of DHHS.[120]
- Establish a salary plan that sets the salaries for area authority employees in conformance with the State Human Resources Act.[121]
- Adopt and enforce a professional reimbursement policy that (1) requires fees for services provided directly by the area authority be paid to the area authority (not to its employees), (2) prohibits area employees from providing on a private basis services that require the use of area program resources and facilities, and (3) allows area employees to accept dual compensation and dual employment only if they first obtain the written permission of the area authority.[122]

In addition to the powers and duties listed above, the area authority may add one or more additional counties to its catchment area upon the adoption of a resolution to that effect by a majority of the members of the area board and with the approval of the secretary of DHHS.[123]

---

that position, is the budget officer for the area authority and the area board need not appoint a budget officer. It is not entirely clear, however, that the area director's budget duty expressed in G.S. 122C-121, by itself, relieves the multi-county area board of the duty, set forth in G.S. 159-9, to appoint a budget officer. Of course, the multi-county area board could choose to impose the duties of budget officer on the area director.

114. G.S. 159-24.

115. G.S. 122C-144.1.

116. G.S. 122C-117.

117. G.S. 122C-115.2(d).

118. G.S. 122C-146.

119. G.S. 122C-117; G.S. 122C-121.

120. G.S. 122C-121.

121. G.S. 122C-156. Approval of the plan by the board or boards of county commissioners is not required unless the salary plan for a single-county area authority exceeds the county's salary plan, or the salary plan for a multi-county area authority exceeds the highest paying salary plan for any county within the area authority's catchment area.

122. G.S. 122C-157.

123. G.S. 122C-115(c1).

The area board has the power to lease and purchase real property[124] and, with the approval of the Local Government Commission, the power to borrow money.[125] The area board also has the power to contract for the purchase, lease, or lease-purchase of personal property, including equipment necessary for the operation of the area authority. The area board may purchase life insurance, health insurance, or both for the benefit of all or any class of area authority officers or employees as part of their compensation.[126] In addition, the area board may enter into a contract to insure the area authority, board members, and employees against civil liability for damages caused by the actions of agents, board members, or employees of the area authority when acting within the course of their duties or employment.[127]

The board also has implicit authority to enter into other contracts necessary to carry out its duty to provide services. Examples of contracts necessary to the performance of area authority functions are contracts for the construction and repair of facilities and contracts for professional or other services not directly related to client services.

Finally, the area board is required to establish informal dispute resolution procedures for (1) persons who claim that the area authority's failure to comply with state laws adversely affected their ability to participate in planning or budgeting processes, (2) clients or contractors who claim that the area authority acted arbitrarily and capriciously in reducing funding for services, (3) contractors who claim that the area authority did not act within applicable law when imposing a particular requirement, and (4) contractors who claim that the area authority imposed a requirement that substantially compromises their ability to fulfill the contract.[128]

Area Board Role

As the governing body for the area authority, the area board bears ultimate responsibility for the execution of all powers and duties conferred by law on the area authority. But, as noted in the introduction to board powers and duties above, the board cannot directly carry out all powers and duties, nor can it perform the many agency functions associated with these duties. What, then, is the board's role beyond discharging those duties that require direct board action, such as adopting a budget or establishing a consumer and family advisory committee? The answer is that the board's role is not to *carry out* all agency responsibilities but to *be accountable* for all responsibilities—in other words, to make sure that the LME/MCO performs as required.

One significant phenomenon associated with area board responsibilities is that many of the subjects warranting board oversight emanate not from statute or published rules but from the area authority's two voluminous contracts with DHHS, which together currently amount to at least two hundred pages of reading. While this might be challenging to officials who need to understand and govern the agency, these contracts also provide the tools for board accountability. These contracts focus not only on LME/MCO functions and the many requirements related to the administration of these functions but also on the collection and reporting of data that the state uses to measure the performance of these functions. Accordingly, the contracts point to some of the operations and activities that area boards should pay attention to as well as the data that may be used to monitor these operations and activities.

In carrying out its responsibilities, the board should look to the statutory and contractual requirements relating to LME/MCO functions described above under "Agency Functions" in the section of this chapter entitled "Today's Area Authority." The board can utilize the performance data that the state requires the area authority to collect and report relating to these management functions, and it should work with staff to determine how this data can be reported to the board in a meaningful way that permits the board to measure the quality and effectiveness of the local service system. (Remember, the *LME Business Plan* is supposed to address how the area authority will carry out its management functions, including how it will ensure the quality of services and measure their effectiveness. Thus, the *LME Business Plan* could include a description of the board's role in evaluating the quality and effectiveness of services.)

124. G.S. 122C-147.
125. G.S. 122C-117.
126. G.S. 122C-156.
127. G.S. 122C-152; G.S.122C-153; G.S. 122C-142.
128. G.S. 122C-151.3; G.S. 122C-151.4.

When monitoring the LME/MCO's service-related functions, the area board, as well as county boards of commissioners and other interested persons, could utilize the following related performance data:[129]

- *Access.* The area authority is required to report to the board, its consumer and family advisory committee, and DHHS access patterns and trends (number of persons requesting services; number determined to need emergency, urgent, and routine care; and number for which access is provided within the time periods defined in state performance standards). This data is helpful in evaluating the LME/MCO's *access* function.
- *Provider management.* The general duty to ensure the provision of services includes the duty to ensure the availability of qualified providers to deliver services, a matter that falls within the scope of the LME/MCO's *provider management* function. The area authority's service delivery reports submitted quarterly to counties include data on types of services delivered, number of persons served, and services requested but not delivered. This data speaks to the question of whether the area authority has adequately developed the capacity of its provider network. In addition, DMA may use the LME/MCO-DMA contract as a means for requiring the submission of other information related to an area authority's provider network. For example, DMA has used contract language to require the area authority to submit to DMA written reports of findings of the area authority's own provider network analyses and, whenever network gaps are identified, to submit to DMA a network development plan within a time frame specified by DMA. This kind of information would be central to any board's performance evaluation of the LME/MCO's provider management function.
- *Service management.* Data that pertains to the LME/MCO *service management* function includes the quarterly reports on service utilization patterns and trends that must be submitted to the area board and reports to DHHS on (1) utilization of services by service type (for example, inpatient, intensive outpatient, emergency department), (2) treated prevalence by age-disability category (number of persons who received treatment for a particular condition compared to number estimated to have that condition) and, (3) percentage of provider service authorization requests processed in the state-required time frame.
- *Quality management.* The area authority's *quality management* committee must review and quarterly report to the area board and CFAC on consumer trends (client outcomes, use of emergency services and state hospitals, perceptions of care), provider trends and performance (service capacity, provider quality), and LME operations (trends in volume and cost of services per consumer, access system data, management of state funds). The LME/MCO contract with DMA requires the area authority to submit data to DMA annually on quality of care measures as well as information on the area authority's performance improvement projects.

The Area Director

The area director, who is the administrative head of the area authority, is appointed by and serves at the pleasure of the area board. The area director appoints and supervises area authority employees, implements area board programs and policies, administers area authority services in compliance with state law, acts as a liaison between the area authority and DHHS, and provides information and advice to boards of county commissioners through the county manager.[130] In addition, the area director must develop the budget for the area authority for review by the area board.

Unless one of these qualifications is specifically waived by the secretary of DHHS, an area director must have a master's degree, management experience, and other related experience. Any area director hired after January 1, 2007, must meet the job classifications adopted for area directors by the Office of State Human Resources.[131]

---

129. This list is intended to be illustrative only, not exhaustive, as other data exists that the board may want to receive as monitoring reports. In addition, dumping huge quantities of data on the board and in a form that is not meaningful or helpful to the board's monitoring responsibilities can be overwhelming and counterproductive. Monitoring reports should present data in a way that is clearly tied to relevant goals and performance expectations. Monitoring is more than simply receiving lots of data. If an entity doesn't know what it is measuring and why, the data is not meaningful or useful.

130. G.S. 122C-121.

131. G.S. 122C-120.1.

The area board must annually evaluate the area director for performance based on criteria established by the area board and the secretary of DHHS. The secretary requires that the director be evaluated for performance in each of the following areas: (1) maintaining an effective relationship with the area board and the CFAC; (2) developing and maintaining effective relationships with the community served and with state and local officials; (3) encouraging consumer and family involvement in system management activities, including program development, quality management, and community development; (4) recruiting, monitoring, and maintaining effective relationships with qualified providers of services; (5) managing human resources; (6) managing fiscal resources; and (7) demonstrating leadership skills.[132] In conducting the evaluation, the area board must consider comments from boards of county commissioners.[133]

The area board must establish the area director's salary in accordance with the State Human Resources Act.[134] An area director may be paid a salary that is in excess of the salary ranges established by the State Human Resources Commission with prior approval of the director of the Office of State Human Resources. Any proposed salary that is higher than the maximum of the applicable salary range must be supported by documentation of comparable salaries in comparable operations within the region and must also include the specific amount the board proposes to pay the director.

The area board is not permitted to provide the director with any benefits that are not also provided by the area board to all permanent employees of the area authority, except that the area board may offer severance benefits, relocation expenses, or both to an applicant for the position of director as an incentive for the applicant to accept an offer of employment. Otherwise, the director may be reimbursed only for allowable employment-related expenses at the same rate and in the same manner as other employees of the area program.[135]

Human Resources Administration

Human resources administration for area authority employees must be conducted in accordance with the State Human Resources Act and the rules and policies of the North Carolina State Human resources Commission.[136] These rules and policies govern position classification, qualifications, recruitment, promotion, dismissal, compensation, personnel records, and nepotism (employment of relatives). For example, area authorities must use a competitive recruitment process that selects employees based on a relative consideration of the applicants' skills, knowledge, and abilities. Employees who have satisfactorily completed a probationary and/or trainee appointment may not be demoted, suspended, or dismissed except for "just cause" or reduction in force.[137] Under the just cause standard defined by the State Human Resources Commission, area employees may not be discharged, suspended, or demoted for disciplinary reasons without adequate procedural due process and a demonstration that just cause for the disciplinary action—unacceptable job performance or personal conduct—exists.

The area board is authorized, but not required, to purchase life insurance and health insurance for the benefit of all or any class of area authority officers or employees as part of their compensation. Other fringe benefits for officers and employees may also be provided.[138]

---

132. The criteria are published in the North Carolina Administrative Code at title 10A, subchapter 27G, section .0507. That regulation also says that area boards may use the area director evaluation as an opportunity to create an annual plan for the area director that includes both policy and programmatic considerations.

133. G.S. 122C-121(b).

134. G.S. 122C-121(a1).

135. G.S. 122C-121(a2).

136. G.S. 122C-154.

137. These and other rules applicable to area authority employees are found in the North Carolina Administrative Code at title 25, subchapter 1I, section .1700.

138. G.S. 122C-156.

Budget and Fiscal Control

Like all other local governments and public authorities, the area authority's budgeting and fiscal management must be administered according to the Local Government Budget and Fiscal Control Act,[139] which prescribes a general system for adopting and administering a budget. Independent of the county governments that are involved in the establishment of the area authority, the area authority is responsible for its own budgeting, disbursing, accounting, and financial management under the direction of a budget officer appointed by the area board and a finance officer appointed by the area director or board.[140]

All area authorities must operate under a balanced annual budget ordinance adopted by the area board. Except for funds used for certain purposes, all moneys received or expended by the area authority—whether federal, state, local, or private in origin—must be spent in accordance with the budget ordinance.

Each area authority also must complete and submit an annual independent audit to the Local Government Commission. Under the audit requirement, an independent certified public accountant examines the area authority's accounting records and other evidence supporting its financial statements to provide independent verification that the financial statements are credible and can be relied upon. This is called a *financial audit.* The accountant also conducts a *compliance audit* to determine whether the area authority has complied with requirements for receiving federal or state financial assistance.

The Role of Consumers and Families

In addition to requiring at least three representatives of consumers of services and their family members to serve on the governing body for the area authority, North Carolina law requires consumers and family members to serve in an advisory capacity on both the state and local levels of government.

Local Consumer and Family Advisory Committee

Every area authority must establish a Consumer and Family Advisory Committee (CFAC) to advise the local management entity on its planning and management of the local mental health, developmental disabilities, and substance abuse (MH/DD/SA) service system.[141] Specifically, the CFAC must

1. review, comment on, and monitor the implementation of the LME business plan;
2. identify service gaps and underserved populations;
3. make recommendations regarding the service array and monitor the development of additional services;
4. review and comment on the area authority budget;
5. participate in all quality improvement measures and performance indicators; and
6. submit to the state CFAC findings and recommendations regarding ways to improve the delivery of services.

139. G.S. Ch. 159.

140. The *multi-county* area authority—because it is considered a *public authority* for purposes of the Local Government Budget and Fiscal Control Act—is responsible for its own budgeting and financial management. Before 2012, a single-county area authority was considered a department of the county in which it was located for purposes of budget and fiscal control (G.S. 122C-116), which meant that the single-county area authority had to present its budget for approval by the county commissioners in the manner requested by the county budget officer, and its financial operations had to follow the budget set by the county commissioners in the county's budget ordinance. In 2012, the General Assembly amended G.S. 122C-116 to delete the language stating that a single-county area authority was a department of the county for purposes of budget and fiscal control. S.L. 2012-151, sec. 2.(a). While it is not clear that this brought the single-county area authority within the scope of the term "public authority" as defined in G.S. Chapter 159, it did signal the legislature's intent that the single-county area authority no longer be a part of the budgeting and accounting system of any county but be independent of county government and under the sole governance of the single-county area board.

141. G.S. 122C-170.

The director of the area authority must provide to the CFAC support staff sufficient to assist the CFAC in implementing its duties. Staff assistance must include the provision of data for the identification of service gaps and underserved populations, training to review and comment on business plans and budgets, implementation of procedures to allow CFAC participation in quality monitoring, and technical advice on rules of procedure and applicable laws.

The CFAC is composed exclusively of adult consumers of MH/DD/SA services and family members of consumers of services. People in each of the three disability groups—mental illness, developmental disabilities, and substance abuse—must be represented on the CFAC, and membership must represent as closely as possible the racial and ethnic composition of the catchment area. Member terms are for three years, and no member may serve more than three consecutive terms.

The law requires the CFAC to be self-governing and self-directed, indicating the legislative intent that the CFAC act independently of the LME staff and board, albeit with staff support, much like LME staff might support the LME board by providing needed information and logistical support. Each CFAC must adopt bylaws that govern the selection and appointment of its members, their number and terms of service, and other procedural matters. At the request of either the CFAC or the governing board of the area authority or county program, the CFAC and governing board must execute an agreement that identifies the roles and responsibilities of each party, the channels of communication between the CFAC and local board, and a process for resolving disputes between the parties.

State Committee

The law also establishes the State Consumer and Family Advisory Committee (State CFAC) to advise the Department of Health and Human Services (DHHS) and the General Assembly on the planning and management of the state's public MH/DD/SA services system.[142] This twenty-one-member body, composed exclusively of adult consumers of MH/DD/SA services and family members of consumers of services, must

1. review, comment on, and monitor the implementation of the State Plan for Mental Health, Developmental Disabilities, and Substance Abuse Services;
2. identify service gaps and underserved populations;
3. make recommendations regarding the service array and monitor the development of additional services;
4. review and comment on the state budget for mental health, developmental disabilities, and substance abuse services;
5. participate in all quality improvement measures and performance indicators;
6. receive the findings and recommendations of local CFACs regarding ways to improve the delivery of mental health, developmental disabilities, and substance abuse services; and
7. provide technical assistance to local CFACs in implementing their duties.

Like the local CFAC, the State CFAC must be a self-governing and self-directed organization, and the secretary of DHHS must provide sufficient staff to assist the State CFAC in implementing its duties. The assistance must include data for the identification of service gaps and underserved populations, training to review and comment on the State Plan and departmental budget, procedures to allow participation in quality monitoring, and technical advice on rules of procedure and applicable laws.

The Role of County Government

After increasing the role of county government in area authority affairs in 2001, the General Assembly has moved in the opposite direction since 2011. The 2001 Act to Phase In Implementation of Mental Health System Reform at the State and Local Level[143] enhanced the role of county government by involving county boards of commissioners in the

142. G.S. 122C-171.
143. S.L. 2001-437.

hiring of the area director, the monitoring of the area authority's fiscal health and service capacity, and the development and approval of the area authority business plan. Counties were given additional administrative options for carrying out their duty to provide mental health, developmental disabilities, and substance abuse (MH/DD/SA) services; they retained exclusive authority to appoint members of the governing board; and every county was represented on the area board by a county commissioner or county manager. Counties had the authority to dissolve an area authority and join with other counties to create a new one. The authority to acquire and hold title to real property used by an area authority was vested in the participating counties.

Since the advent of managed care, and starting with legislation enacted in 2011,[144] the role of county government has receded as much of the authority granted by the 2001 legislation has been eliminated—in some cases directly through statutory amendments, and in some cases indirectly through policy changes implemented by the executive branch of state government. Nevertheless, the law still provides for county responsibility and involvement in certain area authority matters.

Establishing and Dissolving the Area Authority

Counties are required to provide MH/DD/SA services through an area authority.[145] With the approval of the secretary of the Department of Health and Human Services (DHHS), a county, or two or more counties jointly, must establish an area authority to provide mental health, developmental disabilities, and substance abuse services.[146] Because statutory law has recently been amended to require each area authority to serve a catchment area population of at least 500,000 people, most single-county area authorities have had to join other area authorities to meet the population threshold, and the idea of establishing a single-county area authority is a remote consideration for most counties.

Until recently, counties could withdraw from, or jointly dissolve, an area authority if the board or boards of county commissioners determined that the authority was not operating in the best interests of its citizens and the change would not adversely affect the continuity of services. Now, the counties participating in a multi-county area authority no longer have the authority to jointly dissolve the area authority.[147] Only the secretary of DHHS may dissolve an area authority, and he or she is required to do so when an area authority fails to meet particular performance expectations for operating a managed care organization.[148] Individual counties retain the authority to withdraw or "disengage" from an area authority and "realign" with another one, but only pursuant to rules adopted by the secretary that address a number of matters specified by statute.[149] The authority to accept a new county into an existing area authority, once the province of the boards of county commissioners of the counties participating in the area authority, now belongs to the governing body for the area authority itself. Thus, while a board of county commissioners needs to act to disengage from an area authority and to join a new area authority, the counties participating in the area authority receiving that county no longer must act in concert to approve the addition of the new county.[150] A new county can be added by a majority of area board members adopting a resolution to that effect.[151]

---

144. S.L. 2011-264 required each LME to begin operating a 1915(b)/(c) Medicaid Waiver with approval of the secretary by January 1, 2013, and if an LME could not apply for and obtain secretary approval, to merge with an LME that had obtained approval to operate the waiver.

145. G.S. 122C-115(a).

146. G.S. 122C-115.

147. S.L. 2013-85, sec. 5(a).

148. G.S. 122C-124.2.

149. G.S. 122C-115(a3).

150. A contrary interpretation of the applicable law is possible. Statutory law still says that counties must establish an area authority (G.S. 122C-115). Arguably, when a county joins an existing area authority, a new area authority is being established, as the resulting change in the catchment area necessitates a new business plan, a new area board, and a new contract for managed care between the state and the area authority. Thus, it is possible that adding a county to an existing area authority catchment area requires *both* a joint resolution of the boards of commissioners for all of the counties in the new catchment area *and* a resolution adopted by the area board.

151. G.S. 122C-115(c1).

Appointing and Serving on the Area Board

Until 2013, many area boards were appointed by and composed primarily of county commissioners, and the membership of most multi-county area boards included a county commissioner from every county served by the area authority. This was due in part to a desire by each county to be represented by an elected official and also in part to the process used by commissioners for appointing area board members. The board appointment statute provided that each county in a multi-county catchment area would appoint a county commissioner to the area board. This group of commissioner members would then appoint the remaining members of the board, and the requirements for any particular categories of representation were few. As a result, the majority of most area board members were county commissioners, with one commissioner from each county served by the area authority. For example, East Carolina Behavioral Health, a nineteen-county area authority, had nineteen county commissioners on its area board. The Smoky Mountain Center had fifteen county commissioners, one from each of the fifteen counties participating in the area authority.

Changes in the compositional requirements for area boards no longer permit county commissioner representation from every county. Ten of the twenty-one voting members of the area board must be individuals with particular professional expertise or consumers of services or their family members. That leaves eleven board seats for other categories of representation—not enough to accommodate the appointment of a county commissioner from every county in a nineteen- or fifteen-county area authority. Some area authorities, like the eight-county Partners Behavioral Health Management or Sandhills Center area authorities can still accommodate a commissioner from every county. But the traditional practice of having each county represented by a county commissioner on the area board is no longer possible for a majority of counties.

For more on the composition and appointment of the area board, see the section of this chapter entitled "The Governing Board."

County Commissioner Advisory Board

In 2013, the General Assembly established a county commissioner advisory board for each area authority to advise the authority and director on matters pertaining to the delivery of services for individuals with mental illness, intellectual or other developmental disabilities, and substance abuse disorders.[152] Each board of county commissioners within the catchment area must designate one of its commissioner members to serve on the advisory board, and each board of commissioners may determine the manner of designation, the term of service, and the conditions of service for its designee. The advisory board must meet on a regular basis.

Local Management Entity Business Plan

Each county, through its area authority, must develop, review, and approve a business plan for the management and delivery of services and submit the plan for the approval of the North Carolina Secretary of Health and Human Services.[153] The business plan must remain in effect for at least three years and must address implementation of local management entity (LME) functions and other topics specified by statute. For example, the plan must address the area board composition and appointment process, the method for calculating county cash and in-kind contributions to the area authority, resources available and needed within the local area to prevent out-of-community placements, collaboration with other local service systems to ensure access to and coordination of services, and planning for services that identifies gaps in services and methods for filling those gaps. The statute also requires that local service planning related to development of the business plan involve key stakeholders and that the identification of resources available and needed to prevent out-of-community placements include input from other public agencies in the community.

While the business planning requirement is a clearly expressed statutory mandate, it has not been consistently and faithfully pursued by counties and area authorities since the last LME business plans were developed in 2006 and implemented for the three-year cycle beginning July 1, 2007. This is likely due, in part, to the fact that many view the

152. G.S. 122C-118.2.
153. G.S. 122C-115.2.

business planning process as an anachronistic requirement that was developed during mental health reform before the system moved to managed care and therefore as having less relevance now. As well, some may feel that, given the fast pace of change in the system since the implementation of managed care, the expenditure of resources to engage in a time-consuming community planning process among multiple local governments is not appropriate or even possible, and any resulting plan might be out-of-date by the time it is completed. The General Assembly seemed to acknowledge some of these factors when, in 2012, it granted the secretary the authority to waive any requirements of the business planning statute that are inconsistent or incompatible with contracts entered into between DHHS and the area authority for carrying out the 1915(b)/(c) Medicaid Waiver.[154] At the date of this publication, the secretary had not expressly exercised this authority.

For county government, even though its role under the Medicaid Managed Care Waiver is diminished relative to the role granted by the 2001 mental health reform legislation, the development and periodic renewal of the business plan provide opportunities to influence the area authority's planning for such things as service provision and collaboration with other local government service systems. Because county government has no direct control over the governance and management of area authorities, the business planning process provides one of the few vehicles for county input. Moreover, required elements of the business plan not only relate directly to such LME functions as collaboration with other local service systems and planning to close gaps in services but also are intended to address county appointments to the area board and county funding to the area authority, all matters of concern to county commissioners and many of the citizens they serve.

Funding

Counties must appropriate funds to the area authority serving their catchment area without regard to whether any area authority programs are physically located within the county.[155] Cities may appropriate funds to support the area authority. Counties and cities may appropriate funds from revenues not restricted by law, and counties may fund appropriations by levy of property taxes pursuant to G.S. 153A-149(c)(22).

Counties may not reduce county appropriations and expenditures for current operations and ongoing services of area authorities because of revenues available to the area authority from state-allocated funds, client fees, capitation amounts, or fund balance.[156] Counties may reduce county appropriations from the amount previously appropriated for one-time or nonrecurring special needs of the area authority. This "non-supplant" restriction on reductions in county appropriations for ongoing services limits the authority of counties to reduce appropriations to area authorities in response to the availability of funding from other sources.

Oversight

To facilitate county oversight of the community-based service system, area authorities must make regular reports to their participating board or boards of county commissioners regarding the area authority's financial health and service capacity. These reports include quarterly financial reports,[157] quarterly service delivery reports that assess the quality and availability of services within the area authority's catchment area, and an annual progress report assessing the

---

154. S.L. 2012-151, sec. 9.(b), amending G.S. 122C-115.2. "The Secretary may waive any requirements of this section that are inconsistent with or incompatible with contracts entered into between the Department and the area authority for the management responsibilities for the delivery of services for individuals with mental illness, intellectual or other developmental disabilities, and substance abuse disorders under a 1915(b)/(c) Medicaid Waiver."

155. G.S. 122C-115(b).

156. G.S. 122C-115(d).

157. Reports are to be submitted to the county finance officer for each participating county, who in turn submits the reports to the board of county commissioners at its next regularly scheduled meeting. If the report is not submitted within thirty days of each quarter of the fiscal year, the clerk of the board of county commissioners must notify the area director and county finance officer that the report has not been submitted as required. At the request of the board of county commissioners, the report may be presented in person by the area director or the director's designee.

area authority's ability to meet the service needs of its catchment area.[158] As a practical matter, these area authority duties serve informational purposes and, while the board or boards of county commissioners can comment on this information, the county boards have no governing authority with respect to the matters reported. However, the subjects of these reports do relate to elements of the LME business plan, discussed above, which must be developed with the participation of the county board of commissioners for each county participating in the area authority.

Property

Until 2012, the authority to purchase and hold title to real property used by an area authority was vested in the county where the property was located. This authority could be delegated to the area authority, but it required a resolution of the boards of county commissioners of all the counties within the area authority's catchment area. These provisions were deleted in 2012, and now an area authority has the authority to acquire and hold title to real property without needing the approval of county government.[159]

Budget and Fiscal Control

Until 2012, a single-county area authority was considered a department of the county for purposes of the Local Government Budget and Fiscal Control Act.[160] Thus, its administration was linked to county administration in ways not characteristic of the more independent multi-county authorities. The single-county area authority presented its budget for approval of the county commissioners in the manner requested by the county budget officer, and its financial operations had to follow the budget set by the county commissioners in the county's budget ordinance. The ability of the board of county commissioners to approve the budget of the single-county area authority gave the commissioners a substantial role in determining the budget, the scope of services available to county residents, and the number of personnel positions within the area authority. In addition, the county had responsibility for fiscal management and could require that all disbursements, receipts, and financial management of the area authority be handled by the county's finance officer.

In 2012, the General Assembly deleted statutory language that referred to the single-county area authority as a department of the county for purposes of budget and finance, and that statute now refers to all area authorities as local political subdivisions of the state.[161] As a consequence, a single-county area authority appears to have the same status as a multi-county area authority, which is not a part of the budgeting and accounting system of any county but is responsible for its own budgeting, disbursing, accounting, and financial management under the direction of a budget officer and finance officer appointed by the area authority.

Because all counties must appropriate funds to the area authority serving them, boards of commissioners, depending on the size of their appropriations, have the potential to shape or influence the area authority budget and services—particularly services for indigent citizens who would not qualify for services funded by Medicaid or other state appropriations, the two primary sources of revenue for area authority services. To keep counties apprised of the area authority's budget policy and financial status, a multi-county area authority must submit its approved budget and annual audit to the participating boards of county commissioners for informational purposes.[162]

Human Resources

Before 2012, the area board's appointment of the area director was subject to the approval of the boards of county commissioners for the counties within the area authority's catchment area. In addition, a county manager and at least one county commissioner had to sit on the area board search committee involved in selecting the new area director. While

158. G.S. 153A-453; G.S.122C-117.

159. G.S. 122C-147.

160. G.S. Ch. 159. For more about the Local Government Budget and Fiscal Control Act, see Chapter 20, "Budgeting for Operating and Capital Expenditures."

161. S.L. 2012-151, sec. 2.(a).

162. G.S. 122C-117.

these statutory provisions have been deleted,[163] the law still retains a role for county commissioners in the director's annual performance evaluation. The relevant statute does not express any formal mechanism for obtaining county commissioner input on the performance evaluation, but it directs the area board to "consider comments from the board of county commissioners."[164] County commissioner comment seems particularly appropriate when considering that the same statute lists among the area director's duties the obligation to provide information and advice to the county commissioners through the county manager, and the DHHS secretary criteria for evaluating director performance includes the director's performance in developing and maintaining effective relationships with local officials.

Employees under the direct supervision of the area authority are area employees, not county employees. Nonetheless, county personnel policies may apply to area employees in certain circumstances, and counties may pursue statutory options to bring the personnel administration of a single-county authority within the county personnel system. The degree to which county personnel policies may regulate area employees depends in part on whether the area authority is a single-county or multi-county authority and in part on whether a county affirmatively acts to exert authority over area employees.

In the case of a single-county area authority, the board of county commissioners may prescribe for area employees rules governing annual leave, sick leave, hours of work, holidays, and the administration of the pay plan, if these rules are adopted for county employees generally.[165] The State Human Resources Act also appears to grant the same authority to counties that comprise the catchment area of a *multi-county* authority, but the respective boards of county commissioners would have to jointly exercise this authority and apply the rules to their respective county employees, an unlikely course of action given the large number of counties participating in most area authorities. The county rules must be filed with the director of the Office of State Human Resources in order to supersede any rules adopted by the State Human Resources Commission.

The county served by a single-county area authority has the option of bringing area employees within the county system of personnel administration. If the board of county commissioners establishes and maintains a personnel system for all county employees and that system is approved by the State Human Resources Commission as being substantially equivalent to the state's personnel system for area authority employees, then the county personnel system will cover employees of the area authority.[166] In this case, employees covered by the county system would be exempt from the State Human Resources Act, but the provisions on equal opportunity for employment and compensation would continue to apply. In order for the county personnel system to be deemed substantially equivalent, it would have to meet the State Human Resources Commission's basic requirements for recruitment, selection, advancement, classification, compensation, suspension, dismissal, and affirmative action.

As for multi-county area authorities, county governments have no independent authority to substitute a substantially equivalent personnel system for the state rules of human resources administration.

Looking Ahead

While preliminary assessments of North Carolina's Medicaid managed care program for MH/DD/SA services indicate that cost savings are being achieved,[167] and while LMEs are still developing and perfecting the multiple and complex changes required to implement the newly minted managed care program, the future of North Carolina's public system of community MH/DD/SA services remains as uncertain as ever. As has been the case since 2001, the only constant on

163. S.L. 2012-151, sec. 9.(a).

164. G.S. 122C-121.

165. G.S. 126-9(a); G.S. 153A-94.

166. G.S. 126-11.

167. For example, based on the first three LMEs to implement managed care, DHHS reports that the per member (Medicaid enrollee) per month cost for services decreased on average by 10 percent and the state-funded cost of LME administration decreased by 9 percent. North Carolina Department of Health and Human Services, Proposal to Reform North Carolina's Medicaid Program, Report to North Carolina General Assembly (March 17, 2014), p. 28.

the horizon is the prospect for further change. While some proposed changes might be considered a natural or logical extension of prior changes—in a sense, the further evolution of managed care as ever more sophisticated techniques and measures are developed—other proposals involve more fundamental questions about the function, structure, and public nature of North Carolina's managed care organizations, as well as the size of the geographic areas they serve.

The 2014 General Assembly cut administrative funding to LME/MCOs based on the assumption that the nine LME/MCOs will consolidate into seven or fewer entities by June 30, 2015.[168] This action follows the presentation of a Medicaid reform plan by DHHS to the General Assembly on March 17, 2014, that recommends consolidating area authorities into four LME/MCOs, increasing DHHS review and oversight of LME/MCO operations, requiring LME/MCOs to implement more objective outcome and performance measures, and engaging organized groups of health care providers (accountable care organizations) to coordinate and manage physical health services for Medicaid beneficiaries.[169] Under the plan, LME/MCOs and accountable care organizations would collaborate to integrate physical and behavioral health care.

On two fundamental matters—whether to proceed with LME/MCOs as managed care organizations for MH/DD/SA services and whether to create a new department responsible for Medicaid services—the two houses of the 2014 General Assembly could not agree. During the regular legislative session, the House passed a Medicaid reform bill generally aligned with the DHHS Medicaid reform plan.[170] The Senate passed and sent to the House a committee substitute that, among other things, would eliminate the DHHS Division of Medical Assistance and move Medicaid responsibility to a new Department of Medical Benefits run by a board of business, health care, and health insurance leaders. The Senate committee substitute would also, it appears, end LME/MCO responsibility for managing MH/DD/SA services under the state's current federally approved Medicaid waiver and instead require that these services be managed together with other Medicaid health care services by private managed care companies.[171] On July 30, 2014, the House failed to concur with the Senate plan, and the General Assembly adjourned its 2014 Regular Session on August 20, 2014.[172] It is not clear whether these policy issues will arise again in the next legislative session.

Additional Resources

Botts, Mark F. "2001 Legislation Affecting Mental Health Developmental Disabilities, and Substance Abuse Services." *Mental Health Law Bulletin* No. 7. Chapel Hill, N.C.: UNC School of Government, March, 2002.

_____. "2006 Legislation Affecting Mental Health, Developmental Disabilities, and Substance Abuse Services." *Mental Health Law Bulletin* No. 10. Chapel Hill, N.C.: UNC School of Government, November, 2006.

_____. "General Assembly Changes County Requirements for Appointing LME Boards." *Coates' Canons: NC Local Government Law Blog.* Chapel Hill, N.C.: UNC School of Government, July 5th, 2012, http://canons.sog.unc.edu/?p=6736.

Botts, Mark F., and Ingrid M. Johansen. "Mental Health, Developmental Disabilities, and Substance Abuse Services." In *State and Local Government Relations in North Carolina.* 2nd ed., edited by Charles D. Liner. Chapel Hill, N.C.: UNC Institute of Government, 1995.

Douglass, Nam, Jenni Owen, and Lisa J. Berlin, eds. *Children's Mental Health: Strategies for Providing High Quality and Cost-effective Care.* North Carolina Family Impact Seminar, Center for Child and Family Policy. Durham, N.C.: Duke University, May 17 2006.

---

168. S.L. 2014-100 (S 744) and Joint Conference Committee Report on the Continuation, Expansion, and Capital Budgets, July 30, 2014.

169. North Carolina Department of Health and Human Services, Proposal to Reform North Carolina's Medicaid Program, Report to North Carolina General Assembly (March 17, 2014).

170. House Bill 1181.

171. House Bill 1181, Proposed Senate Committee Substitute.

172. Res. 2014-8 (HJR 1276).

Duda, Aisander, and Mebane Rash. "Mental Health, Developmental Disabilities, and Substance Abuse Service in North Carolina: A Look at the System and Who It Serves." *North Carolina Insight* 23, no. 4/24, no. 1. Raleigh, N.C.: N.C. Center for Public Policy Research, December 2012. www.nccppr.org/drupal/content/insightissue/4193/the-state-of-mental-health-in-north-carolina.

The Essential Governing Responsibilities of LME Boards (online program). Chapel Hill: UNC School of Government, 2008. www.sog.unc.edu/node/842.

Gray, Allison. "Reforming Mental Health Reform: The History of Mental Health Reform in North Carolina." *North Carolina Insight.* Special report. Raleigh, N.C.: Center for Public Policy Research, March 2009. www.nccppr.org/drupal/content/insightissue/88/the-history-of-mental-health-reform.

Millonzi, Kara A., ed. *Introduction to Local Government Finance.* 2nd ed. Chapel Hill, N.C.: UNC School of Government, 2014.

MH/DD/SAS Community Systems Progress Reports, prepared quarterly by the Quality Management Team, Community Policy Section, Division of Mental Health, Developmental Disabilities, and Substance Abuse Services. www.ncdhhs.gov/mhddsas/statspublications/Reports/DivisionInitiativeReports/communitysystems/index.htm.

North Carolina Council of Community Programs, www.nc-council.org/.

North Carolina Department of Health and Human Services, Division of Medical Assistance, www.ncdhhs.gov/dma/.

North Carolina Department of Health and Human Services, Division of Mental Health, Developmental Disabilities, and Substance Abuse Services, www.ncdhhs.gov/mhddsas/divisioninfo.htm.

North Carolina Division of Mental Health, Developmental Disabilities, and Substance Abuse Services. *State Plan 2006: An Analysis of State Plans 2001–2005.* Raleigh, N.C.: North Carolina Department of Health and Human Services.

North Carolina LME/MCO Performance Measurement and Reporting Guide. DMA and DMHDDSAS, September 17, 2013.

School of Government, University of North Carolina at Chapel Hill, www.sog.unc.edu/, and particularly the Mental Health website at www.sog.unc.edu/node/152.

About the Author

Mark F. Botts is a School of Government faculty member who specializes in mental health law.

Chapter 41

The County Jail

James M. Markham

Almost all North Carolina counties have a jail. Jails, also known as *detention centers* or *local confinement facilities,* should not be confused with prisons. Jails are local facilities used primarily to incarcerate criminal defendants awaiting trial or serving short sentences of imprisonment, usually for misdemeanors. Prisons, on the other hand, are state-run facilities that house convicted inmates serving longer sentences, usually for felonies.

No specific North Carolina law expressly requires a county to build or operate a jail, but several statutes imply that each county will have access to one. For instance, Section 15-6 of the North Carolina General Statutes (hereinafter G.S.) says that "[n]o person shall be imprisoned except in the common jail of the county, unless otherwise provided by law." Another statute, G.S. 162-56, states that "[p]ersons committed to the custody of the sheriff shall be confined in the facilities designated by law for such confinement, and shall not be confined in any other place." Read together, these laws indicate an expectation that a county will have a jail to house the inmates committed to the custody of its sheriff. As a practical matter, not having access to a jail would impede the smooth operation of the criminal justice system.

Shared Responsibility for Jails

Responsibility for a jail is shared between the board of county commissioners and the sheriff. Generally speaking, the county funds the jail and the sheriff manages it. That division of responsibility is reflected in the statutes. G.S. 153A-218 allows the county to "establish, acquire, erect, repair, maintain, and operate" a jail and to appropriate money to do so, while G.S. 162-22 says that the "sheriff shall have the care and custody of the jail in his county; and shall be, or appoint, the keeper thereof."

The state also has responsibilities related to local jails. Principally, the state Department of Health and Human Services (DHHS) is responsible for issuing minimum statewide standards in the construction and operation of jails, and then inspecting the jails for compliance with those standards. The standards are printed in Title 10A, Chapter 14, Subchapter J of the North Carolina Administrative Code (hereinafter N.C.A.C.). The Construction Section of DHHS's

Division of Health Service Regulation inspects each jail at least twice per year, as provided in G.S. 153A-222. If the jail does not meet standards and the DHHS secretary finds that the conditions put inmates' safety at risk, the secretary may order corrective action or close the jail.

Finally, the court system has a role related to the jail. Judicial officials control admissions to and releases from the jail by setting conditions of pretrial release for arrested defendants and by sentencing convicted offenders. Additionally, the grand jury is required to inspect the jail under G.S. 15A-628.

Construction of Jails

Given the size and diversity of a state like North Carolina, there is no one-size-fits-all approach to jail construction. To illustrate, Mecklenburg County houses over 2,000 inmates in multiple jails and annexes, while the Graham County jail has fewer than a dozen beds. Regardless of the size of the facility, jail construction is expensive. A variety of factors impacts the ultimate cost of a jail. For example, single cells are more expensive than dormitory space. A county also must consider whether it wishes to build a jail with sufficient capacity to house federal inmates or inmates from other counties, both of which can be a source of additional income for the county. But even for counties that have such contractual arrangements in place, local tax revenues are the primary source of funds for jail construction.

Jail construction must comply with DHHS standards, which are set out in the state Administrative Code. Under 10A NCAC 14J, Section .1203, counties must obtain DHHS approval before beginning construction of a new jail or altering an existing jail. The standards include specific requirements for visitation, medical, and housing areas, as well as special requirements for electrical and plumbing systems. The standards are detailed. For example, each single occupancy cell must, under the applicable standard, have 50 square feet of floor space, while a multiple occupancy cell must have 50 square feet of floor space for the first inmate and 35 additional square feet for each additional inmate. In general, the standards emphasize security, fire safety, and the health and welfare of inmates and staff.

District (Regional) Jails

Several counties have, over the years, found it advantageous to share a jail facility, which is allowed under G.S. 153A-219. Under that statute, two or more counties may join together to establish a district confinement facility, providing for an administrator to manage it. Several such facilities exist in North Carolina, including the Albemarle District Jail in Elizabeth City, which is operated pursuant to an agreement between Pasquotank, Perquimans, and Camden counties.

The Jail Population

Inmates in the county jail can be divided into different categories depending on the legal basis for their confinement. These categories are listed and briefly discussed below.

Pretrial Detention

By far, the largest category of jail inmates is pretrial detainees—those who have been arrested on a criminal charge and who are unable to satisfy conditions of pretrial release, such as an appearance bond. Well over half of all jail inmates in North Carolina fall into this category.

Sentenced Confinement

Relatively short sentences for misdemeanors are served in the jail. Many years ago, when there was no state prison system, all criminal sentences were served in jails. The state assumed responsibility for some prisoners around the time of the Great Depression, but short sentences were still served in county facilities. Since then, the sentence-length threshold at which responsibility for an inmate shifted from the county to the state has varied, fluctuating between 30 and 180 days.

Today, under G.S. 15A-1352, most misdemeanor sentences of 90 days or less are served in the local jail. Misdemeanants with sentences in excess of 90 days are housed in a jail that has volunteered to provide space for them through the Statewide Misdemeanant Confinement Program, created as part of the Justice Reinvestment Act of 2011.[1] All active sentences for driving while impaired (DWI), regardless of length, are served through the program. The law includes limited exceptions to these rules for times when the local jail is overcrowded (G.S. 148-32.1), or for inmates who are dangerous or in need of special medical attention (G.S. 162-39).

After 2011, active sentences for felonies can no longer be served in the jail—except to the extent that they remain in so-called backlog status at the jail after sentencing to await transfer to the prison system.

Probationary Confinement

Several forms of confinement that may be ordered as part of a probationary sentence can be served in the local jail. First, special probation under G.S. 15A-1351, often referred to as a split sentence, can be served in the jail, either in a single continuous period or in noncontinuous intervals, such as weekends. Second, jail confinement of up to 90 days can be ordered for misdemeanor probationers who commit certain violations of probation. And third, a probation officer may order a probationer to serve a short, two- or three-day stint in the jail—sometimes referred to as a "quick dip"—in response to a violation of probation.

Contempt of Court

Periods of incarceration for persons held in contempt of court, either civil or criminal, are served in the county jail. Contempt includes things like being disruptive during court proceedings or willfully failing to comply with a court order, such as an order to pay child support.

Public Intoxication

Under G.S. 122C-303, a law enforcement officer may, in certain circumstances, assist a person found intoxicated in a public place by taking him or her to the jail. That statute envisions the jail as a last resort in such situations, to be used only if the person is not in need of immediate medical care and no other facility is available.

Federal Inmates

Some jails house federal prisoners for the Federal Bureau of Prisons, Immigration and Customs Enforcement (ICE), or the U.S. Marshals service. This is permissible under G.S. 162-34 when adequate space is available. The reimbursement rate for such arrangements is set by agreement between the county and the United States government.

Financing Jail Operations

Paying for operation of the jail is primarily a county responsibility, although the state and, to a certain extent, the inmates themselves make some contribution. Under prior law, the state would reimburse the counties $18 per day for inmates serving sentences in the jail of 30 days or more. That provision was repealed in 2009, but some other reimbursements and fees remain. These fees help offset jail expenditures but by no means cover the full cost of housing inmates, which varies by facility but in almost every county exceeds $50 per day per bed.

1. S.L. 2011-192.

Jail Backlog

Beginning on the day after the sheriff has notified the prison system that a sentenced offender is ready for transfer to prison, the state must, under G.S. 148-29, reimburse the county for housing the offender at a per diem rate set by the General Assembly, plus certain medical costs. The current reimbursement rate is $40 per day.

Statewide Misdemeanant Confinement Fund

Counties that volunteer to house misdemeanor inmates pursuant to the Statewide Misdemeanant Confinement Program are paid a per diem rate for each inmate they house. The current reimbursement rate—set by the North Carolina Sheriffs' Association in the terms and conditions of the program—is $40 per day. Out-of-jail medical expenses are also reimbursed. The money comes from a statewide fund that is generated through court costs.

Jail Fees

Certain inmates must pay a fee for each day they are confined in the jail. There are two types of jail fees under G.S. 7A-313.

The first type of jail fee is for time spent in jail awaiting trial. Defendants who wind up getting convicted are liable to the county in the sum of $10 for each 24 hours of pretrial confinement. No fee is assessed if a person is acquitted or the case against him or her is dismissed. The pretrial jail fee is often collected as a condition of the defendant's probation, flowing back to the county through the clerk of court.

The second fee, set out in the second paragraph of G.S. 7A-313, is for "[p]ersons who are ordered to pay jail fees pursuant to a probationary sentence." The exact meaning of this portion of the law has never been crystal clear, but it has generally been interpreted to authorize a fee for every day served in jail as part of a sentence to special probation, also known as a split sentence. The amount of the probationary-sentence jail fee is set at the same per diem rate paid by the state to local jails for maintaining a prisoner, as set by the General Assembly in its appropriations acts. Today, the only such per diem rate paid by the state to the jails is the $40 per day backlog fee, and so that is also the probationary confinement fee.

The $10 pretrial confinement fee is mandatory unless the sentencing judge waives it. The $40 probationary-sentence jail fee, by contrast, applies only when ordered by the sentencing judge.

Work Release Earnings

Under G.S. 148-33.1(f), a jail may collect from a jail inmate's work release earnings an amount of money sufficient to pay for the actual costs of the inmate's keep. The sentencing court determines the amount to be collected.

Administering Jail Sentences

The sheriff and jail administrator are responsible for administering sentences to the jail. Some jails use computer software to aid in sentence administration, and some keep track of time by hand. Whatever the methodology, proper administration of a sentence requires a careful accounting of the time a person has already served and the incentive credits to which he or she may be entitled.

Jail Credit

The jail administrator must reduce an inmate's sentence by the amount of time he or she has already served, known as jail credit. For example, if an inmate sentenced to 30 days of imprisonment for a misdemeanor has spent 20 days in pretrial confinement, then he or she is said to have 20 days of jail credit, and thus only 10 days left to serve. Under G.S. 15-196.4, the sentencing judge is responsible for awarding jail credit and telling the custodian (the sheriff or the prison system) how much credit to apply. As a practical matter, however, the court system will often ask the jail for help in determining how long a defendant was in custody before trial—a determination that can sometimes be difficult when a person has multiple pending charges with varying conditions of release.

Sentence Reduction Credits

Most inmates do not serve every day of their imposed sentences. Many receive sentence reduction credits, which reward work or completion of educational programming with a reduction in the amount of time the inmate must serve. Sentence reduction credits incentivize good behavior by inmates, which is a benefit to themselves, their fellow inmates, and the jailer. Under G.S. 148-13, the sentence credit policies of the state Department of Public Safety (DPS) must be distributed to and followed by local jail administrators with respect to sentenced jail prisoners. Those regulations are available online through the DPS webpage (www.doc.state.nc.us/dop/policy_procedure_manual/b0100.pdf).

For misdemeanor sentences subject to Structured Sentencing (North Carolina's primary sentencing law), the main sentence reduction credit is called *earned time.* State law and DPS regulations allow for up to 4 days of earned time credit per month of incarceration. Thus, an inmate who receives a 90-day sentence could have that sentence reduced by approximately 12 days if he or she were to start a job immediately upon arriving at the jail.

A different rule applies to inmates serving time for impaired driving. They are eligible to receive a sentence reduction credit called *good time,* which is awarded at the rate of 1 day deducted for each day served without an infraction of inmate conduct rules. The practical effect of that day-for-day credit rule is that DWI sentences are cut in half by good time credit for well-behaved inmates.

Work and Education Programs in the Jail

A sheriff may, under G.S. 162-58, have a program to allow sentenced inmates to work during their time in the jail. The work must be on projects to benefit units of state or local government and must be done pursuant to rules issued by the board of county commissioners and approved by the sheriff. Inmates participating in the work program must be supervised by county employees or sheriff's office personnel. A sheriff or jail administrator may also allow a convicted misdemeanant to participate in a GED program or any other education, rehabilitation, or training program under G.S. 162-59.1 (no board approval is required for these programs). An inmate is entitled to a sentence reduction of 4 days for each 30 days of work performed or each 30 days of classes attended, with the caveat that an inmate's total sentence reduction for earned time and work or education programs may not exceed 4 days per month of incarceration under G.S. 15A-1340.20(d).

The work programs described immediately above should not be confused with work release, which is the temporary release of a sentenced prisoner to work on a paid job in the free community. Authorization to participate in work release comes from an order or recommendation by the sentencing judge, and the jail can recover a portion of a work release inmate's earnings to pay for the cost of housing him or her.

Care and Custody of Inmates

The sheriff is responsible for operating the jail. Most sheriffs appoint a jail administrator to manage day-to-day operations, but the sheriff retains final responsibility under G.S. 162-24. A web of constitutional, statutory, and regulatory provisions informs the proper administration of the jail. The jail must have an operations manual with written policies addressing everything from security to food service (DHHS regulations list the required topics). The operations manual must be reviewed and updated annually.

Security

Under G.S. 153A-224, the jail must have sufficient custodial personnel to provide continuous supervision of its prisoners. As a matter of constitutional law, the Eighth Amendment to the federal Constitution's bar on cruel and unusual punishment prohibits detention officers from using excessive force to maintain order and security in jails. When evaluating whether officers used excessive force against an inmate, courts will apply a test set out by the Supreme Court of the United States, asking "whether force was applied in a good-faith effort to maintain or restore discipline, or maliciously and sadistically to cause harm."[2] The Eighth Amendment also requires officers to protect inmates from

2. Hudson v. McMillian, 503 U.S. 1, 7 (1992).

assaults on one another. The jail is not required to guarantee inmates' safety, but officials can be held accountable if they are deliberately indifferent to a known risk of harm.[3] DHHS regulations offer more detailed guidance on day-to-day security requirements. For instance, they require that officers directly observe each inmate at least twice per hour, or more frequently in the case of inmates who are intoxicated, abusive, or who display certain other behaviors.

Medical Care

The jail has a duty to provide medical care for its prisoners—an obligation that can be both challenging and costly. Many who wind up in the jail are not in the best of health to begin with, and being incarcerated can sometimes aggravate preexisting physical and mental health conditions. Nevertheless, the Supreme Court of North Carolina long ago stated that "[i]t is but just that the public be required to care for the prisoner, who cannot, by reason of the deprivation of his liberty, care for himself."[4] Jails satisfy that obligation in different ways—some with in-house medical staff, some through contracts with full-service correctional health care providers, and some by accessing medical providers and hospitals in the local community.

Under G.S. 153A-225, every jail is required to have a medical plan, developed in consultation with local health officials and approved by the local or district health director. When necessary, the jail must provide emergency medical care from a licensed physician according to its jail medical plan. The county must pay for the costs of that care unless the inmate has third-party insurance, although many inmates are uninsured. For non-emergency care, the jail may set and collect a fee not exceeding $20 per incident, but it also must have a procedure for waiving that fee for indigent inmates. The jail is not required to address inmates' every elective or preventative health care issue, but officials must not be deliberately indifferent to inmates' serious medical needs, as that would violate the Eighth Amendment.[5]

Other Conditions of Confinement

Jail inmates do not forfeit all of their constitutional rights when they are incarcerated. Some rights may, however, be limited in the name of security and as part of an inmate's punishment. In general, the jail is justified in limiting a constitutional right when doing so is "reasonably related to legitimate penological interests."[6] For example, to avoid violating an inmate's First Amendment right to practice his or her religion, the jail should be prepared to accommodate special dietary needs, but only to the extent that doing so does not create an unreasonable expense, administrative burden, or security risk. A similar analysis applies to other limitations, such as limits on inmate mail, access to publications, and visitation.

Court interpretations of inmate rights evolve over time. For instance, for decades courts routinely held that a blanket policy of strip searching all arrestees as they were booked into jails violated the Fourth Amendment's prohibition on unreasonable searches and seizures. In 2012, however, the Supreme Court of the United States upheld that practice for inmates entering a jail's general population.[7] That change of course serves as a reminder to jail officials that policies should be reviewed periodically, ideally by legal counsel, to ensure they are up to date in light of recent cases and legislative amendments. At a minimum, DHHS regulations require an annual review of a jail's operations manual by the sheriff or jail administrator.

A background right that ensures the protection of other rights is the right to meaningful access to the courts. To protect that right, a jail should give its inmates access to an adequate law library or assistance from persons trained in the law.[8] According to DHHS regulations, the jail must address inmates' access to legal assistance or legal materials in its operations manual.

---

3. Farmer v. Brennan, 511 U.S. 825 (1994).
4. Spicer v. Williamson, 191 N.C. 487 (1926).
5. Estelle v. Gamble, 429 U.S. 97 (1977).
6. Turner v. Safley, 482 U.S. 78, 89 (1987).
7. Florence v. Bd. of Chosen Freeholders, 132 S. Ct. 1510 (2012).
8. Bounds v. Smith, 430 U.S. 817 (1977).

Managing the Jail Population

Overcrowding can be a problem for some jails—especially on weekends, when inmates serving split sentences typically report to serve the active portion of their time. Though not necessarily a constitutional violation in and of itself, overcrowding can have side effects that lead to liability.

Counties employ different strategies to manage their jail populations. First, when the jail population becomes too high, the sheriff can ask a judge to transfer inmates to another jail or to the prison system under G.S. 148-32.1. Some counties also take a preventative approach, conducting pretrial services programs or providing electronic supervision technology as an alternative to pretrial confinement in the jail. For sentenced inmates, the jail should of course be sure to award all appropriate jail credit and sentence reduction credits.

Jail officials cannot manage or limit the inmate population by themselves. Under G.S. 15-126, the sheriff may not refuse to accept inmates committed to his or her custody by the court system, even when the jail is overcrowded. With that in mind, an interagency approach is often the best strategy for long-term management of the jail population. Some counties have formed planning committees or task forces for this purpose, typically including representatives from the sheriff's department and the board of county commissioners, in addition to local judges, magistrates, prosecutors, defense lawyers, probation officers, the clerk of court, and others. Regular communication between these stakeholders will aid in the efficient administration of justice in the county.

About the Author

James M. Markham is a School of Government faculty member. His area of interest is criminal law and procedure, with a focus on the law of sentencing, corrections, and the conditions of confinement.

Chapter 42

The Courts

James C. Drennan

The framework of North Carolina's court system is established in Article IV, the judicial article, of the state constitution, which was substantially revised in 1962. Article IV created a unified statewide and state-operated General Court of Justice composed of three divisions: the Appellate Division (which includes the Supreme Court and the Appellate Division), the Superior Court Division, and the District Court Division.

Virtually all current operating costs of the General Court of Justice are borne by the state, and it employs all judicial system personnel. (Some local employees, such as bailiffs, assist the courts but are not technically court employees.) However, local governments—primarily the counties—must provide appropriate and adequate space as well as furniture for court system functions carried out at the local level. These functions include practically all operations of the system except central administration and the work of the appellate courts. Thus the court system is a major governmental activity executed largely at the level of the county and housed at its expense.

History of North Carolina's Court System

The current structure of the court system, in its most important organizational principles, dates back to the 1950s and 1960s. Beginning about 1955, a study of the court system was undertaken and a new framework for the state's judiciary was created. This new organizational structure was approved by the voters as part of a series of constitutional amendments and gradually implemented statewide. The transition to the new system concluded in December 1970, fifteen years after the initial studies began.

Several important organizational principles directed and shaped the reform effort.

- The 1950s trial court system was largely a local system, with almost every county having a slightly different structure. The reformed court structure eliminated these local courts and replaced them with a unified system, the General Court of Justice, that is nearly completely state-funded.
- In the 1950s each local court system had unique jurisdictional rules and charged different costs and fees, and the methods of selection for judges and justices of the peace varied by county. The reformed court structure has uniform jurisdictions, cost structures, and methods of selection for all judicial officials.
- In the 1950s many court officials were compensated from the fees they collected, and in criminal cases, only those found guilty were assessed fees. Under the reformed court structure all court officials are state employees, paid only by salaries.
- The 1950s court system had no central administration, since counties and cities provided most of the funding. The reformed court system is administered by a state agency, the Administrative Office of the Courts.

The guiding principle of the system that resulted from this sustained reform effort is that a person who seeks justice from the courts should find that the matter is heard by a judicial official who has the same powers, is selected in the same way, and has no financial stake in the outcome, regardless of where that person may live in North Carolina. In short, the goal is equal justice for all, in small towns and large cities, in the east and in the west, in the mountains and on the coast. The remainder of this chapter describes the organizational structure that is the product of the court reform efforts of the 1950s and 1960s and as it has since been modified.

Appellate Division

The Supreme Court

The supreme court has seven justices (N.C. Gen. Stat. (hereinafter G.S.) Chapter 7A, Subchapter II). Supreme court justices, like all judges, must be lawyers and may not practice law while serving as a judge. They are elected in statewide nonpartisan elections for eight-year terms. Meeting as a body in Raleigh, the court hears oral arguments by attorneys representing the various parties in cases appealed from the lower courts. It is also authorized to meet in up to two sessions per year in the Old Chowan County Courthouse in the Town of Edenton. The supreme court does not have a jury, and it makes no determinations of fact; it considers cases on the written record of the trial only, and it decides questions of law. Its opinions (decisions) are printed in bound volumes and become state law to the same extent as enactments of the General Assembly.

The supreme court primarily decides cases involving questions of constitutional law or legal questions of major significance to the state as a whole or murder cases including a sentence of death. These cases may already have been decided in the court of appeals or may have come to the supreme court directly from the trial court. The supreme court also must hear cases heard by the court of appeals in which one of the judges hearing the case dissents from the position taken by the majority.

The Court of Appeals

The court of appeals is composed of fifteen judges elected in the same manner and for the same term as the supreme court justices. Court of appeals judges, however, sit and render decisions in panels of three. Panels are authorized to convene in various localities throughout the state, although they usually do so in Raleigh. Like the supreme court, this court decides only questions of law, including whether a trial procedure was free of error that would have been prejudicial to the appellant.

The court of appeals was created in 1967 to relieve the supreme court of a portion of its case load, which had become more than it could reasonably handle. Unlike the supreme court (which is required to hear only certain kinds of cases), the court of appeals initially hears and decides all appealed cases, except those that go directly to the supreme court. No matter what the issue, every appellant has a right to be heard by at least one of these appellate courts, except in one instance: a defendant who pleads guilty to a criminal charge in the superior court may have his conviction reviewed only by petitioning the court of appeals for a writ of certiorari. The court of appeals then decides whether to issue the writ and hear the case. Similarly, a person appealing a court-martial proceeding may have the case reviewed only by the court of appeals.

Operation of the Appellate Courts

The supreme court is housed in the Justice Building, across the street from the southeast corner of the capitol. The court of appeals is located in the Ruffin Building, similarly situated, but on the southwest corner. Both courts are supported by the Supreme Court Library, housed primarily in the Justice Building, and each has a clerk, who is that court's administrative officer. The opinions of each court are prepared for publication by an appellate division reporter. Each justice or judge has two research assistants who must be law school graduates.

Vacancies often arise in the supreme court or the court of appeals other than at the end of a judge's term, usually through death or midterm retirement. In this case the governor may fill the vacancy by an appointment effective until the next general election. At the general election, the incumbent appointee almost always runs for the office. Appellate judges may be removed by impeachment or by the appellate courts (the supreme court in the case of a court of appeals judge and the court of appeals for a supreme court justice) on recommendation of the Judicial Standards Commission, discussed later in this chapter.

Supreme court justices and judges of the court of appeals must retire by age seventy-two, but they may do so earlier. A judge retiring before age seventy-two can become an "emergency" judge and may be recalled to active service for temporary duty on the court from which he or she retired (a retired supreme court justice can also serve in a similar capacity on the court of appeals). The governor issues commissions to emergency justices and judges that are valid until the holder is seventy-two. After that age a judge may continue to serve temporarily as a "recalled retired" judge. The compensation and jurisdiction are the same for both kinds of temporary service, with the compensation set at $400 per day as of November 2014.

Superior Court Division

Organization

The Superior Court Division consists of the superior court, which is the trial court for most cases involving a jury. At least two sessions of superior court for the trial of cases involving a jury are held each year in each county; in the busiest counties, several judges conduct sessions each week. The state is currently divided into judicial districts and divisions (G.S. Chapter 7A, Subchapter III).

The district structure for superior courts is complicated. In December 2014 there were seventy districts, and in each of those districts a specified number of judges must reside in and be elected from that district (the number ranges from one to three). Districts are generally established based on geographical considerations, caseload, and population. Some districts are composed of part of one county, others of a single county, a few are composed of parts of two counties, and others of several counties.[1] (The First Judicial District, in the northeastern part of the state, consists of seven counties.) Some of the districts serve only as units for election and are grouped with other districts to form a

1. If a district consists of part of one county and there is considerable disparity in the population of that county's districts, the state must demonstrate that it has a significant interest in creating the district and that the disparity is not substantially greater

Table 42.1. Superior Court Districts

Total	70
Districts with the same boundaries for administrative and electoral purposes	42
Districts that exist for electoral purposes	28
Sets of districts (groups of electoral districts combined to create an administrative unit)	8
Total number of administrative districts	50

single administrative entity. Those grouped districts are called "sets of districts." For more details on the number of districts in each category, see Table 42.1. The largest of those units, District 26A-C (in Mecklenburg County), elects seven judges. Many districts have only one resident judge. The fifty administrative judicial districts are grouped into eight divisions (see Figure 42.1).

Figure 42.1 North Carolina Superior Court Administrative Judicial Districts (Effective January 1, 2015)

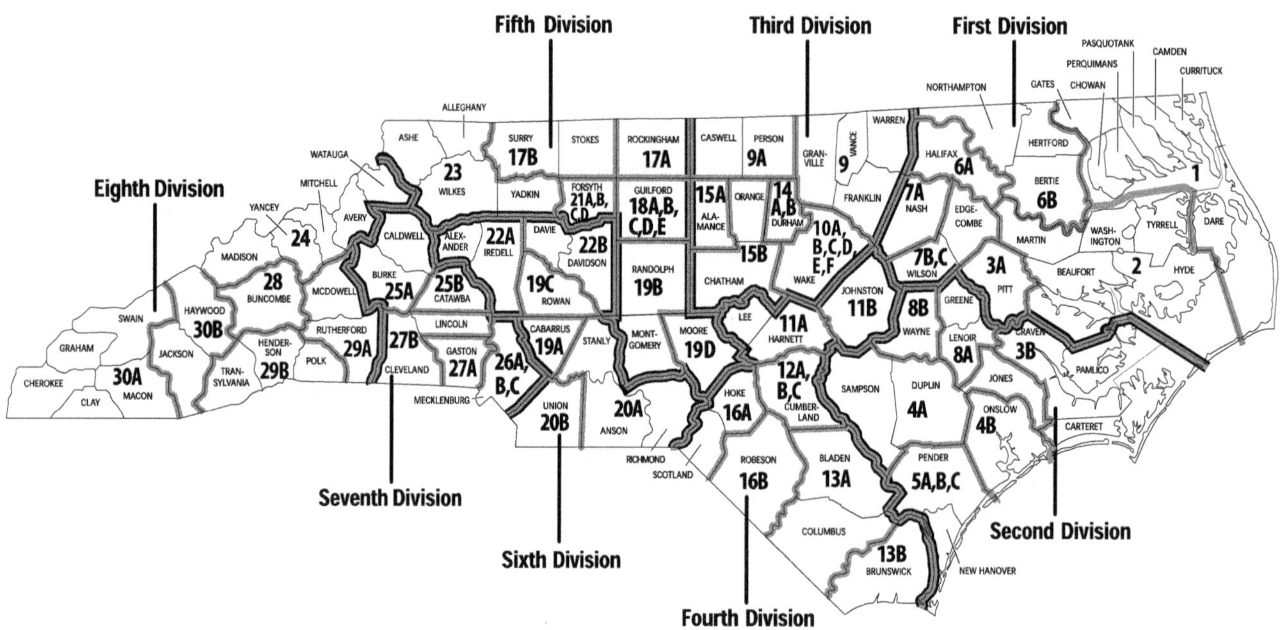

Note: Districts that have more than one letter associated with the district number (i.e., 10A, B, C, D) are divided into separate districts for electoral purposes. For administrative purposes, they are combined into a single district.

Judges

In December 2014 there were ninety-seven regular resident superior court judges. These judges are nominated in nonpartisan primaries by the voters of the district in which they live (see Table 42.2). They are elected in nonpartisan elections by those same voters for eight-year terms. In addition, there are fifteen special superior court judges appointed by the governor, and confirmed by the General Assembly. Three of these special judges are designated by rule of the supreme court as a Special Superior Court for Complex Business Cases, and their caseloads are composed almost exclusively of these cases and assigned to them by the chief justice. The terms of special judges are dependent on the legislative act establishing the judgeship and are currently set at five years. Special judges may reside anywhere in the

than necessary to accommodate that interest. Only Wake County districts have been affected by that ruling so far. Blankenship v. Bartlett, 363 N.C. 518 (2009).

Table 42.2 Numbers of Court Officials, 2014

Superior court judges	112 (97 regular judges and 15 special judges)
District court judges	270
Magistrates	Approximately 650

state. The number of judges at a particular time is specified by the General Assembly on the basis of the volume of judicial business. In each judicial district, the chief justice of the supreme court designates a regular resident judge to serve as the senior resident superior court judge. This judge has many administrative powers and duties related to the management of the superior courts in that district.

All superior court judges, whether resident or special judges, serve full time and may not practice law. Vacancies in resident judgeships are filled by appointment of the governor until the next general election.

North Carolina's constitution requires regular resident superior court judges to rotate from one district to another ("ride circuit") within their divisions. In a rotation cycle, each regular resident judge holds court for six months in each district for each judgeship authorized for the district. Thus the rotation period in a district that has two, three, four, or five resident judges is lengthened accordingly, to twelve, eighteen, twenty-four, or thirty months served in six-month segments. These six-month segments may not be served in continuous order, and the percentage of time served may not be exact due to special assignments either at or away from home. Many regular resident judges thus spend months holding court over 100 miles from their homes. The extent to which North Carolina rotates the judges of its major trial courts is unique among the states, although the distances required were reduced in 2000 when the number of divisions was increased from four to eight.

Special superior court judges are assigned by the chief justice of the supreme court to hold court in any county where needed, without regard to district of residence or rotation requirements. Theoretically, a special judge could eventually sit in each of the 100 counties of the state. In practice, special judges are usually appointed so that they come from all parts of the state; and, insofar as possible, they are assigned to counties reasonably close to their residences.

Retirement rules for superior court judges are similar to those for Appellate Division justices and judges. Those who retire before reaching the mandatory retirement age of seventy-two can become "emergency" judges and as such may be assigned by the chief justice to temporary service on the superior court bench until age seventy-two. An older judge may continue to serve temporarily as a "recalled retired" judge. The compensation and jurisdiction are the same for both kinds of temporary service. A retired judge who engages in private legal practice is not eligible for this temporary service, although many retired judges do serve as mediators or arbitrators and still serve as temporary judges.

Superior court judges may be removed by impeachment or by the supreme court upon recommendation of the Judicial Standards Commission (see the section "Judicial Standards Commission," below).

Jurisdiction

Civil

Civil jurisdiction is concurrent between the two trial divisions (superior and district) of the General Court of Justice (G.S. Chapter 7A, Articles 20 and 22). The "proper" division, however, for cases that involve $25,000 or less in controversy is the District Court Division; for cases over that amount, the Superior Court Division. Normally this $25,000 dividing line is followed, but by consent of the parties and for reasons of speed or convenience, cases may be filed and tried in the "improper" division. No such case is ever "thrown out of court" for lack of jurisdiction, but on request a superior court judge may transfer it to the proper division.

Exceptions to the general rule that the amount in controversy determines the proper forum arise in certain specific subject-matter categories. For example, civil domestic relations matters (divorce and custody and support of children) are properly the business of the district court, while the superior court is the proper forum for constitutional issues, special proceedings, corporate receiverships, and reviews of certain administrative agency rulings. The clerk of superior court (rather than a superior or district court judge) handles probate of wills and appointment of guardians, and in doing so discharges duties performed by probate judges in many other states. Civil cases involving amounts not over $10,000 may, under certain conditions, be assigned to a magistrate for trial. (Clerks of court and magistrates are discussed later in this chapter.)

Criminal

The superior court hears cases involving felonies (serious crimes), misdemeanors (less serious crimes), and infractions (noncriminal law violations such as minor traffic offenses). Misdemeanor and infraction cases are normally heard first by the district court, but trials by jury of those matters, and all dispositions of felony cases, occur only in the superior court. Defendants are tried by a jury of twelve. If the charge is a felony, the process usually begins when a grand jury of eighteen members issues an indictment. A defendant may waive the indictment process, except in capital (potential death sentence) cases. The jury trial may be waived by the defendant, with the consent of the judge; in that case the judge conducts the trial. Trial of misdemeanors and infractions appealed from district court is de novo—that is, the case is tried anew, without regard to the original trial court proceedings. About 30 percent of the superior court's criminal caseload consists of such appeals from the district court.

District Court Division

Organization

The District Court Division is divided into forty-four judicial districts (see Figure 42.2) (G.S. Chapter 7A, Subchapter IV). Most of these districts are established as units for elections and for court administration, except in two places (Districts 9 and 9B and Districts 20B and 20C). These four districts are combined into two sets of districts for administrative purposes (see Table 42.3). Like the superior court, the district court sits in the county seats. It may also convene in certain other cities and towns specifically authorized by the General Assembly. Most counties have no additional seats of court, but a few have several; presently the total number of additional seats is forty (a table in G.S. 7A-133 lists the additional seats).

Figure 42.2 North Carolina District Court Districts (Effective January 1, 2015)

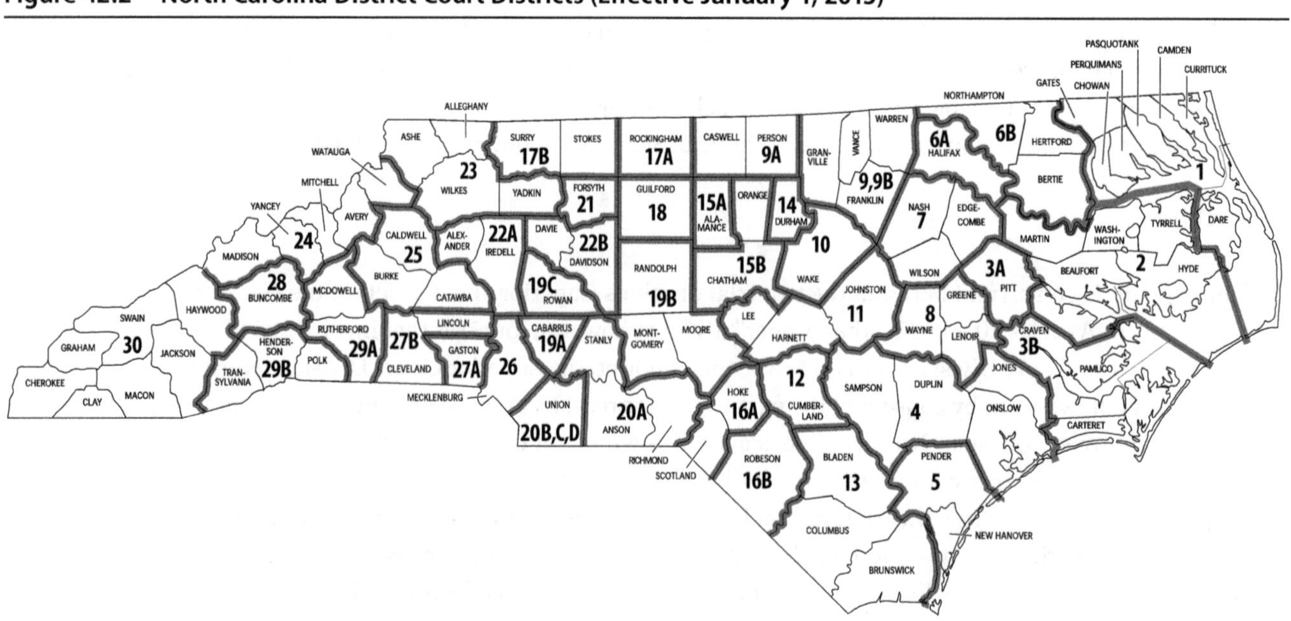

Note: Districts 9 and 9B and districts 20B, 20C, and 20D are districts for electoral purposes only. They are combined for administrative purposes.

Table 42.3 District Court Districts

Total	44
Districts with same boundaries for administrative and electoral purposes	39
Districts that exist for electoral purposes	5
Sets of districts (groups of electoral districts combined to create administrative unit)	2
Total number of administrative districts	41

District court judges serve an entire district. Unlike superior court judges, they do not hold court out of their district of residence unless specially assigned by the chief justice of the supreme court for a particular session of court.

Judges

As of November 2014 the General Assembly has authorized 270 district court judges. They are elected in nonpartisan district elections for four-year terms. They must be lawyers, serve full time, and may not practice law. The state constitution requires that judges be residents of the districts from which they are elected. While that requirement has generally been interpreted to allow residents of any county in a district to seek election for any judgeship in the district, in two districts (11 and 13) the legislature has required candidates for each judgeship to come from specified counties. In District 13, for example, only candidates from Bladen County may run for one of the judgeships assigned to that district, but voters from all three counties in that district may vote for the judgeship.

Each district has from two to twenty-one judges, depending on population and geography. Specialization by subject matter (for example, juvenile or domestic relations cases) is encouraged by law but can be achieved to a significant degree only in districts with several judges; in less populous counties, district court judges must be generalists.

The chief justice of the supreme court appoints one judge in each district as chief district judge. Their responsibilities include assigning themselves and the other judges in their districts to sessions of court, prescribing the times and places at which magistrates will discharge their duties, and assigning civil ("small claims") cases to magistrates for trial. Chief district judges are required to meet at least once a year to discuss mutual problems; make recommendations concerning improvement of the administration of justice; and promulgate a schedule of minor traffic, alcohol, boating, littering, fish, game, and parks offenses for which clerks of court and magistrates may accept guilty pleas.

Vacancies in the office of district court judge are filled by the governor for the remaining unexpired term. The local district bar association provides nominations to the governor, but the governor is not bound to select from that list of nominees. Retirement and removal of district judges are governed by the same principles that pertain to superior court judges.

Magistrates

Magistrates for each county are appointed for initial two-year terms by the senior regular resident superior court judge based on nominations of the clerk of superior court (G.S. Chapter 7A, Article 16). Subsequent terms are for four years. Magistrates are officers of the district court and they are supervised by the chief district court judge in nondiscretionary judicial matters and by the clerk in clerical matters. Magistrates serve only in their counties of residence, subject to special assignments. They are full- or part-time officials, as determined by the chief district judge and the Administrative Office of the Courts (the state agency responsible for court administration), and their salaries, which are paid by the state, vary with their educational levels and length of service. Very few are lawyers. All magistrates appointed after July 1, 1994, must either be college graduates or have an associate degree and four years of experience in a related field. New magistrates must also complete a two-week training course during their first two-year term. As it is for judges, the mandatory retirement age for magistrates is seventy-two.

The minimum number of magistrates allowed for a county is fixed by law. If the minimum quota is inadequate and funds are available, additional magistrates may be authorized by the Administrative Office of the Courts on recommendation of the chief district judge. A vacancy in the office of magistrate is filled for the remaining unexpired term in the same manner as the original appointment was made. After a formal complaint establishing grounds to remove a magistrate (basically the same grounds applicable to judges), a superior court judge may remove the magistrate after a hearing. The magistrate has the right to appeal to the court of appeals.

Jurisdiction

Civil

As noted in the discussion of the superior court's civil jurisdiction, most jurisdiction of this type is held concurrently by the superior and district courts (G.S. Chapter 7A, Articles 20 and 22). Domestic relations cases are an exception, however. They are heard in the district court regardless of the amount of money involved. When large monthly child-support awards are entered or large amounts of marital assets are distributed on divorce, a district court's orders can involve millions of dollars.

Juvenile

The district court also has jurisdiction over juvenile matters. These cases concern children under the age of eighteen (sixteen for delinquent children) who are delinquent, undisciplined, dependent, neglected, or abused. Delinquents are children who have committed acts that, if committed by adults, would be crimes or infractions. Undisciplined children are primarily those who are beyond parental control, truant from school, or both (these two categories are defined in G.S. 7B-1501). The categories of dependent, neglected, and abused are self-explanatory (and are defined in G.S. 7B-200).

The two types of juvenile cases are those in which children have committed an offense, an act of truancy, or something similar (delinquent and undisciplined cases); and those in which children have been, or are threatened with being, harmed, and the court is seeking to protect them (abuse, neglect, and dependency cases). Separate procedures are used for each of the two types of cases; the first type involves procedures similar to those used in criminal court, and the second uses processes designed to promote the protection of the child.

All juvenile court proceedings begin by petition (documents similar to warrants or indictments in adult criminal cases and complaints used in other civil cases). The hearing conducted by the judge on the petition is less formal than in other kinds of cases. Before a hearing to determine either the child's status or what disposition should be made of the case, a court counselor (juvenile probation officer) or a social services official may investigate both the matter alleged in the petition and the child's background and make findings for the judge's consideration. The judge's authority in delinquency cases ranges from placing children on probation to confining them in state institutions. In abuse, neglect, and dependency cases, the judge has wide latitude in deciding how to protect children. No juvenile cases are heard by a jury.

Involuntary Commitment

The district court has jurisdiction over the involuntary commitment of mentally ill persons, inebriated individuals, and alcoholics to mental health and alcoholic treatment facilities.

Criminal

The criminal jurisdiction of the district court is limited in felony cases. Since they must be tried or otherwise disposed of in the superior court, the district court has authority only to conduct preliminary hearings to determine whether there is probable cause (that is, a good reason exists for believing the defendant is probably guilty) to bind the defendant over to the superior court for trial. If all parties (and the judges) consent, a district court judge may accept a guilty plea to the two lowest levels of felonies (Classes H and I) and enter a judgment in the case. In misdemeanor and infraction cases, the district court has exclusive original jurisdiction that, with respect to very minor offenses, it shares with the magistrate.

Magistrate

The magistrate's jurisdiction is both civil and criminal. This official's authority in criminal matters is limited to the following:

- Trying worthless-check cases or accepting guilty pleas when the amount of the check is $2,000 or less
- Accepting guilty pleas to other minor misdemeanors for which the maximum punishment is thirty days' confinement or a $50 fine
- In cases involving minor traffic, alcohol, boating, and fish and game offenses, accepting guilty pleas and imposing a fine fixed by a uniform statewide schedule promulgated by the Conference of Chief District Judges

In addition, magistrates have the important duties of issuing arrest and search warrants and setting conditions for release on bail.

The magistrate is also authorized to try small civil claims that involve up to $10,000, including summary ejectment (landlord's action to oust a tenant) cases, on assignment of the chief district judge. The plaintiff must request that the claim be assigned to a magistrate and at least one defendant must reside in the county in which the action is filed. (If the chief district judge does not assign a small claim to a magistrate within five days after the plaintiff so requests, the claim is tried in district court as a regular civil case.)

The typical small claim is for recovery of personal property, for money for goods sold or services rendered, or for summary ejectment, and the parties are not usually represented by attorneys. Often the claim is uncontested. Simplified trial procedures are followed. The magistrate's judgment has the same effect as that of a judge and is recorded by the clerk of superior court.

The magistrate is also authorized to perform various quasi-judicial or administrative functions. Of these, performance of the marriage ceremony is the most common; magistrates are the only judicial officials in the state who can officiate at weddings. Other authorized functions include administering oaths, verifying pleadings, and taking acknowledgments of (notarizing) instruments.

Judicial Standards Commission

The historical methods of removing judges—impeachment and joint resolution by the legislature—have not been used in North Carolina since the nineteenth century. These procedures are still authorized by Article IV of the state constitution, but that article has been amended to require the General Assembly to provide another method to remove judges from office. In 1973 the legislature created a Judicial Standards Commission (G.S. Chapter 7A, Article 30), composed of judges, lawyers, and nonlawyers. If a judge is charged with willful misconduct in office, failure to perform the duties of the office, habitual intemperance, conviction of a crime involving moral turpitude, or conduct prejudicial to the administration of justice that brings the judicial office into disrepute, the commission is authorized to conduct a public hearing to investigate that charge. If the commission decides the evidence warrants such action, it may recommend to the supreme court that the judge be removed. If the supreme court agrees with the recommendation, it may remove the judge from office. The commission may also recommend removal for physical or mental incapacity, and in any case can recommend lesser sanctions, such as public censure or suspension (which require action by the supreme court), or can on its own issue a private letter of reprimand.

Although this procedure for disciplining, removing, and retiring judges was created fairly recently, a similar one is now used by all the states.

As of December of 2014, the North Carolina Supreme Court has censured or suspended thirty-six trial court judges for professional misconduct and has removed nine trial judges from office. Several other judges have vacated their offices while under investigation (for more details, see Table 42.4).

The grounds for removing a magistrate are the same as for a judge, but the removal proceeding is conducted by a superior court judge rather than the supreme court.

Table 42.4 Actions of Supreme Court to Discipline Judges, 1971–2014

Appellate judges censured or removed	0
Superior court judges removed	2
Superior court judges censured	7
District court judges censured	27
District court judges suspended	2
District court judges removed	7

Court-Related Personnel

District Attorneys

In criminal matters the district attorney represents the state in the superior and district courts (G.S. Chapter 7A, Article 9). This official is elected in partisan district elections for a four-year term. In each prosecutorial district, full-time assistant district attorneys, paid by the state, serve at the district attorney's pleasure. The state also provides part-time assistant district attorneys in districts where they are needed due to case load or geography and compensates them at a daily rate. With two exceptions, the prosecutorial district lines are identical to the district court lines.

A district attorney may be removed from office for misconduct after a hearing before a superior court judge.

Clerks of Superior Court

The clerk of superior court is elected in partisan county elections for a four-year term (G.S. Chapter 7A, Article 12). Unlike trial and appellate judges, clerks need not be lawyers, and relatively few are. Paid by the state on the basis of the county's population and his or her years of service, the clerk is responsible for all clerical and recordkeeping functions of the superior and district courts for both civil and criminal cases. Thus in each county there is only one clerk's office for the two trial courts.

The clerk is also ex officio judge of probate and is thus the first to hear matters relating to the probate of wills and the administration of decedents' estates. In addition, the clerk has jurisdiction over the estates of minors and incompetents and is authorized to hear a variety of special proceedings, such as adoptions, condemnation of private lands for public use, and sales of land for partition or to create cash assets. Depending on the volume of business, the clerk employs a number of assistants and deputies who are paid by the state in accordance with a schedule fixed by the General Assembly (see G.S. 7A-102(c)).

The clerk is bonded by a blanket state bond. The senior regular resident superior court judge who serves the clerk's county may, after a hearing, remove a clerk for misconduct or mental or physical incompetence.

Court Reporters

Court reporters are appointed for the superior court by the senior regular resident superior court judge in each judicial district. Compensation is set by the appointing judge, within limits fixed by the Administrative Office of the Courts. Reporters are required to record verbatim such courtroom proceedings as testimony of witnesses, and orders, judgments, and jury instructions by the judge. Transcripts of courtroom proceedings are required when an appeal is taken, and reporters receive a per-page fee in addition to their salaries for preparing transcripts for appellants. The reporter's original notes are state property and are preserved by the clerk of superior court.

If a reporter is not available, the state will furnish electronic recording equipment on request of the senior regular resident superior court judge. The clerk of superior court is responsible for operating such equipment and for preserving the record produced, and the Administrative Office of the Courts is responsible for transcribing the record if that becomes necessary. In a few counties, video recordings of proceedings are used instead of court reporters.

All civil and juvenile proceedings in district court are recorded by audio recording equipment. No verbatim records are kept of district court criminal proceedings, since they may be appealed for a trial de novo (anew) in superior court, which does keep these records. In 1995 the General Assembly eliminated all court reporter positions assigned to the district courts.

Juvenile Court Counselors

A statewide system of court counselors provides probation and after-care services to juveniles in the jurisdiction of the district court. Each judicial district is assigned one or more counselors. In addition to acting as probation officers, they conduct prehearing studies of children alleged to be delinquent or undisciplined. This program, called intake counseling, attempts to direct the handling of juveniles from the courts to appropriate community-based agencies whenever possible. Counselors also help the court handle cases in which children require detention before or after a hearing.

Office space for court counselors is provided by the county. Court counselors are not court system employees; they are employed by the Department of Public Safety.

Probation and Parole Officers

North Carolina also has a statewide system of adult probation and parole officers (G.S. Chapter 15, Article 20). These officers, who supervise adults placed on probation or released on parole, are employees of the state Department of Public Safety, Division of Adult Correction. Their salaries and program operating costs are paid by the state, but space for local offices must be furnished by the county.

Guardians ad Litem

In child abuse, neglect, and dependency cases, parents are entitled to the services of an attorney and the department of social services represents the state's interest. In 1983 the General Assembly recognized the need for the children affected to have an advocate who represents only their interests. In establishing a statewide program to meet that need, the legislature utilized the results of some privately funded pilot programs that provided that service with volunteer guardians ad litem, who were in turn supported by an attorney and a volunteer coordinator (G.S. Chapter 7B, Article 12). The program is now in place statewide and represents children who are abused, dependent, or neglected. In doing so, it recognizes that while social services departments seek the best interests of children in their representation to the courts, the issues involved are so important and difficult that judges would benefit from having another perspective independent of the agency responsible for implementing the court's decision. The program is run by coordinators who recruit volunteers to work with the children and hire lawyers when they are needed in court.

The county must provide office space for the coordinator and any other employees of the guardian ad litem program.

Community Service Coordinators

In some criminal cases, judges require convicted defendants to perform community service work for public or nonprofit agencies. The state Department of Public Safety administers this program; it assigns a community service coordinator and a supporting staff to each judicial district.[2] These personnel are state employees, but their office space must be provided by the county.

Supporting Staff for Court Officials

Judges and other court officials have support staffs. Trial court administrators or coordinators assist judges with their administrative responsibilities, particularly in matters related to the management of civil cases or the jury system. Family court or drug court personnel or arbitration or custody mediation staff work in locations where those programs are established; they provide professional, clerical, and case management support for the operation of these court programs. Most of these employees are paid by the state, but in some instances their salaries are paid from grants or by a local government. In 2013, the General Assembly eliminated all state support for drug courts, so any drug courts are now funded from other sources.

---

2. N.C. Gen. Stat. (hereinafter G.S.) § 20-179.4; G.S. 143B-475.1.

Bailiffs and Security Personnel

Courthouse security is the county's responsibility. Providing adequate security involves facilities planning and maintenance, security screening procedures, and the staff necessary to implement these functions. The county sheriff usually provides the security staff. Some counties, however, contract with private firms to provide courthouse security. These security officers may be "company police" (private officers licensed by the state to provide law enforcement services in specified locations) or they may be employees without law enforcement powers.

Security inside a particular courtroom is provided by a bailiff, who is employed by the county sheriff for that purpose. Bailiffs may be deputy sheriffs or custodial officers with full arrest powers and the power to possess and use firearms in the course of their duties, or the sheriff may assign the bailiff function to employees who are not sworn deputies or custodial officers and consequently do not have the authority to possess firearms in the courthouse or to arrest anyone.

Public Defenders and Representation of Indigents

Defendants accused of crimes for which confinement is likely and who are financially unable to employ counsel to represent them are entitled to such services at state expense (G.S. Chapter 7A, Subchapter IX). In sixteen public defender districts most indigent defendants are represented by the public defender's office, a staff of full-time, state-paid attorneys whose sole function is to represent indigents. For a list of the counties served by these public defenders, see Table 42.5.

Indigents who are not represented by attorneys in the public defender's office in these counties are assigned to private attorneys, whose fees are paid on a per-case or per-day basis; these private attorneys are used when the public defender has a conflict of interest or an overload of cases. In districts not served by a public defender, legal representation of indigents is provided solely by state-paid private attorneys. Pursuant to a legislative mandate, the Indigent Defense Services Commission contracts with attorneys to handle multiple cases, instead of using a per-case assignment system.

Each public defender is appointed by the senior resident superior court judge serving the district, on the written nomination of the district bar. In one case (districts 1 and 2), a regional public defender serves both districts. Public defenders serve four-year terms and select their own attorney-assistants. The county must provide office space for the public defender staff.

There is also an appellate defender's office. It represents indigents whose cases are appealed when appointed to do so by the trial judge. It is a relatively small office and handles comparatively few cases, but they are usually among the most difficult. The appellate defender is appointed by the chief justice of the supreme court.

Defendants are often ordered to repay the state for their lawyers' fees in one of three ways—as a condition of probation, in lieu of any future state tax refunds, or as a civil money judgment. Even though most defendants never become financially able to pay the entire amount of their fees, the state does recover about 10 percent of its costs each year.

The Indigent Defense Services Commission was created by the General Assembly in 2000 to manage the budget for indigent defense and promulgate standards related to various aspects of the indigent defense system. Funds for indigent defense are provided by the General Assembly and in 2013–14, the budget to provide these services (public defenders and assigned counsel) was around $115 million.

Jury Selection

The law provides for selection of prospective jurors in each county by a jury commission (G.S. Chapter 9). The commission has three members, with one each appointed by the senior resident superior court judge, the clerk of superior court, and the board of county commissioners. The commission's salary and operating costs are paid by the county. Each commission draws from the Division of Motor Vehicles driver's license rolls and the voter registration list for that county to compile jury lists. The Division of Motor Vehicles combines the lists and submits them to the appropriate court officials every two years. Selection is by a random process, with no opportunity for favoritism or discrimination

Table 42.5 Districts and Counties Served by Public Defenders, 2014

Public defender district	Counties served
1	Camden, Chowan, Currituck, Dare, Gates, Pasquotank, and Perquimans (public defender also serves District 2, Beaufort, Hyde, Martin, Tyrrell, and Washington)
3A	Pitt
3B	Carteret
5	New Hanover
10	Wake
12	Cumberland
14	Durham
15B	Chatham and Orange
16A	Scotland and Hoke
16B	Robeson
18	Guilford
21	Forsyth
26	Mecklenburg
27A	Gaston
28	Buncombe
29B	Henderson, Polk, Transylvania

because of race, sex, or any other constitutionally prohibited reason. No one is exempt from jury duty; all qualified citizens, if summoned, are expected to serve. (Inability to hear or understand English, physical or mental incompetence, or conviction of a felony are common grounds for disqualification.) There is no maximum age for jury service, nor is there an age at which a person is automatically excused. Prospective jurors who are seventy-two years old or older may request to be excused without appearing personally, and in practice, they are often excused, but the excuse is not automatic and a person over seventy-two who satisfies the statute's criteria may be required or allowed to serve. Excuses can be granted only by a trial judge, or, if the responsibility is delegated by the chief district court judge, by a trial court administrator (a nonjudicial official in certain counties whose function is to expedite the work of the courts)—and then only for reasons of compelling personal hardship or because service would be detrimental to the public health, safety, or welfare.

Now almost all counties use computers to compile the master jury list and to keep records of those who have already served. When more than one jury session of court is sitting at a time, jurors may be "pooled" (jurors for more than one court session are selected from the same panel), a procedure that saves both money and jurors' time.

Prospective jurors who are not selected for grand jury service usually serve only one week. In some counties (typically the more urban counties) jurors serve for only one trial or one day, whichever is longer. A certain number of jurors (generally nine each six months) are selected to serve on the grand jury. These jurors (whose main duty is to decide whether to charge persons accused of felonies by indicting them) usually serve for a year (six months in some large counties), but are usually "on duty" for no more than the first day of a session of superior court for the trial of criminal cases. Where criminal sessions occur weekly, the grand jury is not needed each week but is convened every few weeks.

The superior court uses a twelve-person jury in both civil and criminal cases. The district court also uses a twelve-person jury in civil cases only; criminal cases are tried by the district court judge without a jury.

Administrative Office of the Courts

The Administrative Office of the Courts, with its central office in Raleigh, handles the administrative details of the court system (G.S. Chapter. 7A, Article 29). Its director is appointed by the chief justice of the supreme court. The director is a nonjudicial officer, responsible for a variety of administrative functions of the Judicial Department. The director's major duties include preparing and administering the Judicial Department's budget; fixing the number of employees in the respective clerks of court offices; supervising the statewide guardian ad litem system; prescribing uniform forms, records, and business methods for the clerks' offices; keeping statistics; and representing the courts in the legislature and other forums.

The Judicial Department budget for fiscal year 2014–15 was approximately $464 million (not including funds for indigent defense services).

Costs, Fees, and Fines

The system the state uses for billing court costs and fees is based on a lump-sum averaging of costs (per type of case and court) (G.S. Chapter 7A, Article 28). In civil actions, special proceedings, and administration of estates, there are only three cost items: a General Court of Justice fee, which accrues to the state for financing the courts generally; a fee to provide phone systems in the county courthouses; and a facilities fee, discussed below. The amount of the fee in each case may vary with the nature of the action or proceeding and with the court in which it is tried. In criminal actions, there are five items in the uniform bill of costs. In addition to the three fees applicable in civil cases, a law enforcement officers' fee is chargeable for each arrest or personal service of criminal process; it is payable to the county or city whose officer performed the service. (Fees for arrests made by state officials accrue to the county where the arrest was made.) The fifth item is a Law Enforcement Officers' Benefit and Retirement Fund fee. Tables 42.6 and 42.7 provide the most recent fee levels.

Besides these basic costs items, in any particular case additional expenses—such as drug testing fees; charges for using a pretrial release program; fees of witnesses; charges for failure to appear; or fees for court-appointed guard-

Table 42.6 Basic Civil Court Costs, December 2014 (G.S. 7A-305)

Civil	Amount
Magistrates (except domestic violence cases)	
General Court of Justice[a]	80.00
Facilities fee	12.00
Phones for courthouses	4.00
Total	96.00
District Court (except certain domestic cases)	
General Court of Justice[a]	130.00
Facilities fee	16.00
Phones for courthouses	4.00
Total	150.00
Superior Court	
General Court of Justice[a]	180.00
Facilities fee	16.00
Phones for courthouses	4.00
Total	200.00

a. There is also a $30.00 service fee for each item of civil process served by the sheriff, as well as additional fees for counterclaims, divorce actions, or any motion filed after a case is begun.

Table 42.7 Basic Criminal Court Costs, December 2014 (G.S. 7A-304)

Criminal	Amount
District Court (including criminal cases before magistrates)	
General Court of Justice[a]	129.50
Facilities fee	12.00
Law Enforcement Officers Benefit Fund (LEOB) and sheriff's pensions	7.50
Misdemeanor Confinement Fund	18.00
Phones for courthouses	4.00
Criminal Justice Training and Standards Commission	2.00
DNA database[b]	2.00
Total	175.00
Superior Court	
General Court of Justice[a]	154.50
Facilities fee	30.00
LEOB and sheriffs' pensions	7.50
Phones for courthouses	4.00
Criminal Justice Training and Standards Commission	2.00
DNA database[b]	2.00
Total	200.00

a. There is also a $5.00 service fee for each arrest or service of criminal process, including citations and subpoenas, applicable to all levels of court, as well as additional fees for motor vehicle cases, failures to appear, and drug lab fees.

b. The DNA fee does not apply to infractions.

ians, referees, interpreters, or commissioners—may be incurred. These charges are assessed along with the basic costs against the party liable for them.

Witness fees are fixed at $5 per day, plus mileage if the witness comes from outside the county; juror fees—paid by the state—are generally set at $12 per day, with no mileage allowance. Juror fees are increased to $20 for the second through fifth days. For more than five days' service, a juror is paid $40 per day. A charge for the miscellaneous services rendered by magistrates and clerks is also authorized, and the charges assessed by the sheriff for serving civil process (legal documents in civil cases) and related costs are included in the five all-inclusive, uniform categories. No charges of any kind other than those specified in the law may be imposed for the use of court-related facilities and services. All fees charged by clerks, magistrates, and sheriffs accrue to the governmental unit concerned; none accrue to individuals. The only fees assessed by court employees that accrue to the person assessing the fee are transcript fees collected by court reporters. Table 42.8 lists the total amounts collected by the court system for the most recent year for which records are available.

Table 42.8 Selected Fees and Fines Collected by Courts and Paid to Local Governments, 2013–14

Facilities fees paid to counties	$13,497,336.00
Facilities fees paid to cities	$288,008.00
Jail fees paid to counties	$4,089,080.00
Jail fees paid to cities	$63.00
Officers' service fees paid to counties	$7,403,222.00
Officers' service fees paid to cities	$1,643,877.00
Fines and forfeitures paid to local school funds	$36,394,509.00

The amount of total fees collected for the state and local governments amounts to approximately 55 percent of the cost of operating the courts (this does not include indigent defense, probation, or other related costs not paid directly by the Judicial Department, nor is the amount of fines collected used in making the calculation) and reflects the policy decision (often debated by the legislature) that courts, like most other governmental functions, should not be supported solely by user fees. When fines are included, that percentage rises to somewhere between 65 and 75 percent. The amount of fines and forfeitures varies significantly from year to year, unlike court costs and fees, which tend to be more stable and predictable.

Fines, penalties, and forfeitures should be distinguished from costs and fees. A *fine* is the monetary penalty imposed by the sentencing judge as part or all of the punishment when a defendant is convicted of a crime. A *penalty* is the monetary payment ordered for commission of an infraction (the most common infractions are minor traffic violations). A *forfeiture* occurs when a defendant, at liberty under bond, fails to meet the conditions it specifies (usually a court appearance), and the bond is forfeited. Forfeitures also may include vehicles seized and sold when driven by persons convicted of alcohol, impaired driving, or drug offenses. Fines, infraction penalties, and forfeitures, by state constitutional mandate (Article IX, Section 7), accrue to the public schools in the county involved and may not be used for any other purpose. In fiscal year 2013–14 fines, penalties, and forfeitures collected by the courts throughout the state totaled $36 million.

Allocation of Financial Responsibility for the Court System

All operating expenses of the Judicial Department are borne by the state (G.S. Chapter 7A, Subchapter VI). These include salaries and travel expenses of all judges, district attorneys, clerks and their assistants, magistrates, court reporters, public defenders, and guardians ad litem. Also included are the books, supplies, records, and equipment in all these officials' offices and the fees of all jurors and witnesses for whom the government is responsible. This arrangement is a direct result of the court reform efforts of the 1950s and 1960s. Before then salaries and other operating expenses for most trial court officials (clerks, lower court judges, justices of the peace, and so forth) were the responsibility of local governments. Correspondingly, most fees collected accrued to local governments or directly to court officials as their compensation. The current arrangement reflects the fundamental policy decisions made during this court reform effort that all court officials should have the same duties and be paid the same salaries. As a result citizens should receive roughly the same services from the courts wherever they live. This rigid commitment to uniformity, reflected in an original policy of requiring all operational funding to come from the state, has, since the late 1990s, begun to erode somewhat. Acting on the request of local court and local government officials, the legislature has authorized local governments to supplement the operations of the courts serving their counties or cities, and in some instances they have chosen to do so by funding temporary positions in the office of the district attorney, the public defender, or the clerk. But this supplementary funding is still the exception.

In the court reform effort of the 1960s, the primary responsibilities counties (and a few cities) retained for court operations was to provide "adequate" physical facilities for the courts. That duty has not changed since. Courtrooms are the most obvious of such facilities, but this responsibility also extends to the provision of office and storage facilities, parking, and related spaces for judges, the clerk of superior court and the clerk's staff, district attorneys, and magistrates. In addition, most of the ancillary personnel described in this chapter are also entitled to county office space, either by virtue of a specific statute or because they are part of the court system. The obligation to provide facilities includes the responsibility for furniture (but not equipment) and the cleaning and maintenance of the courthouse.

Questions often arise about whether particular expenses should be covered by the county or by the state. Often the issue is whether a particular item is an operating expense or part of a facility. How should the cable that connects the state's mainframe computer to the courthouse be classified? (It's probably equipment.) What about cable inside the courthouse? (It's generally considered part of the courthouse infrastructure and thus classified under facilities.) Is a sound system for use in courtrooms an operating expense or part of the facility? (It's probably an infrastructure item and thus part of the facility.) What about court security equipment like metal detectors? (Security is the sheriff's responsibility, and if the equipment is permanent, it is part of the infrastructure.) Sometimes the classification is clear—furniture, drapes, and fixtures are part of the facility, and computers and specialized court equipment are operating expenses. But often the distinction is not clear and is usually resolved through negotiation.

Sometimes the question arises as to whether a facility or the furnishings are "adequate." In such cases the initial determination is made by the county when it allocates and maintains the space allotted to the courts, pursuant to its general authority to control the use of its property. When court officials or clientele question the adequacy of the facilities, they almost always do so informally, and usually the issue can be settled informally as well. But if officials or citizens believe the county's allocation or maintenance of facilities is inadequate, the North Carolina Supreme Court has indicated that the county can be sued to force it to provide adequate facilities.[3] If such litigation results in a decision that the facility in question is indeed inadequate, the court may order the county to provide an adequate facility. The county generally has the discretion to decide how to remedy the inadequacy. If the county fails to take action, or if the action is found to be insufficient, the court could then hold the appropriate officials in contempt, although as of November 2014, no case has ever reached that point. The parties almost always negotiate a settlement before that stage of litigation occurs.

The process described for counties is also applicable if a facility is a municipal district court facility, but the courts have additional options for dealing with this issue. The statutes authorize the director of the Administrative Office of the Courts to forbid the use of a municipal facility if he or she determines it is inadequate.[4] Additionally, a chief district court judge may simply direct that no cases be scheduled in a municipal facility if he or she finds it inadequate.

A facilities fee is collected in each court case as part of the court costs paid by the litigants. This fee is distributed to the counties (and a proportionate share goes to municipalities for cases heard in municipally owned district court facilities) and must be spent exclusively for providing, maintaining, and constructing court facilities for court officials and court-related personnel, as well as for some related functions. Court-related personnel typically include the other employees administratively housed in the Judicial Department, such as family court or drug court professionals, trial court administrators, custody mediation personnel, and so on. Other related functions and services for which facilities must be provided, as listed in G.S. 7A-304, include jails and juvenile detention, free parking for jurors, and law libraries, including books. Sometimes court officials or others ask for an accounting of the use of the facilities fee, and under the public records law, they are entitled to that information. When the state assumed the costs of operating the trial courts in the 1960s, this fee was preserved as a local government source of revenue to help offset the continuing costs paid by the county for court operations. It is rarely sufficient to cover the entire cost of operating a court facility and would never support the cost of construction of new facilities.

Additional Resources

Administrative Office of the Courts. *Annual Reports.* www.nccourts.org/Citizens/Publications/AnnualReports.asp.

Brannon, Joan G., Stevens H. Clarke, and Robert L. Farb. "Law Enforcement, Courts, and Corrections." In *State and Local Government Relations in North Carolina: Their Evolution and Current Status.* 2nd ed., edited by Charles D. Liner. Chapel Hill, N.C.: Institute of Government, University of North Carolina at Chapel Hill, 1995.

Cohen, Thomas H., and Lynn Langton. *State Court Organization, 1987–2004.* Washington, D.C.: United States Department of Justice, Bureau of Justice Statistics, 2007. www.bjs.gov/index.cfm?ty=pbdetail&iid=1205.

Commission for the Future of Justice and the Courts in North Carolina. "Without Favor, Denial, or Delay: A Court System for the 21st Century." 1996. www.sog.unc.edu/sites/www.sog.unc.edu/files/WithoutFavorDenialOrDelayAll.pdf.

3. *In re* Alamance Cnty. Court Facilities, 329 N.C. 84 (1991).
4. G.S. 7A-302.

About the Author

James C. Drennan is a retired School of Government faculty member who specializes in judicial administration and judicial education.

Chapter 43

Registers of Deeds

Charles Szypszak

Registers of deeds are major custodians of county records. The records for which they are responsible include real estate records, marriage records, and other vital records.

Real Estate Records

The register's most consuming responsibility is recording and maintaining real estate records including deeds, deeds of trust and mortgages, financing statements for real estate–related property, and maps and plats. No conveyance of real estate, contract to convey, option to convey, or lease of more than three years is valid against third parties unless it is recorded with the register in the county in which the real estate is located.[1] North Carolina has a "race" type of recording statute, in which the first to record prevails in a contest of priorities, with only very narrow exceptions.[2] Thus, the act of recording, and accessibility to the records, are vital and can have a dispositive legal impact on real estate transactions.

Recording Requirements

Registers are directed to record only after determining "that all statutory and locally adopted prerequisites for recording have been met."[3] Documents submitted for recording must meet statutorily prescribed format requirements relating to size, margins, and legibility.[4] Registers must also review an instrument that requires an acknowledgment or proof to determine if the instrument "appears to have been proved or acknowledged before an officer with the apparent authority to take proofs or acknowledgments, and the said proof or acknowledgment includes the officer's signature, commission, expiration date, and official seal, if required."[5] By statute, a "register of deeds shall not be required to verify or make

1. N.C. Gen. Stat. (hereinafter G.S.) § 47-18.
2. *Id.*
3. G.S. 161-14(a).
4. G.S. 161-14(b).
5. G.S. 47-14(a).

inquiry concerning (i) the legal sufficiency of any proof or acknowledgment, (ii) the authority of any officer who took a proof or acknowledgment, [or] (iii) the legal sufficiency of any document presented for registration."[6]

Maps and Plats

Registers also record maps and subdivision plats, which must meet size, reproducibility, and other requirements.[7] With few exceptions, plats and maps must contain prescribed surveyor certificates.[8] County commissioners are required to designate one or more persons to serve as review officers to review maps and plats submitted for recording.[9] The designation of the review officer must be recorded with the register.[10] Plats and maps must be examined by the review officer unless they are certified to be of existing parcels, streets, structures, or natural features or are control surveys, maps of a municipal boundary or annexation, highway right-of-way plans, transportation corridor maps, or certain types of illustrative maps attached to deeds.[11] Review officers check plats and maps for required information and for subdivision approvals if required; their responsibilities do not supplant the authority of local land use boards.

Financing Statements

Financing statements are used to create security interests in property not classified as real estate under state law. These statements are governed by the Uniform Commercial Code. Since July 1, 2001, registers are custodians only of Uniform Commercial Code financing statements pertaining to real property–related collateral, which includes fixture filings (personal property that has become attached to real estate, such as a furnace), as-extracted collateral (oil, gas, minerals), and timber to be cut.[12] Financing statements usually are submitted on standard forms. To be recorded with the register they must identify the debtor, the secured party, and the collateral; indicate that they cover real property–related collateral; provide a description of the real property to which the collateral is related; and, if the debtor is not the real property owner, state the name of the record owner.[13] The grounds on which a register may reject a financing statement submitted for recording are limited to submissions by a method not authorized, such as electronically to a registry not so equipped, failure to pay the required fee, and omission of specifically required information.[14] Registers index financing statements and subsequent related instruments, such as statements continuing or terminating the security interest, in the Consolidated Real Property Index of all the real estate records.

Excise Tax

Registers collect an excise tax on conveyances of real estate interest except conveyances by federal, state, county, and municipal governments and their instrumentalities. The tax rate is $1 on each $500 or fractional part thereof.[15] When a tax is owed, it must be paid when the instrument is presented for recording. Exceptions from the tax include transfers made by operation of law, such as a survivor's acquisition of full ownership after the death of a tenant by the entireties or a joint tenant; transfers by will or intestacy; leases; and any transfer that is for no consideration.[16] This state excise tax applies to transfers when someone assumes another's debt and when property is exchanged because consideration is deemed paid for the transfer. It also applies to a transfer by deed at foreclosure or in lieu of foreclosure, even if the grantee is the secured creditor.[17] The tax also applies to timber deeds.[18] A few counties have an additional excise tax

6. *Id.*
7. G.S. 47-30.
8. *Id.*
9. G.S. 47-30.2.
10. *Id.*
11. G.S. 47-30.
12. G.S. 25-9-501(a).
13. G.S. 25-9-502.
14. G.S. 25-9-516(b).
15. G.S. 105-228.30.
16. G.S. 105-228.29.
17. G.S. 45-45.2.
18. G.S. 105-228.30(a).

that applies to the same instruments as the state excise tax but not to conveyances to a secured creditor as the result of foreclosure or in lieu of foreclosure.[19]

Registration and Indexing

When documents are registered, they are endorsed with the day and hour at which presented.[20] A document is not considered registered until it is indexed.[21] Registers maintain the records sequentially in order of recording. Records are made available for public use in a variety of formats, increasingly in electronic form. All real property records are indexed in the Consolidated Real Property Index according to standards promulgated by the North Carolina Secretary of State.[22] Registers are required to index documents immediately but may show recently filed instruments for up to thirty days on a temporary index.[23] The usual index is a grantor/grantee index, arranged alphabetically by the names of the parties to the instrument—one index for grantors, such as sellers, and one for grantees, such as buyers—with references to the book and page where the identified instrument can be viewed. Some types of documents are indexed according to specific statutory requirements. Real estate instruments are indexed according to the Minimum Standards for Indexing Real Property Instruments, which are regulations approved by the North Carolina Association of Registers of Deeds and the North Carolina Bar Association and adopted by the North Carolina Secretary of State. These rules contain detailed requirements for index components, name formatting, and sort order, among other things. The rules were substantially revised in 2011 to simplify the formatting of names and to require introduction of computer-assisted search. A few counties maintain a parcel identifier number (PIN) index, in which parcels of real property are assigned unique numbers and references are provided to each instrument affecting the parcel. The county may choose to designate the PIN index as its official index.[24]

When registers index documents, they must use the information in the document to determine the capacity and names of the parties and other information to be indexed. Unlike public filings received in many other government offices, no forms or cover pages are required to assist registers with indexing, and real estate instruments can be drafted in an infinite variety of formats. To facilitate document indexing and make instruments easier to locate, drafters should

- clearly indicate the names of the parties to the document and their capacities as grantor or grantee;
- include all party names in the forefront of the document (not in the middle or in attachments);
- clearly separate from the name to be indexed any additional information about prior names, affiliates, or underlying documents;
- avoid adopting names for real estate title that include symbols, unusual spacing, or punctuation that will force unfamiliar alphabetizing;
- ensure names appear consistently throughout the document and in signatures;
- use a single document title from the common document types listed in the local rules; and
- provide a clear, brief description of the property for indexing reference.

Recording Instruments in Electronic Form

In 2005 North Carolina adopted the Uniform Real Property Electronic Recording Act (URPERA) to facilitate use of electronic documents for public real estate records.[25] URPERA provides that "[i]f a law requires, as a condition for recording, that a document be an original, be on paper or another tangible medium, or be in writing, the requirement is satisfied by an electronic document satisfying" the laws governing electronic records.[26] URPERA also provides a

19. G.S. 45-45.2.
20. G.S. 161-14(a).
21. G.S. 161-22(h).
22. G.S. 147-54.3.
23. G.S. 161-14(a).
24. G.S. 161-22.2.
25. G.S. 47-16.1 to G.S. 47-16.7.
26. G.S. 47-16.3(a).

framework for use of electronic signatures by providing that "[i]f a law requires, as a condition for recording, that a document be signed, the requirement is satisfied by an electronic signature."[27]

Some real estate records must be acknowledged by notaries or other authorized officials before they may be recorded, and URPERA provides that "[a] requirement that a document or a signature associated with a document be notarized, acknowledged, verified, witnessed, or made under oath is satisfied if the electronic signature of the person authorized to notarize, acknowledge, verify, witness, or administer the oath, and all other information required to be included, is attached to or logically associated with the document or signature. A physical or electronic image of a stamp, impression, or seal need not accompany an electronic signature."[28] The Electronic Notary Act allows use of electronic forms of notarization, pursuant to which the North Carolina Secretary of State promulgates standards.[29] These standards describe what a notary must do to perform an electronic notarization, and among other things require that the notary's signature and seal be "attached or logically associated with the document, linking the data in such a manner that any subsequent alterations to the underlying document or electronic notary certificate are observable through visible examination."[30] The Secretary of State also promulgates Electronic Recording Standards that provide guidance to registers and electronic document submitters regarding the format and procedure for electronic record submissions and for the maintenance of electronic records.

Registers who wish to accept electronic documents requiring acknowledgments may do so if they can confirm that the acknowledgments have been completed.[31] Registers can accept electronic documents from two kinds of submitters: the government, or a "trusted submitter." Someone could become a "trusted submitter" only by agreeing to the register's requirements in a memorandum of understanding. When such an agreement is in place, registers are not required by statute to check for originality of electronically submitted documents unless they chose to make it a condition. The submitter is responsible for complying with the originality requirements. The statutes do not require any register to accept electronic submissions nor do they require registers who decide to allow electronic documents to accept them from anyone other than whom the register authorizes.

Documents submitted by trusted submitters must include the following statement, which will appear on the public record:

> Submitted electronically by ______________ (submitter's name) in compliance with North Carolina statutes governing recordable documents and the terms of the submitter agreement with the ______________ (insert county name) County Register of Deeds.

The record will therefore show who was entrusted to comply with the recording requirements for documents submitted electronically by trusted submitters. The statute makes clear that the register may rely on the trusted submitter's representation of compliance with the requirements.[32]

If a document originates in electronic form, submitters are responsible for complying with North Carolina electronic recording and notary statutes and rules. They are also responsible for not electronically recording a document that originated as paper unless the paper document would have been recordable in that form. For example, a submitter could not properly scan a copy of a document and submit it electronically if the copy is not recordable in its paper form. Also, a submitter could not properly record an altered document that does not conform to the paper document rerecording requirements.

Registers also may accept plats submitted electronically. Registers may accept electronically submitted plats only if they are submitted by a governmental unit or instrumentality or a trusted submitter authorized to do so by the registers, as is the case for other electronically submitted instruments. Required certifications must appear on the digitized image of the document as the document will appear on the public record. If the plat is submitted by a trusted

---

27. G.S. 47-16.3(b).
28. G.S. 47-16.3(c).
29. N.C. Admin. Code tit. 18, ch. 07C, §§ .0101–.0604.
30. *Id.* §§ .0401(d), .0402(d).
31. G.S. 47-14(a1), (a2).
32. *Id.*

submitter, it must include the same statement required for other documents submitted electronically. The plat image must otherwise comply with other applicable laws and rules that prescribe recordation.[33]

Redaction

Once registered, a real estate document is part of the permanent public record and a register may not remove it from that record. If a document is registered that causes unlawful harm, a court may issue an order that declares the document void or otherwise addresses its legal effect, and that order when recorded is linked to the original harmful record with the subsequent instrument indexing method. The statutes contain only one authorized basis for removal of information from a registered real estate record: redaction of personal identification numbers from Internet records.[34] Individuals may request redaction of their Social Security, driver's license, state identification, passport, checking account, savings account, credit card, or debit card number or personal identification code or password contained in the public records displayed on the register's Internet website available to the general public. Redaction applies only to the identified personal information—not the entire record—and only to records on the Internet website. A request should be legibly signed by the person to whom the information belongs or by someone with demonstrated legal authority for such a person, such as someone with an applicable power of attorney, and it may be submitted in person or by mail, facsimile, or electronic transmission. It must specify the relevant document and the nature and location within the document of the information to be redacted. Access to inspection of the requests for redaction is restricted to the register of deeds, the clerk of court, their staff members, or to another party by court order. Registers are authorized but not required to redact Social Security and driver's license numbers from the Internet website without a request.[35]

Marriage Records

The register of deeds issues marriage licenses.[36] Couples may apply for licenses on statutorily prescribed forms supplied to registers by the Vital Records Section of the North Carolina Department of Health and Human Services.[37] North Carolina law requires the register to determine whether the applicants are "authorized to be married in accordance with the laws of this State," and the register must make a "reasonable inquiry" into whether the applicants meet the requirements.[38] The form, once completed by the register's office, becomes the marriage license and must be completed and returned with a record of the marriage ceremony.[39]

The register of deeds keeps records of marriage licenses issued and the returns showing the solemnization.[40] The register keeps an index by the names of the intended husbands and wives. The index entries must show the spouses' names, the ceremony dates, and the locations of the original licenses and returns.[41] The register keeps one copy of returned licenses and submits another to the state Vital Records Section on a monthly basis.[42] These are public records.[43] An uncertified copy may be obtained by anyone who pays the required fee, and a certified copy may be obtained by a subject of the license or the subject's spouse, sibling, direct ancestor or descendant, stepparent or stepchild, a person

33. G.S. 47-30.
34. G.S. 132-1.10(f).
35. G.S. 132-1.10(f1).
36. G.S. 51-8.
37. G.S. 51-16.
38. G.S. 51-17.
39. G.S. 51-16.
40. G.S. 51-18.
41. *Id.*
42. G.S. 130A-110(a).
43. G.S. 130A-110(d).

seeking information for a legal determination of personal or property rights, or an authorized agent, attorney, or legal representative of the aforementioned individuals.[44]

Other Records

Other commonly used records for which the register is custodian include birth and death records, military discharges, and records of assumed names.

Birth and Death Certificates

The register files and preserves copies of birth and death certificates furnished by the local health director.[45] County birth and death certificates are public records, and copies must be provided to anyone upon request. The statutes prohibit registers from providing a copy of a vital record to someone seeking his or her own record but who is known to be deceased, in which case attempted fraud is obvious.[46] Certified copies may be obtained by the subject and the subject's spouse, sibling, direct ancestor or descendant, or stepparent or stepchild; an authorized agent, attorney, or legal representative of any of these individuals; someone "seeking information for a legal determination of personal or property rights"; and a funeral director or funeral service licensee.[47] The State Registrar handles new birth certificates in the case of adoption and may direct that the county remove the adopted child's prior certificate.[48]

Military Discharges

Registers are required to keep a separate, permanent book for official discharges from the armed forces.[49] Public access to copies or to the information on the discharges is restricted for discharges received since January 1, 2004, and for discharges kept in separate books prior to that date and that have been on file for less than eighty years.[50] Restricted access is limited to the veteran; the veteran's widow or widower; and the veteran's agents and representatives authorized in writing by the veteran, the veteran's widow or widower, someone appointed by a court to represent the veteran, or by the deceased veteran's executor. Additionally, access to such restricted records is permitted to authorized Agents of the Division of Veterans Affairs, the U.S. Department of Veterans Affairs, the Department of Defense, a court official with an interest in assisting a veteran or a deceased veteran's beneficiaries, and representatives of the North Carolina State Archives.[51] Registers may refuse to accept a discharge if it is submitted by someone other than the aforementioned persons and authorities or if it is not an original, a carbon copy, or a photocopy issued or certified by a state or federal agency.[52] No fees may be charged for filing the documents or for providing certified copies of discharge records to authorized parties. The register may charge standard fees for uncertified copies.[53]

Assumed Names

Any person or partnership that uses an assumed name in North Carolina and any limited partnership, limited liability company, or corporation that uses a name in this state other than the organizational name filed with the Secretary of State must file a certificate of assumed name with the register of deeds in the county in which business is to be

44. G.S. 130A-93(c); G.S. 130A-110(c).
45. G.S. 130A-97; G.S. 130A-99.
46. G.S. 130A-93(g).
47. G.S. 130A-93(c), (c1).
48. G.S. 48-9-107; G.S. 130A-93(d).
49. G.S. 47-109.
50. G.S. 47-113.2.
51. G.S. 47-113.2(b)(1).
52. G.S. 47-113.2(d).
53. G.S. 47-113.2(n), (o).

conducted.[54] Such names may be withdrawn or transferred by the owners.[55] The register keeps an alphabetical index of every assumed name with respect to which a certificate was issued in the county.[56]

Notary Commissions

Registers administer the oath of office to notaries public who live or work in the registers' counties and who have been qualified by the Secretary of State for commissioning. Registers maintain the official records of the notary commissions issued in their counties.[57]

Office of Register of Deeds

The register's office is elective for a four-year term.[58] Before a register may take the oath of office and exercise the office's duties, the board of county commissioners must approve the register's bond.[59] The bond must be for at least $10,000 but not more than $50,000.[60] The bond is "conditioned for the safekeeping of the books and records, and for the faithful discharge of the duties of [the register's] office."[61] If the county provides liability insurance to other county officials, the register must be included in the policy; if the county provides no liability insurance, the register must be informed in writing of that fact.[62] The small amount of the bond makes insurance important for protection against liability for errors and omissions in recording and indexing, which can involve complex transactional documents.

The county must provide the register with at least one deputy and at least a second deputy if the register justifies to the county commissioners that a second deputy is necessary.[63] In most counties, numerous deputies and assistants are necessary to perform the work. The register has the authority to appoint the deputies and assistants, for whose acts the register is officially responsible.[64]

The register's permissible fees are set exclusively by statute.[65] The prescribed fees are designated amounts based on the type of record, as well as designated amounts and guidelines for certified and uncertified copies.[66] Registers may include the cost of purchasing and maintaining related copying and computer equipment in the charges for uncertified copies, which must be uniform and prominently posted.[67] Ninety percent of most fees are deposited into the county general fund.[68] Ten percent of the fees returned to the state by the county must be set aside in a nonreverting Automation Enhancement and Preservation Fund for spending on computer and imaging technology in the register's office.[69]

The excise tax collected by registers upon the recording of instruments transferring interests in real estate is shared between the state and the county. The county finance officer must forward 49 percent of the tax proceeds to the Department of Revenue, and 75 percent of that amount is applied to the Parks and Recreation Trust Fund and 25 percent to the Natural Heritage Trust Fund. The county retains the balance.[70] The impact of the excise tax varies among the

54. G.S. 66-68.
55. G.S. 66-68(f).
56. G.S. 66-69.
57. G.S. 10B-9.
58. G.S. 161-1, -2.
59. G.S. 161-4(a).
60. *Id.*
61. G.S. 161-4(b).
62. G.S. 161-4.2.
63. G.S. 153A-103.
64. G.S. 161-6.
65. G.S. 161-10.
66. *Id.*
67. G.S. 161-10(a)(11).
68. G.S. 161-10.
69. G.S. 161-11.3.
70. G.S. 115-228.30(b).

counties because its amount depends on the value of property conveyed within the county. In counties with valuable commercial and industrial properties, an active real estate market, and new development, the excise tax contributes to the general fund in excess of the register office's operating expenses. In counties without such real estate transactions, the county general fund must supplement register receipts to meet the register's operating expenses.

The office hours of the register of deeds are set by the board of commissioners.[71] In some counties, the commissioners, by resolution, have provided that the register must stop recording instruments a few minutes before the office closes for the day. This arrangement gives the register time to complete the recording process prior to close of business for the documents received.

When a register of deeds resigns, retires, or dies during the register's term, the executive committee of the political party from which the register was elected has thirty days to submit the name of a successor to the board of commissioners. If the committee meets this deadline, the commissioners must appoint the person recommended.[72] This procedure does not apply in Camden, Chowan, Pasquotank, and Perquimans counties; in those counties the board of commissioners selects the replacement. Deputies and assistants continue to serve until discharged or otherwise lawfully relieved by a duly appointed and qualified successor.[73]

Additional Resources

Szypszak, Charles. *North Carolina Guidebook for Registers of Deeds.* 10th ed. Chapel Hill, N.C.: UNC School of Government, 2013.

About the Author

Charles Szypszak is a School of Government faculty member who specializes in real property law, including eminent domain.

71. G.S. 161-8.
72. G.S. 161-5.
73. G.S. 161-5(b).

Chapter 44

Elections

Robert P. Joyce

County boards of elections conduct all elections in North Carolina. These boards conduct the elections for federal, state, county, and city offices. They conduct statewide referendums and local referendums. They conduct elections for special districts, such as school administrative units, sanitary districts, and fire districts.

County boards take voter registration applications, determine the eligibility of applicants for registration, establish precincts and voting places, select and purchase voting equipment, publish the notices associated with an election, employ election day precinct workers, oversee election day activities, canvass the returns, declare the election results, issue certificates of election to the winners, and hold hearings on challenges to voters and candidates and on election protests.

The county board of elections must act within the regulations and directions of the State Board of Elections, and almost all of the county board's actions are subject to review by the state board.

With one large exception and one small exception, the operating costs of elections are paid through appropriations from the county commissioners. City elections are the large exception. Cities must reimburse counties for the costs incurred by the county boards of election in conducting city elections. In addition, a small portion of expenses related to statewide elections is paid from state funds.

According to figures compiled by the State Board of Elections, as of March 2014 there were 6,512,640 registered voters in North Carolina (a million more than in March 2006 and two million more than April 1998), of whom 42.4 percent were registered as Democrats (compared with 45.9 percent in 2006 and 52.7 percent in 1998), 30.7 percent were registered as Republicans (34.7 percent were so registered in 2006 and 33.9 percent in 1998), and 26.6 percent were unaffiliated (the figures for 2006 and 1998 were 19.4 and 13.4 percent, respectively). The rest were Libertarians. Of the registered voters, 70.9 percent were white (whites made up 76.4 percent of registered voters in 2006 and 79.28 percent in 1998) and 22.5 percent were African American (compared to 20.1 percent in 2006 and 18.8 percent in 1998). The rest were characterized as American Indian, Hispanic, or "Other."[1]

Kinds of Elections Authorized

The General Statutes authorize two kinds of elections: (1) elections of candidates to office and (2) certain specified *special elections*. A special election is any kind of referendum on any question other than electing a candidate to office. The range of special elections is limited. (See the discussion of special elections below.)

Election of Candidates to Office

Elections in which the voters choose individuals to fill public offices are the most common kinds of elections. While in nearly all cities elections for municipal offices—mayors and city councils—are held in odd-numbered years (2015, 2017, and so on), elections for just about all other offices are held in even-numbered years (2016, 2018, and so forth). Elections held in even-numbered years include those for federal offices (president and vice president, U.S. Senate and House of Representatives), state executive offices (governor and council of state), state legislative offices (N.C. Senate and House of Representatives), judicial offices (justices and judges of the N.C. Supreme Court, N.C. Court of Appeals, superior court, and district court; clerks of superior court; and district attorneys), and county offices (county commissioners, registers of deeds, sheriffs, and soil and water conservation commissioners). Most school board elections are held in even-numbered years, but some are held in odd-numbered years. Elections for sanitary district governing board members are held in odd-numbered years.

The general election schedule is found at Section 163-1 of the North Carolina General Statutes (hereinafter G.S.).

Partisan Primaries and Elections

Most federal, state, and county elections to fill offices are conducted on a partisan basis. Candidates are nominated by political parties and run under their labels. Two parties—Democratic and Republican—have traditionally and consistently met North Carolina's statutory definition of a *political party*, meaning that their candidates for governor or president have in each election polled at least 2 percent of the total vote cast in the state for governor or president[2] (for many years the requirement was 10 percent). The nominees of these parties are chosen by the voters through primary elections held before the general election. The winner in the primary election is the nominee of the party and appears on the ballot in the general election. If no candidate for nomination receives at least 40 percent of the vote (plus one vote)—a total termed a substantial plurality—in a particular primary, the candidate who finishes second may request a second primary, just between those two candidates. The winner of the second primary is the nominee. Voters affiliated with a particular party are eligible to vote in that party's primary. In addition, a party may permit voting in its primary by registered voters who are not affiliated with any party. That choice is made on an election-by-election basis. Counties bear the costs of primaries, as they do for other elections. The statutes governing primary elections are found at G.S. 163-104 through -119.

A new political party may be formed through the circulation of a petition, signed by registered voters equal to at least 2 percent of the number who voted in the most recent general election for governor. For the first election after it is recognized by the State Board of Elections, the new party chooses its nominees at a party convention, not by a primary election, and is entitled to have those nominees on the ballot for federal, state, and local offices. If the party fails to poll

1. *See* N.C. State Board of Elections, *NC Voter Statistics Results*, www.ncsbe.gov/webapps/voter_stats/results.aspx?date=03-29-2014 (note that these figures are regularly updated and might be different at the time of reading versus the time of writing this chapter).

2. *See* N.C. Gen. Stat. (hereinafter G.S.) § 163-96(a).

at least 2 percent of the vote for governor or president, its recognition is terminated, and it must go through the petition procedure again. The Libertarian Party went through this recognition and termination cycle a couple of times in the last decades of the twentieth century and in the first decade of this century, during a time when the requirement to avoid termination of a party's recognized status was 10 percent. The statutes governing political parties are found at G.S. 163-96 through -99.

An individual who wishes to run in a partisan election as an unaffiliated candidate may do so (if he or she is registered as unaffiliated) through the circulation of a petition. For state offices, the petition must be signed by registered voters equal to at least 2 percent of the number who voted in the most recent general election for governor. For county or district offices, the petition must be signed by at least 4 percent of the registered voters of the district. The statute governing the candidacy of unaffiliated candidates is found at G.S. 163-122.

Nonpartisan Elections

While most elections to fill offices are conducted on a partisan basis, three kinds of elections to office are conducted by a nonpartisan method.[3] The first kind consists of most elections to municipal office—mayor and city council. A few North Carolina cities do, in fact, have partisan elections for municipal offices. These are conducted like state and county partisan elections. The overwhelming majority of municipalities, however, have nonpartisan elections. The second kind of nonpartisan elections consists of elections of judges. School board elections are the third kind of nonpartisan elections. Most school board elections are nonpartisan, but a few are partisan.

In a nonpartisan election, there is, of course, no nomination of candidates in a partisan primary. All candidates stand for election without party identification. Candidates are at liberty to identify themselves by party if they wish, and parties are free to endorse candidates if they wish. What is nonpartisan is the way the election officials conduct the election, not necessarily the way candidates and parties conduct the campaign.

As pointed out above, there are three kinds of offices filled by nonpartisan elections—municipal offices, judgeships, and memberships on school boards. In addition, there are three kinds of nonpartisan elections—nonpartisan plurality elections, nonpartisan primaries and elections, and nonpartisan elections and runoffs. Each is discussed in more detail below.

Types of Nonpartisan Elections

Nonpartisan Plurality Elections

In this sort of election, there is only one vote, held on general election day. Whichever candidate receives the most votes wins, even if no one gets a majority. If several candidates are seeking one seat, the highest vote-getter wins. If two or more seats are being contested as a group (as in an at-large council election) and there are more candidates than open seats, then the number of candidates equal to the number of open seats is elected, based on who receives the highest number of votes.

Nonpartisan Primaries and Elections

In this variety of election, on the fourth Tuesday before general election day, a vote is taken to narrow the field to two candidates for each position to be filled (or if several seats are being filled as a group, to narrow the field to twice as many candidates as there are seats open). If only one or two candidates file for a single seat (or if fewer than twice as many candidates file for two or more seats open as a group), then the candidates who have filed are declared nominated, and no primary is held. If a primary is held, however, then the two candidates receiving the highest number of votes for a single office are declared nominated (even if one of them receives a majority and the second-place finisher receives a minority), and twice the number of candidates as there are seats in a group election are declared nominated. The election is then held on general election day, with the highest vote-getters winning the seats.

---

3. In addition to the three election types discussed in the text, elections for sanitary district governing board members are also held on a nonpartisan basis.

Nonpartisan Elections and Runoffs

With these elections there is an election on general election day only if a runoff is necessary. On the fourth Tuesday before general election day, an election is held among all candidates. A candidate receiving a majority (which, in elections for more than one seat voted on as a group, is calculated by dividing the total vote cast for all candidates by the number of seats and then by two) wins. If no candidate receives a majority, the highest vote-getter is declared elected unless the second-highest vote-getter requests a runoff by noon on the Monday following the election. The runoff is then between these two candidates. In multiple-seat group elections, candidates receiving a majority win.[4] If too few gain majorities to fill all seats, then the highest vote-getters without majorities, equal to the number of remaining seats to be filled, are declared elected unless the next-highest vote-getters equal in number to those remaining seats (or some of them) demand a runoff. The runoff is then between the highest non-majority vote-getters and the candidates demanding a runoff.

City Council and Mayoral Elections

Under the uniform municipal elections law (G.S. Chapter 163, Subchapter IX), a city may elect its governing board and mayor[5] by one of four methods: partisan elections, nonpartisan plurality elections, nonpartisan primaries and elections, and nonpartisan elections and runoffs. Under all four methods, candidates file for election between noon on the first Friday in July and noon on the third Friday in July. General election day is the Tuesday after the first Monday in November in odd-numbered years. Under the first three election methods, there is always an election on that day; under the fourth method there may not be.

Types of City Elections

Partisan Elections

Of the 553 cities in North Carolina, only eight use partisan elections.[6] Notably, those eight include Charlotte, Winston-Salem, and Asheville, which among them encompass more than a million citizens, well more than a tenth of the state's population. The smallest city with partisan elections is Murphy, with a population of about 1,700.

In cities with partisan elections, candidates file to run for party nomination in primary elections held on the sixth Tuesday before the November general election. A second primary, if necessary, is held on the third Tuesday before the general election. On general election day, the nominees of the parties appear on the ballot. In addition, candidates may appear on the ballot as unaffiliated through a petition signed by 4 percent of the voters in the city. The results of partisan municipal elections are determined in the same manner as the results of partisan state and county elections.

Nonpartisan Plurality Elections

Currently, 504 of North Carolina's 553 cities use nonpartisan plurality elections, the simplest of the four election methods.[7] Virtually all towns with small populations use this method. Some larger towns do as well. The most populous of these is Wilmington, with 106,476 inhabitants.

Nonpartisan Primaries and Elections

Only twenty-four North Carolina cities use the nonpartisan primary and election method, but that number includes Burlington, Durham, Fayetteville, Goldsboro, Greensboro, Hickory, and High Point, which together encompass 825,000 people.[8]

---

4. It is possible in a group election for more candidates to receive a majority than there are open seats. In that case, the candidates receiving the greatest number of votes, equal to the number of open seats, are elected.

5. Under G.S. 160-101(8), a city may choose to have its mayor selected by the city council from among the membership of the council, rather than elected by the voters.

6. *See* "Forms of North Carolina City Government: Current Forms of Government," a UNC School of Government webpage (hereinafter *Forms of N.C. City Government*), available at www.sog.unc.edu/node/427.

7. *Forms of N.C. City Government.*

8. *Forms of N.C. City Government.*

Nonpartisan Elections and Runoffs

The seventeen cities in the state using the nonpartisan election and runoff method include Cary, Raleigh, Rocky Mount, and Wilmington, which together have a population of almost 600,000. Under this form, there is an election on general election day only if a runoff is necessary.

The statutes governing municipal elections are found at G.S. 163-279 through -306.

School Board Elections

In North Carolina, there are 115 school administrative units, one for each of the state's 100 counties and fifteen additional units, usually referred to as *city* school units. These fifteen city school units are not part of city government, are typically not coterminous with city boundaries, and function with the same powers and authority as county school units. At one time there were many more city school units, but over time the number has been reduced as these units have merged with county units. The most recent merger, in 2005, of the Cleveland County, Shelby city, and Kings Mountain city units reduced the statewide number of units from 117 to the current 115.

Each of the 115 school administrative units is governed by a local board of education, typically called the *school board.* In three instances—Asheville, Lexington, and Thomasville—the members of the board of education are appointed rather than elected. In the remaining 112 units, board members are elected. Of those 112, fifteen are elected on a partisan basis, and the remainder on a nonpartisan basis. As with city elections, described above, nonpartisan school board elections involve a mix of the nonpartisan election methods—simple plurality, primary and election, and election and runoff.

The general law calls for nonpartisan elections to be held in even-numbered years at the time of the partisan primaries held that year; that is, according to the general law, school board members are to be elected in May. The statute also provides that newly elected school board members are to take their offices in December. Thus, the statute creates a half-year gap between the time a member is elected and the time he or she takes office. A significant number of school boards have secured local acts of the General Assembly to address this problem. In some instances, the local act moves the school board elections to odd-numbered years. That addresses the problem because odd-numbered years are the years for municipal elections, with primaries and general elections in the fall, closer to the December office-taking date. In other instances, the local act keeps the nonpartisan school board election in the even-numbered years but moves it from the May primary election date to the November general election date.

The statutory provision for school board elections is found at G.S. 115C-37.

Judicial Elections

Judges at all state court levels—district court, superior court, court of appeals, and supreme court—are elected on a nonpartisan basis, using the primary and election method described above. Until the mid-1990s, all judges were elected in partisan elections, but the General Assembly changed that in stages, moving superior court judges to nonpartisan elections in 1996, district court judges in 2001, and appellate judges in 2004.

Special Elections

Special elections are all elections other than those in which voters elect candidates to office. They may involve statewide issues, such as the ratification of an amendment to the North Carolina Constitution or a statewide bond referendum. More commonly they are local ballot questions, such as local bond referendums, alcoholic beverage control (ABC) elections, fire district and sanitary district elections, and referendums on restructuring city or county government (such as changing the number of governing board members or moving from at-large to district elections).

Calling Special Elections

Special elections are called in a variety of ways, almost all of which are set by state law. One very common kind of special election—ABC referendums—for instance, may be called as a result of a petition drive or at the request of the governing board of a city or county.[9] Similarly, referendums on changing the structure of city government (such as increasing or decreasing the number of members of the city council) may be called through a petition or by resolution of the city council itself.[10] Corresponding referendums on changing the structure of county government (which are much less common) may be called only by the commissioners.[11]

Bond referendums are perhaps the most common kind of special election. Most new general obligation bond issuances must be approved by the voters. Those referendums are most commonly called by the governing board that is issuing the bonds.[12]

Numerous other kinds of special elections are authorized by the General Statutes but are seldom used. For instance, county commissioners may call a referendum to authorize the levying of property taxes above the normal limit of $1.50 per $100 valuation[13] or a special supplemental school tax.[14] Other types of special elections include elections

- to change the structure of county government (G.S. 153A-58);
- to levy a local sales tax (G.S. 105-465, -484, and -498);
- to levy a sales tax for transportation (G.S. 105-511.2);
- for municipal incorporations (G.S. 120-172);
- for school unit mergers (G.S. 115C-67);
- for city–county consolidation (G.S. 153A-405; 160B-18);
- for a unified city/county government (G.S. 153A-473);
- to create mountain ridge protection districts (G.S. 113A-214);
- to create mosquito control districts (G.S. 130A-353);
- to levy taxes for hospital districts (G.S. 131E-45);
- to create airport districts (G.S. 63-80);
- for airport district bonds (G.S. 63-87);
- for water and sewer authority contracts (G.S. 162A-14);
- for inclusion in a metropolitan water district (G.S. 162A-35);
- for inclusion in a sewerage district (G.S. 162A-68);
- to create/abolish soil and water conservation districts (G.S. 139-5 and -13);
- for soil and water conservation district land-use regulations (G.S. 139-9);
- to levy watershed improvement district taxes (G.S. 139-39);
- to raise the property tax rate above the set limit (G.S. 160A-209 and -542; 153A-149);
- to levy a supplemental school tax (G.S. 115C-501);
- to levy a supplemental community college tax (G.S. 115D-33);
- for certain community development activities by cities (G.S. 160A-456);
- for certain community development activities by counties (G.S. 153A-376);
- to levy taxes to supplement revenue bond projects (G.S. 159-97);
- to levy a public transportation authority special tax (G.S. 160A-583);
- for the sale, lease, or discontinuation of city-owned enterprises (G.S. 160A-321);
- to levy rural fire protection district taxes (G.S. 69-25.1);
- for various actions related to sanitary districts (G.S. 130A-80 through -83); and
- for involuntary annexation (G.S. 160A-58.64).

---

9. *See* G.S. 18B-601.
10. *See* G.S. 160A-101 through -111.
11. *See* G.S. 153A-58 through -64.
12. *See* G.S. 159-50 through -61.
13. G.S. 153A-149(e).
14. G.S. 115C-501.

With a few exceptions, special elections may be conducted only at the same time as regular primary or general elections.[15]

Limits on Calling Special Elections

County officials sometimes want to have a "special referendum" or "straw vote" on a controversial issue. Generally speaking, they are not permitted to do so. Only elections specifically authorized by state statute or by local act of the General Assembly may be held. As then-justice Sam Ervin of the North Carolina Supreme Court said, in *Tucker v. State Board of Alcoholic Control*, "There is no inherent power in any governmental body to hold an election for any purpose. In consequence, an election held without affirmative constitutional or statutory authority is a nullity, no matter how fairly and honestly it may be conducted."[16] If a county wishes to have a vote on where to locate a landfill, or if a city wishes to have a vote on whether to create a beautification district, each governmental unit must receive authorization from the General Assembly in the form of a local act. Without the authorization, the vote simply may not be held.

In some states, citizens may, by a petition drive, force an election on the issue of recalling an elected official from office (a recall election) or adopting or repealing a particular ordinance (initiative and referendum). There are no such provisions in the North Carolina General Statutes. A handful of cities have such provisions by virtue of local acts of the General Assembly. No North Carolina counties have them.

Registration and Voting

To vote in any election in North Carolina, a person must be qualified to vote and must be registered.

Qualifications for Voting

To be qualified to vote in North Carolina, a person must be a U.S. citizen, must be at least eighteen years old by the time of the election (a person who is seventeen at the time of the primary but will be eighteen by the time of the general election may vote in the primary), must have resided for thirty days in the state and in the precinct in which he or she wishes to vote, and must not be a convicted felon (or must have had citizenship rights restored). The requirement of residence is sometimes confusing. Residence means more than simply living in a place. To reside in a place means to make it one's home (to plan to continue to live there, not just to stay there temporarily). For most people, it is easy to tell what place is home. For some others, however, including workers in temporary jobs and college students, determining what place constitutes the residence may be more difficult. The statutes governing voter registration are found at G.S. 163-54 through -90.3.

The North Carolina Constitution contains (in Article VI) two other qualifications for voting that are no longer enforced because they have been held to violate the U.S. Constitution. One provides that a person must have resided in the state for one year before registering to vote.[17] The other requires that to register, a person must "be able to read and write any section of the Constitution in the English language."[18]

Voter Registration

North Carolina employs permanent voter registration. Citizens need register only once to vote in all elections. Voters remain registered and eligible to vote unless they move out of the county, die, or are convicted of a felony.[19] Applications

15. *See* G.S. 163-287.

16. 240 N.C. 177, 180 (1954) (citations omitted).

17. Andrews v. Cody, 327 F. Supp. 793 (M.D.N.C. 1971), *aff'd*, 405 U.S. 1034 (1972).

18. Another provision of the North Carolina Constitution that has been held to be unconstitutional—and so is not enforced—disqualifies from office "any person who denies the being of Almighty God." *See* Op. of N.C. Att'y Gen. to Mr. Clyde Smith, Deputy Sec'y of State, 41 Op. N.C. Att'y Gen. 727 (1972); Gaston Cnty. v. United States, 395 U.S. 285 (1969).

19. G.S. 163-82.1(c).

to register to vote may be submitted to the county board of elections by mail, fax, or email attachment or through a driver's license office or public assistance office.[20] A person may apply to register at any time during the year but must do so by the twenty-fifth day before an election in order to vote in that particular election. An individual who registers after the deadline may not vote until the next election after the upcoming one.[21] A person who moves from one county to another must reregister, but one who relocates within the county need only notify the board of elections of the change of address.[22]

When citizens apply to register to vote, they indicate the party with which they wish to affiliate or indicate that they wish to be listed on the registration rolls as unaffiliated.[23]

Absentee Ballots

Absentee voting is available in all federal, state, and county elections. It is permitted in city elections if the city council adopts a resolution calling for it at least sixty days before an election. That choice remains in effect for future elections until the council rescinds it by resolution adopted sixty days before an election.[24]

Early Voting

Until the first decades of the twentieth century, voting in person on election day was the only option for North Carolina voters. The introduction of absentee voting made it possible for people who were ill or disabled or who were to be away on election day to cast a vote. The process was cumbersome, however. The voter applied for absentee ballots, usually by mail. Elections officials considered the application and, if they approved it, sent the ballots to the voter by mail. The voter then marked the ballots and returned them to the elections officials, by mail.

Beginning in 1977, the General Assembly started a process of expanding absentee voting that led to "one-stop, no excuse, satellite absentee voting," which is commonly called "early voting." That year, the legislature amended the absentee ballot laws to permit a person to come to the county board of elections office and, in one procedure, to apply for absentee ballots and mark the ballots. If elections officials subsequently approved the application, they counted the ballots. This "one-stop" absentee voting, like all absentee voting, applied only to individuals who were eligible under the law to vote by absentee ballot because they were ill or disabled or would be away.

In 1999, the General Assembly authorized "no-excuse" absentee voting in even-year general elections. That is, anyone could now vote by absentee ballot—through the mail or at the board of elections one-stop site—for any reason in those elections. That same year the General Assembly authorized counties to establish one-stop absentee voting sites in locations around the county, not just at the board of elections office. Now, voters in the county who wished to vote by no-excuse absentee ballot had their choice of where to go to vote—and over time boards of elections began to set up one-stop absentee voting sites at non-traditional places, such as shopping malls. In 2001, the provision for no-excuse absentee voting was extended from even-year general elections to all elections. So, by 2001, there was one-stop no-excuse absentee voting at designated sites around the county for all elections. It could be said that "early voting" was by then in place.

In 2001, the General Assembly defined the time for one-stop absentee voting to begin on the third Thursday before the election and to end on the Saturday before the election. It added a local option for counties to include evenings and weekends in the eighteen days before the election.

In 2007, the General Assembly enacted legislation allowing an individual who was qualified to vote but not registered to come to a one-stop site during the early voting period, fill out an application to register to vote, and cast an absentee ballot at the same time. The application would be checked before the final counting of ballots and, if the application was approved, the ballot would count.

---

20. *See* G.S. 163-82.6, -82.19. -82.20.

21. G.S. 163-82.6.

22. G.S. 163-82.15.

23. G.S. 163-82.4(c).

24. *See generally* G.S. Chapter 163, Article 20.

In 2013, the General Assembly enacted two significant changes with respect to early voting. First, it eliminated the provision, enacted in 2007, that permitted individuals who were not already registered to apply to register and to cast a ballot at the same time at a one-stop sight. Second, it reduced the early voting period by one week. Rather than running for eighteen days before an election, early voting now runs for eleven days.[25]

Voter Identification Requirement

Traditionally North Carolina voters have, with a few exceptions, not been required to show identification at the polls. Instead, a voter was merely required to state his or her identity. It has been a felony—the most serious level of crime—to "impersonate falsely another registered voter for the purpose of voting in the stead of such other voter."[26] Beginning in 2016, legislation enacted in 2013 requires voters (with a few limited exceptions) to produce a photo identification. Acceptable forms of identification include a driver's license, passport, or military identification card, plus a few others. The photo identification requirement is found at G.S. 163-166.13.

The State Board of Elections

By statute, the State Board of Elections has "general supervision over the primaries and elections in this State."[27] That provision, G.S. 163-22, sets the framework for the administration of elections in North Carolina: the state board has general supervisory power, and the county boards conduct the elections. The statutes setting out the powers and structure of the state board are found at G.S. 163-19 through -28.

Selection and Organization

The five members of the State Board of Elections are appointed by the governor in the spring following his or her election—that is, in 2013, 2017, 2021, and so on. No more than three members of the state board may belong to the same party. Naturally, the three-member majority is always from the governor's party. The governor chooses the members from lists of five names submitted by the Republican and Democratic parties. No member may serve more than two consecutive terms.[28]

The board's office, in Raleigh, is headed by a full-time executive director.[29]

Duties

The State Board of Elections has overall responsibility for elections.[30] It appoints all county election board members (from lists provided by the parties), conducts training sessions for them and for the county directors of elections, decides what kinds of voting equipment may be used, instructs county boards on what kinds of records to maintain, tells them how ballots should be printed, hears protests concerning the conduct of elections, and performs various other duties to see that elections run smoothly and properly throughout the state.

A chief duty of the state board involves challenges to the way in which particular elections have been conducted. Sometimes called "election protests" and sometimes called "election contests," challenges are usually first heard by the county board of elections and are then appealed, if the protester is not satisfied, to the state board. The state board may also investigate the conduct of elections on its own. As part of an investigation, it may take control of local election

25. *See* S.L. 2013-381.
26. G.S. 163-275(1).
27. G.S. 163-22(a).
28. G.S. 163-19.
29. *See* G.S. 163-26, -27.
30. The powers and duties of the state board are set out at G.S. 163-22.

records. When convinced that irregularities have affected the outcome, the board may invalidate an election anywhere in the state and order a new election. It may also remove any local election official who has acted improperly.[31]

County Boards of Elections

Each of the state's 100 counties has a three-member board of elections appointed by the state board from names submitted by the state chairs of the Democratic and Republican parties. No more than two members may belong to the same party. Because the state board is appointed by the governor, the majority on each county board is also from the governor's party. Elected officials, candidates and their close relatives, campaign managers and treasurers, and political-party officials may not serve on a county board.

County board members serve two-year terms; the appointments are made in the summer of odd-numbered years. The board chooses one of its members as its chair.

The election law requires the county board to meet at certain times for particular purposes: for example, to appoint and train precinct officials; to consider absentee ballot applications; to count absentee ballots; and to canvass the results of an election and declare the results. Other meetings are held as needed.

The statutes setting out the powers and structure of the county boards are found at G.S. 163-30 through -37.

Duties

The county boards of elections conduct all elections. Their duties fall into two categories. The first type consists of administrative duties. The board employs a director to manage its office, chooses other office employees, appoints precinct officials, registers voters, determines precinct boundaries, establishes voting places in the precincts, orders voting equipment, advertises elections, accepts candidates' filings, prepares and prints ballots, issues absentee ballots, supervises the counting of votes, and arranges for the many other activities that are part of registering voters and holding elections. The second type consists of policy-making or quasi-judicial (that is, courtlike) duties. The board hears challenges to voter registrations, determines the sufficiency of petitions, declares election results, hears protests about election irregularities and complaints about election officials, and issues certificates of election (which enable winning candidates to take office). In all of its duties, the county board is subject to the state board's rules and supervision, but most responsibility for seeing that elections are conducted properly rests at the county level. The powers and duties of county boards of elections are outlined at G.S. 163-33.

Directors of Elections

Each county board has a director of elections. The board chooses the person it would like to be the director and forwards that recommendation to the state board's executive director, who makes the formal appointment. The county director has day-to-day responsibility for supervising board employees, ordering supplies, estimating expenses, maintaining records, and attending to the dozens of other tasks that are associated with conducting elections. In fact, only a few specific duties are spelled out in the statutes, and it is up to the county board to assign duties and responsibilities to its director. The board may delegate to the director as much of its work as it wishes, other than its policy-making and quasi-judicial duties. It may not, for example, delegate its responsibility for hearing challenges to voter registrations.

The county board may not dismiss the director on its own. A majority of the board may recommend dismissal to the state board's executive director. The county director must be told the reasons for a dismissal recommendation and must have an opportunity to answer those allegations. The executive director makes a decision on dismissal, which is final unless the state board chooses to consider the matter. If the state board does take the matter up, it holds a hearing and then makes a decision on the dismissal.

In counties with full-time voter registration (which is nearly all counties), the county director is to be paid a salary recommended by the county board of elections and approved by the county board of commissioners. The salary

31. *See* G.S. 163-182.9 through -189.12.

is to be "commensurate with the salary paid to directors in counties similarly situated and similar in population and number of registered voters."[32] In counties where the elections office is open only part time, the director may be paid on an hourly basis. In any event, the director is to be granted the same vacation leave, sick leave, and petty leave as is granted to all other county employees.

The chief statute governing the role of the county director is G.S. 163-35.

Other Employees

In addition to a director, the county board of elections may approve the employment of a deputy county director and other office employees as needed. The statutes are clear that the board is responsible for hiring and firing these employees, but the law governing other aspects of employment, such as working hours, grievance procedures, and job classification, is not so clear. In a strict legal sense, the county board of elections controls the number of employees it employs and what each employee is to be paid. So long as the board of elections spends on salaries no more than the amount appropriated by the board of commissioners, the elections board determines the number of employees and level of pay of each.[33] But because all funds for the board of elections are appropriated by the county commissioners, the commissioners can, as a practical matter, strongly influence the number of employees, their pay, and other conditions of employment, if they wish to do so. In some counties, the board of elections and the board of commissioners have addressed the lack of clarity in the statute by entering into a memorandum of agreement spelling out the extent to which the county's personnel ordinance, grievance procedure, pay plan, and so on will apply to elections board employees. That agreement is, of course, subject to amendment by the parties.

The limited statutory guidance on the status of elections board employees is found at G.S. 163-33(10), which provides that the county board has the power to "appoint and remove the board's clerk, assistant clerks, and other employees."

Precinct and Registration Officials

The county board of elections divides the county into precincts and establishes a voting place for each precinct. On election day, each precinct is staffed by a chief judge and two judges of election. Depending on the size of the precinct, the elections board may also appoint precinct assistants to assist the chief judge and judges.

The board of elections appoints the chief judge and two judges, from names submitted by the county political party chairs, to serve two-year terms. No more than two of these three officials may belong to the same party. For many years the law has required that these officials be residents of the precinct in which they will work. On occasion, however, party chairs and boards of elections have had difficulty locating and recruiting residents willing to serve in some precincts. The law, G.S. 163-41, now provides that when necessity dictates, the board of elections may appoint residents of the county who are not residents of the precinct to serve as chief judge and judge. A similar provision applies to precinct assistants.[34]

The chief judge and judges must work together all day at the polls, from opening to closing through the reporting of the vote count to the elections board. The board of elections may, if it chooses, allow split shifts for precinct assistants.

The election law sets certain minimum wages for precinct officials for working at the polls and for officials attending the instructional meeting before each election. Otherwise, the amount of pay for precinct officials is at the discretion of the board of elections and the county commissioners.[35] In practice, the pay varies from county to county, with the minimum pay being the state minimum wage ($7.25 per hour in 2014). Precinct and registration officials may not accept payment for election-related services from anyone other than the board of elections.

---

32. G.S. 163-35(c).

33. The North Carolina Court of Appeals so held in *Graham County Board of Elections v. Graham County Board of Commissioners*, 212 N.C. App. 313, 324 (2011), saying that "county boards of commissioners have no authority to determine the number of county board of elections employees if those employees can be compensated within the budget established by the county commissioners."

34. *See* G.S. 163-42.

35. *See* G.S. 163-46.

County Boards Conducting City Elections

County boards of elections conduct city elections as they do federal, state, and county elections. Cities must "reimburse the county board of elections for the actual cost involved in the administration" of an election for the city.[36]

County Board Budget

County boards of elections are subject to the Local Government Budget and Fiscal Control Act.[37] The elections board is directed by statute to "prepare and submit . . . a budget estimating the cost of elections for the ensuing fiscal year."[38] Almost all county board funds come by appropriation from the county commissioners. A small amount comes from the state for help with the expenses of statewide referendums and expenses related to the statewide voter registration computer system.[39] Sometimes civic groups and businesses wish to help pay for voter registration drives. They may do so only by donating money to the county general fund; the commissioners may then appropriate that amount to the board of elections. Election officials may not accept funds directly from anyone other than the county.

Many expenses of the county elections board are controlled by state law or regulation, including the minimum pay for board members and precinct officials. The kinds of records that must be maintained, the specifications for certain supplies, the number of notices that must be published, the quantity of ballots that may be printed, the hours of operation for the polls, the days the elections board office must be open, the kinds of voting booths that may be used, the forms that must be available in the board office and at the polling place, and various other matters that affect the county board's budget—all are set by statute or by regulations of the State Board of Elections. The state board determines what kinds of voting machines may be selected by the counties, the county commissioners decide whether to purchase them, and the county board of elections chooses a particular kind.

Most of the elections board's expenses—the costs of maintaining an office and conducting the regularly scheduled elections of public officials—are predictable. Still, not all expenses can be anticipated. When it prepares its budget, the elections board may not know, for example, that citizens will petition for a liquor election, that the decision in a voting rights lawsuit will require a change in election dates, or that the legislature will raise the pay for precinct officials. Expenses for these sorts of things, which may be substantial, may be matters over which the elections board has no control and may require a supplemental appropriation by the county commissioners.

Campaign Finance Regulation

North Carolina law sets limits on who may contribute to candidates for office and to political committees. In general, no one (other than the candidate and certain family members and the state executive committees of recognized political parties) may contribute more than $5,000 per election to any candidate or committee.[40] This limit is adjusted for inflation each year. Contributions over $50 may not be in cash, businesses may not make contributions, and contributions may not be anonymous. The law also sets requirements regarding expenditures by candidates and committees. Expenditures over $50 may not be in cash and all expenditures must show their purpose.[41]

For the enforcement of these regulations, and to inform the voters about the sources of support for candidates, candidates and committees must make regular reports of contributions and expenditures. In races for federal offices,

36. G.S. 163-284(b).
37. *See* G.S. 159-7 through -38.
38. G.S. 163-33(11).
39. *See* G.S. 163-11 through -13.
40. G.S. 163-278.13.
41. G.S. 163-278.14.

reports are filed with the Federal Election Commission;[42] for state, legislative, and judicial offices, they are filed with the state board;[43] and for county and city offices, they are filed with the county board of elections.[44]

At the county level, therefore, the responsibility falls on the county elections board to maintain a list of candidates and committees, to send notifications that required report filing dates are coming up, to receive the reports and review them for apparent compliance, to make the reports available for public inspection, and to send reminders if reports are late.

A candidate may file with the county board a certification that the campaign will not receive or spend more than $1,000. So long as the campaign stays under that limit, the reporting requirement is waived.[45]

If a candidate or committee fails to file a report, or if a filed report appears to show a violation of the campaign finance regulations, then the county board of elections is to report the matter to the state board, which may impose civil penalties or refer criminal matters to the appropriate district attorney for possible prosecution.[46]

Additional Resources

Joyce, Robert P. *The Precinct Manual 2014.* Chapel Hill, N.C.: UNC School of Government, 2014.

About the Author

Robert P. Joyce is a School of Government faculty member whose areas of specialization include the law related to elections.

42. G.S. 163-278.30.
43. G.S. 163-278.9.
44. G.S. 163-278.40A.
45. G.S. 163-278.10A.
46. G.S. 163-278.22.

Part 9

Education

Chapter 45

The Governance and Funding Structure of North Carolina Public Schools

Kara A. Millonzi

Introduction

The importance of public education was recognized in North Carolina's first constitution in 1776. Specifically, Article XLI, Section 41, provided that "a school or schools shall be established by the legislature, for the convenient instruction of youth, with such salaries to the masters, paid by the public, as may enable them to instruct at low prices; and, all useful learning shall be duly encouraged and promoted in one or more universities." The constitution thus required the General Assembly to establish schools staffed by teachers paid from public funds. The legislature took its first step toward carrying out that mandate in 1825 when it created the Literary Fund as a source of revenue for public schools. Public schools began to function as a statewide system in 1839.

The contours and scope of that public education system have evolved over time. The current system is the product of a patchwork of efforts by the state to adapt to changing economics, demographics, and policy prerogatives.[1] It involves an intricate division of policy and funding responsibilities among state and local entities. Each entity plays an integral part in carrying out the constitutional mandate to provide a public education.

This chapter discusses the contours of the constitutional mandate for public education and the structure and funding of elementary and secondary schools. Part I details the current constitutional provisions relating to education and briefly summarizes how those provisions have been interpreted by the North Carolina courts. Part II explains the governance scheme for the public school system and reviews the roles, responsibilities, and authorities assigned to the various state and local government entities, with special emphasis on the role of county governments.[2] Part III describes the funding scheme for public schools, focusing mainly on a county's funding responsibility, and part IV sets forth the local budgeting process. Finally, part V briefly discusses the structure and funding of charter schools and the role they play in public education.

I. Constitutional Mandate for Education

The current state constitution provides that North Carolinians "have a right to the privilege of education, and it is the duty of the State to guard and maintain that right."[3] It further commands the General Assembly to provide "for a general and uniform system of free public schools, which shall be maintained at least nine months in every year, and wherein equal opportunities shall be provided for all students."[4]

The North Carolina Supreme Court has interpreted these provisions to guarantee "every child of this state an opportunity to receive a sound basic education in our public schools."[5] This interpretation has arisen out of a long-running funding dispute, commonly referred to as the *Leandro* litigation. The case began in the mid-1990s as a fight over funding disparities among counties but has since evolved into an argument about what it means to provide each child with the opportunity for an adequate, or "sound basic," education. In 1997, the court described the elements of a sound basic education as follows:

- sufficient ability to read, write, and speak the English language and a sufficient knowledge of fundamental mathematics and physical science to enable the student to function in a complex and rapidly changing society;

---

1. The North Carolina State Board of Education's website provides a brief summary tracing the history of the public education system. It is available at http://stateboard.ncpublicschools.gov/about-sbe/history (last visited Feb. 13, 2014).

2. Postsecondary education is not discussed in this chapter. Statutes relating to the community colleges and the University of North Carolina are codified in, respectively, Chapters 115D and 116 of the North Carolina General Statutes (hereinafter G.S.). *See* Chapter 46, "Community Colleges."

3. N.C. Const. art. I, § 15.

4. N.C. Const. art. IX, § 2(1).

5. Leandro v. State, 346 N.C. 336, 346 (1997).

- sufficient fundamental knowledge of geography, history, and basic economic and political systems to enable the student to make informed choices with regard to issues that affect the student personally or affect the student's community, state, and nation;
- sufficient academic and vocational skills to enable the student to successfully engage in post-secondary education or vocational training; and
- sufficient academic and vocational skills to enable the student to compete on an equal basis with others in further formal education or gainful employment in contemporary society.[6]

To remedy what the court found to be deficiencies in meeting this constitutional standard, at least for some students, in 2004 the court charged the state with responsibility for assuring (1) that every classroom is staffed with a competent, certified, well-trained teacher; (2) that every school is led by a well-trained, competent principal with the leadership skills and ability to hire and retain competent, certified, and well-trained teachers; and (3) that every school is provided, in the most cost-effective manner, the resources necessary to support effective instruction within that school so that all children, including at-risk children, have an equal opportunity to obtain a sound basic education.[7]

Whether or not the state of North Carolina is meeting its responsibility to ensure that every student is given an opportunity to receive a sound basic education is the subject of ongoing judicial interpretation and legislative debate. The succeeding sections of this chapter examine the governance structure and financing scheme currently in place to attempt to carry out this constitutional mandate.

II. Current Governance Structure of Public Schools

The state constitution assigns shared responsibility for public education to the General Assembly, the State Board of Education, and the superintendent of public instruction. The General Assembly has further divided policy, administrative, and funding responsibilities for schools among state and local entities and officials, including the Department of Public Instruction, local school boards, and county governments. This section briefly describes the primary roles and responsibilities of each of these state and local entities.

General Assembly

As detailed above, the constitution assigns to the General Assembly the responsibility for ensuring "a general and uniform system of free public schools" that provides all children a basic education of at least minimum duration, content, and quality.[8] Thus, the legislature's primary authority is to ensure there are adequate funds to carry out this constitutional duty. The constitution allows the General Assembly to assign funding responsibility to units of local government "as it may deem appropriate."[9] Since the Great Depression era, however, the General Assembly has assumed primary funding responsibility for the state's public schools. (The funding scheme is described in detail in the next section.)

The General Assembly also plays a key role in setting global educational policy standards for the state. It accomplishes this through both its funding authority and statutory directives. For example, since the 1980s the legislature has embarked on several educational reform efforts, mainly aimed at increasing the accountability of school personnel for their students' performance. In 1985, it enacted the Basic Educational Program, which called for a rigorous standard course of study and addressed critical components for delivering that curriculum, including staffing levels,

6. *Id.*
7. Hoke Cnty. Bd. of Educ. v. State, 358 N.C. 605, 636 (2004).
8. N.C. Const. art. IX, § 2(1).
9. N.C. Const. art. IX, § 2(2).

class size, and materials and supplies.[10] It prompted the state's public school system to adopt outcome-based education and other accountability measures, and, with adoption of the School Improvement and Accountability Act of 1990, provided local schools greater flexibility in meeting unique local needs.[11] In 1997, the General Assembly enacted the Excellent Schools Act,[12] which was designed to increase student achievement, reduce teacher attrition, and reward teacher knowledge and skills. More recently, the legislature has focused its efforts on literacy, particularly third grade reading proficiency,[13] and increased teacher accountability.[14] In 2011, the General Assembly directed the State Board of Education to "participate in the development of the Common Core State Standards."[15] (Common Core State Standards are a uniform set of educational standards in language arts and mathematics, developed by teachers, parents, school administrators, and other educational organizations across the country to define the knowledge and skills students must have to fully prepare them for college and the workforce.)[16] And in 2013, the General Assembly began phasing out "career status"[17] for public school teachers, principals, and supervisors and replacing it with contractual employment agreements of one, two, or four years.[18]

Most of the time, however, the General Assembly carries out its duty to provide a system of free public schools by appropriating funds and delegating major decision-making authority to the State Board of Education, local boards of education, and other local school officials.

State Board of Education

The North Carolina Constitution provides for the State Board of Education (State Board) in Article IX, Section 4(1). The State Board is responsible for supervising and administering the free public school system and, except for local school funds, all funds provided for it. The board sets education policy for the state and has the power to make all rules and regulations necessary to carry out this responsibility, subject to laws enacted by the General Assembly. The board regulates the grade and salary of school employees, adopts a standard course of study, and develops accountability measures for individual schools. The board's statutory powers and duties are listed in Section 115C-12 of the North Carolina General Statutes (hereinafter G.S.) and include apportioning all state and federal school funds, certifying teachers, and adopting and supplying textbooks.

Superintendent of Public Instruction

In most states, the state school superintendent is appointed by the governor or selected by the state school board. In North Carolina, the superintendent of public instruction is a constitutional officer and is popularly elected for a four-year term.[19] Although not a voting member of the State Board, the superintendent is empowered by the constitution

10. 1985 N.C. Sess. Laws ch. 479.

11. 1990 N.C. Sess. Laws ch. 1066.

12. S.L. 1997-221.

13. S.L. 2012-142, § 7A.

14. S.L. 2013-360, §§ 9.1–9.7.

15. G.S. 115C-174.11. The General Assembly subsequently prohibited the State Board of Education from purchasing or implementing Common Core assessments unless specifically approved by legislative act. *See* S.L. 2013-360, § 9.2(b).

16. For more information on Common Core standards in North Carolina, see N.C. Department of Public Instruction, "Common Core State and NC Essential Standards," www.ncpublicschools.org/acre/standards (last visited Feb. 14, 2014).

17. Prior to August 2013, a teacher or administrator who had been employed by a North Carolina public school system for four consecutive years was eligible for a grant of career status by the local board of education. Such a grant protected the employee from dismissal or demotion, except for certain statutory bases and according to certain statutory procedures. *See* G.S. 115C-325.

18. S.L. 2013-360, § 9.6.

19. N.C. Const. art. IX, § 4(2); G.S. 115C-18.

to serve as the State Board's secretary and chief administrative officer, executing board policies and organizing and managing the Department of Public Instruction as the State Board directs.[20]

The superintendent is responsible for administering the day-to-day operations of the public school system and performing statutorily prescribed duties, subject to "the direction, control, and approval of the State Board."[21] The superintendent also has an important voice in explaining the needs of the school system to various constituencies and recommending changes to improve the public schools.

Department of Public Instruction

The Department of Public Instruction (DPI) is a statutorily created state agency that operates under the policy direction of the State Board of Education.[22] The superintendent of public instruction organizes and administers the DPI, while all appointments of administrative and supervisory personnel are subject to State Board approval.[23] In spite of some reorganization and downsizing in recent years, the DPI continues to provide important leadership and assistance to local school boards in such areas as instructional support, media and technology, research and testing, and personnel. And the DPI collects, compiles, and disseminates important statistical and financial data about school units.[24]

Local School Administrative Units

The local school administrative unit is the legal entity that operates directly below the State Board in the public school organizational hierarchy. In most states the school administrative unit is called the school district, a term frequently used informally in North Carolina as well. By statute, each North Carolina county is classified as a school administrative unit, and its schools are under the general supervision and control of a local board of education.[25]

Some counties have multiple school administrative units. In these counties, there usually is a county school administrative unit and one or more city administrative units. A city administrative unit is a school system established within a county, or within adjacent parts of two or more contiguous counties, that the General Assembly has approved to operate as a separate school unit.[26] In most cases, a city administrative unit is not connected with the city government; the unit merely draws its name from the municipality with which it is geographically associated. Local funding for a city administrative unit comes from the board(s) of county commissioners of the county(ies) in which the unit lies. With very limited exceptions, cities are neither required, nor authorized, to appropriate any funds to support public schools.

Local Boards of Education

Each local school administrative unit is governed by a local board of education. The local board of education is a corporate body created by the General Assembly with the power to sue and be sued[27] and the authority to exercise "[a]ll powers and duties conferred and imposed by law respecting public schools, which are not expressly conferred and

20. G.S. 115C-19; G.S. 115C-21.

21. G.S. 115C-19; *see also* G.S. 115C-21.

22. G.S. 143A-44.1

23. G.S. 115C-21(a).

24. Many of the financial and statistical reports prepared by DPI are available at www.dpi.state.nc.us/data/reports (last visited March 14, 2014).

25. G.S. 115C-66.

26. *Id.*

27. G.S. 115C-40.

imposed upon some other official."[28] State law requires each school board to provide an adequate school system.[29] In doing so, a local board performs five major duties, as follows:

1. hiring and firing of school employees,
2. setting education policy within the guidelines of state education policy,
3. preserving the school unit's assets and managing the local school budget,
4. informing county commissioners of the school unit's fiscal needs,
5. serving as a hearing board for local education disputes.

School boards in most other states have the authority to levy taxes to help finance the schools they administer; North Carolina boards do not have this authority. They derive almost all of their revenue from state and county appropriations.

Boards of County Commissioners

The board of county commissioners (county board) is an integral part of the legal structure of public education. The county board is the local tax-levying authority for the school units within the county's territorial boundaries.[30] Although county commissioners are not official educational policy makers, they nonetheless influence policy through the local budgeting process.

The contour of a county board's funding responsibility for its local school(s) and the local budget process is discussed in part III of this chapter. In addition to its funding role, the board of commissioners has a few other statutory duties, including approving certain school board contracts, conducting special school elections, approving the amount the school board proposes to spend to purchase a school site, mandating the merger of all school units in the county, issuing bonds for school construction, and, by agreement with the local board of education, constructing school facilities.

Approving Certain Local School Board Contracts

A local school board must obtain consent from the county board before entering into several different types of contracts. The county board's approval typically commits the county to providing sufficient funds to meet the local school board's obligations under the contracts.

Continuing Contracts for Capital Outlay

School administrative units may enter into continuing contracts for multi-year capital improvement projects or outlays, even when the school unit's budget resolution for the current year does not include an appropriation for the entire obligation incurred. Three conditions for these continuing contracts must be met: (1) the budget resolution must include an appropriation authorizing the current fiscal year's portion of the obligation, (2) an unencumbered balance of that appropriation for the current fiscal year must be sufficient to cover the unit's current fiscal year obligations under the contract, and (3) the board of county commissioners must approve the contract by a resolution binding the board to appropriate sufficient funds to pay the amounts falling due under the contract in future fiscal years.[31]

Installment Finance Contracts

Under G.S. 115C-528, local boards of education may use installment finance contracts to fund the acquisition of certain kinds of equipment: automobiles and school buses; mobile classroom units; food service equipment; photocopiers; and computers and computer hardware, software, and related support services. The contract term may not exceed the

28. G.S. 115C-36.
29. G.S. 115C-47.
30. There are a few situations in which the governing body of a municipality levies a supplemental tax for a city administrative unit.
31. G.S. 115C-441(c1).

useful life of the property being acquired. The school unit must give the seller a security interest in the property being financed under the installment contract. The school board must obtain the commissioners' approval of an installment finance contract if the contract term is at least three years and the total amount financed under the contract is at least $250,000 or an amount equal to three times the local school system's annual state allocation for classroom materials and equipment, whichever is less. Even if a contract does not require county board approval, a school board must submit information concerning these contracts as part of the annual budget it submits to the county board.

Guaranteed Energy Savings Contracts

G.S. 115C-47(28a) authorizes local school boards to use guaranteed energy savings contracts to purchase an energy conservation measure—such as a facility alteration or personnel training related to a facility's operation—that reduces energy consumption or operating costs. These contracts for the evaluation, recommendation, or implementation of energy conservation measures in school facilities are paid for over time, and energy savings are guaranteed to exceed costs. Local boards of education may finance energy conservation measures by using installment finance agreements under G.S. 160A-20. Such agreements are subject to county approval. A county board must certify to the North Carolina Department of State Treasurer that the payments under a guaranteed energy savings contract are not expected to require any additional appropriations to the local school board or cause an increase in taxes.[32] A county board also must indicate that it does not intend to reduce appropriations to the local school unit based on a reduction in energy costs in a manner that would inhibit the ability of the local school board to make payments under the contract. A county, however, is not legally obligated to appropriate funds to cover contract amounts due or to make payments directly under the contract.

Operational Leases

G.S. 115C-530 authorizes local boards of education to enter into operational leases of real or personal property for use as school buildings or facilities.[33] Leases for terms of three years or longer, including optional renewal periods, must be approved by the board of county commissioners. Approval obligates the commissioners to appropriate sufficient funds to meet the payments due in each year of the lease; the school board's budget resolution must include an appropriation for the current fiscal year's portion of the obligation as well as an unencumbered balance sufficient to pay the obligation.

Also, under G.S. 115C-530, school boards may make improvements to leased property. Contracts for repair and renovation must be approved by the board of county commissioners if they (1) are subject to the competitive bidding requirement in G.S. 143-129(a) (the current threshold for which is $500,000) and (2) do not otherwise constitute continuing contracts for capital outlay.

Capital Leases

A local school board may enter into capital leases of real or personal property for use as school buildings or school facilities.[34] A capital lease is a lease that has the economic characteristics of a purchase. Under a capital lease, ownership of the asset typically transfers to the lessee at the end of the lease term. Alternatively, a capital lease may contain a nominal purchase option for the lessee at the conclusion of the lease. A capital lease is subject to county approval if it meets the criteria in G.S. 115C-441(c1) for a continuing contact. However, even if a county approves a capital lease, payment is always subject to yearly budget decisions by the county board. Furthermore, no deficiency judgment may

32. *See* State of North Carolina Department of State Treasurer, Application for Approval of Guaranteed Energy Savings Contracts, www.energync.net/Portals/14/Documents/Utility%20Savings%20Initiative/PC/lgc-gescnew06-01-12.pdf (last visited Feb. 14, 2014).

33. In an operational lease the lessee obtains no ownership interest or option to obtain an ownership interest in the leased property.

34. G.S. 115C-531 and -532.

be rendered against the local school board or against the county in any action for breach of a capital lease.[35] The capital lease authority currently is set to expire on July 1, 2015.

Conducting Special School Elections

Under G.S. 115C-501, special school elections may be held to vote on proposals to

1. authorize a local supplemental tax,
2. increase the supplemental tax rate in an area that already has a supplemental tax of less than the maximum rate set by statute,
3. enlarge a city administrative unit by consolidating areas of a county unit into the city school unit,
4. supplement and equalize educational advantages by levying a special tax in an area of a county administrative unit enclosed within one common boundary line,
5. abolish a supplemental school tax,
6. authorize the county to issue school bonds,
7. provide a supplemental tax on a countywide basis pursuant to merger of all administrative units within a county,
8. annex or consolidate school areas from contiguous counties and provide a supplemental school tax in such annexed or consolidated areas, or
9. vote school bonds and taxes in certain merged school administrative units.

Involvement by the board of county commissioners begins when it receives a petition from a county or city school board requesting a special school election. The petition, which must be approved by the school board, need not originate with the school board itself. It can be submitted also by a majority of qualified voters who have resided for the preceding year in an area adjacent to a city administrative unit; these voters may petition the county board of education for an election on the question of annexing their area to the city unit. For other types of special elections, 25 percent of the qualified voters in a school area may initiate a petition and submit it to the board of education. The school board must consider the petition and decide whether or not to approve it.

If a petition is approved by the school board, it is submitted to the county commissioners; G.S. 115C-506 requires the commissioners "to call an election and fix the date for the same." In *Board of Education of Yancey County v. Board of Commissioners of Yancey County*,[36] the North Carolina Supreme Court held that, if a petition for an election on authorizing a special supplemental tax is properly presented, the duty of the board of commissioners is ministerial and not discretionary; it is obliged to call the election. This rule likely applies to the other kinds of special elections listed above.[37] The school board may withdraw a petition at any time before the election is called. All school elections, whether for county or city school administrative units, are held and conducted by the appropriate county board of elections.

If an election is held on any of these issues and the proposition is rejected, under G.S. 115C-502 another election on the same issue in the same area may not be called for at least six months. An election on whether to abolish a local tax district may not be held any sooner than one year after the election establishing the district or after an election on the issue of dismantling the local tax district.[38] If a local tax district is in debt or has unmet obligations, no election may be held on the issue of abolishing that tax district.

---

35. G.S. 115C-531(e).

36. 189 N.C. 650 (1925).

37. It is not entirely clear whether or not the rule applies to petitions for school bond elections because of inconsistent provisions in the laws regulating local government debt. However, in 1975 the North Carolina attorney general issued an opinion letter stating that a county must hold a bond referendum if a proper petition is submitted to the county board. Op. N.C. Atty. Gen. (Feb. 10, 1975) (on file with author).

38. G.S. 115C-505.

Approving Expenditures for School Sites

A school board may not execute a contract to purchase a site or to make any expenditure for a property without the county commissioners' approval "as to the amount to be spent for the site." The requirement applies whether the county has made a blanket capital outlay appropriation or has allocated moneys for this particular project. In 1975, in *Painter v. Wake County Board of Education*,[39] the state supreme court considered an earlier version of this statutory provision; its ruling indicates that this approval requirement applies only when the school board is using funds from the county.

If the two boards disagree over a site purchase matter, they may, under G.S. 115C-426(f), settle the dispute through the judicial procedure used to resolve budgetary disputes (found in G.S. 115C-431). If they do so, the issue to be determined is the amount to be spent for the site, not its location. The school board has the sole authority to choose school sites; if the court finds the amount it proposes to spend reasonable, the school board will most likely prevail.

Mandating Merger of School Units within a County

As discussed above, some counties have both a county local school administrative unit and one or more city school administrative units. The propriety of having multiple school administrative units within one county is the subject of much study and debate among county and school officials. The number of school administrative units has decreased substantially over time. In 1960, there were 174 separate school units; as of 2013, there are only 115. The General Assembly merged several of the school units through local acts. Some mergers, however, came about at the behest of county governments in which the administrative units are located. The General Assembly has authorized a board of county commissioners to compel a merger by adopting a merger plan for all school units in the county. In subsequent years, the county must provide the merged school unit local funding based on average daily membership[40] at a level at least equivalent to the highest level received by any school unit in the county during the five fiscal years preceding the merger. The boards of education do not participate in preparing the plan and need not agree to it. A merger plan developed by a board of county commissioners cannot be made subject to voter approval.[41]

There are two other statutorily authorized ways to merge school units without legislative action. A city board may force a merger by dissolving itself. In that case the State Board of Education must adopt a merger plan. Plans developed in this way cannot be subject to voter approval. Boards of education and boards of county commissioners do not participate in preparing such a plan and need not agree to it.[42] Alternatively, the school systems themselves may bring about the merger. The merging units adopt a written plan of merger, which becomes effective if the board of county commissioners and the State Board of Education approve it. The plan may make the merger contingent on approval of the voters in the affected areas.[43]

Constructing School Facilities

A county board of commissioners bears primary funding responsibility for public school infrastructure and facilities. However, state law assigns to each local school board the duty to provide adequate school facilities.[44] G.S. 115C-521(c) also directs that the "building of all new school buildings and the repairing of all old school buildings shall be under the control and direction of, and by contract with, the board of education for which the building and repairing is done." And all school buildings must be located on a site that is "owned in fee simple" by the local school board.[45]

For some capital projects, a county appropriates money to the local school unit and school personnel perform the work or contract with private entities to complete the work. A county board has no legal authority to require that a

---

39. 288 N.C. 165 (1975).

40. Average daily membership is a calculation of a school unit's student population. For more information on that calculation, see the N.C. Department of Public Instruction's *School Attendance and Student Accounting Manual, 2013–2013*, www.dpi.state.nc.us/docs/fbs/accounting/manuals/sasa.pdf (last visited Dec. 18, 2013).

41. G.S. 115C-68.1.

42. G.S. 115C-68.2.

43. G.S. 115C-67.

44. G.S. 115C-521(a).

45. G.S. 115C-521(d).

school board hire a particular contractor or otherwise proceed under a particular process (such as design-build or capital lease). A county and school board may prefer to have the county contract for and oversee school construction and repair projects. In this case, the county and school board must enter into a carefully crafted interlocal agreement in which the local board assigns its contracting rights to the county but retains ultimate oversight authority.[46] Furthermore, if a county issues installment finance debt to fund a school construction project, the county may need to obtain temporary ownership of the school property for the life of the loan.[47] Again, a carefully drafted interlocal agreement should allow the county to perform the construction or repair work while not running afoul of the statutory provisions.

III. Funding Public Schools

Funding public schools is a responsibility of both state and county governments. (The federal government also provides limited funding for certain targeted programs.) In 1839, the first year that North Carolina's public schools began to function as a statewide system, the General Assembly made $40 available to each school district that raised $20 locally.[48] That was the legislature's first stab at dividing the fiscal burden of public education between the state and local governments. The struggle to find a proper division while ensuring fairness in the financial burden, equity in educational opportunities, and quality in education has continued for the ensuing 175 years.

In the early to mid-1930s, largely as a reaction to the fiscal chaos of the Great Depression—a significant number of local governments had defaulted on debt and were in rough financial shape—the state adopted the current fiscal framework of centralizing policy-making and funding responsibility for public education at the state level. It enacted the School Machinery Act,[49] which made the state responsible for paying all current expenses necessary to finance a minimum six-month school term, leaving the counties responsible for constructing and maintaining school buildings.

The basic structure of school finance has not changed since the 1930s. The state continues to be responsible for current expenses necessary to maintain the minimum nine-month term, while counties are responsible for financing construction and the maintenance of school facilities and may supplement state funding for current expenditures. In this respect, North Carolina's approach to financing its public schools differs from that of most other states, where the basic financial backing for public schools comes from local rather than state revenues. Thus, in North Carolina, state income and sales taxes, rather than local property taxes, constitute the primary revenue sources for financing schools.

It is also the case, though, that there has been a blending of funding responsibilities over time. The state often appropriates funds for school construction, and school boards continue to rely on counties to provide funds for current expenses. In fact, the county share of funding has increased significantly in recent years.

State Funding

The primary funding source for public schools is the state income tax. The state allocates this money to the public school system in a few different ways. The majority of the funds are used to cover the operational expenses of each local school administrative unit. The General Assembly, however, typically provides some funds each year to fund school facility projects.

---

46. Counties and local school administrative units have broad authority to enter into interlocal agreements under G.S. Chapter 160A, Article 20.

47. *See* G.S. 160A-20.

48. 1839 N.C. Pub. Laws ch. 8.

49. 1931 N.C. Pub. Laws ch. 728.

Operational Funding

The state appropriates its operational funding for schools in its annual budget. North Carolina differs from most other states in that it does not distribute money for the general education program on the basis of the local unit's financial ability to operate schools. The bulk of state funding for public education is essentially a flat grant to a school system based on the number of students enrolled and the general costs of operation. The primary unit of allocation is average daily membership (ADM). The ADM for each school month is calculated as the "sum of the number of days in membership for all non-violating students in individual [school units], divided by the number of days in the school month."[50]

ADM dollars are typically allocated among counties and school units through three different methods—position allotments, dollar allotments, and categorical allotments.

Position Allotments

The largest component of the state budget for schools is teacher salaries. Each year the state appropriates funds to pay teachers, instructional personnel, and school administrators. Salaries are funded on a position basis—the state allotting a certain number of teachers and support personnel to each school unit based on grade-level ADMs. For fiscal year 2013–14, for grades 1–3, the state allocated one teacher position for every eighteen students. For each position allotment, the state pays the costs to fund a particular person in a particular teaching position, based on the State Salary Schedule. That allows a school unit to hire experienced teachers or instructional support personnel based on the unit's needs without being limited to a specific dollar total.[51] A school unit also has some flexibility to use the allocated funds to cover other expenditures.[52]

Dollar Allotments

Each school unit also receives a per-ADM dollar allotment that may be used to fund textbooks, supplies, materials, and some personnel, such as teacher assistants and central office administration positions. For example, in fiscal year 2013–14, the state allocated $28.58 per ADM for instructional supplies and $14.26 per ADM for textbooks. A school unit may use dollar allotments to cover certain other expenditures.[53]

Categorical Allotments

The General Assembly has targeted some state appropriations to aid smaller and lower wealth counties and to assist school units that serve student populations with unique needs. These moneys are not allocated on a straight ADM basis. Instead, they are disbursed according to detailed formulas set forth in the state's annual budget. Common categorical allotments are for children with disabilities,[54] academically gifted children,[55] low-wealth counties,[56] small school systems,[57] and disadvantaged students.[58] Some of these allocation formulas factor in a county's appropriation to the school unit. For example, the low-wealth formula is based in part on the county's wealth and whether a county's appropriation to the school unit meets a certain minimum-effort threshold.[59] Furthermore, the low-wealth funds may not be used to supplant county appropriations.

---

50. N.C. Department of Public Instruction, *School Attendance and Student Accounting Manual, 2013–2014*, at 27, www.dpi.state.nc.us/docs/fbs/accounting/manuals/sasa.pdf (last visited Feb. 17, 2014).

51. The North Carolina public school personnel *Employee Salary and Benefits Manual, 2013–2014* (State Salary Schedule), is available at www.ncpublicschools.org/docs/fbs/finance/salary/salarymanual.pdf (last visited Feb. 17, 2014).

52. *See* G.S. 115C-105.25. A local school unit must publish information on its website about its state appropriations and any allotment transfers.

53. *See* G.S. 115C-105.25. A local school unit must publish information on its website about its state appropriations and any allotment transfers.

54. S.L. 2013-360, § 8.1.

55. S.L. 2013-360, § 8.2.

56. S.L. 2013-360, § 8.3.

57. S.L. 2013-360, § 8.4.

58. S.L. 2013-360, § 8.5.

59. *See* S.L. 2013-360, § 8.3.

The state also provides funds to local school units to replace buses according to a statutory replacement schedule.[60]

Capital Funding

Counties have been responsible for financing school construction since the state's public school system was established. Over the years, however, the state has offered direct and indirect assistance for construction costs—through state general obligation bonds, local sales and use tax authority, and direct appropriations of corporate income tax and state lottery proceeds.

State Bonds

Over the years, the state has issued numerous bonds to finance construction grants to local school boards. In recent years, however, the state has chosen other forms of funding assistance for school construction. The last state bond for school construction was in 1996.[61]

Local Sales and Use Tax Authority

The state has also provided alternative relief. In 1983, it authorized counties to levy a one-half-cent sales and use tax[62] with a specified percentage of the resulting revenue earmarked for school capital outlay, including retirement of existing school indebtedness (30 percent of the proceeds are currently so earmarked). In 1986, the legislature authorized counties to levy another one-half-cent tax, this time with 60 percent of the revenue earmarked for school capital outlay expenses.[63] Because traditionally sales and use taxes have been a state revenue source, these local sales taxes may reasonably be viewed as a form of state revenue sharing for school construction. All counties levy both taxes.[64] Counties may hold the moneys generated from the earmarked portion of the taxes in a capital reserve fund for future projects; any interest earned must be earmarked for school capital outlays.[65]

State School Construction Funds

In 1987, the legislature enacted the School Facilities Act, which created the Critical School Facility Needs Fund (CSFNF) and the Public School Building Capital Fund (PSBCF).[66]

The CSFNF, funded by corporate income tax proceeds, aided counties and school units with the most pressing needs in relation to their resources, as determined by the CSFNF commission. Moneys were distributed to high-need counties from 1988 through 1994, at which time the fund was abolished.[67]

The PSBCF was established to provide aid to all counties for school construction projects. It too was originally funded by a portion of the state's corporate income tax proceeds,[68] which were allocated among the one hundred counties on the basis of ADM. A county and its local school administrative unit(s) could jointly apply to the Department of Public Instruction to use the county's allocation for capital outlay and technology projects. A county was required to match moneys allocated for capital outlay projects on the basis of $1 of local funds for every $3 of state funds.

---

60. *See* G.S. 115C-249; S.L. 2013-360, § 8.11(a) & (b).

61. *See* 1995 N.C. Sess. Laws ch. 631.

62. G.S. Chapter 105, Article 40.

63. G.S. Chapter 105, Article 42.

64. Counties have additional sales and use tax authority. All counties levy a one-cent tax pursuant to G.S. Chapter 105, Article 39. Several counties also levy a quarter-cent tax pursuant to G.S. Chapter 105, Article 46. Neither of these taxes is earmarked for school funding, though.

65. A county may petition the North Carolina Local Government Commission (LGC) for authorization to use part or all of the earmarked revenues for other purposes. The LGC will approve a petition only if the county demonstrates that it can provide for school capital needs without the earmarked revenue. A local board of education also may petition the LGC if it believes that the county has not complied with the intent of sales and use tax laws. G.S. 105-502 and -487.

66. 1987 N.C. Sess. Laws ch. 622.

67. 1995 N.C. Sess. Laws ch. 631, § 14.

68. G.S. 115C-546.1(b) (repealed 2013).

Beginning in 2005, the legislature also allocated a portion (roughly 40 percent) of the state's lottery proceeds to the PSBCF.[69] These funds could be used to fund capital outlay projects for school buildings and were allocated among the counties according to a detailed statutory formula.[70] No local match was required.

In 2013, the General Assembly repealed the statutory distributions of both corporate income tax proceeds and lottery proceeds to the PSBCF.[71] Although the PSBCF has not been abolished, funding for it will be subject to yearly state budget appropriations. According to G.S. 115C-546.2(d), if funds are appropriated to the PSBCF from the state lottery, those moneys must be allocated for school construction projects based on ADM.[72] A county and its local school administrative unit(s) will jointly apply to the Department of Public Instruction for a distribution of the moneys "to fund school construction projects and to retire indebtedness incurred for school construction projects."[73] No county matching funds are required. For fiscal year 2013–14, the legislature appropriated $100 million to the fund.[74]

County Funding

Another significant difference between North Carolina's funding scheme for public education and that in other states is that local boards of education do not have authority to levy taxes to support schools. Instead, this authority resides with county governments. Although the state bears primary responsibility for establishing and funding a public school system, the constitution authorizes the General Assembly to "assign to units of local government such responsibility for the financial support of the free public schools as it may deem appropriate."[75] It further provides that the "governing boards of units of local government with financial responsibility for public education may use local revenues to add to or supplement any public school or post-secondary school program."[76]

The legislature has not been entirely clear, however, in delineating the public school funding duties of the state from those of county governments. Significant confusion about the contours of a county's obligation for public schools has resulted, forcing counties and local school boards to turn to the courts for guidance.

G.S. 115C-408 specifies that "it is the policy of the State of North Carolina to provide from State revenue sources the instructional expenses for current operations of the public school system as defined in the standard course of study. It is the policy of the State of North Carolina that the facilities requirements for a public education system will be met by county governments." On its face, this statute articulates a clear demarcation of funding responsibility between the state and county governments. The statute, by its terms, is merely aspirational, however. It does not actually assign any specific funding responsibilities. Neither does it reflect funding realities.

A handful of statutory provisions assign funding responsibility to counties for specific expenditure items. These statutes assign to counties responsibility for funding most capital outlay expenditures, including school facilities, furniture, and apparatus;[77] buildings for bus and vehicle storage;[78] library, science, and classroom equipment;[79] water supply and sanitary facilities;[80] and maintenance and repair of school buildings.[81] In addition, the statutes explicitly assign

69. G.S. 18C-164(d) (repealed 2013).

70. G.S. 115C-546.2(d)(1) & (2) (repealed 2013).

71. S.L. 2013-360, § 6.11.

72. G.S. 115C-546.2(e) allows the State Board of Education to use up to $1.5 million of the funds appropriated each year to support positions in the Department of Instruction.

73. G.S. 115C-546.2(d)(4).

74. S.L. 2013-360, § 6.11.

75. N.C. Const. art. IX, § 2(2).

76. *Id.*

77. G.S. 115C-521.

78. G.S. 115C-249.

79. G.S. 115C-522(c).

80. *Id.*

81. G.S. 115C-524(b).

to counties responsibility for funding some operational expenditures—specifically, school maintenance and repairs,[82] instructional supplies and reference books,[83] school property insurance,[84] and fire inspections.[85]

If the funding framework ended there, it might not be such a knotty issue. A county would be required to fund the public school capital and operational expense items explicitly delegated to it by statute. And, a county could choose to supplement its required appropriations in any given year, within the discretion of its governing board. The state would be required to fund any other expenditure necessary to enable a local school administrative unit to provide a "sound basic education" (considering, of course, money the local school administrative unit receives from other sources, such as the federal government).

However, the funding framework does not end there. The statute that sets forth the uniform budget standard for public schools requires that a local school administrative unit maintain at least three funds to account for budgeted moneys.[86] The statute identifies the types and sources of funds that must be appropriated to each fund. One of the funds, the capital outlay fund, includes appropriations from, among other sources, "revenues made available for capital outlay purposes by the State Board of Education and the board of county commissioners."[87]

Another fund, the local current expense fund, must "include appropriations sufficient, when added to appropriations from [the State], for current operating expense of the public school system in conformity with the educational goals and policies of the State and the local board of education, within the financial resources and consistent with the fiscal policies of the board of county commissioners."[88] It further indicates that the appropriations must be funded by, among other revenue sources, "moneys made available to the local school administrative unit by the board of county commissioners."[89] Thus, despite the "policy" statements in G.S. 115C-408, it appears that the state is to provide at least some funding for capital expenses and that counties are to provide at least some funding for operational expenses. But the uniform budget statute still leaves ambiguity as to what the state is responsible for and what is left to counties.

To further complicate the analysis, G.S. 115C-431 authorizes a local board of education to initiate a dispute resolution process with the county if the local board of education determines that in any given year "the amount of money appropriated to the local current expense fund, or the capital outlay fund, or both, by the board of county commissioners is not sufficient to support a system of free public schools." There are several stages to the dispute resolution process, including a mandatory meeting of the two boards, followed by mediation. If both steps fail to produce a satisfactory outcome, the local board of education may file an action in superior court against the county. And, according to the statute, the issues to be determined by the court are (1) the amount of money legally necessary from all sources "to maintain a system of free public schools as defined by State law and State Board of Education policy" and (2) the amount of money legally required from the board of county commissioners. In making the finding, the judge or the jury must "consider the educational goals and policies of the State and the local board of education, the budgetary request of the local board of education, the financial resources of the county and the local board of education, and the fiscal policies of the board of county commissioners and the local board of education." The North Carolina Supreme Court recently interpreted G.S. 115C-431 to "itself assign to the local government responsibility for funding 'a system of free public schools' . . . ."[90] Thus, in any given year, a county may be required to fund operational and capital expenditure items in addition to those explicitly specified by the statutory provisions listed above. Furthermore, what expenditures a county is legally required to fund (and at what level) will depend, at least in part, on the amount of funding a local school administrative unit receives from other sources.

---

82. G.S. 115C-524.
83. G.S. 115C-522(c).
84. G.S. 115C-534.
85. G.S. 115C-525(b).
86. G.S. 115C-426.
87. *Id.*
88. *Id.*
89. *Id.*
90. Beaufort Cnty. Bd. of Educ. v. Beaufort Cnty. Bd. of Comm'rs, 363 N.C. 500, 507 (2009).

Unfortunately, the constitutional and statutory frameworks for public school funding do not provide much guidance for county and public school officials wrestling with tough budgetary decisions. What a county is required to fund (and how much it is required to spend) will depend on the unique facts and circumstances facing the county and its local school unit(s) in any given fiscal year. The amount a county appropriates for public school capital or operational expenses may increase, decrease, or remain unchanged from year to year. Based on the constitutional and statutory framework described above (and case law interpretations of the various provisions), there are, however, several identifiable factors that influence the amount that a county is legally required to appropriate to its public schools for capital and operational expenses. They include

- the budget request for capital and operational expenses from the county's local school administrative unit(s),
- the amount of funding a county's local school administrative unit(s) receives from other sources—including the state and the federal government,
- the educational policies of the state and the county's local school administrative unit(s),
- the size and composition of the student populations in the county's local school administrative unit(s),
- the financial resources of the county, and
- the fiscal policies of the county's board of commissioners.

Note that the listed factors are in no particular order—presumably they are all equally important. The factors simply provide some rudimentary guidelines for county officials as they work with their local school board officials to make difficult appropriation decisions relating to public schools.

Local Funding Sources for School Units

As stated above, a school unit receives most of its capital financing and at least a quarter of its operational financing each year from counties. The local funding is composed primarily of county appropriations of unrestricted general fund revenue (for example, property tax proceeds) and earmarked local sales and use tax revenue. A local school unit also may receive revenue derived from locally collected penalties and fines and a voted supplemental school tax.

County Appropriations of Unrestricted Revenue

A county may appropriate any unrestricted county revenue to fund the capital and operating expenses of its school unit(s). At least to some extent, a county's governing board has discretion in determining the amount of unrestricted revenue to appropriate to support its schools. A school unit, however, may challenge a county's appropriations if it believes that the amount allocated for either capital or operating expenditures (or both), when combined with moneys made available to it through other sources, is not sufficient to support a system of free public schools.

As discussed below, a county board may exercise some control over how the appropriated funds are spent by the local school unit(s).

County Appropriations of Earmarked Local Sales and Use Tax Proceeds

As discussed above, a portion of a county's local sales and use tax revenue is earmarked for certain public school expenditures.[91] A county has discretion to determine how much of these earmarked funds to appropriate each year and for what capital projects. A county board may appropriate all of the available funds each fiscal year, or it may place the money into a capital reserve fund for future expenditure. This allows a county to save moneys over several years to finance large capital outlays for its school unit(s). As with county appropriations of unrestricted general fund revenues, a county board may exercise some control over how its local school unit(s) expends these funds.

A county may seek permission from the Local Government Commission (LGC) to use part or all of the earmarked local sales and use tax proceeds for any lawful purpose if the county demonstrates that it can satisfy all of the capital

91. *See* notes 62–65 and accompanying text.

outlay needs of its school unit(s) from other sources. In order to apply to the LGC for an exemption from the statutory earmarks on the Article 40 and Article 42 tax proceeds, a board of county commissioners must adopt a resolution and then submit it to the LGC. The resolution must indicate that the county can provide for its public school capital needs without restricting the use of part or the entire designated amount. The LGC must consider both the school unit's capital needs and those of the county generally in making its decision. The LGC must issue a written decision detailing its findings and specifying what percentage, if any, of the earmarked proceeds may be used by the county for any lawful purpose.

Local Fines and Penalties

Under Article IX, Section 7, of the North Carolina Constitution, "the clear proceeds of all penalties and forfeitures and of all fines collected in the several counties for any breach of the penal laws of the state, shall belong to and remain in the several counties, and shall be faithfully appropriated and used exclusively for maintaining free public schools." Several locally collected fines and penalties are subject to this constitutional mandate.[92] If a county collects penalties or fines that are subject to this constitutional requirement, it must remit the clear proceeds (gross proceeds minus up to 10 percent in collection costs) to the local school unit(s) within the county within ten days after the end of the month in which the money was collected.

A county does not include these funds in its appropriations to the school unit(s), and the county board has no control over their expenditure. The board of county commissioners, however, may consider the amount of fine, penalty, and forfeiture revenue received by a local school unit when determining the county's annual appropriations.

Voted Supplemental Tax Revenue

Voters within a local school administrative unit may approve by referendum the levy of supplemental taxes for any item of expenditure in the school unit's budget.[93] Under general law, the maximum supplemental tax rate voters may approve is $0.50 per $100 valuation.[94] Once a supplemental tax is approved by the voters, a local board of education may request that the county levy a tax each year up to the maximum rate approved by the voters. The county decides whether or not to levy the tax and at what rate (the rate is capped at the level requested by the local board of education).

The county does not have any control over how the supplemental tax proceeds are spent by the school unit. That decision rests with the local school board, subject only to the terms of the ballot measure under which the tax was approved. The board of county commissioners, however, may consider the availability of the supplemental tax revenue when determining the county's annual appropriations.

Federal Funding

Although public education is a state and local responsibility, since the 1950s the federal government has assumed a significant role in public education, primarily by providing funds to states. Congress generally conditions a state's receipt of federal funds on the state's compliance with federally defined conditions.

For example, the No Child Left Behind Act of 2001[95] created rigorous testing, reporting, and academic progress requirements for all states receiving Title I funds (all fifty states). Title I, which is aimed at raising the academic achievement of low-income children, is the largest source of federal education funds. Significant federal funding also

92. *See* G.S. 115C-437. For a detailed discussion of the categories of locally collected penalties and fines that are subject to this constitutional provision, see Kara Millonzi, "Locally-Collected Penalties & Fines: What Monies Belong to the Public Schools?" *Coates' Canons Local Government Law Blog* (UNC School of Government, Nov. 17, 2011), http://canons.sog.unc.edu/?p=5991.

93. G.S. Chapter 115C, Article 36.

94. The maximum supplemental rate is $0.60 per $100 valuation for a local school administrative unit, district, or other school area having a population of at least 100,000. Some local school units have higher maximum rates authorized by local legislation.

95. 20 U.S.C. §§ 6301 *et seq.*

goes to programs for children with disabilities and to the school breakfast and lunch program. More recently, the U.S. Department of Education initiated the Race to the Top[96] program, which provided competitive grants to spur innovation and reforms in state and local education. States were awarded points for satisfying certain educational policies, such as performance-based standards for teachers and principals; complying with Common Core; lifting caps on charter schools; turning around the lowest-performing schools; and building data systems. North Carolina received a Race to the Top grant of nearly $400 million in 2010.

Most federal moneys are categorical funds, which means they are appropriated by Congress to the states for specific educational purposes. These funds are channeled through the State Board for distribution to local units, but the board has little control over the programs themselves. In general, poorer school units receive more federal dollars relative to their enrollment than wealthier units do.

IV. Local Budgeting Process

Each year, a county engages in a detailed budgetary process to estimate revenues and make appropriations for the forthcoming fiscal year. A county must include its appropriations to its local school unit(s) for capital outlay and current expenses in its annual budget ordinance. The Local Government Budget and Fiscal Control Act,[97] as supplemented by the School Budget and Fiscal Control Act,[98] prescribes the procedural and substantive requirements for adopting the county's budget ordinance and appropriating money to its local school unit(s).[99] The budgeting process is fairly straightforward and can be broken down into the following ten steps:

Step 1: County Board and Local School Board(s) Communicate on an Ongoing Basis
Step 2: Superintendent Submits Proposed Budget
Step 3: Local School Board Considers Superintendent's Budget
Step 4: Local School Board Submits Budget Request to County Board
Step 5: County Board Makes Appropriations to Local School Unit(s)
Step 6: Local School Board Initiates Dispute Resolution Process (optional)
Step 7: Local School Board Adopts School Budget Resolution
Step 8: Local School Board Amends School Budget Resolution (optional)
Step 9: County Board Monitors Local School Unit's Expenditures of County Appropriations (optional)
Step 10: County Board Reduces Appropriations to Local School Unit(s) during Fiscal Year (optional)

Each step is analyzed more thoroughly below.

Step 1: County Board and Local School Board(s) Communicate on an Ongoing Basis

A county board and school board must work together to ensure that each board's statutory requirements are met. The board of county commissioners and local board(s) of education should engage in ongoing communications during the

96. The Race to the Top Program was funded as part of the American Recovery and Reinvestment Act of 2009, Pub. L. No. 111–5, 123 Stat. 115.

97. G.S. Chapter 159, Article 3.

98. G.S. Chapter 115C, Article 31, Part 1.

99. See Chapter 20, "Budgeting for Operating and Capital Expenditures," for more information on adopting, enacting, and amending the annual budget ordinance.

fiscal year.[100] Leading up to the budget process, they should communicate about the fiscal needs of the local school administrative unit and the fiscal resources of the county. Doing so will prevent surprises to either board at budget time and will help make the budgeting process work more efficiently and effectively.

Some county boards and local school boards agree to adopt multi-year financing formulas for operational expenses, indexed to such things as enrollment growth, percentages of low wealth or special needs students, or state funding averages. These funding agreements are not legally enforceable, but they can serve as a useful tool for financial planning.

Step 2: Superintendent Submits Proposed Budget

By May 1, the public school superintendent must submit a budget and budget message to the local board of education (superintendent's budget).[101] A local school board may direct the superintendent to follow certain specified guidelines and processes in preparing the proposed budget. A copy of the superintendent's budget must be filed in the superintendent's office and made available for public inspection.[102] The superintendent may publish notice that the superintendent's budget has been submitted to the local board of education, but the superintendent is not required to do so.

Step 3: Local School Board Considers Superintendent's Budget

The local board of education may hold a public hearing on the superintendent's budget, but it is not required to do so.[103] With or without public input or support, the board is free to make any changes to the proposed budget before submitting it to the county for consideration.

Step 4: Local School Board Submits Budget Request to County Board

By May 15, the local board of education must submit its entire proposed budget (not just its request for county funding) to the board of county commissioners.[104] The county's budget officer must present the local board of education's requests to the county board, even if the budget officer's proposed county budget recommends different funding levels for the school unit.

The board of county commissioners may request further information from the local school administrative unit about its proposed budget request. In fact, the county board has broad authority to obtain from the local board of education "all books, records, audit reports, and other information bearing on the financial operation of the local school administrative unit."[105] It also may specify the format in which the financial information must be presented.

In addition, a county board can (and often does) invite the school unit's superintendent or the local school board to present the school's budget proposal at a county board meeting or during the public hearing on the county's budget. This affords the county board an opportunity to ask questions about certain expenditure items and to obtain further clarification on a local school board's policy goals and needs.

100. *See* G.S. 115C-426.2.
101. G.S. 115C-427.
102. G.S. 115C-428.
103. *Id.*
104. G.S. 115C-429.
105. G.S. 115C-429(c).

Step 5: County Board Makes Appropriations to Local School Unit(s)

The board of county commissioners makes its appropriations for capital and operating expenditures to the local school administrative unit(s) in the county's annual budget ordinance.

Budgeting Factors

In making its appropriation decisions, the county board must carefully consider the local school board's funding request. The county is required to make appropriations for operating expenditures that, when combined with revenues to the school unit from all other sources, are sufficient to allow the school to meet its constitutional mandate to provide a sound basic education.[106] Other revenues available to a school unit for operating expenses include supplemental taxes levied by or on behalf of the school unit; state money disbursed directly to the school unit; moneys made available to the local school unit by the board of county commissioners; moneys accruing to the local school unit from fines, penalties, and forfeitures pursuant to Article IX, Section 7, of the N.C. Constitution; and any other moneys made available or accruing to the local school unit for the current operating expenses of the school system.[107] Of course a county board also has to balance the needs of the school unit with the needs of all other county departments, particularly those that provide state-mandated services, such as public health, social services, and elections. Recognizing this, the statute requires that a county board consider its fiscal resources and financial policies when making school appropriation decisions.

A county also is required to appropriate sufficient funds to meet a school unit's capital needs for the fiscal year.[108] The state makes some funds available to a county and its local school unit(s) to help with school construction, but most of this need must be met with county resources. A school unit's capital needs vary from year to year. It may be helpful for a county board to engage its local school board(s) in the county's capital planning process or capital improvement program (CIP).

Fund Balance

Questions often arise at budget time about the propriety of a local school unit maintaining a fund balance. Most state funds to school units revert at the end of a fiscal year if not spent. Thus, a school unit's fund balance is comprised primarily of county appropriations from previous years. There is no prohibition against a school unit maintaining a fund balance. School units, however, do not need a fund balance to meet cash flow needs to the same extent that counties and municipalities do.[109] And, unlike for counties and municipalities, the state's Local Government Commission does not prescribe a minimum fund balance level for local school units. A county board may not force a school board to expend its fund balance for capital or operating expenditures. And a school unit is not authorized to return all or a portion of its fund balance to the county. A county board, however, likely may consider the amount of fund balance available to the school unit when making its yearly county appropriations for operating expenses.[110]

---

106. *See* G.S. 115C-426.

107. *See* G.S. 115C-426(e).

108. *See* G.S. 115C-426(f).

109. The most significant revenue source for counties and municipalities is property tax proceeds. Although property taxes typically are levied at the beginning of the fiscal year (July 1), they may be paid without penalty until the following January. Thus, counties and municipalities rely heavily on fund balance to pay expenses during the first half of the fiscal year. Local school units do not have the same cash flow needs because they receive revenue disbursements from the state and county governments on a more regular basis throughout the fiscal year.

110. G.S. 115C-426 used to provide more explicit authority for a county to consider a local school unit's fund balance when making its budget appropriation to the school unit for operating expenses. That is because fund balance was considered to be part of the local current expense fund. And G.S. 115C-426(e) required that each year the local current expense fund include appropriations from the county that, when added to appropriations from the state and other local sources, are sufficient to provide for "the current operating expense of the public school system in conformity with the educational goals and policies of the State and the local board of education, within the financial resources and consistent with the fiscal policies of the board of county commissioners."

County Authority to Direct School Unit Expenditures

Generally, appropriations for operating expenses are made to the local current expense fund. A board of county commissioners may appropriate a lump sum to the local current expense fund to support operating expenses. If a county appropriates moneys to the local current expense fund with no further direction, the local board of education has full discretion over the expenditure of these moneys.

A county is authorized, however, to allocate part or all of its appropriation for operating expenses within the local current expense fund by purpose or function, as defined in the uniform budget format.[111] The uniform budget format (now the uniform chart of accounts)[112] defines "purpose code" to include the activities or actions that are performed to accomplish the objectives of the school unit. Function codes are first-level subdivisions of purpose codes and represent the greatest level of specificity to which a county may allocate funds for operating expenses. County appropriations may be allocated to the following purpose and function codes:

- **Purpose (first level) and Function (second level) Codes**
  - 5000—*Instructional Services.* Includes the costs of activities dealing directly with the interaction between teachers and students.
    - 5100—Regular Instructional Services
    - 5200—Special Populations Services
    - 5300—Alternative Programs and Services
    - 5400—School Leadership Services
    - 5500—Co-curricular Services
    - 5600—School-Based Support Services
  - 6000—*Supporting Services Programs.* Includes the costs of activities providing system-wide support for school-based programs, regardless of where these supporting services are based or housed.
    - 6100—Support and Development Services
    - 6200—Special Population Support and Development Services
    - 6300—Alternative Programs and Services Support and Development Services
    - 6400—Technology Support Services
    - 6500—Operational Support Services
    - 6600—Financial and Human Resource Services
    - 6700—Accountability Services
    - 6800—System-Wide Pupil Support Services

In 2010, in reaction to a series of cases involving apportionment of funds from the local current expense fund to charter schools, the General Assembly amended G.S. 115C-426(c) to state that "the appropriation or use of fund balance or interest income by a local school administrative unit shall not be construed as a local current expense appropriation included as a part of the local current expense fund." The impetus behind this amendment was clear. The legislature intended to shield a school unit's fund balance from being apportioned to a charter school pursuant to G.S. 115C-238.29H(b). However, in adding this language, the legislature arguably created an ambiguity as to whether or not a county board may consider a school's existing fund balance when making budget appropriations to the local current expense fund for operating expenses.

However, G.S. 115C-426(e) allows a county board to consider "other moneys available or accruing to the local school administrative unit," which provides some justification for a county board to consider a school unit's uncommitted fund balance when making its yearly appropriation decisions.

111. G.S. 115C-429. The county board may specify that the local school board submit its budget request according to these purpose and function codes.

112. A list of the chart of accounts for fiscal year 2013 is available at www.ncpublicschools.org/fbs/finance/reporting/coa2013 (last visited November 13, 2014).

- 6900—Policy, Leadership, and Public Relations Services
- 7000—*Ancillary Services.* Includes activities that are not directly related to the provision of education for pupils in a local school administrative unit.
  - 7100—Community Services
  - 7200—Nutrition Services
  - 7300—Adult Services
- 8000—*Non-programmed Charges.* Includes conduit-type payments to other local school administrative units in the state or in another state, transfers from one fund to another fund in the local school administrative unit, appropriated but unbudgeted funds, debt service payments, scholarship payments, payments on behalf of educational foundations, and contingency funds.
  - 8100—Payments to Other Government Units
  - 8200—Unbudgeted Funds
  - 8300—Debt Services
  - 8400—Interfund Transfers
  - 8500—Contingency
  - 8600—Educational Foundations
  - 8700—Scholarships
- 9000—*Capital Outlay.* Includes expenditures for acquiring fixed assets, including land or existing buildings, improvements of grounds, initial equipment, additional equipment, and replacement of equipment.

A board of county commissioners may request that a local board of education refrain from using county appropriations for certain items of expenditure within a purpose or function code. However, it may not legally restrict these expenditures at the line-item level. Furthermore, if a county board allocates its appropriations according to a purpose or function code, the local school board may modify up to 25 percent of an allocation for operating expenses. The board of county commissioners may reduce the local school board's discretion to modify allocations if it so specifies in the county budget ordinance, but not to less than 10 percent.[113]

According to the uniform budget format (now the uniform chart of accounts), there are three categories of expenditures to which a county may appropriate capital funds to its public school(s). A county may appropriate moneys for Category I expenditures for a specific capital project or projects. Moneys appropriated for Categories II and III expenditures, however, are allocated to the entire category, not to individual expenditure items.

The following details the authorized capital outlay expenditures in each category:

- **Category I**
  Acquisition of real property and acquisition, construction, reconstruction, enlargement, renovation, or replacement of buildings and other structures for school purposes.
- **Category II**
  Acquisition or replacement of furnishings and equipment.
- **Category III**
  Acquisition of school buses, activity buses, and other motor vehicles.

If the board of county commissioners allocates part or all of its capital appropriations by project, the local school board must obtain approval from the county for any changes in the allocation for specific Category I expenditures—acquisitions of real property for school purposes and acquisitions, construction, reconstruction, enlargement,

113. G.S. 115C-433.

renovations, or replacement of buildings and other structures.[114] However, a local board of education has full discretion to reallocate funds within categories II and III.

Apportionment of County Funds among Multiple School Units

If a county supports more than one local school unit, county appropriations to the local current expense funds of the local school administrative units (to support operating expenses) must be apportioned according to the average daily membership of each unit.[115] There is an exception for appropriations funded by voted supplemental taxes levied less than countywide. These funds do not need to be apportioned equally among local school administrative units.

This uniform apportionment requirement does not apply to capital funds. A county may allocate unequal amounts of capital funding to different school units within a fiscal year. Furthermore, under certain circumstances a county may appropriate moneys to special funds for particular programs at one local school administrative unit without appropriating an equivalent amount to other units. The local school administrative unit must maintain any special funds that are applicable to its operation.

Interim Budget

The Local Government Budget and Fiscal Control Act requires adoption of the budget ordinance by July 1.[116] However, sometimes county boards are unable or unwilling to adopt a budget ordinance by this date. In such a case, a county board must adopt an interim budget that appropriates money to cover necessary expenses for county departments and the local school unit(s) until the budget ordinance is adopted.[117] In an extreme situation, the state's Local Government Commission is authorized to assume the financial duties of the county board and to adopt the budget ordinance.[118] If the county's budget is delayed beyond July 1, a local school board also must adopt an interim budget resolution to pay salaries and the "usual ordinary expenses" of the unit(s).[119]

Step 6: Local School Board Initiates Dispute Resolution Process (optional)

If the local school board "determines that the amount of money appropriated to the local current expense fund, [for operating expenses] or the capital outlay fund, or both, . . . is not sufficient to support a system of free public schools," it may initiate a dispute resolution process with the board of county commissioners to challenge the appropriation (dispute resolution process).[120]

There are a number of steps in the dispute resolution process. First, to trigger the process, a local school board must so notify the county board within seven days of the adoption of the county budget ordinance. The boards then are required to meet and make a good faith effort to try to resolve their differences. A mediator presides over the meeting and acts as a neutral facilitator.

If the meeting is not successful, the boards proceed to official mediation. Unless the two boards agree otherwise, the participants in the mediation are the chairs, attorneys, and finance officers of each board; the public school superintendent; and the county manager. The compensation and expenses of the mediator are shared equally by the local school administrative unit and the county. The mediation is conducted in private, and statements and conduct are not discoverable. The mediation must end by August 1, unless both boards agree otherwise. If the mediation continues

---

114. G.S. 115C-433.
115. G.S. 115C-430.
116. G.S. 159-13; G.S. 115C-429.
117. G.S. 159-16.
118. G.S. 159-181.
119. G.S. 115C-434.
120. G.S. 115C-431(a).

beyond August 1, the county must appropriate to the local current expense fund a sum equal to the local appropriation for the previous fiscal year.

If mediation ultimately fails, the local board of education may file an action in superior court. The action must be filed within five days of the failed mediation. Either side may demand a jury trial. The judge or jury must determine (1) "the amount of money legally necessary from all sources" to maintain a system of free public schools "as defined by State law and the State Board of Education policy" and (2) "the amount of money legally necessary from the board of county commissioners."[121] A recent amendment to G.S. 115C-431(c) clarifies what the judge or jury must consider in making the determination.

> In making the finding, the judge or the jury shall consider the educational goals and policies of the State and the local board of education, the budgetary request of the local board of education, the financial resources of the county and the local board of education, and the fiscal policies of the board of county commissioners and the local board of education.

This statutory directive largely codifies the North Carolina's Supreme Court's holding in *Beaufort County Board of Education v. Beaufort County Board of Commissioners*.[122]

If the school board succeeds in the litigation, the court will order the board of county commissioners to appropriate a specific amount to the local school administrative unit and, if necessary, to levy property taxes to cover the amount of the appropriation. Any payment by the county may not be considered or used to deny or reduce appropriations to a local school administrative unit in subsequent fiscal years.

Either board may appeal the superior court's judgment in writing within ten days after the entry of the judgment. Final judgments at the conclusion of the appellate process are legally binding on both boards.

Although the statute directs the trial court to take up the matter as soon as possible, it is silent as to the timing of appellate review. And, in practice, the appellate review process often takes over a year or more to complete. Thus, even if a judge or jury determines that a local school board needs additional funds from the county to meet its constitutional and statutory educational responsibilities for a particular school year, the school unit may not receive those additional funds that school year. In fact, the school unit may not receive the funds until well into the following school year. And, from a county's perspective, it may end up paying more money in a future fiscal year to its local school unit than is needed to support the school unit that year. In addition, both boards incur the (often substantial) costs of litigating the issue. For these reasons, most dispute resolution processes do not proceed beyond mediation.

Step 7: Local School Board Adopts School Budget Resolution

If the local board of education does not formally dispute the county's budget appropriations, or upon successful resolution of any dispute, the local board of education adopts a budget resolution.[123] The budget resolution reflects the county's appropriations for capital and operating expenses as well as those from the state and federal governments. G.S. 115C-432 imposes several requirements and limitations on a school unit's budget. Among other things, the school unit's budget must conform to the county's budget allocations. The budget resolution must be entered into the minutes of the local board of education. Within five days of adoption of the budget, copies are to be filed with the public school superintendent, school finance officer, and county finance officer.[124]

---

121. G.S. 115C-431(c).
122. 363 N.C. 500 (2009).
123. G.S. 115C-432.
124. *Id.*

Step 8: Local School Board Amends School Budget Resolution (optional)

A local school board is free to amend its budget resolution any time after its adoption. The budget resolution must continue to meet the requirements specified in G.S. 115C-432, and if the county board has allocated funds by purpose or function code, the school board must continue to honor those designations except as allowed by statute.

Occasionally during a fiscal year a local school board will want to move moneys from its capital outlay fund to its current expense fund, or vice versa, in order to cover unexpected expenditures. A local school board is prohibited, however, from transferring money between these two funds, except under limited circumstances. A transfer may occur if all of the following conditions are met: (1) the funds are needed to cover emergency expenditures that were both "unforeseen and unforeseeable" when the school budget resolution was adopted, (2) the local board of education receives approval from the county board of commissioners, and (3) the local board of education follows certain procedural requirements.[125]

A local board of education may initiate a transfer between its capital outlay and current expense funds by adopting a resolution that states (1) the amount of the proposed transfer, (2) the nature of the emergency, (3) why the emergency was unforeseen and could not have been foreseen, (4) what objects of expenditure will be added or increased, and (5) what objects of expenditure will be reduced or eliminated.

The local board of education must send copies of the resolution to the board of county commissioners and any other local school administrative units in the county. The board of county commissioners must allow any other local boards of education to comment on the proposed transfer. The board of county commissioners must then approve or deny the request within thirty days. If the board of county commissioners does not act within the thirty-day period, its approval is presumed, unless the local board of education that submitted the request explicitly agrees to an extension of the deadline.[126] The board of county commissioners must notify the requesting local board of education and any other local boards of education in the county of its decision.

Step 9: County Board Monitors Local School Unit's Expenditures of County Appropriations (optional)

The board of county commissioners has broad discretion to request information from the local school board relating to the expenditure of school funds. Pursuant to the annual budget process, the board of county commissioners is authorized to inspect "all books, records, audit reports, and other information bearing on the financial operation of the local school administrative unit."[127] The board of county commissioners also may request, in writing, that the school finance officer make periodic reports about the financial condition of the local school administrative unit.

In addition, the board of county commissioners automatically receives a copy of the annual audit report for the local school administrative unit.[128]

Finally, the board of county commissioners and the local board of education are authorized and encouraged to "conduct periodic joint meetings during each fiscal year" to discuss the implementation of the current public school budget and assess future capital and operating needs.[129]

---

125. G.S. 115C-433(d).

126. Note that if a board of county commissioners and a local board of education seek to use the local sales and use tax proceeds that are specifically earmarked by state statute for capital outlay expenses to fund operating expenses, the county also must seek approval from the Local Government Commission according to the procedures set forth in G.S. 105-487 and -502.

127. G.S. 115C-429(c).

128. G.S. 115C-447(a).

129. G.S. 115C-462.2.

Step 10: County Board Reduces Appropriations to Local School Unit(s) during Fiscal Year (optional)

A county may reduce its appropriations to a local school unit only under limited circumstances. The board of county commissioners may not reduce its appropriations for capital outlay or operating expenses after it adopts the county budget ordinance unless (1) the local board of education consents to the reduction or (2) it is pursuant to a general reduction in county expenditures due to prevailing economic conditions.[130] If the board of county commissioners reduces its appropriations to its school unit(s) pursuant to a general reduction in county expenditures, it must hold a public meeting and afford the local school board an opportunity to present information on the impact of the reduction and then take a public vote (that is, a vote in an open session of a public meeting) on the decision to reduce the appropriations.

V. Charter Schools

In 1996, as part of its educational reform efforts, the General Assembly authorized the establishment of charter schools, public schools that operate under a charter from the State Board but are free from many of the restrictions that affect other public schools.[131] According to the legislature, the purpose of charter schools is to

> provide opportunities for teachers, parents, pupils, and community members to establish and maintain schools that operate independently of existing schools, as a method to accomplish all of the following:
>
> (1) Improve student learning;
> (2) Increase learning opportunities for all students, with special emphasis on expanded learning experiences for students who are identified as at risk of academic failure or academically gifted;
> (3) Encourage the use of different and innovative teaching methods;
> (4) Create new professional opportunities for teachers, including the opportunities to be responsible for the learning program at the school site;
> (5) Provide parents and students with expanded choices in the types of educational opportunities that are available within the public school system; and
> (6) Hold the schools established under this Part accountable for meeting measurable student achievement results, and provide the schools with a method to change from rule-based to performance-based accountability systems.[132]

Although a statewide cap was originally set for 100 charter schools, in 2011 the legislature removed the limit.[133] In 1997–98, 34 charter schools began operation; by 2013, 123 were in operation.[134]

As long as a school meets the terms of its charter, it is not bound by most of the state statutes and regulations that apply to other public schools. However, unlike other public schools, a charter school may be closed by the State Board's revocation of its charter if it fails to live up to the terms of that charter.[135]

---

130. G.S. 159-13(b)(9).

131. *See* G.S. 115C-238.29A through -239.29I.

132. G.S. 115C-238.29A.

133. S.L. 2011-164, § 2(a) (June 17, 2011) (amending G.S. 115C-238.29D by repealing subdivision (b)).

134. For a list of current charter schools, as well as charter schools scheduled to open in the next school year, see Office of Charter Schools, N.C. State Board of Education, Department of Public Instruction, at www.ncpublicschools.org/charterschools/schools (last visited Feb. 21, 2014).

135. G.S. 115C-238.29G.

Any child who is eligible to attend public school in North Carolina is eligible to attend a charter school.[136] A student is not limited to charter schools located within his or her school district or even his or her county. A charter school may set an enrollment cap but may not limit admission to students on the basis of intellectual ability, scholastic or athletic achievement, disability, race, creed, gender, national origin, religion, or ancestry.[137] A charter school may not charge tuition or fees, except for those also charged by the local school administrative unit in which the charter school is located.

State Funding for Charter Schools

For every child who attends a charter school, the state board of education must allocate to that charter school an amount equal to the average per pupil allocation for average daily membership from the local school administrative unit allotments in which the charter school is located (with the exception of allotments for children with disabilities and children with limited English proficiency).[138] That means that state funding for operational expenses follows the student to the charter school.

State funding may be used for a charter school's operational expenses. It also may be used to enter into operational and financing leases for real property or mobile units utilized as classroom facilities.[139] A charter school may not use state funds to purchase any interest in real property or mobile classroom units, however.

Local Funding for Charter Schools

Under current law, a county is not required, and, in fact, is not statutorily authorized, to provide funding directly to charter schools for either capital or operating expenses.[140]

Operating Expenses

A county does, however, indirectly fund some operating expenses for charter schools. For each student within a local school administrative unit who attends a charter school, the administrative unit must transfer to the charter school an amount equal to the administrative unit's per pupil local current expense appropriation for the fiscal year. The local current expense appropriation includes direct appropriations by the county for operating expenses; revenues from local fines, penalties, and forfeitures; state moneys disbursed directly to the local school administrative unit; and the proceeds of supplemental taxes levied by or on behalf of the local school administrative unit.[141] It does not include fund balance. It also does not include moneys that are properly accounted for in funds other than the local current expense fund, such as moneys resulting from reimbursements, fees for actual costs, tuition, sales tax revenues distributed using the ad valorem method pursuant to G.S. 105-472(B)(2), sales tax refunds, gifts and grants restricted as to use, trust funds, federal appropriations made directly to local school administrative units, and funds received for prekindergarten programs.[142]

136. G.S. 115C-238.29F(g).

137. G.S. 115C-238.29F(g)(5).

138. G.S. 115C-238.29H. The state must allocate an additional amount for each child attending the charter school who is a child with disabilities or a child with limited English proficiency.

139. G.S. 115C-238.29H(a1).

140. *See* Sugar Creek Charter Sch., Inc. v. State, 214 N.C. App. 1 (2011), *rev. den'd*, 366 N.C. 227 (2012).

141. *See* G.S. 115C-238.29H and -426. Note that revenue derived from supplemental taxes will be transferred only to a charter school located in the tax district for which the taxes are levied and in which the student resides. G.S. 115C-238.29H(b).

142. G.S. 115C-426(c). If a local school administrative unit budgets or accounts for any of these moneys in the local current expense fund, however, the moneys must be distributed to the charter schools in accordance with G.S. 115C-238.29H. *See* Sugar Creek Charter Sch., Inc. v. Charlotte–Mecklenburg Bd. of Educ., 195 N.C. App. 348, *appeal dismissed and disc. review den'd*, 363

Conclusion

The North Carolina Constitution guarantees each child in this state an opportunity for a sound basic education. Responsibility for setting educational policy and standards rests largely with the state legislature, state board of education, and local board of education. The state also funds the majority of the public school system's operating expenses. Counties have traditionally been responsible for funding school facilities. Over time, however, county boards have assumed an increasing role in funding operational expenses for school units and, thereby, in influencing educational policy.

About the Author

Kara A. Millonzi is a School of Government faculty member specializing in the areas of municipal and county finance law, special assessments, utility finance law, solid waste finance law, and public school finance law.

This chapter updates and revises the previous chapter, "Elementary and Secondary Education," authored by Laurie L. Mesibov and Ingrid M. Johansen, whose contributions to the field and to this publication are gratefully acknowledged.

N.C. 663 (2009); *see also* Thomas Jefferson Classical Acad. v. Rutherford Cnty. Bd. of Educ., 215 N.C. App. 530 (2011), *review den'd*, 724 S.E.2d 531 (N.C. 2012).

In 2009, the Department of Public Instruction (DPI) established a separate fund, Fund 8, to which local school units may deposit moneys designated for restricted purposes. According to DPI, the fund allows local school units to "separately maintain funds that are restricted in purpose and not intended for the general K-12 population" within the school unit. *Thomas Jefferson Classical Academy*, 215 N.C. App. 530 (detailing Dec. 16, 2009, memo from DPI establishing Fund 8). Examples listed include state funds for a targeted non-K-12 constituency, such as More-at-Four funds, trust funds for specific schools within a school unit, federal or other funds not intended for the general K-12 instructional population, and certain reimbursement funds. Moneys budgeted and accounted for in Fund 8 are not shared with charter schools.

Conclusion

Chapter 46

Community Colleges

Robert P. Joyce

Each year, one North Carolinian in twelve attends the state's community college system. The fifty-eight community colleges serve 840,000 students at an annual operating cost far exceeding $1 billion. That cost is shared by the state and counties in much the same way the costs of running the public elementary and secondary schools are shared—the state pays the bulk of the expense of providing the educational programs (the state appropriation alone exceeded $1 billion in 2013–14) and the counties pay most of the expense of providing and maintaining facilities. Tuition brings in another $300 million to the individual colleges. As with the public schools, in the community college system the operating authority and decision-making power are shared by the state (chiefly through the State Board of Community Colleges) and local government (chiefly through the local community college board of trustees).

Brief History

Both the University of North Carolina and the system of free public schools are provided for by the North Carolina Constitution, and both have roots that reach back to the nineteenth century and earlier. The community college system, by contrast, is not mentioned in the constitution and is strictly a creation of the General Assembly in the twentieth century.

In 1927 Buncombe County Junior College opened as the state's first tuition-free public junior college. Shortly afterward the Asheville board of education started the College of the City of Asheville, also tuition-free, open to any high school graduate in the city. Because of the financial difficulties of the Great Depression, the two colleges merged, in effect, into Biltmore Junior College. Under the names Biltmore College and then Asheville-Biltmore College, the institution remained the sole public junior college in North Carolina until 1946.

At the end of World War II, North Carolina was overwhelmed with former GIs eager for higher education, along with the regular complement of new eighteen- and nineteen-year-olds. Enrollment at existing campuses, such as UNC Chapel Hill, far exceeded capacity. In response, the extension division of the University of North Carolina opened twelve off-campus freshman centers around the state in the fall of 1946. Most of the centers closed when student enrollment numbers abated, but local taxpayers assumed responsibility for two of them: Wilmington College (destined to become the University of North Carolina at Wilmington) and Charlotte College (later the University of North Carolina at Charlotte) joined Asheville-Biltmore College (later the University of North Carolina at Asheville) as public junior colleges.

About this time the notion of "community college" was gaining acceptance nationally, due in part to the 1947 report of the Truman Commission, more formally known as the President's Commission on Higher Education. In 1950 the state superintendent of public instruction authorized a study of the need for community colleges in North Carolina. In 1952 the resulting report, adopting the philosophy of the Truman Commission report, called for the creation of a system of tuition-free institutions designed to meet all the post–secondary school needs of each community, including both academic preparation and practical vocational and technical training.

In 1957 the General Assembly passed the state's first Community College Act, but the act did not create the community college system envisioned by the Truman Commission or by the North Carolina study. The act instead provided funds for public junior colleges—that is, the institutions at Asheville, Wilmington, and Charlotte—to offer a freshman and sophomore curriculum in liberal arts and sciences. The vocational, technical, and adult education aspects of their curricula faded away.

As the public junior colleges moved away from vocational training, the General Assembly appropriated $500,000 to create industrial education centers, under the auspices of the State Board of Education, devoted entirely to vocational training. Soon thereafter the Burlington center enrolled 2,400 students, and by 1963 a total of twenty centers enrolled 34,000 students statewide. To serve the needs of their vocational students, the industrial education centers began offering liberal arts courses in English, mathematics, and the like.

The duplication of effort between the public junior colleges and the industrial education centers motivated Governor Terry Sanford to establish the Governor's Commission on Education Beyond the High School in 1961, which called for the creation of "community colleges" offering not only freshman and sophomore college-level courses, as did the public junior colleges, but also technical, vocational, and adult education courses for both college and noncollege students. Instead of expanding the 1957 version of public junior colleges into true community colleges, North Carolina started from a base of noncollege, industrial education centers and, in effect, transformed them into a community college system. The General Assembly's Omnibus Higher Education Act of 1963—codified at Chapter 115A of the North Carolina General Statutes (hereinafter G.S.) and since replaced by Chapter 115D—authorized the community college system that exists today. Within five years the system comprised fifty institutions. Through the 1970s eight more were added, with the last, now known as Brunswick Community College, joining the system in 1978.

Education Philosophy

The education philosophy of the community college system embraces four elements that distinguish it from more traditional academic institutions of higher education: the "open door," low tuition, convenience of location, and a comprehensive curriculum.

- **The "open door."** The institution is available to anyone who wishes to take advantage of the opportunities it presents, without rigorous entrance obstacles. The North Carolina Administrative Code provides that "[e]ach college shall maintain an open-door admission policy to all applicants who are high school graduates or who are at least 18 years of age."[1] To fulfill this mission, the community college system offers three types of instruction. First, in curriculum programs, the colleges grant certificates, diplomas, or associate degrees designed to prepare individuals for entry-level technical positions in business and industry (such as nursing and computer technology) and offer college transfer programs designed to prepare individuals to move to the junior-year level of study at four-year universities. Second, in continuing education programs, students are not seeking academic credit but are furthering their occupational or academic goals through nondegree courses (such as adult literacy, high school diploma equivalency, or English as a second language). Third, colleges cooperate with local industries to provide specialized training, often targeting the economic development of the community. In any particular program—nursing, for example—a community college may impose entrance requirements. The general philosophy, however, is that the college will offer educational opportunities for all adults who wish to pursue them.

- **Low tuition.** Expense should, to the fullest extent possible, create no barrier to a community college education. In 2014 in-state tuition for North Carolina residents was $1,140 per semester.
- **Convenience of location.** North Carolina's community colleges are not residence colleges as are the campuses of the University of North Carolina. The vast majority of students live at home, many working to support families.
- **A comprehensive curriculum.** These colleges provide educational opportunities for all adults, at whatever educational level the adults may be. Course offerings range from rigorous health technology programs to basic literacy training. Academics and technical and vocation training coexist in the same broad-based institution.

Relationship with the Public Schools and the University of North Carolina

Of particular concern to a community college are (1) its relationship with the public schools in its area and (2) its relationship to the University of North Carolina.

Relationship with the Public Schools

Community colleges have deep and historical links to the public schools. The vocational education centers from which the community colleges grew were established as parts of the public school system under the State Board of Education. The community college system operated under the State Board of Education from its creation until 1980. Also, local boards of education elect members to the board of trustees for each community college.

Generally, the community colleges do not exist to serve public school students; high school students have been encouraged to stay in their high schools until graduation. But high school students have become an increasingly important part of the community college system. For many years these students have been permitted to enroll in community college courses either on a concurrent enrollment basis or through Huskins Bill programs. Two newer, more extensive initiatives—the Learn and Earn and early college high school programs—have increased high school student enrollment at community colleges even further. These four programs are detailed below.

Concurrent Enrollment

A particular high school student may be admitted to courses at a community college, to be taken concurrently with high school courses, upon the approval of the college president and the school superintendent. Admission is on a space-available basis and must not displace adult students. Once admitted, the student earns credit at the community college as does any other student. Concurrent enrollment is an individualized case-by-case matter and requires no approval at the state level.[2]

---

1. 1D SBCCC 400.2. "SBCCC" refers to the State Board of Community Colleges Code, the successor to Title 23 of the North Carolina Administrative Code, which codifies the rules of the State Board of Community Colleges.
2. *See* 1D SBCCC 200.95 and 300.99.

Huskins Bill Programs

Huskins Bill programs are so named because of the statutory provision authorizing them.[3] They are more formalized programs of cooperation between a community college and the local public school system that offer enhanced educational opportunities for high school students that these students would not otherwise have. In contrast to individualized concurrent enrollment, a Huskins Bill program will involve the enrollment of a number of local high school students in one or more community college courses. It requires a formal agreement between the school system and the college and approval by the State Board of Community Colleges.

Learn and Earn

In the Learn and Earn Program, students enrolled in high school can take specified community college courses online. Among other advantages, this program can create additional educational opportunities for students in rural areas.

Early College High School

Early college high school programs bring community colleges into the closest contact with the public schools. Community colleges and local boards of education cooperate in the creation of special high schools, physically located on the community college campus in most cases. High school students take some courses offered by the school board and others offered by the community college. In many of the programs, a student enters as a ninth-grader and attends the school for five years, earning simultaneously a high school diploma and a college associate's degree. Some of these joint high school–college programs have a unique focus, such as health care. The state's first thirteen early college programs opened in 2005, enrolling about 1,500 students. In 2014 seventy-seven such programs enrolled 15,000 students in seventy-one counties.

Relationship with the University

All fifty-eight community colleges offer college transfer programs in the liberal arts and sciences, but the General Assembly has required that "[a]ddition of the college transfer program shall not decrease [the community college's] ability to provide programs within its basic mission of vocational and technical training and basic academic education."[4] Nonetheless, community colleges are reasonably quite concerned about the ability of their college transfer students to gain admission to four-year institutions and obtain credit for work undertaken at the community college.

To address that concern, community colleges over the years worked out "articulation agreements" with four-year colleges that spelled out how course credits would transfer when a community college student gained admission to the four-year college. The welter of such agreements eventually exceeded 300. The complexity of that arrangement provided the impetus for the creation in 1997 of the Comprehensive Articulation Agreement between the community college system and the university, detailing how credits will transfer from community college transfer programs to any of the sixteen campuses of the university—Asheville, Boone, Chapel Hill, Charlotte, Cullowhee, Durham, Elizabeth City, Fayetteville, two in Greensboro, Greenville, Pembroke, Raleigh, Wilmington, and two in Winston-Salem. In general, no community college transfer student is guaranteed admission to any particular UNC institution; the admission decision is made by the UNC institution on a student-by-student basis. The agreement does guarantee, however, that students who complete two years of study at a community college, gaining an associate's degree and meeting certain standards, will be admitted to some UNC institution. Once the student is admitted, the Comprehensive Articulation Agreement governs the transfer of course and grade credit. Legislation enacted in 2013 directs the UNC Board of Governors "to adhere fully" to the agreement.

The individual community colleges are still free to enter into individual agreements with private four-year colleges to spell out how course and grade credits will transfer between the community college and the private college. A number of private colleges simply follow the Comprehensive Articulation Agreement.

---

3. *See* N.C. Gen. Stat. (hereinafter G.S.) § 115D-20(4).

4. G.S. 115D-4.1.

State Governance Structure

The Omnibus Higher Education Act of 1963, creating the community college system, placed the Department of Community Colleges and the individual institutions under the State Board of Education. The community colleges were an adjunct of the state's public schools, providing thirteenth and fourteenth grades, in a sense. But in 1979 the General Assembly established the State Board of Community Colleges and transferred the department to its control. This transfer was made with the enactment of Chapter 115D of the General Statutes to replace Chapter 115A and was effective July 1, 1980. In 1999 the General Assembly changed the name of the Department of Community Colleges to the North Carolina Community College System Office.

State Board of Community Colleges

The State Board of Community Colleges has broad authority over the operations of the community college system and the individual institutions. Since its creation, however, it has exercised its powers with restraint, granting flexibility to the colleges themselves.

Appointment

The State Board of Community Colleges consists of twenty-one members. The lieutenant governor and the state treasurer are ex officio members. The remaining members serve six-year terms. The governor appoints ten members, four from the state at large and one each from the six regions of the community college trustees' association. The General Assembly elects eight members, four each by the House of Representatives and the Senate. The president of the North Carolina Comprehensive Community College Student Government Association serves as a nonvoting member.[5]

Powers and Duties

The General Assembly has by statute granted power over the community college system very broadly to the State Board, providing in G.S. 115D-5(a) that

> [t]he State Board of Community Colleges may adopt and execute such policies, regulations and standards concerning the establishment, administration, and operation of institutions as the State Board may deem necessary to insure the quality of educational programs, to promote the systematic meeting of educational needs of the State, and to provide for the equitable distribution of State and federal funds to the several institutions.

In addition to this broad and general grant of authority, the State Board is authorized to approve the budget of individual colleges, approve building sites, approve building plans, approve the selection of the president for a college, establish and enforce financial accounting procedures, approve a college's adoption of a college transfer program, set pay scales for community college employee salaries, remove local community college trustees, set tuition and fees, and, if necessary, withdraw state financial support from a college if the local county or counties fail to provide adequate support.

The State Board has been reserved in exercising the broad authority over individual colleges granted to it by the General Assembly. It has, in fact, adopted a rule specifying that "[a]ll power and authority vested by law in the State Board which related to the internal administration, regulation, and governance of any individual college . . . are hereby delegated to the board of trustees of such college."[6] At the same time, mindful of its ultimate responsibility, the State Board has also adopted a rule providing that "[t]he State Board reserves the right to rescind any power or authority as it deems necessary."[7]

By 1978, the community college system had grown to fifty-eight institutions, its current number. Establishment of new colleges is subject to the approval of the General Assembly upon the recommendation of the State Board.

---

5. G.S. 115D-2.1.
6. 1B SBCCC 300.1.
7. 1B SBCCC 300.1(b)(3).

System Office and the State President

The System Office is defined by the statutes as a principal administrative department of state government under the direction of the State Board of Community Colleges. Chief among its duties are the allocation of state funds to the individual colleges on an equitable and lawful basis and the financial accounting oversight.

The State Board elects a president of the North Carolina System of Community Colleges to act as chief administrative officer of the System Office. The president's salary is fixed by the State Board from funds appropriated by the General Assembly. Neither the statutes nor the administrative code provisions spell out specific duties of the president.

Local Governance Structure

Each community college is governed—under the authority of the State Board of Community Colleges—by a local board of trustees and is administered by a president, employed by the board of trustees.

Local Board of Trustees

Appointment

Each community college board of trustees is composed of four different sets of members. In the first group are four trustees elected by the board of education of the public school administrative unit located in the administrative area of the college. If there are two or more school units in the administrative area, the four trustees are elected jointly by all the local boards, with each board having one vote. In the second group are four trustees elected by the county commissioners of the county in which the college is located. If the administrative area of the college consists of two or more counties, the trustees are to be elected jointly by all the boards, with each board having one vote. (If a community college has established a satellite campus in another county, the commissioners of that county may elect an additional two members to the board of trustees, if the board of trustees agrees.) Only one trustee elected in this group may him- or herself be a county commissioner. In the third group are four trustees appointed by the governor. In the fourth group is the president of the student government, as an ex officio, nonvoting member. All trustees except the student government president serve four-year terms and must be residents of the administrative area of the college.[8] No one who has been employed full time by a community college within the past five years may serve as a trustee and no spouse or child of a current employee may.

A trustee may be removed from office in one of two ways. First, the board of trustees may declare a seat vacant if a member misses three consecutive scheduled meetings without excuse or fails to participate in the trustee orientation program sponsored by the trustees' association. Second, if the State Board has reason to believe that a trustee is incapable of discharging the duties of the office, or is not discharging them, or is guilty of immoral or disreputable conduct, it may bring the matter to the attention of the local board of trustees. The trustees may then investigate and hold a hearing and, by two-thirds vote, find the charges true and declare the seat vacant.[9]

Powers and Duties

The broadest grant of authority to the local community college board of trustees comes from the State Board, which has provided by rule that "[a]ll power and authority vested by law in the State Board which related to the internal administration, regulation, and governance of any individual college . . . are hereby delegated to the board of trustees of such college."[10] In addition, specific statutory grants of authority empower the board of trustees to do the following things:

- Purchase and hold title to land, easements, and rights-of-way
- Sell, exchange, or lease real and personal property

8. *See* G.S. 115D-12.
9. *See* G.S. 115D-19.
10. 1B SBCCC 300.1.

- Acquire land by condemnation
- Elect a president (subject to the approval of the State Board)
- Employ employees (or delegate the employment authority to the president)
- Adopt rules and regulations for the disciplining of students
- Enter into contracts
- Sue and be sued
- Adopt rules for the use of campus streets, alleys, and driveways, including setting speed limits
- Purchase liability insurance and thereby waive sovereign immunity

These grants of authority are found variously in G.S. 115D-14, -15, -20, and -21. In addition, the trustees are authorized by statute to "exercise such other rights and privileges as may be necessary for the management and administration of the institution" and "perform such other acts and do such other things as may be necessary or proper for the exercise of the foregoing specific powers, including the adoption and enforcement of all reasonable rules, regulations, and bylaws for the government and operation of the institution."[11]

Service Areas, Administrative Areas, and Alternative Trustee Selection

The State Board assigns to each community college a service area for providing educational and training services.[12] A college may offer services in an area assigned to another college only by written agreement between the colleges. Community college service areas are not student attendance zones; any citizen of the state may enroll in any community college in the state. (Figure 46.1 lists the system's service areas.)

The college's service area may be exactly coterminous with its *administrative area*—the county or counties directly responsible for providing financial support for the college. Or the service area may be broader. A college may establish a satellite campus in a county that is not in the administrative area—with the approval of the commissioners of that county—and that county must accept the maintenance and utility costs of the satellite campus.[13]

If a college's administrative area includes two or more counties, the boards of commissioners of all the counties may establish the terms for providing the financial support of the college by contract, and they may provide for an alternative structure for the selection of trustees. The contract is subject to approval by the State Board.

College President

The president of the community college is selected by the board of trustees "for such term and under such conditions as the trustees may fix."[14] The selection is subject to the approval of the State Board. The trustees may delegate as much administrative authority to the president as they deem prudent. Two statutes provide explicitly for significant delegation. The first authorizes the board of trustees to delegate to the president the authority to make hiring decisions for all college personnel.[15] The second authorizes the board of trustees to delegate to the president the authority to transfer moneys from one appropriation to another within the same fund.[16]

Financial Responsibility for Community Colleges

The state and the counties served by a community college share the duty of paying for the college. By statute, the state pays for salaries and other costs of administration, instructional services, and support services (called *current operations expenses*). It also pays for furniture, equipment, and library books, and, when the appropriations are made by

11. G.S. 115D-20(7).
12. *See* 1A SBCCC 300.1.
13. G.S. 115D-32(d).
14. G.S. 115D-20(1).
15. G.S. 115D-20(2)
16. G.S. 115D-58(c).

Figure 46.1 Institutions and Service Areas

Institutions	Service Areas
Alamance Community College	Alamance County[a]
Asheville–Buncombe Community College	Buncombe and Madison counties
Beaufort County Community College	Beaufort, Hyde, Tyrrell, and Washington counties[b]
Bladen Community College	Bladen County
Blue Ridge Community College	Henderson and Transylvania counties
Brunswick Community College	Brunswick County
Caldwell Community College and Technical Institute	Caldwell and Watauga counties
Cape Fear Community College	New Hanover and Pender counties
Carteret Community College	Carteret County
Catawba Valley Community College	Alexander and Catawba counties[c]
Central Carolina Community College	Chatham, Harnett, and Lee counties
Central Piedmont Community College	Mecklenburg County
Cleveland Community College	Cleveland County
Coastal Carolina Community College	Onslow County
College of the Albemarle	Camden, Chowan, Currituck, Dare, Gates, Pasquotank, and Perquimans counties
Craven Community College	Craven County
Davidson Community College	Davidson and Davie counties[d]
Durham Community College	Durham and Orange counties
Edgecombe Community College	Edgecombe County
Fayetteville Technical Community College	Cumberland County
Forsyth Technical Community College	Forsyth and Stokes counties
Gaston College	Gaston and Lincoln counties
Guilford Technical Community College	Guilford County
Halifax Community College	Halifax and Northampton counties (townships of Gaston, Occoneechee, Pleasant Hill, and Seaboard)
Haywood Community College	Haywood County
Isothermal Community College	Polk and Rutherford counties
James Sprunt Community College	Duplin County
Johnston Community College	Johnston County
Lenoir Community College	Greene, Lenoir, and Jones counties
Martin Community College	Bertie County (townships of Indian Woods and Merry Hill), Martin and Washington counties[b, e]
Mayland Community College	Avery, Mitchell, and Yancey counties
McDowell Community College	McDowell County
Mitchell Community College	Iredell County[c, d]
Montgomery Community College	Montgomery County
Nash Community College	Nash County
Pamlico Community College	Pamlico County
Piedmont Community College	Caswell and Person counties[a]
Pitt Community College	Pitt County
Randolph Community College	Randolph County
Richmond Community College	Richmond and Scotland counties

Figure 46.1 Institutions and Service Areas (*continued*)

Institutions	Service Areas
Roanoke–Chowan Community College	Bertie County (townships of Colerain, Mitchells, Roxobel, Snakebite, Whites, and Woodville), Hertford and Northampton counties (townships of Jackson, Kirby, Rich Square, Roanoke, and Wiccacanee)[e]
Robeson Community College	Robeson County
Rockingham Community College	Rockingham County[a]
Rowan–Cabarrus Community College	Cabarrus and Rowan counties[f]
Sampson Community College	Sampson County
Sandhills Community College	Hoke and Moore counties
South Piedmont Community College	Anson and Union counties[g]
Southeastern Community College	Columbus County
Southwestern Community College	Jackson, Macon, and Swain counties
Stanly Community College	Stanly County[f]
Surry Community College	Surry and Yadkin counties
Tri-County Community College	Cherokee, Clay, and Graham counties
Vance–Granville Community College	Vance, Franklin, Granville, and Warren counties
Wake Technical Community College	Wake County
Wayne Community College	Wayne County
Western Piedmont Community College	Burke County
Wilkes Community College	Alleghany, Ashe, and Wilkes counties
Wilson Technical Community College	Wilson County

a. Caswell County is assigned to Piedmont Community College, which is authorized to offer all courses in Caswell County.

b. Martin Community College is authorized to offer in Washington County all adult basic education, adult high school/GED, fire training, emergency medical training, and in-plant training.

c. Catawba Valley Community College is authorized to continue offering the furniture training program at the Iredell Prison Unit. This exception shall be reexamined periodically by the State President, with his findings reported to the State Board.

d. Davie County is assigned to Davidson Community College, which is authorized to offer all courses in Davie County.

e. Bertie County is divided between Roanoke–Chowan Community College and Martin Community College as stated in the service area assignments. In the case of offering courses within the town or township of Windsor, Martin Community College has exclusive authority for offering curriculum and adult basic education courses, and both Martin Community College and Roanoke–Chowan Community College are authorized to offer other continuing education courses.

f. Cabarrus County is assigned to Rowan–Cabarrus Community College, which is authorized to offer all courses.

g. South Piedmont Community College is a multicampus community college authorized to serve Anson and Union counties.

Source: Curriculum Procedures Reference Manual, March 13, 2012, North Carolina Community College System, www.nccommunitycolleges.edu/programs/docs/CPRM/Section18_13Mar2012_Service%20Area%20Assignmentsv2.pdf.

the General Assembly, provides matching funds (to be paired with local funds) to buy land and to construct buildings (collectively called the *plant fund*). The counties served by community colleges must pay for maintenance and repairs to buildings and equipment, rent, utilities, costs of custodians, insurance, and legal fees. In addition, acquisition of land, erection and alteration of buildings, purchase and maintenance of vehicles, and maintenance of grounds are local responsibilities.[17]

The State Appropriation

The total state appropriation for the operations of the System Office and the individual institutions for 2013–14 was $1.021 billion.[18] The General Assembly bases its appropriation (in part) and the System Office in turn bases its allocation of the appropriation to the individual colleges (in part) on the concept of the FTE, or full-time equivalent. An FTE is a statistical picture of a "typical" student. This hypothetical student spends sixteen hours in class each week of each semester, totaling 256 hours per semester and 512 hours in a full school year.[19] Two students who attend eight hours each over the forty-four weeks of the school year together count as one FTE. If a college should (in a very unlikely event) offer a one-hour course that was attended by 512 people, that crowd together would generate one FTE. For 2013–14, the total systemwide community college FTE was 241,776, out of a total head count attendance of more than 800,000, reflecting the fact that many community college students do not attend full time.

Because the amount of money appropriated by the General Assembly varies from year to year, the appropriation-per-FTE and the actual dollar amount paid to each college per FTE also vary. If the General Assembly fails to increase its appropriation in a proportion corresponding to enrollment increases, then the colleges do not receive FTE funding at the previous level. Across the system as a whole, the majority of total funding comes from the state appropriation. The bulk of the remainder is an even split between county appropriations and tuition receipts. In 2013–14, tuition receipts systemwide totaled $360 million.

The County Appropriation

While the state, through General Assembly appropriations disbursed by the System Office, provides the overwhelming majority of funds for community college operating expenses, the counties in the administrative area of a community college provide the appropriations that permit a college to do the following:

- Acquire land
- Erect and alter buildings
- Maintain buildings and grounds
- Purchase and maintain vehicles
- Acquire and maintain equipment necessary for the upkeep of buildings and grounds
- Purchase furniture and equipment for administrative and instructional purposes not provided by state funds
- Pay the salaries of custodians and maintenance workers
- Pay for fuel, water, power, and telephones
- Rent land and buildings
- Pay for insurance for buildings and their contents, motor vehicles, workers' compensation for employees paid by county funds, and other necessary insurance
- Pay tort claims resulting from employee negligence
- Pay the cost of bonding employees for the protection of local funds and property
- Pay legal fees in connection with local administration and operation of the college

---

17. *See* G.S. 115D-31 and -32.
18. S.L. 2013-360.
19. *See* 1G SBCCC 100.1(4).

Two statutory provisions make state funds available in particular circumstances to assist counties with these expenses. The first applies to community colleges whose service areas include three or more counties.[20] A formula found in the statute provides matching state funds to help the host county, in recognition of the fact that students from other counties benefit from services paid for by the host county. The second, similarly, makes some state funds available for the operation of physical facilities for colleges where more than 50 percent of the enrollment at the main campus is composed of out-of-county students.[21]

The Role of the Commissioners

The college board of trustees is required by statute to submit its proposed budget for the upcoming fiscal year to the county commissioners by a date set by the commissioners. By July 1 (or a later date agreeable to the board of trustees, but in no event later than September 1), the commissioners determine the amount of county revenue to be appropriated to the community college for the budget year. The statute permits—but does not require—the commissioners to allocate all or part of an appropriation by purpose, function, or project within guidelines provided by the State Board of Community Colleges through its uniform budget manual. Some counties combine all their appropriations into one lump, while others make one appropriation for current operations and one for plant maintenance and operation. If the commissioners allocate their appropriation by purpose, the board of trustees is bound by the allocation.[22]

The Role of the State Board

The State Board of Community Colleges, through its staff in the System Office, sets budgetary and accounting guidelines for the community colleges. As an example, the format for the budget request that the trustees submit to the commissioners is set by the State Board.

Once the college receives notification of the commissioners' appropriation, it must submit its entire budget to the State Board for approval of the budget's provisions with respect to the spending of state funds.[23] If the State Board determines that the appropriations made by the county commissioners are insufficient to provide the required local financial support of a college, it may withdraw or withhold state financial or administrative support.[24]

Adoption of the Budget and Amendments

Once the State Board has approved the budget, the trustees adopt a budget resolution authorizing expenditure of the available money. The resolution must comply with the State Board approvals and the county commissioners' allocation.

Consistent with rules adopted by the State Board, the trustees may amend the budget resolution during the year or authorize the president to transfer moneys from one appropriation to another within the same budget fund. The chief limitation on budget amendments concerns funds allocated by the county commissioners to certain purposes. To change the budget resolution concerning such funds, the trustees must obtain the commissioners' approval if the amendment increases or decreases the amount of the appropriation allocated to the purpose by 25 percent or more. (The commissioners may reduce this threshold to as low as 10 percent.)

About the Author

Robert P. Joyce is a School of Government faculty member whose areas of specialization include the law related to higher education.

---

20. G.S. 115D-31(a)(3).
21. G.S. 115D-31.2.
22. *See* G.S. 115D-55.
23. See *id.*
24. *See* G.S. 115D-6.

Printed in the USA
CPSIA information can be obtained
at www.ICGtesting.com
LVHW012121031123
762994LV00010B/643